HANDBOOK
OF
INFORMATION TECHNOLOGY AND OFFICE SYSTEMS

HANDBOOK
OF
INFORMATION TECHNOLOGY
AND
OFFICE SYSTEMS

Edited by

A. E. CAWKELL
CITECH Ltd.
P.O. Box 565
Iver, Buckinghamshire
England

1986

NORTH-HOLLAND
AMSTERDAM · NEW YORK · OXFORD · TOKYO

ISBN: 0 444 87907 2

Publishers:
ELSEVIER SCIENCE PUBLISHERS B.V.
P.O. Box 1991
1000 BZ Amsterdam
The Netherlands

Sole distributors for the U.S.A. and Canada:
ELSEVIER SCIENCE PUBLISHING COMPANY, INC.
52 Vanderbilt Avenue
New York, N.Y. 10017
U.S.A.

Library of Congress Cataloging-in-Publication Data
Main entry under title:

Handbook of information technology and office systems.

Includes index.
1. Electronic data processing. 2. Information storage and retrieval systems. 3. Office practice -- Automation. I. Cawkell, A.E.
QA76.I5792 1986   004   85-25435
ISBN 0-444-87907-2 (U.S.)

PREFACE

What is Information Technology? One definition, reflecting what the writer (J.M. Richardson) would like it to be rather than what it really is, was proposed in 1979:— "Information technology means the collection, storage, processing, dissemination and use of information, but acknowledges the importance of man and the goals he sets, the values employed in making choices, and the assessment criteria used to decide whether he is controlling the technology and being enriched by it".

Theorising, social research, and agonising about the Information Society are to be commended, but this is an easier activity than getting down to the nitty-gritty of dealing with specific financial, engineering, political, and human problems which are the lot of the person who implements an IT project and who may later be faced with the responsibility for the pay-off, or lack of it. The unwary may be taken in by the huge range of "easy to install and use" devices which will "revolutionise your activities". It will usually be wiser to find out first from a friend who has tried it, employ a consultant, let the "experts" in the Data Processing or Electrical Engineering departments do it if they are available — or, of course, you can refer to this book.

Here I have attempted to prune the jargon and mystique and put together the component parts of a very wide field in explanatory chapters for "do-it-yourself" people, for teachers to refer to, for businessmen — or for that matter for anyone who wants to find the topic wrapped up in one place. I have enrolled a capable corps of guest authors whose approach, in some cases, is more advanced, to deal with policy and new developments in the fast-moving sectors. However, the subject is so wide that people already occupied in a branch of IT may find something in this book — librarians can find out about telecommunications, office managers can learn about indexing, scientists can read about personal information systems, and sociologists can consider the possibilities of online information systems.

As part author and part editor, a major difficulty has been what *not* to include since the boundaries of IT are blurred. I have attempted to include enough about each topic, with a sufficient number of references, to form a comprehensive survey of one of today's most important activities.

Tony Cawkell, Ickenham, England.
May 1985

CONTENTS

Section 6: THE LEADING EDGE

Section 1: INFORMATION TECHNOLOGY EXPLAINED
By A.E. Cawkell

CHAPTER 1. REFERENCE DATA

Numbering systems

No matter whether a digital computer user is working with numbers, text, or images, the data will be processed internally as binary numbers by the machine's binary (on or off) circuits.

Where a value is represented by a string of digits, each digit increases by one power of the base as you move from right to left. Thus in the decimal system, the value of the right hand digit, d, in a string of digits is d x 10^0, the next digit to the left is a value of 10^1, the next a value of 10^2, and so on, where 10^0 = 1, 10^1 = 10, 10^2 = 100, etc. Thus the number 4303 means 3 units, no tens, 3 hundreds and 4 thousands.

In the binary system (base 2), the right hand symbol is a value of 2^0 = 1, the next 2^1 = 2, the next 2^2 = 4, etc. Thus binary 1101 expressed as a decimal number is, from right to left, one 1, no twos, one four, and one 8 = 13

In the hexadecimal system (base 16), the right hand symbol is a value of 16^0 = 1, the next 16^1 = 16, the next 16^2 = 256, etc. The 16 symbols used are 0 to 9 and then A to F for 10 to 15. Thus DE6F Hex, expressed as a decimal number is 15 ones, 6 sixteens = 96, 14 two five sixes = 3584, and 13 four zero nine sixes = 53248, a total of 56943.

More details about the binary and hexadecimal systems are given in Chapter 3. Here is a conversion table.

Decimal		Binary		Hexadecimal	
	0		0		0
10^0	1	2^0	1	16^0	1
	2	2^1	10		2
	3		11		3
	4	2^2	100		4
	5		101		5
	6		110		6
	7		111		7
	8	2^3	1000		8
	9		1001		9
10^1	10		1010		A
	11		1011		B
	12		1100		C
	13		1101		D
	14		1110		E
	15		1111		F
	16	2^4	10000		10
	17		10001		11
	18		10010		12
	19		10011		13
	20		10100		14
	21		10101		15
	22		10110		16
	23		10111		17
	24		11000		18
	25		11001		19

Decimal		Binary			Hexadecimal	
	26		11010			1A
	27		11011			1B
	28		11100			1C
	29		11101			1D
	30		11110			1E
	31		11111			1F
	32	2^5	100000			20
	40		101000			28
	50		110010			32
	60		111100			3C
	64	2^6	1000000			40
10^2	100		1100100			64
	128	2^7				80
	255					FF
	256	2^8			16^2	100
	511					1FF
	512	2^9				200
	1024	2^{10}		"1K"		400
	2048	2^{11}		"2K"		800
	8192	2^{13}		"8K"		2000
	8193					2001
	16383					3FFF
	16384	2^{14}		"16K"		4000
	32678	2^{15}		"32K"		8000
	65536	2^{16}		"65K"	16^4	10000
	131072	2^{17}		"128K"		20000
	4294.97M	2^{32}		"4295M"	16^8	100000000

TABLE 1.1. DECIMAL, BINARY, AND HEXADECIMAL NUMBER EQUIVALENTS

<u>Communication Theory</u>

The constraints limiting information transmission were first expressed by Shannon in 1948 as follows –

$$C = W \log 2 \ (1 + S/N)$$

where C is the maximum number of bits per second receivable through a communication channel with an arbitrarily small number of errors, W the bandwidth in Hz, and S and N are the average signal and noise powers respectively. This equation provides a performance yardstick for all communication channels. C is a theoretical maximum which can be approached but never reached. The design of systems to convey the maximum amount of information with a given bandwidth and the selection of a media where wideband channels are available are of prime importance.

<u>Decibel</u>

A Decibel or db (one tenth of a Bel, a rarely used unit), is simply a ratio – in the case of electrical measurements 10 x the logarithm of two powers or 20 times the logarithm of two voltages. The following table shows a few values –

Power ratio	Voltage ratio	db
4	2	6
10	3.16	10
100	10	20
10,000	100	40
10^6	1000	60

<u>TABLE 1.2. DECIBEL RATIOS</u>

Thus -20 db is a voltage loss of 10 times or a power loss of 100 times).

A db can signify an absolute value if a reference level is known. For example if db levels are with reference to 1 volt (1 volt = 0 db), "6 dbs" means 2 volts.

The db is also used in another area of communication – hearing. In this case it is used to indicate a sound pressure level above an internationally agreed reference pressure level of 2×10^{-5} Pascals (or in the older notation 0.0002 dynes/cm^2) equivalent to the threshold of hearing at 1000 Hz.

The following table shows the levels of some typical sounds:-

Sound pressure level (SPL) db	SPL: number of times greater than level at threshold	Representative sounds having this level
140	10m	Pain level
120	1M	Jet aircraft takeoff at 60m
100	100K	Rock group (audience level)
80	10K	loud conversation
60	1000.0	office background noise
40	100.0	
20	10.0	just audible whisper
10	3.16	
6	2.0	
3	1.4	
0	0	Threshold of hearing

<u>TABLE 1.3. SOUND PRESSURE LEVELS</u>

1000 Hz is specified as the reference frequency because the sensitivity of the ear varies with sound frequency. It drops considerably at low frequencies, and to some degree at higher frequencies. The effect is particularly marked for quiet sounds. For example the SPL of a quiet sound of, say, 40 Hz, would have to be increased by about 50 db above the level of a 1000 Hz sound for it to appear to be equally loud. To overcome the problem of expressing the loudness of a sound - a subjective matter - a unit of measurement called the Phon is used. A 1000 Hz sound reference source is adjusted until it appears to a listener to be equally loud to a sound to be measured. The loudness of the sound in Phons is then numerically equal to the SPL of the 1000 Hz sound in Dbs.

<u>Magnitude of units of measurement</u>

<u>Unit prefix</u>	<u>Symbol</u>	<u>Power</u>	<u>Examples</u>
Exa	E	10^{18}	
Peta	P	10^{15}	
Tera	T	10^{12}	Terahertz (THz)
Giga	G	10^{9}	Gigahertz (GHz)
Mega	M	10^{6}	Megahertz (MHz)
kilo	K	10^{3}	Kilohertz (KHz)
Hecto	h	10^{2}	
Deka	da	10^{1}	
Deci	d	10^{-1}	
Centi	c	10^{-2}	
Milli	m	10^{-3}	Millisecond (ms) Millimetre (mm)
Micro	u (Greek u)	10^{-6}	Microsecond (us) Micrometre (um)
Nano	n	10^{-9}	Nanosecond (ns) Nanometre (nm)
Pico	p	10^{-12}	Picosecond (ps)
Femto	f	10^{-15}	
Atto	a	10^{-18}	

<u>TABLE 1.4. UNITS OF MEASUREMENT (SI INTERNATIONAL SYSTEM)</u>

<u>Frequency, wavelength, and use</u>

<u>Use</u>	<u>Frequency</u>	<u>Wavelength</u>		
	1 Hz	300,000	KMetres	
	3	100,000		
VLF	10	30,000		
(Very Low	30	10,000		
Frequency	100	3,000		
Communications)	300	1,000		
	1 KHz	300		
	3	100		
	10	30		
LF	30	10		
(Low Frequency)	100	3		
MF	300	1		
(Medium Freq.)	1 MHz	300	metres	
HF	3	100		
(High Frequency)	10	30		
VHF	30	10		
(Very High Frequ.)	100	3		Satellites:-
UHF	300	1		
(Ultra High Frequ.)	1 GHz	30	cms	UHF band
SHF	3	10		S band (2.5-2.7 GHz)
(Super High Frequ.)	10	3		C band (4 - 6 GHz)
EHF	30	1		Ku band (12 - 14 GHz)
(Extra High Frequ.)	100	3	mm	
	300	1		
	1 THz	300	um	
	3	100		
Multimode fibres	10	30		<u>Angstrom Units:-</u>
	30	10		
	100	3		Visible light:-
Monomode fibres	300	1		10,000 (Infra-red 7700)
	1,000	300	nm	3,000 (Ultra-Vi. 4700)
	3,000	100		1,000
	10,000	30		300

<u>TABLE 1.5 FREQUENCY AND WAVELENGTH</u>

<u>Type faces</u>

Type face sizes are specified in <u>Points</u> - the height of the type from the top of a capital letter to the bottom of a descender. One point is 0.01384 inches or 0.3515 mm. Printers also use the <u>Pica</u> (pronounced pie-ca) which is 12 points or 0.166 inches or 4.22 mm. The <u>Em</u> is a measure of type width (after the letter m) also equal to 12 points, but the actual space occupied by the type will depend on whether proportional spacing is used. An <u>En</u> is half an Em. A <u>Font</u> or <u>Fount</u> is the term used to describe a set of type of a particular style.

In practice the point size is often somewhat smaller than the nominal to avoid descenders touching the top of capitals with normal interline spacing. For example a 24 point type which should measure 8.44 mm overall vertically, may measure about 7mm.

Point size	Inches (nearest fraction)		Millimetres
2	0.0277	(1/32)	0.703
4	0.0554	(3/64)	1.406
6	0.0830	(3/32)	2.109
8	0.1107	(1/8)	2.812
10	0.1384	(9/64)	3.515
12	0.1661	(5/32)	4.218
14	0.1938		4.921
16	0.2214		5.625
18	0.2591	(1/4)	6.328
20	0.2768		7.031
22	0.3045		7.734
24	0.3322		8.437
26	0.3598		9.140
28	0.3875	(3/8)	9.843
30	0.4152		10.55
40	0.5536	(1/2)	14.06
50	0.6920		17.58
60	0.8304		21.09
70	0.9688		24.61
80	1.107		28.12

TABLE 1.6 TYPE FACE SIZES

International Paper Sizes

Dimensions (trimmed size)
(Inches equiv. to nearest 1/8th)

Type	Millimetres	Inches
4A	1682 x 2378	66 1/4 x 93 3/8
2A	1189 x 1682	46 3/4 x 66 1/4
A0	841 x 1189	33 1/8 x 46 3/4
A1	594 x 841	23 3/8 x 33 1/8
A2	420 x 594	16 1/2 x 23 3/8
A3	297 x 420	11 3/4 x 16 1/2
A4	210 x 297	8 1/4 x 11 3/4
A5	148 x 210	5 7/8 x 8 1/4
A6	105 x 148	4 1/8 x 5 7/8
A7	74 x 105	2 7/8 x 4 1/8
A8	52 x 74	2 x 2 7/8
A9	37 x 52	1 1/2 x 2
A10	26 x 37	1 x 1 1/2

TABLE 1.7 INTERNATIONAL PAPER SIZES

Ascii Code

The 7-bit American Standard Code for Information Interchange (ASCII) code
has become an internationally used code for computer telecommunications. Many
terminals use ASCII to enable the 7-bit code generated when a symbol is
communicated by depressing a key to be converted back to the symbol again. For

example when the "A" key is depressed, 1000001 is generated, "a" generates 1000011, etc., as shown in the table below. Codes are also provided for non-numeric keys and instructions. Thus ESC (Escape), DEL (Delete) etc., generate ASCII code. Other ASCII codes are provided for software controlled instructions generated during data transmission such as EOT (End Of Transmission), RS (Record Separator) etc. The ASCII 7-bit hex codes are also widely used within computers to represent alpha-numeric characters.

DEC	HEX	CHR	DEC	HEX	CHR	DEC	HEX	CHR	DEC	HEX	CHR
0	0	NUL	32	20	SP	64	40	@	96	60	
1	1	SOH	33	21	!	65	41	A	97	61	a
2	2	STX	34	22	"	66	42	B	98	62	b
3	3	ETX	35	23	#	67	43	C	99	63	c
4	4	EOT	36	24	$	68	44	D	100	64	d
5	5	ENQ	37	25	%	69	45	E	101	65	e
6	6	ACK	38	26	&	70	46	F	102	66	f
7	7	BEL	39	27	'	71	47	G	103	67	g
8	8	BS	40	28	(	72	48	H	104	68	h
9	9	HT	41	29	)	73	49	I	105	69	i
10	A	LF	42	2A	*	74	4A	J	106	6A	j
11	B	VT	43	2B	+	75	4B	K	107	6B	k
12	C	FF	44	2C	.	76	4C	L	108	6C	l
13	D	CR	45	2D	–	77	4D	M	109	6D	m
14	E	S0	46	2E		78	4E	N	110	6E	n
15	F	S1	47	2F	/	79	4F	O	111	6F	o
16	10	DLE	48	30	0	80	50	P	112	70	p
17	11	DC1	49	31	1	81	51	Q	113	71	q
18	12	DC2	50	32	2	82	52	R	114	72	r
19	13	DC3	51	33	3	83	53	S	115	73	s
20	14	DC4	52	34	4	84	54	T	116	74	5
21	15	NAK	53	35	5	85	55	U	117	75	u
22	16	SYN	54	36	6	86	56	V	118	76	v
23	17	ETB	55	37	7	87	57	W	119	77	w
24	18	CAN	56	38	8	88	58	X	120	78	x
25	19	EM	57	39	9	89	59	Y	121	79	y
26	1A	SUB	58	3A	:	90	5A	Z	122	7A	z
27	1B	ESC	59	3B	;	91	5B	[	123	7B	{
28	1C	FS	60	3C	<	92	5C	\	124	7C	¦
29	1D	GS	61	3D	=	93	5D	]	125	7D	}
30	1E	RS	62	3E	>	94	5E	^	126	7E	~
31	1F	US	63	3F	?	95	5F	–	127	7F	DEL

<u>TABLE 1.8 ASCII CODE</u>

EBCDIC code

Extended Binary Coded Decimal Interchange Code (EBCDIC) is an IBM code fulfilling a similar purpose to ASCII, but it provides 256 alternative codes using an eight bit binary number.

CHAPTER 2. SEMICONDUCTOR TECHNOLOGY AND ELECTRONICS

INTRODUCTION

The foundations of today's information technology, based on the use of the electronic valve as a high speed switch or amplifier, were laid during the 1939 to 1945 war. Semiconductor versions of many of the ideas and circuits of those days, originated by people like F.C.Williams, Alan Blumlein and others, are still easily recognisable.

Two events in the post-war pre-sputnick period may be singled out for special mention - Claude Shannon's work on communication theory which, in 1948, established the criteria for data transmission, and the invention of the transistor by Bardeen, Brattain and Shockley in 1949. The pace accelerated notably in the US space and military spheres following the launch of Sputnik 1 in 1957, but it was not until about 1976 that the "chip" started to impact the general public.

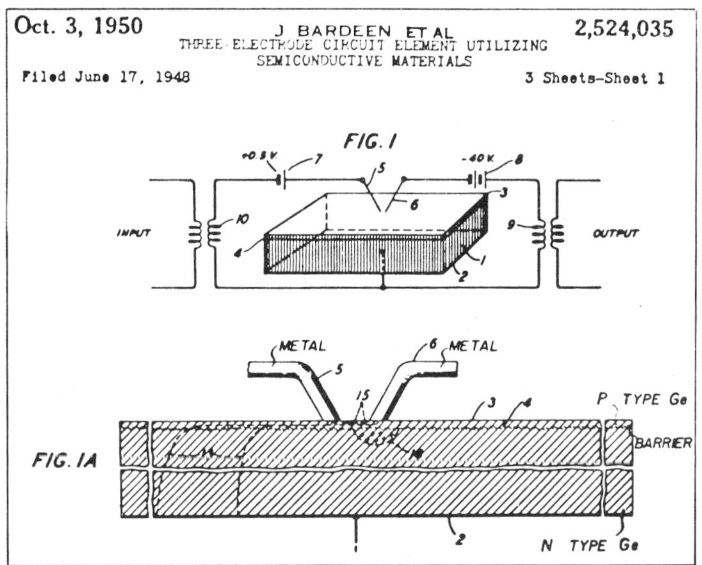

FIGURE 2.1. THE FIRST TRANSISTOR PATENT

The semiconductor chip, which embodies transistors and many other formerly discrete components and their interconnections, enables information to be processed rapidly, reliably, and cheaply using very little space and without generating appreciable heat. Numerous examples have been given to try and convey the rate of advance - for instance the EDSAC computer (1949 vintage), housed in a large room, contained 3000 valves, a 2000 byte (1 byte = 8 bits) memory, and consumed 15 Kilowatts of power. The 8080 microprocessor (1977 vintage), housed in a few square centimetres of plastic package, contained 5000 transistors, can control a 65 Kilobyte memory and consumes a few milliwatts.
Logarithmic scales always have to be used on growth curves.

Figure 2.2 shows how the number of transistors used in microprocessors increased in a ten year period.

Transistors are manufactured out of semi-conducting ("near-insulating") materials which are made more conductive in two different ways by doping with impurities. The impurities possess either one more or one less electron in an atom than the host material so two kinds of doped material become available. One, "p-type", will accept electrons from the other "n-type".

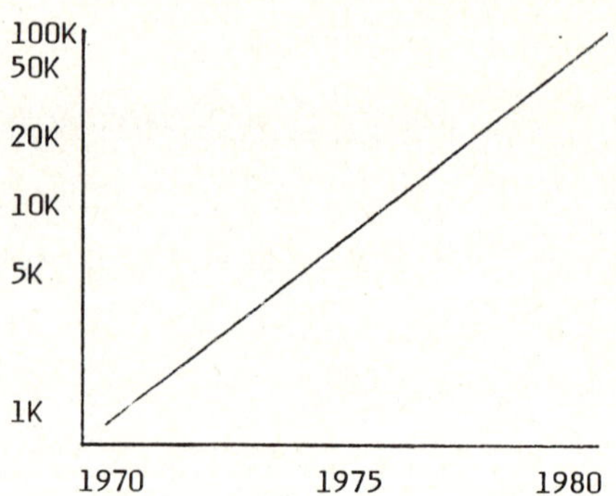

FIGURE 2.2. TRANSISTORS IN MICROS

The earliest types of Junction Transistor consisted of two layers of p-type material separated by a thin layer of n-type. If the operating conditions are set by applying suitable fixed voltages to the layers, say by batteries, a small change in current caused by a signal applied to the middle layer will cause a larger current to flow through the sandwich and the output circuit so the device amplifies. The middle n-type layer plays a similar role to that of the controlling "grid" in a thermionic valve.

The main requirement in computers is for circuits which can produce binary symbols - strings of 0's or 1's - represented either by current flow or no current flow. The arrangement just described, or more suitable ones to be discussed shortly, can be used for that purpose - the output current can be cut-off or switched-on by a signal current applied to the middle layer.

MANUFACTURE

There have been three major changes in methods of manufacturing and assembling electronic circuits. For many years all components such as thermionic valves (vacuum tubes), capacitors, resistors, switches, plugs and sockets etc., were produced by specialist manufacturers. The job of the manufacturer of the complete product - radio or television receiver or other electronic instrument - was to design the circuits needed to do the job, purchase the individual components , fix them on to a metal chassis, and interconnect them by insulated wiring soldered to connection points on each component.

The next phase, which gathered pace in the late 1940s, was a reduction in the cost of this labour-intensive activity by the introduction of printed circuits (PCs). The feasibility of PCs was improved by a steady reduction in the size of components. The circuit interconnections and component sites were drawn and an image of the drawing was projected on to a board of insulating material covered with a thin layer of copper. The pattern was masked with an etch-resistant material and immersed in an etching chemical which removed the surplus copper leaving a pattern corresponding to the image, in copper. Component connecting wires, often also supporting the component, were then soldered on to appropriate points on the copper circuit pattern.

The development of transistors without heat-producing filaments for generating electrons, and without the need for high operating voltages, eased the problem of heat dissipation near the surface of the PC board, formerly assisted by dissipation in the metal chassis. Heat-generating power transistors were fixed to appropriately sited finned metal radiators. Multiple-wire cables were used to interconnect printed circuits; the cables were soldered to strip sockets pushed on to projections on each PC board. The projections carried a strip of copper stubs matching the strip sockets, often gold plated for better contact, formed simply by including them on the original "wiring" drawing.

Later, cage-like containers were introduced with socket strips arranged one above the other at the back. The PC's edge-connectors pushed into the sockets so they also stacked one above the other. The sockets in each strip were connected to the same socket in every other strip e.g. number 1 on socket 1 to number 1 on socket 2, to number 1 on socket 3 etc., number 2 on socket 1 to number 2 on socket 2 etc. This "bus" standardisation took care of all inter- board connections.

The arrival of the Chip

This form of construction prevails today with one dramatic difference. A new type of component has been developed embodying hundreds, thousands, tens of thousands, and in due course a million or more hitherto discrete components.

This development has come about in consequence of two major driving forces - technology advances and information processing requirements. The new technology has enabled circuit complexity of quite a different order to be mass produced so that the end-product manufacturer's task has become very different. The manufacturer of an end-product capable of carrying out most complex tasks can now order components of a far greater complexity than the complete end-products which he previously manufactured, sometimes in arrays on boards ready to interconnect in whatever permutation he needs, and quite possibly with their own on-board programs.

The manufacturer can buy components capable of carrying out sub-tasks with which he need not be concerned in detail, to be organised so that they jointly meet the required specification for his new end-product. He will mainly be concerned with supervisory programmes, physical containment, and the provision of external transducers, displays, peripheral devices etc., designed to enable the buyer to set up the machine to do the job it was designed to accomplish. The trend is expected to accelerate as VLSI is developed (as described below).

This change has been made possible by the development, from the 1950s onward, of methods for the mass production of interconnected transistors with other circuit elements on a small slice of silicon to provide more uniform and more reliable performance, more components packed into a smaller space, and faster switching speeds with less power and less heat to dissipate. This is the "chip" or Integrated Circuit" (IC).

Figure 2.3 shows a micro-photograph of a chip containing nearly 300,000 memory elements. Far greater magnification of a small part of the chip would be needed to show detail. However this picture of the whole chip - one of the densest yet manufactured - conveys some impression of the complexity. Figure 2.4 shows trays of silicon wafer discs, each containing hundreds of chips with all circuitry and components in place, about to be lowered into an electron beam evaporator in which further metallic deposition processes will take place.

Mass production and uniformity have been achieved by steady improvements in the design of photo-mask techniques, and in the chemical vapour deposition of thin films, ion implantation, and diffusion on silicon wafers (the "planar" technique). Patterns of different materials can be built up on the oxidised silicon surface by deposition through stencil-like masks in a series of separate photo-etching processes. Impurities which change the properties of existing materials can be diffused into areas not protected by masks to a pre-determined depth by heat treatment. The properties of materials can also be changed by ion implantation; this involves the ionisation of an impurity material and the application of a high voltage to accelerate its ions so that they penetrate the surface of the host material to some required depth.

Each circuit, 0.05 inches square or less, is subsequently cut from the wafer and sealed into a small plastic container. Fine wire connections are made between the IC and pins protruding from the container. The pins match mating sockets which themselves contain prongs for soldering on to the copper conductors on a PC board, or the pins are sometimes directly soldered to the board.

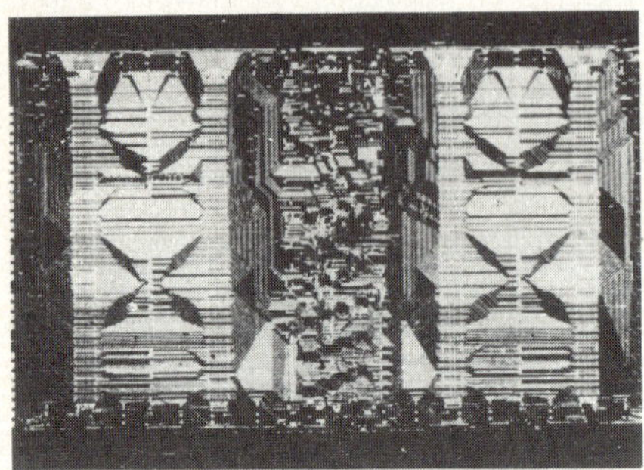

FIGURE 2.3 (ABOVE). HIGH DENSITY
MEMORY CHIP.   (Courtesy of IBM)

FIGURE 2.4 (RIGHT). SILICON CHIP
MANUFACTURE.
(Courtesy of British Telecom)

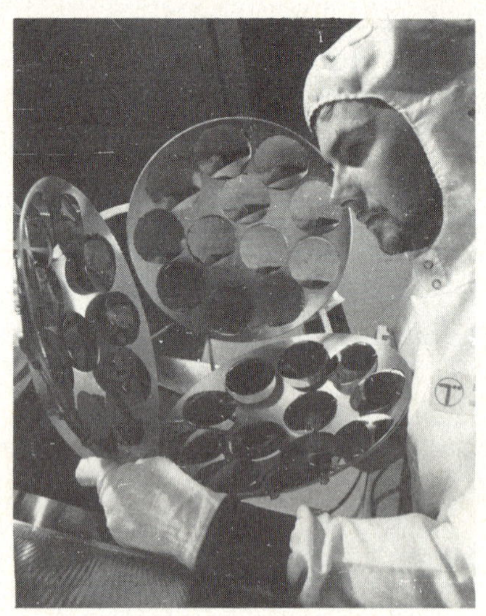

CIRCUIT PERFORMANCE FACTORS: PROCESSING SPEED: DIMENSIONS

Integrated circuits have enabled more and more information to be processed faster at lower cost. Information is represented not by the information-rich words of human communication but by apparently inefficient strings of "bits" - 0's and 1's. The word "information" requires at least 77 bits to be thus represented. Processing speed depends on the rate at which bit-processing circuits can be switched on and off.

Speed contraints

Quite apart from the need to keep down the size, weight, and cost of packages containing thousands of transistors, unwanted electrical capacitance - which absorbs energy and reduces speeds - is proportional to the size and nearness of circuit elements. Capacitance can be reduced by using very small elements connected by very short wires.

We are used to assuming that electricity is conveyed "instantaneously" at about the same speed as light. In terms of today's circuit performance nanosecond (1 ns = one thousand millionth of a second) delays are important. The voltage required to switch a circuit must be generated by a flow of current from the switching source. An electrical current travels about 30 cms along an ideal conductor in 1 ns, but in practice delays are introduced by unwanted capacitance and possibly some inductance, increasing the delay to about 2 ns .

A good analogy of electronic switching is a water tank which must be filled with water before you can take a shower from the sprinkler connected to an outlet at the top of the tank. The way to get a shower quickly when the tank is empty is to fill it up from a hose whose diameter is so large that it offers little resistance to water from the supply which comes rushing through it at a great rate.

In electronic terms the voltage required to switch the circuit has to be raised to the required level (the change in water level) as quickly as possible by a flow of current (the water through the hose) into the circuit's capacitance (the volume of the tank) as shown in Figure 2.5 with its accompanying equation. The major factor limiting the switching speed is the <u>rise time</u> of the voltage to the switching value.

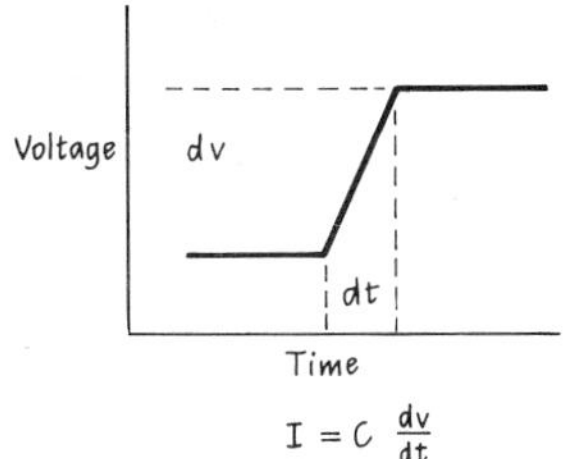

$$I = C \frac{dv}{dt}$$

<u>FIGURE 2.5</u>
<u>PULSE   RISE-TIME</u>

An aproximate figure for the rise time can be calculated from $Tr = EC/I$ where Tr is the rise time in nanoseconds (ns), E is the voltage in volts, C is the capacitance in picofarads (pf) and I, current in milliamps.

Values in a microcomputer circuit could be 2 volts for the switching voltage, 100 pf for the circuit input capacitance (which will include the capacitance of interconnecting wiring), and 1 ma for the current. From the above equation the rise time then works out at a "rather slow" 200 ns.

To repeatedly switch a circuit – for example to move a stream of data from computer storage on to a Cathode Ray Tube (CRT), sufficient time must elapse for the control voltage to switch the circuit, for the circuit to remain switched, and for the circuit to recover ready for the next switching voltage. If these events took, say, 400ns, at least that time interval must elapse between clocking (synchronised switching) impulses. The clocking rate to accommodate successive switching could be no greater than 1 sec/400 ns = 2.5 million times per second or 2.5 <u>Megahertz</u> (MHz). This is not particularly fast by today's standards.

IC TECHNOLOGY

Bipolar and MOS

Until comparatively recently there were two major planar technology products – Bipolar and MOS (Metal Oxide Silicon). The elements of Bipolar transistors in ICs function rather like the original junction transistor. In the MOS an aluminium "Gate" electrode controls the conductivity of the silicon between two p-type regions. The basic MOS is often called The MOS "field effect transistor (FET) because it is the field created near the gate which changes the conductivity of the silicon locally between the "source" and "drain" regions. There are several variations of both types – for instance MOS devices may be called PMOS or NMOS according to the type of silicon used near the gate. In general, bipolar are faster, but most ICs used in computers have been MOS devices because they are easier to manufacture and consume less power.

The first microprocessors used PMOS; the pioneering Intel 8080, still in widespread use and to be described later, uses NMOS. NMOS is widely used in today's microprocessors such as the Intel 8086 and 80286.

CMOS

In 1974 RCA manufactured the Complimentary Metal Oxide Silicon (CMOS) 1802 microprocessor and this technology was introduced by others as improved manufacturing techniques enabled CMOS to be re-considered. Until then this technology, invented in 1962, was thought to be too complex and expensive to make. One driving force was the need for low power in small portable applications like digital watches. In CMOS a current of less than 0.1 microampere (ua) is drawn when one of two complimentary MOS transistors is "on". No current is needed periodically to maintain this condition. Appreciable current flows only for the brief period when the transistors are switched from "on-off" to "off-on".

The voltages in a memory bank of CMOS transistors used to represent either 1's or 0's, do not gradually decay. Data remains stored so long as power is applied unlike memories using earlier transistors which required "refreshing" every few milliseconds by a charging current. CMOS transistors consume little power when used in portable battery-operated equipment. The equipment can be switched off leaving only the memory connected to the battery without losing stored data.

The reduction of the current required by each of the thousands of active circuit elements in an IC is important not only because of much lower drain on the battery in portables, but also because of a substantial reduction in the power dissipated in the form of heat. More elements can be packed into a smaller space without overheating.

HEMT - MESFET and MODFET (GaAs)

Semiconductor development is always accompanied by bigger and better acronyms - here are the latest - High Electron Mobility Transistor, MEtal Semi-conductor Field Effect Transistor, MODulation Doped Field Effect Transistor, and Gallium Arsenide respectively.

Gallium Arsenide devices were demonstrated in the United States in 1978 based on the earlier work of Esaki and Tsu. A number of manufacturers have recently produced experimental circuits, considerable manufacturing problems are being overcome and GaAs is expected to become widely used during 1985. So far most devices have been MESFETs or MODFETs with a source and gate about 4 micrometres apart and a deposited metal gate one micrometre (0.001 mm) wide between them. The acronyms describe different methods of manufacture, superiority being claimed for MODFETs.

GaAs electrons have low mass and high mobility. GaAs devices operating at lower voltages and lower powers than silicon will switch at much higher speeds, and will work over a wider range of temperatures. A GaAs gate switches in about 10 picoseconds with the theoretical potential of being clocked at about eight thousand million times per second (8 GHz) compared to a maximum of about 200 MHz for silicon circuits.

To realise anything like this potential, stray capacitance has to be further reduced by using the shortest thinnest connections. With dimensions down to the micrometre region the state of the manufacturing art is being stretched to its limits.

Charge Coupled Devices (CCD)

A CCD device resembles a long multi-gate MOS transistor. A positive depletion layer is created in the silicon immediately beneath each gate, rather like a well, by applying fixed voltages to the gates. The depth of the layer is proportional to the applied voltage. When a voltage is applied to the first gate the well is filled up or charged according to the applied voltage. This charge can be moved along the semiconductor towards the output end just beneath the surface by pulsing successive gates. A voltage proportional to the charge delivered to the output element will be developed across a series resistor.

Alternatively a set of voltages may be applied to each gate creating a set of charges which may be moved along the device and read out in terms of a voltage across the output resistor.

The ability of the device to store a charge proportional to an applied voltage in a cell, and to preserve the magnitude of the charge or charges as they are moved along and are eventually read out as a voltage, means that it can be used either for analogue or digital storage. The maximum shifting or "clocking " speed of CCDs is about 10 MHz.

CCDs cannot be used for random access storage but they are useful for another purpose. The light sensitive properties of many semi-conductors which is usually not utilised can be used in a CCD device by manufacturing a strip of elements to allow light access to each element. The "wells" are now filled in proportion to the local incident light and the device may be used as a strip of light sensors.

VLSI

Very Large Scale Integration (VLSI) is not material-specific - it is a phrase used to cover methods of producing even greater numbers of circuit elements on one chip - say 250,000 gates with dimensional control down to 0.5 micrometres. In the US a project called the Very High Speed Integrated Circuit (VHSIC) program to try and achieve these goals is in hand for military equipment, no doubt with Japanese-competitive spin-offs also in mind. The program seems to be based on an extension of mature silicon technology rather than on riskier GaAs.

The Intel 80286 commercially available microprocessor embodies 130,000 semiconductor elements on a square chip with sides of little more then 1/4 inch. The un-named CPU used by Hewlett-Packard in their 32 bit microcomputer uses nearly half a million elements on an even smaller chip. An electron beam is used to make the masks required for its manufacture to enable conductors to be spaced 1 micrometre apart with 1/4 micrometre tolerance.

Later in the 1980s the target will probably be raised to one million transistors per chip. It has been suggested that an advance of this kind will require three major ingredients - hierarchy, regularity, and design tool automation. Design hierarchy means splitting up the design into manageable portions which are then joined together in a complete design. Regularity refers to the need to use the same kind of circuit element with the same interface as often as possible. Design tool automation means the computer generation of layouts for standard functions as used in memories, gates, etc.

However VLSI has more profound consequences. It has been suggested that it will bring within reach the possibility of millions of autonomous communicating processing elements operating concurrently in parallel. Architectures and algorithms will become inseparable.

DESIGN AND FUNCTIONS OF COMMONLY USED CIRCUITS
(in alphabetical order)

Circuit developments in mainframe computers continue, although they have, perhaps, been overshadowed by overall design concepts and software. It is of some interest to note that Gene Amdahl, having been responsible for some major IBM designs, moved on to Amdahl and then formed another company Trilogy, Inc., primarily to develop a super-chip using a technique called "wafer scale integration" to out-perform all others in mainframes. The introduction of this chip has been put back to 1987 and Trilogy's stock, issued at $12, stood at $2 after the announcement in June 1984. Sinclair in UK is currently trying to finance production of similar devices.

It remains to be seen whether the Transputer, being developed by Inmos Ltd, can be moved into a viable computer. The transputer is a multi-function chip embodying processing, storage, and communications with its own language, Occam. It is claimed that a parallel processing computer using the transputer, being developed at Imperial College, London, will be introduced before comparable Japanese machines. It is hoped that it will have an operating speed 100 times faster than existing machines.

The remainder of this section wil be mainly about the less esoteric but more widely units commonly used in in microcomputers. For a more detailed treatment of some units see Chapter 3.

Buffer

A buffer is simply a temporary storage device often used between digital devices working at different speeds rather like a tank with water flowing in and out through pipes of different diameters. Its capacity must be adequate to store the largest expected volume of data caused by different input and output data rates.

Cache memory

A cache memory is programmed temporarily to store that information which is most likely to be wanted first. It is relatively small and can be accessed faster than main memory. The art of programming it is to design algorithms which guess what to fetch from main memory, when to bring it into the cache, and when to replace it. One criteria of performance is the "hit ratio" – that is the percentage of cache memory cycles versus the percentage of main memory cycles. For example the net memory cycle time with cache memory in the Texas 99000 is claimed to be 190 ns with a 9:1 hit ratio compared to 330 ns without the cache.

Comparator

A circuit that generates an output voltage when two input voltages reach the same value or when each reaches some pre-determined value. It often embodies some form of multivibrator so that the point of equality is indicated by a regenerative fast transition.

Counter

A circuit which generates a pulse after receiving n input pulses. Thus a counter can also be an exact time _Divider_ - if a decade counter is pulsed once per second it will emit an output pulse once every ten seconds. Counters are used in digital watches and other timers to divide down from some accurate master oscillator, sometimes crystal controlled to ensure stability. The sub-divided impulses are equally accurate. A counter often consists of a string of flip-flops each of which must be triggered before the last generates an output pulse.

Decoder

A decoder is a circuit which executes the function $\log_2 n$ to n. The need for this function is that addresses are carried round computers in 8 bit bytes, or words of n bits, on a single line which must be decoded to the lines 0, 1, 2, 3, 4, 5,....n, which connect to the wanted destinations. For example if there are 8 possible destinations their binary addresses can be carried as a $\log_2 8 = 3$ digit binary number. The 8 binary numbers required are 000 (0), 001 (1), 010 (2)......111(7). Thus a "3 to 8" decoder would have one input line for a 3 digit binary number, and 8 output lines going to 8 different destinations.

A decoder consists of a number of appropriately interconnected gates. One of its most common uses is to decode a memory address to a particular row and column in the array of storage elements.

Gate

A gate is a circuit which produces a binary digit at its output (that is one of two possible voltages) when two or more binary digits are applied to its input. Gates are used for binary logic functions and are rightly called the building bricks of computers. For example a gate with two input terminals which produces a 1 only when a 1 is applied to both inputs is called an AND gate. Several other arrangements are possible and combinations of gates can provide a whole range of calculating and control functions as discussed in Chapter 3.

Current trends are to manufacture arrays of inter-connected gates of the smallest possible size with the fastest possible switching speeds on a chip using the materials and techniques described earlier.

Several integrated circuit arrangements known as Transistor Transistor Logic (TTL), Emitter Coupled Logic (ECL), Diode Transistor Logic (DTL) and Integrated Injection Logic (I^2L) are manufactured using bipolar transistors. Multi-electrode transistors with an input connected to each electrode are sometimes used. In another arrangement Schottky diodes are associated with the transistor to clamp or limit the level of each input voltage. A Schottky diode is characterised by a low voltage drop across its electrodes. High input impedance amplifiers may be included in a gate circuit to reduce the load on preceding circuits with low impedance emitter followers at the output to reduce the effect of loading capacitance.

Memory

Semiconductor Memories can be divided into two major classes - Read Only Memories (ROM) and Random Access Memories (RAM).

ROMs are divisible into three classes according to programming - those programmed irreversibly by the manufacturer (Masked ROMs), those programmable once irreversibly by the user (PROMs), and those which can be erased and re-programmed by the user (EPROMs). "Black Boxes" are commercially available for programming or erasure. The PROM or EPROM is plugged into the box which is connected to a computer by a cable plugging into a standard RS232 port (socket on the machine for peripheral devices).

RAMs are divisible into two classes - Static or Dynamic. A static RAM storage element consists of a flip-flop which stores a 0 or a 1 for as long as the supply voltage is switched on. In a dynamic RAM, a charge or its absence,is held on the leaky capacitance of the gate, usually in an MOS transistor, so the charge has to periodically be renewed or "refreshed".

Developments in memories have been towards increasing the number of elements per chip from around 4K capacity to 16, 32, 64, 256, 512K and 1 Mbyte, each occupying less space and costing less per bit than its predecessor. Manufacturer's "Keep ahead policy" announcements go through curiously diffused processes, rather like their products, which makes it hard to determine whether you can have it now or much later. The late 1984 situation seems to be that 64K RAMs are just coming into use in actual end-products, 256K are in sample production, and 512K and 1 Mbyte are just emerging from the laboratory. In February 1984 Toshiba claimed a six month lead with a 256K static RAM on a 7 x 9 mm (0.28 x 0.75 inch) chip containing a total of 1.6 million circuit elements.

It now costs about $2 per K of dynamic RAM memory when purchasing up to 128K on a ready to use memory board, and about $1 per K to plug in extra chips into the empty sockets provided on the board for expansion.   Memory access times have been substantially reduced - a small bipolar RAM can be accessed in about 40 ns.

If the memory forms part of a microcomputer it will be controlled by the CPU. Signals on the Chip Select/enable (CS) lines and Read/Write (R/W) lines consist of a change of voltage to a high or low value for a specific period of time. A typical memory cycle starts with CS going low enabling the memory to be written or read. For large memories CS may activate a specified part of the memory only. The address of a wanted data byte is then output to the address bus from the CPU as the column and row number of the required storage location. This is followed by one byte of data being written to or read on to the data bus as controlled by the CPU. Finally CS goes high, ending the cycle, and only then can another cycle be initiated. The cycle length has been reduced to less than 200 ns on the fastest currently available microcomputers.

<u>Microprocessor</u>

The term Microprocessor is usually reserved for a single chip Central Processing Unit (CPU). The earliest was the 4004 developed by M.E.Hoff at Intel in 1970. It contained 2000 transistors on one chip and was later developed into the 8080 and the 8080A, the first widely used microcomputer CPU. Its circuit elements and major functions are still used in many of today's microprocessors.

The 8080A is an MOS technology chip internally programmed by code stored in its own read-only memory to perform arithmetic and logical functions. It circulates information internally as 8 bits in parallel on an 8 line bi-directional <u>"Bus"</u>. A bus is simply an interconecting line carrying the same information to or from a number of different circuits. The 8080A contains a number of <u>Registers</u> which are simply small storage units, an <u>Arithmetic Logic Unit (ALU)</u> to perform the operations required by instructions stored in the registers, an <u>Instruction Decoder</u> to decode external program instructions and an <u>Accumulator</u> register temporarily to store the results. More information about the functioning of these circuits is given in Chapter 3.

The 8080A also contains a <u>Multiplexer</u> ("Mux"). An eight line mux is used to connect a selected register to the internal data bus. The Timing and control unit receives timing pulses from the external clock and controls the machine cycles. It also generates signals to control external operations at the right instant.

An 8 bit register can store up to 256 decimal numbers so that when used to indicate an address - say a memory location - the memory could have up to 256 locations. This is too small for many purposes. In the 8080A 16 bit numbers can be represented by using registers in pairs; one out of 2^{16} = 65,636 ("64K") addresses can be located. 16 connections for external addressing are provided so that 16 address bits can be moved in parallel via a 16 line address bus.

Control over the 8080A is exerted by an <u>Instruction Set</u> of over 50 commands or instructions (OP codes), recognised by the instruction decoder, such as ADD (Add contents of register to accumulator) and LDA (Load accumulator from memory). A program consists of a sequence of OP codes each followed by supplementary data which are stored in external memory and called into the CPU when the program is executed. For example LDA 1134H means "Load the accumulator with the contents of memory at the address 1134 hexadecimal". The actual movement and control of data between registers and other elements within the microprocessor after decoding by the instruction decoder is controlled by "microprograms" inherent in the way the circuits are connected together.

Data is processed and conveyed to other parts of a microcomputer in short bursts when all circuits are periodically switched by impulses generated from a master timing clock.

8080A machine cycles are synchronised from clock impulses at about 0.5 us intervals (2 MHz). A clock is an oscillator running at a constant frequency usually determined by a crystal, from which a continuous train of precisely spaced impulses is derived. Some of the more complex instructions may take up to five clock cycles to complete. This does not mean that all activities in a machine controlled by an 8080A are limited to a repetition rate of 0.5 us (500 ns). For example even in vintage 1977 microcomputers a 14 MHz clock oscillator was fitted with dividing circuits to generate impulses at 2 MHz for 8080A timing. The display of characters on the CRT was controlled by a character generator chip to which the 14 MHz clock output was directly connected. This chip stored a character set as dot patterns and was programmed to feed out the dots at 14 MHz (70 ns intervals)) to represent a character on a CRT.

Since the 8080 the major developments have been increases in clock speeds, number of elements per chip, and number of bits per word. Clock speeds have not gone up that much - for example to 5 MHz in the Intel 8086 and up to 8 MHz in the Motorola 68000. The increase in word length means that more information is moved per cycle. 16 bit microprocessors are already being overtaken by 32 bit, although the amount of software available for longer word microprocessors limits the rate of introduction.

The number of instructions in an instruction set have increased, so has the power of instructions. A single instruction replaces several previously separate instructions. In the 16 bit Motorola MC68000 there are two levels of instruction enabling internal microprograms, stored within the chip on a 22K store, to be installed by the manufacturer. With the NCR 32000 32 bit 4 chip microprocessor, external microprogramming is possible enabling mini or mainframe instruction sets to be emulated. Extra sophistication has been introduced by <u>"pipe-lining"</u> meaning that the next instruction is fetched in the same machine cycle used for the execution of the previous one. 32 bit busses with pipelining enable bit transfer rates at 36 Mbytes/sec.

A major benefit of using a longer word is the larger addressing capability. A 32 bit microprocessor, or a 16 bit using two registers, can potentially address 2^{32} storage elements which is over four thousand million. In practice the address range provided is usually up to 16 Mbytes.

The most popular microprocessors fitted in microcomputers available in 1984 were the Intel 8080 series (including the 8085, 8086, 8087, 8088). Next came the Zilog 80, followed some way behind by the The Motorola 68000 and 6800, and the Zilog Z8000. Microprocessor cycle times are 330 ns for the Texas 99000, and 400 ns for the 68000 or 8086. However the actual "performance", "speed", "work done", or "instructions per second" of a microprocessor/memory combination also depend on other things such as instruction efficiency and transmission delays.

<u>Multiplexer</u>

A multi-pole semiconductor switch. A multiplexer or "mux" is used in a microcomputer when one of two or more alternative signal sources require to be connected to a bus. For example it may be that a 16 bit address must be output to the 16 lines of an address bus from any one of several address registers. The mux connects the bus to the required register and also supplies the power to drive the bus capacitance plus the capacitance of the recipient device in order to complete delivery of the signal within the required minimum time interval.

<u>Multivibrator</u>

The multivibrator in some shape or form is one of the most frequently used circuits in computers. The circuit was the subject of intense development and improvement during the 39-45 war at MIT in the US, and at TRE at Malvern and by

F.C. Williams and others at Manchester University in the UK where they were (and are now) known as free running, bistable, and monostable or one-shot multivibrators, Eccles-Jordan circuits, flip-flops and Schmitt triggers. The circuit action developed for valves has been applied to transistors. Most "electronic switches" are based on some kind of multivibrator and so are Gates.

In brief, a multivibrator consists of two valves or transistors coupled to each other by various type of positive regenerative feedback circuit. An input triggering voltage alters the stability of the arrangement and a rapid change of output voltage, voltage step, or impulse is produced. The output voltage may remain at the new level, change continuously between two levels (oscillate) or return to its original level after a time interval determined either by its own circuit components, or when it receives another input trigger. The use of flip-flops in computer circuits is discussed in Chapter 3.

Its important functions are either to <u>switch</u> or control another circuit or to generate a <u>timing</u> voltage. According to its interconnections, circuit values, or triggering arrangements - hence all its different fancy names - it will generate a voltage change - an impulse - at an exact time t1 and a second voltage at a time t2. t2 can follow t1 after a precisely known interval of any required duration. Alternatively it will continuously generate pulses at exact time intervals. <u>Event Timing</u> is all important in digital circuits. An array of multivibrators, some triggered by a master "clock" pulse, and some triggering others can produce as many control or timing pulses as may be needed at whatever intervals or instants may be required.

Operational Amplifier

An operational amplifier is a direct coupled amplifier with negative feedback. The performance of the amplifier is mainly a function of the amount of feedback and the way it is applied. Sometimes an amplifier has a gain of one and is used as a high to low impedance convertor to minimise capacitive effects; a circuit called an "emitter follower" is such an amplifier.

Shift Register

A shift register is a long string of connected flip-flops each of which may be either on or off and so constitute a store. Each FF can have an input and output terminal and can be connected to the next one. All F-F's can be connected to control lines. There are several ways the circuit can be used. For example each F-F's input terminal can receive a succession of digits for storage, and these digits may be shifted along the device to the output terminal by control signals. The shift register has been used as a <u>parallel to serial convertor</u>. Alternatively data can be shifted into the first F-F in the chain and along the register, and when the sequence is stored all digits can be read out simultaneously from the output terminal of each F-F - it has been used as a <u>serial to parallel convertor</u>. Modern shift registers will clock at nanosecond speeds.

Three State Buffer

This circuit is needed when, as is often the case in computer systems, a number of devices required to send or receive information connected to the same data bus are of necessity also connected to each other. At any instant, devices may be at a high or low potential. In the absence of device isolating circuits, devices may be attempting to force the potential of the line in opposite directions. Three state buffers, connected between each device and the common bus, can be set to one of three conditions, high, low, or open (isolate), according to the role of the device. As a result communications on the common line can proceed without conflict.

FURTHER READING

Beynon, J.D.E.
  Radio & Electronic Engineer, 50(5), May 1980, pps 201-204.
    Charge coupled devices: concepts, technology and limitations.
Cannon, Don L.
  Texas Instruments Learning Centre, PO Box 225012, MS-54, Dallas, Texas 75265,
  USA.
    Fundamentals of microcomputer design. 1982.
Clements, Alan.
  Microprocessors & Microsystems, 8(7),September 1984, 324-337.
    The 68000 and its interface.
Eden, Richard C., Livingston, Anthony R., Welch, Bryant M.
  IEEE Spectrum, 20(12), December 1983, pps 30-37.
    Integrated circuits: the case for Gallium Arsenide.
Fullagar, David.
  IEEE Spectrum, 17(12), December 1980, pps 24-27.
    CMOS comes of age.
Gupta, A., Toong, H.D.
  Proc IEEE, 71(11), November 1983, pps 1236-1256.
    Microprocessors - the first twelve years.
Heffer, D.E., King, G.A., Keith, D.C.
  Edward Arnold, London.
    Basic principles and practice of microprocessors. 1981.
Miller, Alan R.
  Byte, November 1984, 143-154.
    Introduction to semiconductors.
Pohm, A.V, Smay, T.A
  Computer, October 1981, pps 93-110.
    Tutorial series 13: Computer memory systems.
Smith, Alan Jay.
  Computing Surveys 14(3), September 1982, pps 474-530.
    Cache Memories.
Zorpette, Glenn.
  IEEE Spectrum 22(1), January 1985, 53-55.
    Microprcessors.

CHAPTER 3. PRINCIPLES OF DIGITAL COMPUTING

INTRODUCTION

Semiconductor manufacture, types, and functions of circuit elements are discussed in Chapter 2 and Microcomputers in Chapter 17 and 18. This chapter overlaps with these three chapters to some extent. It covers basic digital computing with particular reference to microcomputers in information technology - that is with reference to <u>data processing</u> rather than to <u>number crunching</u> (computers were originally mainly used in scientific applications for high speed calculations). Microcomputers in information technology are usually used for data processing, file handling, word processing, etc.

HISTORY

The machines made by a Frenchman, Blaise Pascal in the 1640s are often considered to be the ancestors of digital computing. In one example each gearwheel in an array of coupled gearwheels registering units, tens, hundreds etc., could be rotated by inserting a peg. To carry tens a weighted ratchet was gradually raised as a wheel was rotated from 0 to 9 and then the ratchet dropped on to the next wheel to advance it by one unit. Some years later Leibnitz developed the idea using complex gearwheels in a machine capable of addition, subtraction, and multiplication.

However some would say that Charles Babbage's machines were the true ancestors. Babbage, Professor of Mathematics at Cambridge University, was fascinated by the new technology like many other Victorians. He was involved with Post Office systems, printing, pin-making, and railway trains but soon became absorbed with calculating machines. In 1822, having constructed his three-register Difference Engine which could handle quadratic functions, he obtained a grant for something much more elaborate in order to compute tables to twenty places of decimals (A register is a device for storing the digits of a number).

Support was withdrawn after considerable expenditure and Babbage turned to something yet more ambitious - his Analytical Engine - which was intended to carry out many kinds of calculation, a tremendous advance on the special-purpose Difference Engine. Columns of wheels, gears, and linkages would be used with control rods operated by the holes in punched cards as were used in Jacquard looms, invented some years previously. Results would be output as moulds from which print could be cast. The machine was far ahead of its time and was never built.

Ideas for programming the machine were developed by Ada, Countess of Lovelace, only child of the poet Byron. Babbage's machine and Lady Lovelace's programs were to embody the essential functions of today's computers by having the sections -

A <u>control unit</u> to actuate a sequence of operations.
An <u>input mechanism</u> for feeding in instructions and data.
An <u>output mechanism</u> for delivering results.
A Mill (Babbage's word for the <u>Arithmetic Unit</u>) for performing
operations on numbers.
<u>Stores</u> for retaining data and ongoing results.

Lady Lovelace described in her programming notes ideas which were not realised until a century later. They included the notion of repeating a set of instructions again and again and, at some point, jumping to alternative instructions.

Computer-like machines continued to be developed, notably the Hollerith punched card machines used in the 1890 US census, but it was not until 1944 that the first operating universal calculating machine – the Automatic Sequence Controlled Calculator – was completed by IBM in 1944 to the designs of Aiken of Harvard University. This electro-mechanical machine used registers made out of sets of wheels, received data on punched cards, and read out data on cards or on a typewriter. Very soon afterwards Eckert and Mauchley built an all electronic machine, ENIAC, at the Moore School of Engineering, University of Pennsylvania which contained 18,000 valves and consumed 150 Kilowatts, most of which had to be ducted away as heat. Based on ideas by von Neumann, it was first used in 1946, mainly for calculating shell trajectories.

Obsessive British secrecy (for more see Chapter 27) put paid to any claims that a machine called Colossus may have been the first electronic computer, since its existence was not even admitted until 30 years later. The machine was smaller then Eniac but was used in 1944 at Bletchley Park for breaking coded messages originated on the German Enigma machine. Colossus, of which several versions were built by a team led by Professor Flowers at the old Dollis Hill research laboratories of the Post Office, contained all the basic sections found in modern machines except that it did not run on a stored programme – the programme had to be keyed in.

BASIC OPERATIONS

On-off circuits and binary numbers

Most of the instructions, and many of the operations and results obtained in a computer are achieved by the systematic control of very large numbers of individual inter-connected circuit elements, so that acting like switches, they are either on or off. The system starts to function when a timing pulse is applied simultaneously to all the circuits which then act on information received in order either to stay as they are or to switch to the opposite condition. This new state having been established, the next timing pulse arrives, and once again the circuits re-set according to new instructions, and so on.

In this manner thousands of small processes are set up and then simultaneously executed, a second set of processes are set up and executed, then a third set, etc., at precise intervals of perhaps 0.5 microseconds – that is at the rate of two million different sets of processes per second – until such time as the flow of information to the circuits ceases.

The on-off states represent information in the binary notation. Thus if the low voltage from an "on" circuit signifies a "1", and the high voltage from an "off" circuit signifies a "0", a row of four circuits in on-off-off-on states signifies the binary number 1001. The binary and other numbering systems are described at the end of this chapter.

Floating point numbers

Large numbers are processed using the <u>Scientific Notation</u> as used in many pocket calculators. Thus 7.53×10^{10} means "the number 7.53 with the "point" (radix) shifted 10 points to the right, that is 75,300,000,000. The digits of the number (7.53) are called the <u>Mantissa</u> and its magnitude (10^{10}) the <u>Exponent</u>. When a number using zeros simply to indicate the position of the point is replaced by the mantissa/exponent method of indicating its position, the number is said to be a <u>Floating Point</u> number. Binary numbers can be expressed in this notation, and it is of course these which are actually processed within the computer.

Handling symbols

All symbols are coded so that the computer can process them as binary numbers. The 7-bit ASCII code (given in Chapter 1) is almost universally used as a symbol code. For instance, if the "A" key on a keyboard is pressed, associated circuits will always generate 1000010 - the ASCII code designated for a capital A - and these 7 bits will represent "A" during processing. When an "A" is displayed on the screen it will have been converted by appropriate circuits into a set of bright dots representing an "A" from the code 1000010.

Logic Circuits

Most forms of digital processing are carried out within networks of inter-connected logic circuits. The usual form of a logic or _gate_ circuit accepts one, two, or sometimes more, electrical impulses representing 0's and/or 1's and outputs a 1 or a 0 impulse according to the signals applied to the input.

The basic electrical arrangement of a gate often takes the form of a diode clamp-transistor combination connected to a fast transistor switching pair. The first part of the circuit is designed to generate a pulse only when the potential representing the desired combination of input 0's and/or 1's is reached. At that instant the pulse applied to the transistor pair causes it to switch very rapidly generating the required 0 or 1 output pulse.

The switching action often involves positive feedback typical of biased multivibrator circuits, which makes the transition proceed at nanosecond speeds, once initiated.

The basic types of logic functions and the symbols used to represent them are shown in Table 3.1

An extraordinary range of processes can be carried out simultaneously at high speed by interconnecting tens, hundreds, or thousands of gates. Huge numbers of them with all connections in place are laid down in integrated circuits of a few square millimetres.

All that the circuits do (except the inverter) is generate a single 0 or a single 1 in a particular order from the four possible input combinations of 00, 01, 10, or 11; these are the most frequently used arrangements but not the only ones possible. In microcomputers the switching action of a huge block of circuits is enabled at the beginning of each machine cycle - often about every 400 nanoseconds - and then a sequence of switching events occurs. These events are completed before the end of the machine sequence and stored as described below in readiness for a further set of processes to be performed during the next

INPUTS	OUTPUTS	SYMBOL
AND		
0 0	0	
0 1	0	
1 0	0	
1 1	1	
NAND (Not AND)		
0 0	1	
0 1	1	
1 0	1	
1 1	0	
OR		
0 0	0	
0 1	1	
1 0	1	
1 1	1	
NOR		
0 0	1	
0 1	0	
1 0	0	
1 1	0	
XOR (Exclusive OR)		
0 0	0	
0 1	1	
1 0	1	
1 0	0	
NOT (Invert)		
0	1	
1	0	

TABLE 3.1 COMBINATIONAL LOGIC

cycle.

Combinational Logic circuit operations

The way in which logic circuits can be connected together to perform an actual job of work is shown in Figure 3.1. In this example it is required that a 1 be generated only when the two input symbols match. This could be a very useful arrangement.

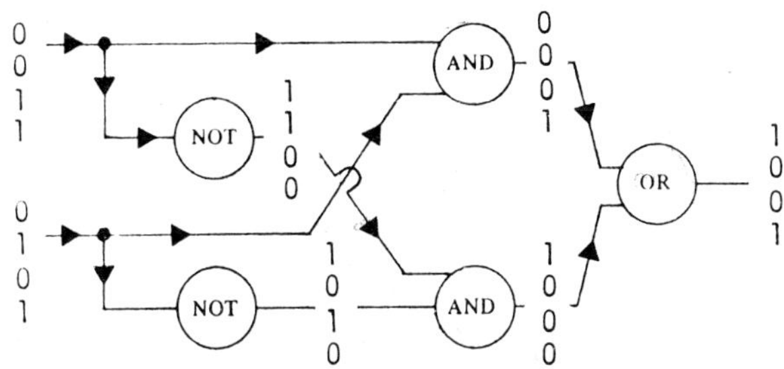

FIGURE 3.1
COMBINATIONAL LOGIC CIRCUIT

For example if the computer was asked to find records dated 1981, and a series of records carrying the years were passed through the circuits, the machine could be programmed to "try the second digit" whenever the first digit of the record's year was a 1. It would then check for a match against 9 and if found, check the next digit of the year for a match, and so on.

In practice, of course, the machine would have to match each **binary** digit representing 1981. Figure 3.1 shows, by following through the action of each circuit for its inputs, how this particular network will only output a 1 when the inputs match - that is they must be 1 1 or 0 0.. Notice that the arrangement is really a continuation of the series shown in Table 3.1. It produces the opposite result to XOR which is sometimes called "Not EQUal" or NEQ because a 1 is output only when the input symbols are **not** the same.

Output Symbol	TTL	ECL	CMOS
1	>+2v	>+0.2v	>+3.5v
0	<+0.8v	>-0.2v	<+1.5v

TABLE 3.2 VOLTAGE OUTPUT
OF LOGIC CIRCUITS

Several different kinds of component arrangements are used in logic circuits, the most popular being Transistor Transistor Logic (TTL), Emitter Coupled Logic and CMOS - terms which are design-implicit and imply information about the pulse voltage output levels as shown in Table 3.2. The benefit of using CMOS (See Chapter 2) to provide a bigger safety margin between the 1 and 0 potentials is obvious.

The **combinational** circuits described so far generate output impulses only as a response to some pattern of input pulses. When the input ceases so does the output, and no memory circuits have yet been mentioned to store the information implicit in the state of the circuits. That information must be available and ready for the ongoing processes in the next machine cycle, as mentioned in the introductory paragraph above.

Sequential Logic

Sequential logic requires both combinational logic **and** storage circuits. Information can then not only be stored ready to be acted upon but can also be the result of the order in which a sequence of processes was carried out. One type of simple circuit to store a 0 or 1 is called a D-type bistable flip-flop. The circuit consists of a two-transistor back-coupled biased multivibrator. A pulse applied to either transistor causes the on-off states to change over to off-on, the output voltage level indicating a 0 or 1. One input is connected to a logic circuit and the flip-flop stores its 0 or 1. This is read out during the next machine cycle, and the flip-flop is reset by a pulse applied to the other input ready to store the next symbol from the logic circuit.

<u>Arithmetic</u>

The rules for binary addition are 0 + 0 = 0, 0 + 1 = 1, and 1 + 1 = 1 with 1 to carry. Thus the calculation 3 + 6 is performed as follows:-

```
        Carry >   1 1
                  0 1 1  (3)
            +     1 1 0  (6)
                  1 0 0 1  (9)
```

For subtraction the rules are 0 - 0 = 0, 0 - 1 = 1 (borrow 1), 1 - 0 = 1, and 1 - 1 = 0. Borrowing is a nuisance in binary subtraction. There is a convenient way out by using the "2's complement" method. The rule is add one to the inverse of the number to be subtracted and then add, ignoring the last carry. Thus 25-16 is performed:-

```
                  1 0 0 0 0  (16)
                  0 1 1 1 1  (Inverse)
                          1  (Add one)
                  1 0 0 0 0
                  1 1 0 0 1  (Add 25)
   ignore carry   0 1 0 0 1  (9)
```

Multiplication and division can be performed using the same rules and procedures as for decimal numbers. It is of interest to note that AND logic, to be discussed shortly, in not to be confused with arithmetical "and"; in an AND logic circuit, 0 AND 1 generates 0. Circuits for AND and other logic are used to perform operations in Boolean algebra. However AND logic, <u>in conjunction with</u> other logic circuits under the control of simple programs, is in fact used to perform arithmetical operations.

<u>DIGITAL PROCESSING SYSTEMS - THE CENTRAL PROCESSING UNIT (CPU)</u>

The three major functions in a digital processing system are:-

1. The reception, processing and delivery of data under program control to and from specifically addressed storage, processing, and other units.

2. The step by step manipulation of data by arithmetical and logical operations to achieve the results demanded by the program.

3. Methods of handling information input and output to external devices most of which provide the means for humans to input data, interact with the machine, and view or read processed data.

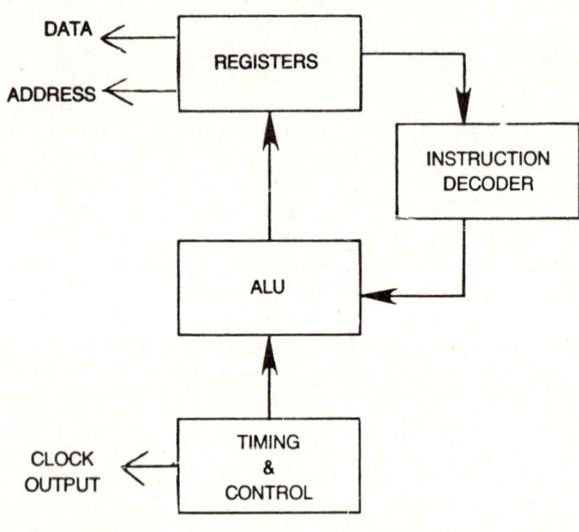

<u>FIGURE 3.3. THE BASIC CPU</u>

We are mainly concerned with paragraph 2 in this part of the Chapter.

The basic CPU is shown in Figure 3.3. A <u>program</u>,stored in the memory, proceeds by as many fetch-execute instructions as may be needed during clocked machine cycles as explained in Chapter 17.

The CPU delivers and receives information to and from a <u>memory</u> or memories (of which there may be several types and sizes in one machine) and communication <u>ports</u> with plugs and sockets connecting to peripheral units such as keyboards,printers, displays, magnetic tape or disk storage. The information is usually sent or received through multiple wires called <u>Busses</u>. "Data" covers both program details and information to be processed which have been placed in memory via one of the ports, perhaps from disk storage.

The <u>multiplexers</u> are electronic switches which connect 8, 16, 32, etc lines (depending on the length of machine words) to the particular units which are required to be connected at some instant in the program.

The functions of the major CPU units shown in Figure 3.2 are as follows:-

<u>Clock, Timing, and Control</u>

The clock continuously generates impulses accurately spaced at, say, 250, 167, or 100 nanoseconds, assuming that its frequency is either 4, 6, or 10 MHz respectively. Some processors embody clocks running at up to 40MHz. The control unit routes these impulses directly, or accurately divided (to provide, say 1 microsecond impulses), to all parts of the machine so that operations are driven periodically and synchronously during the execution of a program. Instructions for doing this are received from the Instruction Decoder.

If the clock frequency is sub-divided to provide, say, a 5 microsecond machine cycle, then a large number of events will be triggered every 5 us under program control. Several series of processes, synchronised by faster impulses from the control unit - say at 200 nanoseconds - each composed of a large number of relatively simple steps - may be triggered during the 5 us period. There may be one or more overlapping processes proceeding at the same instant in different parts of the machine. Thus at time 0 a process is started to be completed 5 us later, at time 0 + 500 ns, another process is started to be completed at 5.5 us from start, another is started at 0 + 2 us, to complete 7 us from start, etc. Moreover some processes may take many machine cycles to complete - for instance a process triggered at time 0 might not complete until 0 + 50 us.

In short, the various processes are triggered at precise instants by timing pulses derived from the clock. Suppliers often provide diagrams showing the time relationships, that is the delays, between pulses which periodically trigger certain routine functions and may "open an electronic gate" for a fixed period. <u>LATCH</u> is the term usually used to describe an electronic gate (not a logic gate) - that is a circuit which generates a gating waveform of fixed duration when periodically triggered by a pulse derived from the clock. For example a one microsecond LATCH could allow a fixed number of bits to be clocked out from RAM - that is the read out would be controlled by fast clock pulses - to form a character on the CRT. The constant length of the LATCH ensures that the same number of bits are always read out for every character.

<u>MEMEN</u> - another term used to describe a memory event - could allow a fixed time for READING from or WRITING into RAM. <u>CAS</u> would be a pulse sent to all RAM columns so that a column can only be written or read at the correct instant in a machine cycle. <u>RAS</u> would perform the same function from RAM rows.

<u>Intruction Decoder and Register</u>

The instruction decoder usually contains its own memory in which the <u>Opcodes</u> comprising the <u>Instruction Set</u> for controlling the CPU, permanently reside. Each code can initiate a complete process - for example "SBC" in the Z80 processor instruction set means "subtract contents of register from contents of accumulator with borrow"; "LD A 1223H" means "load the contents of memory at address 1223H into the Accumulator". The Instruction Register stores the instruction, which it has received from memory under program control, while it is executed. Since the instruction may include one or more data addresses (e.g. the "1223H" above) making it too long to be stored in the Instruction register, more than one memory ready operation may be required.

Program Counter and Address Register

This unit contains several registers and is responsible for storing the memory address of the next instruction and of sub-routine instructions which will have been routed to it from memory under program control. It will send the instruction to the Instruction Decoder. The register/counter can be incremented by one each cycle enabling the address which it stores to access successive locations in memory for new instructions. This unit also contains registers for storing sub-routine addresses.

Data Address Registers

Contains the addresses in memory for data, and registers for the temporary storage of data bytes routed to it from memory under program control.

Arithmetic Logic Unit

The ALU contains the programmable logic circuits for arithmetical and logical operations and accumulator registers for storing temporary results. It is within the ALU that the actual processing of data occurs. The ALU contains registers for holding frequently used addresses or data for immediate access, and a number of flip-flops for parity, sign, "carry" etc.

PROGRAMS

Low Level languages

Computer programs used to be written in machine code, that is in binary digits - an extremely time consuming and error-prone process. Later a kind of building block method called Assembly Language was introduced where the programmer could use symbols (Mnemonics) like SUB for Subtract and LD for Load. Every time a Source Code like this is used the computer automatically translates it into binary digit Object Code for direct use by the machine using a program called an Assembler.

Assembly Language is an enormous improvement but program design and writing is still very laborious. An Assembly program consists of a series of single machine instructions, address assignments, and housekeeping details. However a Listing File, which is a line by line record of how the Assembler handled the program, may be printed, and Assembly Language overcomes the need for a laborious re-write if a change is required; instructions can be deleted or added rather easily.

An Assembly Language is peculiar to the particular processor for which it was written and is the means of putting together the Instruction Codes to form a program. A program consists of lines of code each typically consisting of several fields. For example the first field may be a Label which is simply a name by which the code line is identified, the second an Opcode - that is an instruction from the instruction set - and the third an Operand - that is a quantity or function upon which the operation is to be performed.

For example in "A1 MOV R2,R6" , A1 is the label, MOV is the OPcode for

"Move the contents of register....to register....", and R2,R6 are the identities of the registers.

High Level languages

Two popular examples, Basic, and Pascal will be discussed. These are machine-independent lang- uages which are easier to recognise by any program- mer than the processor- specific instructions in Assembly language.   In such languages English- like statements are auto- matically translated into a large number of machine instructions   so   that where, say, ten lines of code would be needed in Assembly, one suffices in High Level. Thus although programmes will be much faster to write,   they will also be more rest- rictive   since   direct access   to   all   the features of the machine, as is provided by an Assembly language,   is denied.

Interpreters and Compilers -   software packages used to trans- late the High Level lang- uage into the language of the machine in question - are discussed in Chapter 18. Although the actual lanquage used in a High Level language may   be machine independent, the means by which it   is translated for use is not - each type of   machine requires its own trans- lation program.

BASIC, an acronym for Beginners All pur- pose Symbolic Instruction Code, was developed for the purpose described by its title by Kemeny and Kurtz at Dartmouth Col- lege in the USA in 1964.

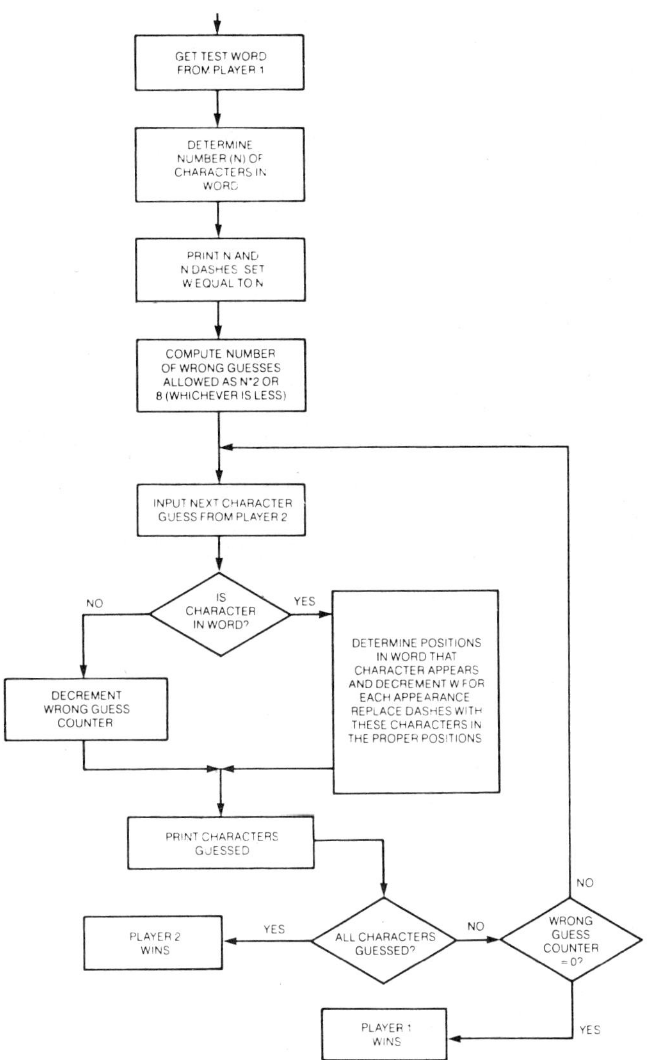

<u>FIGURE 3.4. FLOWCHART FOR "HANGMAN"</u>
(Courtesy Texas Instruments)

Microsoft provided a version in 1975 for the 8080 CPU. Later as MBASIC, and as various other improved versions, it became far more widely used than just as a beginners software. By 1980 it was being used in over 300,000 microcomputers of 55 different makes with several different operating systems.

Figure 3.4 shows the <u>Flowchart</u> which describes the <u>Algorithms</u> for the computer game "Hangman", and Figure 3.5 part of the BASIC program for this game. A flowchart is used to map out the main ideas to be contained in the program in a logical way as a series of "modules" so that the program can be written in inter-related stages. An Algorithm is simply a description of the steps needed in a problem to produce the desired result. The BASIC program shows how quite complicated requirements can be expressed in short BASIC statements.

<u>PASCAL</u>, named after the French mathematician Blaise Pascal was developed by Nicholas Wirth in 1970 but did not start to be used in microcomputers until about 1978 when compilers were introduced by the University of California (San Diego). Pascal is diplacing BASIC as the "serious programmers" language because having the advantage of a well defined standard it is reliable and maintainable and is considered to have a better structure than BASIC.

Another advantage of PASCAL is the provision for the creation of data types with listing of variables. For example Sunday, Monday,....Saturday, could be a list under the Type "Day" with the variables today, yesterday, tomorrow, enabling program statements like "<u>If</u> yesterday = Monday <u>then</u> tomorrow = Wednesday".

```
  5 REM SET UP VARIABLE STORAGE FOR WORD GUESS GAME
 10 DIM C(5), D(5), A(5), N(2), DS(2), GS(10), PS(2), P(1)
 20 $DS(0) = " - " : $D(0) = " - "
 25 REM INPUT PLAY WORD FROM PLAYER #1
 30 INPUT "WORD?"; $C(0)
 35 REM DETERMINE AND DISPLAY THE NUMBER OF CHARACTERS IN THE WORD
 40 K = 1
 50 $N(0) = $C(0,K),1
 60 IF $N(0) = $PS(0) THEN GOTO 90
 70 K = K + 1 : $D(0) = $D(0) + $DS(0)
 80 GOTO 50
 90 K = K - 1
100 $A(0) = $D(0),K
110 PRINT K
120 PRINT $A(0)
125 REM DETERMINE NUMBER OF WRONG GUESSES ALLOWED
130 G = 2*K : W = K : L = 0
140 IF G>8 THEN G = 8
150 PRINT "YOU HAVE"; G ; "GUESSES LEFT"
155 REM GET NEXT CHARACTER GUESS FROM PLAYER #2
160 INPUT "NEXT GUESS?"; $P(0)
165 REM CALL SUBROUTINE THAT DETERMINES IF CHARACTER IS IN WORD
170 GOSUB 600
180 PRINT $A(0)
185 REM UPDATE THE NUMBER OF WRONG GUESSES AND CHARACTERS GUESSED
190 IF L = 0 THEN $GS(0) = $P(0)
200 IF L>0 THEN $GS(0) = $GS(0) + $P(0)
210 L = L + 1
220 PRINT "YOU HAVE TRIED THE LETTERS:"
230 PRINT $GS(0)
240 IF J = 0 THEN GOTO 270
250 IF W = 0 THEN GOTO 310
260 GOTO 150
270 G = G + 1
280 IF G>0 THEN GOTO 150
290 PRINT "YOU LOSE"
300 STOP
310 PRINT "YOU WIN" :STOP
```

a.Program

```
600 J = 0
610 FOR I = 1 TO K
620 $N(0) = $C(0;I), 1
630 IF $N(0)<>$P(0) THEN GOTO 690
640 $D(0) = $A(0)
650 $D(0;I) = $P(0)
660 $D(0) = $D(0) + $A(0;I + 1)
670 $A(0) = $D(0)
680 W = W - 1 ; J = J + 1
690 NEXT I
700 RETURN
```

<u>FIGURE 3.5. PART OF BASIC PROGRAM FOR "HANGMAN"</u>
(Courtesy Texas Instruments)

<u>REFERENCE INFORMATION - NUMBERING SYSTEMS</u>

A conversion table for numbering systems is provided in Chapter 1.

<u>Binary</u>

It is the use of the binary numbering system (to the base 2, that is using only the symbols 1 or 0) instead of a system to the base 10 (the everyday decimal system), that enables basically simple computer circuits to handle information. The decimal number 135 is composed as follows:-

$$
\begin{aligned}
5 \times 10^0 &= 5 \times 1 &=& 5 \\
3 \times 10^1 &= 3 \times 10 &=& 30 \\
1 \times 10^2 &= 1 \times 100 &=& \underline{100} \\
& & & \underline{135}
\end{aligned}
$$

The same number in the binary notation, 10000111, is composed as:-

$$
\begin{aligned}
1 \times 2^0 &= 1 \times 1 &=& 1 \\
1 \times 2^1 &= 1 \times 2 &=& 2 \\
1 \times 2^2 &= 1 \times 4 &=& 4 \\
0 \times 2^3 &= 0 \times 8 &=& 0 \\
0 \times 2^4 &= 0 \times 16 &=& 0 \\
0 \times 2^5 &= 0 \times 32 &=& 0 \\
0 \times 2^6 &= 0 \times 64 &=& 0 \\
1 \times 2^7 &= 1 \times 128 &=& \underline{128} \\
& & & \underline{135}
\end{aligned}
$$

Thus we could store binary numbers up to 255 (11111111) if we had eight circuits, each capable of being switched to the "on" or "off" state. (256 is 100000000). Because of the great difference in the "on" or "off" output voltages held in associated storage circuits, the digits can be "read" without errors at a later time.

<u>Hexadecimal</u>

Programmers and computer buffs need to know about the Hexadecimal system, but most other people do not, although it may useful to know the meaning of the word.

The length of the number 256 in binary, while being no problem to a computer, is already becoming inconveniently long for human handling, and numbers - for example to specify addresses in a large store - have to be keyed and used by programmers. A numbering system to the base 16 - the Hexadecimal ("Hex") system - is often used instead of binary for convenience, and most machines are able automatically to translate a Hex number into Binary which is the system that the machine can work with. Hex uses the numbers 0 to 9 as in the decimal system, but then A to F for the numbers 10 to 16. 135 in Hex is 87 which is much more convenient to handle. It is composed as follows:-

$$
\begin{aligned}
7 \times 16^0 &= 7 \times 1 &=& 7 \text{ decimal} &=& 7 \text{ Hex} \\
8 \times 16^1 &= 8 \times 16 &=& \underline{128} \text{ decimal} &=& \underline{8} \text{ Hex} \\
& & & \underline{135} & & \underline{87}
\end{aligned}
$$

The decimal number 65536, which is 2^{16}, is a popular byte-storage capacity for microcomputer memories. It is a number in the series of rounded off numbers corresponding to 2^{14}, 2^{15}, 2^{16} etc., usually referred to as "14K", "32K", "64K", etc. 65536 is 16^4, so the Hex symbols for it corresponding to 1×16^4 and 0×16^3, 0×16^2, 0×16^1, and 0×16^0, is 10000. This is much more convenient than the binary 1000000000000000.

To make the system, I hope, quite clear, here is the composition of the Hex number E60B:-

$$
\begin{array}{llllll}
E(15) & \times\ 16^3 & = 15 \times & 4096 & = 61440 & \text{decimal} \\
6(6) & \times\ 16^2 & = 6 \times & 256 & = 1536 & .. \\
0(0) & \times\ 16^1 & = 0 \times & 16   & = 0   & .. \\
B(11) & \times\ 16^0 & = 11 \times & 1   & = \underline{11} & .. \\
      &   &   &   & 62987 &
\end{array}
$$

Binary Coded Decimal

This system, which again will only be of passing interest to many readers, is used when fixed length binary codes are needed. Each decimal digit in a number is coded as a four bit binary number. Thus, since the binary codes for the digits in the number 709 are 0111, 0000, and 1001, BCD for 709 is simply 0111 0000 1001.

FURTHER READING

Cannon, Don L.
  Texas Instruments learning Center, Dallas, Texas. 1982.
    Fundamentals of microcomputer design.
Coles, Ray.
  Newnes Technical Books, Butterworth, London. 1979.
    Microprocessors for hobbyists.
Heffer D.E., King, G.A., Keith D.C.
  Edward Arnold, 1981.
    Basic principles and practice of microprocessors.
Vincent, Geoff; Gill,Jim.
  Texas Instruments Learning Centre, Dallas, Texas. 1981.
    Software developmemt.

CHAPTER 4. INPUT AND OUTPUT TECHNOLOGY

INPUTS

"Inputs" as used here means the alternative ways by which characters, images, etc., may be changed into machine-readable or electrically transmissible form, then usually called "data". The devices used include Keyboards, Optical Character Recognition (OCR) machines, Image Processors, etc. "Information" fed into a machine may, of course, already be in the form of "data" - that is a conversion process may have taken place at some remote point and data is being fed into the machine via a telecommunications link. Voice recognition is discussed separately in Chapter 11.

keyboards and Tablets

A series of experiments have been reported in which the conventional QWERTY typewriter keyboard gave better results compared with other possible arrangements including an alphabetically arranged keyboard. QWERTY was the result of some Victorian ergonomics in the 1870s, the most frequently used keys being clustered near the centre. It seems that an alphabetic keyboard may need a human memory search to locate the position of a key and then a visual search to find it, while QWERTY usually only requires a small area visual search.

Keyboards are available for non-roman characters including Japanese Kanji characters, and "Audioline" keyboards have been developed which produce audible feedback for the blind. Several other forms, of hand generated non-QWERTY devices are in use - in fact keyboard alternatives seem to be a peculiarly British development.

The Microwriter, invented by a film director, owes something to the Palantype machine - a small machine used: in US courts with a limited number of keys to type a form of shorthand. The Microwriter, available from the company of that name, is a hand held battery-operated five key device plus a control key, with on board storage for up to about 8,000 characters. A 12 character LED display is incorporated which scrolls to the left as typing proceeds.

Characters are typed using a key combination code which has to be learned. Key combinations also control functions like backspace, delete, skip, etc. End of line "CR" is not needed. The machine is connected to a printer when you return to the office.

At least three devices are available for digitising written characters, made by Micropad, Image Data (Data Tablet) and CTS Recognition-(Telepad) in the UK.

With Micropad, hand printed writing is entered using an ordinary ballpoint pen on to a pressure sensitive surface. A writing grid for 11 x 28 or 17 x 32 rows and columns is provided. The output is ASCII code delivered at up to 1200 baud, derived from microprocessor controlled recognition circuits.

Image Data also provide a pressure sensitive surface, but working on a different principle with a special pen which plugs into the device. A4 paper is normally used for hand printing, but in the graphics mode it also recognises drawings. On either side of the pad a touch-table keyboard is provided for left or right handed people. Output is ASCII code up to 9600 baud.

The CTS Telepad accepts paper of any size up to foolscap. It recognises handprint or graphics, but uses a special pen which generates a low

frequency signal whose co-ordinates are recognised by a backing surface
detector. An associated LED line-display is provided so the user can verify
that input has been correctly recognised. Output is ASCII code up to 9600
baud.

<u>OCR and other symbol recognising machines</u>

At a more sophisticated level, the most advanced Optical Character
Recognition (OCR) machines can now convert almost any clear printed information
into digital data. The Kurzweil KDEM data entry machine can read printed or
typed font or mixture of fonts from 6 to 24 point. It scans and reads at
rates from 50 to 100 characters per second. Standard OCR machines read faster
but permit only one preferred font. Several can be read in more expensive
machines.

Since hand printing can be used both on the tablet-type machines
described above and on documents later to be read by OCR machines, the <u>kind</u>
of print which can be written fastest and still be recognised by the machine is
of some interest. Tests are reported in which groups of people were employed to
try out a range of printing styles, but were constrained to shape the
characters to various degrees. Obviously totally unconstrained printing is the
easiest and fastest, but it is also most likely to cause recognition errors.

Very recently a more sophisticated type of symbol recognising machine has
been developed of which two commercially available models are known to me. The
first, from Palantir in the US, contains an optical scanner (of a kind similar to
that used for facsimile (see Chapter 9). A digital bit-map of the page is
generated by the scanner at 300 dots per inch. Each character is then put
through a recognition process which extracts its topological features and
compares it against a reference stored directory of characters. The machine is
said to be capable of reading good quality print in any normal font with or
without serifs from 6 to 32 point (See Chapter 1 for type face sizes) at a rate
of 10 seconds per page with an error rate of 1 in 300,000. Output is in ASCII
code. 10 to 1 data compression is used to help to make this speed possible.

In principle the system is no different from advanced OCR machines except
that advantage has been taken of the processing capacity and speed now available
in consequence of developments in Integrated Circuits by including far more
complex recognition algorithms.

A second machine, from Optiram in the UK, takes this principle further. I
had considerable doubts about the claims made for it until I tried it out for
myself. One way of inputting data to it is via a document put through a Group 3
facsimile machine - the Optiram can work from Group 3 fax code. This machine
pre-processes the image data to provide better images, and if the image includes
hand-written script, to separate the characters. Feature extraction follows for
comparison with a stored directory of characters, as in the Palantir, but this is
followed by comparison with a word directory.

The machine works at between 180 and 400 characters/sec according to the
variability of the material being input. It is able to store samples of
particular handwriting for better comparision with incoming material from the
same user, and dictionaries in a variety of languages. My writing is not good and
I provided a document containing handwritten script and some German 6 point text
with umlauts, etc. It reproduced it without an error although no sample of my
writing nor a German dictionary was in its store, nor did the machine possess any
other information about what kind of text to expect. The umlaut, being part of
standard ASCII, was recognised and correctly reproduced on the printer connected
to the machine.

This is the first universal symbol reader that I am aware of. It requires a

relatively powerful minicomputer and is only available as a processing service
-the software cannot be purchased.

OUTPUTS: DISPLAYS

One of the earliest attempts to present large displays continues in use
today in the form of banks of electric light bulbs along which
advertising text or news appears to run. There used to be one on a building in
Milan near the cathedral - a monster composed of thousands of bulbs
capable of displaying a low definition animated TV-like picture as well as text.
These signs used to be (and some still are) operated by loops or rolls of
punched paper tape somewhat like the long extinct Pianola mechanical piano. At
one time all rolls or tape had to come from the supplier but now it's done by a
keyboard, microprocessor, and add-on banks of LEDs in three foot lengths. Type a
message of up to 32,000 characters if you like, and off it will go on its
travels to small LEDs for exhibition adverts, or on big ones on buildings.

Most electrically conveyed information has, until recently, been
displayed on the ubiquitous Cathode Ray Tube. Now the CRT has been joined by
devices which favourably compete with it in specialised areas. Progress in
displays is of great importance because the development of both small,
reliable, portable displays, and large high capacity ones, remove a major barrier
in the progression towards a display which compares favourably with the printed
page.

Back in 1945, Vannevar Bush envisaged a universal information storage
and retrieval device which he named Memex. It included "a translucent
screen on which material can be projected for convenient reading...he (the
user) has several projection positions, hence he can leave one item in
position while he calls up another...he can add marginal notes...adding or
erasing quite readily". Associated indexing would enable him to "...build a trail
with items in adjacent viewing positions".

Pursuing Bush's ideas further, such a machine should have a very large
display of ordered broad information about the area of interest from which
specific selections can be made using the rapid scanning and
information-processing power of the eye-brain. The contrast between the
"window-size" represented by present-generation CRTs and print-on-paper is very
marked. What is needed is a screen displaying at least 50,000 characters at a
time so that the viewer can scan and absorb what is required from a mass of
material.

Cathode Ray Tubes

Display devices fall into several groups - Cathode Ray Tubes where the
symbols are traced out by controlling the co-ordinates of a beam of
electrons, large area devices, often of matrix construction, capable of
displaying a relatively large number of individually controllable symbols,
for example Plasma panels, and small area devices, such as Light Emitting
Diodes (LED), Liquid Crystal Devices (LCD), or Gas Discharge Tubes, which can be
assembled to form symbols or banks of symbols.

The cathode ray tube has existed in more or less its present form
for at least 50 years, and although it continues to be improved in detail, the
limits must have been nearly reached in reliability, resolution, optimum size
and shape, brightness, economics of manufacture etc. Considerable research is
in progress to find substitutes which perform better in a particular respect or
in all respects but the CRT still reins supreme for general purpose use. Years of
accumulated manufacturing experience with high volume production have resulted in
a time-tested more or less suitable inexpensive device. Colour tubes are a major
example of what can be achieved in high precision mass production.

The factors which control the appearance of information displayed on a CRT terminal have been discussed in detail by McArthur. They include character spacing, row spacing, and the shape of characters which, by evolution, seem to have become generally preferred. 25 rows of 80 characters are about right for a 15" (diagonal) CRT. Other factors of importance include CRT spot size and defocusing; scan line spacing; dots per character cell; number of characters on screen; line and field frequency, flicker and interlacing; physical parameters; distortion and image stability; contrast and reflection from the surface and choice of phosphor. if you want the high quality resulting from the proper choice with, in many cases, the higher cost of those choices, then you will get them by paying more for the terminal.

The things which should be included on a high quality terminal are —

A relatively flat screen.
Cursive scan — that is the CRT beam traces the character
outline. (only on very expensive terminals).
At least 7 x 9 dots per character cell.
Almost no flicker, high brightness, high contrast, and
very little reflection from the glass surface.
No wobble (produced by stray magnetic fields from the
mains).
Refresh rate (that is frequency at which the whole field
is repeated in order for it to appear permanent) greater
than 52 Hz.
A type P31 phosphor. The phosphor is a powder deposited on
the inner face of the tube; it emits light when excited by
the electron beam.

One method of providing a very large display is to use projection CRTs but inconveniently high voltages and high beam currents are needed to give adequate brightness, tube life is relatively short, and the cost is high. An alternative is to generate light with a xenon lamp and project it via a liquid crystal light valve controlled by a high resolution CRT. A much better performance is obtained by separating the control function and the light source.

Plasma panels

A typical experimental A.C. Plasma panel has been described by Pinsky. It displays 51 rows of 85 characters per row using a 5 x 7 matrix. The characters are displayed on a flat, thin, distortion-free panel, flicker free with a high contrast ratio. Reliability is greater than a CRT, with much better resistance to shock and vibration.

Driving electronics to control the huge number of elements in these devices has always been a problem. Here, the number of components has been reduced by the extensive use of integrated circuits. Texas Instruments has designed a family of peripheral IC's to support the 32 gate plasma drivers. The new IC's would allow an OEM to buy plasma panels and build a plasma equivalent to a CRT monitor. What we are not told is what the cost is likely to be, nor whether, in the event of mass production, there is a prospect of a CRT replacement at the right price.

LEDs and LCDs

LEDs are very inefficient (99.9% heat energy loss) although improvements are being steadily introduced. LCD production was 33 million units in 1977, 150M in 1980 and is expected to rise to 250M in 1985, calculators consuming about half of the production. Almost uniquely in electronics, production is dominated by European companies which also almost totally control the supply of chemicals. Device assembly, particularly for watches, is increasingly carried out in South East Asia.

Large displays based on very small display elements are being widely researched. Currently available devices typically consist of a 48 x 480 dot display panel suitable for graphics or characters which should be capable of being improved in order to display 12 lines of 80 characters, each formed from 5 x 9 dots. Improvements in these displays with larger screens and colour are imminent.

Special display applications

A team at Sussex University developed a system for the high quality display of quickly up-dateable maps in colour. A small computer handles two separate kinds of data - that describing geographical features, such as contour lines, and that specifying symbols and text overlaid on the features. Although it was developed for military purposes, the principle has been used for other applications.

The problem here is to design software which is simple to use and can handle large amounts of data. For example each of 262,000 pixels (picture elements) is required to be displayed in any one out of 4096 different colours. To manage this problem a microprocessor controlled "colour palette" is used which limits the range of colours to 256 at any one time. Furthermore a novel form of run length encoding is employed for data compression. Large areas of background colour are infrequently changed, so new information is not required about those areas every time the picture is changed. Instead of communicating a new colour "specification" for each pixel, a short code is used to specify, for instance, that the next 125 elements in the row should be red.

Evidently the tremendous advances in storage, communication, and processing technology are insufficient to cope with man's thirst for more and more information. Compression techniques - to minimise storage space, expensive bandwidth for data transmission, and system costs - continue to be developed.

These factors are inefficiently handled in domestic television systems. Television has to be able to cope with bursts of information requiring a data transmission rate equivalent to many megabits per second for very short periods of time. Such bursts occur when the picture contains fine detail in motion - for instance a horse-racing shot in which a jockey wearing a coloured chequered cap crosses the screen. For most of the time the information needed to reproduce entirely satisfactory TV pictures requires only a fraction of the bandwidth needed for the moving jockey. However the fact that today's electronics could enable the whole domestic TV system to be replaced by something much less costly is still of academic interest. The present system is too firmly entrenched and the overall cost of obsolescing it would be enormous. Even so, experimental work is in progress.

The information/bandwidth/information capacity equation is nowhere better demonstrated than by experiments carried out in the US by Sperling. All the necessary information was conveyed using American Sign Language (The "deaf and dumb alphabet") on a television channel with a bandwidth of only 20 KHz. This suggests the possibility of a small transmitting camera connected to a telephone line, with a line interfaced to a domestic TV receiver. The images would be viewed by a deaf person in a "box" in a corner of the screen. This idea has just been further developed at Essex University in the UK where they are planning to develop the "viewphone" along similar lines.

OUTPUTS: PRINTERS AND PLOTTERS

Introduction

Many types of printers have become available in recent years stimulated by microcomputer requirements. There is a wide price range from about $200 up to $2000, continuing upwards for special facilities. Perhaps the buyer's first considerations will be price and whether fully formed or dot-matrix type is required, primarily because dot-matrix is rarely acceptable for publication and most people would probably regard it as unsuitable for correspondence.

Another consideration is noise - impact printers are usually noisier, sometimes a lot noisier, than non-impact printers. Next, there is speed, specified in bits, bauds, characters, or lines per second, or even in lines per minute. For most users a printing speed of 10 characters per second or 30 ch./sec., will be adequate, or possibly up to 120 ch/sec., corresponding to the data transmission speeds of 110, 300 and 1200 bauds respectively - available from most microcomputer ports. It is within this range that the majority of recently developed inexpensive printers lie.

Reliability and the availability of quick maintenance are also important although printers seem to be relatively reliable devices. The best way to find out about the reliability of a contemplated purchase is, of course, to try to find someone else who uses it.

At the bottom end of the price range come non-impact (and quiet) thermal or electrosensitive printers operating at 10 or 20 ch./sec, selling for around $200. A good daisy wheel impact printer producing fully formed type at 30 ch./sec., starts at about $1000. The mark-ups on imported printers are as high as with microcomputers. In England a good imported daisy wheel printer cost over £1000 even when the exchange rate was 2 dollars to the pound. Other considerations include a built-in power supply so that the printer is ready to operate on the local A.C. mains voltage; paper thickness control for copies; type of ribbon, and its ease of replacement, life and cost; type face interchangeability and cost of print-head; availability of feed for continuous stationery, and cost of paper, particularly if special paper is needed.

Printers within the price/performance range of most microcomputer users include Thermal and Electrosensitive Non-Impact Matrix printers, and Impact printers of the Dot Matrix, Daisy Wheel and Drum Impact types. Inkjet printers are now within the price range of micro users and doubtless other new types of printer soon will be.

Pen Plotters produce clear line drawings with smooth diagonal lines and are still widely used particularly for good colour. Addressable ink-filled pens are used and they produce excellent results but are very slow for complex images. Small flat bed plotters are available for less than $1000 and prices increase with size - huge plotters are available.

Non-impact thermal printers

In one type of thermal non-impact dot matrix printer the print head contains a vertical strip of 8 very small heating elements. The head is in contact with chemically treated paper and is stepped across the paper to the required position. The dots required for, say, the first vertical strip of a character 8 dots high are printed together by switching on the required elements. The head steps to position the next vertical strip and so on. Thus to form an "H", all print head elements would be switched on to form the left upright, the horizontal part would be formed by stepping successively with one element on, and the character would be completed with all elements on for the right upright.

In thermal printers the heating elements are mounted on a composite substrate designed to cool down the elements quickly ready for the next print, and the heating current determines the dot size. Some types of thermal printer will work at up to 120 ch./sec and are quiet and inexpensive (uncased miniature versions around $200). The special paper needed is a disadvantage.

Non-impact electrosensitive printers

Electrosensitive non-impact dot matrix printers work on a similar principle except that the print elements are small electrodes, and aluminium coated paper is used. A dot is formed by passing current from electrode to paper which causes a discolouration. These printers can print slightly faster than Thermals, are quiet and inexpensive (uncased miniature versions around $150), but the paper is quite expensive.

Non-impact inkjet printers

FIGURE 4.1.THE HEWLETT PACKARD THINKJET PRINTER

The first designs of inkjet printers used a continuous spray of ink broken up into small electrically charged drops directed towards the paper. The drops then came under the deflecting influence of a controllable deflector plate field in an arrangement resembling electron deflection control in a cathode ray tube. Drops were allowed to reach the paper to form characters or were deflected away to a reservoir.

More recently ink-on-demand printers have been introduced like the HP Thinkjet shown in Figure 4.1. Some examples of the type it reproduces are shown in Figure 4.2. The machine was introduced in 1984 at a UK price of £399 with disposable print-heads at £5 each. The printhead consists of 12 vertically

Compressed (142 characters/line)

Normal (80 characters/line)

Expanded compressed (71 characters/line)

Expanded (40 characters/line

FIGURE 4.2. HP THINKET TYPE EXAMPLES

aranged ink nozzles which are stepped along the paper to produce matrices of 12 x 11 characters. When the back of a nozzle is heated an ink bubble grows almost instantaneously and fires a drop of ink in the front

of the nozzle at the paper. Ink sufficient for 500 pages of text is stored in a small collapsible bladder within the printhead. Pressure from the bladder refills the nozzles and the printhead is replaced when the ink runs out. The machine prints very quietly at 150 characters per second.

Non-impact laser printers

Laser printers are hardly within reach of microcomputer users at present, but who would have thought that the price of inkjet printers would have dropped so rapidly? Perhaps lasers will follow. Laser printers are probably the most versatile printing machines available today. They are capable of a quality virtually as good as that created by solid type. Honeywell, Xerox, and IBM produced laser printers in the 1970s and most, if not all, use a controlled extremely fine laser beam to write on to charged paper with a rotating-mirror for line scanning. The image is fixed by a Xerographic-like process.

The flexibility of laser printers was clearly demonstrated by the Xerox 2700 laser printer working with the Xerox Star workstation. The trend is evident from the introduction in 1984 of the Imagen 8/300 laser printer in the US at $10,000 and shortly afterwards the Hewlett Packard Laserjet printer at $3495. The HP machine prints with a resolution equivalent to 300 x 300 dots per inch at 8 pages per minute and the whole of the disposable print unit comprising rotating drum assembly, toner and developer is replaced when the chemicals run out.

Both the above machines were made possible by the introduction by Canon in 1984 of a complete laser printing system with electrical interface costing little more than $1000 in production quantities to Original Equipment Manufacturers (OEMs) and operating at about 500 characters per second.

Impact printers: introduction

Impact printers, except the dot matrix, use variations of the principle of pressing the complete shape of a character against plain paper via a ribbon. The dot matrix impact printer is the least expensive and most widely used. Prices are in the range $300-1000 and the operating principle is similar to the thermal printer except that a strip of extendible print needles are used instead of heating elements. A vertical line of dots is printed according to which needles project from the head and are pressed against the ribbon. The needles are "fired" to produce the required pattern as the head steps across the paper.

Other impact printers discussed below produce fully formed characters.

Impact drum printers

A drum printer contains a row of hammers, corresponding to the position of a line of characters, with a complete character set embossed round the circumference of a steel drum opposite each hammer. A line of characters is printed by rotating the drum to the first character to be printed by the first character set. The first hammer then presses the paper on to the drum via a ribbon. The drum then rotates to present the second character required from the second character set and the second hammer fires, and so on along the line. Drum printers seem to be on the way out.

Impact cylinder printers

In cylinder printers a vertically rotatable moveable cylinder traverses the paper. The cylinder has characters embossed round its surface in rings. To print, the cylinder stops in the required position, rotates to present one character from each ring to the ribbon, and is then raised or lowered to bring the ring containing a particular character into position. The cylinder then presses against the ribbon and paper.

Impact daisy wheel printers

The daisy wheel printer is perhaps the most successful of the impact types. Each embossed character is mounted at the end of one of a series of spokes projecting from a central hub. The assembly rotates until the required character is opposite a hammer which then pushes the flexible spoke against the ribbon and paper.

Impact band printers

A band printer is rather like a drum printer. A plastic or metal band carrying embossed characters rotates horizontally and a bank of hammers strikes the paper against the band via a ribbon at the appropriate instant. Band printers are the most popular fast impact printers, operating at over 1500 lines per minute, but prices start at around $8000. The IBM 4248 band printer prints at 3600 lines per minute.

Train and Chain printers

These printers are variations of the drum and band printer. The characters are on individual metal slugs which slide round a track.

PRINTERS: NEW DEVELOPMENTS

Developments in more sophisticated printers, plotters, and graphic printers continue. One trend is to add "intelligence" by incorporating microprocessors in the printer itself with storage for functions like the setting up of form layouts, logo printing, etc.

Colour printers

Colour printers are not particularly new but it is only recently that prices have dropped to make them attractive - low enough for them to be considered for use with a micro. Small plotters for line drawings with colour are another alternative.

Colour printing is achieved by combining red green and blue inks. Appropriate combinations result in the selective absorption of incident light, the reflected light being of the required colour. Most of the types of printer described in this chapter have been adapted for colour printing by filtering out each primary colour and printing three superimposed primary colour images.

Since information about the primary colours is already available in colour raster terminals (which closely resemble the display section of colour television sets) the filtering required for printers has often already been done. Inkjet and impact colour printers are available at from $700 upwards. The Colourjet inkjet colour printer for microcomputers is available in the UK for £500.

Thin film magnetic printer

The Ferix company introduced a new type of printer in late 1984 using 128 thin film heads in its type 800 printer, operating at 10 pages per minute and selling to OEMs at $2500. The heads generate a local field which passes through the paper and is retained on a drum. The image is fixed as in photocopiers.

The unique features of this printer are the structure of the heads on a strip 0.5 inches wide which moves across the paper providing a 240 x 240 dot resolution, and the ability of the machine to produce copies from only one image. The magnetic drum retains the image enabling up to 14 copies of it to be printed.

The Fujitsu M3071 integrated printer

This machine indicates another undoubted trend, also discussed in Chapter 9, and that is reprographics using converged technology. The machine is a combined printer/copier for reproducing optical or digitised images. It sells for under $8000 to OEMs.

The machine accepts image or character data from a computer into its controller memory. Information scanned out from the memory modulates a semiconductor laser diode with the light deflected by a rotating scanning mirror, the image being held on a drum, and reproduced as in a photocopier. Resolution is 300 dots per inch.

For document copying the machine uses the same drum and photocopying-type reproduction, but the document to be copied is held on a sliding tray and illuminated by a halogen lamp. Alternatively reflected light from the halogen lamp can be read by a CCD scanner which digitises the image and despatches it in 6 seconds to a remote receiver via a telecoms link. The reverse process is used to receive images fax-style.

This is the kind of multi-purpose machine which will be used in offices to replace functions currently executed by different technologies and machines, more conveniently and presumably at a considerably lower cost.

FURTHER READING

Evans, Peter W.
  Program 17(3), 160-171, July 1983.
    Barcodes, readers, and printers for library applications.
Gavaldon, Edward A.
  Laser Focus & Electro-optics, October 1984, pps 120-126.
    The electronic printing systems market.
McArthur, I.D.
  In Proc. Electronic Displays Conference. London 1981. Network, Buckingham,
  England 1981.
      Birds, Bs, and CRTs.
Morozumi, Shinju; Oguchi, Kouichi et al.
  Optical Engineering 23(3), May/June 1984, 241-246.
    Latest developments in liquid crystal television displays.
Oakley, D.
  Displays, October 1984, 229-234.
    Raster graphics display technology: a review.
Ohya, Jun: Tokunaga, Yukio.
  J. Imaging Technol. 10(2), 57-63, April 1984.
    Grey scale printing on plain paper using thermal ink transfer imaging.
Pinsky, D.D
  In Proc. Electronic Displays Conference. London 1981. Network, Buckingham,
  England 1981.
    Plasma display panels.
Sperling, George.
  Science 210(4771), November 1980, 797-799.
    Bandwidth requirements for video transmission of American Sign Language and
    finger spelling.
 Warren, Carl.
  Mini-micro systems, July 1984, 163-178.
    Graphics software schemes enhance peripheral interfacing.
Watkins, Harry S; Moore, John S.
  IEEE Spectrum 21(7), July 1984, 26-37.
    A survey of colour graphics printing.
Willis, P.J.
  Displays, July 1983, 147-151.
    High fidelity pictures for digitizing tablets.

CHAPTER 5. TELECOMMUNICATIONS AND INFORMATION TRANSMISSION PART 1: HISTORY, PRINCIPLES, AND METHODS

"The initiator has the enmity of all who would profit by
the preservation of old institutions and merely lukewarm
defenders in those who would gain by the new ones"
Machiavelli (The Prince, 1513)

HISTORY

Although William Watson demonstrated electrical transmission using an electrostatic source in 1747, Wheatstone in England and Morse in the United States implemented the first practical telegraph system nearly one hundred years later. It took Samuel Morse several years to convince the US government that his ideas were worth supporting. It is not clear whether it was Morse who used the famous test phrase "What hath God wrought?" in 1843 when he completed the Washington-Baltimore telegraph circuit; some say Marconi used the phrase when he first spanned the Atlantic by radio from Poldhu, Cornwall, early in the next century; maybe they both used it.

Events contemporary with the above developments include the first arrest made as a result of the then new technology. It was made in Baltimore (1844) half an hour after the receipt of telegraphed information. The first radio arrest was made in 1910 when, to his total surprise, the murderer Crippen was caught as he stepped off the Southampton-New York boat to what he thought was complete safety.

The first transatlantic telegraph cable was laid in 1866. It took 67 minutes to transmit a 90 word message from Queen Victoria to President Buchanan. The price was about seven shillings per word. In the unlikely event of a bill being sent to the Queen it would have been for over £600 at todays's prices.

Following Bell's patent case victory in the Supreme Court in 1888 American Bell became the "Bell System" private telephone monopoly with AT&T as the holding company and R&D and manufacturing carried out by Bell Laboratories and Western Electric respectively. Bell Labs employ 22,000 people, half of them graduates, centred at Murray Hill, New Jersey; they count seven Nobelists amongst them and operate with a $1.6 billion research budget. The organisation was split up following the legislation of the 80s described in Chapter 25.

Private companies provided telephone services in England until 1912 when they were taken over by the Post Office (except for the system at Hull, Yorkshire). The same pattern was followed world-wide and telecommunications is a state monopoly in many countries today. There are strong pressures to change this situation and there have been substantial changes in the United States and the UK mainly to permit the introduction of competing new services by entrepreneurial companies prepared to move quickly and take risks. There are few signs of "deregulation" in other countries as yet.

CONSTRAINTS AND MEDIA

Analogue and digital signalling

For many years the telephone system - using electrical power varying in proportion with the human voice - has been, and still is, the most widely used long distance method of communication. However amplifiers have to be used at intervals along telephone cables to compensate for losses. Electrical noise, present in all circuits, is amplified each time with the signals. For this reason voice and data signals are digitised when possible - information is

conveyed as periodic relatively large sudden pulses of voltage which can be
regenerated. Noise voltages, small by comparison, are not cumulated.   There
are also a number of other reasons for digitisation to be discussed later.

Transmission rate – bauds, bits, and bandwidth

     Signalling may be carried out by using a key to connect or disconnect, say,
a 32 volt battery to the line. We will assume that 32 is the maximum
voltage that the line can withstand. There is no risk that electrical noise
voltages of, say, 0.5 volt will be mistaken for a "mark". If the sender
holds the key down for 1 second, releases it for one second, and so on, he is
said to be signalling at a rate of 1 Baud – that is one signalling element
per second.

     Say the sender is able to connect a battery to the line for one second,
immediately connect a battery of a different voltage for the next second, and so
on. A code could be devised so that a 1 volt battery could indicate an A, 2
volts a B, etc., easily providing for the whole alphabet within the 32 volts
permitted maximum. Signalling at one baud, the sender can now transmit any one
of 32 different symbols at an information rate of log2 x 32 = 5 bits per second

     A communication channel possesses capacitance and inductance and
if the signalling rate is increased there comes a time when these
characteristics affect the shape of the pulses; they become distorted and
elongated and errors occur because of inter-symbol interference. The transmission
speed is related to the frequency response of the channel. The early work on
this topic was done by Nyquist who showed, back in 1928, that the maximum
signalling rate achievable over a communication line of W Hz bandwidth is 2W
distinguishable signalling elements per second. In other words, at least in
theory, for every 1 Hz of bandwidth, 2 bauds or 2 or more bits per second ("1"or
"mark" and "0" or"space") is the maximum that can be transmitted.

     Note that the bit rate corresponds to the baud rate only when there is no
recourse to additional coding. The earlier example above showed how at a
signalling rate of 1 baud the information rate could be 5 bps.

Noise

     In the single battery example the receiver could not fail to detect the
difference between 0 and 32 volts in the presence of 0.5 volts of noise,
but with additional coding it was required to detect 1 volt differences at that
noise level – a possible, but harder task. If an attempt was made further to
increase the signalling rate – say by arranging 0.5 volt levels – then it
would not be possible to differentiate betwen signals and noise.

     If you use a code and the noise is not severe, a 2000 Hz channel capable of
transmitting signals at 4000 bauds might be able to carry, say, 3 bits per
signalling element, which would be 12000 bps. So far I have been talking about
theoretical maximum rates. The gains brought about by coding have not been so
great in practice but information rates over noisy channels such as telephone
lines have steadily improved by using better equipment and multi-state
signalling.

Channel capacity: trade-offs

     When using a communication channel, best "value for money" is obtained when
the maximum possible amount of information is being passed along it. We have
already noted the limitations in the battery system – the maximum permitted
power and the noise level, and also the bandwidth limitations.

These constraints were first expressed in 1948 by Shannon as follows:

$$C = W \log_2 (1 + S/N)$$

where C is the maximum number of bits per second receivable through a communication channel with an arbitrarily small number of errors, W the bandwidth in Hz, and S and N are the average signal and noise powers respectively. This equation provides a performance yardstick for all communication channels. C is a theoretical maximum which can be approached but never reached. Noise is a natural phenomena and power levels are dictated by channel design and cost. The design of systems to push the maximum amount of information through a given bandwidth, and the selection of a media where wideband channels are available then becomes all important in a world where communication traffic is constantly increasing.

From the above equation it is obvious that to maintain a constant rate (C), the bandwidth (W) can be increased and the signal to noise ratio (S/N) reduced (or vice versa) provided their product remains constant. Trade-offs in these parameters according to circumstances are an important factor in data transmission system design. For example a single frame in a television transmission which is transmitted in 1/30th sec. (US standards) at normal scanning rates can be transmitted along a telephone line by slowing down the scanning rate so that the frame takes 60 secs to transmit; the component frequencies then lie within the bandwidth of the telephone channel.

<u>Bandwidth compression</u>

The incentive to use compression systems may be illustrated by discussing an A4 page in a journal which carries about 2000 characters. Once the text is keyed this could be transmitted as 2000 bytes of an 8-bit code. The information in this form would take about 13 seconds to transmit at 1200 bps. For facsimile transmission the page has to be considered in terms of an area of 600 square centimetres transmitted as bits when the page is scanned strip-wise. Each strip has to be narrow enough, and its length has to be sub-divided into small enough parts in order to resolve and transmit as much fine detail as may be required. For good quality about 2 Mbits per page must be resolved which would take about 28 minutes to transmit at 1200 bps.

The transmission rate required for a digitised colour television picture (UK standards) is about 120 Mbit/sec, so again there is a strong incentive to compress.

There are many ways of compressing text, graphics, or TV pictures. Run Length Coding is one well known method; it is based on the fact that many images consist of areas containing no change in information - for instance white space in a page of text, or blue sky in a TV picture. One bit is generated per picture element scanned in a normal television system whatever its information content, but in a Run Length Coding scheme a code is generated according to the length of the strip of the unchanged picture elements.

Examples of run length coding are to be found in the so-called CCITT Standard Modified Huffman Code (SMHC) used in facsimile image coding as described by Mitchell. This method is also used for compressing television pictures, described, together with other methods used for TV compression, as explained by Camana. The transmission of images of a person sending American Sign Language along a 20 KHz channel was mentioned in Chapter 4.

The frequency spectrum

The comunication of nearly all information is accomplished via physical changes in the media between a source and the eye or the ear of the recipient.

It may be necessary to trans-
duce the information (e.g. with an electro-optical transducer) to change electrical into optical signals at some point or change its frequency (e.g from audio frequencies into higher radio frequencies). You will note from Figure 5.1 (for more details see Chapter 1) that the first decade marked on the left of the spectrum runs from 3 to 30 Hz, a bandwidth of 27 Hz. The last decade on the right - the part within which lies visible light - is marked with the wavelength in Angstrom Units (1 Au = 10^{-10} metres) because of the

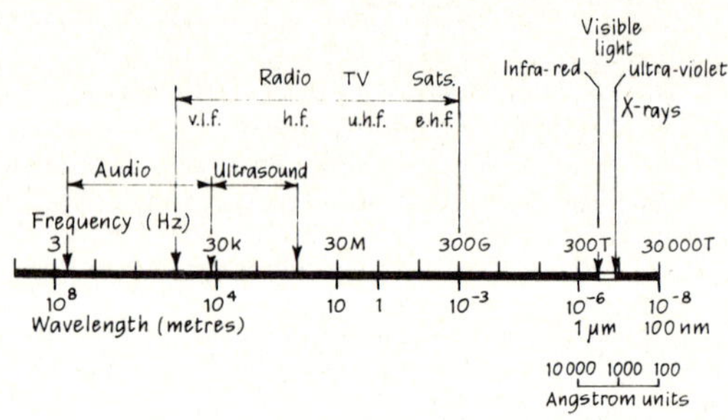

<u>FIGURE 5.1. THE FREQUENCY SPECTRUM</u>

unwieldiness of the figure for frequency. Visible light lies in the decade between 300,000 and 3 million GHz, a bandwidth of about 2,270,000,000,000,000 Hz. It should be remembered that Frequency = Velocity/Wavelength where the frequency is in KHz, the velocity is 300,000 metres (186,000 miles) per second, and the wavelength is in metres.

Whatever the nature of the information or of the transmission media, amounts of information are measured in bits, so the quest for bandwidth inevitably means a greater utilisation of areas towards the right of the diagram. Quite apart from the availability of bandwidth, radiated energy is subject to different effects from the environment according to its wavelength, or there may be engineering considerations which influence the choice - for example the effect of ionised layers surrounding the earth on radio waves, the effect of water particles at SHF (Ku band) in satellite communications, and dispersion and absorption in glass fibres.

METHODS OF TRANSMITTING DATA

Baseband digital signalling

The simplest method of transmitting on or off pulses is called baseband signalling - for instance by connecting a battery to a cable via a switch, sending "ons" or "offs", and observing a voltmeter at the other end. In practice impulses are generated and received by specialised equipment.

An ideal multi-purpose communication system would be one where impulses corresponding to voice, key depressions, computer output etc., were actually generated in the microphone, keyboard, or computer and conveyed by baseband signalling. A device called a Codec (coder-decoder) built into a telephone, with a SLIC (Subscriber Line Interface Circuit) enables this to be done for voice. Manufacture of these transformerless semiconductor devices has been made possible by further advances in integrated circuit technology.

Baseband signalling can be and is used for data transmission provided a simple pair of wires unconnected to any other equipment is available between two points - as could be arranged within a building or between buildings in an enclosed site. It is a cheap, satisfactory, and simple solution; directly generated digital data is exchanged between, say, terminals and a computer. But the frequency components of baseband signalling impulses extend from 0 Hz (direct current) upwards. Any pair of wires longer than about one hundred yards possesses properties of resistance, capacitance and inductance in a large enough degree to affect changing electrical voltages or currents. The faster the change and the longer the line the more pronounced the effect – energy is absorbed in the invisible but real circuits made up of the channel's distributed electrical properties.

If either wideband cables, such as coaxial cables, or repeaters to regenerate the signal, or a combination of both are used, baseband signalling can be carried out over long distances.

<u>Modulation</u>

Telephone network channels of one kind or another, designed for analogue (voice) transmission, are still the main highways used for data transmission. The international switched telephone network has a bandwidth of about 300-3000 Hz; speaking into the microphone simply generates a current fluctuating in proportion to changes in the voice.

<u>Modulation</u> as used for data transmission in analogue channels is a process whereby some property of a steady "carrier" waveform is varied in proportion to a signal carrying information such as a baseband signal. The frequency of the carrier waveform lies within the passband of the transmission channel. Amplitude, frequency, or phase modulation may be used. A carrier wave is shown in Figure 5.2 and diagrams of the appearance of the waveform for each method of modulation follow. These methods of modulation are simply noted. This is sufficient for the occasional reference to them which may be required here.

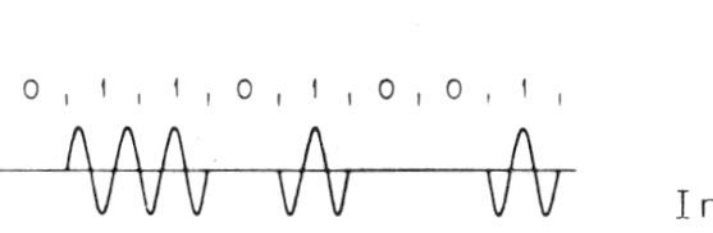

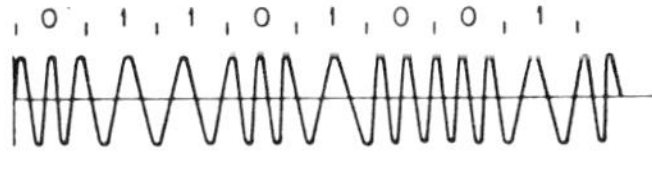

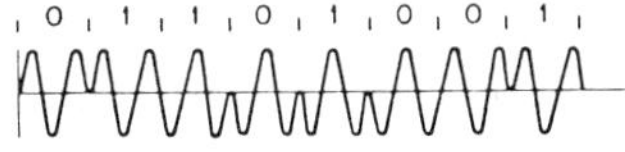

<u>FIGURE 5.2.   FORMS OF MODULATION</u>

The need for using a modulated signal occurs because telephone channels cannot convey frequency components below about 300 Hz, but can carry the information in a baseband signal which modulates a higher carrier frequency. Secondly, in analogue channels of wider bandwidth, several carrier waveforms with frequencies spaced across the passband can be used, each being modulated by a different baseband waveform. A series of bandpass filters, each allowing only the frequency band containing a particular carrier to pass can be used to ensure separation. In this way one circuit can be used to carry a number of information channels.

One widely used method for data transmission over the telephone network called "frequency shift keying" is to signal with two carrier waves of different frequencies, both well within the passband They could be heard as two audible tones. One or other is switched on to signal either a 0 or a 1. Two filters, tuned to the two frequencies, are used at the receiver which detects the presence or absence of the carriera at the outputs.

PRACTICAL DATA TRANSMISSION

modems and terminals

A modem (modulator-demodulator) changes data fed into it, often in binary code, into a form suitable for transmission along a particular type of communication channel - for example as two tones. It also changes the signals received from the channel back into the form of the original data. When the Public Switched Telephone Network (PSTN) is used it is connected directly to it. In most countries these modems must be connected by the telephone authority. Sometimes they are available only from that authority.

An acoustic coupler is a relatively inexpensive portable modem which is not directly connected to the telephone line; the inter-connection is made by pushing the telephone handset into two receptacles made to fit the microphone and earphone. A cable from the coupler is plugged into the terminal. The coupler converts data impulses from the terminal into a tone which is sent down the line via the microphone. Tones received from the earphone are converted into data impulses and passed to the terminal. Because an acoustic coupler is relatively simple it is less able to cope with the adverse conditions sometimes experienced on long distance lines.

A terminal is a device for displaying and converting data fed into it (for instance from a keyboard) into a form suitable for electrical transmission, or for receiving data and displaying it in human-readable form. The "display" part of the terminal may be a printer (e.g. a teletype machine), or a Cathode Ray Tube (CRT in which case the terminal is often referred to as a Visual Display Unit VDU).

Data is transmitted in the form of electrical "on" or "off", "mark" or "space" or "1" or "0" impulses. Information is conveyed by sending separated binary coded groups of impulses or "bits". For example if a group contained 4 bits, each of which can be either on or off, there are 16 possible combinations enabling 16 different symbols to be transmitted. To provide enough codes for all the symbols needed in practice, an 8 bit code called a "byte" is usually used. 7 of the bits provide for 128 different symbols - letters, numerals, punctuation, etc., - and the eighth, called a "parity" bit, has a special purpose to be described later. Each time a key on the keyboard is depressed an 8 bit code is generated.

To decode a message the receiving device obviously has to know the code and so standard codes are used for international signalling. The best known is the ASCII (American Standard Code for Information Exchange) 7 bit plus parity bit code giving 128 combinations for alpha-numeric characters, punctuation and control signals. The code is the US version of the ISO (International Standards Organisation) code. EBCDIC (Extended Binary Coded Decimal Interchange Code), is another 8 bit code, usually used in IBM equipment. For more details see Chapter 1.

With the advent of databases accessible on line, and later, microcomputers, the widespread use of acoustic coupler modems, which could be rented from manufacturers far more cheaply than PTT modems, and which are adequate for many requirements, were grudgingly tolerated outside the US by the PTTs in some countries. Until there was a need to provide compact TV sets, with decoders and a modem included, at the lowest possible price to encourage Prestel useage, modems were not permitted within a TV receiver in the UK. This rule was soon abolished by British Telecom when the practice became in their interest, but, in general, modems in Europe have been far more expensive than in the US, where more liberal conditions encouraged an industry which is now extremely competitive.

A modem can be purchased in the US for $100, and a auto- dialling/auto answer modem for around $250. Texas Instruments offer a modem chip for $30 to form the heart of simple plug-in modem-on-a-PC board. Devices like the Hayes Micromodem 100 have been available for some time. This modem comes on a board ready to plug into the S-100 standard microcomputer socket within a machine, includes programmable auto-dialling and answering, and may be directly connected to the telephone system.

Until 1984 the only auto-dialling modem available from a UK manufacturer came in a separate box from Case and cost £695. Following the privatisation of British Telecom, price reductions and alternative offerings have appeared. At higher speeds special modulation techniques and several bits per baud are used in order to send information at a faster rate within the same bandwidth. 9600 bps modems are now available for use on the PSTN, and these employ adaptive equalising - that is circuit elements in the modem are used to improve the effective characteristics of the line. Special modems are used for the very much higher speeds possible in wider bandwidth channels - for example for satellite circuits.

It ought to be a simple matter to connect a modem to a terminal or microcomputer using the cable and plugs and sockets provided. The functions of the interconnecting wires within the cable and the pin numbers on the plugs are covered by standards. Users might reasonably expect that at least this area would be straight forward. It is not. Most manufacturers omit many of the connections, and leads may be reversed.

Terminal or computer ports for communications - which as far as most users are concerned means a socket at the back - usually operate with serial data. Bits follow each other along the same wire. Parallel ports may be provided, for instance for inter-conection with a Printer. In this case the bits in a byte may be transmitted simultaneously along 8 wires.

The flow of data has to be controlled by special signals between terminal or computer and modem. A number of extra connections in addition to the data connection are needed - usually provided within a 25 pin plug. Control signals must be interpreted by the remote machine; for instance a signal must be sent to the remote person in order to light a bulb or display a message to tell the person that transmission has begun, has been interrupted, or has ended. Consequently Standards have been agreed so that the signals/pins on the plug in your machine match those on a modem, and control signals are routed to the right place at the remote end and are not simply treated as normal text.

It's as well to check whether a particular modem will plug in to your machine. There is more than one standard. The major standards are the 20 milliampere (ma) current loop, CCITT, and Electronics Industry Association (EIA). (It is unlikely that you will meet the current loop). Bell Telephone led in this field and a number of CCITT standards enabling inter-continental data transmission to be carried on, are compatible or nearly compatible with the American EIA standards. The most important is CCITT V24 which is compatible with EIA RS-232C and defines the interchange circuits between terminal and modem. EIA RS-449 has been introduced recently to define more control lines for signalling at higher rates.

Information will be provided by terminal or microcomputer suppliers. For example the Cromemco digital interface, Apple communications card, TRS-80 interface, and many other microcomputers specify RS-232C. An RS-232C acoustic coupler modem can be plugged in to any of them if the manufacturer of the terminal and the coupler had the same ideas about pin connections.

For a modem wired directly to the PSTN, the communication authority supplying the modem will usually ask whether your equipment has the correct interface. The modem may be within your equipment already - as with Prestel television sets or Viewdata intelligent terminals capable of handling bulk data (both in the UK). You may possess a microcomputer embodying the modem on the communications interface card within the machine - for instance the D.C.Hayes Micromodem 100; if you do you will almost certainly be a US resident. In these cases the connection problem will have been dealt with on your behalf. For more information about microcomputer communications see Chapter 17.

According to Predicasts, the US information provider, US 1982 shipments of modems, of which the 2400 bps modem was the most popular, were about $575M, and all other types $65M. By 1992, these figures are expected to be $2500M and $356M repectively, fulfilling the connection requirements for 61 million home and 37 million business terminals. The major manufacturers are Western Electric, which is losing ground in consequence of deregulation, Racal (incl. Milgo and Vadic), Motorola (incl. Codex and Universal Data), Paradyne, Gandalf, and M/A-Com, and for personal computers, D.C. Hayes.

Currently, the introduction of chips into modems is causing prices to fall - for instance Texas markets a 300 bps chip for $30 and low-priced chips for videotex modems are expected.

Speeds and modes

To ensure that modems used on the international telephone network can satisfactorily exchange data, specifications have been laid down by the Comite Consultatif Internationale de Telegraphie et Telephone (CCITT). Recommendation V24 covers the "interface" or interchange conditions such as wiring connections, control signals etc. Particular recommendations cover modems operating at specified speeds as follows:- V21 200 baud, V23 600/1200 bps (bits per second), V22 1200 bps and V26 2400 bps for the switched telephone network; V27 4800 bps, V29 9600 bps, both for special 4 wire telephone lines which have to be leased from the telephone authority.

Since characters are usually coded as groups of at least 8 bits and certain control information may have to be transmitted as well, the character transmission rate will usually be about 1/10th of the bit rate. For equipment, for instance a printer, designed to work at 30 ch/sec., a modem operating at up to the lowest standard rate needed to accommodate that speed would be selected - in this case 600 bps. The mode of transmission may be simplex, half duplex, or full duplex. Simplex means one way only transmission, half-duplex means transmission in both directions but not at the same time, and duplex means in both directions at once. The advantage of full duplex is that the receiver can interrupt the transmitter at any time; data transmission at higher speeds may require that duplex be used for technical reasons.

Until recently a full duplex system required a four wire connection - one pair for each direction; however a device called a "split frequency band" modem was introduced in 1979, capable of operating over one pair of wires at 1200 bps. The frequency band is split into two parts and communication can take place in both directions at once without mutual interference.

Timing

The receiver must know "when to look" as soon as the first information bit appears: if it gets out of step with the transmitter or looks at a moment of transition, errors will appear. A <u>synchronous</u> transmission system is one in which electronic circuits controlling the transmission rate ("clock") at the receiver run continuously. When the transmitter starts up, "padding" bits are automatically transmitted, and the receiver clock is pulled into exact synchronism by these pulses; the transmission of real data follows and by then and thereafter the receiver is held synchronised to the transmitter.

In an <u>asynchronous</u> system a special "start" bit is transmitted before each byte starts, to tell the receiver that is must start looking at the bits which follow. Another "stop" bit is transmitted to tell the receiver that the byte is finished. Clocks running at the same speed are still needed at transmitter and receiver but the receiver clock is synchronised afresh at each byte and need not be a precision device with long term accuracy.

The asynchronous or "start-stop" system is the simpler and cheaper. However a speed penalty is paid because two extra bits have to be transmitted with each byte.

Errors

The error rate and error detection and correction in a data transmission system are important considerations. When text is being transmitted, some errors can be tolerated because of redundancy in the language, but information, such as a number, may or may not contain redundancy. 1285 will usually mean 1985, but if 4 o'clock is received instead of 5 o'clock it may be accepted as correct.

Consider, for instance, the message "Guido Fawkes will light a fuze at 4 o'clock this afternoon, causing barrels of gunpowder to explode beneath the houses of parliament", received garbled as "Guodo Fawkes woll light a fuze at 5 o'click this afternoon caxlong barrels of ginpowder to explide beneath the hojses of parliament". The meaning is rather clear in spite of errors, but there is no redundancy in the time if the recipient has no prior knowledge about it. If the message had been sent electrically to the law-and-order brigade - which was not quite feasible on that occasion - zero redundancy in the time would have given them no chance to detect the error and they might have arrived after a big bang.

In many systems a character is displayed to the person transmitting the message only after "echoing back" - that is it has gone up and down the line so almost certainly the receiving person has seen it correctly. In automatic systems, however, the human decision-making capability is absent. The parity bit which is used within most bytes can be used to detect a single error. If "odd parity" is used the eighth bit is added automatically so that the total found by adding the ones in the byte always gives an odd number. If each byte is totalled automatically at the receiver, an even number indicates an error.

In some systems this event can cause the transmitter to interrupt and ask for a repeat. More complicated systems exist wherein more than one bit is added according to certain rules, and circuits at the receiver can actually correct the erroneous bit. The penalty paid is speed, since it takes longer to transmit the extra bits. Errors are caused by noise in the communication channel.

The probability of errors is specified by the telephone authority. It usually lies somewhere between 1 in 1000 (switched telephone network) and 1 in 100,000 (leased lines, lower speeds). Unfortunately noise tends to occur in bursts with infrequent but noticeable effect unless error detection is in use. More information is given in specialised publications such as Doll or Handbook of Data Communications.

<u>Pulse Code Modulation</u>

Pulse modulation is a method of sending a message by a code representing changes in the amplitude, duration, or position of pulses.

<u>Pulse Code Modulation</u> (PCM) - information transmission by binary coded pulses - is the most widely used method, PCM was invented by A.H. Reeves of Standard Telephones & Cables Ltd in 1936. It enables speech to be transmitted in digital codes for greater efficiency. The principle is illustrated in Figure 5.3. Textbooks about data transmission often provide lengthy mathematical explanations about pulse transmission. Pulses are analysed as if they were continuous waveforms in the tradition of pre 1939 communications. Developments in pulse techniques associated with the work on radar in 1939-1945 point up the inconvenience of this approach. Digital transmission now being the norm it makes sense to talk in terms of discrete waveforms. Professor Cherry, an eminent academic, but also a skilled practitioner, put it like this. "There is no need to consider `continuous' waveforms at all in signal analysis. These functions are the creation of mathematicians; all observable signals must be observed through some finite bandwidth, f, however large. Such signals are completely represented by complete data, 2f per sec".

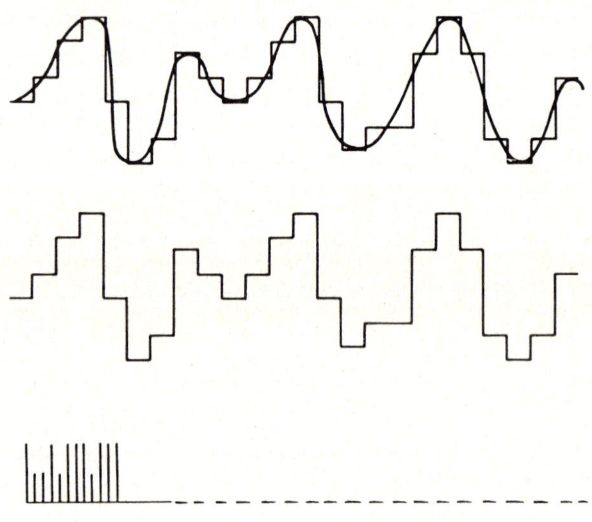

FIGURE 5.3. PULSE CODE MODULATION

Pulse waveforms consist of the fundamental frequency, corresponding to the repetition rate of the pulse, and an infinite series of harmonics. To transmit the pulse perfectly the bandwidth of the channel should also be infinite to accommodate these components. In practice if the upper limit of the pass band is ten times the fundamental frequency the pulse can be transmitted sufficiently well for most purposes.

In PCM the level of the fluctuating speech waveform is measured at frequent intervals; in the figure the smoothly rising waveform on the left has become represented by levels at the moments of measurement - say 5,7, and 8 volts - staircase-wise. If the system is designed to handle eight different levels, each level may be represented by three pulses (3 bits) per "sample" as shown on the bottom line. In other words information about the speech waveform is transmitted as a series of binary coded numbers.

Passing from a simplified example to reality, we know that sampling at the rate 2f, where f is bandwidth in Hz, is sufficient to provide all the data needed (Nuyquist). "2f" is sometimes written as "2wt" where w is bandwidth and t time in seconds. A 4000 Hz bandwidth is adequate for good quality speech, indicating a sampling rate of 8000 per sec. The question is how much data, or how many levels, must be used in practice? Will the "jumps" be audible? In fact <u>quantisation</u> into 128 (2^7) levels is sufficient to reduce quantisation noise (the jumps) to a negligible level, so we end up with a code of 7 bits plus one parity bit, that is 8 bits transmitted 8000 times per second or a transmission rate of 64,000 bps. This is the rate often used for digitised speech transmission.

A binary transmission rate of 64,000 bits per second (64 Kbps) requires a bandwidth of 32 KHz, whereas the original speech only required a bandwidth about 3 KHz. This apparently wasteful exercise will be discussed shortly.

<u>COMMUNICATION ECONOMICS AND CHANNEL AVAILABILITY</u>

Although fast pulses are attenuated in ordinary pairs of wires such as those used for telephone connections, their bandwidth is much greater than is implied by the fact that they are used as 3000 Hz voice channels.

Communication authorities are imprisoned by their enormous investment in the voice telephone network; various items of equipment such as loading coils, transformers, etc., required for voice services are connected to it; the "natural" bandwidth of a pair of wires is unavailable except for baseband signalling within an organisation using its own cables. Even the voice network as it stands has a wider bandwidth than is necessary to accommodate a single voice channel, and this bandwidth can be used in association with special equipment.

If all "attachments" are removed it is possible to signal at least 500,000 bps (500 Kbps) over 1000 yards of a wire pair. If a repeater (pulse regenerator) is used every 1000 yards, a rate of one and half million bps (1.5 Mbps) is possible over long distances. Such a channel could be used either for digitised voice communication or for communication between, say, computers generating digital signals directly.

Provided the communications authority knows that a channel is to be used exclusively for digital transmission then economics dictate the use of the cheapest suitable circuit; the grossly under-used bandwidth of a wire pair - the wires already in place for 4 KHz voice - could be used for PCM. The apparently "wasteful exercise" of conversion to PCM turns out to be - so far as local lines are concerned - no more than the utilisation of existing bandwidth. It is not clear when potentially useable direct digital facilities will actually become available. In the US it is not unusual for at least four conversions to be necessary when two digital machines are connected via the Bell T carrier system because the carrier network cannot be directly accessed by digital signals.

"A significant economic breakthrough for data communications users will occur when they can exploit the fact that conventional leased voice-grade lines use 56,000 bps of carrier digital capacity, whereas the use of 56,000 bps of digital capacity for data applications currently costs customers anywhere from two to five times more than a leased voice line. It would certainly appear that competitive considerations are vastly more important factors than actual costs in determining price structures" said Doll back in 1978 (with reference to the US). This situation is becoming resolved in the U.S., since de-regulation is introducing new competitive considerations.

Users of Information Technology will often be users of communications. These techno-political matters directly effect their bills. It is to be hoped that real price reductions will be passed on to users when systems like System X (UK) come into widespread use. Current publicity emphasises improved services, not reduced prices. In fairness to the PTTs their dedication of resources to the development of voice services, the inevitable inertia of such large organisations and the relatively recent demand for data services is bound to restrict the rate of change.

With the British Telecom's System X and other like systems, digital switching will be used at local exchanges so machine-to-machine direct digital connection becomes possible. Duplex 64 Kbps channels to premises will be provided so inter-connection between machines anywhere in the country should become feasible eventually. The backbone of the system will be a microwave digital relay bulk data transmission network between centres with each link carrying 6 140 Mbps channels.

A good technical overview of the system down to the local exchange level is given by Martin. In principle all the circuits - local and national - could be used for direct digital transmission. A long distance digital circuit includes not only copper in the ground, microwave links etc., but also a lot of associated engineering; special equipment is needed at the interface between customer's various devices and the network. These extra costs will be offset by lower maintenance costs and the costs of digital-analogue-digital conversion will disappear. The UK case exemplifies what is happening in varying degrees in many countries. According to Martin - presumably at the 1979 planned investment level - System X would cover 50% of the trunk network by 1990 and 70% by 2000 at best. The need is now.

Wide bandwidth channels

In recent years the trend has been to pack a number of hitherto separate "circuits" - say telephone circuits - into a single "channel". This is much more efficient than adding more individual circuits - there would be a prohibitively large amount of expensive copper in the thousands of pairs of wires needed to convey transatlantic telephone calls. It is technically feasible to collect together data arriving from many circuits, transmit it over one long-distance wideband channel, and separate it into separate circuits for distribution at the other end in conventional pairs of wires. The technology of 1950 permitted about 36 telephone circuits to be carried in one cable; by the early 70s about 2000 could be carried and by the late 70s over 5000. The PENCAN III Spain-Canary Islands cable, laid in 1978, carries 5,500 circuits.

Wider bandwidth cables containing one or more glass fibres are starting to replace copper cables. Electrical pulses are changed into light pulses by an electro-optical transducer and transmission rates of some hundreds of Mbits/second can be achieved. A practical example is the single chip transducer, developed by IBM, for computer communications which can operate at 165 Mbit/s. A single fibre can easily carry data at this rate over long distances without repeaters. Fibreoptics are discussed in Chapter 7.

Satellite channels of very wide bandwidth are also available. The major difference between satellite and other telecommunication systems is that no switched or other kind of terrestrial connection is needed for every user. A transmitter on one satellite can potentially provide a service for one receiver on one third of the world's surface. Chapter 8 provides more details.

Packing data into communication channels

Communication channels are expensive so the incentive to fully utilise them at all times is high. This can be done in two ways; first, by packing in as many individual data circuits as possible into each channel and second, by arranging that gaps in the flow of data are occupied with information.

Lines carrying a single telephone circuit are under-utilised in terms of bandwidth. The first possibility is to use such a line with appropriate equipment at either end for many relatively slow speed data circuits. This is done by arranging that the data in each channel modulates a carrier wave and the frequencies of the modulated carriers are sufficiently spaced over the bandwidth of the line to avoid mutual interference. The process is known as <u>Frequency Division Multiplexing (FDM)</u>. A "guard" space has to be left between each frequency band occupied by data.

FDM, developed during the "all-analogue" age, is still widely used and may still be the most efficient method of multiplexing in certain cases for technical reasons. However a more sophisticated method for multiplexing digital signals called <u>Time Division Multiplexing (TDM)</u> is replacing it as the cost of the associated technology falls. With TDM, individual pulses or pulse trains representing characters from a number of circuits are interleaved and transmitted in one channel. They can be reformed into individual circuits at the remote end because the interleaving is controlled on a time basis.

TDM techniques have been further developed into <u>Synchronous Time Division Multiplexing (STDM)</u>, <u>Statistical Time Division Multiplexing (STATDM)</u>, and <u>Packet Switching</u>. The last two exhibit <u>Concentration</u> (and are sometimes called <u>Concentrators</u>) wherein the channel bandwidth is less than the sum of the individual circuit bandwidths; the term <u>Intelligent Time Division Multiplexing (ITDM)</u> is also used for these techniques because a microprocessor is used to make decisions about interleaving and timing.

In STDM, time slots for pulses are allocated on a pre-determined basis; consequently if a circuit is idle, unfilled slots exist in the channel. With STATDM the slots are allocated on a dynamic basis. Associated with STATDM is a process called <u>buffering</u>. Say that the bandwidth of the channel is sufficient to accommodate 10 circuits when transmission is continuous but in fact transmission occurs in bursts so that the bandwidth required at the mean rate of transmission is lower. With STATDM, 15, (say) circuits could be connected to the channel, and time slots are allocated by the microprocessor to channels only when they are active.

The buffer, or storage device, temporarily stores pulses when the total tranmission rate exceeds the mean. When a particular circuit stops transmitting, pulses from a waiting circuit stored in the buffer are inserted into the time slots now vacated. With correct design, queueing - that is noticeable waiting time for a circuit because the channel is full - can be avoided.

<u>Muliplexers</u> or "Mux" are available from a number of suppliers. A Multiplexer is the device which performs any of the functions just described. An input/output mux accepts data from a number of circuits and, organises it for transmission in a single channel or receives data from a single channel and re-distributes it to the appropriate circuits. The use of multiplexers in a different way in digital computers is discussed in Chapter 3.

<u>Packet Switching. Circuit & Message Switching</u>

Packet switching takes STATDM a stage further in communication networks. A number of geographically spaced nodes, sometimes in different countries, are interconnected by at least two circuits. A node is a store and forward switching centre forming the hub of a cluster of terminals or computers. The node handles the traffic from the terminals, routing it via another node or by hops from node to node until it reaches its addressed destination. Each node checks the data for correctness and forwards it when a circuit is available.

At a node a message to be transmitted from a terminal or computer is broken up into packets, each containing, say, 2000 bits, preceded by an address header, and ending with a tail containing checking data. At the terminating node the address and header are removed and the packets re-assembled into the original message. Each packet of a message could be transmitted to its destination by a different route or by the same route according to circuit availability. The node handles the various transmission rates at which the terminals or computers connected to it may be operating by buffering. It also manages transmissions through the high speed wideband links of the network.

The   objective   of this complicated arrangement is to make the most efficient use of a national or international communications   network. Multiple interconnections improve reliability. Although wideband circuits are required for the network links, concentration minimises the bandwidth needed so transmission costs are also minimised.

Packet switching is now being widely used in spite of some controversy about its   cost-effectiveness   versus   Circuit Switching (CS). With CS a physical path is established between devices and there is little delay. Extra complication is needed for packet switching to ensure that there are no noticeable   delays. Both methods are superior to Message Switching for computer communications because fast interactive response to short messages is often essential. In Message Switching, also a store-and-forward system, delays are greater because the message is handled in one piece.

Packet switching certainly seems to have established itself as the most efficient way of handling data in bulk, particularly when it is bursty" - as is much of today's data traffic. For example when a remote database is searched by an operator using a keyboard, percentage bandwidth/time occupancy is very low. The most efficient way to use a communications channel is to use all the bandwidth all the time. The benefit is maximised when expensive long distance channels are fully occupied all the time - hence the widespread adoption of packet switching for public data networks.

<u>FURTHER READING</u>

Bleazard, Bernard.
  Published for the UK Post Office by NCC Publications, UK National Computing
  Centre Ltd., Manchester England. 1982.   Handbook of Data Communication.
Camana, Peter.
  IEEE Spectrum, 16(6), 24-29, June 1979.
  Video bandwidth compression: a study in tradeoffs.
Cherry, Colin.
  MIT Press, Cambridge MA, and London, 1966.
  On human communication. Chapter 4, The analysis of signals.
Doll, Dixon R.
  John Wiley 1978.
  Data Communications: facilities, networks and system design.
Martin John.
  In 3rd World Telecommunication Forum, part 2, Geneva, 1979. Pub. by
  International Telecommunications Union (ITU), Geneve, Switzerland. Pps
  2.1.4.1 to 2.1.4.6.
  Technology and system design in telecommunications.
Reeves, A.H.
  IEEE Spectrum 2(5), 58-62, 1965.
  Past, present and future of PCM.
Shannon, Claude E.
  Bell System Technical Journal 27(3), 379-423, July, and 27(4), 623-656,
  August 1948.
  A mathematical theory of communication.

CHAPTER 6. TELECOMMUNICATIONS AND INFORMATION TRANSMISSION PART 2: NETWORKS, PROTOCOLS AND SYSTEMS.

LARGE NETWORKS

Introduction

J.K.Kelly, an engineer in charge of the telecommunications network of a large company, describes communications arrangements appropriate in the stages of growth of an organisation :-

1. No centralised management. Lines and equipment leased by user departments.
2. Centralised planning and management of corporate telephone facilities. Optimisation of separate data networks by data processing managers.
3. Combination of separate data networks into integrated data networks possibly including message switching networks.
4. Management of data and voice facilities as an overall information system.
5. A study of all forms of corporate communication including mail, executive travel and use of information sources.
6. Cost optimisation of all forms of corporate communication.

Growth of data networks

Until quite recently the trend has been to centralise computer power and bulk information storage. Consequently there has been a need for the transfer of data between computers and the exchange of information between computers and people via terminals situated within the same building or at a distance from the mainframe machine. Storage costs have declined steadily and the size and cost of computers have also dropped rapidly. Communication costs have dropped more slowly and inter-connection problems have not eased noticeably - some would say that they have become worse in certain cases.

It now seems likely that there will be some shift of location for electronically stored information. Just as frequently used paperwork is kept in a user's desk or nearby filing cabinet, and less-used is stored in the basement, so frequently used information will be stored locally, perhaps in a desk microcomputer storage. Very large files which are infrequently accessed will be kept in "archival" storage, not necessarily locally. Locally held files which are subsets of large centrally managed files - for instance those containing product data, scientific information, etc., relevant to one user - will be up-dated from remote databanks.

There already has been a shift towards distributed processing in which some computer processing power is moved into "intelligent" terminals. Furthermore the considerable power which would otherwise be needed in host computers required to handle transactions from a range of terminals, printers, etc., connected to them and operating at different speeds, has been relieved by "front-end" machines to handle "intelligent" communication networks. The PSTN has been and is continuing to be squeezed for the maximum possible data transmission capacity. It is used for local point to point transmission, for long distance transmission and increasingly for access to special long distance services. Some imaginative proposals have recently been made for subscriber to exchange local line multiplexing with greatly increased digital data transmission capacity using PCM.

<u>Public data networks - Europe</u>

Public data networks are in service in many countries, earlier circuit-switched networks having usually been replaced by packet-switched. In 1979 about 393,000 devices were connected to all networks in Europe. In 1983 854,000 were expected. There were nearly twice as many terminals in the UK as in the second in the table - Germany. Two of the reasons are heavy useage by UK banks and the attitude of BT which has been somewhat less restrictive than its continental counterparts. Very comprehensive information on a country by country basis, with rates, notes about new developments and a great deal of other very detailed information is contained in the Euronet Directory.

Kelly has described how experience gained on the European Informatics Network was used when Euronet was formed in consequence of co-operation between 9 PTTs and the European Commission. Euronet has been used mainly for the inter-connection of host computers, each running a variety of bibliographic or data banks, with interactive access from terminals in several countries. By October 1980, 2177 hours of Euronet use were billed by PTTs, headed by France , Germany, Netherlands, and UK as the major users. A number of other European public data networks such as TRANSPAC, DATEX and NPDN have also been described by Cardarelli.

In the UK there was a flurry of activity paralleling the passage of the British Telecommunications Bill through parliament. In particular, a competitive network was built up by Mercury, a consortium composed of British Rail, Cable & Wireless, Barclays Bank and BP. Mercury is following a US precedent for using the railway's strips of land criss-crossing the country for telecommunication lines. The US Southern Pacific Railroad Company earned $150 million in 1980 from its specialised common carrier services.

The development of services competing with AT&T has been a US phenomena because of a liberal telecommunications policy in that country. Tymnet and Telenet are of particular interest because of their forays into Europe. At one time is was possible to connect a terminal/modem to the PSTN in the UK, dial a London number, and be connected to the Tymshare service for interactive access to databases run by Companies in the US. The service was simple to use, efficient. and inexpensive.

This arrangement infringed BT's monopoly and it was replaced by a service in which users dialled in for a connection to the International Packet Switching Service's (IPSS) Packet Switching Exchange connected to ITT, RCA, or WUI exchanges in the US which in turn connected to Telenet or Tymnet networks. The service was more difficult to use and more expensive than its predecessor.

The Californian company Lockheed, which offers access to a wide range of databases, leased a line to the UK and charged about 50% less than BT for telecommunications. There was a simple flat range communication charge for database subscribers of $10/hour.

<u>Public data networks - USA</u>

In the United States much of the original work on large networks was carried out, notably in the Advance Research Projects Agency (ARPA) network set up to provide access by government and other agencies to inter-connected host computers by Licklider and others.

Although AT&T is a corporation, its activities were regulated in the manner of a PTT. The major data services were provided via the PSTN with tariff reductions on the Wide Area Telecommunications Service (WATS) for multiple inter-state calls at reduced rates. Bell developed the Dataphone

Digital Service (DDS) for AT&T, comprising various interconnected transmission facilities and microwave links covering major population centres. PCM is used at speeds between 2.4 and 56 Kbps.

Deregulation of telecommunications in the United States has enabled a number of organisations to set up services competing with AT&T, but it has also freed AT&T to move from common carrier activities into data-processing. To limit the ability of the company to overwhelm the competition by diverting its immense resources into other areas, it has been forced to set up arm's length subsidiaries to conduct the new business. The increase in business telecommunications, the blurred distinction between "carriers" and "processors" leading to liberalisation of ownership (deregulation), and the increasing availability of satellite circuits have all played a part in network expansion.

Xerox proposed its XTEN nation-wide intercity microwave/satellite network which was to provide comprehensive message services, and AT&T its Advanced Communication Service (ACS), again providing a complex of facilities aimed at businesses. Subsequently Xerox withdrew XTEN, although it had been widely advertised and staff had been recruited. AT&T passed through a period of great uncertainty and no ACS offerings were made.

Meanwhile Satellite Business Systems (SBS), a consortium of IBM, COMSAT, and Aetna Insurance, successfully launched satellites manufactured by Hughes to provide a satellite rooftop-to-rooftop wideband multi-media communication service primarily for large businesses.

More recently AT&T formed a company to offer a new service throughout the United States called the Intelligent Shared Data Network. It plans to double the capacity of the network every 6 months so that in the fifth year it will consist of up to 200 nodes on a packet switched network throughout the country. A node is quite a large affair requiring a building of up to 15,000 square feet. From it, customers will be offered network inter-connection, communications processing, data storage and data transmission.

One part of the system will enable customers to use information processing resources more economically than might otherwise be possible. For example to operate a growing large database it is hard to optimise resources at each stage of growth. AT&T will offer resources distributed around the country as appropriate.

Another application would be to enable organisations with different systems normally unable to talk to each other to inter-communicate by using the network's reformatting resources. The objective is to provide inter-connected processing power on tap with a degree of flexibility that will make potential customers think hard before they set up their own tailormade systems.

The second largest US telephone company, GTE, purchased Telenet, a well-established commercial network and is obviously prepared to provide strong financial support for its geographically widespread network services.

ITT operates an international communication service with several associated services for Companies. This includes a 960 port private line message switching service, a store and forward telex switching exchange, and a store and forward facsimile service.

<u>Private leased line networks</u>

Many private networks have been assembled by organisations with common interests or by large companies for intra-company communications.

Organizations able to set up leased line networks seem to be reasonably free to connect a variety of devices and operate a range of services for their own use so long as their equipment satisfies the PTT's criteria for physical connection.

This is not to say that the setting up of such a network in the first place is easy. PTTs usually do not admit that users have any right to be provided with a leased circuit. The user must first convince them that his requirements cannot be met by often inadequate public networks.

The PTTs are in a position to manipulate users towards public networks or leased lines by a pricing policy (since they control both) not necessarily related to the efficiency of these alternatives. To the credit of BT in the Lockheed case, no price manipulation appears to have occurred - on the contrary, BT seemed prepared to allow market forces to apply.

The most noteworthy of the very large consortia-operated services are probably SITA, operated by the airlines described by Hirsch and SWIFT by the banks described by Lapidus. The options for setting up business communication networks and the methods used by several large organisations (3M, Massey-Ferguson, Dupont, British Steel) to set up their communications have been described by Mc-Ewen King.

LOCAL AREA NETWORKS (LAN) AND PRIVATE AUTOMATIC BRANCH EXCHANGES (PABX)

Introduction

LANs are the latest fashion in business and university campus telecommunications. Flint lists their characteristics as:-

Transmission speeds of from 100 Kbps to "over 1 Mbps"
(in fact some operate at much faster rates).
Device interconnection range of up to 5 miles.
Digital transmission only (some possibility of including
analogue).

Manufacturers are rushing into print (and maybe into production) in many IT areas, but the activity in LANs is more hectic than most. One objective is the establishment of de facto standards. The climate is indicated by McQuillan "the potential in distributed office systems....is enormous....there is confusion and disagreement about the fundamentals - be forewarned. If there is a bias it is hereby revealed to you. Ethernet is the answer; what is the question?....the reason is to leverage* voice, video, terminal, workstation and mainframe information".

* Related to English LEVER (verb) - "to prise or move with a lever" and LEVERAGE (noun) - "the action of a lever". Hence the US verbonoun TO LEVERAGE = "to lever", but with more vigour.

The concept of picking off data circulating within a ring main - in addition to numerous other ways of implementing a LAN - has introduced a technology with some new rules. Coupled to the rate of activity, this both advances and retards "universal" communication. It advances it because the ring main idea is probably a good one and it retards it because over-hasty introduction and inter-network compatibility problems introduce yet another dimension into the search for standards. A further complication is the complimentary or competitive (according to whether you do or not make them) nature of the digital Private Automatic Branch Exchange (PABX).

According to McQuillan "Networks have been designed backwards... higher level protocols have not been successful yet...In response to user's "just plug right in" pressures, many network vendors have introduced ad hoc....undesirable expedients....Two major failings of packet networks – higher level protocols and host interfaces are once again being neglected, this time in the context of local networks".

In 1980 local networks and message systems generally, were sold and installed by each vendor with his own set of protocols, codes and specifications. Each vendor's equipment was unable to communicate with another's equipment. Even so predictions were made, with the customary exponential curve, showing $700M as the value of local nodes installed by 1985 and $3000M by 1990.

LANs – development and types

LANs are the outcome of early 1970s technology with some ingenious modifications and extensions. Cotton has written a concise review of two major types – Ring networks and Contention networks. They resemble the ring mains in a house, but data exchange instead of electrical power consumption is the objective. Communication costs have not been dropping as fast as computer costs, but these new LANs embody methods for data interchange between different devices without special switching, using cheap wideband cable.

Rings

Pioneering work on rings was done by Farmer et al., and later a working ring at University of California at Irvine was described by Farber (with a b). The idea was taken up elsewhere, and a version developed at Cambridge University by Wilkes and others has been further developed at a number of places in the UK. Farber's work, although published back in 1973, is a useful key to current developments. Later researchers often cite it. Thus Hopper and Wheeler, reporting the Cambridge ring in a paper with an unspecific title cite Farber's earlier work, enabling it, and other more recent work, to be located simply by looking up Farber's cited paper in the Science Citation Index

In ring systems empty data packets circulate like containers in a pneumatic tube system, but at Mbit/sec speeds. When a station wants to transmit it detects an empty packet, enters addresses and data, and empties it after the message has been received when it comes round again. All stations examine all packets and accept only those addressed to them. The electronics is inexpensive and twisted pair or fibreoptic cable can be used. The Cambridge ring cost about $2000 per station in 1980. Reliability may be a weakness since packet use is determined by a control "token", and if that is erroneous the packet will not be recovered. The basic transmission rate is 10 Mbps. Typically a one thousand character message is transmitted in 10 ms (0.01 secs).

Each station connects to a ring via an interface which may embody a microprocessor (typically a Z80) programmed to suit the requirements of the data processing machine connected to the station. The interface must take care of factors like data rate conversion and flow control by buffering (temporary storage), enabling machines operating at different speeds to communicate. It must also handle conversions to accommodate differences between machines in codes, character sets, line lengths etc.

Contention networks

In Contention Networks a station wanting to transmit waits until traffic ceases and then broadcasts a message in packets waiting for each to be acknowledged. If several stations are waiting and there is a collision of messages, each station backs off for a random time period and then tries again. The first contention network was developed at the University of Hawaii by Abramson and christened ALOHA.. The best known contention LAN is probably ETHERNET manufactured by Xerox Corp. In Ethernet, machines are connected to a coaxial cable via a transmitter-receiver. Stations can connect to the cable anywhere and the cable can be extended by using repeaters.

In the prototype Ethernet a cable lKm long, running along ceilings, interconnects 250 small computers. The method used is known as "Carrier Sense Multiple Access with Collision Detection" (CSMA/CD) or sometimes "Collision Avoidance" (/CA), first described in 1976. Conversions of the kind mentioned in Ring systems take place under microcomputer control at the interface. Data transmission is by packets at 10 Mbps and a station will accept only those packets addressed to it. At the end of 1980 Xerox made a strong attempt to establish a de facto standard by teaming up with DEC and Intel thus creating a strong vendor/marketing group.

Several other organisations have developed similar LANs including the National Bureau of Standards and the Mitre Corporation. Network Systems Corp. are introducing a 50 Mbps version for fast inter-machine processing.

<u>Baseband and Broadband systems</u>

The Ring and Contention systems use baseband transmission - that is data is transmitted through a single channel behaving as if it were many channels by a time-division process.

A baseband signal may be made to modulate a carrier waveform of chosen frequency. Several carriers of different frequencies may be used on the same cable, with bandpass filters to avoid mutual interference as discussed in Chapter 5. Thus a number of quite separate baseband/carrier communication channels can be used simultaneously within the same cable. These "broadband" LANs appeared on the market later than Ring and Contention systems and used wideband cables - up to about 300 Mhz - easily capable of carrying video information.

The bandwidth may be "carved up" according to requirements - for example into a hundred dedicated channels for 1200 bps terminals, a LAN CSMA channel, a television channel, channels for digitised voice etc. Broadband systems are more complex and expensive, but less so than might be expected since they can use components mass produced for cable television. They first became available in 1982.

<u>LAN Suppliers</u>

A large number of suppliers are offering LAN components, obviously believing that LANs will have a key role in the office of the future. LANs are intended primarily for the inter-connection of office machines such as word processors, printers, central files etc., within a distance of about 4 Kms.

The leading suppliers of Ring LANs include Acorn Computers (Cambridge Ring), Cambridge UK, and Xionics (Xinet/Xibus) London Wl. Nestar's (Palo Alto Ca) Cluster/One (CSMA) is available from Zynar, Uxbridge, UK. Other multivendor supported LANs include Econet (CSMA) from Acorn Computers, Cambridge UK; Ethernet (CSMA), Xerox, Stamford Conn; Hyperbus (CSMA), Network Systems, Minneapolis & Tesdata, Slough, UK; Net/One (CSMA), Ungermann-Bass, Santa Clara Ca.,& Thame Systems, Thame, UK. Tesdata can also supply Network System's Hyperchannel high-speed LAN.

Broadband systems include Localnet, from Network Technology, Reading; Sytek from Sytek, Sunnyvale, Ca and Wangnet from Wang, Lowell, Mass., & Wang, London Wl. For more see the Product Data section in this book.

Current and future developments

The next problem will be to interconnect LANs at a distance from each other via national or international networks. Since the techniques used in long distance networks are different, a "translation" problem exists. One way of solving it will be by a "gateway" at each node on the long distance network to which the LANs are connected. The gateway takes care of data re-formatting.

Appletalk is an example of a recent inexpensive LAN products. It allows interconnection of up to 32 machines, such as Macintoshes, or peripherals, on up to 1000 feet of cable. The January 1985 price was $50 for a network connector and a length of cable. Traffic control is by CSMA/CA software. A new peripheral for shared used on the network is a high resolution laser printer, the Laser Writer, at $7000. Gateways are said to be available for network interconnection to Ethernet or IBM PC networks.

A book by Cheong lists the major suppliers and includes a great deal of other useful information. Another comprehensive source is the IRD 1982 report; it also suggests a future scenario in consequence of the somewhat greater range made possible with broadband systems - perhaps 50 miles, the existence of wideband cable TV networks in the US serving local communities, and the possibility of inter-connecting these networks via gateways and satellite or coax/repeater links.

In this scenario, businesses, homes, and workers-at-home, are interconnected by cable carrying broadband LANs, are served over the same cable by national data distributors, and are provided with online access to remote databases. A foretaste of things to come was provided in 1981 when the Viacom San Francisco cable network and the Manhattan New York network were connected in an experiment conducted with SBS and Tymnet. The Cable TV circuits were used as a local network for data distribution.

The PABX

An alternative or perhaps complimentary method of local traffic control can be implemented using a Private Automatic Branch Exchange. It is easier to connect the local traffic to the outside world with a PABX, and such an exchange can be used to connect any digital or analogue device to any other internally. PABX's are well proven for reliability and ease of expansion, and could be connected to a LAN in order to gateway the slower LAN terminals to public networks.

There is some doubt about handling voice - that is digitised voice - on a LAN, and about the effectiveness of a LAN for interconnecting relatively slow terminals through an external networks to remote computers. One difficulty is that variable delays exceeding about 0.2 seconds, inherent with packet systems, may produce unacceptable effects during conversation. Perhaps solutions will appear using the best features of LANs and PABXs, interconnected, and under software control, so that traffic is automatically optimally routed. From the data rate viewpoint this would make some sense, because the LAN would be used primarily for circulating wideband data, freeing the PABX which would be clogged up with it, for voice and terminals which need to be connected to external channels.

A useful list of the PABX's available in Britain is given by Cooper. The table summarises the feature of each and includes a price list. Work is in progress within the European Computer Manufacturer's Association (ECMA) for standardisation of interfaces and inter PBX signalling.

PROTOCOLS 1. THE REQUIREMENTS FOR "UNIVERSAL" COMMUNICATIONS

Figure 6.1 will be used to discuss wider requirements. Consider, for instance, the case of Organisation C (whose facilities are represented on the left of the dotted line in the figure. "Person J", assumed to be operating a microcomputer at position "V", wants to communicate with a person in a branch of the same organisation at position "W".

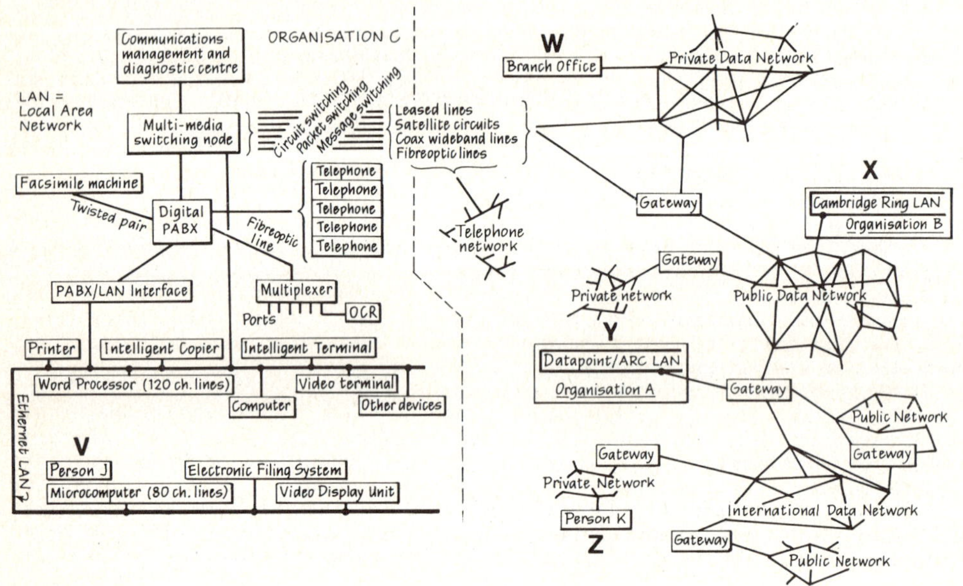

FIGURE 6.1 A "UNIVERSAL" NETWORK?

Organisation C generates enough communications traffic to justify comprehensive facilities including a private data network using PTT leased lines. Let us also assume that a sufficient number of C's employees use microcomputers for C to have ensured that machines connected to its Ethernet Local Area Network, installed at headquarters, are able to "talk to" similar machines at branch offices via a private network – in particular the office at "W". Person J, then, can obtain the address of the person at W by calling up a directory file on his machine, and the system's protocol will take care of data links, message formats, and message interchanges provided that J first types in the correct address.

The amount of intra-organisational traffic must justify the cost of device installation, protocol software with automatic link connection, and pre-arrangement of compatible equipment, with compatible ports, operating systems, and programs for this kind of communication; doubtless C will have a permanent wideband connection to its private network as shown.

Consider next the case of data communication between "Person J" and a person at point Y (within a different organisation and connected to a Datapoint LAN), or X (Cambridge Ring LAN) or "Person K" at Z (directly connected to a private network in an overseas country). In these cases J will presumably be able to obtain addresses for these persons but, considering for example communication with "Person K" at point Z, J must assume that the following facilities exist:-

A. His Ethernet LAN is capable of being switched to the
   "gateway" to connect with the Public Data Network.
B. The Public Network is capable of being gatewayed to
   the International Data Network.
C. Appropriate capabilities exist to gateway to "Person
   K's" network in the overseas country.
D. K's Local Area Network embodies a "compatibility box"
   which becomes operational when signals from a different
   type of LAN are received.
E. K's equipment is capable of indicating to its owner
   that an overseas call has been received, that it can
   decode and display messages because its operating system
   and programs are compatible with those used by J, and that
   it can reply with signals which can be interpreted by J.

No useable arrangements are currently generally available of anything like
the comprehensivity needed for "J's" requirements. To create an effective
scenario like this a struggle is in progress to establish <u>de facto</u> protocols
and standards for various facilities. No "winner" has yet emerged. I suggested
that "Person J" "must assume that routeing and other facilities were ready, but
unless his organisation had established an international private network
with comprehensive compatibility arrangements he could make no such assumption.
The organisation needed to arrange events A to E listed above would be
economic nonsense unless communications betweeen parties were very frequent.
The "Universal Communications" enabling "J's" requirements to be routinely met
are non-existent.

Protocols 2. Needs and objectives

Data Communication Protocols are rules or conventions agreed between
at least two inter-communicating stations engaged in data transmission in
order that communication can be established, messages exchanged, and
communication terminated. If National, or better still, International protocols
are agreed, this is obviously a big step towards universal orderly
telecommunications. Conventions for voice telephone communication – an early
form of protocol – have been developed over the years, culminating in those
required for International Subscriber Trunk Dialling. Unknown to subscribers
when a series of digits are dialled, a range of instructions and
acknowledgements are exchanged between telephone exchanges as the dialling
proceeds; other instructions are needed for ringing, and for appropriate
circuit changes when answering, disconnecting etc. The equipment in the remote
country must operate according to an agreed procedure. CCITT International
Signalling Systems have been internationally established for this purpose as
described by Welch.

Although the world's telephone network has been developed and expanded
fairly rapidly over the last ten years it grew comparatively slowly in
earlier decades. At all terminating points on the network the input/output
device (the telephone) is almost identical and system negotiation and
agreement proceeded in a stately fashion. The CCITT arrangements for what,
by modern standards, may seem to be a rather simple technology, are in fact
very complex, but there has been time to allow them to settle down.

Imagine a set of rules to accommodate th communications situation depicted
in Figure 6.1. The technology mostly exists but the rate of implementation
will depend on factors to be now discussed. The figure is made to appear
spidery and untidy in an attempt to indicate complexity but the actual situation
is far more complicated; it will serve to illustrate some of the points to be
made although no single organisation would necessarily use the facilities in
exactly the way shown.

"Communication needs" have been driven by a market-oriented technology in a world dominated by slow-moving communication monopolies. Consequently development has proceeded by a series of ingenious extemporisations in contrast to the step-by-step planned approach of the telephone system. Many new developments sit uncomfortably on top of the telephone system simply because it exists and provides access to a huge customer-base (It is not possible to show this in the Figure). Maybe this is the way it has to be – when developments are occurring at an exponential rate, new applications and requirements are discovered and new ideas are tried out to be quickly discarded in favour of better ones. Premature agreement and standardisation could fix the situation at a point in time when the next wave of developments would make that situation obsolete and unenforceable.

Although today a huge range of communications options exist, only some of them can be implemented cost-effectively and that can only happen when circumstances are particularly favourable. Presumably the world is large enough for there to be a sufficient number of favourable circumstances to support a New Industry because that Industry – The Data Communications Industry – certainly exists. Gradually the options will be widened, simplified, and reduced in cost so that new forms of communication will become widely adopted.

Protocols 3 – The OSI 7-layer model
==

Communication protocols are described in terms of a "layered" format – a singularly unhelpful idea if you are trying to visualise the occurrence of events when (in Figure 6.1) "Person J" contacts, say, "Person K". Layers are in fact a way of representing different functions, the "bottom layer" representing the "plug and socket" level, and the "top layer" representing the fine detail of applications e.g. how many characters are to be displayed in a line.

An almost ideal "layered" set of protocols – the Open Systems Interconnection (OSI) – has been under discussion for some time. It is instructive to consider it because it embodies features of most other arrangements. If adopted it would provide for most of the "A to E" processes previously listed. The model was agreed under the auspices of the International Standards Organisation (ISO), Comite Consultatif Internationale de Telegraphie et Telephone (CCITT), the Institute of Electrical and Electronics Engineers (IEEE). It is a considerable step forward, at least in principle.

From bottom to top the layers are –

Physical.   Physical and electrical connections to a
                 network.
Data Link.   Data transmission and error correction.
Network.   Switching and routeing functions.
Transport.   End-to-end path construction by node to node
                 best route method.
Session.   Connection between co-operating end-user
                 processes.
Presentation.   Data presentation functions.
Application.   User functions.

Not altogether unexpectedly I have failed to find a comprehensible explanation of this model amongst the huge number of articles that have been written about it. A major article by Pouzin appeared at an early stage of OSI which is heavy going – perhaps because it is aimed at the already knowledgeable. In that case its title is a misnomer. Another equally authoritative heavy article by Tenenbaum appeared later which also fails to provide a picture – at least to me – of exactly what a "layer" is. You simply cannot see the wood for the trees. A number of articles, mainly with self-evident titles, about various aspects of the problem, by Schindler, Mier, Jones, Von Studnitz, and Blauman were published. I can't award prizes for ease of comprehension to any of them.

I will attempt to explain what it seems to be all about - without guaranteeing complete correctness. I'm not sure that the "experts" have themselves got an overall understanding of it. The OSI model is usually presented as an abstraction in the form shown in Figure 6.2. It con- contains the essence of what will be needed for Mr.Dupont to generate some information - for example the message "Gone to lunch; back at 2pm GMT" - on system Y, and send it to Mr. Singh using system Z when they are both connected to a vast international OSI network.

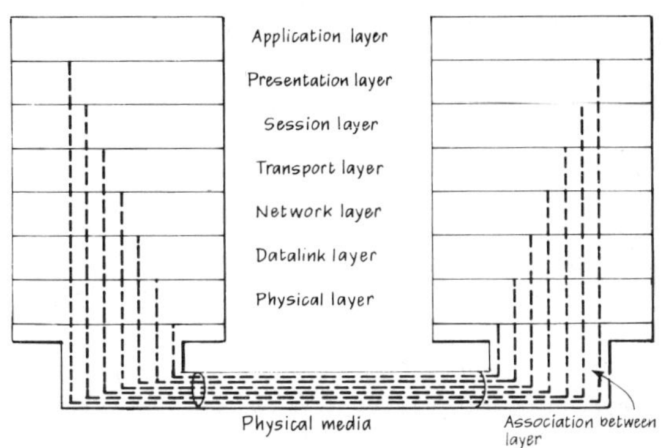

FIGURE 6.2   THE OSI 7-LAYER MODEL

A layer represents one of the seven functions needed to accomplish this, or any other communications activity,   each function having its associated rules and procedures (protocols). It will probably work like this.

Having composed his "Gone to lunch" message, Dupont will prefix it with Singh's address; the only other thing he will need to know is that Singh has a system of some kind capable of receiving messages. Dupont types the message on his work-station and presses the "electronic mail" depatch key. This message will then have a series of seven sets of coded instructions added to it automatically, some in the local system, some en route. Each set will be recognisable only by the equipment/software box responsible for handling the related functions - for instance the "application layer" box will only recognise and execute "application" instructions.

For example, the lunch message will have a "mail" code attached. The remote application layer box will recognise "mail" and know that it must be read into a file called "mail" in Singh's machine. At another level, say the Transport layer - the layer responsible for selecting a route of the required quality for the information being conveyed and checking and maintaining it - a device installed somewhere along the way and triggered by the appropriate code will be standardised with a set of "transport expectations".

In other words the system will be able to take action by reference to a set of codes, any one of which it may receive, to take care of some sub-function. For instance if it receives an error checking code which is wrong it will automatically ask for a re-transmission of a block of symbols.

The IT unit at the UK Department of Trade and industry co-ordinates information on standards and other IT topics. In a January 1985 communication they say "OSI standards are prospective standards in that they are being developed in advance of any widespread experience of the modes of computer use with which they are concerned. The aim is to allow modes of inter-working between computer systems which are currently difficult or impossible to achieve, except, in some cases, between computers from a single supplier. In consequence there is only limited and unrepresentative experience upon which to draw in preparing the standards, and the work involved is as much about learning and the development of understanding as it is about standardisation".

The ISO committee charged with the work is TC97 with a sub-committee SC21 reposnsible for the top 4 layers and another, SC6, for the bottom 3. "Effective agreement" on draft standards for most of the layers is scheduled for the end of 1985. Following that, the step-by-step introduction of the standards into general use will have to be preceded by international and national R&D work, pilot projects, and education and training.

Protocols 4. Current achievements

The first major event we need consider introduced the concept of interactive Distributed Processing whereby Remote Job Entry (RJE) was handled at remote terminals with some "intelligence", connected to a mainframe computer. Binary Synchronous Communications was introduced by IBM in 1966 as a half duplex link control protocol primarily for communication between remote terminals and a computer. Because of IBM's dominance it almost became a de facto standard. All devices were restricted to only one code.

BSC was later extended for Polled Multi-drop operation - a central computer scans round a number of terminals connected to the same line. Each in its turn transmits a burst of data. High Level Data Link Control (HDLC) protocols were subsequently introduced by several manufacturers including IBM's Synchronous Data Link Control (SDLC), Burrough's Data Link Control (BDLC) and Digital Equipment Corporation's (DEC) Digital Data Communications Message Protocol (DDCMP). HDLC procedures have been embodied in an ISO specification.

HDLC represents a considerable step forward because it embodies four-wire duplex operation, potentially doubling traffic capacity. It also provides for the continuous check of character errors block by block with error correction by Automatic ReQuest for repeat (ARQ); this can cope with the delays encountered due to propagation time in satellite transmissions. Futhermore HLDC treats data on a bit by bit basis which means that it is not restricted to a particular code.

IBM's Systems Network Architecture (SNA) was introduced in 1977. The protocols previously described deal with Data Link Control - only a small part of a "universal" communication system. SNA goes much further in an attempt to impose a de facto standard. SNA path control has been discussed by Atkins. SNA uses packet switching and embodies an equivalent of virtually all the OSI layers with the possible exception of the topmost. It ties in users to expensive up-grading of IBM equipment or alternative equipment plus special software. SNA is a considerable step forward towards implementing the "A to E" list above - a kind of criteria for "universal" communications.

(It seems necessary to enclose "universal" within quotation marks because most of the world's population will not be able to afford nor be interested in communication devices or systems except for the telephone. Even in developed countries, many people who could afford the equipment and running costs probably won't bother. Communication and Information go hand in hand, and Information is not a need which ranks high in the man in the street's budget - in fact, apart from buying a newspaper, many people somehow expect free materialisation of the information they need. In spite of that the number of people who will pay for occupational information needs is still very large).

X25 is a protocol which was developed co-operatively in parallel with SNA under CCITT auspices as described by Rybczynski and Folts.. It is an important advance and has been adopted by PTTs for public networks e.g. by PSS (UK), and Transpac (France), by Euronet, by major private networks e.g. Telenet & Tymnet (US) and Datapac (Canada), and by ISO to form part of OSI.

X25 specifies RS-232C at the Physical level. The data link control procedure in X25 is compatible with HDLC and embodies the bottom four layers of OSI - i.e. Physical (RS-232C), Data link (HDLC), Network, and arguably Transport. Therefore any user or manufacturer with a packet mode RS-232C terminal can eventually be assured of end-to-end communications using a wide choice of networks and so a larger number of addressees with whom to communicate.

While the X25 transport layer protocols mean that terminal to terminal compatibility is assured it is possible that OSI may require some transport enhancements (hence the word "arguably" above) Further enhancements have been added to X25 - for example provision for <u>Datagrams</u>. A Datagram provides for a message up to a certain length to be delivered as an intact unit; this avoids certain overheads, inherent in packet switching, which become significant for short messages. Very short messages are frequently used in certain types of interactive operations.

No SNA layer will interface the CCITT X25 protocol - now coming into general use for public data networks (PDN). Presumably some kind of SNA-PDN interface will be introduced in due course; meanwhile SNA can only be used on a leased line network.

To summarise on SNA versus X25. The former provides a sophisticated all-IBM packet-switched communication service on a leased line network, with protocol layers resembling the 7 OSI layers. The latter will eventually provide for end-to-end packet-switched communications on a number of public and private networks, compatible with the 4 lower layers of OSI; if a service embodying the intent of the top 3 OSI layers is required to avoid the installation of a system which will not be compatible with others when ISO becomes more widely adopted, there is enough information available about the intent of those layers at least to try.

<u>Digital Network Architecture (DNA)</u> was introduced in 1975 by DEC as described by Wecker. It provides facilities and protocol layers for the DEC range of minicomputers, performing roughly the same functions as SNA for a "DECNET" network. However it is less restrictive than SNA since the design will interface with X25. DEC also produces an emulator program which enables its PDP11 machines to work with an IBM host computer and SNA network. An emulator is a program which enables a computer to execute programs written for another computer.

Protocols 5. LANs

An IEEE LAN committee was formed at the beginning of 1980 to attempt to formulate IEEE standard 802 specifying a layered protocol to correspond with ISO. It has been forced to recognise two methods of data access - CSMA/MD and "token" (ring). It completed its work in 1984 and was due to announce three standards early in 1985 - on CSMA/MD, Bus token passing, and Ring token passing. Work is continuing on standards for LAN management and inter-networking.

The important matter of gateways to interconnect local area and long haul networks has been discussed by Elden. Such gateways are shown in Figure 6.1. It is proposed to add IEEE 802 to CCITT X25; the effort needed to get this to a stage when it will have an impact on "universal" communication is obvious from reading Elden's article.

<u>TELEPHONE & OTHER DATA SYSTEMS & NETWORKS</u>

<u>Evolution of the Integrated Services Data Network (ISDN)</u>

The advantages of a digital versus an analogue communications system have already been discussed. At the present time the whole international telephone system, representing a colossal investment, is analogue locally, but the signals are often converted into digital form for transmission over long distances. If the telephone instrument itself generated digital output when spoken into, and the line, the exchange, and the remainder of the network could handle digital signals, then either the telephone or any other device generating a digital output could be used as the source - limited to some data rate according to the design of the system.

This, or something resembling it, is currently the objective of many major PTTs including the UK, Japan, Germany, France, Scandinavia, Australia, Italy, Canada, and the USA. PTTs usually start by setting up a "data network" which consists of terminals connected to an analogue telephone line via a modem, and then via the local exchange to a node on a network accessible by a dialled number. The signals are then routed through the network, probably a packet switched network, cobbled together by the PTTs from whatever exists in the way of cable, microwave, or satellite links.

Private network organisations such as Telenet, Tymnet, etc., offer data network facilities which are cobbled together in the same manner. For higher speeds, direct lines to a network can be leased to bypass the local line/telephone exchange narrow-band bottleneck. It behoves an organisation which wants to set up an intra-site network in the most efficient way to take on a communications manager who can expertly do the cobbling with equipment, and publicly available or leased links, for minimum acquisition and running costs.

To convert the world's telephone/data system to an ISDN is a mammoth task which has to be done without interrupting existing facilities. For example British Telecom is changing the UK system to an ISDN by overlaying and gradual substitution as described by Hughes. Ultimately all subscribers will be able to use digital data or voice equipment from their home or business at up to 140 Kbps using the existing pair running from their telephone to the local exchange. Existing cables are quite capable of handling these speeds.

Subscribers will be able to use equipment running at various bit rates up to the permitted maximum. The ISDN must be able to work at a range of speeds and pack the data into lines up to the limits of their capacity to minimise costs. This will entail modifications - hence the word "overlay". For example at exchanges, variable bit rate switches will be required. Initially they will run in parallel with existing equipment. Eventually all subscribers will be provided with the new facilities and at that time the old equipment can be removed.

<u>DATA AND VOICE TRANSMISSION IN THE OFFICE</u>

<u>Information-flow and bit-flow</u>

Ellis equates the flow of data during half an hour per day spent on the telphone with the retrieval of 4000 pages of coded text or 400 pages of image data. It's worth reflecting upon the difference between "communication-theory information" - which is to do with the amount of correctly received bits - and "human-information" - which is to do with data representing a potential increase in the recipient's knowledge.

The maths behind Ellis' remarks is about right. A data transmission rate of 64 Kbps a second is needed in order to transmit digitised speech which will be heard as good quality speech when "reconstituted" at the receiver. The new technology telephone network (ISDN) will handle this, so 64,000 x 60 x 30 = 115.2 Mbits will be transmitted during 30 minutes of conversation (more or less). 115 Mbits also represents about 14 million 8-bit characters, so that would allow 14M/4000 = 3500 characters to be transmitted or say 600-700 words, for each of the 4000 pages mentioned by Ellis. This is equivalent to about 40 images (assuming that each image requires roughly 100 times as many bits as a page).

The same number of bits flow in the above three cases, but is the "value" of the data - potentially an increase in knowledge - the same? That question cannot be answered. Who can say whether 40 images is comparable with half an hour's telephone conversation? The old saying "a picture is worth a thousand words" is nice, but not quantitatively significant. Conversation may dominate the network for various reasons but not necessarily because it is intrinsically superior for information transmission.

Some work has been done by Stamp (private correspondence between C.Stamp, Westport and A.E.Cawkell) resulting in the conclusion "the eye is seven times faster than the ear". Tests showed that people can take in information by reading at least seven times faster than they can take it in by listening. The problem is how to measure the actual amount of information gained in the two cases.

So far as the business world is concerned there is a need for information in whatever media or format is convenient at the time, preferably unconstrained by devices which are hard to use.

Handling voice and data in the office

"Data under voice" means the use of a single office telephone line carrying voice and data on to the office desk, eventually leading to an integrated data-assisted telephone. "Store and Forward Voice and Data" is associated with PABX's, Teletex, and the Message Handling Facility Standard emerging as X400 which covers Teletex as well. X400 is an attempt to standardise facilities such as message addressing by name, storing one message and sending it to multiple addressees, etc. The convergence of voice and data handling with the software on personal computers is making progress hard to follow. In this area manufacturers are trying out various gadgets but it is hard to find out what people are buying and using. The conflicting claims made for LANs and PABXs doesn't help.

The incentives are to try to find products in a supposedly large market for voice text and image electronic mail, electronic diaries and telephone directories, information retrieval systems, etc.

The main features of a PABX include a number of lines to the local exchange, and more recently direct dialling to and from extensions which have their own telephone numbers. Small PABXs have ten extensions and the larger ones have hundreds or thousands. Stored program control in PABXs enables facilities like last number recall, automatic call re-direction, conference calls etc.

For example in Datapoint's Information Switching Exchange (ISX) a Central Switching Unit (CSU) controls and interconnects several facilities:- A; external communications via public or private lines, B; remote switching units (RSU) which look after clusters of telephones and low speed data devices and C; interfaces to Datapoint's ARC local network to which are connected high speed data devices.

The CSU automatically ensures that data is conveyed by the route best suited to it. For example a user served by a particular RSU (the PABX part of the system) can have a digital telephone and a work station on her desk. Internal and external telephone calls use a low speed route, but the work station is routed through to the ARC network for access to a word processing system. A lengthy report, created using this facility, might be printed by retrieval from storage on to a high speed printer, the store and the printer being interconnected by the ARC network.

This kind of PABX is fairly typical of many. The PABX is a development of the old Private Manual Branch Exchange. One of the major improvements that came with it was the "cordless" exchange which did away with a spider's web of cords, plugs, and sockets. PABXs were used in the 1960s to carry low speed data, and presumably will in due course become ISPBXs embodying the necessary signalling arrangements for connection to the ISDN through 2 Mbit links, providing a block of 30 64 Kbs circuits.

The leaders in this field seem to be Northern Telecom (Bell) who introduced the SL1 digital PBX. The IBM 3750 and the Mitel SX200 followed and then a number of other PABXs followed in Europe from Philips, Plessey, GEC, ITT, Thorn-Ericsson and others. British Telecom supplied its own small PABX - the Monarch which included microprocessor control and PCM.

The newest PABXs handle digitised voice and data in the same way and in theory no extension ever gets an engaged or busy signal because all outside lines are being used. In 1984 the Cygnet Cosystem integrated computer/telephone was announced followed by Rolm's Cedar and Juniper and in 1985 Northern Telecom's Meridian. The first idea was to supply an IBM compatible micro for connection to the local PABX, and the models from Meridian can be used this way although one of them - the DV-1 - is a self contained data/voice system for offices needing up to 100 extensions but connecting straight to outside networks and providing extensions to workstations running at over 2 Mbps.

It is far from clear at present whether this trend to nothing less than dispensing with the services of conventional telephone operators altogether will be to the taste of the office community, nor whether any of these new machines are sufficiently easy to use for there to be any real move in this direction.

CELLULAR RADIO

The trouble with CB radio

Citizen's Band (CB) radio has not caught on at the predicted rate in Britain for a reason that should not have been unexpected. The availability of bandwidth or, in radio terms, "radio channels", and the permitted range, have been inadequate. CB radio stations, are not, of course, interconnected via the telephone system; the links are direct station-to-station radio links. People jam each other's conversations trying to communicate on the same channel; the actual benefit for most people, once the new toy syndrome has worn off, is small; thousands, or perhaps a few tens of thousands, rather than the expected millions, of CB radios are in serious use.

The range is only 5 to 15 miles depending on the effects of line-of-sight obstacles on the low power 27 MHz radio waves. Some would say that this is all the fault of the Home Office - notorious for being niggardly in handing out channels on the grounds of "classified requirements". In the US, much more space is available - particularly in the newly allocated 900 MHz band - but this is still not enough. Bandwidth limitations   may diminish as the technology makes the economics of using higher and higher frequency bands come right, but, for the time being, the wavebands available below about 1 million MHz (1 GHz) are at a premium.

The mobile business radio-telephone is often regarded as a rich man's toy - an impression supported in films and on television, as the tycoon picks up the phone in his Roller (Rolls Royce) and buys some more gold shares. There is some justification for this impression - in 1983 there were less than 4000 such telephones in the Greater London area, using BT's system.

A change for the better?

But, we are told, all this is changing - or at least the means of changing has appeared, and the pundits seem to think that the demand is there.   In a cellular radio system an area is divided into small cells, each with a low power station, for handling telephone calls from mobiles - that is, in the main, cars - in its area. As the user moves out of range a central control system detects this, and the radio link is automatically transferred to the station handling users in the next cell. The beauty of the idea is that if the number of mobiles exceeds the the number that each or any cell can handle, you simply decrease the size of the cell or cells, which is rather easily done.

Methods and systems

In the "narrow band" system, a complete cellular radio net uses several low power channels, but stations in the adjacent cells operate at a different frequency. The power of the stations in more distant cells, operating at the same frequency, is insufficient to cause interference.

The main alternative method is called "frequency hopping" or "spread spectrum", not yet commercially available. In this method, one band, at least as wide as the total bandwidth occupied by the several frequencies of narrowband channels, is required, on which all stations operate. Each station rapidly hops from one frequency to another. This is done so that each available frequency receives about the same amount of use. For several reasons which I won't discuss here, the system works using less bandwidth than might intuitively be expected. Stations hop in a pre- determined pattern; spectral efficiency is limited by the amount of interference which is tolerable.

The razzmatazz accompanying the cellular radio push is typical of the new technology. Incidentally that word - quite out of reach if you play Scrabble - means "noisy or showy fuss or activity; a spree or frolic as in the phrase "on the razzle-dazzle"". It is not derived from the US "razz", (a raspberry) but from the Moorish habit of embarking upon a "razzia", or raid for beautiful slaves. Unfortunately the word is becoming dated.

Returning from slaves to cellular radio , until quite recently there were only three small scale systems or experiments in existence. One was in Chicago, an experiment with a few thousand participants by AT&T using a system called AMPS. Another was the Nordic Mobile Telephone (NMT), operating in Scandinavian countries using the Ericcson SRA CMS 8800 system. The third was the NTT system operating in several Japanese cities manufactured by Nippon Electric (NEC). All use variations of the narrowband system.

Spread spectrum systems are widely used for military purposes, but seem to be just a gleam in the eye for civilian use. The variations possible in narrow band systems have given rise to intense competition; each variation appears to have certain advantages under certain conditions.

The US scene

In the US, developments were held up until June 1982, when the FCC decided to issue licences to telephone companies in major cities for half of the available 40 MHz bandwidth, and to others for the remainder. This ruling survived the outcry about "uncompetitive practice" which followed. In spite of that there were many applications for licences. In fact this ruling

probably will favour AT&T which in spite of the anti-trust arrangements is
ensured a large market for its subsidiary. Anaconda-Ericsson's MT system is also
expected to do well.

     Cellular radio services are expected in 30 selected locations by the end of
1985. The first operational system is being run by Metromedia in the
Washington-Baltimore area. Although voice is the main application, data
transmission is also a possibility. However there is some doubt about
interruption, followed by computer disconnection, caused by edge of area fading
or when a mobile station is switched between control stations.

<u>And in the UK...</u>

     Towards the end of 1982, the UK government decided to licence two
competitive networks, one to be run by British Telecom/Securicor (Cellnet), the
other to be decided. In December 1982 the other was awarded to Racal/Hambros
Bank and Millicom (Vodafone), who defeated a Ferranti led consortium and Cable &
Wireless/Telephone Rentals. Several technical alternatives were considered,
particularly AMPS and MATS-E developed by Philips. In the event, TACS a UK
manufactured version of AMPS, is being used by both UK services. This version
conforms to what is hoped to become the European standard, providing up to 1000
channels separated by 25 KHz in the 890-960 MHz band.

     The Racal award provoked a response from   Philips who suggested
that an opportunity to create a European system had been lost, and Europe
would end up, once again, as a good market for US exports. In spite of
that, optimistic forecasts about job creation in the UK followed in the
expectation that there would be a demand for cellular radio in the
hundreds of thousands. Although the competing systems had been introduced and
were being heavily advertised in January 1985 we will be unable to see what
happens until 1986 when the equipment will be available in volume.

     The purchase price for a car installation is £1275 for Vodafone and £1350
for Cellnet. Estimates for 1985 sales are up to 25,000 which seems optimistic.
For the time being there is a flat rate charge of 43*p* a minute to call to a car,
and 25p a minute for a call from a car, regardless of distance. This compares
with 5p for 2 minutes (local calls), 15p up to 35 miles, and 40p over 35 miles
(all at standard rate) for normal PSTN calls. Both services started up in the
London area and are gradually extending to the rest of the country, with
expectations of covering most of it by the end of 1986. The areas of the two
services often overlap, but where they do not, each service accepts traffic to
or from another's subscriber.

<u>FURTHER READING</u>

Abramson, N.
  In Computer Communication Networks. Prentice-Hall, 1972. Chapter 14.
    The ALOHA system.
Anon.
  International Resource Development Inc. Report 193, March 1982. Published
  by IRD, Norwalk, CO, U.S.A.
    Local networks and home information systems: the cable connection.
Anon.
  NCC Ltd., Oxford Road, Machester, England (on behalf of the IT Standards
  Committee for Private Users, Department of Industry).
    The User View of Communications Standards, 2nd edition March 1983,
Atkins, James D.
  IEEE Trans. Com-28(4), 527-538, April 1980.
    Path control; the transport network of SNA.

Authors, various.
  In Williams, M.B.(Ed), Pathways to the Information Society: Proc. 6th Int.
Conf. on Computer Communications, London, Sept 7th, 1982. Published by
North-Holland 1982.
    Sections on Architecture and Protocols. Pps 753-987.
Blauman, Sheldon.
  Data Communications, 111-121, September 1982.
    Setting standards takes user, as well as vendor, input.
Bleazard, G.B.
  National Computing Centre Ltd., Manchester, England. 1982.
    Handbook of Data Communication.
Camana, Peter.
  IEEE Spectrum, 16(6), 24-29, June 1979.
    Video bandwidth compression: a study in tradeoffs.
Cheong, V.E.,Hirscheim, R.A.
  John Wiley. 1983.
    Local Area Networks: issues, products, and developments.
Cherry, Colin.
  MIT Press, Cambridge MA, and London, 1966.
    On Human communication.
    In Chapter 4, The analysis of signals, especially speech, page 190.
Cochrane, P.
  Proc. IEE, 131(7) Pt F, 669-683, December 1984.
    Future trends in telecommunications transmission - a personal view.
Doll, Dixon R.
  John Wiley 1978.
    Data Communications: facilities, networks and system design.
Elden, Walter L.
  In Local Networks & Distributed Office Systems. Online publications,
  Northwood Hills, Middlesex, England. 1981.
    Gateways for interconnecting local area and long haul networks.
Ellis C.W.H
  Online Publications Ltd., Northwood Hills, England. September 1981
  for IT Standards Unit, Department of Trade and Industry, London.
    Transcript of the Business Telecoms conference, London.
Farmer, W.D.; Newhall, E.E.
  In Proc ACM Symp. on problems in optimisation of data communication
  systems, Pine Mountain Ga., 1969. Pps 31-34.
    An experimental distributed switching system to handle bursty computer
    traffic.
Flint,David
  In Local Networks & Distributed Office Systems. Pub.by Online Publications
  Ltd., Northwood, Middlesex, UK. 1981. Page 573.
    The European market for local area networks.
Folts, Harold C.
  IEEE Trans. Com-28(4), 490-500, April 1980.
    X25 transaction oriented features - datagram and fast select.
Hughes, C.J.
  In Williams, M.B.(Ed), Pathways to the Information Society: Proc. 6th Int.
Conf. on Computer Communications, London, Sept 7th, 1982. Published by
North-Holland 1982.
    The long term future of circuit and non-circuit switching in multiservice
networks.
Hirsch, Phil.
  Datamation 20(3), 60-64, 1974.
    SITA - rating a packet switched network.
Jones, Thomas C.
  Data Communications, 123-131, July 1982.
    Paving the way for universal document interchange.

Kelly, J.K.
  In Micros in data processing: Online monograph no.4. 1980.
  Pub. by Online Publications, Northwood, Middlesex,
  England. Pages 25-40
    Communications.
Kelly, P.T.F.; Lee, E.J.B.
  PO Elec. Eng. J., 70, 208-215, January 1978.
    The telecommunications network for Euronet.
Lapidus, G.
  Data Communications 5(5), 20-24, 1976.
    SWIFT network.
Licklider, J.C.R.; Vezza. A.
  Proc IEEE 66(11), 1330-1346, November 1978.
    Applications of information networks.
Martin John.
  In 3rd World Telecommunication Forum, part 2, Geneva, 1979. Pub. by
  International Telecommunications Union (ITU) Geneve 20, Switzerland. Pps
  2.1.4.1 to 2.1.4.6.
    Technology and system design in telecommunications.
Mc-Ewan King R; Watkin, P;: Kunz M; Barber T.G.W.
  In Business Telecommunications, Amsterdam, 1977. Online Conferences,
Northwood Hills, Middlesex, England.
    The PTTs and common carriers.
McQuillan, John M.
  Computer Networks, 4, 235-238, 1980.
    Local network technology and the lessons of history.
Mier, Edwin E.
  Data Communications, 71-101 July 1982.
    High-level protocols, standards, and the OSI reference model.
Pouzin, Louis; Zimmerman, Hubert.
  Proc. IEEE 66(11), 1346-1370, November 1978.
    A tutorial on protocols.
Reeves, A.H.
  IEEE Spectrum 2(5), 58-62, 1965.
    Past, present and future of PCM.
Rybczynski, Antony.
  IEEE Trans. Com-28(4), 500-510, April 1980.
    X25 interface and end-to-end virtual service characteristics.
Schindler, S.
  Computer   Networks 6(4),   291-298, 1982.
    The new ISO standards for communications and office automation.
Shannon, Claude E.
  Bell System Technical Journal 27(3),   379-423,   July,   and
  27(4), 623-656, August 1848.
    A mathematical theory of communication.
Simmons, Brian.
  Communicate 5(6), 62-64, June 1985.
    Digital network signalling.
Tanenbaum, Andrew S.
  Computing Surveys 13(4), 453-489, December 1981.
    Network protocols.
Von Studnitz, Peter.
  Computer Networks 7, 27-35, 1983.
    Transport protocols: their performance and status in international
    standardization.
Wecker, Stuart.
  IEEE Trans. Com-28(4), 510-526, April 1980.
    DNA; the digital network architecture.
Welch, S.
  Peter Peregrinus, London, 1979.
    Signalling in telecommunications networks.

CHAPTER 7. FIBREOPTIC TECHNOLOGY AND TRANSMISSION SYSTEMS

Introduction

Fibreoptic communication is achieved by modulating a light source such as a Light Emitting Diode (LED) or for greater energy a laser, with electrical signals. The modulated light is propagated along a fibre and detected at the other end by a photodiode which generates electrical signals when light falls upon it.

Fibreoptic cable transmission has a number of advantages. The transmission loss is much lower than in coaxial cable until recently the only kind of cable used for wideband transmission except over short distances. This brings with it the advantage of fewer repeaters (amplifiers) - of particular importance for undersea cables. The bandwidth can be over 100 GHz per Km. Fibreoptic cable is thin , light, and flexible. Unlike metallic cables there is no possibility of induced noise or interference from close parallel cables. Manufacturing materials are cheap and abundant.

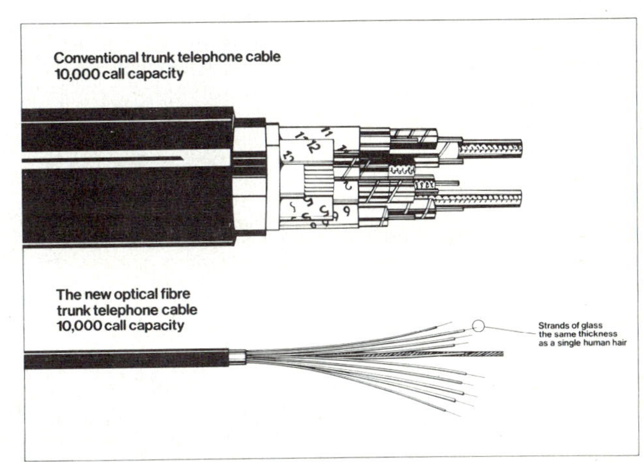

FIGURE 7.1. COAXIAL AND FIBREOPTIC CABLE
(Courtesy British Telecom)

There are also some disadvantages. Excessive bending may fracture the glass and long term changes in cable, particularly when strained, are unknown.

The connectors used for fibreoptic components are expensive but the total cost of a fibreoptic link is competitive with coaxial cable for some purposes with the probability that coax will be displaced by fibreoptic for many purposes in the near future.

The phenomena of the total internal reflection of light within a curved glass rod, and so transmission along it, was demonstrated by John Tyndall at the Royal Institution, London, in 1870. Tyndall was conducting a scientific public lecture - a tradition which continues at the RI to this day. In 1880 Wheeler applied for a US patent to conduct light round a building through glass tubes. The work leading to today's fibres really started with experiments in optical communication using a laser for line-of-sight communication in 1960 by S.E.Miller and others when working lasers first became available.

In 1966 two engineers, Kao and Hockham, working at Standard Telephones & Cables (STC) in London put forward the idea of "Dielectric fibre surface waveguides for optical frequencies" and predicted that fibres could be made with a transmission loss of about 20db/Km..."with an important potential as a new form of communications medium". This paper was the forerunner of modern fibreoptics. It stimulated research at Corning Glass in the US where in 1970 an optical fibre with a loss of 20db/Km was produced by Kapron and others according to those predictions and fibreoptic communications looked like becoming a practical proposition. (See Chapter 1 for an explanation of "db").

Progress has been rapid. In 1977 STC installed a fibreoptic link between telephone exchanges in Hitchin and Stevenage, England - a distance of about 15 Km - capable of a data rate of 120 million bits per second (Mbps). In that same year Bell telephone used an 11Km length of fibreoptic cable for the transmission of some thousands of telephone conversations in Atlanta, USA.   In 1983 the Japanese achieved a transmission rate of 446 Mbps through a single fibre 134 Kms long without intervening repeaters (amplifiers). Jumping to the near future, the next transatlantic cable TAT-8, to be laid shortly, will be fibreoptic. Its capacity will be 560 Mbps equivalent to about 48,000 telephone channels.

Fibreoptic cables

One method of manufacturing an optical fibre consists of depositing layers of a silicon compound from a vapour on to the inside of a silica tube to produce the cladding. When a sufficient thickness has been built up, chlorides of phosphorous or germanium are added to the vapour to deposit what will become the core. The composite tube is then heated and collapsed to form a rod which is drawn out into a thin fibre. A number of fibres are usually carried within the same cable.To give strength, steel strands are included and the cable is protected by a strong outer sheath.

Total internal reflection of a light beam takes place at the cladding-core interface - provided that the angle of the introduced light does not exceed a critical value - because of

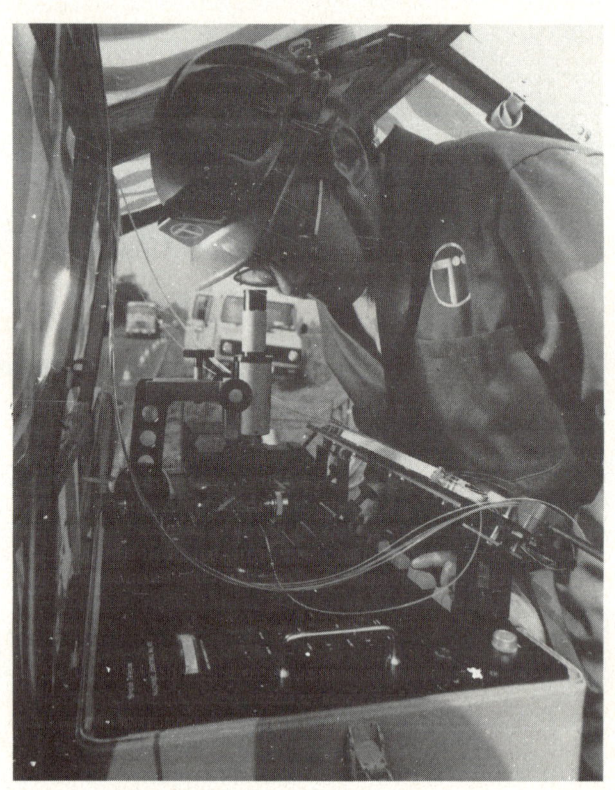

FIGURE 7.2. JOINING FIBREOPTIC CABLE IN THE FIELD
(Courtesy British Telecom)

the differing refractive indices of the two regions. There is some loss of energy by dispersion in the cladding.

When the diameter of the core is small compared with the wavelength of the transmitted light, light rays proceed along the tube zig-zag fashion and emerge out of phase. This causes inter-symbol interference problems during pulse (data) transmission at fast transmission rates so the rate must be slowed. In other words there appears to be a _bandwidth_ limitation; until recently it was believed that phasing problems would limit the pulse rate to about 150 Mbps. "Multi-ray" fibres of this type are called _Multimode Fibres_.

The effects of velocity and phase differences can be reduced by using a core with a refractive index which changes slightly from surface to centre - a _Graded Index_ fibre. But if the diameter is comparable with the light wavelength the mode of propagation changes and can only be explained in mathematical terms   outside the scope of this book. Fibres of this type are sometimes called "optical waveguides". In effect, a single ray proceeds along the core with no phase problems and little loss of energy. Such fibres are called <u>Monomode Fibres</u>.

If light sources generated a narrow beam of light with a single wavelength then the ray inter-phasing problem would be non-existent; the invention of the laser was a huge step forward towards an ideal energy source. The latest lasers generate light over a narrow band of wavelengths, but even in a laser generating red light of only 6 nanometres (nm) spectral width, light from one end of the emitted spectrum will arrive several nanoseconds later in a 100 Km cable than light from the other end of the spectrum. (A micron or micrometer (um) is one millionth of a metre. 1 nanometre is one thousandth of a micron).

Developments are in hand to improve fibre performance by special modifications of the fibre's refractive index characteristics, and some recent claims have been made for very fast transmission rates. Unless new announcements differentiate between laboratory tests and field use, and the application and the error rate is stated it is difficult to assess the claims. In any fibre, inter-symbol interference will cause transmission errors if the transmission rate is increased towards the limiting value and any further rate increase may result in an unacceptable performance for a particular application. Early in 1984 AT&T announced a transmission rate of 1 Gigabit per second (Gbps. 1 Gigabit = 1000 Megabits) in a cable well over 100 Kms in length.

Although the 1970 experimental fibres used monomode transmission, the technology was insufficiently advanced for the manufacture of complete monomode systems and for the next few years multimode cables were used with core diameters typically 50 micrometres (um) and a theoretical maximum data rate of about 600 Mbps per Km for the best graded index fibres. By 1976 advances prompted a move towards monomode fibres with core diameters of around 1.4 um.

Another important practical aspect of fibreoptic cables was how to manufacture them to withstand the stresses encountered in the manufacturing processes and afterwards during the handling and cable laying. Other problems included devising low-loss splicing tecniques and producing junctions, plugs and sockets etc. Solutions were found and the basis for a new industry was established.

Although Corning in the US pioneered manufacturing processes the Japanese started to catch up in the 1970s. NTT developed a process called Vapour Phase Axial Deposition (VAD) which enables high quality fibres to be produced faster than at Corning using their Chemical Vapour Deposition process. An extremely long fibre can be drawn out from the preform made by this process. Prices per unit length are expected soon to compare with the price of conventional cable. The Japanese have been able to undercut Corning in within-US bidding for contracts.

To summarise, improvements in performance, which, for most purposes, means longer distances without repeaters at faster transmission rates, have been achieved by three processes - accumulation of manufacturing know-how, change of light wavelength, and mode of propagation. The first systems operated at light wavelengths of around 0.8 um. A small increase in wavelength reduces dispersion and attenuation and when single-mode fibres became available it became possible to use the so-called "long" wavelengths up to about 1.65 um and move towards the ideal single frequency zero dispersion light beam.

<u>Costs</u>

A fibreoptic system - that is the cable and the terminating equipment - seems to have an undisputed advantage for long-distance wideband communications mainly because the cost per unit length of cable is lower and fewer repeaters are required than for coaxial cable. As the distance decreases so does the cost differential. Somewhere below the distance at which the first repeater becomes necessary in a coax system, probably now well below it, and possibly at a distance of only 1000 metres there is a crossover point where the costs are roughly equal. It is arguable whether coaxial cable will be able to compete over any distance before long because below about 500 metres it is not used much anyway - twisted pairs suffice for many purposes.

At least until very recently, the cost of items like fibreoptic connectors and transducers were higher than their coaxial equivalents and at distances below, say, 2000 metres, these items formed the bulk of the cost. However for shorter distances cheaper fibreoptic transducers and plastic instead of glass cable can be used so the future for coax look like being squeezed out where short range fibreoptics ends and twisted pair starts.

Light transmitters

LEDs

Light Emitting Diodes (LEDs) or Lasers are used as electrical to optical transducers for fibreoptic systems. Both emit light which can be coupled into a fibre and which can be modulated by electrical impulses.

The surface-emitting LED was first used by Burrus in 1969. It was made by diffusing Zinc into n-type Gallium Arsenide (GaAs) on a small chip (See Chapter 2 for more about semiconductor technology). Light is emitted at a p-n junction when current is passed through the device and is coupled to a fibre which is fixed close-up to the junction by etching a well in the surface and fixing the fibre with epoxy resin.

In later developments layers of GaAs and Gallium Aluminium Arsenide (GaAlAs) have been used and a more directional transmission has been obtained by radiation from the edge instead of from the surface of the chip. Theoretically a few milliwatts of power can be launched into a fibre by greatly improving the coupling with a tiny lens between the etched well and the fibre. In practice up to about 150 uw is obtained with an applied current of up to 150 milliamperes (ma). Current research seems to have moved on to experiments with Indium Gallium Arsenide Phosphorous (InGaAsP) chips emitting light with a wavelength of 1.3 um. The major advantages over Lasers is lower cost and longer life.

At the end of 1984, LEDs cost from \$100 to \$1000 in singles with higher prices for shorter wavelengths. These include the STC LH01-10, RCA C86013E and Plessey HR1310.

Lasers

All lasers contain a long cavity with partially reflecting mirrors at either end, called a Fabry-Perot cavity. A semiconductor laser consists basically of a sandwich of appropriate p-type and n-type semiconducting materials. Current in n-type semiconductors is carried by mobile negative charges (donated electrons), and in p-type by mobile positive charges (holes) characterised by the absence of an electron. Between the sandwich there is a narrow "depletion zone" across which a small potential exists and within which the charges neutralise each other. These electrical conditions are virtually identical to the conditions existing in a semiconductor diode (A transistor consists of a three-layer n-p-n or p-n-p sandwich).

When a "forward voltage" is applied across the sandwich - that is the p-type material is made sufficiently positive to overcome the resident potential -

electrons move from n to p and some combine with holes moving in the opposite direction. In contrast to conditions in normal semiconductors, the material used in semiconductor lasers is chosen to encourage radiation at a particular wavelength when holes and electrons combine. To better confine and control this radiation a third layer of semiconducting material in inserted between the p-n sandwich and it is this layer which forms the filament or waveguide cavity with mirrors at either end.

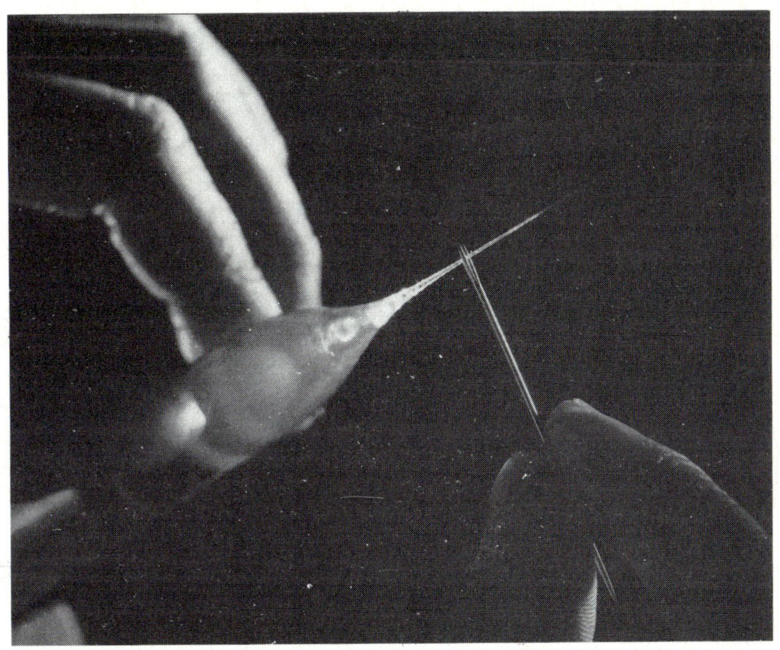

FIGURE 7.3. A PARTLY DRAWN FIBRE
(Courtesy British Telecom)

The dimensions of this cavity are chosen for resonance at the wavelength in question - that is radiated light at that wavelength only is reinforced as it is reflected to and fro across the cavity.

P.A.Kirby, who is involved in developing lasers for long-haul undersea and landline fibreoptic transmission systems at STC, Harlow, England, has described a laser typical of those currently used. This laser is a chip 300 um (0.3 mm) long made of layers of semi-conducting InP and GaInAsP alloys with oxide insulation. Very small facets at either end of the central active layer form partially transparent reflecting mirrors. Laser oscillations resulting in the emission of light take place in a narrow filament of the material between the mirrors, and a narrow intense beam of light is projected through one of them. Several milliwatts of light power are generated, the narrow beam providing higher coupling efficiency to a fibre than is possible with an LED.

Later developments on similar striped double heterostructure chips, as they are called, aim at producing narrower inter-mirror filaments to promote a single mode beam by ensuring that the filament behaves as a waveguide.

The latest advance in special purpose lasers, believed to be not yet available commercially, is the double injection-locked laser. The light output from one laser is focused on a second which is forced into oscillation at the same frequency and is pulsed on or off to generate the information-carrying signal. The second is designed specifically to generate an extremely narrow beam. Widths of less than 0.003 nm have been claimed. Such a beam would exhibit hardly any spreading in cables over 100 Km long. In experiments at BT, transmissions at 140 Mbps with 1.52 um light using a laser of this type took place in 1982. There was a 0.5db loss in a monomode cable over 100 Kms long.

Long wavelength lasers include Siemens SFH 428 5 mw laser and Power Technology CL200 for which a power of over 75 mw is claimed at 1.2 um. The so-called advanced lasers with filaments of 3 um or less include AEG-Telefunken CQX20, Hamamatsu G308 and NEC 3205. Lasers cost from $3000 upwards in singles.

Light receivers

PIN or avalanche photodiodes are used as receivers. PIN stands for the semiconducting structure of the device which consists of an n substrate, with deposited p and intrinsically n regions.

PIN diode materials consist of Germanium or InGaAs. Electrons are generated from incident photons, and satisfactory operation is obtained with light of 1.5 um wavelength.   An avalanche photodiode uses similar materials but is arranged to operate with a higher field gradient from a higher applied reverse bias voltage. Impact ionisation produces a higher photocurrent so the avalanche diode produces a current gain at the expense of some increase in noise.

Because of the low signal levels, improved designs for the required transistor amplifiers have been developed. The important factor is that the detector circuits which follow should be able unambiguously to decide between signals and noise.

APPLICATIONS

PTT wideband services

A number of experimental fibreoptic cable laying and testing experiments took place in the late 70s in several countries using multimode fibres at transmission rates up to about 100 Mbps.

In the period 1975 to 1977 British Telecom and the BBC carried out tests at 120 Mbps both for data and digital transmission. STC laid a fibreoptic cable between telephone exchanges at Hitchin and Stevenage, a distance of 9 Km. This was a 4-fibre cable 7mm in diameter. In January 1984 BT brought into regular service a 17 Km link between Luton and Milton Keynes claimed to be the first in use anywhere using monomode fibre operating at 140 Mbps.

The first major real application was in the Japanese Hi-Ovis "wired city" project which started in 1978. Fibreoptic cables were laid to individual house to provide wideband video services including two way video and facsimile services. Similar experiments followed at Biarritz in France and at Milton Keynes in England.

Since then fibreoptic systems have come into use for PTT junction or inter-exchange use where distances are often less than 12 Km and speeds of up to 30 Mps are required. For greater distances fibreoptic cables are now widely used. AT&T are reported to have laid 200,000 miles of fibreoptic cable in 1983 and plans to spend $2 billion during 1985/6 on fibreoptic networks.

British Telecom had spent £40 million by the end of 1982 and expected to interconnect all major cities in the UK with fibreoptic cable during the eighties. The Japanese spent about 60 billion Yen on PTT fibreoptics during 1984. In 1983/1984 NTT contructed a fibreoptic network using 3000 Km of cable interconnecting a number of islands in Japan.

The TAT8 transatlantic cable will cost around $335 million with AT&T getting the lion's share and STC and a French company also participating. The basic capacity will be 8000 telephone conversations using 1.3um monomode cable, but this can be increased to 40,000 when needed by multiplexing.

Cable services

The use of fibreoptic cable for these services is discussed in Chapter 22. The particular problem in 1985, where cable does not already exist, is whether to install an all-fibreoptic or partly-fibreoptic cable system now, or await further developments in technology and lower prices. Alternatively if coaxial cable is used now with its low-risk well-established technology, will this lower-bandwidth non-interactive arrangement become so well established that the fibreoptic potential won't be realised for many years?

One "play-it-safe" compromise has been adopted by British Telecom who placed a £4m contract with STC in May 1984 for components for a "switched star" cable TV system. Fibreoptic cables radiate out from the head-end to switches in street cabinets scattered throughout the franchise area. The repeaterless cables can easily handle the multi-channel bandwidth/distance requirements.

Each switch connects to up to 300 subscribers by co-axial cable. Presumably the distance/cost/tested termination equation indicated coax in this part of the system. The short length of repeaterless coax is not required to carry all the channels. A subscriber will dial through to the switch where his coax is connected to whichever "channel box" he selects. Channel boxes are the devices tuned to each of the channels emanating from the fibreoptic cable.

Local communications

LANs

For local communications such as with LANs, the advantages of fibreoptics are ease of installation (since the cables are extremely thin), very high data capacity, immunity from interference (which may be important if IIf industrial electrical equipment is in the vicinity), and immunity from electronic eavesdropping - that is high security. The black art of optical eavesdropping hasn't arrived yet.

Against fibreoptics, at least until very frequently, has been the cost of the bits and pieces which swamp the lower cost of the cable which is needed only in small quantities, and the losses introduced by joints, plugs and sockets, etc. This is likely to change because the disadvantages are being steadily overcome.

One way of overcoming the disadvantage of lossy interconnections is to connect stations in a star arrangement with a passive distribution device at the hub so that when anyone transmits all other stations receive the signal but only the one to whom it is addressed decodes it. Anti-collision arrangements are incorporated as normally (see Chapter 6).

One system of this kind called Codestar (made by Codenoll) is compatible with Ethernet and can be connected to an existing Ethernet network. One star arrangement can handle 64 stations, but a "superstar" system can be set up in which any leg can be connected to the hub of another star from which further connections radiate out to more stations. In this way 1024 stations can be interconnected. The system is said to be capable of covering an area sixteen times greater than Ethernet.

A somewhat similar system is available called Fibrenet which is the fibreoptic version of Ethernet. In this arrangement signals from a transceiver bus are connected to a central amplifier and multi-way distributor for individual fibreoptic cables to each transceiver. This arrangement reduces by some 60 db the losses which would otherwise occur in the couplers which would be needed in a conventionally connected system.

<u>Inter-equipment links</u>

A number of manufacturers can supply fibreoptic communication links often consisting of electrical to optical interfaces at either end of a length of fibreoptic cable ready to plug in to so-called "standard" electrical input/output sockets. One of the earliest in this field was Hewlett-Packard. Currently (January 1985) three systems are available - a short range system using plastic cable, and a longer range "Miniature Link" in standard and high performance versions. An evaluation kit for the plastic system consists of electrical/optical transducers (LED for transmission, PIN for reception) and a length of cable (maximum length 20 metres for a 5 Mbps rate) at £28.50 in the UK. The cable can be cut to length and no special precision is needed in connecting it at either end.

The Miniature Link also uses LED/PIN transducers but with a glass fibre link which can be up to 2 Km long for 40 Mbps. In this case special care is required for the fibre terminations. An evaluation kit with 10 metres of cable costs £154 in the UK. For a longer distance it would be necessary to buy a pair of transducers which cost £60 plus cable from a specialist supplier such as Pilkingtons in the UK.

In these Hewlett Packard systems, connecting plugs are not provided. Wires emerge for the customer to make his own arrangements. The electrical input/output is TTL (Transistor-Transistor-Logic) compatible - that is the electrical on/off pulses must be +5/0 volts. H-P can offer a ready to use RS232 fibreoptic multiplexer system consisting, in effect of 16 cables with plugs for RS232 interfaces. Cables lead to a "black box" from which a single fibreoptic cable emerges for connection to a remote box of the same kind from which 16 cables fan out to RS232 connectors thereby providing a 16 channel system.

<u>Further reading</u>

Carter. A.C.
  The Radio & Electronic Engineer 51(7/8), 341-348, July/August 1981.
    Light emitting diodes for optical fibre systems.
Kao, K.C., Hockham, G.A.
  IEE Proc. 113(7), 1151-1158, July 1966.
    Dielectric fibre surface waveguides for optical frequencies.
Kimura, Tatsuya; Yamamoto, Yoshihisa.
  Optical and Quantum Electronics 15(1983), 1-39.
    Review: Progress of coherent optical fibre communication systems.
Kirby, P.A.
  The Radio & Electronic Engineer 51(7/8), 362-376, July/August 1981.
    Semiconductor laser sources for optical communication.
Schwartz, Morton I.
  IEEE Communications Mag. 22(5), 38-48, 1984.
    Optical fiber transmission. From conception to prominence in 20 years.
Wilson, Brett.
  Wireless World 90(1580-1583), May-July 1984, 10pps (not continously
  numbered)
    Fibreoptic communications.

CHAPTER 8. SATELLITE COMMUNICATION TECHNOLOGY

A geostationary satellite does not fly off into space; the effect of its velocity is exactly balanced by gravitational pull. If the satellite's height is 22,282 miles and it is travelling at a speed which maintains it above the same spot on the rotating earth beneath, it is said to be in geosynchronous orbit.

Satellite communications have come a long way since Clarke's 1945 prediction that transmitters on three correctly positioned geostationary satellites could broadcast to receivers anywhere on the whole of the earth's surface. A portion of Clarke's famous article is shown in Figure 8.1.

The unique advantage of satellites versus cable for point to point teleommunications is that if n receiving aerials are visible from one satellite, the potential for two way communication exists between n(n-1)/2 receivers by up-down satellite relay. In other words any station can communicate with any other without an in-place terrestrial cable and switching network.

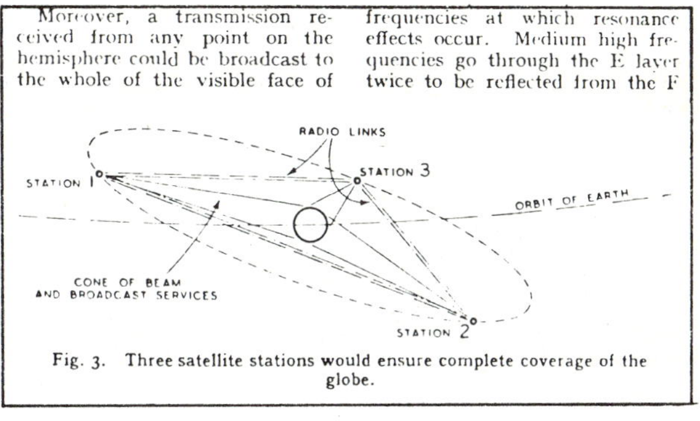

Fig. 3. Three satellite stations would ensure complete coverage of the globe.

Frequencies and Bandwidth

FIGURE 8.1 PART OF CLARKE'S PROPHETIC ARTICLE
(Courtesy Wireless World)

The frequencies used for satellite communications are above about 500 MHz.At these frequencies, transmissions pass through the ionosphere – a region above the earth containing free electrons produced by radiation from space – instead of being reflected by it as are lower frequency transmissions. Transmissions take a line of sight path.

A bonus from the adoption of these very high frequencies and short wavelengths is that because the dimensions of efficient aerials (antennae) are related to wavelength they are very small. A searchlight-like structure containing the aerial at the focal point of a parabolic metallic reflector can be constructed of manageable size. The energy can be concentrated into a narrow beam projected on to an area of the earth's surface.

The upper limit of the satellite communication spectrum is around 30 GHz where energy absorption by water vapour in the atmosphere becomes high. Thus the available bandwidth lies between 500 MHz and 30 Ghz – about 29 Ghz. A digitised telephone circuit occupies about 32 KHz, and a TV channel about 36 MHz, so this bandwidth, if occupied by transmitters radiating in all directions (isotropic), could accommodate about 900,000 telephone channels or 800 TV channels without mutual interference. However satellite transmitters are not isotropic. The energy is beamed, and one beam need not interfere with another. Consequently the available bandwidth is much greater since a number of transmitters can use beams on the same frequency without mutual interference.

Ramani points out, with reference to parts of his own country, India, where public networks do not exist, that satellite channels working at 64 Kbps are often more than adequate. For many types of communications the effective throughput averages only 100 bits per second, being limited by the keyboarding and reading speeds of users. He discusses special requirements in satellites which can provide economic facilities for this speed instead of at the usual very high speeds.

Satellites require to be spaced in orbital "slots" and for geosynchronous satellites there are only so many slots available in positions for optimum coverage of the areas of greatest demand. In spite of the huge bandwidths potentially available, the slot limitation offsets the beam advantage, and slot positions are at a premium. The allocation of slots is a matter for intense international haggling.

<u>Transponders</u>

Typically, signals are beamed up from a narrow beam ground station, changed into a different frequency, and beamed down using a beam designed to cover a specific area of the earth by a receiver-transmitter called a <u>transponder</u>. A transponder may be designed to receive data from more than one ground station, and may re-transmit the data singly, or with data from other stations spaced out over a frequency band, from one aerial, or may re-transmit from one or from several different aerials beamed to cover particular areas.

The latest satellites embody on-board switching to arrange for various combinations of aerials for particular areas of the earth. Earlier satellites incorporated less flexible arrangements - for example one transponder per TV channel, with a possible alternative of 1000 telephone circuits.

A "one-hop" up-down signal to and from a transponder on a satellite at a height of 22,282 miles takes about a quarter of a second to make the round trip. The adverse effects of this delay have been much less than expected, and provided the design and application of a system using a satellite link takes proper account of it, it is unlikely to present much of a problem for most applications.

Martin's book on the subject is highly recommended. It covers the field comprehensively and provides technical details and yet is very readable. The current edition is dated 1978 - a new edition is overdue. An overview of current general developments has been provided by Dusio, Courault, and Rothblatt.

<u>Development of Satellites</u>

Non-military satellite telecommunication applications have been, in chronological order, in the areas of public telecommunications (particularly voice), business telecomms, television/cable systems, and Direct Broadcast Satellites (DBS).

A corporation was set up in 1963 - the Communications Satellite Corporation - to manage the INTELSAT series of satellites, provided by its engineering subsidiary COMSAT on behalf of many participating countries. More satellites of increasing sophistication, greater capacity, and falling costs have characterised this system, used mainly by PTTs. The impact on the public has been the increasing coverage and falling costs of long distance telephone calls, and the relaying of TV programmes of high quality in real time.

In satellite as with cable technology, entertainment is the big market to provide the incentive for the capital investment - an incentive which the information market is unable to provide. We have to follow the entertainment-led growth and wait for information services to start riding on the infrastructure - blurred as the entertainment/information dividing line may be.

In consequence of a change from a restrictive to an "open skies" policy during the Nixon administration, commercial satellites started operating in the US with ground stations scattered round the country. For example the WESTAR satellite had 12 transponders each capable of handling 60 Mbps, hired for a variety of purposes including remote publication of the Wall St. Journal, oil rig communications, Sports TV links, telegrams and telex.

More recently, Satellite Business Systems, with IBM as one of the partners, became fully operational with the addition of its third satellite in 1983. It offers digital intra-organisation communication services (CNS) using a network of ground station and leased lines. A wideband data service for high volume customers called DNS was announced in 1982 but postponed perhaps because the demand did not materialise.

In 1985 a further de-regulatory step is being contemplated by the FCC - a request by five applicants to start transatlantic satellite services competing with Intelsat. This follows a Presidential decision last year that such competition would be in the national interest. This step will require co-operation from abroad both from partner-entrepreneurs and from governments ready to allow them to operate.

The USA: cable television

Transponders, usually one per channel, have been in high demand for cable TV programme distribution, over a hundred now being used on a number of different satellites. Table 8.1 shows the assignments, which were often changed, which existed in 1981 on RCA's Satcom 1. The satellite channels shown are used for distributing programmes to cable TV ground stations for further distribution through terrestrial cable networks.

Trans- ponder	Leesee	Trans- ponder	Leesee
1	Warner-Amex Nickleodeon	13	not used
2	People That Love	14	Cable News network
3	United Video (WGN Chicago)	15	Warner-Amex
4	not used	16	Showtime (Compact Vid)
5	Warner-Amex Movie Channel	17	Showtime (East. Micro)
6	South'n Systms. (Atlanta)	18	Reuters
7	Education & Sports Netwk.	19	Times-Mirror movies
8	Christian Broadcasting	20	Home Box Office (Cx.E)
9	USA Black Network	21	Home Theatre Net.
10	Showtime (Western feed)	22	Home Box Office (West)
11	Warner-Amex music channel	23	Home Box Office (Cx.W)
12	Showtime (Eastern feed)	24	Home Box Office (East)

TABLE 8.1. TRANSPONDER ASSIGNMENTS ON SATCOM 1

The USA: DBS

Direct Broadcast Satellites (DBS) are a more recent development based on entertainment and information distribution by satellite direct to homes. The prelude to this idea was the de-regulation of receive-only earth stations from restrictions by the FCC in 1979. The Holiday Inn chain immediately ordered 200 earth stations for its major hotels. By 1982 TVRO (TeleVision Receive Only) steerable dishes started to sprout in the US. They are cultivated by status seeking TV freaks who aim them at cable relay satellites and beat the system by obtaining free (having paid some thousands of dollars for the equipment) reception from dozens of transponders. A new journal caters for the demand by providing a "guide to satellites" with a schedule of all the programmes.

According to Beakely, TVRO prices stood at about $16,000 in 1974. By 1977 a few thousand had been sold at $8000, by 1980 a good many more at $3500, but prices have now dropped to around $1800 and are expected to drop to $1000 with sales in the hundreds of thousands.

Billings has reported on the plans of his company, Satellite Television Corporation for 1985/6 in the US. It will cost $100 to buy the small 0.75 metre diameter dish aerial/antenna and $24 a month to rent the rest of the electronics and programmes from 3 channels. The satellite's transmitters will embody high power (185w) travelling wave tube amplifiers and will radiate in the 12.2 to 12.7 GHz band.

The Mum's and Dad's of the TV freaks may well have been the radio freaks ("hams") who made a considerable difference to the development of communications. They were forced to use high frequencies, believed to be unuseable for long distance work, because licences were not granted for lower, tested, frequencies.

The move towards DBS in the US was accelerated by the award of FCC licences in 1983 to CBS, RCA, American Communications, Western Union, and Graphic Scanning, who are expected to be in the risky business of transmitting programmes direct to households by 1986. The potential advantages versus cable TV are obvious but the regulatory and recovery of the overall cost problems are not. However the probable cost of the dish and receiving adaptor seems to be fairly clear, as just stated.

As Billings points out satellite television will reach not only subscribers having other choices of TV, but also an estimated 25 million homes in the US to which it will not be feasible to lay cable. He also claims that minority viewers scattered around the country who prefer special programmes could be singled out and aggregated into an audience large enough to support the programmes they desire ("narrowcasting"). Perhaps this approach could be applied in the UK by a satellite/cable combination and the fears about "only wall to wall Dallas" will turn out to be unfounded.

Europe;Satellite development

The European space industry was a joke for some years.Then it grew gradually characterised by grudging cooperation delayed by national aspirations and national/commercial jockeying for leadership as the importance of the communications potential became

FIGURE 8.2
SATELLITE DISH ON A NORTH SEA OIL PLATFORM
(Courtesy British Telecom)

evident. Britain, once the leader, faded out following political wrangles. Latterly things have picked up. Nationalism was supressed to some degree when it was at last realised that resources would have to be pooled to make progress.

Currently the major actor is the European Space Agency (ESA) which supports the French Ariane rocket launcher, and a later more powerful version, and provides hardware for use by EUTELSAT, a consortium of European Telecommunication Administrations.

Europe; telecomms

The Orbital Test Satellite (OTS) was launched in 1978 as a Telecomms testbed. It is being followed by the European Communication Satellite (ECS) series of five satellites from 1983 onwards. Another larger multi-purpose satellite was started - the H-SAT - supported particularly by Germany, but it was stopped in 1978 apparently because the Germans wanted to jump to an operational phase more quickly. The special requirements of ship communications led to the MARECS satellite, working in conjunction with INTELSAT satellites, a successful project with the first satellite placed in orbit in December 1981. In addition to these ESA activities, France is launching a series of three TELECOM satellites for its own communication purposes, starting in 1984.

European television - broadcasting

Satellite television activities also rely on ESA services, but national and commercial forces seem to take over at the operational stage. The work on H-SAT spawned three successors.

L-SAT is a large multi-purpose satellite - the first to have spot beams with on-board switching - to be launched in 1986. Under the aegis of ESA, it is of particular UK interest, with British Aerospace as the prime contractor. The commercial possibilities have re-awakened long overdue UK interest. It will be used for Italian TV and may be used for direct TV broadcasting. The other two satellites which followed H-SAT are the Telediffusion de France (TDF), and the German TV-SAT, with transponders for at least three TV channels on each, possibly to be used for direct broadcasting. They should be operational in 1985.

The Franco/German TV-SAT will be launched by the Ariane rocket in 1985 followed by two years of operational trials, but there have been strong and serious warnings about the risks of introducing, without any limitations, direct satellite broadcasting which could undermine the national regulations of broadcasting. Presumably this indicates that the Germans do not wish to see any cracks appear in their regulatory arrangements - arguably the strictest in Western Europe. There is some doubt about the activities of Luxembourg RTL which at one time was contemplating private TV broadcasting over central Europe. This would upset the control of content maintained by the state monopolies.

Larry Blonstein of British Aerospace has provided us with some sums to consider for providing TV broadcasting satellites. The essentials of his sums are $600M for constructing, launching, insuring and operating 3 satellites providing 5 channels for 10 years. In order to provide the revenue to cover 70% utilisation at costs + 40% profit, the satellite provider must charge $24M per channel per year. He estimates (showing breakdowns) that the total annual production costs to operate a TV service (including satellite costs) to be $165M. After estimating advertising revenue for 6 minutes per hour per 12 hour day, and sale of programme royalties, Blonstein comes out with a loss of $55M. The break-even comes if 185,000 UK and European subscribers pay $25 per month for the service.

<u>UK television - DBS</u>

In the 1977 World Administrative Radio Conference (WARC) the UK was allocated a position at 31 degrees West for a satellite operating in the 12 Ghz band with provision for 5 TV channels radiated with a specified power, polarisation and earth footprint. A report was published in May 1981 setting out options for DBS in the UK. The service area for reception using a 0.9 metre aerial dish in a satellite to the WARC specification is shown in Figure 8.3.

A UK consortium of British Aerospace/Marconi/GEC/Brit. Telecom with some US participation as well, called UNISAT, contracted to make three satellites for BBC DBS ready in 1985/6. The BBC proposed to lease two channels, one providing national TV and radio services financed from licence fees, the other a subscription TV service based on the BBC/Visionhire experiment currently running in London. Services were expected to start in 1985/6. Technical details of household receivers are discussed by Phillips with an estimated volume production cost estimate at £200 in the UK.

In August 1983 IBA asked for channels on UNISAT for a service competing with the BBC. The cost was too high for the BBC alone anyway. Little real progress was being made with the project. A rapidly changing technology may change the satellite power/receiving aerial balance - perhaps economics and convenience will be better served with a more expensive higher powered satellite enabling smaller receiving dishes to be used.

It is embarrassing for the UK government, anxious to encourage the UK space industry, to be confronted with another factor as well - a preference by the club of 21 television

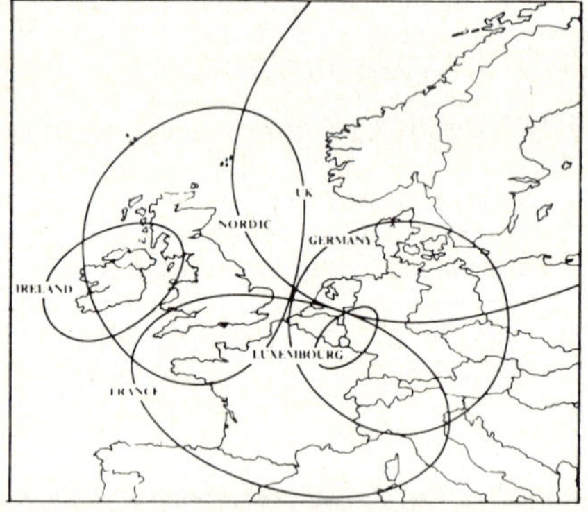

<u>FIGURE 8.3</u>
<u>DBS 0.9 METRE AERIAL SERVICE AREA</u>

TV and other companies who want the channels for a foreign satellite. The new proposal, with the patriotic name of Britsat, is to put up two satellites from RCA and charge a £40M year rental - far less expensive than UNISAT. As at May 1985 this is still being mulled over.

<u>European television - standards and de-regulation</u>

Following the UNISAT proposal a decision was needed about upgrading the picture quality to take advantage of the wider bandwidth available - the major restriction on the quality of terrestrial TV. During 1982, discussions started about the virtues of the BBC's improved system, extended PAL, or a system claimed to be better in several respects, developed by the Independent Broadcasting Authority and called C-MAC, the "C" designating the type of sound and the "MAC" meaning Multiple Analogue Component. At the end of 1982 the government accepted the recommendations of the Part committee and decided on C-MAC.

Attempts were made in 1983 to convince other European countries, through the European Broadcasting Union (EBU), that C-MAC should be the European standard. Agreement could not be reached. However in May 1985 the EEC industry ministers were again seriously considering a single standard with C-MAC as the front runner.

Meanwhile the UK de-regulated satellite reception rules. In May 1985 hotels, flats, and block of houses were allowed to erect dishes for DBS reception. It is not clear what effect whis will have on the cable industry which is struggling to establish itself. There will soon be a range of programmes receivable from two satellites - The European Communications Satellite or Intelsat 5. Special decoders will be needed for those destined for cable TV earth stations. The following programmes are or will be operating in 1985 requiring a two-position receiving dish of at least 1.2M diameter :-

Children's TV (UK from intelsat 5).
European Broadcasting Union channel.
Filmnet Dutch film channel.
Luxembourg TV channel.
Music Box UK pop music channel.
Premiere film (UK from Intelsat 5).
RAI Italian national channel.
Sat 1 and 3 (German). German entertainment programme.
Sky European entertainment/advertising channel already received by over 3 million viewers via cable.
Teleclub Swiss film channel.
TEN (UK film from Intelsat 5).
TV5 (France) entertainment and the Arts.

Direct Broadcast Satellites versus cables

Belton, in an article about this subject, takes care to avoid the controversy about the relative real costs of satellites and cable. He stresses the complimentary nature of these media. Satellites possess the advantage of multi-destination area coverage while cables have the advantage of very high point-to-point capability.

Satellite capacity has been growing and costs have been falling much more rapidly than cable in recent years, but cable economics are now stabilising with the overall effect of fibreoptics remaining uncertain.

Satellites and new jobs

According to Rolf Arnim, projections indicate that 2000 permanent new jobs will be created in the European space industry by DBS, and 85,000 new jobs in the electronics industries of France and Germany alone.

The general arrangement of a system called "Project Universe" is shown in Figure 8.4. It included OTS links and connections between the participating groups via the U.K. package switching system and the Science and Engineering Research Council network. The project was to be a modest job-generator requiring about 70 man years of effort in the period 1981 - 1984. Participants included groups from the UK and Australia. Some preliminary work was done but the project

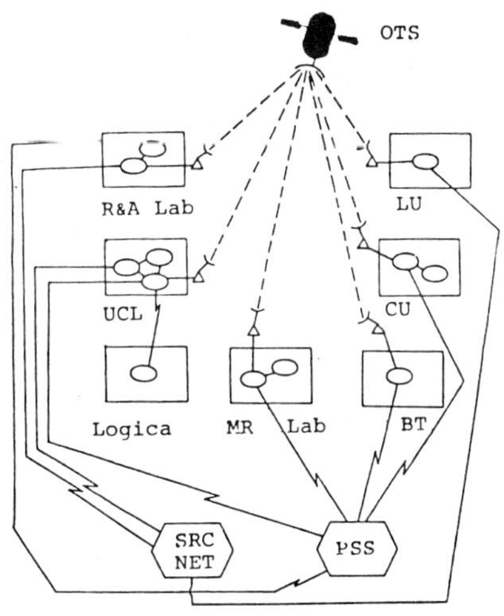

FIGURE 8.4. PROJECT "UNIVERSE"

was later cancelled. However there now seems to be a possibility that it will be revived. Networks of this kind could eventually create many jobs.

<u>FURTHER READING</u>

Anon
  HMSO 1981. Report of a home office study.
    Direct broadcasting by satellite.
Arnim, Rolf.
  In Proc Int. Colloqium Space Coms. and impact new technologies Biarritz,
    France, 20-22 October 1981. Published by Eurospace, Ave Bosquet, Paris 1981.
    Page 240. Establishment of markets and employment at industrial level.
Beakley, Guy W.
  IEEE Trans. Aerospace and Electronic Systems AES-20(4), 455-464, July 1984.
    Overview Of commercial satellite communications.
Belton, R.G.E.
  In Proc Int. Colloqium Space Coms. and impact new technologies Biarritz,
    France, 20-22 October 1981. Published by Eurospace, Ave Bosquet, Paris 1981.
    Page 96. Current status and envisaged trends in international cable and
    satellite communications.
Billings, G.H.
  In Proc Int. Colloqium Space Coms. and impact new technologies Biarritz,
    France, 20-22 October 1981. Published by Eurospace, Ave Bosquet, Paris 1981.
    Page 210. Direct TV broadcasting by satellite: an American viewpoint.
Blonstein, Larry
  In Proc Int. Colloqium Space Coms. and impact new technologies Biarritz,
    France, 20-22 October 1981. Published by Eurospace, Ave Bosquet, Paris 1981.
    Page 237. The social-economic aspects of satellite TV broadcast: costs,
    investment, and financing methods.
Churan, G.G., Leavitt, W.E.
  Comsat   Technical   Review   11(2), 421-321, Fall 1981.
    Summary of the SBS satellite communications performance specifications.
Clarke, Arthur C.
  Wireless World 51, 305-308, 1945.
    Extra-terrestrial relays.
Courault, R., Smith, G.K.
  Microwave Journal   25(1),   83-90, January 1982.
    Technologies for the next European satellites.
Dusio, Emilio W; Murphy, Thomas P., and Cashman, William F.
  Computer 16(4), 21-34, April 1983.
    Communications satellite software: a tutorial.
Gavaghan, Helen.
  New Scientist 105(1440), 41-44, January 1985.
    Europe's space odyssey 2000.
Martin, James.
  Prentice-Hall Inc., 1978.
    Communications Satellite Systems.
Phillips, G.J.
  Proc. IEE 129(7), 478-484, September 1982.
    Direct broadcasting from satellites.
Ramani,S., et al.
  In Williams, M.B. (Ed). Pathways to the information society. Proc. Conf.
  Computer Com., London 1982. North Holland 1982.
    A new type of communications satellite needed for computer based messaging.
Rothhlatt, Martin A.
  The American Journal of International Law 76(1), 56-77, 1982.
    Satellite communication and spectrum allocation.
Rudge, A.W.
  Proc. IEE 132, Part F(1), 1-12, February 1985.
    Skyhooks, fish-warmers, and hub-caps. Milestones in satellite
    communications.

CHAPTER 9. THE ELECTRONIC PROCESSING & DELIVERY OF DOCUMENTS AND TEXT
PART 1: DESCRIPTION AND USE OF FACSIMILE EQUIPMENT

MACHINES: TECHNICAL BACKGROUND

History

A form of electro-mechanical facsimile was used over telegraph circuits by a Scotsman, Alexander Bain, in the 1840s, but the pioneer of modern facsimile was Arthur Korn, an American. Korn used a system very similar in principle to modern machines for transmitting photographs early this century. Later, machines made by RCA were in use by the US newspaper industry and for disseminating weather maps, but the wider applications of facsimile did not start until the 1970s.

In the early 70s there was a small specialised demand for facsimile equipment. The market leader in the United States was Xerox. In Britain Muirhead had been producing machines for some years for specialised requirements, particularly for the Press. Following the recession of the mid 70s the use of facsimile equipment in offices increased in the US and two companies came to the fore - Qwip and Rapifax.

In Japan, a different kind of need was forcing developments. Facsimile transmission was an obvious way of by-passing the problems associated with the coding of kanji characters for bit by bit transmission. Impetus was also given to facsimile in other spheres - notably in the US space programme, in weather forecasting, and in the transmission of specialised data for the oil industry. The Alden Company in the United States and Muirhead in Britain were the market leaders for special equipment.

In the late 70s talk about "electronic offices" started. The cost of transmitting a business letter in about six minutes (a speed which had been used for some years) over the public switched telephone network (PSTN) was too great and it took too long for general office use. New incompatible machines started to appear prompted by cost reductions on two fronts - rapid developments in cheap semiconductor technology, and faster, cheaper, transmission made possible by coding and data reduction.

For a time it looked as if leading manufacturers would attempt to establish de facto standards, but eventually there was some agreement that the common interest would best be served by collaboration in developing new standards to cope with new situations. Consequently standards for group 2 and group 3 machines were born; standards for group 4 machines are still under discussion. There was controversy during the introduction of these standards by the protagonists of new machines and new data reduction codes. The Japanese, emerging as a major force, had already developed codes which were different from those developed in Europe and America.

The wide adoption of CCITT recommendations has been an important factor in the expansion of the industry although the efforts of pressure groups on standardisation committees resulted in several compromises, notably the inclusion of "options". Quite a number of manufacturers now include with the CCITT recommended facilities and options a number of non-CCITT options.

The potential problems that this might introduce have to some extent been overcome by the adoption of CCITT recommended "hand-shaking" procedures which establish, at the time of inter-connection of two machines, which of the available facilities and options will be used for the current "conversation". Some manufacturers, doubtless in the belief that they can tie in a sufficiently large number of users to their own equipment, are still offering quite sophisticated machines without making any claims to CCITT compatibility.

What a facsimile machine does

A facsimile machine converts an image, usually text or graphics printed on paper, into electrical impulses suitable for transmission over a communication channel, usually the public telephone network. The impulses are converted back to a virtually identical image by a remote machine of a similar kind, connected to the same channel. One machine can convert an image into impulses, or impulses back into an image, functioning either as a transmitter or receiver according to the operator's requirements.

The human eye/brain can survey most images almost instantaneously, assessing the whole area. Facsimile machines work by scanning on a narrow line by line basis whatever the nature of the image, generating a stream of electrical impulses at a rate limited to match the capacity of the telecommunications channel. In modern machines, each element in a strip of photosensitive elements wide enough to span the paper, generates a voltage proportional to the intensity of light reflected from a small area beneath it. Impulses corresponding to these voltages are transmitted down the line,the strip is discharged and moved a fraction of an inch up the image, senses another horizontal line, and the process is repeated until the entire image is scanned.

Each element surveys an area about 0.1mm in diameter, so information about fine detail may be "resolved" and transmitted. As well as sending information about the image, the transmitting facsimile machine also sends synchronising information to control the timing of the reverse process at the remote receiver so that line-by-line reproduction is in step with transmission. To reproduce the image, received voltages are applied to a strip of printing elements of similar size to the photosensors at the sending end. Thin-film thermal elements are commonly used, and in this case incoming data for one line are stored and then simultaneously applied to a strip of elements. A line of marks appears on the special printing paper and printing continues on a line by line basis.

Analogue and Digital Transmission; Half Tones

In the foregoing explanation, digital transmision is implied because images have been described in terms of the "picture elements", or pixels – the minute area surveyed by one photosensor. The voltage output may be proportional to the reflected light intensity, or may be converted to generate only one of two outputs – say 0 volts if the photosensor generates from 0 to 0.5 volts, and 1 volt if it generates from 0.5 to 1. The tonal gradations represented by a range of voltages have been reduced to either 0 or 1, black or white, or in computer parlance "one bit".

Speeds are described in terms of "bits per second", and images in terms of the number of bits they contain, both implying that one bit represents an area determined by the size of a photosensor element. A modern machine using a strip of 1728 photosensors stepped up an 11" (279 mm) page in 0.26 mm increments (typical figures) would generate up to 1.85 Mbits per image. It is usually considered that this ability to cope with fine detail – say 2 Mbits – is sufficient for quite exacting fidelity requirements in picture transmission.

It should be remembered that these numbers apply to black and white images without halftones, and certainly without colour – a yet more exacting requirement. To transmit halftones in a digital system the range of voltages needed for a range of halftones must be represented as discrete steps.

We might decide to represent halftones by four bits, enabling one out of 16 shades of grey to be transmitted per picture element. In this case associated circuits would transmit a four bit number for each picture element. Appropriate decoding would be included at the receiver to convert the number into a shade of grey using a special printer. The information content of the image is correspondingly increased to 8 Mbits taking four times as long to transmit as for an otherwise identical black and white picture. Yet more information is needed for colour transmision.

In reality, images are not composed of discrete areas or discrete shades of grey - they possess continuous y variable shades as sensed by the eye, although providing the discontinuities are fine enough a discrete representation is quite acceptable. In older facsimile equipment continuously variable information about shades was transmitted and received and still is on some machines (analogue system); a single moving photosensor scans the page, stripwise fashion, generating a continuously varying voltage which is sent over the telephone line.

Digitisation presents a number of engineering advantages in storage, transmission, use of circuit chips mass produced for computer (digital) use etc., which far outweigh the basically simple analogue method, as described in Chapter 5.

<u>Coding, resolution, and bandwidth</u>

The electrical impulses derived from scanning the image are coded to make them suitable for transmission and to minimise the effect of errors (for instance from telephone line noise). Additional coding may be used for data reduction (compression); for example a short code group could be substituted for a long succession of identical elements to indicate an "all black" strip of the image or a short code could be used as an instruction to the receiver "skip the next line which is blank ("all white"). When decoded at the receiver a black strip or an extra blank line is inserted.

No matter whether a scanning light spot, photosensor, or strip of sensors is used for scanning, each element must be small in comparison with the smallest detail of the image which is required to be resolved. This may impose a requirement of up to nearly 2 Mbits per image, as previously explained.

To transmit the entire contents of a page in an acceptable time, the stream of impulses generated from successive lines must be transmitted at the required speed, and must be received and reproduced without distortion. Higher frequency components are generated as the speed of impulse transmission is increased. A communication channel has a finite bandwidth - that is it can accommodate a given band of frequencies. Fast impulses containing frequency components outside the passband will be distorted when received and errors will occur.

If the Public Switched Telephone Network (PSTN) is to be used as the communication channel, the impulse speed must be adjusted to run within the limits of its bandwidth. We then have a <u>tradeoff</u> situation as discussed in Chapter 5. In images without fine detail, the scanning speed can be increased to enable the entire image to be transmitted in, say, 2 minutes. But if fine detail is present, the speed must be decreased to, say, a 6 minute transmission time; this enables three times the number of elements to be transmitted without generating high frequency components outside the passband.

If special circuits of wider bandwidth can be used (available at special prices from the telephone authority in most countries), another tradeoff is possible, since doubling the bandwidth halves the transmission time. For example if you are fortunate enough to have access to a satellite channel (and the right equipment) the very wide bandwidth enables pictures to be transmitted in 1 second or less.

The transmission rate over the PSTN is typically 2400 bits per second, but in some circumstances higher speeds may be possible. Machines fitted with "automatic shift down" test the line with a 9600 bps signal and reduce speed in steps down to whatever speed will give satisfactory results. Others have special circuits to "equalise" line response and the manufacturers claim that higher speeds can consistently be obtained on the PSTN. Private lines will always be faster than the the PSTN.

STANDARDS

Facsimile machines are available in three groups according to performance standards. The CCITT recommendations for facsimile apparatus are T2 analogue (Group 1 machines taking 6 minutes to transmit an A4 size page of text using frequency modulated (FM) transmission), T3 analogue (Group 2, 3 minutes, amplitude modulation (AM)), and T4 digital (Group 3, 1 minute). A standard for Group 4 machines (less than one minute) is under discussion.

The details are as follows:-

Group 1

Analogue transmission, 6 min. per A4 page. 3.85 scan lines/mm vertical resolution, and equivalent for horizontal. FM 1700Hz 400Hz.

Group 2

Analogue transmission, 3 min. per A4 page. Resolution as for Group 1. AM 2100 Hz vestigial sideband with encoding of baseband signal. (Redundant information contained in sidebands produced by modulation is supressed in vestigial sideband transmission, thereby reducing channel bandwidth requirements).

Group 3

Digital transmission, 1 min. per A4 page, 4800 bps, 20 ms per scanning line. Resolution 3.85 scan lines/mm vertical, 1728 Pels in a 215 mm horizontal scan line. Tonal gradation levels quantised to black or white. Data reduction by modified Huffman code (a form of run length coding). A further recommendation, T30, covers handshaking procedures over the PSTN and also includes a control procedure whereby the calling station can identify whether any of several options (over and above the basic requirements listed above) are available at the receiver, and if so can have them automatically brought into use.

Group 4

It will take a long time before Group 4 machines become generally available. A Group 4 specification is likely to be adopted in the fax part of multi-purpose reprographic machines embodying fax with other technologies.

Discussions on the new standard started in 1981. Later it was stated that there would be three classes of machine in Group 4 - 1. Fax only 200 x 200 pels, 2. Fax only transmission but mixed-mode reception 200 x 200 pels , and 3. Mixed-mode transmission and reception 300 x 300 pels. Mixed mode means character (Teletex protocol - see Chapter 10) and fax coded data combined on the same page.

Rates over data networks can be from 2400 up to 48 Kbps. At the faster rates data will be sent through appropriate high speed lines or packet switched networks at speeds enabling an A4 sheet to be reproduced in 4 seconds. PSTN rates are as yet not known. "Hangover options" have also been suggested in order to allow Group 3 scanners to co-exist with Group 4 apparatus on a "grandfather" basis for 4 years. This seems to be an attempt to put off solving various difficulties associated with different US and ISO paper sizes and will allow Group 3 machine owners to extend the life of their machines.

By far the most difficult part of the standard will be an attempt to include facsimile in the ISO communications protocol (See Chapter 6). This protocol will hasten convergence by enabling machines hitherto regarded as belonging to different technologies to intercommunicate.

COST OF TRANSMISSION; SPEED

Once an organisation has arranged for a private leased line, at a fixed cost, between A & B for its various telecommunication requirements, the communication costs to transmit one fax message a day are not much more than the cost of transmitting messages continuously. In theory the cost of fax transmission will be the cost of the line multiplied by the fraction of the time it is used for fax traffic, but few organisations will incur the accounting costs of identifying and logging messages for internal charging purposes. The most likely procedure is that the line costs will be recovered with other general overheads in the usual way.

For PSTN users, an out of pocket cost is directly incurred each time a call is made; the cost may well be recovered in general overheads like the private line. Regardless of whether a private line or the PSTN is used and the way costs are defrayed, machines which embody methods of minimising transmission time obviously cost less to run. This will be a factor for consideration when buying a machine. A purchaser might decide that a department's needs can be met by one fast instead of two slow machines.

<u>DAILY COST</u>

TABLE 9.1:

Equipment type	Pages per day		
	10	50	200
4-6 min.	£4	£11	£37
2 min.	£6	£9	£20
1 min.	£10	£12	£19

TABLE 9.2:

	50 pgs/day	200 pgs/day	1000 pgs/day
	Network or PSTN + 1 min machine.	Leased line + 1 min/ 2 min mach.	Leased line + 1 min mach.
	£20	£34	£68
which gives the cost per page:-	40p	17p	6.8p

<u>TABLE 9.1. UK TRANSMISSION COSTS</u>   <u>TABLE 9.2. CHEAPEST DAILY COST (UK)</u>

Some useful information about costs has been provided by Kirstein. He considered labour costs - that is for machine operators - and the cost of paper, machines and communications. Machines are divided into three classes - 4 to 6 minute at £2.5 per day rental, 1 minute/2 minute at £5 per day, and 1 minute at £10 (1978 figures, although relatively they are still valid). Labour for attended machines is charged for the transmitting end only at £2 per hour. The daily cost of running a fax machine including rental, labour, and paper, but excluding communications, is then worked out as shown in Table 9.1 .

The table shows how the cost advantage of a slow machine at low volumes swings to a cost advantage for the fast machine at high volumes. The costs of communication by the PSTN, networks (PSS, Transpac, etc) and private lines (250 Km in length assumed) are then taken into account and added to the daily cost table in 9.1, producing the result shown in Table 9.2 for prime telecommunications time.

In 1982 the data given in Table 9.3 was provided by Brobst for the equipment and communication costs for facsimile between between London and New York.

	Group 1	Group 2	Group 3 (4800 bps)	Group 3 (9600 bps)
Equipment	0.34	0.68	0.91	1.02
Telephone charge	6.50	3.20	1.10	0.50
TOTAL	6.84	3.88	2.01	1.52

TABLE 9.3. COST ($) FOR 10 PAGES A DAY IN EACH DIRECTION LONDON-NEW YORK

The figures in Table 9.3 emphasise the point that when the PSTN is used the decrease in telephone charges with higher speed equipment is much larger that the increased cost of that equipment. Labour costs are not included in these figures.

Further information has been provided by Davis as shown in Figure 9.1.

FAX IN THE OFFICE - RESULTS

As part of a 1982/1983 project for the British Library I was able to find out how fax machines were used by a number of major organisations in the UK. Some of the information which follows is derived from that work and is reproduced with their permission. A number of new machines have been introduced since this work was done, but the comments which follow are still applicable. The "test base" of machines used and the type of application is shown in Table 9.4.

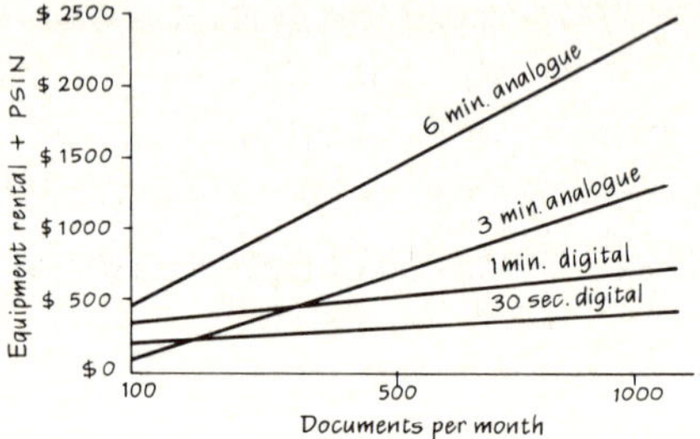

FIGURE 9.1
TRANSMISSION COSTS IN THE US

In table 9.4, second column, figures like "1/2 or "2/3" indicate that most machines can be set to function to one or other of the two CCITT standards. The figures in the fourth column indicate the type of telephone line used for inter-connection (British Telecom terminology). Some organisations have networks employing all types.

Speed considerations

The departmental manager and the fax operator will be more interested in speed than in running costs since speed directly impacts their work while running costs may well be handled as a general overhead. Speed also affects operator's waiting time assuming that the operator has to attend the machine during transmission. There is a big difference in the cost of the sender's time/salary between waiting for 6 minutes while a group 1 machine sends a document, for 1 minute for a group 3 machine, and perhaps for 30 seconds or less if a group 3 machine transmitting at 9600 bps is used.

Type of Organisation	Number and type of machines	Locations	Inter-connecting link	Type of use
Government Offices	16 3M 2346 (1/2) 10 Dex 1100 (1/2) 4 Dex 4200 (1/2)	HQ to regions	PSTN	Urgent data
Magazine Publisher	Qty Muirhead D900 (-) 1 Infotec 6000 (-) 2 Panafax UF520 (2/3))	Hq to printing Co.	S2 (2 wire)	Printer's copy
HQ Large Retailer	1 NEC 3500 (2) 3 3M 2346 (1/2) 1 ITT 3520 (2/3) 2 Xerox 400 (1) 5 Infotec 6000 (-)	HQ to regional depots	PSTN	Orders Loading lists etc.
Patent Office	2 NEC 3500 (2)	Office to library	PSTN	Orders
Local Newspaper Publisher	3 Panafax UF520 (2/3)	Head Off. to regional Offs.	S2 (2 wire)	Advt. Orders
Multi-Nat. Company.	Qty Xerox 400s (1) & 485s (1/2)	Head Off. to overseas offices	PSTN S2,S3. wideband	Financial & other data
National Newspaper	3 Panafax UF520 (2/3)	HQ to Northern Office	T (4 wire)	All kinds of typing/ writing.

<u>Notes</u>

Number(s) in brackets in the second column indicate group numbers. "-" indicates not normally CCITT compatible.
Meaning of data in fourth column is as follows:-
PSTN Public switched telephone network.
- S2   Private leased line. Response, mid-range group delay, and noise and crosstalk levels all specified. (Now re-named "schedule B" by British Telecom).
- S3   Private leased line. Improved version of S2. (Now re-named "schedule C" by BT).
- T   Private leased line. Frequency response and group delay over whole range specified. Lower noise levels specified (Now re-named "schedule D" by BT).

<u>TABLE 9.4</u>

Some machines can be loaded with a stack of papers. The sender presses a button and goes away to do other tasks, coming back later to find all papers sent. The sender knows, either from a stamp placed automatically on each sheet, or from a printed log of operations, that all papers have been sent and presumably have been received.

This useful stacking facility was used at several of the UK test sites with NEC 3500 and Panasonic UF 520 machines. An alarm rings if the machine jams. Occasionally two papers get fed through together but the absence of logging print on the back of a copy shows if this has happened.

Transmission time: speed adjustment automatically

A speed compatible with that of the other facsimile machine connected is automatically selected by the 3M EMT 9160, ensuring that the machine operates at the fastest speed possible. If Group 2 mode is in use this is shown on the panel. The EMT 9160 automatically monitors the quality of the telephone line and adjusts the transmission speed accordingly. The specification for some Group 3 machines contains detailed information about the transmission rate. Table 9.5 is an extract from the leaflet describing the EMT 9160, a comprehensive Group 3 machine introduced in 1982 at £7950 in the UK.

Before considering this specification we need to know more about communication lines. Private lines offer a much lower noise level, a more uniform frequency resp- onse and wider bandwidth, and a more uniform group delay . In the UK the lines available, in order of increasing performance are Schedule A(S1), B(S2), C(S3) and D(T). The symbols in brackets are the old symbols now discontinued. These lines were designed for speech communication and are far from ideal for data. The bandwidth ranges from 200 -3000 Hz, implying a theor-

Modem Specification

CCITT V29 9600/7200 bps
CCITT V27 4800/2400 bps
CCITT V21 300 bps
Group 2 - 2100 Hz carrier
AMPM VSB function

Transmission Speed

Group 3 - data dependent
CCITT No 1 chart (A4 letter)
35 seconds - normal resolution
54 seconds - fine resolution
G3 control overhead 20 seconds

TABLE 9.5
PART OF THE 3M EMT9160 SPECIFICATION

tical signalling rate (numerically) of twice the upper limit in bauds i.e. around 6000 bauds, and a bit rate, depending on a number of factors discussed in Chapter 5, considerably greater.

The controlled group delay means that signal components of different frequencies travel more nearly at the same speed - a requirement for the proper operation of high speed modems. Other lines with improved characteristics are available to special order. In the PSTN the controls on these factors are less stringent and vary according to the route picked up when dialling, just as with noise.

The hand-shaking overhead

The 3M specification introduces the term "control overhead" - something rarely given by manufacturers. This means that during first connection the two machines exchange information about themselves and switch themselves to become mutually compatible in a "handshaking" operation. In the 3M case, when the machine is operating in the 35 seconds mode, this means that it will actually take 55 seconds to complete the transmission of the first message - i.e the user is paying for 55 seconds of telephone time.

The second and subsequent messages in the session are not loaded with this overhead if they follow on immediately. It is possible to measure the handshaking time by watching a machine in operation. Nothing apparently happens for a period after first connection. You can then hear the machine printing and the paper starts to move. On a Panafax UF520 machine the elapsed time between the telephone ringing at the receiving end and the start of printing the first copy was about 45 seconds. On a Xerox 485 the period was about 25 seconds. Private lines were used in both cases.

<u>Realising the speed potential</u>

A machine will perform at its best when used with a private line, but we may not be in a situation where the traffic between two points will justify such a line. "Automatic Speed Selection" enables the machines with that facility to transmit as fast as line conditions will permit but neither the 3M information nor the information provided by any other manufacturer tells us (as far as I know) whether high speeds can be achieved over the PSTN, or whether a private line is necessary. Some manufacturers, including Muirhead and 3M, provide modems with adaptive equalisers on some machines. Before sending fax information the machine sends a "training signal" to the other. The modems then automatically connect equalising circuits to the line which, in effect, reduce the peaks and boost the troughs in the line's characteristics for best possible reproduction and fastest speed.

Machines fitted with these modems provide a better chance of faster communication when confronted with the variable characteristics of the PSTN. PTTs, including British Telecom, are conservative, and do not specify data transmission performance with the PSTN. The only CCITT recommendation for 2400 bps is V26 which calls for four wire inter-connection.

If you buy a machine capable of 9600 bps, claiming 35 seconds for transmission of the CCITT standard A4 letter (as in the 3M specification) with the intention of using it on the PSTN, will it promptly step down its speed so that its maximum speed is never realised? No, say Muirhead. Their adaptive equalisers do permit speeds of 9600 bps most of the time. I was unable to find a test site using 9600 bps machines on the PSTN. The sites using the Panafax UF 520, of which there were several, all used private lines.

The UF520's on private lines were probably working at 9600 bps at the sites visited and provided very good quality under these conditions. Figure 9.2 shows an image transmitted between the offices of a local newspaper by a UF 520 over a private line about 15 miles long. Figure 9.3 shows part of an A4 size advertisement before and after transmission between the same offices as in Fig. 9.2. This image, which is packed with information, took 95 seconds to send, excluding handshaking. The UF 520 was set on "fine density" and to send the amount of information shown within this period was probably working at 9600 bps. Both pictures are photocopies.

Figure 9.4 shows an image before and after transmission by a UF 520 working at 9600 bps at another site. In this case the telecomms manager had arranged for a four-wire private line from London to Manchester to be looped back to a similar line from Manchester to London. The "before" image was taken in London from the machine on "copy", and the "after" from the same machine after the London- Manchester-London trip. The small type is the equivalent of 7 point. The quality of the reproduction shows that very good results can be obtained with a modern machine working under good conditions. There is absolutely no trace of noise on any part of the image.

FIGURE 9.2. PANAFAX UF520. 15 MILE PRIVATE LINE. BEFORE AND AFTER SENDING

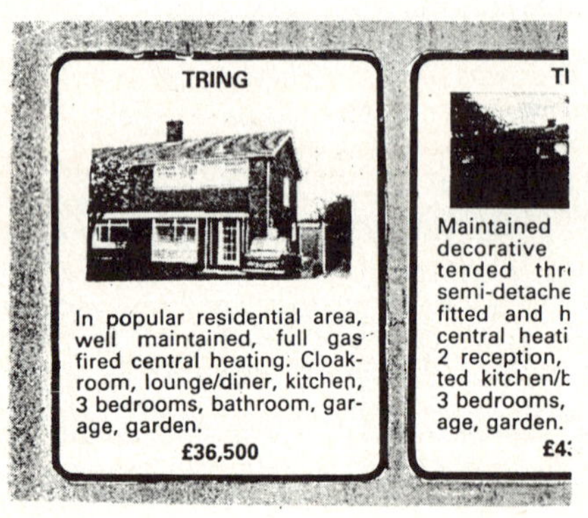

FIGURE 9.3. PANAFAX UF250. 15 MILE PRIVATE LINE. BEFORE AND AFTER SENDING

```
Cosmopoln.Gth.Fd. |18.6    19.6| .....|  5.00
Do.Income Fd. ....|49.0    52.1| .....| 11.24
Craigmount Unit Tst. Mgrs. Ltd.
9/10 Foster Lane, EC2V 6HH            01-606 9262
High Income ..........|47.1  51.4| +0.2| 10.00
North American .......|48.9  52.5| +0.3|   —
Mid Mount High Inc ..|48.6  50.9| .....|  9.00
Crescent Unit Tst. Mngrs. Ltd. (a)(g)
4, Melville Cres., Edinburgh 3.       031-226 4931
Cres. Amer. Fd.......|23.8  25.5| +0.3| 1.62
Cres. Internat'l. ...|60.4  64.8| +0.4| 1.00
Cres. High. Dist.....|45.3  48.6|     | 9.39
Cres. Reserves ......|40.0  42.9| +0.1| 5.22
Cres. Tokyo .........|25.7  27.6|     | 1.89
Discretionary Unit Fund Managers
22, Blomfield St., EC2M 7AL.          01-638 4485
Dis. Inc. Dec. 29 ...|176.7  188.5| .....| 5.07
E. F. Winchester Fund Mngt. Ltd.
Old Jewry, EC2.                       01-606 2167
Great Winchester ....|18.5  20.2| .....| 4.79
Gt. Winchester O'seas|18.1  20.2| .....| 4.40
Emson & Dudley Tst. Mngmnt. Ltd.
20, Arlington St., S.W.1.             01-499 7551
Emson Dudley Tst. ...|68.7  73.9| .....| 6.00
Equity & Law Un. Tr. M.♥ (a)(b)(c)
Amersham Rd., High Wycombe.           0494 33377
Equity & Law ........|67.7  71.2| +0.3| 4.30

‡‡Charibond Jan. 2 ...
‡‡Charifund Jan. 2 ....|145.7
(Accum. Units)..........|190.0
Pens Ex. Jan. 8 ........|140.7
ManuLife Managemen
St. George's Way, Stevenag
Growth Units ...........|57.0
Mayflower Manageme
14-18, Gresham St., EC2V
Income Dec. 19.........|106.2
General Dec. 19........|69.2
Internl. Dec. 19.........|43.5
Mercury Fund Manag
30, Gresham St., EC2P 2EE
Merc. Gen. Jan. 3......|192.8
Acc. Uts. Jan. 3........|259.1
Merc. Int. Jan. 3 .......|68.2
Acc. Uts. Jan. 3........|74.4
Merc. Ext. Dec. 28....|244.8
Accm. Uts. Dec. 28....|296.7
Midland Bank Group
Unit Trust Managers
Courtwood House, Silver
Sheffield, S1 3RD.
Commodity & Gen. ....|66.8
Do. Accum. ...........|78.9
Growth ...............|36.7
Do. Accum. ...........|39.7
Capital...............|26.0
Do. Accum. ...........|28.7
```


```
Craigmount Unit Tst. Mgrs. Ltd.
9/10 Foster Lane, EC2V 6HH            01-606 9262
High Income ..........|47.1  51.4| +0.2| 10.00
North American .......|48.9  52.5| +0.3|   —
Mid Mount High Inc ..|48.6  50.9| .....|  9.00
Crescent Unit Tst. Mngrs. Ltd. (a)(g)
4, Melville Cres., Edinburgh 3.       031-226 4931
Cres. Amer. Fd.......|23.8  25.5| +0.3| 1.62
Cres. Internat'l. ...|60.4  64.8| +0.4| 1.00
Cres. High. Dist.....|45.3  48.6|     | 9.39
Cres. Reserves ......|40.0  42.9| +0.1| 5.22
Cres. Tokyo .........|25.7  27.6|     | 1.89
Discretionary Unit Fund Managers
22, Blomfield St., EC2M 7AL.          01-638 4485
Dis. Inc. Dec. 29 ...|176.7  188.5| .....| 5.07
E. F. Winchester Fund Mngt. Ltd.
Old Jewry, EC2.                       01-606 2167
Great Winchester ....|18.5  20.2| .....| 4.79
Gt. Winchester O'seas|18.1  20.2| .....| 4.40
Emson & Dudley Tst. Mngmnt. Ltd.
20, Arlington St., S.W.1.             01-499 7551
Emson Dudley Tst. ...|68.7  73.9| .....| 6.00
Equity & Law Un. Tr. M.♥ (a)(b)(c)
Amersham Rd., High Wycombe.           0494 33377

(Accum. Units)..........|190.0
Pens.Ex. Jan. 8.........|140.7
ManuLife Management
St. George's Way, Stevenag
Growth Units ...........|57.0
Mayflower Management
14-18, Gresham St., EC2V
Income Dec. 19.........|106.2
General Dec. 19........|69.2
Internl. Dec. 19.........|43.5
Mercury Fund Manage
30, Gresham St., EC2P 2EB
Merc. Gen. Jan. 3......|192.8
Acc. Uts. Jan. 3........|259.1
Merc. Int. Jan. 3 .......|68.2
Acc. Uts. Jan. 3........|74.4
Merc. Ext. Dec. 28....|244.8
Accm. Uts. Dec. 28....|296.7
Midland Bank Group
Unit Trust Managers
Courtwood House, Silver
Sheffield, S1 3RD.
Commodity & Gen. ....|66.8
Do. Accum. ...........|78.9
Growth ...............|36.7
Do. Accum. ...........|39.7
Capital...............|26.0
```


FIGURE 9.4. PANAFAX UF520. 300 MILE PRIVATE LINE. BEFORE AND AFTER SENDING

ORIGINAL AND AFTER-TRANSMISSION FACSIMILE IMAGES IN FIELD TESTS

NOISE

Input noise

Although light detecting elements in scanning heads may be very small, they integrate the light reflected from a finite area of the image. The "noise factor" inherent in this arrangement is built into the system and is not related in any way to circuit noise. Figure 9.5 shows the effect of reproducing a ragged-edged boundary when the edge variations are small compared to the size of scanning

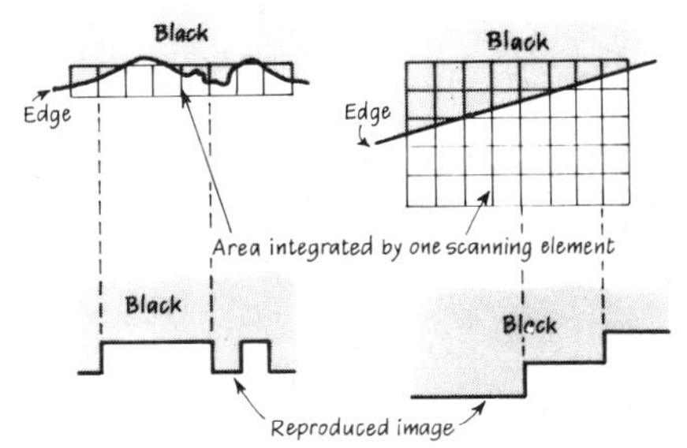

FIGURE 9.5
"RAGGED EDGE" AND "OBLIQUE LINE" NOISE

elements. A "smoothed" effect is produced, which, in a sense, is added noise because detail has been obscured. Figure 9.5 also shows how an oblique straight line is reproduced as a zig-zag line for the same reason. At some point along the line an element integrating over a small area, "decides" that it is receiving black. Figure 9.6 shows the effect on a real image, actual size, and enlarged.

FIGURE 9.6. "NOISE" INTRODUCED BY EDGES. ACTUAL SIZE AND ENLARGED

Circuit noise

"Thermal", "Gaussian", or "White" noise is a fundamental property of all electrical circuits. It is caused by the random fluctuations of electrons in conductors. This type of noise manifests itself in audio-frequency circuits as a steady background hiss which may be almost inaudible, but often becomes obvious on long distance circuits. The voltages generated by this kind of noise are normally small compared with "signal" voltages — that is those conveying information - and do not cause trouble.

The telephone network is a complex of cables, switching devices and other equipment some old, some new. Bad contacts at switching points cause noise, so do the impulses caused by dialling which can break through by inductive coupling from one line to another. Non-telephone electrical equipment and electrical storms can also cause impulsive noise. It is this kind of noise, heard as clicks and crashes which may go on intermittently in the background, or may make conversation unintelligible, which causes problems when telephone lines are used for data transmission.

One remedy is to "dial again", in which case you may get rid of the fortuitous string of "noise generators" present along the first chain of connections. The newer the equipment along the way the less the impulsive noise. One reason is that the metal-to-metal sliding contacts which have been used for many years are being replaced by better devices or "contactless" switches - e.g. semiconductors.

The PSTN was designed for voice and not much useful information about

impulsive noise is available. Speech may be acceptable in the presence of
noise because of context and redundancy in the language, or you can ask for
a phrase to be repeated. That same noise level could well result in an
unreadable word, line, or lines of facsimile print if the circuit is being
used for fax data transmission.

On private lines leased from the PTT noise levels are lower. The number
of inter-connections is smaller and in the case of UK Tariff T (Schedule D),
the impulsive noise limit is specified at a lower level. But it is not as
simple as that because in the UK BT specifies impulsive noise as "not more than
18 impulse noise counts to exceed the threshold limit in any period of 15
minutes" for its private lines. Presumably any or all of those impulses could
cause trouble. No information is provided about impulses on the UK PSTN
where noise is likely to be much worse.

The same information from BT is provided in the current edition of "The
Handbook of Data Communications" as was provided in the 1975 edition under the
heading "Time distribution of erroneous blocks on the PSTN in Chile".
Perhaps this implies that the UK PSTN is no better. Chileans are chatting at
their hardest at 10.30 a.m. at which time 0.065% of 50 bit data blocks are in
error - that is about 1 in 1500. Impulsive noise on the UK PSTN certainly varies
with the time of day, being at its lowest in the middle of the night. It
also varies with a subscriber's position in the network and the route that is
picked up when dialling.

A telecommunications manager at one of the companies I visited said that
he was very near a modern exchange where the uni-selector switches had been
pensioned off. He believed this to be the reason for his low noise levels. These
switches, invented in 1879, had been honourably retired. The inspiration for
their introduction was due to the unreliability of making funeral
arrangements in Kansas City - the home town of a Mr. Strowger, local
undertaker and inventor. Unfortunately his legacy lingers on in many
telephone exchanges.

When you dial on the UK STD system you are routed through a maze of
Transit, District, and Main Switching Centres which account for the variability
of the impulsive noise level. What is the average effect on facsimile data
likely to be? Are facsimile systems designed so that they can cope
satisfactorily with the highest noise levels likely to be encountered
on the PSTN?

Noise and coding

Little has been reported about the effects of noise upon PSTN facsimile,
implying that its effects are not significant. Since group 3 and all future
types of machine will use digital transmission associated with coding systems,
this discussion will be confined to these methods.

Fax data is coded for transmission through a noisy channel. Data is
transmitted as on or off pulses, the "on" voltage being at the
highest possible level. Noise levels usually permit faster multi-level
signalling, used as explained in Chapter 5. The. receiving decoder should not
often have to deal with noise impulses, which it might interpret as signals,
because such impulses should be received below the detection threshold
level. The effect of noise on synchronising data should be limited to one row of
data since each row is synchronised.

In other data transmission systems, additional techniques are often used
for dealing with errors caused by noise. Information is added to the
transmitted data which can be used to correct erroneous groups of data by
the action of special circuits in the receiver. This method is often used for

character by character transmission but rarely or never for facsimile. Such a method was offered for consideration by British Telecomm to   CCITT (The international organisation charged with agreeing facsimile standards) but was not taken up.

Experiments on the effects of noise

Work was done by Mussmanm to find out how received images with different data reduction codes look when noise is introduced in a controllable way. It would not be helpful to adopt an efficient data reduction code if its adoption resulted in worse effects from noise than previously. Recordings of noise bursts from telephone lines were made and used for test purposes. Figure 9.7 shows the appearance of an image sent by a machine using a Huffman code similar to that specified for group 3 machines. This is for a vertical resolution of 7.7 lines/mm. Severe noise bursts cause the destruction of two or more lines. A sufficient number of good lines remain per character for the text to be understandable in most places.

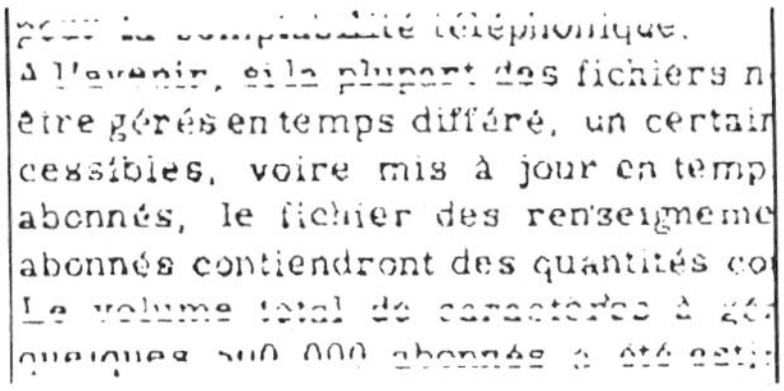

pour la comptabilité téléphonique.
A l'avenir, si la plupart des fichiers n
être gérés en temps différé, un certain
cessibles, voire mis à jour en temp
abonnés, le fichier des renseigneme
abonnés contiendront des quantités co
Le volume total de caractères à gé
quelques 500 000 abonnés a été esti

FIGURE   9.7
EFFECT OF NOISE ON A CODED IMAGE

Noise may sometimes occur in a place which does not affect the user's understanding of text, either because it occurs in white space or in text where missing information can be deduced from context. The same noise occurring an instant later might necessitate a retransmission request. Noise which might erase a line from text in Figure 9.8 might not affect the writing in Figure 9.9 simply because a noise strip across the latter would not make the large characters illegible.

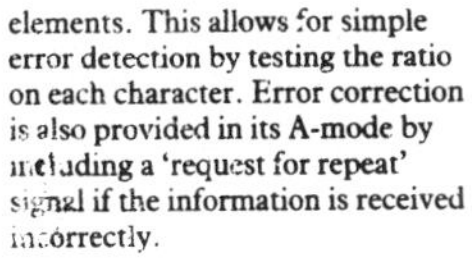

elements. This allows for simple error detection by testing the ratio on each character. Error correction is also provided in its A-mode by including a 'request for repeat' signal if the information is received incorrectly.

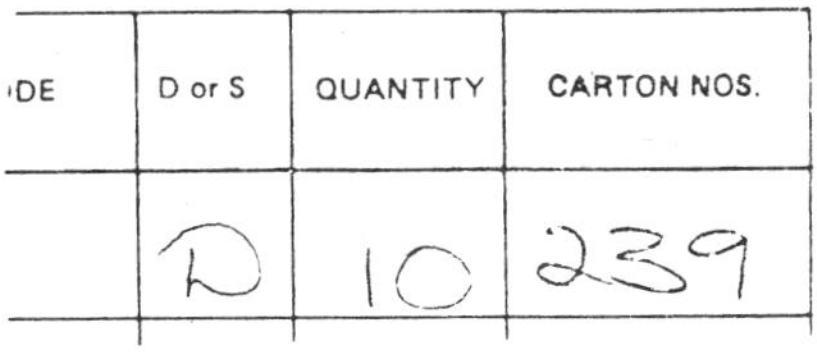

DE	D or S	QUANTITY	CARTON NOS.
	D	10	239

FIGURE   9.8
8 POINT TEXT SUSCEPTIBLE TO NOISE

FIGURE   9.9
LESS SUSCEPTIBLE LARGE CHARACTERS

Observed effects of noise

Field tests carried out during the British Library project provide a fairly clear picture of what may be expected when facsimile machines are being used with the PSTN or private lines. Examples of the effects of noise on received fax images are shown in Figure 9.10.

In these tests, several users were unconcerned about what I thought was unacceptable noise. They regarded the need occasionally to ask for a re-transmission as a small penalty to pay for the substantial overall benefits brought about by facsimile compared with their previous methods. The subjective effect of noise depends upon document contents.

No users complained of noise on any type of private leased line. PSTN users got to know by listening whether a PSTN connection would be unacceptable. They then re-dialled. If a line adjudged to be "noisy" had been

used, reception would, in fact, have been unacceptable, but sometimes "quiet"
lines turned out to be unacceptable. A noise burst occurred during transmission
although the line was quiet at the time of listening.

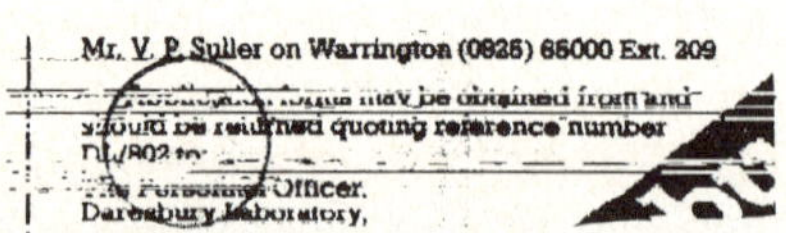

FIGURE 9.10. ORIGINAL AND MAGNIFIED PORTIONS OF TEXT SHOWING NOISE EFFECTS

     For example one user, who was transmitting facsimile images of
newspaper text from the editorial to the printing departments sited on
opposite sides of Greater London via the PSTN, said that noise was much
greater in   the periods 9.30 – 12.30 a.m. and 2 – 5 p.m. On a bad day he said
that 50% of the material contained errors. Not all errors required a request
for re-transmission as the correct version was sometimes obvious from
context. At another site where fax was being used for the reception of order
forms completed in bold handwriting, the users did not complain about noise.
When it occurred, the writing was large enough for noisy characters to be read.

     At yet another site, also in central London, I was allowed to conduct a
series of test transmissions during the afternoon to offices in Kent. After the
first attempt, when the connection was re-dialled because of noise, a very
quiet circuit was picked up. It behaved like a private line circuit.

Conclusions on noise effects

     1. Noise in the UK PSTN system varies with the time of day, the geographical
location of the site, and the circuit route picked up when dialling. It does not
have much effect on most images. Noise on private lines is much lower.

     2. Facsimile systems of the types observed in these tests, and quite
probably all commercially available facsimile systems, are unable to provide
images which are unaffected by noise bursts.

     3. The number of noise bursts per hour likely to produce errors is
unpredictable.

     4. Information in information-rich areas of images without redundancy is
most likely to be destroyed by noise. The vulnerability of text is inversely

proportional to its size. Graphics is usually less vulnerable than text unless parts or all of a graphics image are information-rich. For example all parts of a survey image of the earth's surface produced by the Landsat satellite could contain important fine detail with zero redundancy.

5. It would seem that the value of unattended store-and-forward auto-dialling systems, to be expected in the near future, would be diminished in the absence of noise immunity. In critical applications it would be necessary to implement correction sessions with operators at both ends. The receiving operator would demand re-transmissions and the transmitting operator would be required to maintain a file of recently transmitted documents in order to fufill requests for repetition. The machines would require operators in attendance.

<u>BUYING</u>

A recent article about facsimile applications was entitled "The simple, human problems with Fax". The "person -to-fax, fax-to-fax, and fax-to-person" problems are described. Claims made that the "machine will work unattended" depend upon the user's expectations of unattended operations. For organisations who wish to send a continuous stream of traffic to different addressees, the real solutions are not yet on offer. However, time-wasting problems often associated with facsimile operations have been reduced. The old load-the-drum equipment has been largely replaced by enclosed transceivers, automatically accepting single or small stacks of paper; received information is delivered on sheets cut to the right length from a roll.

There are several other important practical questions to ask before adopting fax as follows-

1. How much fax traffic is expected, and what will the capital
   and annual communications and running costs be?

2. How easy is it use a facsimile machine?

3. Arising from question 2, should a trained operator be
   employed for the machine, or can it be made available on a
   more general basis, like an office copier?

Different machine purchasing costs and different tariff/distance charges will vary from country to country. In the UK a machine capable of operating as Group 1 or 2, costs, on average, about half as much as a Group 2/3. A decision about which to buy is largely determined by speed/volume considerations. The cost of a local dialled call in the UK (1985) is 5p per minute during peak periods. A facsimile machine does not start sending as soon as you have dialled - there is an "overhead" start-up during each session while machines carry out "handshaking".

Ignoring the overhead (on the assumption that several sheets will be sent per session), the transmission costs per A4 sheet will therefore be 5p using a Group 3 machine set to "one minute", 10p for a Group 2 on "two minutes", and 30p on a Group 1 at "6 minutes". For other situations multipliers apply to these costs as follows. For peak periods up to 35 miles x 2.5, and for distances over 35 miles x 5. International calls (peak) Europe x 12, US x 18 (All approximate). It can be seen that as soon as the number of copies per day goes up to about 20 (assuming that a few are over long distance), a Group 2/3 machine is the best buy.

Questions two and three can be taken together because the cost of employing a "dedicated operator" arises which in turn depends on an assessment of ease of use. From the field test referred to previously I concluded that cheaper

machines were fairly easy to use. When more expensive machines are
purchased two kinds of facilities are included - those which provide tangible
benefits, and those which are of the "bells and whistles" variety. This is
where good judgement is needed.

If a machine is required for routine use in an office, speed and
simplicity will be the main requirements. But in situations where images may
include small type, diagrams, etc., some knowledge about the optimum settings of
the controls will be needed. Many people find that machinery is not easy
to work with and in this second situation it may be necessary to employ a
trained operator.

In addition to the basic requirements of enabling images to be
transmitted over a long distance and acceptably reproduced with a choice of
speed/resolution, and for the user to know, by reason of agreed standards, that
the remote machine is compatible with her own, a number of other facilities have
gradually been added. These include Multiple Sheet Feed, Duplex Signalling,
White Line Skip for increased speed, Store and Forward, Automatic Logging as a
check on transmission and reception, Fast Transmission with Automatic Shift-down
to a slower speed when conditions become poor, and Polling - that is a request to
an unattended machine to transmit.

A representative selection of machines available on the UK market today are
listed in a comparison table in the Classified Product List elsewhere in this
book.

Comments on the table in the Classified Product List

Most of the machines currently available in the UK are listed in the
table. "-" in a column means either that the data is inapplicable to the machine
in question, or that the information is not supplied by the manufacturer.
Prices given are "list prices". The degree of competition in the industry is
evident when enquiries are made about prices. Suppliers want to know who you
are, what you want the machine for, and where it will be used. You will receive
a follow-up telephone call soon after your enquiry. Prices are given
reluctantly by some suppliers over the telephone, the emphasis placed on the word
"list" obviously indicating that they would be happy to "negotiate".

The column "Max.speed/copy (secs) & trans. rate (bps)" shows the maximum
speed at which the modem (the device handling signal transmission) will operate
(bits per second) and the manufacturer's claim for the time it takes to send one
copy at the fastest speed setting. In every case where a bps figure is given,
the machine will attempt to transmit at that rate, but if the line is
inadequate the rate will automatically be reduced in steps down to the
"reliable under most circumstances" rate of 2400 bps. This facility enables high
speed to be used if the very variable quality of the intervening PSTN
permits it. If a 4-wire private line is available quite reliable 9600 bps
transmission can be expected.

The   CCITT recommends A4 sheets containing a range of "typical"
material for fax testing, but it is not clear which of these documents, if
any, is used when specifying the quoted speed. The capacity regularly and
reliably to send each copy quickly is obviously important since the lower
running cost then incurred is one of the most important factors justifying
the cost of a higher priced machine. When speeds of less than one minute are
quoted they may have been achieved using a "business letter" with only one
third of the surface occupied by text and a machine using standard coding
methods. Another machine may be using highly sophisticated methods of
compression and the quoted speed is for a page full of text.

When buying a machine the manufacturer's specification needs to be read carefully for the details of high speed transmission - some give much more information than others. Better still, using your own chosen test document, ask the supplier if you can try the machine over a PSTN circuit.

With respect to printers, the quality provided by a good electrostatic printer is much the same as a good thermal printer. Electrostatic copies are claimed to endure better. An important factor is the cost of the paper and any associated chemicals - another factor affecting running costs. Paper for electrostatic printers typically costs 4.5p per sheet, and for thermal 3.5p. Note, in the paper feed column, that some machines will accept paper wider than A4. Most machines cut copies to length from a paper roll when transmission ends so will reproduce long sheets.

"Logging" is the provision for printing information about time, date, etc., either generated as a list on a separate sheet, or printed by the machine at the edge of an actual page. The last column shows the manufacturer's claim for reproducing half tones or "grey scale". In practice there is only one way to find out how well the machine does it - try it on your test document.

Buying policy

When you buy, discriminate between "bells and whistles" and essential features. Consider complication with respect to the intended users. Check paper costs and maintenance arrangements. Try out machines for speed and quality of reproduction under real conditions. Try and find out who else uses the machine and with what result. Fax can bring great benefits when the right machine is chosen; if you want to send images containing graphics quickly and in some quantity fax has no rivals. The same remarks may apply to other information - for instance completed information-rich business forms - particularly if these forms have to be produced for internal use anyway and need to be circulated quickly, say between different sites of the same organisation. Fax does not require keying like telex or computer systems.

If a fax machine has already been purchased for graphics then it can also be used for text communication or "electronic mail", competing very favourably with telex, inter-computer communications and perhaps with teletex (yet to become widely available). The purchase of a fax machine solely for non-graphics purposes - for instance electronic mail - is likely to make sense only for high volume applications. Fax is expensive for short messages.

USING FAX

Many people are not machine oriented and some facsimile machines are daunting for people who do not use them sufficiently often to get to understand them. Infrequent users are unlikely to open the instruction manual. The occasional user will feel disposed only to learn just enough to get by and is likely to be defeated by anything unusual. It may be necessary to designate one person as the fax operator. An organisation which is a heavy fax user and has a number of machines, may employ an operator/engineer who oversees the machines, understands them, and can cope with any problem, possibly including repairs.

Large organisations may employ a telecommunications manager or equivalent person, who considers the economics of communication links and equipment, and organises installation. Three out of the four telecoms managers at the organisations which I visited were not much involved with the users. Once the fax machines were installed, personnel, and the manner of use were mainly left to the using department. Only one telecoms manager seemed to be also involved at the daily operational level.

Facsimile machines are quite reliable. Some faults such as paper stoppage, can usually be rectified. When machines go wrong, maintenance is quite good. No users had complaints on this score about any make of machine. The Muirhead D900, which looks like a museum piece and is simple to use, is still giving good service. Muirhead left the business facsimile market for more specialised activities. They have recently returned to it with Japanese machines made by Oki.

An exchange of facsimile messages usually requires two operators – one sending, one receiving – although newer machines will work unattended for some of the time. The work in progress which I watched was dependent on correct action by both operators. There may have been a skilled man at one end, but the person at the other end was not necessarily skilled. I noted several problems being solved because the skilled man was able to inform the remote operator by telephone how to take the right corrective action.

<u>Operational problems</u>

The inside of a fax machine is a mystery to most operators and they seem to accept mysterious happenings as inevitable.

At one site in central London, Xerox 400 machines are used for traffic to New York where compatible machines are installed. They usually receive documents from London satisfactorily except that New York often asks for a re-transmission when something is missed because of differences in the length of paper at each end of a message. However when I was there a session was intitiated by a telephone conversation and an apparently normal transmission took place. After an interval New York telephoned saying that nothing had been received. A second attempt was made and the same thing happened. The document was received at the third attempt, but no reason was discovered for the previous failures. Another company using a CCITT compatible Rapicom machine, tried to communicate with a Xerox 400 without success. The 400 is certainly not one of the latest machines, explaining perhaps the rather crude facilities for dealing with the kind of problems encountered.

<u>User attitudes and work flow</u>

The fax operators I met were not very concerned about the problems just described. This may seem strange since these were not experimental sessions, but a routine day's work. People seemed resigned to problems with machines. Problems were few when I was watching and I was told that problems did not occur often enough seriously to delay work.

The work flow did not seem to match the capacity of the machines at any of the sites I visited. It tended to be irregular and for most of the time the machines were inactive. It would be interesting to find a site where fax was in continuous use so as to discover whether it is necessary to have spare machine capacity in hand for down time. The ability to send urgent messages for quick action and to be able to send a batch knowing that they would be dealt with at once seemed to be a major benefit. Under-useage in these cirumstances is acceptable.

The messages now sent by fax had previously been sent by courier in several of the organisations visited. The urgency of some messages, plus the volume of less urgent messages, is the reason why couriers are used for traffic between the offices of the same organisation, and sometimes for urgent and heavy traffic between different organisations. Couriers usually provide same day service, but by the time a message is generated, has awaited the next courier trip, and has been delivered, consequent action overlaps into the next day.

One alternative is to have couriers standing by for special trips on demand - a more expensive arrangement. With fax, a message can be sent almost at once at any time of day for same day attention. This seems to be a major reason for its adoption in businesses. For organisations with overseas offices the time benefits are even greater.

<u>Control & Mechanical problems</u>

Problems associated with paper feed seem to be the most common mechanical difficulty.

If the document to be transmitted is on thin paper and the edge offered to the roller-feed mechanism (used in many machines) is not flat, the paper may become skewed or crumpled if allowed to continue into the machine. Another problem is the jamming of blank paper - stored in most of the newer machines in the form of a roll - as an incoming message is being received, or if the machine is being used in the copying mode. The ease of re-establishing paper feed depends on the machine and the handiness of the user. For example an engineer-user said he usually had no difficulty with his Panafax UF 520 in clearing a blockage. However when his remote users had the same problem with the same machine they were unable to cope even when he took them through the procedure over the telephone.

Operation of the controls of the UF 520 is of interest because although not a very new machine it was the newest and most expensive of the machines encountered at the test sites. Is also has the most complex set of controls. This machine produced high quality facsimile in the tests. Some people at the test sites were prepared to pay the necessary attention to the controls to obtain the results of which this machine is capable. Others were not.

One user complained that he knew that the contrast of the pictures he was receiving could be much better if the sender had adjusted his machine properly. Another user took advantage of the machine's flexibility for a special reason. Reconciled to the inability of the person at the other end to set the controls properly, he told him to load the machine with papers ready for transmission, ensuring only that he had the machine set to be polled.

The UF 520 can accept a stack of up to 50 papers of the same size. During the handshaking procedure the receiving machine will automatically shift its major operational characteristics to match the machine at the transmitting end. In this case the controlling user took advantage of these facilities, knowing that when he polled the remote machine to commence sending the stack, it would take care of itself.

It is not clear whether a machine supposed automatically to adapt itself to receive transmissions from a CCITT compatible machine of another make will always do so. For example an NEC 3500 should be able to receive transmissions from a 3M 2346 without the need for the receiving operator to make adjustments. However on one site the NEC 3500 had to be set manually to "3 minutes" before it could receive the 2346's 3 minute transmission.

There is a rough correlation between the number of controls and the price with fax machines. The same remarks apply to the number of indicator lights which range from about 5 in the less expensive machines, increasing to 28 in the most expensive - at the time the Infotec 6350 An increase in the number of controls and indicator lights is usually accompanied by a proportional increase in difficulty of use.

For example in the NEC 3500 machine, a control labelled "copy" provides the useful extra facility of copying a document placed in it, with or without transmission. This requires very little extra comprehension by the operator.

The same machine embodies a setting labelled "Neefax-CCITT". A proper understanding of the function and correct use of this control does require extra comprehension. Extra comprehension may not be needed in proportion to the number of extra indicator lights. Of the large array of lights offered on the Infotec 6350, some simply provide confirmation that a button has been pressed. Others require an explanation.

FAX SERVICES

British Telecom seem to be one of the leaders in offering fax services with their Intelpost system. PTTs in Europe, and the United States Post Office (USPS) have not pushed their services so strongly.

BT offers services to many countries from well over 100 offices around the country to home and foreign city centres for collection, or for same day or following day delivery. Kalle Infotec KI 6400 machines have been adopted. The charge for the first side of a document to the US is £6, with £3 per side thereafter. Fax to the US is handled at a UK centre with special equipment capable of automatically transmitting at 15 seconds per page via the Comsat satellites. BTs selling point is that on many occasions the fax cost can be recouped versus the other major express service, telex, because keying time is often eliminated.

The Japanese also made rather slow progress although a photograph and specification for the "Minifax" terminal was published in 1980. It was hoped that a public service in Tokyo and Osaka would be operational early in 1981 in which this machine would play a part. Eventually two machines based on this design were introduced into a fax networked service operated by NTT commencing in September 1981 - the MF-1 for A5 size and the MF-2 for A4 size paper. Progress was then rapid. Over 30,000 terminals were inter-connected by the end of 1982. Nakajima has described an advanced all-digital network scheduled for mid-1984 with conversion protocols for fax and data.

The French started a service in 1981 using a CIT-Alcatel version of the Burroughs 5100 machine, charging the equivalent of U.S. 75c per page, dropping to 25c at volumes over 4800 pages a month.

The U.S. service Faxpak, has not been very successful although it supports 60 different kinds of machine. One problem, in spite of fall-back modes and supposed inter-machine compatibility, is that analogue and digital machines cannot easily be mixed. Faxpak, in effect, has to operate separate analogue and digital networks. Another service, the NSF sponsored AIP Spin /Dialog experiment using Rapifax machines, gave mixed results with disappointingly low useage. A lack of understanding of behavioural factors seems to have been a major problem.

NEW DEVELOPMENTS; CONVERGENCE

Ergonomic and operational requirements

Ergonomics - the study of the relationship between humans and their environment - has been well covered in Shackel's handbook although a new edition of that work would be welcome. Many Fax machine designers have obviously not read the part about panel design advising that controls and displays should be laid out in order of sequence of operations.

With currently available machines, facilities added to make them capable of operating satisfactorily over a wide range of conditions are usually accompanied by more controls. There is a limit to the amount of information that people can deal with at one time; more controls usually mean more settings to make, more to learn and remember, and a greater need to arrange for one trained operator rather than to allow many occasional users.

A multi-facility machine would not need a trained user if the added facilities were automatic. What is needed is a machine which is loaded with documents, runs with automatic address selection, and then transmits the lot. It should then return itself to "Auto-Receive", meaning that it would reproduce a succession of documents when polled by remote transmitters. Out-of-paper or a fault would actuate an alarm signal and the machine would switch off and await maintenance, also indicating its "down state" to any remote machine connected, or trying to connect, to it.

All other adjustments such as the correct settings for speed, resolution, transmission rate, contrast etc., could, at least in theory and probably in practice be made automatically. It would not be easy to automate contrast and resolution settings because the machine would have to assess the document content before transmitting it. Unless this facility is developed, machines accepting a stack of papers will continue to be limited to papers for which the same resolution and speed settings can be used.

Ergonomic and operational achievements

The degree of automaticity is increasing - for example unattended operation is feasible for foreseen sessions between machines of the same make. Unattended reception when a machine calls up another of a different make, nominally compatible, without pre-arrangement, seems much less likely to be successful. Transmission speeds have been automated to a degree. Some group 3 machines start fast and reduce their transmission rate to match line conditions.

Convergence

Group 3 machines are the current preference. The price is dropping faster than telecommunication costs and the speed of these machines outweighs first cost in most situations as discussed above. At the present time a good Group 2/3 machine costs about £2500 in the UK. Fax is now being used in a variety of situations where the potential is not being realised - it is often isolated from mainstream office procedures. This is an administrative problem and will continue until people find a way to integrate facsimile with other office services.

Facsimile equipment is passing through a period of transition. Until recently it was the basis for relatively low volume, slow transmission, specialised service. In due course the present generation of single-purpose machines will be replaced by multi-function machines which include fax. The rate at which this happens will depend on some mix of cost, convenience, and the capacity of humans to accept bigger bells and louder whistles. Adoption will certainly be much slower than some of the purveyors of equipment and services would have us believe.

Equipment design is changing rapidly and the latest machines reflect the hope that facsimile will find its place in the"office of the future". At one time the various techniques and methods by which information could be input, processed, communicated, stored, retrieved, and displayed, were progressing in more or less mutually exclusive boxes. Around 1982 things started to change. Facsimile signals can be merged into data streams, fed into the various networks which are becoming available, and utilised in mixed-mode reprographic machines.

The rate of the transmission itself need be no problem provided that the traffic density warrants the provision of special communication facilities. For example facsimile pages can be stored and transmitted in bursts at the rate of one page per second over satellite links - as proposed by Satellite Business Systems, the US consortium. For the vast majority of users for whom special circuits are not justifiable, communications are unsatisfactory.

It is not yet clear how facsimile will fit into the office external "electronic message" or "electronic mail" concept. Several PTTs are now operating point to point facsimile services but the link between the originator and the PTT transmission point, and the PTT receiving point and the user rarely exists.

<u>The shape of machines to come</u>

A new type of "photoelectric conversion" scanning head has been developed in Japan in which a strip of the image is illuminated by a row of minute Light Emitting Diodes of the same length as the strip and almost touching the document. A fibre optic array, each fibre being about 18 mm long and very close to the document, picks up the reflected light and conveys it to a diode on the strip like sensor. Higher resolution can be obtained because of the one-to-one size relationship between the document strip and the sensor and the absence of critical focusing.

In late 1981 Siemens announced two machines using ink-jet printers - the HF2040 and HF2050 (unattended), selling at around $6500, and using plain paper which in the U.S. is 13% of the cost of the special papers used in other facsimile machines. Since the same recording mechanism is used in Siemens printers a facsimile/copier/printer machine would be a logical development. Machines like this and the Panasonic MV3000 (discussed below) may well take their place amongst the other resources connected to Local Area Networks during the next five years.

Some manufacturers are fitting a socket to their fax machines for receiving code from a computer so that it can behave like a computer printer. The details for this "port" are the subject of a widely used standard - RS232. This makes it unnecessary for the user to buy two separate machines.

Matsushita experimented with a four colour ink jet fax machine for large pages but no product was announced. Datapoint were developing a machine which will accept ASCII code, or character data from existing analogue or digital facsimile machines converting the analogue into digital facsimile Group 3 format, for storage on disk. The characters may be reproduced on a laser printer or on a Group 3 fax machine.

The Panafax MV3000 "transverter", announced in 1982 embodies a computer, scanner, printer, modem, character generator etc., in one box costing about $8000. The MV3000 can accept facsimile or ASCII coded text at 9600 bps, making it a competitor in some respects to copier-based printers, although it is relatively slow. It includes page size adaptation and reduction - the size range is 3" x 5" to 11.5" x 120", with reductions up to 77%. The machine will use software for handling communication protocols such as BISYNC, HDLC, etc., and can accept Facsimile, Telex, and possibly Teletext. This could bring facsimile into a more central position in offices by embodying it with a general purpose intelligent copier.

It is hard to discover how successful this machine has been. It has not been made available in the UK although a few have been imported unsupported by Panasonic and not approved for connection by BT. What Panasonic has made available in the UK is a machine, just becoming available in June 1985, called the UF400, which contains a socket, some chips, and some resident software enabling it to receive ASCII code and able to work either as a Group 2/3 fax machine or as a remote computer printer. This much more modest attempt sells at an equally modest price - £2793. Perhaps this is an indication or market readiness both in respect of technical useability and price.

Various kinds of data reduction are employed in certain image processing systems such as some kinds of television systems, Group 3 facsimile systems, some pattern recognition systems, etc. Siemens have put together some yet more advanced ideas in their experimental Textfax work station. Data reduction is inherent in the scanning processes used in this machine because areas of data are digitized in proportion to their information content. The amount of data stored, transmitted, and converted back to an image is no more than is necessary for resolving each area.

Images containing illustrations, graphics, line drawings, and text are composed at a special work station. Illustrations and graphics , previously digitised, are available from storage. Half-tones have been quantised into 256 levels and then coded as eight bits per pixel. Areas containing different kinds of information are "windowed" with the cursor, and stored as co-ordinate information ready to be transmitted together with data about the image information they contain. Once the image has been composed it is scanned out for transmission.

Areas with multi-level pixels are identified as illustrations and are transmitted facsimile style as 8 bit codes together with their page co-ordinates. Two level areas are recognised as either text or drawings by special processing. Drawings are transmitted facsimile style. Each area of text, identifiable in storage by reference to its co-ordinates, is ASCII encoded, and transmitted in that form. The picture is reconstructed and reproduced area by area at the receiving end at the appropriate resolution - an approach similar in principle to that used in the Xerox Star office information processing system. The net effect on composite illustration/drawing/text images is a substantial data reduction of up to 10 to 1 depending on the information content of the areas. The method is cumbersome and probably expensive at present but is indicative of things to come.

Rather similar ideas have been discussed by Maekawa but with a more comprehensive explanation about how the software might be organised in a multi-media machine when the latter is connected to a LAN for receiving data for its internal database and for organising that data in a chosen manner for transmission via the LAN to other devices or for printing. Two kinds of storage are envisaged - optical disk and magnetic disk. Each is used for the purposes for which it is best suited.

The software includes a menu-driven format selector via which a user can layout text, graphics, and sound streams from data items called from his database. The main feature of this software enables data formatted appropriately according to its type to be called into a window for layout purposes. Pre-formatted text, images, forms, etc., can be moved about for page construction. Automatic interaction spreadsheet-style between windows enables a change in one window to be automatically made to associated data in another window.

In this proposed machine, convergence has been taken a stage further to a workstation containing its own database with the means of making transformations on stored data of any kind, including image data, and outputting the results in digitised ready to view or print form.

<u>Entry of the gladiators</u>

In the last two years big companies outside the fax industry have also had the feeling that fax has a place in the converging processes leading to the automated office. A more mundane but equally likely reason is that they know that print-on-paper will be around for many years to come, so if you want to generate a standard code to get it into the computer system, albeit using a lot of storage in the process, fax is a good way of doing it.

The economics and technology also makes sense. Storage is getting cheaper and cheaper and "bit-mapping" - that is the bit-by-bit method of displaying high resolution information - is gaining ground. Microcomputers are already being used with image digitisers to display images and before long Group 3/4 circuit boards will probably be introduced so that even if a machine does not include an image digitiser, it can be used as a fax display-receiver. By that time cheap very high quality printers may have arrived too. Whether this will be before 1990 is open to question.

The IBM Scanmaster is a component of the DISOSS office system which enables documents to be digitised and stored in a mainframe. In this way, at a heavy premium on storage, paperwork coming into an organisation from the external world can be converted, filed, and retrieved - that is it can be handled together with the information generated within the organisation in electronic form in the first place.

AT&T is another late entrant - ready, no doubt, for whatever may come up in integrated office systems, and with a huge sales force in place to shift the product. Xerox provides software which enables its Microcomputer to output text in Group 3 fax code for printing on its fax machines. Wang provides equipment with its new PC both to input information from a document via its image digitisor and to output the document in Group 3 code.

Very high speed fax

A typical A4 facsimile page contains up to 1.8 million bits when composed at 3.8 lines/mm; this reduces to 300,000 bits when Huffman encoded, and could perhaps be further compressed to 100,000 bits for many types of image. An AM International subsidiary at Bedford, Mass., developed a laser transceiver for SBS, capable of transmitting one page per second. Documents are fed in from a stack interleaved with address sheets specifying the destination. A helium-neon laser digitises at 12 x 12 lines/mm - about 8.5 million bits per page before compression.

A controller receives and stores data from one or more machines pending the establishment of a data link. Communication then proceeds   at 10 Mbps and the laser printer at the receiver prints up to 70 pages a minute. The arrival of "Wideband" or "Broadband" networks by AT&T, Satellite Business Systems (SBS) and others will make it possible to convey pages at this rate.

Engineers   at Toshiba report the transmission of A4 facsimile images in 3 seconds over a 1.5 Mbps link on the Sakura communications satellite. Normal and high resolution pictures with a 4 bit grey scale were transmitted. The system also allowed for control signals to be exchanged with up to 24 ground stations. The bit error rate for this circuit is less than 10^{-7} on fine but 10^{-4} on rainy days. This means that there could be up to 50 bit errors per page which would not affect picture quality that much.

A machine announced in January 1982 by the Terminal Data Corporation, Woodland Hills, Ca, USA, may have to wait for a supporting document-feeding and communications infrastructure to catch up with it. "Docuscan", will handle both sides of documents ranging from 3" x 5" cards, to A4 pages inclusive of book pages. Book pages are automatically turned by a vacuum transport system - and it is this part of the system which probably imposes a limitation on the remarkable speed. Just over 1 second for both sides of a page is claimed, providing about 3000 pages an hour - assuming that a 10 Mbps communication channel is available to accept the 9.25 Mbps output of the machine. The resolution is 200 pels/inch equivalent to about 8 lines/mm.

Speeds of this kind are accomplished by combining a range of techniques made possible by circuit complexity which would have been absurd to contemplate until recently. Yoshida and others have described the development of a machine for handling an A4 document in one second at a horizontal and vertical resolution of about 12 pels/mm, which is about 8 Mbits. It compresses this information by 4 to 1 with a run-length two-line coding technique using parallel processing with PROM controlled wired logic. Much faster processing is needed than conventional microprocessor clocking techniques can handle. Scanning and printing processes are carried out at constant speed, being separated from variable speed coding/decoding functions by large buffers. Printing is done with a laser printer running at over 8 Mbps.

INSTALLED BASE AND SALES FORECASTS

Table 9.6 shows an estimate for the installed base in Europe as at late 1982.

Type of machine
(Figure in brackets is %)

Country	Group 1	Group 2	Group 3	Total
UK	5500 (34.4)	8700 (54.4)	1800 (11.2)	16000
Germany	2000 (14.3)	10000 (71.4)	2000 (14.5)	14000
France	500 (6.3)	6500 (81.2)	1000 (12.5)	8000
Italy	2500 (35.7)	3000 (42.9)	1500 (21.4)	7000
All other Europe	5000 (21.0)	17000 (71.3)	1850 (7.7)	23850
Total	15500 (22.5)	45200 (65.7)	8150 (11.8)	68850

TABLE 9.6. INSTALLED BASE OF FACSIMILE MACHINES IN EUROPE

By 1982 Group 3 machines were only just starting to have an impact on the market. The US and Canadian installed base was about 330,000, and the Far East 266,000. The installed total, including Europe (from the above table) was thus about 665,000 machines. However Table 9.7 from a different source, showing totals supplied, gives a figure of 447,400. According to this estimate 55% of all machines in use world-wide were supplied by the 6 companies shown.

Area

Supplier	US & Canada	W.Europe	Far East	Total
Xerox	95000	19000	8000	122000
Matsushita/ Panafax	15000	5000	58500	78500
3M	59000	16000	–	75000
Exxon	69000	–	–	69000
Burroughs	55000	1000	–	56000
Nippon	3900	5000	38000	46900
Totals	296900	46000	104500	447400

TABLE 9.7. THE TOP SIX SUPPLIERS BY AREA

During the last five years many of the major established facsimile suppliers have almost given up manufacturing themselves, and are marketing bought-in Japanese equipment. About 80% of world production in sub-minute facsimile machines, worth $270M, were produced in Japan in 1981. By the end of 1984 this had increased to over 90% with total world sales at over $400M. Japan's concentrated production has driven down prices and quite complex high speed machines are produced for a market claimed to be growing at an annual rate of around 30%.

Another estimate puts the total number of machines in use at nearly 800,000 by the end of 1982 split into three roughly equal parts of Groups 1,2 and 3. 1985 sales in the US alone are expected to be 100,000 worth $408M with at least 90% manufactured by the Japanese, nearly all of them Group 2/3 machines. Of these 12% will be supplied by Ricoh, 9% by each of Xerox, Burroughs, NEC, Exxon, 3M, Pitney Bowes and AT&T, and the rest by others. The total installed base worldwide, acording to these figures, would seem to be approaching 1.5M machines by the end of 1985.

In common with other figures available for information technology markets, all these estimates need to be taken with a grain of salt.

FURTHER READING

Anon.
  Communicate 3(1), 23-39, January/February 1983.
    Facsimile review.
Brobst, Paul L.
  Paper delivered at the Institute for Graphic Communication
  (IGC) Digital Facsimile Revolution conference, Amsterdam,
  October, 1982.
    Digital facsimile systems: overview.
Cawkell, A.E.
  British Library R&D Report Number 5719, August 1982.
  Published by BL Lending Division, Boston Spa, West Yorks.
    An investigation of commercially available facsimile
    systems.
Cawkell, A.E.
  British Library R&D Report Number 5753, February 1983.
    Facsimile machines: a field study of human factors and operational
    effectivenesss
Hata, Hidetoh; Ishikawa, Sadayoshi et al.
  Jap. Telecomms. Rev. 22(4), 325-326, October 1980.
    An outline of the public facsimile communication systems.
Huffman, D.A.
  Proc.I.R.E. 40, 1098-1101, September 1952.
    A method for the construction of minimum redundancy codes.
Inagaki, Hiroya; Kamiya, Kenji, et al.
  Japan Telecomms Rev.,24(3), 219-226, July 1982.
    Recent progress in facsimile technology.
Kirstein, Peter K.
  Computer Networks 2(1978), 179-190.
    Choice of data communication media for transmission of
    facsimile information.
Maekawa, Mamoru; Sakamura, Ken; Shimizu, Tohru.
  In Mason, R.E.A. (Ed). Information Processing 83 (IFIP). Elsevier Science
Publishers. 1983.
    Multimedia machine.
McCullough, T.L.
  In Medley, Don (Ed); Proc AFIPS Nat. Comput. Conf.,
  Anaheim,   May   1980. AFIPS Press. 1815 N.Lynn St.,
  Arlington, Va 22209, USA. Pps 409-413.
    CCITT standardisation for digital facsimile.

Mussman, Hans Georg., Preuss, Dieter.
  IEEE Trans. Com., COM-25(11), 1425-1433, November 1977.
    Comparison of redundancy reducing codes for facsimile
    transmission of documents.
Nakajima, Hirohito.
  Japan Telecommuniucations Review, 25(3), 156-165, 1983.
    Recent trends in the development of facsimile and visual communications
    systems in NTT.
Nakano, Kazuo; Nakaya, Shigehisa et al.
  J.Appl.Photog.Eng. 7(1), 21-29, February 1981.
    Review of recent facsimile developments in Japan.
Ochi, Hiroshi; Matsumoto, Mitsuji.
  Rev. Communic. Labs. 30(1), 115-128, 1982.
    A high speed facsimile apparatus for satellite link and
    communication experiment.
Shackel, Brian (Ed).
  IPC Press, Guildford, England. 1974.
    Applied ergonomics handbook.
Schaphorst, R.A.
  Paper delivered at the Institute for Graphic Communication
  (IGC) Digital Facsimile Revolution conference, Amsterdam,
  October, 1982.
    Digital facsimile systems: techniques, standards, coding.
Schmidt, A.C.
  Paper delivered at the Institute for Graphic Communication
  (IGC) Digital Facsimile Revolution conference, Amsterdam,
  October, 1982.
    Advanced digital facsimile and applications.
Winterbauer, C.E.
  In Proc. Internat. Conf. on Electronic Image Processing,
  University of York, July, 1982, pps 144-148. Published by
  the Institution of Electrical Engineers, London, 1982.
    Facsimile data compression for military applications:
    definitions and performance.
Yoshida, Shigeru; Okada, Y., et al.
  Fujitsu Sci. Tech. J. 19(3), 323-339, September 1983.
    Development of compressor and expander for one second facsimile.

CHAPTER 10. THE ELECTRONIC PROCESSING & DELIVERY OF DOCUMENTS AND TEXT
PART 2: OTHER METHODS OF DELIVERING TEXT AND IMAGES ELECTRONICALLY

Other document delivery systems

Documents in the public domain, particularly those published in scientific journals following the tradition established with Journal des Scavans and Philosophical Transactions in the 17th century, can be obtained from a library if the bibliographic reference is known. The cost per photocopied 10 page document, delivered through the normal mail in 4 to 10 days from order through the library system in many countries, costs around $5. About 25 million loan requests were handled in the US in 1980.

The British Library Lending Division handles loans or photocopies either via the inter-library loan network in the UK, or by receiving direct requests on prepaid forms through the mail or by telex. It holds over 4 million volumes of books and periodicals and also other items like conference proceedings, microformed reports, translations, and music. With a staff of 750 it handled about 3 million loan requests in 1980 of which one sixth came from abroad.

In addition to access and delivery of these kinds of documents, a huge range of print-on-paper documents of all kinds are exchanged though the mail, by courier etc., and the private requirements for intra- and extra-organisation document circulation are enormous. The incentives to replace time-honoured methods come from needs for higher speed, lower cost, and more compact storage. Conversion into machine-readable form or the direct acquisition of information in that form also comes high on the requirement list.

Facsimile is the foremost document delivery technology but others have started to appear including networked Word Processing, Teletex (without a "t" at the end) and Optical Disk Based Systems (ODBS). Several large-scale co-operative attempts are being made in Europe using one or more of these technologies including Adonis, Hermes, Apollo, and Docdel and in the US ODBS at the Library of Congress.

Terminology problems - word processing, text, messages, mail, teletex, teletext

We think we know what words mean even if they sometimes sound slightly different. How can we be expected to believe that there are two completely different services in the same area one called "teletex" the other "teletext"? Only a fool would choose such similar words. When someone says "text processing" of course they mean "word processing" don't they? An "electronic message" is of course, a rather short item of "electronic mail" isn't it? Yes, no, and yes and no. This is the zany world of Information Technology, ladies and gentlemen.

Word Processing software, used on a computer, enables text to be created on a CRT screen using a typewriter-like keyboard and many compositional aids such as overtyping with erasure, auto-line return with right justification, electronic cutting and pasting, storage and retrieval, etc. Text processing is occasionally used as a synonym for Word Processing but is usually used to describe software packages where the emphasis is on searching and retrieving records containing text as discussed in Chapter 14. Teletex is like high speed Telex, while Teletext is a kind of Videotex. Electronic Mail? Well, please refer to the glossary. You can see now why I used the words "delivering text and messages electronically" above. I believe (without enormous conviction) that the sections which follow have headings with the correct meaning above them.

Word Processing

The use of Word Processing (WP) machines in medium/large organisations as a replacement for typewriters in the old "typing pool" has received considerable attention and has been mentioned incidentally in other places in this handbook. It has not been accorded whole chapter status because it is gradually becoming just another function to be carried out on multi-purpose terminals, microcomputers, or work-stations. Dedicated WP machines are also being eroded at the "bottom end" by electronic typewriters which include some WP functions. Word processing software is increasingly provided for micros as part of combination packs with spreadsheet, communications and other items. The low incremental cost of adding WP in this way is yet another advantage. However enough special design features may be needed still to justify limited ongoing manufacture of dedicated WP machines.

Two very important factors are ease of use and flexibility - that is ability to switch between standard functions, text/image combinations, downloading from a mainframe computer etc. A buyer can reasonably expect comprehensive performance from a dedicated WP machine, with great attention accorded to instructional and design details to make the facilities easy to use. In the past, even with quite good performance, cut-throat competition for WP microcomputer software has meant minimum attention to ease of use and instruction books. However the micro-software people are now doing better and the human-factors credibility gap between dedicated and micro WP is narrowing.

Wordplex, a leading WP machine supplier, recognising the trend, decided to go in for computers and office systems at the beginning of 1984. However they continue to sell WP machines arguing that the special features required for efficient use cannot so readily be incorporated into multi-purpose machines.

Inter-connected word processing machines or micros with WP software which possess or have access to sufficient storage, and incorporate file retrieval facilities, provide the means for document delivery, usually within one organisation on one or more sites. WP manufacturers call them "shared logic" systems if the workstations depend on certain functions perfomed by a central minicomputer, but "shared facility" if the workstations, normally connected to a central machine, can function autonomously if the central system breaks down. The machines generate standard code for the limited num- of symbols needed for text so no graphics can be transmitted in this method of document delivery. The usual software, equipment, and protocol problems, so often mentioned elsewhere in this book occur if machines made by different manufacturers are inter-connected.

<u>Telex</u>

Telex is to text what the the PSTN is to voice. It is a dial-up international system in which text is typed on a QWERTY keyboard in (until very recently) a special transmitter/receiver machine and appears on paper rather like a typewriter, also appearing on paper on the remote machine which you have dialled. Many machines contain a paper tape punch which can be used with the keyboard offline. The tape emerges during typing with holes punched in it representing the 5 bit Baudot code. When the remote number has been dialled and the machine is ready to transmit, the end of the tape is fed in and transmission proceeds automatically at 50 bits/sec whic is equivalent to about 60 words per minute.

     Alternatively text can be typed and transmitted at the same time. A typist can usually transmit at about 40 to 50 words per minute, observing the paper emerging from the local machine for correctness. Incoming international telexes are sometimes headed with the originating carrier's name e.g. Western Union TWX or ITT, but they have will have been transmitted using the same code and the same speed. A telex machine left switched on will work unattended and record any incoming messages.

     Telex is changing. Machines are available to integrate telex into office systems. Until recently the rather old-fashioned looking telex machines were often housed in their own little room with a trained operator. Wordplex can supply a unit made by Hasler for use with one of their WP machines. The software provides telex prompts and stores incoming telex messages on disk.

     Telex 80-0-80 volt signalling is being replaced by Single Channel Voice Frequency (SCVF) signalling. The signals look like those emerging from low speed modems (CCITT V21 standard). Private systems used in the UK will normally use this form of signalling over wires leased from BT: speeds of up to 300 Bauds are possible. The big users of telex can have a multi-line message switching unit on their premises and that will use SCVF signalling.

Teletex

     Teletex is a higher speed text interchange system working at 2400 bits/sec over public networks enabling an A4 page of text to be transmitted in about ten seconds. Teletex text is composed using a QWERTY keyboard which is then stored in memory. Transmission and reception proceeds between machines on a memory to memory basis. It is almost as if everyone had standard WP machines able to communicate over public networks.

     Politically Teletex may be regarded as an attempt by the European PTTs to offer an inter-office hassle-free text transmission service using their today's communication channels in association with commercial equipment suppliers, up-gradeable for use with tomorrow's channels and equipment. It uses a protocol conforming to the bottom three layers of the OSI architecture (see Chapter 6) for "universal compatible telecommunication networks and equipment". If it is seen to meet the need of today's electronic text delivery requirements it could bring about the unification of control, coding, and character sets. It would also make the task of encipherment relatively easy.

     It remains to be seen whether PTT clout will be enough to make Teletex take off. So far the omens have not been propitious, probably because the PTTs have been unable to convince suppliers to set up manufacturing facilities to produce equipment at an attractive price. This may have been because extensive development work has been needed to deal with the OSI requirements and the arrangements to handle the character set/letter reproduction requirements and cram everything into the PSTN bandwidth.

     Little interest has been displayed in the US, but then the US has never been all that interested in Telex - a major message system for most other industrialised countries. However considerable US interest has been displayed in the proposed CCITT protocol standard X400 which provides for the inclusion of certain coded information in documents which will be acted upon by equipment installed in store and forward telecommunication networks. The kinds of information which can be entered seem to replace some of the functions performed by teletex. For example the owner of an appropriate microcomputer will be able to interrogate a mailbox somewhere on the network, and a user will be able to insert one or multiple addresses on one message for automatic delivery to those addresses.

The Teletex leader has been Germany, where over 10,000 terminals are said to be in use, followed by Sweden. One of the leading manufacturers is Siemens who offer their T4200/40 text terminal (shown in Figure 10.1) at £4350 in the UK. The terminal includes facilities for Teletex and Telex, with a keyboard, daisywheel printer, modem, and electronics with dedicated software - that is it will not run any other software.

FIGURE 10.1. SIEMENS T4200 TEXT TERMINAL

The WP which is provided is said to be easy to learn but it does not provide the comprehensive facilities provided on most WP machines.

Teletex was officially launched in the UK in April 1985 presumably because a plausible selection of terminals and telecoms facilities existed by then. The big advantage versus telex is, of course, the cost per page of text. 4.4p will buy transmission time for between 15 and 82 A4 pages according to the time of day, and 13.2p will buy between 3 and 25 pages for trunk calls over 56 Km.

As with most new systems when first introduced, it is not clear when the promised facilities will be implemented. A user whose terminal may be connected to the PSTN or to PSS, dials another machine using a special code. The PSTN and PSS are interconnected by a gateway called Interstream which is addressed by the code and routes the caller to the network to which the called terminal is attached. This facility is available from launch date.

Later there will be a telex-teletex gateway which will enable these two different kinds of machine to interconnect, automatically raising the number of subscribers available to receive teletex-generated messages by up to about 1.8 million when world-wide inter-conections are in place. Some countries will be unavailable or there will be varying degrees of complication when trying to connect internationally. International inter-networking will be introduced as equipment and arrangements are introduced between countries.

There were 21 suppliers or potential suppliers of teletex equipment for UK use in April 1985. Equipment ranged from the Siemens machine mentioned above to the GEC Centex shared-resource Teletex unit incorporating a 26 Mbyte disk and printer and capable of handling up to eight "dumb" terminals at once (8 ports), or of course a much larger number on a dial-up shared basis via, say, a PABX. Its value for money at £30,000 would depend on the time occupancy per port; it could be low on a per terminal basis.

DOCUMENT DELIVERY: SPECIAL PROJECTS AND THE NEW MYTHOLOGY

In a short review Gates summarises some possible document delivery scenarios:

1. A Teletex system, suitable for documents containing text only. If graphics are needed they must be handled by an auxiliary system.
2. A facsimile system, suitable for containing text and graphics.
3. A combined Teletex and graphics system in which the text of the document will be handled in the form of coded characters while the graphics will be handled by facsimile techniques.
4. A satellite system, suitable for text and graphics, making use of satellite transmission for the actual delivery of the document.
5. A digital optical disk system suitable for text and graphics. It is envisaged that both central and local document delivery services will be developed.
6. A magnetic tape system suitable for documents containing text only. It is envisaged that both central and local document delivery services will be developed.

Gates suggests costs (1983), presumably development costs, for a 400,000 document system, at less than £500K for a text only coded character system, to over £12M for a 200 line/inch fax system for rapid online access to text and graphics. The terminal cost would be in the £4K-£8k range, and transmission costs about 20p for 5 pages transmitted at 1200 bps.

Our old tradeoff friend Bandwidth/speed/cost (See Chapter 5) is once again the problem, particularly as between the text requirement for the coding, transmission, and decoding on a pre-arranged basis, of some tens or hundreds of alternative 8 bit signals, and the image requirement for the transmission of bit patterns about which little is known in advance. Thus, compression techniques excluded, a full A4 page of text at 1200 bps takes about 5 seconds to transmit and requires Kilobytes of storage, while an A4 size high resolution image takes 20 minutes when transmitted at the same rate, and up to 2 Mbytes of storage.

Line has put his finger on another important practical factor which has not received much consideration in what often turn out to be rather abstract discussions about this topic. For online scanning of material enabling you to decide what you <u>do not want</u> in full text, a typical CRT layout/quality may suffice, but for <u>actually reading</u> articles you want not only hard copy but <u>decent</u> hard copy. "Decency" is apt to be expensive!

A number of document delivery projects have been or now are in progress. The hopes implicit in their high-flying Greek names have not always materialised.

Hermes

Project HERMES was an attempt conceived by the National Physical Laboratory and the Printing and Packaging Industry Research Association (PIRA) with Scicon participation, to be sponsored by the Department of Trade and Industry (DOI) in the UK, in order to test the feasibility of a Teletex-based document delivery system. It would embody a database and the capacity to receive requests and despatch documents. Later it was hoped to add some form of parallel facsimile operation from a database stored on optical disk. Selected users - about 100 were said to be interested in 1983 - were expected to buy a terminal and commit themselves to the trial for 12 months during 1984 when the BT Teletex launch was expected.

HERMES just faded away at the end of 1984, probably because of a combination of circumstances. Teletex was delayed, there seemed to be nobody in the driving seat, and the marketing incentives to push it were absent.

Adonis

ADONIS was seen in one publication as "a beauty of a specialised electronic mail network...which will revolutionise the entire system". I don't think its originators - a publisher consortium of Elsevier, Springer Verlag, Pergamon, Blackwells, Acadata , and John Wiley - saw it quite like that, although in October 1982 they announced that it would be operational in 1984 and that they would be approaching major libraries about it.

The Article Delivery Over Network Information Systems was an Elsevier inspired project maybe working on the assumption that technology has reached the point when we can cut out the photocopying-royalty-bypassing types like BLLD, and collect the royalties ourselves. Curiously, the British Library Lending Division (BLLD) was "participating" perhaps on the basis that in case you can't beat 'em join 'em.

ADONIS was to be an optical disk database system containing the significant scientific and medical article digitised output of these large publishers. The response to online requests would be full text plus graphics delivery to distribution centres via satellite to the appropriate ground station, or via an appropriate network. The centres would organise their own digital-to-hard copy conversion and most expeditious method of local or regional delivery.

Bold assumptions about the high volume of expected business indicated that the cost would be competitive with today's steam-driven photocopying-and-mail methods, with the additional advantage of removing the middleman and collecting his erstwhile revenue.

Alas it was not to be - at least not yet. To coin a mixed metaphor it is currently in a wound-licking ticking-over phase perhaps with a view to a quiet start in a high-demand area when the technology gets cheaper.

Great stuff these swashbuckling have-a-go-approaches, but there may be one false assumption behind them - a supposed demand for speed. All other things being equal, presumably a same-day service would scoop up the business from a weekly-turnaround system, or would it? Some years ago the National Bureau of Standards conducted a <u>free</u> document delivery by facsimile experiment to a number of centres. No doubt the quality and "database" could have been better but that wasn't the point. The speed at which people turned up to collect their articles was not compatible with the speed of the service! The speed for the average occupational need was counted in days not hours.

The message may be that the speed-needers are the rather small number of people at the white-hot leading edge where a few days sooner meets a real need even although the production cycle for the material will have already taken, at minimum, weeks to progress from author to publication. The high speed information for which people are really prepared to pay for, is that which does not go through this kind of cycle - it is data concerning stock market prices, exchange rates and the like.

Apollo

Next we come to APOLLO – A Project Of Lots of Lovely Opportunities. Perhaps it's not an acronym at all, like HERMES. It was just borrowed from NASA who borrowed it from Zeus. Perhaps APOLLO was designed to show that a satellite is a Good Thing. I'm sorry about this disgraceful levity – I hope it will turn out to be misplaced and that APOLLO is a success. Destined originally for the OTS European satellite, but then shifted to to ECS, APOLLO is backed by no less than EUTELSAT, the PTTs, and the CEC. However the funding of £1M, allocated to APOLLO in 1983, does not encourage it to be taken seriously, although the real cost may emerge in due course.

The project was set up to test ordering through available media with delivery from a store of digitised full-text documents via satellite and was planned to be operational in 1984. High resolution $10,000 terminals were to be provided at sites for high speed or intermediate speed delivery.

Alas again – APOLLO is said to have been bogged down by political wrangling but the latest is that it is to be a multi-purpose low-tariff system not only for documents but also for newspaper remote printing, electronic mail, computer file transfer etc. Even so, a recent paper about it (Vernimb, December 1984) starts with "probably all of us have already been in a situation where we desperately need a document within one hour or overnight for which we would have been prepared to pay a substantial sum of money". Quite right, I can truthfully reply to that, but not,I fear, the kind of document likely to be available from APOLLO databases.

Docdel

The most recent project was also described in December 1984 (Mastroddi). Eschewing the Greek connection it is called simply DOCDEL or sometimes EURODOCDEL , and is far more ambitious than anything mentioned before – APOLLO will simply be one its transport systems.

Europe needs to get it right this time since the continent needs some market-driven information technology if it is to have thriving industries in this field and does not simply become a yet bigger buyer of dollar and yen products coupled to the waning political clout accompanying such a trend.

DOCDEL, allocated $16M by the CEC, is a test of an integrated system embodying text and graphics preparation and handling, storage, electronic publication, and distribution and marketing. Development has been contracted out – a consortium called Transdoc which includes CNRS, Telesystemes and Electricite de France will organise the storage of 100 scientific journals and the full text of French patents. Europe Data and Machine Bull will deal with reception on special machines, and a number of German research establishment users will test effectiveness using a database of German patents. "Electronic journals" will be tried out by various European publishers.

A second programme is being considered which will have a go at almost everything – economic aspects and administration, standards, transmission systems, automatic indexing, multi-mode receivers, expert systems and whatever.

OPTICAL VIDEODISK AND OPTICAL DIGITAL STORAGE DISK SYSTEMS

Introduction

Optical videodisks were developed for the consumer market to compete with Video Casette Recorders (VCR) as a method of recording and reproducing television pictures. From the information rather than the entertainment viewpoint, optical videodisks represent a competitive method of image storage, but since images simply consist of data arranged in a particular way they could also be used for storing data representing text or other kinds of information.

Friebus is credited with the invention of the optical digital data storage disk in the US in 1929, but the leader in bringing it into use has been Philips who demonstrated a working system in 1978. Later Philips developed a method called DRAW (Direct Read After Write) for writing a block of data and then verifying if by immediately reading it and re-writing in the event of an error. Optical digital data storage disks are now starting to compete with magnetic disks for computer data storage. Philips developed the Compact Disk for audio digital recording during the same period. The digitised audio data normally recorded on a compact disk could just as well be other kinds of information. This media has in fact now been further developed for digital data storage.

<u>Light as a digital information media</u>

The position of light in the spectrum of electromagnetic radiation (See Chapter 5, Figure 5.1) makes it a prime target for exploitation as an information carrying media, given the appropriate technology. In Chapters 5 (about telecommunications) and 7 (about fibreoptics) the emphasis was placed on the information capacity inherent in wideband channels. "Information" is conveyed by transmitting data at the limiting rate of two signalling elements per Hertz of bandwidth in a communications channel. The wider the bandwidth the faster the signalling rate and so the capacity for conveying more information.

Light occupies about 300 THz in the decade of the frequency spectrum between 100 and 1000 TeraHertz (See also Chapter 1, Figure 1.5). The spectrum occupied by all the other major channels used for conveying information extends from very low frequency waves at about 16 Khz to the highest frequencies useable by satellites, currently about 30 GHz. The whole of this bandwidth of about 30 Ghz is about one ten thousandth of the bandwidth available in the light "channel".

However if the properties of light with its enormous information-carrying capacity are going to be harnessed in some way for information transmission, processing, and storage, other requirements must be considered - storage space, transmission methods, and modulation by data. Obviously there must be a detectable physical space between the storage elements in any storage device. If light is to be used for detection the elements must be spaced at least one wavelength apart. The wavelength of light is around 500 nanometres (that is considerably less than one thousandth of a millimetre) so an array of at least one million storage elements per square millimetre is feasible.

Thus, so far as storage density is concerned, it is the wavelength (related to the frequency as w = velocity x 1/f) rather than the frequency, which is of particular interest.

The invention of the laser - capable of transmitting an extremely narrow light beam modulated by data - enabled optical storage to be organised. A mechanically and optically manageable way of doing it is to use a laser for storing information by burning small pits in a rotating disk the smallest possible distance apart to indicate, say, "0" by a pit and "1" by a flat - a form of modulation - and then, as the disk is rotated beneath the laser beam, to retrieve the information by detecting the absence or presence of light reflected or not reflected from pits and flats.

In practice pits representing non-erasable bits of data spaced at about one or two micron intervals (millionth of a metre) are formed by the localised melting action of a laser on a disk coated with a thin film of a Tellurium alloy, a substance found to have the appropriate properties. The surface is protected by a transparent polymer layer after writing. Disks are up to 12 inches in diameter and carry up to 50,000 or more tracks with between 100K and 300K bits per track. The total capacity of one side is typically 8000 Mbits - that is 1000 Mbytes or 1 Gigabyte.

The laser beam is reflected through a mirror on to a lense which focusses it to a spot about one micron in diameter. The lense can be moved radially across the disk on a sledge for track selection, and up and down for focussing. Disks typically rotate at 1200 rpm and the lense head-unit is accurately kept above a track by a servomotor regardless of concentricity, wear etc. A servomotor rotates under the control of an amplified error voltage derived from the device it is positioning, if that device moves out of position. When the voltage becomes zero in consequence of the device having been driven to the correct position, the motor stops. The action is exremely rapid.

Optical and other Videodisks: principles and application

Optical Videodisks were developed as a consumer product for selling recorded television and feature films. Players and disks are available in the shops as an alternative to VCRs, but they are for read-only purposes - you have to buy programs on disk; you cannot record from the TV. Program content and technical methodology have been the factors influencing the growth rate of this media, apart from the all-important factor in the consumer market - price.

Recording is on a continuous spiral track as with gramophone/phonograph recordings. Two forms of recording have been used - Constant Angular Velocity (CAV) and Constant Linear Velocity (CLV). With CAV, each recorded TV frame starts in the same angular position on the disk which permits "freeze frame", slow motion, and random access which are not possible with CLV.

There are two major competitive consumer systems since RCA dropped out of the market with its cheap but limited grooved capacitance system. These are the non-optical Video High Density (VHD) system supported by JVC and Thorn-EMI, and Laservision supported by Philips, Pioneer, and Sony. VHD is a grooveless capacity system while Laservision is a laser operated system which reads light reflected from pits or flats, representing digital data (but see remarks below about modulation), on the disk's surface. Both are CAV recordings.

Philips Laservision, using CAV recordings, is the market leader. In this system, standard PAL (most of Europe) or NTSC (USA) television signals are passed through a convertor (pulse width modulation) for "digital" recording by the laser beam as variably spaced pits or flats on the surface of the disk. The data is read from reflected light interrupted by this pattern and a convertor changes the data back to television format.

It is of interest to note that true digital storage is not used in Laservision since information is contained not only by the presence of pits or flats but also by the variable distance between the pits. In other words additional coded information has been incorporated per pit/flat just as it was added per signalling element in the basic form of multi-level coding described in Chapter 5, and for the same reason - bandwidth reduction. Fewer pits/flats used at slower speeds are needed to convey the same amount of information.

In the PAL version (PAL uses 625 lines, 50 fields per second, with two interlaced fields producing 25 complete TV pictures (frames) per second) the disk rotates at 1500 rpm or 25 times per second. Each frame, consisting of two picture fields and sound, is recorded on one of the 54,000 spiral tracks. The playing time is therefore 54,000/25 = 2160 seconds, or 36 minutes. The disks are double sided providing one hour twelve minutes playing time. The NTSC version rotates at 1800 rpm to provide 30 frames per second.

A long-playing disk, using CLV recording for continuous entertainment, and so not suitable for IR purposes is also available. A playing time of one hour per side is achieved by recording 3 complete frames per revolution on the outside track, decreasing to one on the inside.

The standard consumer model sells at £229 (tax incl) with disks at from £10 to £26 in the UK. Currently there are over 500 disks covering all kinds of entertainment in the catalogue.

<u>Optical videodisks for image information storage and retrieval</u>

Videodisk players for the consumer market contain the basic technology for image IR applications but add on gadgets or "professional model" versions are needed to do an IR job. However it should be remembered that the resolution is "TV set" resolution equivalent to about 400,000 pixels compared to the 2M pixels, or thereabouts, considered necessary for high quality pictures or the reproduction of small text (See Chapter 23).

The gadgetry consists of the means of controlling the position of the head and/or of merging locally generated information to be displayed as if it was actually recorded on the disk. The head can be computer-controlled through an interface, usually the RS232C, so that by keying a number the head is located over a particular track. This "random access" takes 5 seconds on average. The head is stepped back once per revolution so that an apparently still picture is generated by the continuous repetition of the same frame. Other control functions include fast forward/reverse, pause, and go to a selected segment of the disk – that is a part of the disk bounded by two specified picture numbers – and play that segment.

Another activity has recently been gaining ground as described by Daynes and Jarvis, using microcomputer controlled disk players, or using other Philips Laservision models containing the necessary facilities – and that is "Authoring". Authoring means the overlaying of text and/or graphics on videodisk frames so that the result is a composite of the images permanently recorded on the disk and the images stored in the computer which is controlling the system, previously created by the local author. The composite "TV programme" can be repeated by simply replaying the disk under software control. These programmes are being used for education and training purposes.

The Philips Laservision model VP835, available in the UK at £1945, for example, enables teletext images to be created and overlaid on disk material. The Philips ILVAS system is more comprehensive. It is really a TV programme management computer software system, offered at £3000 for use with an IBM PC and Laservision model VP835 for the creation of a complete programme, probably in conjunction with the user's own audio-visual material. This material will have been supplied to Philips, say on VCR tape, for the creation of a master disk. The computer and software runs a menu-driven program enabling the user to design one or more programmes combining disk and overlay material. Philips operate a service for the creation of Laservision disks from a customer's material usually supplied on videotape.

Pergamon Infoline announced a system in 1982 for searching US Patents called Video Patsearch, using videodisks. For an annual fee of £7000 a user was provided with microcomputer, videodisk player and a set of disks, periodically up-dated, with one screen for viewing text and one for images. The patent database was searchable online at BRS in the US or at Pergamon Infoline in London. Normal search procedures were used to obtain "hits" and abstracts (text) of the patents found were displayed. The microcomputer automatically retrieved drawings associated with the hit patents from the videodisk and displayed them on the second screen. The service was discontinued in 1984.

More recently the BBC announced that in conjunction with the UK Department of Trade and Industry and Philips it would be organising a 1985/1986 computerised-videodisk version of the Domesday Book on the 900th anniversary of the original version. Schools and various local groups will collect data about their locality which will be collated at regional centres all over Britain and keyed on to floppy disks. The disks together with diagrams, maps and photographs will be sent to the BBC who will organise recordings on to two Laservision disks. This will provide space for up to 2M pages of text plus tens of thousands of maps and photographs. Together with an index this will form a comprehensive record of the country as it is today.

<u>Optical digital storage disks: principles and application</u>

Optical pseudo-digital storage is used in one of the major <u>video</u> storage sytems for the general consumer market as just described. The other application is for high density random access computer storage competing with magnetic disk so there need be no limitations in order to conform to television standards.

The potential of this method of digital storage was realised in the late seventies and RCA, Philips, and others devised experimental systems. In 1979 the estimated cost of storage per gigabyte was $50,000 for magnetic disks and $8000 for read-only optical disks. This ratio has remained about the same in later years - one late 1983 estimate was $6000 per gigabyte for small optical disk systems (e.g Shugart and Optimem), $60,000 for small Winchesters, still hardly feasible at this capacity level, and $15,000 for IBM 3380 disks.

By 1985 about ten manufacturers had announced digital optical storage disks with data transfer rates of 1 Mbyte/sec or more. They will probably soon become adopted for large databases and archival storage. Another advantage is disk compactness. Optical disks occupy far less space/volume than other forms of storage, microforms excepted.

One of the first major systems announced was for the US Library of Congress as described by Wood. The first system was installed in 1982 for the storage and production of catalogue cards. Wood goes on to discuss the use of optical disks as a document delivery system to replace library photocopying under various input supply and input cost conditions, including participation in ADONIS as originally conceived. He concludes that the price will probably be higher during the next 5 years and that "there is no evidence that users will routinely pay these higher prices for copies available a few hours or days sooner than the turnaround they normally receive".

However in 1984 a system was delivered to the Library of Congress by Integrated Automation using Thomson-CSF disks in a carousel with a capacity of 2.5M A4 pages and less than 15 seconds random access time. This system includes a high speed high resolution digitising CCD camera for "photographing" documents and a number of online searching and viewing terminals and printers. The system costs between $500K and $4M according to the facilities provided and was accorded the usual puff by the supplier about its "awesome implications". The storage cost is said to be $150 per gigabyte or 2000 600 word pages per $.

Another major system is available apparently as a "production" item rather than as a "special" - the Philips Megadoc - at £85,000 in the UK with single sided 1Gbyte disks at £250, double sided at £320. Megadoc has been adopted by Gruner and Jahr (a Bertelsmann Company) who are transferring some 3 million items in their archives to Megadoc, previously stored as newspaper cuttings or on fiche. It is also being used by the Dutch land registry of properties, and by LBS Munster to replace a COM system (See Chapter 24). The Italian insurance company Reale Mutual are using it for the processing and storage of insurance claims - for instance sketches of car accident situations can be stored together with all the other images/text relevant to the claim.

Megadoc is a kind of computerised facsimile database system. Its CCD scanner processes print-on-paper pages input at 10 pages/minute using the proposed fax Group 4 standard (See Chapter 9). Digitised page images are bit- stored on the optical disk by a writing laser. The user keys in page indexing data to a conventionally organised record/field database (Chapters 13 and 14). To retrieve an image the user searches the database's inverted file. Index records contain pointers to the disk image index, and the asociated page images corresponding to the hit records appear on the screen as hit images. The display unit uses one of the highest resolution CRTs available - the Philips M38-200 - capable of displaying 4M pixels, so with the Group 4 input resolution also approaching 4Mbits, the system is capable of processing and displaying very high quality images.

Average database retrieval time is 6 seconds with a further 2 seconds for image retrieval. A "jukebox" type 64-disk magazine is available with the system and a maximum of three magazines can be used providing a total capacity of nearly 400 Gbs. Maximum acess time is then 15 seconds. The Megadoc system can be used on its own, as just described, or it can be used as a shared "resource" connected to a network - for example as a central filing system.

During 1985 the so-called CDROM 5.25 inch digital optical storage disks with players based on the Philips compact audio disk will become available. The same method of recording and playback with a laser is used but the disks have a relatively small capacity of 600 Mbytes. However the extraordinary success of the compact disk has meant that mass production of its laser unit and other parts, also used on the CDROM, have enabled the latter to be cheaply manufactured.

<u>Erasable optical digital storage disks</u>

Mansuripur provided a list of 40 papers describing research on erasable disks early in 1985. In April Matsushita announced that it was on the way to producing something which would be commercially viable. The principle used in most experiments is to use a laser beam to write on a rotating disk coated with an amorphous film of a material (rare earth transition metal) having special magnetic properties. If the material is heated in a magnetic field the heated area remains magnetised in a particular direction when the heat is removed. When the laser is switched on for 50 ns, local heating in the spot of material immediately beneath the beam is sufficient for magnetisation. In that extremely short time period the disk moves less then a micron.

When the disk is rotated beneath a laser light beam which has been polarised, the polarisation of the light reflected from a magnetised spot is changed and that change can be detected. A previously written-on track can be "cleaned" by continuous laser writing in a magnetic field having a direction opposite to the direction used when recording. The whole of the track area is then changed back to the "unwritten" magnetised state ready for localised laser heat-induced changes when the field direction is again changed for writing. No information seems yet to have been released about when an erasable system is likely to be commercially available.

<u>FURTHER READING</u>

Anon.
   Report 83405 to DG13 of the CEC, April 1980. Arthur D. Little Inc., April 1980.
   Artemis - a system for document digitalisation and tele-transmission.
Daynes, Rod; Holder, Steve.
   Byte 9(7), 207-228, July 1984.
   Controlling videodiscs with micros.

Gates, Yuri.
  Aslib Proc. 35(4), 195-203, April 1983.
    User needs and technology options for electronic document delivery.
Jarvis, Stan.
  Byte 9(7), 187-203, July 1984.
    Videodiscs and computers.
Line, Maurice B.
  Aslib Proc.35(4),167-176, April 1983.
    Document delivery now and in the future.
Mansuripur, M; Ruane, M.F; Horenstein, M .N.
  Indus. Eng. Chem. Prod. Res. Dev. 24, 80-84, 1985.
    Erasable optical disks for data storage: principles and applications.
Mastroddi, Franco A.
  In Proc. 8th Int. Online Information Meeting, London, December 1984, Pps
  179-194. Learned Information, Abingdon, England.
    Integrated electronic publishing - some pointers for the future.
Vernimb, Carlo.
  In Proc. 8th Int. Online Information Meeting, London, December 1984, Pps
  541-545. Learned Information, Abingdon, England.
    Apollo - a catalyst for full text delivery in Europe.
Wood, James L.
  Interlending & Document Supply 11(4), 127-130, 1983.
    Document delivery and new technologies.
Yates, D.M.
  Aslib Proc. 35(4), 177-182, April 1983.
    Project Hermes.

CHAPTER 11. SPEECH SYNTHESIS AND RECOGNITION

INTRODUCTION

I have lost count of the number of times that I have read or heard about The Imminent Arrival of the Listening and Talking Machine during the last ten years. The accomplishments of Hal in the film "2001" seem to have been accepted as being quite reasonable by that date although Raj Reddy, one of about half a dozen people who lead the major research projects and who have spent most of their lives working on it said in 1983 "Machines that can recognise isolated words from large vocabularies independent of the speaker may be commercially available in the next decade". He also guessed that "systems capable of taking limited dictation may well be possible in the 1990s.

Experience in a number of fields shows that even the most eminent engineers who devoted their lives to a project forecast a rate of progress which was not achieved. They were almost invariably optimistic and who can blame them for that? I do not think, therefore, that Reddy will be surprised if his "limited dictation machine" is not with us until the first decade of the next century at the earliest. However its arrival largely depends on something which is even more difficult to forecast - the money and resources which will be allocated to research in this field during the next twenty years.

Speech synthesis is much easier to achieve than speech recognition. Some examples follow of what you can actually buy, or what exists in the laboratory today.

SPEECH RECOGNITION

Methods

For practical applications at an acceptable price, isolated-word speaker-adaptive systems are today's choice. These systems accept any language and will work in industrial surroundings. Three processes are involved. A "preprocessor" accepts spoken word waveforms, which will be used later for reference purposes, from a microphone and shapes and filters the waveform. A "feature extractor" determines the spectral (frequency distribution) and phonetic events (that is pauses, intensity of phonemes or word elements, etc) of the words, and creates a matrix (pattern) of binary signal codes representing these characteristics.

Finally a "classifier" handles the duration of elements and their storage, and the "training" electronics makes matching decisions when a speaker who intends to use the machine speaks the set of words which he will be using to "train" the machine to his voice.

When the machine is used to recognise an incoming word, a matrix is created for it, as before, and this is compared against the codes in the matrices of reference words for the best fit.

For connected word speech recognition Linear Predictive Coding (LPC) has been used (as described later for speech synthesis). Reference speech is divided into 10 millisecond segments and passed through an electrical representation of the human vocal tract. The electrical output is a stored pattern against which incoming speech is matched. Nippon Electric made a commercially available system in 1980 which recognized a string of up to 5 words. It adjusted the rate of the stored speech to match that of the incoming speech during the comparison process, and applied the comparison twice - once for each word and again for the string of words.

In more advanced research the effort is directed towards getting the maximum information from speech waveforms. Beyond that, and presumably in order eventually to conquer the problem, consideration is being given to the "sources of human knowledge" of speech - that is prosodics, syntax, semantics, and pragmatics.

Major research was done some time ago in the ARPA five year speech understanding systems programme. The protagonists were Harpy and Hearsay 2 (Carnegie-Mellon), HWIM (Bolt Beranek & Newman), and a system developed by a System Development Corp/Stanford Research Institute group.

Harpy was considered the most successful. The astronomically large possible number of combinations of 1011 words (about computer technology) in Harpy (as described by Robinson) was purposely limited. A computer generated a graph structure (which took 13 hours of computer time to plot) containing 15,000 nodes represented the allowable combinations. In Hearsay 2, a number of paths were combined in one model equivalent to a set of co-operating parallel processors. Information from one path which might be useful to another was communicated to it. The model included semantic and syntactic information.

Only at Carnegie-Mellon, with probably the most ambitious system, has research continued. The biggest research effort today is at IBM (non-participants in the earlier "competition"). In October 1984 IBM announced an experimental machine for recognising a large number of words, which must be spoken quite separately, and displaying them on a CRT screen. The machine has a 5000 word vocabulary and also has a look-up predictive system built into it containing information about word combination probabilities. In other words it can select the most likely sequence from a given combination of words. No attempt is made to recognise continuous speech.

In the UK a group was formed in 1980 at the National Physical Laboratory, and is working on the auto-correlation of phonetic features using a DEC LSI-11 machine in real time. The aim is to make a commercially available machine for dealing with continuous speech at a price (assuming quantity production) of a few thousand pounds (personal communication from NPL).

<u>Systems available - Speaker Verification</u>

The general objective with speaker verification is to enable a caller's voice to be verified in order that a locked door may be opened, to permit the reading of a bank balance to a caller over the telephone, or similar applications where the machine's output is one bit - yes or no, true or false.

The speaker first identifies himself by a code - say by inserting his card into a slot. The verification system then calls up a phrase previously recorded by the same speaker and matches it against the same phrase, now spoken into a microphone, pattern against stored pattern, in terms of pitch, intensity, and frequency distribution. Even if an imposter speaks the same phrase it is likely that it will fall outside the required matching tolerance. Note that the system is not required to identify any speaker who has not first made himself known to it. A system of this kind is in experimental use by the Bell Telephone Co for voice verification over the switched telephone network. It is based on earlier experiments which showed that machines can do better than humans in voice verification.

<u>Systems available - Recognition of isolated words</u>

Typical of one of the earlier inexpensive units for controlling a microcomputer was a speaker-programmed isolated word recognition device available on a plug-in board to fit into an Apple computer. The user must first speak a word or phrase of up to 1.5 seconds duration three times to enable the system to store a representative record - it has to be "trained" to recognize that word and carry out whatever control function is programmed with it when the same person speaks it again.

The device will recognize up to 64 different words programmed into it. A received word is compared with the stored words, and an output signal is generated when the best match is found a fraction of a second later. The words may be stored on floppy disk for use when needed and 4k of Apple's Random Access Memory (RAM) must be made available for the program.

In a microcomputer the speed of the central processor unit (CPU) and the memory size limit the size of the vocabulary. The output signal initiated by an incoming word can be used by the computer to control a programme, or it can be used to actuate external relay contacts - for instance to control a model railway; the 1979 price for the board (excluding microphone, relay controller, or other accessories) was $259. This kind of performance for a device of this kind, perhaps at a somewhat lower price, still seems to be typical of what is available today.

Similar but more comprehensive facilities were available from Threshold Technology Inc; this Company had sold more than 250 systems by 1979. Insterstate Electronics had sold about 40 by that date. The cost was in the $5000-$80,000 area. These prices can be justified in some circumstances, and a number of applications have been described. Control words may be spoken during hands/eyes-occupied quality control operations. In another application an operator observing assorted items passing along a production line can switch them to different destinations by voice commands.

In 1983 an experimental single chip recogniser was decribed by Kimura et al. It was claimed to recognise 200 different words from one speaker after training. The chip works by LPC analysis followed by a whizzo technique known as "flag-bit controlled dynamic time warping". This is a refinement added to pattern matching where the timing of separate parts of the incoming word are checked for best match against the timing of the same parts in reference words.

Systems available - recognition of connected words

It is difficult to design a speech recognition system capable of deciding when one word ends and another begins particularly with continuously spoken words such as "did you", or for recognising digits spoken without intervening pauses. Systems for recognising 120 four or five fixed-order word utterances cost at least seven times more - say $50,000 - than comprehensive devices only capable of recognising the same number of isolated words. Recognising words spoken in any order is yet more difficult. Research in progress on this problem was described in Reddy's 1976 classic article. It is probably true to say that no device is likely to be available ln the near future enabling a machine to be controlled, even by restricted continuous speech, at a price which makes the idea feasible.

A system capable of understanding speech from any speaker is a far future concept; it may require a crossing of the blurred border from analytical techniques into artificial intelligence on which much work requires to be done. Computer power and storage requirements will need to be colossal even in terms of the projected advances in this field. A team at IBM (where intensive research is in progress led by Jelinek and others) developed a system for use with the 370 computer which can convert speech with a 1000 word vocabulary into print. However it takes 100 minutes to deal with a 30 second sentence, and requires each speaker to endure a two hour training session.

Speech Systems Inc, at Tarzana, California, is aiming to introduce a machine for continuous speech recognition selling for $35,000 within the next two years. Trying to resist the temptation to remark that this is mere jungle gossip, I have

to say that this seems rather unlikely. However Speech Systems
expect to do it with about 80% accuracy on a speech-activated word processing
machine.

Votan introduced a system in 1984,
the VPC 2000 voice card for plugging in
to an IBM PC. The system can recognise
short commands from one speaker after
training up to about 30 characters long
consisting of words from a vocabulary
of 75 words.   It sells for $2500
including software and microphone.

Also in 1984 Matsushita, sometimes
calling itself National Computer or
Panasonic, introduced the JH600 voice
recognising machine which looks like a
portable microcomputer. It will recognise up to 60 phrases not exceeding 1.2
seconds in duration when trained by up
to two speakers, but not exceeding a
total stored duration of 42 seconds.

The user can then type a short memo and arrange to associate it with
any spoken phrase - for instance memo number 39 would be associated with phrase
39. When a phrase is spoken the asociated memo is displayed on the screen.

<u>Systems available - voice controlled telephone systems</u>

A system using the spoken voice instead of a telephone dial has been
described by Blomberg but the recognition accuracy and response time of   the
system were not satisfactory. The man-machine training procedure which would
be required by a user of the system was also considered to be too complicated. A different kind of machine was developed later using the MCS 68000
microprocessor and the NEC 7720 speech processor chip, subsequently
incorporated in an Ericsson 180 line intercom exchange system.

Users of the system first key the control unit for a training session and
can record up to 30 names so that the machine will subsequently recognise
those names when they are spoken again. After this has been done a user can call
up the exchange from his extension and simply ask for the name, whereupon the
machine will dial the number.

Karhan considers that the best that could be done in the near future with a
voice activated telephone service would be a speaker independent service capable
of recognising the digits and a few control words. This forecast recognises the
realities and difficulties of getting a word recognising system working under
field rather than laboratory conditions.

<u>SPEECH SYNTHESIS</u>

In the Plato computer-based educational system a playback head may be
directed on to the particular track of a disc containing a required message.
Systems of this kind will not be discussed here since they can only reproduce
pre-recorded messages. A computer controlled speech synthesiser can generate
any message limited only by the facilities provided and the ingenuity of the
program. In the simpler systems speech can be formed only from a limited number
of words.

Speech synthesisers can be used to speak information which would otherwise
have to be viewed on a CRT screen. A machine operator in a factory might have to

perform certain functions according to the flow or type of materials through the machine. The need for him to watch the machine might make it impossible for a CRT to be watched as well. The kind of thing that could be done, to give a simple example, would be to arrange sensors connected to a computer to monitor the flow of parts being fed to a machine for an assembly operation. If the number of parts passing a sensor fell below the needed supply rate, the computer could cause the synthesiser to announce to the operator "Tell George in sub-assembly shop 10 that his units will be in short supply in 30 minutes time".

Optimistic belief in the progress of man-machine speech has been encouraged by progress in speech synthesis - a different and relatively easy problem. The idea of developing a machine which listens and speaks, Hal fashion, is further encouraged by demonstrations, tv programmes etc., wherein machines emit speech ranging from the weird to the almost acceptable. Stevie Wonder has been seen operating a text-reading speech-synthesising machine (probably a Kurzweil) on television. This is a technical tour de force emitting very reasonable prosodic - that is rhythmically intoned - speech, but it recognizes print, not speech.

While it may be relatively easy to synthesise acceptable speech, it is probably as hard to pass it off as human speech, or something near it, as it is to achieve continuous speech recognition. Only by the incorporation of a "knowledge" of syntax and semantics could the correct emphasis and intonation be applied to a spoken phrase or sentence.

Methods

The earliest, but still widely used method, is called Waveform Digitisation. Words to be processed for later synthesis into speech are spoken into a microphone and the speech is digitised - that is a binary code number proportional to the amplitude of the speech waveform is generated at frequent intervals. Provided this is done at the correct rate (Nyquist sampling) all the information in the speech can subsequently be reconstituted from the samples. The numbers are stored as binary digits. Improved methods for digitisation or digital quantisation have been described by Flanagan - for example using ADPCM - Adaptive Differential Pulse Code Modulation, an improved type of PCM (See Chapter 5).

To digitise or re-generate continuous speech a bit rate of about 64 Kbits/sec is required; however male-voice speech can be quite acceptable if processed at a slower rate; it turns out that a typical word can be compressed into about 1000 bits for storage. Word sounds (phonemes) or complete words are stored and can be later retrieved from known storage addresses.

To synthesise speech from the stored information a program is required which calls up a stream of digits from selected addresses, strings them together to form words or phrases, passes them through a "de-digitising" process (a digital to analogue converter - the reverse of the original process) and plays the result through a loudspeaker. This process of stringing phonemes or words together without their original in-context expressive variations would result in the reproduction of a dull monotonic voice. Some degree of prosody can be restored by building a variable frequency generator into the system. Under program control a word with a rising or falling pitch can then be generated.

The other major method of synthesising speech depends upon "formant synthesis" - that is the synthesis of words from internally generated electrical waveforms, not from stored data derived from previously recorded words. The idea is electrically to modify simple waveforms generated by oscillators by passing them through circuits which simulate the human voice tract. In the Texas "Speak & Spell" a random frequency or "white noise" oscillator is used for generating unvoiced sounds and a second oscillator generates impulses whose frequency may be varied according to the desired pitch; the combined waveform then passes through a complex filter network.

The parameters of the network can be set to shape and filter the waveform in order to produce a characteristic sound waveform. The parameters are changed frequently and the number of times they are changed per second (the Frame Rate) is important – the faster the better, particularly when speech sounds are rapidly changing. Typically the parameters are changed every 20 milliseconds. The relationship between the parameters and the required sound can be determined by a   mathematical procedure known as Linear Predictive Coding – LPC. (The inverse of this process has already been mentioned   for speech recognition). Smoothly changing sounds will be heard from the loudspeaker because the small high speed parameter changes cannot be heard individually.

Systems available

A range of equipment providing speech of different qualities is available but it cannot easily be divided into divisions or classes as with speech recognising equipment. The Votrax Company has been a leader in this field. It produced the ML-1 multilingual voice system which converted a bit stream from a computer into synthesised speech of unlimited vocabulary in any language. Votrax also makes the VS-6 from which has been developed a simpler version for use with the Radio Shack personal computer. The Votrax single chip synthesiser, the SC-01 ($12 each in quantity, 1980 prices) is manufactured in association with Silicon Systems Inc; particular speech suitable for toys and games can be programmed into the SC-01 using a $10,000 development system which accepts keyboarded text.

A number of speech-generating toys are available pioneered by Texas Instruments with its "Speak and Spell". Texas makes a synthesiser for microcomputers with a 100 word vocabulary – the TM990/306. It has also developed a hand-held language translator (£90 at 1980 prices in the UK) which speaks its vocabulary; separate plug-in modules were available for different languages at £35. Texas offered a programmable speech chip for toys – the TMS5100 – with a 128 Kbyte memory chip, for 100 words at $13 (1980) in quantity.

Later Texas developed the TMS5220 and 5220A chips for use with microcomputers which currently (1985) sell for about $14 per chip in small quantities. Their performance is typical of those available from a number of suppliers. These chips generate speech at about 1 Kbps with a frame rate of 25 ms and 60 levels of pitch. A vocabulary of separate words can be purchased in a separate Read Only Memory (ROM) chip which requires a program to be written to produce connected speech, or you can write programs to generate your own words and speech. Since the chips must be wired into a printed circuit board and connected to the appropriate lines, and programs must be written, the job cannot be done on a "plug in and go" basis.

A good "how to do it" article has been published by Ciarcia using one of the new generation chips – the Silicon Systems SS1263 phoneme-based speech synthesiser which will produce continuous speech from an unlimited vocabulary. The programmer is required to write a programme which strings together words which have been constructed by using codes to call up the required phonemes. A text-to-speech algorithm is also described which analyses the ASCII code, used in the computer to represent the letters of words, in the words typed by the user, and generates speech. The rule tables used in the algorithm can be changed by the user if he wishes to try and improve the realism – for example by word stressing.

By 1985 quite a number of text-to-speech conversion systems had become available ranging from prices of a few hundred dollars upwards. For example

Votrax's "Personal Speech System" which speaks at over 100 words per minute costs $400, while "Dectalk" from DEC speaks at up to 350 wpm and costs $4000.

Good results have been claimed from some of the comprehensive systems which can be purchased such as the Votrax ML-1. The ML-1 is controlled from externally derived 12 bit command words which need be transmitted at less than 300 bits/sec, so the commands can come from a small computer or via a communications network. A command word is used to select one of 122 phonemes at one of 4 durations and one of 8 inflections (pitch). The language or vocabulary is virtually unlimited by reason of the enormous number of possible combinations of the attributes provided. The result will be dependent on the ingenuity of the person who writes the programs for the computer generating the 12 bit words.

Some interesting special applications of speech synthesisers have been reported. In one system for reading printed text aloud the image of the text to be read is viewed by a vidicon camera, digitized, processed in a PDP-11/45, and read by a Votrax synthesiser. Algorithms (sets of problem solving rules) have been written for the Votrax VS-6 for synthesising speech received from a machine which reads text in Esperanto, Spanish, Russian, or English.

CONCLUSION

A great deal of work has and is being done both in speech recognition and synthesis. It is a pity that credulity has been strained by silly claims for superb performance because the lower performance which is available from systems you can buy off the shelf can be very useful. Steady progress can be expected, but all claims about much better performance in the recognition of continuous speech than has been reported here will need plenty of substantiation. This is simply because speech recognition, like visual recognition, lies in the "very hard" area of information technology. You cannot bundle the whole of IT together and pile it on to a general bandwaggon labelled "rapid advances and falling prices".

FURTHER READING

Blomberg, M; Elenius K; Lindin F.
   In Proc 10th Internat. Sympos. Human factors in telecoms., Helsinki, Finland
   June 1983, Pub. by PTT of Finland, Helsinki, 1983. pps 233-238.
   Voice controlled dialling in an intercom system.
Ciarcia, Steve.
   Byte, 28-40, March 1984.
   Build a third generation phonetic speech synthesizer.
Flanagan, James L.
   Proc.IEEE 64(4), 405-415, April 1976.
   Computers that talk and listen: man-machine communication by voice.
Green David J.
   Data Processing 26(5), 13-15, June 1984.
   Voice recognition - still a long way to go.
Hunt, Jonathan A; Handa, Michael K.
   High Technology, 30-32, June 1984.
   Speech recognition struggles to life.
Kaplan, Gadi; Lerner,Eric J.
   IEEE Spectrum 22(4), 32-37, April 1985.
   Realism in synthetic speech.
Karhan, Cynthia K.
   In Proc 10th Internat. Sympos. Human factors in telecoms., Helsinki,
   Finland   June 1983, Pub. by PTT of Finland, Helsinki, 1983. pps 247-254
   Human factors issues in applying automatic speech recognition to network
   services.

Kimura, Takashi; Yano, Takao et al.
  IEEE J. Solid State Circuits SC-18 (3), June 1983.
    A single chip self contained speech recogniser.
Kuhn, Michael H; Tomaschewski, Horst H.
  IEEE Trans. Acoust., Speech & Signal Proc. ASSP-319(1), 157-167, February
  1983.
    Improvements in isolated word recognition.
Reddy, Raj D.
  Proc.IEEE 64(4), 501-531, April 1976.
    Speech recognition by machine - a review.
Reddy, Raj, and Zue, Victor.
  IEEE Spectrum 20(11), 84-87, November 1983.
    Recognising continuous speech remains an elusive goal.
Robinson, Arthur L.
  IEEE Trans. Prof.Communic. PC-22(3), 159-167, Sept 1979.
    Communicating with computers by voice.
Scott, Brian L.
  Computer Design, 67-70, January 1983.
    Voice recognition systems and strategies.
Schalk, Thomas B; Frantz Gene A; Woodson, Larry.
  Mini-micro Systems 15(12), 146-160, December 1982.
    Voice synthesis and recognition.
Simmons, Joseph E.
  Computer Design, 95-101, June 1979.
    Speech recognition technology.

CHAPTER 12. EXPERT SYSTEMS AND ARTIFICIAL INTELLIGENCE

TERMINOLOGY

This branch of IT is not unusual in having its share of synonyms and over-grandiose terms to describe undeserving systems. The words "Expert Systems" "Knowledge Engineering", "Artificial Intelligence", and even sometimes "Decision Support Systems" etc., may simply indicate that the system described falls within a field customarily known by another name. The addition of the fashionable words hypes up the topic so that it rides on the research front. On the other hand the system may deserve its title, and may be one of many representing some significant diverse aspect of a fast developing and controversial field.

One trend is noticeable in the literature, and that is retention of the term "artificial intelligence" for machines which apparently possess real "intelligence" - for example those able to "understand" language or "see" images. The machine solves problems in these areas by referring to a body of stored knowledge. The term "Knowledge-based System" also seems to be coming into use as a more specific term avoiding the more general connotations of other terms.

It is quite difficult to draw the diverse IT applications in this field together at present. A number of different approaches are being explored in the four major areas of pattern recognition, representation (descriptive conventions), problem solving, and learning.

HISTORY AND DEVELOPMENTS

Although nothing much happened for some years following Turing's 1950 paper "Computing Machinery and Intelligence", his interest and reputation directed attention to the subject. He suggested a game which would demonstrate the existence of machine intelligence. A human was required to interrogate a machine and another human by posing a series of questions to both of them. If the machine was able to fool the interrogator by its answers into believing that it was the human, its intelligence would have been demonstrated.

In 1956 a meeting was held at Dartmouth College in the US to discuss the subject and this meeting is considered to be a milestone since it inspired the early work. One ambitious early system was called General Problem Solver, capable of solving theorems and puzzles, but it did little to demonstrate machine intelligence.

The first demonstration of the real possibilities was the DENDRAL system developed at Stanford University by Lederberg, Feigenbaum, and Djerassi in 1966. DENDRAL used a computer language for describing the structures of organic compounds and was able to generate structures and postulate tests compiled from data about a compound for comparison with the structure and test results known from the actual compound.

Most of the early experimental work involved continuous close "hand-made" attention by the expert who was attempting to move his knowledge into the system in a useable form. During the development of another system called MYCIN by Duda and Shortliffe in the 1970s at Stanford, Davis, a co-worker, developed some software, called TEIRESIAS, for debugging purposes. It separated the software concerned with the expert's knowledge - the Knowledge Base - from the part concerned with problem-solving (inference), and turned out to be the first important step in decoupling the human expert from the system. It then became possible for a wider range of knowledge to be added, not necessarily by the same expert.

Perhaps the most important potential of AI/Expert Systems is the easing of communication between man and machine. Eventually Natural Language (NL) schemes will make computer systems available to a wide public using the English language instead of only to those who understand formalised computer language. One of the earliest investigations in this area was Weizenbaum's (MIT) Eliza NL system. Eliza's apparent understanding of sentences was achieved by matching against a library of sentence meaning patterns. The machine then asked a relevant question to acquire more information.

Other milestones were Quillian's (University of Sydney) semantic network representation scheme, later embodied in an algorithm called ID3, and Winograd's NL system. Quillian's scheme consists of a tree-like data structure of nodes and links and an inference program which operates on this data to find a solution - a part of the system often called the Inference Engine. A major feature of the data structure is the "is a" link connecting the nodes which represent concepts - for example a node "mammal" connecting to node "whale" by an "is a" link. Inferences can be drawn from the information contained in the network. An excellent explanation of this and other schemes and of the work at Edinburgh and elsewhere is given by Michie in Chapter 42.

Winograd's (Stanford) SHRDLU, and Schank's (Stanford & Yale) systems which use "sentence primitives" were another important development. Winograd's NL system enabled English commands to be given to a simulated robot called SHRDLU which moved solid shapes such as blocks or pyramids about and could be asked how they were arranged.Its expertise, which appeared to be considerable, lay entirely in its knowledge of the domain of solid objects - in other words, unlike some other more generalised systems, its specialisation enabled it to do one thing well. This set a precedent for concentrating AI effort into domain knowledge research. Subsequently ambitious attempts were made to design systems capable of handling a number of different domains as described in the next section.

Shells and chaining

By 1985 attempts were being made to devise domain-independent inference systems or "shells". If this was made possible a subject expert could be presented with ready to use rule-making software enabling him to insert his own knowledge base, do some tests to check that the rules worked, and complete the design of an expert system in far less time than previously with less attention to "housekeeping" procedures.

Some combination of "forward and backward chaining" is often used in the inference engine. Forward chaining uses various rules, particularly those based on "if then...." statements, to move to a conclusion. If the conclusion is known but the sequences to arrive at it are not, then backward chaining can be used to deduce the set of conditions needed to arrive at the conclusion. In the MYCIN example which follows later in this chapter, backward chaining enables the known conclusion to be reached from questions about a manageable number of relevant medical symptoms. To reach a conclusion, unknown in advance, by forward chaining, a prohibitively large number of questions would have to be asked in an attempt to diagnose one out of all possible diseases.

Forward chaining may be preferred in other circumstances, for example for form filling procedures required, say, for obtaining a car licence. In this case alternative replies are limited to the small number which are feasible in response to questions already selected for their relevance to the conclusion.

A combination of forward and backward chaining may be used in an exploratory procedure which steps back to look at the evidence available to confirm that the last step forward was reasonable. At the present time there seems to some controversy about whether or not it is over-ambitious to attempt to design inference engines which can cope with a range of different applications.

Here is a simple example of forward chaining (after Winston) as used in

LISP-based software (more about LISP later) to move from facts to conclusions. In an Animal Recognition System it is assumed that rules already in the system enable assertions to be made about facts about animals stored in the knowledge database -

> Robbie is a mammal because Robbie has hair.
> Robbie is a carnivore because Robbie eats meat.
> Robbie is a Cheetah because Robbie has dark spots and is a tawny colour
> and is a carnivore and is a mammal.

Then the rule -

> "IF animal A is a P type AND IF animal A is a parent
> of X child THEN X child is a P type"

- already in the system, can be manipulated by LISP in an expression-matching procedure against all the available assertions to move to a conclusion in response to the question "What type of animal is Bozo if Robbie is a parent of Bozo?", as follows -

> Bozo is a mammal because Robby is a parent of Bozo and Robby is a mammal.
> Bozo is a carnivore because Robbie is a parent of Bozo and Robbie is a
> carnivore.
> Bozo is a Cheetah because Robbie is a parent of Bozo and Robbie is a
> Cheetah.

Semantics

One general difficulty with AI, as pointed out by Lee, is presented by the degree of reliance of information system semantics on natural language semantics. Natural language semantics are based on an implied sociological reference which is very difficult - perhaps overwhelmingly difficult - to provide within a machine. In plain language this means that machines do not possess the background information possessed by humans which can be called up at high speed from a colossal reservoir of stored knowledge in the brain to assist in assessing each new situation.

Lee uses an example provided by another AI researcher to make the point that whether a thing is, or is not, that which is implied in its label, involves discrimination based on a social background which is constantly changing.

"Being a poor cook my concept of lemons is fairly elementary - I can't tell a lemon from a lime, yet I manage quite well. I go to the fruit section in the supermarket and look for a case labelled lemons. I rely on their knowledge to know what lemons are. They, in turn, order "lemons" from a distributor, and he knows that he can get them from lemon growers. How do they know a lemon? Eventually the chain goes back to botanical criteria for a lemon. Turning to another object,the concept of "a chair" can be followed back to manufacturing companies who specify that their products are chairs. A company manufacturing chairs of stiffened cardboard might specify their products as "throwaway chairs".

Because mechanical inference relies on stable, fixed, semantics, the utility of an idealised, fully integrated, knowledge-based inference system will be limited to stable environments, AI systems in some environments such as management decision support systems, may be hard to implement because of continuing changes in the semantics of organisation language.

Software and Hardware trends

The software used in a shell inference engine is likely to be written in LISP or PROLOG. This software is used to search a knowledge database and enables retrieved data to be used in conjunction with decision making rules according to the requirements of the programmer.

There appears to be some US-European rivalry in the adoption of these languages, LISP, supposedly better for practical applications but requiring efficient programming, having been developed at MIT in the 50s, and PROLOG, supposedly better for research work and easier to use, developed later in Europe. PROLOG is being adopted by the Japanese in their fifth generation systems, and attempts are being made to provide software combining the best features of both. Foster has described and compared the two languages.

It has not yet become clear how portable are the two languages or whether they differ in portability. Neither seems yet to have progressed to the point where versions are available for, and will run equally well, on several different computers. For smaller systems the IBM PC is emerging as the preferred machine.

It is interesting that performance improvements that really matter - that is the improved speed, cost, and efficiency required to get a job done on a machine - proceed much more slowly than the rate of what seem to be substantial technical advances. A classical case is the progression of micros from 8 to 16 to 32 bit machines. From the user's viewpoint improvements have undoubtedly been made but they do not appear to match the apparent potential inherent in the increased word length. So it is with AI and parallel processing.

With AI systems a major requirement, as in other areas of IT such as speech recognition, is to be able to use the power of parallel processing. The techniques of arranging for a number of operations to proceed simultaneously via multiple processors has been known for some time and has been used for special purposes. AI is not one of them.

In an excellent article, Deering points out that it is difficult to realise an increase in computing power which is directly related to the number of processors used. The problem is in writing the software so that the work can be divided into parallel paths with equal workload distribution and in organising the overhead facilities - e.g. memory transfers and communication facilities - which must be available to support the system. The state of the art and the incentives have only just improved to the point where it is worth making the effort.

When the demand for AI systems reaches the appropriate size special parallel-processing hardware, perhaps with its own operating system, will appear specifically to accommodate the special needs of AI.

INTELLIGENT MACHINES

A system which attempts to model visual images is an example of an Intelligent Machine system. Information is contained in a TV-like representation of an image fed into the machine via its camera-eye. A set of stored rules will have been worked out in order to display an image reconstructed from information received by the machine's "eye". At the present state of development the rules enable it to "know" something about just one type of scene - for instance the interior of a living room. The machine examines edges contained in the electrical image - it might test for vertical edges consisting of a sequence of more than n elements where there is an abrupt change of contrast. Any found might be labelled "wall boundary". The machine might then explore long, not necessarily continuous, edges which join the wall boundary in order to construct the outline of the complete wall.

EXPERT SYSTEMS

The term "Expert System" seems to be displacing "Artificial Intelligence"

in computer applications where modelling of the brain's activities are not
involved - - the word "Intelligence" is perhaps then considered to be
unacceptably pretentious. For example a set of rules could be devised for a
relatively simple expert system automatically to connect an online searcher to
the one database most likely to contain the answer to his question. The words
or phrases in the question would be matched against a vocabulary of words each of
which had been previously labelled with a code representing the database most
likely to cover the subject. Thus the words "Coherent Radiation" might cause the
user to be logged on to the INSPEC database as first choice.

However, unambiguously clear useage of the terminology does not seem to have
progressed very far. I prefer "Knowledge-based System"for general use, and for
the obvious reason mentioned in the next paragraph. One way of identifying
knowledge-based systems is to know how they differ from other computer systems.

EXAMPLES SHOWING HOW KNOWLEDGE-BASED SYSTEMS DIFFER FROM ORDINARY SOFTWARE

Ordinary computer software consists of a set of instructions incorporating
the writer's knowledge in lines of code in order to control different parts of
the machine to execute a task. The lines are written with reference to the
attributes Input Data, Algorithm, and Output Data. In an expert system an
additional separate part of the software, the Knowledge Base, contains the
know-how of one or many people, and also any rules which may have been developed
by the machine as a result of learning by example. Additional rules can be added
to the knowledge base as necessary. The Inference Engine takes the input data,
the rules, and the information it contains about applying the rules, in order to
find the shortest and so the most rapid path to a solution.

In the already-mentioned task of reconstructing a room interior from the bit
patterns of a TV image, the control software might link a rule and stored data in
this fashion "IF an edge is vertical AND is more than 200 elements long THEN
store its coordinates AND label this information Wall Boundary".

More information about current thinking and the way Knowledge-based Systems
work is given by Michie in Chapter 42.

In a recent review, Garfield uses an example from MYCIN, a diagnostic tool,
which illustrates the functioning of a Knowledge-based system very well. MYCIN
elicits information from a doctor by a question-and-answer dialog and then
applies the rules previously entered into it by experts to this information using
the classic IF-AND-THEN procedure as follows:-

    IF the infection which required therapy is Meningitis
    AND the patient has evidence of serious skin or soft tissue infection
    AND organisms were not seen on the stain of the culture
    AND the type of infection is bacterial
    THEN there is evidence that the organism, other than those seen on
        cultures or smears, which might be causing the infection is
        staphylococcus-coagpos (.75) or streptococcus (.5)

Waterman describes an expert system called LDS designed for evaluating
claims in civil courts. Although the application area is quite different from
MYCIN the general priciples are quite similar. At first glance in both MYCIN and
LDS it looks as if the main benefit has been to concentrate the mind on
assembling sufficient information to make rational decisions and then to assemble
the data in a way which forces a consideration of it in logical steps. A computer
is helpful but not essential for this process.

However the extra dimension added by the machine's software is to apply the
rules in accordance with experience gained. Systems with this dimension seem
deserving of the title "expert system". So-called expert systems without this

ability to "improve themselves" without human intervention hardly deserve that title.

As Waterman explains - "Every time the system finds a rule that matches the case facts it treats the conclusion of that rule as a new fact in the case. For example if a product liability claim includes two facts - that the product is a machine and that it is over ten years old - then a stored rule might conclude that the implied warranty of fitness no longer applies to the product.
Thus a new fact is added to the case - "the implied warranty of fitness does not apply". The system continues to select other rules and conclusions of previously selected rules that are called for by the facts of the case. It stops when it reaches a conclusion about the likely value of the claim".

<u>PRODUCTS AVAILABLE</u>

<u>General</u>

3000 people attended an important AI meeting in San Francisco at the end of 1984 and 1000 were turned away. However according to Anderson there was a dearth of good papers, except about the ethics of AI. It is unusual to hear that researchers themselves feel (as was reported here) that expectations about results in their field have been raised to an unreasonable levels by their peers. In Information Technology the hype is more often the prerogative of the sales people when the product reaches the market.

A number of AI/Expert System products have been announced, but little information is yet available about their effectiveness either for immediate use, or to provide the shell for creating systems which will perform useful jobs.

A knowledge system called Insight is available on floppy disk at $95 from Level 5 Research, 4980 South AlA, Melbourne Beach, FL 32951, USA. It runs on an IBM PC with a 128K memory. It contains a set of general purpose rules and provides the means of using facts supplied by the user in a limited manner for solving small problems. SPL at Abingdon, Oxford UK, has sold a number of its Sage expert systems at £8000 each. It was demonstrated early in 1984 using a model for disease diagnosis. Presumably the user's expectations will be in proportion to the price differential once he has read the specifications.

In 1984 Microsoft announced a version of LISP for running on micros with the MS DOS operating system such as Act Sirius, IBM PC, Vectorgraphic 4, etc. The software, called mu-LISP-82, is an Artificial Intelligence Development System, of limited performance, probably most useful for research work. Texas Instruments developed a product called Personal Consultant in 1984 to run on its Professional micros. It is a LISP-based shell capable of generating a complete Expert System using the development system also provided, for around £7500.

DEC is known to be active in Expert System work possibly because it may be able to capitalise upon the success of a system called XCON used within the company on a VAX machine for working out computer system configurations to fulfill customer orders.It is said that use of the system has cut down errors in delivered equipment to a very low level.

<u>Database information retrieval applications</u>

An expert online system which draws upon stored information to assist a person who is searching a large remote database using complex query procedures has been described by Meadow. It embodies an instructional program to take a user through procedures for performing searches on databases in the Lockheed Dialog system. When a user is online to Dialog using this system, called Individualised Instruction for Data Access (IIDA), the "expert" part comes into play. It monitors the man-machine dialogue and intervenes when problems

come up or errors are made. For instance IIDA will detect procedural single
errors in commands or errors in a string of commands. In the case of a string it
will intervene if the user exceeds the permitted number of commands.

The system will also intervene if syntactical errors are made and will
provide the user with information about the nature of the error. To do this a
software module called a _Parser_ is used. _Syntax_ is a set of rules about the
grammatical arrangement of words, while parsing is the resolving of a sentence
into its component parts. Parsing software must therefore have access to
information about the grammar used, in this case in the query language. The IIDA
parser is able to check the validity of the arrangement of words in user's
messages to the database computer by reference to the stored
information about the limited grammar of the system. If IIDA was used in a
system with a different search language, major changes would have to made in
parser software and stored information. However if another searchable
database was introduced into Dialog, accessible via Dialog commands, only
minor changes would be needed.

The concluding remarks in the second part of Meadow's article are of
considerable interest. The authors summarise the difficulties in testing the
effectiveness of such a system. They discuss such matters as the size of the
test population, and the collection of data from users before and after
sessions in order to find out whether the assumed benefits of the
machine have turned out to be actual benefits. In experiments of this kind it is
hard to decide whether tasks should be undertaken as they arise during the
subject's normal work, or whether they should be standardised and are therefore
"the same for all even if possibly real for none".

The authors are also refreshingly frank about the outcome of the
experiment. "In light of the intent of this study i.e. to provide a set of
diagnostic benchmark criteria to assess the performance of IIDA trained and
assisted searchers, it was surprising to discover a lack of significant
differences between the two groups of searchers" (that is between the IIDA
group and control groups who did not use it). But "There is a sizeable class of
search problems for which end users do not need a human intermediary should
they choose to do their own searching. In fact it is entirely likely that the
development of IIDA and other systems that enable direct end user access
will increase the need for highly trained professional intermediaries who
will exercise their skills on the difficult, the highly spcialised, or the
particularly challenging search problems where a high level of expertise is
required".

Other possible applications of expert systems in information retrieval have
been discussed by Smith, Novak, Williams, Pollitt, and Armstrong.

<u>FURTHER READING</u>

Anderson, Ian.
  New Scientist 104(1430), 18-21, November 15th 1984.
    AI is stark naked from the ankles up.
Armstrong, C.J.
  In 8th International Online Information Meeting, London, December 1984.
  Published by Learned Information, Oxford and New Jersey. Pages 161-169.
    Command languages and the intelligence factor.
Curnow, H.J.
  Information Age 7(1), 10-14, 1985.
    Artificial intelligence - a survey.

Deering, Michael F.
  Byte, April 1985, pps 193-206.
    Architectures for AI.
Foster, Edward.
  Mini-micro systems, May 1984, pps 119-125.
    Artificial intelligence faces a crossroads.
Garfield, E.
  Current Contents numbers 49 and 50, December 5th and 26th, 1983.
    Artificial Intelligence: using computers to think about thinking. Part 1.
    Representing knowledge. Part 2. Some practical applications of AI.
Lederberg, J; Feigenbaum, E.A.
  In Kleinmuntz.B., (Ed), Formal representation of human judgement, pps.
  187-218. John Wiley, New York, 1968.
    Mechanization of inductive inference in chemistry.
Lee, R.M.
  Soc. Sci. Information Studies 1985(5) 3-10.
    On information system semantics: expert vs. decision support systems.
Meadow, Charles T., Hewett, Thomas T., et al.
  J. Amer. Soc. for Info. Sci 33(5/6), 325-332/357-364, 1982.
    A computer intermediary for interactive database searching
    1.Design/2.Evaluation.
Nowak, Elzbieta J., Szablowski, Bogumil F,
  J. Info. Science 8(1984) 103-111.
    Expert systems in scientific information exchange.
Pollitt, A.S.
  Aslib Proc. 36(5), 229-234, May 1984.
    A front-end system: an expert system as an online search intermediary.
Smith, Linda C.
  In Williams M.E.(Ed), Annual Review of Information Science and Technology,
  Volume 15, 1980. Published by Knowledge Industry Inc., White Plains, NY,
  USA. Chapter 3, pps 67-105.
    Artificial intelligence in information systems.
Waterman Donald A; Peterson, Mark A.
  Expert Systems 1(1), 65-76, 1984.
    Evaluating civil claims: an expert systems approach.
Williams, P.W.
  In 8th International Online Information Meeting, London, December 1984.
  Published by Learned Information, Oxford and New Jersey. Pages 139-147.
    A model for an expert system for automated information retrieval.
Winston, Patrick K.
  Byte, April 1985, pps 209-218.
    The Lisp revolution.

CHAPTER 13
THEORETICAL AND APPLIED INFORMATION SCIENCE IN LIBRARIES AND OFFICES

> Names or descriptions cannot be discovered
> by examining the things named or described.
> They are not discovered; they are bestowed.
>   Robert Fairthorne

Definition

Is there really such a thing as "Library and Information Science" or is this a fancy name for ordinary happenings? But thereby hangs a tale. Shortly after joining The Institute for Scientific Information I was working in their Philadelphia office and wanted an old article quickly. Old journal issues were stored on miles of shelves in the basement. The man in charge was running errands all day to find them.

He was a black man with the job title of "The Keeper of the Archives". He took a pride in his knowledge of the system and the speed with which he was able to return, triumphant, with the articles in less than five minutes.

I suspect that the archive keeper's opposite number in the UK would have grudgingly performed what he believed to be a menial task. I doubt if the management would have thought of the value of a title in recognition of the value of his job. Consequently he would not do it so well. You have your answer to the question "What's in a name?"

In Collins encyclopaedic dictionary, Library Science is defined as "The study of the theory and practice of library administration, bibliographic skills, and information retrieval". Information Science is "The science of the collection, evaluation, organisation, and dissemination of information, often employing computers". Information" is defined as "Knowledge acquired through experience or study; knowledge of specific and timely events or situations".

Using or ignoring Information Science in Offices

The basic procedure usually used by a user - through an intermediary in a library and often directly in an office - is shown in Figure 13.1.

The intermediary is needed when an organisation gets to a certain size, and someone decides that the flow of information is such that an Information Officer or Librarian is required. At that point some Information Science is introduced - that is specialised knowledge about the now numerous information sources and ways of extracting information from them is needed. At about this time the organisation way well start using external databases and this activity is likely to come under the aegis of the information Officer. As yet, with the possible exception of financial information systems, few information users wish to acquire the knowledge required for searching on line systems efficiently.

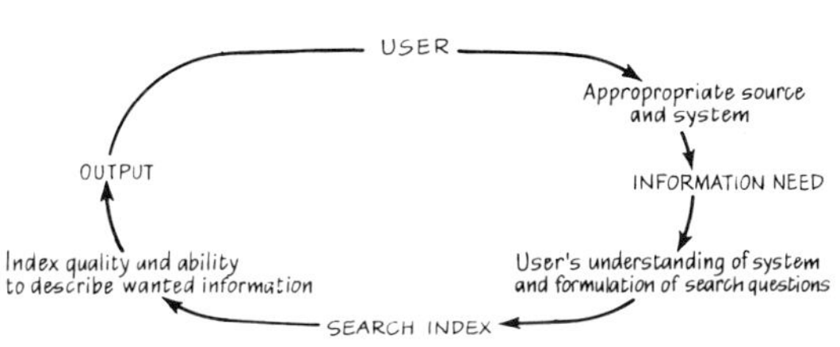

FIGURE 13.1. FINDING INFORMATION

People in many non-electronic offices have been able to ignore any need for Librarians or Information Officers. In small to medium organisations, office work seems to be concerned mainly with purchases, stores, sales and deliveries, and salaries and accounts. Some people in offices accumulate information for decision-making purposes. There will be some differences in the nature of the work if the organisation is providing a service, rather than an end-product, but in either case the work is done by managers, clerks, secretaries and typists. The information store is the filing cabinet, box- file, and folder.

Paperwork is ordered by name of person in personnel files, name of organisation in correspondence files, order number in order files, etc. At the management level there is a requirement for information contained in reports about competitor's activities, financial information, information about the industry, etc.

Lester criticises a UK proposal to provide public funds for "User education". "Users" are people who use, or more particularly do not use libraries and information services....despite all our effort libraries will remain difficult to use....the publications we handle come in such a variety of logical and physical forms and the commodity they carry - information - can be so difficult to pin down, to index and classify....we librarians should not say to our users "I have searched through the literature and these items should be relevant" but "Here is a state of the art summary of the best that has been written in the literature"".

That last most laudable sentiment depends, of course, upon whether the management appoints librarians who are sufficiently knowledeable about a range of subjects that they are able to decide what is "the best that has been written", and are then permitted by their masters to write state of the art reports.

Lester then extracts from the Aslib 1984 Conference Handbook (his article started life as a paper at that conference) this interesting quotation. <u>"Suddenly the skills of those who "know" about indexing and classification are in high demand</u> (my underlining). After one or two disasters the creators of our "offices of the future" have realised that there is more to information retrieval than was at first thought. We cannot pour all our information into a great database cauldron, inject one or two commands into the database furnace and - hey presto! - out comes the information we need.

Or can we? If our database systems are sufficiently "expert" might not this be just what can be achieved? And what need then for "user education" - when all users need to know is how to enter a few commands into their computer work stations? That only takes five minutes to demonstrate".

Lester comments:- "Anyone can write at that sort of level. But to go further and define precisely who should do exactly what, for whom, when, where and how, let alone why, as regards "user education", is extremely troublesome: at least I have found it so".

The underlining emphasises the interesting bit. Unfortunately this is wishful thinking. Indexing is dismissed as too boring to be associated with the glamour of the electronic office. Reference to it in office systems is almost non-existent.

The skills mentioned certainly <u>ought</u> to be wanted - indexing is an essential time-consuming chore in any paper-filing system. In a computer-filing system, retrieval of wanted items <u>depends</u> on it. If indexing is properly understood the chore can be minimised and the usefulness of the information system maximised.

<u>Performance of information systems: Recall & Precision</u>

An investigation was carried out some years ago which transformed people's ideas about information systems. New basic principles and results were introduced and although it takes a little while to explain them, they are, in the main, rather obvious and expected. Like many other discoveries it's easy to say that with hindsight.

In 1968, Robert Fairthorne, arguably the first real information scientist, discussed the difficulties of finding the information you need. A theoretically perfect information retrieval system is one which retrieves documents which match the question posed by a user; the retrieved documents are relevant, irrelevant documents ("noise") are not retrieved, and no relevant documents are missed.

When discussing information systems, "relevant" means that a retrieved document has a direct bearing on the question. Whether or not the document is "interesting" is another matter since it is not unusual for serendipity to play a part. I scan Current Contents for articles about information technology but I enjoyed the articles entitled "Why do bedouins wear black robes in hot deserts" (Nature) and "How to run a meeting" (Harvard Business review) when I obtained them. However this interest has nothing to do with the effectiveness of Current Contents as a source of information about information technology.

In formal information systems the performance depends critically on the method of indexing used. In 1954 Cyril Cleverdon, librarian at The Royal Aircraft Establishment, Farnborough, reported on some experiments using the then new "Uniterm" system devised by Mortimer Taube in the United States. Later he moved to the Cranfield Institute of Technology, and in those far off days when research grants were plentiful and Sputnik had concentrated US minds on the need for better dissemination of scientific information, he obtained a grant from the National Science Foundation to compare the effectiveness of several different indexing methods.

Retrieval performance tests were carried out on a collection of 1400 aeronautical research papers indexed in different ways, by searching with 221 different questions, and judging the relevance of the retrieved articles. Subject experts participated in the work and some 300,000 test results were examined. The results of this research have withstood the test of time well.

It is important to remember that two forces are at work in information systems - the intrinsic performance of the system and the way in which a user adjusts his questions in order to find the information he wants. The major factors in which he is likely to be interested are the <u>subject area covered</u> by the system, the <u>effort required</u> to use it, the <u>retrieval performance</u>, and the <u>response time</u> - that is how long it takes to get the wanted information.

The degree of success achieved when a searcher retrieves some relevant documents is called the <u>Recall Ratio</u> - defined as the percentage of relevant documents actually retrieved out of the total number of relevant documents in the collection. Thus 10 documents retrieved out of the 20 in the collection which are known to be relevant is a Recall Ratio of 50%.

The Recall Ratio tells us how well the system releases wanted documents. It can be measured if we know how many relevant documents are <u>missed</u>. Normally it is not practical to measure it because the number of relevant missed documents can only be discovered by examining the entire collection.

The <u>Precision Ratio</u> is the percentage of relevant documents retrieved out of the total number retrieved; it tells us how well the system stops the release of unwanted documents. Thus if 50 documents are retrieved of which 10 are relevant the Precision Ratio is 20%. The user has to expend effort in separating the 40 unwanted documents from the 10 relevant ones.

Recall and Precision are related by a curve of the shape shown in Figure

13.2. If the user broadens the search question to try to ensure he does not miss anything, that is he wants high Recall, he will indeed get it, but he will also get more unwanted documents - i.e lower Precision. But if the question is narrowed in an attempt to retrieve only relevant documents, fewer unwanted documents will be retrieved but fewer wanted documents will be retrieved as well - higher Precision is accompanied by lower Recall.

100% Recall and 100% Precision means that every relevant document is found unaccompanied by any un- wanted documents. This may be real- isable for some kinds of office documents e.g. a January 10th memo from Moggs to Bloggs.If the memo is stored electronically and the date originator and addressee are ent- ered for every memo and are inc- luded in every question, then perfect retrieval is possible.

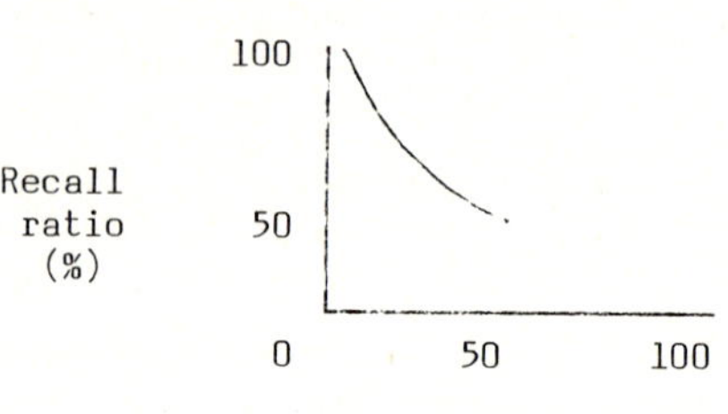

FIGURE 13.2
RECALL-PRECISION RELATIONSHIP

Such perfection could be ach- ieved in a machine-based system because of the way it can be organised as will become evident in a moment, but in a paper-based system the wanted memo will be filed by a single attribute, such as date. You would go to the date-ordered "Internal memos" file, go to those dated January 10th, and look through 20 memos to find the one to Bloggs. The elements of Recall and Precision are here, but the response time dominates.

<u>Indexing conceptual and factual information</u>

In the case of collections of articles, books, or reports in which many subjects may be covered, the indexing problem is more difficult. <u>Surrogates</u> - that is descriptions - with perhaps a brief abstract - representing the item are often searched, and a note is provided with the surrogate about the location of the actual document, perhaps a shelf number. A library card is an example of a surrogate.

Much of the work done on information systems has been concerned with scientific information, where a user may not wish to find all the possibly embarrassingly large number of relevant articles about a subject. He will be considering his reading chore. He may want a few informative articles.

Moreover the desired information may be conceptual rather than factual, making indexing and retrieval more difficult. For example an article entitled "Effect of human leukocyte interferon on hepatitis B virus infection in patients with chronic active hepatitis", not only embodies several concepts in the title, but there might be details of diagnostic or analytical methods of interest <u>per se</u> in the text which require to be indexed.

In contrast, an office searcher may often want to find, without fail, one unique item - for example the memo from Bloggs to Moggs dated January 10th.

Office information may be factual rather than conceptual, and may be easier to index - in a personnel file the name of a person is an unambiguous indexing term. Records in such a file can be completed using a standardised form filling procedure. The field into which an "age" figure is entered will always contain a two-digit value for the attribute "age". Few problems can be expected when posing questions to such a file of the kind "find all persons who are over 50".

Virtually no work has been done on indexing methods and retrieval performance for"typical" collections of office "documents", nor on the performance of systems containing such documents. The principles put forward by Cleverdon, discussed earlier, would seem to be generally applicable, but are less important for files containing simple records such as Bloggs to Moggs.

<u>"Personal" and "public" indexing: free and imposed (controlled) vocabularies</u>

The nuances of the problem have been nicely illustrated by Broadbent with reference to filing things in drawers but with a view to using a personal computer-based system:-

"If many files are kept, we might have a filing cabinet devoted to industrial relations with one drawer concerning wage negotiations, different sections of the drawer for the different unions, and individual files within each section representing particular categories of worker belonging to the union.

The difficulty of such a system is that material placed under one heading may contain some parts which are relevant for a completely different purpose; wage negotiations may include some matters which are relevant to health and safety, agreements reached with one union may affect relations with another, and so on.

The problem is, of course, a familiar one to librarians who have traditionally used a hierarchic classification but find that it produces difficulties. They may therefore use an alternative system in which each book possesses a set of descriptive words, and all possible combinations of these words are allowed.

The labelling words are usually known as "descriptors". For practical reasons, however, a retrieval system based on descriptors usually makes use of a fixed vocabulary, the descriptors assigned to each book being chosen from the prescribed vocabulary by the person cataloguing the book; the person making a search employs the same vocabulary to make up the enquiry he wants to pursue.

In personal systems, the individual makes up descriptors of his own choice for each item and the vocabulary is likely to be peculiar to the person. It is not clear what the consequences of this would be in practice; would the individual pick so many descriptors that a small and realistically cheap computer system would be overloaded, and is the advantage of a personal vocabulary of descriptors worth while?"

This succinct discussion contains the essence of the indexing problem - the controlled index brings a measure of uniformity when the indexer is working for the benefit of others, as in the case of the librarian. For example the index lists synonyms which lead to the preferred indexing term which must be used. When the indexer and the user are the same person, he has only to cater for his own "peculiarities".

Broadbent conducted a series of experiments in which subjects were asked to choose a set of descriptors for 100 objects suitable for Christmas presents in pictures cut out of a mail-order catalogue. Later they were asked to choose a Christmas present for a person described in such a way that one particular present out of the 100 was the most suitable for that person.

The experiments were designed to show the effects of classification upon retrieval according to the numbers and kinds of descriptors chosen,and the differences resulting from freely chosen or imposed vocabularies.

It was concluded that retrieval is better when people use their own descriptors, rather than choosing from an imposed vocabulary, also that they find a hierarchic system limiting. Given an imposed vocabulary they use more different words and more words for each object. These are, of course, Broadbent's findings for a "personal" not a "public" system.

An imposed vocabulary, sometimes called a thesaurus, is sometimes used in computer-based systems, but it must be up-dated to accommodate new words, and it occupies considerable storage space.

<u>Classification and Indexing methods</u>

Some notes about this subject follow,but space does not permit a thorough explanation of this complex topic. Aristotle (384-322 BC) sub-divided the animal kingdom into birds, fish,insects, etc., a system later developed by Linnaeus into the Phylum, Class,.......Genus, Species classification system.

As Sokal says in a classic work about the subject, <u>classification</u> is "the ordering or arrangement of objects into groups or sets on the basis of their relationships". An <u>index</u> is an ordered list of descriptive terms.

Fairthorne retells an anecdote, said to come from Germany towards the end of the last war, which illustrates with black humour a traditional method of classification.

"A German with a starving wife and family sought help from the Winter Aid Fund. Entering an imposing building he found himself facing two doors, one marked "Party members", the other "Non-party members". Going through the second door he was faced with two more doors, one marked "Subscribers to the fund", the other "Non-subscribers to the fund". Going through the latter he found two more doors,and so on. After an hour or two he reached two more doors marked "Family men", the other "Non-family men". Opening the last he found himself out in the street where he had started. A friend asked him if he had received any help. "Oh no", he replied, "but what a marvellcus systems"!

The story illustrates traditional indexing with supposedly mutually exclusive selectable categories which can, in practice, be violated. For instance in the Universal Decimal Classification (UDC), indexing terms are hierarchically arranged. Thus "Apparatus with Wheel Mechanisms" includes the Subset "Calculating and Adding Apparatus" which in turn includes "Slide Rules". The latter are certainly not a sub-set of "Apparatus with Wheel Mechanisms"!

```
Mercury                        125
MICROCOMPUTER   -S
  CPUs                         177
  files, moving                187
  forecasts                144,169
  hardware
    ACT                        167
    Apple Lisa                 167
    Hewlett Packard            168
  SEE ALSO Disks
Modem -s
  SEE Telecommunications
```

"Prestel" indexing, using 10 choices per step, is an extension of the two-choice (binary) German door system. A more flexible system, similar to the layout of the index in this book, is shown (above right) to illustrate simple indexing principles.

The index is alphabetised and major subjects such as Microcomputers are capitalised, sub-divided, and set out in up to three levels as shown on

```
MICROCOMPUTER -S
    hardware
      Apple Lisa
```

the right. To keep down the size of the index and to lead a user to related subjects, SEE entries are included. Thus "Disks", perhaps sub-divided into several topics, are detailed under "D" but have a SEE reference under "Microcomputers". This arrangement also anticipates where a user might look - e.g not necessarily under "Microcomputers" for "Disks". All Disks may not be microcomputer disks.

Such an arrangement has to do with the <u>specificity</u> (see below) of an indexing term and the number of postings beneath it. For example "Telecommunications" has many facets; "Satellite Telecoms" is more specific, and "Transponders used in Satellite Telecomms" is yet more specific.

The generality of the term "Telecommunications" is such that the user would have to refer to many pages before an article about, say, "Satellite Transponders" is found on, say, page 91. Thus the arrangement shown (above right) would be unhelpful.

Telecommunications 1, 2, 57, 58, 69, 70, 84, 91, 103, 104-108, etc.

The index arrangement previously described limits the <u>frequency</u> of postings per term and so the number of lookups needed to check each item.

Turning to another aspect of indexes, alphabetisation is not quite as straighforward as you might think. The London telephone directory uses the arrangement shown above right. However the alphabetisation rules would arguably be more helpful, if they were altered to provide the arrangement shown below right.

S.W.Trading
Sacre K.J.
Sacred Heart Convent
Saint G.V.
St. Agnes Youth Centre
Society for Underwater Technology
Society of Aviation Artists

Exhaustivity and Specificity

These two indexing parameters are the main factors controlling the Recall and Precision of an information system. <u>Exhaustivity</u> is the degree or depth of indexing accorded to the topics in a document. Using the earlier example, the terms "leukocyte", "interferon", "hepatitis" and "virus infection" plus terms describing diagnostic and analytical methods - say "Lowry's method" - might be used exhaustively to index the document in question.

Sacred Heart Convent
Sacre K.J.
Saint Agnes Youth Centre
Saint G.V.
Society (of) Aviation Artists
Society (for) Underwater Technology
S.W.Trading

The potential for high Recall now exists because if a user wants high Recall, and he is interested in articles described by the above four terms, he can get it. Unfortunately high Exhaustivity reduces Precision because there is no means of knowing the <u>treatment</u> of the subject in the article. There may be 50 articles mentioning Lowry's method, but a complete description of the method is given in only one.

If low Exhaustivity indexing is used, "Lowry's method" will be used as a term when the article is substantially about that topic. for instance its use could hardly be avoided for an article entitled "Lowry's method for protein determination". In this case a searcher using that term would be led only to such articles and not to articles in which Lowry is merely mentioned.

<u>Specificity</u> is the degree of precision of indexing terms. Thus the terms "hepatitis A" and "hepatitis B" are more precise then "hepatitis", just as "Telecoms", "Telecoms: satellites", and "Telecoms: satellite transponders" represent increasing degrees of precision. As might be expected, indexes containing many specific terms provide the potential for high Precision, while indexes with fewer, more general, terms do not.

The number of articles described by each specific term will be relatively small, so if the specific term "Resolution" is used, aspects of that subject contained in articles about "Image processing", had this broader term been used, will be missed by a searcher unless it occurs to him to look at articles indexed by that term. Over-specificity - that is using a very large number of different terms for indexing - is likely to reduce Recall, although the average number of terms used to index each document does not much effect performance according to Cleverdon.

Another of Cleverdon's findings came from experiments using an average of from 7 up to 60 terms per document. It seems that if you want good Recall, the allocation of a few well-chosen indexing terms (making the indexing chore less onerous) for each document provides much the same results as using a much larger number of terms. Presumably this must have something to do with the limited number of topics above some arbitrary level of importance that are discussed in most articles. Review articles may be an exception.

Efficiency of a computerised index

In computer-based systems where the index is the only link between a user and files of information, good organisation becomes very important. A user can scan a huge amount of ordered information quickly in a paper-based index and the only cost of homing in to wanted information is the cost of his time; a major disadvantage is that the index must embody expensive intellectual effort and can only be up-dated by printing a new edition. However although the index may be expensive to compile, the cost per lookup will still be small if it is heavily used.

It takes more time to home in to a wanted item in a computer-based index, and there is an additional cost per lookup - information has to be electrically transmitted from store to terminal, often in successive chunks, because of the size/resolution limitations of a Cathode Ray Tube. The transmission cost may be quite small if store and terminal are close, but will be appreciable if the store is distant - for instance as when searching a database in another country. Trends in telecommunications (cost independent of distance) are reducing this difference.

As Garfield and Zunde have shown, information theory can tell us something about the right way to organise indexes to minimise the amount, and so the costs, of transmitted information. In brief, if the number of postings per term are arranged in order of frequency, it can be shown that the maximum amount of information transmitted per term occurs when there is a particular frequency distribution function of the postings/terms.

Indexing in online systems

Typically when browsing the index in an online system, article titles or abstracts containing the wanted word and variants will be displayed. The hit frequency - that is the number of articles containing the word - provides a clue about the next step to take. Should an alternative or additional words be used, or is the chosen word insufficiently specific, for instance. In the example, Enkephalin on its own is too broad and in a computer system this information would encourage the searcher to consider what

WORD	HITS
Enkephela	1
Enkephalin	1188
Enkephalinamide	61
Enkephalinamides	4
Enkephelinase	42
Enkephalinases	3
Enkephaline	2
Enkephalinergic	23
Enkephalinol	1
Enkephalins	250
etc.	

aspect of the subject is of interest. He might try "Enkephalin/ AND Naloxone" to retrieve items containing the string "Enkephalin but only if "Naloxone" appears in the item as well.

But consider an informed indexer's representation of Enkephalin such as that shown on the right. In this case a user is led to the aspect of interest to him in a one-step process because intellectual indexing has been brought to bear. The user does not now need to proceed step by step to decide how to put the question. The great advantage of a computerised index is that it can be up-dated automatically each time new "documents" are added to the database without intellectual intervention, in a way which is no more and no less satisfactory than the rules, currently rather crude, put by a human into the controlling software to determine the words to be selected for indexing terms.

```
Enkephalin -s
  behavioural effects of-
  Naloxone, interaction with-
  secretion stimulation in:
    dogs
    man
    rats
  structure of-
```

Progress with automatic indexing in which information is processed according to certain rules in order to generate indexing terms in a way which approaches the results of a person-compiled index has been slow. However words are not the only terms which can be used as indexing terms as will be shown later in this chapter.

Full text considerations

Developments in technology have enabled database suppliers and host computer bureaux to offer full text searching of articles, books, newspaper reports etc. In many cases every word is searchable, so the text is self-indexed. In cases where the text is structured, some organisations such as the American Chemical Society and the International Research Communications (IRCS) System, divide the text into individually searchable fields - for example "Introduction", "Materials and Methods", and "Results". This helps to reduce the retrieval of irrelevant parts ("false drops") of the text. WESTLAW, a US legal full text database, adds indexing terms in the form of separately searchable keywords and summary notes.

The full text of every article has been "indexed" to some degree by its author, and to some degree by the act of directing searchers to databases containing collections of articles covering subjects in the general area of interest to them. Thus a person searching free text in the full text online version of the Harvard Business Review using the words ECONOMIC INDICATOR/ is much more likely to find a number of articles which have some relevance than he would find in, say, the IRCS medical article database. However it seems unlikely that the principles of information retrieval appertaining to the searching of article indexing terms, as discussed earlier in this chapter, can be readily applied when searching every word in an article.

The retrieval performance of full text databases has been reviewed by Tenopir. Tenopir quotes from an investigator who uses words which seem to sum up the situation "all the problems of lack of vocabulary control and bulk which might be anticipated are encountered with the obvious advantage of speed and completeness as tradeoffs".

It would be expensive for database suppliers to introduce some form of indexing in order to reduce user's expenditure on expensive computer time. Suppliers emphasise the need to adopt practices which are different from those applied to indexed material. Proximity indicators are an important aid. In many systems searchers can specify that search words should be spaced apart by n or not more than n words. For example the phrases "banks have decided to increase their interest rates", "the government has decided that bank interest rates....", "Barclays Bank, unlike other banks, has decided to maintain its interest rate at 12.5%" and "the bank rate is now 10%" occurring in articles, would be retrieved by the question BANK/ (8) RATE/ meaning "find all articles in which the words BANK/ and RATE/ occur separated by up to 8 words".

Other necessary precautions are to anticipate the synonym problem in free text and restrict the search to specific fields when they are available.

Tenopir concludes that full-text searching is potentially an answer to the document delivery problem and there is a market for full text databases with numbers of satisfied users prepared to accept the disadvantages. A major disadvantage at present is the absence of the graphics which come with printed versions.

<u>Indexes in electronic office systems</u>

If computerised files are to be introduced into smaller offices, it would appear that the organisation, classification, and indexing arrangements, at least for most of the "routine information" such as correspondence, memos etc., need be no better than they were for paper-based operations.

In fact that is not the case. Electronic files are not nearly so easily browsed or scanned as paper-based files. You cannot use physical aids such as box-files, drawers, coloured folders, notes, annotations, tags or whatever. The information is now intangible but it still must be at least as accessible as before. Personal information systems are discussed in Chapter 14.

In larger offices the volume of some kinds of paper-based information and most computer-based information will justify the supervision of an Information Officer or Librarian. This person will make the initial intellectual effort to devise a system which is no more onerous to operate than it need be to handle the flow of material to be indexed.

<u>Enter computers (almost): Coordinate indexing.</u>

One of the earliest attempts to apply multi-aspect co-ordinate indexing methods was with "Batten cards". The idea was to get immediate answers to questions like "how many red 1979 Jaguar XJS cars offered for less than £10,000 and fitted with anti-pollution exhaust systems have I got in stock?"

A glimpse of what might be forthcoming when mechanisation got under way was provided by the card systems developed during 1948 to 1960. These included "Batten card", "Uniterm", "Peek-a-Boo", and "Edge-notched card" systems.

The significance of these devices can be understood by considering a car dealer's stock reference system. Say he wants to classify cars in terms of their brand name, model, year, engine size, colour, and type.

If one stock card listing these attributes is made out for each car, he could file the cards alphabetically by brand name, then alphabetically by model, then in year order etc. Thus the cards would be ordered as in Fig. 13.3.

To find a red Jaguar XJ6 he would go to Jaguar and flick through the cards observing the second attribute, model, until he came to the XJ6's and then check through those cards for a red car. But suppose he wanted to know how many red 1981 1200cc sports cars he has in stock. He has got to sort through a large number of cards to find those containing the three required attribute values — a time consuming process. This

```
Austin: Allegro: 1981: 1400cc: red: saloon
Austin: Allegro: 1981: 1400cc: red: sports
Austin: Allegro: 1981: 1400cc: white: saloon
Austin: Allegro: 1981: 1600cc: blue: estate
Austin: Allegro; 1981: 1600cc: white sports
etc.
Ford: Cortina: 1980: 1200cc: blue: saloon
Ford: Cortina: 1981: 1200cc  red: saloon
etc
Jaguar: etc etc.
etc.
```

<u>FIGURE 13.3. CARD INDEX ORDERING</u>

is called a <u>Pre-coordinate</u> indexing system because the "attributes" (e.g colour) and the attribute "values" (e.g red) have been indexed and filed in a fixed order before use and the cards must be accessed by reference to that order.

Peek-a-Boo cards

The card systems named at the beginning of this section embody a facility for <u>post-coordinate</u> indexing. For example in a "peek-a-boo" car stock system, the dealer would arrange for master cards to contain all the details of each car, and would file these cards in numerical order.

He would also possess a set of peek-a-boo cards capable of having holes punched in specific positions. If he knows he will have up to 1000 cars in stock he would have a set of cards with 1000 positions for holes, with each position numbered. Each card represents the value of an attribute. Thus there would be a card for "Austin", another for "Allegro", for "1979", for "red", etc. These cards are kept separately in alpha-numeric order.

When a car arrives - say a Ford Fiesta 1980 1200cc red saloon - the dealer makes out the next master card - say 427 - and enters the details of the car on it. He then gets out the Ford peek-a-boo card, and punches a hole in position 427. He also gets the Fiesta card and punches that at 427 and so on.

Suppose now he poses the same question as before: "how many 1981 1200cc sports cars have I in stock?". He pulls out the peek-a-boo cards marked "1981", "1200cc" and "sports" and aligns them. The number of any holes in the same position on each card - visible because light can pass through the three cards at that point - will indicate the numbers of the master cards listing 1981 1200c sports cars to which he can then refer.

This is called "post-coordination" because the coordination of terms is performed not at the time of indexing but at the time of selection. When this principle is applied to conceptual information, a degree of pre-coordination is often performed in order to avoid "false drops" (co-ordinations which are spuriously generated and do not match the query) or to reduce the need to use a large number of indexing terms. For example a person interested in "The production of uranium in Canada", using the terms "production","Canada", and "uranium" to retrieve documents about this topic would also retrieve an article about "The effect of uranium radiation during the production of fuel rods in Canada".

One way of dealing with this is to pre-coordinate word pairs or triples which occur frequently, as done in the Permuterm Subject Index published by the Institute for Scientific Information, and shown on the right. The benefits of coordination (indicated by hyphens) to more easily locate an article by C.W.Myles entitled "Crystal field and magnetic field effects on nuclear spin lattice relaxations in solid H2" are self-evident.

```
NUCLEAR-SPIN-LATTICE
   CRYSTALS            Prager GR
   MAGNETIC-FIELD      Myles CW
   RELAXATION          Clark LG
                       Edwards JD
```

Edge-Notched cards

Returning to the days when computers were still expensive and mysterious instead of cheap and mysterious, a variation - edge-notched cards - were quite widely used for personal collections. Experiments for the machine sorting of cards in larger collections were being carried out in the same period.

A detailed description of an edge-notched card system for a collection of electronics papers in 1962 is given by Cawkell. Information about an article, including, say, its number in an article file, is written on the card, and the aspects of interest are coded by converting numbered holes round the edge of the card into notches with a clipping tool. To find a paper of interest, needles are inserted into the holes at the edge of a pack of cards, corresponding to the codes symbolising the topics of interest. The cards describing articles containing those topics will fall out since appropriate holes will have previously been turned into notches. The corresponding articles are then found in the article file.

This method was a significant advance on indexing cards filed in order of a single attribute - say major subject. Articles embodying a particular combination of required attributes could be found, and articles containing a combination of items not anticipated as being a requirement at the time of indexing could also be found. Unlike conventional indexing cards, edge-notched cards do not have to be maintained in any particular order.

A variation on this idea, as put into practice (also in 1962) for a personal collection of references to the Psychology literature has been described by Broadhurst. Further variations were reported in 1980 by Cooney.

<u>The Humpty Dumpty syndrome</u>

All indexing systems, have to face up to problems associated with the subjective meaning of words - the "Humpty Dumpty Syndrome" picturesquely described by Lewis Carroll:- "When I use a word" Humpty Dumpty said in rather a scornful tone "it means just what I choose it to mean - neither more nor less".

In systems where a number of different people share an information system and each is free to insert his or her own indexing terms the problem becomes acute. User A might consider that the word "Production" unambiguously specifies his information requirement, being unaware that user B indexed articles about that topic but used "manufacture" for his indexing term. One way out is to accept the additional cost of a controlled indexing system - a "thesaurus" which forces useage of preferred words.

<u>Thesauri</u>

Indexing problems have not changed much with the advent of computers. The HD syndrome remains - a wanted item in a computer file may be missed because the searcher's choice of words to describe it differ from those used by the indexer. You have only to look in Roget's Thesaurus to appreciate the richness of the English language in synonyms and shades of meaning.

There's the American language to cope with as well and of course the huge area in other languages which defy exact translation - how can you convey the elegance and nuances of <u>cherchez la femme</u> or <u>fin de siecle</u> in English?

A thesaurus contains lists of synonyms and other words, referring the indexer and the user to the preferred words which he must use. An example is shown in figure 13.4.

This would be helpful in coal research, but in other disciplines a thesaurus might look quite different. In medicine, synonyms are a major problem. A thesaurus covering drugs would need to take account of the equivalence of chemical, generic, and trade names.

In a thesaurus a time overhead is transferred from users to the human compiler. The compiler has to add new words to the thesaurus when they appear. Alternatively a "new word list", automatically created when adding information to

a database in a computer-based system with the appropriate software, will have to
be examined and edited. This may require a considerable effort with a complex
nomenclature - as, for instance in medicine. If it is not done quickly a user
will not find items about newly named subjects entering the literature.

GYROSCOPES
RT   MEASURING INSTRUMENTS
RT   PRECESSION
RT   ROTATION

H CODES
BT   COMPUTER CODES

H-COAL PROCESS
BT   COAL LIQUEFACTION

HABITAT
RT   ENVIRONMENT

HAEMATITE
USE   **HEMATITE**

HAFNIUM
BT   REFRACTORY METALS

HAFNIUM ALLOYS
BT   ALLOYS
NT   HAFNIUM ADDITIONS

HALIDES
BT   HALOGEN COMPOUNDS
NT   CHLORIDES
NT   COPPER HALIDES
NT   FLUORIDES
NT   IODIDES
NT   ZINC HALIDES

HALL EFFECT
RT   ELECTRIC CONDUCTORS

HALL GENERATORS
USE   **MHD GENERATORS**

UF	Used for (indicates the non-preferred term from which reference is made).
UFC	Used for (indicates the non-preferred term for which the main term is one of the substitute descriptors).
SF	Seen for (indicates the non-preferred for which the main term is a more specific substitute).
BT	Broader term (indicates a more general term, one level higher in the hierarchy, which defines and limits the use of the narrower terms).
NT	Narrower term (indicates a more specific term, one level lower in the hierarchy, which helps to define the broader term but which does not limit its use).
RT	Related term (indicates an associative relationship between terms not related hierarchically).

FIGURE 13.4. EXAMPLE OF ENTRIES IN A THESAURUS

From the Coal database (an Assassin based system) thesaurus
by courtesy of IEA Coal Research, London.

Search philosophy

The results of a search for information contained in one or more "items"
somewhere within a "collection", depends on the contents of the collection, on
the indexing and search facilities that are provided, and on the way the searcher
uses the system. An "item" may be a letter, a product data sheet, a journal
article, an electronically stored report, etc.

The searcher can exercise some control over the results by posing a "broad",
or "narrow" question, or a question somewhere between these extremes. Most of the
relatively small number of items retrieved from a narrow question will be of
interest but a number of interesting items within the collection outside the
range of the question will be missed. On the other hand nearly all the items of
interest in the collection will be retrieved by a broad question but they will be
accompanied by many of marginal or zero interest ("noise").

This is just another way of expressing the Recall/Precision relationship
discussed earlier - even more important for computer-based information systems
because of the huge amount of information which can be searched, the tendency in
some systems to include everything in case somebody might want it, and the
potentially huge amount of unwanted information ("noise") which may be
communicated to the user.

When the searcher ends up with a number of information-containing items
she/he will be able to rank-order them by "importance", "relevance" or useful

"interest" to her/him. First will come the item containing the "best" information, and last will be an item containing very little or perhaps no useful information.

In the case of the "broad question results" the searcher will have to decide on a point of cut-off below which he believes that time spent in reading will be unrewarding.

In personal systems the same principle applies, but the problem is usually less severe because of the small size of the database, the user's intimate knowledge of it, and the fact that if he is both indexer and user the effects of the Humpty Dumpty syndrome will be much less severe.

ON LINE INFORMATION RETRIEVAL SYSTEMS: COMPUTER FILES

Searching for information can be done by <u>batching</u>, or <u>interactively online</u> Batching means collecting together all the queries from a number of users and putting them on to cards or tape. These data are matched against the data records in a database (usually on tape) by a "pass" in a computer. When a match occurs, the matching record or <u>"hit"</u> is printed, and hit data records are sorted at the end of the run and sent to the appropriate users. If a question is badly formulated a user has to change it, have it re-inputted, and await the results from the next occasion the database is passed through the computer.

In interactive online searching a user sits at a terminal connected to a computer on which a database is mounted, usually on disks. He types queries and the matching process is rapidly carried out, hits being displayed or printed at the terminal. If the results are unsatisfactory the query may be re-formulated, perhaps more narrowly, and the user tries again, and so on until she gets it right. Matching usually involves comparing "strings". A string is a sequence of characters and spaces. Thus COMPUT is a string, and if that term is used as a question all records containing COMPUT (e.g COMPUTING, COMPUTER, COMPUTERS, etc., would be hits). ELECTRONIC MAIL SYSTEM is another string.

It seems unlikely that batch searching will be used much in the office. Most people will want to get at "paperwork" quickly and expect an almost immediate response in the form of a display of text. The rate of that response will depend upon many factors, but the ones with which we are here concerned are the ways in which the files are organised for ease of searching and the way in which they are indexed. Lancaster's book is recommended for further reading.

Computer files

Conventional computers are still based on Von Neumann architecture as reviewed by Burks. They are designed for arithmetical computation with relatively small amounts of stored data. Applications in text searching require character string comparisons on large amounts of stored data. Some new ways of organising computers for database searching are described by Su, but most of the software is still written for Von Neumann machines since the vast majority are still based on this architecture.

One way of searching files - collections of textual data - is to arrange for the computer system to search serially through the records for strings matching the query string. Hits, in the form of complete records will be transferred to the user's terminal for viewing, or to his printer if he wants a permanent copy. This involves searching through the complete text of records so very high speeds are essential. If the items containing the actual wanted information document are represented by a <u>surrogate</u> - that is a short representation of it - of, say, one hundredth of its length - then the search will obviously be completed more quickly.

The surrogate must contain the essence of the document. The document may be of a simple kind e.g. a letter for which addressee details may be considered sufficient, or it may be a report whose essence may have to be a brief description of the subject - its title, keywords or an abs_r In short, the document will have been indexed. If the title only is used then that is the index - an index which won't work unless the originator has given some thought to it or it has been supplemented by an indexer. Thus the words "The wiring of Britain" would be unhelpful in a title-based retrieval system for a searcher looking for information about cable television.

A "hit", in the case of searching surrogates, will be a display of the the hit surrogate so that the viewer can decide whether to get the whole document. Obviously some arrangement must be made for each record in the searcheable surrogate records to be connected to its associated complete document containing the wanted informaion.

Inverted file systems
____

File structures are discussed by Meadows, Hallaar, and Lefkowitz. Until quite recently, serial searching of full text online has been unacceptably slow, and searching of suitably arranged surrogate records has usually been used. The inverted file and the multilist or threaded-list file are the most widely used out of several which have been developed for medium to large databases.

The inverted file seems to have gained widest acceptance. It is a directory to the keys used in records. A key is simply a search term such as a word, an author's name, a chemical formula etc. Note that we have seen this idea before - the peek-a-boo cards were an inverted file system. For example a database might comprise a series of records describing company reports. Each record might be a surrogate with report titles and added keywords, author, date, and a shelf number indicating where the print-on-paper report itself is kept.

In an inverted file system it is the relatively small key directory which is searched by the computer not the relatively large totality of surrogate text in records (or the full text in systems where each record contains the complete document). Inverted files are often searched using Boolean expressions - for instance in "Find records containing ELECTRONIC MAIL and MICROCOMPUTER" the machine has to identify the addresses of records containing both keys in a keyword list in order to locate hit records.

The number of hits resulting from this directory search can be displayed without the need for the records themselves being retrieved so that the user can quickly re-formulate his question if necessary. The records can, of course, be retrieved as needed because their addresses are stored in computer memory as a result of the search.

Penalties are paid for the convenience and operational speed of an inverted file system in the form of software complexity and storage space. When a new record is added to the record file, information must also be added to the separate key/record address directory (the inverted file). If its keys are already in the directory, the address of each new record must be included with the other records containing those keys. If the record contains new keys, those keys and the record's address must be added to the directory.

The key directories occupy considerable storage space. Depending on the diversity of the file this space can approach that needed for the records themselves . In a batch system, a series of new records are added periodically and the necessary re-organisation process for that batch of new records is carried out at some convenient time. Until that time, use of the new records is

denied to users. If the system is simultaneously useable for information
retrieval and record up-dating the software and power of the system must be
capable of coping with both without much degradation of performance. For
more information see Lefkowitz and Cardenas.

Sequentially ordered computer files

    A sequentially ordered file consists of records each containing all the
information needed to identify and retrieve a document. Records are ordered
by some common attribute, and if searching is usually by one particular
attribute then the file may be ordered by that attribute - that is the
physical and logical order are the same.

    For instance if an author's name appears on each record, the ordering
could be alphabetically by the author's surname. When a new record is entered
the computer reads the name and stores the record in its proper place. Searching
for all items by Bloggs will be fast because all the hit records are together
in one place.

    If it is required to search the file by <u>any</u> attribute then a new record can
be added at the end. Records are then stored in chronological order of
input so the record number could be used as a key - e.g. a search requirement
for "records only if input this week (number 4978 onwards)" could be
quickly fulfilled.

Indexing and searching sequentially ordered files

    In a sequential file the computer searches through the full text of the
surrogate records which also serve as the index, not through a separate
directory of indexing terms. In an inverted file the keys will be selected
according to certain rules - for example there may be a "stop list" of
trivial words ("the", "of" etc.,) which are not used as keys, but which are
present in sequential file records.

    For sequentially ordered files no elaborate "loading" software is
required since there is no key directory to be created when new records are
added. Nor is there any need, in an online system, to arrange for searching
operations to proceed simultaneously with up-dating operations. In sequential
file searching the problem avoided in the inverted file system remains - How can
the computer find records containing, say, the strings ELECTRONIC MAIL <u>and</u>
MICROCOMPUTER with an acceptable response time after the question is posed when
it has to search the whole of each record?

Rapid searching of a sequential file

    If special methods for searching a sequential file are not introduced, the
machine will simply search serially through the records until it finds a hit.
Assuming that the records are stored on disk, the machine will transfer a block
of records to the CPU and match them, character by character, against the
query string. It will continue to do this until all records have been tried.
The response time will probably be unacceptably long on most mainframe
computers and will take several minutes on most microcomputers even if only
a thousand records of, say, 300 characters each, are stored on disk.

    Various methods of overcoming this problem are available, and all require
some additional software. The principle is usually to represent the
contents of records by encoding them, to use the same code to encode the search
query, and then to carry out the search by matching the encoded query against
the encoded records (See Lefkowitz). If the system is for online interactive use
it must be possible to enter a new record into the system and then carry out
a search in which the new record is immediately available as a potential hit.

This is not an article about computer software, but it will be obvious to the reader that the response time will depend upon the rate at which the machine can match the encoded queries and records. That, in turn, will depend on the effectiveness of the code in compressing the records, and the way the records are distributed on the disk. An example of what is possible has been described by Cawkell. In the microcomputer system described, about 1500 records each containing, say, 300 characters stored on floppy disk, or 10,000 or more stored on Winchester disk can be full-text searched at a rate approaching 30,000 characters per second. When a new record is typed, online up-dating is almost instantaneous.

In addition to sophisticated ways of speeding up sequential file operations, advances in computer power seem likely to bring them back into favour. Several recently introduced techniques are of interest. With these, the advantages of sequential file processing are introduced without the disadvantages and they should eventually find their way into office systems. The "backend" computer described by Su is an almost self-contained machine which is controlled by a "host" computer and can get on with time-consuming operations, particularly database operations, in parallel with operations in the host. Information about Parallel Processing and Associative Arrays is now appearing in the computer literature to describe faster processing by arranging for banks of processors to process data under collective control instead of having it done by one processor.

An example of this trend is the ICL Content Addressable File Store (CAFS) which came into use during 1980. CAFS is a disk system with its own processing hardware which handles sequential files. In this system all fields in a record are not searched. The machine only searches those fields containing the values of the attributes specified in the query. Queries are processed in one pass and many operations are carried out in parallel.

For example the results of a search for a hit record from a query of the form "ELECTRONIC (OFFICE OR MAIL) and MICROCOMPUT" accumulate as the record is processed. Bits are set when query and record keys match, but only if the bit pattern matches the whole query is the record sent to the main machine as a hit.

Dealing with electronic documents/records in the office

```
Cat. No:   6085
Date:      May 1985
No.Pages:  5
Source:    Metheus Corp., PO Box 1049, Hillsboro, OR 97123, USA
Tel:       503 640 8000
Details:   Omega 500 Display Controller. 1280 x 1024 pixels. 8 x 24 lookup
           table for 256 different colours. DEC, HP, IEEE1978, and RS232C
           interfaces. Single board construction in container. 110/240v
           60/50Hz 200w.
```

```
System: Telecom Gold              Time/Date: 0930 June 9th 1985
To:     All C6 Engineers          From: Dir. Engineering
```

Prepare to substitute TELRAD standard k-5 module for 3-602 in all 4800bps modems on EUR10 network. Bit key being sent all depts. by courier. First use will be 0800 GMT July 1st 1985. Acknowledge.
Encryption

<u>FIGURE 13.5. RECORDS IN A COMPUTERISED OFFICE SYSTEM</u>

An example of the kinds of records that might appear in an office system are shown in Figure 13.5. It is imagined that the first record describes catalogue number 6085 in a catalogue collection stored on a shelf in order of serial number. The record number is the same as the serial number. The document has been described by the value of several attributes - Catalogue Number, Date, etc. Someone will have been appointed to look after the collection, enter records into the system and describe the subject matter.

The second item is supposed to be a message electronically circulated within a Company and just displayed on the CRT of an office work-station. The system software dictates that certain attributes must be entered for such messages, namely System name; originator; addressee(s); time and date; message. The user, who may wish to file the message, has no control over the words used in the subject matter - they were the originator's choice.

There are several points of interest here. The originator's use of a collective address should present no problem in electronic mail systems provided that the collective address list used is correct and up to date. The names of the people covered by the collective term will be stored and the system will arrange for distribution automatically.

It is imagined in the figure that one of the recipients has looked at her terminal and has considered how to file this message. She thought that the message did not contain sufficient indexing terms and has added one keyword "encryption" anticipating that it might be used for retrieval. She will also be considering where to file it. A policy will presumably have been agreed for local and central filing. This kind of message would be filed locally but where? Has the organisation of electronic files followed precedents set by paper files or are different methods or principles called for in electronic office systems? No doubt she will have typed a note for insertion in her diary, stored in the same system, as a reminder that a new encryption key must be in place by the due date.

In a tangible print-on-paper system, no "backup" is necessary. What backup has been arranged for electronic information stored as so many electrical impulses? Is a second copy of each file periodically made as a matter of routine? What has been done to allow for the possibility of the whole system going down?

It seems very obvious that there will be quite a range of matters to attend to when office systems come into wider use, a few of which have been discussed here. Are office managers aware of them or are they in a state of new technology euphoria? There would seem to be some opportunities coming up for librarians and information scientists to switch their skills to offices and probably to become better paid for them.

INDEXES USING OTHER SYMBOLS OTHER THAN WORDS

We are accustomed to using descriptive words to find a document, but other words or symbols can be used. For instance articles may be filed alphabetically by Author (as in a collection of scientific reprints). The Author's name acts as a subject indexing term when it is synonymous with a particular subject.

A citation index uses article citations as subject symbols. Figure 13.6 shows part of the Science Citation Index.

This is an index to enable the user to find published scientific articles likely to be of interest. Descriptions of earlier articles are followed by later articles which cite them. A searcher enters the index at a known article of interest and is led to later citing articles.

```
SUTTGEN G
   77 Havtarzt       26   277
      Reimer G            Arch Derm R   270    313   81
SUTTIE JW
   72 J Dairy Sci 55   790
      Ekstrand J          Act Pharm T   488   433   81
   77 Physiol Rev 57    1
      Gottschalk KE   Theochem            1   197   81
      Walsh PN        Fed Proc           40  2086   81
SUTTKUS RD
   etc., etc.
```

<u>FIGURE 13.6.ENTRIES IN THE 1981 SCIENCE CITATION INDEX</u>
(By courtesy of the Institute for Scientific Information)

In the example,the 1977 article by Suttie in the Physiological Review, vol. 57, page 1 is cited by the Gottschalk and Walsh articles. Its subject "The biochemistry of vitamin K" is unambiguously symbolised by "SUTTIE JW 72 Physiol Rev 57 1". It is an article of repute about that topic. It is assumed that the searcher knows about it and uses it as an entry point to the index. Entering the 1981 index at those symbols he is led to the two 1981 citing articles. The Walsh article is entitled "Platelets and coagulation proteins" (this information can be obtained from a different section of the index which provides details about all the 1981 citing articles).

Neither the Suttie nor the Walsh articles include "vitamin K" in the title – the Humpty Dumpty syndrome is avoided in this index. Vitamin K plays an important role in blood clotting. The information is arranged in such a way that questions like "Has any further investigation of Einstein's unified field theory been pursued in the last few years?" should be answered with fairly high recall and precision. Any author researching this subject can reasonably be expected to cite the foundation paper.

<u>COMPUTERS IN LIBRARIES</u>

<u>Introduction</u>

A large library, like many other enterprises, has certain business activities common to all businesses such as accounting, budgeting, forecasting, purchasing, receipts and payments etc., and computers may be employed in this area as in other businesses and offices. Also like other businesses, libraries are involved in specialised activities, to be reviewed briefly here. The most important are to do with the acquisition of books, creating and using library catalogues, the control of circulation, the purchase and control of serials, the organisation of library networks, integrated library systems, online searching, and the use of micrococomputers in libraries.

Interest in all these aspects, including SDI – online searching's predecessor – started during the sixties when data processing equipment started to become available at lower prices. Although one of the earliest publications surveying computer applications in libraries came from Cox et al in a US/UK team at the Newcastle University library in 1966, The UK took perverse pleasure in claiming a much slower rate of progress than anybody else. At the 1966 Brasenose conference one speaker said "If Oxford has gone less far than the British Museum, Cambridge has gone less far than Oxford". The speaker described the catalogue in his library as an "archaelogical deposit". In spite of that the quality of UK library computer activities had reached that of the US by 1969 according to Kilgour, a well known US practitioner.

<u>Acquisition control</u>

Computerised acquisition processes do not seem to have been widely
introduced although ordering, catalogue card production, label production, etc.,
are computerised on an ad hoc basis. With the increasing adoption of
microcomputers in libraries some attempts have been made to use database
management software such as Dbase II for this purpose. The control of serials is
handled online by the copilers of commercial databases and some large libraries
operate online acquisition systems.

Adams has described an inter-library loan control system called AIM
demonstrated at Leicester Polytechnic in the UK either for borrowing from British
Library Lending Division (BLLD), or lending to or borrowing from other libraries.
The DMS system produced by Compsoft using CP/M, MS-DOS, or CBM operating systems
on micros was selected. Commodore and later Cifer 2684 micros were used. BLLD
loans can be ordered by telex but protocol problems require to be overcome before
AIM can be used to place orders by telex.

<u>Library catalogues - the standardisation of bibliographic descriptions</u>

Early work included Kilgour's computer generated catalogue cards at Yale and
Buckland's machine readable catalogue on tape by typing bibliographic records
using a perforated tape typewriter at the Library of Congress. This library's
Machine Readable Cataloguing (MARC) project, started in 1966, was destined to
become probably the most important library computer project ever undertaken. The
growing catalogue was sent weekly on tape to a number of participating libraries.
The improved MARC II format appeared in 1967. In 1969 a standard for biblographic
information exchange on magnetic tape was proposed and in that year was
considered for use in the UK.

MARC was developed to cater not only for a standardised biliographic
representation for books, but also for serials, and eventually for reports and
almost anything else that might need to be exchanged between libraries.

MARC continued to be developed in the late 60s and in 1969 an attempt to
develop an Anglo-American code by modifying MARC II was made by the British
National Bibliography (BNB). By 1970 agreement was reached to make MARC records
used by the BNB and Library of Congress almost identical, leaving minor
differences is sub-field codes. Many other countries in Europe and elsewhere
started to adopt MARC type formats. By 1973 18 major libraries in the UK were
using BNB/MARC tapes on IBM 360 or ICL 1900 series computers.

An international MARC format was proposed in 1975, later called UNIMARC, by
the US and major European countries and by 1980 a second edition of this
internationally agreed format was published called The Anglo American
Cataloguing Rules 2nd edition (AACR2).

However this cooperative effort failed to prevent other formats for
describing published material coming into widespread use, presumably either
because MARC was ignored or because other formats were considered more suitable
for other purposes. Most machine readable databases do not use a MARC format. An
attempt to standardise database formats was made by UNISIST with the publication
of a Reference Manual in 1974, and persisted with in the 1981 second edition. A
further attempt was made under the aegis of UNESCO in 1978 to develop yet another
format which could be used for all purposes. These efforts do not seem to have
made much progress.

<u>Circulation control</u>

The data processing equipment which became available in the early sixties
was not readily adopted for circulation control purposes mainly because the

methods were thought to be too costly. A real time system was working at Illinois State University library in 1967 using an IBM 1710 and a disk file for circulation transactions. By 1979 several systems were running in the UK. An online system for library-desk transactions was in operation at Queen's University, Belfast. A control system for serials should be able to deal with budget, renewals, check-in, routing, and listing holdings.

In recent years circulation control seems to have become merged with multi-functional library systems as discussed in later sections of this chapter.

<u>Library networks</u>

A "Library Network" often means a library resource-sharing cooperative, not necessarily a number of libraries connected to a computer network. Library networks in the general sense have been functioning for many years simply because few libraries can supply the needs of clients from their own stocks and it makes sense for smaller libraries to make their combined stocks available to all their clients.

Computer-networks were the tool adopted by library networks to make their task easier and in due course enabled other resources to be shared as well as book or serial stocks.

A small network, NELINET, was operating between five New England University libraries in 1968. Requests to a computer in a central office were made from terminals in outlying libraries for catalogue card production, book labels etc.

The Library of Congress has been a library-systems leader in the US, but its activities have been matched by the Ohio College Library Center, now known as the the Online Computer Library Center (OCLC Inc.) which has aggressively introduced several innovations. Another leader in the US is Research Libraries Information Network (RLIN). Both these organisations have been active in developing library systems and networks.

The arrival of computer-based integrated library systems, discussed in the next section, is likely to encourage the use of within-site LANs for sharing various resources, and the use of LANs in a small number of libraries in the UK and US has been reported by Levert. Several libraries were using the LANs with an integrated library system. Several others were using them for circulation management purposes only. Other applications included a large public library supporting the services at its branches, the provision of special software access for clients, and arranging for access to a catalogue from networked microcomputers.

<u>Integrated library systems</u>

The first attempt at an integrated library was an ambitious scheme implemented at the Massachusetts Institute of Technology (MIT) called The Information Transfer Experiment (INTREX), planned to start in 1965. It was to be nothing less than a project to provide computer-controlled access to the university's total information resources, including the library, departmental files, reports etc., using touch-tone telephones, keyboards, displays, copying facilities, etc., with a communications network connecting to outside sources and users.

INTREX continued until 1973. A whole range of ideas were tried out but the experiments centred on an online catalogue to information stored full text on microfiche with computer-controlled fast access to the fiche. The project ended with some curious results. It was reported that microfiche was preferred to hard copy whether the latter was charged or supplied free. However in the final report it was stated that no economical method was found to provide rapid access to the full text of documents electronically - a situation which prevails to this day. From this there seems to be an implication that if an economic method of supplying fiche could be found, then it would be used for full text delivery. This seems to be the opposite of the conclusions reported in Chapter 24 of this book.

At about the same time as INTREX was started, another more modest project called project SHARP was in use on an IBM 7090/1401 computer at a US naval establishment. Catalogue cards, report and serial accession lists, and periodical subscriptions were handled by the machine.

Today several complete commercially available packages are available as discussed by Powell et al. Powell proposes a searching examination of several aspects of a system before choosing one - software and operating system, size and type of computer, disk storage capacity, interconnections and telecommunications, proposed terminal and printers, installation details, training, growth plan, and hardware and software maintenance. Nine competitive offerings are listed.

<u>Online searching</u>

Online searching is frequently considered to be in the province of the library partly because many online systems provide bibliographic references to publications which are already in the library or can be obtained through library loan schemes, and partly because online searching is an alternative way of finding information which would otherwise be found through other library services.

So far, online searching has not become the simple tool useable by anyone that was once expected. Searching is usually carried out on behalf of an end-user by a librarian or information scientist who has the appropriate background knowledge and who is trained in the use of the various systems and databases available. Since it is often a library-based operation, the recovery of the costs has also to be considered by the library.

Costs and other aspects of online systems are discussed in Chapter 16.

<u>General use of microcomputers in libraries</u>

Software of several different kinds available for libraries has been listed and tabulated by Burton and Gates, including text information retrieval, online search assistance, cataloguing and card production, acquisitions, serials control, and circulation control.

Batt's review confirms that micros have been widely adopted in UK libraries. The use of micros has followed widespread computerisation experience, with more than two thirds of 169 library authorities operating computer-based circulation methods by the end of 1983. The favoured machines in order of precedence are BBC Model B, IBM PC, Sirius 1, CBM Pet, ICL DRS, Torch, Apple, Spectrum, and Hytec. The first three named contribute to more than half of the total. Applications, again in order of precedence, are general housekeeping, indexing, online access, Prestel, and other.

The same kind of progress is reported from the US by Berry who states that 45,000 microcomputers were in use in US libraries in 1984. Apple micros were the leader, followed by IBM PCs and DEC micros, of which Apple accounted for more than half. This review seems to take in general office use as well as library applications since word processing is the most popular appplication followed by database management and statistics.

But do libraries experience the same difficulty in acquiring the knowledge to cope with micros before they can be usefully used as has been asserted several times elsewhere in this book?. Yes, says Carlson - "...enthusiasm is usually based solely on experience with a personal computer...many of the converted often have little perspective and little in the way of broad knowledge from which to draw informed conclusions and make critical assessments".

FURTHER READING

Adams,Roy.
   Program, 19(1), 48-58, January 1985.
      Development of the automation of interlending by microcomputer (AIM) system
      Leicester Polytechnic.
Batt, Chris.
   Program, 19(1), 39-47, January 1985.
      Microcomputers in UK public libraries: a review of current trends.
Beckley, Robert F.; Bleich, Howard L.
   Computers and Biomed. Research 10, 423-430, 1977.
      Paper chase - a computer based reprint storage and information retrieval
      system.
Berry, John.
   Library Journal, 48-49, February 1, 1985.
      Library use of microcomputers: massive and growing.
Broadhurst, P.L.
   Amer. Psychologist 17(3), 137-142, 1962.
      Coordinate indexing: a bibliographic aid.
Broadbent, Donald E., Broadbent, Margaret H.P.
   Ergonomics 21(5), 343-354, May 1978.
      The allocation of descriptor terms by individuals in a simulated retrieval
      system.
Burton, Paul F; Gates, Hilary.
   Program 19(1), 1-19, January 1985.
      Library software for microcomputers.
Cardenas, Alfonso F.
   Communications of the ACM 18(5), 253-263, May 1975.
      Analysis and performance of inverted database structures.
Carlson, David H.
   Library Journal, 50-55, February 1, 1985.
      The perils of personals: microcomputers in libraries.
Cawkell, A.E.
   Wireless World 68(8,9), 352-357, 432-434, August & September 1962.
      Classification and retrieval of technical information.
Cleverdon, Cyril W.
   Aslib Proc. 19(6) 173-194, June 1967.
      The Cranfield tests on index language devices.
Cleverdon, Cyril.
   J.Documentation 30(2), 170-180, June 1974.
      User evaluation of information retrieval systems.
Cooney, S.
   J. Information Science 2, 81-90, 1980.
      A standard procedure for generating personal classifications and indexes.
Cox, N.S.M; Dews J.D; Dolby, J.L.
   Archon Books and University of Newcastle 1966.
      The computer and the library.
Fairthorne, Robert A.
   In Towards Information Retrieval. Archon Books 1968. Chapter 12.
      Delegation of classification.
Garfield, Eugene.
   J.Chem. Doc. 1, page 70, 1961.
      Information theory and other quantitative factors in the code design for
      document card systems.

Lancaster, Wilfred W.; Fayen E.G.
  Melville Publishing Co., Los Angeles. 1973. 597 pps.
    Information retrieval on-line.
Lefkowitz, David.
  MacMillan, 1969. 215 pps.
    File structures for on-line systems.
Lester, Ray.
  Aslib Proc. 36(2), 96-111, 1984.
    User education in the online age.
Levert, Virginia M.
  Information Technology & Libraries, 9-18, March 1985.
    Applications of local area networks of microcomputers in libraries.
Meadows, Charles T.; Meadows Harriott R.
  In Cuadra, Carlos A. (Ed). Annual review of information science and
  technology, Volume 5, 1970. Published for ASIS by Encyclopaedia
  Britannica, Chicago.   Chapter 7, 169-191.
    Organisation, maintenance, and search of machine files.
Powell, James R; Slach, June E.
  Online, 30-36, March 1985.
    How to evaluate integrated library systems.
Sokal, Robert R.
  Science, 185(4157),1115-1123, September 27th, 1974.
    Classification: purposes, principles, progress, prospects.
Su, Stanley Y.; Chang, Hsu, et al.
  In Proc AFIPS May 1980, Anaheim CA, USA. Pub by AFIPS Press 1815 North Lynn
  St., Arlington Va 22209, USA. pps 191-208.
    Database machines and some issues on DBMS standards.
Tenopir, Carol
  In Martha E.Williams (Ed), Annual Review of Information Science & Technology,
  Volume 19,1984. Chapter 7, pps 215-246. Published by Knowledge Industries.
    Full text databases.
Vickery, Brian C.
  Butterworths 1973. 350pps.
    Information Systems.
Wallace, Everett M.
  Proc. Annual Meeting Amer. Doc. Inst, Vol 3, 73-80, 1966.
    User requirements, personal indexes, and computer support.
Zunde, Pranas; Slamecka, Vladimir.
  American Documentation, 104-108, April 1967.
    Distribution of indexing terms for maximum efficiency of information
    transmission.

CHAPTER 14. PERSONAL INFORMATION SYSTEMS

INDEXING AND RETRIEVAL IN PERSONAL INFORMATION SYSTEMS

For a more detailed treatment of indexing, refer to Chapter 13.

Indexing philosophy in offices

Most people are quite prepared to put up with a relatively crude system for locating paperwork. In offices correspondence, reports etc., may be filed in date order, by name of addressee, or by subject content. In science and technology, collections of reprinted articles obtained from authors or information services are often used as an information source; reprints are filed alphabetically by first author's name.

People tend to recall fragments of information when trying to find paperwork – for instance "I'm sure Bloggs wrote to me about widget inertia in '78 or was it '79, and didn't that fellow from Wigan University write a piece about it in the New Scientist last summer?" The time consumed in finding the papers, or perhaps never finding them, from these fragments of information will depend a great deal on the way the files are organised.

People seem concerned about the inadequacy of their filing system but don't do anything about it because it works after a fashion. The cost of not turning potential information into actual information (because the searcher is unable to find what he wants or finds only some fraction of what is contained in the file) is unknown. The cost of implementing a better system and the benefits and time saved are also hard to calculate. It is always difficult to justify a cash outlay in order to change an intangible loss into an intangible benefit.

Most textual information is only potential information unless it is retrievable, and that usually means that it must be indexed. Indexing means labelling an object, page in a book, report, letter, or other item so that it may be retrieved conveniently from, or identified in a stored collection. The store can be a book, filing cabinet, magnetic tape or disk, videodisk, etc.

"Documents" marked with symbols - usually text, graphics or other data – may exist permanently on paper, or may be stored in electrical form to be retrieved and displayed or printed when needed. An index is an essential requirement and the compiling of a successful index is a skilled laborious process. A good indexer anticipates the descriptive words that a user might employ and also takes account of synonyms and the way the index is designed so that it can be up-dated more easily.

Indexing can be considered at two levels - that which concerns the professionals, and that which concerns the rest of us on almost every occasion that we handle a piece of paper (or in due course a CRT page). The professionals are interested but we are not. Most of us file things in some kind of order and are prepared to accept that we will not always find what we want. Perhaps some of us rarely find what we want. Indexing done for self, or for those in the office or group is often done rather nonchalantly.

If you, the indexer, are also going to be the user, then you have to anticipate where only you might look. If you are indexing for a wider audience you have to anticipate where they might look. The first is hard enough (a year later your ideas may have changed) but the second is very hard.

Indexing skills and requirements become more important if you buy an office system which provides facilities for file storage - the equivalent of papers in a folder, folders in a cabinet etc.

Indexing is a time-consuming necessity - sellers don't want to talk about it, and buyers don't appreciate how much time and effort it takes - that is unless they have been trained as librarians or information scientists.

A substantial part of a librarian's training is to do with indexing. Do office workers receive a comparable training? Will they need it when large computerised central filing systems become commonplace? The answer is yes. Have equipment manufacturers made appropriate arrangements with friendly software to assist? Regrettably the answer is usually no.

Serial ordering

A collection of papers ordered by serial number can be used as a record of completeness or as a backup file. I find it convenient to order outgoing paperwork by serial number (which, conveniently, also means chronologically ordered) and keep them in a drawer within reach. A second copy of outgoing letters, reports, etc., is kept, together with incoming letters and other papers, in a separate drawer, ordered by name of organisation.

Provided there is no break in the numbers I know that a copy of all paperwork that I generate must be in the serial file. Such a file works quickly when a phone caller says "Thanks for your letter last week. Regarding the second paragraph....etc". At the same time the file is organised to respond to a question like "To which firms did I write concerning disk-drives about three weeks ago?".

(This little problem of finding things has a lot to do with office protocol. You busy executives will say "my secretary deals with all that". Does she do it in such a way that it is conveniently to hand and easy to use when she is out, or on holiday? Is this because you have not bothered to be interested?)

Copies of the same items are also kept in the organisational file, but the trouble is that some people have addresses like-

> Dr. Abdullah Jones,
> MRC Research Unit,
> Institute of Child Health,
> University of Bishop's Stortford,
> Herts HC1 6BC
> England

Well now, if you lack the luxury of the serial file, should you look under MRC, Institute, Child Health, University, or Bishop's Stortford? Does your secretary ever file under such generalisations as "University" and "Institute"? What kind of an impression is created when you tell the caller that you will phone him back when you've found his letter?

Computer-based personal information systems

For computer-based information systems the principle used in Batten and edge-notched cards can be extended subject only to the ingenuity of designers. One of the earliest systems, called SURF, was in use in 1966 on an IBM 1401 machine. It printed an index from a user's personal choice of terms. When minicomputers, particularly DEC PDP machines, became available, a number of systems were reported.

Beckley and Bleich's "Paper Chase" system, implemented in 1976 primarily to find articles in a collection, is a good example. The program is written in MUMPS for running on a PDP11 or PDP15 machine, and is said to run also on Nova and Eclipse computers. 20 people can use the system simultaneously by time-sharing and the software permits "string matching" – that is any sequence of characters can be searched – for instance COMPUT would find text containing COMPUTER, COMPUTING, TELECOMPUTING etc., and ELECTRON MICROSCOP would find ELECTRON MICROSCOPE, ELECTRON MICROSCOPY etc.

Brief descriptions of articles are input to the machine; during a search, the machine will retrieve those descriptions which match the questions typed in by the searcher and will provide the accession numbers for the corresponding articles. Each user inputs his own material online – the machine calls for information in several <u>Fields</u> – that is the <u>Values</u> of several <u>Attributes</u> must be inserted. The fields are Accession number, Author's names, Title of item, Journal, bibliographic reference, and subject words. Thus the "value" of the "attribute" "Author" might be "Einstein, A.". The accession number is the user's next serial number to be written on to the reprint. He then files the reprint in a drawer by number order.

Any user can search in any collection; the machine will indicate (by accession number) whether a reprint containing the required information is in the user's own office, or whether he has to obtain it from a colleague.

<u>A brief review</u>

Before falling costs made it feasible to consider systems running on a personal computer, people with easy access to mainframes or minicomputers, often in universities, were able to experiment with personal systems and many of their ideas were later implemented on microcomputers. Some early examples are "Paper Chase", just discussed, Famulus, used on CDC, IBM and Univac machines, as described for the indexing and retrieval of information about viral diseases of insects by Matignoni, and Shoebox used by Glantz for office desk-files. A system using a Hewlett Packard 2100 minicomputer for personal indexes in a pharmaceutical laboratory is discussed by Parker and Leggate discusses personal file searching on a PDP 11/20.

Microcomputer systems first caught on in the late 70s. Ideas for moving files about Economics from minicomputers to microcomputers at ILO, Geneva, were outlined by Thompson, and Van Stuyvendale described an RNA phage bibliography of 2000 papers running on a Tektronix 4051 32K micro using magnetic tape storage.

Medical personal information systems have received quite a lot of attention and general applications were discussed by Freamo with many caustic comments about unreliability. Freamo complained that one program had 75 serious errors in it and also complained about the inadequacy of microcomputer servicing arrangements. In another early attempt an Altair 8800 was used by Trobridge, a physician, to maintain patient records and for billing purposes. Another doctor, Glinka, devised a system using an Apple II for displaying the patient schedule over the existing hospital television system and to provide "a dynamic notice board".

Disk storage was soon adopted and used on most post-1979 micros for example with Refles on a TRS80 for an information system in a library, by Bertrand with a bibliographic reference-searching system on an Imsai 8080 micro, one of the first machines with effective disk storage, and by Ross with the LITER Literature reference information retrieval program written in Wang BASIC, on a Wang 2200C.

The PRIMATE/SCIMATE personal information system to be described in greater detail embodies some special features but the facilities exemplify many of the general features of such systems in current use and of the wider class known as "text retrieval" systems.

<u>PRIMATE</u>

In 1977 I developed a system called Primate for the Institute for Scientific Information, intended ultimately for commercial sale and general personal use, particularly for records describing scientific articles. It was first used in 1978 on a Processor Technology Sol machine with a 64K memory, and 750K dual disk drive - one of the first machines made in quantity at what was then considered to be a low price.

The software specification for Primate as described by Garfield amd Cawkell was agreed in order that ideally it -

1. Should be primarily for finding information contained
   in a serially numbered associated collection of papers.
2. Must be very easy to use by people with no interest in,
   or familiarity with, microcomputers.
3. Must provide the means of inputting/editing
   self-indexed records with 1500 records per disk (or
   later with 10-20,000 records per Winchester disk).
4. Must indicate all records matching search questions
   with a response time of less than 5 seconds.
5. Must be useable with questions comprising words,
   strings, or word phrases in various combinations.
6. Must embody telecommunication facilities.
7. Must provide for that minimum amount of indexing which
   provides a just acceptable retrieval performance.

<u>Indexing (yet again)</u>

Indexing time is an overhead which must be minimised in a small office otherwise it will be treated as a chore to be done "when time is available". Since time never is available, a quantity of papers will always be in limbo which defeats the object of the system, particularly for fast moving fields. Because Primate was required for a collection of papers of any kind, no fields, forms, divisions, etc., were provided - the inputter was presented with unformatted space in which to insert a document record in whatever format best suited the application. The machine searched all character strings in all records when responding to a question, so the record formed both an index and a description of the article to help the user assess relevance before getting items from the files of papers.

In conventional information systems it often takes rather a long time to find a wanted item so it pays to devote sufficient time to indexing, question formulation etc., in order to minimise time wasting iterations. With Primate the number of hits was indicated very quickly so it was immediately obvious whether the question posed was too narrow or too broad. Since the question could be rapidly re-formulated it mattered less that the first attempt was ill-conceived. The onus of "classical" indexing methods - too time consuming and of little interest to most users - has been transferred to a relatively crude but practical "look and try again" procedure. Even so, it is as necessary as ever to consider synonyms, shades of meaning etc., because the system won't work unless some consideration has been given to these problems.

It was also intended to provide facilities on Primate to assist in accessing large remote databases - such as Science Citation Index, Chemical Abstracts, Biological Abstracts etc. This could be followed by <u>Downloading</u> "hit" records into local storage following a search carried out via a telecommunications link, or, when such services became available, by receiving disks containing relevant information by post.

<u>SCIMATE</u>

     Later Primate was re-written in a transportable language for generally available operating systems to form the basis for a more comprehensive system called Scimate with the following specification -

<u>Personal Data Manager</u>

RECORD   INPUT
 From keyboard or remote computer (via "work" file).
RECORD SEARCHING RATE
 25,000 ch/sec. (Average).
RECORD SEARCHING METHODS
 Searches full text.
 String searching (words with right, left, internal, trun-
   cation; word phrases).
 Boolean AND, ANDNOT, OR, ORNOT. Proximity choice (term A...n words...term B).
SPECIAL FACILITIES
 12,000 words of on-screen "help".
 User-designed field layouts ("templates") selectable from
   stored or newly created layouts.
 Annotatable ("flag") records; print status of annotations.
 Sort by any field.
 Sort/print contents of a selected file using a printable columnar report
   format selectable from format store.

<u>Universal Online Searcher</u>

COMMAND METHOD
 By keying number from menu choice.
AUTOMATIC FACILITIES
 Automatic dial/logon to ISI, Dialog, SDC, BRS, NLM host
   computers.
UNIVERSAL MENU SEARCHING for the above hosts.
 String and Boolean searching (as in offline section).
 Select stored statement from store and search with it.
 Limit search to recent database up-dates.
DOWNLOADING
 Transmit hits back to data manager section.
OTHER FACILITIES.
 Search above hosts using their own search languages.
 Search other hosts using conventional terminal logon and
   own search languages.

     Scimate will run on several popular microcomputers - IBM personal, TRS80, Vectorgraphic, Apple, Kaypro etc., and can also be made to run on other machines   using   CP/M or MSDOS operating systems by <u>Customising</u>. A customisation page displays a series of questions about disk drives and hardware. The answers typed in by the user are permanently incorporated into the software so that each time she switches on, Scimate will run on that machine. The online software includes facilities for auto-dialling via a communications network to access a remote computer and to transmit automatically log-on codes, passwords, telephone numbers, etc., previously placed in local storage by user customisation.

     In the United States, telecomms is relatively well unified and various kinds of modem are available in a highly competitive market, so the autodial and logon facilities can be used. In Europe the situation is different but changing for the better in respect of competitive modem offerings, so the same automatic facilities are gradually becoming feasible.

Menus or direct-entry commands?

This subject is also discussed in Chapter 15. Computer people recode English so they can talk to each other in time-saving jargon and surround themselves in an inpenetrable mystique. They find it particularly hard to ask the question "what level of knowledge can I assume exists in the potential customers who will use my software?" Wrong assumptions about this point or little attention to it are the main reason why people have problems with microcomputers.

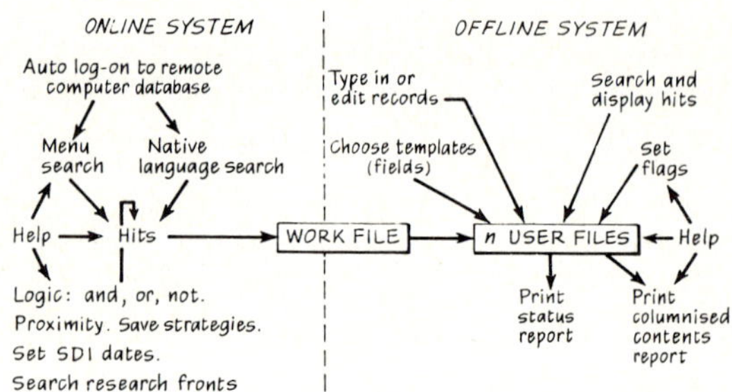

FIGURE 14.1. SCIMATE SOFTWARE ARRANGEMENT

In computer-based information systems designed to be used by information scientists, or by people who are prepared to become trained users, a certain background knowledge plus a desire to get to grips with the software can be assumed.

Instead of the menu arangement designed for the non-computer-buff-non-expert, on which the sofware shown in Figure 14.1 is based, the software could have been designed to respond to direct

    Offline RETURN
    Search Expert or Artificial RETURN
    Display hits RETURN
    Type Report no. 1 RETURN

commands, a sequence of which is shown on the right. The user must then be trained in the use of the format and language permitted, and must type statements precisely in the right order. To the extent that a menu-driven system slows down the expert and does not capitalise on his expertise, menus are time-consuming. Systems are needed which provide "expertise options" so that short cuts are available when the procedures are known.

When carrying out searches on remote databases, a user requires further expertise because he must know the language requirements for the particular software used for each remote database. The Scimate Universal Online Searcher obviates this expertise because a standardised menu language is provided for searching the major databases. The expertise required to cope with this situation has, until now, discouraged users from doing their own searching. They usually ask for it to be done by someone in the library - assuming, of course, that there is a library and there is a someone. But a personal information system is a do-it-yourself service. It may not be needed every day. When it is needed it should deliver the goods with minimum effort. Most people don't care how it's done - they want speed, convenience, and simplicity.

The principle of "menu-driven" operations should be evident from the illustrations in Figure 14.2. The user progresses from the general command "I want to use the Personal Data Manager" to the specific "I want to find a record containing the word "computer" in the file I last used named "Kent"". Computers only recognise exact symbol sequences. If you don't know the required form of command words or miss out a comma, the machine won't work. But in Scimate the user does not need to know that he is required to type "Personal Data manager" or "Pers Dat Man" or "PDM", or "Offline". The objective of the "menu-driven" system is to avoid the need to know about the endless trivialities, jargon, and what-do-I-do-next problems that occur all too often in computer systems.

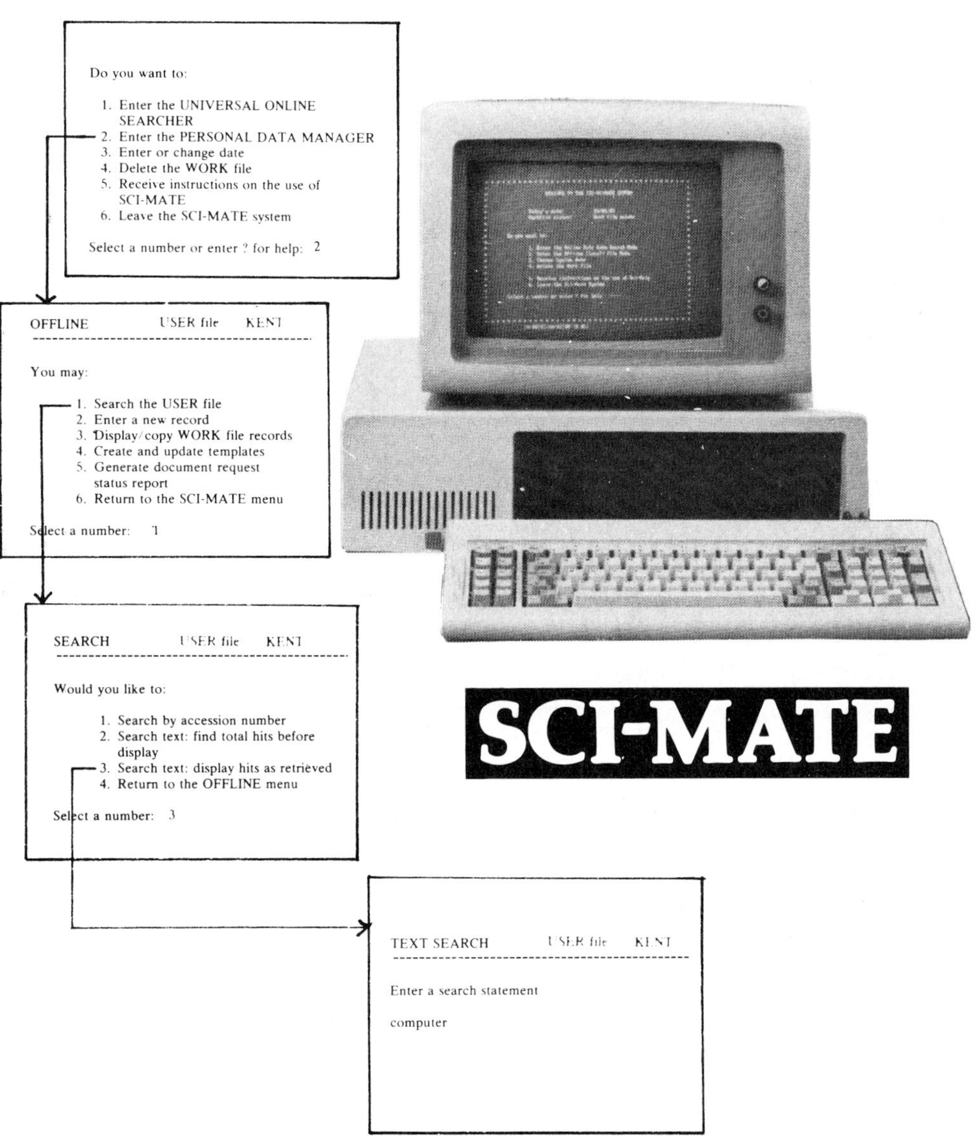

FIGURE 14.2. EXAMPLE OF SCIMATE MENUS

However the lower the user's assumed background of knowledge is set the more the menu becomes cluttered with explanatory material. The Scimate compromise is to back up each menu with "help" material retrieved when "?" is typed. If the user wants more information about the choices offered in the first menu he can type "5". But time consuming simple procedures like this are not needed by the expert who wants to use his knowledge to do rapid searches. More sophisticated user-adaptable software requires more disk space and may also require more space in main memory. This is likely to become available because this space is becoming available in today's micros at a low price.

<u>Searching a remote database; managing "hits"</u>

A "hit" is a record selected from the database for the user's inspection because a term or terms in it match the term or terms in the user's question. When a search is completed a menu appears giving the user various options for hit disposal e.g. sort, display and edit, etc. Meanwhile the hits are stored temporarily in a hit file. A "file" is of course a named addressable space which may be empty or may be occupied with data usually organised in a series of records.

Hits may simply be displayed for inspection, printed in lists, or transmitted down the line into the "Work file" for storage in the microcomputer pending further operations. Once they are in the work file, the line connection can be broken.

<u>The Workfile</u>

The Workfile is reserved for data on its way into or out of the Personal Data Manager ("Offline") section. For example it is used to receive the hits downloaded during an online search. Hits can later be moved into a particular named user file for more permanent storage. The content of a hit varies from database to database. The fields may consist of a number of attributes with their values. Titles, abstracts, or the full text of articles may be included.

<u>User files and associated facilities</u>

User files are collections of records created by the user for various purposes. For example one file, named CATS, might be the owner's index to his collection of manufacturer's catalogues stored in number order on a shelf, each number corresponding to a CATS record number. Each record, might contain four fields - Publication date, manufacturer's name, product name, description. Another, named ENDORPH, might contain records associated with the owner's reprint collection about Endorphins. Yet another, named ADDRESSES, could contain an address list, each record being arranged by fields e.g. name, organisation, street, telephone number etc., maintained on the machine for ease of sorting, printing out an ordered list, or creating hit files e.g "Do I know anyone who works at the University of Wigan?

<u>FURTHER READING</u>

Beckley, Robert F., Bleich, Howard L.
   Computers & Biomed. Research 10, 423-430, 1977.
    Paper Chase; a computer-based reprint storage and retrieval system.
Bivins, Kathleen T.; Palmer, Roger C.
   Online Review 4(4), 357-365, 1980.
    Refles: an individual microcomputer system for fact retrieval.
Bertrand, D.; Bader C.R.
   Int. J. Biomedical Computing, 11, 285-293, 1980.
    Storage and retrieval of bibliographic references using a
    microprocessor system.

Cawkell, Anthony E.
  In 4th International Online Information Meeting, London,
  December 1980. pps 377-386. Pub. by Learned Information
  Ltd., Besselsleigh Rd., Abingdon, Oxford OX13 6EF.
    A personal microcomputer for office use.
Freamo, B.E; Landry M.G.
  CMA Journal 120, 706-708, March 22 1980.
    Do microcomputers have a place in medical practice?
Garfield, E.
  Current Contents, No. 29, July 17, 1978.
    Introducing Primate: personal retrieval of information by
    microcomputer and terminal ensemble.
Glantz, Richard S.
  In Proc. AFIPS 1970 Fall Joint Computer Conference, 37, 535-546, April
  1970.
    SHOEBOX, a personal file handling system for textual data.
Glinka, Steven J.
  J. Family Practice 11(4), 643-645, 1980.
    Use of a microcomputer in a family practice residency.
Leggate, P., Eaglestone, B.M. et al.
  Aslib Proc., 29(2), 56-66, February 1977.
    An on-line system for handling personal data bases on a PDP 11/20
    microcomputer.
Martignoni, Mauro E.; Williams, Patricia; Reineke, Dorothy E.
  J. Invert. Pathol. 22(1), 100-107, July 1973.
    Computer-based catalog of viral diseases of insects: a FAMULUS
    application.
Parker, Ian M.; Thorpe, Peter.
  Program 13(1), 14-22, January 1979.
    GRIP - a personal online indexing system using a minicomputer.
Ross, John D.
  Agricultural Engineering 60(10), 16-17, November 1979.
    LITER: A literature reference information retrieval
    program.
Thompson, George K.
  J. Information Science, 1, 203-207, 1979.
    Data entry using microcomputers: an experimental file of the International
    Bibliography of Economics.
Trobridge, G.F.
  CMA J. 119, 770-772, October 7th, 1978.
    Use of a microcomputer in a three physician practice.
Van Styvendale, B.J.H.
  Meth. Inform. Med. 18(3), 158-164, March 1979.
    The making of an RNA phage bibliography with personal information
    retrieval by micromputer.

CHAPTER 15. THE MAN-MACHINE INTERFACE.

Eight years ago a review article appeared in Science by Holt and Stevenson which is as relevant today as when it was written. The authors refer to the three problem areas cited by Licklider, computer communications pioneer, back in 1960 - the speed-cost/response-time problem, the physical interface (terminal), and the language mismatch. While there have been many improvements in the first two, there are still major problems with the third. The preparation and debugging of programs is still in the category of a cottage craft and the machine-to-user sub-system is left to the last minute and given little or no consideration. In the worst cases the software is simply turned over to the clients who attempt to fit in the people functions in some way, often with disastrous results.

Miller et al have commented on a different aspect of human-computer interaction. The target user is primarily someone who is not a computer professional, but one who interacts with a computer to achieve specific goals of any nature - in fact your general man-in-the-street user. There are two kinds of human activity of particular interest - routine tasks, and problem solving. Great attention must be given to behavioural issues when nothing is known about the user. The variability of response time delays, not their magnitude, is often the most distressing factor.

Defaults

The allocation of default values is a concept which should be extended. The use of defaults constitutes an agreement between user and computer as to what his "normal" or "usual" working environment might be. A default setting is an arrangement which automatically sets up a number of parameters to make the machine ready for the required average task.

Users can have separate profiles of defaults which are appropriate to different tasks. An example of a default profile for writing this book on the machine I am using now, would be for it to be set to 12 pitch characters, 9/64th inch interline spacing, 80 character columns and 60 line pages. When switched on it always sets itself to these "normal" characteristics, any of which can be changed later as necessary. Moreover I can call up a file from the word processor package's dictionary which I have previously created, to set up the machine with a different set of characteristics - for example to print a two column format with columns of specific widths. This kind of thing is a great time-saver because the page layout for a particular requirement need be worked out only once and may be immediately recalled for use at any time.

Incomprehensible instructions

Human - machine communication problems have been well described by Hayes et al who provide examples of the kind of thing with which all computer users must be familiar. The user wants to find out whether he has received any messages from Robertson since May 15 on his electronic mail system. He selects the "headers" command which makes the machine print out incoming messages, by typing:-

"Headers from ROBERTSON since May 15"

The system responds that this message is "illegal" but it is moderately informative about the details, stating:-

"illegal sequence at "from" - missing quoted string
from ROBERTSON since MAY 15".

What this supposedly helpful information turns out to mean is:-

            Put quotes round "ROBERTSON"
                and "MAY 15".

The user does this having first unsuccessfully put quotes round "ROBERSON since MAY 15" with no result, and the machine responds with:-

"illegal sequence at since junk at end from "ROBERTSON" since "MAY 15".

The user is now so intimidated that he really does need " help!". He calls up the help screen which is voluminous, particularly in connection with "since". He reads it all, can't understand what to do and goes off to talk to someone better versed in the folklore of the system. It turns out that the correct version is:-

        "Headers from "ROBERTSON" intersect since "MAY 15".

The "ideal" (but non-existent) instructions (claim Hayes et al in their article) which the user really needs are:-

"Two message set descriptors must be separated by a binary set operator:-

        1. Intersect - only the messages in both sequences.
        2. Union - all the messages in either sequence.
    3. Difference - the messages in the first set but not the second.

            Which one? (1, 2, 3, abort)."

But for whom are these "ideal" instructions? Hayes is (presumably) referring to a university audience but I don't believe these instructions will be understood by the majority of that audience. They are certainly far from ideal for ordinary people, businessmen, etc. What percentage of these audiences understand what a "binary operator" is? The above sequence of exchanges shows how much care is needed in just this one narrow area of the man-machine interface.

Software to enable a user to address a machine in conversational English is not yet available. Users have usually to take a course of instruction on the necessary procedures, and most are evidently not prepared to take time out for such a course. For instance scientists usually ask someone skilled in the procedures to handle online database sessions to locate articles about research topics.

<u>Forcing formal communication</u>

Some attempts have been made to ease this problem for the more stereotyped kinds of questions. For example IBM offers a package based on Zloof's "Query by Example" work. This system is an attempt to simplify the data entry problem in offices, and also to instruct a machine automatically to take action when it receives certain types of information, eliminating the need for some kinds of user-machine sessions.

Information is conveyed to a user by the display of a form containing column headings already completed, or blank spaces for headings to be inserted. If a user enters a "constant" element such as "P" (Print) and an "example" element <u>N</u> (meaning names) in the form shown in Figure 15.1 (top), together with the "example" element "Lee" in the "MGR" column, this is equivalent to typing the request "Print a list of the names of the people who work in Lee's department"

In some word processing machines, a letter or memo can be sent to different people, addresses from a stored list being successively transferred to copies of the letter which are then printed. In Query by Example, form filling can be used to perform this same function, as shown in Figure 15.1 (bottom). The machine has already generated a list of names and addresses of people in Lee's department, and a memo has been typed into the machine as shown. The machine then "maps" data from one form on to a prescribed position on another – in this case a succession of names and addresses from the list into a heading position on successive copies of the memo.

An additional feature of the system is its ability to take action when certain conditions are met. The action to be taken is specified by a "Trigger Expression". Query by Example forms part of an office system, including, say, an electronic mail and inventory control system and Figure 15.2 shows a form which has been completed, embodying a "Trigger Expression" TR1. The meaning of the form is "Check the quantity of pens in stock daily, and if the quantity falls below 500, send an order for 500 more to Henry". Although the form layout implicitly conveys much information, the user must know of certain rules to be able to compose such a form, and the system must include both the means of monitoring stocks, and a communications system to deliver messages.

Although procedures of this kind will save time and reduce costs and a lot can be done to make systems easier for office workers to use, training will be needed for people to be able to cope with relatively complex operational sequences.

NAME	MGR
P.$\underline{N}$	Lee

NAME: $\underline{N}$

LOC: $\underline{L}$

Subject: Vacation plans

This is to inform you that I'll be going on vacation from 5/5/79 to and including 5/15/79. David Jones will be Acting Manager in my absence, and all questions should be directed to him.

Earl Lee

FIGURE 15.1 "QUERY BY EXAMPLE" FORM

INVENTORY	ITEM	QUANTITY
TR1(DAILY)	PEN	<500

ORDER

Please order 500 Pens

Lee

SEND (TR1) ORDER TO HENRY

FIGURE 15.2 "QUERY BY EXAMPLE" FUNCTIONS

Presumably the cost of the system is justified partly by the reduced knowledge/skill needed by users, and the shorter time needed to do a job, and partly because the inclusion of inventory and communications automates time-consuming work which costs money. These days Zloof would probably go with the fashion and re-title his work "Query by Example - An Expert System for Office

Use". More information about expert systems is given in Chapter 12.

<u>Words and meaning; Novices and Experts</u>

The designer who is responsible for writing the software must obviously make some assumptions about the user's behavioural and linguistic ability but it is not helpful when he assumes, as is often the case, that the user understands computerese and is an experienced terminal operator. In fact most people won't normally use words like "module", "spool", etc., or may attribute to them quite a different meaning. Communication requires that an appeal is made to some assumed body of underlying knowledge that will enable the user to fill in the missing parts.

As soon as possible but certainly before making final decisions on manuals, prompts, and menus, at least one or two representatives of the intended user population should read through the material and mark every word they do not understand. This sounds incredibly obvious but does not seem often to be done. It must have something to do either with the computer man's need to cultivate a jargon mystique, or his arrogant attitude towards non-computer-buffs whom he thinks should speak computerese instead of English.

Apart from the language itself the intent of a displayed message should be clear. A message may be meant to inform about an error, or about the state of the operation, or it may be a prompt or is intended to provide feedback . For example the terseness of the message "Display Device Number" may lead to ambiguities. Is it a prompt to enter a number? Is the system about to display a number? Did the user input something now classified as a device number? Has the user inadvertently chosen the menu item "Display Device Number"? etc.

Dean suggests how a computer should talk to people. One reason why some systems contain bad messages may be that "message" has come to mean a terse one-liner that people are not expected to understand without an explanation. But a message whose meaning has to be explained does not communicate - it fails as a message. Owen provides some good advice about setting human goals for messages, but does not mention a likely reason for the use of one-liners. System designers are constrained by storage/programming considerations, particularly with microcomputers, and these constraints outweigh user-friendly considerations.

Designers of computer/software application packages need to ask themselves by what kind of people is the package likely to be used? For example the people likely to use an hotel-desk room availability system could be narrowly defined. On the other hand the range of knowledge and needs of users of a statistics package would be hard to assess.

Explanations and language which may have been helpful initially may later seem to be over-long or devious. The design of many current computer systems is based on the assumption that there is a single ideal system which can satisfy all users, but it is doubtful that any single system can achieve this ideal.

There appear to be two distinct groups, one containing sophisticated or frequent users and the other unsophisticated, infrequent, or novice users. These groups differ in both their competence and their demands on the computer system. Black and Sebrechts point out that there are two types of flexibility that need to be considered - between-group and within-group flexibility. The first concerns the extent to which the system is capable of differential response to two groups of users, but for an unsophisticated within-group user a highly constrained system might be the best: such a user may simply be unable to deal with a large number of options.

It would be worthwhile to have a system which could respond to different levels of user ability. The design of such systems, however, first requires an analysis of how the "level" of a user can be determined. This is an area within which there has been little experimental research in either applied or basic psychology.

<u>Menus, commands, and ikons</u>

A menu is a list of command choices displayed on a CRT screen. The user is asked to select one. Often the choices are numbered and the user is simply asked to key the number. Figure 15.3 shows menus used with one experimental small database out of about 100 available on Prestel in its early days. The user has no chance to generate commands which may not be understandable to the machine. The machine proceeds from menu to menu down the tree. Whether the words chosen for presentation to the user are unambiguous and convey to him or her what was intended by the "indexer" (yes, there still is one, because this is a menu-driven index) is another matter.

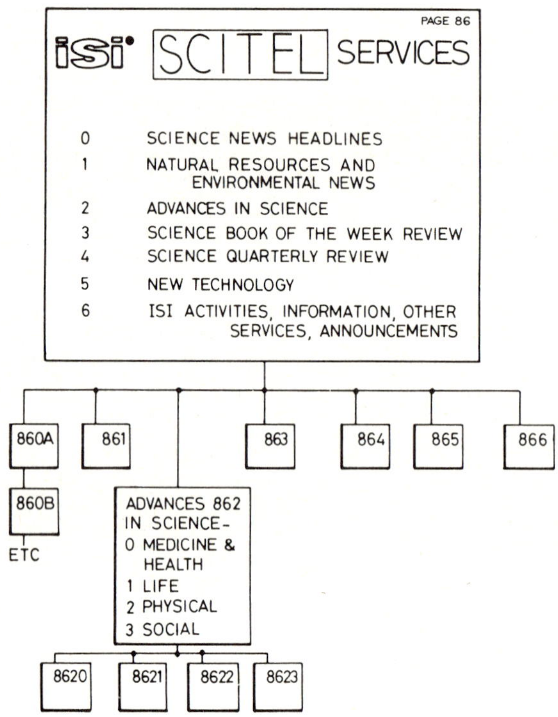

<u>FIGURE 15.3. INDEX AND MENU TREE IN PRESTEL SCITEL SERVICE</u>

This is a simple way of forcing unambiguous selections to proceed from the general to the particular. The viewer will have started with a menu sub-dividing the entire database into 10. Having selected 8 – "science", and then, from the alternatives offered, 86 for Scitel, the first page shown in figure 15.3 appears. Keying 2 takes the viewer to 862 "Advances in science", and 2 again to 8622 "Physical Sciences" comprising 10 headlines. A choice of one of these leads to the required information itself – on pages 86221a, 86221b, 86221c....etc., 86222a...n, 86223a...n, etc., (not shown in the figure). Thus the viewer gets to the page he wants by 5 1-out-10 choices to pinpoint one out of 100,000 pages. Alternatively if he already knows that "Physical Sciences" is on 8622, he can key that number direct.

WHAT BOOK DO YOU WANT TO RESERVE?
? least of the mohicans

'LEAST OF THE MOHICANS' IS NOT IN OUR CATALOG.
TYPE 'QUIT' OR GIVE ANOTHER TITLE.
? last of the mohicans

WHAT IS THE PATRON'S NAME AND ADDRESS?
? natty bumpo
  25 sycamore street
  wilderness, ny 00010

RESERVATION NOTED.
BOOK SHOULD BE AVAILABLE BY 09/28/82.

TYPE 'MORE' TO RESERVE ANOTHER BOOK, OR
TYPE 'DONE' TO END THIS SESSION.
?done

FIGURE 15.4. MENU DIALOGUE AND MODEL

Figure 15.4, after Casey et al. is more typical of the kind of menu encountered in information service systems. In this case the user is invited to choose one of five library services. The user, rejoicing in the name of Mr. Natty Bumpo, then enters into a brief dialogue with the machine.

If the designer creates a model in the manner shown in the figure, it will focus attention on the necessary functions. One requirement is the need for "validity checkpoints" during the dialogue, such as "correct title".

Menus are largely replaced by a different technique in the software supplied with machines like Star, Lisa, and MacIntosh. The comments made earlier about novices and experts may need to be revised for these systems.

Ramsey and Grimes consider that in object/action systems where graphical ikons are used to represent manipulable objects, the user simply selects the object desired for manipulation and proceeds to manipulate it; the many studies to do with cursor controlled keys, fonts, selection of command names, length and breadth of menus etc., may be rendered obsolete by these changes in technology.

More difficult abstract studies may be needed. Cognitive modeling - that is the way in which a human perceives, processes, and stores information, may be the way to go. They regard the work being done at Xerox by Stuart Card and others as being particularly interesting. The so-called "user conceptual" model is another promising example of psychological models leading to the possibility that the relationships between the user's mental model, the user conceptual model, and the actual system design might be

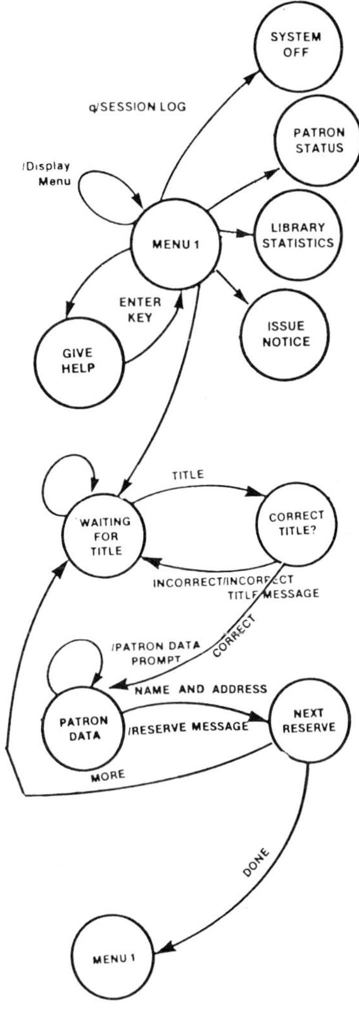

subject to analysis and even stimulation.

Menu design, and the presentation of text on a CRT generally, has received particular attention in word processing systems. Menus need to be simple and consistent in layout. Thus in Figure 15.5 (from Helander), the available commands are displayed for the most frequently used requirements and bear a logical relationship to the user's experience. The arrangement of the display is always consistent - instructions top left, commands in two half display columns,status line near the bottom and a "services line" at the bottom.

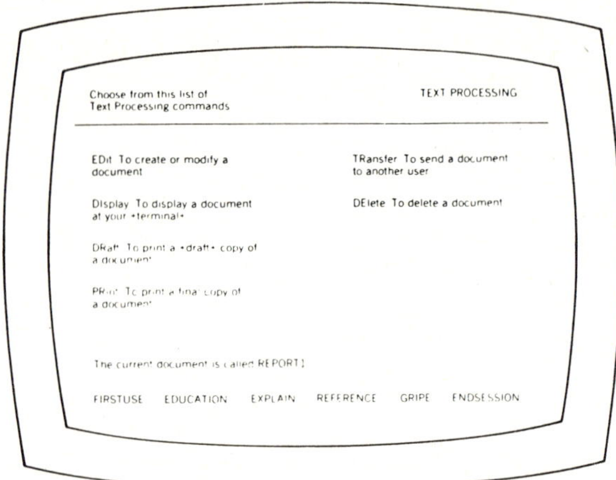

FIGURE 15.5. WORD PROCESSING MENU LAYOUT

A user types a command-object phrase - for instance "ED REPORT 1". If she cannot remember the name of the object with which she wishes to work she uses a "*". Thus to edit such an object the command "ED *" produces a display of document names previously allocated. The author goes on to describe displays packed with more information for experienced users. The kind of menu and the procedure just described would probably irritate the user as she becomes more experienced.

Response times

Response time is an important consideration. Response times are usually a compromise between system complexity/cost and user tolerance. "Acceptable" response times could be written on to the model in Figure 15.4 as a design reminder. These days users expect rapid response of not more than a few seconds in a dialogue situation, or some indication that "something is happening" if the machine is processing a large volume of data and will take longer.

For some functions which take a relatively long time - for instance housekeeping activities like disk copying - the user may be able to do something else if he knows that the operation will exceed a minute or two. It may be possible to present monitoring information so that the user can stop the processing if the information indicates it is unsatisfactory so that he does not need to wait for completion. An example is the display of a runnng count of "hits" during online searching.

In most large information retrieval systems, response times depend on the efficiency of the software, the size of the database being searched and the number of people searching it at one time. At peak periods the system may be unacceptably slow - a problem usually resolved by spending more money on disk storage and the means of accessing the contents. The same remarks apply to communicating office systems which include LANs, and shared resources such as message services and central filing systems.

It may not be clear whether annoyingly long delays are to be expected in PBX or local network systems either at first installation, or when more users and resources are added later. This will depend on the method

adopted for communication control, the bandwidth of the channel, the number
of users, and the extent to which each user has local storage or relies
extensively on centralised remote storage.

Human factors

Humans interact with machines at several levels all of which have
received considerable attention. These levels start with physical contact with
machines, but then move away to subtler and more important emotional effects
like values, expectations, and hopes and fears.

First, there is the direct contact with Cathode Ray Tube terminals and
keyboards. Various keyboard designs have been tried, so have writing tablets.
Many aspects of CRT displays have been investigated including screen size
and capacity, character size, shape, and spacing, the use of colour and
graphics, screen phosphors, resolution, focus, contrast, brightness and flicker
as discussed in Chapter 4.

Next, various so-called human factors have been studied, such as visual
and postural strain, stress, amd the effect of the working environment. It
turns out that the X-ray radiation scare from high voltage CRTs was probably
unfounded. It seems that working at a terminal produces no effects that do
not also characterise other forms of sedentary work requiring concentration.
However these effects have been looked at in more detail because more and
more people are working with machines. Many of them are covered in a short
clear review article by Wheatley.

Displays

There are several factors which contribute to the presentation of
electronically generated data in a pleasing, familiar, legible way, drawing
inevitability from the accumulated experience with print on paper. Since the
CRT is still so widely used, this discussion will be confined to CRT viewing,
although some intensive work is in progress to replace it by other forms of
display.

For characters, size, shape, colour, form of construction, contrast and so
background versus character colour, height to width ratio, and brightness all
play a part. For other images, resolution – that is the size of each element of
the image, and the reproduction of half tones or colour, are important.

The devising of algorithms which can be used to transform
continuous tone and half tone images into coded representation for computer
storage and processing – in other words "image digitisation" or "picture
processing", an important subject, has been reviewed by Stoffel and Moreland.
Images present special problems in terms of standardisation of formats and
information retrieval. They are usually generated in one of two formats –
vector or raster. Vector means line plotting – for instance in geographic
images, areas are represented by their boundaries. Raster is the result of
the more familiar line by line scanning process.

An image database presents special retrieval problems which are being
solved using relational database techniques or hierarchical systems using
attributes like shape, symbolic description, and relationship with other
objects, as very well reviewed by Chang and Kunii.

The cheapest form of display uses only one colour as determined by the
choice of the fluorescing phosphor deposited on the glass screen. The phosphor
glows with a colour according to its chemical composition when struck by
electrons. Popular colours include white, yellow, blue and green. A
variation, without the addition of an extra colour, can be produced by

reversal e.g. white characters on a black background can be changed to black on white.

Another technique coming into quite wide use, particularly for office systems, involves the generation of symbols such as folders, mailboxes, etc., - the "ikons" mentioned earlier - together with paper-like areas of the screen which can be stored and retrieved by the "sheet" and produce a familiar print-on-paper effect. These developments, which nearly always require that more data (bits) be displayed at one time, have been accompanied by other improvements such as smaller CRT spot sizes, higher resolution, more storage, faster information processing, and faster throughput (i.e. wider bandwidth).

Further information is provided in Chapter 4, and the whole question of handling and displaying information is discussed by Smura in Chapter 43 of this book.

<u>Displaying text and graphics</u>

10 or 12 point type is commonly used for typewriters and computer printers, but the usual 7 x 9 element characters in CRT displays are somewhat larger.

Experiments have been carried out to see if these characters - typically about 0.135 in. high - could be reduced to 0.1 in. approximating to 12 point type without errors arising from legibility. A statistically significant increase in errors was found when reading lower case characters of the smaller size but this could probably be ignored in practice; it would be counterbalanced by contextual clues in normal text. Presumably a still smaller size would result in an excessive error rate.

The comprehension of displayed messages has also received attention. For example sequences, "chunks", or lines have been tested. How many units of information should there be in a message and what should be the presentation rate - the time allowed for reading a word? This question was considered in the context of drivers looking at computer generated displays on motorways, but it could be applicable when considering the best form of presentation for rapid CRT viewing.

A chunk is a complete thought understandable without reference to another part of a message. It usually consists of about four words con- taining two units of information e.g. "Lane closed at Borden". To complete the message a second sequence might follow, say "Use A37 instead". As an alternative, a message composed of line sequences consisting of a series of separated two-word noun-verb combinations such as "Merge right" "At Dover" "Traffic exit" could be used. Combining words and presentation time it was found that two-unit messages of four words could be recalled following 1 second exposure times. However messages twice as long (four-unit messages) required 4 seconds exposure time.

Speed and accuracy tests have also been carried out, this time using CRTs, on several kinds of presentation - narrative, tabular, and half tone and black and white graphics. Questions were displayed one at a time at the bottom of the screen for which an answer existed in the main body of the display. Subjects responded by pointing to the answer with a light pen.

The response times for graphics were significantly faster than they were when the same information was displayed in narrative and tabular format. Colour added to the graphics made no difference; the response accuracy was about the same for all formats. Seven out of eight subjects said they would prefer to work with colour graphics. However it was concluded that tabular or structured text was the best compromise between costs and human performance. Further tests on carefully arranged textual data with key information shown prominently, and other data logically chunked produced improved performance, but at a considerably lower cost than the preparation and system cost of the graphics.

<u>Scrolling</u>

For <u>scrolling</u> or <u>windowing</u> two different techniques are used to look at text "beyond the limits of the edge of the screen". In most systems, more text is moved from disk to memory than can be displayed on the screen at one time and so is immediately available for scrolling or windowing. Scrolling is usually defined as apparently moving the text behind a stationary aperture. Windowing is apparently moving the aperture over a stationary area of text. Which technique is usually expected, how should instructions, the use of arrowed keys etc., be explained, and which is usually preferred?

In tests carried out with a large number of subjects arrowed keys indicating up, down, left and right were provided. If a subject pressed the left pointing arrow to view data concealed off-left, then that is windowing. Pressing the right pointing arrow is scrolling. The tests were quite detailed and the results showed that with windowing, data was found faster and with fewer moves.

<u>Effects, attitudes and aspirations</u>

<u>Stress</u>

Computer systems should be designed to minimise the stresses in a working day. The length of a time cycle associated with a job and the anticipation of system delays are said to be factors affecting stress. This leads to the possibility of allowing for, minimising, or even introducing delays in self-paced and computer-paced tasks.

In an attempt to determine the requirements for office work stations, the work of secretaries and their preferences were investigated by Bullen. Secretaries are involved in two kinds of work - set tasks standardised through policy, tradition, or equipment constraints, and self-initiated work reflecting increased responsibility and creativity. In contrast to the conventional findings, it is claimed that manager's secretaries work on self-initiated tasks more than half the time, and other secretaries for 10 to 50 per cent of it.

Of the work requiring typing, 90% prefer a WP/terminal system for most work, but all prefer a typewriter for form filling or short jobs. Of the things they would like changed or easing for terminal work, first came training, then response time, printer problems and the need to have the printer close by, then difficulties in proof reading vertically displayed text and a need for less cumbersome portable terminals occupying less desk top space. One of the things secretaries like best is the computer-based message system with which they inform each other when they are away from their desks, request printed documents to be collected etc.

<u>Social politics</u>

Mumford et al feel that the notion of having a computer system imposed upon you at your place of work may invoke some kind of Big Brother syndrome. They present a plea for the participative approach as opposed to imposition by management dictat.

"System design can be improved through the participation of the people who will eventually use the system if they can be provided with the necessary skills...people have a moral right to influence the organisation of their own work situations and if that right is conceded then there is likely to be both job satisfaction and efficiency gains...we are suggesting that the technical and user groups associated with the introduction of a new computer system are unlikely to have a complete identity of interest and may have major conflicts of interest".

The laudable aims of these ideas are accompanied by a degree of naivety. The tentative comment about technical and user groups could be replaced by the comment "it is unlikely that the technical and user groups will have anything in common". However the article does contain much good advice which, highly compressed, means "you are likely to do better if you consult, pursuade, and carry people along with you, than if you impose without consultation.

The "failure of a management information system" (Fernandez) supposedly introduced according to the principles of maximum involvement and minimum disruption, supports this advice. Two years after implementation of the system in question, 27% of centres involved had adequate records compared with 80% 6 months after starting. Regional directors rarely, if ever, used the data to facilitate a decision.

When clerical staff became unable to input the required volume of data "the computer programs were converted and moved from one type of machine to another...leading to delays and errors in the production of reports with the result that feedback was considerably disrupted". The causes? "If any single cause had to be pinpointed as a major contributor to the failure of the MIS it would be the lack of support from management. Many of the other difficulties could have been worked out or weathered if management had maintained a commitment to getting and using the data - with the emphasis on using.

Typing; reading from a CRT

In an IBM establishment, which may not be typical, referred to by Bullen, there was no reluctance to use the new technology nor, says the author, was there any reluctance by professional staff to enter their own documents into the system, presumably implying that most of them could type. This question of the need to acquire the ability to type seems to be rarely mentioned. Perhaps it is possible to obtain sufficient benefits out of a computer system by one finger pecking;, anything in the way of text typing is simply passed on to a typist.

The question of division of "input" labour is an interesting one. If an executive learned to type and had the necessary equipment to hand, would he/she consider greater use of that equipment an efficient use of his/her time?

Turning to reading text from a CRT, this is a matter about which there seem to be differences of opinion. Visual fatigue has been reported by Mourant et al. Viewing a CRT is more fatiguing than using hard copy. 2 to 3 hours produces fatigue which is "readily reversible when breaks are provided". However Mourant et al conclude that people can read continuous text on a television screen for two hours without undue discomfort, although they read more slowly than people reading the same material in book form. For reading from the TV the presence or absence of proportional horizontal spacing made no difference to speed or comprehension.

Another result of this experiment was that there was no difference in people's preference for reading a book or a CRT. This seems extraordinary. One explanation may be that there was too much scientific and insufficient humanistic consideration in this investigation. The questions were addressed to reading per se - but other factors such as convenience, aesthetics, browsing, scanning and skipping, cost, availability etc., will affect people's conclusions in a real world. Nor can I imagine how the imaginative, meditative, or pensive state induced by a book could be induced by a Cathode Ray Tube. Nor is a CRT with rows of titles projected upon it a replacement for the promise conveyed by rows of books on their shelves.

In mundane terms, reading may be regarded simply as a means of acquiring information. Personally I find that the reading of print on paper is better in this respect as well.

Social consequences

The realisation that much more work needs to be done on the human-machine interface has certainly dawned and there are commercial incentives to drive the work along. However if machines become really easy to use, the potential for their use by everybody, not just the 0.1% of computer buffs, raises the possibility that knowledge could become more readily available, thereby diminishing the information have and have not division. However it seems more likely that this division will be brought about by economic differences, and there is little evidence to suggest that these will be solved by clever machines. The inability of people to pay for information obtainable via easy to use machines will be the reason if this division becomes pronounced.

FURTHER READING

Black, John B., Sebrechts, Mace M.
  Applied Psycholinguistics 2(2), 149-177, 1981.
    An invited article: facilitating human-computer communication.
Bullen, C.V., Bennett, J.C.
  IBM Syst. J. 21(3), 351-369, 1982.
    A case study of office workstation use.
Casey, Bernice E., Dasarathy, B.
  Software Pract. & Exper. 12(6), 557-569, 1982.
    Modelling and validating the man-machine interface.
Cawkell, A.E.
  In 4th International Online Meeting, London. December 1980. Learned
  Information, Abingdon, England. 377-386.
    A personal microcomputer for office use.
Chang, Ski-Kuo; Kunii, Tosigyasu, L.
  Computer 14(10), 13.21, October 1981.
    Pictorial database systems (73 references).
Dean, M.
  IBM Syst. J. 21(4), 424-453, 1982.
    How a computer should talk to people.
Edwards, Sam.
  Byte 8(12),127-230, December 1983.
    Why is software so hard to use?
Fernandez, Don.
  Admin. in Mental Health 8(4), 286-288, Summer 1981.
    The failure of a management information system: a case study.
Hayes, Phil; Ball, Eugene: Reddy, Raj.
  Computer 14(3), 19-30, March 1981.
    Breaking the man-machine communication barrier.
Helander, G.A.
  IBM Syst. J. 20(2), 294-305, 1981.
    Improved systems useability for business professionals.
Holt H.O., Stevenson, F.L.
  Science, 195, 1205-1209, March 18th 1977.
    Human performance considerations in complex systems.

     Information and Library Science

Lueder, Rani K.
   Human Factors 25(6), 701-711, December 1983.
     Seat comfort: a review of the construct in the office environment.
Miller, Lance A., Thoams, John C.
   Int. J. Man-Mach. Studies 9, 509-536, 1977.
     Behavioural issues in the use of interactive systems.
Monk, Andrew F.
   Int. J. Man-Mach. Studs. 21, 269-277, 1984.
     Reading continuous text from a one-line visual display.
Mourant, Ronald R., Lakshmanan, Raman, et al.
   Human Factors 23(5), 520-540, 1981.
     Visual fatigue and cathode ray tube display terminals.
Mumford, Enid; Hawgood, John.
   Impact Sci. on Soc. 28(3), 235-253, 1978.
     A participative approach to the design of a computer system.
Muter, Paul; Latremouille, Susanne A., et al.
   Human Factors 24(5), 501-508, 1982.
     Extended reading of continuous text on television screens.
Ramsey, Rudy H., Grimes, Jack D.
   In Annual Review of Information Science and Technology, Volume 18, 1983.
   Edited by Martha E. Williams. Knowledge Industry Publications, White Plains,
   NY, 1983. Chapter 2, pps 29-59.
     Human factors in interactive computer dialog.
Rich, Elaine.
   Computer, 39-47, September 1984.
     Natural language interfaces.
Rissland, Edwina I.
   Int. J.Man Mach. Studs. 21, 377-388, 1984.
     Ingredients of intelligent user interfaces.
Zloof, M.M.
   IBM Syst. J. 16(4), 324-332, 1977.
     Query by example: a database language.

CHAPTER 16. ONLINE INFORMATION SYSTEMS AND DATABASES

Computer-based information searches

Searching for information in a computer-stored database can be done by batching, or interactively online.

Batching means collecting together all the terms in queries from a number of users and storing them on cards, tape, or disk. These terms are computer-matched against the terms in database records. When a match occurs, the matching record or hit containing the query term is printed, and hit data records are sorted at the end of the run and sent to the appropriate users. If the results show that a question has been badly formulated, a user has to change it, have it re-inputted, and await the results from the next occasion the database is passed through the computer.

In interactive online searching a user sits at a terminal connected to a computer system in which a database is stored, usually on disks. He types queries and the matching process is rapidly carried out, hits being displayed or printed at the terminal. If the results are unsatisfactory the query may be re-formulated, perhaps more narrowly, and the user tries again, and so on until he gets it right.

Matching usually involves comparing "strings" in questions against strings in database records. A string is a sequence of characters and spaces. Thus COMPUT/ is a string, and if that term is used as a question all database records containing COMPUT/ (e.g COMPUTING, COMPUTER, COMPUTERS, etc.) would be hits. ELECTRONIC MAIL SYSTEM/ is another string.

It seems unlikely that batch searching will be used much in offices. Most people will want to get at "paperwork" quickly and expect an almost immediate response in the form of a display of text. The rate of that response will depend upon many factors, but the ones with which we are here concerned are the ways in which the files are organised for ease of searching and the way in which they are indexed.

Serial searches: surrogates: indexing

Conventional computers are still based on Von Neumann architecture originally designed for arithmetical computation with relatively small amounts of stored data. Applications involving text searching require string comparisons and large amounts of stored data. Most of the software is still written for Von Neumann machines.

One way of searching a database file - a collection of records usually containing textual data - is to arrange for the computer system to search serially through the records for strings matching the query string. In online systems, hits, in the form of complete records, will be transferred to the user's terminal for viewing, or to his printer if he wants a permanent copy. The computer searches through the complete text of records so very high speeds are essential if the database is large. Many databases contain short records describing the actual documents containing the wanted information which the user has to obtain once he has been notified of their existence; the document is represented by a surrogate - that is a short description of it, say one hundredth of its length, consequently the search will be completed relatively quickly.

The surrogate must contain the essence of the document. The document may be of a simple kind e.g. a letter for which addressee details and date may be considered sufficient, or it may be a report, scientific article, or even a

book whose essence must be expressed through its title, keywords, or abstract.
In short, the document will have been _indexed_. If only the title is provided
in the database record, then that is the index - an index which won't
work unless the originator has included explicit words in it or it has been
supplemented by an indexer. Thus the words "The wiring of Britain" may be
satisfactory for a topical magazine article but unhelpful in a title-based
retrieval system for a searcher looking for information about cable television.
Indexing problems are discussed in Chapters 13 and 14.

When searching surrogates, a "hit" is the retrieval of a surrogate
containing elements which match the search question. The viewer has to decide
from the surrogate whether to get the original document. The record containing
the surrogate must contain information about its location. If the document has
been published then the included bibliographic data will enable the user to get
it from the nearest library covering the subject area in question. In a
comprehensive office system the full text of the "document" may be stored
elsewhere and can be "delivered", "page by page" at the user's terminal, in which
case the user will need to know its address. In a microcomputer-based surrogate
personal information system, the "address" of the document could simply be the
serial number of a printed document kept with others on a shelf.

Inverted file systems

Until quite recently, serial searching of full text has been prohibitively
expensive and unacceptably slow. The searching of large surrogate databases has
also been expensive and slow. The inverted file and the multilist or
threaded-list methods are the most widely used out of several which have been
developed for medium to large databases in order to reduce costs and provide
acceptable response times. Lefkowitz has discussed filing systems in depth. The
inverted file seems to have gained widest acceptance and will be described here.

An inverted file is a directory to the keys used in records. A key is simply
a search term such as a word, an author's name, a chemical formula etc. For
example a database might comprise records containing both titles and added
keywords to describe internal company reports, each record containing a shelf
number indicating where the print-on-paper report itself is kept. The principle
was first used in "Uniterm" and "peek-a-boo" manually searchable cards as
described in Chapter 13.

It is the relatively small key directory linked to the records which is
searched by the computer, not the relatively large totality of records. Boolean
searching is often used to make the question more specific - for instance with
a query like "Find records containing ELECTRONIC MAIL _and_ (COST/ _or_ PRIC/)" the
machine is not required to find all records linked to the key ELECTRONIC MAIL,
only those linked to a specific aspect of the subject, namely ELECTRONIC MAIL and
COST, COSTS etc., or ELECTRONIC MAIL and PRICE, PRICES, PRICING, etc. Boolean
algebra, named after mathematician George Boole, is a method of expressing
logical relationships. It is characterised by AND, OR, and other operations for
which computers are eminently suited as described in Chapter 3.

The number of hits found can be displayed without the need for the
records themselves being retrieved so that the user can quickly re-formulate
his question if necessary. For example ELECTRONIC MAIL might retrieve two hundred
hits when the user only wants a few articles about, say, costs and prices.
Re-formulating the question as shown in the preceding paragraph produces, say,
only ten hits. The associated records can be retrieved when wanted because they
are linked to the keys by _"pointers"_. A pointer is simply an address, thus a key
in the directory will consist of the key-symbols (e.g. author's names, subject
words) and the addresses of the records containing those keys.

Penalties are paid for the convenience and operational speed of an inverted file system in terms of software complexity and storage space. Every time a new record is added to the record file its address must also be added to the record addresses already listed with each key in the key directory. If the record contains new keys not already in the directory, these must be entered together with the address of the record with each new key. The key directories occupy considerable storage space. Depending on the diversity of the file this space can approach that needed for the records themselves.

In a batch system a series of records are added and the necessary re-organisation process for all new records is carried out periodically at some convenient time. Until that time the new records are unavailable to users. In inverted file systems which are up-dateable on line there is additional complexity. If the system is simultaneously useable for information retrieval and record up-dating the software and power of the system must be capable of coping with both without much degradation of performance.

STI services: online versus print

The transitional period in the movement from print-on-paper to electronic information is of great interest. This trend has been often heralded.

Online Scientific and Technical Information (STI) services have received considerable attention. The "end product" of most of the larger STI services is a document record. The record may be a short bibliographic description of an article, an abstract, or possibly the full text of the article. Until about 1974, that record, stored at the service centre on magnetic tape and used to ease production processes, was reproduced and sold only as print on paper. Later, the same record might appear in an SDI service offered by the centre , now using the tape for record searches. These services are still available. Later still these machine-readable records on tape, loaded into random-access disks, provided the opportunity for yet another service - an online information service.

Figure 16.1 shows the operational steps originally used by one provider to generate a database from scientific journal articles. The printed products and the SDI service (ASCA) derived from the database are shown.

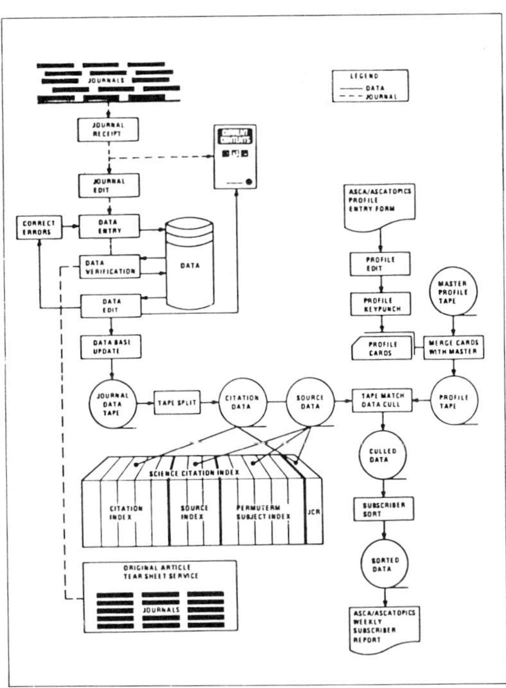

FIGURE 16.1
PRINTED AND SDI SERVICE PROCESSES
(Courtesy of ISI)

The growth of online services has been fostered by bureaux connected to communication networks offering access to databases supplied by a number of different information providers. Collectively these databases represent a large fund of information conveniently available from one source. Each information provider supplies tapes to the bureau who transfers them to disk. Providers earn royalties passed on to them from the bureau from users who log on to their databases. In the first phase of these operations the royalties provided extra revenue at low cost. The costs of data preparation had already been recovered in the sale of printed products. During the second phase, now in progress, users are realising that buying specific information, available on a pay-as-you-go on-demand basis, may be more effective and more convenient than buying that same information as part of a print on paper service for shared use (say in a library).

Several factors need considering if the two alternatives are to be evaluated - timeliness, convenience, availability of current year's and earlier year's data, individual cost recovery for on line searching versus communal cost recovery for large printed indexes etc. If there is no net loss of revenue to the information provider in consequence of any shift from print to online, then he need have no cause for concern. However losses seem to be occurring although it is controversial whether this is solely due to "migration" from print. Perhaps providers have been slow in facing up to this situation and bringing forward remedies.

Table 16.1 compares prices for looking up items in a printed and online directory, excluding the cost of the user's time. Online scores heavily for occasional use. Assuming three minutes of online time is paid for at each lookup, about 50 lookups could be carried out for the price of buying the directory. For heavier use the printed directory obviously wins because of its once-only purchase price. Timeliness is not considered, but for a directory of changeable airline departure times, the frequency of the need for a new edition becomes a consideration. The online user has the assurance of currency.

One million word directory: number of lookups per year/Price $

Database (at 3 mins. per lookup)	10/27.6	30/82.8	50/138.0
Printed version.	10/140	30/140	50/140

TABLE 16.1. PRINT VERSUS ONLINE PRICE COMPARISON

Information about useage and growth of online services and databases is given in the database section later in this chapter.

Using an online system

Unless you are professionally occupied with the activity, online systems, like many other Information Technology (IT) activities, are a hassle. True to form, the popular representation of "information from all over the world at the touch of a button" is, for most people, nonsense.

The basic question that the non-professional must ask himself is "how long in the first place will it take me to get my system to work and understand how to do it?" ("it" is shown in Table 16.2). For most people, the actual time/cost of this exercise, if realistically costed, is likely to be far higher than the running costs of the equipment. Of course some people will not enter the field "cold". A friend or colleague who is doing it may be a short cut to the acquisition of knowledge. Even assuming that all equipment, software, and telecommunication problems have been solved, someone is on hand to tell you what to do, and you only need to connect to one database running on one host computer, it will still take time to find out how to pose the right questions in order to get the right answers.

These comments may be an over-generalisation because it depends what online system we are talking about. The phrase "online system" now covers a very wide spectrum. Looked at from another viewpoint, and bearing in mind your occupational needs, the benefits to be obtained from using a system may easily outweigh your investment in equipment and knowledge acquisition.

<u>Explanation</u>   <u>Online dialogue</u>
                                              (Underlined items typed by user)

Activate telecoms software.
Dial number of PSS node.
Place telephone in acoustic coupler.
Press RETURN twice, then terminal
          identifier and RETURN -   <u>CR CR D1 CR</u>
Alternatively to above, use auto-
  matic facilities if you have them.
PSS Pad acknowledges -   LON/A03-92200404
Network user's identifier code -   <u>NUBD1RP896HK CR</u>
Invitation to continue -   ADD?
Network and Host computer address -   <u>A942203030002 CR</u>
Acknowledgement -   3410203030002+
Host connects -   216 18 CONNECTED
Password echoed back but obliterated   Enter your Dialog Password
          for security reasons -   <u>XXXXXXXX</u>
User asks for file 7 -   ? Begin <u>7</u>
Alternatively to above, use auto-
  connect software if you have it.
Host computer logs on and confirms   1Apr85 14.30 User 5702
          database is available -   File 07 Social Scisearch
User asks how many records   Set items description
          containing the word Aged? -   ? <u>$ Aged</u>
Computer replies to first question -   1 893 Aged
How many containing Elderly? -   ? <u>$ Elderly</u>
Item 2 786 -   2 786 Elderly
                                             ? <u>Combine 1 or 2</u>
                                             3 1679 1 or 2
                                             ? <u>$ Isolat</u>
                                             4 1060 Isolat
How many containing (Elderly or   ? <u>Combine 3 and 4</u>
          Aged) and Isolat? -   5 15 3 and 4
Type, using format 3/5, the first   ? <u>Type 3/5/1-2</u>
          two records -   1 711447 Editorial Oats order CX481
Machine sends the records down the   2 refs.
          line -   Congregate housing can shield eld-
                                             erly from isolation while keeping
                                             them out of institutions
                                             Geriatrics V32 N2 P16 1977
                                             2 690054 Article Oats order CK269
                                             13 refs
                                             Hospital home health-care program
                                             aids isolated
                                             Brickner PW; Janeski JF; Duque T
                                             Chelsea Village Program, New York,NY
                                             J Amer Hosp Assoc V50 N21 P67-86 1976
User ends session -   ? <u>Logoff</u>
Host supplies details -   1Apr85 14.40 User 5702
                                             $3.50 0.08 Hrs File 7
                                             Logoff 14.40

<u>TABLE 16.2. A COMPLETE SESSION ONLINE TO A REMOTE DATABASE FROM THE UK</u>

The example of a complete small online session in Table 16.2 shows what happens when you put questions to the Lockheed Dialog host computer in

California. Dialog runs a very large number of databases covering a huge range of subjects. It is assumed that you possess a terminal or microcomputer and modem, that it has been correctly connected to a line to the PSTN, and that you are a UK resident who has already made the necessary prior arrangements with British Telecom to access the Packet Switched System (PSS), and with Lockheed. It will be much cheaper to use PSS than to dial Dialog direct.

The database used provides bibliographic information about any articles containing the strings which match the question strings. The user can order the actual articles from the database supplier through a tearsheet service (once called OATS, now called The Genuine Article — hence the reference number for ordering), or get them from a library.

The knowledge which the user must possess to participate in this session will be fairly obvious. You may also have noticed that the user has made no mistakes which prompt a corrective response. In fact a wrongly typed code will be followed by some kind of request to repeat, and wrong procedures in database questions may or may not be followed by a helpful response. However it is not this kind of mistake which is the problem. the real problem is contained in the "what do I do next" syndrome when nothing happens and it appears that you have done everything correctly. You must then know how to proceed through a process of elimination in order to locate the fault.

On one occasion I could not get a response from PSS. Everything seemed to be OK. The modem "data" and "carrier on" indicator lights showed that my micro was outputting pulsed data and that "handshaking" with PSS had taken place. I then systematically worked through everything — baud rates, parity, procedures, re-check on telephone number, telecoms software etc etc. After an hour's work with no result I telephoned BT to ask if they would check at their end for data coming from my telephone line. I was told, with BT's regrets, that there was a technical problem at their end — but the <u>real</u> problem was that BT's problem did not result in the transmission of a message stating that there was a problem!

<u>Expert systems</u>

The term "expert system" in the online area is analogous to calling a man who repairs watches a horological technologist. However this phrase and another which is sometimes used, "gateway software", has apparently come to stay.

Shepherd and Watters, in describing their own attempt at easing the man-machine problem, briefly review other similar systems such as the MIT Conit, Scimate, Messidor, and Userlink. They also mention C.T. Meadow's comprehensive exposition about his experiments with an expert system. These systems assist a user to login, transmit commands, and search, by storing a collection of frequently used code sequences which may be recalled and transmitted by depressing one or two keys. They also store information about the commands needed to search a range of databases in order to translate the variations into a standard language available to the user. Consequently the user does not have to learn about the pecularities of each database when he searches it.

These systems are designed for information-conscious people who are already library users and would like to use online systems from time to time without the benefit of an intermediary person. Although the intermediary may be technically adroit and able to cope with database idiosyncracies there is nothing like using a tool yourself.

The major features usually provided in online expert system software are telecommunication aids, universal search language, offline search strategy formulation, save effective search strategy command routine, downloading facilities (discussed later), and online help screens. The communication aids are auto-dialling and re-dialling to pre-selected numbers, and automatic

transmission of the pre-logon routine as set out in Table 16.2 . For
auto-dialling a special modem is required, controllable by the expert system's
software loaded into the user's computer. These are cheap and usually fitted
within the machine in the US, but expensive and usually supplied in an external
box in Europe.

It is cheaper to compose and type the questions offline, particularly if the
search statement is likely to be elaborate. They can be checked for accuracy and
stored ready for rapid, accurate, transmission online when needed. If the same
questions are going to be asked periodically - say when a new month's information
is loaded into the host computer - again it is a time/cost saver to be able to
fire off the questions whenever needed.

Downloading
____

Developments in technology enable the results of the online session shown
in Table 16.2 (there were 15 hit records in the search shown of which only two
were requested) which come down the line in reponse to the "type" command into
local storage. Downloading means the act of moving data online from the host
computer (whose owner is often an agent acting for the vendor who is the owner of
the database) to be stored in the user's computer.

Downloading has both technical and commercial ramifications (which will be
briefly discussed here) and copyright ramifications discussed in Chapter 29. It
is of interest to note that "we" (used with reference to a pre-1980 myself
employed by the Institute for Scientific Information) were the first database
owners to appreciate the implications of this situation and the first database
vendor implicitly to encourage the idea by offering microcomputer software
(Scimate) for doing it. Since hard-to-police illegal downloading was already
being practiced somebody said to me shortly after its introduction that it may
often be a good idea to act on the axiom "if you can't beat 'em join 'em!"

The commercial problem is how to devise a method of compensation. At least
three user scenarios come to mind. First, the user may simply select relevant
records and store them for his personal re-use. A record could, of course, be a
surrogate as in Table 16.2, or it could be self-contained full text information -
ultimately, perhaps, a book. Second, the user could periodically download with
the intention of building up a retrospectively searchable cumulated relevant
subset of a database or databases for his personal use. Third, the user involved
in either of these activities, but more likely the second, could make this
material available to his colleagues or re-sell it for a profit to others - say
by offering the subset database on a disk to suit a range of machines.

Obviously there are degrees of impact on the vendor's business depending
upon his database re-packaging policy. Those vendors who have created and priced
an information service solely for online access will be in a different situation
from those who created the database for generating printed products and those
whose price for online services is fixed on the basis of earnings from some
product mix. In the second case it is possible that the online service earnings
will ultimately be the major method of recovering costs in view of the
diminished demand for printed products.

Technical developments will increase the user's propensity to download. In
the US a 9600 baud telecommunication network called Dialnet is likely to spread
nationwide. Present day norms are 300, 600 or 1200 baud, although 2400 is now
rapidly gaining ground. It has been reported that Dialog will be offering a
service using Dialnet in parallel with their slower speed services currently
running over the Tymnet and Telenet networks. Inexpensive modems will be
developed for reception purposes, storage costs continue to fall,and large
amounts of data will be accessed, communicated, and stored cheaply.

In October 1984 The Institute of Electrical Engineers, publishers of the INSPEC physics, electrical and electronics database, produced a policy statement about downloading, perhaps to ensure that nobody should have any illusions about the application of the Copyright Act to this activity. They define three categories of use - temporary storage with limited use only by the user and his colleagues at no extra charge, long term storage and use only within the user's organisation subject to a special agreement including additional payment in advance of $96 for 300 records with shortfall or excess adjustment at the end of the year, and thirdly, use of INSPEC material for resale, payment terms to be negotiated.

Migration from print to online services

Once again we have controversy. According to Lancaster (1981), "the availability of online services has had rather a minor effect in causing libraries to cancel subscriptions to print on paper". But "loss of subscription income to publishers as a direct result of online exceeds that due to cancellations alone since the availability of a database online may prevent the initiation of new subscriptions by certain information services" and "cancellations may occur at an accelerated pace in the future".

Following a point made about the sensitivity of profits to cancellations in printed subscriptions, Trubkin takes up the question of migration from print to electronic information. She points not only to the profit-sensitivity of print cancellations but also to the effect on another very profitable product - the cumulated index. Cumulated indexes "made obsolete by online searching" are low cost products, and if they also are not taken up, profits will need to be recouped by considerable increases in online royalties.

These discussions about migration were criticised later by Summit on the grounds of undue attention to a single aspect of a complex situation. For example to what extent have subscriptions to printed products not available online been affected? A focus on the expanding market is required with strategies for maintaining and increasing growth. A similar view is advanced in one of the most thorough examinations of this problem by Williams (1981) . "In many industries, or in companies within industries, competing products are marketed, and it is very likely that one form may outstrip the other....the existence or non-existence of migration is immaterial". The writer stresses the need to analyse costs and revenues by product and discusses ways in which information providers might cope with trends in terms of efficiency, pricing, marketing, new products and so forth.

Note that I have said nothing about information which is created directly for online access, and is not simply a by-product of the production process used to make it available in print. The full cost of preparation would have to be passed on to users in online pricing unless there is a subsidy. The reason why this subject is not discussed is probably because the problems are simply normal commercial ones. Nobody is going to create data for sale unless they have done some homework on the market. If they decide to sell it they do so because they think that users will pay the relatively high prices needed to cover the preparational costs. In other words such special data creation is performed for the specialised needs of people who value information highly.

Databases

Several machine readable databases were started in the early 60s including Medlars, Biosis, and Chemical Abstracts, followed by Inspec, ISI and others. In due course these were made available for online searching. Selective Dissemination of Information systems (SDI) were the precursors of online searching. One of the earliest SDI systems was operated on a Univac machine by the US army's Fort Detrick laboratories which received Medlars tapes periodically. Terms from the profiles of scientists were matched against Medlars article terms and the scientists were provided with abstracts of the matching articles.

A database is a set of records held in computer storage and structured in such a way that records can be retrieved using a suitable query language. Most databases started life as compilations used for the production of ordered printed publications for information retrieval such as indexes. Today many databases are still used for this purpose but they are also run to provide online information retrieval services to remote users. Another major trend in recent years has been the re-packaging of database data so the compilation costs may be recovered in other ways.

Databases now exist covering every conceivable subject. Not only are the major scientific disciplines such as Chemistry, Physics, Medicine etc., comprehensively covered, but also subjects like Architecture, Banking, Cars, Child abuse, Cosmetics, Music, Taxation, Urban planning and the Yukon. By the end of 1983 Cuadra Associates estimated that there were 210 Science, 341 Technical, 446 Business, 178 Social Science and Humanities and 139 other publicly available <u>online</u> databases - a total of 1314. They included two main types - referral, that is the source information has to be obtained elesewhere, and source, that is the source information is contained in the record.

Scientists apparently do not have as great an incentive as businessmen to pay for information since information services for the latter have grown at a faster rate without government subsidies. Knowledge Industries state that the US online business grew by over 40% in 1984 led by Dow Jones with 160,000 subscribers (online passwords) followed by Quotron, Reuters, Dunsprint and Telerate. Dialog, the leading biblographic service, has issued about 50,000 passwords. Other major online services/users mentioned include The Source 60,000, Prestel 48,000 and Dialcom, 80,000. It is interesting to note that Prestel is way ahead of any other comparable service. The US Viewtron service, the largest in that country, issued 2700 passwords. According to Frost & Sullivan, 75% of "electronic publishing" (which is not quite the same thing as online services) European earnings come from business information including credit ratings.

EURIPA, a European providers association (quoted in Diane News) states that "The Electronic Information Industry", whatever that is, reached a turnover of $700M in 1983, making it about 20% of the size of the US industry. In 1982 it employed about 16,000 people. For-profit organisations, accounting for over 70% of the industry, have much higher growth rates than not-for-profit.

Cuadra lists the major host computer bureaux at the end of 1983 as shown in Table 16.3 .

<u>Referral (databases available)</u>		<u>Source (databases available)</u>	
Dialog	(180)	IP Sharp	(84)
SDC	(67)	Chase Econometrics	(83)
BRS	(65)	DRI	(78)
ESA-IRS	(36)	Geisco	(37)
Inka	(31)	Control Data Corp	(34)
Dimdi	(30)	ADP	(30)
Telesystemes Questel	(30)	SIA	(12)
Datastar	(21)		
Blaise	(20)		
Pergamon Infoline	(15)		

<u>TABLE 16.3.   PUBLICLY AVAILABLE ONLINE DATABASES 1983.</u>

<u>Local databases: Text retrieval</u>

A number of software packages, sometimes called "text retrieval packages" are available for the creation, maintenance, and searching of local databases. Some, such as ASSASSIN from ICI, have comprehensive facilities intended for running on computer mainframes and managing large document collections in companies. Others are aimed at people having smaller databases on microcomputers - for example scientists with reprint collections. The demand has been stimulated by the possibility of downloading records (discussed earlier) from large remote databases into the local database, and the need to manage them.

Most records in these systems will be searchable surrogates associated with print-on-paper documents. Packages for larger machines could be used for full text records. Several of these packages have been reviewed by Ashford.

<u>Useage and growth of databases and online searching</u>

Databases came to the fore in the United States after the launching of Sputnik 1 - an incentive to maximise the use of scientific information. Later, financial and business databases were developed, the incentive being the supply of information to a market with the highest occupational need for it, coupled with the ability to pay. The number of characters per database record steadily increased as the costs of the technology dropped. Originally database records contained short descriptions linked to information stored separately as print on paper. Later the descriptions became abstracts, but now the full text of the paper version is available in some cases. Notable examples are LEXIS, a legal database, produced by Mead Data Central and NEXIS from the same organisation which provides full text coverage of major newspapers and magazines.

There is no doubt that interactive online use has grown steadily and will continue to grow, although as is usual with statistics of this kind, the rate of growth is unclear. According to Lindquist after rapid growth from 1970 to 1975, and forecasts of 30% a year thereafter, the growth in the author's opinion would slow to 12%. However Williams (1979) estimated the number of searches for all countries to have increased from 700,000 in 1974 to 2.67M in 1978 and 4M estimated for 1979 - a four year increase at nearly 40% compound, and to about 50% for the projected year.

Lancaster believes that bibliographic database service revenues in Europe only, were $31.5M in 1980, expected to grow to $310.4M in 1985 - a growth by value of 58% per annum. (Note the impression of accuracy for 1985 conveyed by the ".4" in the projected figure). The rate of growth of all types of online databases for the same period is projected at 63% p.a. but the European situation is stated to be "5 years behind" the USA. However an estimate from another source, "Monitor", gives the bibliographic online figure for Europe as "$7.5M" in 1980. Compare this with the Lancaster figure of $31.5M" for 1980!).

In yet another 1980 estimate, European revenues were estimated at $120M with business information predominating at $77M followed by bibliographic data at $32M. At that time it was estimated that the 1985 revenues would have soared to $1400M with business information contributing about half, bibliographic about the same proportion as before, but two new sectors would emerge - industry specific information expanding, from $8M in 1980 to $224M by 1985, and marketing information, increasing from $5M to $132M.

The US figures for 1980 and 1985 were estimated at $1440M and $4300M respectively, with the proportions rather similar to Europe except that the relative proportion of marketing information in the US would be over twice that in Europe. The 1985 figure for business information was forecast at $1660M.

By 1983 various other forecasts for 1985 (tabulated by Knowledge Industries) had appeared varying between $400M to $4000M for the US and $460M to $4000M for Europe. Obviously different forecasters define online databases differently. Once again it seems that we must be content with saying that this field is growing but the rate seems to be pure conjecture, and we may well ask how such figures are collected. The question is "is this growth at the expense of print-on-paper information services?" - a hard to answer question discussed earlier in this Chapter.

FURTHER READING

Ashford, John.
   Program 18(2), 124-146, April 1984.
      Information storage and retrieval systems on mainframes and
      minicomputers: a comparison of text retrieval packages available in the UK.
Kruzas, A.,and Schmittroth J. (Eds).
   Encyclopaedia of information systems and services. 4th edition,1981.
      Gale Publishing, Book Tower, Detroit, Mich 48226, USA
Lancaster F .W.; Goldhor, Herbert.
   Online Review 5(4), 301-311, 1981.
      The impact of online services on subscriptions to printed
      publications.
Lefkowitz, David.
   Macmillan 1969.
      File structures for online systems.
Lindquist, Mats G.
   Online Review 1(2), 109-116, 1977.
      An explanation of the coming stagnation of information
      search services.
Meadow, C.T.; Hewett T.T.; Aversa, E.S.
   J.Amer.Soc.Info. Science 33 (5,6), 325-332 and 357-364, 1982.
      A computer intermediary for interactive database searching. Part 1 design:
      Part 2 Evaluation.
Shepherd, Michael A.; Watters, Carolyn
   Online Review 8(5), 451-463, 1984.
      PSI: a portable self-contained intermediary for access to bibliographic
      database systems.
Summit, Roger K.
   Online Review 5(6), 496, 1981.
      Online and print.
Trubkin, Loene.
   Online Review 4(1), 5-12, 1980.
      Migration from print to online use.
Williams, M.E.
   ASIS Bull., 7(2), 27-29, 1980. Published by the American
   Society for Information Science.
      Database and online statistics for 1979.
Williams, Martha E.
   Information Proces. & Manag. 17(5), 263-276, 1981.
      Relative impact of print and database products on database
      producer expenses and income - trends for database
      producer organisations based on a thirteen year financial
      analysis.

CHAPTER 17. MICROCOMPUTER SYSTEMS PART 1:
HARDWARE DESIGN AND CHOICE OF MACHINES

INTRODUCTION AND HISTORY

Microcomputers, as opposed to mini-computers - the "next size up" - are probably most easily defined in terms of price; it is becoming increasingly difficult to distinguish between micros and minis. The price of a micro starts at a few hundred dollars and extends upwards to about $5000, or even to $10,000 or more if various power-extending add-ons and peripheral units, which are steadily becoming available, are added. At the lower end the distinction between micros and programmable calculators is blurred.

A microprocessor consists of the parts of the Central Processor Unit (CPU) brought together as an integrated circuit of components and connections deposited on a very small slice or chip, usually of silicon. The CPU comprises interconnected circuit elements,to be described, such as gates, electronic switches and local storage (registers) for adding, subtracting etc. Together these circuits execute a program of instructions. The trend is to bring associated circuits which were formerly on separate chips on to the CPU chip.

A microcomputer consists of a CPU with peripherals (e.g. keyboard, display unit, etc) that can perform useful functions under program control.

In the 1980s hardware development showed some signs of slowing up as the physical limits of optical resolution in chip layout were approached. The problem of the man-hours required to write software capable of capitalising on the hardware also started to receive increasing attention. Some machine language software is now being built into the chips. The software writer can use a terse statement where previously lines of code were needed.

Most microcomputers being purchased in Europe are still being imported from the United States. The selling price is often nearly double the equivalent US price. Obviously costs are incurred in importing and supporting procedures,, but a differential of nearly two to one seems excessive. At least this differential often applies to software which may pass through the hands of various middlemen before reaching the customer.

Few technologies have moved from first experiments to widespread use in so short a time. Favourable political, economic and engineering factors have combined to beat the "10 year rule" which says that a period of at least ten years will pass before a major new technology will take off.

The devices mentioned and the terms used in this potted history of the microcomputer will be explained later in this chapter.

The PDP-8 minicomputer, sold by the Digital Equipment Corporation in 1965 at about $20,000, provided a foretast of what would soon become possible. The arrival of microprocessors in 1971 for Central Processing Units (CPUs) was a major event providing the impetus for the first commercially available machine to be produced in any quantity - the Altair 8800 - supplied as a kit by MITS in 1975.

Other developments which made that possible were the transistor (first patent filed 1948); improvements in photolithography and diffusion techniques enabling transistors and other circuit elements to be manufactured as integrated circuits (Fairchild 1959); M.E.Hoff's invention of the Intel 4004 microprocessor containing over 2000 transistors on a chip, further developed into the 8080 in 1973; US government subsidisation of semiconductor developments amounting to about $1000M in 1958-1974, and a large local computer market capable of absorbing and encouraging improved devices.

For a period the Altair and its successors were limited by small memories and the absence of disk storage, to a market composed of enthusiastic hobbyists. Software for useful applications was non-existent. Demand increased with increasing software availability, improved reliability, and falling costs, but two further related developments may be singled out as major contributors to the explosive demand which started around 1978.

IBM introduced a terminal incorporating the FD-11 floppy disk providing cheap bulk storage in 1971. Competitors announced copies almost immediately, but in September 1972 IBM announced the 3740 data entry station incorporating a "diskette", and a host of competitors followed.

FIGURE 17.1. APPLE MACINTOSH
(Courtesy Apple Computers)

FIGURE 17.2 IBM 3270 PC
(Courtesy IBM Corp.)

In 1975 Gary Kildall wrote some software for controlling files stored on a floppy disk. He was asked by Imsai, a floppy disk supplier, to design an "operating system" (to be discussed later) and the first version of CP/M, labelled 1.3, became available. Hardware dependent functions were concentrated in one section of it enabling it to be adapted for use with any microcomputer using the widely adopted 8080 and later the Z80 CPUs. Kildall founded Digital Research in 1976 and more versions were released later, including one for 16 bit machines, CP/M 86.

Microcomputers with CP/M and floppy disks offering 250 Kbytes and later up to 1 Mbyte Random Access Storage were manufactured at reasonable prices and the "business microcomputer" was born. In 1977 Commodore, Apple, and Radio Shack/Tandy introduced personal computers selling complete with Cathode Ray Tube display, cassette tape data recorder, keyboard and Basic software for below $1000.

Parallel developments of larger disks started with the IBM Ramac "hard disk" introduced in 1956, and in 1973 IBM announced the 3340 "Winchester Disk" a sealed unit with the heads flying 20 microinches above the disk surface. In due course engineering devlopments were put in hand to miniaturise and mass produce Winchesters and in 1978 Shugart announced the SA4000 Winchester for microcomputers. In 1980 Seagate introduced a 5 Mbyte 5.25 inch Winchester selling for $925. Tandon replied in 1982 with the same unit for $400 and microcomputers can now be purchased with built-in Winchesters to store 10 Mbytes or more for around $3000. These machines can deal with sophisticated information storage and retrieval, word processing, etc.

WORD LENGTHS

Addressing

A "word" in an 8 bit device is a sequence of 8 bits, in a 16 bit device, 16 bits etc. 8 bits = 2^8 and 16 = 2^{16} so 8 bits can represent 256 different numbers, and 16 bits 65536 (often called "64K") numbers.

Microcomputer word lengths started at 4 bits, then 8 bits became widely adopted to be followed by 16 and now 32. This has become possible because improvements in technology, particularly in the packing density of semiconductor elements, have enabled the extra complexity needed to handle longer words to be introduced without proportional increases in cost, space or unreliability.

Longer word lengths are needed in order to be able to address each cell of the larger memories which are now available in microcomputers. The address word can be formed from smaller words - for example in 8 bit microcomputers the 16 bit word needed to address the 65,536 locations of a "64K" memory is composed of one 8 bit word for the 8 "lower order" bits and a second 8 bit word for the 8 "higher order" bits. The 16 bits of the two words are transmitted simultaneously along 16 lines to memory as if they were one 16 bit word. A 32 word potentially can address over four thousand million locations.

8, 16, and 32 bit machines

One advantage of machines working with longer words is that single word addressing of larger memories become possible without the extra complexity and cost of organising two or more words for the purpose. Larger memories can accomodate more sophisticated programs and more of the user's data which otherwise would have to be accomodated on disk which takes much longer to access than semiconductor memory.

Another advantage is that data can be moved about in larger chunks. If each 16 bit data word is moved around at the same speed as an 8 bit data word, any task involving the movement of numbers of data words will be completed in a shorter time, and if 32 bit words are used in a still shorter time. For example, a row of 32 pixels (picture elements) representing black or white parts of an image will be processed in four cycles by an 8 bit, 2 by a 16 bit, and in one by a 32 bit machine - i.e. four times more quickly by the latter.

In some computer system applications it may be necessary to allocate a unique code to describe each item in a collection of n different items. The shortest single code word to uniquely describe each item must contain 2^n bits. Thus an 8 bit word can describe up to 256 items, 9 bits 512 items, 16 bits 65536 etc. Again there is an advantage if the word length is long enough to describe each item in a large collection with one word.

The penalty to be paid is the cost of the extra bandwidth (for buses this means more lines) needed to move longer words at the same speed as shorter words and of the additional circuits and storage. However improvements in manufacturing techniques and rapid adoption on a big scale enable these performance improvements to be incorporated into microcomputers with the machine selling for less than the previous generation of machines which it displaced.

MICROCOMPUTER HARDWARE

Figure 17.3 shows the general layout of a microcomputer, shorn of detail, typical of the simpler types of machine currently available. The CPU controls the other parts of the microcomputer and is itself controlled by a sequence of instructions from a stored program. A single instruction may cause hundreds or thousands of semi-conductors to change state, so to ensure that the instruction is correctly executed changes are synchronously switched by impulses from a "clock" as discussed in Chapter 2.

Data is transmitted in a series of bursts at the clock rate, or at some exact sub-multiple of it. The program controlling the CPU causes instructions to be fetched from memory, accepts data input from other parts of the machine, manipulates the data according to the instructions, and outputs or communicates the results to some other part. There are two major sections within the CPU - the arithmetic and logic unit where the instructions are marshalled and data is manipulated, and the con-

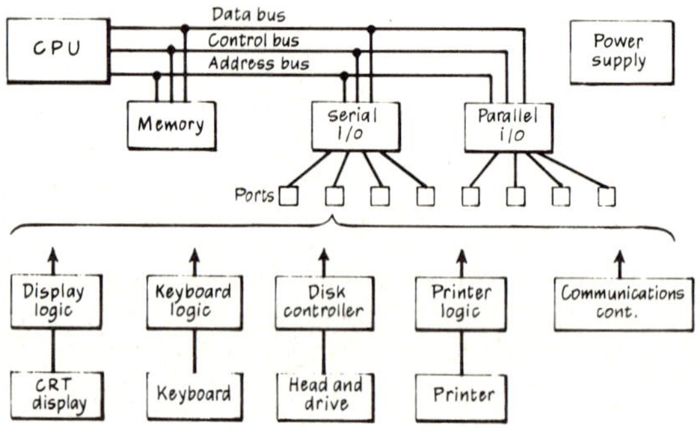

FIGURE 17.3. MICROCOMPUTER BASIC LAYOUT

trol,distribution,and addressing circuits for receiving and distributing information and controlling events in all parts of the machine. At intervals determined by the clock, bursts - usually of 8 or 16 bits in parallel - are received or despatched by the CPU.

Buses

The other major parts of the microcomputer, such as Random Access Memories (RAM) into which program instructions and data are fed, stored, and extracted as operations proceed, and the ports via which data is conveyed to and from the peripheral units such as display, printer etc., are connected to the CPU and to each other by a "bus". A bus is simply a set of interconnecting wires, often arranged in groups as shown on the figure.

In an 8 bit microcomputer the address bus typically consists of 16 lines along which flow 16 bits to identify a particular memory cell, data from which will be read into an 8 line data bus. There may also be a multiple line control signal bus.

With this mass of interconnecting lines it would obviously make sense to standardise the purpose of each line, together with its identification, numbering and connection. If this was not done each type of machine would need a different program simply to distribute information correctly to the right place. A degree of standardisation has in fact occurred, notably in the adoption of a set of 100 lines called "S-100" defined by the US IEEE in specification 696. Another is in the process of adoption to cope with the increasing use of longer words - the IEEE-P796 Multibus with 146 lines. DEC have adopted their own - the Unibus.

A popular method of construction has become associated with the adoption of buses - the "backplane"- in the case of the S100 backplane a line of 100 sockets fixed in a long thin plastic strip. Several of these socket-strips are often fixed above each other along one side of a "cage" and each socket on a strip is wired to the same socket on every other strip - e.g. if there are six strips, each socket numbered 83 will be connected to every other socket numbered 83. The printed circuit boards carrying the microcomputer's components have 100 gold plated flat connection pins arranged along one edge, each of which fits into a socket on a socket-strip. The completed assembly consists of a number of boards plugged into the socket strips and retained in the cage, with each bus line carried round to all boards via the described arrangement. Any board may be plugged in to any socket.

CPU fetch-execute cycle

The CPU runs a succession of "fetch-execute" cycles initiated by a series of instructions called "opcodes" together with "operands" forming a program, which has been loaded into memory usually from a disk. The opcodes in the Instruction Set for a microprocessor, say an 8080, are the repertoire of operations available to the program writer for that microprocessor. Operands are supplementary data associated with the opcode. The CPU is concerned with program sequence control, control of system operations and information input or output to other parts of the microcomputer or peripheral devices, and the transfer and modification of data.

Say that the first one-byte opcode is an instruction to move a data byte into register A in the CPU, and it is followed by a two-byte operand which is the address of the memory cell where the wanted data is stored. The first stage of this operation is to fetch this information into the CPU to enable it to be ready for the execute stage.

When a program is initiated, say by a typed command from the operator, the CPU fetches the first opcode byte from Memory, stores it in the Instruction Register and also moves it to the Instruction Decoder and Control Unit. The Control Unit acts on the decoded instruction, passes a "read" control signal to Memory followed by the two-byte operand (via the address bus) - the address from which data is to be read, and routes the data stored at this address, itself an address to be used in the execute stage of the operation, to the Memory Address Register in the CPU. Thus the situation at the end of this fetch cycle is that the opcode is stored in the Instruction Register and the address of the byte to be moved is stored in the Memory Address Register.

Several details have been omitted from this sequence. The appropriate buses will have been switched to interconnect the appropriate units during data transfer, and a Program Counter is keeping track of each step. At this point the required number of steps in the fetch cycle have been completed and the Program Counter calls up the first step of the execute stage.

This second stage is simply to execute a read cycle, route the address stored in the Memory Address Register to Memory and move the data at that address into register A in the CPU.

The next part of the program may require that a byte of data be moved from memory to some other part of the machine - say to a port. In this case control circuits in the CPU would make an address register ready to receive the address of the next byte required from memory. Subsequently the byte would be moved to the required peripheral device. Alternatively the byte might have to be moved into the CPU to, say, be added to another number stored in the arithmetic circuits as the result of an earlier instruction.

The CPU can also interact with peripheral units. It can "poll" - that is periodically switch round to each peripheral - to check readiness to transfer data and if readiness is indicated, complete the current instruction, branch to a program for data transfer, and then return to the interrupted program. Alternatively a peripheral may generate an interrupt signal to indicate readiness. The CPU will then allow a routine program to run to transfer the data according to pre-arranged priority rules.

There is one other facility that should be mentioned in this necessarily short attempt to explain program functions. If a lot of data has to be transferred in a short time it is clumsy to go through a series of CPU-controllled byte by byte processes. Many microcomputers include the means of Direct Memory Access (DMA) so that a stream of data can be transmitted to and from memory directly from a peripheral device, once the CPU has handled the initiation processes.

<u>Semiconductor storage</u>

In the above remarks no distinction was made between different kinds of memory. In Figure 17.3 Random Access Memories (RAMs) are lumped together in one block for simplicity; in reality there may be several separate memories of the same or different types in the same machine.

One kind of memory, called a non-volatile Read Only Memory (ROM), has data permanently written into it which does not disappear when the power is switched off. The data is usually supplied in the ROM with the machine. Programs are "hard-wired" into the ROM chip at the design stage; the program resides in the design of a circuit complex in which electrical impulses are manipulated to generate the required instructions.

Later, Programmable Read Only Memory (PROM) was developed. A PROM is a chip containing a number of fuseable links interconnecting a large number of possible circuit arrangements. The links are individually addressable. To implant a permanent program, the "fuses" can be selectively blown leaving a permanent particular kind of circuit arrangement, and so a "hard wired" program. PROMs were then followed by Erasable PROMs (EPROMs) in which the "fuses" are replaced by electrical charges sited to block or unblock "gates". Gates can be blocked by impulse addressing in order to arrange the circuit network as required. The charges can be removed (making the device ready to receive a different program) by the energy contained in ultraviolet light. A window is left in the chip for exposing it to UV.

The major application of ROMs and PROMs is to retain program instructions and control data when the microcomputer is switched off, ready for use when power is again applied. ROM is also used to hold a small start-up program which is loaded into the machine to set it ready for a particular purpose. Actuating this program is called "Booting". It is usually executed simply by pressing keys - say B followed by O.

Volatile read-and-write RAM is used in the main memory for storing programs and data which continually change as the microcomputer carries out its tasks. The contents of the memory disappear when the equipment is switched off. Its contents also disappear relatively slowly even when power is applied, rather like the slow discharge of a voltage stored in a capacitor. To combat this the memory is automatically refreshed periodically by scanning all its elements in order to reinforce whatever state they may be in - that is either "on" or "off".

One of the reasons for the increasing use of micros is the rapid development and falling costs of memory chips. Memory used to come as "1K" per chip, but 16K chips were soon developed. Beyond that, new problems were encountered in manufacturing the extremely small transistor cells required. In 1980 three manufacturers were producing 64K chips in quantity but at a higher price per bit compared with 16K chips. 256K RAMs were introduced by the Japanese experimentally in 1980 with 100 nanosecond access times and connections about 1 micrometer wide. One Japanese company even produced a 1Mbit chip which is about twice the physical size of a 64K.

<u>Keyboard functions</u>

In capacity-actuated keyboards each key operates a variable capacitor, and all capacitors are arranged in a matrix. The rows and columns of the matrix are continuously scanned and counted. When, say, the "H" key is depressed, the capacitance change at the row/column intersection is detected by the scanner and the row and column counters "note" that a change has occurred at the point "H". The same principle is used in other types of keyboard.

The scanner/counter is connected to a small ROM in which is permanently stored the ASCII code for each character. In this case the code for H is extracted and moved into a register ready for transmission. Information about the position required for the character on the display is derived from cursor movement. The cursor, displayed as a bright blob, is stepped along each time a key is depressed or may be placed anywhere on the screen by using special "arrowed" keys to indicate direction. Cursor positioning keys control up-down counters which provide coordinate information for positioning the cursor. If the H is required to be the second character in the third row, and the cursor is placed in that position, keying H will cause it to appear in the same position as the cursor.

<u>Display functions</u>

Bright dots can be formed on the screen by electronically switching on the electron beam of a CRT as it reaches particular positions during its traverse. The beam scans continuously, generating closely spaced rows of dots, sweeping out the entire pattern repeatedly at a high speed so that the eye sees an apparently permanent image. Microcomputers are often designed to display 24 rows of 80 characters per row - a total of 1920 characters - built up by a pattern of dots formed line by line as the beam traverses. To be easily readable a character requires to be about 9 dots high - that is 9 scanning lines are required - and 7 dots wide. "G", "H" and "E" formed in this manner would appear as in Fig. 17.4

There has to be a space between characters and a two-line space between each
row requiring a total number of 8 x 11
= 88 dots per character. A screenful of
1920 characters therefore requires over
169,000 controllable dots.

Since a "page" of characters has to
be displayed for as long as the viewer
needs it, about 170 Kbits of storage with
associated control circuits would apparently be required just for this purpose,
quite apart from additional memory needed
to store dot patterns representing each
character. Various techniques are used to

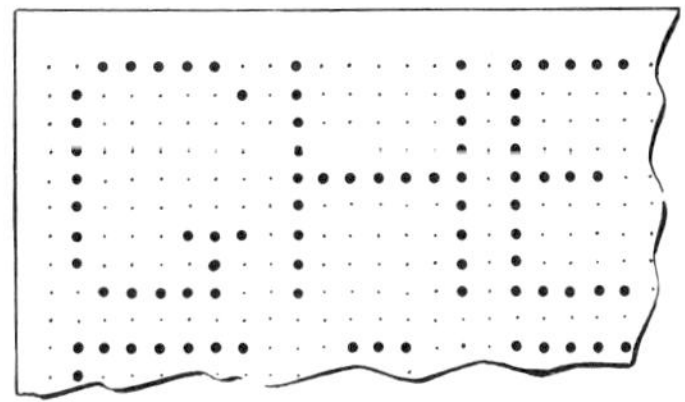

<u>FIGURE 17.4</u>
<u>BRIGHT-DOT CHARACTER DISPLAY</u>

reduce this complexity. The most popular works by scanning out permanently stored dot patterns which form characters.

An 8K Display RAM is provided to receive and temporarily store in the form of 7 bit ASCII code as many characters received from the keyboard as may be needed up to a screenful, together with data about cursor co-ordinates to determine where each character is to be positioned.

A character set, usually of at least 128 characters to include upper and lower case, numerals and symbols, is permanently stored, each character as a 7 x

9 dot pattern, in 8 rows of 16 characters within an "8K" bit Character
Generator (CG) ROM (7 x 9 x 8 x 16 = 8064 bits). It is these patterns, read out
when needed and forming bright dots on the CRT screen, which represent displayed
characters.

The addresses of the characters to be successively displayed are called by
the program as the CRT beam proceeds. The time taken for the beam to reach any
position on the screen is accurately known, so provided character information is
released for spot brightness control purposes from the CG ROM at the correct
moment by the Display RAM (which contains all the data for a current screen) all
will be well.

The CRT beam is initially cut-off so several lines may be traced by the spot
with the screen remaining black. Eventually the moment comes for a line to be
scanned which will carry some bright blobs representing the top strip of the
first row of characters. Say there are just three characters in the first row –
G,H,E, as in Figure 17.4. The program calls the address in Display RAM where data
about the first character is stored. The data is ASCII code for G – in other
words the address of the matrix representing G in the CG ROM. The dot pattern for
the top of the G – five dots – is clocked out from the CG ROM to the CRT beam as
fast successive switch-on pulses.

The beam then cuts-off for a time interval corresponding to two spot-clocked
intervals for inter-character spacing, and then the second character matrix, H,
in display RAM is addressed. One switch-on pulse, five clocked off intervals,
and then another switch-on pulse are clocked out from the H matrix in CG ROM,
forming the the top of the H as two spaced bright blobs.

The beam continues, having switched on for very short intervals to produce a
succession of bright spots, until the scan line is complete, flies back, and
starts on the next line. The same sequence occurs to produce the next strip of
blobs for the same characters with the next scanning line and so on. After nine
lines (See Figure 17.4) the characters are complete.

All that is present on the screen at any instant when the beam is on is a
single spot which stays there for 50 nanoseconds or less. To produce an image
which is visible to the eye the whole screen is scanned usually 50 (UK) or 60
(US) time per second. The blob pattern is continuously overlaid so the tube
phosphor glows continuously at each point where the beam is switched on to form
rows of visible characters.

<u>Disks and information storage</u>

For many applications the advent of disks of large capacity for
microcomputers heads the list of factors which have moved them from an
interesting device for computer buffs to a machine for regular use in an office.

The economic upper limit of semiconductor storage capacity falls far short
of the capacities needed for random access information storage and retrieval with
files of reasonable size. Unfortunately the word "file" has several meanings. It
usually means a collection of related papers in, say a "filing cabinet". In
computerese a file is simply data or a programs given a name and an address so
that it can be retrieved for storage.

There is less ambiguity about the words <u>"record"</u> and <u>"field"</u>. A record is a
collection of data fields. For example a library system might consist of a
collection of records, each record describing a book in a collection of 500
gardening books. A record would consist of a title field, an author field, a
publisher field and a shelf location field. Thus each record would contain
information about the same attributes of each book, and the records, numbered
from 1 to 500, form a <u>file</u> called GARDENING.

Records and fields can be of fixed or variable length. Fixed length may be convenient for processing but is wasteful in storage space. For instance the length of an author field might be 100 characters to allow for the listing of joint authors. If the average number of authors is 2, most of the field is usually blank space; however the constant field length simplifies data processing.

The first magnetic media for storing quantities of machine readable records was magnetic tape, but it may take seconds or minutes to retrieve a particular record from somewhere on a long tape. If finding a record on tape is rather like finding a particular frame on a reel of cinema film, then finding a record on disk is like finding a record groove on a gramophone (phonograph) with a groove-calibrated pickup. A disk is a random access device, but its mechanical action results in a slower peformance than all-electric semiconductor storage.

Disk systems for microcomputers

With large computers one or more rigid magnetic disks are mounted on a drive in a clean air environment and hundreds of megabytes of information can be recorded on each disk. Inexpensive disk drives with small flexible ("floppy") disks to work in a normal environment were later developed for use with microcomputers. Storage capacity is in the range 100 Kbytes to several Megabytes per disk. During the last four years the "Winchester" disk (so-called because it was the code name used by IBM when it introduced the principle in 1973) has been introduced at a price and in a form suitable for micros. Until then the head was in physical contact with the disk.

A Winchester head embodies two rail-like projections which entrap a small volume of air, with a rail embodying the head element between them. The aerodynamic forces created when the disk rotates beneath the head causes the latter to hover less than a millionth of a metre above the surface and in consequence there is no wear. Higher recording densities also become feasible. In the microcomputer version the whole assembly is enclosed in its own clean air, and storage capacities extend from a few megabytes up to 40 megabytes or more.

Floppy disk systems; general description

A floppy disk, typical of those in general use until recently, is shown in Fig. 17.5. It consists of a plastic envelope with cut-out portions, permanently housing the disk, which is inserted through into the disk drive through a slot in the front of the microcomputer. Within the drive is a motor-driven projection which fits a hole in the centre of the disk. Driven by the projection, the disk rotates within its envelope against the light friction of a soft material inside the envelope. The read/write head moves to-and-fro along the disk radius, making contact through an elongated aperture cut out of the plastic envelope.

Typically data is recorded in 77 concentric tracks, each track being sub-divided into 16 sectors with each sector capable of storing 256 8-bit bytes with a 64 byte intersector gap.

Data is recorded in variable length blocks which may occupy less than one sector, or continue over several sectors. In the typical single-sided 8 inch disk being described here, storage capacity is therefore $77 \times 16 \times 256 = 315,000$ bytes (approx). Smaller disks are available, and both sides of a disk are often used with appropriate drives to double the storage capacity.

Each disk will contain a directory of its contents - that is the address for the first block of each named file, its size, and other information. The directory is always loaded into memory when the disk is in use. The files stored on the disk may contain user's data or they may be programs - such as the operating system program which is always transferred to memory when starting up, or special"driver" programs associated with the control of peripheral devices, or programs for applications such as word processing, etc.

In the so-called "hard sectored" disk, each hole in a circle of small holes in the disk becomes visible through a hole in the outer plastic envelope as the disk rotates. The presence of a hole is detected by a light beam shining through it on to a sensor enabling the rotational position of the disk to be accurately determined. In a "soft sectored" disk there is no such facility and rotational position is determined by control circuits from timing data recorded on the disk.

IBM introduced the soft sectored FD-33 system, and some manufacturers followed this design with "IBM comptible" disks. Rather more data can be recorded on a hard-sectored disk, the penalty paid being some additional electromechanical complication.

The read/write head must first be directed to and make contact with a particular track. For disks rotating at 360 rpm this may take 100 ms maximum, 33 ms average. It must then wait 166 ms max., 83 ms average, for the disk to rotate to the position of the wanted byte. At that instant data transfer commences.

For maximum convenience the response time during a question-and-answer interactive session or the finding and presentation of text should be fast. This depends on a number of hardware and software factors of which the floppy disk mechanics is only one. The data transfer rate in systems of the kind being discussed here is about 660 Kbytes/sec using Direct Memory Access (DMA) which is very fast compared with access time.

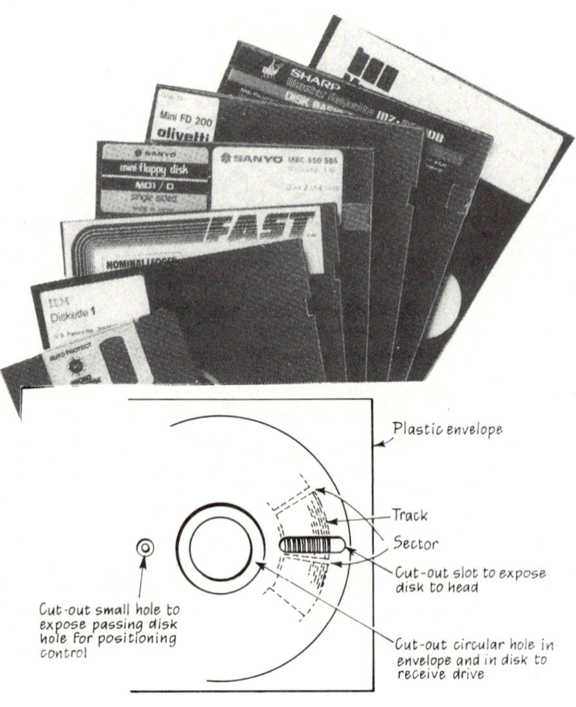

FIGURE 17.5 FLOPPY DISK CONSTRUCTION

Floppy disks - density

The importance of storing the maximum amount of data on a floppy disk at minimum cost with reliable operation has stimulated research into pushing up recording density, improving precision in production, and reducing disk and drive size so that drives can be housed within the microcomputer casing. Progress has been from single sided single density 8" disks, to double sided double density, then to 5.25 inch with up to 1.6 Mbyte capacity and 3.5 inch with up to

1 Mbyte capacity.

In single density recording, bits are recorded as a flux reversal on the surface which is composed of fine magnetisable particles. The interval of a few microseconds between each recorded bit is accurately controlled by the microcomputer's master clock. Clock impulses are also recorded on the disk which are checked when the disk is being read to ensure synchronisation. If a bit had to be recorded at a precisely timed instant the system might be upset by variations caused by various mechanical imperfections in the drive/disk assembly. To allow for this, recording is permitted anywhere within a short time zone between clock pulses. So long as the bit impulses do not wander right outside this zone, write/read performance is unaffected.

One way of accomplishing double density recording is doubling the recorded bit rate by cutting the time period allowed for data and clock impulses by half and eliminating clock pulses when Os are recorded. This calls for more complex timing and control circuitry.

<u>Floppy disk system arrangements and backup</u>

When disk systems started to become widely used they often consisted of dual drives for two single sided double density 8" floppy disks with a total storage capacity of around 700 Kbytes. with functions of the system sections as follows -

1. Drive electromechanics and control system.

This section, directly associated with the drive motor and heads, consists of arrangements for motorised disk insertion, retention and ejection; a motor for rotating the disks with speed control; a form of motor for moving the heads across the disks from track to track. (This "motor" may be a coil which actuates a rod-like armature upon which the heads are mounted combined with a servo-mechanism for accurate positioning); a motorised head loader (for holding the disks against the heads); optical index and sector sensing; clock and data recording, writing, and data separation electronics.

2. Formatter.

The formatter, a program supplied with every microcomputer with disk drives, lays down the track structure on the blank disk's surface in readiness for its first use. The details of this procedure and the differences between different formats is of considerable interest because disks of the same size and same recording density are not necessarily interchangeable between micromputers made by different manufacturers. In fact disk format compatibilities are yet another infuriating problem in exchanging data between machines. The subject is rarely discussed so the article by Thompson (See "Further reading") is most useful .

3. Controller.

The controller circuits are concerned with selection, control, addressing and data arrangements, acting on instructions received from CPU. The controller usually incorporates FIFO (first in first out) buffering - that is temporary storage up to the capacity of one block, to cope with transfer rate differences between disk and CPU. It also manages Direct Memory Access. Another function is series/parallel or parallel/series conversion of data, as required by various parts of the system.

4. Software.

Management of the head movements, reading and writing, and management of track and sector data is controlled by the disk operating system software which resides on disk but is loaded into memory as needed for operations in progress.

In the absence of a hard disk, two disk drives offer substantial if not essential benefits over one, quite apart from the additional storage capacity. Software and user's data may reside on both or either disk; a usual arrangement is for one disk to contain software and archiving space (see below) and the other user's data. This is operationally convenient because different software packages may be interchanged independently of user's data, or any one of a collection of user's data disks can be interchanged without re-loading the common software.

A most important function of a dual drive system is the provision for backup and disk copying. The possibility exists of a crash (severe fault) which results in a loss of some or all disk data. Another problem is the loss of a small but critical part of the software - for instance any part of the "boot" software which is stored on disk not in ROM. Yet another problem is the loss of one or more pages of text, when a word processing software package is in use, by pressing a wrong key. Backup is insurance against loss. The frequency and inconvenience of doing it must be balanced against the probability of loss.

Reference was made to "archiving" earlier. This is a very useful first stage of backup available with some software packages. It consists of copying, a file from the data disk (in,say, drive 1) to an area designated for the purpose on the software disk (in, say, drive 0). This will take typically about 5 seconds per "page" in older systems and perhaps 1 second in newer ones. It should be carried out periodically while adding to a file as an insurance against losing data on the drive 1 disk. Each time it is done, data previously stored in archive is overwritten.

FIGURE 17.6 ICL
ONE PER DESK (Courtesy ICL)

FIGURE 17.7   RADIO SHACK
TRS80/100 (Courtesy Radio Shack)

Newer systems, requiring more storage space, have automatic creation of a complete backup file somewhere on the same disk. For example in some word processing systems two versions of all files reside on disk - B, the current version, and C the version which existed before it was revised and became B. When the file is needed version B is copied into temporary storage as version A. When the instruction is given to write A to disk, C is erased, B is re-named C, and A is named B. A only exists while the file is being worked on.

Archiving or same disk backup copies do not insure against a severe crash or problems with drive 0 on a dual disk system. Disk copying provides almost total insurance. Dual drives permit the contents of one disk to be copied on to a scratch (empty) disk. This usually takes a few minutes and should be done daily. If a malfunction occurs on the following day, the worst that can then happen is that work done up to that time on that day is lost. Copying also provides the

opportunity, which should certainly be taken, of storing copies of all disks of
value away from the work position.

Care of floppy disks and drives

Older types of disks and drives repay care more then any other part of a
microcomputer. The arrival of enclosed hard discs and 3.5" disks in a plastic
pack which are exposed only when inserted into the drive have removed some of the
handling and dust problems. The points worth noting are;-

1. Clean the air filter and mechanical parts of drive liable
   to be affected by dirt.

2. Clean the heads by occasional running of a special slightly abrasive
   cleaning disk.

3. Always store disks in a sealed container when not in use.

4. Always handle disks very carefully and never finger
   exposed surfaces.

5. Copy and discard disks showing signs of wear before wear starts to give
problems. The disk surface gradually changes from a perfectly uniform
appearance to a lined appearance proportional to the frequency of use of a
particular track.

6. Read the technical information put out by disk manufacturers and note their
test methods and certification (if any). Exchange information with other   micro
users. Treat disks like car tyres; play it safe by paying a bit more   for the
best available.

Microcomputer disks - current developments

Many microcomputers are available with built in Winchesters. The great
advantage is that a large amount of data can be used or searched without the need
for proceeding through a collection of floppies of equivalent capacity. The
problem with a collection of floppies is whether always to add new data on the
nth disk - that is serially on to the most recent disk - or whether to adopt a
scheme in which the data is spread over a number of disks, plenty of space having
been left on each disk for new data.

There is no problem if the subject content of each disk is mutually
exclusive, since there is a certainty of retrieval when a particular disk is
selected. If this cannot be done then each disk will have to be searched.

Microcomputers incorporating hard disks include a floppy disk drive for
loading software and for running data from hard disk to floppies for backup
purposes. Potentially the best arrangement for backup is probably the "streaming
tape drive". It consists of a high speed tape system capable of accommodating the
Winchester's contents by writing "on the fly" at up to 100" per second.

Floppy disks for micros have passed through various stages of development.
The 8" disks were originally low-capacity single-sided devices of doubtful
reliability. They were steadily improved; double-sided double-density versions
were introduced and a hub-reinforcing ring was introduced for more accurate
consistent centring on the driving boss. Further improvements in heads and
magnetic media enabled the capacity to be increased with up to 80 tracks/inch and
630 Kbytes capacity for a double sided disk. One manufacturer (Drivetec) has
managed to cram 3.3 Mbytes on to his size of disk by using 192 tracks per inch.

8" disks have a notch at one edge which actuates a lever in the drive when inserted. To prevent the disk being accidentally over-written or erased the notch must be left <u>uncovered</u>. When the 5.25" was introduced, the user was ignored as usual, and he must somehow remember that the notch has to be <u>covered</u> for write-protection.

Now we have the 3.5" disk and yet smaller drives. One single-side version in wide use stores 270 Kbytes at 135 tracks per inch. The disk has a solid centre with a centre-hole for fitting over the drive-boss which does not provide the rotating torque. This is provided by a spigot on the drive which projects through an off-centre hole in the solid centre area of the disk. The read-write slot - the vulnerable area where the rigid plastic holder is cut away to allow head access - is protected by a shutter which slides back when the disk is inserted.

The 5.25" multiple-platter Winchester disk drive has been the subject of even more intense competition than the floppy; starting at 5 Mbytes it soon went up to an incredible 60 Mbytes with 35 ms access time. Before this could be digested, out came the half-height Winchester with a capacity of up to 40 Mbytes and 40 ms access time. This was closely followed by the 3.5" with 12 Mbytes capacity.

<u>Reliability</u>

The reliability of microprocessors has steadily increased. Motorola claimed 9 years as the Mean Time Between Failures (MTBF) in 1974. By 1979 this had become 1900 <u>years</u>. The problems involved in detecting causes of failure, and in producing meaningful statistics are considerable. For example in one case the equivalent of three thousand million hours (nearly 350,000 years) of testing was needed to produce 30 failures.

It is nice to know that chips are reliable, but a person buying a microcomputer wants to know something about the overall reliability of a machine under typical operating conditions before he buys it. This includes any kind of failure which interrupts work. We have become so used to the reliability of typewriters or print on paper that we forget the importance of reliability. Information about this subject is inadequate.

<u>HARDWARE AND SOFTWARE - CHOICE AND AVOIDING DISASTERS</u>

<u>Choice</u>

These remarks apply to microcomputers for business and possibly home use when applied to file management, information storage and retrieval and text processing but not to more specialised applications such as "number crunching", process control, robotics, etc.

Microcomputers suitable for office use cost from about £500 or $500 upwards, but at this price the size of the memory and disk storage would be rather small. How can a sensible choice be made if you want to buy one?

You can narrow down the choice simply by eliminating those machines outside your price range and those which have a performance which is either superior (on paper) or inferior to your requirements. This assumes that you know enough about micros to know what to look for in the manufacturer's blurb. If you don't, there are lots of books for beginners available in most bookshops.

Weekly and monthly magazines abound and some have unbiased reviews and lists of machines with performance and price data in them - for example Which Computer and Personal Computer World in the UK and Byte in the US. Some list the machine reviews which appeared in earlier issues and will provide reprints.

When searching a UK magazine recently I found I could buy Apples all over the place - from Claisse-Allen at £8,000, Parr Computer Services at £4,000, and Action Computers at £2,000. Parr offer 9 application packages - the maximum number which where inclusively listed by any supplier, but it is hard to compare like with like because there are so many variations and extras for the same model.

<u>Maintenance</u>

If you've chosen a machine and programs which do the job well you may become more and more dependent upon them, so a breakdown will become more and more of a nuisance or even a disaster. A good, fast, maintenance service is important. Find out about this from others who use the same service.

A good maintenance agreement is expensive - it may cost up to 12.5% of the machine's purchase price per year - or are you prepared to find out enough to be able to diagnose the area in which a fault probably lies and do repairs at least on a "plug in a new board and try it" basis (if the form of construction permits it)? Is it worth buying a spare set of plug in circuit boards for this purpose? Find out the cost of spares and consider the idea.

Alternatively, is the acquisition of enough knowledge to quickly eliminate most faults in this way the right use of your time? Some people like being "handymen/women", others prefer to pay someone else to do it, particularly if they, personally, don't have to pay!

If you use floppy disks buy the best. I use long life disks for heavy use and cheap ones for copies kept as insurance. The latter may only get used twice. Wear and dirt are the enemies. The cost of a good disk easily outweighs the agro and cost of time wasted in only one "incident".

<u>On the acquisition of knowledge</u>

Although 60% of a sample of people in Britain over 14, when asked by Gallup in late 1983 whether they understood the words "software" and "micro" said "never heard of them", the business community can hardly escape them. The well cultivated "progressive" Information Technology image makes us feel inefficient, or even fossilised, if we do not adopt it. The UK Sunday Times "Living with the Computer" supplement dated May 13th 1984 contained an article headed "Instant information: tidy, efficient, paper-free", which is typical of thousands of such publications.

Surely small and medium size businesses should be able to find something to match their requirements from an enormous choice of hardware and software packages, and rejoice in the benefits? The answer may well be yes, but to get to the operational stage, time must be spent absorbing new knowledge for a two-stage process - purchasing and using. But there is a chicken and egg problem.

In order to ask the right questions at the time of purchase, knowledge which can best be gained from experience following hands-on operation is needed. You can ask people who you think may have the required knowledge and experience before buying, but beware of computer buffs disguised as bona fide users. These people love messing about with computers regardless of time. Their attitude towards doing anything useful is beside the point. Fiddling with the thing is an obsession in itself. They will never admit to having had learning problems or unreliable equipment. Their job is to purvey the mystique using a language designed to conceal. Don't listen. To them, experimentation and achievement is rewarding fun, and time rushes by. For you, fiddling about time will soon exhaust your budget and ruin your schedule.

Buying and installing a system needs sufficient knowledge both about the job to be done <u>and</u> computers to be able to ask the right questions about hardware/software performance, operating systems, etc., and assess the value for money of suitable offerings.

When you buy a car, vendors will be pleased to take you for a trial run. There is no way you can take a comparable trial run on your computer. You require suitable software, an appropriate volume of on-board data resembling your own, and your accumulated expertise in order to try out some typical tasks. In the absence of such a test you will have to assess the suitability of the software available; it may need modifying. You will also need to consider reliability, the storage requirements, backup, and maintenance arrangements, and the probability that the vendor will be in business next year. You may require communications (Note. All communications are a hassle). Having purchased the system you will have to learn how to get everything to work, polish up your perception of the strengths and weaknesses of paper-based and machine-based systems, understand computer file organisation, and organise work methods combining paper and machine based data.

There are three aspects which I have found particularly important when attempting to assist people with computer problems at work. They do not usually receive much attention in "proceed carefully" or "which one to buy" publications.

Firstly, try and get a software package ("application program") which is known to work well on the chosen machine and which will do your job, or the best part of it, without modification. The intensely competitive software market brings with it "bells and whistles" salesmanship. 50 "features" look better than 25 in advertisements, but are the extra 25 any use to you?

Have a good look at the Instruction Manual before purchasing. A good manual is worth its weight in gold and it's well worth spending some time in examining it. A good, easily understandable, manual is an exception.

Don't ask someone to write a new software package if it can be avoided. Some people possess one kind of occupational knowledge (e.g. Accountants, Librarians, Chemists, etc.). Others (computer software writers) have another kind. These two groups find it very hard to communicate. For a chemist it is a great advantage to go to a computer person who knows some chemistry - each can then understand the other's jargon.

If you must get a package modified or get a new one written, go to someone with a proven track record for software for your kind of application. It won't be cheap. Negotiate a satisfactory arrangement inclusive of "complete" (an unsatisfactory word, but I cannot think of a better one) documentation including an instruction manual, ideally with enough leeway to add a bonus for adherence to delivery date. Try and get all the details down in writing and avoid changing your mind later (it may give rise to unquoted cost-uncontrolled modifications).

The designer may later become "unavailable" for any one of a number of reasons and if after delivery something doesn't work properly, or if a modification is later required, it's unhelpful if all the relevant information resides only in the designer's head.

Take every precaution against getting into a situation where the software, almost complete, requires an unforseen change and you have to decide whether to put good money after what may already be bad money. Never have there been so many "software experts" about. Modifying someone else's software is often very difficult; if good documentation does not exist it may be well-nigh impossible. Unfortunately it may be impossible to get documentation for proprietary packages, since providers don't want to reveal how their software works for commercial reasons.

Secondly, the current situation regarding operating systems needs some homework. An operating system is software which manages machine functions and allocates the resources of the machine for the job to be done by the application program (the one which does your specific job).

Most microcomputers run on an operating system which is a de facto standard such as CP/M or MSDOS. Your application program will be written to run in conjunction with a designated operating system. The practical effect of this arrangement is that application program writers, knowing that the "housekeeping" will be taken care of by the operating system, can concentrate on the job in hand without needing to spend time on other problems. Consequently there is a large choice of programs, some very cheap, designed to run with designated operating systems.

You will need to acquire two kinds of knowledge - about the application software and about the operating system. Operating system commands are used for general organisation. For example you will discover that two quite different procedures are needed for hard to floppy disk backup depending upon the size of your files and floppy disk capacity.

The newer, faster, 16 bit CPUs enable more sophisticated software to be introduced but larger memories may be needed - 64K must now be reckoned as "small", and floppy disk storage is becoming insufficient for some activities. A recently introduced microcomputer database package (Dayflo) occupies 1 Mbyte (that does not of course include any provision for the user's records). Visi On, with multiple "windows" allowing several tasks to be viewed at the same time, requires 256K of RAM memory and 5 Mbytes of disk. Many people will go for a minimum-cost 8 bit solution for today's job. Another £500-£1000 might just buy you an 8/16 bit machine with Winchester add-on facilities for next year's job as well. Special operating systems and application programs are provided for some of the newer machines - Apple's Lisa and Macintosh machines are examples. But you must then choose from a limited (but rather good) number of programs - the huge CP/M choice is closed.

The third, and perhaps least publicised aspect, is the one which requires most attention in information retrieval applications. Information storage and retrieval can bring great benefits (regardless of occupational specialty) in small/medium sized offices - the biggest market for microcomputers. This aspect really has two parts - adjusting your ingrained paper-based information habits to cope with machine files, and a re-consideration of indexing principles.

Nobody has yet succeeded in designing computer software which follows the curious ways in which paperwork is shuffled about and the way people interact, decisions are made, and office work gets done. This system has evolved over many years and somehow creaks along. A computer-based small-office system on the other hand - let us say a combination of file management, personnel and customer record storage and processing, word processing, information retrieval, accounting and invoicing - is an exercise in systematic formality. It forces concentration upon and changes in working methods which can be beneficial in themselves. It takes some time to re-organise, face up to ways of combining paper and machine-based operations, and appreciate how to make the most of new possibilities.

Unless software is going to be used regularly its complication may require it to be learnt all over again. For instance, try remembering the significance of the way you set up a "spreadsheet" financial model (e.g. Visicalc) when you want to use it again with some different figures after an interval of a few weeks. Rudimentary indexing suffices for some office paperwork. Other papers - for example reports - may require as much attention as scientific articles. Many clues are available about the contents of papers. Visible shelves, drawers, the colour of covers, and even strategically placed piles all help.

Few office software people have heard of Indexing. It is a boring overhead which is never listed among the "features" in glossy software leaflets. Tangible clues are lost when information is electrically stored. Good indexing becomes essential in personal information systems, but vital in central filing systems to avoid the unacceptable penalty of many people's idiosyncratic indexing. Indexing in offices is rarely considered to be a professional activity. It is usually someone's incidental chore. This notion will have to be changed.

<u>FURTHER READING</u>

Information about micromputer hardware and software often overlaps. Further reading about both these topics is listed at the end of Chapter 18 about software.

CHAPTER 18. MICROCOMPUTER SYSTEMS PART 2
SOFTWARE, SYSTEMS, AND MARKETS

Operating system functions

An operating system enables housekeeping jobs to be executed, usually in
conjunction with an application program. An example of a job is the printing of
a line of type; to print a line, data must be transmitted from a specified
address in storage at a specified rate through a specified port to the printer
until the line is complete.

An operating system is a set of programs stored as named files. Programs are
loaded as needed into memory from floppy disk. The operating system disk is kept
in the drive. In micros with hard disk drives the operating system will probably
be loaded initially via the micro's floppy disk drive into the hard disk where it
will be permanently stored and called into memory as needed. The floppy disk is
removed after loading.

If a microcomputer user possesses a machine with a "standard" operating
system the probability of finding a program for the application in hand which
will work is greatly increased. The operative words here are "standard" and
"which will work".

There are no actual standards but certain operating systems are in
widespread use - as _de facto_ standards. A machine capable of running on one or
more operating systems should also be capable of running on the application
programs supported by those operating systems provided that the version of the
machine which is available embodies the right hardware.

Every operating system supports one or more popular high level languages -
that is the operating system and a program written in that language can be used
together. To use a program supplied on a disk in the language, or to write a
program in it, Compiler or Interpreter (see Glossary) programs for the language
must also be available on disk and be called into memory so that the machine can
execute data in machine language. Thus a program in the language can be stored on
disk in a named file which can be manipulated by the operating system and
executed, provided the Compiler or Interpreter programs have been loaded.

A development system (a term which is gradually becoming irrelevant because
of the the increasing comprehensivity of micro-computers) is a microcomputer with
a number of features under the general control of the operating system for
developing application programs - that is the programs designed to actually do
the work for which the machine was purchased. Most microcomputers can be used
only by one programmer at a time, but some are now available for time-sharing -
an arrangement by which it appears to each programmer that he has almost
independent and unrestricted use of the machine. Other multi-user systems of
lesser sophistication are available which enable each user to use different
programs simultaneously, but not the same program simultaneously.

Most operating systems were originally designed to handle the resources of a
particular CPU. Often, modified versions were designed later for other CPUs or to
accommodate the change from 8 bit to 16 bit words in the same CPU family. They
became particularly important when microcomputer disk systems came into
widespread use and a number of them embody the words Disk Operating System (DOS)
into their name for that reason. An operating system is designed to respond to a
user's requirements via a command language and much depends on the repertoire of
commands which can be displayed on the screen and executed. Commands are usually
self-evident words e.g. "CREATE".

To an operating system almost everything is a "file". That means that a file
is not only a set of your records or your text stored on disk - it is an entity

which can be manipulated via the operating system. A file may also be a software routine to control some part of the system – for example an "output file" which is a program for managing the diplay of characters on a CRT or for managing a printer.

An operating system command (OSC) may often itself be a file because when the command is typed a small program must be called up in readiness to handle any of a number of symbols expected to be typed to follow the command. OSC's are words like COPY (copy contents of one named file to another named file) or FILES (display a directory of the names of the files in storage). Other commands are available for the use of a person who may wish to change the software, for example EXEC (execute code at a named address).

As an example of the functioning of an operating system, say you want to write a short program in the assembly language of the machine. After booting (starting up and loading software automatically) the machine, a "*" appears meaning "ready to accept a typed OSC". The appearance of the "*" also indicates that a file has already been called up – namely the keyboard, (an input file) so the machine is ready to accept data from that source. Another file will have been called up automatically as well – the display output file – in order that typed characters will be displayed in the right places.

When CREATE is typed the machine expects instructions in a certain order from the current input file – in this case the keyboard. The first expected item is the file name – let us call the file for the new program TRIAL. The disk directory is first searched for a file called CREATE containing the CREATE program, which already exists and is loaded into memory at an address specified in the file's heading. At the same time instructions are sent to the CPU to arrange for the CREATE program to be in control. When the name TRIAL is typed, a special file on disk which contains data about available disk space, is called from disk into memory. This file is up-dated to show that space has been allocated to TRIAL at a particular address, and is then read back to disk.

The disk directory file is now called into memory, the data required to up-date the directory about TRIAL is added to it and it is then read back on to disk. The CREATE program is still in command and any data typed into TRIAL will be read on to that disk file. The machine will possess facilities to execute programs in the Assembly language of the particular CPU fitted – say an Intel 8080. The programmer now enters his or her program into the TRIAL file. It will consist of line numbers for reference purposes with program source code (8080 assembly language which is described in the manual supplied by Intel) on each line.

Upon completion of the program the operating system command ASSM is typed followed by the file name TRIAL. The assembler software is now loaded into memory and processes the source code in order to translate it into the machine readable binary object code. When that is done the programmer can use another OSC – DEBUG which calls up a special program for debugging the code previously input on the TRIAL file.

As another example with the CP/M operating system, still the most widely used, following the prompt ">A" (indicating that drive A is in use), the command "TYPE LISTC.MEM" would call up a command program named "TYPE" and display the contents of a user's file called "LISTC.MEM". The "TYPE" program, executed by typing "TYPE" is one of many commands/programs available in the operating system. "TYPE" followed by a file name will cause the named file to be rapidly displayed on the screen, line by line, for checking purposes.

Operating systems in general use

Operating systems are closely associated with the instruction set available on the microprocessor used in the Central Processing Unit (CPU). The designer of the operating system will probably have written it in a high level language which has been translated into machine code by a special program (compiler). The compiler uses appropriate codes ("opcodes") selected from the instruction set for the particular microprocessor, followed by data, addresses etc., specifying what has to be done. The microprocessor uses its permanent internal micro-instructions to translate the opcodes into operation sequences.

The 8 bit 8080 and Z80 microprocessors use similar but not identical instruction sets. The CP/M operating system was designed to be used originally with the 8080, and later the Z80. The instruction sets for 16 bit processors such as the Intel 8086 or 8088, Motorola MC-68000, and Zilog Z8000 are larger and different. CP/M 86, Concurrent CP/M 86, MS-DOS, MSX-DOS - a variation of MS-DOS written by Microsoft for Japanese micro manufacturers, Unix/Xenix, and UCSDp are the best known operating systems for use with machines containing these CPUs.

Versions of any of these operating systems seem to be available for use on machines with any of the CPUs just mentioned, although it will always be necessary to check just what runs on what. For example although the MC-68000 is associated particularly with Unix, the new CP/M 68K is now available for MC-68000 machines.

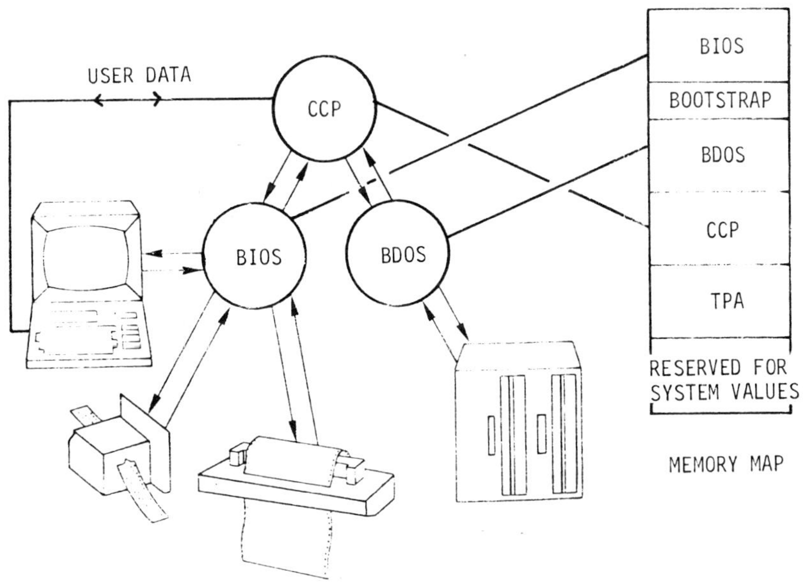

FIGURE 18.1. ORGANISATION OF THE CP/M OPERATING SYSTEM

CP/M, usually believed to stand for "Control Program for Microcomputers" originally stood for "Control Program Monitor". It is organised by modules as shown in Figure 18.1. It was developed by Gary Kidall, founder of Digital Research, in 1975, who own and licence the use of the system. The advent of floppy disk drives following the introduction of the 8080 and Z80 CPUs prompted the production of low cost microcomputer systems which needed a control system.

CP/M arrived at the right moment for mass adoption in the rapidly growing micro business.

Referring to the figure, CCP, the Console Command Processor, does some processing, but is primarily to interpret commands received from the keyboard. It calls up the resources of BIOS and BDOS as necessary. BIOS (Basic Input/ Output System) handles the communication routines carried out by driver programs, and BDOS (Basic Disk Operating System) manages disk files. Different zones of the memory (minimum 16K) are allocated to modules. Programs are loaded into TPA (Transient Program Area). The 16K memory space is arranged as shown in the figure. Each additional 16K of memory purchased by the user is made available for programs (TPA) at the bottom of memory, the top being reserved for the system.

To maximise storage utilisation, the memory is re-arranged when the micro is running a program. For instance after a command has been received and a program is being executed, CCP is emptied and that space is made available as an increase in the capacity of TPA. CCP is made available for its original purpose when the program is finished by calling it in again from disk. Some micro manufacturers purchased CP/M and modified it - for instance Cromemco amd Processor Technology (now defunct) - but the major functions will still be as just described.

CP/M 80's adoption as a <u>de facto</u> standard - at least 100 machines use it - was accompanied by the development of compiler software for many languages including Basic, Fortran, Cobol, Pascal, APL and Pl/1. At one time CP/M became standardised at version 1.4, but further enhancements were soon introduced - 2.2 is a widely used version.

<u>MP/M</u>, a multi-user version of CP/M allowing a single machine to be used for several tasks, followed later and later still came <u>CP/M 86</u>. for the 16 bit 8086 CPU. MP/M was partly superseded by <u>CP/NET</u> for networked distributed processing - for instance for the use of a master computer and its resources, files, etc by any of a number of micros each with its own private files.

At a simpler but still useful level, files can, in principle, be transferred from one CP/M machine to another without MP/M or CP/NET provided they have identical disk drives, by inter-changing disks. If they do not have matching floppy disk drives, two machines, with appropriate local communications software, can be interconnected by means of their RS232 ports and the files transmitted as ASCII code. In practice, differences in application programs may require that software changes be made before this can be done.

Although the different versions of CP/M are compatible the rapid introduction of improvements may mean that if you possess a machine with an early version and purchase a program designed for use with a later version, you may not be able to use some or all of the facilities. It's advisable to check before purchase in case limitations of this kind exist.

The versatility of the various versions of CP/M 86 is certainly considerable. That part of CP/M which needs to be changed to suit the hardware of 8 bit Z80, 8080 or 8085 machines, or 16 bit 8086 or 8088 is located in the BIOS section occupying 12K of memory. This is "easily" done - but not by your average user. The difference between 8 bit and 16 bit systems is well illustrated by the difference between CP/M 80 and CP/M 86. CP/M 80 can manage up to 64K of memory and 64,000 records occupying up to 8 Mbytes in a single user database system. CP/M 86 can manage up to 1 Mbyte of memory and 16 disk drives each containing 8 Mbytes. With multiple users. CP/M plus, yet another new version, is said to increase disk access speeds by five times.

<u>Multi-task windowing with CP/M</u>

Several software vendors are releasing software capitalising on the multi-tasking facilities now available on micros. Multi-tasking means that several programs can be running instantaneously on one machine - as with Concurrent CP/M 86. This enables several "windows" to be displayed on the screen, the data in each being controlled by a different program. Although Apple Lisa is excellent on graphics, and pioneered the use of windows, it cannot function in this manner.

For example one window might be handling telephone numbers, blown up to a size capable of containing a scrollable list of names and numbers large enough to read, or reduced at will to a size just large enough to contain the title "telephone directory". When the number is selected and auto-dialled - perhaps simply by pointing at it, WP software is loaded so that the main area of the screen is available for electronic mail messages. The new software from Visicorp ("VisiOn"), Microsoft ("Windows"), and Digital Research will offer facilities aiming at greater convenience - perhaps a step forward to the long touted "executive work station". We shall see whether an "executive" is also required to be an expert typist/electronics engineer/telecoms person.

MS-DOS

The selection of Microsoft's MS-DOS as the standard operating system for the IBM-PC encourages the belief that it must be a front runner. For MS-DOS version 2.0 it is claimed that special attention has been paid to ease of "transportability" between different hardware arrangements - particularly to take care of apparently similar machines which do in fact have differences between methods of display, cursor codes, and input/output arrangements. This may well have been done as a piece of one-upmanship over CP/M. With MS-DOS a table of "drivers" provided for a range of hardware can be selected. A driver sounds like an electronic device; in fact it is a small program.

Another feature of MS-DOS is the adoption of ANSI standard terminal codes describing terminal types. MS-DOS recognises the identity code from a terminal and adapts itself to suit the one being used - another idea to improve transportability. A formatting standard was not introduced when 5.25" disks started to be used. Consequently you cannot necessarily use any disk. Microsoft was strong enough to establish a de facto standard for MS-DOS. MS-DOS maintains files in a hierarchical structure for ease of organisation and indexing and the directory is particularly easy to use.

Integrated program windowing systems with MS-DOS

Microsoft has already introduced "Microsoft Windows" which uses the mouse and the bit mapped graphics potential of 16 bit machines. This package enables information from unrelated application software packages to be viewed in different windows, and information may be cross-transferred and merged. Microsoft Windows arranges for application programs to be brought into memory so that inter-package operations are fast. In late 1984 it became available on DEC Rainbow, Wang Professional, Zenith Z100, HP 150, and certain Altos and NCR machines.

Another windowing system is competing against Microsoft - DesQ from a US company called Quarterdeck (Santa Monica). General principles and facilities are similar to Microsoft Windows. To be effective such systems require substantial amounts of memory and disk storage. DesQ code takes up to 150K of memory, and the user may wish to have simultaneous access to several application programs. Speed and effectiveness will depend on the amount of memory in his machine. Using an IBM PC, an absolute minimum of 250K memory, with 512K preferred, and a 5 Mbyte hard disk are required. DesQ includes a zoom and unzoom feature - that is identifiable windows/programs can be available on the screen for blowing up, working on, and "pushing away to a corner of the desk" as required.

The potential of systems like this is enormous. Put it on a big screen and in theory, at least, this is real progress. The question is how easy are they to use, and how much better would they be for office tasks? How much ingenuity in software selection, task design, and related paperwork changes are needed to make them really useful? Once you get to grips with them, will you wonder how on earth you managed before, or will they become a new toy syndrome casualty because you need a course on them each time you use them?

UNIX was developed by K.Thompsons at the Bell Telephone Laboratories in 1970 specifically as a time sharing system for the popular 16 bit DEC PDP-7 minicomputer - a machine which was in widespread use in Universities and research establishments. He found that a widely used system called Multics was too complex for small machines - hence the name UN (single user) + IX (borrowed from Multics). Unix is licensed by Western Electric, both Bell and WE, being, of course, AT&T affiliates, at prices the market can stand from $30,000 for big users to $300 for universities. It is supplied by WE on disk for PDP11s but by others in various ways. For instance, Cromemco offers a variation of it with its machines, and Onyx computers offers another variation, ONIX, for its machines.

Since Unix was a 16 bit system from the outset, not a conversion from something else, and because it has many very useful features it may become the 16 bit *de facto* standard operating system. Although it started as a single user system, a multi-user version was soon developed and a huge fund of experience with Unix has accumulated - by 1974 it was already used on over 600 PDP11 installations. Since then it has been modified to run on 16 bit 8086, Z8000 and 68000 CPUs. Unix's strong feature is the hierarchical structure of its file store and directories, with a facility for moving file stores to different levels in the tree structure. This has particular significance in a multi-user system where each file has an owner with unique password access; any file owner can be linked to any other file if he has permission from the owner.

The flavour of Unix becomes obvious when reading the specification for one version, Microsoft's Xenix 3.0, by arrangement with Western Electric, offered at about $250 to individual users and available from Logica in the UK. It includes a software development and text processing system with commands such as "typset mathematics", "permuted index", and "find spelling errors". An inter-Xenix machine electronic mail system is also provided. Xenix is a multi-user system with time sharing software included as part of the package. MS-DOS directories and files can be read and written.

Xenix is the up-market microcomputer operating system. It requires 512K of memory and a 10 Mbyte disk, assuming that time sharing is to be used with a small number of users. When 16 bit micromputers emerged, Unix was already a sophisticated well tested 16 bit operating system backed by the clout of Bell/ AT&T. AT&T's policy of low-fee licencing for Unix at Universities looks like paying off.

In May 1983 Intel and National Semiconductor followed Motorola in announcing microprocessors suitable for Unix machines. Later, Hewlett Packard and NCR stated that Unix would be the operating system for their new micros. As experience accumulates it will be interesting to see how the relative virtues of CP/M, MS-DOS, and Unix/Xenix influence the saleability of micros.Already manufacturers are hedging their bets by fitting two CPU's and offering two operating systems on the same machine.

Another major virtue claimed for Unix is its portability; two of the steps required when modifying it for use with a particular machine - recoding and debugging - are carried out in the high level language. C is well known as being a "programmer's" language, containing special features for software development, and the same may be said for Unix.

The most popular general purpose operating systems used in microcomputers available in 1984 was CP/M followed by MSDOS. A number of other Operating systems available for specific machines were also widely used because the machines were market leaders. They include Apple DOS, Apple SOS, IBM's PC DOS and various TRS80 operating systems.

Software costs and prices

A line of program code fully debugged and documented costs up to $100. Productivity for a simple program tested and documented is about 9 lines of code per hour (LC/H) and for a transportable program which can be run on several types of machine only 3 LC/H. To write an Operating System, productivity is about 1 LC/H for a single-machine system, and 0.33 LC/H for a transportable one. These figures are gradually being out-dated because more sophisticated programming aids are being introduced, badly needed because of the increasing complexity of programmes.

If productivity is 3 LC/H for tested documented code at $40/hour for salary and overheads, the cost of a very modest word processing program in Basic of 3000 lines requiring 24K storage would be $40,000. Marketing, advertising and support would cost at least another $40,000 so 400 copies at $200 each would have to be sold to break even at $80,000. If the purchaser takes one week of learning time before he can start creative work $1000 (say) is added to his start-up costs.

There is a huge difference between manufacturers in the presentation of instructional information, either by screen tutorials and "help" aids, or by Instruction Manuals. Few manuals are written by professional writers – they usually seem to be written by engineers with disastrous results. At the low prices often charged for some software packages no margin is available for a decent manual. Fortunately producers of business microcomputers are just starting to assume that the buyer might not be a computer buff and manuals fit for ordinary people are starting to appear. Table 18.1 shows typical US and UK prices for some popular software.

The popularity of integrated software, such as Lotus 1-2-3 and Symphony now joined by Jazz designed especially for Macintosh, is growing rapidly. The next development – too new to appear on the table – will be multi-tasking software such as IBM's Topview and DEC's Gem which will enable different programs running concurrently to be viewed on windows at the same time. After that will probably come multiprocessing on a number of processors with advanced pipelining – that is fetching and routing instructions for co-ordinated processors. The hardware and software for multiprocessing on micros will not be available for some time to come.

	$	£
Bstam (Coms)		135
DBase II	269	280
DBase III	339	325
Easywriter II	219	
Framework	339	350
Lotus 1-2-3	229	325
PC Draw	259	
Smartcom II (Coms)	109	
Supercalc	199	261
Symphony	419	425
TK! Solver	269	
Wordmac		171
Wordstar	199	260

TABLE 18.1 TYPICAL SOFTWARE PRICES

Microcomputer Languages

BASIC. (Tiny Basic, Basic, Extended Basic, MBasic and other variations). BASIC was developed in 1964 by Kemeny and Kurz at Dartmouth College in the United States and generally introduced by Microsoft Inc., in 1975. It is easily the most popular microcomputer language, being suitable for first-time users and for more advanced work with subroutines, strings etc. A version of it, often in the form of an Interpreter program on disk, is available for nearly all microcomputers and operating systems.

FORTRAN (FORmula TRANslation) was introduced many years ago for scientific and engineering numerical applications in batch mode for mainframe computers. Later, interactive versions became available, and later still microcomputer versions for numerical work. Available on a number of machines, it is efficient in terms of machine code generated per statement and strong on arithmetic routines.

COBOL (COmmon Business Oriented Language) also introduced years ago for mainframe computers, is more suitable for "information" handling (that is for "human" information not "data" information). Cobol is structured to handle business applications and is generally available for most microcomputers as Cobol-80.

PASCAL is named after the French mathematician Blaise Pascal who invented a calculating machine in 1642. Pascal's sister stated that he discovered for himself most of Euclid's theorems when he was 12 years old. Developed by Wirth and confined for some time to academia, it was made available for microcomputer use at the University of California (San Diego) in 1970 and versions are now available from Intel, Zilog, Texas and others.It is favoured by some teachers in preference to Basic, as a starting language for newcomers and is becoming increasingly popular for micros, allowing problems to be solved in the way natural thought problems are solved - from the top downwards.

C a language closely associated with the UNIX operating system, which owes some of its origins to BCPL - a high level language originated at Cambridge University. The language was called C by Bell Laboratories when developed for use with Unix on their own PDP machines. C is very suitable for general work, is economic to use and easy to write and is likely to come into wide use in view of the increasing popularity of Unix.

By 1981 Basic was supported on 75% of the available operating systems (meaning that it could be used on microcomputers in conjunction with those operating systems) although it was starting to be displaced by other languages. Fortran had spurted from 35% to over 50% presumably because of the increasing use of small machines for scientific purposes in universities. Pascal's operating system support had grown from 45 to 50%, and Cobol from 22 to 33% reflecting the growth of business applications.

The most popular language used in microcomputers in 1984 was Basic (all versions) followed by Pascal, Cobol, and Fortran.

Comparing 8 and 16 bit machines

The maximum size of memory fitted to most microcomputers is around 1.05 Mbytes usually known as "1024K". The most popular 16 bit processors are the Intel 8086 and 8088, Motorola 68000, and Zilog Z8001 and Z8002. The realisation of the potential of either an 8 or 16 bit machine is strongly dependent upon the operating system which manages the facilities provided. For instance Microsoft's MSDOS will provide access to a memory of 1000K maximum size and can control up to 1000 Mbytes of disk storage. Microsoft's Xenix will also access 1000K memory, and up to 230 Mbytes of disk. It will not support the Pascal high level language which can be used with MSDOS. Motorola's Versados will access 16000K, and up to 192 Mbytes. Versados and Xenix are multi-user multi-task operating systems, while MSDOS is single user single task.

At present there is nothing like the volume of software available for 16 bit machines as there is for 8 bit. The 16 bit software doesn't necessarily capitalise on all aspects of 16 bit potential - it may have been developed from 8 bit.

It seems that the benefits of 16 bit machines are the ability to address larger memories for those applications where it is needed, and faster, but not as fast as might be expected, operation than is possible with 8 bit machines. Other benefits are more subtle. For example in certain applications with large files where sorting operations or string matching is required,the rate of execution will be faster with larger memories because larger amounts of data can be transferred from disk at a time into memory for processing.

Microcomputer "power" is sometimes expressed in another form - number of Instructions Per Second (IPS). The higher the IPS the faster the execution of a program, but it won't be pro rata. In late 1982 two machines appeared claiming very fast operating speeds. A Danish machine, Unimax, produced by Dansk Data Elektronic, embodies 8 MC68000 processors interlinked by a 32 bit 4 Mbyte/sec bus, each with its own memory, and capable of operating at nearly 5 million instructions per second. Another machine, the Sage II from the US, incorporating one 68000, claims 2 million instructions per second, part of the speed being due to the use of RAMs operating at 150ns with no waiting time.

One result of this is that auxiliary operations become very fast - for example it takes only one second to load a 20K program from disk with the Sage. A Sage II (which will take up to a 500K memory) with 128K memory and one disk drive costs $3600. If the Apple II's instruction rate is 1, the relative rates of the machines discussed are IBM personal 3.5, Sage 14, and Unimax 35.

But, in plain language, what does all this mean for the user? Is a 16 bit system better than an 8 bit, and if so by how much? Let us forget, for the moment, that CP/M and 8 bit systems enjoy the advantage of having been around for so long that there are many more ready to use programs available. Say you want to buy a micro and you must have an application program specially written because nothing suitable exists; what then?

The clock and cycle times in 16 bit CPUs are usually higher than 8 bit. Clock oscillators run at up to 12 MHz, compared with up to about 4 MHz. This provides cycle times of less than 100 nanoseconds (0.1 microseconds or over 10 million cycles per second) compared with 250 ns, in theory.

Since data can, presumably, be moved around in 16 bit chunks, and 16 bits can convey numbers up to over 4 million instead of up to 65000, surely this ought to result in much faster processing of more information, shorter response times etc?

The most popular programs are Word Processing, Financial and Spread sheet packages, and Accounting, and if true 16 bit programs were available they would not be substantially better then 8 bit ones. These applications are conceptually familiar, imitating paper-based systems more or less and are not seriously limited by technical factors.

The benefits of 16 bit systems seem to be mainly in the wider number of applications which become possible.

First, 16 bits remove the 8 bit addressing bottleneck, enabling many more stored items to be addressed. Semiconductor memory and disk storage is now quite cheap. Consequently 125K, 256K, and upwards directly addressable memories can be fitted at low cost. This large memory enables effective multi-user and multi-task systems to be used. New operating systems, such as Concurrent CP/M, capable of running several jobs simultaneously, have been developed in consequence of the availability of larger useable memories.

Second, certain single user applications benefit from large memories - notably image processing and high resolution graphics.

Third, since large amounts of data can now reside in cheap Winchesters, but data must be brought into memory for high speed processing, larger quantities of data can be brought in at one time. This should enable faster processing to be carried out in certain applications as, for instance, when strings of text fetched from disk are matched against query strings stored in memory during database searches.

When memory gets still more compact and yet cheaper, all data could reside in memory and this would result in yet faster processing and shorter response times.

The protagonists of the various microcomputer operating systems argue continuously about their merits. The field is very competitive and each system is being steadily improved. One which is leading one day may be lagging the next.

The difference between 8 bit and 16 bit systems is well illustrated by the difference between CP/M and CP/M 86. CP/M can manage up to 64K of memory and 64,000 records occupying up to 8 Mbytes in a single user database system. CP/M 86 can manage up to 1 Mbyte of memory and 16 disk drives each containing 8 Mbytes, with multiple users. CP/M plus, yet another new version, is said to increase disk access speeds by five times.

<u>Microcomputer communications</u>

One of the simplest requirements is to communicate with another machine of the same type, say via the Public Switched Telephone Network (PSTN). Given the appropriate hardware, interface, modems etc., for the two machines, you must possess software to enable you to establish contact, do the preliminary electronic "handshaking" that is always needed, obtain access to, or transfer information from, the other machine, exchange messages with its user etc. The software should be self evident in operation - that is, since you are not (I assume) a computer buff, it should prompt you for its requirements by displaying messages or alternative choice menus.

Your next most likely requirement would probably be to communicate with a remote machine from which some service is available - for instance the facilities for searching a remote database. In this case you will need to be able to make your machine look like a terminal of a type with which you know that the remote machine can communicate, and then use your own telecommunications and possible database search software.

Nearly all the publications about this matter give the impression that it is simple. The author of a recent article describes how a home microcomputer might be connected to Euronet - the European network to which are also connected a number of host computers with access to databases. "It is a trivial matter to program these home computers to recognise any key depression....in addition the local processing power could be exploited...etc". This is a gross over-simplification.

Unfortunately there is no way to avoid part or all of the Protocol issues discussed in Chapter 6 just because you are using a micro. Similar methods are required for similar communication requirements whatever the machine.

You will also need to know about how physically to arrange modem interconnections (supposedly "standardised" but in practice not) and you must be made aware by the resident software of what you have to do when you want to communicate with another like machine, a machine of a different make, a remote host or bureau mainframe computer, or a local or remote particular minicomputer or mainframe. When you type something the software at both ends must enable a replica of your text to be viewed on the remote machine, or it must enable the desired action to be executed, say to move some text which you already have on disk to the remote machine.

Very occasionally the awful truth emerges from an author who has no vested interest in pursuading you that communications is simplicity itself. "First the hardware doesn't necessarily work right away. Even though we had owned our micro for a couple of years the addition of the RS232 interface revealed an addressing problem. Then it took some fiddling with the little switches....... before the speeds and codes matched...All in all it took three or four weeks before everything was squared away....To start you want to be able to input and output characters....it can be done using BASIC... novelty with which you may want to experiment....that leaves Assembler...but where are the ROM routines which BASIC uses to drive the IEEE interface and how can I access them from Assembler?"

Where indeed. This author, writing in the publication EMMS, then provides a program listing and if you use it and it works you can actually output a character!

You may be able to buy a   machine which does exactly what you want but if you are unable to ask the right questions and get true answers it is unlikely that you will find the required   information spelled out in the Manual and extremely unlikely that you will be able easily to carry out what you quite reasonably expect to be a simple operation.

In August 1984 I wanted to move   some text from an old microcomputer to a new one. Since text is transmitted as ASCII code by both machines and both use the CP/M operating system it would seem to be rather easy to stand the machines side by side and interconnect their RS232 telecommunication ports. The old machine would be

Cartoon by S.Harris from Science Goes To The Dogs, ISI Press (By permission). A flowchart used for somewhat more serious purposes is shown in Chap.3.

commanded to transmit a text file, created using its word processing software, into the new machine so that it would be useable with the new machine's word processing software. In my usual sceptical manner I approached this apparently simple requirement with trepidation.

A search revealed that no software existed which could be used on the old machine to handle port to port transmission. Proprietry software did exist for the new machine which would put it in a "waiting" condition ready to receive code when the old machine was commanded to transmit, and would load the text into a word processing file on the new machine. I was assured by the dealer that it would work, but double checked with the manufacturer who gave a guarantee that it would. My kindly dealer allowed me to add a clause to my order stating that if it did not, he would return the money. It did not and the money was returned.

I reasoned to myself that since both my old and new machines could inter-communicate with the same printer for printing text, why couldn't I simply buy a software package to install in the new machine to make it look like a printer? If a cable from this machine was then plugged into the socket on the old machine normally used for the printer and the old machine was commanded to print, it would happily communicate believing it was connecting to the usual printer.

Unfortunately the software fraternity are unable to think in such simple terms and no software of this kind exists. I realised that I would have to get someone to write it. Eventually I discovered a person who could provide something like it and, much more important, was entirely prepared to cater for a disbeliever. Certainly my concept was feasible; he would modify his existing package, bring it to my office, and would not consider the job done until it was tested and conformed to my specification. Cost? Not more than £400. At that price it made no sense to take time off to acquire the degree of detailed knowlege needed to do the job myself, so I accepted.

What a gentleman! There really are such men in the computer business! (See under "Wordmongers" in "Further reading" at the end of this chapter). He was as good as his word and charged me £340, but he had problems. For example the underlining in underlined words created using the old system was the result of an instruction which could not be interpreted by the new system. Each time it appeared there were problems. He simply modified his software there and then so that each time the underline code appeared it was ignored. He did not leave until the software worked perfectly.

The moral of this story is clear. Never assume that anything to do with computers is simple. If you are forced to get software written <u>caveat emptor</u> and then <u>caveat emptor</u> again!

<u>Microcomputer networks</u>

Hams and CB radio enthusiasts became interested in networks in the US in 1976. A Personal Computer Network (PCNET) group of volunteers started to investigate the exchange of messages over the PSTN in 1977. This culminated in the Chicago Community Bulletin Board System in which software and protocols had been sufficiently well agreed for a kind of electronic mail system to be established early in 1978. Users call a central unattended machine to which they "deliver" a message, or they can find out whether anybody has left one addressed to them. Also in 1978 New York (Buffalo) University announced plans for a packet switched network using DEC LSI-11 microcomputer nodes for research purposes.

By 1981 microcomputer manufacturers had started to offer bits and pieces for various kinds of networks.

Zilog offer Z-net - a coaxial cable Local Area Network (LAN). It consists of the Z80 based MCZ series microcomputers, a network station transmitter/transceiver, and network protocol software. Nestar have adopted Apple II machines in their Cluster One 16-wire connected system, using 8 bits in parallel transmission. They feel confident enough to publish a table comparing it with Ethernet. It includes packet switching and sophisticated protocol but operates at 240 Kbps compared with Ethernet's 10 Mbps.

Digital Research, originators of the CP/M operating system, offer the CP/NET network operating system to enable microcomputers to access common network facilities. The cost of expensive programs, databases, etc., can be shared among the users.

The Micro to Mainframe connection

The realisation by many organisations that they possess micros scattered around the place, usually purchased on a departmental basis without the knowledge of the Data Processing (DP) Department, has forced consideration of centralising resources in a mainframe computer using micros as connected intelligent terminals. By the time they wake up to this idea, incompatibility problems have become horrendous. However special micro-to-mainframe software connection packages are now available which are alleged to deal with this situation. Such packages may also be needed if micros are purchased centrally for use with the organisation's mainframe, not supplied by the manufacturer of the mainframe, but selected for reasons of cost or performance.

The problem of inter-computer communications is widespread because of machine incompatibility brought about by rapid advances in a highly competitive field with little regard for standards. Some would say that if there had been a regard for standards - a notoriously difficult area in which to obtain a consensus - then the rate of advance in price/performance would have been much slower. Predictably a very large number of software offerings are available claimed to enable files to be transferred between machines. The golden rule is to check whether somebody else has successfully used a particular software package in exactly the same situation as contemplated by yourself - a piece of information likely to be worth a good deal of time and money.

MICROCOMPUTER HARDWARE AND SOFTWARE: SELECTED EXAMPLES

The IBM personal computer

IBM's entry into microcomputers late in 1981 made micros respectable. The IBM PC was developed in just over a year, is being marketed through retailers, and uses operating systems written by other companies - IBM realised that the "all home-grown treatment" accorded to its other products was inappropriate and acted accordingly. The PC was launched in the US first, and people in the UK realised something unusual was going on when IBM turned its attention to this country in 1983. Regular full page advertisements in the national press followed by extensive TV advertising for microcomputers was something new.

What other microcomputer manufacturer can operate an advertising budget to compare with a company with a turnover of $44KM (44 billion dollars)? We must hope that indigenous industries will continue to be able to offer choices.

The IBM PC uses the Intel 8088 16 bit processor. It is similar to other currently available 16 bit machines, selling at about the same price. There are a number of machines at £3000 - £4000 in the UK when compared on a like-with- like basis - that is which includes 128K memory, hard disk, and operating system at about the same price. The PC will run on several different operating systems, but a preferred system is emerging - Microsoft's PC/DOS which IBM sells for £32. CP/M 86 from Digital Research is available at £200.

A range of application programs are available from well known houses such as Peachtree, and versions of Visicalc, Wordstar and other well known programs are available for it. The colour graphics facilities are good, and the instruction manuals, in several volumes, are an example of what can and should be done.

Hard disk units up to 27 Mbytes, a huge range of plug-in alternative boards and disk drives, and all sorts of accessories and software are available from dozens of suppliers hanging on to IBM's coat-tails. Thus you can buy 512K memory, clock calendar, IBM asynch ports, printer port, disk emulator and spooling on one plug in board; special communication boards; 5 Mbyte Winchesters which fit inside it; 27 Mbyte Winchesters with tape backup; specially made lock-up cabinets to keep it in, and printers which not only work with it but are styled like it. If you want very high resolution - no problem. You can buy a 690 line colour monitor which plugs into it.

The advent of this machine had, and is having, a strong influence on other microcomputer manufacturers who advertise their machines as "fully compatible with the IBM personal computer", "IBM circuit board compatible expansion slots" etc. IBM has recently moved further making it obvious that the PC is also designed to gather in to the fold any of its mainframe users who might also be using micros dotted about the place manufactured by somebody else.

The 3270 PC, recently announced in the US at $5600, eliminates the need to buy additional bits and pieces to enable the IBM PC to look like an IBM 3270 terminal in order to connect to and exchange information with IBM mainframe. Until now this had to be done in two stages. Emulation was done by buying a communications card and some software, available from several suppliers. This made the PC look like a 3270 terminal. Next you needed more software to move files between the mainframe and micro, and to use them with word processing, spreadsheet or other programs. The 3270 PC provides all this ready to go, plus a display of 7 windows simultaneously, 4 of them variable-size and able to display different applications by direct connection to the IBM host computer. High resolution colour is included.

Yet another new version - the XT/370 PC - includes a 655K (4 Mbytes max. option) memory, 2 Motorola 68000 processors, and an 8087. With this power the machine can run on the VM/CMS (Virtual Machine/Conversational Monitor System) IBM mainframe operating system.The capability of bringing mainframe software down on to a desktop machine will enable programme development for micros/mainframes to be carried out by people without an IBM mainframe who previously had to use a time-sharing bureau.

IBM also tackled the home computer market with the PC Jr, offered in the US at $669 64K basic, or $1269 128K with double density disk drive. The keyboard communicates with the machine by an infra-red link, TV control unit style, and so may be used at a distance from it. It was not a success.

Radio Shack/Tandy

Radio Shack were the first major manufacturer to respond to IBM with a complete competitive machine - the TRS80 model 16 - using a Motorola MC68000 32/16 bit processor. It also embodies the same processor - the Z80 - as is used on earlier TRS80 models so it will run all the software written for them. Tandy enjoys the considerable advantage of its well established Radio Shack computer shops which should help it to withstand IBM competition.

.Tandy has also introduced the TRS80 model 2000 with the same operating system as IBM - MS/DOS from Microsoft. It uses the 80186, a later version of the 8088 used in the IBM PC and embodies twin floppy disks providing 720 Kbytes storage - twice the capacity of the IBM PC. With a 128K memory it sells for $2750 substantially undercutting the PC. It is said to be three times faster.

Apple Lisa and Macintosh

The Xerox Star was a truly innovatory machine. It embodies the "look, point, and select" concept under the control of a "mouse" hold-in-the-palm slide-about-on-your-desk device. The position of a screen cursor follows the movement of the mouse exactly. When you point to a menu item, overlaid paper-like "sheets", containing black-on-white print, appear on the screen. Smaller windows with narrower choices can be opened at convenient positions to enable more specific point and select commands to be executed. These facilities are also incorporated in Lisa and its smaller brother Macintosh.

Apple designers have provided bit-mapped facilities under software control, meaning that information is displayed by controlling individual pixels, as opposed to moving stored patterns of pixels en bloc - for instance to represent characters.

The mouse is a ball mounted under a small hand-held box. The ball rotates as the mouse is moved across a surface driving two small rollers at right angles to each other which provide the positional information for the screen cursor. A single button on the mouse enables two commands to be executed from one cursor pointing. One press selects a window, and a second press will open it for viewing the next level.

When first switched on, Lisa displays a set of small objects called ikons, to take care of preliminaries. This set is the pictorial equivalent of a menu. Instead of an invitation to initiate an action by reading several numbered lines of text, and then keying a number, you move the cursor over an ikon and press a button on the mouse to indicate selection.

The major choice on the introductory "pictorial menu" is "profile" - a pictorial directory. When you point and select "profile", you get the first screen display. This is a disk directory presented in a novel way. In most micros you type the name of the file you want. With Lisa you see ikons with titles.

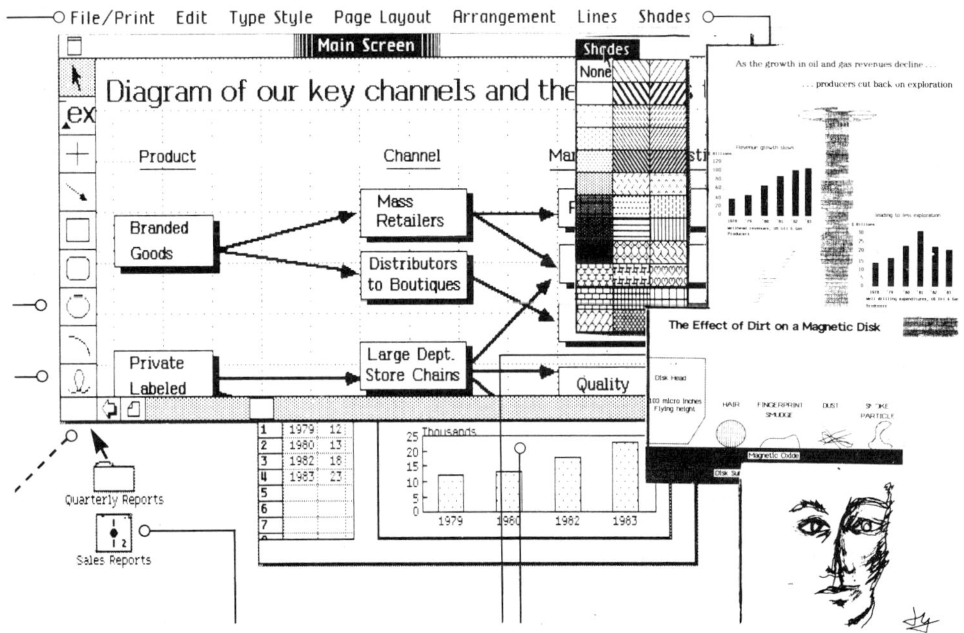

<u>FIGURE 18.2.   LISADRAW DISPLAY AND SOME SKETCHES DRAWN WITH IT</u>

The designers of Lisa chose menu-driven software in an integrated microcomputer cum operating system cum application software package, - the designers had control over every part of the system. What they chose to do was to provide a number of software packages with standardised self-evident presentation and command procedures, any of which may be called up to be used on the work in progress as the situation demands.

A window resembles a menu in that behind it lies a structure resembling a tree where the roots branch out to finer detail. Thus, pointing at "Edit" opens the "Edit" window and further choices are available. Another set of narrower options may appear for each choice in such a window in much the same way as in a hierarchy of menus, where more detailed choices appear each time a number is keyed.

Options such as Cut, Copy, Paste, or Select All, enable selected or all parts of the work area to be moved and merged with work called up from storage under the control of the current program, or, if a different program is called up, under the different control facilities which then become available.

Having looked at the directory the user will probably point to one of the different kinds of "stationery" - for example "Lisawrite paper" if he wants to do this kind of work. This does not mean that he is committed to the word processing program (Lisawrite). If he wants to include some graphics he can shift to another program, and the menu information in the area surrounding the work changes to relate to the graphics software aids.

With Lisadraw, great flexibility is provided by an array of symbols on the left of the screen which can be selected and moved into position for building your own drawings in conjunction with a facility for stretching or contracting a symbol to properly connect to another symbol (point, stretch, or contract) see Figure 18.2. With this array of choices coupled to the recall of bits of text, columns, or anything else which may be retrieved from some earlier activity the possibilities are enormous. Because the system is bit-mapped at the pixel level, even freehand sketching can be done, the main limitation here being the user's ability to sketch with a mouse instead of with a pencil.

Lisawrite is a Word Processing package and Lisalist is a list-oriented personal database. A variety of forms/lists can be stored, retrieved, regularly up-dated, sorted and columnised in different ways if necessary, and then printed. Row entries are typed from the keyboard, and a wide range of sorting/ re-arranging options are provided. Search criteria for information retrieval is specified by filling in a small table. Fields may be specified and operators such as "less than" "greater than" etc., may be used.

Apple cut the US price of Lisa in September 1983 to $7000 without its six special software packages and $8200 with them. The UK price was dropped to £6500 with software. Its earlier selling price in the UK was £8000, then equivalent to around $12,000.

Apple cancelled software being developed by Cullinet to enable Lisa to interface IBM mainframes. However in November 1983 Apple stated that IBM's PC-DOS operating system would soon be available for Lisa. Apple planned to introduce new versions of Lisa in mid-1984 using the Motorola MC-68000 CPU. Also in November 1983, Apple announced an add-on unit for Apple II's to enable them to run programs designed for the IBM PC.

Apple did bring out Lisa 2 in 1984 with 512K memory and a 3.5 inch 400K disk drive at $3495 for the basic model and $5495 for the top of the range model with 10 Mbyte Winchester disk. At the same time it introduced the Macintosh with MC-68000 CPU, 128K memory and 3.5 inch disk drive at $2495.

The Macintosh is a scaled down version of Lisa and incorporates many of the facilities described above. Early in 1985 a Macintosh with a 512K memory was introduced selling for $3495, and a whole range of improvements were announced aimed at the office market including the Zilog 8530 SCC chip with Appletalk software enabling Macintoshes to communicate on a twisted pair LAN at up to 230 Kbps, with a laser printer and file printer for added resources. Finally (or at least as far I can go in this edition of this book) Apple announced in May 1985 that it would phase out Lisa.

All these measures indicate the traumatic effect that the IBM PC and the steady introduction of more and more powerful versions of it have had on the business micro market. Apple's draconian measures have not saved it from getting into the financial difficulties experienced by many other manufacturers. Currently it is implementing drastic cuts in its work force.

However Macintosh has been very well received and a wide range of software is offered for it by from competing suppliers.

Vectorgraphic

Vectorgraphic (sometimes shortened to Vector, but not to be confused with Victor) is not in the same size league with the above companies, but I include it here because a Vector 4 was my choice in 1983 against several other competitive offerings. The 8/16 bit Vector 4, currently costing around £4000 in the UK, has a 5 Mbyte Winchester disk on board and both Z80B and 8088 CPUs. When loaded with the 8 bit CP/M operating system the Z80B is used and any of the many CP/M-compatible application programs can be run on it.

In the 16 bit/8088 mode, 8 bit programs can still be run. For instance Vector's excellent Memorite WP software will run either with CP/M 80 or CP/M 86 but the user will not notice much difference. The advantages of true 16 bit application software can be realised if such software is available.

The MS-DOS operating system, to work with the 8088, can be loaded into the Vector. The machine will then run most programs written for the IBM PC. Most, but not all IBM PC programs will run with either MS-DOS or PC-DOS. Subsequently Vector introduced the 4/60 with CP/M 86 including a double shock mounted 46 Mbyte Winchester disk.

Vectorgraphic Inc., has been restructured following the resignation of its founder, Lore Harp. I hope that it will survive.

ACT

ACT (Advanced Computer Techniques) is the most successful UK Company in the business machines market. In 1981 it recognised the trend towards 16 bit machines and concluded a 3 year agreement with Victor, at that time one of the few manufacturers of such machines. It sells a Victor machine, re-named the Act Sirius 1, for £2895 in the UK with 256K memory and twin double sided 5.25" floppy disks providing 2.4 Mbytes storage. The Sirius SX includes a 10 Mbyte Winchester and sells for £3995. The ACT Sirius is estimated to have captured about 18% of the market for machines of this type in the UK.

The Sirius uses the 8088 CPU with CP/M 86, Basic, Cobol, Fortran and Pascal, and a comprehensive set of application programs for word processing, mailing,financial spreadsheet, etc., including its own Pulsar accounting package are provided. ACT have recently introduced a communications/protocol software module enabling files to be transferred at up to 9600 bps between two different microcomputers when each is loaded with the module. So far the module is available for inter-working between Act Sirius, Act Apricot, IBM PC and Apple IIE.

ACT launched the Apricot microcomputer, manufactured in Glenrothes, Scotland (but with sub-assemblies made in the Far East) in the US and UK in December 1983, aiming for UK 1984 sales of up to 40,000 machines. ACT hoped to sell 20,000

Apricots in the US in 1984 through distributors. Target revenue for Apricot in 1984 was £25M. Apricot is a portable 16 bit machine with 256K memory and two processors - an 8086 cpu and an 8089 chip for handling ports, peripherals, and comunications. It has several disk options, all with the new Sony 3.5" disk, from 1 single-sided drive (315 Kbytes) up to 2 double-sided (1.44 Mbytes).

The minimum-disk version sells for £1690, the largest for £1890 including the 80 character x 25 line (320K pixel) monitor. The price also includes CP/M 86 and Concurrent CP/M 86 operating systems and Basic. All other software is extra - for instance Wordstar £295, Pulsar business system modules £195 each, Supercalc 3 £195, Database II £395, etc. MS-DOS and UCSD operating systems are also available together with the usual high level languages.

ACT is currently trying to maintain its 80% annual growth rate record, having exceeded its forecasts (current sales are £80M a year), by expanding into the US and Europe. The price of its shares continues to fall in spite of its success, reflecting the general uncertainty in microcomputer futures.

Wang

The Wang Professional Computer sells for around £3000 in the UK and will operate as a stand-alone, as a work-station in Wang multi-user office systems, or in distributed computing operations emulating IBM 2780 and 3780 connected to a mainframe. The machine uses the 8086 16 bit processor, includes 128K memory, and can be supplied with 320K up to 720 Kbyte floppy disks and a 10 Mbyte hard disk. It will run on MS-DOS or CP/M 80 operating systems. Software includes Basic, the usual high level languages, and various utilities and work-station emulation packages.

However Wang has made a bigger impact with its announcement of the Personal Image Computer (PIC). This was very timely in view of IBM's domination of the microcomputer news headlines. The PIC can digitise a picture held in a stand and viewed by a form of TV camera. The machine comes with 512 Kbytes of memory and a 10 Mbyte disk with storage for 100 images. This implies about 800 Kbits per picture - quite a respectable resolution. The WP software supplied with the machine enables an image to be reproduced as an inset with text. Text consisting of annotations, captions etc., can be prepared for overlaying a picture, the result being stored as a composite picture/text file.

It will be sold in the US for around $15,000 excluding the laser printer - needed to do full justice to the stored pictures. Database software is included so text/pictures may be indexed, stored, processed,locally reproduced or transmitted. This gives the currently unique advantage of keeping illustrated pages in one place ready for serial transmission as a bit-stream, to be reconstituted by a remote receiving machine back into a text/picture format.

It will be interesting to see how this machine finds applications which it can do better than current alternatives - for instance Apple Macintosh, fax systems, separate photos-from-a-drawer-of-photos with text (estate agent style) etc. But Wang is no exception in being hit by current uncertainties.

Hewlett Packard

Bill Hewlett and David Packard started up in a garage workshop. In 1938 they managed to get an important order - some oscillators to be used by Walt Disney for special sound effects in Fantasia. Further successes followed and HP moved into computers in 1966. The company's turnover is now over $4 Billion. Until recently HP have been up-market at the scientific end of computing and their advertisement "Merging science with business" for the HP 200 model 16 personal technical computer still reflects this. The software includes computation & analysis, computer aided engineering, and R&D/business management packages.

Context MBA software, embodying spreadsheet, graphics, WP, database management and telecoms with windowing in one package is also available. This machine uses the Motorola 68000 16 bit (32 bits internally) CPU, and comes with 256 Kbytes of memory and twin 3.5" disk drives for disks totalling 540 Kbytes capacity, at around £3000. This includes HP's own operating system and their improved Basic. CP/M and Unix are also available.

A large range of add-on units are optional for the 200/16 including higher capacity floppies, Winchesters, various kinds of printers and plotters, and additional plug-in boards for use with other software such as Statistics Libraries, Waveform Analysis, Filter Design etc.

In 1984 HP announced the HP 150 with touch-screen control achieved by interruption by the finger of narrow vertical and horizontal light beams in the CRT frame. It uses MS-DOS with an 8088 CPU. Special software is included - for instance a file can be opened by touching the indexing tab of files displayed as if arranged in the drawer of a filing cabinet. The machine has a high resolution screen. Price in the UK is around £2500 (excl.VAT) inclusive of 256K disk storage.

Portables

At present, display size and storage capacity are the main items sacrificed when using a truly portable battery operated microcomputer such as the Tandy TRS80 Model 100 or the Convergent Technologies Workslate. The advantages are that these machines can be used anywhere by sales reps., travellers, and others in planes, cars, trains, hotel rooms etc. The Model 100 displays 320 characters at a time on a liquid crystal display. The machine is designed primarily for word processing. The Workslate is primarily for financial/spreadsheet work and displays 736 characters.

The same Japanese designer, Kyocera, who designed the Tandy also designed the NEC 8201A, another portable which you can use on your lap. Fitted with alkali batteries providing 18 hours work-time before recharging, it includes a full size keyboard, memory up to 64K, CMOS 8085 CPU, and a liquid crystal display of eight 40-character lines. Since the operating system and some programs are stored in a 32K ROM, all but 4k of the RAM (into which the operating system needed for WP is loaded) is available for storing text - 60K is equivalent to about 20 A4 pages of text. When you get back to the office you print it. As in other portables the RAM incorporates CMOS technology (See Chapter 2) so that stored information remains so long as the batteries are connected. The more usual nMOS dynamic RAM requires fast periodic refreshment of the decaying stored charge. The NEC 8201A costs £475 (excluding VAT) in the UK.

The Sharp PC-5000 portable includes 128K of RAM expandable to 256K for user's files, a 192K ROM for software, full size keyboard, and incorporates the 16 bit 8088 CPU with MS-DOS operating system. An 8-line 80-character liquid crystal flat display is included. Optional extras with the Sharp include a 320K floppy disk unit and a 128K bubble memory.

Computers on a chip or on a single plug-in board

A "computer on a chip" has often been talked about, but it depends what you mean by a computer. The phrase cannot be true literally because to most people a "computer" includes "peripherals" - that is the means of inputting information, for instance a keyboard, and the means of outputting it, for instance a CRT with its associated circuits and adjustments.

A "computer on a chip" may turn out to be simply a microprocessor although more and more of the supporting circuits are being incorporated on to the chip which contains the CPU.

The Intel 8051 is an example of an 8-bit one chip device. It contains 60,000 transistors on a silicon wafer 0.023 inches square. Included on the chip are the CPU with 128 8-bit registers, crystal controlled oscillator and timing circuits, 4096 bytes of program memory, 128 bytes of data memory, two 16 bit timing and event counters, duplex Universal Asynchronous Receiver and Transmitter (UART), and 32 programmable input/output lines.

"Computers" on one circuit board are readily available. To turn them into a microcomputer you need to add a CRT unit, keyboard, power supply and disk drive. A board costs around $400, so you should be able to put together a complete machine for around $1000 in the US. Such a machine could have quite a good performance because boards are available which run on the latest version of CP/M and include a Z80 cpu, 64K RAM, real time clock, serial and parallel ports, floppy disk controller capable of handling up to 4 8inch drives, and sophisticated display controller.

<u>Image digitisers</u>

If you don't have a Wang PIC a US company called Micron offers a complete outfit consisting of camera with tripod, a RAM store at the camera end so you can connect a remote camera to your machine with ordinary wire, and instruction manual. It costs about $500. This is no toy. The camera sends 256 line pictures at 20 frames per second, and includes freeze frame facilities and automatic iris. The control is from software supplied on a floppy disk to suit Apple 2, IBM, TRS 80 and other microcomputers.

<u>Memories</u>

A 16K dynamic 8-bit memory device now costs about $16 in the US, which implies that a 64K memory would cost $64 - in other words $1 per 1K. Once a pattern of voltages indicating the presence or absence of bits is established in a dynamic RAM it consumes no power. However the voltages gradually discharge. Each charged element is re-charged to the original level by a periodic "refresh" voltage pulse at intervals of about 2ms.

Each element in a static RAM is composed of several components including transistors which are "on" or "off" indicating 1 or 0. A static RAM is therefore more expensive than a dynamic RAM and consumes more power. To produce a working memory the memory chips must be inserted into sockets on a printed circuit board connecting them to control circuits, and to a multiplexer which receives address data "in bulk" from the address bus and distributes it around the memory chips.

The whole assembly must be mechanically strong, and will contain a row of gold plated contacts along one edge so that it can be plugged into a strip-like socket within a microcomputer. Thus the actual cost of a working memory assembly will be much more than just the cost of the memory chips.

You can buy a 64K dynamic RAM board ready to plug in to microcomputers with the standard S100 backplane connections for about $400 in the US. A memory with 8 times the capacity (512K) costs about twice as much money. You can also buy static RAM boards which incorporate a lithium battery with a life exceeding 5 years. This type of RAM does not require refreshing, and the bit pattern remains in place, held by battery powered "on" circuits, when the mains is switched off. These boards sell at about double the price of a dynamic RAM boards of equivalent capacity.

<u>Telephone enhancement terminals</u>

PC/tele-terminals (PCTs) are microcomputers with a built-in telephone and modem, forming a "telephone services" terminal. A PCT developed by Bell may be marketed by one of AT&T's de-regulated subsidiaries. Bell anticipate that the first menu presented to a user (Alex) will offer a choice by pressing a single key as shown on the right.

This provides for single key dialling by keying - e.g. by pressing 4, 5, or 6 - for presenting a second menu listing 10 most used numbers each obtainable by single keying, or for freeing the keys for dialling any number . "General Directory" would be provided by the telephone company "Personal Directory" would have been previously input by Alex. and "Mail/Diary" would generate another menu as shown below right. If Alex wants to call Susan he lifts the phone and presses 4. The Machine displays "calling Susan " but Susan does

Choose	by pressing
General Directory	1
Personal Directory	2
Mail/Diary	3
Susan	4
George Jackson	5
Home	6
Top 10 numbers	7
Dial	8
Help	9
Lock	0

not reply. He presses 3, gets the second menu, and presses 5. His machine then sends the message "Please call Alex Jackson on 7654 858687" and displays "return call memo sent"

When Susan returns she sees the message displayed "you have new mail" under the first menu. She presses 3, gets the second menu , presses 3 again, reads Alex's message, presses 6, and then presses the "Alex" key again which she will have previously allocated on her menu.

To day's appointments	1
Diary	2
Read mail	3
Send mail	4
Send return call memo	5
Return to first menu	6

Note that this scenario calls for far more than simply a piece of telephone/micro/modem hardware. A complete system is envisaged with special services, a simple form of electronic message/mail, connection to a remote machine without the need for its owner to lift the phone, etc. "Convergence" is at work yet again. A number of devices, some incorporating most of Bell's ideas, are now available in the US. They extend from the Tymeshare Scanset ($795), to the Zaisan ES1 ($850), Northern Telecom Display-phone ($1300), GTE XT300 ($1600), Cygnet Cosystem ($1845) Rolm Cypress ($1950), to the Ambistation ($2,200). The ES1, for instance, has all the facilities of a small micro, two line telephone operation, and personal support software.

The Cygnet Cosystem is designed for use with the IBM PC via its RS232 port. It includes a software module which can work with the MS-DOS operating system in the PC and so make direct use of the PC's facilities. For example it can directly call up a file in the PC's WP directory, the file being, for instance, a personal telephone list. The Cosystem can perform as an electronic mailbox and could receive telex messages; it can also set up teleconferencing between itself and another Cosystem.

The ICL One Per Desk described earlier provides similar facilities to these machines.

<u>MARKETS AND GROWTH</u>

<u>Forecasting new product growth</u>

How widely are microcomputers used in homes and businesses and how fast is the market growing? After the dazzling debut of microcomputers for the home there seems to have been something of a reaction. One 1979 question (with the answer provided) was "Does the consumer really want to pay $500 to $3000 to balance the cheque book, educate the children and turn on the sprinklers? At this point the answer would seem to be "no", and continuing "when the hobby product need for enthusiasts is satisfied the market will have been saturated .....virtually all manufacturers are now moving expeditiously toward the professional, educational, and very small business markets".

Initially a new product is bought by innovators: momentum is increased by imitators as the innovators spread the word. The process is amenable to the kind of analysis which has been used for epidemics. Other factors which must be considered include the rate of re-purchasing by second-time, third-time buyers etc., because of obsolescence or a change of needs, divisions of the market, assessment of estimates made by others, and so on.

The earlier a forecast is made in the life of a new product the lower the probable accuracy because of the short length of the track record and uncertainties about the more distant future influences . Grey and Carlson consider that the Bass model used for other consumer products, and successfully used to predict colour television set sales, is appropriate for microcomputers.

Microcomputer applications and growth

The microcomputer market has three components - homes, small businesses and professional offices, and large organisations. Grey and Carlson give the consensus of a number of annual microcomputer growth estimates at 83% compound from 1977 onwards but doubt whether this can be sustained over a ten year period. They estimate that about half US households will possess a personal computer by the end of the 1980s, and that is 43 million units!

How do you define a personal computer? The complexity of some hand-held calculators now entitles them to be called personal computers. Some machines, once defined as minicomputers, have shrunk in size and price to become micros. Whatever the definition this seems an extraordinary forecast. It must imply that either micro computers will become very easy to use for a wide range of applications which have not yet been thought of, or that people's educational level and information requirements have soared, or perhaps both.

The average person's computer and information requirements has been discussed by Vail. The sub-title of his article is "transforming the household of tomorrow". A picture on the first page illustrates domestic bliss - a smiling lady of the house, posed by the food mixer in the kitchen, with a baby on one arm operating the micro keyboard with the other (No, not a herculean child prodigy - I mean the lady). The implication is that she is checking recipes. I have often discussed this idea with my wife. A consideration of the way people find and use recipes, the classification method to be adopted, and an estimate of the input chore quickly put both of us off the idea.

Gray & Carlson's estimates for business are based on the expectation of 50 million information workers in the US by the late 80's. The microcomputer saturation level for information workers is estimated at about 18 million units, with a three year replacement cycle. Two thirds will be in large businesses and one third in small.

From these considerations Gray & Carlson's estimate cumulated US sales at about 3 million by 1983, 9 million by 1985, and no less than 40 million by 1990. I hope G & C have not been influenced by Joe, boss of Debbie, departmental clerk at Chemical Bank (as quoted in a computer magazine) "We simply showed Debbie the Visicalc matrix and she wrote the program in an afternoon". Visicalc is a useful piece of business software but it will take most people several hours to learn, probably a week of hard work to master, and longer still to marshall the information to feed into it. Tell us the whole story Joe.

Predictions made in 1981 are much lower. Installed systems will reach 10 million by 1990, says a report from Strategic (San Jose, US). Distribution will be increasingly through franchised or company owned shops, following the absorption of shops into chains. From the forecast mentioned above it might appear that this one is way out. Most microcomputer forecasts have been wild under-estimates, or did Strategic know something in advance about the 84/85 slump that we didn't?

Back in 1980 there was one market trend about which everyone seemed to agree. That was that boundaries between the home and business markets are disappearing led by the workaholics. These people work at home on machines purchased by the company. Other employees of larger companies use company money to buy machines for use in their own department. I suspect that frustration from delays in the company's data processing department are replaced by frustration when finding out that with the micro it takes a long fiddling-about time to reach the benefits.

The overall consensus of opinion in 1982 seemed to be that US cumulated sales would be not less than 2.5 million by 1983, Europe 1 million, UK 300,000, and the rest of the world 500,000. By 1985 this would have risen to 5 million, 2 million, 600,000, and 1.5 million repectively. In May 1984, IRD forecast that shipments by the end of the year would be nearly 6 million units, 43% by IBM. This is greater than the cumulated sales in the 1982 forecast! This total included Japanese machines specifically but not British or indigenous machines from any other country who together are shipping much more than the Japanese.

However a forecast made in 1984 about 1984 is more likely to be accurate than earlier forecasts so we might conclude that the microcomputer figures for annual sales are still progressing along the exponential part of the classic sigmoid or flattened S-shape curve, but have not reached the flatter part of the curve inevitably reached sooner or later by all products. However from events during the last six months we might conclude that home computer growth rate _is_ now on the flat part, and that business micros are getting near it.

The mystery about what people do with "home" computers remains a mystery. A huge number were purchased in the 1983 Christmas period. An IBM spokesman, pondering the potential of the PC Jr, said "I like to describe a personal computer as a productivity tool, but when I tell my neighbours that I get a blank stare. They are quite happy with their typewriter, they have no problems balancing their cheque books with paper, pen, and calculator, and they are quite comfortable with shoebox files". The demise of the PC Jr indicates that their happiness was not misplaced.

Home computers are used by keep-up-with-the-Jones's-kid's-parents according to Apple (the Jones believe that all kids must be able to write Basic programs) for some kind of job-related activity (but what?), or by hobbyists. People who play games - the area at which much advertising is directed - don't get a mention.

FURTHER READING

Anon.
   (Central computer agency guide No. 10), 1979. 52pps, £2.25. Available from
   HMSO High Holborn, London, WC1V 6HB.
      Microcomputer operating systems.
Bass, F.M.
   Management Sci. 15, page 215, 1969.
      A new product growth model for consumer durables.
Cannon, Don L.
   Texas Instruments Learning Centre, Dallas, Tx, USA. 1982.
      Fundamentals of microcomputer design: system hardware and software.

Carpenter, James; Deloria, Dennis; Morganstein, David.
   Byte 9(4), 234-264, April 1984.
      Statistical software for microcomputers.
Cawkell, Anthony E.
   In 4th International Online Information Meeting, London, December 1980. pps
   377-386. Pub. by Learned Information Ltd., Besselsleigh Rd., Abingdon,
   Oxford OX13 6EF.
      A personal microcomputer for office use.
Clements, Alan.
   Microprocessors & Microsystems 8(78), 324-337, September 1984.
      The 68000 and its interface.
Dickerson, Connie J. (Ed)
   Elsevier Science Publishing, Published twice each year.
      The software catalogue: microcomputers. (28,000 software packages).
Gray, Paul; Carlson, Ray,
   IEEE Trans. Syst. Man. & Cyber. SMC-10(8), 484-501, 1980.
      Analysing the future impact of personal computers.
Gupta, Amar; Toong, H.D.
   Proc IEEE, 71(11), 1236-1256, 1983.
      Microprocessors - the first twelve years.
Guteri, Fred et al.
   IEEE Spectrum 22(1), 43-55, January 1985
      Personal computers; software; microprocessors.
Krajewski, Rich.
   Byte 10(5), 171-198, May 1985.
      Multiprocessing - an overview.
Lemmons Phil, et al.
   Byte 9(12), A3-A138, December 1984
      Guide to the Apple personal computers: Apple IIE, Apple IIc, Macintosh,
      Lisa.
Moran, Tom.
   Mini-micro Systems, 47-49, June 15 1984.
      Personal computer spotlight shifts to portables.
Nirmal, Barry; Nutter, Jean.
   J.Syst. Management, 12-15, March 1985.
      Present state of personal computing - challenges and concerns.
Raskin, Jeff., Whitney, Tom.
   Computer, 62-73, January 1981.
      Perspectives on personal computing.
Schofield, Jack et al.
   Practical Computing 8(6), 96-106, June 1985.
      The IBM PC success.
Slater, J.A.
   In Microsoftware - A symposium, University of Sussex, England, July 1980.
   Published by the Institution of Electronic & Radio Engineers, 99 Gower St.,
   London WC1E 6AZ. Pps 113-127.
      Software quality assurance.
Thompson, Lester E.
   Byte 9(9), 147, 436-443, September 1984.
      Floppy disk formats.
Vail, Hollis.
   The Futurist, 52-58, December 1980.
      The home computer terminal: transforming the household of tomorrow.
White, Webster, Bruce F.
   Byte 9(8), 238-251, August 1984.
      The Macintosh.
Wordmongers are at
   32 Redlands Road,
   Reading, Berks 2RG1 5HD
   England.   0743 867855

CHAPTER 19. OFFICE SYSTEMS PART 1.
METHODS, MANAGEMENT, AND CASE HISTORIES

Everyone knows how to transform a "1970 model" organisation into the office of the future. First, of course, you hire an interior decorator who knocks down walls and hangs a lot of plants to make it <u>look</u> like the pictures of the office of the future. Then you do away with private secretaries and install word processing machines, order a few more computers, and add the latest fillip - an electronic mail system. However none of this should touch top management - they should be left in their private corner offices dictating to their private secretaries and never clouding their brains by interacting with a computer in any way

> Murray Turoff and Roxanne Hiltz
> in "Structuring communications
> for the office of the future"
> Office Automat. Conf. Mar. 1980

INTRODUCTION

"The Automated Office", "The Electronic Office", and "The Office of the Future" have received the full sales hype treatment. A vision of bustling productive activity in a futuristic environment instead of today's image of a rather boring workplace makes a superb sales platform. Inevitably an anti-technology backlash followed the ballyhoo. Worse still the subject is media "news" which only comes in two varieties - good and bad. An attempt will be made to separate truth from fiction in this chapter but if it turns out to be gloomy this will be because the good news is hard to obtain. The cynic may say that perhaps this is because there isn't any.

However there are at least two reasons why "I've got a super system" stories are in rather short supply. A technological industry has raised expectations of immediate advances which bear little relationship to the speed with which people can change their ingrained habits; consequently a sufficient number of systems have not yet been installed for a valid assessment to be made. Secondly, the people who are pleased with the progress they are making are not inclined to tell us about it. In part this may be because "success" often means a reduction brought about by economies in the labour force - a subject about which they may not wish to enthuse.

DIVIDED OPINIONS

Those in favour....

The office equipment industry's enthusiasm can plausibly be reinforced by figures showing that investment and productivity in the office is comfortably outstripped by almost any other commercial or industrial activity. Suppliers think that one way or another offices must be "ripe for development". The costs of computer power were about 1% of their 1950 value in 1970 and since then may well have fallen to 1% of that value again. Employment in the "information sector" increased 108% between 1950 and 1970 but productivity only a few percent. A yawning opportunity gap for office information systems apparently exists.

Further plausibility comes from the steadily increasing adoption of word processing systems which undoubtedly have a lot to offer. I am writing this piece using a microcomputer's WP software and the benefits from doing it this way are numerous and obvious. Very soon, it was said in a 1977 article, ".... the typewriter and filing cabinet will be things of the past. With satellite communications and high speed data transmission, data will be moved about over the face of the earth at an unheard of rate. The use of computers in the office will reduce many of the laborious manual tasks associated with office work, leaving people time to use their skills to better advantage".

In a 1983 study, users rated electronic filing as the item of greatest importance in automated office functions, closely followed by electronic mail/voice. Next came information retrieval and decision support systems followed by telephone functions, then, some way behind, colour graphics, electronic funds transfer, and picturephone.

A whole range of diverse views, some diametrically opposite to others, have been expressed about office systems. Some would not withstand even the most cursory examination. A few samples from those in favour, usually from manufacturers or businessmen, but with a sprinkling of academics, follow:-

"Software architectures that integrate many new jobs are making computer systems at home with top management and clerical workers alike."...."Handling correspondence is fantastic - I average 20 letters a day incoming and outgoing. In strictly offline mode I could never handle that amount of communication".... "The knowledge worker professional, skilled in the application of specialised computer systems, and the knowledge-worker support person will have interesting jobs and our capability for human-directed knowledge work will be extended, rather than churning out our invoices with production line efficiency".

Apparently the larger companies had already made it back in 1964 (according to a Fortune article in that year):- "The computer organises and processes information so swiftly that computerised information systems enable top management to know everything important that happens as soon as it happens in the largest and most dispersed organisations. The general staff can bypass many intermediate functionaries, dispense with much subordinate judgement, and even plan and create for the whole organisation by asking the computer to simulate the company's activities in dozens or hundreds of hypothetical situations in order to choose the best course".

But twenty years later, according to a 1984 Frost & Sullivan report, we haven't made it yet, so you had better make haste:- "Companies would do well to introduce electronic mail systems for internal use today in order to be ready for the inter-company and public electronic mail services which will be commonplace later in the decade". However the headline in a 1984 UK Sunday Times supplement feature about "Living with the computer" tells us that we can all _now_ have "Instant information: tidy, efficient, paper free"

<u>Improved working conditions</u>

Olsen thinks that the location and temporal definition of work may be altered; people will work at home and enjoy increased flexibility and savings in commuting time; managers will monitor and control employees remotely. (This was how Orwell's "Inner Party" managed its affairs).

Giuliano suggests that office work can be divided into three evolutionary stages. First came the pre-industrial small office with little attention being paid to work flow or productivity. It was a friendly place with most people doing their own thing. Next came the "industrial" office - a much larger affair embodying work simplification and time and motion study not unlike a mass production line.

In the third stage "The company can expect dramatic savings in personnel costs. Staff reductions of as much as 50% have been common in departments making the change-over to a work station system. Those employees who remain benefit from a marked improvement in the quality of their working life". Giuliano also dwells on the developing "virtual office" - that is an office which is anywhere that the remotely connected worker happens to be.

These stages were echoed by a British Telecom TV advertisement. Masses of men are seen synchronously rubber stamping papers, as they transfer them from an "In" to an "Out" tray. Eventually the piles reach the roof, and a hand appears round one of them reaching for the telephone, followed by a suggestion that you should jump to Guiliano's third stage of evolution. The next scene in the advertisement (after the transition) shows one person sitting at a work station dealing with a whole range of activities.

If a company calls Executrade has its way, the virtual office will come a little nearer when its proposals to offer various facilities from business centres in various parts of the UK gets off the ground. The idea is to provide offices complete with technology for small companies which will have access to services via Plessey digital IDX exchanges at the centres. People working at home will be able to use the services as well.

A better life for secretaries

Niels Bjorn-Andersen identifies three possibilities for the traditional secretarial role in "the changing roles of secretaries and clerks". If technology takes over routine tasks the secretary might become the "office wife" providing general support, passing on gossip etc. But "changing social attitudes and the elimination of the legitimacy of using a secretary as a status symbol means that the office-wife role is unlikely to grow significantly".

More likely the secretary will become a "girl Friday" taking on responsibilities such as information retrieval, telephoning and other PA activities. However the big jump is to the "manager's co-worker" - for example at Copenhagen Business School some secretaries do tasks like administering student's duties, negotiating with publishers over books and papers, and do some teaching. Lecturers on the other hand are actually writing letters!

Those not in favour....

The main line taken by this school of thought, usually comprising academics or sociologists, is either disbelief that changes, particularly for managers, will come quickly, or belief that for many the work will become "deskilled".

"If the cost of the technologies soon approached zero dollars I don't believe that any organization would be able to make use of more than 30% of the capabilities until well past 1985"....."Management represent by far the largest element of office expense....until office automation is able to address the entire communication function of managers and professionals it will fail to increase the productivity of office operations significantly".

"Pollock has seen the future and so far he wants no part of it" (reports the Wall Street Journal about a bank executive)..."with the touch of a button he can command memos, view data, and respond to letters, but he doesn't. He hates to type"..... "Watch out, vendors are there for one reason and one reason only - they are there to sell. They will sell as much as the floor will bear without collapsing"..... "The convenience copier has proved to be a mixed blessing..... many people found themselves inundated in a sea of paperwork without which they would have been better off".

Even IBM is not always too ebullient about the prospects for executives:- "Current implementations of office systems, centred around the workstation, are most appropriate to the secretarial worker but less appropriate to clerical, professional, and managerial people. The clerical worker is normally concerned with the filing and retrieval of records or repetitive operations such as validation and calculation. The professional worker is concerned with skills such as giving investment advice or performing engineering design. The manager is concerned with the financial, time related, and people aspects of getting work done."

Managers cam manage without personal computers

A similar line is taken in an article in the Harvard Business Review:- "If a manager does not want to use a personal computer his or her performance will not be adversely affected. This conclusion is based on the following observations.

1. The computer has not added to the important information required by top managers.

2. The important information required by top managers can best be supplied by staff personnel. It is not necessary for a manager to query a computer directly.

3. Computers with the same characteristics as the personal computer have been available to top managers of large and medium sized businesses for over fifteen years. If few top managers have been using these computers there is a considerable question about their utility".

James Driscoll, a Professor at the Sloan School of Management at MIT at the time, heads his chapter in a book about the subject:- "Office automation: the dynamics of a technological boondoggle" and continues:- "The boss decides what tasks must be done....and asks the systems analyst to prepare the program. The rest of the workforce picks up the garbage which is left over at the edge of the programmed tasks....you will either like or dislike the picture depending on whether your present position makes it likely that you will be a boss/systems analyst or a garbage collector". Chapter 45 later in this book by the same author further justifies this opinion.

A worse life for secretaries

Driscoll's comments are based, in part, on an extrapolation of the limited changes already introduced - for instance by word processing which has "..increased the separation between boss and secretary...to create a new breed of even more menial office workers. Little improvement in the jobs of non-word processing secretaries has resulted, despite the advertising claims of the vendors about career paths for women. The separation of secretary from boss will dominate future systems...one way or another product designers are seeking ways to keep the boss from having to type...he will sit in an easy chair with both hands on pressure-sensitive armrests allowing him to zoom across a wall-sized projection of a desk top by pressing down either hand. The standard form of input for text from such high-status users, be they hunt-and-peckers, mice, pointers, or zoomers, is by dictation to a typist".

Driscoll's words remind me about the mass of people, about whom one hears very little, who replaced quill-pen clerks on high stools. Some of them do word processing but many more try and satisfy the immense appetite of computers for data to sort and process. His words also prompt a response, and my first is that if I did not do everything on a microcomputer I would probably not be in business. The benefit is the throughput of work obtainable by being able to quickly interact with existing information. I have little doubt that I would have to employ two or three more people if a machine was not used for general office work. For creative writing, provided you can type properly, a WP machine also provides many benefits.

If I had not adopted this method of working I would have provided some badly needed jobs. However I have to compete with others who are treading the same path. If I took on existing people and mothballed the micros the new jobs would not last for long - I would be out of business.

However you won't find many computers in the Indian civil service. The Indians are more interested in retaining clerical jobs for some of their huge population. They have made remarkable progress in that country in many fields but probably feel that the economic and political consequences of efficiency through the widespread use of data processing equipment are too high a price to pay for the resulting unemployment.

Returning to word processing, my impression is that there are probably at least as many typists reasonably content with their word processing lot as there are typists who are discontented with it. The reason for the discontent is almost certainly the office environment and the way the work is organised. Properly managed, it seems that WP work can be made tolerable. Above all it means a job. The adoption of word processing is one factor in the struggle to remain competitive. If the alternative is going out of business, there may be more jobs to be had by adopting it and other technologies.

PLANNING AND INTRODUCING OFFICE SYSTEMS

Some definitions

Message. A communication, usually brief, from one person or group to another.

Electronic Message. The transmission of messages of any length by electrical means. The phrase usually implies the existence of an Electronic Message and Switching Network in order that the message can be sent to selected remote addressees.

Mail (also called "post"). Letters, packages, etc., that are transported and delivered by the Post Office or by competing oranisations such as couriers.

Electronic Mail. Messages communicated by electrical or optical means, particularly as an alternative to information transmitted as print-on-paper through the mail.

Electronic Office. An office within which management, administrative, and transactional activities based on printed information have been largely displaced by activities based on information electrically or optically processed, transmitted, stored, and retrieved.

By using the phrase Electronic Mail indiscriminately, it becomes impossible to distinguish between systems which may displace the public postal systems as we know them, and a related but different field - Electronic Message Systems. The latter is about communications within and between offices.

If word processing machines possess communication ports and can be used with other kinds of software, and if they can be connected to an electronic message and switching network, then this is a step towards the electronic office. In most so-called electronic offices, items of equipment have been introduced piecemeal This may have resulted in some displacemenent of labour but it has not so far much affected management or organisational procedures.

Office system progress in the UK

According to a sample census taken in 1980 by Industrial Market Research there were 1.7 million work places in Britain at that time, of which 17,000 employed 200 or more people. The Policy Study Institute sampled 1060 establishments in 1982 which were known to have an established computer base. Since this was not a random sample it cannot be used as the basis for an estimate of the penetration of office technology in the UK, but it is still of some interest.

The Word Processor is probably the most popular symbol of "office automation" and 62% of the sample used these machines. 39% of the companies employing up to 200 people used them, 64% of companies employing between 200 and 500, and 83% of companies employing more than 5000 people were users.

After photocopiers and electronic typewriters/WP machines came micro-computers, used in 80% of the offices sampled – double the proportion that were used 3 years previously. Next came microfilm/microfiche, used, surprisingly, by nearly 66% of the sample followed by PABX's (64%) , and fac-simile machines (39%).

1. Compatibility problems.
2. Limited budgets.
3. Unsuitable systems.
4. Current economic climate.
5. Lack of mananagement planning.
6. Scepticism about benefits.
7. Lack of management commitment.
8. Other management problems.
9. Inadequate national telecoms.
10. Staff or union resistance.

The main obstacles to the introduction of office systems according to users are shown rank ordered in Table 19.1.

TABLE 19.1.
OBSTACLES TO OFFICE SYSTEM DEVELOPMENT

Out of 194 respondents who replied to a question asking who was responsible for the introduction of the electronic office systems, 63% said Management Services, 35% DP staff, 11% Office Services, and 21% other.

The reaction of office staff to the introduction of word processors was generally favourable, the stated resistance being about 3% average from all types of staff. In most cases the introduction of word processors did not produce any job changes. The number of cases where there were no changes averaged about 75%, while only an average of about 20% of the respondent organisations reported a decrease.

Managing the people-machine change.

Discussions about people, information technology, and machines are usually in the context of large offices in large organisations involving large numbers of people.

Eason stresses the need to involve the users at the planning stage of a new information system, and to carry them along with every stage thereafter. Evolutionary design – "with the possibility that parts of it may be modified, withdrawn, or elaborated" may well be necessary for large systems designed for use in areas where behavioural factors are poorly understood and many people are involved.

These methods, together with good Budgetary Control – the rarely mentioned item (particularly in academic circles) which must get a mention – together with committed management support plus a certain amount of faith that it will be worth it in the end are essential ingredients. This is echoed in a booklet published by the Institute for Personnel Management – "communication should involve planners, designers, installation and production staff, as well as personnel specialists and employees as a whole throughout the process of change"

Bair suggests that the cost of a properly performed assessment may be 25-35% of the cost of the installed technology. Such an assessment should include comparisons between a prototype office embodying the technology, a similar office with optimised manual work, and an unchanged office.

Keen stresses the need for a definition of office productivity. He cites plans made by 25 American organisations with a commitment to technology, the main objective being an increase in the productivity of white collar workers. In only five cases were methods for measuring productivity suggested, although in all cases things like return on investment, application priorities etc., depend on having clear productivity criteria.

"Specialists involved in applying computer-based systems thrive on words that rarely get defined such as "productivity", "user involvement", and "top management commitment". They are used almost as magic spells, as if to use the labels is to create reality. These are of little value unless "productivity is translated into something concrete and meaningful".

Keen lists six basic resources: hardware; software; technical development staff; project control staff and methods; support staff; business planners. "A key element is handling the culture gap between users and designers. This requires participation of hybrid individuals who are fluent about the technology and literate about its applications.Most studies of successful computerised systems show the importance of skilled hybrids - facilitators, change agents, educators, and consultants.

He continues:- "The studies of unsuccessful efforts attribute the negative consequences of a technocentric design focus or user departments which have no

BE SELF JUSTIFYING. Be seen to contribute to productivity.

MAKE SOMEONE HAPPY by solving someone's problems or creating opportunities.

BE PHASEABLE with short phases and firm delivery dates.

TEACH designers and users.

DON'T PUT AT RISK morale, stability, and efficiency.

<u>TABLE 19.2. KEY FACTORS IN INTRODUCING OFFICE SYSTEMS</u>

way to support the user and bridge the culture gap". In discussing the question of leadership and authority Keen says that "the leader must be an innovator, able to focus on problem solving, having a high credibility which allows risks to be taken and a degree of pragmatism which prevents extreme risks. Innovators are different to ideas people - they focus their energies on results, and show a readiness to seek out new ideas and know how to use ideas people". Keen's ideas about tackling office automation are shown in Figure 19.2.

Chen criticises the omission of the evaluation of intangible benefits. It's hard to believe that any serious study could be carried out without this kind of evaluation, which, he might have added, is very hard to carry out. The quantification of intangibles is notoriously difficult. Time saved can of, course, be costed, but it is difficult to bring credibility to estimates of the amount of time that might be saved.

Landau refers to another field from which we might learn a lesson - Management Information Systems. He refers to "the promises that could not be kept", and says "what we have discovered is that the computer has made significant and cost-effective contributions to the more routine operations of an organisation".

A manager has the option of behaving somewhere between two extremes when faced with implementing changes of whatever kind. He(she) can lean over backwards, even to the extent of almost total appeasement, to accommodate employees and implement change only by consent. On the other hand he can impose change without notice or consultation.

Obvious this may be, but the point is made in interesting ways by Lasden.

"Human reluctance to move from the comfortable status quo to the unfamiliar new creates management problems. Understanding the problems is the first step to solving them. Today the reality of most change situations is one of negotiation. There is a recognition of different interests and a more equal distribution of power within organisations....it is questionable whether a systems change involving the bulldozer approach is really successful if it retards future change and uses up any goodwill that may have resided in the organisation in terms of tolerance for change".

And some further comments:- "The most crucial ingredient in implementing a system is winning the support of users who will take a leadership role........ I'm sceptical of those approaches that call for a long drawn out process of participation. Everyone wants their own bells and whistles and they'll never forgive you if they ask and you can't deliver". And another viewpoint "Some managers prefer the participatory approach but are prepared to turn the screws if necessary. This escalator approach might start with the gentlest of measures and step by step become increasingly firm." But in Japan "When it's all over and a decision is made the workers are required to sign a document that stipulates approval for what's being done".

Is there going to be cooperation or confrontation with the Unions? Are these changes going to be so slow that there will no feeling that anything dramatic is occurring? Perhaps they will occur in a series of very small steps, each representing a degree of change which is easy to manage, or is there bound to be a large step at some point which generates fierce opposition?

The change which at the moment seems to be generating greatest speculation is the flexibility of choice of the place of work enabled by work-at-home terminals. Speculation about the replacement of face-to-face by remote management has also appeared. Does this make any sense? Presumably it will be possible to say "The first really major changes in office work and management occurred in the period 19?? to 19??" - but when will that period be upon us? Has it already started?

According to Wainwright the answer, so far as the UK is concerned, appears to be "slightly". Once again most of the discussion seems to be about possible ways of doing it rather than the results of having done it, although some comments are made about organisations who have tackled office systems in four basic combinations of the options Centralised or De-centralised design with and without user participation. Curiously enough the two design options without user participation are suggested as being appropriate in certain circumstances.

Managing Information

Is Information a resource in its own right requiring separate management? If it is, and because no part of an organisation can function without information, the acceptance of this idea means that an "outsider" - the new Information Manager - may have to interact with the Managers of all departments, probably including Production, R&D etc.

Should the Information Manager simply be brought in to rationalise the mechanics of information - that is to organise the equipment, telecommunications, etc? This line was taken by Dickinson at Exxon. The Information Manager was given corporate responsibility for DP, office technology, and telecommunications. He carried out studies and provided consulting services worldwide including functional surveillance of new technology, coordination and information dissemination. He addressed problems of incompatibilities, considered standards, developed simple transportable electronic filing packages, and evaluated electronic mail services.

Do the properties of information make it amenable to unified management, or are the different kinds of information handled in the separate departments of an organisation better handled within those departments?

There have been some cross-department trends such as the provision of Management Information Systems, the setting up of Data Processing Departments, and suggestions of a wider role for Information Officers - hitherto a library based activity.

Levitan poses this question in the electronic office context:- "The rapidly improving cost/performance ratio of computer hardware and the proliferation of available technologies, especially those under the umbrella of "office automation" require an enlightened management to connect technology budgets to the values and objectives of the organization".

Management should "organize technical resources to fit the objectives of a corporation...focus on people as well as technology for improving services.... ...emphasize the team approach and lateral relations...develop information services more in tune with business needs...recognize the importance of training".

Levitan, who works for a company providing Information Resource Management (IRM) services continues:- " IRM involves the administration of all corporate information, of all manual and automated data, and of all methods used for the communication, manipulation, and presentation of information used. What does the balance sheet look like for IRM? Is it a substantive area of management or just another slogan? On the plus side is the fact that more than 85% of the references that support this view express the belief that IRM is a substantive area. But IRM will not happen unless senior management wants it to happen".

It should be beneficial to provide unified management of the means - computers, microcomputers, office equipment and communications. This should result in buying economies and equipment compatibility. Most departments in an organisation would find that acceptable and would soon see the benfits.

However when it comes to the wholesale adoption of office systems,local networks, shared resources, and centralised filing, small departmental empires will crumble and the new Information Overlord is unlikely to be received with rapture. Should the Information Manager be involved with the information itself as recommended by Levitan? Could he do the job properly without such involvement? It seems unlikely that the Information Manager could successfully fufill his role unless he gets involved with the requirements of different user classes which must also cover the information itself. He may need to have rather wider responsibilities that merely those of an integrated technology implementor, and that will make it doubly difficult for him to obtain cooperation. He will need very strong backing from top management.

Rockart forcefully exhorts top management to become involved "It is time for top management to get off the sidelines. Recognising that information is a strategic resource implies a clear need to link information systems to business strategy and especially to ensure that business strategy is developed in the context of the new IT environment. In short, senior executives are feeling the need to become informed, energized, and engaged in information systems".

His recipe for management involvement contains a three stage process. First should come a consideration of strategy objectives culminating in a "focusing workshop"; next complete familiarisation and evaluation concluding with a "decisions scenarios workshop: then comes the prototype design, systems development, and evaluation and institutionalization.

Effects of information laissez-faire

Anthony Hopwood of the London Graduate School of Business Studies provides an example of the danger of failing to investigate the organisational impact of unofficial information.

The management of a British company which had survived a turbulent period with difficulty was about to disperse two thirds of its head office staff to a surburban site, with an expansion of its existing computer based management information system.

The move was abandoned following the examination of information flow in the company by a consultant. He found that the company had survived the crisis which had hit the industry primarily because of the close proximity of key members. Information was transmitted and acted upon very quickly - a role which had not been recognised in the plan for removal.

Michel Crozier recounts how an experimental computer-based system, commissioned by management, worked well on an experimental basis in a company. In production it was a complete failure "not because technical flaws emerged, but because there was an unexpected problem related to the social system of the plant. The computer was a kind of time and motion study machine which regulated production of paid workers. The problem was that it interfered with previous informal secretive arrangements which had helped both managers and workers".

A tacit agreement between foremen and employees had allowed the "time worked figures to be falsified. Workers received more than the agreed rate which they felt was commensurate with the relative importance of the plant and the bargaining power of their union. The transparency introduced by the computer in the information gathering and processing routines meant that this arrangement could no longer be continued.

The subsequent analysis proved that the whole supervisory system at the plant had relied on the arbitrary leeway gained by the supervisors through tolerating the "cheating" by the workers. The wheels of the entire endeavour were oiled because the secret arrangement enabled all parties to have a margin for negotiation or the potential for making many other subordinate arrangements. Supervisors could use their bargaining power to obtain the co-operation of workers and their willingness to adjust quickly to crisis situations.

Conversely, shop stewards were able to maintain a strong influence on the workers because they would seem to be their natural partners in the constant bargaining with the supervisors. The advantages gained by the secret agreement meant that none of the parties wanted to accept the obvious solution, which would have been to adjust the rates of pay so that they could use the actual hours worked to achieve the required level of wages".

So much for the best laid computerised plans of mice and men!

Technology and People

So far as people's ac-tivities are concerned, Figure 19.1 shows some rather well known information about how office time is spent. Secretarial time is shown on the left and managerial on the right. It is managerial time-saving which receives the most attention and where least progress has been made. What is not shown is the time spent by people doing routine tasks, to be discussed in Chapter 20, where the greatest potential for office automation exists.

A stand-alone microcomputer with WP or other software will be many people's first introduction to office systems. The temptation to be (supposedly) master of your own destiny is a strong one. Why wait in the queue to the Data Processing

(DP) department when you can (supposedly)- easily do it yourself?

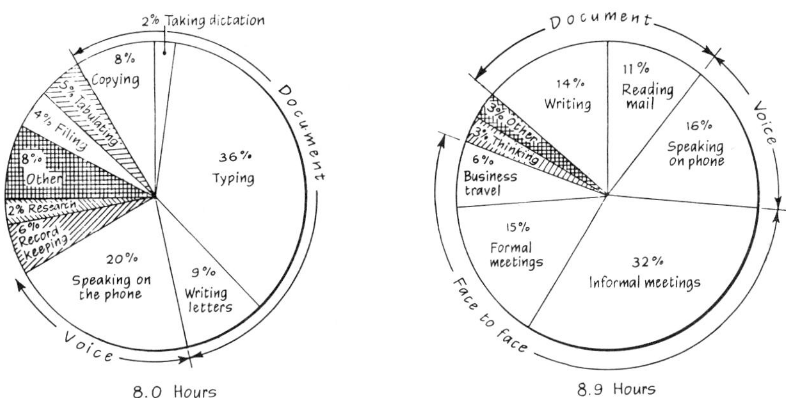

<u>FIGURE 19.1. OFFICE TIME: LEFT SECRETARIAL, RIGHT MANAGERIAL</u>

Peter Keen, late of MIT, discusses the role of DP departments. He claims that in 1980 about one third of major organisations carrying out office technology innovation had assigned it to the DP department, one third to Administrative Services and one third to a new unit often called Office Systems.

Since that time the DP department has increasingly come into favour on the grounds that they have the skill and experience of planning and project management. Behavioural skills can be acquired - perhaps more easily than the acquisition of technical expertise by behavioural specialists.

A contra argument is that the DP Department is isolated from the mainstream and is often bureaucratic, inflexible and unresponsive. Technical expertise can be obtained from outside but knowledge of the organisation cannot be brought in.

<u>Getting to the point of doing something useful</u>

Is there a single microcomputer supplier who does not claim that his machine is easy to use, or in whose sales blurb the phrase "user friendly" does not appear? Sometimes they are - for computer-buffs, "handy" people, or people who are prepared to acquire some technical knowledge. Most people are not in one of these categories.

It is suggested by Eason that developments in software now enable the service that the user receives to be changed with relative ease. Indeed the interface can be "personalised" so that the same system provides tailor-made services to a variety of users", and yes, it is certainly possible to change things provided an engineer/instructor is available. Users cannot and do not want to cope with systems. In the case of micros, software designed to run on a particular machine can be made to run on another by a "customisation" procedure provided that the operating systems of the machines are not too different.

It is also common practice to personalise software in the sense that "form filling" may be carried out to fulfill "personal" requirements. For example information can be typed in specifying the printer and disks to be selected, listing the required telephone numbers of hosts/databases or other organisations, selecting baud rates, detailing logging on codes etc.

However Eason's "tailor-made service" is in the area of evolutionary design and the linking together of microcomputer systems - provided that the company is properly implementing this kind of policy and has the expensive expertise on hand. Without that expertise communications is a hassle even at the most elementary level. The "standard" interconections between micro and modem are nearly always different because the standard is hopelessly out of date. One wrong pin interconnection and it won't work. How does the non-computer-buff find the right one and can he/she use a miniature soldering iron? Most people will make the "standard" connections and when nothing happens look for the trouble somewhere else, while it is those very connections that are probably incorrect.

Since many people find it hard to connect up their electric iron to a mains plug, they find it daunting to interconnect, say, a micro, a modem and a printer, probably all made by different manufacturers. If everything was purchased at the same time from one friendly dealer all may be well. If everything was purchased at different times from different unhelpful dealers it won't be. The cost of getting software changed is high and will greatly depend upon how well it is documented and whether the original designer is still around.

Lord Rayleigh said (about advances in science) that it may be easier to discover it again in the laboratory than to find it in the literature (or words to that effect). Likewise it may be easier to get the software re-written than to modify what somebody else has written.

<u>Modelling Office Systems</u>

An excellent review of modelling work then in progress was published in 1980 by Ellis. In it a description of the ancestry of the Xerox Star - the "Officetalk" software - first implemented on the Alto computer - is given, with not a word about the Star presumably for commercial reasons. Information flow and processing considered as a tree structure with nodes at which activities are performed has also been discussed by Smith, also of Xerox.

Ellis comments:- "The problem of retaining social contact among workers is yet unsolved; the trend toward automation works against the goal of maintaining a social structure...there is a danger that informal conversation will be destroyed...with the possible exception of some word processing centres, most current automated office centres have not developed to the point where they have endangered channels of social conversation...the next steps in automation will probably require more effort toward maintaining informal communication channels".

Ellis published a further review in 1984 summarising the work at the Xerox Palo Alto Research Centre (PARC) with Information Control Nets covering information flow, electronic mail, and organisational needs. Since PARC is one of the leaders, if not <u>the</u> leader, in this field, this article, containing a good bibliography, is well worth reading.

The SCOOP system has been described by Zisman (MIT). It uses augmented Petri Nets a formalised model for depicting information flow in an office, as discussed earlier by Peterson. Zisman's comments about what he calls "automating goal producing functions" - the testing stage of which is at least 5 to 10 years away (from 1978) in his opinion - are worth quoting at length in view of his reputation.

"It is the manager of an organization who has a notion of process. From a very simplistic viewpoint, the devices in the office are resources of the secretary, and the secretary is a resource of the manager. By mechanising devices we are addressing the resources of the secretary, but, by and large, not those of the manager.

However, when we attack office processes we are automating office functions, not office tasks, and are addressing problems of the manager. We are not suggesting that secretaries will be replaced, but we do suggest that some of the more structured, routine, and mundane responsibilities of the secretary and manager will be (almost) completely automated at this stage, thus making this group of workers available for more productive activities.

Zisman expresses the hope that as workers are relieved of mundane and routine functions which are turned over to computer control, there will be less employee alienation and quicker acceptance of the technology.

Although Zisman delves into behavioural matters to some degree, not a word is written about the possible unemployment consequences. Like the majority of automation practitioners he cuts off at this point, and his remarks about "job enlargement" may indicate that he thinks unemployment is unlikely. He seems to believe that a smooth evolutionary transition will occur. Time will show whether he is right.

An IBM office model for automatically managing an operation such as accounts receivable has been described by Hammer. As machine readable forms pass through stages of processing, information from input "documents" is absorbed, e.g. receipt for goods, and other "documents" such as invoices are generated at the output. Similar work has been described by de Sousa where "print" and "control" data streams embody information about documents which may be processed and distributed.

Work has been in progress at IBM since about 1974 on a high level management language, now an IBM product, called "Query by example" <Zloof 1977 and 1980>. The objective is to enable a user directly to express the equivalent of a lengthy program in order to manipulate data without having to acquire the skills of a programmer. Options are selected from menus which set up the program parameters.

Information may be mapped from one form to another or on to other objects such as letters – for example a name and address can be mapped from a form on to a letter in the correct position. The system enables a variety of objects such as charts, letters and facsimile documents to be created, edited, and communicated to others.

Another model called POISE has been described by David Croft and implemented at the University of Massachusetts. It uses a so-called intelligent interface for handling several kind of information. For example the "Procedure Library" contains form filling procedures. When a user enters certain details he is referred to the "Semantic Database" containing forms for completion. The objective, as in other similar systems, is to force formalisation amenable to computer manipulation. Poise also includes components for formalising procedure specifications and planning.

<u>FURTHER READING</u>

A list of references and further reading will be found at the end of the companion Chapter 20.

CHAPTER 20. OFFICE SYSTEMS PART 2.
USING CURRENTLY AVAILABLE SYSTEMS AND SERVICES

IBM

The major supplier on the scene is IBM. IBM possesses immense resources and is devoting a large fraction of them to the development of new office systems. Surely it must be trying them out in real situations, which will ensure that these trials are carried out as quickly as possible and will broadcast the results immediately because they are in business to sell the products?

Gardner discussed some of the problems in 1981. IBM has been developing an Office System - OFS - for trials in its Poughkeepsie offices, since 1970. In that year it installed a 360/67 for the purpose; it was superseded by a Virtual Machine facility - the 370 (VM/370) operating system. What has been accomplished in ten years by this leading organisation?

This work drew upon some earlier work at IBM's data processing division described by Engel. During this period there was considerable staff turnover. Also there were "many unexpected operational problems. Cables had to be restrung, new phones were installed and electrical outlets had to added to the area. These problems and those associated with training and education need to be taken into account when planning an automated office". Indeed they do but such naivety seems extraordinary.

Gardner's objectives, lugubriously discussed, are clear. The first stage is the use of stand alone word processing machines. The second is "a structured systems solution...highlighted by its structured control and procedural operation nature...in areas of administrative control that are highly proceduralized". The third is the "implementation of a functionally rich user environment....applicable to the needs of professionals and decision makers.....VM/370 appeared to be an ideal operating base on which to begin structuring a total office systems interface".

The system was used in offices by 400 programming and engineering professionals, 80 clerks and secretaries, and 40 managers, but for what? If you are expecting to hear that the nature of office work was substantially changed by this system you will be disappointed. The author claims the following outcomes "improvements in the quality of business memos and reports....timely distribution of weekly status meeting information....online calendar and scheduling facilities.....and valuable means of staying in contact...by online mailboxes".

Garner also states that "many other benefits are difficult to measure specifically but are of obvious value to the overall performance of the organisation". All this represents substantial progress, but it does provide a sober reminder of how far we have to go, and is in marked contrast to the supposed radical changes which many equipment purveyors of office systems would have us believe are just around the corner.

IBM have adopted a step-by-step try-it-and-see approach which convincingly demonstrates that they are in a long term development programme, which, after ten years, was still at an early stage in terms of many people's publicity-induced expectations. As the author says "with every new insight several new questions surface". If we were dangerously to draw conclusions from only one article, then they would be that significant changes in office work which will seriously affect management are unlikely to be at all widespread for at least five years. We are not discussing developments in technology, proceeding at a breakneck speed. We are talking about a change in people's ingrained behaviour which, in offices, has changed little in the last hundred years.

Stanford/Bell

For every practitioner there seem to be hundreds of academic theorists - articles about what might happen in the office of the future and what we should do about it are ten a penny. However there was another fairly large experiment, conducted at Stanford Research Institute by Douglas Engelbart and others which has been reported upon by Edwards and Uhlig - the oN Line System (NLS) - which started in the 1960s. NLS was made available on PDP-10 computers via the ARPANET network in North America in 1974. It provides facilities for a user to conduct many on line office tasks from his terminal.

A survey on the impact of NLS upon 100 users in 13 subscribing organisations is discussed by Edwards. These users of which 30 were managers, commented mainly about three aspects - benefits of electronic message facilities with associated reduction in phone calls, advantages of the document production facilities with elimination of drafts, and flexibility of working hours with the development of a "portable office". There were mixed feelings about privacy.

Management by remote control

The phrase "remote management" appears in this article. If some form of remote management beomes possible then this would certainly have a profound effect on office organisation. According to the article "Distance was irrelevant...if a manager had memos to send to his or her subordinates, a request for budget proposals etc.,... it made little difference whether the manager was at a terminal in the office, at home, or conducting business in another city".

Users commented "A major impact is the electronic and remote management through the use of message systems" and "Remote personnel management" (no examples are given). The above quotations are the only ones associated with "remote management" but the author returns to the subject in the concluding sentences :- "group meetings on trivial administrative issues have almost been eliminated...less misunderstanding due to forgotten oral agreements ....verbal communication has diminished 50%"...can easily respond without face to face contact...less requirement to converse in person.... one impact is certain to be of greater permanence - changes in management style. Line of sight management will move into obsolescence, requiring new measures of productivity". And finally:- "Meanwhile the private secretary will become increasingly difficult to justify. As the productivity of each professional increases, their number may also be reduced, especially at the middle management level".

Nothing is said about time. No doubt things will be different in fifty, twenty, or even ten years, but most of us don't look ahead much further than next year. Regardless of the rate of change, are the conclusions about the "obsolescence of line of sight management" reasonable?. This idea is the antithesis of conventional management methods. Certainly we can do without "meetings on trivial administrative issues", but is it possible to imagine office management with progressively less conversation and face-to-face meetings?"

Of course it is - Orwell did - in the offices of his "Inner Party" they probably managed without any conversation at all. I think and hope we can dismiss this figment of the imagination. Fewer face-to-face meetings there will be, and this will be discussed in other chapters under "Teleconferencing", "Computer Conferencing" etc., but, so far as I am aware, remote management has made very little progress.

Xerox

Xerox is engaged in office system development across the board from total communications (XTEN, from which it seems to have withdrawn from the moment),

Local Area Networks (Ethernet, Star, etc.,) to items of advanced office machinery such as "intelligent copiers". According to Uttal, several Xerox systems have been used at their Palo Alto Center (PARC) and at over 1500 other Xerox offices, with several large installations at Boeing, U.S.Congress, The White House, and in Sweden.

Xerox has invested heavily in this area no doubt to try and recover from the inroads into its copier business by competitors. In 1981 this resulted in its deletion from Fortune's list of companies with oustanding growth. Presumably because this effort is too recent for experience to have accumulated I can find nothing of interest to report about the effects on management. Nutt and Ellis have reported on office modelling and other work somewhat similar to IBM's research.

Citibank

Citibank was one of the early leaders in accumulating practical experience. They hived off a new company, Axxa, to manufacture office systems, being unable themselves to engage in this kind of activity because of US regulatory conditions. There then seems to have been a hiatus, and Axxa was sold. Progress was described in optimistic terms back in early 1977. 12 prototype "Management Work Stations" interconnecting Citibank managers in New York City, were in place in November 1976. I went to see Axxa's System 90 being used at their offices in Woodland Hills, Los Angeles, in January 1982.

Each Citibank manager's terminal was connected to its own PDP-8A. The main features were an appointments calendar, electronic message system, word processing system, and a following up file. The Management requirements of the integrated electronic office were stated to be "...the provision of planning, monitoring, and control support...later this year we will interface a system that monitors and forecasts operations expense and staff levels versus budgets...and tie in to Citibank's system which....will have access to product by product transaction and dollar volume figures for customer market segments".

Experience seems to be confined to those manager's secretaries who were trained to use the system. There has not been much effect upon managers. Citibank reported:- "Our secretaries have so far shown far more flexibility and adventurousness than the managers have...they will become free to assume more administrative tasks...the position we refer to as "secretary" today will become an entry-level management job...the keyboard won't suffer from a clerical stigma because office managers will be keyboarding too..this question will probably be made academic by the development of voice entry technology... The most important lesson we've learned so far is to make the system function as analogous as possible to the paper-based routines that people are accustomed to". Not much has been heard from Citibank since. Either they are not telling because they have accumulated a substantial competitive advantage, or interest in the system has lapsed.

Continental Illinois Bank

The office system developed at this bank was described by Mertes although no details of the equipment were given. The bank first captured, stored, and indexed "all its information" in a central computer-based library. It then developed four office systems to handle word processing and remote dictation, electronic mail, information retrieval, and audio mail.

At that time the electronic mail system was available to 3000 people on the staff in the US and overseas out of a total of 12,000. Breakdowns are stated to be not more than 5-10 minutes per day on average, with the benefits of distance and time-zone barriers removed, multiple address messages easily handled, and portable terminals enabling people who are at home or travelling conveniently to keep in touch with the bank. Other components are IRIS, a database and information retrieval system available to 22% of staff and a telephone answering system with prompting to encourage messages of any length.

Comments about the effects on managers are as follows "....workaholics are few....not everyone holds the same values for work, travel, and leisure time...one question as yet unanswered is whether managers will be less effective if they cannot come out of the confines of their offices to see their subordinates performing assigned tasks at work stations" The article continues with a discussion about what people _may_ do rather than what they do _now_.

A reader is once again left with the impression that while the new systems have added considerable convenience and save time, the organisation has not changed much. There is considerable speculation about what _may_ happen, including comments about the difficult transition to a different kind of organisation, without much discussion about even more difficult problems associated with the radical changes required in people's behaviour.

Exxon

A comprehensive integration of data processing, telecommunications and office technology was commenced in January 1979 at Exxon on an international basis as described by Dickinson. It called for the installation and evaluation of three to five large scale system prototypes per year covering conferencing, information storage and retrieval, electronic mail, text processing, project status, calendar and diary etc. The information provided in the article is interesting, but again things were at the developmental stage at the time it was written.

TRW, Torrance

Harold Borko, well known in the information science world, describes a project to "gather and analyse objective data related to the actual use of an Automated Office Information System; to study the manner in which an AOIS will change the behaviour, functions, procedures, and attitudes of knowledge workers....and to provide a more efficient work environment". The project was carried out at TRW, Torrance, as arranged by the the University of California at Los Angeles.

A VAX 11/750 was used with the DEC "All-in-one" office software providing electronic mail, word processing, calendar management, action item reminders, phone directory and personal calculator facilities. Eight months after the system became operational a 10 day study of user's activities was undertaken. "The time spent in arranging and attending meetings, information gathering and planning activities, and in telephoning did not change at all. There was a slight reduction in the percentage of time spent in document preparation and supervising activities.

The measurable changes which took place are slight and inconclusive. We had hypothesised that the introduction of an AOIS would result in significant changes....but the changes were not statistically significant. Nevertheless the users are pleased with the systems and especially the electronic mail functions. They want the system to continue, and they are learning to depend on their terminal to help accomplish their daily office tasks".

Immediately following these remarks The article ends with a dry, terse, one line comment. "On this note the project was terminated at the end of 1982". Other information given in the article makes me think that the operational period was not long enough and the number of people involved not large enough to lend full force to these results. However the project organiser obviously felt enough was enough.

<u>Seaqas</u>

Alf Collins of South Eastern Gas, UK., has described the experiences of that organisation over the last seven years. He claims to have worked out that "the profit generated per computing employee used in Segas during 1982/83 was £9,000". This was achieved mainly in three areas "avoidance of recruiting extra people for what would otherwise have been an extra workload, decreasing staff needed for current workload, and improving cash flow, reducing interest charges, etc." The "people saving" aspect accounted for 67% of the benefits to Segas, but contributed no benefits, of course, to those people. Findings like this reinforce the views of the IT pessimists about IT and jobs - a topic which has been discussed several times in these pages.

Segas adopted the old IBM ATMS Word Processing software back in 1976 together with some AES stand-alone WP machines. In 1978/79, a business systems planning study was undertaken, the organisation already being committed to IBM's SNA for networked communications. Following "disappointing experiences with equipment from several vendors" Segas narrowed their future requirements for WP and other office requirements to IBM or Wang. Wang were given 14 days to demonstrate inter-working with an IBM mainframe and certain other functions. This was achieved and Wang equipment was adopted.

An Amdahl machine and software enables workstations connected to Wang VS computers to be linked to IBM mainframes and provides other inter-networking facilities based on SNA. At that time 1100 DP stations, 150 scientific/engineering stations, 100 Wang WP stations and 65 Apple II and IBM PC micros were in use. The system permits a work station to be connected to the type of service required by its user, but "the current network handles the basic transactions of the Segas region's day to day operations. It does not, at present, give truly adequate support to professional/ managerial staff except in a few specific and isolated areas".

The system serves about 1 in 4 of Segas' 6000 office workers - a major segment of the 11,000 strong workforce. The organisation has a £550 million turnover and 1.9 million customers in the south east corner of Britain. Although the micros are used by professional staff with software like Visicalc, the system is used primarily for transaction processing - that is customer's accounts etc., and the associated correspondence. Thus DP and WP predominate. Although this is an impressive sales, accounting, and general operations system it does not seem that much can be learnt about office re-organisation resulting from office automation, or about changes in the habits of executives from it.

Questions are only now being asked about facilities like electronic mail and "management network" facilities. (the media would have us believe that these services would surely already be in place in an organisation as committed to computers and telecomms as Segas). It seems as if Segas put first things - that is the things likely to provide tangible benefits - first.

<u>Rowntree Mackintosh</u>

With reference to a particular part of office systems - the communications network - Ron Pontefract has described this company's activities. The company plumped for a PABX based system - the "message switch" shown in Figure 20.1. The bit rate required by the average person using it is between 7k and 24K, well within the capacity of PABX extensions. In Pontefract's opinion the sheer number of terminals to be handled indicate that the only likely solution is a current generation PABX such as a Plessey IDX or Mitel SSX2000 - "a LAN has an important complimentary role diminutive with that for which it is often portrayed".

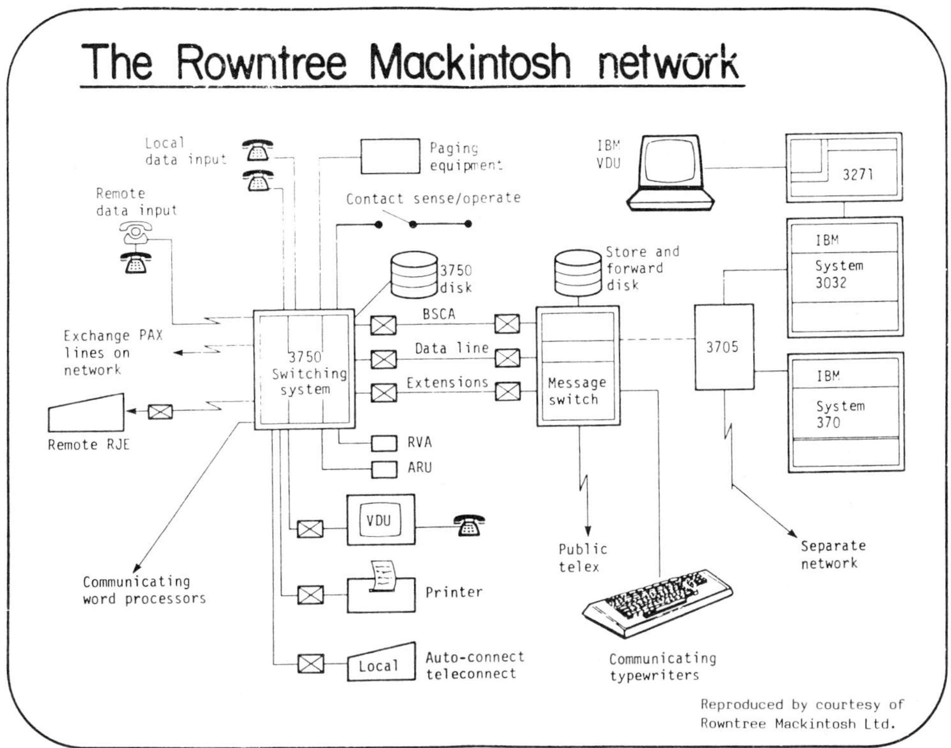

FIGURE 20.1

ICI (WITH DIGRESSIONS)

Management commitment

The planning and systems being used at ICI are of considerable interest. In view of earlier remarks about the need for top management commitment some remarks about this aspect are in order.

In the book "Wealth From Knowledge" Langrish and others examined success factors in 40 case histories of British Companies who had won the Queen's Award for Technological Innovation. These included Beecham's antibiotics, Ferranti's microcircuits , the Chorleywood dough-improving process (which revolutionised bread making), ICI's Procion dyes, the Martin-Baker ejector seat, and many others.

Following the success ingredient which Langrish lists first - "Top person: the presence of an outstanding person in a position of authority", he continues:- "The starting of a successful project was in many cases the result of a top person identifying a useful area to work in. The top person can generate enthusiasm for a project by making sure that resources are available, taking personal interest in the results of the workers, and in general being the spokesman for the project".

A Start from Scratch and an Act of Faith are also of importance. Many companies fail to get started in office technology because they cannot or will not think about these factors. Clearly if you have the resources to set aside the old office technology bits and pieces, probably purchased on an ad hoc basis, and plan your system knowing the current state of the art, there can be a better chance for success with no later excuses for having to press the old stuff into use.

An Act of Faith is needed because of the absence of hard information about the success of Integrated Offices - by no means the only business resource requiring this Act. A degree of faith is needed whenever benefits are likely to be hard to quantify. Basic research, and that curious resource, Information, are examples. The intangibles of the Integrated Office are in some measure due to the intangibility of Information itself, and to the hard to measure benefit of access to the right information at the right time.

The impact of office systems on higher management is particularly important in view of the higher salaries involved and the potential for improving decision-making. This is where faith is really needed - it is the area which has been exposed to advertising loaded with superlatives by an industry which thinks it has a winner without a shred of evidence to back the claims. The executive work station is aimed at a person who is assumed to be an expert typist, telecommunications expert, and information scientist - or at least those are the virtues that this improbable individual must possess until we understand how to match the machine to the executive's behaviour.

In the "remote management" concept, an equally improbable individual sits at his terminal, deduces what needs to be done from various forms of information display, and issues a flow of instructions. Face-to-face and behavioural aspects play no part in this extraordinary scenario. I believe that the integrated office is likely to expedite certain aspects of routine office work, may well reduce some time-wasting activities and add value to others, and should improve information flow. Beyond that - well it's fun to speculate.

In most big companies, large-scale information processing is carried out in the Data Processing (DP) department. This department is inclined to be unavailable for dealing with the information needs of individuals; it does its own thing for the corporate benefit. The wide adoption of micros in companies is only to be expected. People like to be in a master- of-their-own-destiny situation. They are less happy with a   terminal connecting to a cable which disappears through a hole in the wall to a central filing system. Information on paper, or the contents of the dog-eared blue folder on the left, has a comforting tangibility embodying crude indexing, as discussed elsewhere in this book.

The Chinese Restaurant Syndrome and Zipf's Law

Indexing requirements have been discussed in several parts of this book. I am reminded of a problem in the medical literature in describing the effects of Monosodium Glutamate. You couldn't find half the articles about it because people would keep referring to the effects - the dizzy feeling experienced by some people after an oriental meal - either as "Kwock's disease" or the "Chinese Restaurant Syndrome".

Even when good central information services exist, human nature will out - as with University libraries. Faculties and professors operate their own private libraries with much "wasteful" duplication of information. It's too far to walk to the usually excellent central facility. Zipf's law (the principle of least effort) operates.

<u>Information was Power</u>

Position, power, and empire-building activities in the organisation may depend on the possession of, and access to, information. At some point in the automating of an office presumably decisions must be made about central versus local computer storage, classification, access limited by password, etc. This requires that the contents of inner sanctums will be phased out so that they may be handled in the "most efficient" computerised manner.

This must stop at some point otherwise some rather useful customs may disappear. Custodians well-known throughout the company as being the best, perhaps the only, information sources in certain fields may be swept away. When you ring them up in the future they will politely refer you to the computer – but will it be better? Perhaps people always will retain a fund of their own information in their office for this reason.

<u>Early work at ICI</u>

By 1979, ICI's Mond Division at Runcorn, Merseyside, already had extensive computer experience and in that year a group of three senior managers was formed to investigate office networks. Of the two who were users of computers, one came from Management Services Department, but the man chosen to head up the effort came from the Chemical Products Division – he did not have a computer or data processing background. The project team decided that it was absolutely essential for the users to be consulted at every stage – the system had to be matched to their requirements.

An office network typically consists of various resources made available to many users at their work-stations via some kind of reliable telecommunications network. A typical resource could be a mainframe computer running a management database. Office automation is beset by equipment compatibility problems and telecommunication hassles. The alternatives are to commit yourself to one manufacturer, wait until the standards arrive, or do what is necessary to sort out the incompatibilities yourself. Most large organisations will not be starting from scratch and will have to decide what to do with what they already have.

Mond already possessed resources purchased from various manufacturers. The project team decided to undertake the difficult task of buying a network and using it to interconnect workstations, existing resources, and new resources. Management Services would provide a customer support service for consultation and assistance from the start.

Experience acquired at ICI during the widespread introduction of word processing provided evidence about the need for a "user first" approach. During that operation, attention to training, people's preferences, working conditions and salary grades had enabled this first exposure to the technology to go through reasonably well. A policy of no dismissals had been adopted even although the typing staff had been reduced by one per WP machine introduced. This was during the late seventies when the chip had just been introduced to a marvelling public and something akin to a Victorian interest in technology had been aroused.

The team decided that a new office system would have to provide reliable service to workstations used for handling text and sending messages. It would have to accommodate improvements such as colour, image processing, and voice annotation. Additionally the stations would be used as intelligent terminals connected to mainframe computers. Above all the system must be easy to use. It was anticipated that a terminal would be on every desk within five years.

Having formulated the policy, one of the first major steps was to acquire the network. Mond could not find what they wanted off the shelf, but a small company in London, Xionics, was developing a fast network, Xinet, including a control system, multi-purpose workstation software, and communication adaptors (interfaces) to enable different kinds of machine to be connected to it. Mond put one of their own systems people to work on Xionic's premises in the early stages. The major features of the Mond system as it is today, using this network, are shown in Figure 20.2.

The network and main disk storage are duplicated for reliability. There are no floppy disks at workstations – user's storage is centralised. The decision to work backwards from the user's requirements instead of forwards by imposing the technology is paying off as I saw when I visited the site. To use the system you go to your workstation, enter your password, and the main menu is displayed inviting you to choose one of the facilities offered.

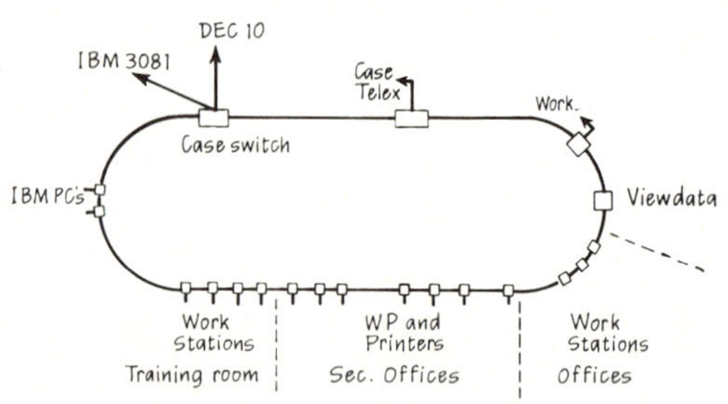

FIGURE 20.2. ICI MOND SYSTEM

They include word processing, electronic mail and messages, telex, personal computing, financial modelling, personal filing and retrieval, professional services, access to central computers, and routine data processing. Amortisation and operational costs per user were estimated at £3000 per annum in 1984 but what are the benefits in monetary terms? Do the results justify this cost? Answers to these questions are what everyone interested in office systems wants, but ICI are quite clear that there can be no simple answer. The conventional wisdom has it that benefits can be counted in salaries saved, time saved, or value added in better, more efficient services.

The company know that time has been saved. There has been a considerable reduction in the number of people employed on the site over the years but it is hard to say what fraction of them can be attributed to office systems. ICI Mond have been using their system long enough to be convinced that there are real, if intangible benefits.

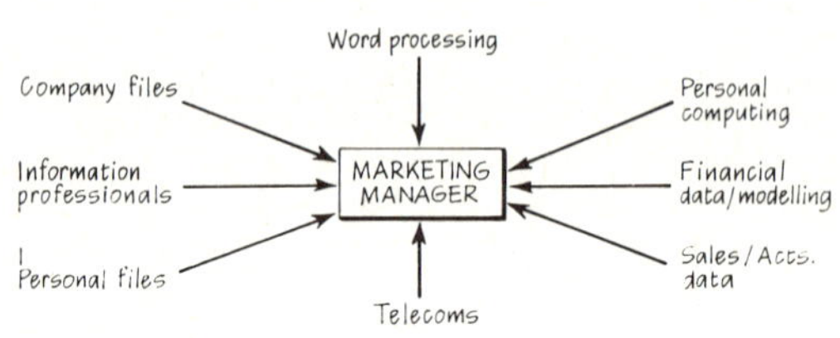

FIGURE 20.3 ICI MOND SERVICES

Another way of representing the system is in terms of user support as shown in Figure 20.3 A marketing manager is shown at the centre since he is probably more dependent than anyone else on a continuous flow of information. A diagram of this kind could be drawn with any other user at its hub.

During a visit to Mond I saw how the information available via a work station is made accessible. The user is invited to choose a service from the first menu by pressing a single key. Another menu will usually follow offering a narrower choice within the selected service. In other words the usual advantages of a menu-driven system are provided. ICI can draw upon experience obtained with this system when proceeding towards a more general installation of office systems throughout the company. Other Divisions are providing complimentary experience, notably Agricultural (Videotex and Database

Management) and Wilmslow (Computer Systems Research).

<u>Office systems at ICI head office: effects of the Chairman's interest</u>

The current technology push at head office owes much to the Chairman, John Harvey-Jones, appointed in April 1982. Harvey-Jones is well aware of the importance of the right information at the right time. The story is told that following a presentation in Los Angles, a guest observed "Mr Harvey-Jones, we've not only enjoyed listening to you, but have also enjoyed looking at your tie". Harvey-Jones promptly replied "I must tell you that my secretary, who knows I like interesting ties, recently informed me "Sir, I happened to see this revolting tie, and immediately I thought of you".

Harvey-Jones decided to go ahead with the installation of an integrated office system at Thames House, Millbank, London very soon after he became Chairman. He possesses or has access to three factors which will maximise the chance of success - he is Chairman, his company has the necessary resources to set aside what exists and start and run a large experiment from scratch, and his position enables him to pursue an Act of Faith. The objectives of the office installation are to assess the benefits and demonstrate the system to other Divisions in the expectation that similar systems will be installed and networked through the company.

The operation is being performed beneath the umbrella of a "Corporate Management Services" function for liason purposes. The task of Dr. Armitage, the project manager,is made a little easier because he is catering for the 350, or so, head office staff remaining when several departments currently working at Millbank are dispersed elsewhere. Although the system draws on Mond's experience this change presents the opportunity for starting from scratch.

The selection of major components and external services is interesting. Some come from manufacturers who are already established suppliers to ICI, but others do not. The Racal Planet Local Area Network (LAN) - which is not amongst the most widely known at present - has been chosen to inter-connect workstations and resources. Planet is based on a Cambridge University design (The "Cambridge Ring") in

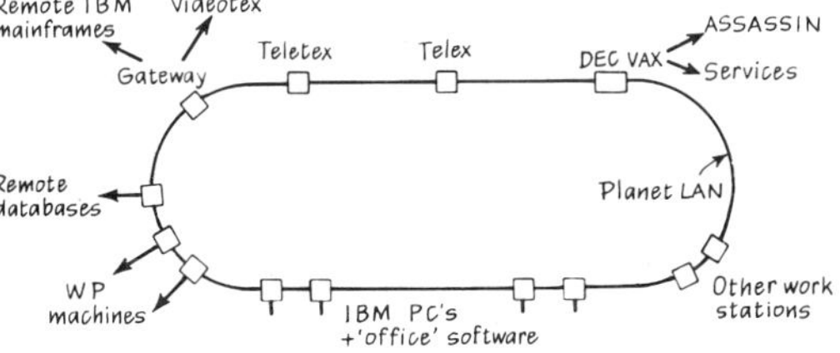

<u>FIGURE 20.4 ICI HEAD OFFICE SYSTEM</u>

which "message slots" continuously circulate at 10 Megabits/sec on a cable ring to which intercommunicating stations are attached as described by Carrington. A transmitting station detects an empty slot and fills it with symbols and an address as it passes, for action by the addressed station somewhere else on the ring. Figure 20.4 shows the arrangement

Planet was probably chosen because of its advanced facilities, its development potential, and because it has Racal, one of the most progressive telecommunications companies in the world, behind it. Up to 500 different devices may be inter-connected on one Planet ring but 64,000 different stations can be addressed. A user could communicate with any station on any of a number of other Planets when the Planets are inter-connected through long distance links. Unlike some other LANs, Planet can handle voice as well as data, and includes ring duplication with an automatic self repairing function in the event of a break. In due course a fibreoptic ring should be possible. Planet is not cheap; the cost for a 40 station installation would be about £16,000.

<u>System software</u>

Another interesting decision is the selection of Digital Equipment Corporation's (DEC) VAX 11/780 to handle the main resources on the network although IBM apparently dominates the electronic office scene.

IBM offers its Professional Office System (PROFS) and Distributed Office Support System (DISOSS) software for running on 370 and other machines. Soon after the introduction of its personal computer (IBM PC), which had a dramatic effect on the microcomputer market, it introduced versions of it for use as "intelligent terminals" connected to the IBM mainframes possessed by a very large number of organisations. Because of its domination of the mainframe market, the company has a captive audience for its compatible micro. IBM has also developed its System Network Architecture (SNA) to enable a wide variety of different items to be interconnected for purposes of remote control, exchange of information files, etc., on the same site or on sites in different countries.

However DEC has also been beavering away with office systems, the strength of the company having been founded on the PDP range of minicomputers which established it as a world leader for this type of machine. Later it introduced the more powerful 32 bit VAX range of computers. When DEC introduced its office systems software, the company seemed less concerned about trying to ensure that it would always be used with equipment of its own manufacture. DEC's equivalent to IBM's SNA - Digital Network Architecture (DNA) - to be used with whatever collection of telecom links may be available (collectively called DECNET) - exemplifies this philosophy. DECNET enables DEC equipment to be used together with items from other manufacturers. This may have been an important factor in ICI's choice.

Earlier choices made by ICI for use in the head office system include the Aregon IVS3 videotex (viewdata) system, and Wordplex word processors. Although videotex is best known in its Prestel form, it can be regarded as simply a rather different kind of computer software, and versions of it are available for corporate use on several different computers. Videotex can be used rather easily as a message system, or for finding information on a database without the need for users to have to take a course on how to do it.

<u>ASSASSIN - unique perception of a need?</u>

Perhaps uniquely in office system installations, ICI have taken account of indexing problems by providing a software package called ASSASSIN which will be run on the VAX machine accessible via the Planet network. ASSASSIN was developed at ICI's Agricultural division at Billingham and is used there and at many other organisations for text indexing, processing, storage, and retrieval by trained specialists. Recently it has been re-designed by Robin Clough and his team so that it can be used directly by office staff or managers. Menu selection is provided. Text in various forms - for instance enduring memos, reports etc., can be indexed by the author, simply by marking significant words or phrases.

If the author-selected terms are already in the stored imposed-vocabulary (thesaurus) when new text is typed into the system, it is indexed under those terms. New terms are placed in temporary storage and checked by indexers to become either new terms in the thesaurus or to be listed under an existing preferred term - for instance "Chinese Restaurant Syndrome: see under Kwok's disease". If a searcher chooses a term but there is no information associated with it, the words alphabetically near to it may be displayed.

I have seen the new version - ASSASSIN 6 - being used. Information science has been applied to an office system product. If it can be sold - as all such systems must be "sold" (using that word in it's best sense) - to office people already receptive to new ideas, an important barrier which inhibits effective use of office systems will have been removed.

OTHER RECENT CASE HISTORIES

Pilot systems in the UK

The Department of Industry is sponsoring an experiment in which 21 pilot systems are running in government offices, local authorities, nationalised industries and other places. To give a few examples of systems and places, Xionics have fitted out the Cabinet Office; Philips the Department of Transport; IBM, Cambridgeshire County Council; Office Technology Ltd., British Rail Engineering; Logica, Wales Gas; Wang, the National Coal Board; ICL, The Science and Engineering Reseach Council, and Racal, the BBC Personnel Department. The systems were discussed at a 1984 meeting as summarised by Grieves.

The cost of each of these systems never exceeeded £250,000 and users are obliged to supply information about the trial for 2 years. The investment cost in the six completed trials was about £7000 per work station with supporting costs from £2000 to £5000 per work station. In the most recent progress report of the trials to hand (May 1985) the usefulness of the systems is not unexpectedly found to be far less than the claims made in much of the general literature. The trials themselves did not start with rosy expectations and the objectives were modest.

"Direct savings were not widely sought......improvements in management effectiveness were only infrequently sought....the overall balance of benefits sought appearing, as it may, to be somewhat unconvincing.....staff reductions would have made it more difficult to establish the goodwill and co-operation of users and trade unions". Surely we cannot be in the same world that shines out from the sales literature?

However five out of the six organisation whose trials are complete decided to continue with their systems and some are enlarging them, so even if the achievements were modest they are enough to encourage continuation.

Current work in the US

Having checked the activities in a large number of offices in banks, hospitals and general administration, Panko divides them into two categories - Type 1, where accounting, payroll, billing, WP and reprographic work is carried out, that is _routine_ information processing, and Type 2, the offices of line managers, legal people, corporate planning, marketing, and engineering where _non-routine_ information processing goes on.

Panko concludes that most current work is concerned with only one type of support - the creation of tools to automate office procedures only in Type 1 offices. "Type 2 offices present a major problem to designers of office methodologies. Traditional procedural analysis skills taught in systems and office analysis methodologies are not likely to be central to the needs of the office. Rather the strategies that must be designed and supported are likely to depend very heavily on the professional content of the work being done in that office".

Kriebel provides some facts and comes to some interesting conclusions having surveyed 48 major companies. Centralised decision making and centralised systems, as in most of these companies, go together, but leading edge companies are moving to a "more distributed environment". What this means is that in quite a number of companies, employees are allowed to access corporate computers, portable terminals are being provided for travelling employees, mainly for data entry and computations, and more use is being made of external databases. Kriebel hypothesises that the primary justification for home terminals is to allow employees to work extra hours at home ("allow" seems a curious choice of words), and that although electronic mail systems are not common at present, their use will increase with this trend towards decentralisation.

CONCLUSIONS ON OFFICE SYSTEM PROGRESS

The automated office is a technology/sales led phenomenon where the success of word processing has raised the hopes of manufacturers and users that WP was a just a start and that low productivity in other parts of the office will soon be changed by the introduction of something called "office systems".

At present the evidence that there will be substantial changes in these areas lags way behind manufacturer's optimism. The role that special systems may play in assisting non routine office work will become clearer as organisational and behavioural factors become better understood. The complexity of current generation machines and their software and the state of the man-machine interface also need to become much better matched to human understanding and working practices.

However, although expectations seem to be higher than probable outcomes the present state of personal computers, workstations, etc., to be used mainly for routine tasks, is good enough for the current growth to continue. The kind of figures suggested for the US are that the great majority of a white collar workforce of about 60 million people will be sitting in front of workstations in the 1990s with a saving of up to about $6000 per person per year (Sniger).

A figure of $270 billion dollars is forecast for 1986 office product sales, and that is already very big business. Unquestionably this is a growth field but thre is no reason to believe that the 1990s forecast will turn out to be any more accurate than other forecasts which have been discussed elsewhere in this book.

Presumably the opportunity to automate was open to Harold Geneen, president of ITT, before he retired, but there is no hint of it in his article "In praise of the cluttered desk". On the contrary, executives with clear desks - presumably those with a propensity to automate - were objects of suspicion. "If you are in the firing line" says Geneen "you are going to have 89 things on your desk, ten others on the floor, and eight more on the credenza behind you". (Note for the uninitiated - a credenza is an up-market foreign-type table). In short, "a good cluttered-desk executive...is vital to the success of the enterprise". I wonder if IBM selected the position of their two-page Charlie Chaplin advt for the PC in Fortune magazine where Geneen's article was published? It was exactly in the middle of this article.

EXAMPLES OF AVAILABLE OFFICE SYSTEMS

Xerox Star

Xerox Star: Concept and Design

The design of the Star system, now referred to as the 8000 Network System, appears to have started at the office user and worked backwards. Such a procedure is as necessary as it is rare; it is much easier and cheaper to adapt or project something from the existing fund of equipment and software and expect the user to behave like a computer buff.

Xerox took eight years over this project, a development of their "Alto" system, so even if they had a team averaging only ten well-supported people to develop all the units of the Star system, that would have cost them around £8 million. Add as much again for prototype construction and testing, and treble it to include drawings, production engineering and launching costs, and Xerox will see little change out of £25M in 1980 dollars. My guess is that it has cost them much more than that - which no doubt accounts for the high price of this system. Further work has continued on it since the first launching in 1981.

A black-on-a-white background high resolution CRT screen with familiar looking objects displayed ("icons"), and an effect resembling overlaid sheets of paper emphasises the Star's radical design. Paperlike pages of text, messages. etc., with graphics can be composed, stored, retrieved or circulated to others electronically. The impact of the PARC approach (an acronym meaning the Xerox Palo Alto Research Centre) on the industry has been substantial. Apple's Lisa and Macintosh owe much to it. The general philosophy is described by Smura in Chapter 43.

Work stations on the desks of clerks and "professionals" connect to a data highway (Ethernet coaxial cable). Common-resource items such as file servers (electronic filing cabinets) print servers (laser printers), and communication servers (electronic mail and gateway to external communication channels) also connect to it. It is not clear whether "professionals" is intended to mean managers, executives, and others who can't or won't type. Some of the work for which the Star is designed does not require typing expertise.

For people who do more than some arbitrary amount of creative writing - and that could include some executives - there is a real incentive to do your own typing. The greater the power of the text processing device to assist you the more you will benefit. The assistance provided by the Star is very considerable. Perhaps some executives will supress their conservative ideas about the division of labour and the social hierarchy in the office and consider the undoubted benefits of typing a finished piece of writing. "Finished" of course covers not only subject content but presentation - that is an aesthetically pleasing combination of type faces, headings, white space, and perhaps graphics.

Another benefit is the replacement of the much-corrected written-on-paper or typed draft disaster which is exchanged between the executive and his secretary, by a text that is always legible and correct. Moreover that final polish for which there is never enough time in normal circumstances can be made with a flourish on the Star.

<u>Xerox Star: The work station - word processing and graphics</u>

The model 8011 work station consists of a keyboard, display unit and mouse, 16 bit 512K memory, processor, and 10Mbyte disk. To connect a work station to other work stations or shared resources via an Ethernet LAN, suitable cable with terminator and a transceiver is required. Figure 20.5 shows some of the available fonts and shapes which can be assembled, stretched or shrunk to fit the required area. Figure 20.6 shows some text and simple graphics composed with the system and the same after columnising and shrinking the graphics to fit one column - the work of a few moments.

These pages were printed using the laser printer and you can see that the sophistication provided by the control system, software, and printer are of a different order to conventional equipment. Shapes, lines, etc., can be selected from an existing collection by a "point, move, and assemble" process so no artistry except for some feeling for design is needed. The equipment could be used to compile a very acceptable textbook complete with line drawings, headings, special fonts etc., ready to go to the printer.

These effects have become much more familiar with the advent of Apple Lisa and later systems.

This is an example of Modern 12. *... and Modern 12 italic* ... **and Modern 12 bold**

This is **an** example of Modern 10. *... and Modern 10 italic* ... **and Modern 10 bold**

This is an example of Modern 8. *... and Modern 8 italic* ... **and Modern 8 bold**

This is an example of Modern 14. *... and italic* ... **and bold**

This is an example of Modern 18. *and italic* **and bold**

This is Modern 24. *italic* **bold**

This is an example of Classic 12. Classic 10, and Classic 8.

This is an example of Classic 12. Classic 10, and Classic 8.

This is an example of Classic 12. Classic 10, and Classic 8.

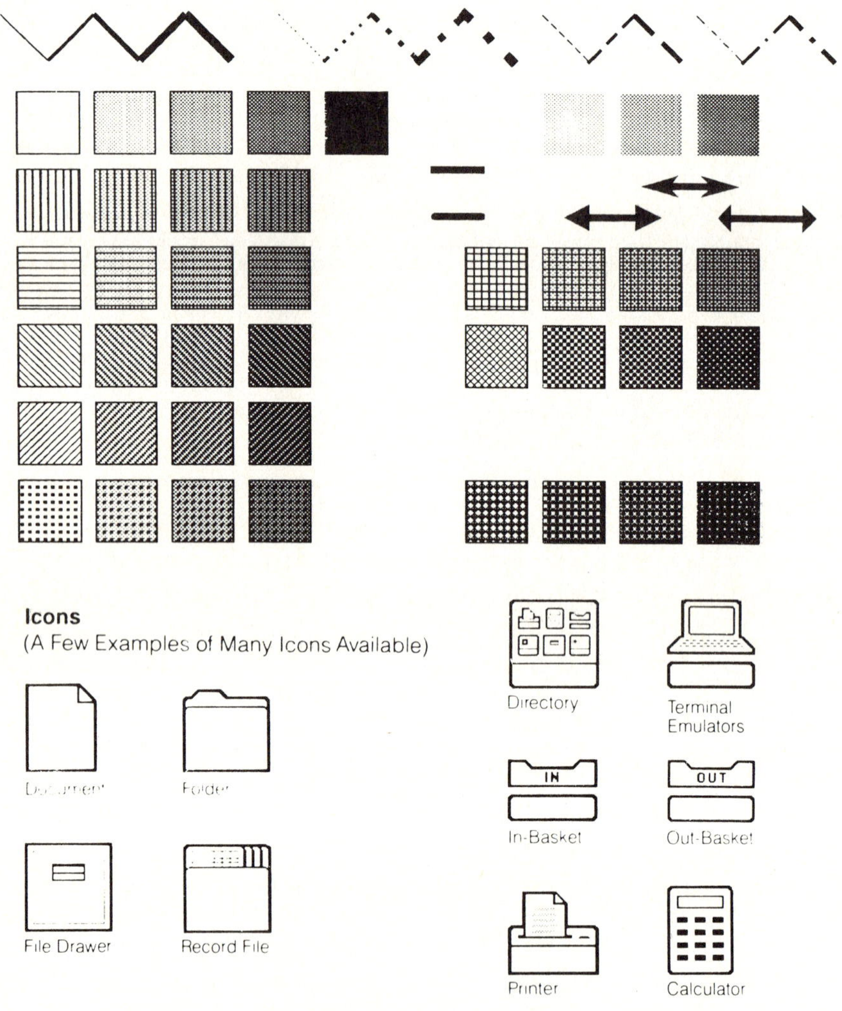

FIGURE 20.5. XEROX STAR: FONTS, GRAPHICS, AND ICONS

But it appears that it was worth the wait. The machine which embodies all that has been learned from the earlier experimental systems is finally here, and our first reaction is that it is even better than we thought it would be.

Xerox was going to call the new device the Professional Workstation, but it was code-named Star through most of the long development cycle. and, in the end, this name seemed to capture the spirit

goodness product.

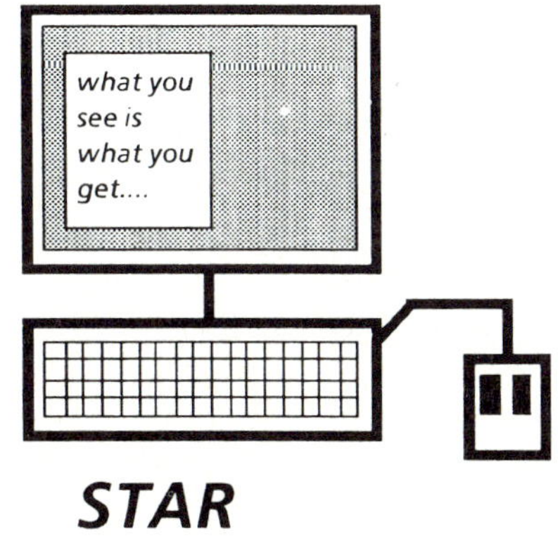

But it appears that it was worth the wait. The machine which

range of capabilities than anything which has preceded it; and different becuase it introduces to the commercial market radically new concepts in human engineering. It is almost certain to engender some quite spirited discussion as people try to sort out just what it is, what it can do and where and how it should be used.

Enter Star

In early 1975, Dave Liddle (vice president of office systems within the Office Products Division) was assigned the task of turning Alto into a product which the company could market. He began to gather together a small team

FIGURE 20.6. XEROX STAR: MANIPULATING TEXT AND GRAPHICS

General control and display system

The control system is quite simple. It consists of special keys surrounding
the conventional Qwerty keyboard, labelled MOVE,   AGAIN,   OPEN, CENTER,
LARGER, SMALLER, etc; the mouse; displayed forms, and displayed objects. The
mouse, since widely copied, is a small trolley which fits in the palm of the hand
so that the fingers rest on two keys - "SELECT" and "EXTEND SELECTION". A
displayed arrow can be pointed at any object because its motion and
direction on the screen exactly follows the motion and direction of the mouse
as you move it across the surface of the desk in front of you.

The whole concept is based on "look, point, and press the SELECT key"
(instead of "type and remember"). To aid the process, familiar objects (icons)
such as filing cabinets, folders, in and out baskets, etc., are displayed on a
designated part of the screen. Each can have a name superimposed on it. Nearby,
another area is reserved for either "option sheets" or "property sheets" -
overlaid forms requesting options completion, or listing typographic attributes
of an associated document (e.g. typeface and size) respectively. These may
appear following icon selection. To the left of the screen is the text
composition area.

A user feels at ease with this system because the black-on-white
format, icons, framed forms with contrasting fonts, shaded areas etc.
produce the familiar appearance of print on paper. For example if you want
to know what's in one of the folders look at the picture of the named folder you
want, point to it, point to the picture of a printer, press the MOVE key and
"pull" the printer icon on to the folder. A list of the "documents" within
the folder will then be printed.

The construction of a diagram, insert, line drawing etc., is carried out by
pointing to and moving graphic bits and pieces. The EXTEND SELECTION key on
the mouse, used with other facilities, enables graphic elements to be
selected,lines to be drawn, a set of graphic elements to be clustered and moved
thereafter as a cluster, shading, cross hatching etc., to be added, items
broken out of a cluster, and stretching, shrinking, framing and moving, to be
carried out. In short, a fluid rubber-like quality is imparted to an area of
graphics to enable it to be re-arranged, moved, and fitted in as needed.

Documents can be filed, stored and retrieved from a file server by their
originator, or by others at different work stations with due authorisation.
Incoming and Outgoing messages - the "electronic mail" facility communicated
via Ethernet - are depicted as letters in the "In" and "Out" baskets on the
screen. Operations on this mail are arranged using menus displayed nearby when
they are needed.

Xerox Star: Prices

A completely equipped ten-station office system with
shared resources would cost at today's prices about:-

	$	£
	<u>$</u>	<u>£</u>
One Laser printer	21237	23059
One File server	13285	14425
One Communication server	<u>10761</u>	<u>11685</u>
	10(45283	49169
	4528	4917
One Work station (inc. Ethernet)	9685	10515
Total, per Work station	<u>14213</u>	<u>15432</u>
(Total cost of system	<u>$142133</u>	<u>£154320)</u>

The market is presumably the medium to large organisation with two or more office complexes on separate sites. This would enable the full communications potential to be realised with electronic mail, shared information storage and retrieval etc.

Xerox Star: Justification for purchase

Can this cost be justified in terms of increased productivity, or is that too narrow a viewpoint since there will be intangible but possibly major elements of added "quality"? Can it be justified for carrying out in-house work which might otherwise have to be contracted out?

Say a 10 station system is to be installed for the use of ten professions/clerks with salaries averaging $25000. To total annual salaries of $250,000 add 100% overheads so total costs without the system are $500K per annum. There will be a once only delivery, installation, and learning cost to be accounted for which could easily amount to $50,000. Let us spread that over three years at, say, $17,000 annually. A $142,000 10 station system could be leased for, say, $40,000, plus maintenance at, say $17,000, totalling $74,000 annually. The annual costs of the "department" are now $574,000 annually so productivity would need to increase by 15% to pay for the system.

But will all the work of the 10 people be amenable to productivity increases? Alternatively can the machines be reserved for, and used all the time for the kind of work for which the system will generate productivity gains? This may not be the case so perhaps we are looking for a productivity increase of 20 to 25% for the work actually done with the machines, according to this admittedly crude accounting assessment. A productivity increase ofthis order seems not unreasonable .

No allowance has yet been made for possible overhead reductions. For example if the electronic mail system is used for communicating with a similar remote installation and the traffic is large, reductions in postage and telephone bills would more than offset the cost of a leased telecoms line. Other savings can be expected for eliminating the physical handling, storing, filing, and retrieving of documents. More intangible savings could include general improvements in "quality". Well illustrated reports with a professional appearance, which would otherwise have to be produced elsewhere, could be created in the office.

The high cost of this equipment puts it out of court for most small offices, but from the above rough and ready sums it seems likely that Star could be a good investment under the right conditions. Most of the current applications reported involve information collection by networked workstations and word processing, but it is the originator's ability to assemble that information in camera-ready or ready printed form without an intermediary that gets most mention. The originator can experiment with his own concepts and get it exactly right for his reader or customer.

To convince the management at Boeing that an 8000 (to give the system its current name) installation was needed the project team chose special people known to be innovative to be the first users. Subsequently the preparation of special documents for contract support by engineers became a major application. At Allen-Bradley a major application is the preparation of technical publications and instruction sheets. Another is the direct production of documents with charts and graphs by the management information systems department which were previously prepared by intermediaries. At Upjohn the company's photo-typesetter in the print shop receives copy direct from workstations via Ethernet.

<u>OTL Information Management Processor (IMP)</u>

<u>Office Technology Ltd.</u>

OTL is not as well known as Xerox. It started up in the 60s as Computer Technology Ltd., manufacturer of the Modular One minicomputer. In 1980 the company was re-formed as Information Technology Ltd (ITL), with Office Technology Ltd as an operating subsidiary specialising in office automation, plus two other subsidiaries. Tony Davies became chief executive. At that time four men from IBM's Hursley Labs, including Dr. Bob Remington, human factors specialist, joined OTL's office systems venture at Winchester and the Imp was conceived. It was born less than two years later at the end of 1981.

Growth has been steady and 1980/81 turnover was £8.7M, an increase of £1.3M; profit was £604K. From 78/79 to 80/81 revenue increased by £2.4M, but profits by only £64,000; By 1984 turnover had gone up to £25M with profits up to £1.05M and £9M orders in hand. ITL now employs 650 people and has provided installations for major companies and public authorities such as Shell, Pilkington, ICI, Lloyds Bank,British Rail, The Metropolitan Police, etc.

<u>OTL: The Imp</u>

The Star and the Imp are aiming their products at the same market – the offices within medium to large companies. Both started the design from the user's needs and worked backwards, rather than adopting the more usual and much less expensive method of improving what exists. The Imp units are Controller and Filestore, Workstation, Principal Workstation with voice facilities (an important innovation) and Printer, plus the necessary software. For workstation/controller communications a star arrangement is used – that is connections radiate from a controller to a cluster of workstations. A workstation may be up to 600 metres from a controller; communication is at speeds up to 1.07 Mbps. Controllers communicate with each other at up to 312 Kbps on a LAN basis using HDLC ports.

The design trend in large office systems is to interconnect a workstation with immediately adjacent information resources – for instance disk storage – by a short link whose bandwidth is adequate for data exchange with short response times. Shared resources – for example a laser printer or a central file store – and workstations are interconnected by a LAN able to cope with maximum traffic demands – such as when a number of workstations are simultaneously using the central filing system. If the network cannot accommodate this traffic, users may experience erratic or unacceptably long response times.

Electronic Office machine vendors, will, no doubt, continue to try and obtain competitive advantages by offering new goodies such as electronic mail, image processing, and voice transfer. It is not clear at what point LANs may start to behave erratically because of the above limitations. Buyers should ascertain what the limits are before they start adding large numbers of work stations and shared resources. As with most of the new technology it is necessary for the buyer to possess, or to obtain the necessary expertise to enable him to be sure that his purchase really will work under the conditions contemplated. The Imp designers seem to have taken a conservative view. They have specified the maximum number of work stations per cluster, so that the above problem should not occur.

<u>OTL: Imp Workstations</u>

A principal workstation consists of a terminal with a high-resolution black-on-white tilting and rotatable 15" (diagonal dimension) display. The supporting plinth houses a small loudspeaker. The screen contents can be smoothly scrolled in any direction and graphics or characters are exceptionally

clear although the claimed resolution is considerably lower than is claimed for
the Star.

The keys on the detachable keyboard (which includes a telephone handset) are
grouped according to functions; see details in Figure 20.7.   Many keys are
shift-operated dual-function engraved on top and on the front vertical face. It
will be evident from the figure that functions usually requiring several key
depressions, or which are menu-driven on other machines, are here handled by a
single key depression. Each workstation contains an 8086 microprocessor with 8K
ROM and 128K RAM. A 40 character/sec or fast draft printer may be connected to a
workstation; font selection is provided.

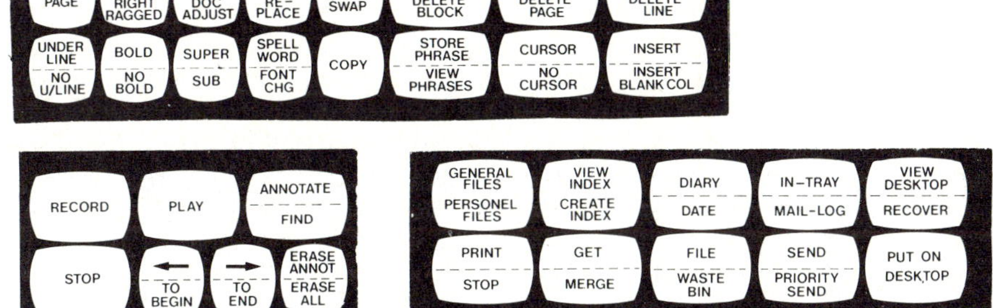

FIGURE 20.7. SOME OF THE OTL IMP'S SPECIAL KEYS

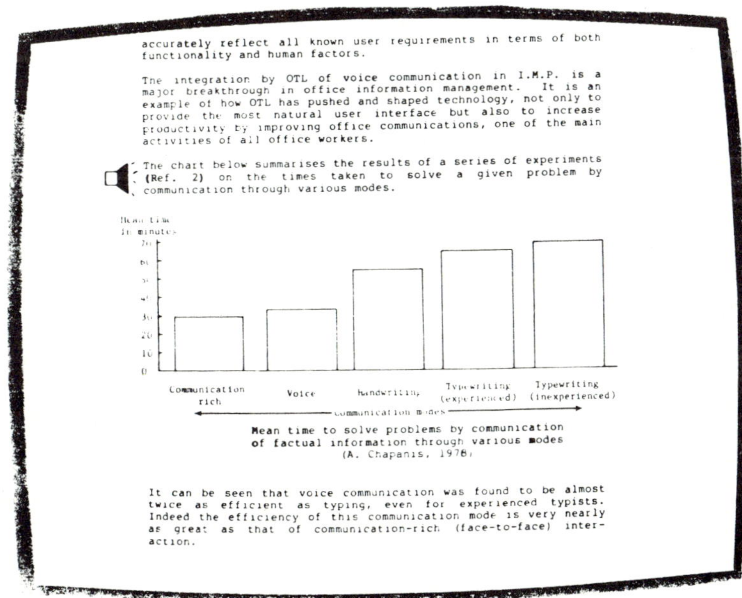

FIGURE 20.8. OTL IMP DISPLAY WITH VOICE RECORDING INDICATED

OTL: Imp software

Depression of the key "View Desktop" causes a list of frequently used "paperwork" to be displayed - e.g. diary, address list, phone numbers etc. This is a "digression key" because if I interrupt current work to go to desktop I can return to that work by pressing "Recover". On the other hand I could, or course, select any desktop file for detailed examination - e.g. diary for next Tuesday.

The preparation of simple graphics is quite effective. Lines can be drawn by holding down keys. Illustrations such as organisation diagrams etc., can be constructed. Electronic mail with the usual facilities is provided.

Voice recording and transmission is the most interesting part of a principal workstation. The keys controlling voice facilities are shown in Figure 20.7 (bottom left). Voice comments associated with a particular "document" can be recorded (a symbol appears on the screen as shown on Figure 20.8). This recording is available to anyone viewing the document by using either the loudspeaker or handset. I used this facility during a demonstration, having imagined that I needed to draw my secretary's attention to a diary change by "voice annotating" the "cover page" of my diary. It worked well, was simple to do, and the playback quality was quite good. This is a letout for the executive who won't, can't, or doesn't want to be seen typing - an obvious requirement for office equipment.

Many applications of voice come to mind - for instance the first draft of a report can be viewed and edited by recording voice instructions for re-typing. When a recording is made the voice is digitised using PCM techniques at 64 Kbps and compressed to around 20 Kbps. Thus about 1 Mbyte of storage is required for 50 seconds of continuous speech, or 10Mbytes per 8 minutes. Clearly, this is an incentive to be brief.

OTL: Imp Controllers

Office system controllers are available for up to 6, 16, or 32 workstations. 160 or 80 Mbyte Control Data MMD disk drives are fitted and maximum capacity is 640 Mbytes. Disk backup, archiving, or software additions are by streaming tape cartridges of 13 Mbyte capacity which run at 192 Kbits/sec. Two microprocessors are fitted - one for workstations disk control and one for main control. Each controller includes two 312 Kbps controller- to-controller ports, two local printer ports, and except in the case of the smallest controller (there are three slightly different models), four programmable ports for external communications (e.g. with auto-dialling).

OTL: Imp price and justification for purchase

If a 10 station system is to be purchased, prices (1985) would be as shown below.

Thus the average price per workstation using the mix shown and with one printer between two workstations, would be £6460.

This compares with the cost per Star workstation of £15,432, but it is hard to assess the relative merits of the two systems. Buyers would need to go and see some installations of both types, and the "Act of Faith" syndrome will probably be needed as well in view of the difficulty of evaluating intangible benefits, as discussed elsewhere in this chapter.

The Star's graphics is a <u>tour de force</u>. Imp's approach is less revolutionary, but it is very well done.

£

```
One OSC B controller with
160 Mbyte disk filestore          16,000
3 principal workstations with voice   15,000
7 workstations                    25,200
3 40 ch/sec printers               8,400
                                 £64,600
```

New office layouts for new systems and circumstances

Office layouts are changed whenever a company re-organises its structure – which these days may be quite often. In their office of the future, Stone and Luchetti abolish the need to relate the office layout to an organisational chart of the company. Their new office is based on "activity settings" which make no concessions to status, but some areas do provide privacy.

The idea assumes that "the electronic cottage", where people work at home from a terminal, will not appeal to most managers because of the removal of face-to-face contact. The activity settings office consists of areas designed for particular tasks so an employee will locate him/herself in the area most suited to the task in hand, not in one office which cannot meet the requirements for a variety of tasks. Human territorial habits are retained with quite small cubicle-like "home bases" (personal offices), but most work is done in areas designed to match the nature of the work. In this new layout it is assumed that electronic systems will increase and print-on-paper will decrease. The whole question of doing work in an office is examined and some alternatives are suggested.

One thing not discussed is office design in respect of trunking and concealment of cables, design of office furniture to take account of inter-connecting desk units and accommodating such units, and considerations regarding the movement of furniture and partitions when each item of furniture contains a number of devices requiring multiple connections. This problem needs attention.

WHERE TO BUY OFFICE SYSTEM COMPONENTS

Wharton Publishing have produced a very useful handbook covering dictating machines, electronic typewriters, WP machines and packages, printers, professional micros, facsimile machines, LANs, PABXs, modems, multiplexers, etc. Most sections consist of a short explanatory review followed by a table of equipment with a compressed tabulated specification for each item. The publication ends with a supplier's address list and glossary. According to this handbook nearly half a million electronic typewriters were sold in Europe in 1983 and 250,000 microcomputers bringing the value of the intalled total to £5 billion. The leaders and market share (prices for WP software), were;-

Electronic Typewriters		Professional Micros		WP software	
Olivetti	41%	IBM	27%	Lexicom	£350
Olympia	25%	Apple	23%	Superwriter	£295
Triumph Adler	13%	DEC	16%	Peachtext	£250
Rank Xerox	4%	Triumph Adler	16%	Easywriter	£153
Canon	3%	Olivetti	11%	Wordstar	–
Others	14%	Others	7%	Spellbinder	–

ELECTRONIC MAIL SYSTEMS

Some Statistics

The following figures and forecasts have been extracted from various reports:-

Equipment in use in Western Europe

	1978/1979	1986/1987
Network termination points	393,000	1,500,000
Data communications equipment	$720M	$1400M

Mail per day (1980, millions of items)

France	GDR	UK	US
23.6	24.7	24	146.8

Text, facsimile, text & graphics (millions items/day transmitted)

1978 2.82   1987 26.2

Resources Investment

$4000 per office worker (productivity +0.4%/year)
$25,000 per industrial worker (productivity +2%/year)

Taken together these figures and projections have convinced the Electronic Mail Industry (whatever that may be) that it is on to a good thing.

What is Electronic Mail?

"Electronic Mail" (EM) is used to describe Viewdata public or private message systems, terminals networked to a computer bureau/mailbox such as Comet, facsimile transmission between Wigan pier and Acapulco, and numerous other things. The phrase seems to be used without regard to economic, time, or volume considerations of the message. Thus an electrically communicated and displayed message from a French company to a visitor from its London office "Car will meet AF612 arrivals at Charles de Gaulle to take you to office" may be called EM, as may be inter-bank funds transfer, a parts list of car spares, a 6 page report, or today's dollar/sterling rate.

The cost, traffic, protocol, switching and communication considerations, and the degree of the effect upon people's activities in offices between the extremes mentioned above is so grossly different that it helps not at all to lump them together beneath one buzzword title. I shall try to stick to the definitions provided in the Glossary elsewhere in this book.

Electronic Message Systems: Driving forces

Electronic Message Systems (EMS) started to be discussed many years ago; by 1977 hundreds of articles on the subject were being published. The prestigious journal Science – usually dedicated to advances in biochemistry, molecular biology etc., saw fit to publish a review article entitled "Electronic Mail" in that year by Potter. Potter informs us that "The concept of organised mail is believed to have emerged in about 4000 BC in the Persian Empire. Queen Elizabeth I issued a proclamation in 1591 which prohibited carrying of mail except by messengers authorised by the Master of the Posts. In America, the first postal system was authorised by the colonial legislature of Massachusetts in 1639.

The sub-title of that article proclaimed "electronic communication of information is more rapid than conventional transportation of documents". I take it that this is not supposed to be humorous - perhaps it's intended as a quiet rebuke to some of the more assertive contemporary articles, one of which was brashly entitled, "Electronic mail comes of age". The Science article clearly summarises the background; It lists types of mail in the US as follows -

<u>% of total mail</u>

Transactions (checks, bills, account statements, orders, etc>)	40%
Advertising	27%
Correspondence (personal 13%, business 5%, government 4%)	22%
Magazines and newspapers	11%

<u>TYPES OF MAIL IN THE UNITED STATES (1968)</u>

Businesses originated 73.6% of the total, and the bulk of the mail flowed in three directions - 47% from businesses to households, 26% from business to business, and 14% from household to household. Several advantages are claimed for electronic mail. Transmission time is measured in minutes while traditional mail takes days. In 1977 the transmission cost of a letter was 6.5 cents a page. 4.5 cents per page was claimed to be the transmission cost when terminals inter-communicated at 1200bps. The author reviews the technology and provides the diagram of a hypothetical electronic mail and message system shown in Figure 20.9

Potter, a Xerox man, sees few problems ahead - "the evolution is inevitable" although "since the sociopolitics and economics are complex, it is beyond the intent of this article to address the question of who should own or operate the electronic mail system". It is interesting that he thinks that EM will be developed as an integrated system; having mentioned the Post Office he finds it obligatory to back away from the contentious problems of the ownership of publicly available systems.

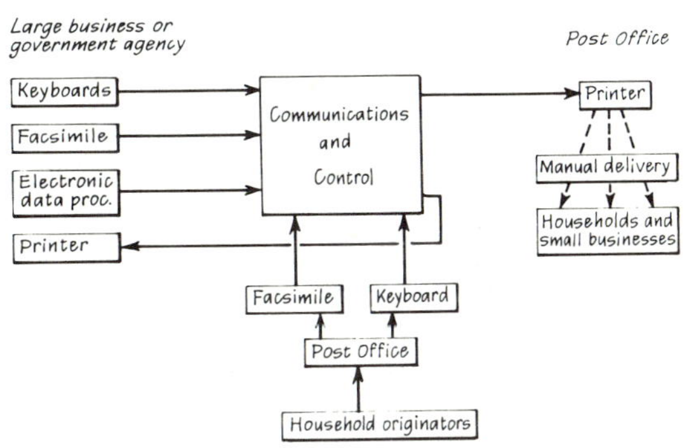

<u>FIGURE 20.9. POTTER'S EM SYSTEM</u>

The whole field was covered in great detail in a 1978 report from Kalba Bowen which describes a number of systems and deals with regulatory and legal matters from the US viewpoint. It is also covered in detail in a Mackintosh (consultancy) report, this time with the emphasis on the European and International traffic, costs, and business applications, together with a policy and market analysis and a brief survey of the major suppliers.

The amount of intra-organisational mail is a significant fraction of the total. The report considers that:- "In the early 1980s, the most likely traffic will be intra-organisational, since general penetration of electronic mail terminals will be low. However "hybrid" services will be developing rapidly during the early 1980s and their availability will affect the usefulness of electronic mail for external mail". We are now in the mid-eighties and those remarks still apply.

Public Electronic mail in the United States

"Electronic Mail" in this section means "alternatives to the post". Useage of the phrase in this context is becoming increasingly common. In 1975 the United States Postal Service (USPS) asked the National Research Council to study EM, and a study report was published in 1977. The US Department of Commerce, and the Congressional Commission on the Postal Service also studied the subject. The unanimous conclusion was that the USPS should undertake the provision of electronic services almost as a matter of survival.

The USPS enjoys a letter-post monopoly with access to public funding. To offer EM services, various policy options needed consideration. The monopoly could be extended to cover EM services, or both postal and EM services could operate competitively without monopoly. Since the need for certain kinds of mail would exist for a long time to come, yet another option would be to continue with the present mail, but enter into co-operative arrangements with the private sector for EM. Changes of this kind require public discussion in the US and tortuous involvement with the White House and Congress, the courts, and various commissions and commercial and public pressure groups.

Unlike changes in European services where the procedure is almost dictatorial by comparison (for instance the provision of Prestel in the UK), great care is needed before launching a particular policy so that there can be some hope of achieving a consensus within a reasonable period of time. In 1978 the USPS proposed EM services competing with the private sector, without seeking to become a common carrier, to which private services could connect. This aroused strong opposition on the grounds of the impossibility of competing with an organisation with such huge resources, or of negotiating with such a dominant partner.

The in-fighting took place against a background of deregulation of communication services and in 1979 private companies with allies in the Carter administration forced USPS to think again. They obtained a ruling from the Federal Communications Commission (FCC) to stop the introduction of the USPS' ECOM (Electronic Computer Originated Mail service) system.. This service would enable large mailers such as insurance and credit card companies to connect to a USPS system which would receive information electrically and change it into hard copy for delivery using the existing mail distribution system. The USPS found itself involved in a battle against Washington and big business.

Following much manoeuvering, a considerably revised form of ECOM was implemented. In February 1980 the USPS proposed that common carriers, with standards imposed upon them, would accept customers input, and would connect to USPS printing centres for onward conventional mail distribution. Apparently the FCC did not intervene. Communication common carriers could also collect electronic messages as a service to lower volume mailers and re-package and sort them for transmission to post offices with ECOM printing equipment.

Two day service was guaranteed at a cost of 26 cents for the first page (1200 characters average) and 5 cents for the second, with a $50 annual fee. Common carriers, operating mainly for a number of lower volume users, were required to add a 10 cents surcharge. It was thought that ECOM could be successful, even with the specified limited objectives. Existing quite successful EM services such as GTE/Telenet, Dialcom, Compuserve etc., could connect to ECOM and help to make it successful.

In 1984 ECOM was virtually ended. It was never widely used and attempts made by the USPS to sell it to a private operator failed.

"Public" Electronic mail in the UK

Since BT is no longer "publicly owned" (it never was really) "public" here means BT operated.

In June 1980 BT (then called the Post Office) opened a facsimile service called Intelpost to Toronto, charging £4 for the first A4 page, and £2 for subsequent pages. It operated from one centre in London. Although USPS was an original proposer the FCC disallowed a US connection. Since then the system has been greatly expanded. Now called Bureaufax, it is available from 15 centres around the UK to many countries in Europe, Canada, USA, and some Caribbean islands at £2 per A4 page, and to many more countries at £4 per page, plus £2 per address for all transmissions.

BT is operating an experimental system in the Midlands for the same day or overnight delivery of packages using a combination of the telephone, dispatch riders, and a small computer which handles billing and labelling. If successful it will be extended to other regions. In December 1981, BT started a six month trial of a system somewhat like ECOM. Customers provide an address tape for bulk mailing and the format of a promotional piece. It is printed by a laser printer (currently Hewlett Packard) at the distribution centre, placed in envelopes, and distributed with the post. At present the system is working between London and Manchester.

BT also concluded an agreement with Dialcom to run the Dialcom software on Prime computers in London as an experimental electronic mail service. Later it introduced the Telecom Gold service for general use using PSS for telecommunications with cheaper rates than PSTN direct dialling.

People don't want to mess about with long strings of log-on characters if they are online professionals, let alone if they simply want to send an EM message. This is a leftover from the days when the services were designed by engineers without marketing or customer consideration. But this arrangement still applies with Telecom Gold. The Telecom Gold software is good but not only is log-on a nuisance but telecom error rates are high. A major claimed virtue of PSS is low error rates. For some reason an extra piece of equipment is needed at exchanges, said to be under development, and to be installed one day.

Electronic mail in Europe

There does not seem to have been as much interest in electronic mail in continental Europe as in the UK.

In France the communications system lagged behind systems in other countries until the recent huge injection of funds. The country has rapidly caught up and has become a leader in communication satellite experiments and in the widespread introduction of data transmission networks. The Transpac packet switched network was the first to adopt the X25 protocol and is available throughout the country, although hopelessly overloaded at the time of writing (June 1985).

The French PTT also operates a system called Colisée for interconnecting the Private Automatic Branch Exchanges (PABX) of geographically separate divisions of the same organisation - a suitable arrangement for inter-company messages. The means therefore exist for some form of EM.

The German PTT probably exercises its monopoly more rigidly than any other European PTT. However it looks as if it is starting to adopt a more adventurous policy. It is embarking on trials of services to households in seven cities by fibreoptic interconnection. The Germans are also pressing ahead with Teletex - a high speed message system to be later discussed.

So far as is known, no particular EM systems are being developed in other countries although many have or are about to introduce data transmission networks.

<u>A typical electronic message system</u>

EM procedures are illustrated in Figure 20.10 with an example showing messages based on the Comet system facilities.

(First dial the number. Underlined items are typed by the user, the remainder by the system).

```
COMET message service - BL31  5 -  Tuesday,  February  9,
1982, 13:08:24 GMT.
Please type your name: Bill Bloggs
Password:__________(not printed)
Thank  you. Your last login was Tuesday, February 9, 1982,
12:58:37 GMT. You have 2 new messages.
Command: REA 1        (Command means "press Return")
                      (REA 1 means "display 1st message").

To: Bill Bloggs
From:       Jane Jones
Date:       Tue 9-Feb-82 12:58:37 GMT
Subject:    New Comet Customer
Would you please note that William Woggs from  BLT  at  LB
joined today. You can also now contact  Henry  Higgins  on
his mailbox.
Command:  Compose (Compose means "I want prompts in
                    order to compose a message)


To:         William Woggs
cc:         H.Higgins
H.Higgins  is  not  a  valid  Comet name, do you wish to see 2
similar names? (Y or N):  Y

Henry Higgins
Herbert Higgins

Corrected name: Henry Higgins
Subject:        Rumblers
Text:
Welcome  William.  Are  you  the  same  Woggs who invented
four barelled rumblers?
Command:  Send
BLSL 9-Feb-82 12:59:50  160 1

Message sent
Command:  File in  Woggs, rsvp
```

<u>FIGURE 20.10. EXCHANGE OF MESSAGES ON AN ELECTRONIC MAIL SYSTEM</u>

This illustrates many of the features typical of the systems available today. Comet correctly calls itelf a "message system" with gratifying modesty. It consists of a computer bureau which uses multi-port PDP-11 computers. A customer dials a number and his VDU, teletype machine, or possibly microcomputer, is then connected to a Comet port for inter-communication at 30 char/sec. Used thus, a "mailbox" cost £30 per month in 1982. (Current comparative prices for EM systems are given in the Classified Product Lists later in this book). Alternatively the system can be run privately under licence - for example an organisation could provide a service for some hundreds of users using a PDP 11-34 with 16 ports and the Comet software.

Note the following points:-

1. The system is reasonably easy to use and it embodies some helpful facilities e.g. a name look-up check.

2. A customer can either use it from his office, or if he is travelling, from any telephone booth using a portable terminal and acoustic coupler.

3. The fee covers 500 messages per month of any length and a maximum access time of 9 hours.

4. Other facilities not shown in the example include editing, help, message retrieval from named files, and scanning of message headings.

COSTS, BENEFITS, AND LIMITATIONS OF INTER-PERSON EMS

Cost of time saved.

BL Systems claim that the following problems are eliminated by EMS. Only about 26% of telephone calls placed go through first time because the person is "at a meeting", line is busy, person is out etc., telephone calls during office hours to foreign countries are limited by time zone differences, and EMS provides a printed record of the "conversation". However a telephone conversation not only enables a discussion to take place but also includes additional information in the recognition, tone, expression, or stress of the voice. EMS requires that the user invests in additional equipment or software on which information is transmitted by typing. Most people can't convey information by typing at anything like the rate they can by speech.

The economics of EMS are hard to work out. Obviously time saved in money terms will be greater for more highly paid people, but such people will usually have secretaries, so it is mostly their time which is saved. Within a company many kinds of communication could be carried out more speedily by EMS than by phone calls or typed memos, but that still leaves quite a number requiring the cut, thrust, and feedback of discussion. EMS enthusiasts will claim that it eliminates the inefficiency of long-winded social chat etc. This claim may be seen to be dubious by considering a situation in which conversation is entirely replaced by EMS - an efficient but intolerably impersonal situation.

Say a person earning £15,000 a year, himself makes 10 telephone calls per day of a kind which could be adequately handled by an electronic message system. The caller's time, based on an 1800 hour/108000 minute year, is worth about £0.14 a minute.

If the called parties themselves answer all calls reasonably quickly, the average time taken by the caller from lifting the phone up to the moment someone replies would be about 30 seconds. However for the US it has been claimed that only 10% of all calls made in the United States are successful first time - a much more pessimistic figure than BL System's. Usually the person called is unavailable, engaged, away, the caller is asked to hold, etc. The average time the caller is actually on the phone trying to make the call averages about 2 minutes, plus the 30 seconds "contact" time. In this event, the preliminaries would cost £0.35 or £3.5 for 10 calls.

Let's assume that the costs of typical UK/US time wastage not incurred with EM per 10-call day are £0.7 for 5 minutes "contact" time plus £2.1 for 15 minutes time wasting - that is about £2.8 per 10-call day.

Telephone costs saved

The cost of 15 extra minutes per day wasted telephone time depends on distance and tariffs in a particular country. In 1985, the time allowed in the UK for the first 3 minutes of a dialled local call is 10p in business hours, 20p for up to 56 Km, and 46p over 56 Kms. Thus the cost of the 15 extra minutes for our executive's 10 calls per day could range from 50p (all local) to £2.30 (all long distance). If they were all international the extra cost would be much higher.

Let's assume that the average extra cost not incurred with EM is £1.5 per day.

EM costs

Because of complex tariff structures it is extremely difficult to work out the price of an electronic mail service. EMMS, experts in this area, estimate about $2 per call, but the distribution of figures contributing to that average is very wide.

It was assumed earlier that the 10 calls per day (out of all the calls that the executive might make) would be suitable for EMS - that is that the equivalent EM messages would be reasonably brief.   So far as I am aware, nobody has compared the telephone time taken to telephone a terse message with one sent by EMS, where both have about the same information content which is not necessarily the same as the number of words. Presumably an EM message is usually shorter since it carries no "conversational redundancy".

Someone has got to cope with the composition and typing of an EM message and go through the ease or difficulty of getting it up on the terminal and connected through to the computer mailbox. There is no activity comparable to this one when making a telephone call.

Different services make different charges for EM calls. This seems to depend on the computer mailbox distribution, not on distance. For example Telecom Gold charges 30p more per A4 message (approx) for calls to US addressees. The Geisco charges are almost identical for UK, Europe, or US.
More information about prices is given in the Product Data section in this book.

Little is known about user behaviour or whether people find EM comfortable and convenient. If they are uncomfortable in using mainly CRT screens instead of paper, in typing, in general operation at a terminal, in using the system etc., they may defect to the telephone.

Conclusions on costs/prices

While it is more or less clear that there will be certain savings because of time wasting when using the telephone, it is not at all clear what the all-cost/price difference is between telephone and electronic mail.

EXPERIENCE WITH LARGE ELECTRONIC MAIL SYSTEMS

Several systems operational for some years, mainly in companies, have been described.

In 1971 the Texas Instruments network linked 50 plants in 19 countries, handling 10,000 messages per day at 8 cents each. In 1981 there were 9000 terminals on the network handling 100,000 messages a day at 4 cents each, with a switching system which can select any addressee in 10 seconds. The kind of messages passed via this network are not described nor are we told what costs are included or excluded from the 4c per message. What is clear is that a successful company has steadily developed a comprehensive intra-company communication system. It would be interesting to know what alternatives were considered, and what savings have been made with the present system.

Hewlett Packard used a number of its COMYS networks consisting of terminals connected to a minicomputer via dial-up telephone lines handling 240,000 messages a day. These were mainly formalised messages dealing with product availability, orders, credits, shipping dates, etc. Costs inclusive of message preparation, amortisation, etc., varied from $1 to $4 per message.

Another system, apparently devised to fulfill a real need by a non-computer company, was developed jointly by Cook Industries, a large US grain purchasing and exporting company, and Quotron Systems. Cook had become overloaded with paperwork produced by a paper tape communication system which generated over a ton of message copies monthly. The messages, mainly dealing with transactions associated with a range of grains, were formalised and circulated via store and forward message switches situated in Memphis, Hong Kong and Paris, with leased lines radiating out from each switch. The message switches are controlled from the corporate message switch - a Nova 1200.

The Nova also connects to an electronic mailbox computer which is available to a number of multi-terminal "user computers" situated in various parts of the US, and to an IBM 370/158 host computer from which various services are available. The system had the backing of upper management in the face of objections while traditional methods were disrupted during implementation. It is cautiously claimed that savings from abandoning the old copying/messenger arrangements have balanced the costs of the new system, but the latter provides a much faster service.

Intra-company message systems are attractive for companies which are widely dispersed and have sufficient traffic to justify the costs of setting up their own private network with compatible equipment of their own choice. The introduction of EMS will have a trivial or considerable effect upon an organisation according to the range and purpose of messages and the degree to which EMS alters established procedures. So far there seems to be little evidence of the effects dramatised in the "Electronic Mail" literature where the executive sits at his terminal effortlessly conducting his day's business with the rest of the world, also seated at terminals.

There is an additional cost-uncertainty about EMS and EM. The continuing covergence of information systems makes it hard to forecast changes in transmission media and equipment. The communications costs of facsimile has greatly decreased because of advances in compression, scanning systems, and compact electronics. Recently very reasonably priced facsimile machines have been introduced which also accept ASCII code so they can be used like conventional printers as well. If fax machines are already installed for other purposes and a message service is needed, then the add-on cost of that service would make it attractive. The installation of intra-company fax machines specifically for an EMS could not be justified unless traffic was very heavy.

<u>USING WHAT EXIST NOW</u>

What is the simplest and least expensive system to use if you decide that there is sufficient traffic between a set of offices to warrant organising an electronic message system, and how do you quantify "sufficient"?

According to EMMS (back in 1979) EM was already a $3 billion business, but that seemed to include revenue from virtually every kind of non-telephone electrical message system. "Beware of cost justification" says EMMS, "users must expect to pay substantially more for their information handling than they do today....many users embracing the new technology....may fear that failure to use it will become the hallmark of the old fashioned or declining organisation". Perhaps EMMS found, as I have, that EM costs/prices are very difficult to work out.

But if you can back up your act of faith by some cost justification, so much the better. Better still you may be able to press into service equipment which may not be ideal but has the great advantage that it is already installed for other purposes. Extra "stations" may be added as necessary.

<u>Telex</u>

Telex is now included under the fashionable Electronic Mail heading. There are about 140,000 US and 300,000 European telex subscribers. If you wish to use this network for an inter-office EMS and some of your proposed respondents are not on it, they can soon get on to it. If your offices are dispersed nationally or internationally, telex has the great advantage that it is PTT supported and there are no equipment compatibility problems.

A "bulk mailing" machine can be purchased enabling you to prepare a message on a VDU for despatch to hundreds of telex users whose addresses are stored in the machine. The machine will then autodial each addressee and automatically work through the list, printing a log of completed "deliveries" as it goes. This kind of machine is a far cry from the older telex machines which are noisy, slow, and subject to "busy line" frustrations for the caller - particularly if the called machine is one of the older types which is "engaged" while the operator is preparing a tape. Telex is not that easy to operate - many companies employ trained telex operators. For more information see Chapter 10.

<u>Facsimile</u>

Facsimile machines, discussed in Chapter 9, are still relatively uncommon and until recently have been beset with standardisation problems. The standard becoming most widely used as machine costs fall and new facilities are added is the CCITT Group 3. A Group 3 machine digitises the image for transmission and is capable of communicating an average A4 pageful of text in one minute to another group 3 machine over the PSTN.

Fax is passing through a stage of intensive development. Innovations, coming mainly from Japan, include automatic transmission speed adaptation to line conditions, unattended operation, auto-dialling for successive transmission to a number of addressees, data compression and higher speeds, and the possible standardisation of a Group 4 machine in the next year or two. Fax machines possess a unique advantage, of course, - exact reproduction of an image at a remote point - but we are here considering electronic message systems. Fax is rather expensive for this purpose although prices are falling. Group 1 and 2 machines are less expensive but slower.

Group 3 machines are not as "operator friendly" as manufacturers would have us believe, although they are available in desktop form. However if compatible fax machines of whatever kind are already used in the single-site or dispersed offices of an organisation, obviously they could be used for inter-office messages.

<u>Videotex</u>

A relatively small number of people possess videotex terminals capable of being used for EMS (a message system is available for Prestel users in the

UK.) Wider use of videotex gateways - a networking development - will enable more people to use it for EMS.

Home Computer message systems

System details, communications, and behavioural circumstances make all the difference to cost and convenience. If you are a home computer owner living in the United States you may well already possess all you need to hook up to a network which runs an electronic message system designed for home users. Your capital outlay may only be the acquisition of a communications board with an RS232 port and modem incorporated at a cost of around $200.

You can then dial up Compuserve via the PSTN to whom you will pay $5 an hour for the use of various services, including an electronic message service. The hourly cost (assuming local calls to a network node) including the telephone bill is unlikely to exceed $10, and that would cover quite a few messages. Your home computer behaves like an electric typewriter - you press a key in response to choices presented on a menu such as "Read Mail", "Send Mail", "File Mail", and you type a message. The perceived cost will probably not include computer amortisation because that is your hobby so the out of pocket cost per message will be, say, $1.

The perceived value will include a consideration of the number of people with whom you wish to exchange messages who are connected to the system. In the home situation it seems unlikely that it will also include a consideration of the elimination of the cost of postage stamps, assuming that some of your electronic messages would otherwise be letters. They would probably be phone calls anyway. The "time is money" consideration will probably not enter your thoughts. Of course it could be that you use the system as a business "out of office hours" facility, paid for by the company, in which case your considerations may be different.

In the United States EMS services are offered by bureaux for home computer owners. Forum-80, a videotex-like software package used on home computer networks in that country, is now available in Europe, thanks to the enterprise of "Fred the Shed" (Fred Brown, in a garden shed in Hull). Suitable for TRS-80, Apple, Atari, Commodore Vic and other machines, Mailbox-80, Fred's UK version, is said to have users in several European countries.

The absence of integrated software modules for home computers is a severe limitation, but Apple are going in the right direction with Micro-Telegram - a package which integrates an EMS system with word processing and a filing system.

Communicating terminals

The piece of equipment which is most likely to be possessed by the greatest number of people is a CRT terminal - perhaps in the form of a microcomputer, as an on-line computer terminal, or as part of a word processing system. Some may already be interconnected, some may already have communication facilities fitted and may require a modem or acoustic coupler, and telecomms software and some may have no communication facilities.

The ease with which communication facilities can be added to terminals without ports, software etc., will depend on the method of construction and the availability of software. Many microcomputers and some terminals contain plug-in boards with space for extras. The manufacturer may be able to supply a communications board with interface and plug and socket, and suitable software. For terminals which form part of a proprietary system - for instance a stand alone word processing system - the addition of telecomms may be difficult or impossible.

<u>Teletex</u>

	A new method of communicating text has been introduced, christened Teletex
- a name which, of course, confuses it with Teletext the name for services in
which picture data, broadcast with entertainment television, is captured by
modified TV receivers. This is the odd man out in this section ("using what
exists now") since it is only partially implemented (April 1985). Teletex brings
relatively fast telex-like communications to word processing. If CCITT standards
can be widely implemented in machines as well as in telecommunications, then
teletex will be free from incompatibility problems. The rate at which this occurs
will depend mainly on PTT politics and manufacturer's perception of the market.
More information is given in Chapter 10.

<u>FURTHER READING</u>

Anon.
   Department of Trade & Industry, London.
      Bulletin of office automation pilot projects. Number 7. May 1985.
Anon.
   Wharton Publishing, 12 Eton St., Richmond, Surrey, England. 1984.
      The internatioal office automation guide.
Bair, James H.
   In Landau (1982). Page 149.
      Productivity assessment of office information systems technology.
Bjorn-Andersen, Nils.
   In Otway (1983). Page 120.
      The changing role of secretaries and clerks.
Borko, Harold.
   In Vondran, Raymond F. et al (Eds). Proc ASIS 46th meeting, Vol 20. Published
   by Knowledge Industries, White Plains NY. 1983.
      The effect of automated information systems on knowledge worker
      productivity.
Chen, Peter P.
   In Landau (1982). Page 223.
      Fundamental issues in cost benefit analysis of office automation systems.
Croft, W.Bruce; Lefkowitz, Lawrence S.
   ACM Trans. Office Info. 2(3), 197-212, July 1984.
      Task support in an office system.
Crozier, Michael.
   In Otway (1983). Page 86.
      Implications for the organisation.
de Sousa, M.R.
   IBM Syst. J. 20(1), 4-22, 1981.
      Electronic information interchange in an office environment.
Dickinson, Robert M.
   Industrial Engineering, 50-55, July 1980.
      Exxon. How a major corporation is coping with the pressures of an office
      automation program.
Driscoll, James W.
   In Landau (1982). Page 259.
      Office automation: the dynamics of a technological boondoggle.
Eason, K.D.
   Behav. & Info. Technol. 1(2), 197-213, 1982.
      The process of introducing information technology.
Edwards, Gwen C.
   Telecomms. Policy 2(2), 128-136, 1978.
      Organisational impacts of office organisation.

Ellis, Clarence A.
  Proc. Conf. ACM on Simulation, Measurement and Modeling of Computer systems
  1979. pps 832-840.
    Information control nets: a mathematical model of office information flow.
Ellis, Clarence A.; Nutt, Garry J.
  Computing Surveys 12(1), 27-60, March 1980.
    Office information systems and computer science.
Ellis, Clarence A.
  In Information Processing Proc.IFIP, Paris 1983. 11-22. Elsevier/North
  Holland.
    Formal and informal models of office activity.
EMMS (Electronic Mail & Microsystems). Published fortnightly by EMMS, 6 Prowitt
St., Norwalk CT 06855, USA. Caswell,Stephen A. (Ed).
Engel, G.H.; Gropusso, J., et al.
  Proc. Office Automation Conf., Atlanta Ga, March 1980, pps 301-313.
    An office communications system.
Engelbart, Douglas C.
  In Landau (1982). Page 287.
    Evolving the organisation of the future: a point of view.
    Page. 297. Integrated evolutionary office automation systems.
Gardner, P.C.
  IBM Syst. J. 20(3), 321-345, 1981.
    A system for the automated office environment.
Geneen, Harold.
  Fortune, 89-98, October 15, 1984.
    In praise of cluttered desks.
Giuliano, Vincent E.
  Scientific American 247(3), 149-164, 1982.
    The mechanisation of office work.
Grieves, M. (Ed)
  British Library R&D Report 5827. British Library, Boston Spa, UK. 1984
    Information handling and the office of the future: report of a seminar.
Hammer, Michael; Howe, W Gerry et al.
  Comm. ACM 20(11), 832-840, November 1977.
    A very high level language for data processing applications.
Hopwood, Anthony G.
  In Otway (1983). Page 37.
    Evaluating the real benefits.
Kalba, Konrad A.; Surbu, Marvin A.; de Sola Pool, Ithiel.
  Report, 300pps, April 1978 Published by Kalba Bowen Associates, 12 Arrow
  St., Cambridge, Mass., 02138, USA, in association with the Centre for Policy
  Alternatives, MIT.
    Electronic message systems: the technical, market, and regulatory
    prospects.
Keen, Peter G.W.
  In Otway (1983). Page 51.
    Strategic planning for the new system.
Kriebel, Charles H; Strong, Diane M.
  MIS Quarterly, 171-178, September 1984.
    A survey of MIS and telecommunications activities of major business firms.
Landau, Robert; Bair,James H.; Siegman, Jean H. (Eds)
  Published by Ablex Publishing Corp., Norwood, N.J. 07648, USA. 1982.
    Emerging Office Systems.
Langrish, J; Gibbons M. et al.
  MacMillan, London, 1972.
    Wealth through knowledge; a study of innovation in industry.
Lasden, Martin.
  Computer Decisions, 92-100, January 1981.
    Turning reluctant users on to change.

Levitan, Karen B,
  In Williams. Martha E. (Ed). Annual review of information science and
  technology. Volume 17. Knowledge Industries, White Plains NY. 1982. Chapter
  8. Page 227.
    Information Resources Management.
Mertes, Louis H.
  Harvard Business Rev., 59(2), 127-135, March/April 1981.
    Doing your office over electronically.
Mumford, Enid.
  In Otway (1983). Page 68.
    Successful system design.
Nutt, Gary J.; Rucci, Paul A.
  Computer 14(5), 41-57, May 1981.
    Quinault - an office modeling system.
Olsen, Margarethe H; Lucas, Henry C.
  Comm. ACM 25(11), 838-847, November 1982.
    The impact of office automation on the organisation; some implications for
    research and practice.
Otway, H.J; Peltu, Malcolm. (Eds)
  Francis Pinter, London, 1983.
    New office technology: human and organisational aspects.
Panko, Raymond R.
  ACM Trans. Office Info. 2(3), 226-234, July 1984.
    38 offices: analysing individual needs.
Peterson, J.C.
  Computing Surveys 9(3), 223-252, September 1977.
    Petri Nets.
Potter, Robert J.
  Science 195(4283), 1160-1164, May 1977.
    Electronic mail.
Rockart, John F.
  Sloan Management Rev. 3-16, Summer 1984.
    Engaging top management in information technology.
Smith, Stephen A.
  IEEE Trans. Syst. Man & Cybernetics SMC10 (5), 232-242, May 1980.
    Minimising processing costs in an automated office system.
Sniger, Paul.
  Mini-micro systems, 89-92, December 1984.
    Office systems struggle for user acceptance.
Stone, Philip J; Luchetti, Robert.
  Harvard Business Rev. 102-111, March/April 1985.
    Your office is where you are.
Uttal, Bro.
  Fortune 103(10), 44-52, May 18 1981.
    Xerox zooms toward the office of the future.
Uhlig, Ronald P; Farber, David J., et al.
  In "The Office of the Future". ICCC monograph volume 1.
    North Holland, 1979. Chapter 1, pps 50-52, 68-75.
Wainwright, Judith.
  Personel Review, 13(1), 2-10, 1984.
    Office automation - its design, implementation and impact.
Zisman, Michael D.
  Sloan Management Rev., 1-16, Spring 1978.
    Office automation - revolution or evolution.
Zloof, Moshe M.
  IBM Syst. J. 16(4), 324-343, 1977.
    Query by example: a data base language.
Zloof, Moshe M.
  IBM Research Report RC8091 (No.35086) Jan 24th 1980. IBM Watson Research
  Centre, Yorktown Heights, NY 10598, USA.
    A language for office and business automation.

CHAPTER 21. INFORMATION TECHNOLOGY IN BANKING, RETAILING, AND PUBLISHING

BANKING AND RETAILING

Electronic Funds Transfer (EFT)

We do not hear a great deal from the two kinds of organisations who are deeply involved in the new technology, and who pioneered large telecommunication networks. They are airlines and banks.

Banks were among the earliest pioneers of big network with the Swift system which started in 1977. It interconnected banks in 15 countries including the U.S., Canada, and major European countries. Later the whole of Western Europe became connected and the system is now being extended into Eastern Europe, South America, The Middle East, Africa and Asia. Swift has about two thousand member banks in 46 countries, with 1200 actual banking locations. The system handles over 350,000 transactions per day.

In the UK, a number of clearing banks are interconnected by the CHAPS EFT network for the direct transfer of amounts exceeding £10,000. For example the contract formalities and funds transfer for a house purchase could be a same-day transaction replacing the notoriously slow procedures which usually apply. These banks each operate a Tandem backed-up computer gatewayed to PSS with "a closed user group" arrangement, fully protected by encrypted communications. Other smaller banks and corporate customers can arrange to use certain facilities by arrangement with the clearing banks.

The automation of cheque clearance processes has received an on-going effort culminating in a new standard to extend the usefulness of schemes like the well known E-13B standard for machine readable characters on cheques. Inter -Bank Standard 3, part 2, caters for banks using Optical Character Recognition schemes (OCR) for clearance as well as those using E-13B.

The mind boggles at the consequences of the instant transfer of all funds electronically. The implications of releasing the enormous sums of money at present more or less in limbo during the cheque clearance process are enormous.

Retail EFT

Apart from inter-bank transactions and cheque clearance there is another trend of even greater significance - the move towards the "cashless society", starting with EFT between retailers and banks. Foster thinks that if EFT is introduced at the point of sale and if all cheque transactions are replaced by EFT debit card transactions eliminating vouchers, then retailers could expect a 50% saving in payment time and almost 20% in costs. This analysis assumes there will be no shift away from cash transactions. It would be interesting to know whether an allowance for "running-in investment time" is included in this calculation. There is bound to be a fairly long expensive period during which a complete system is being operated on behalf of a small growing number of retailers and their customers. For more about this see Chapter 50.

EFTPOS (Electronic Funds Transfer at Point Of Sale) means that a buyer inserts a card at the check-out desk in a shop to pay for goods purchased by immediate funds transfer from his or her bank account to the shop's. The transaction proceeds via a telephone line connection.

Banks and retailers stand to benefit from the arrangement because of reductions in paperwork handling compared with, say, credit card payment, as mentioned above. The customer benefit is the price reduction on goods which will

occur because of this cheaper more efficient method of payment - but don't take
this remark too seriously. The first thing they will lose is the credit part of
the credit card.

Britain may be the first country to embark on a system of this kind on any
scale. British Telecom, the clearing banks, and IBM are believed to be ready to
start. The Banks are prepared to make the equipment investment if the government
agrees to the go-ahead in this politically sensitive operation. The subject is
well covered in Chapter 50.

The idea of total EFT based on terminals in shops is a big collaborative
venture not so much concerning people as technology. It will certainly require
the involvement of many planners, and once installed there will be some
changes in the work of the person running each point of sale station.
Presumably there will still be a need for about the same staff/customer ratio
to handle the checking, totalling, and registering of purchased goods.

Clearing banks, and more recently smaller banks, have been discussing ways
of launching a nationwide system in the UK for some time. A pilot scheme
scheduled for use in Southampton early in 1983 was shelved on the grounds of too
high an initial cost. It's the usual problem of financing until a critical
mass is reached. It won't be long before something happens. Various bits of new
technology keep appearing: taken together they will make the whole thing
possible.

Another parallel development in banking is the so-called "Smart Card" - that
is a credit card carrying a passive magnetic strip for wiping credit or debit
data on or off when inserted in a machine, or containing a microprocessor for
more sophisticated operations. One advantage is that the micro-card is said to be
very secure. Smart cards could be used for cashless shopping. French Companies
are the leaders in the field and are hoping to establish a de facto standard. US
banks have ordered cards from France for experimental purposes. The first major
application in France is for pay-telephones - 200,000 cards have been ordered
from Bull.

<u>Banking services - banks of the future</u>

Although new High Street Banks keep appearing, for the time being the need
for a row of people behind the counter remains whatever is going on behind
the scenes although current activity in the further development of cash
dispensing systems may change that. For example Barclay's have introduced, on an
experimental basis, the counter equivalent but much cheaper version of the ATM
(Automatic Teller Machine), now to be found outside many banks.

The customer, using her PIN (Personal Identification Number) keys the amount
required; the teller on the opposite side of the counter observes the operation
and hands over the cash. The point is that the customer is doing all the bank's
associated "paperwork" while keying.

However a large investment is being made by all major banks in connecting
the machine outside the bank to a communications network enabling it to do much
more than simply identify a customer, pay out cash, and debit his account. In the
US nearly 50,000 ATM's have been installed compared to a few thousand six years
ago. Major networks such as Cirrus link over 5000 terminals. In January 1985 21
UK banks and Building Societies started to connect ATMs to the Link network
planned to extend into airports, shopping centres, and connect to foreign
networks.

In February 1985 NCR announced an ATM incoporating cash withdrawal and
deposit facilities, loans, insurance, buying and selling shares, and providing
investment and other advice via an interactive videodisk machine and display

tube. The machine is of modular construction so that semi custom-built variations can be supplied according to the requirements of any bank. Typical price is £23,000.

New developments in "Home Banking Systems" are annnounced almost daily, but the mix of resources needed seems to be inhibiting take-off as with point of scale schemes. In the UK the best known is probably the Nottingham Building Society/Prestel system called Homelink. In addition to account management, such as switching cash into a deposit account to minimise interest loss, bill paying, statement check etc., Homelink has provided other services to make the whole idea more interesting.

The services include regular auctions with bids accepted from terminals for goods, buying goods for delivery at home, flights and holiday arrangements, etc. Homelink has been followed by similar services - Midland Bank in 1984, and Bank of Scotland in 1985. Some information about home banking in the US is given in Chapter 25; since the Knoxville experiment several banks including Chemical Bank and Bank of America offer home banking services. Compuserve operates one of the largest services in the US for which software for all major personal computers is available. Banks in many parts of the US allow Compuserve to be used for bill payments, and Compuserve now offers hundreds of different services. Evening connect rates (September 1984) are $6 per hour.

It seems likely that labour-intensive banks will attempt to mechanise all banking transactions and they will be handled by machines outside the bank or in special within-bank areas. Most of the labour force will be working behind the scenes or in a comfortable personal service area providing consultation and advice. A bank of this kind is already operating in Sweden - the Sveavagen branch in Stockholm of Gotabanken.

<u>Communications: security</u>

Hebditch thinks that if communication costs are going to increase over the next ten years to meet the high convergent costs of digital technology, then it is going to be increasingly important to design systems to minimise dependency on telecommunications. "The less data you transmit the less bandwidth you require and the less cost you will incur.... further reinforcing the trend towards distributed processing".

"The localisation of computer power will make it increasingly feasible to employ office automation procedures well established in the commercial sector e.g. word processing, electronic mail etc., to be employed by banks without putting additional and unwelcome pressure on the communications network".

The phrase "as safe as the Bank of England" is a reminder of the major concern of banks with all aspects of security. D.W.Davies clearly explains the general principles and degrees of security obtainable with different arrangements for the transmission of data and starts with a description of the "RSA" method (the initial letter of the names of its three MIT inventors in 1978).

In this method the sender computes a number called the "Authenticator" derived from the content of the whole message, using a secret key.   The recipient possesses a secret key and also computes the Authenticator, comparing it with the sender's which is included with the message. Fairly large keys are needed and Davis recommends 512 bits for the RSA system. "The best known method (for breaking) would then occupy 200M years". The computation in RSA is of course done automatically and quite quickly. A chip designed for the purpose can do it in about one second, and Davis says that designs for doing it in 20 milliseconds are being investigated. See Chapter 27 for more information.

Other security requirements

Davies continues with a description of security considerations in cash
dispensers with reference to the personal identification number (Pin) and
discusses "Electronic Cheques" - that is information about money which is
telecommunicated accompanied by a secret key. For example the Chase Manhattan
Bank has developed a microprocessor "data authentication" device to be used
in telephone line transmission of funds data from remote terminals. It greatly
reduces the possibility of transmission errors and fraud by an automatic
exchange of keys between the remote terminal and the host computer.

Personal identification is of course an essential factor in cash transfer,
the time honoured method being a signature on a cheque. The whole edifice behind
cheque schemes can still be retained, if a human teller is no longer present,
by the use of automatic recognition systems. Developments in pattern recognition
enable the unique information describing a particular fingerprint to be
encoded in 200 bytes. A system called "Finger-matrix", has been developed in
the US, for use alongside keyboards.

The customer places the index finger on a pressure plate, and the machine
scans the image comparing the resultant code with codes held in a central
store. Signature verifying devices are available working on a similar principle,
although the matching of the pattern derived from a scanned signature with one
held in a central store is said to be less reliable than the fingerprint system.

ELECTRONIC PUBLISHING

> Reading maketh a full man, conference
> a ready man, and writing an exact man.
> Francis Bacon.

Introduction

Electronic publishing is a catch phrase coined for the same purposes as
Electronic Mail - sometimes the items described by it deserve the accolade,
sometimes it is applied to something vaguely electronic to hype up its image.

The aspects of it which seems worthy of discussion are the computer-aided
production of printed or never-in-print material, and the electronic distribution
of information, including the so-called "electronic journal". While these matters
are of considerable interest to authors, journalists, and writers, as opposed to
publishers, part of the production process is of special interest to them - the
keying of their ideas directly into publishable form.

Bishop has published a short review which covers many of the issues and
possibilities of electronic publishing.

Computer aided production

Information technology intrudes into the production of printed material at
every stage. In some parts of the industry it achieves notoriety because of
friction between employees and management as old crafts are rendered obsolete
and the old camaraderie engendered by tough working conditions disappears.

Areas which have been transformed include information inputting, sorting and
layout, and composition. Keying directly into a computer with disk storage is a
different proposition from typing on to paper. The software can include a variety
of aids to reduce the work chore, in addition to normal Word Processing aids.

For example at the Institute for Scientific Information where information about hundreds of thousands of articles are input annually a dictionary of article bibliographic references is available. When an operator inputs the references to earlier articles contained in a current article, there is a high probability that an earlier article will have been been previously input. As soon as the operator has typed a sufficient number of characters to uniquely identify the item, the machine checks the dictionary and displays the complete reference corrected if necessary. The operator goes on to the next reference, a substantial amount of keying time having been saved.

STEPHEN HARRIS'S VIEW OF PROBABILITIES
(Reproduced by courtesy of ISI)

Developments in photo-typesetting have revolutionised printing, particularly for very large runs of frequently repeated publications such as telephone directories. These machines work at very high speeds from computer tape. Their precursor was the 1966 Digiset where the page image was reproduced on a CRT, replacing the old photographic master.

<u>Author directly-generated printing</u>

This subject is discussed by Holloway in a most useful publication. Many authors type into a WP machine or microcomputer and can print camera-ready copy or despatch a disk to a publisher. However this information cannot be directly used by a phototypesetting machine unless the disk can be read by the particular machine owned by the publisher. Furthermore a phototypesetter requires codes embedded in the copy to tell it what to do e.g. end line, change type face, etc, and it must strip out codes before printing.

The codes must be inserted in the text or tags must be inserted to be converted into instructions by the phototypesetter using a look up table. Different machines require different codes so there is a standardisation problem. Holloway describes the more or less inconvenient ways of getting the codes inserted.

However the arrival of "what you see is what you print" microcomputers such as a Macintosh with a Laserwriter printer enables very good camera-ready copy with different fonts and graphics to be produced. But an even more significant advance is to use Apple's PostScript software, which runs on the Macintosh, to include codes in the text which enables it to be directly read and printed by a Linotron 101 typesetter. This system removes much of the encoding hassle for the author because most of the codes are generated automatically and inserted by the software. For instance when the author changes a font or underlines the software inserts a code.

The cost of the Apple system is under $12,000 but the author must, of course, be prepared to buy and use that machine and the publisher must have a Linotron 101.

To try and break the whole problem Xerox, in conjunction with a number of computer companies (excluding IBM) is pushing its Interpress page descriptor language as a standard. IBM may well be working on a language for its PC. When software becomes available for a number of WP machines/microcomputers, readable by a number of phototypesetting machines, then the author type-to-publish revolution will have arrived.

<u>The Electronic Publishing Industry</u>

Commercial publishers are experimenting with electronic publications which bear some resemblance to those in print, aimed at people who are already using terminal/communication facilities because they are engaged in "electronic" information-seeking or other activities requiring a terminal. Some or all of these people are the ready-made potential customer base.

Other publishers, often with large conventional publishing interests, already generate text and graphics in machine readable form as part of their printed product production processes. These publishers are also experimenting with electronic forms of publication for the general public particularly the business community. They are accumulating experience and testing the ground ready to participate in the expected growth, and to be ready to shift from their printed product base as and when it starts to be undermined.

Gurnsey provides a lot of information in a most useful compact publication. US publishing revenues exceeded $33 billion in 1980. Deregulation has enabled publishing to become a multi-media industry. For example only a third of Time Inc's $3 billion comes from print, compared with 90% for Bertelesman, Europe's biggest publisher, with a similar revenue. Data is provided in appendices showing how widely diversified some of the larger US publishers have become.

The companies which receive special mention for having moved into electronic publishing are Dow Jones, Standard & Poors and VNU/Arete. The ten major companies in Europe and the US whose main business is conventional publishing and who are, no doubt, watching every move made by others into electronic publishing are shown on the right in order of revenue.

Bertelsman/Grunner & Jahr	Germany
Times Inc.	US
Times Mirror	US
S.Pearson/Pears.-Longman	UK
Axel Springer Verlag	Germany
Gannett Inc.	US
Knight Ridder Newspapers	US
Thomson Organisation	UK
McGraw Hill	US
Associated Newspapers	UK

Gurnsey suggests that "The keys to success in electronic publishing are probably a vertically integrated corporate structure, a good revenue base from which to fund capital investment, a clear indication of the needs of users, and the ability to react quickly and positively to new technological and marketing opportunities".

The answer to the publisher's dilemma - should he jump in a particular direction or wait and see for a bit - is probably evident from the present actions of publishers who are probing new areas cautiously. Gurnsey concludes that electronic publishing is in a mess:- "...a long way from user aceptance" and "suffering from a plethora of misinformation and false claims".

<u>Fringe activities</u>

This is a question of definition. The label "electronic publishing" is sometimes used to cover what I call fringe activities because many publishers are involved in, or have diversified into, the Entertainment Industry, or because entertainment and information are lumped together. For example Gurnsey includes the 100 television stations (I'm sure that figure is a gross under-estimate), 4370 cable operators, and nearly 10,000 radio stations in the US as part of the electronic publishing infrastructure. This leads to the idea of dominant national information providers - CBS, NBC, and ABC - and a number of local information providers. Another example is the 200 private TV stations in Italy.

The Electronic Scientific Journal

There is some anxiety about the survival of the scientific journal, paticularly small specialised journals, which has evolved from two publications which first appeared in the 17th century, the Philosophical Transactions and the Journal des Scavans.

The electronic journal idea is usually attributed to Senders. In 1976 he suggested that printed scientific journals might become extinct because of increasing costs, falling subscriptions, and general problems of distribution and finding the information published in them. His feeling was not so much that electronic substitutes were desirable but that economic pressures would force their birth. He suggested a plausible scenario and the idea sparked off much new technology whizz-kiddery.

I have in front of me a whole page advertisement from the New York Times of May 21st 1979 about the "Alpex 900 Information Network". It contains the headline, in 144 point type, "Publishers: your information network is ready". According to the blurb, a publisher types copy into a special terminal from which it is transferred to the Alpex data centre. A subscriber to the service "places a phone call and sees the information displayed on his own TV set". The service "fulfills publisher's urgent needs for a fast and economical method of electronic transmission to subscribers". I don't recall hearing about this service again. Perhaps the cost of the whole page ad. was just too much.

Commencing in 1973 The National Science Foundation (NSF) funded Westat Inc., and Aspen systems to study the feasibility of an Editorial Processing Centre (EPC – see Berut). Later it also funded SRI International, who considered the role of an EPC in a complete electronic scientific information system. An EPC is a system designed for use co-operatively by small/medium size publishers and authors, editors, and referees, (particularly for scientific journals) who would exchange "electronic manuscripts" which would be published in "electronic" or conventional journals. It would also connect to a network for disseminating information derived from the EPC database.

There was quite a kerfuffle about this idea at the time. Costing was done showing that it was economically feasible for a group of small publishers. It seemed to be a way out of the higher-cost declining-subscription problems being experienced by many of the smaller scientific journal publishers, offering both computer-aided publication with paper end-products, and provision, in due course, for electronically displayed information. Having financed the venture, the NSF withdrew saying, in effect, "there you are lads, it works, now get together and try it". So far as I know there were no takers.

The next attempt was the Electronic Information Exchange System (EIES), based on a computer at the New Jersey Institute of Technology, with MIT also involved, and participants with their terminals interconnected via Telenet (See Turoff). This was a large scale experiment in computer conferencing but also included two actual electronic journals – <u>Chimo</u> and <u>The Mental Workload</u>.

In a later article about this system, published in 1980 (Guillaume), it seemed that it had not been very successful. At the end of the evaluation period "only 1 paper had been submitted to the electronic journal, a single author production. Conference activity was still dominated by a select few, many participants ceasing completely to contribute. Maintenance functions were missing and task functions were still ineffectively carried out".

Incidentally the British Post Office helped to put a blight on the system by ruling that the use of Telenet by third parties infringed its monopoly. The third parties were the substantial UK contingent of contributors and editors proposed for the <u>Mental Workload</u>. In the event they contributed nothing.

EIES is discussed in more detail by Hiltz in Chapter 46 who takes the view that there is much more to be learnt and would probably disagree with the more limited view expressed by Guillaume about just one part of the experiment. Teleconferencing or Computer Conferencing, as discussed by Hiltz, is a near relative of the Electronic Journal since it has been used to place scientists engaged in a similar research area in ongoing contact with each other.

According to Freeman this idea too has some way to go. An experiment which started in 1978 involved a number of social scientists interested in social networks. The conclusions are not very definite - indeed "perhaps the most important conclusion is that there are no true conclusions". However the computer conference, it was felt, had a considerable impact.

Nothing daunted, the UK universities of Loughborough and Birmingham, supported by the British Library, decided to have another go, building on the EIES experience. Once again it seems that the economic problems of the scientific journal system are the driving force. The BLEND experiment, described by Shackel and Pullinger, is exploring various forms of communication between scientists using terminals connected to a DEC 20 central computer. Amongst other things the electronic journal <u>Computer Human Factors</u> will be generated.

Wilson has described the joint authorship of a paper by five "distributed authors" using the BLEND facilities. In particular he discusses the possibility of "active mailboxes" wherein certain secretarial functions could be performed on incoming messages/documents received in one mailbox from a number of different people.

In an earlier paper describing this project it was said that "Even if electronic journals are obviously efficient for transmitting information, there remains the possibility that users none the less do not like this medium of communication. Therefore questionnaires, interviews..etc...will be used to establish measures of acceptability". That does indeed seem to be a necessary measure.

Virtues of the Printed Scientific Journal

The main objective of present experimental electronic journals is the efficient dissemination of information. Information dissemination is only one of the functions of printed journals and it will be a very long time before they are displaced.

These other functions include the benefit provided for the author in building up his reputation both at the time of publication - particularly in establishing his priority for a new discovery - and in knowing that his collected works are solidly accessible today and for future generations through the reference library process. For the reader, they include the benefit of being able to assimilate information provided by the most knowledgeable people in their field, and of reading the editorials, the letters, the news items, the book reviews, the advertisements, and the situations vacant - a comprehensive blend of professional information requirements.

The importance of the printed journal in the efforts of Watson & Crick to stay ahead of Pauling is clearly evident from Watson's account of their discovery.

"It seemed almost unbelievable that the DNA structure was solved, that the answer was incredibly exciting and that our names would be associated with the double helix as Pauling's was with the alpha helix". Just prior to publication Watson expresses his delight that Pauling was "still way off base", but Watson cleared the decks for publication just in case. In fact Pauling was hot on the same track.

Francis Crick and he "stood over her (his sister) as she typed the article. On Tuesday it was sent up to Bragg's office, and on Wednesday April 2, it went off to the editors of Nature". It was published in that same month (1953). This rapid action was taken in order to establish the earliest possible publication date by submission to a prestigious fast-publishing weekly journal, via an influential scientist (Bragg). Watson & Crick later received the Nobel prize.

Electronic Books

Some years ago a device called the Izon micrographics reader was developed, supposedly to sell for about $100. It used an optical compression system with a form of Fresnel lense housed in a book-size box, with the expectation of breaking the portability barrier imposed by normal microfiche readers. It disappeared without a trace.

The "electronic book" is not dead. A new version is proposed, based on the VLSI (Very Large Scale Integrated) circuits now starting to appear, according to Murray. It would be book-size with a flat screen display, the words being encoded as 12 bit numbers stored, together with coarse graphics, in a memory of about 14 Mbytes.

The method of compression would enable the text of a novel to be stored. "Books" would come in small plug-in memories, and an on-board microprocessor would handle decoding and presentation. The device would include a keyboard and string-searching capabilities for "publications" requiring that facility. It is suggested that the electronic book would "alter the nature of libraries, increase the efficiency of the scientific, legal, and medical professions, minimise information access time in industry, and modify the operation of the educational system".

Electronics versus print on paper

Inefficient as the paper journal maybe, the fact is that at the display-human interface the print-human match is far better than the machine-human match, both in information transfer and behavioural terms. For general browsing, book reading, scanning news items, appreciating pictures or drawings, and being generally entertained, print on paper is superior. It can be written on, carried about, and digested in aeroplanes, on trains, or in the bath. It looks nice on shelves, makes a very acceptable gift, and can be used for wrapping up fish and chips.

Referring specifically to books, "there is simply no experience in life that matches silent reading....readers make everything happen just the way they want it to. The actions, scenes, and voices in a book come to life entirely in the reader's mind" says Jennings. "Sometimes when I can't go to sleep I see the family of the future. Dressed in three-tone shorts and shirts of disposable papersilk they sit before the television wall of their apartment; only their eyes are moving. After I've looked for a while I always see - otherwise I'd die - a pigheaded soul in the corner with a book; only his eyes are moving but in them there is a different look".

Unquestionably the economic pressures have got to be very strong to dent the print-human relationship. Quite apart from the aesthetics and other pleasant or convenient aspects of print, electronic information distribution on any scale awaits the placement of a communications and terminal infrastructure with a customer base of critical mass. The prospect of profits in consequence of mounting the nth service at relatively low cost will provide the incentive for further expansion as discussed elsewhere in this book.

But the advantages of print diminish and may be superseded when searching for and retrieving a specific chunk of information, knowing that when found it will be completely up to date. This is when easily up-dated information on a machine comes into its own and this is the area where innovations are appearing. Online encyclopaedias, stock exchange prices, airline schedules, and news items are examples.

After the item has been located, it is convenient to be able to read it on the self-same machine. Machines can display most kinds of information likely to be needed in this situation. That convenience must be balanced against adequacy of presentation. For some items it still may be necessary to introduce the inconvenience of referring the user to a place where the wanted information can be seen in print - i.e a library.

This requirement will gradually disappear as electronic input, storage, and reproduction and display techniques improve and costs decrease. The current practice of providing an information surrogate when the amount of information is too expensive to store and transmit will also gradually disappear to be replaced by the complete text.

FURTHER READING

Anon.
  Proceedings of the Electronic Banking Conference, London, October,
  1982. Published by Oyez Scientific and Technical Services Ltd., Bath House,
  56 Holborn Viaduct, London, EC1A 2EX, England.
Anon.
  Financial Times, October 22nd 1984.
    FT Survey: computers in banking.
Berul, Lawrence W; Krevitt, Beth I.
  In Zunde, Pranas (Ed). Proc 37th ASIS meeting, Atlanta, Ga.,USA.   October
  1974. Published by American Society for Information Science, Washington DC.
  pps 98-102.
    Innovative editorial procedure: the Editorial Processing Center concept.
Bishop, Claude T.
  Quarterly Rev. Biol. 60(1), 43-52, March 1985.
    Electronic publishing: to be or not to be.
Davies, D.W.
  In Anon. Banking Conf. 1982.
  The potential of public key ciphers and signatures in banking.
Foster, Eric.
  In Anon. Banking Conf. 1982.
  The future of electronic point of sale systems.
Freeman, Linton C.
  Social Networks 6, 201-221, 1984.
    The impact of computer based comunication on the social structure of an
    emerging scientific specialty.
Guillaume, Jeanne.
  Can. J. Info.Sci. 5, 21-29, 1980.
    Computer conferencing and the development of an electronic journal.
Gurnsey, John.
  Learned Information, Oxford, 1982.
    Electronic document delivery. III: electronic publishing trends in Europe
    and the United States.
Hebditch, David.
  In Anon. Banking Conf. 1982
  Impact of network technologies on banking automation.
Holloway, Henry L.
  Elsevier, Oxford, EIB Report no.7., for Primary Communications Centre, Univ.
  of Leicester, England, 1985.

Author-generated phototypesetting: author-publisher printer links.
Jennings, Laura.
  The Futurist 17(2), 5-11, April 1983.
    Why books will survive.
Murray, John M., Klingenstein, Kenneth J.
  IEEE Trans. Indust. Electronics IE-29(1), 82-91, February 1981.
    The architecture of an electronic book.
Read, Charles N.
  Long Range Planning 16(4), 21-30, August 1983.
    Information technology in banking.
Senders, John.
  Amer.Sociol. 11, 160-164, August 1976.
    The scientific journal of the future.
Shackel, Brian; Pullinger D.J et al.
  The Computer Journal, 26(3), 247-254, 1983.
    The Blend-Linc project on "electronic journals" after two years.
Turoff, Murray;
  Bull. Amer.Soc. Info. Sci 41(1),9-10, 1978.
     The EIES experience.
Watson, James D.
  Weidenfeld & Nicholson (1968).
    The double helix.
White, Nick.
  Data Processing 26(3), 29-32, April 1984.
    Network management of integrated banking systems.
Whitby, Oliver.
  J. Research Communic. Studies 2(1979/80), 9-23.
    Computer architecture for external editorial processing.
Wilson, P.A; Maude, T.I. et al.
  In Smith, H.T. (Ed), Computer Based Message Services, North Holland, 1984.
  Pages 137-165.
    The active mailbox - your online secretary.

CHAPTER 22. CABLE SYSTEMS AND MARKETS

A cable network has two great advantages - information can be moved in both directions (unlike broadcast television which has wide bandwidth but not the two way facility), and the bandwidth is wide (unlike the telephone which has the two way facility but not the bandwidth). Current general interest in cable systems is centred on home television entertainment based on experiences in the United States. However once cable connections are made to large numbers of premises of any kind, a highway for the flow of any kind of information is in place.

The feasibility of cable information networks and associated devices, like many other systems, is based upon the availability of reliable, compact, cheap semiconductor storage and processing electronics, now a fait accompli.

THE TECHNOLOGY

Schemes for implementing cable systems are shown, shorn of all details in Figure 22.1. The distributing station comprises the means of inputting information, typically television pictures, into a number of channels.   In this case four kinds of input are shown each having a bandwidth of 8 MHz for good quality colour. This is called the "head end" of the system which sends data "downstream" to subscribers.

The programmes could come from TV studios, telecine machines - that is machines capable of running 35mm film and converting it to TV images , or from a remote source - the satellite transmitter RT in the figure and the satellite-receiver link SL1. The head end station distributes the programmes to its local audience.

The four television programmes, separated by appropriate guard bands of relatively narrow bandwidth, are combined in the device C> and distributed via a trunk line with repeaters, R, to boost the signals at suitable intervals. The trunk line may be wideband coaxial cable or fibreoptic cable. If the latter, the device EOC (electro-optical convertor) will be required.

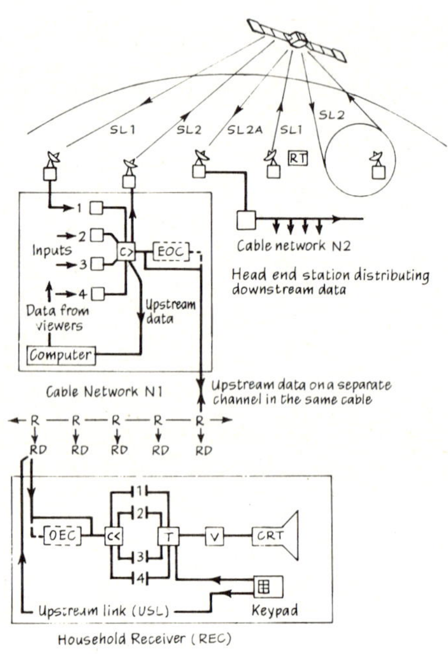

FIGURE 22.1. CABLE NETWORK

Local distribution lines, RD, are tapped off to feed groups of subscribers from repeater/distribution points R.   The distribution network may be part co-axial and part fibreoptic as dictated by traffic and economic considerations. Its bandwidth must be adequate to accommodate the combined bandwidth plus guard bands of the individual channels - 300 MHz or more is needed to accommodate 24 or more TV channels.

A receiver, REC, is fed from the local cable passing along the street. If fibreoptic transmission is used it will incorporate an opto-electric convertor, OEC. For electrical transmission, incoming signals will be fed directly to C<, a device performing the inverse function to >C at the transmitter. At the receiver the frequencies used for distribution are shifted to come within the range of the tuning circuits available in standard TV receivers (shown as 1,2,3,4 with the tuner T). The tuned signal is passed to the CRT via video circuits V. If two optical fibres are used channel switching can be arranged with an electro-mechanical switch which moves the face of the common receiving fibre against the face of either fibre,

Another method of distribution is shown in the figure. This is a Direct Broadcast Satellite (DBS) not a cable system – probably cable's major competing technology in the future. The sending station could broadcast information direct to individual receiving stations using its own transmitting dish to transmit signals to a transponder on the satellite. The signals are re-transmitted to a selected area on the earth's surface wherein lie the cable company's subscribers, via the link SL2. Alternatively signals could be relayed to another area distribution station and into the cable network, N2, via path SL2A.

A DBS system has been described by Haldeman. Programmes for 40 channels contained in a band 800 MHz wide would be radiated to earth stations in the 11.7 to 12.5 GHz band reserved for such purposes (in Europe). Reception would be via rooftop dishes 0.9 metres in diameter.

Interactive facilities
===

The basic interactive facilities shown in the figure include the keypad attached to the receiver which may be used to transmit signals "upstream" to the distribution station via the link USL. A computer at the distribution station receives the up-stream signals for processing.

The problem of organising interactive facilities has been well recognised and was described by Kay during the pioneering work sponsored by the National Science Foundation. Seven grants were awarded in 1974 for experimental systems to deliver social and administrative services via interactive cable television.

If n users can transmit signals of some kind upstream simultaneously, the channel bandwidth, w, must be at least w x n. There could also be a requirement for TV pictures to be generated by a subscriber and sent back to the head end – as in video conferencing. In that case a full TV bandwidth will be required on the return link.

Alternatively subscriber data transmission may be no more than a need to distinguish between 1 out of b buttons, as in the Qube system. By 1979 this system had been running for some time in Columbus, Ohio, with 29,000 of its subscribers able to communicate over the cable by depressing one of five buttons. Say 8 buttons are fitted (requiring a 3 bit code), and a communication rate of 3 bits per second is required – i.e there is provision for one out of 8 choices to be made at a maximum rate of one per second. The theoretical bandwidth needed would only be 1.5Hz so the total bandwidth required by 29,000 subscribers would only be 43.5 KHz.

In practice all the subscriber circuits could be packed into one channel as individual frequency bands with intervening guard bands so one 100 KHz channel would, in theory, suffice. In the Qube system, an announcer says to viewers "if you use Gnasher cleaner for your dentures (or words to that effect) press button 1; if you've never heard of it press 2". An arrangement such as that just described is adequate for such purposes. The computer at the head end simply counts the yes/no responses and expresses them to the announcer as, say, percentages of total responses.

If subscribers were to be provided with full alpha-numeric keyboards, each would need a bandwidth of, say, 150 Hz permitting rates of 300 bps or around 30 char/sec. That would require one hundred times the bandwidth of Qube - say 10 MHz, consuming a substantial fraction of the available bandwidth. A flexible cable system (or perhaps I should say a cable system with flexible facilities) could provide some mix of economically feasible facilities for subscribers with different needs. It might provide for some subscribers with non-interactive, some with low-speed interactive, and some with higher speed interactive facilities at different prices. It might embody a channel for Teleconferences available by special arrangement.

Another technique, called "narrowcasting" provides computer control of the channel viewed by individual subscribers from the head-end. This can be used for the selective addressing of programmes or advertising to homes, schools, businesses etc., according to some pre-arranged pattern.

Cable configurations with up-stream facilities

In Figure 22.1 a low bandwidth return path is shown because repeaters (wideband amplifiers) in the normal tree-and-branch distribution arrangement are usually only fitted for downstream signals. Most US systems are of this type, although the latest US tree and branch systems have an upstream channel with its own repeaters having a bandwidth of up to 30MHz.

In some systems, subscribers are "polled" to see if they have any messages. This means that the head-end computer periodically interrogates all subscribers - and there might be 100,000 of them - to see if they have anything stored ready to transmit and if so, gets it transmitted back to the head end. Such an operation may take up to 10 seconds per complete cycle so it's really suitable only for low data rate systems like the Qube. Bandwidth has been traded for time (See Chapter 5).

However multi-star switched systems are now working which deal with the bandwidth problem in a different way. One such system has been developed at British Telecom's research establishment at Martlesham Heath (Fox). It consists of a distribution station at the centre of a web-like network with a number of trunk connections radiating out to Wideband Flexibility Points (WFP). These WFP's in turn radiate local connections to individual subscribers.

The system may be all coax, or fibreoptic for the trunk connections and coax from WFP's to subscribers. With fibres, long distances without repeaters are possible. WFP to subscriber connections are short and don't need repeaters for coax. Consequently a direct wideband path is available between subscriber and head end. If there are any long distance paths then wideband down and up repeaters are fitted.

Typically a system will consist of some tens or even hundreds of wideband trunks with each WFP connecting to up to 300 subscribers by 100 Mhz lines for up or down stream data. Services can consist of TV, radio, and data transmission channels. At least three TV programmes could be viewed by a subscribing establishment on three different receivers. Channel selection would be by a microprocessor-controlled video switch at a WFP. Each subscriber has a low speed data link for controlling his switch.

Alternatively a subscriber could use one channel for an up-stream video link (e.g.for video conferencing) the other two being used for reception. An up-stream connection could be routed into British Telecomm's System-X digital communications system, which is gradually permeating through the country, at the head end. In this case it is likely that the subscriber will wish to originate data at 64 Kbps or 2 Mbps.

In Britain it is hoped that cable operators will install systems of this kind at the outset, because if tree and branch systems are installed, operators will be locked in to a system without the potential for advanced services which may well soon be needed. On the other hand complete fibreoptic systems are more expensive at present.

FIBREOPTIC AND COAXIAL CABLE COMPARED
(Photograph by courtesy of British Telecom)

Current developments: distribution paths

In common with other information systems, cable technology has benefited by a host of technical developments resulting in the production of low cost complex transmission and processing electronic devices whose dimensions and prices decrease every year. Communications developments include wider bandwidth at lower cost by improvements in the design of coaxial cable, the development of fibreoptic systems with yet wider bandwidth, and the availability of wideband transponders for relaying television signals from satellites.

A satellite transponder typically has a bandwidth of 500 MHz and can handle 12 television channels with either horizontal or vertical polarisation, or 24 if it has both. Polarisation simply means the generation of a single-plane electric field. The bandwidth can be doubled if two signals are transmitted with their planes at right angles, each being receivable without mutual interference by an appropriately polarised receiving aerial/antenna.

It may be as well to clearly differentiate between the systems shown in Figure 22.1. Television signals are at present conveyed by :-

1. Broadcasting on different channels "over the air". At a receiver a channel is selected by switching to the tuned circuit for the desired channel.

2. Wideband or fibreoptic cable, where the energy is contained within the cable and, unlike over-the-air broadcasting, does not occupy scarce bandwidth or interfere with other broadcasts. A single wideband cable can contain a number of channels in different frequency bands selected by switching to different tuned circuits at the receiver.

3. Relaying signals from one transmitter to a distant receiver via a satellite or by a succession of hops from one terrestrial microwave tower to another. Thus one studio/transmission facility can relay television signals to one or more earth receiving stations, via satellite, and each station can feed a number of subscribers via cable.

4. Direct Broadcast Satellite (DBS).

Because satellite signals can be sent/received in a narrow beam, somewhat in the manner of a searchlight, interference can be much lower than with conventional broadcasting. Signal power outside the beam is negligible. Incidentally American viewers have a particular incentive to subscribe to cable systems. The NTSC (unofficially known as Never The Same Colour) 525 line system is very susceptible to phase errors caused by multiple reflections. Reception with poor colour is experienced in cities with high buildings. European systems are much less susceptible and have better definition.

New kinds of services

The special qualities of cable seem well suited for other kinds of non-TV services for which the technology exists, such as videotex services. In telephone line videotex the bandwidth for user-generated data is adequate for most applications, but it imposes limits on certain kinds of downstream data.

As discussed in Chapter 23, broadcast-television teletext usually shares a channel with entertainment TV. There is sufficient space only for cyclic magazines with the maximum number of pages limited by the acceptable waiting time between page selection and "frame grabbing". But a cable system may embody a sufficient number of wideband channels for one channel to be dedicated entirely to a teletext service with a large number of pages, and another channel for special control services.

For an installation charge of $800 and a monthly charge of $16, Qube provide special services for 5000 homes including home security, fire protection, and emergencies. The system consists of transducers in the home to change physical into electrical changes, data transmission facilities, and a fraction of the cable bandwidth to carry the data back to a computer at the head end. The computer sends the information to the appropriate place for action - for instance information from smoke detectors goes to the fire department.

In due course services may be introduced by public utilities for meter or gas consumption measurement and billing, energy control, etc.

The Threat - Direct Broadcast Satellites (DBS)

The fourth method of those listed in the previous pargraph, the subject for much speculation, is direct transmission via a satellite transponder which receives the signal from an earth transmitter aimed at it, and re-transmits the signal via another aerial aimed at a specific area on the earth's surface. Within that area, subscribers have rooftop dishes aimed at the satellite.

The satellite-to-receivers beam is deliberately broadened so precautions must be taken to stop mutual interference which could be caused by the overlapping "footprints" of other satellites working at the same frequencies.

In due course, systems involving satellite links could incorporate two-way facilities. Right now a low-speed link, say by telephone line back to the head-end - a rather clumsy arrangement - would be feasible.

DBS systems, as yet in their infancy, are arousing great interest because no terrestrial links are needed. The vested interests in control of those links are bypassed unless those same interests are also enpowered to control satellite transmissions as part of the regulatory policy. DBS subscribers will require a sensitive receiver with an accurately pointed dish, double frequency conversion receivers and special decoding circuits.

There are already (1984) 40,000 TeleVision Receive Only (TVRO) stations in the US. Admittedly these are for computer buffs or stunt-conscious people exhibiting the ultimate (for the moment) POOOJ (Put One Over On the Jones) syndrome - but these are still very early days. These people can pick up a variety of programmes, for which they pay nothing, depending upon the "footprints" of the satellites within which they lie.

There is a possibility that cable - at least for TV entertainment - could be rendered obsolete as soon as receiving equipment costs drop - and they are droppping fast.

In the US in June 1980 the FCC accepted an application to start a DBS service at 12GHz for people with one metre rooftop dishes and the necessary equipment. In 1981 it considered three more contenders, appreciating the lead time needed for frequency allocations and other preparations. Technical considerations are discussed by Pritchard. Early in 1982 British Aerospace announced its intention to launch a DBS in 1986. The BBC would use two of the five channels available in the UK under international allocations of the spectrum. Coincidentally better colour television systems will be considered. The present PAL system is a compromise attempt to get a lot of information into the narrowest possible bandwidth. For more see Chapter 8.

George Valentine of Rank Trident, UK asked in 1983 "Satellites and cable - will they mix?" and then debunks this combination. "DBS system operators have succeeded in creating symbiotic relationships with cable service operators whereby DBS home services provide additional channels...but they don't. There is no significant DBS in the world at present. It won't be operating in the US before 1986 at the earliest. The British government probably created a confusion by publishing a discussion paper called "Direct broadcast by satellite" when the paper ought to have been called "The use of satellites for the distribution of television signals".

DEVELOPMENT OF CABLE TV IN THE USA

A study of events in the USA leading to the current state of cable TV in that country - around 25 million subscribers (1984) - reveals a fascinating struggle between conflicting influences. Many of these forces have parallels in other countries - high cost of entry, the "chicken and egg" situation (without a network there can be no services, without revenues there can be no network), technological readiness, and the regulatory situation.

One influence, unique to the US, is the first amendment to the Constitution about the freedom of the press - and its extension to cover other media.

In 1958 the existence of cable systems, albeit in a small way, prompted an enquiry by the Federal Communications Commission (FCC), but the FCC concluded that there was no need to control programme content. It did, however, control the issue of licences to microwave TV relay systems at that time. A little later a request for a licence at Riverton, Wyoming, was refused because the FCC considered that programme duplication by the proposed relay would result in the demise of the local TV station.

This decision, affirmed on appeal in Carter Mountain Transmission Corp. vs FCC, became the foundation of the FCC's regulatory role. Cirumstances had forced a change of attitude. In 1965 the FCC asserted wide jurisdiction over all cable systems. It established "mandatory carriage" in which a cable system, channel capacity permitting, had to carry the programmes from the local TV stations covering the same area. It also established the "nonduplication concept", prohibiting the cable operator from generating duplicatory local programmes.

The notion of the "top 100 markets" for television broadcasting was introduced at this time – covering the TV broadcasting stations providing for over 80% of the US population. Cable TV might compete with these stations by "importing" distant signals (having made no payment for the programmes) and distributing them locally. It was thought that this might undermine the foundations of US broadcast TV, and it was the FCC rule prohibiting such importation which slowed up cable development.

1968 saw the publication of the Friendly Report advocating cable in cities, particularly in New York. The report contained comments about the "communications revolution" giving widespread publicity to its potential. Later in the year a Presidential report (the Rostow report) defined the place of cable in a national telecommunications policy. In particular it emphasised the need for regulation with the words "policy should guard against excessive concentration in the control of communications media".

These reports, "blue sky" treatment by the press, and the advance of technology in general, fostered the belief that cable TV would take off. It was forecast that 70% of the US population would be receiving cable TV by 1980. In fact nothing like this happened until 1980 when there was a change of climate.

<u>Information in the home</u>

Electronic information services for the biggest mass market – the home – is much more than simply modified TV receivers, home computers, etc. The concept involves "Readiness Potential and an Enabling Infrastructure" as discussed in Chapter 25. This fact was well recognised by Paul Barran (an ARPA pioneer) back in 1975 when he reviewed the cable TV situation. If his article was re-published with minor changes, it would be as relevant today as it was then. Even as late as 1978 expansion was unexpectedly slow. By that date cable had made slow progress into the "Top 100" market; less than 10% of households therein were cable subscribers.

The scope of Barran's article did not include regulation, and his assessment of other problems was as follows-

People at home will only pay very small sums for information. A suitable terminal must do almost everything for everybody but it must be cheap – really cheap. To reduce fixed costs to acceptable levels, uniform standards are required. A good system must have self-instructing capabilities, self-indexing capability, and commonality of input formats. The overwhelming use of this terminal will be for watching the nth rerun of "I love Lucy" (then a highly poular TV programme). The program selection of PORT (Plain Ordinary Rotten Television) should not be complicated by the addition of new services – a comment reminiscent of the continuing overwhelming use of POTS (Plain Old Telephone Service) for information transmission). The 525 line TV standard has insufficient resolution if the designer tries to squeeze in more than 40 characters or 20 lines. It is more likely that each individual service will be provided by separate national or international companies. Local franchised systems will be a common carrier for others. There must be a measure of confidence in reliability,freedom from eavesdropping,freedom from error, and freedom from malicious mischief (a correct forecast of "hackers", then unknown).

For 1975 this was a penetrating analysis. Barran continues "those companies that might logically be providing leadership have been sitting back and waiting. Everyone is waiting for something to happen and nothing ever does...some strong external force is needed to change the dynamics of the game." This was not to happen for another five years.

<u>Why the climate changed in 1980</u>

<u>1. De-regulation</u>

For many years the FCC had been concerned with the situation in broadcasting where bandwidth is a scarce commodity. The Supreme Court, with the First Amendment in mind, upheld FCC action in <u>Red Lion Broadcasting vs FCC</u> (1969). It was considered that viewers and listeners should have access to "an uninhibited marketplace of ideas" and that it was right for the FCC to pursue a licensing policy which encouraged diversity.

In cable television, bandwidth is not a scarce commodity. In the absence of evidence showing a strong demand for better access (for public, educational, or local government programs, as already provided for in earlier FCC rules) there would seem to be a case for the same liberal regulatory conditions as applied to newspapers as discussed by Silk.

This was the view taken by circuit court in a famous case, <u>Home Box Office vs FCC</u> (1977) followed by <u>Midwest Video Corp. vs FCC</u> (1978) upheld in the Supreme Court. The FCC's cable access requirements were defeated. More than this, the FCC had to set aside requirements for the provision of two way facilities and also the rule for a minimum of 20 channels in systems with 3500 or more subscribers. These were a part of its "access" requirement mentioned above. Questions like what is two way capacity, what is two way service, and what operational requirements should there be if this aspect should be a consideration in franchising were discussed.

In 1980, with satellite relays becoming an attractive way of linking up cable distribution systems in different parts of the country, the FCC removed restrictions on the reception and re-transmission of distant signals. The reason why such relays became available was that the Nixon administration reversed the Johnson policy by allowing the operation of commercial satellites in a so-called "open skies" policy within the US. In this new competitive situation with the consequent diversity of choice, the need for regulatory intervention diminishes since the requirements of the First Amendment are satisfied.

Some tidying up remained to be done but these events removed a number of the restrictions responsible for the slow growth of cable TV. They were strongly influenced by the existence of the First Amendment, and to that extent the scenario is unique. However the way in which cable TV subsequently developed in the US may contain some precedents of interest to other countries where cable TV is at an earlier stage of its development.

2. Technical Developments

Rapid advances in telecommunications, particularly satellite relays, made many of the earlier regulatory conditions obsolete or irrelevant.

3. Commercial incentives

Home Box Office initiated pay TV in 1972 but growth was slow until 1976 when about 800,000 subscribers viewed programmes on 250 systems - 7% of all cable systems. Later, the combined effect of the events already described resulted in the take off of cable systems. By 1980 pay TV on 2000 systems was viewed by 7.5 million subscribers - about half the total number. By 1982 the total number of cable TV subscribers was estimated to be 25 million and growing rapidly. Apparently the US viewing public had an insatiable appetite for movies - the supply being led by Home Box Office, followed by Showtime, but anything goes.

On Manhattan cable,Ugly George's claim to fame is that he asks women to undress in the street, and occasionally one obliges. The Rainbow channel advises "send the kids to bed and turn on the Escapade channel to see Naughty Nymphs, Hot T-Shirts" etc. At the other end of the cultural spectrum the Rockefeller Centre (Radio City) announced a joint venture with RCA "to offer high quality entertainment". In May 1981 they reached agreement with BBC enterprises to provide up to 40% of the programmes.

However a CBS system, concentrating on cultural programmes, closed down in September 1982, having been unable to attract the advertising revenue needed for its survival. The movie industry tried to move in in a big way in 1980 when Getty Oil formed a joint venture - Premiere - with Columbia, Paramount, Universal and 20th Century Fox to provide up to 15 films a month. The venture was stopped by the Justice department, on the grounds of violation of the anti-trust laws.

Finance

There are two methods of financing. Cable TV companies offer "basic channel" fare for a fixed monthly charge which includes the cable fee and some programmes. The company, which may have paid a large sum for the area franchise from the local town or city authority, also obtains revenue from paid advertising. A viewer can pay extra for first-run films, sport,or star entertainment supplied to the cable company by programme distributors with the added attraction of the absence of advertising. This revenue is split between the distributor and the cable company.

Cable TV in the US ran into difficult times in 1982 with the industry heavily in debt although it was felt that survivors would be reaping rewards in the second half of the decade. The cost per mile for new franchise equipment was $52,000. With about 75 subscribers per mile this meant an investment of $700 per subscriber, the required revenue per month then working out at about $29. Direct Broadcast Satellite (DBS) TV became a possible threat. Full time employment in 1981 was 51,000 but it is not clear what comprised "the industry". If this figure represents jobs in all parts of the industry, the cable job potential for countries like the UK is not large. Home Box Office was believed to be one of the only pay TV companies making any money and advertising revenue from cable TV has been disappointing. It was $129M in 1981 compared with nearly $13 Billion for the three national TV networks.

New technical developments in the US are now mainly in DBS. Roof top antennas of around 1 metre diameter will receive the 12 GHz 500 MHz bandwidth downlink, and an attached convertor will change the signals to a 500 MHz band centred at 1 Ghz. This will enable a longer cable to be used between the antenna and the receiver. The development of cheap low noise amplifiers at these frequencies and advances in electronics generally should enable the antenna and a receiver with addressable scrambling equipment for 24 channels to be produced for about $600.

However new services continue to appear on cable. Compucard currently operate a service via The Source, Dow Jones, and other systems in the US and in Europe, enabling customers to "go shopping" by checking alternatives from a "catalogue" database, order and pay using a credit card number, and then have the goods delivered. The next stage will be a similar service at an in-store "electronic catalog desk".

The whole system will move on to cable where wider bandwidths will presumably enable "catalogues" to include good illustrations.	Service	Mth'ly Rate($)	Penetration(%)
	Basic	4.50	100
	Expanded basic	+6.25	98
Dutson (1982) has provided	Single Pay	+7.60	96
some figures which illustrate the	Dual Pay	+3.00	70
price/demand for cable programmes	Rainbow	+10.00	20

in the US. They include a breakdown of the expenditure of 136,000 people in Long Island, as shown on the right.

CABLE DEVELOPMENTS IN OTHER COUNTRIES

Europe

About 27% of Europe's 125m households are expected to be cabled by 1992 (best case) with $4.7 billion revenue, and 16% (worst case) with $2.6 billion. 20M people in Europe were connected to some kind of cable TV system in 1984, usually "first generation", licensed to transmit only existing TV programmes, although many experiments are in progress.

Canada

In Saskatchewan, Canada, a fairly large fibreoptic network already exists. Some 400 miles of it existed in 1981 with a link between Regina and Yorktown. Another 700 miles were added in 1982. The trunk cable is fibreoptic, with coaxial links to houses. Installation cost per household is about $700. The system loses money but may break even in the late 80s.

France

In France an interactive wideband 15 channel fibreoptic system was scheduled to be working in 1500 homes in 1983. In 1982 a scheme was announced for 20,000 homes to be wired commencing in 1983 for one basic service providing ultimately 60 channels, with additional telephone, videotex, and home security services. The first phase (83-85) will cost 6 billion francs, 2.5 billion borne by the government, 1.5 billion by local authorities, and 2 billion provided by the programme industry. Nothing is stated about subscriber's costs or revenues.

Germany

Several pilot programmes have been proposed in West Germany for Ludwigshafen, Munich, Berlin and Dortmund. The Dortmund project is, institutionally modelled on the IBA in Britain. The service will pass 150,000 homes and provide 11 channels by the end of 1985. 50 companies have expressed interest in providing programmes. 35M Dm for the four German pilot schemes covering a three year period is being provided by fees from householders.

Japan

The Japanese Hi-Ovis (at Higashi Ikoma) and CCIS (at Tama) projects have received wide publicity. The Hi-Ovis system consists of trunk lines containing 38 fibres per cable, distribution to a subscriber being by one send and one receive fibre. The scheme is government financed to the tune of around $20M. It covers far fewer subscribers (500 households) than originally intended but the services are elaborate with wideband downstream and upstream paths. Upstream TV signals can be generated from homes using TV cameras. The basic services are TV re-transmissions, locally generated TV services, video-by-request programmes, and still picture information services.

The Tama system was just as ambitious. It operated between 1976 and 1980. It consisted of a coaxial cable network with a twisted pair (i.e. ordinary telephone line bandwidth) back to the head end. The services included TV retransmissions and locally originated TV, but also included user response by speech to questions posed in certain kinds of programmes. A flash information service was also provided in which the user could choose a particular kind of information e.g. weather forecast, which was superimposed, when becoming available from time to time, upon whatever was being viewed at that moment.

A hard copy "memo" service was available for users with dot-matrix printers to receive local news, public notices, notices from members of the community, etc. A newspaper was even transmitted by a facsimile machine in Tokyo via a microwave link to the head end which could be received by appropriate equipment hooked on to the cable.

Presumably the Japanese, armed with a wealth of experience from these experiments, are considering the market and the roles of government and private interests in the provision of new services.

Netherlands

Cees Wolzak of VNU describes how cable is run in his country without mincing words. VNU is a large publisher heavily involved in "electronic publishing". It employs 7500 people with annual sales of $550M. "You may have seen our cable magazine from Zaltbommel and you may be thinking that the Netherlands is a paradise for publishers who want to get moving with the electronic media.

Forget it! When it comes to electronic or video publishing in the Netherlands there are only two rules. Rule 1. Eveything is forbidden. Rule 2. Nothing is allowed. It would take me all day to explain why and my blood pressure can't stand the strain. My plea to the politicians is simply this - we are willing to take the risks in the cable TV marketplace - please give us the chance to take them!"

I have not seen any official rebbutal of these remarks. Restrictive Dutch cable may be. The fact remains that the country has the most comprehensive cable network in Europe.

Switzerland

In Switzerland some 2M people subscribe to cable TV - popular because of bad reception of ordinary TV in a mountainous country. About 20,000 people receive a "TV newspaper", operated by two local newspapers in the town of Baden, with the co-operation of the Autophon cable network. Regional and local news is supplied. However it is believed that the "newspaper" is not very popular.

UK

About 2.5M homes subscribe to cable TV in Britain, with a further 2M within connection range. These first generation network are mainly to relay existing television programmes from a receiver at a high point to homes which otherwise would be experiencing poor reception. It seems unlikely that the limited facilities available on these systems, dispersed around the country, would be of much use for forming the core of the proposed nationwide "second generation network".

In 1980 it was expected that a number of companies including Rediffusion, British Relay, Radio Rentals and others would be applying for licences to operate experimental pay TV cable networks at several centres including Reading, Hull, Swindon, Rochester, and Northampton. It was expected that 250,000 homes might be connected in the next year or two. There would be no advertising, and a mix of films, sport, and other entertainment would be offered. Subscriptions were expected to be £5-£7 a month.

In the event something like that has happened, and these systems probably could form part of a national network. For example Philips Cablevision operates a system in Northampton, capable of delivering 30 channels in a 300 MHz bandwidth. At present 7 channels are delivered to 12,000 homes, providing normal UK TV programmes, but for an extra subscription a decoder box can be fitted at a receiver for a viewer to receive films transmitted from the local cable station. Programmes are the responsibility of a separate company, Select TV.

Philips also operate a microwave link for supplying programmes to Milton Keynes, one of Britain's "New Towns", where British Telecomm are operating a small "wired home" experiment. At Milton Keynes a number of homes receive these programmes and Prestel, via optical fibre connections.

There may well be 200,000 people around the country connected to these "second generation" networks (but not by fibres, so far as is known, except Milton Keynes). It appears as if the small nucleus of a national system, operationally resembling the US system in some respects, does exist.

The Big Push

In July 1981 the Conservative government decided to launch a major Information Technology intitiative, believing that the country needed a push into a new industry with a big employment and export potential. The Prime Minister, Margaret Thatcher, appointed a six man team of information technology (IT) advisers - four from industry, one from inter-bank research and one from a university computer centre. An assessment of the cable system potential became one of their priorities.

The government was looking for a network with a potential for non-entertainment services such as online databases, electronic publishing, security, utility, and environmental control systems, EFT, reservations and shopping, electronic mail, education and general business use, together with the creation of a supporting and exporting information industry. But they thought that the most likely near-future utilisation and funding, assuming no government funding, would come from the Entertainment Industry.

The IT group made major recommendations to the government in a report from the Cabinet Office, dated February 1982, including a go-ahead for DBS. They were immediately succeeded by a second group under Lord Hunt which reported on September 1982, and released its report on October 12th.

The Cabinet report received wide comment. A trade newspaper, Computer Weekly, said "Let's back the visionaries" but New Scientist, a widely read magazine said "Plans to wire up Britain are unlikely to go ahead...they threaten vested interests and are technically inept". The leader of the Engineering Union said "it could be an expensive mistake".

Peter Jay, Channel 4 TV-AM chairman, was reported to have compared the birth of cable to the renaissance, but Colin Shaw, Independent Broadcasting Authority (IBA) programme director, thought that cable people were "smilers with knives pretending they are producing the renaissance". Roy Hattersley, Labour MP, thought that cable could "deny viewers programmes they presently enjoy" and Philip Whitehead, also Labour, thought it contained elements of economic nonsense.

A well known oracle of the Arts, Melvin Bragg, emphasised the two-culture problem by giving us a clear definition in the Sunday Times:- "Only a small percentage of people know what cable is. It is, quite simply, a piece of wire". He followed this technical exposition with a clear view of the future "It's goodbye to Auntie (the BBC)", but then "over the past 60 years we have had a broadcasting system based on two major elements: what the producers thought was good and what the audience liked best. The resulting consensus has been envied world wide..... will Auntie be replaced by liberators or barbarians?"

British Telecomm said (in effect) "We are the best people to do it". But the role of British Telecomm was not made clear. Somebody said that the report was rather like a preview of the Pope's visit without a mention of the catholic church, although the report did say that it thought BT should have a competitive but not dominant role. Some would say that one lot of people digging up the roads is sufficient. BT has the right (wayleaves) to dig holes. In many places it would not need to dig any extra ones.

The objectives of the government initiative were to lift restrictions on cable systems, to promote the complimentary development of DBS and cable, and to generate economic activity in information technology. The Cabinet Report thought that the direct market for equipment and services was £3000M or more. This, together with the possibilities for the sale of UK programmes, which already enjoy a high reputation, made it essential for a UK technological lead to be established.

The report suggested that fibreoptic cable would probably be used for trunk lines and co-ax for local links. It considered that the return on capital would be sufficient to encourage private investment, so there would be no need for public funding; cable would not place as heavy a burden of investment on consumers as would an equivalent DBS system.

Programme costs for present UK broadcasting is around £1000M annually, which may provide some idea of the costs of programmes for cable. The IT report thinks that all this would generate considerable economic activity and new employment.

My rough and ready calculations show that (based on 1982 pounds) if the cost can be as low as £250 per house, as has been suggested, the installation cost for 5M households would be £1250M. 15% per annum return on that investment is £190M. That would be £38 per each of 5M households if they rented the installation or borrowed the money in some other way. Presumably users would have to sign, say, a three year agreement. If programmes cost £500M per annum, and are priced to yield £600M, that assumes another £120 per household, making £158 per annum in total or £13 per month, and people might be prepared to pay that much.

This does not assume any participation by information providers or business and home information users. Any activity in this area would assist in spreading amortisation costs. Not does it make any allowance for losses in the early years or what seems to be a very low estimate for installation costs.

Racal, a company which has been exceptionally successful in electronics, had little doubt about cable futures. It proposed to move into distribution as well as being an equipment supplier. Thorn EMI and Granada seemed set to benefit from programme distribution, with BICC picking up installation business, and

Philips a general beneficiary from a further general expansion of technology.

The Hunt Report

The Hunt report included the following recommendations:-

* Four functions - The provider,the operator, the programme or service provider, and the programme maker, the key figure being the operator.

* Competitive franchising with a 10 year term and local participation for not more than .5M homes per franchise, with no restrictions on number of channels, prices charged, programme content (except decency standards) or use of out-of-area or foreign programmes. Revenues from basic subscription, extra programmes and advertising, but no Pay-per-item-TV or exclusivity for popular events.

* No ownership by companies or political, religious, or foreign bodies. Cable companies must carry the programmes of the four broadcast TV channels.

* New supervisory authority and no national common carrier network. Complimentary service from Direct Broadcast Satellite (DBS) from the five channels available to the UK.

At the techical level the hope probably is that Britain will be able to leapfrog into fibreoptic distribution. If it does not it may be installing an obsolescent system based on conventional cables.

At this point a brief recapitulation of US events may be helpful. In 1970 a very rosy future was forecast for cable TV in the US. 80% penetration of US households was forecast by 1980. The forecasters totally underestimated that only the incentive of more or less unrestricted programme franchises would generate the necessary finance. A number of experiments on the benefits of cable TV for programmes catering for communal requirements and social needs, sponsored by the National Science Foundation, had been abandoned. Cable took off in the US because the opportunists stepped in when the FCC first removed some programme controls in 1975 and because of a combination of factors, already described, from 1980 onwards. Since 1975, US expansion has been based on the public's propensity to pay for old or blue movies, and some quality programmes have followed.

Reaction to the Hunt report

The British media overwhelmingly selected the possible effects on programme content as the most interesting aspect of the report. A BBC spokesman is reported to have said that cable operators will be free to offer either "wall to wall Dallas" or "wall to wall Starsky & Hutch" (according to whether you read the Telegraph or the Financial Times).

The Daily Telegraph carried a headline claiming "Cable TV may cost viewers £20 a month" (rental). In the same piece it reports Richard Dennis of Rediffusion as claiming a cost of between £5 and £6 a month. It considered that the report was a traditional British fudge. While feeling that the UK has from time to time a standard of television programmes the world envies it asks why any organisation should claim a monopoly for fathoming a consumer's obscure needs.

The Financial Times said that the report was "a fiendishly clever web of British compromise" - which seems to be a distinct improvement on British fudge. Lex, the FT's financial columnist thought that "the package is just what the budding industry wanted...only one major criticism levelled at the report.. the franchise period should be more than 8 years to allow a longer period for investment write-off period".

The IBA thought it was much worse than a fudge - "an Exocet sent into the sides of the BBC and ITV (Independent Television)". Lord Thomson, IBA Chairman, suggested in his own newspaper, the Sunday Times, that the report was "Pie in the sky". "We do not believe that Britain should be floated into the brave new world of push-button shopping and banking on an unregulated flood of cheap imported entertainment and soft porn films".

UK Technical standards

Another committee under Dr Edward Eden was required to make technical recommendations by March 1st 1983. The committee is said to have considered that this speed was "unprecedented" - of course it was, and quite right too.

There is certainly some danger that an obsolescing technology may be standardised in consequence of a decision made too early. On the other hand with a rapidly advancing technology there is always something better round the corner; at what point do you say "stop - we'll settle for this"? This is a notorious dilemma for R&D Directors. If the UK is going to have an inter-connectable wideband network it is necessary to set the standard now otherwise there will be a drift into the general chaos which characterises other telecom networks.

The technical recommendations were eventually published in Cmnd 8866, an April 1983 "White Paper". They were weakly reasonable. Switched-star networks were "encouraged" by offering 20 year licences when they were used, but only 12 years would be offered for tree and branch licences; the ducts used must allow for later conversion to star. Switches are already available - BT has a switch for 300 users and Plessey has proposed a 1500 user switch.

Recent developments

1983 was a year of hope and negotiations. Eleven of the proposed twelve franchises, limited to 100,000 homes each, were granted in cities around the country. But in 1984 a series of pessimistic announcements and reports appeared about costs. In one report (McKinsey April 1984) it was suggested that the franchises as then contemplated would never make a profit. The whole idea that launching of the UK network should be based on entertainment only was questioned. The network should be treated as a data highway and inter-business communications plus entertainment should enable franchises to break even in the 1990s.

Other discouraging events were the abolishing of first year capital allowances which would have been helpful to the franchisees and the possibility that competition from DBS would come sooner than had been thought. It was becoming realised that the government's attempts to impose programme control, influenced on the one hand by the anti-porn/violence lobby, and on the other by its desire to protect the BBC and ITA quality programs, might leave the cable companies with an unappealing programme mix. It was also felt that the limitation of 100,000 homes per franchise might be too small for profitability and that technical standards had been set too high.

The Plessey/Scientific Atlanta company, developing video switches for cable, shut down. Rediffusion, BET and Visionhire moved out of cable and Robert Maxwell bought Rediffusion Cablevision. The franchisees were experiencing financial and marketing problems. In contrast to the flood of applicants for the first round, only one application per franchise was received in the second round of franchising completed in May 1985. The cost of cabling an area of 100,000 homes is now estimated at around £30M. This round was managed by the new Cable Authority, appointed in January.

However some good news started to appear in 1985. In March it was claimed that in areas taking cable more people watched cable programmes than the BBC. The most popular programmes on Cablevision were Movie Channel, Music Box (pop) and Sky (general entertainment). Over one million homes were passed by the first eleven franchisees and over half a million by the second five. It was planned to advertise for five new areas every four months.

The first new multi-channel franchise to become operational was Swindon, but the initial demand from homes passed was disappointing. Charges for the 13 standard channels were reduced to £5.95 per month. The demand from other areas was also disappointing. The first subscribers at Swindon were delighted by the wide choice offered and it was hoped that their enthusiasm would be contagious.

Discussion on UK Futures

Unfortunately, government push instead of market pull is probably needed if the country wants to establish a new kind of information industry instead of being a follower and importer. It is unfortunate because this is second best to a market driven approach. Inevitably people point to an earlier advance by dictat - Prestel - which seemed to be a very good idea, but was not market driven.

The UK no longer has either the resources, the entrepreneurial access to finance, or a sufficiently developed market place to enable Information Infrastructures to "just grow" at a speed appropriate to the general pace of the eighties. The UK government has got the general approach right - first, vigorously raise the issue, then get the debating over at a rate compatible with the 1980s rather than with the Edwardians, then pass the enabling legislation with minimum delay.

However it looks as if the attractions for cable investors will have to be increased. As Veljanovski points out, cable is risky, technology changes are hard to predict and the market is uncertain. "The uncertain nature of cable expansion and the complexities of its output make any attempt to subject the industry to detailed regulation counter-productive".

The question of falling programme standards is a tough one. The wisdom of Solomon is required to set the regulatory conditions at the point which will attract the necessary investment and yet ensure a probability that we shall have more like The Ascent of Man, The Jewel in the Crown etc. Is that compromise possible? Is it not possible to generate a high quality programme at, say, £25,000 per hour instead of at the current rate of £50-100,000 and upwards? Of course some would ask why should anyone presume to be an arbiter of capricious public taste? Let the public demand what it wants and let the programme makers supply it.

FURTHER READING

Anon.
   Cabinet office: IT advisory panel. HMSO, London, February 1982.
      Report on cable systems.
Anon
   Cmnd 8866 ("White Paper"). HMSO April 1983.
      The development of cable systems and services
Anon.
   IEEE Spectrum, 21(9), 57-62, Septemeber 1984.
      Direct broadcast satellites: television stations in orbit.
Barran, Paul.
   IEEE TRans. Com. 23(1), 178-184, January 1975.
      Broadband interactive communication services to the home. Part 2: impasse.

Clement-Jones, Tim
  Telecommunications Policy, 7, 204-214, September 1983.
    Cable and satellites TV in the UK and Europe: the emerging legal issues.
Estrin, Deborah L; Sirbu, Marvin A.
  J.Telecom. Networks 103-115, 1984.
    Cable television networks as an alternative to the local loop.
Fox, J.R
  Report 374-16 BT Research Labs , Martlesham Heath, Ipswich IP5 7RE, England.
    Fibre optics in a multi-star wideband local network.
Hatamian,M; Bowen, E.G.
  AT&T Tech J. 64(2), 347-367, February 1985.
    Homenet: a broadband voice-data-video network on CATV systems.
Hunt of Tanworth, Lord (Chairman).
  The Home Office. Cmnd 8679, October,1982. Published by HMSO, 49, High
  Holborn, London WC1V 6HM.
    Report of enquiry into cable expansion and broadcasting policy.
Kay, Peg; Gerendasy, Stanley.
  NSF Report NSF/RA-760161, National Science Foundation, Washington, 1976.
    Social services and cable TV.
Litman, Barry; Eun, Susanna.
  Telecommunications Policy 5(2), 121-135, June 1981.
    The emerging oligopoly of pay TV in the USA.
Mccron, R,.
  J.Educ.Television 10(1), 7-18, 1984.
    New technologies, new opportunities? The potential of cable in educational
    and social action broadcasting.
Page, John R.U.
  In Proc. 6th Online Information meeting, London. Learned Information, Oxford.
  1982 Pps 155-160.
    Broadcast satellites in association with other broadband techniques for
    innovative methods of information distribution.
Veljanovski, Cento.
  Telecommunications Policy, 8, 290-306, December 1984.
    Regulatory options for cable TV in the UK.

CHAPTER 23. VIDEOTEX SYSTEMS AND MARKETS

"Videotex" was a word chosen to cover a particular kind of information system using a particular communication channel (The PSTN). The Comité Consultatif International de Telegraphie et Telephone (CCITT), a section of the ITU concerned with standardisation, introduced it. (The International Telecommunication Union (ITU) is a United Nations agency to promote international telecommunications co-operation).

New developments occurred far beyond those contemplated at the time and "videotex" seems to have now become a more general term. It is the generic name for special kinds of data storage and transmission systems in which pages of information are retrieved and displayed in response to simple commands, on "terminals" such as a modified television receiver. Videotex usually meant receive-only information systems. Only the people who supplied the information pages used send-receive terminals. Latterly interactive systems for more general purposes have come into wider use. Videotex systems are usually simpler to use and less expensive than other kinds of computer based information systems. Some of the special terms used in this technology are explained in the Glossary.

THE TECHNICAL BACKGROUND: VIDEOTEX IN THE UK

First steps

Although videotex in various guises was talked about earlier, 1972 must be considered a milestone year - discussions then commenced with a view to taking a bold step to cut short the birth pangs of a new technology. Some would say (with easy hindsight) that it might have been wiser to allow a more natural birth. The step was taken in a relatively dictatorial manner - the participants were the British Broadcasting Corporation (BBC) and the British Post Office, monarchs (at that time, and still more or less today) of all they surveyed. The Independent Television Authority (ITA) and the British Radio Equipment Manufacturers Association (BREMA) were the other parties. You do not have to hold public debates about communication adventures in the UK, even when the monopoly carrier launches out into something radically different.

The idea was to standardise a method of digital transmission and display of a page of text on a modified 625 line television receiver containing decoding circuits and storage for one page of data. Development work could then commence on systems for the storage, retrieval, and dissemination of information in the form of pages of text or graphics for inexpensive use in the home. The decision would provide a stable period for investment free from the usual technological hassles and attempts at <u>de facto</u> standardisation which occur in a more competitive situation. A document was published in October 1974 specifying the method for inserting the data into the spare lines of a broadcast television frame.

Teletext

Development then proceeded along two paths. One system was called Teletext and two similar services were developed by the BBC and ITA called Ceefax and Oracle respectively. For reasonable quality, even under adverse conditions, it was decided that a page of text on a TV CRT should consist of 24 rows of 40 characters per row - 960 characters in total. To transmit this information, one row of characters with the usual 8 bits per character is coded as 360 bits, but some control bits are required so one row takes 400 bits, and one page 9600 bits.

A television channel for the UK television standard requires a bandwidth of around 5.25 MHz. Such a channel could equally well be used for digital transmission at a maximum rate of 10.5 Mbps (or more precisely 10.5M signalling elements per second - see Chapter 5). The reliable rate achievable in practice turns out to be about 7 Mbps, and UK teletext signals are transmitted at about that rate so the teletext page rate per second could be 7M/9600 = 729 if a dedicated channel could be made available for the purpose.

Such a channel was not made available, but there are brief periods in each frame of existing occupied TV channels during which no TV information is transmitted - the so-called "spare lines". In a 625 line system the duration of one scanning line is around 60 microseconds (us) so up to about 420 bits could be transmitted in that period at the 7 Mbps rate. The 400 bits needed for one row of characters can be comfortably accommodated and 400 bits per line is technically convenient.

In the event, two of the available spare lines in each field were used in the first system to be adopted, and as 50 fields are transmitted per second in the UK system, the 100 rows of characters or about 4 pages are transmitted per second. Thus transmission occurs in bursts - 800 bits representing two rows of characters are transmitted on two spare lines in a field and then teletext data stops while the rest of the field containing TV picture information is transmitted. After 1/50th of a second another two line burst of teletext data is transmitted, and so on.

Teletext page "magazines" - a sequence of pages - are repeated again and again. A sequence of 100 numbered pages takes about 25 seconds to transmit. Receivers incorporate a circuit for capturing and storing the data in one numbered page. A viewer selects a number on a dial and the receiver grabs all the rows constituting the page next time it comes round in the cycle. The average delay before he sees it will therefore be 12.5 seconds. If the size of the magazine was doubled then the waiting time would be doubled - but an average wait of 25 seconds would be inconveniently long.

To summarise, in the UK teletext system, the whole magazine sweeps past continuously at a rate determined by the number of pages, the bandwidth of the channel, and the percentage of the total transmission time for which the channel is occupied by teletext data. The system is relatively inexpensive to set up. One computer is needed with inputs from editing terminals for changing pages, with an output to an existing TV transmitter.

The cost to be recovered per subscriber is relatively small. The up-dating costs of the relatively small number of pages is also low. In the UK there is no need to recover costs by useage monitoring and invoicing. They are recovered either through the TV licence fee (BBC) or from advertisers (ITA).
Television receivers with teletext decoders and circuits are now mass produced and cost about 20% more than an ordinary receiver.

<u>Viewdata</u>

The   other   path, strongly influenced by its control over the PSTN and its potential for information transmission, was taken by the British Post Office (now British Telecom). The same data format and display already described for teletext are used so that most of the special unit within a TV receiver is the same. With viewdata the modified TV set receives the data from a telephone line instead of from the TV aerial/antenna as in teletext. A subscriber dials up a local multi-port computer - that is a machine capable of handling many calls at once.

Such an arrangement presents the following opportunities and advantages, described by the pioneer Fedida:- Low cost terminals; virtually unlimited information capacity from random access computer storage; small amount of computation per transaction so relatively simple software; information distributed by network-connected local computers; users can dial the computer and transmit commands; simple page selection system.

The user dials the computer's telephone number, and if she knows the subject covered on, say, page 56,720, she requests that page. The data is then returned once only at a rate limited by the bandwidth of the line. The data rate chosen is 1200 bps, fairly well within the bandwidth of the PSTN (about 2600 Hz), so a complete 9600 bit page takes about 8 seconds to be completely received.

If the page number is not known the user selects the first page of the index which displays the ten major subject areas covered by the database. He presses the chosen numbered key on the keypad and then sees the selected subject area, again sub-divided into ten parts and makes another selection. This procedure continues until the last one-out-of-ten menu is replaced by a page of information about the wanted subject. Thus if the database contained one million pages, 6 successive key selections would be needed to pinpoint a wanted page. There is no need to provide high speed facilities on the user-to-computer channel. This data is transmitted at 75 bps.

Compare this with teletext transmission in a shared TV channel where one out of a relatively small number of pages is captured after an interval, and then quickly received by a succession of high speed bursts of transmitted data.

The computers chosen for the Prestel service were GEC4080 machines comprising a cpu with a 16 bit instruction set having a repertoire of 180 instructions, 256K store, communication controllers, and 9.6 or 70 Mbyte disk storage units. Control of the ports into which subscribers may connect by dialling is managed by multi-channel controllers which also operate the automatic answering facilities. The system can rapidly respond to interrupts at any port to provide fast service. The basic operation is to accept characters/messages, and queue them ready for a task such as to identify the frame to be output and request it from disk, retrieve from disk, and route the frame back through the appropriate port.

Originally two computer centres were set up in London and both handled input from information providers and served Prestel users. As the network expanded into the regions, dedicated machines were used for inputting, the up-dated pages being distributed to regional centres.

Data Transmission

In the case of teletext, the data impulses transmitted as part of the TV signal may be corrupted by noise. Ignition interference from a car which produces a snowstorm effects on a TV picture does not disturb viewing too much, but it might cause one bit of teletext data to be received as a "0" instead of a "1". If the receiver is near the edge of the TV transmitter's service area, noise is more likely to over-ride weaker signals. Accordingly special measures are taken to combat noise particularly for critical codes which specify things like page header data which could ruin an entire page if wrongly received.

Extra bits are inserted into the transmitted codes in such a way that they may be examined in special circuits in the receiver, a mathematical check performed, and various kinds of error may be detected and corrected before the code is passed on to the display circuits. This technique has been described by Hamming.

The signal level is relatively high compared with the noise in the PSTN connections used for viewdata. Asynchronous data transmission is used with a modem at the computer end and another built into the TV set. A simple form of error detection is provided; a blob is displayed on the screen if a wrong character is detected. If necessary a page re-transmission can be requested.

Receiving and displaying data

The major parts of a combined teletext/viewdata receiver are shown in Figure 23.1. The Figure and the following description relate to general principles. Actual receivers may perform the functions described in different ways.

The Character Generator Read Only Memory (CGROM) contains a set of 5 x 7 storage blocks. The characters to be displayed are permanently stored as a pattern of on or off bits in these 5 x 7 bit stores. Thus for a "T", the top line of 5 bits would be "on" representing the cross stroke of the T, with a vertical column of "on" bits representing the upright part of the character. Each character contained in its store is addressable by the store's column and row number in the CGROM.

A page of incoming data which comprises the CGROM addresses of all the characters required for that page is stored in a Random Access Memory (RAM) until over-written by the next incoming page data.

To display the page the codes are read out sequentially from the RAM to address the corresponding characters in the CG ROM. The "on" bits in the matrix for that character are then fed to the CRT gun as bright-up pulses when the CRT scan reaches a position on the screen corresponding to the required position of that character. That position corresponds to the position of the character in the page stored as a code in the RAM since the scan which reads out the RAM page is synchronised with the CRT scan.

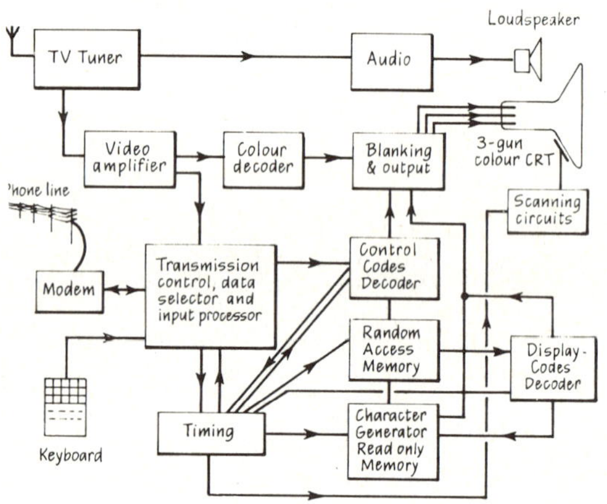

<u>FIGURE 23.1. VIDEOTEX RECEIVER LAYOUT</u>

The start of the TV scan and RAM read-out scan is controlled by a pulse from a clock-pulse generator. The position of the CRT beam at any time is n clock pulses from start. Thus a dot produced by unblanking the CRT beam can be produced at any point on the basis of timing – for instance by controlling unblanking with a counter set to operate after n clock pulses. The unblanking control comes from the RAM as just described.

Viewdata page preparation (editing)

A viewdata editing terminal contains special facilities for compiling pages using a typewriter keyboard. The pages are transmitted along a telephone line connected to the viewdata computer. When editing, an "echoing back" function operates. Each symbol is displayed after having made a go and return trip along the line. The receiving computer checks parity before either storing a code and echoing it back or, if the received code is incorrect, by echoing back a "blob", indicating that the page should be sent again.

In some types of editing terminal, pages can be created offline and stored. A "bulk transmission" facility to the viewdata computer can be used to send the pages rapidly en bloc. Error correction is automatic; the viewdata computer checks blocks of characters and asks for a re-transmission if an incorrect block is received.

Later Prestel/Viewdata developments

As in other new technology areas it is often hard to tell whether pronouncements are wishful thinking, are simply a gleam in the eye, a laboratory experiment, a small scale test, or a fully operational happening.

British Telecomm have come out with some enhancemements such as gateways. These certainly are operational and will be discussed later in this chapter. Relatively large organisations are likely to benefit most from gateways. They will be able to afford the software and systems people which they will probably need to get it right.

BT have also introduced a number of improvements in the Prestel software. In March 1982 BT announced that they could accommodate 32000 instead of 50 Closed User Groups (CUGs). These can be used for self-contained private information and message systems for companies, or for an "electronic publisher" to deliver pages only to paid up subscribers. At the same time the price for this facility was reduced from £2500 to £250.

A number of ambitious schemes have been proposed, and some have been demonstrated in experimental form, to increase Prestel's information capacity. No doubt some of these have been prompted by the intensive foreign competition to show that Prestel can adapt and is not just an entrenched first generation system.

BT have demonstrated Dynamically Redefinable Character Sets (DRCS - in plain language different fonts and picture elements). Clarke <1982> claims results as good as Telidon without actually naming it.

"Prextend" is a keep-up-with-or-ahead-of-the-French/Canadians extension of Prestel using parallel coding which "offers overseas customers the option of starting a service with existing UK equipment and extending later". By exploiting existing Prestel facilities, it is claimed that animation effects should be possible.

"Picture Prestel" has been described by Nicol and Clarke <1982>. The system is designed for the display of high definition colour puctures (without motion) on a Prestel receiver by a suitable combination of additional within-receiver storage and decoding circuits under microprocessor control. A compressed picture is transmitted at a within-channel-capacity rate resulting in a gradual build up in the definition of the received picture. The rate of picture build-up, the area it occupies on the screen, and the transmission rate are chosen to fit the circumstances.

For example with a 24K within receiver store and the existing Prestel transmission rate of 1200 bps, a high definition picture occupying one ninth of the screen takes 1 minute to build up. Its form is recognisable in seconds so unwanted pictures could be rejected fairly quickly. When System X arrives with speeds of 64 Kbps generally available, such a picture would build up in 1 second, or a larger picture would take a few seconds. Demonstrations of the arrangement have been given showing high definition pictures embedded in advertising text.

Well over one million Teletext receivers have been sold but Prestel lags. By 1985 there were 44,000 Prestel terminals in use with 62% business and 38% home users. Micronet, with 9000 subscribers, has been mainly responsible for increased home use; it provides computer users with information, news, and software for downloading. There were 1200 information providers, 317,000 accessible frames, and 14M accesses were made per month - an average of about 75 per terminal/week. The Prestel network embodies 17 gateways to external computers and is accesssible to 94% of the population with a local call.

Prestel shopping is also gaining ground. A Tokyo-based Japanese retailer and bank joined forces in March 1985 to offer an international home shopping service with an on-screen catalogue of consumer goods to be ordered, paid for by credit card, and delivered to Prestel users.

But receiver costs, plus phone and page costs are still too high for public useage to take off. Private viewdata systems gatewayed to Prestel are becoming more widely used for business purposes, but Prestel has not been able to compete with the real-time high-volume processing requirements of businesses. However this may change with new services like Viewdata Gold - software which makes the system appear to a user much more like a conventional interactive system with a fast response time. Moreover the software protocol accommodates the CEPT, Telidon, and Prestel standards, and could be implemented at a cable head-end distribution centre.

BT plans to install a new Prestel network with X25 packet switch/multiplexer technology and one second response time as part of its value-added network services using PSS. PSS already supports X25 protocols and will also probably support IBM protocols eventually although there has been a political setback to direct BT/IBM network installation.

Videotex systems are starting to find particular niches - for example Vauxhall Motors dealer's private system. BT's Kilostream/Megastream high speed data transmission facilities will be used for image transmission. Meanwhile dealers are provided with microcomputer videotex terminals so that they can not only download car information from the company's database but also use the micro for offline accounting and other work.

Later Teletext developments

Since the first system was introduced, two more spare lines have been used in the UK for teletext data, so a magazine of 200 pages can be used with the same delay.

A series of improvements similar to those just described for Prestel have been proposed for broadcast teletext in the UK. These are described by Vivian as "5 levels of compatible enhancements". Level 1 is the present system; Level 2 provides an additional "G0": selectable character set with accented and underlined characters and improved graphics symbols. Level 3 is DRCS, Level 4 alpha-geometric coding, and Level 5 a system similar to Picture Prestel.

DEVELOPMENTS IN OTHER COUNTRIES

The French Antiope/Didon system

The system developed at the Centre Commun d'Etudes de Telecommunications (CCET) at Rennes in France is called Antiope. Titan is the name given to Antiope-based services, first tried experimentally via a packet switching network for stock exchange information in 1976. The name now generally used for viewdata-type services is Teletel. The broadcast teletext system is called Didon. Networked demonstrations were given at the Berlin fair in 1977 where according to Marti "quite by chance our network philosophy of the videotex service was born".

25 rows of 40 characters and alpha-mosaic coding are used and Antiope uses an 8 bit code to specify characters and other symbols like Prestel, but a further 8 bits are associated with each character code to specify its attributes. This 16 bit code, used on both the viewdata and television broadcast versions, can potentially specify over 16,000 different meanings, compared with 128 for an 8 bit code. (7 and 14 bits in these codes respectively carry information, the others are parity bits). The 16 bit code addresses two stores in parallel, so requirements for storage space in the receiver is doubled. Each character can

have, in theory, 128 different independent attributes if needed,as opposed to
the total of 128 characters-cum-attributes possible with an 8 bit code.

It is not clear whether it is essential to include a microprocessor in an
Antiope receiver to handle the greater complication, or whether it is an
advantage to include one to take full advantage of the potential. In one design
provision is made for the control of graphics mapping at the pixel level of
detail. Presumably a special coding scheme would be needed to control this
facility.

French developments were discussed in 1982 by Roy Bright, sometime sales
director of Prestel but then at Intelmatique. Bright forecast that by early 1983
"videotex terminals in France are projected to pass the 70,000
figure...representing nearly double the total in the rest of the world" Several
services are mentioned including Agritel for farmers, Cititel for hotels and a
service for Banks (Francitel ?). The banking system is for major corporate
clients mainly outside Paris rather than for home banking. Bright considered
that national access via the Transpac packet switched network was one of the most
significant developments.

The French Minitel terminals were expected to be rentable at £6 per month,
and would result in a huge expansion of videotex sevices. They were said to be
in mass production, 1.2 million units having been ordered. While this was
over-optimistic there has in fact been substantial growth and by 1985 there were
claimed to be over half a million minitels in use. They cost £130 to produce and
are now provided rent-free. In consequence the French Teletel public videotex
service is widely used, a number of commercial providers offer services, and many
banks provide home banking services. There are more services now than were
predicted. For example credit card validation can be carried out with a small
card reader attached to a Minitel. It reads a magnetic strip and presents a
response on the screen.

The Japanese Captain system

Captain is an acronym for Character And Pattern Telephone Access Information
Network - a viewdata type system - in which the most significant word is,
perhaps, pattern. Patterns are needed to display Kanji characters and Japanese
Hiragana syllables. Characters are constructed from 527 sub-blocks each
containing 8 x 12 elements, stored in a character generator ROM at the
transmitter. Alternatively fine-detail graphics may be composed and transmitted
as a dot pattern. At the receiver, the bits representing one picture are stored
and scanned/refreshed at the standard TV rate to present an apparently stationary
image on the CRT.

A screenful of data can be composed of 120 standard characters (4
sub-blocks) in 15 rows of 8, or 480 small characters (one sub-block) in 30 rows
of 16. Characters containing two sub-blocks can also be formed. Each page is
preceded by a header row of 16 sub-blocks.

Data transmission is at 2400 bps or 3500bps with terminal to computer
transmission at 75 bps. A complete picture display, including the header row and
certain other data, is composed of 527 8 x 12 sub-blocks = 50,592 elements. At
2400bps it would appear that 50592/2400 = over 21 seconds would be required to
transmit a picture. It would also appear that a 50592 bit store is required at
the receiver. However data reduction by run-length coding is used and only new
information is transmitted. When successive frames differ only partially, parts
common to both are not re-transmitted. This considerably reduces transmission
times and storage requirements. The computer centre comprises terminals for image
database composition, database storage, and image conversion and information
storage units from which data is fed into the line.

Extensive trials were carried out between 1979 and 1984 with an experimental service, and a service was made available in the Tokyo and Osaka areas in 1985 with nationwide expansions expected in 1986. During this period there were general advances in digital transmission techniques and Captain anticipates the trend by working at 64 Kbps. Its widespread use will therefore depend on the availability of new telephone equipment.

Europe

Videotex host computers and terminals embodying European standards may be connected to Euronet. In 1982 it was estimated that 50 million videotex frames were available on 13 operational systems in Europe. They were available to 12,000 public users, expected to increase to 1 million by the end of the year but it was far from clear where the 50 million frames were, nor how this huge number of people were to be provided access to them within this very short period.

West Germany

According to the head of the Bundespost's text services about 400,000 subscribers were expected by 1985, and 1 million by 1986. Apparently if the Bundepost ordered 400,000 modems, access costs were expected to be less than 5 Dm a month, but it is not clear why the cost should be qualified in this manner.

In fact these predictions for West Germany's Bildschirmtext have been as wildly out as BT's for Prestel. By the beginning of 1985 only 20,000 receivers were in use. This is in spite of the fact that over one hundred external computers are inter-connected to it. The price of receivers is again considered to be the main delaying factor.

The Canadian Telidon system

The CRC system, called Telidon, is considerably more ambitious than viewdata/Prestel or Antiope. It was developed by the Communications Research Centre (CRC) of the Department Of Communications (DOC). It was first demonstrated in 1978, and by 1979 a small scale trial was in progress. Data transmission is by 8 bit coded Picture Description Instructions (PDI) to a microprocessor within the receiver; the microprocessor plots the displayed picture according to those instruction which act together with information permanently stored within the receiver - there is no transference of symbols to the display from a character generator store.

Positional co-ordinates of PDI's are specified to one part in 2048 and basic shapes such as, polygons, arcs, lines etc., are drawn between points specified as displacements projected from the PDI position. This requires 4 8-bit bytes, i.e 28 bits and 4 parity bits. The creative effort to draw graphics with quite fine detail using these facilities will depend on the software-aided skill of the creator. Complexity and cost is higher than Prestel or Antiope.

So far as is known, videotex services in Canada are still in the experimental stage.

The United States - AT&T NAPLPS

At the Toronto videotex conference exhibition and politicking jamboree in May 1981, AT&T announced its intention to adopt something called the 709E/Presentation Level Protocol (PLP) for videotex, usually called NAPLPS (North American Presentation Level Protocol Syntax). AT&T have plumped for Telidon (709E is the reference number used for Telidon), but the first code received addresses a control character, the effect of which is to divert incoming codes to a microprocessor with enhanced Telidon software. This is claimed not only to provide Telidon's graphics potential described earlier, but also to display graphics in a huge range of colours, of which 16 may be included in any one picture.

Poulter Compuvision makes a machine claimed to enable an editor to take advantage of these facilities. It comprises a digitising drawing tablet, a PDP 11/03 microcomputer with 1 Mbyte floppy disk storage, two colour monitors, keyboard, RS232 communications interface and software.

It can send or retrieve files from devices conforming to the NAPLPS standard. Resolution is 212 x 256 pixels = 52742 plus 16 colours (4 bits per pixel). This is a far cry from the 1 to 2 Mbits needed for high resolution graphics, but much better than Prestel's 24 x 40 6-section graphic elements. But this machine seems to offer more than straight Telidon meccano-set graphic construction. As well as the provision for graphics by pointing, marking co-ordinates, amd having the machine draw arcs, lines etc., on demand, it offers a "freehand sketch mode".

An image derived from a TV camera can be displayed on the screen for copying. This, of course, would be a big time saver, and could draw upon the enormous graphic effort already put into the illustrations available from printed material.

Other developments in the United States

The lack of much original development work in the USA, and of any "US videotext system" until comparatively recently is easily explained in terms of the market and regulatory conditions in that country. Virtually all the initial development work elsewhere has been funded by the establishment - i.e. by governmental or statutory bodies. These bodies are non-market-driven monolithic or monopolistic organisations. Their activities are, for the most part, not subject to open discussion or subject to incentives or constraints from competition, lobbying, or pressure groups.

In market-driven USA, few organisations perceived an immediate market for videotext and the regulatory situation made it far more difficult to create a national infrastructure. A number of experiments took place to test the market using adapted foreign technology and the question of adapting the UK technology to US television standards received some attention.

US television works on the National Television System Committee (NTSC) standard of 525 lines, 60 frames per second (30 fields/sec by interlacing the alternate scanning lines of two frames to form one complete field). In the UK the Phase Alternation Line (PAL) standard of 625 lines, 50 Hz (25 fields) is used.

Using a rule of thumb expression, Bandwidth = $0.56N^2$ x n, (where n = fields/sec and N = lines), the nominal bandwidths needed for USA and UK television signals which carry the teletext data work out at 4.6 and 5.5 MHz respectively. The bit rate used in UK teletext is about 7 Mbps, well below the maximum rate possible for the UK bandwidth, and somewhat below what is possible for the US bandwidth. The information that can be included in a 40 x 24 = 960 characters/page is little enough. However in 10 systems listed which were proposed or are running experimentally in the US, 5 use 512, 1 640, 3 800, and 1 1920 characters.

The 1920 character system is The Source, using a standard 80 x 24 terminal display, but this information is transmitted by ASCII code and is not true videotex. The appearance of 1920 characters on a modified US television set type of terminal would be unsatisfactory.

It is hard to estimate the actual number of videotex receivers in use because videotex is often only one of several services provided by a single organisation, and the figures available apply to users of all its services. Thus The Source, Compuserve, and Dow Jones News claim to have nearly 90,000 users between them. WFLD radio station, which runs teletext, claims 70,000 and San Francisco State University on Viacom cable network, 40,000. The majority of other systems, of which there are 16, number 150 users on average. The number of potential users, if they had receivers, on services like SSS CableText, Reuters, Dow Jones Cable, etc., who are running some videotext services, run into several millions.

AT&T is continuing to gain experience with two experimental systems - "Viewtron" jointly with Knight-Ridder Newspapers, and "Venture One" with CBS. Viewtron experiments started in 1981 and by 1984, following a reported expenditure of $12M, had attracted less than 2000 subscribers. Expectations are higher for 1985 with more micros, such as IBM PCs and Commodore 64s becoming available to receive the signals. 13 other new trials were planned in 1983. According to Truxal the total number of US videotex users in 1982 was 11,700, excluding the 100,000 subscribers claimed by Dow Jones, Compuserve and The Source which are not videotex services as usually defined.

The nearest thing to a US service comparable to Prestel, although for a specialised market, is probably Agridata, an online videotex system for farmers and dairy farmers in the US and Canada. However its operations are very different showing a typical US entrepreneurial collaboration. Radio Shack, with computer shops throughout the continent, does the marketing, Agridata is a private company, and the National Dairy Herd Improvement Association processes dairy management records and provides users of this part of the service with free Zenith terminals.

Although a _de facto_ standard for telephone/viewdata may have emerged, the is not the case for TV/teletext. Keycom Electronic Publishing, the Centel/Honeywell/Field Enterprises group, used British teletext technology for their trials, CBS and NBC are planning to use NAPLPs, while Zenith and Sony are considering both. Keycom is put out on WFLD, Chicago, using "Keyfax", its teletext magazine compiled by ex-BBC Ceefax employees, amongst others, on a small scale trial. However it transmits all night movies on a service called "Nite Owl" interspersed with advts and Keyfax pages of general interest, receivable on ordinary TV sets.

Thus Keycom capitalises on its database which earns real money. "Now is the time for UK industry to manufacture a 525 line teletext decoder" says Peter Winter, ex-Ceefax man with Keyfax. "The market is there for the taking" Keycom's Keyfax service is part of larger electronic publishing activities. Field Electronic Publishing has access to a network of 14 PDP11/34 computers with a large database of editorial and advertising information owned by the Chicago Sun Times. The teletext part of the system runs on Logica software which provides a wider range of facilities than is available on BBC Ceefax (from which it is derived), reflecting various interconnect and service packaging requirements.

Zenith's videotex manager, William Thomas, claims that mass produced NAPLPS decoders will cost $300-$500 against British 625 line decoders currently available at $100-$150, but Greg Harpe of Antiope US, claims that NAPLPS decoders will cost $200. "98% of teletext decoders in use in the world today use British Technology" says Truxal. That sounds as if British Industry must really be on the ball, exporting all over the place. Not so - 90% of them are in use within the UK where teletext is doing well.

Truxal continues, quoting Francois Olibet of Videodial a French videotex subsidiary, "people enjoy graphics at first, but get annoyed when they have to wait for an umbrella to appear on the screen before a weather forecast". In a US teletext trial service, this point was rubbed in when people had to wait for a nicely drawn skull and crossbones to be displayed each time before they could get poison treatment advice - information that might be needed in a hurry.

A home banking experiment is being carried out within the Knight-Ridder/AT&T trial, already mentioned, in conjunction with a bank in Florida. This is more recent than the Knoxville experiment dscribed in Chapter 25. The service provides transfers beween current and savings accounts, bill payments, and account information. If the experiment proves a success, investment, at-home shopping, and other services may be offered on a paying basis.

IBM, CBS, and Sears Roebuck announced a joint venture in 1984 called Trintex to be aimed at home computer users for a home videotex service, presumably with the intention of automating Sears huge shop-from-home catalogue. Videotex software is available for the IBM PC ($250) but a colour graphics adaptor is also needed which sells for $400 (1984 prices).

An interesting system is operated by Reuters in the US for the delivery of continually up-dated financial information. The information is transmitted from New York by microwave link to an RCA ground station and from there up to the Satcom 1 satellite for distribution to those cable networks connected to ground stations receiving from it in various parts of the US.

The bandwidth of the system enables data to be transmitted at 3.2 Mbps or about 30 million characters per minute. At the ground station a cablehead data reformatter organises the data into groups of pages which are cyclically renewed by up-dates. The cablehead reformatter also enables paid-up subscribers to access pages to which they are entitled by a system called "IDR row-grabbing" - teletext by another name. Reuters have organised their pages into 1000 groups of 1000. Users with appropriate facilities can compile their own magazines by pulling out a pre-selected set of pages.

Videotex services produce revenues which are negligible compared to other US information services. In 1981 consumer newspapers magazines and books produced $12,000M, Business magazines, books, and other publications $4,000M, movies and cable $4000M, Database services $2,600M and Business seminars, exhibitions, and other services $2,000M. The price per page of a business publication is much higher than a consumer publication.

Predictions for Videotex growth in the US vary. Predicasts thinks that by 1987 revenues will reach $2 billion, but Arthur Andersen considers that by 1992 it will have grown to only $500M. Other estimates go up to the wildly optimistic figure of $30 billion by 1995. This simply confirms doubts about new technology forecasting, expressed elsewhere in this volume. Clearly a track record of some years must be established before forecasts become credible.

TECHNO-COMMERCIAL POLITICS

The different approaches of Prestel, Antiope, and Telidon demonstrate changes brought about by technical developments and nationalistic politics.

Devious tactics are a regular feature during the introduction of a new technology for commercial reasons and tactics of the same kind have been practised in other fields. For instance some extraordinary technical claims and counter claims were made during arguments about the international introduction of television systems, electronic navigational schemes, and later about aircraft landing aids. The protagonists on these occasions, normally concerned with technical matters and the publication of more or less objective technical papers, behave like politicians and all claims have to be taken with a grain of salt.

A standards struggle simmers in the US. Outside the US a battle has openly raged between the protagonists of the British, French, and Canadian systems with one eye on the US market potential. A three part article by Jackson, Reid, and Clarke, viewdata/Prestel supporters, was published in 1980. It was followed by a debate, also published, between Wells and Clarke. The first article contained trumpet-blowing comments which were too much for Wells, a Telidon supporter, who reacted like a bull to a red rag.

Wells refuted Clarke's article point by point, concluding with a most non-technical comment "Mr Clarke's paper is confusing, biased, and incorrect. I am extremely disappointed to see a paper with such a biased view in the presumably refereed contents of a journal as prestigious as Spectrum". Spectrum is a major journal published by the US Institute of Electrical and Electronics Engineers.

A graph in Clarke's piece caused unrestrained fury when it was used on a earlier occasion. It showed that parallel coding, as used by the French, allows more characters per page but only at the expense of larger receiver memory. For example there is a probability that at least 25% of parallel coded pages will have about twice as many characters as serially coded pages. However Spectrum allowed Clarke - from British Telecom's research department - to have the last word. His acidic response commenced with "The debate on viewdata is the most bitter controversy about communications standards since the arguments about colour television 20 years ago". He could find no points of agreement with Wells.

Clarke was again to the fore in criticising AT&T for failing to table its NAPLPS proposals for consideration at the next appropriate CCITT meeting, having launched them earlier in a blaze of publicity at Toronto. AT&T had, in fact, been engaged on videotex trials for some time together with CBS. It was attempting to establish a _de facto_ standard, so arguments (which nearly always lead to a compromise) within the CCITT were the last thing it needed.

Another different kind of controversy was reported in late 1982. Senator Moynihan tried to introduce a Bill preventing US companies from charging Telidon-based videotex systems as a business expense. This was an attempt to pressurise the Canadians, who had prohibited Canadian companies from charging across-border advertising from US TV stations as a business expense.

Many of the broadcasts came from the State of New York, the home state of - guess who - Senator Moynihan. His local TV stations had a few words with him because they lost around $20 million in Canadian advertising! Canadians have long been up in arms against cultural influences from across the border.

<u>METHODS FOR CONTROLLING CHARACTERS AND GRAPHICS</u>

This topic was the technical subject which the "bitter controversy" just discussed was all about. At the time BT was seeing its pioneering viewdata efforts failing in the market place and was anxious to keep down receiver costs. In the UK, receivers were already too expensive for the general public. BT's objective was to stick to something simple and as cheap as possible, primarily for the display of text. Organisations in other countries capitalised on the weakness of viewdata/Prestel's graphics by offering something more complex but better.

However the cost differential between the systems has steadily decreased with the drop in cost of integrated circuits. Ingenious software has removed many of the problems of actually using the more complex graphics facilities. On the other hand it appears that nice graphics do not have sufficient appeal for the world at large to drop the original arrangement. The systems in use are overwhelmingly based on the original BT design. Both sides can find some comfort for their pride.

a. (above)
4 x 7 pixel space for a character. Characters within allocated space with 3 pixel inter-character and inter-line spacing.
b. (below)
8 x 10 pixel space for graphic shape. Division of shape into 6
elements. A chosen shape. The chosen shape repeated 2 x 2.

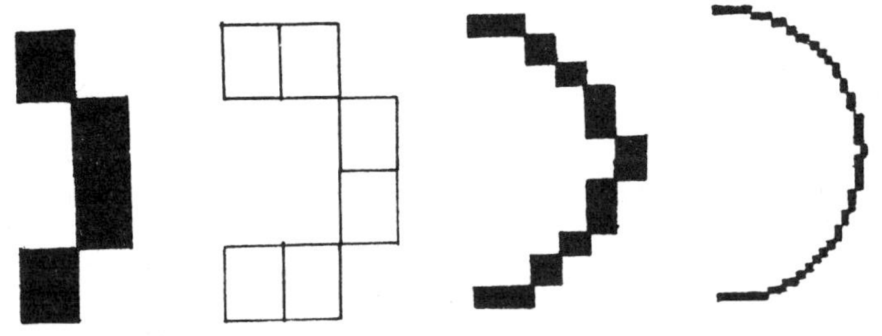

c.
"Best curve" that can be formed by 4 solid graphic shapes.
Position of 6 shapes for a better curve. The 6 shapes with
"best curve" elements selected. Curve formed by individual
pixel selection. (pixel scale same as in a. & b.)

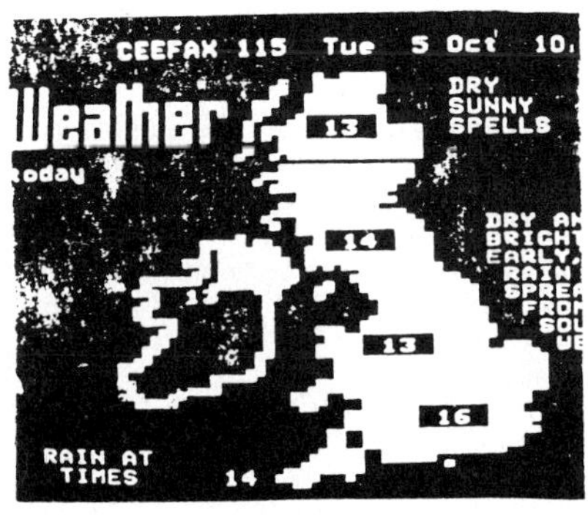

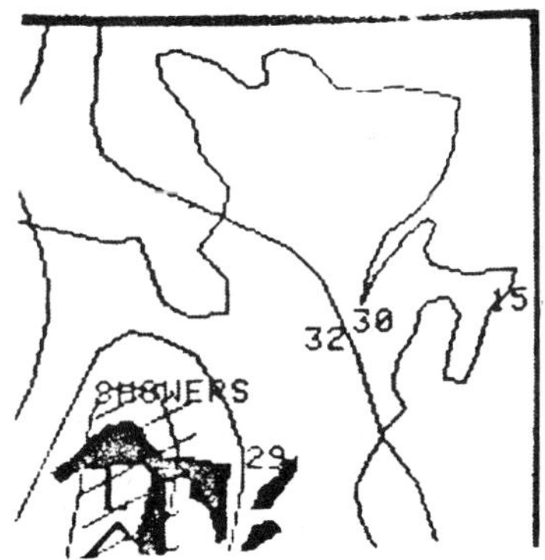

d. Teletext/viewdata graphics.   e. Telidon graphics
(Not on the same scale as a,b, & c. Also
telidon is on larger scale than teletext so its
structure is better (relatively) than shown.

FIGURE 23.2. VIDEOTEX CHARACTER AND DISPLAY STRUCTURES

Character structures are shown in Figure 23.2 (a). A character is composed of bright dots within a 5 x 7 dot pattern with 3 dots between each character and between each row of characters. Maximum possible vertical resolution is achieved by using one picture element (pixel) per TV line. This enables 24 40-character rows with a suitable border and space for a header row conveniently to be displayed on a standard 625 line TV display. (Not all of the 625 are available "active" lines).

In Prestel, the 7 dots in a character are pixels displayed on 7 successive TV lines, with 5 horizontal pixels to provide the right proportions as shown in the figure. Graphics are built up from "building blocks" composed of shapes within an 8 x 10 block of pixels as shown in Figure 23.2 (b).

To compose a curve using one of these graphic shapes, solid shapes may be arranged as shown in figure 23.2 (c, left). This produces the relatively coarse picture shown in (d). Alternatively shapes could be combined with appropriate elements switched on, as shown in the next diagrams in (c), to produce a finer structure. If curves can be composed by controlling individual pixels, as in Telidon, a finer curve, as shown on the right of (c) can be obtained. Figures 23.2 (a) to (c) are on the same scale of resolution.

An idea of the relative effect of Prestel/Viewdata/Teletext and Telidon pictures can be obtained from (d) and (e). The Telidon picture should be shrunk by about three times for a true comparison with the Ceefax picture. The relative difference would then be about the same as between the last two diagrams in (c). In Telidon, shapes can be drawn by issuing instructions - for example to draw an arc of a given length in a particular position. This might automatically manage the "switching on" of, say, 100 pixels.

For data transmission, 8 bit codes (7 + 1 parity bit) have been almost universally used for years. 7 bits provide 128 different combinations or, if you like, numbers from 0 to 127, or 1 to 128, etc., normally quite sufficient for all the letters, numbers and punctuation marks needed for textual information.

If CGROMs are used in a receiver, as described earlier in this chapter, this would enable 128 different patterns to be addressed as column number and row number in, say, an 8 x 16 matrix or table. This does not provide a sufficient number of positions for videotex requirements because as well as dot patterns forming letters and numbers, a large number of patterns which can be used to form illustrations, mosaic style, have also to be addressed. So also do control characters which are not displayed; when addressed by an incoming code group, these cause special functions to be executed.

One of these special functions is to provide for the selection of extra columns in the table - see Figure 23.3 which shows the table used for Prestel. To choose any item in the table, 5 bits are transmitted (in the order shown in the top left hand corner of the figure) to select 1 out of 15 rows. These are followed by 3 bits to select one out of the 8 columns.

To select, say, the inverted L graphics pattern in column 3a, a control character (SO "shift out"), allocated the meaning "from now on select column 3a instead of column 3", is first addressed. To revert to column 3, another control character (SI "shift in"), meaning "from now on revert to column 3", is addressed. Thus to address the inverted L followed by the pattern immediately below it, the code sequence 0111000 1110110 0001110 would be transmitted.

bit/s b7 b6 b5 b4 b3 b2 b1	Row (Col)	0	1	2	2a	3	3a	3b	4	4b	5	5b	6	6a	7	7a
b7 b6 b5 →		0 0 0	0 0 1	0 1 0		0 1 1			1 0 0		1 0 1		1 1 0		1 1 1	
0 0 0 0	0	NUL	DLE	Sp	▦	0	▦		@		P		—	▦	p	▦
0 0 0 1	1	SOH	Cursor DC1 On	!	▦	1	▦	Set Verity Mode(1)	A	Alpha^n Red	Q	Graphics Red	a	▦	q	▦
0 0 1 0	2	STX	DC2	"	▦	2	▦	Set Verify (2)	B	Alpha^n Green	R	Graphics Green	b	▦	r	▦
0 0 1 1	3	ETX	DC3	£	▦	3	▦	Set Verify (3)	C	Alpha^n Yellow	S	Graphics Yellow	c	▦	s	▦
0 1 0 0	4	EOT	Cursor DC4 Off	$	▦	4	▦	Set Programme Mode	D	Alpha^n Blue	T	Graphics Blue	d	▦	t	▦
0 1 0 1	5	ENQ	NAK	%	▦	5	▦	Tape Pause on Playback	E	Alpha^n Magenta	U	Graphics Magenta	e	▦	u	▦
0 1 1 0	6	ACK	SYN	&	▦	6	▦	Tape Start	F	Alpha^n Cyan	V	Graphics Cyan	f	▦	v	▦
0 1 1 1	7	BEL	ETB	'	▦	7	▦	Tape Stop	G	Alpha^n White	W	Graphics White	g	▦	w	▦
1 0 0 0	8	Cursor ← BS	CAN	(	▦	8	▦		H	Flash	X	Conseal Display	h	▦	x	▦
1 0 0 1	9	Cursor → HT	EM	)	▦	9	▦		I	Steady	Y	Contig Graphic	i	▦	y	▦
1 0 1 0 (A)	10	Cursor ↓ LF	SUB	*	▦	:	▦		J	End Edit	Z	Separated Graphics	j	▦	z	▦
1 0 1 1 (B)	11	Cursor ↑ VT	ESC	+	▦	;	▦		K	Start Edit	←		k	▦	¼	▦
1 1 0 0 (C)	12	Cursor Home & Clear FF	SS2	,	▦	<	▦		L	Normal Height	↖	Black Background	l	▦	‖	▦
1 1 0 1 (D)	13	Cursor ← CR	SS3	—	▦	=	▦		M	Double Height	→	New Background	m	▦	¾	▦
1 1 1 0 (E)	14	SO	Cursor RS Home	.	▦	>	▦		N		↑	Hold Graphics	n	▦	÷	▦
1 1 1 1 (F)	15	SI	US	/	▦	?	▦		O		⊞	Release Graphics	o	▦	▬	▦

FIGURE 23.3. CODE AND SYMBOL TABLE USED IN PRESTEL
(The bit order in code groups is shown at bottom left)

7 + 1 bit codes are used by everybody for data transmission, so if international agreement could be reached on the address of control characters (the "CO" set) a shift to alternative graphic table sets G0, G1, G2, etc) containing different sets of graphics, characters, etc, according to national or individual requirements could be arranged. Thus the receivers for all users could be almost identical, with the resulting mass-produced low-cost benefits which would follow. The only differences would be small plug-in storage units containing the the required G0 set selected by using a designated control character. For example in French receivers, symbols like £ would be omitted and a range of accented characters would be added in a G0 set stored in those receivers.

Furthermore, instead of an alternative G0 set, a microprocessor capable of performing special functions, could be actuated by a code addressing a special control character. The received codes, diverted thereafter into the microprocessor, could consist of commands executed by the microprocessor's software. This is more or less what happens in the Telidon system.

To reconcile national differences a compromise Standard was eventually agreed between the European PTTs — the CEPT (Conference of European Posts and Telecommunications administrations) Videotex Standard TCD6-1. (See Childs). It is in line with the OSI 7-layer standard (presentation layer) and so equipment made to this Standard will be able to exchange information within the OSI framework, as gradually introduced. See Chapter 6.

The Standard specifies a "Presentation Protocol Data Unit" an 8-bit code which contains instructions about what the receiver must do to set itself up to understand, implement, and display the information, as well as being used to send and receive the data containing information about the symbols to be displayed. A succession of 8-bit codes may be needed for a complete instruction. For example 32 bits are required to specify all the required functions. To manage all these functions a microprocessor is necessary.

The Standard provides the rules necessary to implement the procedures described above — that is it specifies codes to enable the receiver to bring into action the "G" sets with which the receiver is fitted. For example in a Prestel system the first codes transmitted tell the receiver that what follows will be Prestel data. The codes which follow simply address the character set which is fitted within the receiver. In a more expensive "universal" receiver, should such a receiver be required, additional chips containing sets for all the other systems could be fitted. In that case (at least in principle) the receiver recognises from the first code groups that, say, DRCS is coming up.
It will then direct the incoming data codes into its microprocessor.

The more sophisticated receivers are likely to contain additional storage for the more complex symbols that the receiver can handle so that they may be recalled from store instead of being constructed each time using the DRCS procedure. For example the symbol "1/2" including an oblique stroke which really looks like one, symbols such as "@", etc, could be stored, quite apart
from much more complex shapes for picture construction.

The components for such a receiver would consist of a modem and keyboard, microprocessor, program memory, page/DRCS memory, a special display controller chip such as the Mullard Eurom SAA 5350 as well as the usual other TV receiver circuits. The SAA 5350 handles all the character/colour/size/flashing/boxing etc., effects.

OTHER ASPECTS OF VIDEOTEX

Circuit components

The problem for receiver manufacturers in a changing technical and political situation is how many receivers of a particular design can they sell at a particular price and how many must be laid down in a production run to achieve that price? The problems for the videotex chip designers/manufacturers are similar although they are one step away from the ultimate market.

They must decide from their assessment of the receiver manufacturer's requirements whether they dare design and manufacture   all videotex circuits on one chip. If the demand is large enough that will provide the lowest cost solution. Alternatively should the functions be broken down into, say, 5 chips on a board which includes interconnections and a few discrete components? The production costs will be higher than the one-chip solution, unless the demand is relatively small.

If the manufacturer thinks he will make only n units before he is
forced to change the design, and provided he segregates the functions of the 5 chips correctly, the new design may call for a change in only one chip. The board and the remaining chips being unchanged, the cost of re-design and new production will be much less than re-design of the 1 chip all-eggs-in-one-basket option. The widely used Mullard Lucy/Lucinda chip set, for example, shown in Figure 23.4, consists of modem, auto-dialler, ports and filters, ready to form the front end of a videotex receiver.

FIGURE 23.4. MULLARD ON-BOARD CHIP SET FOR VIDEOTEX RECEIVER
(Courtesy Mullard Ltd)

At least two all purpose videotex chip solutions have been described. Presumably some have been manufactured, but the current production situation is not known. Both are far from a single chip solution, but both claim to enable "universal receivers" to be designed around them. Both were exhibited at the New York Videotex 82 conference in June 1982.

One is the joint development of Texas Instruments and Telediffusion de France. It contains decoding, display processing, microprocessor and 64K RAM. It can be used in either broadcast TV/teletext systems, or phone/Viewdata type systems and contains a modem on a chip for the latter. It is claimed that this multi-chip set will handle Antiope/Didon NAPLPS, and European CEPT (Conference of European PTT) systems.

The other, developed in Austria at the University of Graz by Herman Maurer, is more like a microcomputer with software. The software handles decoding and systems conversion, and editing and terminal facilities. It can perform all the other functions already described for the multi-chip set, contains RAMs for software and picture frame storage, and was expected to be available from the Austrian manufacturer Elektronische Gerate in Florian at $500.

However a solution along the lines of the Mullard design, mentioned above, seems more practical, and the components are now (1985) available as standard production items.

Private viewdata systems

A private viewdata system is based on the same technology as earlier described but the computer and the data stored in it is privately owned and accessible only to particular people. A basic system consists of a central computer with disk storage for information pages, input (editing) terminal(s), user's viewing terminals, and terminal-to-computer inter-connections by appropriate (e.g. dial telephone) links. A number of organisations are selling private viewdata systems in the UK including GEC, Honeywell (Incoterm), IBM, ICL, Rediffusion, and other smaller companies.

The market grew slowly – for instance Incoterm (since taken over by Honeywell) although offering a system for only £17,000 complete, sold only 10 systems in two years. For some time only Rediffusion, Aregon, and Incoterm could name more than a couple of customers. ICL's Bulletin failed to win any large scale success. GEC's idea of the private viewdata electronic office is shown in Figure 23.5. The advantages claimed for such systems compared to other private computer-based information systems is relatively low cost, convenient rapid information up-dating,

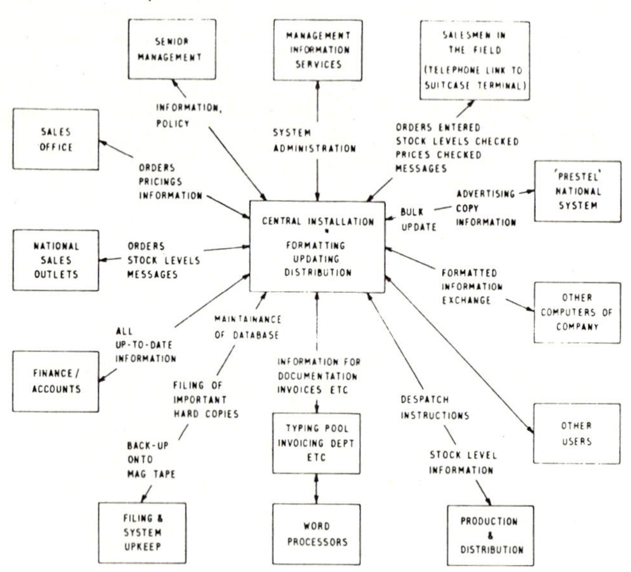

FIGURE 23.5. GEC'S PRIVATE VIEWDATA FUNCTIONS

fast information retrieval, and ease of operation for non-technical users. A typical small private system is offered by Metrotech in the UK. It consists of a central microcomputer with editing terminal and keyboard connected by cable to a number of terminals in other parts of a building. The terminals consist of a colour television receiver in a box with three connections - from the cable, to a keypad, and to the aerial lead of the TV set, also capable of normal TV reception. The smallest system comprises a microcomputer with software and disk storage for 250 information frames at £5500. A user terminal equipment (excluding the TV set) costs £500. Larger systems, for example the GEC 4000, comes in versions from 4 ports with storage for 4000 frames to 200 ports and 200,000 frames. Prices start at around £50,000.

Similar systems are available in other European countries, notably France and Germany.

IBM had an early interest in videotex and installed terminals at 30 recruitment agencies in the UK for use by potential employees of Aramco. They also operated a bureau to which terminals could be connected by dial telephone. IBM announced its latest private viewdata system in September 1984 to a market estimated to be worth over $3 billion by 1990. The system enables users in an organisation with an IBM mainframe and SNA network remote communications controllers to dial-in to a controller in order to access the database. Alternatively users can dial in to the system via a Prestel gateway.

Gateways

A Gateway is a communications processor connected to at least two networks which enables messages to pass between stations connected to different networks. To a user, it appears as if he is sending a message to another station on his own network. Shelzer suggests that to provide an efficient communications service, gateways should provide switching node functions such as adaptive routing, flow control, and network monitoring.

When a user keys a command to the Prestel computer in order to retrieve an information frame from his private computer, the Prestel computer links the command through to the user's host computer and links the block of frame data back from the host to the user. The Prestel computer is able to supervise the exchange of data between a private terminal and a host in a "form-filling" data collection procedure. In this case the Prestel gateway protocol fetches a "form frame" from the host and displays it to the user, checks and prompts the "filling in" activity by the user from his terminal, and forwards correct data filled in by the user to the host.

This is an economical method because only data representing new information travels the whole journey - the format and text of the form is stored in the Prestel computer during the exercise. A user can, of course, dial up his private computer and receive data via the PSTN. A simple example of data collection would be the entering by the user of keywords (assuming he has a full keyboard) for search purposes once he has been connected to the desired database on the private host computer.

To do this he would have to be presented with a "form" with a displayed prompt such as ENTER KEYWORD. The host computer, having "issued" the form via the Prestel computer, will be expecting keywords, will act upon them, and can send back the retrieved frames to the user's terminal.

Viewdata networks

A number of possible arrangements for viewdata interconnections are shown in Figure 23.6. A system like this would depend on the facilities required, transmission costs over given distances, and the volume of traffic. For example

PSS charges are independent of distance, PSTN charges are not. The figure shows different ways of interconnecting equipment, networks, etc. It is not intended to represent an economically designed layout, nor are the X25 networks shown the only type which could be used.

However the X25 interface, a CCITT recommendation, is receiving international support and may be widely adopted. The host-Prestel data exchange described above is accomplished by means of a host/PSS/Prestel interconnection like that shown in the figure. A host computer will require software to run a communications protocol so that it can transmit and receive messages, using the X25 interface, via the PSS. It will also require software to run Prestel gateway protocol for handling transactions between a calling-in terminal and the Prestel computer.

"Interface" is a term which was first applied to the specifications for a plug and socket connection for data exchange between two systems. The specification includes pin numbers, voltage levels for control or data signals, and the functions of the control signals. Provided the manufacturer of the equipment associated with the plug and the manufacturer of the equipment associated with the socket follow an agreed specification, data can be exchanged between equipments. However the meaning of "interface" has been widened. It can now be synonymous with "protocol". A protocol is a set of rules. Thus the "X25 interface" may be referred to as the "X25 protocol". It specifies interconnections and their functions, and a whole range of software functions needed, for instance, to "packetise" a stream of data code.

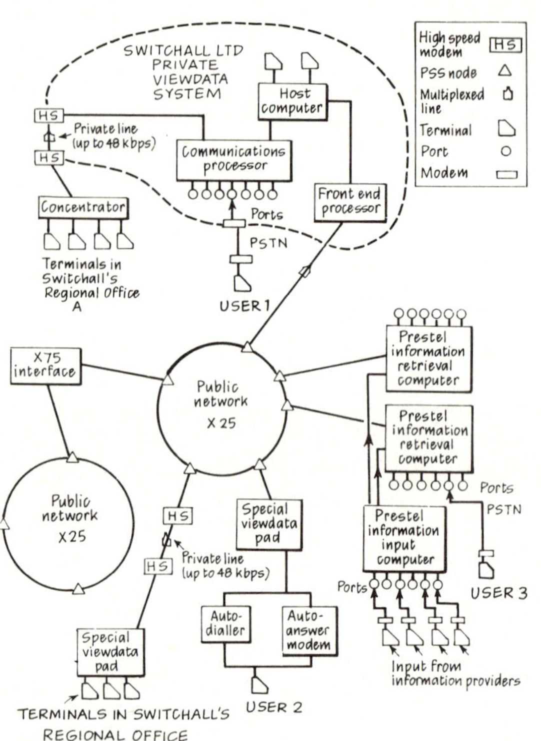

FIGURE 23.6. A VIEWDATA NETWORK

Various facilities and interconnections are shown in the figure. Some actually exist, some are feasible now, and some will become feasible according to the rate of introduction of standards. A front end processor (FEP) arranges for messages from the host computer to other devices connected to the network to be packetised, and for incoming packets to be assembled into messages that the computer can handle. X25 includes provision for multiplexing, so a number of messages may be almost simultaneously in transit along a line of suitable bandwidth between a PSS node and the FEP of a host.

In the UK, private lines of up to 48KHz bandwidth can be arranged with BT. Wider bandwidth lines are available in BT's special services. At present (so far as is known) most users connect to their private computer via the PSTN — like User 1 in the figure. If User 1 wants to communicate with Prestel he does so via the host, PSS, and a Prestel Information Retrieval (IR) computer.

A user - such as User 2 - should be able to communicate with his host and the Prestel computer via PSS. A Packet Assembler/Disassembler (PAD) at the nearest PSS node must be available for this to be done. A node is a point on the PSS where connection facilities are available. The PAD can packetise asynchronous terminal data. Connection from terminal to PAD could be by dial up to a PAD port, or by direct connection via a private line. A Concentrator is another name for a communications processor handling data for a number of devices by multiplexing in one communication channel. Such a processor could be used to service a number of terminals in a regional office of an organisation having a private viewdata system at Headquarters.

X25 networks may be interconnected via an X75 interface. Networks of this kind, providing "transparency" for messages exchanged between terminals or computers on different networks, are in their infancy. User 3 in Figure 23.6 is an ordinary Prestel user who can dial up his local Prestel IR computer. User 2 is the proud possessor of an autodialler enabling him to dial one or more telephone numbers by pressing one key on his terminal.He also possesses an auto-answer modem so that his terminal can respond to callers automatically in some pre-arranged manner.

<u>Response times: menus: keywords</u>

In BT experiments, when the response time exceeded 6 seconds, half of the population of test subjects thought that their work was being slowed down. When viewdata is used as an access to other computer systems, delay times may become a problem. BT has also experimented with keyword indexing. Prestel, of course, currently provides for searching with the aid of either a succession of menus of ever increasing specificity, or for going direct to a page if the page number is known. Ambiguities can arise with a tree system as with any indexing system.

Experiments have been carried out with a full size keyboard and a 22 inch Prestel television set. In one set of experiments, subjects had 70 successes and 11 failures with a key word search, compared with 49 successes and 27 failures with a menu search. From these and other experiments it was concluded that there would be a clear benefit in providing a key word search facility on Prestel.

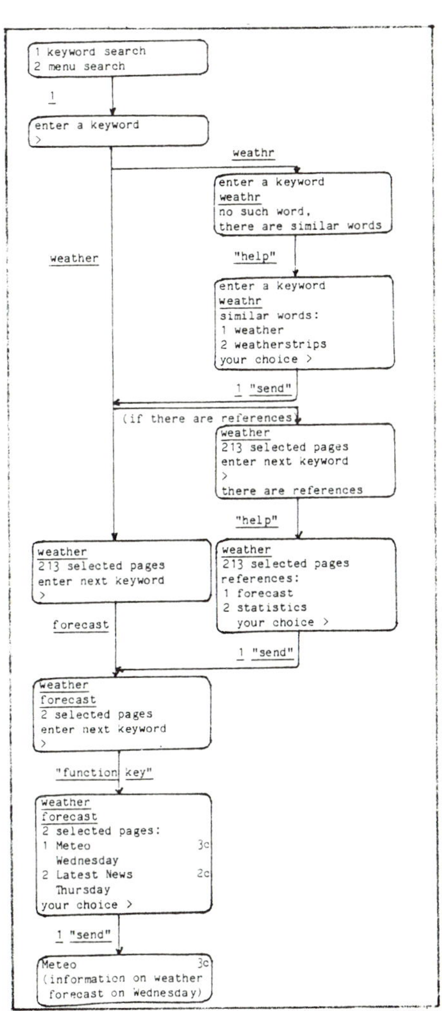

<u>FIGURE 23.7 KEYWORD FLOWCHART</u>

Experiments on the same subject have also been carried out in the Netherlands by Viditel and by the MRC Applied Psychology Unit at Cambridge. Figure 23.7 shows a succession of keyword menus used to provide choices with added help when finding out about the weather, suggested by Toon (Viditel). A

spelling aid is incorporated. Note how "hits" are used to direct enquiries
towards more specific terms. "Weather" produced 213 hits, but the note "there
are references" (the phrase "press help for common associated words" would
have been better) prompts the user to key "Weather forecast".

FURTHER READING

Anon.
  Joint Publication by BBC London, IBA and BREMA, October 1974.
    Specification of standards for information transmission by digitally coded
    signals in the field-blanking interval of 625 line television systems.
Anon.
  Booklet, 1982. Available from Prestel Gateway Dept., Telephone House,
  Temple Ave., London EC4Y OHL.
    Welcome to Gateway.
Anon.
  In Proc. Videotex 84 International, Amsterdam. Published by Online
  Conferences Ltd, Pinner, Middlesex, England. Pps 395-418, 1984.
    A quick guide to the the Videotex universe.
Baird, D.D.
  Aslib Proc. 37 (6/7), 257-265, June/July, 1985.
    Managing Information on a viewdatabase.
Ball, A.J.S.; Bochmann, G.V.; Gecsei, Jan.
  Computer, pps 8-14, December 1980.
    Videotex networks.
Bown, H.G.; O'Brien, C.D.; Sawchuk, W; Storey, J.
  IEEE Trans. Consumer Electronics CE-25(3), 256-268, July 1979.
    Telidon: a new approach to videotex system design.
Buscain, Alison.
  Aslib Proc. 37 (6/7), 249-256, June/July, 1985.
    Videotex systems and data access methods: a state of the art review.
Chambers, John P.
  IEEE Trans. Consum. Electron. CE-26, 527-554, August 1980.
    Enhanced UK teletext moves towards still pictures, Appendix A "A draft
    amended UK teletext specification".
Childs, Geoff.
  Computer Communications 5(5), 226-233, October 1982.
    The European videotex standard.
Clarke, K.E., Childs, G.H.L.
  In Proc. 4th Internat Online Mtg, London, December 1980, published by
  Learned Information, Besselsleigh Rd., Abingdon, Oxford, OX13 6EF. Pps
  137-145.
    The future of videotex.
Clarke, K.E.
  Radio & Electronic Engineer 52(2), 59-66, February 1982.
    Videotex display technology.
Ettema, James S.
  J.Broadcasting 28(4),383-395, Fall 1984.
    Three phases in the creation of information inequities: an assessment of
    a prototype videotex system.
Fedida, S.
  PO Research Dept. report No. 564, October 1976. Published by the Post Office
  Research Centre, Martlesham Heath, Ipswich, England, IP5 7RE.
    Viewdata and teletext as complimentary information systems.
Fedida, S.
  In Elton, Martin C.J; Lucas, William A., et al (Eds). Evaluating new
  telecommunications services. Plenum Press 1978. pps 531-561.
    Viewdata networks.

Fedida S.
  Wireless World 83(1494,1495,1496,1497) pps 32-36, 52-54, 65-70, 55-60,
  Feb-May 1977 (Note non-sequential page numbering in issue 1497). 84(1508),
  44-48, April 1978.
    Viewdata: the viewdata computer.
Fedida, S.
  In Viewdata 81. Published by Online Conferences Ltd, Pinner Middlesex,
  England. pps 523-536. 1981
    Videotex gateways: commercial significance and economic
    criteria.
Frandon, P.; Chauvel, G.
  IEEE Trans. Consumer Electronics CE-25(3), 334-338, July 1979.
    Antiope LSI.
Hamming, R.W.
  Bell System Tech. J. 29(2), 147-160, 1950.
    Error detecting and error correcting codes.
Hunter, P.N.
  Aslib Proc. 37 (6/7), 277-280, June/July, 1985.
    Trends in private viewdata systems.
Jacobs, C.H.
  Aslib Proc. 37 (6/7), 273-276, June/July, 1985.
    Fourth generation videotex.
Keith, Michael;.Siracusa, Robert.
  Report from RCA Laboratories, Princeton, NJ, USA. 1984
    Design and implementation of NABTS teletext decoder software.
Kinghorn, J.R.
  IEEE Trans. Consum. Electronics CE-30(3), 437-441, August 1984.
    New features in world system teletext.
Marti, Bernard.
  Telecommunications Policy 2(2), 60-64, April 1979.
    Videotex developments in France.
Metcalf, A.J.
  Aslib Proc. 37 (6/7), 267-271, June/July, 1985.
    Installing and managing an in-house viewdata system.
Mochizuki, Tamotsu, et al
  Rev. Elec. Comm. Labs. 32(6), 1044-1050, 1984.
    Digital videotex system.
Nicol R.C., Fenn, B.A., Turkington, R.D.
  Radio & Electronic Engineer 51(10), 514-518, October 1981.
    Transmission techniques for picture Prestel.
Sheltzer, Alan; Hinden,Robert; Brescia, Mike.
  Data Communications, pps 111-122, August 1982.
    Connecting different types of networks with gateways.
Shimell, Paul F.
  In Videotex 84, pps 283-298. 1984.
    Gateways, road blocks, access points, and a route guide to better
    internetworking.
Tateki, Inada,
  In Proc. Videotex 84 International, Amsterdam. Published by Online
  Conferences Ltd, Pinner, Middlesex, England, 1984. pps 1-10. 1984.
    Captain progress & prospects in Japan.
Truxal, Carol.
  IEEE Spectrum 19(11), 52-56, November 1984.
    Americanizing videotex.
Vivian, R.H.
  Proc. IEE 129 Pt.A (7), 545-548, September 1982.
    Enhanced UK teletext: level 4 alphageometrics.
Wells,James M., Clarke, Keith E.
  IEEE Spectrum, 18(1), 14-15, January 1981.
    Forum: videotex debated.

CHAPTER 24. MICROFORM SYSTEMS AND MARKETS

DEFINITIONS, HISTORY, AND PRELIMINARY REVIEW

Although the first patent for microfilm was granted in 1859, and was used in an often quoted episode during the Franco-Prussian war to send carrier pidgeon messages from besieged Paris in 1871, little use of the technique was made until microfilming was carried out in libraries during the first world war to ensure the preservation of important material. Wider use came with the Kodak Recordak continuous microfilm recording camera developed in 1927. This camera was used in 1928 to photograph cheques. Microform images were viewed in a US court to identify endorsements in a fraud case in the following year.

In the 1930s an American, Eugene Power, realised that microfilming could be used to bring copies of documents in European libraries to US libraries. He founded University Microfilms, still thriving today, to do the job.

Atherton Seidell used film strips called Filmstats in a microform system in 1935 and in 1939 he microfilmed periodicals at the US Army Medical Library, later to become the National Library of Medicine. During the 1939-45 war, microfilming of air-letters was extensively carried out for weight-reduction purposes, but microforms did not become generally used until well after the war.

<u>Micrographic Systems</u> provide for the creation, processing, retrieval, and reproduction of small images for viewing. <u>Microforms</u> are photographs of images, often from printed pages, which have been reduced in size for easier storage. Special machines are available for photography which usually operate on a step and repeat basis using either a flat bed or rotary method.

Film

Microforms may be produced as image frames on 35mm roll film typically 30 metres long, contained in a cassette or cartridge. The film can be run through a motorised viewing machine which may have facilities for frame selection using a code, such as a bar code, signifying indexing terms which were filmed with the image. The machine stops at those frames containing terms selected from a keyboard and a frame is reproduced at a convenient size for viewing by means of a light source, optical system and viewing screen. Some machines provide for the printing of a copy of the image.

Fiche

Alternatively microforms may be produced in flat film format. With <u>Microfiche</u>, the most common, a number of images are stored on a piece of photographic film, typically as a 6 x 4 inch film card. A popular reduction size is x 42 with 208 frames per card. Size reductions have been used down to about x 140 providing 3200 frames per card (NCR PCMI ultra-fiche).

In a manually operated fiche-viewing machine the wanted fiche is roughly identified visually and the card, mounted on a movable carriage, is moved around beneath the viewing machine until the required frame is positioned for the projection of a magnified image, usually on a screen which is part of the machine.

Colour fiche

Colour fiche and colour fiche viewing equipment are available although not yet widely used. A x 24 reduction fiche at a processing cost of 2 cents per frame will probably become the most popular.

Computer Output Microfilm (COM)

The rate of production of microfiche has been increased by the Computer Output Microfilm (COM) technique in which images on a Cathode Ray Tube are successively microfilmed by a step and repeat camera at 250 frames per minute or more. The CRT is driven by a computer with software to control the generation of the images at high speed from data on tape. Alternatively a film image may be created by a computer controlled laser beam writing on to thermally dry-processed film. COM fiche cards usually contain 270 images at x48 reduction, or 208 at x42. An eye-legible title is provided at the top of each card.

There are probably some thousands of COM users in Europe, and perhaps 20,000 or more in the US, the majority using COM bureaux production services. COM catalogues are fairly widely used in libraries where space saving and up-dating convenience may outweigh user resistance.

Computer Input Microfilm (CIM)

CIM is a term usually used to describe equipment which scans microfilm and converts the images to analogue or digital data to be telecommunicated for reconstruction remotely or stored for further processing. Compuscan, Digiscan, IBM and others manufacture equipment for this purpose.

Fiche retrieval systems

In the late 60s and 70s, the microform world received the impact of convergence, integrated circuits, compact reliable electronics etc., and this led to the production of a number of automated viewing systems. Typically these systems consisted of an electrically operated magazine, "carousel" style, for holding a number of fiche cards, and a computer based indexing and retrieval system for selecting a fiche by means of a code associated with it. The fiche was then rapidly selected and projected from the computer-controlled carousel.

The computer, operator's terminal and fiche machine could be in the same room or on different sites with the machine accessible from several remote viewing CRT terminals. The selected image would be transmitted to a terminal CRT, television fashion, via a telecoms link. One such machine, the Automated Microfiche Terminal, developed by GEC-Marconi, embodied a magazine housing 128 x 3500 fiche frames – a total of 448,000 A4 frames. The machine responded to a seven figure instruction which caused a particular frame on a particular fiche card to be positioned under the optical system within a few seconds.

A somewhat similar system was developed by Stabletron in the UK and marketed by Antone. The system comprised a carousel and an electronic image storage arrangement. An image of a frame selected by the computer-controlled carousel could be viewed remotely over a high resolution TV system beside terminal 1 while another frame was being selected by terminal 2. With storage for several images the "store and hold" facility meant that the carousel was freed for on-going selection by any terminal while other viewers were gazing at their stored pictures, selected earlier. Interconnection was by high resolution TV over a wideband link. The device also embodied facilities for overlaying separately generated text on to fiche images.

A carousel manufactured by Image Systems became quite widely used in a number of automated systems. For example the Daily Mirror newspaper group used ten carousels controlled by a Univac computer for a morgue file. About 15 "Telefiche" systems, made by Planning Research Corp., were in use in the US in 1979. In this case characters from a fiche were digitised, the fiche having been selected from a remote terminal. Data was sent along a telephone line to be displayed near the remote terminal.

Various combinations of microform image systems, computers, telecommunications systems etc., have since come into use in which the microform element has become one component in several converging technologies.

ADVANTAGES OF MICROFORMS

Information can be stored on microform very cheaply. The comparative costs of media storage for 1 Mbyte (1979) were estimated as in Table 24.1. Since then disk storage has become cheaper but still leaving microform with a clear advantage. 1 Mbyte represents a page of text/graphics of fair quality. However even if the quality was

	$
Microfiche	0.3
Floppy Disk	20
Mag.tape	5.2
8Mb diskpack	9.6

TABLE 24.1. COSTS OF STORAGE.

improved for the reproduction of high quality, the fiche cost would not increase much, always assuming that the costs of preparing the master fiche are defrayed over a number of copies.

Huge amounts of information can be stored in a small space. Fiche is cheap to store, cheap to airmail, and rapidly produced. With optically viewed fiche the expense of high resolution and inherently wide bandwidth needed for comparable transmission and reproduction in electronic systems is absent.

However it is the complex mix of cost, convenience, competition and social and behavioral factors which determine whether a particular technology becomes widely adopted. It would seem that fiche could replace images on paper for many applications. Badly needed storage space could be released for other purposes in offices, libraries etc. I still have a 2" x 2" fiche, used at one time as an advertisement by a fiche supplier, containing the 800,000 words of the Bible on 1245 pages - an area reduction of 62,500 times. At this reduction the contents of the British Museum library could be stored in a few filing cabinets.

You would think that a fiche cabinet surrounded by microform viewing machines would by now be commonplace in libraries and offices. This would result not only in space economy but also in many fringe benefits such as ease of handling, low cost of storage space, easier administrative control etc. The fact is that such a scenario is not commonplace.

DISADVANTAGES OF MICROFORMS

The reasons for the unpopularity of microforms compared to print on paper seem to be as follows:-

1. Some microform originals or some viewers produce fuzzy images. Some are difficult to use or cannot be viewed off-axis.

2. The wanted image may take time to find. Special attention must be paid to the overall speed of microform retrieval because unlike print on paper, images are not immediately visible. Perhaps the special need for good indexing does not receive the attention it deserves in some systems.

3. You cannot annotate or make marks on microforms.

4. Microforms are not portable. You cannot read them in the train or the loo (UK/US translation = john).

5. Cross referencing, scanning, browsing etc., is not so convenient. This indicates an even greater need for good indexing.

The unpopularity of microforms for users have prompted many articles. At a

conference of the National Micrographics Association, the audience was asked to
indicate personal possession of a microform viewer. Disastrously, only two hands
went up. Pawsey, a librarian at the Rolls Royce research centre, published a
report which gave the reasons for the limited use of US government reports
supplied on fiche. It included some of those given above.

FURTHER REVIEW

Now that you have read about microform techniques, I can bring the
preliminary review at the beginning of this chapter up to date.

The Annual Review of Information Science and Technology prepared under the
aegis of the American Society for Information Science includes chapters about
basic techniques and technologies. A chapter about Microforms appeared in 1969,
and in 1970, 1971, 1973, and 1976. The decreasing frequency of the chapters and
then their absence from 1977 onwards and the decreasing number of references to
microforms in the comprehensive index provided with each edition are interesting.
In the 1969 review chapter, the writer concluded "Microform technology is not
well. It is a field riddled with unsystematic disconnected collections of
gimmicks masquerading as systems".

In the most recent (1976) review, the writer concluded "Microform has almost
disappeared. The most important trend has been and will continue to be the
interaction of microforms into larger information systems...the real growth will
come from the "disappearance" of microforms by integration into systems where
they are appropriate". He forecasted, possibly correctly, the greater use of
COM, and incorrectly, its increasing use for document delivery in conjunction
with online retrieval systems.

In 1980, Bernard Williams, the leading UK microform authority, wrote a
defensive article in the face of what he called "microchip jitters". He claims
that the steady growth of about 20% per annum continues and that microforms have
come into widespread use for the storage of business documents, providing several
examples, and citing situations where microforms score –

1. For storage and retrieval of engineering drawings, maps, plans, and
similar documents.
2. As a third mode of computer output complimenting paper and online
access.
3. For publications where demand in printed format would make production
uneconomic.
4. For utility publishing of items like parts lists, patents, theses, etc.

Williams admits that although viewing devices have improved they need to be
better but considers that neither print nor microfilm will be easily displaced.
However he anticipates inroads from videotex and videodisk.

The various comments cited above were made a long time ago in ITT
(Information Technology Time). As much happens in one IT year as in two ordinary
years, so things obsolesce twice as fast. IT time = Real Time x 2. The number "2"
is called Cawkell's multiplier (Maybe it should be 3, but did I hear you say "I
never heard of it?"). Thus in 1985, a 1984 reference is not one year but two years
out of date.

Paradoxically, the rate of change in Microforms, almost alone in IT, has
proceeded in real, not IT time – the comments cited above are not <u>that</u> out of
date. The applications of "stand alone" Microforms, as opposed to microforms with
a small m, converged with computer-based systems, are not greatly different today
to what they were five years ago. Microforms seem to have found their niche
where there is a requirement for the distribution of reference data which
needs to be periodically up-dated at intervals greater than a day or two. The

up-dating costs are low; massive quantities of information on cheap fiche
cards are simply replaced by massive quantities of information on new ones sent
by post. People will put up with reading a few lines of references or
component data on a viewer, knowing that it is up to date.

For page by page reading, microforms are sometimes used in libraries
to provide access to a very large collection of documents or books. It may
not be possible to justify the storage cost of print on paper for massive
volumes in city centres for public useage when the demand is relatively small.
A cabinet of fiche and a viewer may be a cost-effective substitute if the once
only filming and indexing cost can be justified; the filming job may, of
course, already have been done elsewhere. Library clients, confronted by the
decision that they can have access to a collection - for example of UK House
of Commons proceedings (Hansard) - which otherwise could not be on site, have to
use the microform viewers.

In a well argued article, Blick discusses the standard library problem about
what to do about the constant pressure for more shelf space for journal issues.
He decided to subscribe to the fiche edition as well as to the hard copy of each
journal, discarding the hard copies after 3-5 years; he provided manually
operated readers for library users and a reader-printer for library staff for the
supply of hard copy of old journals to users when requested.

Most journals can be purchased alternatively on fiche. The cost of hard copy and
fiche editions for some typical journals
are shown in Table 24.2 (after Blick).
The net extra cost of this policy was 7.5%
on to the primary journal budget excluding
the reduced costs of inter-library loans
and saved space. Positive fiche (i.e.
black print on a white background) was
preferred. Blick stresses the need to
carry users with you when introducing
fiche and states that not only will the
library now have substantial back runs
but it will not require additional space for ten years. The majority of users
realised the need for the new policy and accepted it.

Journal	Hard copy	Fiche
Brit.J.Canc.	£ 85	£ 8.77*
Experientia	£122.15	£ 12.34*
J.Physiol.	£315	£ 40.26*
Bioch.Pharm.	£307.35	£146.34x
Tetrahedron	£460.98	£219.51x

*from University Microfilms
xfrom Pergamon Press

TABLE 24.2.   JOURNAL/FICHE COSTS

Public libraries use COM produced fiche for book catalogues, banks use
them for current account balances, and garages use them for parts catalogues.
Although Com/fiche systems in libraries will be around for some years, they
will gradually be replaced by terminals on-line to remote computer databases.
Computer based on-line library catalogues are one out of many services available
via the same terminal/telecoms facilities. Similarly COM and other computer
assisted microform systems will continue to be fairly widely used in Banking,
Government, Insurance, and Utilities, for accounts, correspondence, computer
assisted graphics, and micro-facsimile.

<u>EQUIPMENT</u>

<u>Today's viewing equipment</u>

Modern manual fiche viewers are compact and many produce clear images,
provided the filmed images are properly recorded, but it is not easy to produce
a really portable high quality viewer. In 1972 an ingenious attempt was made to
overcome the portability problem by Izon. The Izon book-size viewing machine
used 500 tiny lenses spaced about one inch from an image on film reduced 25
times. The screen was 7" x 9" and the lense system eliminated the need for the
usual long optical path which determines the minimum size of conventional
viewers. It was thought possible to mass produce the viewer and sell it for

around $5. By 1978 $6M had been spent on R&D, and the selling price was expected to be $250 when mass produced. Alas, the machine has not been heard of since.

Cheap hand held viewers are available and briefcase size viewers were pioneered by Visidyne in the US with its rear projection 14 inch wide screen model. One of the most popular general purpose viewers was the German CUBE, later manufactured in the US. In the UK the Saul LG16 FCA at £235 for the basic model is a good general purpose machine.

Reader-printer 35mm roll film machines have been available for many years. The film is motor driven and is rapidly passed through the machine, stopping as instructed at a selected frame. Bar codes, sensed by the selection mechanism, are recorded along the edge of the film. The selected frame is either magnified and projected for viewing and can be printed.

Automatic fiche retrieval systems have also been available for some years, as mentioned previously. A portable microprocessor controlled machine made in Germany called FACTS and sold in the UK as HYDRA for £2250 by Eurocom in the UK is an example of today's equipment. This machine embodies a large screen, keyboard, and cassette-loading retrieval system. A cassette will take 30 standard COM fiche cards so up to about 9000 frames can be stored. Normal method of use is to call up an index frame which provides a fiche number, and key that number to get the desired fiche. Retrieval time for any fiche is less than 4 seconds.

However the expected growth of automated systems of the kind described earlier, or for that matter for all types of microform systems, did not occur at anything like the rate of CRT-based image reproducing systems. From the viewer's aspect this is difficult to understand because the aesthetics, convenience, portability, and text capacity of the CRT leave much to be desired. The advantages of the printed page in respect of layout, captions, variety of fonts and information capacity are present in most fiche images, since they are usually reproductions of paper pages.

It may have something to do with people's familiarity with the CRT in another guise – the telly, the flashier (metaphorically) image of a computer terminal, or the terminal's multi-function advantage. You cannot manipulate text or blend information called from storage into the required format in a fiche system. The relatively low resolution CRT-based system is satisfactory for manipulating text, and text is more widely used than high resolution graphics. Fiche excels for the page by page reproduction of graphics.

Displacement by the Optical Storage Disk?

In mid-1984 a Kodak representative claimed that optical disks (ODs) would not displace microforms in the forseeable future. He pointed out that equipment was available for digitising microfilm so the advantages of digitisation did not lie exclusively with ODs. However his argument was mainly cost-based.

Placing the UK cost of today's optical storage work stations at £50,000, which is far higher than microform equipment with the same capacity, he also compared OD costs at £200 for 10,000 A4 documents with a £5 roll of microfilm capable of storing 50,000 A4 documents. However bearing in mind the above mentioned relationship between real time and IT time, what must be watched is the all-costs system differences when the relatively new OD systems get into quantity production. It is hard to predict a date or a cost for this event.

The MNEMOS system 6000

Large automated microform systems have been used in a limited number of applications where the need to move quantities of images outweighs first costs

- for instance for the retrieval and transmission of engineering drawings to
remote sites. However further developments in low cost electronics plus some
interesting lateral thinking have prompted the development of an entirely new
form of automated microform equipment. This device will be considered in some
detail as an example of an exercise in convergence.

     Following an R&D programme said to have cost £5M, a company owned mainly by
Combined Technologies Corporation (COMTECH) called Mnemos launched a new kind of
system in 1982 and expected to commence UK deliveries in June 1984 from
sub-contracted production carried out in the United States. The Mnemos 6000,
shown in Figure 24.1 is a work station comprising a keyboard, microcomputer,
40 character digital display strip, optical disk drive and head, and a rear
projection screen for viewing magnified microform images.

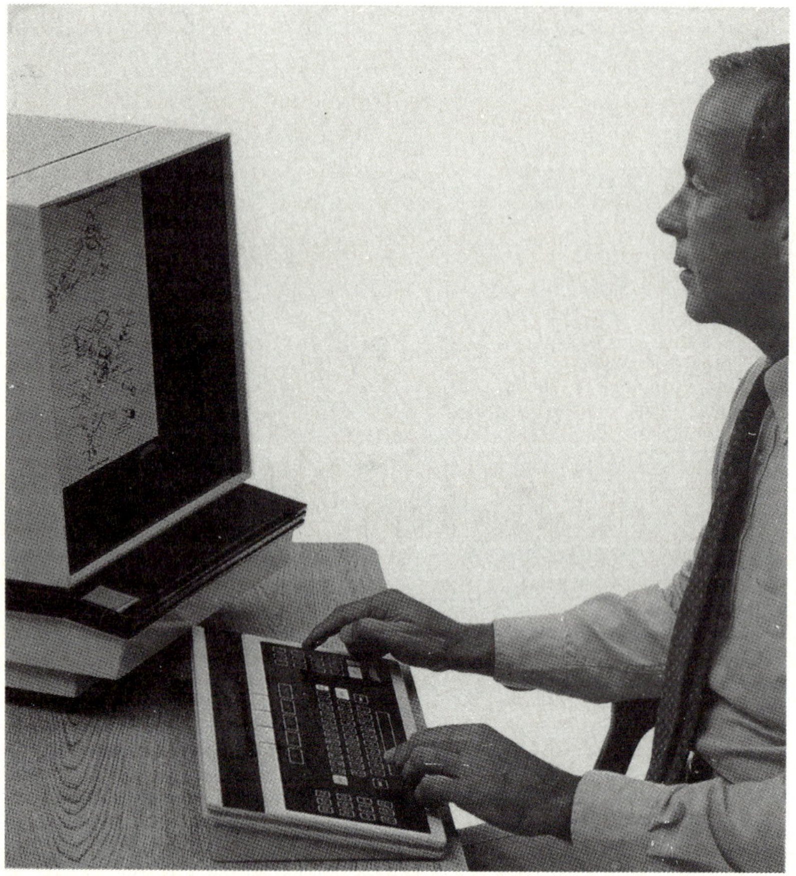

FIGURE 24.1. THE MNEMOS 6000 WORKSTATION

A different kind of optical disk

     The flexible transparent disk is housed in a jacket with a radial slot
for optical access, looking rather like a large floppy disk, ready for loading
into the work station. The outermost ring (annulus) on the disk contains moiré
fringes - a "watered silk" pattern of lines spaced with great accuracy which
are detected by a light beam projected through a hole in the disk cover. This
provides a reference for very accurate disk positioning. Glass master disks   are

prepared from customer taped data at Mnemos using a computer-controlled electron beam. Replicated plastic disks can be cheaply generated from them; Mnemos claim a fifty year life for these disks. Only Mnemos can make the master disks. A set of concentric rings in the middle area of the disk contain transparent microform frames recorded at x 88 reduction from which an image under the Reading Head (RH) may be projected on to an integral viewing screen.

The innermost set of rings (see Figure 24.2) contain optically readable bar codes from which indexing, software, or other data may be read. Bar codes are scanned, when illuminated, by a 2048 element Charge Coupled Device (CCD). Up to about 6000 microform frames plus 150 Kbytes of bar code data can be stored on one disk; alternatively fewer images, say 4000, with more data, say 2 Mbytes, can be stored. The positioning of the CCD scanner and light source relative to a particular bar code or microform frame is set by controlling the angular rotation of the disk and the radial movement of the CCD/ light source head.

The user proceeds by successive choices from menus on the work station until the required microform page is projected - a retrieval principle used in many information systems. Instructions, prompts etc., are presented on the digital strip display. Retrieval is effected under the control of "housekeeping" software and indexing data contained in the bar codes.

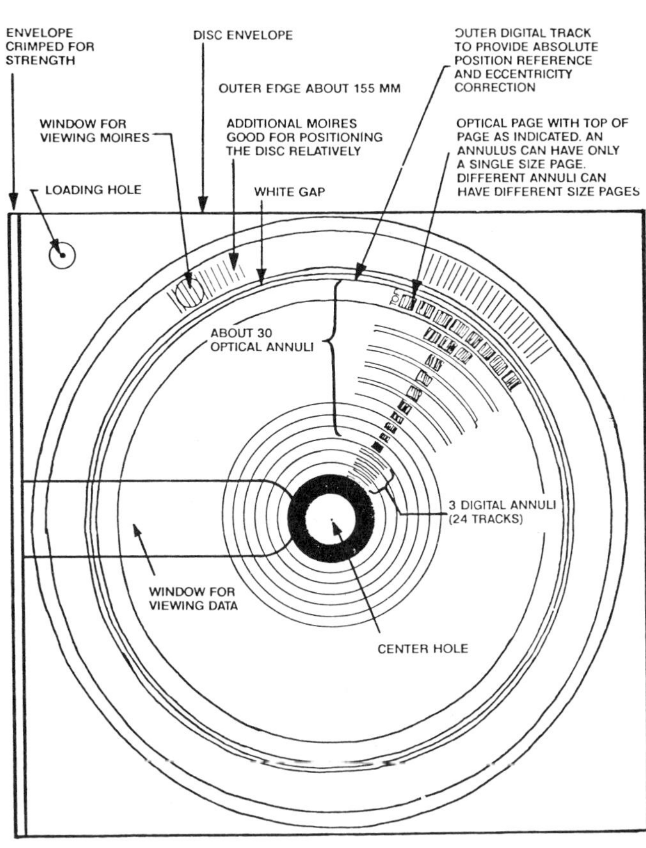

FIGURE 24.2. THE MNEMOS DISK

When switching on, the CCD reads data from the "starting" codes which cause the microcomputer to generate an appropriate message on the work station. The user types a command which causes the disk to rotate through an exact angle of up to 360 degrees; it then stops, presenting a radial line under the CCD. The CCD moves radially across the disk to the selected bar code instruction which controls the next event – a disk/head movement to home on to a microfilm image. The image is automatically focussed and projected on to the screen with a resolution equivalent to 200 lines per inch. The user views the projected image and presses keys accordingly. The machine then proceeds through another similar cycle. A selection cycle following a key depression takes about one second.

With conventional microform or automated microform systems indexing is tied to the indexed item. To find an item in a manually operated fiche system, items can only be ordered by one attribute - e.g. alphabetically by first letter. An eye-visible header is provided on each card e.g AA-AF, AG-AK etc. With an automated fiche or roll film system, optically readable marks are made on each frame. This causes the film to run until the wanted frame is detected.

The Mnemos 6000 provides the well known benefits of microforms e.g. access to a huge volume of graphics or text with high resolution occupying a very small space. Information can be changed at low cost (provided overhead disk preparational costs are spread across a large number of users) by a disk re-issue.   The additional dimensions are the separate index, also changeable by a disk re-issue, with   fast menu-driven information retrieval from a large database without telecommunication costs or hassles, but with telecom interconnections to other systems if needed.

This arrangement permits a synergistic set of operations associated with, say, the identification and ordering of a spare part from a captioned engineering drawing. Menu driven access to areas of, say, a car, shown as a series of drawings would be simple. The user would first key a number on a menu listing a choice of major areas of a car which would take him to an exploded drawing showing numbered component parts. The strip display would prompt "type the reference number of the wanted part". The user would then be taken to the parts list page on which a description and reference number for the part is given with a prompt "type the reference number, and press ORDER". The user would type the number and order the part by pressing a key pre-programmed either to display details to a person working at the storage racks (or to have it brought to him by a automated stock selection/conveyor system) or to enter it into the ordering system if not in stock.

Note that two different kinds of access are provided - from menu choice, or from keying a string of characters (when ordering a part by reference number). The mind boggles at the time which could be saved by such an operation compared with the sequence of operations needed on every occasion that a customer goes to the stores in a garage to obtain a part.

For, say, drug manufacturers, special secure indexing and search pre-programming could be provided for each manufacturer to a common database, all provided on one disk. If a database with graphics is required, the Mnemos system obviously has a unique edge - for example structural diagrams and other illustrations could be included in the drug manufacturer's database.

The Mnemos 6000 is aimed at organisations which need to distribute large volumes of information to many users, for example by publishing complex parts catalogues, timetables, patent legal or financial abstracts, price lists, engineering drawings, academic or research papers, rate tables, directories - in short, any high volume information with widespread distribution. The selling price per work station was originally expected to be $3000 in small quantities. At £1200 per master disk and £12 per copy the total price per copy for 500 stations would be $15 per disk.

It takes time to pursuade one of the relatively small number of potential customers for a system on this scale that it meets their needs. By the end of 1984 not one order had been received and Mnemos's recorded a loss of £2.26M in the first half of the year. Manufacturing for pilot installations started and an agreement was concluded with Sperry for selling to the US military market. The company remains confident of success and seems to be prepared to continue to fund the project. Meanwhile there is always the possibility that a competitor may emerge who has adopted cheaper, newer, technologies. Perhaps a customer will be using the system this year - an event awaited with great interest.

Rank Cintel Retriever

The latest example of convergence at work in the microform business comes from Rank Cintel, world leader in the production of telecine machines and earlier pioneer of electronic timer/counters. Rank Cintel have returned to the higher reduction factors of former microform systems by adopting a x 215 reduction and recording on 8 inch long 35mm film strips with over 3000 frames per strip. 300 or more strips are housed in a drum-type magazine so that the capacity of one magazine is one million or more micro-images of A4 originals.

The Retriever, announced in late 1984, uses a 1728 element CCD scanner shifted up the image to generate 2287 lines to produce a 4 Mbyte very high resolution display. The required image is selected by keyboard command which causes a film strip to be pulled out of the magazine on to a platen for scanning. The image is presented on a raster graphics CRT workstation in about six seconds and is identified by a code recorded with it which provides its column and row number on the film strip.

CCD scanning has become almost the standard method in facsimile machines and although the Retriever can produce higher resolution pictures than are called for in the Group 3 fax standard (see Chapter 9), the machine can be set to generate Group 3 code. Disk storage sufficient for several hundred pages will be provided for at leisure viewing while the machine is being used by someone else.

The machine itself is expected to cost around £50,000, but not unexpectedly a work station with this order of resolution will be expensive - around £10,000. Clearly the required resolution is pushing the CRT display to its limits. Photographic recording, to be carried out at Crawley, Sussex, will cost about 3.5p or about 4 cents per image.

FURTHER READING

Blick,A.R; Ward S.M.
   Aslib Proc. 36(4), 165-176, April 1984.
   A microform policy to reduce the physical growth of industrial libraries.
Grimaldi, John E.
   J. Imaging Technology 10(4), 143-145, August 1984.
   How does one store color business graphics? - computer generated color microfice.
Pawsey, Gwyneth
   Report number RR(OH) 233, December 1965. Published by
   Rolls Royce Ltd., Advanced Research Dept, Old Hall,
   Littleover, Derby, England.
Spang, Lothar; Collier, Monica; Thompson, Donald D; Dwyer, James R; Boss, Richard..
   ASIS Bulletin, 7(1), 11-30, October 1980
   Special section on micrographics.
Williams, Bernard.
   Communication Technology Impact 2(7), October 1980, 1-6.
   Microfilm: a future in the age of the microchip.

CHAPTER 25. THE INFORMATION SOCIETY: TECHNICAL, POLITICAL AND SOCIAL ISSUES

> Machines are worshipped because they are beautiful and
> valued because they confer power; they are hated because
> they are hideous and loathed because they impose slavery.
> Bertrand Russell

INFORMATION, TECHNOLOGY, AND RATES OF CHANGE

In 1978 I wrote an article about forces controlling the introduction of new technology. At that time the arrival of the silicon chip, just introduced to a marvelling public, was being discussed with both optimism and foreboding. The article was entitled "The paperless revolution" and featured a machine called the Consumersole (Figure 25.1), an information interface between man and the world outside to become a reality, perhaps, by the year 2000; universal data communications were assumed to be in place. Reading this article again, I see that I took a rather gloomy view of the technological future.

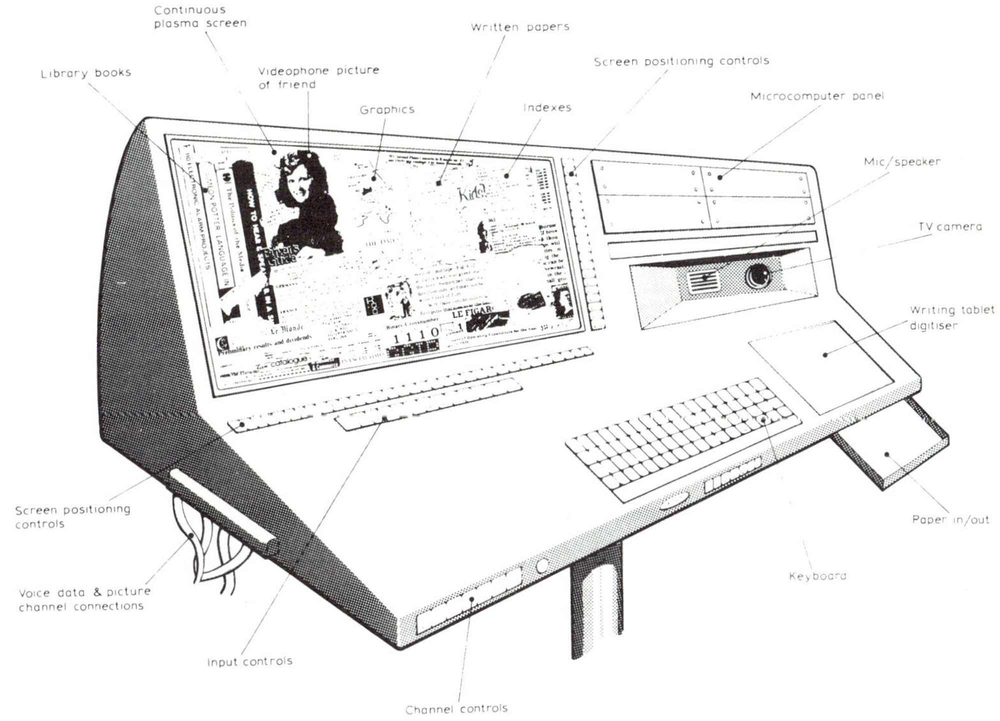

FIGURE 25.1. THE CONSUMERSOLE: A 1978 FIGMENT OF THE IMAGINATION

Information is a curious and unique resource. It is unsatisfactory to call it a commodity. You cannot evaluate it until you have obtained it; once you have it, it may be almost impossible to evaluate in monetary terms, but on other occasions there may be no doubt about its value - ask a dealer on the money market about the value to him of timely accurate information. The value of a

train time-table to a man standing on Victoria station who wants to get to Dover
is obvious. It is equally clear that the same information displayed to a Martian
is valueless. Information is destroyed when consumed and so has no scarcity value
in the usual sense, and yet the meaning of the phrase "there is a scarcity of
information about the effects of video nasties on crime" is perfectly clear.

Information is obtained for pleasure and entertainment, for monetary gain or
the acquisition of power, or simply to satisfy curiousity. Nearly always it has
to be moved before it is changed from mere data into knowledge. These days
transference often involves the use of an electrical rather than a paper-based
system.

The idea of an "The Information Society" was implicit in Fritz Machlup's
1962 work. In 1974 Marc Porat, in an unpublished paper, analysed occupations in
the United States and concluded that 50% of the labour force was engaged in
information processing occupations. Parker & Porat discussed political issues and
headed part of a 1975 article with the phrase "The Information Society".

The concept of an industry centred on a resource more important than oil -
Information - was introduced later. In the UK, Information Technology Year "IT
82" was launched to rub in the message "Britain Needs Information Technology".
We managed to get through 1984 which turned out to be rather better than Orwell's
forecast. Before considering the outlook for the rest of the decade, let me
establish my forecasting credentials, if any, by conducting a brief post mortem
on the 1978 article.

Semi-conductor technology has advanced and costs have droppped at about the
rate predicted. Expectations for bubble memories and holographic storage have not
materialised. In 1979 I made an appointment to visit the supplier of a
holographic storage device (referred to in the 1978 article) at an address in Los
Angeles. When I got there a few days later the office was closed; they were no
longer in business. Holography has recently emerged again on "smart" bank cards,
although the belief that it would be impossible to forge them is, surprisingly,
false.

The mismatch between the information processing capacity of the eye/brain
and the amount actually provided by the CRT screenful is being improved. Larger
display devices will be available rather sooner than I predicted. Teletext is
successful but Viewdata/Prestel flags, although private Viewdata-type systems are
making progress. Teleconferencing is still in its infancy and so are electronic
journals, but electronic publishing is advancing.

Electronic mail was much discussed in 1978 and it still is today; peering
through the hype I do not observe a very remarkable rate of progress. Speech
Recognition is moving slowly, also as predicted; optimistic forecasts about the
recognition of continuous speech are much the same now as they were then.

I think my end-of-term school report should read "Forecasting - very fair;
Cawkell should try harder". However it is no worse than most other forecasts, and
rather better than those mentioned below.

Wild forecasting
================

Before considering the likely rate of formation of a telecommunications
infrastructure - the backbone of the Information Society - it is instructive to
consider the development rate of other technologies. Usually they had to contend
mainly with technical and less with social and political problems - but it is the
latter which will control the infrastructure's growth rate.

In the July 1966 issue of Datamation it was stated that "economies of scale
are swinging increasingly in the direction of large computers" and in a 1970

issue of Computer Decisions "small businesses are not going to have small computers; it's not a practical way to go". In 1972 it was forecast that "40-60% of American homes will have cable TV by 1980" and at the end of 1979 a UK forecast of "100,000 Prestel sets in 1980 equally split between domestic and business" was made.

In 1979 it was anticipated that "By 1983 all the 220,000 telephone subscribers in the Ille et Villaine department of Brittany will possess desk-top video terminals costing £33 each providing access to a local and national database of telephone numbers".

All these forecasts were wildly off target.

As recently as late 1981 one pundit said that the world total for <u>all</u> types of microcomputer in use by the end of 1983 would be 4 million units costing $3550M. In 1983 another considered, presumably with up to date information, that it would be 17 million units costing $79KM (79 billion dollars). In May 1984 it was estimated that world shipments of <u>business</u> microcomputers would be nearly 6 million units (International Resource Developments). Perhaps we must be content with saying that there are now very large numbers of micros about.

The delay factor 1. Rates of change

The title of the late Arthur Koestler's book "The Ghost in the Machine" refers to the human mind dependent upon, but also responsible for, the actions of the body. These title words could be used equally well to apply to the presence left within a computer by its human programmer. But it is not the ghost who is blamed either by a customer, who gets an electricity bill for one million pounds, nor by the employee of the company who despatched it. The convenient scapegoat is "The Computer". In fact the machine is rarely at fault. There are as many human errors in bills now as there were when they were manually handled. The programmer or data keyer is responsible instead of the clerk in the billing office.

Koestler says in his book "The uncanny properties of exponential curves reflect the uniqueness of our time - not only the population explosion, but also the explosion in power, communications, and specialised knowledge". He might have added Rate of Change to that list - an aspect of modern life which has also increased exponentially to a level which is becoming unacceptable to many. Robert Lucky, a well known engineer with the Bell Telephone Labs, wrote "I myself feel blameless for all this turmoil/progress. As I look about me it occurs to me that all my friends also seem innocent. Somebody else must have done it". Ogburn, the sociologist, stated the obvious when he said that beliefs, customs, and social institutions change more slowly than the material aspects of society.

It has been suggested that the reasons for the slow introduction of IT in the UK include the recession, ignorance, difficulty of realising the benefits, suspicion of salesman, financial caution, human problems, and wariness of Trade Union activity. In the Soviet Union "the methodology of determining the national socioeconomic effect of new consumer goods must include such elements as additional costs of measures for attaining the normative socioeconomic result". Quite. But "the sharp increase in expenditure on new technology measures in a given branch (of industry)...is often accompanied by a decline of effectiveness of these measures" - and the Soviet author provides all kinds of statistics to prove it.

In the US that notable optimist H.A.Simon tells us that "thinking is a characteristic shared by man with other species, including artificial species like the computer" - a statement which I find hard to take. Simon continues poetically "as we design new technology...we will realise that we will have to apply it in a way which keeps man's peace with the universe in which he lives, instead of conceiving it as a weapon with which man can wage war on the rest of nature". Perhaps we will, but the fact is that although the rate of change is increasing there is still quite a long interval between the invention and its general use.

<u>The delay factor 2. The 10 year syndrome</u>

Forecasters are often misled by manufacturer's announcements about development work which may or may not be followed by production, limited application, and more general application. For technical and political reasons the interval between these events may be many years, but new technology announcements fuel speculative articles in the press which prompt discussion and awareness, and new products or services get talked into existence.

Euronet, already merged, and a set of separate European PTT telecommunication networks are expected to become a unified network by 1990 - 20 years after the pioneering work with ARPANET in the US. It took about 10 years before working Local Area Network (LAN) systems were installed in any quantity following the development of the ALOHA network.

The next transatlantic cable will be fibreoptic. The idea of fibreoptic communications was first mooted in 1966 and the development of more efficient monomode cables accelerated their use. Such cables started to be installed in 1980 - an interval of 14 years after the early work.

Many years passed before Clarke's 1945 forecast that global communications using three geostationary satellites would be possible. By 1980 satellites were being routinely used as relay stations in the United States. In this case it took 18 years for the idea falteringly to be realised, a further 10 years before satellites became used as telephone relay stations in the Intelsat network, and several more years for TV relay satellites to become commonplace.

The "Electronic Scientific Journal", was suggested in 1976, pioneered with mixed results in 1979-1982, and is the subject of further experiments today. It seems unlikely that the final form will replace the scientific and social functions of the conventional journal for many years.

It has turned out to be extremely difficult to design an electronic device which can recognise continuous speech from any speaker. A very large research effort seems to have produced rather limited results, reflecting the difficulty of the problem. The interval between the first substantial research work in the 70s and the application of continuous speech recognition may well be 50 years.

A recent television programme described progress with synthetic speech - a much easier achievement - and then showed the recognition of single words and short phrases by a machine which had almost certainly been preceded by a human/machine training session which was not mentioned. This led naturally to speculation and an interview, firstly with an equipment supplier about this "here and now" technology, and then with a lay audience about how comfortable they would feel when conversing with machines. This kind of "logical extension" from one thing to another against a background of impressive rows of knobs and CRT screens encourages false expectations.

Very large screen displays may become generally available during the next 5 years, 60 years after the CRT, not much changed today, was first introduced by Von Ardenne in the 1920s. Technical advances have been rapid in image processing systems but Facsimile machines of rather low resolution have been available since the 1930s. After the war, machine compatibility was the problem. The interval between the introduction of the first useable machines, the evolution of standards, and fairly widespread use in business was 50 years. The development of Teletex, (not Teletext) a system for transmitting text rapidly between

telex-replacement/word processing machines, is progressing slowly, and microforms
- around since the Franco-Prussian war - are still not very widely used.

I conclude that a significant new development in information technology
usually takes at least 10 years from point A in time to point B, where B is
useful small scale application. Point A - the "starting date" is hard to define.
It is not so much that something significant actually happens on that date, but
that a preliminary announcement about Widgetisors gets transformed into a report
that "Colossus Systems Ltd are believed to be considering the construction of a
new factory for the production of Widgetisors". The information technology
industry is skilled in convincing us that only fossilised people can afford to
ignore "imminent" developments which may still be a gleam in the inventor's eye.

However technical developments, falling costs, and a combination of other
circumstances sometimes enables something new to be offered and applied rather
quickly. If political, human acceptability, and economic factors are favourable
the offering will catch on faster - an exception to the ten year rule appears.
The micromputer is such an exception. Its brief history was described in Chapter
17.

INTERACTIVE INFRASTRUCTURES

Component parts and players

In order to discuss some of the wider issues it may be helpful to refer to
Figure 25.2 which is an attempt to look at the information world as an
interactive infrastructure.

Technical advances are a necessary but far from sufficient requirement for progressing towards an information society. The rate of advance will be much more dependent upon the interplay of the factors shown in the figure. Exceptions like the microcomputer may arise in special cases where successful applications can be independent of most of the delaying factors.

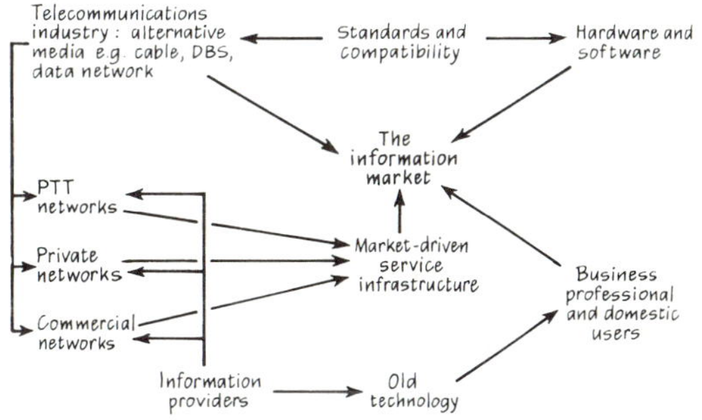

FIGURE 25.2. INTERACTIVE INFRASTRUCTURES

Two prime forms of information transport are shown - the "old technology", that is print-on-paper in the form of written letters, typed reports, printed newspapers, magazines and books, and by
the "new technology", that is radio, television, tape or disc recordings,
videotex, databases and information banks. Associated with these systems and
information channels, is the hardware and software required to put the
information into machine-readable form, process it, and convert it back into
human-assimilatable form.

The old technology is well entrenched. It has been developed by trial and
error since 1455 - when Gutenberg demonstrated the feasibility of moveable type.
A set of compromises in compilation, distribution, storage, display, aesthetics,
convenience, accessibility and cost has emerged which serves us quite well.

The new technology has been developed during the last 50 years, but 90% of
it during the last 15. In that time radio, television, automation and computers
have been followed in quick succession by pocket calculators, home computers,

online systems, word processing machines and video and optical disks, backed by a semiconductor technology proceeding at an unprecedented speed.

The general momentum of all this encourages the belief that almost anything is possible by the introduction of more technology. There is no shortage of people with vested interests in fostering that belief. However application takes time, as has been discussed already. Ordinary people get in the way. They have contra-beliefs generated both by innate conservatism and, in some areas, by well-founded scepticism. This scepticism is in part a reaction to sales razz-matazz, to the observed general mismatch between men and machines, and to the fact that for every prediction which turned out to be an under-estimate, there are several which turn out to be unduly optimistic or completely wrong.

Some years ago the phrases "Readiness Factors" and "Enabling Forces" were used with reference to teleconferencing. The similar phrases "Readiness Potential" and "Enabling Infrastructure" are apt when referring to the information infrastructure. For a new undertaking to be feasible the state of the various ingredients needed for success must be considered. A Readiness Potential exists when the development of those ingredients, considered collectively, seems to indicate that the time is ripe for launching the undertaking. They include:-

    * Processing technology (hardware & software)
    * Appropriate telecommunication facilities
    * Encouraging experimental work
    * Credible advocates and publicity
    * Optimistic forecasts
    * Apparent economic viability
    * Apparent need (Markets)

Figure 25.2 shows the factors which then control success - the factors with which the driving force - a group of manufacturers or services, or perhaps one only - must successfully contend. They seem to be :-

    * Human Factors associated with
      the use of machines
    * Reliability
    * Standardisation/compatibility
    * Success momentum
    * Political reality
    * Service infrastructure

Success momentum continues if the earlier hot air can be backed up by success in practice, with circulation of the good word, favourable technical articles and reviews, further purchases with wider useage etc. Success breeds success.

Political reality means both concentration on the art of the possible with operations managed to take advantage of PTT or government policy instead of clashing with it. Current attitudes and actions in communications deregulation, particularly in the US and UK, obviously need close attention. What should governments do and what will they actually do? You may take the view that the less a government does, the better, you may think it should have a limited role, or you may think it should intervene at all levels.

Personally I see little evidence that any government has had much success in intervening at the market level. It may result in a disaster - witness the rise and fall of Nexos in the UK. In this area of rapid changes and emerging markets, bureaucratic involvement seems unhelpful.

All governments are more or less involved with several of the areas shown on

Figure 25.2 - particularly employment in the industry, control of telecommunications, and additionally with privacy and security. Involvement in communications - because of the importance of what is communicated, particularly news - spills over into topics like data protection, the flow of information across borders, and the concern of undeveloped countries about this topic.

The government has a role in co-ordinating national and international standards. Perhaps it can best continue to do that by supporting organisations like NPL, British Standards and ISO in the UK, National Bureau of Standards and ISO in the US, and similar activities in other countries.

In the US the IEEE has succeeded in establishing standards which have become international such as the RS232 communications interface. Some manufacturers have established de facto standards such as Digital's CP/M microcomputer operating system software and IBM's SNA communication protocol. Europe often follows the US in this field although a recent attempt by IBM to formally establish SNA in the UK by an alliance with British Telecom was frustrated by one of the first major acts of the newly established UK regulatory body, OFTEL. In Europe German DIN standards have been adopted in some fields (not in information technology).

Telecommunications and the Market

A telecommunications service infrastructure will be the technological backbone of an information society. Digitised information (or, for the purists digitised data, which may be one person's information but another's noise) will flow from source to recipient. I am not referring to "service" in the "maintenance" sense (although an efficient service network in these days of increasing dependence upon machines is extremely important) but services for supplying information.

The components of a service infrastructure are;-

*   A communications network accessible to a large
    customer base offering cheap time, independent of
    distance.
*   A customer base possessing a range of compatible
    machines using standardised processing and
    communications software.
*   A number of information providers feeding information
    to the network.

When compatible terminals connected to a growing network reach a critical mass and assuming that an adequate customer base for the nth service also exists, the incremental cost to a supplier mounting that service will be low. It will ride on the infrastructure so his direct investment involves only the injection of information.

THE CREATION OF THE MARKET-DRIVEN SERVICE INFRASTRUCTURE

The economics and politics of telecommunications

Governments are of course concerned about roads, medical services, police, railways, telecommunications etc., and the question of state control has always been controversial in democratic countries. In the US, telecommunications has been in the public eye for many years. In the UK, interest is more recent. Governmental interest in information technology has grown because it is seen as a way of generating new industries and services, increasing exports, and providing new jobs to replace those lost in decaying industries. UK governmental interest in cable systems is a particular example.

The present UK government takes more of an arm's length view than has formerly been the case - in other words it is attempting to set a climate which it thinks will encourage development, rather than becoming directly involved in it - hence its action in first liberalising and then privatising British Telecom, in granting licenses for cable franchises, and so on. In the US the trend is similar with the de-regulation of AT&T. There are some signs of a move in this direction in continental Europe.

Inevitably governments have been and will continue to be involved in the provision of telecommunications through the PTT's (a European acronym which I shall use to describe all telecom authorities). Thus the creation of a suitable PTT network in Figure 25.2 depends upon the actions of PTTs/governments.

The great advantage of the international PTT telephone network is that it exists. It is far from ideal for data transmission but can be pressed into service for that purpose. Most PTTs have also created, or are in the process of creating, purpose designed national data networks. They also collaborated in Europe under EEC auspices in setting up Euronet, a network consisting of interconnected host computers in different countries running databases for information storage and retrieval (mainly scientific information) for terminal-connected users.

The conversion of telephone networks into Integrated Service Digital Networks (ISDN) - a long term objective of many PTTs - will (subject to bandwidth limitations) remove the distinction between the analogue telephone network and digital systems using a "pressed into service" telephone network.

The "Private Networks" shown in Figure 25.2 are composed of lines leased from the PTTs for inter-connecting the different sites of an organisation within a country, or may be to provide intra-organisation services for large companies, airlines etc., requiring international satellite or cable links.

The "Commercial Networks" in Figure 25.2 at present refer mainly to the Value Added Networks (VANs); developed by private telecommunication companies in consequence of de-regulation in the United States, to offer special services using lines leased from AT&T, or using satellite or terrestrial microwave communications. Some private companies have been accorded the status of "common carriers", meaning that they are permitted to carry traffic for others without having to qualify as VANs. Some companies have "nodes" - that is connection points - in Europe and elsewhere.

If these three kinds of network were interconnected so that any service available on any of them was available to all in such a way that there appeared to be a single network, then a big step towards universal communications would have been made. The critical mass of customers needed to encourage more services would appear, the system would grow, costs would fall and home services would become viable.

There are some technical problems to overcome but the main obstacles to this kind of common sense have been political. The PTTs have rigidly applied their carrier monopoly. No other organisation has been permitted to arrange communication links between service and customers. This may be a desirable objective for a universal telephone system, but the requirements for a universal network for information transmission are quite different as discussed in Chapter 6.

The question is can the existing networks be coalesced to provide the needs of the Information Society and how long is it likely to take? The "critical mass" problem mentioned previously could of course be resolved by further separation rather than coalescence. New separate networks can appear for inter-connecting a specific information source and its customers because the value of the specific information is believed to justify a specialised service.

The services available to stockbrokers in the City of London are an example.

A possible compromise would be multiple interconnected networks, each free to innovate (a huge unified network would tend to adopt communications new technology rather slowly), but with common interconnection standards and a payments clearing-house mechanism.

<u>Growth of infrastructure services</u>

Private industry is unlikely to introduce networks or services unless it considers that the market will return an adequate short or medium term profit. For PTT monopolies this aspect is less important, consequently marketing skills are also of less importance to them.

The potential advantage of the activities of government agencies in establishing a network is that the system is imposed on the population by dictat which means that it ought to be possible to install it quickly. Whether it <u>is</u> done quickly is another matter - Euronet progressed very slowly. However the launching of Viewdata/Teletext in the UK and the associated standards was done relatively quickly. There was no public consultation. The disadvantage is that in the absence of control by the market the taxpayer's money can be invested more or less continuously. Shut-down may become politically unacceptable and good money follows bad money.

It may be necessary to start up in this manner, but without commercial criteria, success yardsticks are absent. The Prestel (originally Viewdata) service would have been long since shut down had it been a commercial system since it turned out to be based on wrong expectations. Alternatively it may be argued that the foundations were set for a valuable public service.

At the end of 1983 the total number of installed local area networks and PABXs in the UK was estimated at 700 and 100 respectively. A local area network can be anything from a few microcomputers with communication software and twisted pair inter connections, to a major network.

Consider now the situation in the United States. In that country it is almost impossible to do things by dictat. Prolonged public discussion, lobbying, etc., is necessary before anything can be done. Considerable reliance is placed on market forces. That country also possesses a strong electronics industry, has a propensity to innovate, and contains a large number of people with disposable income. Together these factors may enable service infrastructures to get off the ground.

In 1980 communication networks for home computers were being operated by two companies, The Source and Compuserve. Compuserve's Micronet was interconnected with Tymnet. Charges were $5 per hour plus $2 for Tymnet. The Source and Compuserve then had about 8000 subscribers, mainly with TRS80's or Apple 2's. Compuserve offered micronet terminal programs for both machines and a videotex program for TRS80s.

The Source and Compuserve are also Information Providers. Compuserve provided a range of services included with its $5/hour fee - for instance an electronic mail service for all listed users - but charged extra for special services like access to 32,000 continuously updated stocks in its Microquote service. Detailed information about a stock cost 5c. Compuserve had also signed up other information providers, including 13 daily newspapers ,to provide current editorial information. A special service from AP was included.

Perceiving that it might have a customer base, a bank in Knoxville concluded an agreement with Compuserve and Radio Shack who supplied TRS80 microcomputers, and offered banking services for viewing statements, paying bills etc., by the page (videotex) at \$5 per hour. Users also required the TRS80's videotex program. The service included the provision of a special modem for use with a TRS80 into which a magnetic card carrying an encryption key had to be inserted. This provided a secure channel between the user and the bank. For those who did not already possess a TRS80, a service Company associated with the bank (UASC) would rent a TRS80 with the special modem at \$25/month. At that time about 300 people used this service.

It was not clear whether prices for domestic users had dropped to a level which made success probable. The fact is that a structure has been gradually assembled in which operational costs were shared by many. Consequently an information provider or customer could join at a low incremental cost. There was no public financial burden. The foundation of the undertaking was the existence of a corps of people with a common self-interest - they were computer buffs. However there is no reason why business and professional users could not use the common resource and some did. A company called UASC was offering a banking service for businesses using rented IBM displaywriters.

This kind of approach seems to be prospering. By 1983 The Source, now owned by Reader's Digest had expanded greatly and Compuserve, a subsidiary of H&R Block, had over 20,000 subscribers. Each runs a "Chat" service with a directory of subscribers, for the exchange of typed messages with any other subscriber, also classified situations vacant and news services. Compuserve offers an online encyclopaedia, and both have shop at home services listing 30,000 items in an online catalogue. The all-in price is about \$21 per hour dropping to \$6 per hour at off peak periods. Software on floppy disk for different microcomputers is available for auto-dialling, communications, moving data in or out, and printer control.

Confirmation of the prosperity of the US information industry is given by the following estimates of the value of its sectors (1980 data, figures in brackets are \$billions). Communications channel and technology providers (69.48), integrating technology e.g. packet switching (2.1), Broadcast channel (10), Information services and packages (39.6), Agencies and bureaux (25.9), Information technology providers e.g. word processors (36.8).

PAST AND PRESENT TELECOMMUNICATION POLITICS

Telecommunication Monopolies

The usefulness, modification, convergence or fusion of the networks shown in Figure 26.2 will obviously be affected by control, administration, and investment. The best way of administering a telephone system is controversial. The consensus of opinion was, and still is in countries where information technology is less advanced and in some advanced countries as well, that a regulated monopoly is the best answer.

The classical condition for a "Natural Monopoly" is a service or industry in which economies of scale make it cheaper for one organisation to produce a product or provide a service then for two or more to do so. Regulations can be imposed by the government to set prices which are in line with costs. The result, says the conventional wisdom, is a service provided at relatively low cost, obtained by regulating the prices charged by a single organisation which is able to operate at the scale needed to achieve maximum economies.

However in the case of AT&T, investigated by Meyer et al, econometric evidence is presented to show that this factor is not as important as was thought; there is little evidence of scale economies in the production and distribution of customer equipment, although there are such economies in long distance links. The effects upon scale economies by considerable competitive penetration of the market would increase estimated AT&T 1985 costs by no more than 1%. These costs could well be offset by the savings from diminished regulatory administration amounting to $100-$500 million per year.

"Cream skimming" is one of the major factors used in pro-monopoly arguments. Competitors could provide new profitable business services, eroding the incumbent's (until recently British Telecom (BT) in the UK and AT&T in the US) revenues needed to fulfill its social obligation to provide loss making rural telephone service. However "Predatory Pricing" can be introduced - a practice which may be important during a period of de-regulation - because the incumbent can afford to charge a price for a particular service at or below costs for a long enough period to drive out a less substantial newcomer who is offering a competitive service. An event which may be an example of this was AT&T's response to long line services offered by Datran in the late 70s. AT&T quoted rates claimed to be profitable, but Datran went bankrupt because these rates were intolerably low.

Meyer et al., claim that Bell did not enter rural areas originally and have not since to any great extent. By 1940 there were fewer farms on the telephone than there were in 1920. Subsequently low interest loans and technical assistance were afforded to co-operatives and local telephone companies under the 1949 amendments to the Rural Electrification Act. This assistance raised the telephone penetration level to 90%. In short, there is little evidence to show that rural phone services are receiving disproportionate help from AT&T. Even more surprisingly Mayer et al present evidence to support their claim that unit costs are not substantially higher in rural areas than in other areas.

Telecommunication monopolies are under scrutiny in developed countries. Some are making dramatic changes for reasons to be discussed.

Changing the system

The terms deregulation, liberalisation, and privatisation are used to describe the changes that are going on to change telecommunication monopolies - a difficult and controversial attempt to pursue an ideal beautifully described nearly two thousand years ago (Horace, Odes 3);-

> Who so cultivates the golden mean avoids the
> poverty of a hovel and the envy of a palace.

Deregulation means a decrease or abolition of the rules laid down by a government for the conduct of the telecoms authority. Liberalisation usually means some relaxation in the rules, particularly in regard to diminishing or removing a monopoly and allowing competition. Privatisation usually means that the telecoms authority, hitherto wholly or partly controlled by the government, will be converted into a Company controlled by its shareholders.

The major goal of people charged with formulating policy is to decide on service, commercial, and social objectives, and legislate accordingly. But as Morgan says, what is worrying is that, as yet, politicians have not on the whole understood the implications of the telecommunications revolution and are ill-suited to deal with these issues with sufficient subtlety and vision. The problems require timely and intelligent government action, whether at a national or international level.

Telecommunication monopolies: advantages

In many countries the telephone system is part of the established order of things. There has never been an alternative for comparison purposes. It works more or less adequately - major changes in such a large organisation are a step into the unknown.

In the US it was perceived that good progress was being made towards a universal telephone service from a fragmented system by regulated monopoly policies. Services improved because of the widespread adoption of standard well tried equipment. Services previously provided by a number of competing companies were at best variable and at worst incompatible.

Furthermore, regulation enabled telephone pricing policies to be dictated by a mix of demand and social considerations, rather than solely for commercial reasons - for instance to subsidise rural telephones by charging business customers more.

Telecommunication monopolies; retarding effect upon "progress"

"Progress", you understand, is what comes after what went before. My dictionary says almost the same thing - "forward or onward movement", carefully avoiding any implication that it means moving forward to something better. We must hope that it never means moving forward to something worse.

In the US the view was taken that the nature of the telephone/information transport business and the computer/information processing business are so different that they could not both be handled by a regulated monopoly.

The necessarily conservative carriers were not geared to set up new systems for businesses. Even after a considerable degree of liberalisation in the 70s permitting more attachments and competitive networks, the arrangement was still considered to be unsatisfactory.

For example in 1977 AT&T wanted to supply its customers with terminals made by its Teletype subsidiary. Competitors argued that it was entering the processing business. There was a long delay and eventually the FCC agreed with the competitors. The major benificiaries were the lawyers.

Cartoon by permission of S.Harris

In the UK, some of the problems of the Post Office (now British Telecom), were discussed by one of its strategy directors back in 1977. The absence of competition "removes information about markets which could otherwise be inferred from competitors". Government policies, which may be changed at short notice, "influence the amount of investment and borrowing...the levels of tariffs...the procurement of equipment...and the boundaries of business". The UK Post Office "...lays down procedures for its 237,000 staff in 112,000 separate instructions varying from 1 to 100 pages in length...whose working lives are spent usually in a single organisation. Size, complexity, plant life of 40 years etc., all "militate against rapid change".

Telephone authorities may be required, at the same time, to break even or be profitable, and yet to pursue policies, however desirable, which are designed to lose money. According to one report it cost the Post Office an average of £400 to provide a new telephone line, yet in the interest of universality, the installation charge was £40.

Egalitarianism requires the generation of wealth to support it. The wealth generators have to compete internationally, and for them a poor telecomms system is an expensive overhead. The competitiveness of UK and European industry depend in part on the efficiency and related costs of the telecommunications services at their disposal, especially compared with the US and Japan. The UK and European computer, telecommunications and electronics industries need to expand at a rate to match world demand so as to provide substitute jobs for those being abolished in declining industries.

<u>The United States; governmental style</u>

Deregulation in the US has been in progress for some years. The methods chosen, were, of course, closely linked to the style of government.

Freedom of speech and of the press referred to in the first amendment to the US Constitution extends to electrically transmitted information (<u>Winters v. New York</u> 1948). The court held that one person's entertainment may be another's doctrine.

In the communications area, issues set out in the 1934 Communications Act were, as one report put it, "adjudicated, investigated, prosecuted, negotiated, settled, or informally acted upon" by the Federal Communications Commission (FCC), and are reviewable by the court of appeals and ultimately by the Supreme Court.

The FCC was set up by Congress in 1934 to regulate communications, an action which must have been influenced by the earlier important <u>Smith v. Illinois decision</u> (1930). This made it mandatory to recover some of the cost of local calls by charging higher prices for long distance calls. The FCC now handles broadcasting, cable, common carrier, and safety and service matters in the United States. With the increasing complication of communication issues the regulatory procedures are laborious, costly, and time consuming.

<u>The United States; winds of change</u>

In the 1960's the US telephone network started to be pressed into service for data transmission since it was the only ubiquitous network available. New requirements prompted the following questions. First, would consumer's needs be best fulfilled by entrusting all services to the traditional carriers, and second, was it rational to extend the monopolistic structure to the closely associated information processing technologies covering devices and services like modems, terminals, private line and microwave facilities, special data services, communication satellites etc? The FCC held its first and second computer enquiries in 1971 and 1976. These enquiries had a great effect on the formulation of policy.

It became evident that the convergence of communication and computer technologies required that the business of a "common carrier", and the regulation applied to it under the 1934 Communications Act, needed re-assessment. Not only had it become extremely difficult to determine where communications ended and processing began, but carriers and processing companies are different animals.

The carriers adopt long periods over which to depreciate their equipment (the British Post Office depreciates plant and equipment over 25 years). The organisation's finances and price structures are arranged accordingly. Obsolescence in the computer/data processing industry, on the other hand, operates on a five year or less cycle, not because equipment has by then come to the end of its useful life, but because it needs to be replaced by something better and cheaper. Steady as you go and reliable service are the watchwords of the carriers. The computer industry's are pace, rate of change and attention to marketing.

The wind of change which first blew in the United States, was not generated so much because the regulated monopoly principle for a telephone network was found wanting, although it had its critics, but because of converging technology. The answer to the question "Where have all the boundaries gone?" was "Stolen by engineers - every one!"

The telephone system, once a definable entity, had become an information system. The interwoven issues are complex and the outcomes are of the greatest importance, but, it was said, "commercial considerations indicate that the role of government lies in formulating generous and international telecommunication policies.

The United States: action

A huge opinionated literature exists about ways to provide satisfactory communication services for all. One opinion, unsurprisingly from IBM (Branscomb), is that "any entrepreneur should be permitted to purchase these facilities (electronic highways), utilize them to support any end application he has in mind, and offer the entire application to the public without any form of regulatory impediment".

The outstanding problem in the US has been in differentiating between data transport and data processing in order to formulate a regulatory policy appropriate to different kinds of organisation. Common carrier monopolies have a capital to annual turnover ratio of about 3:1 (Hartley's first law). The ratio for most industrial and commercial organisations is about 1:3. US tax laws relating to amortisation in the two cases is quite different.

Two paths to a solution have been sought. First, the monopoly of the carriers was allowed to be eroded. In 1968 the FCC allowed competitive devices to be connected to the existing telephone network (The "Carterphone" decision) and events were set in motion to allow Microwave Communication Inc. (MCI) to offer long distance links with distribution through local telephone lines. Liberalisation with cream skimming safeguards to ensure that the carriers offered a universal telephone service continued.

Second, several attempts were made to re-write the 1934 Communications Act, but only relatively minor amendments were enacted until the passage of the Telecommunication Competition and Deregulation Act through the Senate in October 1981.

The relatively minor changes made during the period preceding the major changes introduced by this Act were highly controversial. For example AT&T's chairman of the board John de Butts said "By fragmenting responsibility for service, those (FCC) decisions jeopardise its quality. By encouraging wasteful duplication of facilities they add unnecessary costs to the nation's telephone bill. A continuation of these policies....will produce significantly higher charges - primarily for 68 million telephone users".

Raymond Kraus, an ex-Bell employee turned consultant, waxes almost lyrical:- "The Bell Laboratories is the most unique, prestigious, and efficient communications organisation of its kind by several orders of magnitude. It has produced more Nobel and other award winners, more scientific discoveries and breakthroughs, more new apparatus developments, and more new systems and subsystems than all the other telephone laboratories in the world put together".

On the other hand ex-FCC bureau chief Walter Hinchman thinks that "The Bell system companies - under AT&T management - collectively enjoy control over every aspect of U.S. telecommunications service; equipment manufacturing and supply, local exchange service, long-distance service. This bottleneck control is a major and growing threat to the increasingly vital information handling component of the American social, economic, and political system".

And with respect to allegedly selfish system development, Carlson Agnew remarked "AT&T favoured a low orbit (satellite) system...the equipment used in such a system would have been part of the company's base rate, thereby enabling it to earn a larger return than on a geostationary system...AT&T and Bell Labs had a substantial financial and even personal commitment to the low orbit technology (some would see this as evidence of the not-invented-here syndrome)...much of this behaviour is consistent with more general predictions as to the behaviour of regulated firms".

In August 1982 a Justice Department/AT&T anti-trust suit was settled by a decree issued after lengthy hearings under Judge Harold Green. It provided for the divestment by AT&T of its 22 operating companies. AT&T was allowed to provide equipment and services for the computer and data processing business, although it was not allowed to provide electronic publishing services, such as videotex, for 7 years. A number of other conditions were included, but the general effect is to allow others to compete in areas where AT&T had a monopoly, while allowing AT&T to compete in fields which it was not allowed to enter previously.

This disentangling operation is the largest since the dismantling of the Rockefeller Standard Oil Empire decades ago. AT&T's revenues were nearly $65 billion in 1982, with assets at around $150 billion. The privatisation of AT&T's local operating companies placed $120 billion in the hands of shareholders during 1984.

One effect is expected to be an increase in the charges of local calls since the latter will no longer be automatically subsidised. There have already been some repercussions. A gentleman's agreement between AT&T and ITT was established many years ago whereby AT&T would not compete in ITT's overseas markets. In the new situation each is now turning its attention to what has been, until recently, the other's preserve. AT&T's chosen method of doing this relatively quickly is to join forces with Philips with the objective of joint production of a digital telephone exchange. BT may now find it even harder to make any progress with exports of System X, aimed at the same market.

As Mayer says "This is an industry in a state of change with many attendant uncertainties best resolved by proceeding with the market tests that have been started during the last decade. So far the industry has not crumbled because of these experiments....many ways can be identified, moreover, to remedy any adverse developments if, by chance, they do occur....there is considerable reason to believe that the market test will end up where free markets usually do, with the most efficient producers, and therefore consumers as well, all benefiting". This last phrase suggests that Mayer's political pursuasions, are, shall we say, to the right of centre - a thought confirmed by the complete absence of any mention of the future for AT&T's employees. Perhaps Mayer may consider that this is so assured that it needs no mention.

Any UK investigator dealing with this topic could hardly ignore the views of over 400,000 highly unionised employees in British Telecomm and the Post Office or the view of the Labour Party which would probably try to undo any undoable parts of the present administration's deregulation attempts if returned to power.

The United Kingdom: governmental style

Quite apart from the absence of a written Constitution, the styles of government in Britain and in the US are quite different.

The country remained outside the International Telegraph Union (ITU) for a long time because the system was privately controlled. The Telegraph Act was passed in 1863 to prevent a monopoly. At that time Britain was one of the few countries in which telecommunications were still private, although the government was closely interested. For example in 1844 the Admiralty paid half the cost of the London-Portsmouth telegraph link. This policy was completely reversed by further Acts in 1869, when communications became a state controlled monopoly on the European pattern.

The Secretary of State was responsible for the Post Office but rarely issued directives. The liability of the Post Office was limited and it had extensive monopoly rights, little changed until it was split into the Post Office and British Telecom (BT) when the 1980 British Telecommunication Bill became law in October 1981. In a way this was a return to the policies of the 1850's.

The 1981 Act did not bring with it anything resembling regular public hearings as in the USA. The opportunity to exert influence on BT was small and few people were well informed about the issues.

Another relevant factor - particularly with respect to the issues discussed in Chapter 27 - in the UK is the baleful influence exerted by the Official Secrets Act passed on the nod in 1911. There is nothing like it in the US. It covers all governmental affairs, not just national security. The government can take refuge behind it as it wishes. The scene remains Victorian in the sense that the impression conveyed by the government, of whatever party, is "we <u>know</u> what is good for you". Fortunately the administration is backed by the permanent, experienced, mainly honest civil service, so the system works much better than might be expected, but extensive public discussion, as in the US, is absent.

This climate permeates the system. For example British Telecom, then the Post Office, for better or for worse, was able with others to clear all the standardisation, regulatory, planning, system design, and implementation issues for Viewdata/Prestel quite quickly in the late 70s. There was no public discussion.

The United Kingdom: winds of change

In a press release describing the year's results just before privatisation BT claimed a number of successes. One critic disagreed using the standard anti-monoply argument; "I love to see people making money but monopoly profits are something else. A monopoly profit is the difference between how much they can get away with charging and how much they can get away with wasting. If you can't take your business elsewhere then there is no market, no competition, no price mechanism, no measure of anything. This leaves you with the last choice - the market of misery, take it or leave it".

Various criticisms were levelled at BT. Its charges for telephone services have consistently been near the top of inter-country comparison tables. Its differential pricing policy has been questioned; it was reported that the cost of a PABX per extension in London was £650, but £198 in Dublin for a similar PABX. It was suggested that this was because BT's specifications for home suppliers are unecessarily tight.

At a 1983 London conference organised by the Yankee Group, British Telecom came in for some heavy criticism. Only 16% of users thought their installation services were good, but 37% thought it   poor. Maintenance was better regarded, with 27% considering it good and 15% poor. There were several comments on the poor service associated with BT installations such as "we have lost an incalculable amount of revenue due to BTs inability to provide service" and "intolerably slow on delivery of lines". A few users made favourable remarks; for instance " we have never encountered any problems with BT in any respect".

Calculations were made showing that a London-New York private satellite link, if it was allowed, would cost £53,000 a year, compared with the BT tariff of £565,000 for a similar link. The BT price for a single circuit leased link between London and New York was £49,900 a year, while a coast to coast link of about the same length in the USA cost £4500 a year. A Financial Times correspondent complained that increases of 17% and 7% announced by BT in 82/83 were misleading. Charges in the writer's Company increased from £80,000 in 1980 to £150,000 in 1982, a compound increase of 37%.

In 1979 an "Electronic Journal" was running in the United States, and the organisers planned an experiment to connect terminals for editorial services and contributors from the UK to the system. British Telecom (BT) could not provide the interconnection, and it was planned to use the commercial network, Telenet, which had a node in the UK which needed to be connected to user's terminals via BT lines. The experiment had to be abandoned because BT vetoed the participation of Telenet as a "third party" carrier. If Telenet had been offering an Electronic Journal to UK participants - that is if it had owned the Journal's computer and facilities in the US, and was using its network to link its own customers to the system - then it would not have been acting as a third party and the veto could not have been applied.

Government policies for the Post Office "protect inefficiency, remove incentives to self-improvement, penalise consumers and lower the gross national product" - according to De Sola Pool, a well known authority, writing in 1975. For example BT added a high surcharge to certain services provided via Tymnet, an efficient US network with a London node (access point). Tymnet would not agree to it, so users had to dial the Tymnet node in Paris at a cost almost as great as the surcharge. By its action BT gained a small amount of revenue but lost the goodwill of its customers by its heavy handed action which was perfectly justifiable under the old Post Office Act. Having a captive market it did not need to be concerned with goodwill. There was no freedom of choice and so no redress.

The United Kingdom; action: A better way of doing it?

A Conservative government was returned to power in May 1979, having released a document proposing policies for information technology in the previous month. It presented the British Telecommunications Bill in November 1980, proposing to split Postal and Telecommunications services as recommended in the earlier Carter report and to allow telecoms competition controlled by the Department of Trade and Industry (DTI). Connection to the BT network would be allowed by others who could set up their own networks or services.

BT would retain its monopoly over the Public Switched Telephone Network (PSTN). The government would dispose of its shares in Cable and Wireless, the state owned overseas telecoms organisation. Competitive equipment would be introduced gradually to protect UK industry. The secretary of the Post Office Engineers Union said that its 126,000 members were fully prepared to take industrial action in order to prevent any relaxation of BT's monopoly.

In the Beesley report of April 1981 it was said that the consumer benefits of allowing competition would outweigh any BT loss of revenue. BT should be free to set prices and compete for non-voice services, subject to DTI regulation. It seemed likely that cream skimming and leased line price increases would follow.

The bill became the British Telecommunications Act on October 1st 1981.   The
Labour opposition stated that it would re-possess BT's assets without
compensation if returned to power.

The UK: Mercury

In June 1931 a consortium set
up by Barclay's Bank, Cable & Wireless and British Petroleum   sought
permission to set up a communication
network to be called Mercury, in the
first instance to link up a number
of UK cities. This would be BT's
first major telecom competitor. High
capacity fibreoptic cables would be
laid alongside British Rail lines
and the system would include microwave and cellular   radio communications with satellite extensions to
other areas. The government granted
a 25 year licence to Mercury in February 1982.

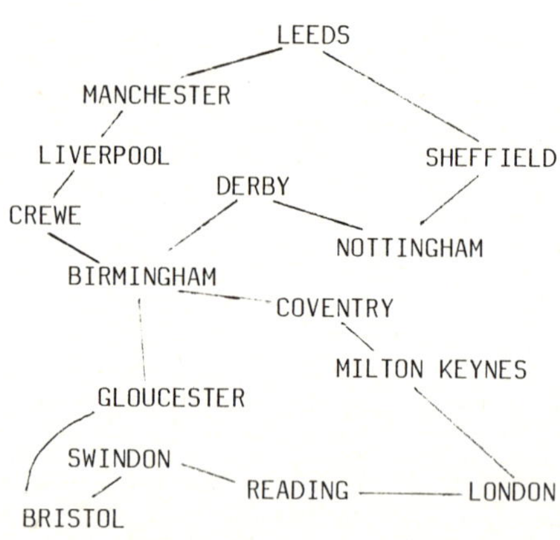

FIGURE 25.3. MERCURY'S FIRST NETWORK

Mercury started preliminary operations in the City of London during
April 1983 with a point to point
microwave service. Its proposed net-
work is shown in Figure 25.3. Later Mercury announced that it would establish a
transatlantic link via a spur from its network to an earth station in the London
docks and an Intelsat satellite.

The UK 1982 Bill and 1984 sale of BT

A new Telecommunications Bill was introduced in October 1982. Its main
purpose was to sell 51% of British Telecom - in other words to "privatise" it.
The government also proposed to set up an Office of Telecommunications (OFTEL)
early in 1984, and to grant an operating license to BT as its first act. The
Bill was lost in the general election of June 1983, re-introduced when the
Conservatives were returned to power, and received its second reading in
July 1983. It became law in 1984 and BT became a public company in August.

In 1983, Professor Littlechild, an advocate of free markets, reported as
requested to the DTI. In responding to terms of reference including "regulation
with a light rein" he said that new competitors should be encouraged, and that
for five years after privatisation BT should be required to keep its price
increases for certain services, particularly local calls and domestic rentals,
below the rise in the retail price index.

The threat of deregulation and then privatisation produced a remarkable
effect. BT concluded an agreement with SBS for a transatlantic business service
and joined a UK private consortium to provide a direct broadcast satellite (DBS).
The 18 month waiting time for services in the City of London was cut to 3 months.
BT became an agent for a multiplexer manufacturer and also became associated
with a local company in the north east for turnkey office systems.

BT started taking full page advertisements in the national press in October
1983 to advertise Teletex, satellite, facsimile, business system, Prestel, and
digital overlay services. It said it would offer complete packages to companies
for external and internal private services, the latter using Local Area Networks
(LANs) - strong competition for Mercury. Some wag suggested that all that was
needed to get the right services was simply to keep up the threat of

privatisation without actually doing it.

Also in October 1983 the government announced that BT's operating licence would include obligations to provide rural telephone services, kiosks, and emergency services, which are lossmakers. Competitors have no such obligations.

Opinions have been expressed about the timing of liberalisation, a relatively non-controversial issue, and privatisation, a controversial separate issue, but linked with or merged into liberalisation in the minds of many people. Perhaps it would have been better to let the liberalisation dust settle before risking the general muddiness produced by the rain of privatisation; no doubt the government's timing was dictated by a desire to get the job done within its present term of office.

The case against privatisation has been well presented by BT's management trade union - the Association of Telecom executives. They think that it offers no economic advantages, no benefits to the consumer, and that it will damage the British communications industry. They also think that it would offer little but insecurity to BT's employees.

FIG. 25.4. EXPERIMENTAL VOICE-CONTROLLED TELEPHONE SYSTEM AT BT RESEARCH LABS

BT after privatisation

An organisation which has for so long not needed to take much account of its customers will take time to re-orient itself. The intent is there, but the proof of ability to sell into a competitive market, if such a market really develops, is awaited.

BT's 1983/84 results showed assets at £8500M, an income at £6.87M and profit at £990M, with a return on capital of 17.7%. A 1985 profit of £1400M is forecast. In 1984 The sheer size of the share offer, expected to raise nearly £4000M was expected to cause problems - it was the largest equity offering ever made anywhere. However the sale conditions, share price, and state of the market enabled £3900M to be raised without difficulty - in fact the share price turned out to be too low.

BT ranks after AT&T and the West German and French PTT's in size. The French were way behind, but by a concentrated effort in recent years they have overtaken BT and now have more lines and more investment per line, but slightly lower revenues. BT also has a lower equipment investment per line than the other networks, a long term debt of over £3 billion, and a pension liability of over £1 billion.

Since privatisation BT has lost no time in spending some of its money on acquisitions the most significant of which is perhaps its offer to buy 51% of Mitel for £180M. Mitel is an important Canadian manufacturer of telecoms equipment and has been very successful with its PABX's. This action is currently under consideration by the UK Monopoly Commission since BT already dominates the PBX market. BT's attempt to introduce SNA on a big scale into the UK by doing a deal with IBM was frustrated by OFTEL.

It looks as if the British telecoms industry is going to pay the penalty for its protected "Buggins' turn" equipment sales relationship with BT over the years. BT orders are being placed overseas since it is now free to purchase where it likes. An important major order for new telephone exchanges has, for the first time, gone to a foreign manufacturer - Ericsson. Alternative suppliers considered were all foreign.

BT and the UK government, mainly through OFTEL, will now be playing out a balancing act. Unlike the AT&T arrangement, BT has a virtual monopoly of the voice network - a base from which to launch forays into the business telecoms area where it will meet its competitors, including the British telecoms industry. The ideal outcome would be for the UK industry to be rejuvenated by the tougher competitive climate, while the country's telephone system becomes better and cheaper. It will be interesting to see how this very large scale experiment turns out.

TELECOMMUNICATIONS; TECHNO-COMMERCIAL POLITICS

Standards

The big telecom and IT users whose traffic justifies a nationwide or international private telecommunications network can employ managers responsible for ensuring reliable service. These people lease lines, purchase equipment, organise software etc., and can control the whole system and purchase equipment in such a way that protocol and equipment incompatibility problems are avoided. These are the people who use the "Private Networks" shown on Figure 25.2 for intra-organisational communications and who are likely also to use the facilities offered by VAN vendors on "Commercial Networks". However when it comes to inter-organisation or inter-person communications they are no better off than the rest of us.

A coalescence of networks transparent to the user enabling him to send and receive data on any machine as easily as he now direct dials and talks to a friend in Hong Kong, may well be 20 years away. Incidentally the politics,technicalities, and investment needed to establish direct dial communications between users with one simple standard instrument - the telephone - took many years to complete.

Communication between machines brings in another team of players - the commercial suppliers - active in the techno-commercial political arena which is somewhat different from the "higher level" politics discussed in the previous section. Each player is trying to establish his own rules (protocols) for running a system using machines of his own manufacture so that other suppliers will have to play by those rules if they want to join the game (a <u>de facto</u> standard). At the same time he co-operates with his competitors in hammering out a consensus standard for the general benefit of the community, but without trying too hard.

Commercial suppliers have less inertia than PTTs and some are more enterprising than others. If one supplier jumps in with a system while the PTTs are still thinking about it, penetrates the market, and the system is seen to work, he can hope that the others won't re-invent the wheel and will adjust to his fait accompli. Other suppliers and PTTs can, of course, think of all kinds of reasons for ignoring this pushiness. The system may be geared to the proposer's own data processing equipment, it may be considered to be too complex or already out of date, it may give the proposer an unacceptable commercial advantage, or it may be incompatible with such standards as already exist.

The development of machines for inputting, storing, processing, and retrieving information, and methods for tranferring data from one machine to another has been carried out in a very short time in a highly competitive environment with the larger companies introducing major advanced systems incompatible with others. The sale of a number of systems is followed by the introduction of add-on bits and pieces, the whole being controlled by proprietary software. Suppliers hope that customers faced with the option of writing off their first investment and starting afresh with another supplier, or buying and using the new compatible offerings from themselves more or less painlessly, will choose the second course.

The opportunities for IBM, the most thrusting supplier, have increased with the splitting up of AT&T. Its policy - already becoming communications oriented in recent years with SNA, SBS, the PC linked to mainframes, and the purchase of Rolm, a major telecoms equipment manufacturer - has moved further in this direction with the unification of communications activities in a new division, Information Systems Communications.

For the French, and the British who rebuffed IBM's offer for SNA co-operation, further entrenchment by Big Blue was too much. Their natural support is for OSI (see Chapter 6) telecommunication and equipment standards, already way behind SNA which <u>is</u> a fait accompli. Official encouragement for SNA would put European companies at a further disadvantage. Already IBM has several big telecom projects in hand in Europe including a BT-SBS link-up and the possible adoption of SNA for inter-bank EFT purposes.

<u>The UK industry - equipment and VANs approval</u>

The industry has been strongly influenced by BT's equipment procurement policy. Until recently BT favoured well-tried exchanges of ancient design, and after some false starts put its weight behind System X, an advanced system, which eventually will enable almost anybody in the UK to couple voice or digital equipment to the network from homes or offices. It is not generally known that the existing pair of wires from a telephone to the local exchange are capable of carrying much more information than is implied from their normal use of conveying intelligible speech.

Under the old policy, uncompetitive equipment was made, and the hopes for System X have not been realised - no major overseas orders have yet been received during a period in which a number of major systems have been ordered overseas. UK exports in this area have steadily declined.

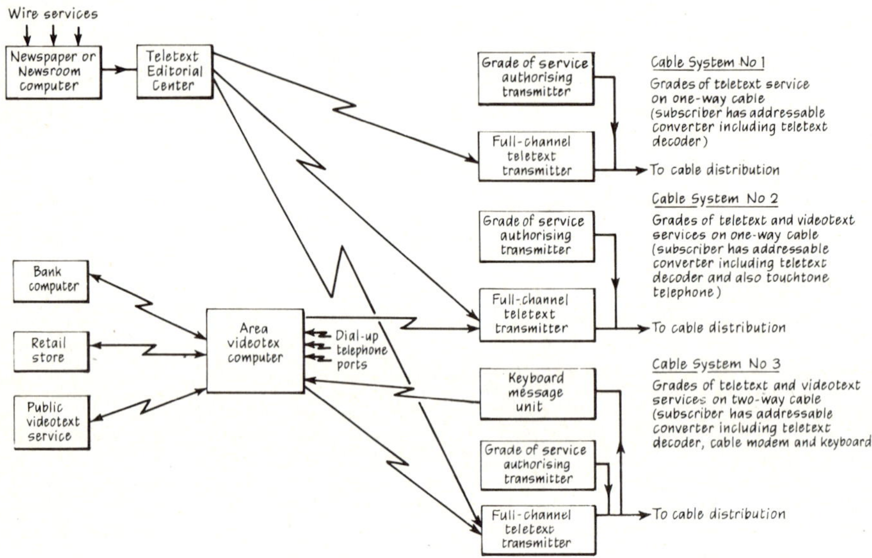

FIGURE 25.5   ONE POSSIBLE LAYOUT FOR A FUTURE VALUE ADDED NETWORK

(In this scheme different ways of delivering and/or demanding
different services on a page-by- page basis are shown)

In the US you can purchase an auto-dial modem ready to plug in to a microcomputer for $250. General purpose modems are available for $100, and the major elements of a modem can be purchased in chip form for $30. Approval of new equipment for connection to the telephone network is rapid. In the UK the only modern auto-dialling modem available in 1984 sold at £650. General purpose modems cost around £250. Action taken to enable equipment to be approved in the UK was inadequate. To start with, BT was the approval authority since nobody else could do it - rather like having the jury appointed by the prosecution. The British Standards Institute (BSI) was asked to publish needed standards.

In August, 1982, BT was accused of "time-wasting" tactics. The British Approval Board for Telecommunications (BABT) was set up to test equipment, independently of BT. By October, five BSI standards had been written. By August 1983 it was alleged that BABT had approved only one device - a telephone. Standards often take years to finalise, and there is little doubt that gearing up to quick approval will take time. Testing is expensive - some thousands of pounds for a telephone and well over £100,000 for a PBX. However by 1985 things were much improved and many telephones, modems, and other items had been approved although of 9 PBX's submitted only 1 had been approved.

The terms of a general licence for Value Added communication Network Services (VANS) were announced in 1982. Licences would run from 10 years up to 25 years from October 1st 1982 and would cover services, other than ordinary message services, such as conferencing, database services, electronic mail etc., offered to third parties (customers) by suppliers connecting to BT or Mercury networks.

The UK: response of the industry; the outlook for users

There are many subsidiaries or agents of foreign telecommunication/data processing/computer companies in Britain, but not many sizeable all-British companies. These include GEC, Plessey, Racal, ICL, Ferranti, Case, Inmos, Muirhead, Sinclair, Cable & Wireless and Rediffusion. The major UK software houses such as Logica and Scicon might also be included in the list. A number of others have foreign connections such as Rank-Xerox and STC.

Sir John Clark, chairman of Plessey, is quoted as saying "you can't turn an industry on its head after years in which the Post Office has entirely dominated the market". Sir Arnold Weinstock, chairman of GEC, said in July 1983, that he could not see how you could have anything other than a monopoly running a national communication service. In 1981 a report by Pactel was harshly critical of the British information technology industry, competing in a world market estimated at $50 Billion. Only Racal, it said, could compete strongly on an international level; GEC, a major exporting company was too closely tied to the home market, and it was dismissive of other companies. Pactel estimated the 1983 UK market to be worth £230M - that is for special telephones, facsimile machines, answering machines, PABX's, and other systems.

By October 1st 1983, 58 applications had been received by the DOI for VAN licences - in other words the applicants wish to offer for sale a service of some kind, using BT or Mercury lines - for example an electronic mail service. Perhaps this is indicative of the direction of UK activities - it would not be surprising if the effort goes into services rather than into manufacturing. In general, the UK service industry is growing, while manufacturing is not.

If British Industry cannot, or does not wish itself to create new products for communications and related areas on any scale at present, it does seem to be involved in setting up arrangements with foreign companies for licensing, know-how, importing etc., and several link-ups have been reported. These include Plessey with Scientific Atlanta (which was ahead of its time), Racal and Oak (cable TV), Racal and Millicom (cellular radio), and GTE and Ferranti (PABXs).

Since the UK "enjoys" more microcomputers per head of the population than any other country, there would appear to be a potential for microcomputer communication software, modems, and inter-machine services. The question is what for? A communicating micro is likely to require additional facilities - for example disk storage and file handling software needed for storing and processing worth while amounts of information. This prices it out of the "home" computer market at present.

For businesses or "business at home" users, there will be a growing market for telecoms. The growth rate will be limited by horrendous compatibility problems awaiting the application of agreed standards. The nature of this problem is such that it will take years to solve in spite of current efforts to introduce the ISO 7-layer communication standards concept. The most likely near future requirements are for the intra-organisation interconnection of microcomputers, terminals and mainframe computers in "distributed processing" applications between sites, particularly if the "worker at a terminal in his home" idea develops. Communication problems will limit the expansion rate of information services, particularly low cost home services.

UK Futures

The most predictable effect of deregulation plus the privatisation of

British Telecom is that domestic telephone charges will increase unless held down by government action - the stated intent of the present administration. If US precedents are any guide, better equipment should become available for businesses - for instance in PABX's - and there should be some appreciable improvements for organisations with sufficient traffic to justify deals with VANs; most of that traffic will still be voice.

New services will become available for business use. There will be opportunities for innovative UK manufacturers able to compete with imports from US and Japanese manufacturers already manufacturing in volume. The UK track record indicates that there are unlikely to be many of them - they will find it easier to import. The opportunities would seem to be greatest for services, for example for intra-company use, and possibly in the area of electronic publishing, discussed in Chapter 21. The impact of Cable and DBS services is hard to predict.

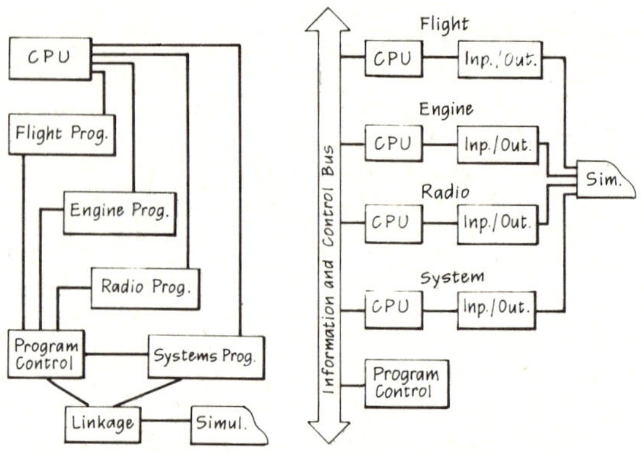

Old system with central processing   *New system with distributed processing*

FIG. 25.6. DISTRIBUTED PROCESSING EXAMPLE
(The diagram clearly shows how, in a
flight trainer, a central processing
design was changed into a series of
autonomous processes)

The evolution of universally available networks will not proceed smoothly. The PTTs have introduced packet switched networks with approved X25 network access protocol to try and reduce the penetration of systems such as SNA. The information service suppliers are developing new value added network services and special intra-organisation offerings such as message and information services. BT's strategy will be to exploit a digitised main network and to develop text, image, and data services in a much more vigorous manner than was ever applied to the telephone system.

THE INFORMATION SOCIETY

Is "The Information Society" a plausible concept?

By focusing on Information we force ourselves to consider the route along a thorny track towards an inevitable outcome - a world where the production of goods and many services are performed by machines provided with the necessary information. The claim has already been made that 50% of the US labour force (and by implication a substantial percentage in other countries) is engaged in information processing. What does that imply?

Crawford stresses the importance of Fritz Machlup's seminal 1962 book in which he defined the knowledge production areas in the US as R&D, education, printed and communications media, information technology and computers, libraries and information services, creative works, and those parts of government heavily dependent on information handling. Machlup's statistics created quite a stir - the aggregate knowledge production in the US was 29% of

GNP, its growth rate would become 2.5 times the average growth rate of other GNP components, and would soon reach 50% of GNP, and if full time students were included the labour force involved was already 42.8% of the total".

Drucker took the theme up in 1969 to be followed by Bell's book "The coming of the post-industrial society" in 1973. Porat and Parker, whose work is described below, developed Machlup's statistics further.

Crawford poses the question "has there been a shift from the service economy to the information economy?" she concludes "although we may disagree in some aspects with Machlup and Porat, we cannot fault them on the introduction of powerful new ideas". The phrase "The Information Society" has been picked by many others and this idea has been talked into existence with suggestions that we are moving on from the Industrial and the Post-Industrial (service) economies. An examination of the concept reveals a certain fragility.

The figures produced by Porat and discussed by Parker & Porat in 1975 encouraged the belief that a very large number of people are generating Information, a resource having very different properties from the goods and services on which the economics of many countries are based, with the result that there may be a dramatic change of some kind which justifies the claim that we are moving into an Information Society. The figures were based on 1967 data and were later up-dated to 1972 which give similar results – there was little change in that period in the percentage of US labour involved in information processing.

About 29.5 million people in the US were engaged in information processing according to Porat. Nearly 80% of this total can be aggregated into the general occupations shown in Table 25.1 from the detailed categories given in the   original table.

Occupation	Number (millions)
Office workers	8.52
Managers	5.57
Teachers	3.1
Professions	2.94
Communication & Computer people	1.76
Engineers & Draughtsmen	1.42
	23.31

The other smaller groups include people like Buyers, Public administration officials, Sales representatives etc. We can immediately see that nothing

TABLE 25.1
<u>INFORMATION PROCESSING PEOPLE IN THE USA</u>

dramatic can be expected. This is simply another way of recognising long term trends in the official records of many countries showing a decline in agricultural employment to about 8%, industrial employment to 40%, and an increase in service employment to over 50%.

What is new is the splitting of services into those with a low and high information processing content. For example Porat's service people with a low content include Truck drivers (1.4), Waiters (1.1) and, oddly, Janitors and Sextons (1.2) (Figures in brackets are millions of US employees); these are not in the above table. It is not clear why Retail sales clerks (2.2) and Miscellaneous sales clerks (1.2), are excluded from the table. Nothing unexpected is likely to happen because Teachers, Managers, etc., are now seen to be generating Information – a hard to evaluate resource which is difficult to handle for economists. There may be more of them but their activities haven't change much.

The reason why there are no serious evaluation problems is because these people provide labour intensive information services evidently of determinable value – there seems to be no great difficulty in deciding what the level of their salaries should be. Some of the concerns of economists seem to be unfounded. They bring the concern with them from economic theory where there is much discussion about demand and price-setting for products in a market where consumers possess imperfect information.

There are, however, other factors to be discussed. Labour was displaced by machines plus the information they needed to carry out an automated task, and by the increasing information content in computerised or computer-assisted tasks. Wages and salaries could be increased without price rises because of the increased productivity. But another part of the information sector - office services - grew as well without much improvement in productivity, and the increases in the salaries of these people which was coupled to the "deserved" increase awarded to diminishing more productive numbers of their colleagues was followed by price increases.

In many cases the "information sector" is an artificial division, previously considered to be part of the overhead. For example the largest "information sector" in a plastics company would be its office staff.

<u>Information per se - demand and value</u>

The validity of the Information Society concept would be helped if the existence of an Information Source Industry meeting an increasing demand for information could be demonstrated. This is where the current buzzwords "The Information Industry" or "The Knowledge Industry" must be introduced. Relatively few people in the Porat table are recognisably a part of this industry, about 400,000 in fact - people like Authors, Editors, Librarians, and some Computer people - and many of these are working in other "industries".

Further published discussions about the number of "information workers", with attempts to define what a person has to do to come into that category have taken place betwen Gleave and Cawkell.

Products of this Information Industry include both information and the means of manipulating it such as home computers and software, books and magazines, advisory and consulting services, television and radio programmes, private educational services and "electronic publishing" such as information provided via databases, computer networks, videotex, videotape, television, radio, and cable.

The difficulty here is drawing a line between entertainment and information. Entertainment is valued highly - witness the popularity of TV and videotape machines, but the evaluation of information is much more difficult.

The actual value of timely relevant information to people with obvious occupational need of it - for example the money market people - can be expressed in monetary terms. At the other end of the scale is the domestic market. People will pay for a daily paper and may subscribe to a magazine - partly, at least, for their information content. They receive a good deal of information without paying for it - for instance magazines and newspapers supported by advertising, bus, train and flight timetables, advice from citizen's advice bureaux and library services etc. They do not seem to want to pay for very much other information.

In between these extremes lies a grey area composed of professional and business people who may need information but may not want it enough to pay much for it. Evidently the intangibility of the information makes it hard to evaluate. You would imagine that doctors would be prepared to pay for medical information; however Physicians in the US, who are certainly not short of money, were provided with a free online computer-based information for six years which was quite widely used. The introduction of a $5 charge caused demand to fall by 77%. See Chapter 28 for more about this subject.

I conclude that the Information Society's (if and when it exists) demand for information can be summarised in this way. Many people in industry, commerce, and services are now seen as "information workers" - they always have been. There are now more of them and Information Technology provides them with better tools. They are demanding better communications and machines and use external information services. They mainly handle internally generated and transactional information, and are striving for better productivity. Additionally the Information Society will consume information and information products, often hard to distinguish from entertainment. The demand will be variable with business information predominating. There is little evidence to suggest that the general public want more information for which it is prepared to pay.

Social aspects

The many aspects of the widespread dissemination of information by telecommunication and new forms of display as they gradually replace paper-based information may be grouped under the following headings:-

* The man-machine mismatch
* The effects on people's behaviour at work and at home
* Privacy, secrecy, security, and freedom
* Work, leisure, and unemployment
* The differential distribution of information - the
  "information rich" and the "information poor"
* The generation and distribution of wealth from
  information

The man machine mismatch 1. The desirability of print on paper

The man-machine interface is discussed in Chapter 15, but there are some additional aspects of it which should be mentioned.

Certain "de-humanisation" effects have been discussed by Fondin and Escarpit. "Je deteste ce qu'on pourrait appeler le "Macluhanisme", c'est a dire l'utilisation que l'on a faite des idées de MacLuhan pour justifier des choses injustifiables".

How many people find microform viewers or CRT screens acceptable substitutes for print on paper? Escarpit sees no merit in the possible abolition of the written word. So far as reading from a CRT screen is concerned he is driven to use an English phrase - Miller's "chunks of sense" - in order to emphasise his disgust. A Frenchman only lapses into English when he is 'abérrant'. " Le processus de lecture ne progresse pas regulierement ligne apres ligne, page apres page. Cela n'est pas possible avec l'écran".

Other problems have been discussed by Hayes et al "If a speaker or writer makes a syntactic slip or spelling error his listener or reader does not normally fail to understand but instead makes the obvious correction. The inability of current interactive systems to make such corrections is very frustrating for their human users".

The man-machine mismatch 2. Engineers and codes

Gilb complains that "Computer systems, and the abstract codes, detailed forms, unreadable reports and documents which they produce too often, are clearly a form of environmental pollution". Many computer people are insensitive to the fact that the tools that they design have to be used by non-computer people.

Gilb cites the preferences of Bell personnel for codes conveying a meaning. It was hardly surprising that the Bell people's preference rating for "732681 8518" as the code for "Canton, Ohio" was 2, but for "MK PHILA PA" (Market St, Philadelphia, Pennsylvania) it was 9. He also points out that "The BBC radio/TV

licence number of about 38 digits is an example of the ridiculous lengths
technologists will go to (and defend it in the Times!) when management does not
pull the strings properly".

It is hard to understand why the old UK telephone numbering system for
London exchanges - for instance ABB 1234 (ABBEY 1234) - was replaced "for
technical reasons" by all figure numbers. For UK postal codes such a changeover
was not made (for "non-technical reasons"?). When more symbols were required,
"WCl" (West Central 1), for instance, was extended to "WCl 2AA". A just
sufficient number of symbols was added to exisiting meaningful information to
provide the extra information needed.

If the UK owner of a terminal wants to obtain information from one of the
many databases running in Europe or the United States, he can connect to it via
the Public Switched Telephone Network (PSTN), British Telecom's International
Packet Switched Service (IPSS) and a US network.

The most convenient arrangement for an engineer and the least convenient for
a user is to string together the codes which the user has to type on his terminal
to establish the through connection. The number of symbols which you have to type
correctly - one mistake and you have to start all over again - before you reach
your database turns out to to over 30. The string of alphanumeric symbols
required to be typed allows about 9.5×10^{32} host computers/databases to be
addressed. Numbers like this may be of interest to astronomers but in this
context they somewhat exceed requirements. (The world's population is about $4 \times
10^9$).

In an exchange of correspondence between myself and British Telecom back in
1979, my suggestion for "a single small program to translate, on behalf of all
users, many symbols into a few key-strokes" was ignored. I was told by a BT (then
Post Office) gentleman that "we consider the IPSS log-on procedure to be
relatively simple... and adopted to follow CCITT (another lot of engineers)
recommendations". In consequence a hundred different versions of the small
program needed to compress this procedure now sits inside people's intelligent
terminals doing a job which could be done once only in the central system.

Information, change, and unemployment

The effect of technological change on people's lives is much more frequently
discussed than the changes bought about by different ways of generating,
distributing, and using Information, enabled by new technology. It seems to me
that Information is at the heart of the matter more often than not.

Consider the man who loses his job on a car production line because painting
is done by a jet-spraying machine controlled by a programme on tape. In
machine-efficiency terms the correctness of the decision to change cannot be
challenged. Why use a human - an incredibly powerful multi-task information
processing machine which can do a million other things and is expensive to
maintain, when you can use a single-task machine which simply requires an
occasional squirt of oil? Simply represent the Information possessed by the man
about manipulating the jet as electrical impulses on tape instead of in his
brain, thereby releasing him to do a job that really needs that power - in other
words match the information processing capacity to the job requirement.

The problem which arises when a policy of information transfer from man to
machine is widely implemented was succinctly expressed over a century ago by
Robert Owen's son "If we can imagine a point at which all the necessaries and
comforts of life shall be produced without human labour, are we to suppose that
the human labourer is then to be dismissed to be told that he is now a useless
encumbrance that we canot afford to hire?".

Another viewpoint was given by Shubik many years later - " even with our ingenuity for coding, the information overload grows, especially if we wish to maintain values that stress individual men not as small component parts of the social intelligence, but as individuals".

The question of unemployment has received very wide discussion. Trends are hard to discern firstly because the net medium-term change in consequence of technology introduction is hard to measure in the face of shorter term changes as people are displaced from a job and then, possibly following re-training, settle down in another job, or remain unemployed. Secondly, changes in growth rate, economic conditions generally, import-export policies etc., mask the effects of technology.

<u>Jobless growth and work distribution</u>

What is known is that increasing productivity may not be accompanied by a decrease in unemployment. During the period 1950-1965 an average annual increase of 7% in the industrial output of EEC countries was accompanied by a 1% job increase, but during 1973-1978, industrial output increased by 1% annually while jobs decreased by 1.8%.

Unquestionably new technology creates new jobs as anyone who has been to the area between San Jose and San Francisco along the Bay can see, but it seems unlikely that they are enough to balance job losses in other areas. The consensus of opinion seems to be rather pessimistic. A call is made in a well argued article by Godet for far-reaching changes :-

"We perhaps need to prepare for the coming of a societal structure in which only part of the working population will be needed at any given point in time, to produce all the goods and marketed services - an extension to the entire economy of a phenomenon which already exists in agriculture. In this light, is it possible that we would accept a dual or a single society structure in which a minority would be at work and the majority condemned to idleness? Or must we learn to share out available work in a different way? Would it not be better to use productivity as a lever to free time and to reduce the working week with a view to enlarging free time activities? Our answer is clear: we must do away with the single, salaried and full-time job syndrome and promote a society based on a pluriactivity for those involved".

This proposal must be countered with the remark "Is it politically possible to carry through such ideas, and what would be the effects on a particular country if it was out of phase with the others during this period?".

The same counter could be used in response to Cherns who wrote:-"A society which relies so heavily on employment as a means of distributing material and moral resources (respect, prestige, etc.) is gravely shaken by the impact of too little employment. The microprocessor is feared not because it will lead to the production of less wealth but because it will enable wealth to be produced with less employment. Of course that wealth has to be distributed but why do people need to be "employed" for that purpose? At once the litany of objections is recited. "Somebody will have to work: if people can get what they want without working who will want to work? Without everybody at work how is the wealth to be created?"..."the creation of goods and services will never again require 65,000 hours of everyone's life, we shall need to acquire the values that go with the sequestration of a mere 35,000 or 25,000 hours".

Employment is discussed further in Chapter 26, and that discussion includes quite a different viewpoint which holds that there is no macro evidence that more technology means fewer jobs.

The quality of the Information Society

The social pros and cons of advancing technology on people's lives has been variously argued, notably by Simon, Weizenbaum, and Bell. We are told that "computer technology can show man how to live in harmony with nature" or alternatively that "The use of large-scale computer based information systems induces an extremely poverty stricken notion of knowledge and fact...such systems necessarily induce recoding of data into information-rich chunks denuding the original data of the subtleties which accompanied them and determined their meaning while still in ordinary language".

Bell discusses the "Intellectual foundations of the revolution in communications" and argues that attempts to discipline human knowledge and create a vast and unified edifice, as Delgano and even Leibnitz sought to do, were bound to fail. "The effort to formalise knowledge or create artificial languages has proved inadequate. The scholastic orderings of Mortimer Adler may help an individual to trace the bibliographic cross-references of ideas, but if the purpose of a library or knowledge based computer program is to help a historian to assemble evidence or a scholar to re-order his ideas, then the ambiguity of language itself must be confronted. Terms necessarily vary in different contexts and lend themselves to different interpretation, and historical usages shift over time making the problem of designing a "knowledge" program quite different from designing an "information " program".

Weizenbaum attacks Bell for his preoccupation with computer-based information systems, and the use of computers generally, which he considers may "amplify and intensify problems and exacerbate effects". Bell responds by stating that "a change in the techno-economic order (and that is the realm of information) does not determine changes in the political and cultural realms of society but poses questions to which society must respond".

The wider use of communications and information distribution may produce various effects according to your viewpoint - it may bring with it a utopian home of the future or widen the knowledge gap between the information rich and the information poor. Mason becomes almost poetic-"a home once more will be a place to live, not just a place to stay. The communications revolution will make it increasingly easy to perform many kinds of work from remote locations - including home - rather than requiring people to work at a central office or plant. The addition of telecomputing capabilities to radio, TV, phonograph, and other home entertainment devices will transform today's family room into a media room. A home computer will tie separate systems together and provide the central focus or "electronic hearth" around which the family will gather for work, play, and fellowship". But more than that, sensors will recognise the mood of the occupants, leading to the introduction of "white noise to mask out street sounds or relaxing raindrop or soft wind noises".

I've often wondered what the millions who buy home computers do with them. According to Dickerson, information processing is not one of the major incentives for buying. "Home-computer adopters are characterised as having a higher income since the financial risk of the purchase is smaller; a higher status occupation is likely to mean that the individual has more work-related experience with computers". Users may be logical introverts. "Information- seeker" comes some way down the list of "discriminant functions" of computer adopters after "Video TV games", "programmable pocket calculator", and "computer attitudes and home ownership", but above "self-designated opinion leader", and "culinary and aesthetic enthusiast".

Gandy thinks that "The popular mythology that sees the avalanche of new information technologies as heralding a new democratic, egalitarian age, is little more than a cruel hoax - the product of marketing hype or self-delusion....the distribution of benefits flowing from the new technologies will widen the information gap between the rich and poor...the transformation of information into a commodity traded in an unregulated marketplace will mean that the poor will simply not be able to afford access to most of the new technologies or their software".

Sociologists vs. Businessmen

In the movement towards an Information Society each country feels the need to develop its own technology, partly to become independent of foreign dominance, and partly to provide employment in new industries and services to offset decline in other areas - a major consideration in Europe. But there are fears that an uncontrolled market-driven business-oriented technology will seriously affect the quality of life and produce a division between the information-rich and the information-poor.

The pro-technology people sometimes include with their "information-technology-will-bring-a-better-life" comments, rather vague misgivings about human rights unaccompanied by positive suggestions for safeguards, thus:- "I believe that we must expand the citizen's right to acquire information and to express himself through the existing media system, as well as to be protected against the misuse of information about him. With the advent of widespread access to the media which people will have to be assured of in the future, I think that information technology will be able to guarantee these fundamental rights of equity and privacy, and to re-define them for inclusion in the codes of our future society" (Branscomb, IBM).)

Vinken (Publisher) strives to convince us that business and culture make perfectly good bedfellows - "A year ago Mr. Edward Ploman dealt critically with the proposition that information and communications are economic commodities. He found this market-oriented attitude, captured in the phrase "the market-place of ideas", both denigrating and demeaning. He observed that with such a proposition, the social, political or cultural dimensions of information are conspicuous by their absence. This is a view with which I must disagree. Surely no one can fail to see the social, cultural, and political aspects of information. In all probability they are more evident than with any other product.

Of course information (perhaps all information) has social, political and cultural connotations. To take but one example our entire educational system is a cultural and social structure of the first order and what is it but an immense information system? But having said this it does not follow that it is immune from the normal laws of economics. Do not teachers have to receive a salary and do not parents exercise value judgements where they can between private and state schools? Have we reached the point where schools and laboratories can be built and maintained without cost? Do members of an orchestra perform for nothing?"

Line sums up the situation well, but does not attempt to offer solutions- "Optimistic faith in technology is a thing of the past, except for those directly involved in technological developments. A feeling almost of despair on the part of many people, due partly but certainly not solely to technology and its misuse, is leading them to take up extreme positions. This is a dangerous trend: society rarely progresses by extremes or fluctuations between them".

Conclusion

We have a long way to go before anything like an "Information Society" can be said to exist - there may be a movement in that direction but it is slow. The effects of technological change on people's lives is much more frequently discussed than the changes bought about by different ways of generating, distributing, and using Information enabled by new technology, although

Information is at the heart of the matter more often than not.

To what degree do the developing and converging media - described at length
in other parts of this volume - directly influence the Information Society?.
McLuhan is remembered for his comment that Media are Messages in the sense that
they determine and embody what is to be considered the appropriate social
organisation; a new media provides human beings with new psychological-
structural equipment. It will be interesting to see whether Gronbeck's comment
(regarding McLuhan) that "it is perhaps typical of very creative minds that they
hit very large nails not quite on the head" is appropriate, or whether McLuhan
got it absolutely right.

FURTHER READING

Anon
   Society of British Telecom Executives, 102-104 Sheen Rd., Richmond,
   Surrey TW9 1US, England. July 1983.
      Liberalisation, privatisation & regulation. What future for British
      Telecom?
Anon.
   Booklet published by the Inst. of Personnel Management,
   Central House, Upper Woburn Place, London WC1H OHX. 1981.
      Personnel policies and new technology.
Baker, T.W.
   Electronics & Power, 447-450, June 1982.
      The evolution of private communication.
Bell, Daniel.
   Basic Books, New York, 1973.
      The coming of the post industrial society.
Bell, Daniel.
   In Forester, Tom (Ed). The microelectronics revolution. Basil Blackwell,
Oxford. 1980, pps 500-549.
      The social framework of the information society.
Branscomb, Lewis M.
   Science 203(4376), Jan 12th, 1979, 143-147.
      Information: the ultimate frontier.
Branscomb, Lewis M.
   IBM Sys.J 18(2), 189-201,1979.
      Computing and communications - a perspective of the evolving environment.
Cawkell, A.E.
   Wireless World 84 (1511/1512), 38-42 69-74, July/August 1978. Reprinted in
Forester, Tom (Ed), The microelectronics revolution. Basil Blackwell 1980, and
(in Russian) in Communication with databases. Znaniye publication No.12,
Moscow 1979.
      The paperless revolution. Forces controlling the introduction of
      electronic information systems.
Cawkell, A.E.
   J.Info.Sci 8(1), 42-44, 1984.
      Economics of the information society.
Cawkell, A.E.
   Aslib Proc. 37(6/7), 287-288, June/July 1985.
      Inter-group connections in a structurally changing information society.
Cawkell, A.E.
   Aslib Proc. 37(8), 339-340, August 1985.
      Inter-group connections: the debate continues.
Cherns, A.B.
   Int. Labour Rev. 119(6), 705-721, December 1980.
      Speculations on the social effects of new microelectronics technology.
Crawford, Susan.
   Bull. Med. Libr. Assoc., 71(4), 380-385, 1983.
      The origin and development of a concept: the Information Society.

Cronin, Blaise.
  J. Info. Sci. 7(1) (1983) 1-14.
    Post-industrial society: some manpower issues for the library/information
      profession.
Debons, Anthony.
  Marcel Dekker,1981.
    The information professional: survey of an emerging field.
de Sola Pool, Ithiel.
  In Proc. OECD Conf., Paris, February 1975. Published by OECD, 2 Rue Andre
    Pascal, Paris Cedex 15, France. Pps 281-308.
    Social implications of computer and telecommunications systems:
    background report.
Dickerson, Mary D., and Gentry, James W.
  J. Consumer Res. 10(2), 225-235, 1983.
    Characteristics of adopters and non-adopters of home computers.
Drucker, Peter.
  Harper & Row, New York, 1968.
    The age of discontinuity.
Gandy, Oscar J.
  Ablex Publishing Co., Norwood, NJ, 1982.
    In Beyond Agenda Setting. Chapter 9 Information inequality.
Gleave, D; Angell C; Woolley K.
  Aslib Proc. 37(2), 99-133, February 1985.
    Structural change within the information profession: a scenario for the
    1990s.
Gleave, David.
  Aslib Proc. 37(6/7), 289-291, June/July 1985.
    Inter-group connections in a structurally changing information society:
    reply.
Godet. Michael.
  Futures 15(4), 251-263, August 1983.
    Crisis and oportunity: from technological to social change.
Gronbeck, Bruce E.
  J. Communication, 31(3), 117-128, Summer 1981.
    McLuhan as a rhetorical theorist.
Hinchman, W.
  IEEE Spectrum 16(12), 42-48, December 1979.
    On Bell 1. Time for a change.
Kraus, Raymond.
  IEEE Communications, September 1975.
    Kraus responds to "another view of the AT&T anti-trust suit".
LeDuc, Don R.
  J.Broadcasting 27(2), 99-112, Spring 1983.
    Parallel policy patterns in Europe and the United States.
Line, Maurice B.
  J. Libr. Automat. 14(4), 252-267, 1981.
    Libraries and information services in a post technological society.
Littlechild, S.C.
  Peter Peregrinus, Stevenage, England, for the IEE, 1979.
    Elements of telecommunications economics.
Machlup, Fritz.
  Princeton University Press, 1962.
    Knowledge: its creation, distribution, and economic significance.
Mason, Roy; Jennings, Lane.
  The Futurist, 16(1), 35-43, February 1982.
    The computer home: will tomorrow's housing come alive?
McLuhan, Marshall; Fiore Quentin.
  The medium is the message: an inventory of effects.
    Bantam Books, New York, 1967.

Meyer, John R., Wilson, Robert W., Baughcum, Alan., Burton, Ellen., Caouette, Louis.
  Oelgeschlager, Gunn & Hain, Cambridge, Mass. USA. 1980.
    The economics of competition in the telecommunications industry.
Parker, Edwin B.
  Report to the National Commission on libraries and information science.
  Published by the Commission, Washington, D.C., USA, 1973.
    Information and society.
Parker, Edwin.B. and Porat, Marc.
  OECD, Rue Andre Pascal, Paris, France. In Proc. OECD Conf. on Computer &
  Telecommunications Policy. Paris, Feb. 1975, pps 87-131.
    Background report.
Parker, Edwin B.
  Telecomunications Policy 1(1), 3-20, December 1976.
    Social implications of computer/telecoms systems.
Pierce, John R.
  IEEE Spectrum 16(12), 48-50, December 1979.
    On Bell 2. The system is sound.
Porat, M.U.(with M.R. Rubin for some volumes).
  Government Printing Office, Washington D.C., USA. 1977.
    The information economy (7 volumes).
Rothwell, Roy.
  Int. J. Management Sci. 9(3), 229-245, 1981.
    Technology, structural change, and manufacturing employment.
Rubin, Michael Rogers; Taylor, Elizabeth.
  Information Processing & Management 17, 163-194, 1981.
    The US information sector and GNP: an input-output study.
Simon, Herbert A.
  Computer 14(11), 69-74, November 1981.
    Prometheus or Pandora: the influence of automation on society.
Stapley, Barry.
  Telecommunications Policy 5(2), 149-151, June 1981.
    Managing communications - the value of choice.
Vinken, Pierre J.
  Euripa brochure no.1. Published by the European Information Providers
  Association, 79 Great Titchfield St., London W1P 7FN. 1982.
    Information economy, government, and society.
Weizenbaum, Joseph.
  In Forester, Tom (Ed). The Microelectronics revolution. Basil Blackwell 1980.
  pps 550-570.
    Once more the computer revolution.

CHAPTER 26. UNEMPLOYMENT, WORK, AND LEISURE

There will never be a system invented which
will do away with the necessity for work
Henry Ford

Maslow's statement about human needs would seem to be a good introduction to this Chapter. In order of priority they are food, sleep, and other physiological needs; safety; social - such as belonging and affection; self esteem; self development. On the assumption that, at least in the developed countries, the first priorities are usually fulfilled, the lesser priorities are dependent to a considerable degree on having a satisfactory job.

EMPLOYMENT - FACTS AND TRENDS

General employment trends in industrialised countries can be deduced from official records. They have been well summarised by Rothwell. The replacement of men by machines started to accelerate from around the middle of the eighteenth century - Arkwright invented his water-powered weaving machine in 1769. Although there were periods of unemployment from then onwards, the demands of a growing population and the creation of new industries and services generated new jobs about as fast as men were replaced by machines until the first world war. Much later scares about automation seemed to be unfounded.

Current viewpoints are usually based on the analysis of post second world war trends. These trends are very obvious. In the period 1955 to 1975 agricultural employment continued to diminish ending at an average of about 8% of total employment in Japan, France, Germany, Sweden, Canada, US and UK. Industrial employment declined slowly to about 40% with the exception of Japan, but Service employment increased steeply from around 40% to 55%. Productivity in the period also changed. In all EEC countries 1950-1965 was characterised by 7% annual average increase in industrial output and 1% annual average job creation, but in 1973-1978 there was an average 1% increase in industrial output but a 1.8% _decrease_ in employment annually.

In the UK the need for new jobs is particularly important because, regardless of the effect of world conditions or government policy, the birth rate, retirement age, school-leaving age etc., has generated a net requirement for about 1.5 million jobs during the eighties.

EMPLOYMENT - THEORIES

Keynes proposed methods for stimulating demand to create employment _(The Aggregate Demand Theory)_ but it appears from the above data that increased industrial output would not be accompanied by more jobs. Growth is now Jobless Growth. In the _Structural Change Theory_ it is suggested that jobs are lost partly because industry in the home country cannot compete against imports, particularly technically advanced imports, and partly because the home industry responds by increased mechanisation of production.

In a more speculative idea called The _Kondratiev Wave Theory_ it was suggested that the formation of capital, investment in major technologies, growth, peak, obsolescence and depression, runs in 60 year cycles. There is some evidence to suggest that peaks occurred around 1813, 1872, 1918, and 1976. This idea received some support from Schumpeter who identified cyclic clusters of activity such as steam power, railways, and cars and electric power. However Kuznets and de Solla Price consider that twentieth century science/technology-based expansion is best explained in terms of a symmetrical sigmoid (S shaped) curve. Growth starts from a floor, passes through a phase of exponential increase, and then inevitably hits a ceiling. Kuznets is interested in production and Price in Science, Technology, R&D and scientists.

Kelly constructs a series of sigmoid curves to demonstrate the progress of several technologies e.g railways, cars, energy, armaments, etc. He concludes we are reaching a unique situation in which a number of dominant technologies are simultaneously losing momentum. A long period of R&D growth is also approaching a ceiling, as predicted by Price; the youngest technology - Information - uniquely offers the best potential, reaching maximum growth rate around the early eighties. Overall the position is bad because the outlook for successor technologies is gloomy, Information Technology excepted.

However the "common sense theory" demolishes these erudite explanations. Unemployment supposedly resulting from automation pre-supposes that there is only so much work available. But say prices come down - as with the pocket calculator. Large numbers of people can now afford to buy one without any increase in their wages. If a whole range of items fall in price because of cheaper mechanised production processes, purchasing power is increased, more goods are bought, so more have to be produced with more people employed to make them. In other words production technology creates demand.

Although many may be out of work because of general economic conditions, it is strongly suspected that a proportion of the 12 million jobless (1985) in EEC countries are jobless because of displacement by automation, so why doesn't the theory work? It is probably because the requirements for re-training re-employment and re-housing in a different location slow up the re-adjustment process so that people are removed from the pool of jobless at a slower rate than the people being added to it. It may also be because £1 Billion of "automated" goods, say, bought because of the released purchasing power, require 50,000 people to make them, whereas 100,000 have been rendered jobless by the decay of old, non-automated, industries. Perhaps the "common sense theory" has some flaws, and things won't come right eventually without some kind of intervention.

Another area which has received attention is the possibility of earlier retirement and a shorter working week. In fact a steady reduction in working hours has been going on since the 19th century - a fall of about 40% in life-time hours spent at work has occurred; since 1930 there has been a drop of over 20%. Suggestions of sharing a job to spread the work over more people is of limited value because it involves wage sharing as well.

VIEWPOINTS

One view about technology and jobs

A letter appeared in Computer Weekly in July 1981 under the headline "Micros will change our lives rather than destroy our jobs". In it the phrase "the threat to jobs nonsense" was used - a reference to the impact of technology. As it seems difficult to separate out from official national or regional employment figures, that fraction specifically attributable to microcomputers, or for that matter to any new technology, I was prompted to reply. My letter appeared later in the same publication:-

"The evidence to support either "the nonsense of the threat to jobs" or "the collapse of work" is nebulous. The availability of work will be determined, amongst other factors, by general economic conditions, replacement of men by machines, and efficiency and productivity of goods and services for internal use and export. History cannot tell us much because current economic conditions have no parallel in the past and the rate of change today is without precedent.

The rate of growth and competitiveness of an individual country and the state of its competitors will probably be a major factor determining the availability of work. The total number of available jobs will be higher in a "successful" country than in a "stagnating" one. Even in the successful country, older people and those unable to contribute the new skills demanded in the new technology jobs becoming available may not find work when they are displaced by machines unless they are mobile and adaptable. In the stagnating country only the highly skilled are likely to find new jobs when displaced.

This generalisation is as about as far as you can go. I cannot see how anyone can separate out the effect of job losses or gains solely due to new technology. Nor can I see how anyone can put numbers to net job losses or gains since this will be the overall result of a wide range of winners and losers in many industries and services. The other uncertainty is the amount of wealth to be created by new industries and services based on new technology and the distribution of it. Nobody, so far as I know, has attempted to quantify this wealth which will probably be accompanied by jobless growth, nor has anyone suggested how it might be distributed without unpalatable side effects".

<u>Other views: 1.The optimists</u>

While there are some notable exceptions, the most optimistic people seem to be technologists, new technology salesmen, or employers. North Americans are more optimistic than Europeans. At the blue sky level, Cater suggests that we will be able to talk back to our information systems and come up with ambitious plans for more diversified entertainment and education programming directed toward more selective audiences. There will be boundless vistas for creating new forms of cottage enterprise emancipated from the congestion of office and factory.

Lepkowski considers that almost every major force in any human society is conservative. It seeks to preserve the status quo. You can look at law, politics, religion, tradition – they are all attempts to keep things the way they were. New technology by its nature is anti-conservative. It's dynamic; it changes things. Every new idea upsets the status quo to some extent. In the long run automation can be an enormous force for human freedom and for liberating the spirit. Without the invention of steam machinery we would still have slavery. Without the invention of the internal combustion engine we would still be on the farm working from dawn to dusk.

In the US, innovative technology has created jobs in the past and that country still enjoys a supremacy and a degree of confidence in spite of Japanese inroads. A comparative study was undertaken during 1978 of six mature (combined annual sales $36 billion), five innovative ($21 billion) and five young high technology ($857 million) Corporations. The number of new jobs created per $M of turnover was 0.7, 5, and 41 respectively.

According to Rothwell (1979), firms had strong connections with universities and government laboratories which also provided a continuous flow of highly specialised engineers. Communication between firms was guaranteed by that peculiarly American habit of job-hopping – job turnover in Silicon Valley was 15-20% per annum at one time. Risk capital was amply and expertly provided by local venture capitalists. Their success may reflect a particularly American phemonenon based on a culture that puts a low value on Company loyalty and a high one on individual entrepreneurial activity. If this analysis is correct it would be unwise to expect too much from similar European efforts. It could be wiser for Europe to concentrate on improving the performance of established firms.

It would be interesting to know how many jobs were created in the US by a local supporting manufacturing infrastructure. Small electronic firms buy out printed circuit boards and cases, get plating and painting done by local contractors, and buy in unit-interconnecting wiring harnesses from sub-contractors. A number of specialised subcontractors are needed for a variety of such services.

Robinson considers that increased productivity arising from technological innovation will, given a reasonably healthy economy, create an increased demand for labour and raise real wages. After the changeover from discrete transistors to integrated circuits in the US, the average output in individual devices per employee did not change greatly but in terms of transistors (or equivalent transistors), productivity per employee skyrocketed. The increased sales stimulated by the resulting lower costs was the foundation for more than a tenfold increase in employment during a 15 year period. While makers of slide rules may have taken a beating, relatively few persons ever bought slide rules in the first place. The hand held calculator on the other hand has so caught the public fancy that practically every kid has one now. The volume of calculators produced has probably more than made up for the number of displaced slide rule manufacturers and their employees.

Government regulatory policy strongly effects jobs in telecommunications. A huge number of devices became available in the US for incorporating in systems competing with AT&T/Bell as liberalisation proceeded. Employment in the data communications industry increased. The deregulation of British Telecom may result in a net job increase provided that British entrepreneurs can outwit foreign importers. Now that private industry can offer telecommunication devices or services for public use, competition and new services could result in overall growth. The total number of people employed by BT and private companies should increase.

The media obviously believes that most people in Britain aren't interested in good news. Strikes and chip doomsday scenarios get special attention. There are probably quite a large number of new technology employment agreements which are quietly resolved and although news about them is hard to find they are occasionally reported. For instance the Herald Tribune was able to change from linotype hot metal composition requiring 180 employees to a computer-based editing and typesetting system manned by only 30 people, over a weekend. Not one hour was lost to any sort of job action any sort of strike or any kind of technical breakdown. What happened to those displaced? We don't know.

In 1981 "no news value"" agreements in Britain went ahead in industry while the strikes made all the headlines. 86 technology agreements were made primarily with members of the APEX and ASTM Unions in the engineering and manufacturing sectors. The main features were discussion before change, use of an agreed disputes procedure if agreement could not be reached, and no compulsory redundancies.

A number of British Companies in the car industry are now using a microprocessor controlled machine which stamps out components. Because it is more efficient than competitive machines they can reduce their labour force and turn out lower cost components. On the other hand the Company which makes the machine - also a British Company - took on 60 more men to make it because of the demand created by its greater efficiency. If this Company had not developed the machine the component manufacturers would have imported foreign ones. This little story contains all the ingredients of the new technology dilemma. It is hard to determine whether the net effect of its many outcomes (most of which are not spelled out here) are likely to be beneficial or whether they create more problems than they solve.

A 1981 OECD report on the subject is rather out of date - the discussions took place in 1979 - but at that time the optimists were in the majority. A Finnish speaker felt that following automation, jobs had become more responsible, varied, and interesting. A Japanese speaker expected that strong economic growth would create new jobs and absorb technologically displaced workers. In a concluding part of this report emphasis is placed on growth and demand. If real economic growth in an economy remains inadequate despite attempts to expand aggregate demand, measures can be taken to reduce the growth of labour supply.

One speaker felt that the development of microelectronics presents a number of unique characteristics which have virtually no precedent in the history of technology. "The occurrence of technological employment on the scale predicted by some analysts would clearly be unprecedented in the world economic history". This point is unclear because there seems to be no reason why unprecedented employment could not be brought about by an unprecedented industry! Microelectronics is dynamic; it pulls an increasing rate of change in other developments in its wake. Let us hope that unprecedented rates of change do not, instead, create unprecedented unemployment.

The report seems to suggest that a responsive control system is available for providing the correct remedies for the economy when the right buttons are pressed. But from actual events I get the feeling that nobody, least of all economists, has any idea what will happen when they push the buttons. Professor Nostradamus sincerely believes that his theory cannot fail to work. However Dr. Weedshoveller, who advocates the exact opposite, is equally certain that his proposals will transform the economy.

The summary at the end of the report is optimistic - if the demand for the products of progressive industries is relatively price elastic, output will increase more than productivity and employment will rise. The development of new products and services based on microelectronics will further increase employment.

In a more recent UK survey by Northcott of 1200 industrial companies, three quarters of them reported little change in employment as a result of the application of microelectronics to products or processes. However in firms applying microelectronics to processes, there tended to be a reduction in jobs; in those applying it to products there was an increase. On the basis of this survey it is estimated that the use of microelectronics in Britain in products may have created about 23,000 jobs, while applications to processes may have caused 7000 job losses.

The Economist, addressing Englishmen in 1982 said "Go West young men", not to California, but to the heady atmosphere along the M4 motorway connecting London with Wales and the west country. The chips are up - high-technology companies in the area buck the trend by showing an average growth of 30% per annum and a similar growth in the work force in the three years ending 1981. The Economist characteristically concludes that this has been happening quietly with more hindrance than help from governments. The marketplace has driven it along. Moral: if planners seek to limit the natural growth of successful technological areas, their prosperity can quickly wither. Coventry was prevented from diversifying. It is now stuck in a ditch with the motor industry. Regional planners mark, learn, digest, and desist.

Stockbrokers H.C.Lumsden estimated in the same year that the UK growth in production of information technology products was 12% per year. The growth rate of application software was likely to grow at 30%, and that must mean more jobs.

<u>Other views 2; The Pessimists</u>

The most pessimistic people seem to be European, particularly British, and particularly trade unionists. Even allowing for the media's enthusiasm for bad news and the over exposure of prophets of doom, such evidence as there is indicates, on average, a rather gloomy picture for the next five years at least.

People cope with a period of unemployment and re-adjustment in a new job following redundancy according to their age and previous occupation. As the rate of change increases, at some point it will exceed people's rate of adaptability and the rate at which institutions and processes can re-adjust.

In 1968-1972 a comprehensive analysis was carried out by Daniel on the occupations of people made redundant following the closure in 1968 of a factory at Woolwich in south east London. In those years unemployment in England was around the 2% level. The factory employed 5500 people who thought they were in a secure job and had not expected changes. Supervisors over 50 fared worst. 28% found jobs of a comparable level, but 20% had to accept jobs as unskilled labourers. Their age and job-specific knowledge were against them. Women fared considerably better than men on average. 11% of all workers remained unemployed 6 months after leaving. Psychological and other effects of unemployment are described in this report.

Very little information is available about the macro effects of the introduction of specific new technology on employment because of the difficulty of isolating this cause from others, and because of the laborious work required to discover what percentage of people made redundant were re-employed, quickly or slowly, elsewhere in the same or in another organisation. But more is available, on a "micro" scale, about the local effect on employment following the introduction of new equipment, and in some cases about the effect on a particular industry. Information about the re-employment of those displaced is not often provided.

A number of cases are given by Jenkins. The big seven Japanese television receiver manufacturers reduced their labour force from 48,000 to 25,000 between 1972 and 1976 while output rose by 25%. The introduction of integrated circuits greatly reduced assembly time. The introduction by National Cash Register of electronic to replace electromechanical machines resulted in a reduction of the labour force from 37,000 to 18,000. After a discussion about the likely reduction in labour because of the introduction of electronically switched telephone exchanges, it is stated that AT&T reduced its labour force from 39,200 to 18,500 between 1970 and 1977.

Robinson presents rather a different picture of what appears to be the identical case - the labour force employed by the telephone switching section of Western Electric - the manufacturing division of AT&T. According to him, employment in the switching division declined from 39,000 in 1970 to 27,172 in 1976 - the period during which electronic switching was introduced.

However the total numbers employed in Western Electric's manufacturing plant was 144,000 in 1963, 178,000 in 1970, and 144,000 again in 1976. There was also a change in the nature of employment with an increased demand for trained testers and analysts, an on-going demand for unskilled people, and a lessening demand for people with middle skills.

Note, en passant, that Jenkins is a trade unionist and Robinson a staff writer on the US magazine Science.

In 1978 pessimism gathered momentum in England following the publication of Hines' "The chips are down" which received wide attention in the media. Hines claimed in it that within the next few years vast sections of the industrial and service sectors would be automated and millions would lose their jobs.

In the following year a book was published by Barron and Curnow which also commanded wide attention. It summarised a study carried out at the University of Sussex in which the possible effect of the widespread introduction of microelectronics was investigated in depth. It was concluded that in a society experiencing low growth and balance of payments problems we may be contemplating levels of unemployment around 10-15% of the labour force. Note the qualification about economic background conditions.

The optimistic remarks quoted earlier from Cater were followed in the same article by the supposed counter-attack of a pessimist who would say that home information centres could trivialise the uses of technology and interactive TV would encourage still further the political impulse for a form of plebiscitary democracy leading to the demise of representative government. Holed up with a home information center away from office and friends, individuals would be further isolated from meaningful communication.

In a 1981 UK Mori poll, 58% of those questioned thought that new technology would increase unemployment, while only 8% thought it would help to reduce it. However 76% thought it was essential for Britain's prosperity. Fears about invasion of privacy or worse working conditions were not widespread. 81% of men and 71% of women thought new technology was "a good thing".

Hull calls for an explanation of earlier work about the effects of levels of automation. Levels 1 and 2 are the effects produced at low levels of automaticity where physical effort is reduced and the operator still has a degree of control and freedom to manage the machine. At level 3 the machine cycles automatically through its processes with self-fed materials, and the operator becomes a machine minder. At levels 4 and 5 the process is automatic and computer controlled. The labour force then includes a good many monitoring operators, maintenance men, engineers, and programmers.

Blauner hypothesised that job alienation increases with increased automation up to some point roughly corresponding to level 3, but then decreases. This idea has been tested by surveying the labour turnover in a number of factories with different degrees of automation. In general it has been found that Blauner's hypothesis is borne out - for example the degree of complexity is positively correlated with the percentage of maintenance personnel and a low turnover of labour.

Printers in New York were almost the only craftsmen to survive into the 1970s. Their activity quickly jumped to level 5 with the introduction of pages read by OCR etc. The re-trained printers consider their jobs are now intellectually more challenging and less physically demanding. The general conclusion from this and other surveys is that more technology in industry may not be more alienating.

However in a series of televised interviews in 1985, the printers in a London newspaper professed mixed feelings. Admitting that things were quieter, cleaner, and easier they still yearned for the sights, smells, and comradeship of hot metal. They preferred the sweaty macho to the up-market typist image.

In most studies of the effects of automation we are not told directly whether the labour force was reduced although this is almost always implied, nor whether those displaced found jobs which were the equivalent or better than the ones they lost.

WOMEN AT WORK

The number of women employed in industrialised countries has grown steadily. The total number of women employed in the USA increased by 60% to 35.1 million between 1960 and 1976 - 40% of the employed total. Of the total male and female "White Collar" work-force of 43.7 million in 1976, about 23 million or two thirds were women. In Britain about 40% (about 10.5 million) of the employed total in 1980 were women. Of those about 3.5 million worked in offices. In 1971 only 17% of them were managers and the increase since then has probably been slow.

Predictions about the effect of new technology on future employment vary widely between countries and with respect to the people affected within those countries. Unions are usually pessimistic, management moderately optimistic and office equipment manufacturers very optimistic. Few predictions are based on analysis and reasoned argument. Differences of opinion are easy to find. In 1980 Mackintosh (Consultant) considered that office employment will continue to increase; Sherman (Trade Unionist) thought otherwise and mentions a German report predicting a job loss of up to 2 million in the German clerical sector.

In a detailed and well reasoned report about women's jobs, Emma Bird and others discuss the situation in Britain. They consider that the introduction of Word Processors in offices will displace 2% of the secretarial work-force by 1985 and 17% of it (projected at 170,000 jobs) by 1990. These figures apparently exclude the influence of economic conditions.

The present and future prospects for women in offices

Since women office managers will continue to be a small minority I will confine my comments to Secretaries, Typists, and Clerical Workers (divisions with blurred edges) and their work. For the forseeable future we need not consider "The Electronic Office", "Electronic Mail", etc., as currently sensationalised. Near future realities (except in very large organizations) include Word Processing machines or microcomputers and the introduction of communicating WP machines. Certain kinds of clerical work may be amenable to greater mechanization and this will be discussed later.

Most office work gets done in curious informal conversational ways which are not amenable to mechanization; the way in which the information necessary for executive decision making may be indexed, stored, retrieved, transmitted and assimilated is not well understood.

Personal Secretaries (PS)

It seems unlikely that the work of personal secretaries will be much affected by new developments. The diverse tasks that they perform, their own status, and the status conferred on an executive who has a PS are an entrenched part of the system. In 1980 it was predicted in EMMS that 200,000 "Executive Workstations" at $6000 (1980 prices) would be in place in the US by 1985, and 1.25 million at $2000 each in 1990. Facsimile message transmission, it was said, would be an important component. The accuracy of forecasts like this cannot be high because little is known about the aspects of an executive's behaviour amenable to machine-help.

Not much more has been found out in the last 5 years. Consequently the specification of a machine/communication system likely to be attractive for executive use, and so its cost, must be largely guesswork. The question of the acquisition of typing skills by an executive or the design of a machine for which they are not needed also arises. The work of a PS seems secure for some years to come.

Secretaries/Typists

Typists, meaning women who spend most or nearly all of the time typing, extend from those who also supervise, or who also do some secretarial work, to full time typists - as in typing pools. Their work first started to change with the introduction of telex machines and special purpose typewriters, for instance for accounts; then came electric typewriters, some with special facilities, followed by stand-alone word processing (WP) machines, later generations of which nearly all embody cathode ray tube or semiconductor strip displays.

Later still came shared-logic WP machines - that is machines with centralised processing power to which are connected a number of workstations. The latest of all - few in number at present - incorporate communication links extending beyond those needed to interconnect work stations and central processors. The links may be between offices within a building or to remote offices, possibly in other countries. Teletex machines which may widen this trend have yet to catch on.

About 170,000 WP machines were shipped in the USA in 1979, a total expected to rise to 750,000 in 1984. In Western Europe about 11,800 were added in 1979 to a then existing total of 70,000; about 18,000 of these were in the UK where the total was expected to rise to 50,000 in 1984. These forecasts are, of course, not necessarily reliable particularly because the forecasters had not forseen the advent of micros with WP software. I have not come across any recent forecasts.

Considering the figures given previously for the number of women office workers, perhaps one in twenty women in US offices are using WP machines (assuming a total of at least one million machines in use). In Western Europe about one in three hundred are using them, and in the UK about one in two hundred. Thus the average woman typist in the US is not very likely to be using a WP machine, and in Europe that event is quite unlikely. However increases in WP in whatever form are expected.

There is another interesting development, at present affecting only a few people, and that is the possibility of working at a machine in the home which is linked by telephone line to a central processing machine ("Telecommuting").

The question of interest here is "to what extent are these developments affecting and will increasingly affect the quality of work, wages, salaries, and promotion prospects for secretary/typists?". Philip Kraft, an American Sociologist, is quoted as saying that the introduction of WP is the continuation of an old struggle to replace skilled people with skilled machines tended by unskilled people. Stupid workers and smart machines are the goal for every manager in the workplace. Philip Dorn, New York consultant, has a different view. The WP workers must be smarter, not less intelligent; we'll see smaller groups of better workers. If automation pushes enough people out the next thing you get is a revolution. In some European countries there is a genuine concern for the workers.

One UK viewpoint, based on extensive analysis, is that the job market will shrink for unskilled and semi-skilled women with a shift towards a requirement for more qualified people: the effect will be slow during the next ten years and there will be wide regional differences.

Clerical Workers

The term "clerk" presumably includes the army of women who are keying accounting and statistical information into computers in offices and also those in banks, building societies, travel bureaux, airlines etc. The usual meaning of clerical worker is "a worker, especially in an office, who keeps records, files, etc". This includes many women whose work involves filling in forms or processing completed forms.

The mechanization of office filing and form movement through an organization is a mundane but important area where mechanization will be felt by clerks long before it is felt by executives - although the "executive's electronic office" excites much greater interest. This is simply because some clerical work is already formalised, and much of it is amenable to formalisation - particularly in cases where a form (for instance an order) sets in motion a sequence of events. Considerable research is in progress in this area.

Most of the remarks made about the effect of the introduction of machines upon typists apply to clerks. The purpose of a "clerical" machine may be

different, but most such machines contain the same operator interface as the
typist's - that is keyboard, screen, etc.

<u>The quality of office work</u>

The results of office automation could be machine pacing, noise, reduced
mobility, repetitive work and de-skilling if human factors are not given
appropriate priority. It may be possible to select a particular type of person
who is likely to do well on a word processing machine. The required attributes
are flexibility, enjoyment of change and autonomy, preference for working with
machines than with people, not distracted by noise, etc., - in other words
select from the available personnel; do not require everyone to conform to the
same type of job.

The quality of work may well depend on the attitude of management which may
lie somewhere between two extremes. The objective may be a reduction of
administrative costs made possible by using centralised machine-aided facilities
with fewer people; there may be a trend towards grey uniformity in this
situation. On the other hand the accent may be on higher productivity from the
same number of people using more machines, accompanied by selection of the right
kind of people for the work and appropriate working conditions; this seems to
have been the objective in the trials carried out in UK Civil Service typing
pools.

The most important factors in these trials were the selection of people
and their work, and proper training; given these factors productivity gains of up
to 100% were recorded for particular kinds of work. The reactions of
employees when asked how they felt about operating WPs were 27.8% very
satisfied, 53.5% satisfied, 14% indifferent, 4.7% dissatisfied. 76.7% wanted
the opportunity of using WPs again (Note: The Civil Service allows a £450 pa
increase for WP operators).

The "VDU bogey" was raised some years ago. It was claimed that X-rays from
cathode ray tubes used in Video Display Units were a hazard to health. Eye
strain, posture problems, etc were also said to occur. These fears seem to have
been unfounded although the subject still gets an airing.

<u>Promotion</u>

New jobs associated with new technology in offices include technicians,
supervisors, training officers and project managers. For computer based
operations a range of opportunities exist including engineers, programmers,
system analysts etc. These conclusions are related more to differences in
education and training than to differences in sex. Opportunities are better for
men than for women because more men have the required educational standards. The
message for women is acquire a better education, or given only an average
education, look out for special training or adult education opportunities.

<u>Information technology and women at work</u>

Driscoll (a contributor to this book) has no doubt about the effects of
office systems. They "will increase the separation between boss and secretary
...to create a breed of even more menial office workers."

Smith also feels that the outlook for women is rather gloomy. In Australia
women in the labour market tend to concentrate in a limited range of occupations
and industries in the economy because of labour market segregation by sex. These
are the jobs where displacement will occur to a significant degree as a result of
advances in microelectronics technology.

Over half the female paid workforce were (1977) concentrated in five occupation - clerical workers, sales assistants, stenographers and typists, housekeepers cooks and maids, and teachers. Over 50% of the female workforce were employed in "at risk" occupations, compared with 25.2% of the male. It is not claimed that anything will happen quickly, but when it does it will be bad for women. Smith urges a policy of a wider range of non-traditional female subjects to be taught at school and a wider range of employment opportunities might also be created for women by the provision of schemes for retraining on re-entry to the workforce.

A case study of the effects of the introduction of word processing in a British engineering consultancy is reported by Buchanan who points out that previous findings have been contradictory. He concludes that the change from copy to video typing reduced task variety, meaning, and contribution to end-product, control over work scheduling and boundary tasks, skill and knowledge requirements (in some respects) and communication between authors and typists. It increased control over typing quality, skill and knowledge requirements (in some respects) and pay and promotion prospects. However video typists were given a salary increase of one grade over copy typists and had the opportunity of promotion to a supervisor. They felt that their job prospects had been improved through their experience with the word processing system.

Eckart starts with a review of reports of previous effects of the impact of microprocessors on female employment. In fact it is a review of that impact on all jobs and includes the hardy annual about the loss of jobs at Western Electric. This review is long on job losses, but short on job gains. Such job gains as are reported refer mainly to men's jobs. The author continues with proposals for action rather similar to those suggested by Smith. However he emphasises the need for speed, particularly in the implementation of "compensatory educational programmes"and asks how important are fathers in limiting the potential of their daughters. The girl's relative lack of interest in mathematics and science may be the result of malleable social influences.

The 1981 OECD report also points out that most routine information handling tasks are carried out by women and states that because of the high degree of occupational segregation any female labour that is displaced will have more difficulty in securing alternative employment. At the same time, relatively low levels of educational attainment, combined with lack of continuity in employment, make it difficult for women to develop market skills. This becomes a still greater disadvantage when previous skills become still more rapidly obsolete.

The same message came across in 1981/82 even more strongly than in 1980, but drew little response. Perhaps the whole climate needs to be changed starting with attitudes at primary schools. The issue does not seem to be getting widespread support led by action-forcing people. Does it command wide support or simply lip service?

THE UNEMPLOYMENT-TCHNOLOGY CONNECTION

Henize comments on the arbitrary analytic methods which have been used as the basis for formulating policy. He rightly states that to determine the employment impact resulting from technological change, two basic problems have to be solved. The first is to determine the effect of change within individual industries. The second is to determine the end effect of all the separate influences. The macro effects which result from the complicated interplay of all the various individual microlevel developments interacting together in various complimentary, conflicting, and continually changing ways are generally not well understood at all.

How right he is. His work should be compulsory reading for the pundits who pronounce about the impact of this or that without the slightest attempt at quantification.

He continues with proposing methods for quantification using the case of the likely future impact of the introduction of automatic teller machines in banks as an example. The idea is to estimate the unemployment impact in the bank, and set it against the employment created by manufacturing, installing and maintaining each machine. The net effect is estimated at minus 1.32 Full Time Equivalent persons (FTE) per machine, but this is offset by machine manufacturing employment, the result being a net labour displacement of 0.6. This is indeed a noble attempt. If it turns out to be correct in the event and sets a precedent for quantifying other situations, then it will have been easily worth every Mark spent in the effort. The question is can such predictions be made, even if great effort is involved, with an accuracy which is good enough to be useful?

In his concluding remarks Henize says that his figures have been arrived at using only rough rules of thumb in several places, but in the light of earlier costs per transaction comparisons, it does appear quite plausible. What he means is that it is plausible with the information he has at his disposal looked at in terms of today's context, terms, and situations projected to the future. This kind of work requires at least three results labelled "most pessimistic", "expected", and "most optimistic" so that we can see how greatly the spread of possible future variations of the component figures affect the results.

<u>PROPOSED REMEDIES</u>

From about 1978 onwards, everybody in the UK wanted to suggest remedies. The government of the day made available very large sums of money for industry, education etc., and a spate of official looking booklets appeared. The Trades Union Congress (TUC) recommended the pursuit of new technology employment agreements, reduction in the working week, more educational effort, more vocational training for young people, re-training of scientists, engineers, and teachers, and a general revision of manpower policy, development of trade union education, and assistance for the microelectronics industry.

The Advisory Council for Applied Research & Development (ACARD) recommended the development of technology strategies, study of how the government can foster rapid development of new industries e.g. information technology and biotechnology, study of transfer of technology into the UK, possible increase of engineers in government posts overseas, how to strengthen industrial R&D, and how to increase R&D in the service industries. The Council for Science in Society, in an excellent publication, provided a historical review, a consideration of the nature and satisfaction of work, a discussion of the current theories, and a range of suggestions for the future.

One factor which receives little mention is the importance of being able to supply and effectively market goods or services which people want. Another approach is to create a need (as did Xerox) and then satisfy it. Employment will follow. It is hard to promote these intangible attributes because people's attitudes towards marketing have to be changed. In England, and to a lesser extent in Europe, salesmen and engineers are barely respectable and this may have something to do with the dominance of the US, and now Japan, in the electronic building blocks of the new technology.

If the opinions expressed by Uttal turn out correctly Europe will probably not catch up. In 1979 Europe manufactured less than one third of its own chip consumption. A European customer who gets an imported chip 6 months after his US competitor will have missed out on so much planning and design work that the product he builds with can be two years behind. The immensity of the American market helps the chip manufacturers slide quickly down the learning curve.

With customers in every nation in Europe using different chip designs, markets are too fragmented to absorb high volume production. Compared with the US and Japanese manufacturers the couple of billion dollars to be spent in Europe over the next five years looks puny. US manufacturers will invest about $1.3 billion just in plant this year.

Scepticism expressed in the same article about Inmos, the Company founded in 1977 with UK government money, may have been misplaced. Inmos seemed to be on schedule and deliveries of its 16K memory chips started in 1983/1984. However in 1985 Inmos is suffering the same production cut-backs as the rest of the industry. Hopes are centred on its "transputer" advanced technology chips which are not yet in production.

The frequently advocated idea of providing government support for radical inventions and innovations in firms during the gestation period is discussed by Freeman. It is suggested that where this idea has gone wrong in the past is in providing support not only for exploratory development but also for full scale commercial development. But what happens if the promising invention gets through the first stage, but then funding for the second is not available from risk-takers? Should the government then say "We gave you every chance lads, but if nobody wants to take it up now, hard luck". It may be politically difficult to abandon the firm to its fate. It may become even more difficult to make the right decision after yet more money has been poured into the enterprise.

Freeman also suggests that job-generation in the UK coulld be provided by cabling the country. He also suggests massive public investment in higher education, training, and re-training and improvements in the importing and diffusion of foreign technology.

The most notable case of government support in information technology is probably that of Nexos. At the beginning of its three year life the headlines were "Nexos poised to scoop the Fax market" (An absurd comment) and "Nexos moves fast on office automation". But on December 11th 1981 we read "A £30 million gamble on the office of the future goes wrong" and "the bold strategy...is now in tatters". It seems that the problem was simply too many bosses - The National Research Development Corporation, the National Enterprise Board, Muirhead, Logica, and Nexos, plus Delphi and Exxon somewhere in the background was hardly a recipe for a single minded thrust into a highly competitive field.

A table is given by Rothwell (1982) showing the employment in the 1970s provided by manufacturing companies with 200 or less workers in 8 industrialised countries. In Japan nearly 70% of manufacturing employment is provided by such companies. The figure for West Germany is 50%, France 32%, and UK 29%. In the US, 66% of net new jobs were created by firms employing less than twenty people between 1969 and 1976. Data for the East Midlands in the UK show that 42% of new jobs were created by wholly new manufacturing establishments between 1968 and 1975.

More detailed examination of job creation by US and European companies shows that while new small firms generate a large number of new jobs, it is the technologically innovative small firms which create even larger numbers. Rothwell concludes that various government schemes to assist such firms are justified but an assessment of them is urgently required.

Idealistic ideas are expressed by Engberg in which the nature of work itself is questioned. What interests are we serving through cementing respect for a work-oriented ethic which is incompatible with the automated society? If we do not get rid of the present competitive mentality focused on material possessions, and turn instead to individual creative use of information, automation may lead to a totalitarian society.

Few people seem to have interested themselves in what seems to me to be an important question. How much wealth is needed to bring about what may well be very desirable changes in work, leisure, retirement age etc., and how is it to be created and distributed? How many more "calculating machine syndromes" are out there waiting to contribute to that wealth?

EFFECTS OF INFORMATION TECHNOLOGY ON THE QUALITY OF LIFE

"The proper study of mankind is man" said Pope, but some people take a jaundiced view of the Social Sciences and Sociology in particular (referred to as the "soft sciences"). It seems better to judge each piece of work on its merits and some very interesting work has been done, particularly in regard to the social impact of computers, by such people as Stone, Kling, Weizenbaum, Simon, Bell, Whisler, Parker, Rule, Kraemer and others. Some of these are primarily computer professionals who have reflected upon the consequences of their activities.

Schools of Thought

All salesmen of ideas or material things are biased although conventionally it is the car, vacuum cleaner etc., salesman who does the hard sell. However no salesman is so assiduous as the academic marshalling his or her material to strengthen the hobby-horse on which the next research grant may ride. In the social sciences subjective assessments and opinions rather than verifiable facts often dominate so it becomes even more important to identify the author's hobby-horse. Usually this presents little difficulty.

In discussing the studies on the use of computers in organisations, Kling identifies two major schools - the "Systems Rationalists" and the "Segmented Institutionalists". You will observe that concepts are recoded into terse jargon in the social sciences, rather like computerese. These schools have their right and left wings. The Segmented Institutionalists include "Class Politicians" with Marxist leanings. The near-equivalents of the Systems Rationalists are the Technocrats and the Social Analysts. The former often take a "hard" line and the latter a "soft".

Although I am over simplifying Kling's view, the types are recognisable; as a matter of fact this classification can be applied to people mentioned earlier in this chapter. On the one hand there is "a continuation of the old struggle...to replace skilled people with skilled machines tended by unskilled people" and on the other ".....there is genuine concern for the workers".

Both groups do a lot of shouting, particularly the Class Politicians. These days you have to shout to be noticed by the media, but probing a little further into the literature there is some good stuff which demands serious attention. "In characteristic American fashion (says Kling) know-how has produced immense improvements in equipment and applications software" but "with the meagre attention given to understanding social repercussions it is hard to believe that important understandings will be reached before inappropriate commitments are made". What he means is that you should talk to the users first.

Kling considers that the technocrats "emphasise the positive roles of computer technology" and "...often examine new capabilities of computer technologies, e.g. computer conferencing.....they assume that there is a marked consensus on major goals relevant to computer use and they often develop a relatively synoptic account of social behaviour". In other words people need convincing. The Social Analysts, on the other hand, "examine both legitimate and illegitimate consequences of computerised technology on social life....they assume that intergroup conflict is as likely as co-operation unless the contrary is empirically demonstrated....they identify as dominant values the sovereignty of individuals and groups over critical values of their lives".

Social Outcomes

Kling makes no claim that his classification is all-embracing - rather does
it consist of "two sweeping labels to help to identify the major choruses and
their principal songs"; he does, however, rather well describe situations which I
know and you know are not untypical in which the computer serves "almost
exclusively symbolic and political functions".

For example in the Riverville welfare agencies in the United States
"...automated information systems did little to improve internal efficiency, but
improved the agencies image of efficient administration to attract funding more
easily". In another case he finds that "...computer modelling does not easily
fit into the fragmented world of public policy making.....it may take several
years to design, programme, and fine tune....but policy makers are often working
with shifting definitions of the dilemmas they face....and the actors may be
voted out of office in a two year period".In the case of Wesco, a multi-national
engineering firm, "calculations were shifted from pencil and paper to computers
to provide the appearance of greater accuracy....and computing was used because
it convinced important parties that decisions were being carefully made".

Kling also cites many cases where the advent of computers was perceived as
beneficial and computer use had perceptible but not dominant effects on those
involved. "White collar workers in several different occupations attributed to
computing clear, often positive influences in their jobs". He also summarises
the findings of others who analysed abuses of personal information "....few
abuses have occurred in the past decade....there were abuses in the National
Criminal Information Centre's files, all of which were rapidly remedied" and
those that did occur "were essentially the random acts of a few individuals".

But with new technology it comes as no surprise to discover that sometimes
things sometimes go badly wrong. It's mainly to do with the way the technology is
introduced, and very little to do with the machines - in other words,
people. Mumford (1978) enquired about attitudes following the introduction of
computer systems into unidentified organisations. In the several cases she
reports the viewpoints of clerks were obtained by interviews, but no interviews
with executives are reported. This may not mean that there were none but we do
not know whether the management viewpoint voiced by Mumford is simply assumption.

Senior management were determined to gain the knowledge to design their own
system as they mistrusted the ability of outside technical experts to
understand the complexities of their business. At managerial level an excellent
adaptation process has taken place but "when I interviewed the clerks who
operated the system, I found that they felt their work had been degraded" and in
another case "When I visited a number of local offices, far from a good fit
being achieved between the technology and the needs of staff, I found a situation
in a turmoil" and (concluding) "...most organisations introducing computer
systems set only technical and business goals and either do not have human goals
or do not make these explicit".

We are now starting to get to the heart of the matter. In a hard
competitive world how near can we reasonably expect to get to (quoting Mumford
again) "...a participative approach in which no one must suffer and as many
employees as possible must gain from the change?". It is pleasant to imagine that
the important matter of wealth creation can proceed in so gentle and laudable an
environment.

A well orchestrated controversy: 1. Goods and Services

Herbert Simon and Daniel Bell (optimists) and Joe Weizenbaum (iconoclast)
are the protagonists in a war of words about the progress of technology.   Bell

is best known for his 1973 book "The coming of Post-Industrial Society". He considers that Science is a "collective good" which has become the major productive force in society. It is the nature of modern technology which frees location from resource site and opens the way to alternative modes of achieving individuality and variety within a vastly increased output of goods. "This is the promise - the fateful question is whether it will be realised".

Bell's major premise is that as societies get richer "people's horizons expand and new wants and tastes develop; they move on from exclusive concern with their immediate material needs - these are largely satisfied - to the more abstract requirements associated with wealth and leisure. These "post-industrial" needs....are more readily met on the basis of the collective provision of services". This is an elaboration of a theory first put forward by C.Engel in the nineteenth century sometimes called "Engel's Law".

The Post-Industrial Society has been discussed so often that Bell's assumptions are infrequently questioned. Gershuny is a dissenter. He examined UK consumption statistics and concluded that although expenditure on services in the period under examination (1954-1974) rose rapidly, the cost of services rose twice as fast as goods and were more affected by inflation. In terms of real money, a given expenditure in 1974 resulted in only half the consumption that the same expenditure would have provided in 1954; there was in fact a net fall in total real consumption of services. Gershuny examines the increase in tertiary (service) employment in the same period. He concludes that about half the tertiary employment is "goods-related". For example although nothing is manufactured in the Distribution Industry, classified as tertiary, it is simply an integral part of manufacture - the movement of goods to the market.

Another trend, says Gershuny, is that "investment is transferred from service industries into households" (as in washing machines for instance) and "there is a trend towards the self-service economy. ....Certainly there has been considerable growth in medicine and education, but why should we assume that consumption of these items should necessarily continue to rise? Can we not imagine the replacement of social investment in educational and medical plant by household investment in educational and medical machines (helped, for instance, by rapidly developing video and storage devices with falling costs)?"

A well orchestrated controversy: 2.Intelligent computers

Simon pursues several ideas in an article in Science. He believes that Artificial Intelligence will progress steadily because "...available computer memory size is increasing rapidly to the point where it may not much longer be an effective limit on the capacity of computers to match human performance". On the subject of work he says "...the sensible response to this problem (unemployment, that is) is not to eschew the benefits of change; it is rather to take institutional steps to shift the burdens of the transition from the individual to society". Referring to the past he continues "The polls provide absolutely no evidence for decrease in job satisfaction....if alienation has been increased by automation the increase somehow does not show up in answers by workers to questions about attitudes toward their jobs".

Weizenbaum, master of devastating criticism, castigates the Systems Rationalists, and generally lays into proponents of the Computer Revolution. With regard to Artificial Intelligence, to him "....the answer seems to be obvious. Truly creative thought gains its power from the combination of hitherto disparate contexts. All the analogical reasoning programs that artifical intelligence has produced so far are given the relevant criteria of similarity they need: that is, the two frameworks which are to be fused. This is not to criticise quite clever programs produced to date: it is rather to illustrate on what profoundly and fundamentally misguided bases some of the most crucial concepts of artificial intelligence are built".

Weizenbaum is quite clear about the future for Home Computers:- "...what fraction of American homes will have them? A standard analogy is to television. Essentially all American dwellings have at least one television set. Indeed many dwellings of the poor and the very poor have, whatever else they lack, a television set. Television is an example of a technological gadget which vindicated the marketeers who think in term of consumer resistance thresholds below which it is possible to duck absolutely.....will the home computer be as pervasive as today's television sets? The answer almost certainly is no.

Continuing with a dry humour "....There are some appliances computers must control: the wall-to-wall carpeting must be cleaned by a robot, roasts are in the oven, and the computer helps "the mother" pay the telephone bill, and so on and on.

We need not credit computers for accomplishments with which they have nothing to do. They can be realistically credited with having made possible some easing of the lives of some people. Modern airline reservation systems, for example, have made it easier for me to travel. Computers have radically transformed many aspects of astronomy and without computers space flight would have been impossible. The computer has done some good."

Effective user-oriented computer operations

Of course computers are widely used for information retrieval, but information is a curious resource. As Parker argues "The distribution of information has a declining marginal cost: the cost of providing information to the n'th user, once it has been produced, is small....this makes it difficult to create appropriate incentives for the original production of information....with a consequent under-incentive for the private sector to produce it....which initially led many governments to their present large involvement in the information sector of the economy". To this Engburg adds "The private investor has to have guarantees against illegal copying. At best, information can be invaluable when it is secret. Once it is made public there is no reason for paying for anything other than retrieval, transmission and presentation".

This theme has been taken up by Stone who starts by criticising the computer industry which "...has shown little comprehension about user co-ordination. He suggests that the strength of a computer based system may be in "....a tailored negotiation which boils down to the user being able to say "here is what I want" or "this is what I am seeking" according to the user's frame of reference, rather than for the user to have to select from among what the supplier chooses to offer in the supplier's terms".

He continues "some examples exist where three components - opportunity assessment, booking, and accounting - have been integrated within an information processing context. In an airline reservation network a clerk can assess travel availability, book a specific travel arrangememt, and clear payment by credit card, all through the same computer. Another domain is found in some of the emerging databank networks. Users may be helped in locating the right databank, to assess whether the desired piece of information is available and how much it will cost, to retrieve it if it is wanted, and automatically having all costs charged to the user's account.

Stone works within a noteable Ivory Tower - to wit, Harvard. He may know something about indexing and computer software. However he wisely abstains from suggesting ways, means, and costs. Even so he makes some pertinent remarks which connect with earlier comments about information economics. "People selling information have always had to be careful not to give the information away in the course of selling it, a task made especially difficult when the customer is unable clearly to specify what is wanted. By integrating the negotiation and retrieval processes the user can retrieve in stages, not taking a full retrieval until it is clearly evident it is the information desired. Only a computer could have the patience or be cost effective in selling information in such a piece by piece basis".

Perhaps this idea has some potential; it seems to integrate several features of many information-seeking activities in which the user gets the needle out of a haystack by successive ever-narrowing homing-in steps.

<u>Limits to rate of change</u>

Everyone knows that the method of broadcasting information in a scientific or technical journal article is rather like advertising; a minute fraction reaches the target. The average number of times an article about turboencabulators or about anything at all is read, seldom exceeds single figures. Thus very few, if any, of you will know that I am a cynic when it comes to the oft-made predictions about the rapid effects of the white-hot technological revolution (Cawkell 1980) - or perhaps you have read enough of this book to have your suspicions.

Thompson distinguishes between intensive interactions with substitution or extrapolation and those which generate real transformations. "...the steam engine replaced the donkey in supplying the motive power for the mine hoist; it could hoist heavier loads faster and cheaper. Taking the same steam engine, mounting it on wheels and having it run along rails produced something quite different. New cities sprang up along the rails in North America and other parts of the world. The higher order impacts turned out to be more important than the first order impacts".

Passing on to the present Thompson suggests that "...It is difficult to find in suggestions for new services (proposed for running on integrated networks) anything that is likely to have higher order impacts of sufficient significance....".

"To be particularly horrified one only has to look at the systems that "aid the office worker". Here the notion of intensification is rampant. Only in the most futuristic projections does one see any seeds of transformation. The underlying theme here is to improve the productivity of document preparation. Surely this can result in nothing but more documents being prepared with a strong tendency to lowering the quality of those documents. Like the Xerox machine this technology merely increases the need for larger IN baskets and waste paper baskets. It is not clear how this increase in lower quality information can help.

The combination of an implicit faith in the value of information technology and the almost complete confinement of this activity to the intensive class of interactions can produce a level of competitive activity that would not necessarily benefit the key actors or the society at large...The return on investment that the society might get under such situations for its efforts in the area of information technology could be one of diminishing returns. It is difficult to develop alternative arguments that do not involve faith, hand-waving and other such emotion-laden techniques".

Indeed it is, but provided there is a return on the investment, a businessman would be unlikely to reflect upon these lofty issues. For example it would be easy to argue that the huge investment in the development of instantly-processed colour photographs could have been used to develop a more beneficial product, but why should such arguments impress industrialists?

Thompson considers one possibility "The rapidly evolving computer graphics field is spawning studies of graphics as a basic means of communication

.....earlier iconic languages could not make use of the time-varying capabilities that our present technology has.....we have the opportunity to develop a visual language based on time varying icons and using an alternative syntax to spoken language".

Direct Benefits Now
----

1. Health, medicine, the elderly

Thompsons's comments about "transformations" - at least up until now - seem to be correct. No dramatic change in most people's lives has occurred as a result of ten years of information technology. Today's discussions seem taken up with speculation - are we heading towards a fulfillment of Orwell's predictions or will new technology "free location from resource site and open the way to alternative modes of achieving individuality and variety within a vastly increased output of goods?"

Despite Weizenbaum's sarcasm there have been quite a few less dramatic developments which most people would subjectively assess as "improvements". Townley appeals for better awareness about the variety of devices being developed independently to help the handicapped - she has accumulated a file of records describing over 300 different devices. Some of them have been described by Aylor. Mobility is obviously of great importance to handicapped people and various micro-processor controlled devices for wheelchairs have been introduced. For instance a joystick control has been developed which extracts the average value of spastic hand movements. A manipulator enabling the occupant of a wheelchair to retrieve objects from shelves, open doors, etc., has also been described.

In 1980 Tesco, a large British stores group, announced an experimental "shopping by computer" scheme for elderly people in Gateshead. Visual display units in homes for old people were connected to a small computer enabling orders to be placed at the local store. IBM announced a talking typewriter for blind operators at the end of 1979. A unit attached to the typewriter monitors the typing and generates synthetic speech as phonemes according to rules stored in the unit's memory. The system sold for around $5300 but was withdrawn in 1984.

Developments in reliable compact microprocessors have been an important factor in rapid advances in medical electronics. A Nobel prize was awarded for work in this area (to Geoffrey Hounsfield for the invention of "brain scanners" - x-ray computer assisted tomography (CAT) - first installed at a hospital in Wimbledon, London). There are many other examples including an artificial larynx, a Braille tactile display, epilectic seizure control by biofeedback and medical data systems.

2. Industrial applications, cars

Motor car manufacturers are now routinely including electronic devices in cars - the original incentive was the anti-pollution drive in the United States. Accurate monitoring of factors like ignition timing and air/fuel ratios not only reduce pollution; they also help in another area where there is a great incentive for improvement - fuel economy.

Ford are incorporating a second generation system controlled entirely by integrated circuits in some car models. This system, the EEC 111, embodies an exhaust gas oxygen sensor, an engine coolant temperature sensor, a crankshaft position sensor and a throttle position sensor. Signals from these sensors are processed in a control box which incorporates a calibration module. The proper operating conditions are calculated for running the car under the prevailing circumstances and control is exercised via the fuel injectors and exhaust gas re-circulation solenoids to reduce pollutant levels).

Other developments in the car industry include the increasing use of diagnostic equipment in garages. Volkswagen and General Motors are the leaders. General Motors fitted late 1981 cars with a small display panel on the dashboard; any of 22 different codes could be displayed to indicate a fault automatically. The local authorised garage decoded and rectified the fault.

Back in 1958 an inventor tried to interest me in making a servo-driven map device upon which a light indicated the position of the car, James Bond style. The driver was supposed to be able to locate his position and follow a route accordingly; it worked after a fashion but appropriate technology was not then available. The device did not rely on externally generated guidance signals. Evidently this was too ambitious because modern systems of a similar kind - for instance those used in aircraft - do depend on such signals.

Volkswagen was reported to be developing an information system for car drivers back in 1979.   Data about road conditions, traffic congestion and routing data was coupled to the car's receiver and micro-control box via roadside sensors. Advice to the driver is displayed on a simplified map.

3.The home

One problem in homes is the routing of information from a computer or control device to the individual machines to be controlled. This can be done without the need for additional wiring or radio control by using the A.C. mains. Modulated signals are circulated between neutral and earth using the mains as a data bus.

Most reports come from the States and it is hard to judge whether anything really useful actually happens, or whether the reports simply reflect the ebullience of that remarkable country. For example "A new concept in central heating and air conditioning control comes from Sensors & Systems Ltd. Programming is performed on a calculator style keyboard.....and all programs can be suspended for 99 days for holidays etc....but the Micro 8 still works to provide frost protection if the temperature falls below 5 degrees ...the unit provides for two different hot water programs each of which can be programmed for any day of the week" - and that was back in 1980.

This device falls far short of my requirements. I would certainly expect a two-barrelled auto-ejector hot-bath re-entry system as well. This device would eject two persons from bed into personalized temperature controlled his-and-her jacuzzi baths, pre-selected to operate at a particular moment in time - a considerable advance on the Alarm Clock. The system should include an auto-dryer, after the style of a clothes washer, to empty the water and blow hot air across the erstwhile bathers, whilst relaying the sounds of egg and bacon frying in the kitchen via stereophonic hydrophones concealed in the solenoid-controlled auto-evacuator (plug hole) and wafting the associated smell through the Pong-o-matic air conditioning system.

Conclusions

What may be concluded from this short survey of opinions? Should any particular action be taken by governments? It seems to me that hard evidence of any particular trend is lacking. There are a few proponents of the idea that the new technology will bring work for all - but pleasanter work for fewer people seems more likely. There does seem to be some evidence that a considerable degree of new technology can be harmoniously introduced into an organisation provided a sincere attempt is made by management to carry employees along with them. That is not a sensational finding but entrenched attitudes may make it very hard to do in practice; traditional strife is a habit which dies hard in some industries.

<u>FURTHER READING</u>

Amber, G.S.; Amber P.
  Prentice Hall. 1962.
    Anatomy of automation.
Anon.
  Pub. by Council for Science in Society, 3/4 St. Andrews Hill, London,
  EC4V 5BY. 1981.
    New technology; society, employment and skill.
Anon.
  No.5 in the ICCP series. Published by the OECD, Rue Andre Pascal, 75775
  Paris Cedex 16, France. 1981.
    Microelectronics, productivity, and employment.
Anon.
  No.6 (Volume 1) in the ICCP series.. Published by OECD, Rue Andre
  Pascal,75775 Paris Cedex 16, France. 1981.
    Information activities, electronics and telecommunications technologies:
    impact on employment, growth, and trade.
Aylor, J.H.; Johnson B.W., et al.
  Computer, 35-40, January 1981.
    The impact of microcomputers on devices to aid the handicapped.
Barron, Iann; Curnow, Ray.
  Francis Pinter, London, 1979.
    The future with microelectronics.
Bell, Daniel.
  In Dertouzos, Michael L. and Moses, Joel (Eds).
  The Computer Age, a twenty year view, Pub by MIT Press 1979. Chapter 9, pps
  163-211.
    The social framework of the information society.
Bird, Emma, et al.
  Report, 1980, by Communication Studies and Planning Ltd for, and
  published by The Equal Opportunities Commission, Overseas House, Quay St.,
  Manchester M3 3HN, England.
    Information technology in the office: the impact on women's jobs.
Blauner, R.
  University of Chicago Press, 1964.
    Alienation and freedom.
Boddy, David; Buchanan, David A.
  Omega 12(3), 233-240, 1984.
    Information technology and productivity: myths and realities.
Buchanan, David A; Boddy, David.
  J. Occup. Psychol 55, 1-11, 1982.
    Advanced technology and the quality of working life. The effects of word
    processing on video typists.
Cater, Douglas.
  J.Communication 31(1), 190-194, 1981.
    The survival of human values.
Cawkell, A.E.
  In Proc Aslib IIS LA Joint Conference, Sheffield, September, 1980; pps
  98-104. Pub. by The Library Association, 7 Ridgmount St.,London WC1E 7AE,
  England.
    The mismatch between converging information technologies and people.
Daniel, W.W.; Stilgoe, Elizabeth.
  Broadsheet 572, October 1977. PEP Press, London.
    Where are they now? A follow-up study of the unemployed.
Driscoll, James.
  In Landau, Robert et al.(Eds). Emerging Office Systems. 1982. Ablex
  Publishing Corp., Norwood. NJ 07648, USA. Chapter 16.
    Office automation: the dynamics of a technological boondoggle.

Eckart, Dennis R.
   Int. J. Women's Stud. 5(1), 47-57, 1982.
     Microprocessors, women, and future employment opportunities.
Engberg,Ole.
   Impact of Science on Society, 28(3), 283-296, 1978.
     Who will lead the way to the information society?
Freeman, Christopher; Clark, John; Soete, Luc.
   Francis Pinter (London). 1982.
     Unemployment and technical innovation.
Godet, Michel.
   Futures, 120-123, April 1984.
     The technological miracle.
Gershuny, J.I.
   Futures 9(2), 103-114, April 1977.
     Post-industrial society: the myth of the service economy.
Henize, John.
   Technol. Forecast.& Social Change 20, 41-61, 1981.
     Evaluating the employment impact of information technology.
Hines, Colin.
   Pub. by Earth Resources Ltd, London, April 1978.
     The chips are down.
Huber, George P.
   Management Sci. 30(8), 928-951, August 1984.
     The nature and design of post-industrial organizations.
Hull, Frank M.; Friedman, Nathalie S., et al.
   Work and Occupation 9(1), 31-57, February 1982.
     The effect of technology on alienation from work: testing Blauner's
     inverted U-curve hypothesis for 110 industrial organisations and 245
     re-trained printers.
Jenkins, Clive; Sherman, Barrie.
   Eyre Methuen, London, 1979.
     The collapse of work.
Johnson, Deborah G.
   J. Social Issues 40(3), 63-76, 1984.
     Mapping ordinary morals on to the computer society: a philosophical
     perspective.
Kelly, Francis H.M.
   Report, Blyth Eastman Dillon Inc., 1221 Ave. of the Americas, New York, NY
   10020. June 1978.
     The Faustian delusion.
Kling, Rob.
   Computing Surveys,12(1),61-110,1980.
     Social analyses of computing: theoretical perspectives in recent
     empirical research.
Kochen, Manfred.
   In El-Hadidy, B., & Horne, E.E.(Eds). The Infrastructure of an information
   society. Elsevier 1984. PPs 26-40.
     A new concept of information society.
Kondratiev, Nicolai.
   Rev. Economics and Statistics, Nov 1935.
     The long waves in economic life. (Translation).
        For an interpretation see-
        Freeman, C.
        In Proc. OECD Conf. Structural determinants of employment and
        unemployment. OECD Paris, November 1977. Pub by OECD Paris.
        The Kondratiev long waves , technical change and unemployment.
Kuznets, S.
   American Economic Review, 30, June 1940.
     Review of Business Cycles.

Lepkowski, Wil; Bova, Ben, et al.
  Computers & People, 17-21, November/December 1980.
    The impact of automation upon people - Part 1.
Maslow, Abraham H.
  Harper & Row 1954.
    Motivation and Personality.
Meade, James.
  J.Social Policy 13(2), 129-146, 1984.
    Full employment, new technologies and the distribution of income.
Moore, Nick; Kempson, Elaine.
  J.Librarianship 17(1), 1-16, January 1985.
    The size and structure of the library and information workforce in the
    United kingdom.
Mumford, Enid.
  In Moneta, Josef (Ed). Proc 3rd Jerusalem Conf. on Information Technology,
  August 1978. Pub. by North Holland, Amsterdam. Pps 239-244.
    Human values and the introduction of technical change.
Northcott, Jim; Rogers Petra.
  Available from Policy Studies Institute, 1-2 Castle Lane, London SW1E 6DR.
    Microelectronics in industry: What's happening in Britain. (1982).
Price, Derek de Solla.
  Columbia University Press, New York, 1963.
    Little science big science.
Robinson, Arthur L.
  Science 195(4283), 1179-1184, 1977.
    Impact of electronics on employment: productivity and displacement effects.
Rothwell, Roy; Zegveld, Walter.
  Francis Pinter (London) 1982.
    Innovation and the small and medium sized firm.
Schement, Jorge R; Lievrouw, Leah.
  Telecommunications Policy, 321-334, December 1984.
    A behavioral measure of information work.
Schumpeter, Joseph.
  Harvard University Press, Cambridge Mass., 1934.
    Theories of economic development: an enquiry into profits, capital,
    interest, and the business cycle.
Simon, Herbert A.
  Science 195(4283), 1186-1191, 1977.
    What computers mean for man and society.
Smith, Andreas W. et al
  Daily Telegraph 10-11, Jan 29th 1985 and 7, Jan 30th 1985.
    Unemployment crisis 25 years in the making: eight proposals for reversing
    the trend.
Smith, Joy.
  The Australian Quarterly, 52(4), 415-431, Summer 1980.
    Developments in microelectronic technology and their impact on women
    in paid employment.
Stone, Philip J.
  Scientia 115(1-4), 125-146, 1980.
    Social evolution and a computer science challenge.
Thompson, G.B.
  Phil.Trans.R.Soc.Lond.A. 289, 207-212, June 1978.
    On the relation between information technology and socio-economic systems.
Townley, Helen M.
  Computer Age, 10-11, October 1980.
    The handicapped.
Weizenbaum, Joseph.
  In Dertouzos, Michael L. and Moses, Joel (Eds). The Computer Age, a twenty
  year view, Pub by MIT Press 1979. Chapter 20, pps 440-458.
    Once more the computer revolution.

<u>CHAPTER 27. PRIVACY, FREEDOM, AND DATA PROTECTION</u>

<u>Styles of government</u>

1984 has come and gone and most of Orwell's vision has not come about. However parts of it have turned out to be sufficiently accurate to cause considerable unease.

<u>The United States</u>

No government can be unaware of invasion of privacy dangers - for instance those associated with access to networked files containing personal information - but actions taken to deal with such dangers depend on style and political climate. Attitudes towards secrecy, or more particularly towards freedom, spread from the top downwards. In the United States freedom of speech and of the press are referred to in the first amendment to the constitution; these rights have been argued and extended into other media - for example in <u>NBC v United States (1943)</u> ensuring the expression of diverse views and in <u>Winters v New York (1948)</u> dealing with entertainment and doctrine.

The climate in the US is further exemplified by the Privacy, Freedom of Information, and other Acts. Problems associated with the FOI Act include the many cases in which one or more of the nine exemption clauses have been invoked, according to Madans. Administrative problems resulting from the 1974 amendments have been discussed by Peterson. The two major "Sunshine" Acts illustrate some of the conflicting requirements in privacy legislation.

The FOI Act provides for an individual or "legal person" (e.g. a corporation) to request and be supplied with any non-exempt government record but not "private" records in certain defined categories. The Privacy Act permits an individual to inspect government records about him or herself, but about another only with another's written authorisation. Neither Act provides for information disclosure by private organisations. Inspection of credit ratings,etc., held in private files, is covered by other Acts.

The upholding of the Freedom of the Press, a related issue of great importance, also has its problems - for instance the delicate matter of "leaks" and the naming of sources as in the famous case of <u>The New York Times v US</u> (1971) (The "Pentagon Papers"). In short, the will exists in the United States to confront information and secrecy problems although more than the Acts mentioned above are needed to clarify rights of access and personal privacy. There has been much criticism about the absence of a national information policy.

<u>The UK: a potted history of inertia</u>

In some countries in Europe, and particularly in Britain, secrecy is pervasive. The UK climate is set by the Official Secrets Act, passed hastily in 1911 during a spy scare, and virtually unchanged since. Conveniently for the government of the day the Press was fully occupied at the time with the Kaiser and the Agadir crisis. Governments take refuge behind this blanket measure, although before every election pledges are given to reform the Act.

Recommendations for the reform of the catch-all section 2 (forbidding government officials to divulge confidential information) appeared in a 1978 White Paper. The Labour government did nothing and was heavily criticised by the opposition. That opposition, now the governing Conservative party, finds reform to be equally unattractive.

In February 1985 events connected with the sinking of the Argentinian warship the Admiral Belgrano demonstrated, once again, the need for reform. The restrictive nature of the Act prompted leaks which, among other issues, highlighted the question of relationships between the government and the civil service. The parliamentary debate reflected no credit on anybody. It so happened that a Labour opposition berated a Conservative government about reforming the Act, but both displayed the same hypocrisy.

While the makers of the US Constitution tried to ensure that their countrymen would not be subjected to the tyranny of the Old Country, the rulers of Britain have never felt that much is amiss. The feelings of our mentors about secrecy in government are enshrined in the Official Secrets Act. Those feelings have been obvious over the years in lip service for more open government prior to elections, and no action when in power.

The Act has become a symbol of government inertia - extreme reluctance in getting to grips with data protection is one of many examples. The Act has been used by successive governments for their greater general convenience. To acknowledge a public "right to know" as opposed to a governmental "right to secrecy" requires a complete change of attitude.

Three bills introduced to the UK parliament in the late 60s to do with personal information and privacy failed to get a second reading. The 1972 Younger report concluded that there was no need legally to establish privacy rights. The 1970 Conservative manifesto contained a pledge to "review the operation of the Official Secrets Act so that government is more open and more accountable to the public". When elected, the Conservatives appointed the Franks committee to review the topic. It argued against a freedom of information law in its report, but suggested some reforms. Nothing was done.

The 1974 Labour manifesto contained almost the same words as the Conservative's. In 1978 Mr Mervyn Rees produced a White Paper with proposals to reform the Act but members of his own party thought it was "completely inadequate". Labour MP Mr Christopher Price said "the secrecy we have in Britain is a cancer which acts against everything which this Labour movement wants to carry out". His government obviously did not agree since again nothing happened.

Having quoted from remarks in the White Paper to the effect that a Freedom of Information Act would completely change the nature of the government's obligations, an article in the Financial Times, dated July 21st 1978 remarked "Of course it would - that is why it was in the Labour manifesto". The article continued "It is claimed that legislation along Swedish or American lines would be inappropriate in the British context, where the policies and decisions of the executive are under constant and vigilant security by parliament. There could be few clearer examples of British hypocrisy than that statement".

The 1978 Lindop report to which the government again paid lip service, recommended legislation, including the establishment of a Data Protection Authority which would bring Britain into line with other countries. It had one encouraging provision although not completely explicit. The Data Protection Authority might have a security-cleared inspector able to check that the government was not evading its responsibilities merely by shifting files into a "security" classification. In 1980 a parliamentary statement prompted the headline "Go-ahead for privacy law". In March 1981 a Conservative Home Secretary, Mr. Whitelaw, announced that "legislation will be introduced when an opportunity offers". Perhaps he had 1984 in mind as an ironically appropriate year.

Unfortunately there seems to be little public concern. The Crichel Down scandal (in which "vigilant scrutiny" was notably absent when civil servants deceived the public in the course of disposing of Crown held farmland) has long since been forgotten.

In the words of an American and an Englishman (quoted in a perceptive discussion of the issues by Michael) "The liberties of the people never were, nor ever will be, secure, when the transactions of their rulers may be concealed from them" (Patrick Henry, American revolutionary). "Persons who carry high responsibility in Britain tend to assume that they cannot be expected to explain their actions fully to ordinary people, who would be unable to understand even if they wished to. This is the residue of old-fashioned aristocratic principle which remains firmly embedded in British democracy." (Andrew Schonfield, English economist).

Archaic English laws

The absurdity of much of English law in this area has been well reviewed by Stevens & Yardley. They point out that while the restraints which exist in the law resemble those in the European Convention (and doubtless the First Amendment too) the absence of a written constitution in the UK in which freedom of expression is afforded a degree of constitutional protection is very clear. The basic assumption is that Parliament may make any laws it chooses - very different from the wording of the First Amendment - and that the courts are obliged to give effect to these laws.

The absence of a yardstick, such as that provided by the First Amendment, has meant that our judges have little to go on and instead have adopted the relatively easy course of simply following, literally wherever possible, the words of parliament, seldom enquiring into their spirit. Stevens & Yardley give two major examples of the way the law does less than credit to the English legal system. They cite first the extraordinary case in which Mrs. Whitehouse tried to prosecute for obscenity those responsible for producing the play "The Romans in Britain".

Because the Attorney General refused to bring proceedings, Mrs. Whitehouse brought a private prosecution against a Director of the National Theatre, where the play was shown, under the Sexual Offences Act 1967. This Act provides for imprisonment of up to 2 years for homosexual acts in public. When the case came to Court the judge felt that an act of gross indecency within the meaning of the Act had been shown in the play, but that having been established, Mrs. Whitehouse declined to bring any further evidence consequently proceedings were abandoned. Mrs. Whitehouse's action demonstrated that Parliament's intention was thwarted since the intention was that the Attorney General should have sole discretion about prosecutions in respect of theatrical performances.

Absurdities of the law had been demonstrated earlier during the "Ladies Directory" case of 1962 concerning a booklet of services with prices. The extraordinary conclusion of the House of Lords was that a person could be guilty of corrupting public morals whether or not he was guilty of an obscene publication, and whether or not his purpose was itself criminal - that is whether or not there was such an offence as "corrupting public morals"!

Earlier still, questions about the obscenity of Lawrence's "Lady Chatterley's Lover" were the subject of a notorious case in which bishops, critics, and experts were required to testify as to the merits of the book. "It is this sort of subjective judgement which gives rise not only to confusion of the law but a tendency for an articulate and aggressive minority to dictate the case of the majority" conclude Stevens & Yardley.

What is Privacy ?

Huff illustrates the character and importance of privacy with the story in Genesis of Noah's reaction in cursing his son, Canaan, upon finding out that Canaan had observed him in a drunken sleep, naked in his tent, and had told his brothers about it. Privacy is to do with our ability to develop social relationships and intimacies enabling us to control what is known about us. This enables us to decide when evaluation of us is appropriate, expected, or invited. Thus Canaan's intrusion and disclosure had violated Noah's code of privacy.

Privacy invasions of this kind are at the heart of the uncomfortable feeling we have when we are treated as an object of gratuitious evaluation by others. Orwell describes The shape of Winston's living room in Victory Mansions. It provided a degree of privacy and enabled him to open his diary out of sight of the telescreen.

Most people's feelings in regard to the government's interest in us are to be found in Brandeis' remarks, made during the <u>Olmstead v United States</u> case, about the intent of the makers of the Constitution. "They conferred, as against the government, the right to be let alone - the most comprehensive of rights and the right most valued by civilised man". The same rights are declared in article 8 of the European Convention on Human Rights "Everyone has the right of respect for his private and family life, his home and his correspondence".

<u>Information technology and privacy</u>

Information technology has added the dimensions of computer-based information storage and retrieval of information about people, and access to it via communication networks. As the complexity of modern society has steadily increased so has the interest of the government in us, for better or for worse. Can we still say that "An Englishman's home is his castle", and, if not, are we prepared eventually to leave the drawbridge down permanently? Where lies the balance between the interests of the individual and the legitimate interest of organisations and society? There is no doubt that people are uneasy about the amount and correctness of information held about themselves in computer storage, and about the number of people who can get at it via proliferating networks.

The ubiquity of computer facilities introduces a tendency to obtain information by consulting records instead of asking. The Privacy Protection Commission (USA 1977) observed "most record-keeping organisations consult the records of other organizations to verify information they obtain from an individual and thus pay as much or more attention to what other organizations report about him than they pay to what he reports about himself".

A different aspect of privacy, reviewed by Salton, summarises the <u>Menard v. Saxbe</u>, <u>Anderson v. Sills</u> and other similar cases in the US. Menard took nine years and spent a great deal of money to get his record and finger-prints removed from the FBI file following his arrest and release without charges being brought. In these cases the opinions and dissensions of judges show that existing US legislation is not clear. In one case the court ruled that the prospect of injury caused by the existence of a personal databank must be a real and immediate threat before a suit is brought; the chilling effect of such a file upon individuals is insufficient to warrant its destruction.

<u>Telephone tapping</u>

Improved technology provides the potential for automating telephone tapping - a once labour intensive activity. Speech can be automatically logged using a voice actuated recorder and many lines can be monitored by scanning (similar to "polling" where one line is used for transmitting data from many intermittently generating sources connected in turn to the line). The recording can be networked from a central interception point to "subscribing" agencies.

In the UK assurances are given from time to time at Westminster that the restrictions and safeguards controlling government telephone tapping are the same today as they were in 1957 - the year of the Birkett Committee's re-assuring enquiry. There were then 159 taps in the entire year.

The value of these assurances can be assessed against the findings in a
piece of 1980 investigative journalism by Campbell. British Telecom operates the
"Tinkerbell" telephone tapping service in a building in Ebury Bridge Rd., London,
manned 24 hours a day for several customers including MI5 and the Special
Branch. It probably has the capacity to monitor 1000 lines simultaneously and
employs 125 executive engineers. The home and office numbers of union leaders are
regularly tapped and during the Grunwick strike the organiser's office was tapped
at the local telephone exchange.

When the Home Office was asked to confirm the role of Tinkerbell, the
Director of Information replied that it was not in the public interest to supply
details and that the Burkitt recommendations were carried out to the letter.
Early in 1985 a former MI5 officer claimed (of course violating the Official
Secrets Act) that Arthur Scargill, leader of the striking coalminers, members of
CND etc., had their telephones regularly tapped.

In reviewing telephone tapping in a 1979 case, Sir Robert Megarry, the
Vice-Chancellor at the time, held that "no right of privacy, either general or
particular existed in English law and it is no function of the court to legislate
in a new field". With regard to the European Convention on Human Rights "he did
not feel that the right to enjoy one's private and family life and one's home and
correspondence was enforceable in the U.K., despite a recent European Court of
Human Rights decision which, some have argued, suggests otherwise. The absence
of the specific grant of any power to tap did not mean that no such power
existed. England is not a country where everything is forbidden except what is
expressly permitted. In his view, the case seemed to make it plain that telephone
tapping is a subject which cries out for legislation".

Benjamin Shieber was motivated to write a 50 page article about telephone
tapping and other methods of eavesdropping in the US entitled "Electronic
surveillance, the Mafia, and Individual Freedom". Shieber takes the view that
"there is no warrant for assuming that eliminating governmental electronic
surveillance will expand individual freedom. On the contrary, its elimination
may contract it by subjecting people to the power of authoritarian criminal
regimes that are not subject to any political controls".

This article demonstrates the dilemmas in the balance of freedom when faced
with a well organised Mafia which according to Schieber, consists of 2000 members
and 20,000 associates grossing 50 billion dollars annually. He concludes that
"judicially supervised electronic surveillance is both constitutional and
advisable".

The extent to which it is considered that "the right to be left alone"
should be eroded was observable in the invasion of de Lorean's privacy when
videotapes of FBI eavesdropping became available to the world's television
stations. This is an extreme example of a trend brought about to combat organised
crime in the US.

A Bill of Rights for the UK?

Without a written constitution or a Bill of Rights in the U.K., it is
necessary for people to "take the long road to Strasbourg as a court of first
instance". Article 26 of the European Convention says that all domestic remedies
must be exhausted before the Commission can entertain an individual's petition.
Remedies seldom exist in this country. To change the situation a Bill of Rights
was introduced by Lord Wade in September 1976. It was reintroduced in February
1981, but not enacted.

The British public do not seem to be concerned about the new-technology Big
Brother Syndrome. In a 1982 Mori poll, two thirds of those asked disagreed with

governmental files designated as "classified".

Transborder data flow, discussed later in this chapter, is admissable if (ideally) equivalent DP laws operate in the recipient country, but in practice it is allowed if a reasonable degree of protection operates there. Burkert, who investigated the matter, did not come across any cases where information transfer has been forbidden, but he is aware of cases where the DP authority has asked companies to reconsider their practices.

Legislation in Europe has created awareness and debate, evolved principles, and shown the need for adaptation of the laws.

<u>The US experience</u>

The main concern in the US has been with the record-keeping activities of the government about private individuals. There is no legislation in the US of the kind favoured in Europe. The 1966 Freedom of Information Act – about the right of public access to government information – was reinforced by the Privacy Act of 1974 which included measures for easing procedural barriers in public access. The 1974 Act is the only comprehensive piece of privacy protection legislation, although there are several other Acts and a number of state laws, and there have been US government initiatives in this area.

Major US corporations were asked in 1981 and again in 1982 to endorse guidelines about the privacy of records covering customers, shareholders, and employees. 157 large corporations and trade associations did so. Senator Edward Kennedy, active in this field, warned against attempts to change the Acts in order to limit freedom of access to government information on the grounds that criminal investigations were impeded. He cites the information uncovered about the My Lai massacre, and about misuse of powers used to investigate political dissidents, tax evasion by Spiro Agnew, and million dollar expense payments in connection with contract lobbying as evidence of the value of the Acts as they stand.

Proposals covering the use of information in databanks and other matters were made by the Carter administration in 1979 but the outcome seems to have more of the same kind of legislation – the 1980 Privacy Protection Act which limits government search and seizure of documents from individuals.

<u>Data protection in the UK</u>

Data protection legislation is not universally approved. Some people think that it will be impossible to enforce. It can be argued that the necessary expensive procedures will be adopted by honest people, but the person who wishes to conceal could arrange for selected print commands to be excluded from a program. The complexity of, say, relational databases, is such that the most thorough inspector could not be sure that there had been no concealment. A speaker at a UK parliamentary computer forum said "I use a computer network with nodes in 27 countries including a public call box in Peru. How can any data protection authority hope to find out what I am doing with my data?"

A number of comments were made at the INFO 82 conference in London at the time the UK Data Protection Bill was going through parliament. One speaker made a plea for attention to ethics by computer professionals when the legislation arrived. He stressed the need to avoid later overkill legislation which might be introduced if professionals do not shoulder their responsibilities. Another considered that the need for protection did not justify the costs which will have to be incurred by those who are required to register their files, and used Swedish experience of costs to back his comments.

He said that a shortened form of registration had already been introduced in Europe to reduce costs, and gave an example of problems in regard to internationally interconnected electronic mail files. If it was feasible to register computer files in the UK why not sensitive manual files? The National Computer Council had so far only unearthed five abuses of computer files. A third speaker said that there was no longer any option for the UK; having signed the European Convention, ratification must follow and the UK would then have to conform with certain minimum standards. A Swedish company had already refused an export license for plastic security cards to a British Company because of the inadequacy of protection in the UK.

In a discussion afterwards questions were raised about unenforceable laws. If it became necessary to prove that files containing, say, data restricted to specific internal use were being exported, presumably it would be necessary first to intercept them. Because of bit stream multiplexing, complex protocols, mixing of facsimile, electronic mail, picture data etc., that would be extremely difficult, it not impossible. Might that not mean that while large reputable organisations would behave properly, small ones intent on earning revenue from such data would ignore the law being almost certain that they could not be found out?

One opinion was that it was not the business of legislators to become involved in enforceability questions; if a law is needed it should be introduced regardless of such considerations.

THE UK DATA PROTECTION ACT

The new version of the Data Protection Bill was published in November 1983. It had already been of immense benefit - to the lawyers who prepared it. It was littered with sub-clauses and sub-sections, encouraging sentences like "(3) where any such notice as is mentioned in paragraph (b) in subsection (1) above contains a statement by the Registrar in accordance with section 10(6), 11(5), or 12(7) above then....etc. Legalese is worse than Computerese. The purpose of the bill was to implement the 1982 White Paper on Data Protection Cmnd 8538) and to enable the UK to ratify the European Convention. Some would say it was grudgingly introduced for that purpose and for no other. It was enacted in July 1984.

The eight principles

The Act establishes eight data protection principles - fair and lawful processing; specific purposes; confidentiality; sufficient but not excessive data; accuracy and timeliness; keep no longer than is necessary; individual right of access and correction if necessary; proper security.

Registration

The Act sets up a Registrar of data users and bureaux who hold or provide services involving personal data. Applicants will be informed within two months of application about acceptance or refusal. Provision is made for enforcement and appeal and a tribunal is set up. Registration must take place by May 1986.

Transborder flow

Transborder flow can be stopped by a transfer prohibition notice from the Registrar if he thinks that the data protection priciples in the country of destination are inadequate.

Rights of access

A person is entitled to find out whether a data user has personal information about him, and if he has, to receive a written copy within 40 days upon payment of the prescribed fee. If the data subject suffers damage because of inaccuracy he is entitled to compensation. Errors must be rectified or the data erased. If a data user cannot supply information to a data subject in response to a request without disclosing information about another, he is not obliged to do so unless the other person consents.

Exemptions

Personal data which is exempt from registration and right of access includes that concerned with national security; family, household or recreational purposes; certain administrative business records; club membership data; addresses-only mailing lists. Exemption from subject access are crime and taxation data; judicial appointments; professional privilege; research or statistical purposes; data already covered by the Consumer Credit Act 1974; backup data; certain data held by statutory bodies.

Cost (1983 estimates)

£650,000 a year at current prices for the DP Registrar and Tribunal with a staff (initially), of about twenty persons. £5.5M for computer hardware/software for government compliance with the Act; annual running cost for access requests about £1M; Up to £13M per year for local authorities and public bodies. One estimate (October 1984) of the cost to UK industry is £250M over the next five years.

Parliamentary changes

Several changes were made to the Bill during its passage through parliament. Data user's accounts and payroll are now exempt. Immigration information is no longer exempt from the provisions for subject access.

What the Act does not include

A number of provisions were hoped for or expected in the DP Act and others were considered by some to be very desirable but were not really expected. These include:-

Exemption safeguards.

There is no provision for a security-cleared inspector to check whether the files specified as "classified" are legitimately so specified, or have merely been shifted into that category to avoid rights of access.

Manual files.

The exclusion of manual files from the Act presents the opportunity for the data user to shift files to paper should he wish to deny right of access. Other European countries (except Denmark) and the US, do not specify the media for files, and the rather small number of enquiries received have applied to printed files. In other words attention is focused on the data, not the method of recording it.

Advice.

Neither an advisory committee for the Registrar nor a code of practice for data users are mentioned in the Act. However a governmental code of practice aimed at civil servants formalising the arrangements for confidentiality was published in June 1984. It emphasised this requirement during the widespread practice of data collection for statistical purposes only. It is hoped that this will allay public distrust.

Disclosure.

     The Act makes no mention of the need for data users to record transfers of
information to other files. An error, found by a person requesting access, may
therefore still be present on the transferred information. Problems have already
arisen by the adoption in the Act of a definition of data as "information
recorded in a form in which it can be processed by equipment operating
automatically in response to instructions given for that purpose".

     The above curious definition apparently applies to WP equipment, any type of
computer and punched card equipment, and microform equipment if it embodies
computer-controlled retrieval, but not if it doesn't .

The UK Data Protection Act: discussion

     A record may contain an address, printable on its own, and also
print-inhibitable data about the addressee. The Bill deals specifically with a
similar problem in a different situation - mailing lists for the distribution of
goods are exempt provided they do not include details of the articles sent. No
doubt we shall hear more as the technology changes about problems generated by
the catch-all definition used in the bill in an attempt to circumscribe the area
without including manual files.

     Questions have been raised about the magnitude of the Registrar's task,
given a limited budget and a small staff. The Registrar may be overloaded to
start with, but it is also thought that the on-going work-load of problems
associated with access rights will be heavy. However if the UK reaction is
similar to that in Europe, this is unlikely.

     A serious objection to the Act has come from the British Medical
Association. The BMA make two points. First, it would be impractical to move the
computerised personal records, used locally by doctors, into centralised systems
presumably to be controlled by a government agency. This would be necessary in
order to comply with all DP requirements. Second, a centralised file not
controlled by those who compile and use it for its intended purpose, could be
used by other agencies without the knowledge either of the compilers or of the
people who are described in the system's records.

     The BMA is particularly anxious that medical record files should not be
routinely used by the police as would be possible under the new Bill, once
control passes to a government agency. At present, confidential medical
information is passed to the police only in very exceptional circumstances.
Knowing that their records are no longer only for the eyes of their doctor, the
public would become wary of giving away details of, for instance, socially taboo
information needed for research purposes.

     However it is the interconnection of databanks which seems to be the main
Big Brother worry in this country. This would be diminished to some extent if a
security-cleared "Ombudsman" type of person was able to check such practices -
as recommended in earlier committees but not included in the Act. The present
policy encourages people to believe, if they need any further encouragement, that
pious pre-election remarks about changes in the climate - for instance by
changing the Official Secrets Act - are unlikely to mean much, and that
pervasive government secrecy is here to stay.

     Wong has summarised the action needed by UK company managers to respond to
the Act. They should review security, ensure that personal data is accurate,
complete, relevant, and timely, and arrange that their computer systems are able
to retrieve those parts of records that should be available to data subjects at
low cost with appropriate keys and indexes. Some set-up costs will have to be
incurred for defining and arranging need to know and rights of access and in

ensuring technically that systems are able to conform with requirements. On-going costs may also be incurred in handling access requests, and satisfying the enquiries of the Registrar.

Assuming that the content and control of personal and other information has been agreed, arrangements have to be made for protecting data from unauthorised access. Precautions must include "conventional" security - that is preventing unauthorised access to the computer room, theft of disks or tapes, etc. Remote terminals, perhaps in other countries, may be connected to the computer so passwords must be issued to authorised users of those terminals. The data could be intercepted en route between computer and terminal by telephone tapping, or by radio interception between terrestrial microwave links or satellite links so this too may require attention. In every case a balance has to be struck between the value of the data, the cost of security, and the inconvenience to authorised users caused by that security.

I received a letter from a computer bureau on Nov 26th 1980 informing me that a former employee had information which could compromise access security. The bureau invited me to change my password. This is an example of new problems posed by using computers. Sophisticated computer crime has received good press coverage and a very plausible novel has been written by McNeil about funds transfer from a bank to the internationally distributed accounts of one of the bank's programmers.

DATA SECURITY

The principle weapon against the interception of data in electrical transit is encryption. Diffie has provided a comprehensive treatment of the subject; the cloak-and-dagger politics and possibilities of code-breaking have been discussed by Sugarman. A code is simply the substitution of codewords for plain language, while the two major types of cypher - transposition and substitution - are operations on individual characters. Cyphers and cryptography (from the Greek kryptos, hidden, and graphein, to write) are used to prepare secret messages.

The two major encryption methods in use today are the DES or Data Encryption Standard and the PKA or Public Key Algorithm. They provide protection against the theft of tapes or disks, or against the interception of data in the course of transmission.

The DES specifies an enciphering algorithm for the high speed processing of data by computer hardware. A 56 bit key is used for multiple permutations of blocks of plain text composed of 64 bits inclusive of 8 error-detection bits. To decipher, it is only necessary to apply the same algorithm to an enciphered block using the same key. Everyone knows the algorithm but only the sender and receiver know the selected key. There are 72 quadrillion possible keys and there has been some controversy about the effort and cost needed to produce a computer capable of breaking the algorithm, with charges of collusion between the US National Security Agency and IBM who developed it - real space age cloak and dagger stuff.

The PKA, however, embodies an additional factor to nullify the possible effect of the security risk inherent in the DES; with DES, information about keys could be intercepted en route to perhaps many correspondents. PKA uses two separate keys - a public enciphering key and a different secret deciphering key. The inverse of the enciphering functions cannot be derived even if the enciphering functions are known.

The distribution of information about keys to the message recipient is not necessary because of the "trap-door" method of using one way enciphering and inverse functions. The PKA also embodies a signature to authenticate the sender as actually being the person he is purporting to be.

A different solution, as described by Walker, is needed for the case when a
large computer, connected to a communications network, contains files of
different security classifications, and it is desired to make the installation
available to a number of people who themselves are within different security
categories. Machines can embody a security "kernel" or interface between the
operating system - that is specialised software controlling computer functions -
and the hardware. The function of the kernel is to check the access rights of
each user to any information-containing system element. It may, of course, be
necessary to encrypt data flowing through the network as well.

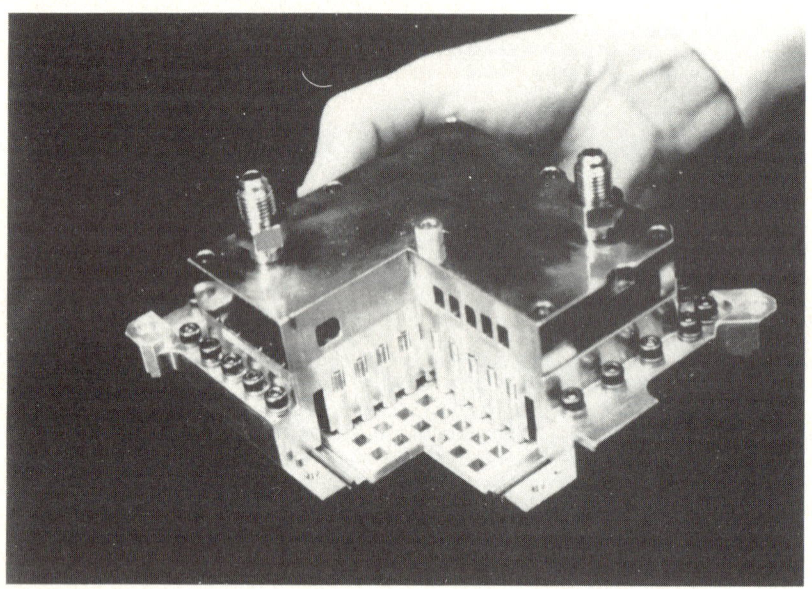

FIGURE 27.1. THE CORE OF A 370/148 COMPUTER

This photograph, by courtesy of IBM, shows a cut-away thermal conduction module
housing nearly one million logic circuits. Chips (bottom front) are normally
in contact with water-cooled metal rods (seen behind the chips). The design
allows compactness with heat dissipation

TRANSBORDER DATA FLOW

The ease of access to a computer in another country via international
communications and the country to country beaming of information via satellites
bring with them many complex new issues.

Consider two simple but dramatic actions which, in a crude way, highlight
new-technology political implications. At a 1978 colloquium a Hughes engineer
admitted that the Indonesian Palapa satellite, Hughes designed and NASA
launched, could be turned off by Hughes or by the US department of defence. The
title of an article by Jacobson about this topic - "Satellite business systems
and the concept of the dispersed enterprise - an end to national sovereignty"
spells out the implications.

In 1979 the British Post Office was successfully demonstrating Prestel at an international exhibition in Paris, but the competing French Didon videotex system was not working. Shortly after a tour by the French telecommunications minister both of the Prestel connections to London were cut off. The exhibition organisers improvised another line but that too was cut off. The exhibition was held at the French PTT headquarters, but a French service engineer was unavailable. No other exhibitors had telephone line problems.

The most important issues seem to stem from the realisation that we are heading for the Information Society (having left the Industrial and Post-Industrial Society behind us), that the United States dominates the technology of information distribution, and that he who dominates the technology can control content and even modify local culture.

"It is ironic that Reuters, the European news agency, once glorified English and French progress, but told the world about lynchings, crime, and the risk of attack from Indians while travelling in the United States, but that now the "free flow of information" is seen as a license to swamp the universe with made-in-America cultural/media artefacts" says Dizard.

It has been suggested that Western agencies (Reuters, AFP, AP, UPI) and the Russian Tass agency generate news about but not for the third world; the distribution technology is also under their control. For example from the Indian viewpoint, that country observes good coverage about its natural disasters and social problems at the expense of news about its doubling of food production and elevation to the eighth largest industrial country.

There are a number of related issues centred round a "Third World Information and Communication Order", and the UNESCO McBride report - an attempt to rectify the West's news domination. Recommendations made in it were considered to be a threat to press freedom by Western journalists.

Fears expressed before the 1979 World Administrative Radio Conference about a reversal of the "first come first served" satellite slot "policy" (in other words appropriation by the US or the USSR) at that conference also bear on the same issue. The fears were that scarce communication satellite slots might be shared out but not taken up because of technological inability or lack of need. In the event, decisions on this issue were postponed. Recommendations about satellite broadcasting have also been made by Unesco but the US foreign service fears international censorship.

Transborder flow restrictions are also seen as a way of curtailing the transfer of lucrative data processing business out of the home country. According to Dunn, European attempts to implement all-embracing privacy laws could be an indirect but perhaps obvious way of curtailing US dominance - "...a tourniquet applied by foreign governments to the data flow essential to modern business". The point here is that privacy laws could be used not to keep out cultural influences but to keep in revenue ".....it's most often discussed in pious terms of concern for individual privacy...but the real issues involve such materialistic matters as balance of payments and the opportunity to tax data transmission".

On the other hand the lack of privacy legislation, as in Britain until recently, could lead to the loss of business because foreign companies will not use data processing facilities in a country which does not provide adequate protection for their data.

The export-import of data brings me back full circle to the man using his terminal from Peru and the datastream complexity problem - that is that it will be impossible to police dataflow. Instead remedies should be sought through enforceable regulations aimed at systematic patterns of illegal behaviour where

many kinds of evidence may be available, thinks de Sola Pool. She also argues
(with reference to Swedish bogeymen) that there is no evidence yet that there is
any need for a bureaucracy to control transborder flow, nor is there yet a single
indication that anyone has been hurt by it.

       Transborder flow takes many forms. Television programme distribution by
satellite in Europe is controversial. West German newspaper companies would like
to transmit to Germany via a Luxembourg based transmitter outside the control of
the German government. This might enable the publishers to gain an excessive
control over the media at the expense of the German public corporation monopoly,
upsetting a carefully preserved balance of the media.

<u>FURTHER READING</u>

Anning, Nick; Connor, Steve; Fitzgerald, Pat.
   New Scientist, 6-7, February 28th, 1985.
     How Britain's economic spies tap the world.
Anon.
   The Home Office. Cmnd 7341. Pub. by HMSO, London, 1978.
     Report of the committee on data protection (Chairman Sir Norman Lindop).
Anon.
   Financial Times, July 21, 1978.
     The government's protection racket.
Anon.
   Pub. by Office of the DP Registrar, Water Lane, Wilmslow, Cheshire SK9 5AX,
   England. February 1985.
     The Data Protection Act 1984.
Beker, H.J.
   Radio & Electronic Eng. 54(1), 35-40, January 1984.
     Options available for speech encryption.
Bosworth, Bruce.
   Hayden Book Co., Rochelle Park,New Jersey, USA. 1982.
     Codes, ciphers and computers.
Campbell, Duncan.
   New Statesman, Feb 1, 1980
     Big Buzby is watching you.
Cawkell, Anthony E.
   In Williams, Martha E. (Ed). Annual Review of Information Science and
   Technology Vol 15, 1980; Chapter 2, 37-65. Pub. by Knowledge Industries
   Inc. New York.
     Information technology and communications.
de Sola Pool, Ithiel; Solomon, Richard J.
   Telecommunications Policy, 3(3), 176-191, September 1979.
     The regulation of transborder data flows.
de Sola Pool, Ithiel.
   Telecommunications Policy, 4(4), 314, December 1980.
     Exporting data - latest paranoia. (Review of Freese, Jan. International
     dataflow. Pub by Student Litteratur, Lund, 1979)
Diffie, Whitfield; Hellman, Martin E.
   Proc IEEE 67(3), 397-427, March 1979.
     Privacy and authentication: an introduction to cryptography.
Dizard, Wilson P.
   Journal of Communication, 30(2), 157-168, Spring 1980.
     The U.S. position - DBS and free flow.
Dunn, Nina.
   Computer Decisions 11(2), 24-30, February 1979.
     Us vs. Them
Hondius, Fritz W.
   IEEE Spectrum, 17(3), 67-70, March 1980.
     Computers: data privacy.

Huff, Thomas.
  Washington Law Review, 55, 777-794, 1980
    Thinking clearly about privacy.
Jacobson, Robert E.
  Media Culture & Society 1, 235-253, 1979.
    Satellite business system and the concept of the dispersed enterprise - an
    end to national sovereignty.
Kennedy, Edward M.
  Harvard Civil Rights - Civil Liberties Law Rev.16(2), 311-317, Fall 1981.
    Foreword: is the pendulum swinging away from freedom of information?
Kline, Charles S; Popek, Gerald J. et al.
  J.Communic. Networks 2(1), 61-81, 1983.
    Digital signatures: principles and implementation.
Lerner, Eric J.
  IEEE Spectrum 21(7), 45-49, July 1984.
    International data wars are brewing.
Madans, Alan S.
  Duke Law Journal 1980, 139-169, 1980.
    Developments under the freedom of information act 1979.
Marchand, Donald A.
  Telecommunications Policy 3(3), 192-208, Sept 1979.
    Privacy, confidentiality and computers.
McCafferty, Maxine.
  Aslib bibliography No.1. (1976). Pub. by Aslib, 3 Belgrave Square, London
  SW1X 8PL, England.
    The Right to Know.
McNeil, John.
  Futura Publications, London 1979
    The Consultant.
Michael, James.
  Social Audit, 1, 53-64, 1973.
    The politics of secrecy, the secrecy of politics.
Nisenoff, Norman; Bishop, Ethelyn, et al.
  Information Processing and Management 15, 205-211, 1979.
    The privacy of computerized records - the Swedish experience and possible
    US policy impacts.
Orwell, George.
  Penguin Books 1980.
    Ninety-eighty four.
Peterson, Trudy H.
  The American Archivist 43(2), 161-168, Spring 1980.
    After five years: an assessment of the amended US freedom of information
    Act.
Salton, Gerard.
  Journal of the American Society for Information Science, 31(2), 75-83, 1980.
    A progress report on information privacy and data security.
Schieber, Benjamin J.
  Louisiana Law Rev. 42(4), 1323-1372, 1982.
    Electronic surveillance, the Mafia, and individual freedom.
Stevens, I.N; Yardley, D.C.M
  Basil Blackwell Oxford. 1982.
    The protection of liberty.
Stone, Eugene F; Gardner,Donald G. et al.
  J.Appl. Psychol. 68(3), 459-468, 1983.
    A field experiment comparing information privacy values, beliefs, and
    attitudes across several types of organizations.
Sugarman, Robert et al.
  IEEE Spectrum 16(7), 31-41, July 1979.
    On foiling computer crime.
Summers, R.C.
  IBM Systems J. 23(4), 309-332, 1984.

An overview of computer security.
Walker, Martin; Large,Peter; Pallister, David.
  The Guardian, Sept 22, 23, and 24, 1980.
    Someone to watch over you. Our lives at their fingertips, Big brother
    arrived yesterday.
Walker, Stephen S.
  Proc. AFIPS National Computer Conference, Anaheim Ca, May 1980. 655-665.
  Pub. by AFIPS Press, 1815 North Lynn St., Arlington Va 22209, USA.
    The advent of trusted computer operating systems.
Westin, Alan F.
  In Mason, R.E.A. (Ed). Information Processing 1983. Elsevier 1983. 733-739.
    New issues of computer privacy in the eighties.
Wigand, Rolf T; Shipley, Carrie; Shipley, Dwayne.
  J. Communications 34(1), 153-175, 1984.
    Transborder data flow, informatics, and national policies.
Wofsey, Marvin M. (Ed).
  John Wiley 1983.
    Advances in computer security management. Volume 2.
Wong, Ken.
  Information Age 5(3), 145-148, July 1983.
    Impact of the UK Data Protection Bill.
Wood, Michael B.
  NCC Publications, Oxford Rd., Manchester, M1 7ED. England. 1982.
    Introducing computer security.

CHAPTER 28. THE ECONOMICS OF INFORMATION

Almost the only group of economists who have much
sense of realism are the agricultural economists,
and these are dealing with a vanishing sector that
is now only 5% of the total economy. The whole
economic profession, indeed, is an example of that
monumental misallocation of intellectual resources which
is one of the most striking phenomena of our times
K.E.Boulding

One should hardly have to tell academicians that
information is a valuable resource: knowledge is power
And yet it occupies a slum dwelling in the town of economics
G.J.Stigler

It is better to remain silent and appear to be a
fool than to open your mouth and remove all doubt.
Abraham Lincoln

Introduction

The first two quotations above, by very well known economists, are clear
admissions of economist's failure to evaluate information. Its nebulous yet
challenging qualities goads them into further efforts, and the rewards may even
include a Nobel prize - Stigler has recently received one. I may prove Lincoln
right in this chapter but I must still open my mouth since the subject should not
escape discussion in a book about information technology.

If a value could be placed on information, information services and
information technology could, to use a mixed metaphor. take their place in the
pecking order for a proper share of the financial cake. At present they often
come under the heading of Acts of Faith and do not compete well for resources
against more tangible items.

The need

Information as an essential resource suddenly came to the fore in 1967 with
the publication of Servan-Schreiber's book "Le défi Americain" in which he
suggests that we (the French) are forced to rethink completely our methods for
transferring information. There was indeed a rethink in the shape of the
influential Nora-Minc report which was followed by heavy investment.

Everybody needs information but some of us have an intense continuing
occupational need of which we are in no doubt. If our occupation depends upon
it, it has a high value which may well be quantifiable. For example a dealer on
the money market could probably calculate the value of a system which instantly
displays current exchange rates. He could certainly make a decision, on a value
basis, between that service and a cheaper one which takes 15 minutes to provide
the same information.

If we prepared a list of people in order of the value they place upon
particular kinds of information, and therefore of their propensity to pay for a
service which provides it, there is no doubt that people like money market
dealers would come near the top.

As we proceed down the list we come to those who need information but do not
particularly want it - and maybe three quarters of the list consists of such
people. It includes the majority of scientists and technologists to whom I once
tried to sell information services. They get information by talking to colleagues

(the "invisible college"), or from the library, which costs them personally nothing. They may already have access to an inexpensive subsidised information service of some kind, and here we have a clue about the degree of their need.

<u>Subsidies</u>

It seems very unlikely that any government would subsidise a money market dealer's information service, but it's quite likely to subsidise an information service covering, say, medical information. It may finance such a service because no other service exists; no entrepreneur believes he can offer a service presenting the opportunity for making a profit because of price/demand/cost considerations. The government believes that public good will come of it and encourages use by arranging for the service to be offered free or at a low price. Under these conditions there will be some demand.

More accurately, even if no charge is made, the service and all other subsidised services are not free. The cost, of course, appears to the user as it does to the rest of the community - as a component of taxation.

Policy varies. R&D subsidies are sometimes provided, and it may be felt that the service should become self supporting in due course. At that point the subsidy is removed with the danger that the service may collapse. It is hard to see the logic of that action, since a public good of this kind is then quite likely to collapse. One reason why no service previously existed was that no private operator thought it could be viable. If the service is a justifiable public good, and an alternative service which costs the taxpayer nothing is unavailable, then the provision of an on-going subsidy may be defensible.

Many subsidised suppliers suffered the indignity of finding out what their subscribers really thought of their services when the subsidy was withdrawn and they had to charge a price which was in line with costs. The subsidisors correctly attributed a higher value to the information than did the users. It is rightly assumed, at least by successive UK governments, that people are not prepared to pay for information even when it's among the most important of their interests. Once a tradition has been established that certain kinds of information are free it's hard to change it.

Of course this simple discussion excludes many side issues. For example Prestel would have been shut down if subjected to normal commercial criteria. However it can be argued that it is a long term investment and that it established a new industry in the UK.

<u>Charging for library and other information services</u>

Andrew Carnegie, wealthy expatriate Scotsman who founded many free libraries, would certainly have had something to say about the current controversy about the imposition of charges for some services by libraries.

Marilyn Gell thinks that "while most librarians react with moral outrage to the suggestion that user fees be levied, the economic argument for such a course of action is persuasive. The imposition of fees provides a mechanism for determining preference through willingness to pay. Those who favour fees maintain that the use of prices helps allocate scarce resources according to the intensity of demand and helps provide a rationale for new investment decisions", and, (loftily, and somewhat as a non-sequitur) "It is of paramount importance that the means of general information should be so diffused that the largest possible number of persons should be induced to read and understand questions going to the very foundations of social order".

Would people be prepared to pay for services rendered at Citizen's Advice Bureaux in the UK, if the real direct cost was charged? Almost certainly the demand would drop substantially. Governments have not succeeded in providing a system of easily understood legislation, services, and benefits aimed at under-privileged people. It would hardly be logical if these same people were charged when they were trying to find out whether they qualified for a particular service for which there was no charge. Questions about the Value of Information are nudgingly close to another topic which is a cause for concern - what are the consequences of creating a society divisible into the information-rich and the information-poor?

The problems of providing information services for people with "middling" needs were well set out by Hislop in the case history of the Metals Information Services, terminated following the removal of a subsidy. The author suggests that the level of subsidy should have been based on the identification of several areas of cost, including marketing costs. In fact marketing received no special mention. It was absurd not to give it special attention because marketing needs to be particularly well done in a service of this kind. Metallurgists are likely to require far more convincing than money market dealers about their information needs. More than one worthy service has perished because the organisers behaved like the mousetrap inventor. They believed they just needed to wait for people to beat a path to their door.

The flow of information about everyday products and their prices to consumers is a part of economics which has received much more attention than the problems of selling products with intangible benefits - information services - to people who do not particularly want them. Markets and price information are discussed in an often quoted article by Stigler. Further discussion about the transmission of information and the power of the market has been provided by another Nobelist - Milton Friedman.

<u>Is Information like anything else?</u>

There seems to be some confusion between information and information services. Information services are perfectly tangible although what they are intended to purvey may not be. Information services are only one of many types of information source for occupational needs. These sources are part of a larger spectrum from which we receive information about all aspects of our environment. Economists are in some doubt about how to proceed. If information is a <u>commodity</u>, it can be examined with the background of economic experience accumulated about commodities.

As Porat points out, a commodity is characterised by a supply and demand function according to price and utility; it is wholly appropriable, there is a scarcity of it and it has a value and a definite price in exchange processes. Information has none of these attributes. Its value to a customer is unknown until revealed, at which point is has no further value. It could only have value if fully appropriable. It is not destroyed during consumption so has no scarcity value.

Porat then discusses information as a public or private good and remarks "entrepreneurs in the information markets today, especially in cable TV, pay TV, database publishing and so on, are acutely aware of the market failures resulting from our inability to fully understand cost and price relationships in information production". He then discusses the source of these difficulties, if not the solution, covering invention, patent and copyright, and governmental and private activities in further sections of his review.

This echoes opinions expressed in an article by yet another Nobelist/economist - K.J.Arrow. "With suitable legal measures information may become an appropriable commodity. Then the monopoly power can indeed be exerted. However no amount of legal protection can make a thoroughly appropriable commodity of something so intangible as information. The demand for information also has uncomfortable properties...."

However some information scientists feel that information definitely can be treated as a commodity. Rorvig turns to one of the foundations of information science - the Cranfield tests (see Chapter 13) - to support this thesis which is central to the arguments in his article. He quotes the comments of people who were involved in assessing the relevance of documents retrieved from a test collection, suggesting that validity of judgement was confounded by consumer variables.

Thus one judge said "None of your definitions (i.e. the project organiser's) fits my attitude towards the documents. All were of considerable interest to me because they showed me what people had done so far, how recently, and by what methods". The thrust of Rorvig's article is that other methods are available to the information system designer in addition to the simple concept that the system should be able to provide the user with relevant information.

He may mean that a user should be able to make assessments using a wider range of criteria than those currently used, and that designers and marketing people should widen the criteria to make the system successful. He quotes Cooper's comments about the need to distinguish between relevance and utility, and goes on to suggest that "the expected utility of an item is a multiplicative function of the novelty value, the credibility of the item, and its relevance".

He describes some experiments in progress to test the effect of people's prior attitudes on their assessment of the utility of a system, but his concluding remarks seem obvious to anyone who has been involved in marketing. It did not amaze me to be told that the most receptive people for Compuserve - a well known US information/communication system - are "young males of high income with above average experience in computers". Nor was I astonished to hear that 100 households found that Compuserve provided "inadequate user instructions". Even so considerations of utility for the target market are clearly important.

A "<u>resource</u>" is one label for information which seems to be gaining some popularity. My dictionary defines a resource as "a supply or source of aid or support: something resorted to in time of need: a means of doing something expedient". This label sounds appropriate for information services, if not for information. Information services, libraries, etc., are certainly a resource, but however appropriate the label a resource has a cost, a potential for exploitation, and a use related to its nature. Oil is a resource. So far as I know resources possess no general intrinsic properties which might assist in our understanding of information.

Although it has always been hoped that Information Theory might shed some light on information itself as well as about the communication of it, little of practical value has emerged. Marschak provides a statistical approach covering this area.

<u>The value of information</u>

We can conclude from the above brief review that a better understanding of the economic and value of information is likely to be slow in coming. Lack of progress has prompted some remarks about the futility of further work on the subject. It has been suggested that the provision of information may be likened to a gaggle of geese which sometimes lays golden eggs. It is impossible to say which goose may lay a golden egg or when, and that perhaps it is time for some research on the economics of further research on the economics of information.

Little heed has been taken of such defeatism and in the late seventies there was a burst of activity by the British Library and later the European Economic Commission.

Some research was sponsored in the hope that it would assist in determining the amount and the direction of support for scientific information services. The conclusions were that further work was needed, such as case studies, because present knowledge of information economics was inadequate. The second sponsored task was an investigation into the price/demand characteristics of online information services. It was hoped that the demand for such services, to be supplied via Euronet, the then new European communications network, might be estimated.

This report was not released, although I managed to obtain a copy. The growth rate suggested for on line services was probably unpalatably low for the sponsors. Presumably they had hoped for better predictions to lend strength to Euronet financing and launching. The reports, by Flowerdew et al, simply reflected, once again, the difficulty in making predictions in a poorly understood area.

Costs and benefits

You and I have little doubt about the cost of things, including information. I know what it costs me to get the information I need - it's a mixture of payments for things like newspapers, journals, and information services plus the cost of my time and overheads like telephone bills etc., in getting and processing the information. The benefit, in monetary terms, of any given item is another matter.

Robert Bickner explains why an economist's definition of "costs" is different from everybody else's. When an economist is talking about the costs and benefits of, say, an information service, he isn't talking just about the cost to the supplier of providing the service, or the user's costs which are relatively easy to determine, or about the hard to quantify benefit to the user. To him, an important cost component is the "benefit lost" or the "opportunity cost" of a decision. Bickner makes the point in an example :-

"The "cost" of stopping at a neighbourhood bar on the way home might be either an expenditure of several dollars, or a chance to watch a stockmarket report on TV, or, finally, a hangover. What would be the real "cost" of stopping at the bar?" In other words it is just as hard to work out costs as it is to work out benefits. I'll buy the logic of the argument, but there's no way I'm going to go through such an agonising decision-making process when dropping in at the local (English vernacular for the local Public House or "Pub").

The example is intended to make a point applicable to more complex activities. Should attempts be made to estimate the resources required for an activity, the alternative use of the resources, the value of the alternative uses, or the dollar cost? The answer is the dollar cost - because and only because, and only to the extent that this helps us identify and evaluate the alternatives. This is a rather neat answer.

I should mention that in articles about how to cost information services, overheads and development costs tend to get ignored. The treatment of R&D costs depends upon whether it's your own money or someone else's - perhaps the remote and impotent taxpayer. In the latter case it's advisable to sweep the usually large sums involved under the mat. If the ultimate cost of the R&D was revealed in advance perhaps most projects would never be launched.

There are two often-used measures associated with the cost of supplying information. <u>Cost   Effectiveness</u> is the cost of achieving a specified goal. For example if the average cost per item retrieved is £2 in service A and £4 in service B, service A is more cost effective than B. <u>Cost Benefit</u> is the value, preferably in monetary terms, of the benefit of the information supplied. Thus if the items received via service B consistently provide information leading to the successful enforcement of patent royalty payments worth £50,000 annually, while service A provides no such information, the better cost effectiveness of A pales into insignificance compared with the cost benefit of service B.

Unfortunately benefits are seldom as clear-cut as this: they may be of various kinds and with different degrees of tangibility. It may be quite impractical to quantify them. A more feasible way of demonstrating that information has value is to describe real cases of benefits derived from the use of Information Service X, and to suggest that similar benefits might accrue in the future to users of that service. This seems to be about the best that can be done because no statement can be made like "if you use service X, you possibly, or may, or probably, or definitely will receive benefits of £50,000 annually for a service cost of £10,000.

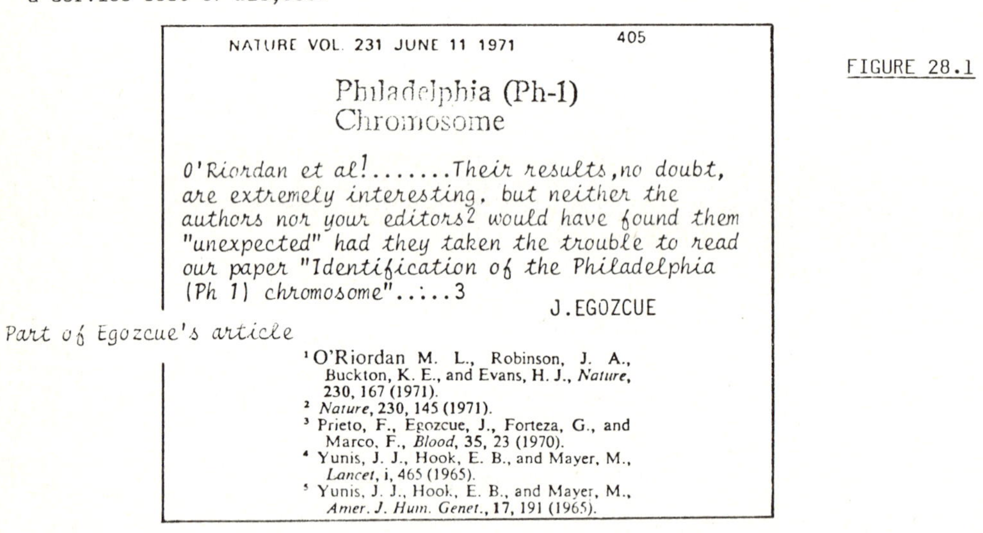

FIGURE 28.1

Part of Egozcue's article

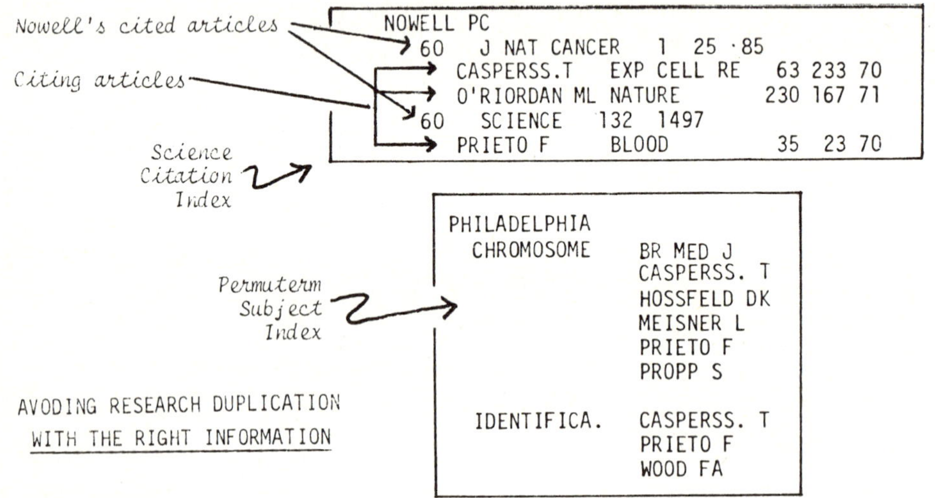

AVODING RESEARCH DUPLICATION
WITH THE RIGHT INFORMATION

I once collected together some actual cases to demonstrate the time-saving effect of possessing the right information at the right time, discovered with the aid of a particular information service. These examples were an attempt to demonstrate potential tangible value when trying to sell the service. A rather typical example, intended to demonstrate the value of a literature search, is shown in Figure 28.1.

Part of an article by Egozcue is shown at the top. Egozcue is saying, in effect, that Prieto and himself had anticipated the research recently claimed to be novel by O'Riordan. We may surmise that the minimum effect on O'Riordan was some embarrassment. It may also mean that x weeks of O'Riordan's time was spent on an unnecessary project. The question is how could O'Riordan have found out about Prieto et al's work and so have received the quantifiable benefit of not incurring x weeks of wasted time? The excerpt from the Science Citation Index (SCI) shows that Nowell was cited by O'Riordan in his Nature article. If O'Riordan had used this index and it had occurred to him that others like himself who cited Nowell could well be engaged on similar work, he would have found Prieto's article in "Blood".

The same information in a different form is available from the words-in-title index (The Permuterm Subject Index, a companion index to the SCI), perhaps rather more obviously. A search by O'Riordan in the PSI under "Philadelphia" would have shown that the article by Prieto was worth investigating because that article (and another by Caspersson), included the word pairs "Philadelphia..chromosome" and "Philadelphia...identification" in their titles.

Christie has given the evaluation problem some careful thought in his interesting book. Taking account of the multi-dimensional nature of the value of information, he suggests an equation for value estimation. Proportions are assigned to programmed planning and orientation activities, behavioural intentions - belief about cost and benefits and other people's expectations - and to estimated actual and potential value. The sum of these factors represents the expected value of the information emerging from a processing operation.

Such a formula might be used during an "Information Audit" where the main aspects are the value of information in relation to costs and needs. His various suggestions focus on many aspects of information in order to give each aspect due weight when striving for efficient information management. This is a step towards the quantification of information value which remains elusive.

<u>Demand and prices</u>

Three price-setting practices are identified by Zais - <u>cost based pricing</u>, <u>demand based pricing</u> and <u>competition based pricing</u>. These categories are more or less self evident. Cost based pricing is a mark-up on costs, demand based is what the market can stand, and competition based is the "going rate".

There are at least three strategies in relating prices to costs. <u>Average cost pricing</u> is one price strategy, as used, for instance, for motorway tolls. <u>Discriminatory pricing</u> is the method of pricing the same product differently in different markets. <u>Marginal cost pricing</u>, the third strategy, supposedly maximises social benefit. It is based on the cost of one additional unit of output. Suppose the total costs of a lawn-mower sharpening business which handles one hundred lawn-mowers is £3000 and its total costs when it handles its one hundred and first lawn-mower are £3020. Its marginal cost, on which the price to its one hundred and first customer would be based, is the difference between these figures.

<u>Elasticity of demand</u>, means the demand sensitivity to a change in price. Demand is elastic if a small change in price results in a relatively large change in demand. Birks has made a number of suggestions about the pricing of information services. He reports cases where imposing a charge on a previously

free service led to a dramatic fall in the level of the demand. One may well question the wisdom of offering a service of this kind for nothing - it lowers the perceived value. Beckwith provides a Friedman-like discussion about free goods with the example that "when bread was sold at a very low subsidised price in Soviet Russia, peasants used it to feed pigs and chickens".

Some detailed information about prices and demand for information services has been provided by Huston. The case of (presumably) affluent American physicians - whose demand for online searches was studied for six years - is extraordinary. The introduction of a \$5 charge in a service hitherto free caused demand to fall by 77%. Lockheed, a major host for online services, reported demand for online searches in public libraries. Following a year's free service, a charge was introduced; more than half the patrons only had to pay \$10 or less. Searches dropped from 2000 to 750 per annum.

It is of interest to note that the demand elasticity judged from a transition from zero to a nominal charge is usually quite different from that adjudged from a change in the existing price of a service. Once people have become dependent upon a service, relatively large price changes seem to have a relatively small effect upon demand.

Price/demand for online and videotex services

According to Collier, from information received from 497 organisations mainly using online database services in Europe providing Scientific and Technical Information (STI), a typical searcher was a science graduate with an information science background earning between \$15K and \$30K dollars. Most of his searches were probably carried out for somebody else because most end-users do not rank their need highly enough to take the time to find out how to do a search - specialists do it for them.

It is hard to estimate the demand at the "market price" for online access to databases (mainly scientific or technical) because many are low-priced (\$15-\$30 per connect hour) governmental offerings. We do not know what the demand would be for them if they were priced to yield a profit. The perceived value of this present generation of online services is certainly greater than that of the Selective Dissemination of Information" (SDI) services which have been available for about 20 years. Speed, convenience, and critical mass are probably major factors.

An SDI service requires a "profile" of a user's interests composed of "terms" which are periodically matched against terms contained in a new batch of information within a database, usually stored on magnetic tape. A list of "hits" - that is items containing terms matching profile terms - are sent to the user periodically. The user observes the results after the receipt of a few lists, and having read the articles cited, then modifies his profile to better circumscribe his interests. SDI systems proliferated in the sixties and seventies, mainly for scientific information, but were only taken up by a small fraction of potential users. It has been suggested by Cole that this was due to wrong assumptions about the nature of scientific communication, and about the motivation for information.

Cole claims that confidence in the highly motivated information seeking behaviour assumed when SDI systems were first developed has recently been undermined. The reluctance of engineers to use technical literature has been understood for some time but there has also been an increasing amount of evidence that scientists also are not highly motivated. However, present generation interactive online services have become much more widely used. The slow modification of the profile for SDI has been replaced by a question and answer dialogue with a database stored on disks. Circumscribing of the subject takes place by trial and error in the course of, perhaps, a 15 minute session. Often many databases are available at an online centre so the user may have several sources for wanted information.

Advances in technology have affected the availability and in one sense the "amount" of information for a given price. Cheaper storage costs, faster searching, and more characters transmitted per second at lower cost have encouraged the provision of full text storage and processing. In other words a user can rapidly obtain a display of the text which contains the original information instead of a surrogate which summarises it, from which the user has to decide whether to obtain a copy of the the complete print-on-paper (usually) original.

Turning to a different kind of information, experiences with Prestel, and Ceefax and Oracle (See Chapter 23), provide some economic data. The demand for Prestel, at the given total price, has been over-estimated from the start. It was designed as a simple to use general information system for home users, but the total price was much too high for mass demand. It included a premium for an expensive modified TV receiver, plus connection time, telephone time, and information frame charges.

Launched as a public service in 1979, there were about 13,000 users by the end of 1981, of which less than 2000 were in the home, and over 40,000 by 1985. A radical change of approach and pricing policies has been undertaken recently to change this situation, but it seems likely that apart from Microline, demand will continue to come from business users.

From what we have seen of online users with at least some occupational needs, it seems likely that demand from the general public for information will be low unless the price is very low – probably well below £100 per year for total costs.

When Prestel was introduced, newspaper publishers clamoured to be consulted, presumably because they thought it might be a competitive threat if not for news, then possibly for advertising. It is hard to equate the value of the information content of a "frame" – say 1000 characters on a TV screen – with that of a newspaper with maybe 20 times that number on one page. It certainly appears as if the screen must contain information regarded as being valuable – for instance airline flight times known to be up to date.

The demand for UK teletext services in the UK – Ceefax and Oracle – reinforces this quantification of the order of information price/demand by the public. About 300,000 teletext sets were in use by the end of 1981, perhaps 200,000 of them in homes, at a rental cost of £15 to £25 per annum over and above TV set rental. There are no other direct costs. By 1985 the number of users had risen to well over a million.

A further convergence of home information systems coupled to cheap wideband communications would, no doubt, encourage a variety of information providers, and create an information infrastructure providing a cheap ride for the nth service – but that is another matter discussed in Chapter 25.

<u>The economics of publishing</u>

Before considering the exchange value of electronic and printed information the economics of publishing, obviously of vital interest to publishers, but perhaps less well known to students of the Economics of Information, are worth stressing.

They have been discussed by Trubkin. Figure 28.2 is similar to a figure in his article. Publishing is labour intensive. Break-even occurs when costs are recovered by the sale of x copies. A profit is made only when copy x+1 is sold and the total profit depends upon the number of copies sold thereafter. Put another way, a small percentage loss of subscriptions means a large percentage drop in profit, so for annual publications a small drop in the number of subscriptions is a serious matter.

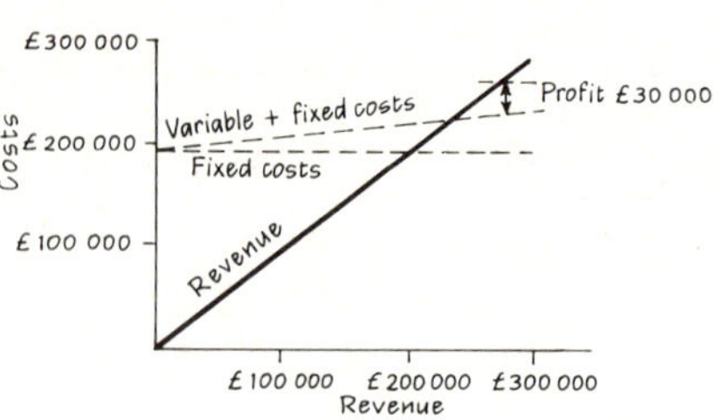

FIGURE 28.2 PUBLISHING ECONOMICS

Exchange value of information in alternative packages

As time goes on, information - much of it the same or similar information - will be packaged and re-packaged in various ways and new ways will be found to enable users to find what they want and deliver it to them more conveniently at lower cost. The people who rate information highly because of its value to them in pursuing their occupations will continue to be willing to pay more for it than those without such a pressing need.

It seems likely that information in an "electronic package" will slowly replace information in a "printed package" in some areas because the shorter time spent in obtaining it in a more convenient form at the price asked is considered to represent better value. These comments are a gross over-simplification because although the perception of "value", will be important, many other factors will contribute such as distribution by "on demand" publishing organisations offering information in print or electronically and human factors such as machine operation and reading preferences. The perceived "value" of different formats and media and the demand at given prices remains to be seen.

FURTHER READING

Arrow, K.J.
  In The rate and direction of inventive activity: economic and social
  factors. Pub. by National bureau of economic research, Princeton University
  Press, 1962, pps 609-626.
    Economic welfare and the allocation of resources for invention.
Barker, Frances H.
  Aslib Proc. 37(7/8), 289-297, July/August 1984.
    Pricing of information products.
Beckwith, Burnham B.
  The Futurist, 307-312, October 1978.
    Free! free! free! The priceless world of tomorrow.
Birks, C.I.
  British Library R&D report 5430, July 1978. Published by the British Library
  R&D Dept.,Sheraton House, Great Chapel St., London W1V 4BH.
    Information services in the market place.
Blick, A.R.
  Aslib Proc. 29(5), 189-196, May 1977
    The value of measurement in decision making in an information unit - a cost
    benefit analysis.
Boyle, Harry F.
  Online Review 6(6), 517-523, 1982.
    The pricing of information - a search-based approach to pricing an online
    search service.

Carter, M.P.
  J.Info.Sci. 9, 117-112, 1984.
    Costing management information - a more formal approach.
Cawkell, Anthony E.
  In Proc. Annual Conf. IIS., Loughborough, April 1978. Selling information
  to the organisation. Published by the Institute of Information Scientists,
  Museum St., London.
    Quantifying the intangible: in what terms can information be evaluated?
Christie, Bruce.
  John Wiley 1981.
    Face to file communication: a psychological approach to information
    systems.
Cole, Elliot.
  J. Amer. Soc.for Information Science 32, 444-450, November 1981.
    Examining design assumptions for an information retrieval service: SDI
    use for scientific and technical databases.
Collier, Harry R.
  Online Review 6(1), 27-37, 1982
    European online users: a mid 1981 report.
Cooper, Michael D.
  Information Proces. & Manag. 19(1), 6-26, 1983.
    The structure and future of the information economy.
Detlefsen, Ellen.
  Government Publication Rev. 11, 385-394, 1984.
    User costs: information a social good vs information as a commodity.
Flowerdew, A.D.J.; Whitehead, C.M.E.
  Report to OSTI on project S1/97/03, October 1974. London School of Economics.
  Available from British Library, Boston Spa, Wetherby LS23 7BQ, England.
    Cost effectiveness and cost benefit analysis in information science.
Flowerdew, A.D.J.; Thomas J.J. et al.
  A report for the EEC, July 1976. Unavailable.
    Demand for online services as a function of the charges.
Friedman, Milton.
  Free to choose. Penguin Books. 1980. Chapter 1.
    The power of the market.
Gilchrist, Alan.
  Aslib Proc. 23(9), 455-461, September 1971.
    Cost effectiveness.
Huston, Mary M.
  Library Journal, 1811-1814, Sept 15th 1979.
    Fee or free: the effect of charging on information demand.
Hyslop, Marjorie R.
  In North,Jeanne B.,(Ed). Proc. 31st meeting American Society for Information
  Science, Vol. 5, 1968. Pub. by Greenwood Publishing, Westport, Conn., USA.
  Page 301.
    The economics of information systems - observations on development costs
    and nature of the market.
Keren, Carl; Schwuchow, Werner.
  J. Information Sci. 3(1981), 249-251.
    Economic aspects of information services - report on a symposium.
King, John L.; Schrems, Edward L.
  Computing surveys, 10(1), 19-34, March 1978.
    Cost benefit analysis in information systems development and operation.
King, D.W; Roderer, N.K; Olsen, Harold A. (Eds).
  Knowledge Industry Publications, White Plains, New York, and Henrietta St.,
  London. 1982.
    Key papers in the economics of information.
Lamberton, D.M., (Ed).
  Penguin Books 1971.
    Economics of information and knowledge.

Lamberton, D.M.
  In Williams, M.E. (Ed). Annual Review of Information Science and Technology,
  Volume 19. Knowledge Industries, White Plains, N.Y. 1984. pps 3-30.
    The economics of information and organisation.
Lancaster, F.W.; Goldhor, Herbert.
  Online Review 5(4), 301-311, 1981.
    The impact of online services on subscriptions to printed publications.
Machlup, Fritz.
  Princeton University Press, Princeton N.J. Volume 1, 1980. Volume 2, 1982.
    Knowledge: its creation, distribution and economic significance.
Marschak, Jacob.
  J. Amer. Statist. Assoc. 66(333), 192-219, March 1971.
    Economics of information systems.
Martyn, John.
  Aslib: Report of a British Library conference, July 1982.
    Studies of the economics of information: a commentary.
Niznik, Carol A.
  IEEE Trans. Communic. COM30(1), 19-26, January 1982.
    Cost benefit analysis for local integrated facsimile/data/voice packet
    communication networks.
Nora, Simon; Minc, Alain.
  Report to the President. Pub. by La Documentation Francaise, Paris, 1978.
    L'Informatisation de la societé.
Parker, M.M.
  IBM Syst. J. 21(1), 108-123, 1982.
    Enterprise information analysis: cost benefit analysis and the data managed
    system.
Porat, Marc U.
  Report, Center for interdisciplinary research, Stanford University, Stanford,
  Ca 94305, USA. 1975, revised 1976.
    The information economy and the economics of information: a literature
    survey.
Servan-Schreiber, Jean-Jacques.
  The American challenge (Le défi Americain).
    Published by Pelican Books, 1969. (Translated from the French by Ronald
    Steele).
Stigler, G.J.
  J. Political Econ. Volume 69, 213-225, 1961. Reprinted in Lamberton, D.M.,
  Ed., Economics of information and knowledge, Penguin Books, 1971, chapter 3.
    The economics of information.
Summit, Roger K.
  Online Review 5(6), 496, 1981.
    Online and print.
Trubkin, Loene.
  Online Review 4(1), 5-12, 1980.
    Migration from print to online use.
Urquhart, D.J.
  J. Documentation, 32(2), 123-125, June 1976.
    Economic analysis of information services.
Wall, R.A.
  Aslib Proc. 36, (7/8), 325-332, July/August 1984.
    Publisher pricing policies and the reprographic copyright controversy.
Williams, Martha E.
  Information Proces. & Manag. 17(5), 263-276, 1981.
    Relative impact of print and database products on database producer
    expenses and income - trends for database producer organisations based on a
    thirteen year financial analysis.
Williams, Martha E.
  Information Proces. & Manag. 18(6), 307-311, 1982.
    Relative impact of print and database products on database producer
    expenses and income - a follow-up.

Williams, Martha E.
   Online Review 6(1), 7-26, 1982.
      An analysis of online database prices and a rationale for increasing the
      price of Medline.
Wills, Gordon; Christopher, Martin.
   Unesco Bull. Libr. 24(1), 9-22, Jan/Feb 1970.
      Cost benefit analysis of company information needs.
Whitehall, T
   Aslib Proc., 32(2), 87-105, February 1980.
      User valuations and resource management for information services.
Zais, Harriet W.
   Report number LBL 4899, University of California, Lawrence Berkeley
   Laboratory, Berkeley Ca., USA. August 1976.
      Economic modeling: an aid to the pricing of information services.

CHAPTER 29. COPYRIGHT AND PATENTS

Introduction

Interest in copyright from the information technology viewpoint centred, until recently, on the rights of authors and publishers because the invention of the Xerox machine (and upon the expiry of the Xerox patents, many other similar machines) has enabled photocopying to be carried out on a large scale. There is also considerable interest in the application of copyright law to the protection of less tangible information resident in a computer as author's text or software, and to the protection afforded to database producers. Information in "knowledge" databases may be in the form of a bibliographic reference, an abstract or as full text.

Interest in patents seems to be mainly centred on attempts to get computer software defined in such a way that existing definitions about what is patentable may also apply to it.

Copyright

Copyright protection goes back to Queen Anne's Statute to protect the rights of book authors in England, introduced following pressure from the Stationer's Company in 1710. Similar laws were enacted in many countries according to the local background - whether based on Roman or Anglo-Saxon tradition - and international agreement came with the Berne Convention of 1886.

Since then there have been many changes, notably in the Universal Copyright Convention, Geneva, 1952, and the Paris 1971 revisions taking special account of the needs of developing countries.

A copyright subsists in an "original work of authorship fixed in any tangible medium of expression" (US Copyright Act 1976), extending for the life of the author, usually plus 50 years, the same term as in the UK.

Patents

A patent or "letters patent" grants a monopoly in an invention for a limited period. The procedures vary in different countries although there was unification in Europe, to which Britain contributed, with the 1977 Patent Act. A major change was the requirement that a patent should exhibit "absolute novelty" involving the furtherance of knowledge by an "inventive step". There is a delay between the filing of a patent and its publication - usually about 18 months in the UK, and until the actual granting of the patent which may take up to four years.

In the USA a patent covers an invention or process for 17 years during which the patentee has a monopoly, and in the UK the maximum period is twenty years.

If a competitor uses the invention between publication and granting, the owner of the patent cannot do anything until the patent is granted. He can then sue the infringer with regard to the infringer's activities back dated to the publication date. It is sometimes considered that the uncertainties, costs, and delays associated with patents make it better, at least for smaller fast-moving organisations, to keep their inventions secret and get into production quickly, preferably with the "Mark 2" version up their sleeves. In other words make hay while the sun shines.

Liebesny point out that patents are useful sources of information per se. Their main purpose is of course to protect inventors who traditionally have a hard time. One irate inventor took out a patent for a rocket designed to package the British patent office and blast it into space.

It is companies to whom employees or other persons assign their patent rights which mainly benefit since production and marketing expertise is required to exploit a patent. During the last war the EMI Company took out a number of patents on circuit inventions by Alan Blumlein. Blumlein was killed while flight-testing one of his inventions. The patents were so drafted that it was almost impossible to construct any piece of digital electronic equipment without infringing a Blumlein patent. At one time EMI employed a large staff, much of whose activity was concerned with negotiating royalties for the use of Blumlein patents.

Figure 29.1 shows a drawing from the patent for Fleming's thermionic valve, a major step towards making radio communication possible. When the Bell Telephone Company came out with its successor - the transistor - the patent was the first of a series which was to prove very remunerative in royalties for Bell. Having collected from transistor manufacturers, they then collected from all the users since they patented many of the circuits in which transistors were used as well.

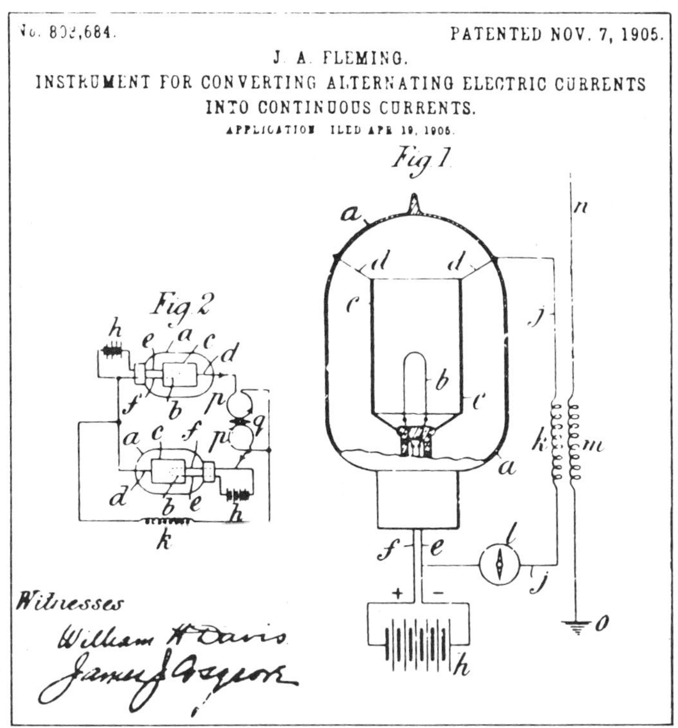

FIGURE 29.1. SKETCH FROM FLEMING'S DETECTOR VALVE

It seems unlikely that a patent taken out in the US in 1895 proved to be remunerative. It described a method for avoiding head-on railroad collisions. All trains had lines running along the top of the carriages sloping down to rail-level at the back and front. In trains running in opposite directions the sloping part at the front was adjusted to be at a slightly different height just above the track. Two trains could not, of course, collide because one would simply run up and over, and down the other side in perfect safety. No information is available about the testing of this device.

<u>Photocopying</u>

In many countries provision is made for taking a copy of a journal article for "research or private study" which is considered to be "fair use". Section 7 of the UK 1956 Copyright Act, for example, says this may be done provided that the person taking the copy signs a declaration that the copy is for this purpose only.

The 1972 Williams & Wilkins v. United States case is a landmark in this area. The US Court of Claims commissioner recommended that a publisher, Williams & Wilkins, was entitled to compensation for the photocopying of its journal articles by the National Library of Medicine (NLM). In 1970, NLM handled 120,000 photocopying requests. 18 months later, in a 4 to 3 decision, the Court rejected the commissioner's recommendation, finding no evidence of economic harm to Williams & Wilkins. This decision was upheld by an equally divided Supreme Court in 1975.

One consequence of this decision was a re-defining and formalising of the manner and extent of photocopying in libraries in the US 1976 Copyright Act. In 1978 the Copyright Clearance Centre (CCC) was set up to handle royalties accruing from library photocopying in excess of the permitted quantity. Journals print the royalty due on the title page of each article. The CCC soon ran into difficulties because the royalties collected did not cover the processing costs. However things improved in 1980 when royalty collection increased to $300,000, compared with $57,000 in 1978.

The same issue – that is the conflict of interest between libraries and publishers – is exemplified in an exchange of articles in the UK in 1976. In the piece by Line from the British Library Lending Division (BLLD) (which photocopied nearly one million articles in 1974) containing many facts and figures, it was concluded that "in the absence of any evidence to the contrary the economic difficulties experienced by journal publishers and the increased demand on the BLLD are unrelated".

This was followed by an exchange of letters between the publishers association and BLLD. The publishers claimed that the BLLD article was an attempt to whitewash large scale free use of articles. This was firmly rebutted by BLLD.

<u>Fair Use</u>

Fair use of copyright material is similar in several countries. It usually covers the limited use of the material for comment, criticism or review, teaching and research. Warwick defines the four tests for fair use in the US and considers those tests as applied to downloaded material – that is data transferred from a database, following a search, to another computer, usually over a telephone line.

The tests are: purpose and character of use, nature of the copyrighted work, amount and substance of the portion used, and the effect on the market for the copyrighted work or the value of the work.

Warwick suggests that after the fair use of the work, the copy of it stored in memory should be erased. With respect to the nature of the work he points out that the effort required to load data into a database having limited specialised use may be just as great as loading it into a heavily used database. Warwick considers that there is no limit to the number of records which may be downloaded but the number of copies which may be made of the records without copyright infringement is not clear. It will be difficult for the downloader to satisfy the supplier that he is not having an effect on the market. For example the user could repeatedly search the downloaded material instead of repeatedly paying the supplier for online searching.

The UK Society of Authors and Publishers suggest that re-publishing of an extract, or multiple extracts of a work not exceeding 10% of the length of the work, might not infringe copyright. If this be so then the re-publishing of short abstracts or bibliographic references certainly would not infringe.

Trends; Possible changes in the law

Copyright reform is pending in the UK, but so too is it in the EEC. The former will almost certainly await the latter. Meanwhile two documents have been published about the subject - the Whitford Report and the 1981 "Green Paper". Whitford was in favour of blanket licensing whereby an organisation like the CCC collects royalties and distributes the proceeds to publishers with no exceptions as are now provided for research purposes. The Green Paper thinks that the exceptions should be retained "with some tightening to control abuse". Neither the British Library nor the Publishers were happy with the Green Paper, the publishers considering that the approach to photocopying was inconclusive.

Problems about protecting the rights of authors in "hard copy" which is photocopied, in information in "soft form, i.e. resident in a computer, and in computer software which does not seem to fit any of the definitions of what constitutes a patent, merge into each other. For example the Green Paper suggests that the act of displaying a work for reading on a VDU is analgous to opening a book at an appropriate page and probably cannot be regarded as making a copy under the present UK law.

Taking a hard copy from the machine may be an infringment of copyright, subject to the usual exceptions, as with photocopying, but the Green Paper then introduces another factor. The copyright owner may have no need of protection since assumptions about user activities could have been made and covered in the initial negotiations when the work was changed into machine readable form. In the future, and maybe already, there could be some works which first existed in machine readable form because they were intended for use via a VDU.

Information does not fit into current laws, framed to cover physical entities. Information can be repeatedly sold yet be retained by the seller. A buyer can become a seller and is then in the same position as the original seller in respect of resale activities.

Software

To make a computer program patentable in the US, attempts were made to define it as a computer component nominated "firmware". In France and Germany programs have been held to be unpatentable, and they were also excluded from patent protection in 1973 by the EEC under the European economic patent grant system. Allowing software to become patentable also poses horrendous policing problems, and it seems that copyright is more likely to be the path chosen in the US.

In 1983 a decision was made in the US heralded as a milestone, and completely opposite to the contemporary British viewpoint that only literary works are covered by copyright. In the <u>Apple vs. Franklin</u> case the Philadelphia appeals court ruled against several Apple II "look-alike" programs. One company admitted that it had copied Apple programs but claimed that software was not copyrightable. It was held that Apple holds the copyright for its software and its operating system stored in ROM.

However the UK public became aware of the need for copyright protection, perhaps as never before, because of the publicity associated with the widespread

practice of pirating videotape recordings. The measures announced in the
Copyright Amendment Act of 1983 were effective in curtailing it. In 1985 a
private member's Bill - the Copyright (Computer Software) Amendment Bill - was
introduced into parliament with the intention of curtailing software pirating by
enabling inspection and penalties to be imposed like the 1983 amendment. It is
expected to become law by September 1985.

A good guide to copyright has been published by UNESCO and a short
review with particular reference to information technology has been provided by
Bull.

Hardware

In 1983 attempts were made in the US to stop semiconductor chip copying by
amending copyright law to apply but several organisations thought that this would
create a precedent for other new technology and what was needed was some new
legislation designed specifically for the protection of new kinds of intellectual
property. Accordingly a Bill was introduced and the Semiconductor Chip
Protection Act became law in November 1984. The Act covers "a mask work" - that
is the series of images used to form the materials of the chip. The interesting
point here is that this is the first time for a century that a completely new
piece of legislation of this kind has been introduced in the US opening the way
for the protection of other new products of the new technology.

Databases

Activities by users of databases focus attention on yet another aspect of
copyright. The information contained in a database may be the full text of
articles, it may be lengthy abstracts, or it may be simply bibliographic
references.

In the US, copyright protection extends to collective works - that is where
a number of independent works are assembled into a collective whole. This is
thought to cover full text databases such as Lexis even although this database is
a compilation of public domain material. If this kind of information is covered,
"electronic journal" type databases, containing the full text of articles not in
the public domain contributed by separate authors, would also seem likely to be
covered. In the UK, if a database contains portions or abstracts of works, and
the law applicable to hard copy also covers such databases, then the
reproduction of portions of works would not seem to be protected by copyright.

Apart from the authors of material stored in databases, there is the
question of copyright in databases whose producers have expended time and money
in compiling them. Such producers, when drawing up agreements with users, spell
out conditions of use in an attempt to make the users believe that they may be
sued if they transgress certain conditions. In particular they warn against the
sale of any part of a database in any form to a third party.

Holmes thinks that producers would find it difficult to obtain redress,
and, speaking on behalf of the producer that he represented, suggested a
different approach. "It is better to know what users are doing, than to encourage
them to hide certain practices" and "users are basically honest and would honour
the rules if fair, clearly defined, and above all, communicated to them".

Downloading from databases

Saksida, from another producer, obviously does not feel that such reasonable
sentiments apply to "downloading" - that is searching databases and running off
subsets down the line into local storage. He entitles his article "The pirates
of online". He believes that "nothing can be done" about users who will use the
tools now available to "manipulate data (retrieved from a database) and become a

"micro/mini spinner in his own right ...Given the four basic ingredients - the
database producer, the spinner(that is the host computer owner), the user, and
technological progress, the simple way is to put them all together, and say,
quite simply, that if a user wants to re-use his data for internal purposes, then
let us provide a service which provides for his specific need..."

This is fine, but it does not cover the case of the user who takes
advantage of such an arrangement, and offers a service for sale using the
"stolen" data. The actions of one producer seem to indicate that he agrees with
Saksida. Having made it convenient for a user to offload data from a database
into his microcomputer, ISI asks each Scimate purchaser to sign an "End user
Agreement" - a one page legal document covering two topics.

First, the user agrees to use the software only on his own microcomputer.
Wider use can be negotiated for suitable fees. Second, the user can download
data from ISI databases and re-use the stored data for his own purposes without
further payment, but other "database vendors and producers may restrict re-use"
and with reference to those other vendors, ISI includes the reminder "end user
must comply with the database vendor's agreement as to end-user's ability to
store downloaded data".

The Institute of Electrical Engineers have recently spelled out the
conditions for offloading fron their database as discussed in Chapter 16.

Further Reading

Anon.
   Cmnd 6732, HMSO London 1977.
     Report of the committee to consider the law of copyright and designs.
     (Chairman The Hon. Mr.Justice Whitford).
Anon.
   Cmnd 8302, HMSO London, 1981.
     Reform of the law relating to copyright, designs, and performer's
     protection ("Green Paper").
Anon.
   Unesco, 7 Place de Fontenoy, 75700, Paris, France. 1981.
     The ABC of copyright.
Bull, Gillian.
   Communication Technology Impact 5(4), 9-11, July 1983.
     Copyright - special feature.
de Freitas, Denis.
   Aslib Proc., 35(11/12), 431-439, Nov/Dec 1983.
     Interpretation of copyright law - looking especially at the situation
     created by new technology.
Holmes, P.L.
   Ibid (See Neal). 1-13.
     The re-use of machine readable data and copyright - a pragmatic approach
     to the problems.
Kutten, L.J.
   Mini-micro Systems, 249-253, September 1984.
     Can copyrights protect all forms of software?
Liebesny, F; Hewitt, J.W; Hunter, P.S. et al.
   Report. School of Lib., Polyechnic of N.London, Holloway Rd., London N.7.
   July 1973.
     The scientific and technical information contained in patent
     specifications.
Line. Maurice B., Wood, D.N.
   J.Doc 31(4), 234-245, Dec.1975
     The effect of a large scale photocopying service on journal sales.

Line,M.B., Wood, D.N.
 J.Doc.32(3), 204-206, Sep.1976
    Photocopying and journal sales.
Martyn, John.
  Aslib information, January 1985. (Supplement). Aslib, 26 Boswell St.,London
  WClN 3JZ.
    Software protection, piracy, and the library.
Miles, Dana E.
  IEEE Software, 84-87, April 1984.
    Copyrighting computer software after Apple v Franklin.
Neal,Peyton R; Slowinski, F.H.
  Proc 4th Internat. Online Meeting, London. Pub. by Learned Information,
  Besselsleigh Rd., Abingdon, Oxford, OX13 6LG. 409-420, Dec. 1980.
    The changing law on proprietary protection for computer databases.
Pegram, John B.
  The Business Lawyer, 34,1251-1282, April 1979.
    Photocopying in profit oriented organisations under the copyright revision
    act of 1976.
Saksida, M.F.
  Proc. 6th Internat. Online Meeting, London, 251-253, December 1982. Pub. by
  Learned Information.
    The Pirates of online.
Slack, Jennifer D.
 J.Comm. 31(1), 151-162, Winter 1981.
   Programming protection: the problem of software.
Van Tongeren, E.
  J.Doc.32(3),198-204, Sep.1976.
    The effect of a large scale photocopying service on journal sales.
Warwick, Thomas S.
  Online 8(4), 58-70, July 1984.
    Large databases , small computers, and fast modems: an attorney looks at
    the legal ramifications of downloading.

CHAPTER 30.

INFORMATION, TELECOMMUNICATIONS, CHALLENGE AND
UNCERTAINTY: A VIEWPOINT FROM THE UNITED STATES

DR.H.DORDICK
Annenburg School of Communication,
University of Southern California, U.S.A.

Waiting for the Information Society

There is an expectancy among the industrial and newly industrial nations of
the world, today. This mood can best be described as waiting for the Information
Society. It is a time of tension and uncertainty, for just what this society or era is
likely to bring with it can only be dimly seen.

One manifestation of this mood is the new interest of many countries in the
study of communications policy issues and an urgency of coming to grips with
them. Increasingly, nations see information and its distribution as a new resource
and informatics as a rational, systematic and necessary way to apply information
to political, economic and social problems. A report to the President of France on
the computerization of society argues that if France does not "respond effectively
to the serious challenges she faces, her internal tensions will deprive her of the
ability to control her fate" (1). Servan-Schreiber, the French journalist-author of
The World Challenge suggests that the future of the Third World does not reside in
low cost labor but in high value knowledge and that the adoption of informatics will
develop their economies in parallel rather than in series with the developed world
(2). Daniel Bell, states the case very succintly: "The computerization of society
will shape, allow, facilitate, determine-which verb will be the operative one
depends upon our consciousness and public policy-an extraordinary transformation"
(3).

Telecommunications and the Political Agendas of Nations

The political economy of telecommunications is of major concern to all of
the advanced nations and of increasing concern to the developing ones.
Telecommunications has moved to the top of their political agendas. New
technology has led to the break-up of the traditional telecommunications
monopolies in the United States, Great Britain and Japan. Pressures for
introducing competition in both broadcasting and telecommunications have
appeared in West Germany and France. The INTELSAT monopoly has been
challenged in Europe by a host of domestic satellites whose footprints spill over the
neighboring nations while in Southeast Asia the Indonesian satellite, Palapa,
provides both telecommunications and broadcast services to ASEAN. Australia has
launched its AUSSAT and ARABSAT will shortly provide telecommunications
services to the Middle East and the Northern tier of Africa.

The growing importance and enhanced political status of telecommunications
throughout the world is the result of three important forces:

1)   Many nations have realized that they cannot compete in the
development of information industries without good telecommunications;
telecommunications has become an important component of a nation's industrial
policy.

2)   Because of the convergence of the computer and communications
technologies, the telecommunications and computer industries see the
possibility of growth lying in each other's territory and, further, have found

that they can develop and profitably market their information products and services domestically as well as globally, and,

3)   Multi-national corporate operations require world-wide round the clock communications, global networks for banking, air traffic control, travel reservations news, and trade.

For these reasons domestic telecommunications policies have become deeply intertwined with international politics as firms expand their markets globally and as nations seek to enter into their information societies.

The World-Wide Network Marketplace

Many information societies have been idealized. In Japan there is the vision of a Computopia, a society that brings about a general flourishing state of human intellectual creativity instead of affluent material consumption. It is a society where people, in Masuda's words, may "draw future designs on an invisible canvas and pursue and realize individual lives worth living" (4).

The American economist Fritz Machlup (5) and Porat (6) after him envisioned an economically driven information society, one that would transform society by way of jobs, industries and trade. Knowledge becomes a form of technology itself, the "intellectual technology" of Daniel Bell and information the basic resource in the post-industrial society. With information as the central capital, indeed, the cost center and the crucial resource in our economy and with modern telecommunications systems for the efficient distribution of that information there will be a major restructuring of our economic base. It is the economist's vision of a society in which efficiency rules and human behavior adjusts. Information work is intellectual work and with computers and telecommunications as the tools of that work will become even more efficient. If less work is required to produce today's products and services, we shall invent new products and services for world-wide markets and the distribution of information products and services will take place on global telecommunications networks. The efficient world-wide distribution of labor will insure the proper allocation of competitive advantage. In the long run, every nation and every person will find their appropriate place in the scheme of things. This is the vision of the information society as a world-wide network marketplace (7).

It is this vision of an economic utopia that the industrialized and newly industrialized nations of the world are seeking, a world of rapid yet equitable economic development through the utilization of knowledge. Indeed, it is their vision on which the hopes of the developing nations also rest for they see telecommunications as the lever that will help them leap into their new era, to take their place among the family of industrialized nations sooner rather than later and in a manner that will overcome the age old inequities of the industrial revolution. Without a modern system for exchanging computerized information--a modern telecommunications network--this dream will not be fulfilled. Modern telecommunications are a necessary condition for rapidly achieving the high levels of industrialization they seek.

We are witnessing a rapid diffusion of the telecommunications technologies throughout the world; optical fibers are spanning the globe competing with satellites which have the capacity to serve earth locations only miles apart. Increasingly intelligent networks and terminals operate over essentially cost-free wired and broadcast transmission systems made so by greater utilization of computer technologies in telecommunications. We are seeing world-wide instantaneous electronic delivery of information in multiple modes, voice, image, data, and video. A new form of global infrastructure is emerging, one that provides both communications and computing and is intelligent. This coherent global system for handling information may explain the revolutionary dimensions

emerging in world business and the resulting political and technological tensions
that are emerging.

Telecommunications and Organizational Restructuring

A truism about modern capitalist organizations, but one which is often
overlooked when examining their roles in the creation of social and political
effects, is their need for constant growth. Firms require growth for any number
of reasons, perhaps the most important of which is to prevent take over by larger
firms. Further, the more firms grow the more benefits are available to be
distributed among those who own and manage the firm. Various arguments have
been advanced about how growth imperatives result in the transformation of
competitive markets into oligopoly or monopoly markets. A major incentive for
growth is the ability of the firm to increase relative control over its various
environments, including markets and to employ governments to socialize risk (9).

In the real world growth comes from a limited number of sources of which
the most important are: the creation of new markets through marginal advantage
gained from greater efficiencies of production and/or distribution which influence
real costs to the firm, (these include the classic factors of land, labor and capital)
and mergers--the utilization of the existing firm and its capacities to grow larger
and thus acquire greater capacity for liquidity, market balance, personnel and
talent mix, market entry, and financial depth.

The post-war decades have seen an incredible concentration in First World
capital with a corresponding increase in the size of the remaining firms, a tendency
which in the United States has been given new force by conservative
administrations which have permitted new levels of combinations to occur. There
are similar pressures in Great Britain, Japan, West Germany and Malaysia.
Simultaneously these same firms have extended their reach into the 500-700
transactional firms which dominate the international economy (10). Estimates vary
but many think that about 80% of the industrial production of the non-communist
world is accountable to their activities.

Critical to these developments are the managers who coordinate, manage and
plan these far-flung and complex operations. In his pioneering work, Chandler has
pointed out how modern management has become the "visible hand" replacing the
invisible hand of the marketplace for the coordination of that marketplace (11).
More efficient coordination and management increases the spans of control of the
firm thereby enabling mergers and other forms of concentration to occur. By
internalizing these operations the acquiring firm removes the acquired firms from
the marketplace, thereby restructuring the marketplace to its advantage.

Intelligent telecommunications networks provides yet another arrow in the
quiver of crucial corporate management skills necessary for achieving these
increased control and coordinating efficiencies with little relative increase in
costs. For telecommunications and computing have proven to be highly productive
activities, becoming even more so with the continued integration of software
packages on multi-media networks. More and more firms, however, are providing
their own telecommunications networks for these coordination and management
tasks. They reason that they can better control their costs, better insure that the
latest technologies will be available to them without delay, and control the
network to meet their own specific requirements rather than depend upon a
network that also serves the less demanding needs of consumers. Many firms in the
United States now perceive telecommunications as a priority investment enabling
them to capture a competitive edge through more efficient and less costly
management and through the more rapid introduction of new products made
possible by the availability of intelligent telecommunications networks (12). There
can be little doubt that these corporate pressures have been significantly
responsible for the restructuring of the telecommunications industry in the United
States, Great Britain and Japan.

Information as Currency

In the enumeration of forces that are creating the information society we often overlook information iteself as we concentrate on the techologies that process and transport this information. In particular, information as money, or electronic money on today's international telecommunications networks is a major factor in creating new enterprise structures throughout the world. Firms can utilize financial resources in ways heretofore impossible or difficult. This ability for intra and inter-firm transactions opens the door to configurations of new business activities effectively breaking down traditional barriers of product and process knowledge and experience.

Finance, insurance, brokering, information processing, the so-called high technology industries so dependent on the rapid transfer of information and the news media among many others are rapidly becoming computerized because of the ability to rapidly transport large volumes of information across nations and continents at costs that are far below the value of the information being transported. The extent to which SWIFT (13) has made possible today's international money crisis is not clear. What is clear, however, is that larger amounts of money have continually moved into the international data net where they are difficult to identify in terms of content or point of origin or the nature of the   terms of transactions. As this phenomenon grows in size, several related aspects grow in clarity and pose important political questions. And at the heart of these issues are the nation's telecommunications system and the global telecommunications networks.

The ability of a nation-state to "manage" or regulate the flow of information as money is decreasing. Inability to "watch" money limits the capacity of the state to tax it. As corporations move into the world, all aspects of the production process are transformed to make use of local advantage in gaining lower costs and higher prices. Thus, speed and ease of transportation and communications become of primary importance. Money, moved through a new medium and encoded in the new and emerging language of international transaction accounting benefit the corporation by contributing to the marginal increment to be gained from local advantage in each transaction, and by framing the transaction to protect it from governmental view and action.

Since governments move more slowly than private business, corporations wish to "free" telecommunications from its place within the bureaucracy. Once outside the rule structure of government deregulated private companies can use the new technology to gain relatively great advantage over their public sector counterparts, further limiting the ability of government to meaningfully regulate or tax the industries.

The blurring of distinctions between information and money is having profound effects on the structure of modern business throughout the entire world. Those firms that can master and integrate the new information technologies have leaped into the world arena utilizing the superior capabilities of the new machines and networks to integrate world production and distribution processes thereby maximizing their local advantage. Further, the distinction between financial and manufacturing firms is becoming less and less clear as virtually all large capital enterprises have sought to institutionalize some aspect of their capability within the information-as-money structure. Sometimes this movement has been from manufacturing to finance as General Motors has done, from retailing to finance, (e.g. Sears), or from traditional money institutions such as banks to other forms of ownership and activities such as bank holding companies with conglomerate holdings. Generally, it has been from one form of financial institution, for example, an insurance company, into integrated financial structures which operate across the spectrum of money and finance. What is important is that these firms are integrated by way of their intelligent networks along which flows the controlling power of information as money or electronic money (14).

Dilemmas for the Postal Telephone and Telegraph Monopolies

Traditionally the nation-state seeks to maintain control over these electronic transactions through their monopoly telecommunications authorities, their Postal Telephone and Telegraph companies. In addition to providing telecommunications services a nation's telecommunications monopoly serves other important functions for the nation; it provides a considerable number of jobs including employment for those very knowledge workers so important to an information society, subsidizes public services such as the post and other non-revenue producing services required by its citizens and is important for the nation's defense. Further, it is a measure of a state's sovereignty to provide its citizens a well managed, modern telecommunications system. As electronic money flows along the telecommunications channels in a nation, serving both national and multi-national interests, a single integrated telecommunications network, the ISDN, (15) as a national monopoly provides a means for maintaining control of money and insuring that revenues do not leave the nation untaxed.

The dilemma faced by today's PT&Ts is that they are under pressures for the reasons we have discussed to "privatize". They are pressured to allow the development of a multiplicity of specialized networks to serve the business and industrial needs of expanding domestic and multi-national firms. Furthermore, globally expanding telecommunications are encouraging firms not primarily in the telecommunication significantly field to increase productivity, thereby requiring fewer workers, including mid-level managers.

Pressures for specialized networks arise not only from the private sector but from the public sector as well. The availability of highly flexible and relatively low cost telecommunications systems is attractive to local, state and federal agencies. The defense establishment itself no longer need depend upon the PT&T for their telecommunications services.

The PT&Ts see their roles eroded. Yet there remains the need to subsidize postal services and other public workers and to provide the mix of job opportunities the PT&T can offer. Privatized firms are not likely to take up the slack. These firms will seek to maximize profit and productivity and are more likely to reduce their labor force, as has been so evident in the United States. Formerly subsidized services will either have to fend for themselves or seek subsidies from general tax revenues. In some countries there are suggestions that these services should seek the competitive route as well. Malaysia, for example, is considering the privatization of their ports as a means for increasing their productivity as well as providing opportunities for Malaysian entrepreneurs.

Telecommunications entities are not standing idly by watching their authorities erode. They have accepted the challenge offered by the new telecommunications and computer technologies by entering the all-digital era via the Integrated Services Digital Network (ISDN). By providing end-to-end digital services, the PT&Ts seek to meet the transmission requirements for the widest possible range of services, from full motion television at 90 megabits per second to telemetering for monitoring security systems of 10 bits per second. While users would pay for only the range of speeds or bandwidths they desire the cost of the system's construction must be borne by all users, indeed the entire nation.

This structure is in contrast with that which has emerged in the United States. In order to preserve the traditional policy of "universal service at affordable cost" and at the same time encourage competition two tiers of services are provided. "Basic" services are regulated voice services and are not likely to be digital for some time. "Enhanced" services are unregulated non-voice services; data, video, facsimile and other specialized telecommunications services likely to be required by business and industry.

Nations see several advantages to the ISDN architecture. It offers them the opportunity to maintain control over the domestic as well as international flow of information. Additionally they hope that the significant structural difference between U.S. telecommunications and their telecommunications could form a trade barrier to U.S. systems and equipments. It should be remembered that PT&Ts are often the primary providers of telecommunications equipment to their nations.

Conclusions

The political consequences of modern telecommunications extend beyond the current uncertainties surrounding the future of national PT&Ts although, as we have seen, these create serious consequences. Nations face challenges to their economic sovereignty as industry structures become increasingly globalized. Nations must learn to deal with the flow of information, labor, and money across their borders via high speed intelligent telecommunications networks, networks over which they have limited control. Just as satellite broadcasting does not recognize national boundaries and, consequently, challenges a nation's cultural sovereignty,international telecommunications networks challenge a nation's economic sovereignty.

In terms of output and employment the telecommunications industry is relatively small when compared to other industries. Nevertheless, it is an industry that greatly influences the management styles and business growth opportunities of other industries. As firms seek to expand their enterprises, both horizontally and vertically across national boundaries they recognize the extraordinary power of computer-communications networks to extend and improve their spans of control, reduce diseconomies of management coordination and increase their economies of scope, in short to achieve more and
better control over ever larger industrial organizations, domestically and throughout the world. The same technology makes possible the free flow of electronic money across national borders, thereby challenging the degree of autonomy nations have for establishing national monetary policy and their ability to tax the multinational enterprise.

References

1. Nora, Simon, & Alain Minc. The Computerisation of Society. Cambridge, MA.: The MIT Press, 1981

2. Servan-Schreiber, Jean-Jacques. The World Challenge. New York: Basic Books, 1976

3. Bell, Daniel. The Coming of Post-Industrial Society. New York: Basic Books, 1976

4. Masuda, Yoneji, The Information Society; as Post Industrial Society. Tokyo: Institute for the Information Society, 1981

5. Machlup, Fritz. The Production and Distribution of Knowledge in the United States, Princeton, N.J. Princeton University Press, 1962

6. Porat, Marc. The Information Economy: Definition and Measurement, Volume 1, Washington, D.C.: OT Special Publication, 77-12 (1), 1977

7. Dordick, Herbert S., Helen G. Bradley, & Burt Nanus, The Emerging Network Information Marketplace, Norwood, N.J.: Ablex Publishing Corporation

8. Galbraith, John Kenneth, The New Industrial State, New York: New American Library, 1967

9.   Lowi, Theodore J. The End of Liberalism: The Second Republic of the United States, 2nd ed., New York: W.W. Norton, 1979

10. Stauffer, Roger   "U.S. TNC's in an Era of Global Challenge: Tactical Responses to Structural Crisis", Research Monograph No. 18, Sydney: University of Sydney, Transnational Corporations Research Project, 1984

11. Chandler, Jr. Alfred D. The Visible Hand: The Managerial Revolution in American Business, The Billings Press of Harvard University Press Cambridge, Massachusetts and London, England, 1977

12. Research in Progress

13. Society for World-Wide International Financial Transactions

14. Moffett, The World's Money: International Banking from Bretton Woods to the Brink of Insolvency, New York: Simon and Schuster, 1983

15. Integrated Digital Services Network

Additional Readings

Youichi Ito, "The 'Johoka Shakai" Approach to the Study of Communications in Japan", in G.C. Wilhoit & H. de Bock (eds), Mass Communications Review Yearbook, Volume 2, Beverly Hills, CA.: Sage Publishing, 1981, pp. 671-698.

Ithiel de Sola Pool, Hiroshi Inose, Nozoma Takasaki & Roger Hurwitz, Communications Flows: A Census in the United States and Japan, Tokyo, University of Tokyo Press, 1984. Japanese-American comparisons are found in Chapter 3, pp. 35-76.

Dan Schiller, Telematics and Government, Norwood, N.J.: Ablex Publishing Corporation, 1982, offers a very comprehensive review of the pressures on A&T beginning in the 1950's on through the Department of Justice anti-trust suit against AT&T.

John Brooks, Telephone: The First Hundred Years, New York: Harper & Row, 1976. This most recent history of AT&T provides an excellent account of AT&Ts squabbles with the Federal Government over the past 70 or more years.

Telecommunications: Pressures and Policies for Changes, Paris: OECD, 1983, pp. 82-107.

Creek Froman, The Two American Political Systems: Society, Economics, and Politics, Englewood Cliffs, N.J.: Prentice-Hall, 1984. See also Murray Edelman, Political Language: Words That Succeed and Policies That Fail, New York: Academic Press, 1978.

Global Research: The Power of the Multinational Corporations, New York: Simon and Schuster, 1974.

Edward Tufte, The Political Control of the Economy, Princeton, N.J.: Princeton University Press, 1968.

Ronald E. Muller, Revitalizing America: Politics for Prosperity, New York: Simon and Schuster, 1980.

Richard Newfarmer, et. al, Transnational Conglomerates and the Economics of Dependent Development, Greenwich: JAI Press, 1980.

Robert Stauffer, "States and TNCs in the Capitalist World Economy: Four Country Studies on Relationships, Sydney: University of Syndey, Transnational Corporations Research Project, forthcoming.

Cheryl Payer, The Debt Trap: The IMF and the Third World, New York: Monthly Review Press, 1975.

Alfred D. Chandler, Jr., Strategy and Structure: Chapters in the History of the American Industrial Enterprise, Cambridge, MIT Press, 1962.

CHAPTER 31.

THE THIRD WORLD; TELECOMMUNICATIONS, GROWTH, AND THE POLITICS OF INFORMATION CONTENT

PROFESSOR ROBERT L. STEVENSON
University of North Carolina, U.S.A.

Introduction

In information-rich North America, there is one telephone for every 1.2 people; in big cities, telephones outnumber inhabitants. Every day, Americans make 800 million phone calls. In information-poor Africa, in contrast, there is one telephone for every 60 people; millions of people there and in other parts of the Third World live and die without ever making or receiving a telephone call.

The disparity in telephones is part of a broader communication gap between the West and the Third world that includes both mass media and "personal" media such as mail, tape recorders and computers. However, telecommunication is at the center of the communication gap because it links all of the other parts. Through telecommunication networks flow news dispatches, radio and television signals, routine business and government messages as well as telegrams and telephone calls. In modern systems, in fact, the signals are converted into packets of binary impulses that obliterate the differences between voice, text and pictures.

For the West, a major task of the 1980s is to adjust from an industrial economy to an information economy, but for the Third World, the question is more basic: can communication, itself a measure of the disparity between rich and poor countries, promote rapid growth in the Third World? And still more basic: should development projects try to incorporate Third World countries into the global information economy that is -- and will continue to be -- dominated by the West? For more than 20 years, most Third World governments have emphasized mass media as the centerpiece of national development efforts while paying relatively little attention to telecommunication. In the 1980s, the priority seems to be reversed, but loud voices object to any development in the Western image. In this chapter, we will examine the traditional role of communication in Third World development programs, a radical challenge to the less-than-successful development schemes, a current renewed interest in telecommunication as an engine of growth and the outlook for the future.

Communication Policy and National Development

Communication has been at the core of efforts to promote rapid Third World development for more than a generation. Of the thousands of projects designed to help poor countries make the leap to modernity, most can be traced to two Americans writing in the late 1950s and early 1960s when the dismantling of the great European empires began. An observer at this moment of historical change was Daniel Lerner, a sociologist at the Massachusetts Institute of Technology and director of a study of mass media and opinion formation in an arc of countries around the eastern Mediterranean. From interviews with people in all parts of this vast area, Lerner pieced together a picture of accelerating change in villages throughout the region.

What became known as the "dominant paradigm" of the role of communication in development was really quite simple. Lerner concluded that countries changed when people changed and that the key to individual change was empathy, the ability to imagine a different and better future, a rejection of the basic tenet of stable village life that the future must be like the past. For Lerner, the traditional means of instilling empathy was physical contact with other ways of doing things; in the age of mass communication, vicarious encounter could do the same thing.

Lerner claimed that mass media -- mostly radio in those days -- could help set spark a revolution of rising expectations among people in the developing countries that in turn would lead to accelerating growth in literacy, the economy and, finally, participant democracy. It was a simple and hopeful blueprint for the new countries emerging from colonialism and anxious to accomplish in decades what had taken centuries in the West. His book, <u>The Passing of Traditional Society</u>, was published in 1958 at exactly the time that the United Nations was urging the developing countries to develop national information policies that would mobilize mass media to promote rapid economic growth.

As part of the United Nations effort, the U.N. Educational, Scientific and Cultural Organization (Unesco) undertook a study to consolidate what it had learned about the role of communication in development. The study, written by Wilbur Schramm, then at Stanford University in California, was something of a how-to manual for the generation of development projects that followed. In it, Schramm laid out a role for communication in the whole spectrum of development but mostly as a multiplier of development efforts. His conclusion was virtually a call to arms to let information become the engine driving rapid growth (1964, 271):

> But we must remember that the full power of mass communication has never been used, in any developing country, to push economic and social development forward. This is the really exciting question: how much could we increase the present rate of development, how much could we smooth out the difficulties of the "terrible ascent," how much further could we make our resources go, how much more could we contribute to the growth of informed, participating citizens in the new nations, if we were to put the resources of modern communication skillfully and fully behind economic and social development?

How much indeed? We do not know the answer to that question because communication was never fully mobilized in the way that Schramm suggested. While most projects had communication components built into them, they were essentially efforts to combat illiteracy, improve sanitation or health or increase agricultural production. They typically made use of existing media or tried to improve the system as the project dictated. In some cases, mass media systems were installed or expanded but they seldom functioned the way the planners had hoped and usually increased dependency on the West for technology and programming.

The development of national communication networks -- that meant telecommunication -- received surprisingly little attention. As late as 1983, the United Nations Development Program allocated only 11% of its resources to communication and transportation. For the years 1969-81, World Bank total loans for telecommunication projects remained steady at about US$100 million annually, but as a percentage of total loans, dropped from 5% to less than 1%. The MacBride Commission, the Unesco Commission appointed in 1976 to examine the whole range of international communication issues, found that developing nations as a whole invested only about .5% of GDP in telecommunication while industrialized nations committed about twice that large a proportion.

From the perspective of the 1980s, it is puzzling to note how little attention telecommunication got from the first generation of development programs. Part of the reason, of course, was that the global system based on computers and satellites that we now take for granted was just emerging then in the West and had not reached the Third World. In the developing countries, simple telephone and telegraph service depended on expensive copper wire lines and high frequency radio that linked cities but seldom extended below the capital or provincial centers. To reach the mass audiences in the countryside -- the target of most development programs -- mass media were more efficient. In countries where physical travel was difficult at best and often impossible, they were often the only way to disseminate information.

A Radical Alternative

It does not take more than a cursory examination of the history of the past two decades, however, to see how the simple optimism of Lerner and Schramm failed to anticipate the turmoil that engulfed so much of the Third World in its first decades of political independence. The revolution of rising expectations that Lerner expected to propel the Third World toward modernity turned into a revolution of rising frustrations as mass media became more of a mirror of the growing gap between the West and the Third World than a magic machine to compress centuries of development into years. In fact, in Unesco where Western mass media were once promoted as the means to speed development toward a Western model of industry and democracy, communication was presented as the new medium of imperial control, maintaining Western dominance of the Third World in the same way that armies had done in earlier centuries.

The theory (or theology) of dependency mostly came out of Latin America and argued that the global system of economic, political and military control was responsible for the failure of the Third World to achieve what the dominant paradigm had promised. In fact, the whole definition of modernity based on a Western model of economic growth was rejected as at best inappropriate for the Third World and at worst a transparent effort to disguise the activities of the (mostly American) multi-national corporations, military powers and political interests. Authentic development, it was claimed, meant disengagement from the West, not further incorporation into a global system that was becoming more and more dominated by information. Development itself, it was argued, should be defined in terms of maintaining a separate cultural identity and independence from the dominant global system. Information policy, of course, then should stress disengagement from the dominant global structure and emphasize the use of all forms of communication -- mass media, of course, but telecommunication as well -- to promote an "authentic" Third World development based on national autonomy and Third World solidarity against the West.

The most influential writer about information as the driving force of neo-colonialism was Herbert Schiller from the University of California at San Diego. For more than a decade, he stridently argued that communication was the heart of a new American empire. As information became the dominant force of the American economy, and its global influence, which had weakened in the wake of a decade of domestic and international setbacks, regained its strength, his attack shifted from the mass media to the new information industries. Here, he said, was the real obstacle to Third World development. In rhetoric more notable for hyperbole than evidence or logic, he had argued (1971, 3):

> A powerful communications system exists to secure not grudging submission by an open-armed allegiance in the penetrated areas, but by identifying the American presence with freedom -- freedom of trade, freedom of speech and freedom of enterprise. In short, the emerging imperial network of American economics and finances utilizes the communications media for its defense and entrenchment wherever it exists already and for its expansion to locales where it hopes to become active.

The controversy about communication took root in the congenial atmosphere of Unesco where a new world information order was debated for nearly a decade. Nobody really could define the new world information order. For the West, it meant a promise to help reduce the information gap by increasing technical and financial assistance to Third World communication development efforts; for others, it meant **redefining the role of mass media to justify their mobilization to promote political development schemes.** When **the issue burned itself out with the approval of an indecipherable declaration on mass media in 1978 and the formation of the International Program for the Development of** Communication (IPDC) two years later, not much had changed. The gap between information-rich West and information-poor Third World remained -- and was perhaps growing -- while the belief that communication could help narrow the gap persisted.

But some things had changed. One was an explosion of radio and television throughout the Third World, especially in those areas where these media were least accessible. The other was a shift from the use of mass media to telecommunication as the linchpin of many development schemes. In the jargon of development experts, telecommunication represented "horizontal" communication rather than the "vertical" communication of mass media. The difference was that electronic media were one-way, top-to-bottom <u>mass</u> media, while telecommunication -- essentially the telephone but including its compatible services such as telex and facsimile -- linked individuals directly and could pass information up and horizontally through a bureaucratic structure as well as from top to bottom. There was some research suggesting that this arrangment produced a much higher payoff in development terms than the ambitious programs of the 1960s using radio and television.

The Third World Electronic Explosion

After examining several studies of the role of mass media on rural Third World development, Emile McAnany (1980) asked rhetorically, is there any village so remote that radio does not reach it? The answer, with a few inevitable exceptions, is "no." Even the casual traveler in the Third World senses how deeply radio and television are embedded in the fabric of daily life. Village markets and urban shantytowns ring with the sound of radio, usually a blend of Western pop music, local dialects and the solemn tones of a government-controlled news reader. A new photo once showed a man in south Asia plowing with a pocket-sized radio tied between the horns of his bullock. The picture seems to epitomize the arrival of the information revolution in the Third World.

No one knows how many radios and TV receivers there are in the Third World. Separate estimates (Stevenson 1983) in the late 1970s put the number of TV sets in Algeria at 39,000, 256,000 and 900,000. Any of the three could be right, but all sources document an exponential increase throughout the Third World that brings all developing regions well above the minimum of 50 radios per 1,000 people established by Unesco as a development goal in the early 1960s. In most regions of the developing nations, the number of TV receivers approaches or exceeds that number as well.

According to annual estimates by the BBC, between 1965

and 1982, the total number of radio sets in the Third World increased from 66 million to nearly 392 million; sets per thousand population grew from 30 to 120. The growth of television was more dramatic: from 8 million sets in 1965 to nearly 100 million in 1982, from 4 sets per 1,000 people to 30. Of course, these numbers must be compared to statistics in the industrialized countries where there is about one radio receiver per person and one TV receiver for every two people. The gap remains.

Still the absolute growth in the Third World is striking, and so is one other comparison. The Third World's share of all radio sets on the planet increased from 13% in 1965 to 28% in 1982; for the same years, the developing nation's share of all TVs grew from 5% to 17%. It does suggest that one part of the information gap between the industrialized North and developing South is closing, although slowly.

In telecommunication, the record of change in the Third World is less clear and, from the information we do have, less dramatic. However, significant growth did take place. In each Third World region, the number of telephones per 1,000 people about doubled between 1970 and 1978, although disparities between the Third World and the West and within the Third World remained. Africa remained the most media-poor region with only 16.7 phones per 1,000 people in 1978. Asia, with 27.6 and Latin America with 59.4 were better. The Middle East, where some of the fastest and most violent change had occurred, reached 74.9 telephones per thousand population.

Telecommunication differs from radio and television

because it is completely dependent on government policies. The decision to get a radio or TV is up to the individual as long as receivers can be bought, given or smuggled; not so with telephones that have to be connected to a government-run or -authorized PTT. Most governments fell farther and farther behind as population growth and urbanization overtook modest efforts to maintain or expand an existing inadequate telephone system. Tanzania's President Nyerere, in another context, once lamented that while the West was reaching the moon, the Third World was still trying to reach the countryside. It was an irony of the information age that a telephone link from the main PTT in a Third World capital around the world was loud and clear; across town, it was often garbled, out of order or non-existent.

Out of the murky new world information order debate came a recognition of the need to improve Third World communication capabilities and a commitment, through the IPDC and other aid organizations, to expand national news agencies, regional exchanges and the like. It turned out **that the single biggest obstacle to these efforts was the high cost of telecommunication and restrictions on the development of news systems outside of the structure of the national PTT. By the mid-1980s, there was growing recognition in organizations such as Unesco, ITU and IPDC that development of telecommunications had to be meshed with development of mass media and, beyond that, a growing interest in the power of telecommunication itself to do what mass media had tried to do but failed.**

Telecommunication and Development

Along with the extraordinary growth of electronic media and not-so extraordinary but steady growth of telephones came a shift in emphasis in development programs. At the same time that many critics of traditional development theory were arguing against the expansion of mass media, others were exploring how telecommunication could promote economic and social growth. There were some differences between the 1980s perspective and that offered by Lerner and Schramm a generation earlier.

For one thing, many of the new communication-oriented development specialists were economists rather than sociologists or traditional communications researchers. They were less caught up in the old arguments about how -- or even whether -- you could demonstrate that a change in X (mass media) <u>caused</u> a subsequent change in Y (economic growth). They preferred to talk about cost-benefit ratios and economic returns on investment instead. And several important studies found that an investment in telecommunication did indeed produce a significant economic return, whereas mass media did not. When social benefits were factored into the equation, the payoffs could be dramatic.

One of the most impressive studies was carried out in 146 rural villages of Egypt by Ithiel de Sola Pool of MIT (in Singh 1983). Pool was in many ways Lerner's successor at MIT; the Egyptian study was one of the last of a long and productive career devoted to various aspects of communication and public policy. He and Egyptian colleagues studied how the full spectrum of residents of those villages used the existing communication network and could make use of a better one.

Consider what an absence of horizontal communication means in such circumstances. Villagers can neither send nor receive mail, neither send nor receive telegrams or telephone calls. Good news of weddings and births, bad news of deaths and routine gossip can be transmitted to family members in nearby villages, provincial towns or the slums of the capital only when someone goes there to pass on the information in person, usually by walking or hiring a taxi. As much as 60% of that travel could have been eliminated if an adequate phone system were available.

Beyond the difficulties inadequate telecommunication imposed on people in their personal lives, the social and economic structure suffered more. Without telephone service, business and government activities were slowed and often interrupted. Efficiency was reduced, initiative stifled and emergencies unmet. Telecommunication seemed to play a key role in the network of activities that bound the villages together and moved them, however slowly, toward modernity. Was the importance of telecommunication to development unique to Egypt?

The answer, of course, is "no." Telecommunication as it evolved in the 1970s and '80s seemed to offer promise as a spur to economic growth that mass media had promised but not delivered a generation earlier. For one thing, as the technical distinctions among media blurred, telecommunication became the core of a total communication system that carried news agency dispatches and radio and TV programming as well as traditional telephone and telegraph traffic. Satellites, which only a decade earlier were used almost exclusively for international traffic, became available for Third World domestic use and eliminated the single biggest barrier to telecommunication development in many developing countries. With traditional landlines, the cost of developing and maintaining even a minimal telecommunication system in a sprawling, unevenly populated country such as Brazil or Zaire was prohibitive. In archipeligos such as Indonesia and the Philippines, it was impossible. A satellite system, however, such as those in use or planned by a half dozen Third World countries, could connect the most distant points in the country as easily and cheaply as it could connect the capital with the rest of the world.

It was easy to dismiss the new interest in the role of telecommunication in development as another step in the long search for a simple way to ease the terrible ascent of Third World countries toward modernity and stability. Telecommunication might be nothing more than a 1980s version of the elusive magic multiplier of development efforts that Lerner and Schramm once identified with radio and then television. True, but recent evidence from an impressive range of macro-level studies supports what Pool and his colleagues found in the rural villages of Egypt.

A survey of studies by the International Telecommunication Union (ITU) and Organization for Economic Cooperation and Development (OECD) for World Communications Year (Pierce and Jequier 1983) found evidence of telecommunication's effects on rural development, industry and public services. Most important were data that supported the argument that investment in telecommunication led to a significant increase in economic growth and that the least-developed countries profited most from telecommunication investment. In Kenya, investments in telecommunication of about 300,000 Kenyan pounds by nine enterprises produced benefits of more than 34 million pounds -- a cost/benefit ratio of one to 115. A separate hypothetical calculation concluded that one simple satellite earth station connected to ten telephones over nine years could contribute from US$4,000 to $15,000 to the gross domestic product of a relatively wealthy Third World country with a minimal existing phone system. In a rural area, the return was estimated to be from $167,000 to $496,000.

A thorough analysis of data from nearly all developing countries between 1970 and 1980 (Ghorpade et al. 1984) tested various assertions about communication and economic, political and social change derived from the original Lerner/Schramm model and the alternative radical arguments. The only factor that clearly showed a direct influence on economic growth was telecommunication. Other analyses at the macrolevel, with better data and better methods than were available even a decade earlier, showed both that telecommunication was a more important factor in development than mass media and that, just possibly, the arrow linking them had been pointed in the wrong direction.

Richard E. Butler, secretary general of the ITU, captured the change of thinking about the importance of telecommunication to the Third World in his preface to the ITU/OECD report. Conventional wisdom, he noted, was that telecommunication growth followed economic development and was a luxury that a developing country could afford only after other needs were met. Now it appeared that telecommunication produced important benefits across the whole spectrum of development goals and probably should be the core of development programs, not at the periphery. This about-face has important implications for the Third World in the 1980s and beyond.

Barriers to Telecommunication Growth

Government bureaucracies resemble the oil supertankers that we learned about in the OPEC embargo a decade ago: once underway, they can change course only slowly and with great effort. Even though the importance of telecommunication is now recognized, many Third World governments seem less concerned with the construction of a modern telecommunication system than with the continued development of mass media as the centerpiece of national development. Indeed, most of the rhetoric of the Unesco debate and the modest efforts of the IPDC still focus on the creation and expansion of national news agencies, regional news exchanges and redefinitions of news to mobilize information to support development. Telecommunication is still largely on the periphery of the development agenda.

Why, after a wide range of studies convincingly demonstrates the importance of telecommunication, does it still get so little attention in five-year plans? And so little money from aid and loan agencies? Part of the reason, of course, is the length of time it takes for new ideas to percolate from academic studies and planning agencies through specific development projects to anything tangible on the ground. The notion that mass media are the key to rapid growth is so well entrenched in development literature and the minds of development planners of both the traditional and radical persuasions that it takes a while to change course. It is hard for people whose careers are built on one approach to development to jump ship in favor of another.

Not that advice from Unesco, the World Bank and Western universities was ever followed very carefully. For years, Unesco had pleaded for comprehensive national planning to harness all of the forces of change into one common effort pulling in one direction. Schramm had done the same, putting communication at the core of the effort. The MacBride Commission, almost two decades later, came to the same conclusion. Yet it was just about impossible, even in the mid-1980s, to find an example of any broad-based development program based on a comprehensive, coherent blueprint, let alone one that followed it.

Change in the Third World in general and growth in communication in particular seem to proceed more from some mixture of internal dynamics and external forces than from specific programs that try to promote education, public health or agriculture. If development is erratic when governments try to promote it, consider what is likely to happen when governments discourage it. One of the reasons why telecommunication receives so little attention was that many Third World governments simply do not want to expand a system that weakens their control.

A common element of many Third World governments is tight control on mass media. In newspaper after newspaper, TV newscast after newscast in Africa, the Middle East and parts of Asia and Latin America, the comings and goings of the national leader are featured in mind-numbing repetition and detail. Use of mass media to promote political leaders in the name of nationalism is not new, of course, but came to prominence in the new world information order debate. The new national development was said to require the mobilization of all communication media in support of political objectives. That meant legitimacy for concepts such as "development news" (information which both promoted and documented progress in development) and the egregious "protocol news" (celebrations of national leaders amid the muffled rhetoric of welcoming speeches, banquet toasts and bland communiques). Information policy was supposed to promote disengagement from the West with its emphasis on "coups and earthquakes" journalism, its independent and critical media that were dysfunctional to the new style of development.

Not surprisingly, the more radical interpretation of development in the 1980s that defends the mobilization of mass media to support political goals is cool to telecommunication. Telephones are powerful tools for getting information into and out of a country and even more powerful for disseminating information horizontally within a country. In short, telecommunication can be a threat to the monopoly of information that some Third World leaders demand.

But there are costs. In all of the discussions, debates and diatribes about the dominance of the West in global information flow, a critical point was often ignored: government information policies restricting telecommunication growth worked against the expansion of mass media, which were still at the center of development programs. Efforts to promote national and regional news services were thwarted because of the often artificially high cost of telecommunication and restrictions on the development of independent distribution systems. UPI told the MacBride Commission that smaller papers in Venezuela had to receive the agency's regional file on erratic and old-fashioned shortwave radio-teletype because of the cost of leasing a landline within Venezuela. UPI charged $100-300 a month for its file; a teletype line to move it from Caracas ranged from $350 to $1,000 a month. Till (1983) calculated that a low-speed teletype line between the United States and Zaire would cost $7,263 a month; the American link to the satellite rented for $1,648; from the satellite down to Zaire, the charge was $5,615. The fledgling Caribbean News Agency ran into similar problems (Cuthbert 1981). A reporter in the French islands could call Paris for less than neighboring islands; a teletype line from Barbados to Venezuela cost $3,000 to month, compared to $1,000 for a link between Venezuela and New York. Despite pleas for reduced rates for Third World news organizations, little has changed.

As the new news services promoted by the IPDC got down to business, the inseperable links between the Third World's news system and its telecommunication system became clearer. Unesco, ITU, IPDC, Intelsat and International Press Telecommunications Council (IPTC) all studied the issue and came, by varying paths, to the same conclusion: the existing international telecommunication system could be adapted to just about any kind of national, regional and global news system the organizations involved wanted. The biggest obstacles? High charges to the customer, usually set arbitrarily and above actual costs, and laws preventing news organizations from developing their own systems. All of these organizations called for special reduced rates for news media. A few countries, mostly in Asia, mapped out rate schedules that encouraged news distribution, but the PTT bureaucracies often operated with different priorities than the news organizations, and change was painfully slow.

The biggest promise for improving the flow of news into, out of and within the Third World, however, was the use of satellites, both the existing Intelsat system and the proliferating domestic systems that were owned outright (India, Indonesia, for example) or based on rented capacity from Intelsat (more than two dozen developing countries). The current Intelsat system has the technical capacity (and offers it to customers, although few use it) to meet virtually all Third World news needs. For Third World mass media, the biggest advantages of satellite systems are single-point to multi-point transmissions, flexibility in accomodating voice, video and text, simplicity in setting up temporary installations, especially in remote areas and, of course, elimination of distance as a factor in cost or reliability. Why hasn't a decade of discussion about problems of communication development produced a chorus demanding the immediate adaptation of the satellite system to Third World needs?

As usual, the answer is a combination of money, politics and inertia. The problems of money fall partly to Third World countries themselves (for keeping costs to customers artifically high) and partly to aid donor organizations (for commiting so little to telecommunication). Politics and inertia are universal problems -- consider the reluctance of Western nations to free telecommunication from public monopoly -- and cannot be overcome by the strongest exhortations from **Unesco**. About the best thing governments could do is get out of the way and let the news organizations themselves set up their own news distribution systems.

Don Till, communications director of the Washington **Post**, laid out the technical possibilities of using satellites to improve news flow around the world but especially in the Third World in a report to Unesco. He concluded with this strong statement: "The deliberate witholding of valuable satellite services, causing a severe impediment to the free flow of information worldwide, particulary to and from developing nations, cannot under any circumstances be justified. Undoubtedly, the reluctance of telecommunication administrations to provide specific new satellite services traces back to a basic two-way, point-to-point tariff philosophy, related perhaps conveniently, but certainly obliquely and with total irrelevance to a unit of telephone conversation."

Till's concern was mostly for news media and his admonition was addressed to governments generally, but the point is germane to the whole range of information policies in developing areas where the uncertainties of new communications technology confound the problems of nation-building. Two decades ago, with Lerner and Schramm as guides, the direction was clear, and the goal seemed to be within sight. Modernity was the West; communication was the magic multiplier of development efforts. With it, the painful evolution of industrialization and democracy that had taken centuries in the West could be compressed into decades.

Now both the direction and goal are unclear. Development is sometimes talked about as disengagement from the West and the preservation of indigenous life even at the expense of foregoing the marvels of the information age. Integration of a national communication into a powerful global system controlled by the West seems to guarantee the continued imbalance in news, popular culture and information technology that inspired the new world information order debate in the first place. Radical critics decry the rejuvenated power and influence of the "imperial" information societies; moderates see continuing Western influence as a threat to their own established ways and cultural values but acknowledge that a policy of building barriers against Western influence would be both unwise and unsuccessful.

Lerner defended the use of mass media to promote Western-style modernity with the argument that only modern Western governments could accomodate the rapid change that characterizes so much of our time. The point is still compelling. Religious fundamentalist nations that try to deny the age and countries that try to monopolize information as though communication were confined to 17th century printing presses are doomed to turmoil. Information policies based on such goals are doomed to failure. Instead, Third World countries need to recognize that information by itself is neither an instant and certain solution to intractable problems nor the cause of them. Policies that encourage the flow of information at all levels within a society and among societies are likely to produce surer steps toward modernity than those that restrict information flow.

It is hard to think of circumstances where ignorance is better than knowledge or where the past, despite its romantic appeal, is really better than the present or the future. The lives of people, of course, not economic growth or social change, per se, are what communication policies are about, and Hudson (1984, 133) captured the real importance of improved communication on the Third World while interviewing a doctor in a remote part of the Cook Islands over a primitive HF radio network. The exchange went like this:

Researcher: "What did you do before you had the radio to get medical advice? Over."

Remote doctor: "Just prayed to God. Over."

References and Further Reading

Cuthbert, Marlene. 1981. "The First Five Years of the Caribbean News Agency." Gazette 28(1):3-15. One of several publications based on a study of one of the first and best Third World regional agencies.

Frey, Frederick W. 1973. "Communication and Development." In Ithiel de Sola Pool et al. (eds.). **Handbook of Communication**. Chicago: Rand McNally. A careful survey of academic studies up to about 1970 examining the influence of mass media on national development.

Gandy, Oscar H., Jr., et al. 1982. **Proceedings from the Tenth Annual Telecommunications Policy Research Conference**. Norwood NJ: Ablex. An important collection of papers, including several directly related to issues of information policy and telecommunication in the Third World.

Ghorpade, Shailendra, et al. 1984. "A Re-evaluation of the Dominant Paradigm of Communication and Development." Presented to the Association for Education in Journalism and Mass Communication, meeting in Gainsville FL. Available in microfiche through Educational Resources Information Center (ERIC). A prize-winning student paper incorporating the best techniques and data available.

Hamelink, Cees. 1983. **Cultural Autonomy in Global Communications; Planning National Information Policy.** New York: Longman. A strong statement advocating Third World disengagement from the West as the only alternative to continued Western dominancee.

Hudson, Heather E. 1984. **When Telephones Reach the Village; the Role of Telecommunications in Rural Development.** Norwood NJ: Ablex. A thorough, up-to-date synthesis of a wide range of technical studies; a key document.

International Commission for the Study of Communication Problems [MacBride Commission]. 1980. **Many Voices, One World.** Paris: Unesco. A wide-ranging examination of the spectrum of communication problems with special attention to Third World development; unreadable but very important; supporting documents are especially valuable.

Lerner, Daniel. 1958. **The Passing of Traditional Society**. Glencoe IL: Free Press. Paperback edition published in 1964. The original study, now out of print.

Lerner, Daniel, and Wilbur Schramm. 1967. **Communication and Change in the Developing Countries**. Honolulu: East-West Center Press. Report on a conference shortly after the publication of Schramm´s famous book; early hints of disenchantment with Lerner-Schramm model.

McAnany, Emile. 1980. **Communications in the Rural Third World; the Role of Information in Development**. New York: Praeger. A technical analysis of several major studies; tries to evaluate opposing theories of communication and development.

Pool, Ithiel de Sola. 1977. **The Social Impact of the Telephone**. Cambridge MA: MIT Press. A useful collection of essays with relevance to the Third World.

Saunders, Robert, et al. 1983. **Telecommunications and Economic Development**. Baltimore MD: Johns Hopkins University Press. More technical analysis, complementing the Heather and ITU/OECD studies.

Schiller, Herbert I. 1976. **Communication and Cultural Domination**. White Plains NY: International Arts and Sciences Press. An impassioned articulation of the cultural imperialism hypothesis.

Schiller, Herbert I. 1984. **Who Knows? Information in the Age of the Fortune 500**. Norwood NJ: Ablex. Cultural imperialism updated to the information age with no diminution of fervor.

Schramm, Wilbur. 1964. **Mass Media and National Development**. Paris and Stanford CA: Unesco and Stanford University Press. The book that launched a generation of communication development, still selling several hundred copies a year.

Schramm, Wilbur, and Daniel Lerner. 1976. **Communication and Change: The Last Ten Years -- and the Next**. Honolulu: University Press of Hawaii. Papers from a second conference with Lerner-Schramm clearly on the defensive.

Singh, Indu B. 1983. **Telecommunications in the Year 2000; National and International Perspectives**. Norwood NJ: Ablex Publishing Co. An exellent collection of readings, including reports on Egypt, India and Brazil.

Stevenson, Robert L. 1983. "The Record of Communication Development in the 1970s." Paper presented to the conference on communication and development, sponsored by Northwestern University in Chicago. Available on microfiche from the university. First results of an extended assessment of Third World communication development.

Telecommunications for Development. 1983. Geneva: International Telecommunications Union. An excellent summary of recent studies; considerable overlap with the Hudson book.

Telecommunication Tariffs for the Mass Media. No date. Documents on the New Communication Order No. 8. Paris: Unesco. Mostly statements from international conferences and bodies; long on rhetoric, short on specifics.

Till, Don. 1983. **A Study on the Feasibility of the Installation and Operation of Satellite Earth Stations for Broadcasting Organizations, News Agencies and Newspapers.** Documents on the New Communication Order No. 10. Paris: Unesco. Invaluable summary by an expert; a clear assessment of technical requirements.

CHAPTER 32.

EUROPE. TELECOMMUNICATIONS AND INFORMATION POLICIES
OF COMPETITION, CRISIS, AND CONFUSION

JILL HILLS
Manchester University, England.

Reaction of "Le défi Americain"

In order to discuss information and telecommunications policy in Europe one must first recognise that Europe is not a unified whole. In terms of markets Europe consists of both the ten EEC countries and the European Free Trade Association (Austria, Finland, Iceland, Norway, Portugal, Sweden and Switzerland). From 1972 EFTA members have each had a free trade agreement with the EEC and they have recently agreed with the EEC that there should be more co-operative R & D in high technology between companies in their respective blocs. But the political divide between the two blocs remains, as do non-tariff barriers and other impediments to trade.

During 1984 the political divisions within the EEC itself came to the fore, with dissension over the EEC budget dominating other policy initiatives. Despite attempts to solve the crisis by cutting back on agricultural subsidies, a permanent solution involving increased funding for the Community has been blocked by West Germany until the accession of Spain and Portugal is finalised. The rejection of the budget by the EEC Parliament in December means that no new policy initiatives may come out of Brussels until a new budget is agreed, and that current programmes, including those on information- technology, will be funded on a month by month basis. Meanwhile pressure from France to further unify the Community, encapsulated in proposals within the Dogue Report, has underlined the differences in political commitment to Europe between the original seven, and Britain, Denmark and Greece, the three who demur at possible further unification. Political differences have also been exacerbated by the reconvening of the Western European Union within Nato and the de facto recognition that the EEC (with Ireland as a neutral member) is an inappropriate forum for the discussion of issues related to procurement and the defence industry - an issue which is of increasing importance to the electronics companies of France and Britain. Such a politically divided Europe has obvious implications for markets which are still predominantly politically controlled.

Historically, in the information and telecommunications markets, it has been the European national governments which have set targets and decided policies. These policies have been based primarily upon a concern in the major nations to avoid a total dependence upon the USA for either products or technology. Governments have attempted where possible to develop competitive supplies under domestic control. Traditionally they also devoted separate policies to separate markets in data processing, telecommunications and microchip components.

From the 1950's, when IBM first entered the data processing business, the promise of a tariff-free market brought American multi-nationals into Europe. By the end of the 1960's IBM alone took a major share of each of the domestic European markets in mainframe computers. At one stage it seemed that both the British and French governments would be willing to allow domination of this market by the Americans, welcoming imports and local manufacture as an outcome of the increasingly specialised world division of labour. But this form of dependence suddenly became untenable when American defence interests refused to allow the use of American computers in French nuclear establishments. There followed a period in which the British, French and West German governments used loans, subsidies and rationalisation, R & D support and public procurement preferences to retain a domestically owned manufacturer in the mainframe computer market - ICL in Britain, Siemens in West Germany and CII in France.

Attempts were made to utilise the extent of the European market by linking national firms together. In the 1960s, Unidata, a joint marketing agreement, brought Philips of Holland, Siemens, and CII together. When that arrangement collapsed, further attempts were made to bring companies together in joint R & D and marketing agreements. When those also failed national governments reverted to supporting their own champion companies. France brought in Honeywell with American technology to rescue CII and Siemens turned to America for its technology. Yet, despite continued support for 'their' companies, IBM continued to take over 50% of the European market.

As the growth in the market has devolved downwards into mini-computers, then desk top micros and personal computers, so European governments have tended to give support to those sectors. But, at each stage they have been faced with the domination of American manufacturers in the market. IBM standards have become de facto standards for the rest of the industry. In 1983 IBM's data processing revenue in Europe was $10bn compared to the $1.3bn of Olivetti and the $1.2bn of Siemens. IBM's turnover in Britain and France was double that of the national champion companies.

Another major area where American companies have predominated is in micro-chip production. Several of these companies set up manufacture in Britain during the 1960s in response to the Labour Government's imposition of a tariff on micro-chips. At this time the French and West German governments supported domestic micro-chip manufacture (without much success) and British companies withdrew from the market. Subsequently, when manufacture was re-established in the 1970s, it predominantly relied upon American technology, either through licensing agreements or through joint ventures with American firms. More recently Japanese firms have entered the EEC, manufacturing in Scotland, Ireland and West Germany. The European companies' share of the world market in integrated circuits has declined from 14.5% in 1977, to 11% in 1982, to 9.6% in 1983. In 1978, Philips, Siemens and Thomson (France) were in the top fifteen world suppliers. By 1983 only Siemens remained, and then only by virtue of its ownership of Signetics of the USA.

Only in the public sector telecommunications market could it be said that Europe retained a considerable amount of autonomy in manufacture and market share until the 1980s. In the private exchange market, in Britain in particular, IBM and Ericson of Sweden were dominant. But, in the public sector, national preferences and standards ensured that in the major West European countries the suppliers were predominantly domestic. Siemens and AEG-Telefunken in West Germany, Italtel in Italy, CIT-Alcatel and Thomson in France, Plessey and GEC in Britain were the major suppliers. But even in this market American multinationals, ITT and GTE were involved in the sector through subsidiaries. GTE played a leading role in the Italian market, whilst ITT had subsidiaries in eight of the West European countries. To some extent, ITT's presence has been reduced over the years, through the sale of its subsidiaries to the French government and by the reduction in its holdings in Standard Telephone and Cables (its UK subsidiary). But worldwide in 1982, with sales of $6.7bn, ITT has been second only to AT & T of America. ITT's System 12 digital exchange is sold in West Germany, Italy and Norway.

Different policies in different countries

There have been differences amongst the national governments' policies. In France the domestic ownership of the electronics industry has been of major importance. Thus the Socialist Government of President Mitterand nationalised Honeywell-CII. Under the new name of Bull it continues to be supported by the government through the posts and tele-communications administration (PTT). The French government has also rationalised the telecommunications manufacturing industry, bringing Thomson and CIT-Alcatel together into one company under state control, against the advice of the PTT - a factor which has been influential in the PTT's search abroad for competitive supplies.

Until very recently the policies of the major West European countries have been mainly concerned with technology rather than with market base. France has been the major exception. In France, the most chauvinistic of the countries, the domestic market has been used as the demand base for domestic supply. This policy has involved public sector purchasing preference in favour of French owned manufacturers where possible. In Britain and West Germany a similar policy preference in the mainframe market operated until 1981, when GATT regulations came into force through EEC law. The EEC directive outlawed preference for domestically owned manufacturers in data-processing contracts over a certain size. Although Britain in particular attempted to obey the letter of the law, and ICL's share of public contracts diminished, in France the regulation was more or less ignored. The telecommunications market, with its linkage to defence, is in any case exempt from the regulation, as are smaller contracts, so for those wishing to evade the provision, avenues have been open for evasion. An attempt in Britain to revive a 'Buy British' policy under the name of a 'Positive Purchasing Policy' was made in the 1980s. The policy has not been a success; micro-computer manufacturers found for instance that the first list of approved central government suppliers contained more American than British names. In 1984, demands came from the National Economic Development Office that the policy be more firmly administered.

The major initiative on these lines in Britain, which has been successful in creating demand for domestic supply has been the micro-computers in schools programme. Publicised by a programme on the BBC, the Acorn computer has been adopted by thousands of both secondary and primary schools, although suitable software has been sadly lacking. A further programme to support the development of educational software was launched in 1984. In France, where the government announced that all secondary schools would have a micro by the end of 1987, a similar policy has not been so successful. Lacking indigenous supply, demand has been met from American and British suppliers, primarily Sinclair (UK) and Apple (US), although the government has not formally agreed to the entry of foreign manufacturers to the market.

Despite this failure the French government has had perhaps the most wide-ranging policy towards the information and telecommunications industries. The Programme D'Action Filiere Electronique, begun in 1982, based on stimulation of the telecommunications market, had as its aim that the French electronic industry should be in the same league as that of the USA and Japan by 1990. Under the plan the electronics and computer industries have received £2000m per annum. Bull and Thomson have each received £90m and CGCT (the ITT subsidiary nationalised in 1982) has received £5m. The plan has not met its target, for instance Bull continues to make a loss, but the industry has grown by 8% in 1983-4 and, in the semi-conductor sector Thomson and Matra have been successful in increasing production by 20% in the same year.

Further action, stimulating both demand and supply is planned through the cabling of France. Whereas the modernisation of the telecommunications network was used as the domestic demand base for the development of telecommunications micro-chips and the development of Minitels (subscriber terminals to give access to videotex systems), the cabling of France, with optic fibre is seen as the means by which the domestic optic fibre industry can expand. Contracts have been shared between two French firms (both medium sized) and foreign manufacturers are to be excluded from the market. Cabling will take place at the rate by which production can be increased, although there is some doubt as to whether domestic supply will be adequate.

In contrast, in West Germany, government policy has given precedence to technological push through massive R & D funding. Although France in 1984 introduced a R & D programme to aid small businesses in linking up in innovatory work with universities, and a similar policy has been adopted in Holland, the scale of the West German commitment to R & D is immense. The government is proposing to spend a higher proportion of its GNP on R & D (2.8%) than its main rivals, the USA and Japan. Between 1984 and 1988, £769m will go from the state to microchip, communications and computer industries. At present West German production of microchips is only 60% of its national market. The micro-computer market is also met mainly by American suppliers. Siemens will be a prime beneficiary of the new policy, but industry is expected to invest twice as much as the state in the programme. Siemens already invests almost £1bn per annum but is now planning to raise its investment in microchip production.

West Germany's R & D programme contrasts with that of Britain. Whereas overall more than 50% of Britain's R & D expenditure is from government and more than 50% of that is devoted to defence, the comparable proportions in West Germany have been less than 40% and 10%. Whilst 30% of the total West German budget goes on support to industry, the comparable proportion in Britain is 17%. In a seven nation analysis done in 1984 of the industrialised West, the British government spent the lowest amount on R & D. Domestic criticisms of the policy have increased recently for its emphasis on defence and for the lack of civilian spin-off to be gained from that defence funding. The policy has had the effect of linking domestic electronics companies more firmly into the defence sector where profits are good, but where competition in exports with French firms is severe. The Conservative government in 1984, also called a five month moratorium on its £120m programme for the support of microchip manufacture and information technology innovation and has cut its funding of the research councils, thereby endangering one of the six specialist facilities on micro-electronics funded by the Science and Engineering Research Council.

However, in 1984, the first projects under the Alvey programme were started. The programme, initiated to compete with the Japanese fifth generation computer project, is designed to bring industry and universities together in a technological leap forward. The government will spend £350m on the project over five years and industry will spend £150m. The project is being run in a centralised way under the direction of an academic and has been criticised both for the slowness of start-up and its neglect of smaller firms. In comparison the West German R & D programme seems to be using a less direct manner of funding projects, specifically so as to avoid the rigidity which tends to go with centralisation. The Alvey project has also been criticised for allowing the entry of multinationals, such as IBM. Critics, who include some Conservative Members of Parliament, point out the difficulty of ensuring that the technology is not transferred overseas and the problems in the ownership of research results.

There have always been two arguments within Europe over what should be the aim of government policy in the information and telecommunications sector. The first argument, particularly popular in the 1960s and 1970s, is that governments need to support domestic manufacture and domestic technology both in order that it should not be dependent upon foreign suppliers, and so that domestic industry should not always be in second best position. The alternative argument has been that the major problem in Europe is caused by lack of competitiveness in its industries and their failure to modernise and invest. For the proponents of this argument the most important factor is the usage of technology and its application, not its parentage. The two arguments have been seen as opposed, rather than as complementary, the one arguing for the support of domestic manufacture, the other for support of domestic demand. When the British Conservative Government entered power in 1979, it continued some of the previous support of domestic manufacturers of the previous Labour government such as support for the Anglo-American chip firm, Inmos. But policies changed to demand side support, bringing in multinational capacity, liberalising the market of telecommunications and supporting innovation in industry - even where the robots used came from Japan. Multinationals have responded to the new environment. ITT alone has increased investment by 70% over four years. But, in its wake this increased investment by multinationals within Britain has brought concern that it will soak up all the available British trained personnel. A serious shortage of engineers is forecast within the immediate future - a problem which the French government has already taken steps to meet.

The informal liberalisation of the private telephone exchange market in Britain in the 1970s brought in Ericsson and Philips and then IBM. The further liberalisation in 1982 of British Telecom's monopoly increased the numbers of multinationals seeking entry. The privatisation of British Telecom in 1984 has further widened market opportunities. BT has announced that it will be seeking a second supplier for its public exchanges from Northern Telecom of Canada, AT & T-Philips (US-Holland) or Thorn Ericsson

(UK-Sweden). Mercury, BT's new competitor, will order its exchanges from Thorn-Ericsson, Northern Telecom or Italcom (a consortium of Italtel, GTE and Telattra of Fiat). BT has also ordered from IBM. There are now more North American multinationals in the British telecommunications market than there were two years ago. British Telecom is itself set to become a multinational force, looking to the USA rather than to Europe. Although the domestic digital public exchange, System X, manufactured by Plessey and GEC has not yet been successful in export markets, an approach by the French PTT to open their markets to System X in return for BT's ordering of their E10 was eventually turned down, amid much French bitterness. And BT's proposed alliance with IBM to run a value added network was finally turned down by the government Minister only after a concerted outcry from equipment manufacturers on the grounds that such a combination would smother any independent supply. The French commented that a similar proposal to themselves had been turned down immediately on the grounds that it used IBM's Standard System Network Architecture not a European standard.

A similar public outcry prevented the sale of the government-backed microchip manufacturer, Inmos, to AT & T, and it was eventually sold to Thorn-EMI. However, ICL, which had been rescued in the early 1980s with government guarantees backing a bank loan package, was sold to STC, a company still partly owned by ITT and still with strong technical links to its parent company. British Telecom's shares were also marketed in the USA and Japan, foreign sales which the Japanese do not intend to emulate in their sale of Nippon Telephone and Telegraph Public Corporation (NTT). The British government seems unconcerned about ownership.

Cable and DBS

A different approach to suppy and demand from that in France or West

Germany is evident in the British proposals for cabling the country. Whereas in France the cabling will take place under PTT control and in West Germany the Bundespost has already spent £2bn on four cabling projects, creating 45,000 jobs, in Britain the government is expecting private capital to pay for the recabling. Few financial incentives have been given. Cuts in tax allowances on capital expenditure in the March 1984 budget hit both cable companies and those in microchip manufacture. During the year it became obvious that cable will not be the financially lucrative venture that was first thought and companies have begun to pull out. The government has been accused of attempting to control the cable enterprises too much, giving longer licences only to those who opted for the switched star technology using optic fibres rather than copper cables. Critics argue that the emphasis on fibre optics has little to do with commercial realities.

Similar criticisms are being hurled at the French government whose cable plans involve joint public/private consortia running local cable companies, but which intends to control the proportion of foreign content in programmes and the proportion of purely local programmes. In West Germany, despite the Bundespost efforts, progress has been held up by the regional nature of broadcasting and, in a federal system, the domination of two important Länder (States) by the opposition SPD Party. North Rhine Westphalia controls the most powerful broadcasting group, WDR. The SPD controlled Länder administration has opposed the introduction of both cable and Direct Satellite Broadcasting (DBS) and has threatened to expand nationwide if the other Länder go ahead with their plans. DBS broadcasts may begin but they will not be seen in the major cities of Frankfurt, Cologne, Dusseldorf, Dortmund or Essen. The Bundespost is prepared to take the matter to the courts.

The confusion over cable policy in Britain, where a joint venture between Plessey and Scientific Atlantic (US) to produce the necessary electronic switch has been disbanded, in France, where the original initial investment of FFR 12bn has been scaled down to FFR 1bn for 1985, and in West Germany, is in contrast to the Netherlands, where 65% of homes are already on cable and in Switzerland, where cable has reached saturation point. In Belgium and Luxembourg cable is also growing, but, in all, only 8% of European homes now receive cable TV.

The confusion over cable is as nothing compared to the confusion over DBS. In Britain, the consortium of BBC, ITV and independent broadcasting companies has reached the decision that the price demanded by Unisat, a consortium of British Aerospace, GEC-Marconi and British Telecom, at £560m over seven years makes the service uneconomic. The government has already announced that DBS would use Unisat, but an alternative supplier, Britsat, using an RCA (US) satellite has offered a cheaper price and the likelihood seems that competitive bids will now be secured. In France it is not at all clear whether DBS will be in conflict or collaboration with cable, or with the new pay-TV channel. France is however committed to DBS in 1986. Nor is it clear how the British DBS service will fit in with that of Luxembourg or of Ireland, if and when that country decides to begin a service. Each of the satellites will have a footprint which covers most of Europe. At present it seems that there may be 10 or 12 satellites each providing a national service, rather than the two or three which would be possible.

In relation to DBS receiving sets one advance was made in 1984. Britain and France agreed on a compromise technical standard which would allow sets to receive either the French or British service. Efforts are still continuing to gain the agreement of the West Germans, so that there may be one unified market.

As can be seen from the above, the problem in this policy area is that governments are retaining traditional nationally oriented policies in the face of a technology which is both international in its applications and needs large markets. Governments are concerned to retain national employment and to compete in exports or to reduce imports. Hence West Germany's research initiative was brought about both by its declining share in high technology world markets and its trade deficit in data processing in particular. France's electronics plan has similar orientations. Its government claims that the plan has raised exports to FFR 3.3bn by the end of 1984 compared to 1.2bn in 1981 (despite the 80% fall in large overseas contracts) with a concomitant fall in the overall trade deficit in the IT sector. In Britain the National Economic Development Office has warned that the country faces a crisis in the information technology sector. Only one British firm features in the list of top ten suppliers of integrated circuits in the UK and manufacture is particularly weak in keyboard products, a prime base commodity in the automated office market. In IT products Britain's trade deficit was estimated to be £2.1bn in 1984. In Europe, as a whole, 75% of small business computers are imported, mainly from the USA, and the Japanese are posing a threat to the electronic typewriter market, taking 50% of it in 1984 - a factor which led to an allegation of 'dumping' by European manufacturers. The Japanese are beginning to market computers in Europe, producing equipment to a common standard MSX and their typewriter market base is seen as a danger in that it can provide them with the base for other automated office sales, including computers.

Privatisation and commercialism

Europe's policies towards information and telecommunications seem characterised by confusion, crisis and competition, just at a time when the IT sector is becoming more crucial to Europe's economic performance. Private actors are taking over from public actors in deciding the development of the market. And, as the chip famine of 1984 demonstrated, Europe is becoming more rather than less dependent for its technology on the USA, just at a time when the Reagan Administration seems prepared to use its power, through the Export Administration Act and the Semi-conductor Protection Act, to contain European and Japanese competitiveness.

Several factors have contributed to this rise in power of private actors and in particular to the rise in power of American capital. The most important has been the coalescing of data processing, office machinery, microchip and telecommunications and the entry of new services via satellite and cable, coupled with image transmission. This coalescing of markets gave the impetus to American companies to break down the legal barriers separating data processing and telecommunications in the USA. The subsequent liberalisation of the American market released AT & T onto the world market. AT & T has responded to its new found freedom by buying into the European market, first with an agreement with Philips to market its digital exchange and then with Olivetti of Italy, the computer and office equipment manufacturer. Under the agreement Olivetti will market AT & T's exchanges in Europe whilst AT & T markets Olivetti's products in the USA. In January AT & T made an unsuccessful bid for Inmos, and it has also been involved in talks with Spanish manufacturers. It has already had a significant impact on European technology with the withdrawal of Philips own large telecommunications exchange.

In addition the liberalisation in America has brought about changes in capital structure leading to further concentration. Companies now need to span a diversity of technologies and where strong companies lack a technology they have been able to buy expertise or form joint ventures. The majority of agreements and links made in the past two years by European electronics companies have been with American, not European partners. Of 200 agreements made during 1983, 50% were with American firms, 30% with

Japanese and only 18% were between two European partners.

To take only some examples from 1984, Thomson of France has an agreement with IBM on semi-conductors. Siemens is co-operating with ITT's West German subsidiary SEL to provide the Bundespost with digital exchanges and to work in a joint Company Gesat, to market complete satellite communications systems. Bull of France has bought into Ridge (US) to make a new powerful mini-computer. Olivetti has bought into 30 US high technology firms over the past two years. Rank Xerox has an agreement with a subsidiary of French state-owned CGE on artificial intelligence systems. A subsidiary of CIT-Alcatel has taken a 20% stake in US Sonitrol and French software firm Telic has an agreement with Honeywell on marketing French teletext in the USA. Many of these links are between French and American companies, signifying a recent change of policy on the part of the French government.

A third factor in the weakening of European resources has been the unleashing of IBM, following the withdrawal of its Anti-Trust case against the company by the Reagan Administration. Since that decision in 1982, IBM has become overtly agressive in its stance towards other manufacturers. It has prosecuted Hitachi, accelerated product introduction, slashed some prices and increased others where users are tied in to the product. In Europe the EEC's Anti-Trust case against the company on the publication of interface connection data was settled in July in an agreement which IBM said would not hinder its activities. Its personal computer sold 45,000 in Europe in 1983 and it is aiming worldwide at 30% growth in its PC sales, leaving little room for competitors. In the US it has bought a controlling share in Rolm, the telecommunications manufacturer, despite its previous undertaking to keep its share at 30%. It has increased its stake in SBS to 60%, through which it has a linkage with British Telecom. It has joined with Merrill Lynch to provide financial services, has linked with CBS and

Sears Roebuck for viewdata and has attempted entry into the VAN networks in Europe through BT and through EARN (a network linking academic research institutes). One of the primary dangers seen from Europe is that IBM may use entry into VAN to impose its standard SNA on other manufacturers.

The final factor in the weakening of Europen autonomous resources has been the general economic recession. With unemployment rates as high as 14% in Belgium and the Netherlands and 13% in Britain and with the unemployed within the EEC now totalling more than 10 million, European governments have welcomed inward investment for the employment it brings. IBM alone employs almost 10,000 in Europe. Of particular importance has been the weakening of the French economy, where IBM employs 21,000 - more than French owned Bull. A combination of economic vulnerability, large-scale advertising by IBM with claims to be a 'French' company and the threat of court action by the EEC, has led the French government to modify its public sector purchasing policy in favour of IBM. The company has been asked to invest more in France, whereas, in contrast British ICL's retrenchment of its French operations and the redundancies created have alienated it from the French government.

Europe tries to close its ranks

The combined threat of AT & T, IBM and the Japanese has had some galvanising influence upon European national governments. In particular France has sought more European co-operation, with its proposls on tele-communications to BT and with an agreement with the Germans to reciprocally open their telecommunications markets in handsets and to co-operate on radio telephones. Unfortunately all three initiatives have so far failed, which may explain the French govermment's new toleration of American links. In Britain the government has announced that all VAN networks must use Open

Systems Interconnection, a standard adopted by European and Japanese companies and AT & T, and not the IBM standard. All government purchasing is now to be on that basis. The British government has also called upon British micro-computer manufacturers to standardise their products and to resist the Japanese MSX standard which has already been accepted by Philips and GEC-Dragon computers. West Germany and France have also agreed that their videotex systems will be able to exchange information via software interfaces on the public network of the two countries.

At industry level, too, there have been successes in developing a European rather than national presence. Philips and Siemens have joined together in the development of a mega-chip, supported by both governments. Philips has also taken over Grundig of Germany, and Thomson of France has 75% of Telefunken of Germany. Thomson and Philips are co-operating on home computers. ICL, Bull and Siemens are co-operating in pre-competitive R & D on knowledge processing. CIT-Alcatel is co-operating with Olivetti, and has also opened an office in Spain. The European Computer Services Association, a fifteen strong group of national software associations is pressing for copyright protection of software against the Japanese alternative proposals.

At EEC level there has also been some progress. A new impetus has been given to the concept of European autonomy in technology by the American Export Administration Act. Europeans have experienced difficulties in obtaining computers and microchips in gaining access to ADA programming language documentation and in gaining entry to academic American conferences. An additional factor has been the recognition at EEC level that R & D, particularly into new telecommunications systems has become too expensive for any one national - market based company. Taken separately national markets in Europe are too small to repay the investment. EEC policy has therefore had two related aims, the one concerned with technology and the other with market pull and the unification of both standards and markets.

Inevitably it has been easier to get the R & D programme off the ground. The EEC has funded a programme to develop the technology for the manufacture of microchips, a programme which meshes with that of R & D in information technology (ESPRIT). Agreed in 1983, ESPRIT was scheduled to cost about £900m over five years. It is under criticism however for allowing the entry of multinationals, particularly IBM, which received 4% of the money in the second round of applications, for its concentration on large companies, for its failure to fund development work and for the numbers of projects agreed which are not central to its aims. The Commission also hopes to fund a similar project in the telecommunications sector, RACE, to develop the next generation of telecommunications networks. The project has been costed at £200m over ten years with matching funds for industry, but there are problems both with the funding, following the Budget rejection, and with decisions on priorities and there is some doubt about its prospects.

Progress on the EEC strategy on standards and markets has been much slower. A £20m project to standardise procurement, research, data privacy and software protection regulations among EEC member countries has been adopted to ease some of the problems in programmes such as ESPRIT. EARN, the IBM backed network , has been held up because it uses the SNA standard. The EEC announced its own data-processing procurement which will be shared by many European manufacturers, but the EEC Parliament has expressed concern at the slowness of standards progress on standards and procurement. Although all the major domestic European manufacturers have now agreed in principle to use Open Network Interconnection, the actual technical discussions take a great deal of time. Meanwhile it is hoped that ESPRIT will bring about some integration of standards. The EEC Commission itself sees European technology, European standards and unified markets as all necessary to save the autonomy of Europe and its domestic Information Technology Industries.

National governments are however still more concerned with the short-term and with gaining competitive advantage over each other. It is only when they feel threatened that they are prepared to co-operate in action. Politically divided as Europe stands, it seems unlikely that governments within it will yet feel sufficiently threatened to forego their traditional autonomy in the information and telecommunications markets. Yet, if they do not, private actors in the shape of both American and Japanese manufacturers are likely to increase their domination of the European market.

Bibliography

Jill Hills, Information Technology and Industrial Policy London, Croom
        Helm 1984.

House of Lords, Select Committee on the European Communities
        New Information Technologies (London, HMSO, 1981)
        ESPRIT Programme (London, HMSO, FEb, 1985).

N. Jacquier, "Computers" in R. Vernon Ed., Big Business and the State
        (London, Macmillan, 1974).

Gareth Locksley, A Study of the evolution of concentration in the UK data
        processing industry with some international comparisons
        (Brussels, EEC, 1981).

NEDO, The Crisis in Information Technology (London, NEDO, 1984).

William Wallace ed., Britain in Europe (London Heinemann, 1980).

John Zysman, Political strategies for industrial order (Berkeley,
          University of California Press, 1977).

EEC Documents

Com (80) 421   Proposal for a Council Regulation (EEC) concerning Community
               Action in the field of Microelectronics Technology.

Com (83) 564   First Report by the Commission to the Council on Community
               Projects in the field of Microelectronics Technolgoy.

Com (83) 661   Proposal for a decision adopting a Community programme for the
               development of the specialised information market in Europe.

Com (84) 264   Amended proposal for a decision adopting a Community programme
               for the development of the specialised information market in
               Europe.

Com (84) 277   Commission communication on telecommunications - progress
               report on the thinking and work done in the field and initial
               proposals for an action programme.

Com (84) 287   Commission communication to the Council concerning Community
               research priorities.

Com (84) 48 Agreement between the EEC & Austria on the interconnection of
the Community data transmission network (Euronet) and the
Austria national data transmission network.

Com (84) 56 Draft Council Decision adopting the 1984 work programme for the
European Strategic Programme for R & D in Information
Technology (ESPRIT).

CHAPTER 33.

FRANCE; TELECOMMUNICATIONS –
INTERVENTION AT THE CROSSROADS

DR.M.DANG-NGUYEN
The European University Institute, Geneva, Switzerland

France is the country where the logic of public monopoly has been carried through to its extreme consequences. This does not mean that the monopoly has been more extended than elsewhere, on the contrary. The attachment conditions for terminal equipment are less stringent than in Germany or in the UK before liberalisation.

But within the range of its attributions, the Direction Générale des Télécommunications (DGT), the French PTT, has been the spearhead of the governmental intervention in Information Technology and Telecommunications. One of the results has been a bias towards telecommunications against information services,and public against private networks.

Two paradoxes lie at the heart of this intervention:
- It is in some sense the consequence of an historical accident, the underdevelopment of the telephone network in France at the beginning of the 70s.

In fact, in 1970, there were only 5 million subscribers, that is about 1 out of 10 inhabitants. After having been able to catch up with the European standards at the end of the 70s, the French governments have judged it worthwhile to continue the investment effort, geared now towards new services and Information Technology.

Had they not embarked on the catching up program, they would have not promoted such a bold policy afterwards.
- The intervention is widely welcome in France, whatever the political color of the govermnent. The debate on deregulation has been completely absent mainly because its upsurge has coincided with the DGT's hour of glory (1975-1980): The French PTT can't be accused, as BT has been, to run inefficiently an obsolete network.

Now, in the mid-eighties, the environment with which the

French policy has to cope has, in many respects, changed dramatically compared to five years ago. The entry of IBM and AT&T, which was expected at that time, shows its first effects. "Telematics", a French neologism, which covered a branch of telephone derived services, is now challenged by technology which has much less to do with the telephone network: Cable TV, Office Automation and, more generally, Information Technology.

The position of PTTs as public monopolies has thus been weakened in relative terms although in absolute it is still strong: Telephone revenues represent 90% of PTTs receipts, and a recent experience in France (July 84) has shown that, given the price inelasticity of demand and the monopoly situation, the DGT was able to raise a large amount of money out of telephone subscribers in order to finance risky investments.

It remains to be seen whether this will be sufficient for France to stay on par with the formidable offensive that the US and Japanese firms have launched in this highly evolutionary sector.

<u>Telecommunications and Information Technology Organization in France.</u>

As said above, the DGT is by far the leading actor in the Information Technology field in France. It is one Directorate of the Ministry of Post, Telecommunications and Telediffusion, the other being the Direction Générale des Postes et de la Télédiffusion de France (TDF). In 1983, the DGT had a turnover of 62 billions FF ($ 8 billions) and a cash flow of 21 billions FF ($ 3 billions); it was able to self-finance 75% of its investments which amounted to 26 billions FF ($ 3.5 billions).

The DGT has 165,000 employees who are civil servants. It has been reorganized many times since the early 70s. Broadly speaking, the structure of the DGT is now more divisional with six major Directorates: The Direction des Affaires Industrielles et Internationales (DAII) is responsible for the relationships with the industry and represents France in the International Organizations (CCITT, UIT, CEPT). From 1974 onwards, the DAII controls the pricing of equipment by manufacturers and negotiates the price formula with them every one or two years, depending on the type of equipment purchased. It has also the ability to sign contracts with companies for R&D projects and in 1983 it signed with the industry a total amount of 1.77 billions FF ($ .25 billion) for 242 so called "marchés d'études".

Directly linked with DAII is the CNET (Centre National d'Etudes des Télécommunications), the main research center of the DGT, with an impressive workforce of 4000 engineers and auxiliary persons, employed in four labs: Issy-les-Moulineaux, Lannion, Rennes and Grenoble. The CNET undertakes fundamental research on network planning and network architecture, electronics, technology of transmission and switching, and now videocommunications.

In 1982, it had a turnover of 900 millions FF ($ .1 billion). It has been instrumental in the conception and design of the first digital exchange, the E 10, which has been successfully produced by CIT-Alcatel in 1972.

The "Direction de la Production" is responsible for network management. The "Direction des Programmes et Affaires Financières" (DPAF) undertakes financial planning, network and traffic forecasting and prepares the budget to be discussed by the Parliament. Internal audit of financial accounts at the local level -with the 22 "Directions Régionales des Télécommunications"- is also made by DPAF.

The "Direction Affaires Commerciales et Télématiques" (DACT) is responsible for the promotion of services, particularly the new ones, like telematics. The tariff policy is also in the hands of the DACT.

Two major "Services" complete the picture: The "Service du Personnel" (manpower management) and the "Service de Perspectives Economiques et Sociales", the latter looking at the long term economic consequences of telecommunications developments.

To understand the way the telecommunications policy is implemented in France, one has to know something about the so called "Grands Corps".

The ruling élite in France is trained through two alternative channels: The first is the Ecole Nationale d'Administration which educates future administrative civil servants like e.g. "Inspecteurs des Finances" or "Diplomates" (members of Foreign Affairs Ministry); the competence of this élite is grounded on administrative knowledge and management. The second is Ecole Polytechnique, which grooms technical civil servants. These specialize further within the so called "Ecoles d'Application" (Mines, Ponts et Chaussées, Télécommunications). The competence of these engineers is grounded on technical knowledge.

Each Ministry and its whole hierarchical structure is the fief of one "Corps": The Ministry of Economy and Finances is in the hands of "Inspecteurs des Finances"; the Ministry of Industry held by the "Ingénieurs des Mines"; the Ministry of PTT controlled by the "Ingénieurs des Télécommunications" etc...

Hence, behind the anonymous and hierarchical aspect of the mighty French administration, there is a strong rivalry among Departments which reflects a sociological antagonism between the ruling groups. This struggle is independent with the usual political one among parties, but has perhaps as much importance, as far as industrial policy is concerned.

Outside the administrative framework, the DGT controls a bunch of private law companies, which are at arm's length with the French administration. The main are:

- France Câbles et Radio (FCR), created in 1945 to operate intercontinental transmission through cables and microwaves.

  Now FCR has extended the scope of its activities and has set joint-ventures with developing countries (former African French colonies) to help them to grow their telephone network.

  In many respects, FCR is identical to UK's Cable and Wireless which was also publicly owned until 1980.

  FCR runs now the large bandwidth services offered to large companies,through the Télécom 1 satellite, launched in August 84.

  The DGT holds 99,9% of FCR's shares. And FCR controls several other companies the activity of which is linked with telecommunications. The most important are:

  a) Entreprise Générale des Télécommunications (99,9% FCR control) which sells telephone answering machines, mobile telephones and facsimile devices. EGT is thus a direct competitor to the industry in the terminal market.

  b) Télésystèmes (96,8% FCR control) which is a software producing company having one of the largest data base in Europe, Questel.

- Transpac is the second company directly controlled by the DGT, with 96,8% of shares.

  Transpac runs the packet switched network although this is owned by DGT. The argument for the existence of private law companies is flexibility to be guaranteed in the field of new services.

Other tools for DGT's intervention are more usual in the European context. These are equipment approval, investment planning (DGT represents 60 to 70% of telecom equipment demand in France) and R&D support through DAII.

Equipment approval is generally considered as liberal in France compared to other countries, but for French manufacturers only. Foreign manufacturers find it hard to enter the market unless they have links with a French partner or are ready to settle a plant in France (Mitel tried this second solution recently without success).

Investment planning is the bulk of DGT's influence on the major French manufacturers. during the 70s, and in particular during the crash program (1975-80), the DGT found a new way to ensure a regular flow of orders to manufacturers, while severely controlling their prices. These were renegotiated every 2 or 3 years and there was a premium for the best offer in terms of order volumes (the so called "tranche libre"). Now this tight control has been somewhat loosened and orders are discussed on a yearly basis.

R&D support goes beyond what is generally done in Europe. Since the changing of political majority in 1981, the rôle of the DGT has been even increased to support what is called the "filière électronique". This means that apart from consumer electronics and chips, which are controlled by the Ministry of Industry, the rest of electronic products (computers, office automation, telecoms, etc..) is supported by DGT which contracts directly with the industry R&D projects.

The other public actor besides DGT is the Ministry of Industry which has been instrumental in the 60s and 70s for the implementation of an industrial policy in the computer and semi-conductor industries.

The Department is divided in several Directorates, among them the Direction des Industries Electriques et Electroniques (DIELI) which, until recently, was not a "strong" Directorate within its Department compared to e.g. the steel one. This, together with a "traditional" conduct of electronic companies in France, has led to poor achievements in the sector.

Information and Telecommunications Policy in France:
The three phases.

We can, roughly speaking, divide the Information and Telecommunications Policy in France into three phases: The catching up period (1970-78), the telematic period (1978-83) and the cable period (since 1983).
Any periodisation has something arbitrary and one can find elements of one period during another. But on the whole there is a noticeable break up in 78 and 83, and it is impossible to understand the present policy if one has not in mind what has happened 15 years ago.
We will present the three periods in succession, and assess, in the last paragraph, the present situation of France after 15 years of bold intervention.

I) The "catching up" period (1970-78):

Although the major achievements of these years could seem unremarkable for a superficial observer to bring France to the same level of telephone equipment as other European countries, they have been fundamental for the shaping of the subsequent policies.
It is the time when the DGT is able to prove its capacity to mobilize resources and energies:
- 140 billions FF (about 28 billions dollars) were invested between 1975 and 1980 by the French PTT.
- The number of main lines grew from 5 millions in1970 to 16 millions in 1980.
- The DGT's manpower, numbering 125,700 persons in 1975, reached the 161,000 level in 1980.
The catching up period can be divided in two subperiods, each corresponding to a French "Plan".
During the Sixth (1970-75), the DGT is freed from its obligation to self-finance its investments and takes the decision to use private law companies as intermediaries to raise funds on the financial markets; this is partly to avoid the Department of Finance's control.
As far as results are concerned, the quality of service is much improved and the objectives of the Plan are reached. But it appears that they had underestimated the demand. Hence the

waiting list grows instead of diminishing despite the DGT's efforts.

The Seventh Plan (1975-80),accelerates the develop-ment of the telephone network. Telecommunications becomes a priority sector, the objectives of which (20 million lines in 1982) should be realized at any cost. The French President, V. Giscard d'Estaing, publicly engages his responsibility on this topic.

In 1980, the challenge has been won and telecommunications are, with the nuclear energy one, the only sector in France which has not really suffered from the two oil shocks and the economic recession.

But the policy does not restrict itself to wire up France. Industrial goals are tackled as well:

- The first major decision is

to develop and install digital switching very early; the first digital exchange was installed in 1972 derived from a prototype produced in 1970 by CNET.Cit-Alcatel produces this exchange, named E 10, and will quickly improve its share in the world market. DGT's plan is to suppress orders for electromechanical systems from 1979 onwards.

- The second major decision in 1976, is to get rid of ITT and Ericsson, the subsidiaries of which in France were bought by Thomson, a company specialized in transmission and defense equipment. As a compensation, Thomson uses Ericsson and ITT licences for producing electronic analog exchanges.

This shake up of the industry shows the enormous power of the DGT, which has piloted Thomson's entry. ITT maintains a foothold in France with CGCT (17% of the switching equipment market).

Other initiatives are also worth mentionning: A packet switched network project, begun in 1972 led to Transpac, marketed in 1979 by a private company controlled by the DGT (see above). Studies on videotex are undertaken at CNET, but the project is less advanced than the UK's. The DGT tries to loosen its public service oriented attitude for a more market oriented strategy. Modern management methods are introduced,like internal audit and accounting practice copied from private companies. The DGT's managers are eager to have it split from the Post Office, butthis faces the strong opposition of Trade Unions.

To sum up, the catching up period reveals to itself and to the environment as well, the power of the DGT.

The task has been both difficult and easy; it has been difficult because nobody could expect from an administration reputed for its lack of management ability and its emphasis on technical rather than marketing achievements, not only to quickly meet the demand requirements, but also to "frenchify" the industry and boost national exports in telecommunications. On the other hand, it has been made easy by the constant excess of demand over supply, and the DGT has never had to take care of demand uncertainties: The major task was to plan investments in order to reach , as quickly as possible, a given level of equipment.

To some extent, the catching up period has shown to the "Ingénieurs des Télécommunications", who, up to 1970, had been superseded by the powerful Ministry of Finances and its armed hand, the "Ingénieurs des Finances", that to promote the policy in which they believed they had to refer directly to the Président de la République and to present the telecommunications outcome as a highly political issue.

It has shown also that a quick and ambitious action was possible, and that both the telecom establishment (i.e. manufacturing companies and also the PTT bureaucracy) and the political one (i.e. local "notables", MPs, etc...) could be shaken with a bold and successful policy.

Besides telecommunications, the achievements in the information sector are much less buoyant. Suffice here to mention the failure of the successive "Plans Calcul".

The first (1967-71) was designed to provide France with a healthy computer company CII, able to build up large mainframes to pilot nuclear weapons. At the end of the Plan, CII had only a 7.5% share of the French market.

The second Plan (1971-75) led to the failure of the European consortium CII/Siemens/Philips, the French government being afraid of a possible hegemony of the two foreign colosses at the expense of the "small" CII.

The third Plan (1975-79), led to a joint-venture CII/Honeywell Bull; in that partnership, the French company was totally dependent on the American technology and, despite a guaranteed access to public orders, did not achieve a great penetration of the national market (17.8% in 1976).

Such a difference of performance between the telecommunications and the computer industries, is easily understandable.

The monopoly position of the DGT, its massive investment

program, and its preference for national equipment, has boosted
the French production while in the computer industry nothing
equivalent happened, on the contrary: The power and marketing
ability of IBM was too high an obstacle to the French industry
which was also hindered by the rivalry between CGE and Thomson,
the two major electronics groups, and the weakness of DIELI.

II) 1978-82: DGT's hour of glory.

1978 is a key year for the development of telecommunications
and information policy in France. At that date, several phenomena
are converging.

First, the catching up program reaches its climax since DGT's
investments cease to grow.

The DGT which had so well monitored the telecom industry revival,
is thus concerned in finding the best way to replace its own
orders by larger exports.

Second, the deregulation movement in the US shows how unstable
the telecommunications and information sector can be, and
observers expect a giants' battle between AT&T and IBM
particularly after the latter's entry, with its SBS project, in
the communication satellite business. This feeling is echoed in
France by the famous Nora-Minc report.

This official document warns against the potential hegemony of
IBM, which after having dominated the data processing sector,
will, according to the authors, control the networks with
satellites. They recommend thus to rely on the only strength of
France to resist this hegemony: The public monopoly over networks.
This report, issued in January 1978, had a tremendous
publicity in France because it suddenly revealed to the political
power the vulnerability of Europe, and France in particular, in
the fast growing and far reaching "information revolution".

Third, the Japanese are showing that the US superiority is
nothing but ineluctable. After having taken a dominant position
in consumer electronics, the Japanese companies are now
challenging the US ones in their homeyard: Semi-conductors and
computers. The Japanese example has struck the French bureaucracy
as the model of a successful State intervention.

As a result of this favorable environment, the French
government adopted in December 78, the so called "Plan
Télématique" which represents the boldest attempt to promote

telecommunications services.

The Plan consists of a bunch of tests to be launched and services to be marketed in order not to leave a potential development area untouched.

For business communications, a telecommunications satellite, called Télécom 1, was announced to be launched in 1983. It will handle some telephone traffic between the Caribbean "départements" (Martinique, Guadeloupe, Guyane) but also offer large bandwidth communications facilities for video-conferencing and high volume data transmission.

Télécom 1 is a direct copy of the SBS project and reflects the conclusions of the Nora-Minc report according to which satellites are an "imperial tool" to dominate the telecommunications market. This is really the first national satellite built in Europe for telecommunications.

Another important decision concerning business communications was not taken within the "Plan Télématique" but has ever been behind the DGT strategy. It is the decision to quickly digitize the network at the level of both transmission and switching.

By 1981, the DGT no longer bought Crossbar exchange, and by 1984 only full digital exchanges are ordered. This enables the French monopoly to plan a wideband ISDN, following the CEPT recommendation (two 64 K bits/sec and one 16K bits/sec channels), for 1987 onwards.

As far as video-conferencing was concerned, the objective was 2000 studios in 1985, while the telex service was also launched and expected to reach at least 80,000 terminals in 1985.

But the most impressive effort concerned the residential user's market.

The hallmark of the DGT's strategy has been the electronic directory, with a small black and white terminal which could allow an on-line retrieval of address and telephone number of subscribers everywhere in France through the telephone network. The terminal was planned to be delivered free of charge, but any transaction will cost the price of a local conversation.

Moreover, the electronic directory was announced to be compulsory. The "Plan Télématique" specified that feasibility would be carried on in Saint-Malo (Britanny), involving 260,000 subscribers.

Besides this, a classical videotex test, called Télétel-3V, was also undertaken in the wake of Prestel's upsurge. It involved

1500 carefully chosen subscribers to whomsome on-line services were offered, like e.g. an "electronic newspaper", games, or information services on trains, planes or financial markets.

The DGT announced that both projects, the electronic directory and the videotex test, were completely different but nobody believed this, and in particular not the Press groups, which were afraid to have their advertisements receipts curbed, once "electronic newspaper" would be available for 30 million telephone subscribers.

To complete the residential user's orientation of the Plan, the DGT launched a public tender for the prosition of a low cost, group 2, facsimile terminal. Several companies enteredthe competition, among them Matra, Secre, Thomson.

In the same domains, several studies were commissionned for a project called "smart card", a credit card embedding a microprocessor and a memory, instead of a magnetic tape, to use as "electronic money".

Finally, a test for a broadband interactive fiber optics network, was launched in Biarritz, involving 1500 subscribers. The test, which was inspired by the Tana experience in Japan, was by far the largest in the world. By comparison, British Telecom undertook such a test at Milton-Keynes with 28 subscribers only! Subscribers in Biarritz would be offered interactive high definition television, visiophony, every quick facsimile transmission and the like.

The idea behind the "Plan Télématique" was quite simple: To reproduce what the Japanese had so well achieved in the consumer electronics sector. They had created a strong home base which enabled them to produce cheap devices, and to sell them, in a second step, in exports markets.
The compulsory electronic directory would obviously create this strong home base but it would have been the same, in DGT's hopes, with the non-compulsory cheap facsimile or the smart card. With such strong bases, the DGT wished that the manufacturers "conquer" the US market. Moreover, it was eager to introduce more competition among French groups, in the same way as MITI does with Japanese conglomerates. Newcomers like Matra or Saint-Gobain were encouraged to enter the telecom and electronic market, while price controls through the DAII were gradually abandoned.

This strategy was the result of the peculiar situation of DGT's managers, both vis-à-vis their own administration and the other ruling élites: To carry out a project as successful as the "catching up program", it was necessary to act quickly and with a great panoply of projects in order to "wrong-foot" all the forces interested in a statusquo . This obviously necessitated the full support of the Président de la République. The strength of DGT's head, Mr Théry, has been to get this support.

Broadly speaking, the DGT's strategy failed.
First the compulsory electronic directory met a strong social opposition from Press groups but also from MPs of the majority parties.
Manufacturers were unable to design cheap videotex and facsimile terminals and have been unenthusiastic about the idea to get a foothold in the US market. They preferred sales of telecom equipment to Third World countries where they benefit from the full support of the French government (e.g. Cit-Alcatel in India). Newcomers in the French market did not succeed very well, and eventually withdrew after the Socialist nationalisations; now only Matra produces terminal equipment.
The Biarritz test appeared to be very costly although it has been carried through.
Several projects of "smart card" competed one against the other, and it was not until the beginning of 1985 that the DGT decided to unify them, with the agreement of the major banks.
Video-conferencing and teletex services were opened in 1984 and they do not seem to have achieved very much since.
Finally, Télécom 1 was launched in August 84 and does not work yet at full capacity. There has been a lot of discussion about the direct broadcasting TDF 1 satellite which is now considered as too "mighty", because there are new small antennas able to receive signals from "medium powered" satellites. After a long hesitation, on whether to abandon the project or to continue it, the DGT decided at the end of 1984 to go ahead.

Paradoxically, it is in "classical" telecommunications that the DGT performed well, both at home and outside.
The packet switched data network Transpac, has been quite successful (13,000 subscribers in 1983) and it is now also used for videotex services. Digitisation of the network which had been undertaken quite early compared with other European countries, went well.
Outside, Cit-Alcatel, benefitting from the early start of its digital exchange, took a significant part of the World Market at

least until 1982. Thomson was less successful although it gained a major contract in Egypt in association with Siemens in 1980. Matra made a breakthrough in the US market with videotex terminals.

The reasons why the bold gamble of DGT brought few results are obvious. There has been an overestimation of the receptivity of the French market towards "telematics" services. These seem to be diffused at a much slower pace than expected. On the supply side, cheap terminals could not bring much value added to manufacturers, who devoted their efforts to the bulky transmission and switching equipment. Their lack of success in the US is mainly due to their complete ignorance of this market, compared for example to Canadian companies. And the support of DGT there, has been highly insufficient.

The changing of political majority in May 1981, brought a new team to manage the DGT. A new program was then designed, not without difficulty.

Outside telecommunications, few things were undertaken. The computer industry remained more or less in the same situation as in 1978, with CII/HB playing the card of incompatibility of its hardware with IBM's. Some efforts were made in the creation of data bases and several were successful. CISI, in particular, which is a subsidiary of "Commissariat de l'Energie Atomique" (Nuclear Energy Agency), designed an internationally accessible data base primarily geared to scientific users; it extended its range of activity when buying Wharton Econometrics models.

The entry of Matra and Saint-Gobain in the data processing sector has been Interesting . The latter in particular was encouraged by the French government at the end of the 70s to set up a strong new electronic group besides Thomson and CGE. Saint-Gobain a glass manufacturer, poured important amounts of money in the sector through the acquisition of small office automation companies (e.g. Logabax), a 20% participation in the capital of Olivetti in 1980, and a technology transfer agreement with National Semiconductor. But the group could not take advantage of this strategy since the change of political majority in May 1981 upset the future of the whole sector.

III) <u>Telecommunications</u> <u>and</u> <u>Information</u> <u>policy</u> <u>at</u> <u>a</u> <u>crossroads</u> <u>(1982-85).</u>

When the Socialists came to power , one of the few things they could not reject from the preceding team's heritage was the telecommunications program.

On the other hand, as we saw , the Telematic Plan did not seem to bring all the expected benefits. Hence, the situation of telecommunications in France was somehow ambiguous.

The industry still benefitted from the momentum given by the catching up program and the telematic Plan, but this was not sufficient to preserve its position in the future. Something new and different had thus to be found.

During the first year, the new government had to manage the transition and took several measures which have had far reaching consequences on the development of the sector.

First, the compulsory nature of the electronic directory was abandoned and this slowed down the diffusion of the so called "Minitels" (the small black and white terminals). Otherwise most of the projects of the"Plan Télématique" were continued.

The second important decision concerned nationalizations. The two major telecommunications groups, Thomson and Compagnie Générale d'Electricité (CGE), this latter owning Cit-Alcatel, were on the list of the nine industrial groups to be nationalized. There was thus a great uncertainty about their future particularly because in their program the Socialists had decided to merge the telecom activity of the two companies in order to create a strong French group. Finally, it took one year to nationalize all the groups and the merger was cancelled. But during that year, the potential clients of the two companies became hesitant whether to purchase French equipment, given the uncertainties surrounding the French industry.

The third event was the nomination of Mr J. Dondoux to replace Mr G. Théry at the head of the DGT. The former, who had been director of CNET until 1975, represented the tradition of "Ingénieurs des Télécommunications" looking at technical excellence and network planning, instead of the bold, service marketing oriented vision of the latter (yet himself an "Ingénieur des Télécommunications").

In 1982, after the transition had been carried through, a new policy had to be designed. First, the government tried to promote the whole "filière électronique" with a five years plan of 140 billions FF (40 billions $), 60 billions (9 billions $) being spent by the State. The idea was to boost the whole sector (components, computers, telecoms, office automation, consumer electronics), in order to benefit from "synergies" from one branch to another (e.g. computers as users of components, public and private networks developing simultaneously, etc...). At the industrial level, this meant a complete reshuffling of the sector: Thomson got most of the activities in consumers electronics and components, Saint-Gobain was pulled out of the sectorandthe participation of Honeywell in CII/HB was reduced and eventually suppressed.

The emphasis was on R&D and the government was ready to support a small bunch of projects large enough to have a "critical mass" and which had the most "synergic" effects. In this plan, the DGT had no longer the leading rôle but had to support some of the R&D projects with financial help. This plan was a clear sign of DGT's loss of influence on the government. No longer were telecommunications the "growth pole", but just a milk-cow for the whole electronic sector.

This can be interpreted as a defeat of "Ingénieurs des Télécommunications" vis-à-vis Ministry of Industry.

But it appeared quickly that the "Plan filière électronique" was something halfway between a propaganda manoeuvre and an ideological ingenuity. It has brought indeed some effects in the sector, but was in no way the spearhead of the State intervention in higher technology. Broadly speaking, its long term orientation could not bring quick results, and the finances of the French State could not support a major effort.

The government had thus to go back to more concrete objectives. Once again, the opportunity was given by the DGT, and with the "Plan Câbles" was renewed the alliance between the political power and the " Ingénieurs des Télécommunications". In fact, only the DGT with its huge budget and its ability to levy taxes through slight increases of telephone tariffs, had the resources to realize a grand design. And its managers had some ideas on this.

The new team was convinced that networks were their business, and that pushing technology in that field (like e.g. fibre optics), could bring more tangible industrial results than the preceding strategy (i.e. massive orders of low cost terminals), "à la japonaise". Cable TV was considered as the meansto carry out this program.

But Cable TV had not only industrial advantages. It would trigger off less social rejection than did videotex the former being associated with TV, a familiar object,   and the latter with computers, which were more disturbing. It would be associated with programs,   hence perhaps with a cultural   policy,   a traditional pet of the French Left parties. Being essentially implemented at the local level, the "Plan Câbles" would give a new dimension to decentralisation, another pet of Socialists in France.

The Plan in itself was very impressive. A Council of Ministers in November 82 announced that 100,000 connexions would be ordered in 1983, and 1 million in 1985.

Between those two dates, the DGT would spend 7 billions FF (1 billion $), and the municipalities, the Industry and the administration around 1.6 billions FF (230 millions $) each.

The objective was to start interactive services (the so called 2nd generation) from 1986 onwards. Thus a star network architecture was necessary.

The   "Plan Câbles" is undoubtly a bold gamble and its implementation has revealed itself more difficult than foreseen.

The investment was reduced in the early phase due to some cash problems faced by the DGT in 1984. Since the municipalities are associated to the project on a counterpart basis, their agreement is needed for its development. Until now many towns seem interested, but very few have already signed a contract with the DGT. The latter, on the other hand, is eager to push the project for industrial reasons. Some know-how must be gained in the construction, installation and running of fibre optics cables.

After   the   announcement   of   the   "Plan   Câbles",   and independently from the difficulties of its implementation several events showed the weakening position of DGT in the political context.

First, in September 83 the merger of the telecommunications activities of CGE and Thomson was made, despite the opposition of the DGT which wanted to maintain the competition between its two major suppliers. The main reason for the merger, apart from pure ideological positions which were less relevant since 1982, was the difficult financial condition of Thomson's group which has incurred   heavy losses even in its telecommunications branch.

Then the Ministry of PTTs was placed under the responsibility of the Ministry of Industry. Regular transfers from DGT's resources to the general budget were made in 1982, 83, and 84 in order to alleviate the public deficit. In 1983 the DGT results were negative for the first time in its history and in 1984 it avoided a similar performance through an exceptional telephone tariff increase of 25% which raised a political issue.

Finally, the DGT had to take a participation in the capital of CII/HB in 1983, after the withdrawal of Honeywell.

The results of the telecom industry in the exports markets were particularly poor, after the great success of India's contract in 1983. The following year no orders were made for the French digital exchanges, while Northern Telecom, Ericsson, ITT and even Siemens, which was a latecomer, made significant breakthroughs.

With the stronger pressure of AT&T and IBM in the European market, after the former's deregulation, the DGT tried in 1984 to promote a European approach to telecommunications development. But most of its initiatives failed, as for example the deal with BT to swap digital exchangesand the common orders to be made with Bundespost for cellular radio.

Last but not least, the "Plan Cables" is threatened, not in its essence but in its prospects, by governmental decisions to introduce private TV in France.

Although no definitive measure has been taken so far, there is now a real threat of diverting potential subscribers to CATV, hence the success of the "Plan Cables".

Conclusions:

In the Information Technology challenge, France has tried to play its only trump: the great capacity of intervention of the DGT. But what has stopped the French PTT from becoming a second MITI, has not been the resources, human and financial, or the decision making capacity, or even the political support of government -although the latter has decreased considerably since 1981-. The missing element has been time.

While MITI has had more than twenty years to prepare Japan's transition to electronics, the DGT had to make crucial choices in less than five years: Technology was pushing quickly ahead and the gap to fill was so huge that the DGT's managers had to rush the industry towards ambitious goals. it is no surprise that it did not succeed completely.

Outside telecommunications, the results have been worse: Before 1981, the backbone of Information policy was an increase of internal competition through the entry of French newcomers; after 1981, there has been a division of labor among specialized and (hopefully) strong groups: CGE for telecommunications, Thomson for consumer electronics, etc...

In the first case, the policy has been implemented too late while in the second, it does not correspond any longer to the conditions of the international competition. One has thus to find new ways to promote a long term policy.

Paradoxically, the DGT still remains the major trump of any French policy. But its relative strength has diminished significantly since no crash program can sustain the industry any longer.

The European option, tried last year, seems thus quite sensible. But one does not see actually what is aimed at: A European market, an harmonisation of PTTs' plans or a genuine common policy.

European PTTs should take account of what is their major strength, the control over the networks, to design a policy which could counterbalance the North-American and Japanese technological lead.

DGT's gamble is still playable, but at the European level now, and on well defined stakes. The French case has shown the importance of the political involvement in that respect.

<u>BIBLIOGRAPHY</u>

Ancelin, C. and Marchand, M. (1984): "Le videotex: contribution aux débats sur la télématique", Masson, Paris.

Bertho, C. (1981): "Télégraphes et téléphones", Le Livre de Poche, Paris.

Cherki, E. (1982): "Le projet télématique: réflexions sur une stratégie industrielle", Bulletin de l'IDATE, n 9, October, Montpellier.

Communications International (1983): "France: The Big Push in Communications", Special Report, June.

Ergas, H. (1983): "Public Utilities and Industrial Policy: the Case of the French Telecommunications", Mimeo,OECD, Paris.

Glowinski, A. (1980): "Télécommunications: Objectif 2000", Dunod, Paris.

Guillou, B. (1984): "La stratégie multimédias des groupes de l'audiovisuel", La Documentation Française, Paris.

IDATE (Institut pour le développement et l'aménagement des télécommunications et de l'économie) (1984): "Le prix des nouveaux médias", 6èmes Journées Internationales, 24-26 October, Montpellier.

Journal des Télécommunications (1979): Telecommunications in France", Special Issue, July, UIT, Geneva.

Le Diberder, A. (1980): "La production des réseaux de télécommunications", Economica, Paris.

Libois, L-J. (1983): "Genèse et croissance des télécommunications", Masson, Paris.

Lorenzi, J-H. and Le Boucher, E. (1979): "Mémoires volées", Ramsay, Paris.

Nouvion, M. (1984): "L'automatisation des télécommunications: la mutation d'une administration", Presses Universitaires de Lyon, Lyon.

Pigeat, H. and Virol, L. (1980): "Du téléphone à la télématique", La Documentation Française, Paris.

Télécommunications (1983): "Vidéocommuniquer", n 47, April.

Vedel, T. (1984): "Les Ingénieurs des Télécommunications: formation d'un grand corps", Culture Technique, n 12.

Verdier, E. (1983): "La bureautique", Maspéro, Paris.

CHAPTER 34.

INFORMATION AND TELECOMMUNICATIONS POLICY IN GERMANY (FRG)

DR. THEODORE IRMER
Deutsche Bundespost, Darmstadt, FRG.

1.   A short historical review

Telecommunications have a long history in the Federal Republic of Germany as in well as its preceding structures of state organizations. Under the monarchy in the middle of the past century, Imperial Germany already operated a telegraph network including international telegraph lines. Recognizing early the importance of international cooperation in telecommunications Germany was a signatory to the International Telegraph Convention set up in Paris in 1865. The invention of the telephone by Alexander Graham Bell and Philipp Reiss (a German schoolteacher whose invention, however, did not receive great publicity at that time) attracted immediate attention in Germany. The legendary Post Master General, Mr. Heinrich von Stephan, one of the prominent promoters of international postal services (amongst other innovations, he created the postcard and was the founder of the World Postal Congress) immediately recognized the potential of this invention and ordered two telephones from Bell. After a successful demonstration in the Ministry of Posts, Heinrich von Stephan started the commercial implementation of telephony in Germany. On 1 April 1881, the first manual telephone exchange was inaugurated in Berlin serving 48 subscribers.

Despite many doubts and criticism the first directory, published in 1881 and listing the 48 subscribers, was dubbed by people "The book of fools". Nevertheless, von Stephan was convinced of the future importance of the telephone, both for business and private subscribers, and he continued his work. The evolution of the telephone proved that he was right: after one year, in 1882, in Berlin already 573 subscribers were connected to the telephone network. Since then progress was rapid: 1908 operation of the first local automatic exchange; 1920 already one million of telephone subscribers; 1923 operation of the first automatic trunk exchange, and so on. Today, a fully automatic telephone network interconnects about 35 million telephones (about 25 million main stations) and provides STD services to about 137 countries worldwide.

Before looking more in detail into the telecommunication services and the networks provided in the Federal Republic of Germany, we must investigate the legal provisions governing the technical evolution of telecommunications in the past as well as at present. The understanding of these legal provisions makes it easy to follow the telecommunications policy in the Federal Republic of Germany as demonstrated in terms of services and networks offered to the public.

2.   The legal framework of telecommunications

Under the Imperial regime up to the end of World War I, postal
services had been regarded as a state matter as they had been for
centuries when they where carried out either by state monopolies or by
agencies licensed by the Head of State. With the advent of
telecommunications at the end of the last century it was logical that
telecommunications (operated by postal staff) should be considered a
state monopoly. For exercising the postal and telecommunications
monopoly, a State organization (Reichspost) was set up under the
direction of the Government.

This principle of State sovereignty in telecommunications is
still valid in the Federal Republic of Germany. In its Constitution
(Basic Instrument) it is stated that:

-   exclusive legislative powers relating to (postal services and)
    telecommunications are vested in the Federation;

-   the Federation enforces laws through its own Federal
    Administration (the DBP);

-   the Deutsche Bundespost is run as a Federal Administration
    with its own administrative infrastructure.

In other words, telecommunications are directly controlled by
the State. Neither the Laender (counties) nor the municipalities have
any direct influence or power of intervention despite the federal
structure of the country. The State´s duties in this field are performed
by the Deutsche Bundespost (DBP) as part of the State Administration;
the DBP is headed by the Federal Minister of Posts and
Telecommunications who, as a Member of the Federal Government, exercises
responsibility for his department within the framework of the policy
guidelines proposed by the Chancellor of the Federal Republic of
Germany.

These constitutional principles have naturally given rise to a
series of laws and regulations aimed at protecting and administering
federal telecommunictions sovereignty and regulating the use of
telecommunication facilities. With a view to organization, the most
important law is the Telecommunication Installations Act (Gesetz ueber
Fernmeldeanlagen), which includes the following provisions:

-   Sovereignty in the matter of telecommunications (the exclusive
    right to install and operate a telecommunication plant) is
    part of the State´s sovereign rights. This sovereignty is
    vested in the Federation and exercised by the Federal Minister
    of Posts and Telecommunictions (the only exception being
    installations serving the purpose of federal defense);

-   The right to set up and to operate individual facilities may
    be delegated (by authorization).

-   However, no authorization is required for installations used
    by official bodies solely for internal purposes, or by
    transport organizations (such as the Federal railways) for
    operational purposes, or within a single property or two parts
    of the same property situated not more than 25 km from each

other. In the case of radio installations, authorization is compulsory.

This is the legal basis on which the public telecommuication network has been established and operated by the DBP. The DBP is also responsible for supervising all telecommunication installations, subject to authorization (i.e. private installations). As·far as the provision of terminals is concerned, the monopoly of the DBP is restricted only to the main station terminating the subscribers´ line, i.e. only for this main station has the DBP an exclusive right. All other terminals are offered either <u>exclusively</u> by private suppliers (e.g. telex/Teletex terminals, mobile telephone stations) or on a competitive basis by private suppliers as well as by the DBP (e.g. PBXs, Telefax terminals). This rather liberal situation in the terminal market should be borne in mind by the reader when the so-called "monopoly" of the DBP is briefly discussed hereafter.

Legal matters are, of course, not the main subject of this paper. But today, where a fierce battle of "deregulation versus monopolies" is being fought, some remarks for a better understanding of the position of the DBP seem to be appropriate because this position has its roots in the socio-economic consensus of the Federal Republic of Germany.

The basic decision in favour of the "social market economy" (free market economy serving the interests of the community) was made in 1949; This basic decision has been accepted and observed by all relevant political groups up to the present day.

It implies that the principle of competition is given priority over state planning and other forms of state intervention. It is, however, equally accepted that the State, in a "social market economy", must also perform important functions – particularly in areas where unlimited competition would disturb the social balance between various groups forming a population.

Generally monopolies (either of the state or large business groups) are not desirable in this economic system. However, competition is not to be the final economic objective <u>per se</u>, but merely a means of accomplishing social objectives. If, in certain branches, such social objectives as for instance a cost efficient production, are best accomplished by a monopoly, then monopolies are justified – even in our economic system. In this case, however, the State must exercise control and regulating functions which would otherwise be performed by the competition mechanism. In such a case, the State may perform this function either by acting as a supplier or by regulating prices and conditions of private monopolies. In other words: under the provisions of the "social market economy" a state telecommunications monopoly is justified if it complies with the social objectives of this economic structure (i.e. provide telecommunication services to everybody, and everywhere in the country and under equal conditions, at equal charges and of identical quality). This social commitment prevails everywhere in the activities of the DBP – a fact which is sometimes disregarded in the discussion about telecommunication monopolies where monopolies are often understood as maximum-profit and market determining organizations.

The DBP tariff policy is another example to highlight the understanding of the role of the DBP: the charges do not, to a large extent, reflect the costs of the individual service which the customer receives. By applying uniform charges throughout the country to everybody, regardless of whether he is a business or private customer, whether he lives in a big city or in a scantly populated area, the DBP makes a significant contribution to structural development politics. The higher production costs for telecommunications in such scantly populated regions are not to be borne by customers in this region. The cross-subsidization of local calls by trunk calls has as well a socio-political objective: private customers (mainly low-income customers) have the advantage over business customers (who are making most of the trunk calls). Even by structuring tariffs to a large extent according to social considerations, the DBP has been able to run a highly profitable business: after delivering every year 10% of its total earnings to the Federal Treasury (as a compensation for tax-exemptions) and subsidizing the Postal Services considerably it has, during the last few years, made an average annual gross profit of about DM 2 billion — an amount which was substantially invested in equipment.

3.   Telecommunication networks in the Federal Republic of Germany

The DBP presently operates several dedicated networks. The most important networks are the telephone, circuit-switched and packed-switched networks. Their technical characteristics are briefly described below:

3.1   Telephone network

The telephone network is by far the largest dedicated network: over 35 million telephones are interconnected with this network, out of which over 25 million are main stations; about 20,000 radio telephones are in operation and over 160,000 public telephones service customers.

The telephone network is structured on four levels:

1.   on the first level, 3,754 local networks are in operation;

2.   the second level is formed by 525 nodal exchanges. These are interconnected with

3.   68 main exchanges which form the third level;

4.   at the top of the network 8 central exchanges are in operation which also interconnect with international traffic.

As many other administrations, the DBP is currently implementing in its telephone network digital transmission and digital switching systems in ever-increasing quantities. We will look closer at the transition into a digital telephone network in the following:

The DBP started the implementation of digital transmission systems in 1970. The first digital transmission system was the "PCM 30" (2 Mbit/s) system, operated on deloaded symmetrical pairs. Since then, the development of medium and high capacity digital transmission systems (in conformity with the hierarchy based on the 2 Mbit/s system, i.e. at

8,34, 140 and 505 Mbit/s)) to be operated on various transmission media (coaxial pairs/optical fibres/radio relay) has progressed steadily and in line with the development of technology. A preliminary ending is marked by the PCM 7680 system (565 Mbit/s) which will be brought into service in 1985. At present, the portion of long-distance exchanges currently terminating digital line paths has already increased to about 40%, and it is expected to grow even more within the next few years.

The implementation of digital transmission systems has been stretched over some 10 years but because of the rapid development of technology, the transistion to digital switching as well as its implementation in the network, is expected within a much shorter time than was the case for digital transmission systems.

The DBP has constantly and carefully monitored progress in digital switching around the world. Digital transit and local switching systems attractive from the cost point of view are commercially available since some years already. At the same time they meet the technical requirements of the DBP stipulated hereafter:

- high reliability, excellent system performance;

- simple operating/maintenance procedures, built-in fault routines to be handled by existing staff after short on-the-job training;

- compliance with latest CCITT-Recommendations (G.- and Q.-Series, CHILL, MML, etc.);

In addition, the progress in digital transmission ("system family" from 2 to 565 Mbit/s available in 1985) necessitates provision of digital transit and local switching systems ready for implementation, thus enabling significant savings through digital interfacing transmission and switching equipment. Finally, for about five years the upcoming ISDN had to be taken into consideration. For the implementation of ISDN both digital transit and local switching exchanges will need some modifications of the telephone switching systems.

The decision whether and how digital switching systems are to be selected and implemented bears a great number of far-reaching consequences: not only technical considerations are to be investigated, but commercial aspects are at least as important; for instance, different system architectures and their consequences for operation and maintenance both for the hard- and software, manpower resources, competition between different manufacturers, as well as the optimal number of various system types to be implemented are only a few items which play an important role prior to taking a decision on switching systems.

Under these circumstances, the DBP decided in 1979 to run a special procedure ("Presentation of world market digital switching systems") in which other administrations showed quite a lot of interest because of its unique character. In order to reach as quickly as possible, and under competitive conditions, a reliable decision on switching systems, the DBP carried out a one-year presentation procedure

for both long-distance and local switching systems. The principal
marginal conditions for industry were the following:

- the DBP did not ask for a system specifically developed for the
  DBP, but for a product readily available on the world market
  and adaptable to the requirements of the DBP;

- the DBP made no stipulations and exerted no influence with a
  view to the development of a particular system;

- a decision on the system chosen was made upon proven evidence
  that the system offered could also be implemented by the
  required deadline, and that it was operationally as well as
  financially suitable;

- system selection (decreasing to two systems which was found to
  be the optimal number for the DP telephone network) will
  remain valid for a long period;

- for regular purchases, competition in price must be ensured.

The applicability of this procedure led ultimately to the DBP
decision in favour of the Siemens EWSD System and the System 12 of
Standard Elektrik Lorenz (ITT) as future digital switching systems
manufactured in series for the DBP network.

Implementation of these switching systems will start in 1985
and increase rapidly within the following years. To ensure maximum
benefits both in terms of costs and performance, this implementation is
closely linked to the implementation of digital transmission systems the
entire product range of which will also be available in 1985. By 1990,
there will already be over 200 exchanges. Digital local exchanges will
always be tied to digital trunk exchanges. Their application will
commence with the replacement of entire switching centers in large local
networks and will then continue with medium-size and small local
networks. Implementation of common channel signalling is also underway
with regard to digital switching. After extensive field trials,
application of the CCITT Common Channel Signalling System No. 7 is
planned for 1986.

The continuous implementation of both digital transmission and
digital switching in the existing telephone network will transform it
into a digital telephone network. In addition to offering economic,
technical and operational advantages, this transition is a prerequisite
for establishing the next major step – the setting up of an Integrated
Services Digital Network (ISDN) which is discussed later on.

3.2   Data networks

The DBP has traditionally been the promoter of telex service
ever since its beginning. A fully automized telex network using

electromechanical switching equipment has been in operation since
long before World War II. But in the early 60s, this network (and more
precisely the switching equipment) had to be overhauled. After over 30
years of successful operation, a new generation of switching equipment
was due to be brought into service.

At that time, the DBP took a far-reaching decision, the
validity of which was proven in the subsequent development. In 1968, the
DBP initiated the development of a new, fully electronic stored-program
data switching system that could be optimized not only for telex, but
also for data transmission requirements which, at that time, had just
started to evolve. This was possible by using EDS (Electronic Data
Exchanges) interconnecting telex and data customers by means of
circuit-switching. This network is therefore referred to as "DATEX-L"
network ("L" stands for "leitungsvermittelt" which is the German
equivalent for circuit-switching). In 1972, the DATEX-L network was
offering bitrates from 50 bit/s (for telex) up to 2400 bit/s. Since
then, it was permanently upgraded through implementation of higher data
rates and in conformity with the development of relevant CCITT-
Recommendations. Today, switched data rates from 50 bit/s up to 64
kbit/s are offered to customers of this network.

The DATEX-L network presently serves some 160,000 telex
subscribers as well as some 15,000 data stations. It is worth noting
that this network is fully digital and it probably was one of the first
fully digitized networks in the world. This was made possible by
interconnecting all 23 EDS exchanges by 2 Mbit/s digital line systems
which were installed on an existing, analogue symmetrical pair network
carrying 120 voice channels per pair. By using a special line code
(which shifts the frequency spectrum of the 2 Mbit/s line signal towards
higher frequencies) it is possible to transmit on each of the phantom
circuits of this analogue carrier network a 2 Mbit/s data stream without
interfering with analogue voice channels carried on symmetrical pairs.

Soon after the start of DATEX-L, the development of packet
switching was fostered. With a view to users' expectations, the
expanding market and possibilities of enhancing circuit switching, the
DBP was prompted in 1980 to set up, once the basic CCITT standards had
been decided upon, a packet-switched data network (DATEX-P) and to
commence with chargeable operation under normal conditions in August
1981, following a one-year charge-free trial period. DATEX-P transmits
data rates complying with all relevant CCITT Recommendations. At
present, some 7,500 data stations are interconnected with this network.

In addition to the two switched data networks DATEX-L and
DATEX-P, customers may use fixed connections between their data
stations. This service, which was already opened in 1974, has so far
attracted some 11,000 customers. A large portion of data communication
in the telephone network is still performed by means of modems (up to
4800 bit/s) concentrating, however, on data rates of 2400 bit/s and
below. At present, there are some 211,000 data stations in operation
which are connected to the various networks mentioned above.

4.   <u>Evolution of telecommunication services</u>

As in many other countries, the telephone service is - and remains - the most dominant of all telecommunication services provided by the DBP. The reasons for this are clear: telephony is a typical mass communication service - inexpensive, easy to handle, meeting both the requirements of business and private customers very efficiently - and still open to introduction of new capabilities and new features which strengthen even more the dominant position of telephony. A brief outlook on the present status as well as on future evolution of telecommunication services in the Federal Republic of Germany is given below.

4.1   <u>Telephone service</u>

In 1984, over 16,000 million local calls and calls in the extended local telephone service were registered; furthermore, over 9,500 million long-distance calls (331 million of which represented international calls) were placed by DBP customers. While customers are making frequent and ever-increasing use of the telephone, another interesting trend becomes more and more obvious: this trend asks for more comfort, more features; customers are no longer content with their role of merely being "talkers" or "listeners". They expect more from their telephone than just listening and talking. Modern technology renders it possible to implement such requirements in the telephone network and, if charges are moderate, customers are willing to pay for and to use such new features.

In order to meet the requirements of this trend and to enhance the conventional telephone services, the DBP already offers a range of new features. The most important ones are the following:

<u>Service 130:</u>   This service offers the same features as in the United States the well known "Service 800" (although the technical provision is different). A customer may call another customer free of charge or at the price of one local call. The called subscriber undertakes to pay the charges for the long-distance calls. This "Service 130" (130 is the access number) enjoys an increasing popularity with companies which operate nationwide, using however centralized booking facilities (for instance airlines, car rental offices, hotel chains, etc.).

<u>GEDAN service:</u> By using this service, a subscriber may transfer incoming calls to his station to another one (call diversion). Thus, a customer who is frequently absent from his office or home (doctors in rural areas, travelling salesmen, etc.) can be reached at any telephone station where he may happen to be.

<u>Telephone conferencing:</u> This service, which is not restricted only to domestic customers, has been available for several years and many companies with representatives at different locations use it to coordinate their activities more efficiently.

<u>Call logging:</u>   The customer may, upon request, obtain a telephone bill
listing all calls made from his station. Owing to strict
rules concerning security as well as individual privacy,
the DBP does not generally implement this service unless
the customer expressly asks for an itemized bill.

<u>Phone card service:</u> Telephone booths are now being equipped enabling
payment of calls by phonecards, thus relieving users from
payment with coins (difficult when making long-distance
or international calls). Furthermore, an increasing
number of telephone booths now have incoming call
facilities, so a user may be called while waiting in a
telephone booth.

<u>Computer-based directory inquiry service:</u> This fully automatic system
(which eventually will replace inquiry operators) is at
present under test and will be introduced from 1986.

<u>Mobile telephone service:</u> A new mobile telephone network ("network C")
will be opened in 1986, offering a basic capacity for
about 100,000 customers.

4.2   Bildschirmtext service

This Videotex service (comparable to Prestel in the United
Kingdom and Teletel in France) has been open to the public since 1984.
Contacts were already made in 1976 with British Telecom (which was at
that time launching Viewdata service), and a close cooperation between
BT and DBP was established during the following years. At the Berlin
Radio and TV Fair in 1977, DBP demonstrated Bildschirmtext for the first
time to the public, using the same software and computer type as BT.
This first presentation of Bildschirmtext was a tremendous success.
Therefore, immediately after the Berlin Radio and TV Fair a field trial
for information providers (non-public) was started in order to
familiarize them with the possibilities of this new service. From 1980
onwards, two large field trials with some 5,000 customers were
successfully carried out. After evaluation of the results of these field
trials and the establishment of the necessary legal provisions, the
public Bildschirmtext service was planned for 1983.

However, two major obstacles meanwhile became evident:

—   the lack of international, or only European, Videotex
standards. DBP, always in favour of international
standardization in all telecommunication fields, did its
best to overcome this hurdle and to contribute towards
this goal; nevertheless, standardization in Europe
progressed much more slowly than originally anticipated.
Divergent opinions between major European Administrations
made the set-up of true videotex standards a painful
effort. Moreover, changing requirements (mainly from
information providers) which were to be incorporated,
contributed to the slow progress of standardization. For
example, a request for better graphical display was
mainly pushed by information providers who were not

satisfied with the rather simple presentation of graphics as provided at that time for both the Viewdata and Bildschirm text systems. (Both systems were mainly text display systems and the display of graphics was, at the beginning, not considered to be essential). Under such circumstances the European Videotex standard ("CEPT standard") was finally agreed upon in 1983 – thus considerably delaying the development of equipment (e.g. the Bildschirmtext codec).

- The second obstacle was the complexity of the Bildschirmtext network and the data bases. The Viewdata concept was based on stand-alone data bases; from the very beginning, the Bildschirmtext concept foresaw the interconnection of all DBP data bases via the DATEX-P network. In addition, the concept included the interconnection of third party data bases (e.g. of mail order houses, insurance companies, etc.) with DBP data bases via DATEX-P. It is evident that the setting-up and operation of such a complex network is extremely complicated as the software complexity is immense.

However, after overcoming all these problems, Bildschirmtext finally opened in 1984 and is now being progressively implemented on a nationwide basis. Some 3,000 information providers are registered, whereas the number of Bildschirmtext customers (about 30,000) is at present lower than originally estimated; the high price of a TV set with build-in Bildschirm codec (about DM 1,000 more than an ordinary TV set) seems to represent the main reason for complaint from private Bildschirmtext customers. Future experience will show whether these are current problems which each new telecommunication service must cope with upon its implementation, or whether forecasts were too optimistic.

4.3   <u>Teletex service</u>

It is not surprising that DBP, operating the largest telex network in the world, has paid great attention to the Teletex service; the DBP may indeed be regarded as having pioneered this service.

The potential of Teletex, compared to telex, is that it provides a quicker and better text transmission than telex. Teletex is furthermore a means of rationalizing office operations. Studies have shown that the efficiency of office operations is greatly improved by Teletex rather than telex. The Teletex terminal is integrated into the office organization and can be operated by each secretary; messages can be sent out and received "at the desk". This is much more efficient than sending them through a separate telex office, and moreover avoids the restricted text representation of a telex message.

Immediately after relevant CCITT Recommendations had been agreed upon, the Teletex service was inaugurated in 1981 on a trial basis. Service is provided by the DATEX-L network operating at 2400 bits/s transmitting, for example, a business letter in just a few seconds at very low cost. Although DBP is quite optimistic about the extension of Teletex, it would only be realistic to admit that the conventional telex will remain in service for quite a long time. For this reason, and also to increase the market potential for Teletex, interworking between Teletex and telex terminals is provided (in which case, however, the restricted text representations of the telex alphabet apply). Since the opening of its service, subscription to Teletex has increased steadily; by the end of 1984, over 10,000 customers were registered. This positive trend will most probably continue in the future, supported by increasing international traffic to and from countries implementing Teletex. For 1992, over 100,000 Teletex terminals are forecasted and this amount does not appear to be unrealistic considering decreasing prices for Teletex terminals which are already being produced by some manufacturers.

5.   The task ahead: Transition to ISDN

Telecommunication networks operated by the DBP and described in this article are "dedicated networks" – dedicated to provide one particular service or sometimes several but inter-related services in one and the same network. The transition from an analogue to a digital telephone network offers, apart from economic, technical and operational benefits for telephony alone, a much wider field of operation: a digital telephone network may be enhanced to an Integrated Services Digital Network (ISDN) carrying literally all telecommunication services in a single network.

It would be beyond the scope of this review to go into detail of exactly how such an ISDN evolves from a digital telephone network. In conformity with international trends and CCITT Recommendations, this evolution will take place in two phases:

- the evolution from a digital telephone network (operating at 64 Kbit/s as the standard bitrate) to a "narrowband" or 64 Kbit/s-ISDN. Such a 64 Kbit/s-ISDN will be able to carry all services up to 64 Kbit/s. Telecommunication services such as sound programmes, videotelephone, TV, etc. require much higher bitrates than 64 Kbit/s. To accommodate these services a second phase is envisaged:

- the 64 Kbit/s-ISDN will, in a second phase, be enhanced to a "broadband" or n x 64 Kbit/s-ISDN which, in addition to all services requiring up to 64 Kbit/s, will also carry services at higher bitrates.

It goes without saying that the operation of one universal network for all services is much more economic than the operation of several parallel running dedicated networks. Not only the network operator will benefit but also the customer who receives more and better services at lower cost.

The DBP was one of the promoters of the ISDN concept for the reasons stated above and it has made a firm commitment to establish ISDN in two phases. The transition to ISDN is a gigantic task – eventually, several billion Deutschmarks will have to be spent. But at the same time it is an excellent example of how a "monopolistic" enterprise such as the DBP is committed to implementing highly advanced technology for the benefit of all its customers.

5.1   Transition to the 64 Kbit/s-ISDN

The digital telephone network of the DBP is expected to grow rapidly as a result of extensive implementation of digital transmission and digital switching systems. In other words, in a few years from now the digital "infrastructure" will have developed sufficiently for the next step to be taken - the transition from a digital telephone network to 64 Kbit/s-ISDN.

By a "declaration of intent" in March 1982 the DBP clearly defined its position on the ISDN. In this declaration the DBP states that it recognizes the technical, operational and economic benefits offered by a uniform digital network for various services (speech, data, text, facsimile, image transmission, telemetry, interactive videotex, etc.) and wishes for more speedy expansion of the digital telephone network leading to ISDN. The ISDN declaration of intent was understood by the German telecommunications industry as a signal to mobilize all available forces to reach this goal.

In this declaration the DBP announced two further important stages for the implementation of ISDN, namely:

-       an ISDN pilot project scheduled for 1986;

-       ISDN operation as a regular service scheduled for 1988.

In order to fully understand the strategies of the DBP, both for the pilot project and the operation of ISDN regular services, some fundamental considerations should be made clear. These considerations are valid for the 64 Kbit/s-ISDN as well as for the n x 64 Kbit/s-ISDN.

Giving reality to ISDN represents first of all a technical problem; the necessary equipment has to be developed and it has to operate in the network satisfactorily. But the best ISDN equipment is useless if ISDN services and ISDN features (ISDN capabilities) are not accepted and used frequently by the customer. The customer is really setting the decision: his acceptance (or non-acceptance) of ISDN capabilities will decide whether or not ISDN flourishes or withers away.

The acceptance of the customer, however, will be determined not only by technical considerations for him. Technical equipment is something that <u>has</u> to function. His decision will be narrowed down to the simple but crucial question: Are the ISDN capabilities sufficiently attractive from the economic viewpoint? Does he get <u>more</u> for the <u>same</u> money as under present circumstances? In other words, the economy of the ISDN capabilities and their consequent use by the customer will be the decisive factor upon which the evolution of any ISDN will depend.

An administration (or any other network provider) will therefore not only have to provide the technical prerequisites (ISDN equipment) but must also create economic incentives to encourage the customer to use ISDN capabilities as much as possible.

For a network provider there are basically two areas where economic incentives for the ISDN may be stimulated:

-   low cost, "user-friendly", terminals;

-   attractive tariffs.

When developing its ISDN implementation strategy the DBP devoted particular attention to these two domains. In principle, the following measures will be executed to back up ISDN implementation:

<u>Low cost and "user friendly" terminals</u> can be expected soon if this market is exposed to competition between many manufacturers; as a consequence, the ISDN terminal market must be liberalized. This liberalization will come as a consequence of many attempts underway in most countries and which we summarize briefly as "deregulation". The expected stiff competition will automaticallly result in availability of the desired low cost terminals designed to customer benefits. Influence on the design by the network provider should be restricted to the technical standards required for interconnection with the network.

The liberalization of the ISDN technical market is from the technical point of view not a problem: the interconnection points (ISDN user/network interfaces) have been standardized in such a way as to anticipate this evolution of the terminal market.

In order to allow further maximum freedom for the terminal design (and consequently for evolution of ISDN services) the DBP is providing the B + B + D (64 + 64 + 16 Kbit/s) structure (basic access) not only at the ISDN user/network interfaces but even transmits this bitstream to the customers' premises. Although for some non-voice-ISDN services (like Teletex, Videotex, etc.) the full bitrate of 64 Kbit/s is not at present required it cannot be excluded that the evolution of ISDN terminals and ISDN services will lead to higher bitrates in the future which will offer many attractive features to the customer. By using echo cancellation for transmission of 64 + 64 + 16 Kbit/s the subscriber network of the DBP is capable of carrying this bitstream (total 192 Kbit/s) to the customers' premises without any modification up to loop lengths of about 4 km; 95% of the loops are shorter than 4 km and longer loops exist only in rural environments where ISDN services are not expected to be needed for the time being.

As far as <u>tariffs</u> are concerned, in the opinion of the DBP the ISDN calls for harmonized tariff structures and a harmonized tariff level in the various telecommunication services. The following marginal conditions must be borne in mind:

-   The telephone service will serve as the basis for establishing

tariffs for all services in the ISDN, since it constitutes the major
part of business turn-over.

-    In the ISDN, all connections will be implemented by way of
accesses, i.e. accesses will be provided for dedicated (leased) circuits
just as well as for switched connections. With his basic ISDN access,
the customer will in future be able to choose between the following:

-    both 64 Kbit/s channels are employed for switched
     connections;

-    one 64 Kbit/s channel is employed for switched
     connections, the other for a dedicated circuit;

-    both 64 Kbit/s channels are employed for dedicated
     circuits;

-    it is also possible for a single 64 Kbit/s channel to be
     employed for switched connections or for dedicated
     circuits.

Initial ideas for ISDN tariff policy deriving from this are:

1.   the monthly charges for providing ISDN accesses will be
     service independent;

2.   features for switched connections in the ISDN
     -    service independence
     -    dependence on distance (tariff zones)
     -    different usage times for a unit fee of 0.23 DM (at present)
          in various tariff zones
     -    normal and cheap-rate times.

3.   feature for dedicated circuits in the ISDN
     -    service independence

Harmonization of the tariffs between switched connections and
dedicated circuits by way of the following measures:

.   dependence on distance (tariff zones) on the basis of the
     tariff zones for switched connections;

.   different usage times for a unit fee in the various
     tariff zones; efforts should be made in the local and
     long-distance exchange zone(s) to achieve as uniform a
     relationship as possible between the time pulse lengths
     for dedicated circuits and those for equivalent switched
     connections;

.   normal and cheap-rate tariffs as for switched
connections;

—   minimum usage times to ensure that fixed costs are covered.

Aligning ISDN tariffs on telephone tariffs will create an
incentive for switching all non-telephone applications to the ISDN.

Bearing in mind these explanations, plans of the DBP for its
pilot project and the operation of ISDN regular services will be more
evident.

The purpose of the <u>pilot project</u> (to begin in 1986 for about
two years) is to test the new components of the ISDN (signalling
D-channel protocol) and transmission system on the subscriber line,
network terminations, terminals, multiplexers for the basic access,
concentrators, inter-exchange signalling adaption of digital switching
systems, etc.) under operational conditions. It is, therefore, not a
market trial or an acceptance test for ISDN capabilities. The DBP holds
the view that the attraction of the ISDN capabilities — provided as
explained above — is self-evident. A market trial in addition would make
sense only if a sufficiently great number of ISDN customers would be
interconnected nationwide — but the digital infrastructure existing in
1986 will not have reached the proportions required for such a project.
Therefore, the objective of the pilot project is to verify that all ISDN
components designed in accordance with DBP specifications (which are
based on the I-Series Recommendations of the CCITT) interwork as
expected so that their serial production can be undertaken without
technical risk.

The pilot project is due to be carried out in Mannheim and
Stuttgart. It is envisaged that around 400 ISDN basic accesses should be
connected to each of the two local exchanges with ISDN capability. The
project will be implemented in several stages:

—   testing and evaluating of the ISDN´s fundamental functional
performance;

—   connection and trial operation of PABXs and other ISDN
terminal equipment (terminals for telephony, teletex, textfax,
facsimile, data transmission, fixed image transmission and
multiservice terminals);

—   testing of CCITT signalling system No. 7, in particular of the
ISDN user part (ISUP) between the digital local exchanges
involved in the ISDN pilot project.

All necessary measures (provision of funds, procurement, etc.)
have already been started and are progressing on schedule.

At its expiry the pilot project will be taken over by the

regular ISDN services. In 1988, the DBP intends to start operation on
the first two ISDN digital local exchanges with ISDN capability.
Furthermore, all digital local exchanges that are placed in service in
1989 or later will be capable of servicing ISDN subscribers. The digital
local exchanges installed in the DBP´s digital telephone network between
1985 and 1988 will then be fitted with ISDN capability.

By 1990, about 100 long-distance and 100 local digital
exchanges will have been installed in the DBP´s digital telephone
network. As some 50% of all telephone terminals are incorporated in the
100 largest local networks and the business terminals – potential ISDN
customers – are primarily concentrated in the cities, these 100 local
networks will permit the majority of future ISDN subscribers to be
reached without crossing local network boundaries. In the initial phase,
it will be possible to tie remote ISDN users to the ISDN local network
as long-distance subscribers. It can be assumed that 5 years after the
commencement of ISDN operations nationwide ISDN coverage will have been
achieved.

Since ISDN accesses only constitute a special class of general
digital exchange accesses, the expansion projects planned each year for
the local exchanges will enable the current demand for ISDN to be
followed. Thus no special overlay network is required for the
introduction of ISDN.

5.2   <u>Transition to the n x 64 Kbit/s-ISDN</u>

So far the strategy of the DBP for implementing the
64 Kbit/s-ISDN. But meanwhile a lot of work is being carried out to draw
up a similar strategy for the next phase, i.e. the implementation of the
n x 64 Kbit/s-ISDN ("broadband-ISDN").

Towards the end of this decade, when optical fibre cables and
optical systems will become economically competitive even in the local
networks, it will be feasible to expand the ISDN with broadband
facilities to an extent that will permit the integration of all switched
narrowband and broadband applications (telephony, data, test and image
communications, video telephony and video conferencing).

The 64 Kbit/s ISDN is a prerequisite for switched broadband
services. Most of the principal components of this ISDN, e.g.
signalling on the subscriber line (D-channel protocol) and between
exchanges (Signalling System No. 7), control of exchanges, call charge
recording, network synchronization, power supply and the transmission
system in the long-distance sector, are also suitable for implementing
the broadband communication of the future. In addition, broadband
services call for the same structure as the ISDN. Hence, it is
recommended to continue with the logical evolution of the ISDN into a
broadband ISDN in which the copper cables are complemented by optical
fibre cables and the exchanges by broadband switching units of the type
that will presumably be available in the late ´80s. This broadband-ISDN will
provide switched services at a point-to-point basis; inclusion of
distribution services (such as cable TV) is envisaged to follow as an
enhancement of the broadband ISDN.

As the 64 Kbit/s ISDN, the broadband ISDN will also call for comprehensive national and international standardization. Only in this way can future-oriented, competitive switched broadband networks be created, as joint use of the ISDN facilities will prevent double investments. Separate switching nodes outside the ISDN would result in special separate networks which, as experience with such networks shows, cannot be operated profitably.

6.   Progressive strategies and concepts

As set out in this paper, the DBP believes in evolution of networks rather than in setting up new networks. In this evolution various phases must be passed through. These phases, leading from the analogue telephone network to the integrated services universal network, are marked by technically consistent, progressive development in a series of integration stages:

- digitization of the network components
  - transmission (since 1970)
  - switching (from 1985 onwards)

- digital telephone network (from 1986 onwards)
  - integration stage 1 (transmission and switching)

- ISDN (from 1988 onwards)
  - integration stage 2 (64 Kbit/s services)

- Integration of broadband switched services into the ISDN (from 1990 onwards)
  - integration stage 3

- Integration of the distribution services into the ISDN (from 1992 onwards)
  - integration stage 4.

To promote this last technical development, the DBP has already implemented BIGFON (German acronym for broadband integrated optical fibre local network) trial networks in seven German cities. For the first time, these permit all forms of narrow-band and broadband individual communication with which we are familiar today, including video telephony, plus broadband distribution communications (TV and sound radio) to be offered on an integrated basis. The trial phase will last until 1986.

There are many opinions about the pros and the cons of the "information area" where nearly unlimited access will be provided to all sources of information and which may change today's work substantially. An administration which intends to remain a leading force in telecommunications must harness itself for the future. The strategies and concepts developed by Deutsche Bundespost will enable new technological opportunities to be used to the full and by everybody.

References:

1. Telecommunication Journal: Special edition on the
   Federal Republic of Germany, ITU Geneva, September 1982;

2. Several authors in "Jahrbuch der DBP 1984", Verlag Georg
   Meidecker, Bad Windsheim

3. M. Schoen: "The Deutsche Bundespost on its way towards the
   ISDN", Zeitschrift fuer das Post- und Fernmeldewesen (ZPF),
   June 1984;

4. W. Kaiser (Editor), "Integrated Telecommunications
   Proceedings", held at a congress in Munich,
   5-7 November 1984, Springer Verlag.

CHAPTER 35.

BRITAIN; THE PROBLEMS AND BENEFITS OF LIBERALISATION

MR. BRIAN V.SIMMONS
Pactel Ltd., London, England.

1   OVERVIEW

The United Kingdom (UK) has made a significant contribution to information and telecommunications technology, and yet many of the commercial benefits have been lost to other advanced countries. The penetration of this new technology into British industry has so far been disappointing and, with few exceptions, the UK has not had the large export success of other countries, such as the USA, Japan and Sweden.

One particular strength of the UK, however, is in software, but its inability to match this with a comprehensive range of viable hardware has created an imbalance. Much basic chip technology is bought-in from other counties, and there are insufficient home-based UK producers to satisfy requirements.

Competing with computer giants, such as IBM and DEC, there is only one UK company of any size, which is ICL. Its performance has for many years been disappointing, although under the direction of Robert Wilmott and latterly Michael Edwards, who previously turned the ailing British Leyland motor company into profitability, its performance has improved. ICL is now owned by STC.

The UK is the fourth largest telecommunications country in the world behind the USA, Japan and Germany, having almost 30M telephones and over 20M lines with a legacy of old electromechanical public exchanges, mostly of Strowger technology, it is now investing heavily in a programme to transform its national trunk network to digital operation and is ordering hundreds of digital local exchanges to replace the remainder of its older exchangesby the end of the century.

In the past the 'ring' of five main suppliers, over which work was previously shared out, enjoyed a relatively stable business without any great incentive to innovate and export. Since the breaking of that ring, many smaller companies are now supplying BT. The major public network switching contracts still go to GEC and Plessey however, for digital exchanges, and to STC for completing the programme of TXE4 public electronic analogue exchanges. Other suppliers, such as IBM, are developing electronic equipment to provide new facilities and features on these systems. One of IBM's contracts, for example, is to supply computer equipment to provide detailed call–charge billing; something which UK customers have been demanding for many years to replace unsatisfactory bulk call charge billing.

With recent moves to liberalise telecommunications in the UK, and the privatisation of BT in 1984, the climate should now favour a much greater innovative approach to the development and marketing of new telecommunications and information technology products and services, to benefit UK users and stimulate exports. The impact of deregulation in the UK is being closely watched by many other countries and their PTTs. Much has already been learned from the USA, but a series of new problems has emerged and has necessitated a further learning process. The UK has had to migrate from a heavy monopolised situation, in which BT had an almost supreme control, in comparison with many European PTTs which already allow privately supplied equipment to be connected to their networks and to be privately maintained.

2   INFORMATION AND TELECOMMUNICATIONS POLICY

Under the promotion of successive UK governments since the early 1970's, Britain's Information Technology (IT) industry has failed to maintain its share of the world market. In a National Economic Development Council report, published in September 1984, it was revealed that the UK's £4 billion-a-year IT industry now claimed only a 4% world market share, with an annual growth rate of only 12% (figure 1). Moreover, parts of the industry were stated to be on the brink of collapse, owing to international competition, lack of investment, and shortage of skilled resources.

Figure 1

UK Information Technology Growth and World Market Share.

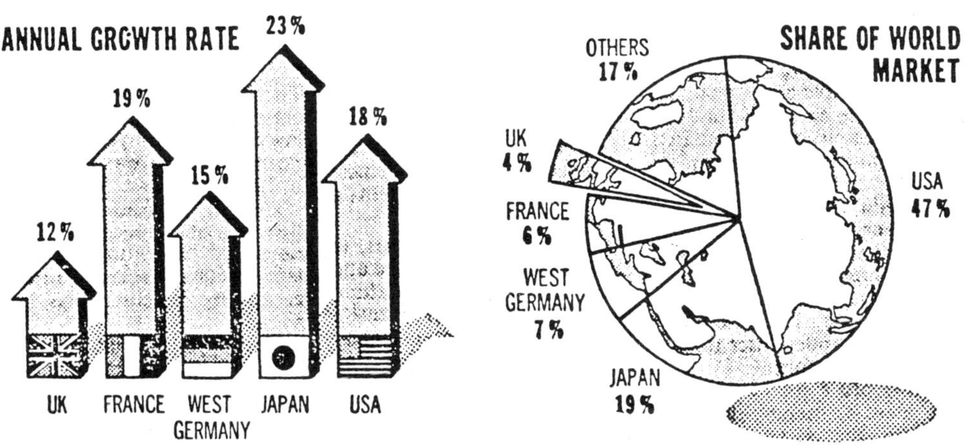

     International Information and Telecommunications Policy

Yet despite this pessimistic review, IT is having an increasing impact on the way we conduct our businesses, and is making available an increasing range of high technology products and software which is crucial to the economic recovery of the UK. Almost 40% of our working population are now in information industries compared with over 50% in the USA.

The UK telecommunications liberalisation programme is of more recent formation and it began with the Conservative Government's 1981 Telecommunications Bill which culminated in August 1984, when British Telecommunications (BT) plc was formed and operated under licence along with Mercury Communications, Hull Corporation, and two cellular-radio consortiums in the UK.

Private suppliers are now able to install apparatus in competition with BT and to offer maintenance service. BT is required to enter into contracts with its 20 million customers in line with common commercial practice, for telephone, telex, private circuit, packet switching, radiophone, radiopaging, and the other telecommunications services which BT operates.

In this chapter we shall examine the developments and implications of the progression into a liberalised telecommunications environment and of IT, dealing in greatest detail with the new telecommunications environment.

3   Telecommunications Liberalisation

British governments have a reputation for changing course in the way they handle important industrial, social and economic issues, sometimes even during one parliamentary period. The Thatcher government however has, since July 1979, pursued a determined course towards the liberalisation of telecommunications in the UK. This administration, now in its second term of office, fervently believes that telecommunications should be at the heart of its industrial policy and has worked to unshackle it from the earlier monopolistic framework which existed under the 1969 Post Office Act.

The key objective of the 1981 Telecommunications Act was not only to separate the telecommunications and postal services, but also to liberate the UK telecommunications market from the long-standing influence of the state monopoly. A rigorous programme was set into motion to liberalise the supply and maintenance of apparatus which could be connected to the public switched telephone and telex networks. This involved:

-   the preparation of standards by appointed committees to be published by the British Standards Institute (BSI) specifying safety and performance requirements of apparatus

-   the testing of apparatus to these rigorous standards for attachment approval

-   the approval of private maintainers to service privately supplied apparatus for connection to BT's, or any other licensed network, such as Mercury.

By 1984, a considerable degree of liberalisation had been achieved. There were, for example, many tens of approved telephones for plug-in attachment to the public network; there was a wide choice of small electronic PABX and key systems; many computer controlled telex machines were approved; and an extensive range of approved call

Figure 2

<u>British Telecom Organisation</u>

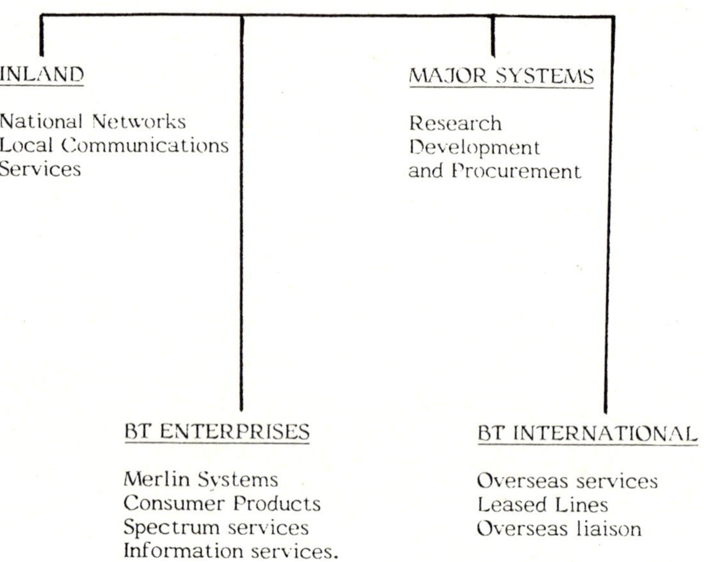

Figure 3

<u>Apparatus approved for connection to BT networks.</u>   The circle is
coloured green.

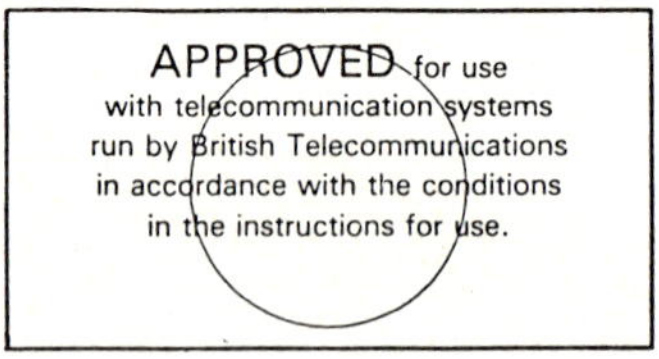

makers, answering machines, and other attachment devices could be privately purchased.

The combined effect was to stimulate BT into a positive response to the challenge and, over the past several years, the image of BT has changed from that of a complacent monopoly to one of an aggressive marketing organisation. A small, but important, indication of this is illustrated by the way BT now refers to users as customers and not subscribers; the term previously adopted.

Massive internal reorganisation within BT has produced a new organisation formed of four main sectors: Inland, BT Enterprises, Major Systems, and BT International, illustrated in figure 2. Local Communication Services, which is a part of Inland, has a staff of over 200,000 persons, who make up that part of the organisation which directly interfaces with BT's customers.

3.1   Approvals

An independent body, the British Approvals Board for Telecommunications (BABT), was established to approve apparatus for attachment to the network. Its function is essentially to receive requests for type approval of apparatus from suppliers, arrange for testing in available laboratories, and to assess the test results with the view to issuing approval certificates. Under the 1981 Act, only apparatus bearing an approval mark (figure 3) may be connected to the network. Unapproved apparatus may be marketed but it must bear a prohibition mark, (figure 4) and it is illegal to attach such apparatus to the network.

Figure 4

<u>Apparatus not approved for connection to BT networks.</u> The triangle
is coloured red.

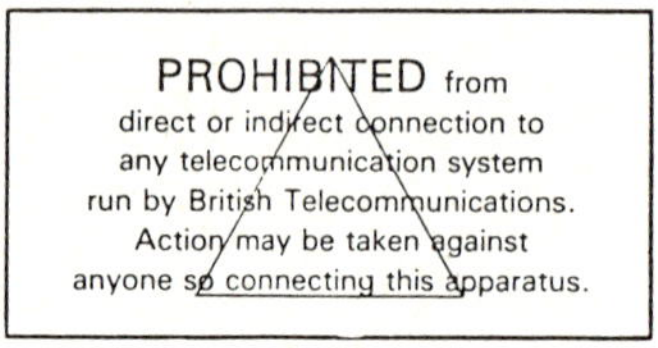

PROHIBITED from
direct or indirect connection to
any telecommunication system
run by British Telecommunications.
Action may be taken against
anyone so connecting this apparatus.

Approval tests are to ensure that:

-       apparatus does not constitute any danger either to the network,

        BT engineers, or users

-       signalling and transmission features of the apparatus are within

        defined limits to ensure satisfactory performance

-       apparatus will be reliable in service and satisfy all the essential

        operational requirements of the specifications.

Following the approval tests conducted on production samples,
field-trial observation of a selected number of similar systems is also
required, before type approval is granted. BABT is also required to
conduct regular inspections of suppliers' production processes to
ensure that standards are being maintained.

Unfortunately, the time to prepare standards has far exceeded the
original predictions of the Government's Department of Trade and
Industry (DTI), responsible for the telecommunications liberalisation
programme. A two-year standards preparation programme was

originally planned which would end in July 1983 with publication of the Private Branch Exchange (PBX) specification, as shown in figure 5.

Figure 5

<u>Programme Set by DTI in October 1981</u>
<u>for the Issue of Telecommunictions Standards</u>

General Safety	July 1982
General Requirements	"
Simple Telephones	"
Modems	"
Plugs and Sockets	"
Private Circuits	"
Simple Teleprinters	October 1982
Packet Switching	December 1982
PBX	July 1983

In fact, it has taken until 1984 to get the majority of these standards published. One of the most important, the new PBX specifications, is still incomplete and unlikely to be fully published in all its parts until 1986.

3.2   <u>Interim Standards</u>

To cover the immediate approval requirements for switching systems, the DTI has, with the cooperation of BT and the various BSI standards technical committees, produced a number of interim standards for key system and PBX approvals.

The principal standards called up in the key system and PBX approval specifications are described in figure 6 for the DTI interim schemes shown below:

        82/006I   Small Call Routing Apparatus I

        84/010I   Small Call Routing Apparatus II

        84/012I   Private Branch Exchanges.

Other interim standards have been produced, such as for Dealer Board connection to the public network.

Figure 6

Principal Telecommnications Standards

Related to Switching Systems

BS   6301   Safety Requirements

     6305   General Requirements

     6312   Plugs and Sockets

     6317   Simple Telephones

     6450   PABX

     6506   Code of Practice for the Installation of PABX

BTR 1050/6   PABX

Note: BTR 1050/6 is the alternative PBX specification based
             on previous BT test requirements which is available for
             selection by a supplier seeking approval under the
             interim scheme 84/0121

3.3   Installing Apparatus

In allowing anyone to connect approved apparatus to the network, the
Government has nevertheless imposed some controls by applying
certain rules of connection. There are two basic connection methods:

-    plug and socket connection

-    hard-wired connection.

In the former, connection and disconnection can be achieved without the use of tools, and this is therefore applicable to single line installations, such as telephones, modems, and simple telex terminals.

In the latter, connection will be hard-wired (permanent connection) from a BT cable. On hard-wired installations (usually multi-line), BT is responsible for connecting the apparatus into service, after first checking that it is in accordance with the approval certificate and the BSI installation code of practice. Pre-connection tests on hard-wired installations are made by BT to ensure that the apparatus complies with the approval certificate.

The installation code of practice published by the BSI contains several mandatory requirements, although the majority are recommendations only.

Installation work may be performed by any appointed organisation, but apparatus can only be maintained by an organisation which has been approved by the Quality Assurance Branch of the BSI. Approval of the apparatus to be connected to the PSTN requires at least one BSI approved maintainer.

As liberalisation progresses, the Government is introducing further relaxations. For example, existing block telephone wiring in a building, owned by BT, must be available to a private supplier of switching equipment at a reasonable price. Hitherto, it was often impossible for a private supplier to compete with BT when supplying a

PABX, owing to the need to install new wiring, because BT was unwilling to sell its own wiring.

Other measures are also being introduced which will permit the connection of subsidiary apparatus, such as key systems to host PBXs, and allow PABXs incorporating Direct Dialling Inward (DDI) facilities to be privately maintained. Yet another easement will permit a supplier to install a limited number of systems after safety tests are successfully completed, provided the supplier can declare that the apparatus conforms to all other test requirements and if insurance cover is provided to cover any claims made against the supplier due to inferior performance. Interim approval schemes operated by the DTI do not however require apparatus to be tested again, when the specifications are finally completed. Following the satisfactory approval testing of apparatus, field trials are conducted before type approval is granted.

3.4   OFTEL

In July 1984, Professor Bryan Carsberg was appointed Director General for Telecommunications, as head of the Office of Telecommunications (OFTEL), a watchdog organisation (figure 7) whose responsibility is to monitor the licences of BT and other operators with the objective of safeguarding the interests of other suppliers and of business and domestic telecommunications users. He will encourage and protect fair competition, and investigate any legitimate complaints. Already he has been lobbied on alleged predatory marketing tactics of BT and the proposed association of BT and IBM to provide a value added network (VAN) based on SNA, IBM's

Figure 7

OFTEL ORGANISATON CHART

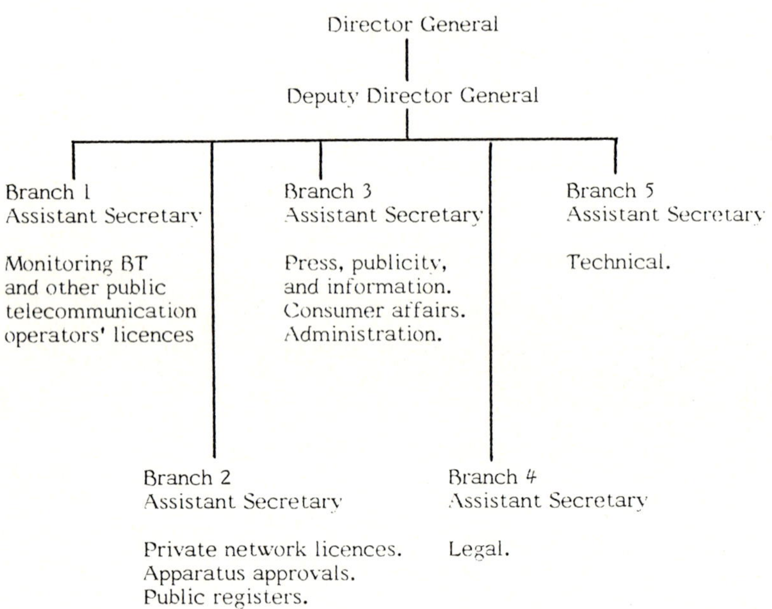

own network architecture, which was disallowed by OFTEL. The effectiveness of OFTEL is of vital importance to private suppliers competing with BT and the industry giants, and OFTEL's early activities under deregulation are being closely observed by industry and users alike.

3.5   Grandfathering

To overcome some of the delays in getting privately supplied systems into the market place in advance of approval testing, the DTI in December 1982 introduced the 'grandfathering' scheme. This permits private suppliers, who already sell equipment to BT which has been type approved, to sell this same specification equipment privately without further testing.

3.6   Competition in Maintenance

As part of the liberalisation plan, the Government published its intentions in July 1983 for private maintenance of telecommunications equipment connected to the PSTN. This was to supercede the existing arrangements which gave BT the right to maintain all call routing apparatus. Equipment already in service would continue to be maintained by BT, but any new installations could qualify for private maintenance to the following schedule:

August 1983   – Key systems having at least two exchange lines

December 1984 – PBXs of up to 120 extensions

July 1985   – PBXs over 120 extensions

December 1984 – Key and lamp units

July 1986   – automatic call distribution systems

November 1986 – plan telephones   and   apparatus   not   elsewhere
                 specified.

Note: digital PABXs with pcm transmission were eligible for private
maintenance from July 1983.

4   <u>1984 TELECOMMUNICATIONS ACT</u>

The UK Telecommunications Act came into effect in early August
1984 with the Government's two main objectives of:

-          introducing fair competition into telecommunications

-          transfering BT to the private sector as a business, to
           be known as British Telecommunications plc (public
           limited company)

Three major changes were introduced which were:

a)   BT's   exclusive   monopoly   to   operate
           telecommunications systems was terminated and new
           arrangements were introduced for licensing BT for a
           minimum period of 25 years to provide services, along
           with other operators, with ten years notice of any
           termination.

b)   BT was made a private sector limited company in

which 51% of its shares would be offered on the open market to its customers, employees and institutions.

c)   The Director General of OFTEL would oversee the provision of telecommunications in the UK and would ensure that BT, and other operators, comply with the terms of their licences in fair trading, and would require public service operators to protect rural services, emergency services, public call-box service, and ship-to-shore communications.

The licence also requires BT to maintain any tariff increases to 3% below the national retail prices index, and changes sections of the law on wireless telegraphy and the supply of cable TV service.

Licences have also been issued to two other public service operators: Mercury Communications and the Kingston-upon-Hull City Council in North East England, which has always been independent of BT. No other licences for public services are to be granted until 1990. In addition, two cellular radio services have been licensed to start operations in 1985, directly interfacing the public telephone network. These are Cellnet and Vodafone and were selected by the DTI in 1982 after evaluation of a number of applicants.

5   <u>BRITISH TELECOM DEVELOPMENTS</u>

When it became clear, in the late 1970s, that the UK telecommunications market would be liberalised, BT had already made extensive plans to develop its own network and services to achieve a much greater impact on business and residential customers' requirements. Liberalisation has, however, hightened the drive, and the will, of senior BT management to streamline their organisation and improve its marketing efficiency. Despite BT's high annual turnover, its profit of £365M in 1983 represented only a 6% return on capital employed.

The UK is the fourth largest telecommunication operation in the world. 1983 statistics revealed that it had:

-           30M telephones

-           21M exchange lines

-           0.1M telex lines

-           21,000M inland calls

-           300M international calls

-           £6,377M total revenue

-           £365M net profit .

Because the majority of UK telephone lines are being served by electromechanical exchanges, customers have suffered a number of disadvantages: long call setting times, noisy connections, insufficient facilities, bulk-unit call billing, long delivery times, and a very limited range of customer apparatus.

An intensive programme of installing digital switches is now underway, based on BT's System X architecture, which is highly modular and evolutionary. By the late 1980s, a digital trunk network of 60 electronic switching centres should be in operation, connected to many hundreds of digital local exchanges. Progressively, the network of some 6,500 public exchanges will be upgraded to System X digital systems and, by the year 2000, almost the entire network will comprise digital exchanges with extensive fibre optic transmission lines linking these together. Whilst ordering the bulk of its System X exchanges from GEC and Plessey, BT intends also to open supply to one other company, and several overseas systems are under review. Not only will this speed up the installation programme, it will also keep it more competitive.

This will be the framework of the Integrated Services Digital Network (ISDN) which is being designed to international standards for providing a common network for all voice, telex, data, message, facsimile and video transmission, replacing the present individual networks for greater flexibility and efficiency. The UK is in the forefront of pilot ISDN operation which will commence in 1985 using an interim access rate of 80Kbps, to be upgraded later to the full 144Kbps standard. BT digital services are shown in figure 8.

6   Mercury

Mercury was first launched by a consortium of Cable and Wireless, British Petroleum and Barclays Merchant Bank, and is the only other nationally licensed network to compete directly with BT. Cable and Wireless now totally owns Mercury. It is the Government's intention that no other licenses will be issued for at least seven years, and the Mercury Communications license will apply for at least 25 years, in which Mercury predicts it will spend £1,000M to develop its network.

Figure 8

British Telecoms Digital Services

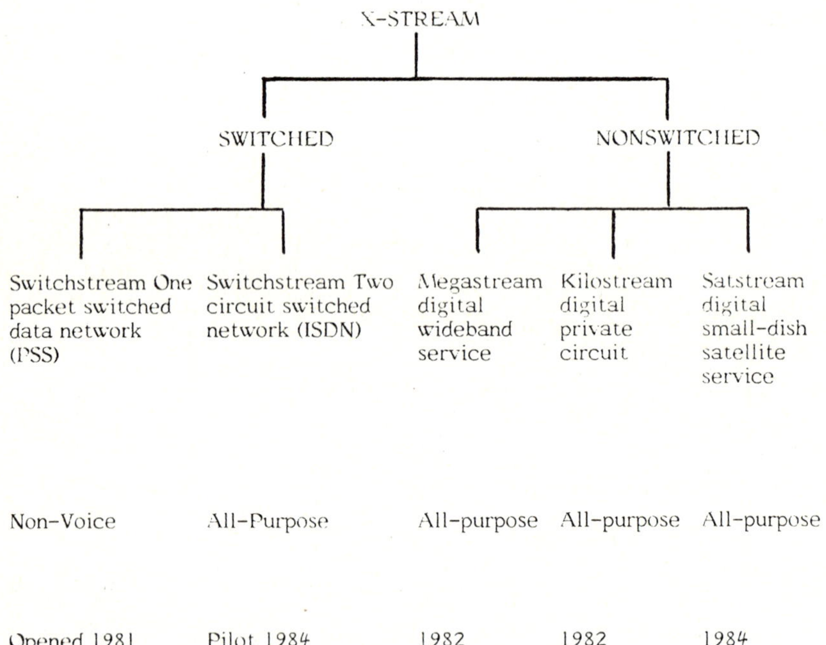

This network is a figure-of-eight formation which will serve the major conurbations in England, with spurs to other more remote locations. In London there will be a more densely provided service which will use cables run in a disused network of old hydraulic pipeline ducts. The main Mercury network is of fibre-optic cable alongside British Rail track. Each fibre, of the 8-fibre cable installed, has a capacity of 140Mbps. A satellite link is also to be used which is located in East London Docklands area. The requirement for interfacing Mercury with BT's PSTN brought initial Trades Union resistance, but connection requirements have now been agreed.

No switched network is presently proposed and customers will use the links as they would private network circuits. Two capacities for transmission are to be used; individual 64Kbps channels and 30 channel 2Mbps blocks of capacity. There may also be intermediate capacities, such as 6 channel blocks. Mercury is designed to carry voice, data and multiplexed voice/data services.

The success of Mercury will depend upon the number of customers it has and the freedom it posesses to interconnect with other networks, including the PSTN. Until these factors have been totally resolved, many potential customers are likely to remain uncertain of whether to adopt the alternative digital service to that which BT offers. This could introduce a serious cash flow problem for the company unless soon resolved.

7   TELECOMMUNICATION SERVICES

7.1   Value Added Networks

By June 1984, the number of Value Added Network Services (VANS) licences in the the UK had reached 370. Most of these are not yet in operation. VANS are services in which circuits provided by carriers are associated with other equipment, including computers, intelligent terminals, and switching systems to provide customer services of added value, including electronic mail, telex access via telephone lines, audio conferencing, and voice messaging. VANS are offering a wide range of new services to customers, who avoid the high cost of providing their own private facilities by using such services.

Other new services which, after an uncertain start, are now gathering considerable momentum are Prestel, the TV based BT information service accessed via the PTSN, for which open and closed user group access is possible; and BT Gold, the electronic mail service which also interfaces with Prestel.

7.2   Teletex Promotion

To speed the introduction of teletext, the 'super telex' text transmission system, the DTI selected five companies for its teletex introductory scheme: Ferranti, GEC, Mitel, Plessey and STC. The programme offered £4M as up to 50% subsidy for customers installing the teletex equipment of any of the above five suppliers between

October 1983 and June 1984.

Teletex transmission in the UK should be only one tenth the cost of telex, and 30 times as fast. Access to the UK's 80,000 telex users would be provided by telex/teletex network interfaces.

7.3   Video Services

BT is establishing a range of video services using 2Mbps, and higher-speed, digital transmission. These provide slow-scan TV, picture quality colour TV , and conference quality services. The latter service uses a special picture replenishment technique so that only the parts of the picture which move, from frame to frame, need to be transmitted. This is quite suitable for slow movement video conferences and provides 625 line quality pictures with only a 2Mbps transmission rate. BTI intends to establish both national and international TV conference links using public and customer-provided private studios.

7.4   Voice Messaging

Voice messaging began in the UK in 1982, when IBM introduced its Audio Distribution System (ADS). This was followed by Wang's Digital Voice Exchange. Other systems such as ITT's Voice Message Service, BT's Voice Bank, Plessey's Ibis Voice Manager, Ferranti's Voice Manager, GEC's Echo, and NTC's Memophone have followed. The voice messaging market has yet to develop, but USA experience indicates that it can offer a very useful service. It may be premature for users to accept the operating principle in the UK, and the extra cost of voice messaging is often difficult to justify.

7.5   <u>Telex</u>

Telex with over 100,000 lines in the UK is still expanding in size. The introduction of Single Channel Voice Frequency (SCVF) operation has opened the way for word processors and other keyboard terminals to access the network via a telex interface and, by using analogue voice frequencies in place of direct current signalling, telex information can be transmitted via the PSTN using electronic mail, Prestel, and other services appropriate for telex management systems.

7.6   <u>New Radio Services</u>

With the release of more VHF frequencies, the DTI has been able to establish a further 20 new mobile radio services in 1984, which will cover all major areas of the UK. The channels lie in the private maritime VHF band.

The 405 black and white TV standard, long since made obsolescent by the introduction of 625 PAL standard colour TV, is now being released for use and will provide many new VHF frequencies. Exploitation of the radio spectrum in the UK for private communication requirements has been greatly hampered by the hitherto unwillingness of the Home Office to release bandwidth.

Cellular radio provides extensive user coverage by repeatedly reutilising a frequency band of radio channels geographically dispersed as a network of cells. This is to feature as a major service in the UK from 1985. Two cellular networks have been licensed and these will connect with the PSTN to permit dial-up access between fixed and mobile stations. Both services were required to start operation by March 1985 and to cover 90% of the UK population by 1990.

Cellnet is the service of TSCR, a joint company owned by BT and Securicor. Racal-Vodafone is the competing service owned by Racal, Millicom and Hambros Bank. Each has a licence to operate lasting 25 years. The system is similar to that used in the USA and is called Total Access Communications System (TACS).

The decision to use this, rather than the Scandinavian Nordic or other European systems, has been criticised as short sighted by opponents who believe that it will restrict export potential and compatibility. It uses the 900MHz frequency band unlike Nordic, which uses 450 MHz.

7.7   Viewdata (Prestel)

Viewdata, named Prestel by BT, was invented in the UK as a cheap method of obtaining information in the home using a standard TV receiver, modem, and dial-up telephone line. Pages of information, held in a data base which can be accessed by the user after making a telephone call, are available from a menu selectable through a keypad associated with the TV and line. Some data is charged for, but much is free as advertising or information services.

Prestel has not been a success story for the home owing to the extra costs involved, and the tendency in the UK not to do 'arm-chair' shopping or access information regularly by this means. It has however been of great benefit to businesses in travel and related services, and for closed user groups. Like several other services which are slow to gain acceptance in the UK, Prestel could take-off when conditions, such as home banking, shopping and education are more readily practiced. The DTI is helping to finance the provision of Prestel in the UK's 7,500 secondary schools, to help pupils gain experience in using modern interactive information systems.

8   LIBERALISATION PROBLEMS

As in the USA, the UK liberalisation programme has not been without its problems and, until all the BS specifications have been published and modified where necessary, interim approval schemes authorised by the DTI are still likely to operate. The Government also intends to set up a body to rationalise specifications so that mandatory requirements are kept as few as possible, and most other requirements are in the form of good practice recommendations with which a supplier is expected to comply, and will ultimately be judged on in the open marketplace by customers. The principal problems which have delayed the arrival of new privately supplied apparatus in the UK telecommunications market place are described below.

Very few switching systems are of indigenous UK design, and most have therefore had to be anglicised from North American, Asian or European mainland designs. In the case of other apparatus such as telex, telephones, data and radio, many more of the designs are of UK origin and there is also less complexity in the specifications.

The delay in compiling specifications has been the result of breaking new ground, the extensive work programme of technical committees, and their staffing from a wide cross-section of industry. The UK network has special requirements for signalling and transmission which have complicated the work.

The standards programme has not been sufficiently well managed to achieve the target timescales. The standards have been written to facilitate a wide range of systems and, as such, incorporate requirements that may not be totally applicable in all cases.

Standards have been written essentially for the existing analogue network. New requirements will need to be considered for digital public and private networks, which are likely to be extensively used in the UK in future and which will include PBX and LAN architectures. The interpretation of the new specifications by suppliers, and even by the test laboratories, has caused considerable difficulty.

The UK standards differ from those aboard in a number of ways, such as transmission levels, which in general have to be higher and to closer tolerances than in the USA. Line length losses and signalling techniques differ, direct inward dialling telephone standards have been revised, safety requirements are complex, and even tones are peculiar to the UK network.

The DTI requires that every system for approval testing must be supported by a UK supplier and a BSI approved maintainer. In the case of systems from abroad, where the UK experience and supplier base is often not well developed, anglicisation problems and modification work often has to take place at arms length with the overseas base. This imposes particular communications difficulties.

Test resources in the UK are inadequate for a large approval test programme, coupled with the delays which are commonplace. Basic system approval of a key system presently involves at least 12 weeks in work stages, whilst a PABX may take as much as six to nine months, and in most cases considerably more. Until 1984, BT was the only approval authority, but now the BSI laboratories are regularly used by suppliers requiring pre-approval testing, as well as for BABT key systems and dealer board testing. BSI is likely also to perform small PBX test work, and other organisations such as the independent Hull City Corporation and Mercury Communications may be required to offer test facilities as part of their licence requirements.

BEAB, whose responsibility is to observe test work, and analyse and evaluate test work reports from the laboratories has, since its formation, been particularly short of resources to handle all approval work. The situation is improving however, and should result in a greater volume of test approval work being managed in future. BABT also has a responsibility to assess and monitor the performance of the suppliers' MDT laboratories conducting approval testing work.

There have been accusations that BT, has acted unfairly:

-	advising customers that certain private equipment was unlikely to gain approval, and offering a BT system in its place

-	cross-subsidising costs between business sectors, such that PBXs could be offered below regular market prices, and connection charges for wiring waived.

The presence of OFTEL should prevent these problems occurring in future.

9   <u>INFORMATION TECHNOLOGY</u>

In 1980, Kenneth Baker, Secretary of State in the Conservative Government elected in 1979, advised the Prime Minister of the vital importance of developing new information based industries in the UK and, as a result, became the world's first Minister for Information Technology. Mr Baker achieved a remarkable revolution in attitude within his area of responsibility at the DTI. As a result, the UK information-technology industry is supported by a carefully devised framework of financial aid and institutional help; yet the results to date have not been very encouraging.

Government spending on IT has risen from £50M in 1979 to £210M in 1984. A special programme of aid, established as the result of the Alvey Directorate report on IT requirements, will involve the spending of £350 on important IT projects. The Government is financing the installation of computers in 33,000 primary and secondary education schools, colleges of further education, and polytechnics. It is computerising the Pay As You Earn (PAYE) tax system using products of the UK computer company ICL.

The UK has the fastest growing microchip industry in Europe, and an increasing number of international IT companies are setting up in Europe. Fibre optics has also had a promising start, although the future of cable services in Britain remains uncertain and has not moved ahead at anything like the pace that was earlier predicted. The UK has a very successful record in software capability and for small companies developing specialised technologies.

Contrasting with this optimistic situation, a mid-1984 report from the

National Economic Development Council (NEDC) painted a gloomy picture. It cited sectors of the IT industry about to collapse owing to lack of investment, skill shortages, and intensifying international competition. Although UK output rose from £2,700M to over £4,000M in only three years, imports of IT goods have increased from 41% to 54%. The IT balance of trade fell from a £89M deficit in 1980 to a projected loss in excess of £1,000M in 1984. Around 40% of employed persons in the UK work in producing, processing, or distributing information, but the numbers employed in the IT industry fell by 10% between 1980 to 1984, and stand at only 120,000 today. As many as 30,000 key jobs in software and technician areas need to be filled, but cannot owing to the worsening skills shortage. The UK share of the IT market has fallen from 10% in 1970 to under 4% in 1984.

The NEDC report predicted that owing to the very small share of IT markets which the UK now has, it can no longer adequately invest either in marketing or production facilities, and that drastic new policies are required by industry and Government to arrest this decline. In the absence of a well defined and implemented national strategy, Britain by 1990 could be reduced to relying upon licensed overseas' supplied technology and on companies which only specialise in particular aspects of IT.

To reverse the trend, measures were called for which would provide:

-       a coordinated training programme for another 30,000 computer-skilled persons

-       more money for research

-       public purchasing to strengthen the civil market rather than concentrating predominently on defence contracts

—	improved means of financing fast growing, medium sized companies, not necessarily seeking to expand their equity base or size.

Clearly, this is an area which the report identifies to be of great national significance and for which urgent and concentrated action is necessary if the UK is to be a strong competitor in the IT market.

9.1   Alvey Directorate

Concerned about the development of fifth generation computers in Japan, the Government commissioned John Alvey, now Director of Research and Development in BT, to study implications and requirements for the UK. In its report, the Alvey Directorate called for massive funds to bring UK technology into line with the developements in other industrial countries. The Directorate has around £350M to spend on projects jointly sponsored with industry over the next five years. Originally recommending that the UK should concentrate on what it was best at, namely software, there has recently been a change of emphasis to include hardware system architecture.

The Directorate comprises five parts which cover: artificial intelligence, knowledge based engineering, man–machine interfaces, software engineering, and very large scale integration.

9.2   <u>ESPRIT</u>

The Commission of the European Communities, of which the UK is a member, in 1984 launched 90 transitional research and development projects as the main phase of a 10 year programme called ESPRIT (European Studies Programme for Research and Development in Information Technology and Telecommunications). The EEC is to commit 200M European Currency Units (ECU), and this investment is to be equally matched by industrial participants in the programme. Total funding amounts to 1.9 billion ECUs. ESPRIT is intended to unify industry, research laboratories and universities in Europe to focus on research into microelectronics, software and advanced information processing in the two main application areas of:

-        office automation systems

-        computer integrated manufacturing.

The objective of ESPRIT is to aid EEC countries in keeping to the forefront of IT in the face of Japanese and North American competition.

9.3   <u>The Office at Home</u>

The extent of the penetration of electronics into homes in Britain has tended to centre on entertainment. Television, video recorders, and high-fidelity record, tape and radio systems account for the majority of the investment.

The personal computer is, however of increasing popularity and the UK, with an installed base of over 1M PCs, leads Europe. This rapid penetration over the last few years has not resulted in any large migration of office work into the home however, and only an estimated 6% of office work is being done at home, and very little of this using computer and telecommunications technology. Yet most predictions for the future offer a scenario which portrays the return of 'cottage industry' to the UK based on computer terminals. One company, Rank Xerox, has run a two-year study with 50 of its staff working out of home using network linked microcomputers.

High transport costs, wasted travel time, expensive office accommodation, and the growing demands of a highly educated work force to regulate hours of work are likely to increase the amount of work done at home. On the other hand relatively few persons have an 'office environment' at home during the working day, free of interruptions and distractions. As terminal and telecommunications costs fall, it will however become increasingly more attractive to operate from home. It is predicted that a complex of systems will be centred in the home of professional persons providing, education, communication, entertainment, energy control, and home services using computer and telecommunications techniques.

9.4   Cable TV Services

The UK presently has four television services: two operated by the British Broadcasting Corporation and two commercial services with advertisements. Several illegal 'private' stations also transmit. Unlike the USA, the UK has until recently seen little demand for cable TV, but the prospects now look more encouraging. Local communities, such as at Greenwich and Milton Keynes, already operate their own services for entertainment. Additional use for viewdata information services and TV shopping is now envisaged.

The Government's plans for cable systems and services was published in April 1983. In November 1983 11 consortia were identified for the issue of broadband licences. Two types of service were envisaged: 'tree and branch' and 'switched star'. Commercial undertakings operating broadcast serices tend to favour the simple 'tree and branch' network using coaxial cable which could be installed now, whilst BT considers the intelligent 'switched star' network to be more flexible and economic for interactive services, providing and controlling these in accordance with individual requirements.

One issue which is commanding increasing interest is whether the proliferation of personal computers will provide the base for extensive interactive services, such as computer interconnection, database delivery, and software downloading. These could predominate in place of transactional services, such as home banking and home shopping that have not materialised.

There is little to report in UK Cable TV at present and clearly the viability of such services remains unproven. Fibre optic transmission is favoured for wideband CATV service, but coaxial cable represents the current technology, although its installation costs are high and it would be expensive to install in UK urban areas.

10   <u>CONCLUSIONS</u>

The UK is nearing the completion of the Conservative Government's plans to liberalise telecommunications and privatise British Telecommunications. Despite many problems and teething troubles, the programme has, on the whole, been successful in providing the UK with a range of innovative telecommunications products and services. The range still falls short of what is available in the US market, but the UK programme has been conducted over the relatively short period of four years and has avoided some of the pitfalls encountered in the USA's liberalisation programme.

The implications for the user and UK suppliers are, however, less well defined. Having been protected for so long under the BT monopoly, many users are not well equipped to make the many decisions required as to which products to buy, from whom they should buy them, and who should install and maintain them. There is confusion also about which technologies to adopt, for example: key systems or small PBX, digital or analogue systems, third or fourth generation switching systems, PABX or LAN, private supplier or BT, private or public networks, packet or circuit switched data, etc. The list of options is extensive and has resulted in a lucrative growth of conferences, publications, and consultancy work.

Uncertainty also exists as to whether a saturation effect will occur in about 1986, when the range of products approved for network attachment could exceed requirements, and the market shares of suppliers may fall below viable volumes. Other fears concern unemployment where, for example, the policy of BT to equip its network with System X exchanges will, according to its Engineering

Union, result in huge job cuts owing to the reduced maintenance requirements of electronic exchanges, cheap expendable telephones, more reliable fibre optic and plastic covered cables, and massive reductions in clerical jobs lost by the installation of more and more computers. With well over 3M persons already unemployed in the UK, further large cuts in the labour force will be opposed by Unions.

The net effect of liberalisation however is likely to be product improvements in price/performance terms, better service and more choice. On the IT front, the future is less certain, because this is already a substantially liberalised worldwide market, dominated by giant industries which are not UK based. The UK will have to decide for example on whether it intends to have an indigenous chip manufacturing capacity, at least one major computer manufacturer, a hardware design and manufacturing capability, as well as software expertise, an R and D programme for expert systems, and 5th generation computers which can make inroads into competitive, markets, such as the Japanese and USA.

With its limited resources, the UK must carefully assess and select a limited number of projects in which to invest capital and manpower, whilst increasing and improving the training of engineers and scientists to fill the many vacancies which exist. Given that inroads can be made into these areas, the brighter future of liberalised telecommunications could be complemented by an invigorated IT industry with real growth prospects. The possible threat of renationalisation of telecommunications does not appear to be a strong possibility, owing to the present low standing of the Labour Party opposition in the UK. BT privatisation and share offering geared to the public sector will buffer against any possible renationalisation measures. In this present climate the DTI will continue to stimulate the development of the British IT and telecommunications industries.

11   BIBLIOGRAPHY

British Standards Institution

British Standards for Telecommunications.

Code of Practice for PBX Accommodation and Installation.

Publications Manager, 101 Pentonville Road, London NW1 9ND

Scheme for Assessment of Telecommunications Apparatus
Maintainers

Hemel Hempstead Centre, Maylands Avenue, Hemel
Hempstead, Herts, HP2 4SQ

British Approvals Board for Telecommunications

BABT Organisation and Procedures Guide.

Approval Mark Regulations.

Approval Symbol Regulations.

Mark House, The Green, 9-11 Queens Road, Hersham, Walton
on Thames, Surrey.

Department of Trade and Industry

Interim Code of Practice for PBX Installation.

Value Added Network Licence.

Technical Requirements for PBX Extension Telephones

The Future of Telecommunications - Government Policy
Explained

Telecommunication Division, 1-19 Victoria Street, London,
SW1H 0ET

Her Majesty's Stationery Office

Telecommunications Bill 1981

Telecommunications Act 1984

Liberalisation of the Use of British Telecommunications Networks

Regulation of British Telecommunications Profitability.

General Liberalisation Information

Ringing the Changes (periodic publication)

Marketing Solutions Ltd, 70 Salisbury Road, Queen's Park, London NW6 6NU

* The Telecommunications Handbook. The 1984 Telecommunications Act and all related areas including the responsibilities of the DTI, Home Office and Oftel.

* The British Telecommunications Act 1981. Covers in detail the provisions for liberalisation, the powers of the Secretary of State, BT charges, finance, assets, and all other details of this Act.

* The British Telecom Licence 140 p. This sets out the operating conditions for BT, covering definitions, interpretations, provision of services, codes of practice, and all the ground rules of the licence.

* The Telecommunications Act 1984. Covers in detail every aspect and requirement of the Act and the responsibilities of BT, OFTEL, and all other parties affected by the legislation.

*   The Telecommunications Trade Directory. Lists 800 organisations in the industry with their addresses, and contains articles covering a wide range of telecommunications subjects. It covers descriptions of all types of telecommunications equipment supplied and services available.

*   Telematic Society – A Challenge for Tomorrow. James Martin 240p Prentice Hall. Designed to promote thought on the impact of communications technology on industry, education, the working week and costs. It also provides useful insight into value added services'.

*   Directory of Telecommunications S J Aries 330 p. Clear definitions of the many terms used in telecommunications.

*   Buying a PABX – How to make a Sensible Choice. R Camrass 100 p. Covers every aspect of the technology, specification and facilities required in order to choose a modern electronic PABX.

*   Telephony Today and Tomorrow. DN Chorofas 290 p.
    Ideal for the director or general manager who requires a sound briefing on modern telecommunication services and technology.

*   Telecommunications Liberalisation – Value Added Network Services.
    Transcript of the Proceedings of the London seminar of Novemeber 1984.

All the above marked * are available from CommEd, Communications House, 137, Dulwich Road, London, SE24 ONG.

COMMUNICATE monthly journal 1983/84. A Series of six articles on British Telecom which describe the transformation of BT in its approach to becoming a private company. COMMUNICATE, for the Telecommunications User. Link House Magazines (Croydon) Ltd, Dingwall Ave, Croydon CR9 9DX, UK.

ISDN. A Description of the British Telecom. Integrated Services Digital Network 1984. Available free of charge from BT's Network Strategy Department, London.

CHAPTER 36.

JAPAN; RE-STRUCTURING THE INFORMATION
INDUSTRY FOR A CHANGING JAPANESE SOCIETY

PROFESSOR MITSURU YOKOI

Kogakuin University, Tokyo, Japan

1. Introduction

One of the great difficulties in making a policy is to forecast probable social impacts which the policy decision will bring in. As the information processing and telecommunications technologies are developing unprecedentally quickly, this difficulty is exaggerated.

The Japanese government has taken policies of stimulating industrial activities only, for examples, research, marketing, production and operation. The Ministry of International Trade and Industry, MITI, and the Ministry of Post and Telecommunications, MPT, are two concerned governmental agencies. Japanese tradition and culture[1][2] naturally underlie their ways of making policy. The "vertical structure" of the society* and "life-long employment" should cause the two ministries to hold their own positions independently[3].

* Note: C. Nakane describes its various aspects in her book by
         such words as vertical principle, vertical relation,
         vertical order, vertical organization, vertical links,
         vertical hierarchy and vertical structure.

As the information processing and telecommunications technologies penetrate extensively into the society, both agencies are strengthening powers and taking influential positions.

Because of them, a transition in making policy begins to emerge. They recognize serious social implications of both technologies.

They tend to take a unified and integrated approach. In addition, enterprises in other industrial sectors, such as transportation, energy, finance, trading and local governmental agencies, are inclined to have concerns on the technologies to jump out of present recessive situation. Now, the society, as a whole, seems to conceive that a comprehensive view on the information society is mandatory.

In the following two sections the author will describe the governmental policies and activities in the information and telecommunications sectors separately. Then, in the final sections social implications will be outlined by introducing words, "information-oriented" (or "informatized") and "internationalization". Readers will be able to grasp a general idea on the recent policy development in Japan. In the reference, materials for further reading will be listed to help understanding it more profoundly.

2. Policy for Information Industries

2.1. MITI's position and laws [4]-[7]

The Ministry of International Trade and Industry, MITI, one of the most influential governmental agencies, has taken various steps towards promoting domestic industries. The information industries, including equipment and software manufacturers and information service providers, are of course not excluded but rather nurtured most carefully.

The MITI's initial step was to enact the Ad-hoc Law of Electronic Industry Promotion, Denshin-ho, in 1957. It was the basic law for electronic industries, demonstrating a guideline for their research and development, plant expansion and manufacturing process improvement. The Ministry formed two divisions in it to realize ideas of the law; Electronic Industry Division and Electric Communication Machine Division were made in the former Heavy Industry Bureau, which is now named as Machine and Information Industry Bureau. Here, the name, the Heavy Industry, implys that such heavy industries as of steel, ship and automobile were far more important than electronic ones in that period. However, some leaders in the industry circle who foresaw importance of electronic industries, initiated to let the government take the step.

To coordinate with the governmental decision domestic electronic industries established two supporting organizations: Japan Electronic Industry Development Association, JEIDA, in 1958 and Japan Electronic computer Company, JECC, in 1961. The former aims at exchanging information and views among domestic manufacturers along the guideline indicated by the Law, while the latter at funding for the computer rental system.

The second step was taken around 1970, when Japan has grown to a leading industrial country, symbolized by the Expo '70 in Osaka. It was also when the third-generation computer, represented by IBM 360, was in boom

and the time-sharing computer service was coming into
business with telecommunications circuits. More leaders
in the government and industries felt that the information
service providers as well as the electronic equipment
manufacturing industries should play a leading role in
near future, and take the place of the heavy industries
that had greatly contributed to increase the gross
national product. The Ministry enacted two ad-hoc laws,
the Promotion Action for Particular Electronic and Machine
Industries, briefly called Kiden-ho, in 1971 and the
Information Technology Promotion Agency and its Related
Matters, briefly called Joshin-ho in 1970. While the
former, Kiden-ho, aims at promoting hardware manufacturing
industries as the continuation of Denshin-ho, the latter,
Joshin-ho is new, mainly assisting software suppliers and
information service providers, both of which began to grow
at that time. Two external organizations were formed
around 1970, Japan Information Processing Development
Center, JIPDEC, in 1967 and Information-technology
Promotion Agency, IPA, in 1970. The former is not
directly related to the two laws but to a conflict[3]
that happened at that time between the two sectors of
information processing and telecommunications. Consequently, two ministries, MITI, as well as the Ministry
of Post and Telecommunications, have subsidized it
jointly to promote information processing activities[8].
On the other hand, MITI has subsidized the latter, IPA,
exclusively to promote software development and distribution, and guarantee debts of software suppliers and
information service providers.

In 1978, a new ad-hoc law for the electronic and

mechanical industries, the Promotion Action for Particular Machine and Information Industries, briefly called Kijo-ho, was enacted to succeed the ad-hoc law, Kiden-ho, with minor modifications. It aims at upgrading machine manufacturing technologies. The MITI's position is now based on the two laws, Kijo-ho and Joshin-ho.

2.2. "Vertical structure" and principle

The above two basic laws, under the MITI's administration, have successfully worked to stimulate developing new technologies, manufacturing new products and services and, further, to provide financial assistances for industries, directly and indirectly. However, questions may arise: how do they work actually and why can they work successfully? The answer should come from a "vertical structure" of the Japanese society that MITI has maintained not only with the information industry but also with other industries.

The structure has three key elements; making national consensus in several committees where most relevant industries' leaders attend, feeding direct and indirect financial assistances from MITI through external agencies to industrial sectors, and maintaining informal contacts between industrial leaders and government staff.

The most influential committees in the information industry sector are the Electronic Industry Council and Industry Structure Council. Both work as advisory groups for the Minister. The chairmen and members are selected carefully with delicate balance among leading persons in industries, academic circles and, sometimes, retired government staff. If conclusions to be drawn in the

Table 1.   Reports issued by the Councils

Date	Title
Mar., 1966	Actions to strengthen international competitive power of electronic computer industries
May, 1969	Actions to promote information processing activities and information processing industries' development
May, 1971	Advices to promote industrial "informatization"
Sep., 1974	Targets and actions for "informatization" and information industry
Jul., 1976	Forecasting "informatization" process and information industry in 1985
Jun., 1981	Targets and actions for "informatization" and information industry in the 1980s
Dec., 1983	Strategic actions to improve basis for sound and smooth development of "informatization" (intermediate)

council are likely to be serious, not only government officers, powerful politicians but also key industrial leaders scrutinize them discreetly. However, once MITI decides items to be discussed and members to attend the council, discussions normally go on smoothly and conclusions are powerful, sometime persuading, although the conclusions are not always explicitly stated. The two councils have issued several reports, as shown in Table 1.

The principle, which the councils have concluded as national consensus, is outlined as follows.

The information industry, which should play a central role to institute the information society, will have to take a strategic position at the very core of the industrially restructuring process, because it has three distinguishing features. First, the information industry is itself material-saving, pollution-free and highly value-added, so that it is the most representative and leading in due course of development towards the knowledge-intensive post-industry society. Second, the information industry is a high-technology industry. Technologies that the information industry has developed could be applied not only to electronic industries but also mechanical, chemical and other ones. Third, the information industry has grown quickly and is expected to grow with a more accelerated rate. Therefore, a sound development of the information industry is a must, to upgrade national welfare and maintain a steady economic growth.

Although MITI provides an amount of funds through a variety of subsidiary entities to the information industry, the total is not large enough to have the

information industry take a risk for new technical
developments (see Table 2). However, MITI has authority
or sometimes power to persuade the information industry
to go toward a goal, even if there is only a sort of
tacit consensus. This is quite Japanese. The "vertical
structure" of the society, "life-long employment" and
the traditional working attitude in group may help to
advance it successfully.

2.3.   Activities[9]

        Within the "vertical structure" of the society, and
based upon the principle, as described in 2.2, MITI and
the information industry have taken various actions
cooperatively. Their prime and common target was to
protect domestic computer manufactures in the domestic
market from U.S-funded ones, such as IBM, UNIVAC and
others, which have been stationed in Japan since the
end of the war. Even in the 1970s, when the Japanese
economy arrived at a mature stage, the domestic computer
market was dominated by U.S-funded suppliers. Let me
describe some actions briefly. .

Technical development

        In 1971, when the computer manufacturers had to face
the 50%-liberalization of foreign capital investment under
pressure from the U.S government, MITI persuaded six
domestic leading manufacturers to make up three groups
each of which could receive an amount of subsidy to
develop one new family of computers. This subsidy,
terminated in 1976, helped them to manufacture the three
families of computers, the M family for Fujitsu and

Hitachi, the ACOS one for NEC and Toshiba and the COMO one for Mitsubishi and Oki.

Since then, a similar subsidizing system has worked for the three targets; developments of ultra-large-scale integrated circuits, operating system and new peripheral units. The amounts of the subsidy for the three targets are shown in Table 3. The subsidizing system has been taken up with due consideration on the 100%-liberalization schedule of foreign investment and trade in 1975 and of information service providing in 1976. Another line of subsidizing is for a new research project, the fifth-generation computer project[10][11], which started in 1982 and will continue until 1991.

The other line has worked for big projects since 1966. The government provides funds to risky R & D projects that need a long period to finalize and a large amount of fund to invest. Now, eight projects are going on. Two of them are for the micro-electronics industry; super-computer for scientific applications, and opto-measurement and control system. The items and the total budgets are shown in Table 4.

In addition to the above, MITI has subsidized soft-ware development and distribution through IPA, which was founded in 1970 under the law, Joshin-ho. The Agency's tasks are: to subsidize development of advanced and general-purpose computer programs, to purchase and distribute such programs, and to survey various applications of information processing. The annual expenses are shown in Table 5, which shows that the governmental subsidy is decreasing, while funds from banks and beneficiaries complement. The 5-year project that IPA

Table 2.   MITI's Budget, Loans and Tax Preference
          for Information Industry

Million Yen

Item	FY 1983	FY 1984
Budget		
Fifth-generation computer project	2,723	5,124
Super-computer project	1,567	2,248
New-media community project	-	96
Medical system project	171	119
Information-technology Promotion Agency	2,620	2,482
International Cooperation for "Informatization"	110	207
Data base and information providers	-	12
Survey for "Informatization"	-	22

Loan

Government Loan via Development Bank of Japan to:

a) JECC		
b) New computer development projects	55,000	Less than 65,000
c) New-media development projects		
d) Electronic machine industries	11,000	11,000

NOTE
1M Yen = $4050 = £3078 (June 1985)

Item	FY 1983	FY 1984
<u>Undertaking Bond for Information Processing Promotion</u>	4,000	3,500
<u>Government Loan via Small Enterprise Loan Corp.</u>	Less than 75,000	Less than 75,000
<u>Loans for "Informatization" Promotion for Small Enterprises</u>		
a) via Small Enterprise Loan Corp.	–	Less than 156,900
b) via People's Finance Corp.	–	Less than 164,500

<u>Tax Incentive</u>

7% of Payment for Information Processing Facilities is tax-deductable or 30% of Special Depreciation Treatment is applied in case of medium- and small-enterprises

Table 3. Subsidies for Computer Developments

Million Yen

FY Target	1976	1977	1978	1979	1980	1981	1982	1983	Total
Ultra LSI	3,500	8,640	10,052	6,906					29,098
OS				1,450	4,910	5,150	4,986	2,360	18,856
Peripheral				250	875	1,050	630	500	3,305

Table 4. MITI   Big Projects

Item	Total Budget (Billion Yen)
1. Compound Production System with Super-quality Laser Applications	13.0
2. Submarine Oil Production System	15.0
3. Opto-Measurement and Control System	18.0
4. Fundamental Chemicals Production with Carbon-dioxide as Basic Material	15.0
5. Super-computer for Scientific Applications	23.0
6. Manganese Nodule Mining System	22.0
7. Automatic Sewing System	N.A.
8. Robot in Extremely hazardous Environment	N.A.

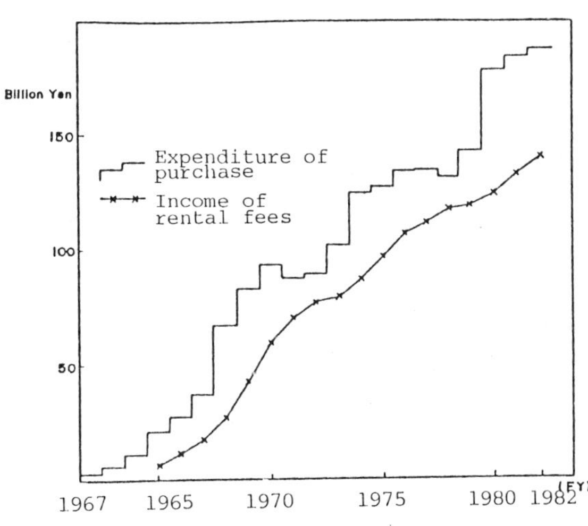

Fig. 1

JECC's Income and Expense

Table 5. IPA's Total Expense, Subsidy and Funds

Billion Yen

Item \ FY	1970	1971	1972	1973	1974	1975	1976	1977	1978	1979	1980	1981	1982	1983	1984
Total Expense	0.30	0.46	0.49	0.95	1.18	1.54	1.99	2.33	2.61	3.05	3.38	3.37	3.46	2.95	2.68
Subsidy	0.30	0.40	0.37	0.79	1.00	1.32	1.73	2.05	2.28	2.58	2.78	2.66	2.62	2.08	1.71
Own Funds	0	0.06	0.12	0.16	0.18	0.22	0.26	0.28	0.33	0.47	0.60	0.71	0.84	0.87	0.97

has supported since 1981 is aimed at developing software
maintenance technologies.

Modernization of Production Facilities and its Finance

The information industry could borrow preferencial
funds from the Development Bank of Japan to upgrade
their production facilities (see Table 2). Further,
industries, other than the information industry, could
also apply to similar funds if they intend to automate
their plants or modernize them by applying computers or
some information processing units (see also Table 2).

The other governmental finance is to provide funds
for the computer rental system, which JECC has managed
since 1961. The total money flows are as shown in Fig.1.

3. Telecommunications Policy

3.1.Monopoly and three organizations[3]

As in most European countries, such as France, Germany
and U.K, the telecommunications in Japan have also been
monopolistic. The governmental agencies have led telecommunications development, since 1885, when the ministry
was founded. Even after two telecommunications operation
agencies, Nippon Telegraph and Telephone Public Corporation, NTT, and Oversea Telegraph and Telephone Company,
KDD, were formed in 1952 and 1953, their monopolistic
nature has been maintained mainly by two laws, the Public
Telecommunications Law and the Wire Telecommunications
Law. NTT owns and operates the telecommunications facilities and provides telegraph, telex, and telephone services
domestically, while KDD does them internationally. The

Table 6.   NTT's Telephone Subscribers

(Ten thousand or %)

Item \ FY	1952	1965	1970	1975	1980
Ordinary Telephone Subscriber	155	730	1,517	3,034	3,849
For residential use	10	185	683	1,926	2,619
For business use	145	545	834	1,108	1,230
Subscribers in a large building	(Start in 1968)		5	21	35
Subscribers in a local group	(Start in 1964)	9	118	115	21
Total	155	739	1,640	3,170	3,905
Rate per 100 population	1.8	7.5	15.7	28.2	33.3

Table 7.   KDD's International Calls

Ten thousands

Item \ FY	1953	1965	1970	1975	1980
Telegraph	343	502	582	525	334
Telex	(Start in 1956)	110	436	1,623	3,798
Telephone	19	52	218	857	2,343

Ministry of Post and Telecommunications, MPT, is the
regulation agency not only for telecommunications, but
also for broadcasting and uses of radio frequencies.
However, as the two telecommunications operation agencies
are formed out of the Ministry, it is quite natural that
the three entities, MPT, NTT and KDD, have co-operated
well even after separation. The laws support them.
Its underlying principle is that the best public telecommunications services are provided only through a
monopolistic organization that owns and operates the
whole telecommunications facilities exclusively.

Given this principle, both NTT and KDD have quickly
expanded their telecommunications facilities, mostly
telephonic ones, to meet tremendous demands[12]-[14].
In 1978, NTT successfully completed its consecutive
5-year development projects which targets were to reduce
customers waiting for telephone installation to the
minimum and to complete the nationwide subscriber dialing
telephone system. KDD has had similar projects to offer
better services internationally, which are still growing.
Both performances are distinguished, as shown roughly in
Table 6 and 7.

While the telecommunications laws allow NTT and KDD
to own the public telecommunications plants monopolis-
tically, ownership and operation of private telecommunications facilities is not so restrictive. Not only
governmental agencies but also a variety of private
enterprises, large or small, could own and operate their
facilities, if they use them only for their own purposes.
Radio communications are used by the police department,
fire agencies, and private agencies of aviation, trans-

Table 8. Private Wire Communication Applications

Sector / FY	Agriculture & Fishery	Manufacturing	Service	Sales	Transportation	Construction	Gas, Water	Others	Total
1978	348	243	100	65	79	70	32	658	1,595
1979	328	241	100	64	80	71	35	587	1,506
1980	316	243	91	73	69	51	47	662	1,552
1981	311	242	97	73	72	56	51	652	1,554

portation, fishery, gas, water, electricity, news, whose
radio stations amount to more than 2 million, about 87%
of the total, as of 1984. The private wire communication
applications are more diverse, as in Table 8.

   Although these systems are normally small and local,
owners or operators have to report them to MPT. Further,
if parties intend either to interconnect each other or
with the NTT's network, or to let "other" parties[15] use
the systems, whether radio or wire, they must obtain MPT's
certifications. In other words, the telecommunications
service provision must be monopolistic. The service
providers are only NTT and KDD, whom MPT, therefore,
should regulate. Any person can own and operate his
telecommunications facilities but must not let "other"
parties   use them as his business. It is the policy.
Therefore, exceptions, if any, depend upon to what extent
"other" parties are public or "specified". For example,
if "other" persons are "specified" as employees of a
company who own and operate its telecommunications
system, and they use the system only for the company's
private business, the company does not need the certification. However, if there is, for example, a coin-
telephone booth in the system, "unspecified" persons
can call any of employees. Then, the MPT's certification
comes. However, an argument could naturally come out
on the words, "specified" or "public" instead of "other",
as there still remains uncertainty. In fact, data
communication, as it penetrates into the society,
 stimulates arguments.   Let me describe it later in 3.3.

3.2. Manufacturing and supplying

Even if the ownership of private telecommunications facilities is not so restrictive, the NTT's and KDD's facilities are dominant, as any communications are inherently not limited among "specified" persons. Therefore manufacturers heavily rely on both operating organizations, particularly on NTT, as those in most industrialized countries. For a period, after the war, MITI and NTT cooperatively encouraged poor domestic suppliers of telecommunications equipment and cable. MITI played a central role as it did for domestic computer manufactures. Denshin-ho, enacted in 1957, was to promote electronic equipment manufacturing, including telecommunications equipment. On the other hand, NTT supported it through its procurement policy. Most leading persons thought it favorable to keep closed relationship between NTT and its family manufacturers like that between AT&T and Western Electric Co. The traditional feature of the Japanese society, the "vertical structure" which is a kind of paternalism, emphasises the relationship.

The NTT's procurement policy had never been announced to the public in papers or other forms. Its custom was not to purchase equipment through the competitive bidding but through negotiation, as done by most leading telecommunications operating agencies in industrialized nations. Reasons are common for all of them. For example as telecommunications equipment and cable need to be standardized ones that can work as components of the nationwide networks, intensive negotiations are mandatory before contracts. As NTT's fund was flowing

to the family manufacturers, NTT could substantially
assist them to expand their production capacities and,
even, their research and development capability through
the NTT's Laboratory.

For a period of time, from 1950 to 1980, NTT's top
leaders could examine the family suppliers' capabilities,
by evaluating their final products, and could allocate
amounts of purchase orders among them with far-sighted
and prudent considerations. It was successful. It
helped domestic manufacturers to stand on their feet,
as far as telecommunications equipment and cable are
concerned[16].

NTT cut into the on-line computer service market in
1966. NTT intended to purchase even computers and their
related products only from the family manufacturers that
had supplied telecommunications equipment to NTT.

Outside of the solid telecommunications party and
NTT's family manufacturers, there are dominant powers in
the computer sector, such as MITI, IBM Japan, UNIVAC and
others. In addition, pressure came from the U.S government to open up the Japanese telecommunication market
under the GATT Agreement, around 1980. NTT and its
family manufacturers had to suddenly face fierce environments, domestically as well as internationally.

3.3. Open-door policy in telecommunications sector

The telecommunications sector has taken three actions
to produce more liberal and open environments.

First, MPT and NTT have decided to let its customers
use the public telecommunications circuits more freely by
relaxing the restrictive term of the "specified" persons.

Accordingly, in 1971, the law was revised to allow NTT's customers to use the public telephone and telex network for data communication more freely than before[3][15]. The restrictions on "shared" use and "third-party" use were relaxed to some extent. Later, in 1982, further relaxation was enacted, as the computer and telecommunications systems had merged more tightly. For example one computer connected to the public network can work to accept, process and transfer data toward some destinations, even if toward "unspecified" persons. Via a computer, several data communication systems may be interconnected to provide comprehensive services to their terminals.

Second, finally in 1981, NTT accepted the open procurement. The new procurement procedures have good agreement to the GATT ones, which include the competitive bidding and the negotiated purchase after open advertisement. Although the NTT's new procurement policy had worked smoothly since then, another reaction may come, because the amount of NTT's purchase orders from U.S suppliers is not yet grown up to a level that they expected and, further, a huge trade deficit exists.

Third, the most drastic change has finally come. It is to introduce competition into the telecommunications service market[17]-[19]. Two new laws were established in December 1984. They are: the Law of Telecommunications Service Agencies and the Law of Nippon Telegraph and Telephone Company. The former substitutes the Public Telecommunications Law, while the latter the Law of Nippon Telegraph and Telephone Public Corporation. Both laws aim at allowing privately owned telecommunic-

ations service providers to set up in the domestic as
well as international market and, further, change the
former NTT Public Corporation to a joint-stock company.
The new NTT company will start in April 1985. The direct
motives which stimulate to make a national consensus of
enacting the two laws are: people's willingness to make
a variety of computer networks in and among various
industrial sectors, which are called here as value-add
networks, VANs, and various industries' intention to
enter into the technology-intensive and rapidly growing
telecommunications service market[20].

In addition, the Ad-hoc Committee of Governmental
Reform, which was working from 1981 to 1983, concluded
in 1983 that less regulatory regimes are preferable to
reduce the government's financial deficit and to promote
competition, even in the telecommunications service
market[21]. Thus, the principle of service monopoly
which had worked since a telecommunications law was
enacted in 1874, finally terminated.

3.4. Competition in telecommunications service market[18]-[20]

Now, let me describe more about the two new laws to
demonstrate conditions under which competition will
take place.

The targets of both the laws are stated as follows.
To meet diverse and sophisticated demands for telecommunications services in future, the unified service-
providing system in existence could not work appropriately. In order that the telecommunications services
play a more leading role in the coming advanced information society, telecommunications themselves should

take a multilayered form. Consequently, it is mandatory
to realize more efficient and vigorous business environments in the whole telecommunications sector, so that
the principle of competition, rather than monopoly, is
the most effective in the telecommunications service
market. Further, to make NTT function more actively
under such circumstances and to produce genuine
competitive environments, NTT should take the form of
a company with more freedom in its business activities,
rather than of the public corporation.

The main items in the laws are as follows. First,
the Law of Telecommunication Service Agencies classifies
the service providing agencies into the two categories;
the primary and secondary classes. The primary-class
agency is one that owns its telecommunications circuit
facilities, while the secondary one does not, renting
circuits from one of the primary-class agencies. The
secondary-class agency is sub-classified into the
special and ordinary ones according to its business
features The special secondary-class agency is one
that provides nation-wide, fundamental or international
services, while the ordinary one is not, providing only
regional and auxiliary services.

Secondly, the law specifies that MPT has the
authority to regulate the primary-class agency, while
it only accepts registration and reporting from the
special and ordinary secondary-class agencies respectively.
Its regulation power on them becomes less in that order.
For example, the tariff system is subject to the MPT's
approval in case of the primary-class, but it is not,
in case of the secondary-class.

Thirdly, any terminal, including an initially connected telephone set, can be customer-owned but is subject to a third party's approval. Fourthly, the Ministry reserves the right to order interconnection between various systems, if required, to ensure fair competitions among service providers. Fifthly, foreign investment to the primary-class service provider is restricted to be no more than one-third of the total. However, no restriction is placed on foreign investments to the secondary-class.

On the other hand, the Law of Nippon Telegraph and Telephone Company provides the new company with more management decision power. For examples, the new company, one of the primary-class agencies, can invest in other business more freely. Although its legal obligation is to provide not only the conventional telephone service but also other sophisticated telecommunications services universally and extensively, the new company may be absolved from it in a region where a competitor begins to provide the same service as NTT has done.

Both the laws are so revolutionary that they have been argued extensively in many quarters. No one could convince others that only the laws can form appropriate competitive environments in the telecommunications service market.

Members of the House of the Representative summarized several resolutions during their arguments. For examples, they are: the resale business should be prohibited, the government has to make up a law which can help promote information-communication industries, and the new NTT company should not enter telecommunications equipment

manufacturing business for the time being. Further, the
Law of the Telecommunications Service Agencies should be
reviewed within next three years.

A new era will start in April, 1985, under the new
telecommunications laws, to institute a competitive
telecommunications service market, which the Japanese
has never experienced before.

4. Policy Toward the Information Society

4.1."Information-oriented" ("informatized") and "Inter-
    nationalized" society

Some newly-invented Japanese words represent the
people's dream, target, or expectation, which are, for
example "information-oriented" (or "informatized"),
"internationalized", "senior-included", and "slower
economic growth". They imply changes and trends in the
Japanese society. These words have appeared on popular
TV programs, newspapers or magazines, and, then, penetrated into the society in fashion. They may make the
Japanese people have ideas, concepts or sometimes feelings,
which underlie their policy-making process. The words
may help the people to constitute consensus, which
normally works as a powerful basis in policy-making.

The two words, the "information-oriented" (or
"informatized") and "internationalized", among them are
most well-known and long-standing, like slogans of the
society. The word, "information-oriented", appeared in
the Dr. Y. Hayashi's book, "Information-oriented Society",
in 1970[22]. He indicated in it that the Japanese
society of mono-value, having had particular emphasis

on its economic activity, will turn toward that of poly-value, as information gains its relative importance among others. The word, "internationalized", came in around 1970. As the Japanese increasingly goes abroad and accepts aliens at the home country, the word has penetrated increasingly into society.

These two words appear even in governmental documents. Let me examine them in two key documents, by MITI's and MPT's consulting committees where discussions were made on their information and communication policy for the 1980s.

In the MITI report in 1981[6], the council's members have summarized their conclusions into eight items, to answer questions from the Minister, "what positions the "informatization" and the information industry should hold and what policy the government should take for them in the 1980s?" The eight items, listed below, may imply their common ideas, targets and underlying principles, though implicitly. They are; deep and broad penetration of the "informatization" into the society, the "informatization" that is a necessity for the MITI's target formation, vigorous economic activities with comfortable lives, information industries which lead others in the 1980s, promotion of the "informatization" and information industries' activities as a part of infrastructure investment, improvement of the basis for the "information-oriented" society, promoting the most advanced technologies that should play leading roles in the world, and active contributions to the world-wide "information-oriented" society.

In the MPT document[19], the committee members
have noted social trends in connection with telecommunications development, by listing four items. They are:
major technical advances, transition to "slower economic
growth", more "information-oriented" society and progress
in international interdependency.

These items, listed above, should indicate what
policy the Japanese will tend to take in the information
and telecommunications sectors, though it may take time
to reach concrete and actual policy-making. However,
most leaders are convinced that more involvement in
information-dependent activities, rather than traditional
large-scale and efficient manufacturing ones, is essential
for more prosperity and happiness.

4.2. New-media community and tele-topia projects[23]-[24]

In December 1983, three subcommittees of the Industry
Structure Council issued an interim report to show
practical actions to be taken. The members concluded,
by introducing a new word, the "secondary information-
oriented revolution", that the "informatization" is
penetrating more broadly and deeply, not only into
industrial circles as before but also individual lives.
It should provide a variety of benefits more to individual
personal lives. They emphasized three items; "new-media"
as a social infrastructure, computer security and legal
protection of software. Here, the "new-media" means
advanced computer-communication systems, such as satellite
communication, video-tex, cable television, computer
networks, local area network etc. for voice, data,

facsimile and video transmission. A remarkable point
in it is, however, that they have shown concern about social
impacts of telecommunications as well as information
processing services on the whole society, in addition
to industries, such as computer manufacturers and
computer service providers. MITI has proposed a new
project, called the "new-media" community, which is now
going on to promote the "information-oriented" activities,
not only in industrial sectors but also social sectors,
such as educational, medical and welfare activities, and
individual lives. The MITI's policy is gradually changing in setting its target, from industry sectors only to
the whole society and from leading industries to local
communities.

On the other hand, in April, 1984, MPT also accepted
an interim report, titled as "Toward local community
development with new-media", from a Minister's advice
group, the "Tele-topia" Consultative Committee. The word,
"Tele-topia", is the hyphened and compressed two words,
telecommunications and utopia, meaning that the "new-
media" that includes information processing and telecommunications systems should assist promoting industrial
as well as social activities in local communities, which
will converge to a utopia eventually. MPT intends to
subsidize projects of local communities along the line
of the Committee's advice . Fortyseven local-state
governments have proposed one hundred and seven projects
that will implement advanced systems, to get benefits of
the "new-media". MPT will select about ten projects
among them in the initial quarter of 1985. The projects
to be selected are expected to produce representative

Table 9.　Probable Tele-topia Projects

Name	Location	Operation Agency	Plan or Target
Port in future 21	Yokohama Beside its port	Residential Town Public Corp. Kanagawa Local Government Yokohama City Government Mitsubishi Real-estate Co.	To form an international, cultural, and high-tech urban area in a newly-produced 186-ha sea-side area
Techno-port, Osaka	Osaka and its port	Osaka City Osaka Local Government Others	To construct an information and telecommunication center like that in New York
Micon-city Development	Kawasaki	Kawasaki City Microcomputer Industry Union	To produce a microcomputer industry center with diverse functions; technical development, education, production, and advertisement
Chiba New-media Town	Chiba	Chiba Local Government Chiba City Government Residential Town Public Corp. Local Industry Circle	To form a new local community with new-media
Kansai Academic Town	Kyoto, Osaka and Nara	Three Local Governments	To make up three nearby blocks for education, research and high-tech and to organize them coordinately

local "new-media" networks each of which can function to upgrade local industrial and social activities and lead their further penetration throughout the nation. Examples of probable projects are shown in Table 9.

4.3. Policy and society to come

Distinguishing features in making policy in the 1980s are: comprehensiveness in technology and impacts on society. Both ministries, MITI and MPT, understand technologies for information processing and telecommunications appropriately[26][27][28]. They are increasingly concerned with total systems or integrated networks that will extend globally, rather than on individual technologies and manufacturing. Both ministries have begun to pay more attention on the social impact of the microelectronics than before. They tend to study relationships between the "information-oriented" activities and social (r)evolution more seriously and vigorously than systems or networks themselves. The words, "new-media community" and "tele-topia" imply a trend.

The governmental policy is gradually converging to an unified target; to maximize the total benefit in the whole society, rather than to distribute them in particular sectors. Then, questions may arise; where will the Japanese society go?   Will they still intend to maintain tradition, even after the information society comes? The author hopes that policy may change the traditional "vertical structure" so that the society will be able to accept heterogeneous value or culture, instead of encouraging it to remain mono-valued or mono-cultured.

The two words in fashion, "information-oriented" and
"internationalized", indicate a change. National consensus seems to direct the policy toward restructuring
the whole society to be more open, international and
multiform. An inherent character of the information
processing and telecommunications networks, forcing
themselves to grow horizontally beyond the barriers of
time and distance, will cause to help restructuring
society   in the geographically and culturally isolated
four islands. The Japanese should welcome it.

<u>REFERENCES AND FURTHER READING</u>

(1) Chie Nakane: Japanese Society, Charles E. Tuttle Co., Tokyo
    1970

(2) Isaiah Ben-Dasan: The Japanese and The Jews, Weatherhill
    Co., N.Y 1972

(3) Mitsuru Yokoi: Agencies and Directions of Japanese Policy,
    Telecommunications Policy, Vol.6, No.4, Dec. 1982

(4) Chalmers Johnson: MITI and the Japanese Miracle, Stanford
    University Press, 1982

(5) White Paper of Trade and Commerce, 1984 Edition (In Japanese),
    Edited by MITI, The Japanese Government Printing Office
    (Okura-sho Insatsu Kyoku)

(6) JECC's Computer Note, 1984 Edition (In Japanese), Edited
    by MITI, Japan Electronic Computer Co.

(7) MITI Handbook, 1984 Edition, Japan Trade and Publicity Inc.,
    Tokyo

(8) White Paper of Computers, 1983 Edition (In Japanese),
    Edited and Published by the Japan Information Processing
    Development Center

(9) James W. Reese: Special Report, Computing in Japan, Asian
Computer Monthly, August, 1984

(10) Japanese Computer Technology & Culture, Computer, March 1984,
IEEE Computer Society. The following 6 articles are
included in the special issue.

  a) Stephen S. Yau: Editor-in-Chief's Remarks, Japanese Computer
  Technology and Culture

  b) Tohru Moto-oka and Harold S. Stone: Fifth-Generation
  Computer System, A Japanese Project

  c) Kazuhiro Fuchi, Shigeru Sato and Edward Miller: Japanese
  Approaches to High-Technology R & D

  d) Masaki Togai: Japan's Next Generation of Robots

  e) Harold Stone: Computer Research in Japan

  f) Denji Tajima and Tomoo Matsubara: Inside the Japanese
  Software Factory

(11) Edward A. Feingenbaum and Pamela McCorduck: Fifth Generation
Computer, Pan Books, 1983

(12) White Paper of Communication, 1984 Edition (In Japanese),
Edited by MPT, Japanese Government Printing Office
(Okura-sho Insatsu Kyoku)

(13) Nippon Telegraph and Telephone Public Corporation 1983/1984
Annual Report, Edited and Published by NTT Public Corporation

(14) KDD Annual Report 1983, Edited and Published by Kokusai
Denshin Denwa Co., Ltd.

(15) Yasuo Makino: Regulation on Data Communication, (In Japanese),
Kikaku Center, 1972

(16) Electronics in Japan, '83-'84 Edition, Edited and Published
by the Electronics Association of Japan

(17) Manri Ishikawa: Law of Telecommunications Service Agencies

and Telecommunications Service Market in Future (In
Japanese), The Journal of the Japan Society of Information
and Communication Research, Vol.2, No.2, August, 1984

(18) Research Group of Telecommunications Issue, 55 points of
the New Telecommunications Law (In Japanese), I.M.I. Co.,
September, 1984

(19) Telecommunications Laws (In Japanese), Edited by Research
Group of Telecommunications Law, Hifumi Book Agency, June
1984

(20) What the Best Telecommunications Policy should be in the
1980s (In Japanese), Edited by the MPT's Consultative
Meeting, Daiichi Hoki Publishing Co., November, 1981

(21) Ad-hoc Committee's Proposals, 1st, 2nd, 3rd, 4th and 5th
(In Japanese), Edited and Published by the Governmental
Administration Research (Gyosei Kanri Kenkyu) Center, 1981,
1982 and 1983

(22) Yujiro Hayashi: Information-Oriented Society (In Japanese),
Mainichi Newspaper Co., 1970

(23) Special Issue of Advanced Information Society (In Japanese),
The Journal of the Institute of Electronics and Communication Engineers of Japan, Vol.67, No.9, September, 1984

(24) Special Issue of New-media (In Japanese), The Journal of
the Institute of Electronics and Communication Engineers
of Japan, Vol.67, No.7, July, 1984

(25) Special Issue of Tele-topia (In Japanese), The Journal of
Telecommunications, Vol.47, No.451, 1984

(26) Industrial Review of Japan/1984, The Japan Economic Journal

(27) Alun M. Anderson: Science and Technology in Japan, Longman
U.K, 1984

(28) Hiroshi Inose (Editor): Scientific Information Systems in
Japan, North-Holland, 1981

Section 6: THE LEADING EDGE

CHAPTER 37.

ADVANCES IN SEMICONDUCTOR TECHNOLOGY

DR. JOHN WHITE
Radar & Signals Establishment, Malvern, England

INTRODUCTION

The microelectronic industry has exhibited the biggest growth rate of any industry this century. It will soon affect virtually every aspect of our daily life. To ignore this key enabling technology , or discover its importance too late will have dire consequences . Yet the key invention , that of the transistor occured as recently as 1947.

How did this revolution start? It really all began with the invention of the transistor in 1947 (Shockley W, 1976). Like most great discoveries it was somewhat of an accident. John Bardeen and Walter Brattain of the Bell Telephone Laboratories were investigating the performance of an early electronic component called a "Cat's Whisker" rectifier. Various electrical probes were applied to the device and it was noticed that when a signal was applied , an amplified version appeared at another connection. William Shockley later explained the operation of this device and all three shared a Nobel Prize for their discovery.

The term transistor refers to "transfer resistor" and permits the controlled transfer of power from one circuit to another . It permits the amplification of electronic signals and represents a considerable advance over the vacuum valve which it effectively replaces.

As early even as the 1930's , solid state equivalents had been proposed and even very slow devices with poor performance had been made. However the Bardeen , Brattain and Shockley device represented the first practical transistor.

These transistors formed the basis of the early electronic developments. It was the requirements of space and defence programmes in the USA towards the end of the 1950's which provided the stimulus which led to the invention of the integrated circuit (Kilby J S, 1976)(For, by producing a number of transistors on the same piece of silicon and interconnecting them directly, it was possible to make whole circuits extremely small), In particular these programmes produced stringent demands for reductions in size, power and weight of digital circuitry. The concept of the integrated circuit was first proposed by Harwick Johnson of the RCA corporation and was later extended by Dummer of the RRE in the UK. Subsequent US Government funding for research and development in the emerging semiconductor companies saw the first commercial devices appear in the early 1960's.

Growth from then on was very rapid. Initially , the drive was concentrated on applying this new technology to military systems under funding from the US Department of Defence, with commercial manufacturers of computer and communications equipment preferring to use hybrid circuits built from discrete components, The emphasis started to change towards the end of the 1960's when companies such as DEC (Digital Equipment Corp) recognised the economics and importance of incorporating complete digital functions on a single chip. This led to the development (in the early 1970's) of a whole series of relatively cheap minicomputers and memory chips (Dennard R, 1984)and paved the way for the commercial exploitation of microelectronics technology.
The latter phase has been characterised by intense industrial competition , particularly between companies in the USA and lately Japan. The defence market, having been the initial key stimulus, now only forms a small fraction - some 6 to 7 % of the total IC production.

Whilst the development of microelectronics over the past twenty years or so has been extremely impressive, its future seems equally assured. Major government programmes are now under way in many western countries which aim to see the rapid advancement of this technology and its application. One example is the US VHSIC (Very High Speed Integrated Circuit) programme, which was announced in late 1978 and whose main goal is the production of high performance chips for digital signal processing applications. This initiative is aimed at providing advanced chip sets for military applications and is necessary to stimulate commercial industry to invest in specialised micron and sub micron processing equipment. Cynics may speculate that the extent of the Japanese competition also may have had some influence! One main objective of this programme is to reduce the feature size of devices to around 0.5 micron (1/40 the diameter of the human hair) and through this to increase the speed and computational capabilities which can be incorporated on a single silicon chip.

Very Large Scale Integrated Circuit (VLSI) technology is central to the so called Fifth Generation Computer project currently underway in Japan. This programme plans a quantum leap in the nature of advanced computer technology . It is hoped that by 1990, systems will be developed that , amongst other things, can reason for themselves, can understand natural languages and are capable of recognising both images and speech. The computational power required to meet these objectives can only be achieved through significant advances in VLSI circuitry. This is because advances in VLSI permit the individual devices to be operated faster, . Also by increasing the number of transistors on a chip it permits more functions to be incorporated at less cost.

TECHNOLOGY ADVANCES THROUGH SCALING

The most important factor in increasing   the   level   of integration and bringing down the costs per function of I C s is reducing the dimension of the minimum feature size on a chip (a general discussion is given by Meindl J D, 1984). Generally the past has shown   that the the penalty in terms of additional manufacturing difficulty has been fairly low and is considerably outweighed by improvements in productivity and performance.

The reduction in size of the circuit element increases the number of devices that can be packed on a given sized chip. Since circuit delay times are directly proportional to device dimensions, the circuit also becomes faster as devices become smaller. The key scaling features are summarised in Table 1

TABLE 1

Parameter	Scaling Factor
Device dimension	$1/k$
Operating voltage	$1/k$
Packing density	k^2
Power consumption (per switch or gate)	$1/k^2$
Chip DC power density (per unit area)	1
Circuit delay (speed)	$1/k$
Power delay product	$1/k^3$

The inverse cubic relationship of the power delay product - the combination of gate power and propagation delay - is a representative yardstick for the performance improvement obtained by reducing chip minimum feature size.

The above scaling principles apply strictly to Unipolar (or MOS) devices. Bipolar scaling is considerably more complicated. This is because not only is there both a more diverse range of bipolar structures , but also the vertical nature of current injection, collection etc., precludes such simple scaling as in   Unipolar devices with their concomitant high performance improvements.   It is very difficult to scale this vertical dimension further, since doping densities and electric field strengths have already reached practical limits. Since supply voltages are already at a workable lower value, constant voltage scaling is employed. This reduces an important degree of freedom viz a viz Unipolar devices. Typically , power dissipation per gate remains constant resulting in chip power density rising as K^2.   This is discussed in more detail in the last section of this chapter . Thus , in general , bipolar does not show the significant advantages as Unipolar, and in many instances will be power limited at the higher gate densities, unless special heat dissipating packages are employed.

   Scaling Problems - Inverse Scaled Features

Application of the principles given in table 1 gives   many advantages   in   terms   of   circuit   performance,   but   some characterisitics exhibit an inverse, detrimental scaling behaviour. These detrimental effects are confined principally to the contact points to the active device and the interconnects between them. Table   2   shows the affect of scaling on contact resistance and interconnect response time.   It has been assumed that vertical thicknesses will scale by an amount equivalent to horizontal dimensions. In practice , the advent of well controlled anisotropic dry etching , together with better lithography on non-planar wafers, will result in thicker layers than would otherwise be possible . Thus this figure probably represents a pessimistic outlook.

Table 2 - Interconnect Scaling

Parameter	Scaling Factor
Interconnection Line Resistance	K
Interconnect Current Density	K
Interconnect Line Response Time	1
Normalised Line Response Time (with respect to gate delay)	K
Contact Resistance	K^2

The delay (RC time constant)   associated   with   fine   line interconnects can provide a significant limitation to the circuit performance. This is because although design rules have shrunk, , chip sizes and hence the length of interconnects have remained nearly constant . Consequently the line resistance and the edge component of the line capacitance, for runners of centimeter length increase sharply as design rules decrease . This is a particular problem for interconnect lines fabricated in polysilicon as opposed to aluminium or metallised lines. The high resistance of polysilicon has led to the development of low resistance silicides (formed by reacting together silicon with , for example, various refractory

metals: molybdenum silicide, tungsten silicide also tantalum or
platinum silicide) for gates and interconnect. In this context, it
should be pointed out that the use of gate material for interconnect
avoids the use of wasteful contact holes , which would otherwise be
required and "waste" considerable silicon real estate.

For submicron circuits , even aluminium metallization may
eventually become a dominant delay element on the chip. Polysilicon
interconnects are completely unacceptable unless used for very short
lengths (less than 0.01 cm) as part of a multi level low resistance
interconnect scheme. Composites of refractory silicide/poly-Si can
lower the RC time constant of straight poly-Si by over an order of
magnitude, allowing longer segments of these materials to be used
and thereby considerably alleviating the layout routing and design
problems. (This represents only a partial solution and in many
circuit applications may not be worthwile or economic - eg In
memory applications ,it will probably be vital but for general
random logic circuits multi level Al may be more efficient)

This problem in inverse scaling of interconnects, affects not
only the direction of technological process innovation, but also
influences the design philosophy. Long,   across-chip, lines. are
avoided and nearest neighbour interactions are "encouraged" wherever
possible (eg systolic arrays - see later).

Two other methods can be used separately or in conjunction with
each other to improve chip complexity; increase of chip area and
use of circuit and device innovation (" cleverness "), where
possible exploiting structural regularity to give enhanced yields
using reduncy techniques, together with reduced interconnect line
lenghts giving higher speeds, and / or simpler processing
technology.

Increasing the chip area is difficult if a sufficient quantity
or yield of devices is to be achieved. Various yield models exist,
but all predict a very rapid decrease in acceptable devices with
increase in chip area. As devices are scaled down by a factor k,
the minimum significant yield reducing defect size also scales down
by the same factor . Since the area density of significant defects
increases by k, considerable process development work has to be
done, simply to maintain yields at no increase in chip size. This is
the principle reason behind the trends in chip making towards ever
cleaner, " dustless " processing environments (Singer P H, 1984).

ADVANCES IN PROCESS TECHNOLOGY

The number of semiconductor processes available to industry has
been steadily expanding and diversifying(Roberts 1984) based on two
main types of transistors: Bipolar and Unipolar (or Metal Oxide
Semiconductor , MOS)). Many different types exist to serve special
purposes and applications.

BIPOLAR

Bipolar in the past was the dominant technology . It was easier to fabricate and due to the high transconductance of bipolar transistors was better for linear applications and for driving high capacitive loads off-chip - the ideal technology for relatively low levels of integration.

However, more recently bipolar technologies have lagged behind MOS in popularity ; one of the key factors being the drive for large memories based on MOS. The other has been its scaling difficulties.

The most recent advances have been directed towards reducing unwanted sideways capacitance by introducing new forms of oxide isolation . The oxide isolated process typically uses a similar emitter base structure to the conventional diffusion isolated device, which relies on reverse biased junctions to achieve isolation.   Oxide isolation not only reduces parasitic capacitance giving higher intrinsic device speed but also increases packing density since designers are no longer limited by junction breakdown phenomena associated with butting ,adjacent diffused regions.

While oxide isolation provides one technique to enhance speed, another has employed enhanced emitter structures to increase the intrinsic bipolar speed. Conventional bipolars are difficult to scale since : a) decreasing the base width will reduce the transit time of carriers across the base - giving a faster device - but also results in punch through / breakdown effects at fairly low voltages - a volt or so. The device is faster but can only operate at low voltages thus reducing its practicality, b) increasing the base and emitter doping density to overcome the above affects are limited by fundamental material properties associated with the solid solubility of dopants in silicon.

Polysilicon emitter technology has been employed in this context both to give a self aligned / high density process (Sakai T, Suzuki M, 1983) but also with a thin interfacial oxide layer between the polysilicon and the silicon to act as a tunnelling barrier , which gives a much more efficient , high gain transistor. The details of both bipolar improvements are somewhat complicated and are discussed in more detail by Cuthbertson and Ashburn, 1984).

In conclusion , bipolars are high speed, generally high power devices which are difficult to scale without major, radically new improvements in process technology (see Soloman , 1982 for a more general discussion). Their market share is predicted to decrease as larger VLSI chips are likely to dissipate exhorbitant amounts of power.   Their main role is likely to be as glue chips for linking together other chips ,where high intrinsic transconductance gives good linear and line driving capability, or for dedicated high speed computing applications where ultimate speed is of vital importance.

MOS

MOS is currently the most important technology and is scheduled to become more so: By 1990 MOS should take over 65% of the total IC market . We have essentially three main contenders: PMOS - P channel MOS, NMOS - N channel MOS, and CMOS - Complimentary MOS. PMOS was developed first , since it is easier to make but is now virtually obsolete with NMOS effectively replacing it. Most of the advanced technology development is now concentrated on NMOS and CMOS with high density RAMs providing the incentive for both.

Whilst the main markets for 64K and 256K DRAM over the next few years are likely to be served by NMOS technology, after this some form of CMOS will be needed to overcome NMOS difficulties ; such as excessive power dissipation, soft error susceptibilty etc.

Complimentary MOS, comprising both P and N channel push pull transistors, only consumes power when switching from one state to another,. It is therefore ideal for chips where low power and high density are required, and analoque applications where the push - pull format gives high gain. In the 1980's, therefore, a definite move towards CMOS technology is occuring . The exact nature of the CMOS process is unclear: whether for example the N channel transistors are fabricated in a P well or in the substrate itself. There are a number of options and the particular applications in mind will determine which polarity is used where.

P well CMOS has been the easiest to implement. Since the old PMOS technology used an N substrate it was a simple extension of the process to add P wells where necessary to provide the complimentary N channel devices. This has resulted in considerable production experience being built up over time . However , N well CMOS based on more recent developments with N channel MOS (which employ a p substrate) has become more popular recently , particularly since it exhibits many better characteristics at smaller geometries (Yu K, 1983).

Recent advances in CMOS technology have involved new isolation techniques . Conventional oxide isolated CMOS , has employed the LOCOS (LOCal Oxidation of Silicon) technique , where thick oxide layers are grown in the non active areas using a silicon nitride layer in the device regions (to prevent oxidation.). Oxidation still occurs at the edges of the nitride masking layer , producing a tapered profile somewhat resembling the shape of a birds beak. This is satisfactory at large geometries (>> 2-3 microns) but at smaller dimensions a more abrupt form of isolation is needed.

A large amount of work has been carried out on various forms of "trench" isolation where a groove is cut (by dry, plasma etching) a micron or so deep into the bulk , and then refilled either with oxide or oxide/high resistivity polysilicon sandwich layers (Rung, 1984). This enables high packing densities to be achieved and gives a flat surface ideal for subsequent layer deposition,

lithography and patterning. If this is combined with an epitaxial
layer /buried layer process, the latch up characteristics associated
with parasitic NPNP thyristors , may be significantly better
controlled (Long D M, 1980) . Although using an epitaxial layer
increases the expense of the process , the advantage of controlling
latch up together with reducing the effect of ionising radiation in
memory (soft error reduction) make it worth while at small
geometries.

GaAs

Advances in GaAs technology are now leading to commercial chip
and wafer manufacture (up to 3") . Most of the applications are
for high speed front ends, in satellites and commercial microwave
receivers where the low noise and high gain arising from the
superior GaAs mobility together with radiation hardness give it the
edge over silicon. The radiation hardness is not implicit in GaAs
rather it is associated with the simple MESFET (a junction rather
than a capacitive device) technology employed in most GaAs chips (
see also Eden R C , 1982 with regard to possible future GaAs bipolar
devices) .   This arises because only with silicon can one grow a
stable passivating oxide layer both for masking and patterning but
also   for   the   thin   dielectric   "filling"   used   in   the
Metal-Oxide-Semiconductor transistor sandwich. Without the stable
oxide employed in silicon technology , junction -type FETs have to
be employed resulting in more difficult , less controlled processing
and more complex device configurations to make simple gates (Long
et al , 1982). Advances in technology recently have involved self
-aligned transistors   - common in silicon for many years - and
enhancement /depletion Junction FETs which give better device and
circuit performance .   GaAs process and material technology ,
however, is still relatively immature , typically relying on gate
lengths 2-3 times smaller than VLSI silicon to give the necessary
performance edge to warrant its use. GaAs will become increasingly
availible for specialist applications in direct broadcasting
applications , opto-electronic links and some ultra high speed
digital computer applications , but is unlikely to be used for
highly complex chips.

ADVANCES IN ARCHITECTURES AND SYSTEMS

Developments in technology have given the designer   the
capability of putting whole systems on a chip with device counts of
100,000 or more in 1 square cm of silicon. There are two problems to
be faced : one , how to deal with and manage the complexity of the
task - a single error in fabrication or design will result in
wastage of the entire chip, two: how to simplify and incorporate
redundant components on chip to give reasonable yield.

With memory, due to its repetive nature extra redundant rows
and columns can be provided , to be connected in place of failed
memory cells.   Polysilicon fusing may be used for selective
interconnection. For 64K DRAMs an order of magnitude improvement in

yield may be achieved in this way.

For general signal / data processing chips based on conventional architectures , this approach is not so easy since these are made up of separate discrete functional blocks.

New architectures are now appearing based on series of processing blocks with regular array structures. Since they are regular , they are easier to design and fault tolerance can be incorporated (Smith K, 1985). Various correlator and convolver chips have been designed based on wavefront processors or "systolic arrays": the name systolic refers to the regular clocking or pumping of signals through the 2D array analagous to the heart beat. Fault tolerance can also be applied to image processing chips such as those under development at Brunel and GEC in England. GEC's GRID (for GEC Rectangular Image and Data Processor) contains 32 identical processors on a chip , while Brunel Universities SCAPE (Single Chip Array Processing Element) has 256 image processors on a single regular chip. The concept of using regular structures either at the chip (above) or at the system level (such as the transputer , ICL Distributed Array Processor) , etc.) is the key to making complex high " powered " systems manageable both in design and manufacture.

The concept can be taken one step further to give wafer scale integration . By exploiting the regularity / yield improvements it should be possible to make a quantum step increase in chip sizes from the typical 1 square cm today , to the whole wafer.
Clive Sinclair is intending to make a 1/2 megabyte mini-Winchester disc with this approach , utilizing self testing logic to automatically detect and switch out failed memory cells. Such wafer scale projects could be considerably cheaper than conventional systems since the bulk of the micro circuit cost is incurred in labour intensive end stages such as testing and packaging . Considerable speed improvements are also likely since on chip delays are typically considerably less than driving long interconnections off-chip.

ADVANCES IN LAYER PROCESSING

Perhaps the most obvious problem of shrinking devices is that dimensions are now approaching the wavelength of light ,hence diffraction and resolution can be limiting factors. However imaging a pattern onto the surface is not sufficient - it has to be reproduced at the correct dimension and in the correct place relative to other patterns . The minimum linewidth that can be used is not the smallest that can be imaged onto the surface , but the smallest that can be controlled within critical limits . [Typically , the minimum is ten times larger than the standard deviation on linewidth variation.]Positional accuracy is also vital and devices have to be made tolerant to two to three times the typical error.

The ever shrinking linewidth obviously makes this more difficult to achieve because whilst one can live with a micrometer (um) error in position with a 5 um linewidth , that obviously would be worse than useless with 1 um features ; you could be completely in the wrong place.

The traditional techniques of pattern delination have been whole wafer optical shadow printing using ultra-violet light to expose a photosensitive chemically resistant layer coated onto the silicon wafer through a mask with the desired pattern. Highest resolution is obtained by having the mask and wafer in contact (contact printing). However this inevitably causes damage to the mask or resist layer reducing or killing yields of good devices. The mask damage often results from spikes that grow on the wafer during certain process steps. Once damaged , the mask then replicates that fault on all subsequent wafers. Some manufactures overcome this by the use of spike crushers - the crushed-spike portion of the wafer almost certainly won't work , but at least saves subsequent wafers. The other way of reducing this damage problem is by having the mask and wafer separated by a small gap (proximity printing). However , the penalty to be paid is loss of resolution due to diffraction effects between the mask and the bottom of the resist . Any variation in this gap due to wafer or mask distortions gives rise to variable resolution and linewidth . The other major problem of both contact and proximity printing is that they are whole wafer techniques and it is increasingly difficult to achieve acceptable alignment over a whole wafer with shrinking dimensions due to mask or wafer distortions or thermal expansion mismatch.

These problems have provided the incentive to improve pattern replication techniques. Resolution can be improved by using shorter wavelength radiation . The damage can be eliminated by the use of projection printing techniques, which permit improvements in alignment accuracy by allowing individual chip or block rather than whole wafer registration. Optical projection printers are capable of micron resolution with an alignment accuracy better than 0.25 um . Further improvements are expected . Reduction projection printers, that is machines which project a reduced image onto the wafer , have the advantage over 1 to 1 printers of: higher resolution, chip by chip alignment, and less sensitivity to dust particles on the mask. But they suffer from increased cost and decreased throughput.

X ray techniques appear to have the advantage of extremely high resolution (0.02 um). There are , however, major problems with producing the specially thin (a few microns thick) shadow masks to use with soft X rays. Special resists are also necessary but , at present, don't have adequate sensitivity to allow the use of stepping techniques which perhaps explains why existing commercial machines use whole wafer exposure. The resist speed problem can be overcome by the use of an intense X Ray source such as a synchrotron, but not every factory has access to one of these on their production lines! It has been suggested , though, that for a very large wafer fabrication facility, it may well be a commercial propostion.

Electron beam machines are used for making the highest quality masks but haven't, as yet , made much impact on patterning directly a whole wafer. Although potentially capable of very high resolution and high alignment accuracy they have been slow and expensive compared with optical machines. High resolution , high accuracy and large area coverage require a variable beam shape for success but another problem is the proximity effect. When an electron beam exposes photoresist , secondary and scattered electrons cause significant changes in the exposure threshold in adjacent regions. When a number of areas are written in close proximity,the cumulative dose on the remaining , nominally unexposed areas may be sufficient for it to fully develop ,resulting in unwanted , incorrect pattern replication. The use of higher energy electron beams reduces the effect but highly sophisticated correction to the electron beam , which corrects for proximity, are nevertheless still necessary.

Ion beams do not suffer from this problem and should have a very high resolution . In addition resists are much more sensitive to ions than electrons thus making ion beam lithography a very attractive proposition. If it is possible to achieve adequate ion beam currents of dopant elements , then device processing could be dramatically simplified since the resist and masking stages could be eliminated and metered doses of dopant be introduced directly into the appropriate areas.

Ion beam lithography is still at an early stage and there are many problems to be solved . However, advanced optical and ion beam techniques are probably the forerunners in the race to achieve commercial production of sub micron circuits.

Having produced a pattern in the resist layer, it then has to be transferred into the underlying layer. This is performed by etching . For exact pattern replication no undercut of the mask should occur, ie the etch should be anisotropic, and should be completely specific to the layer being etched . For the smallest geometries this is necessary but extremely difficult to achieve and the very steep steps produced can cause problems. An abrupt step one tenth of a micron high can cause breaks in a one micron thick metallisation track! The sidewalls of the etched pattern therefore have to be controlled to a fine degree to obtain the best compromise.

Wet chemical etchants can be found which are very highly selective but almost invariably they etch isotropically , ie they etch equally in all directions. For thin layers and geometries of a few microns, this is quite adequate . As linewidths are reduced the problem becomes more serious as in general layer thicknesses are not scaled down to the same degree as the printed down dimensions. Ion beam milling , a dry etching technique which uses a beam of ions to knock atoms off the surface has been available for some time. It is capable of anisotropic etching but unfortunately is unselective, etching virtually all layers at the same rate. It is thus very difficult to stop etching at the required point. It is necessary to find a new etching technique which combines the anisotropy of ion beam milling together with the chemical selectivity of wet chemical etching. The techniques that have recently emerged are plasma etching, reactive ion etching and reactive ion beam etching (Chapman B, 1980) . These are all vacuum dry etching techniques using highly energetic species of ions, extracted from a plasma, directed at the surface.   They use a combination of physical and chemical etching to achieve the required compromise in selectivity and anisotropy. These processes have proved extremely difficult to understand and control. Although considerable progress has been made there are still serious problems with certain combinations of layers, in both achieving the necessary compromise in anisotropy and selectivity and also avoiding the unwanted deposition of certain polymers. In other circumstances these deposited polymers would make excellent non stick frying pans!

These are but a few of the problems to be solved for the fabrication of the smallest geometry devices and circuits. There are many others including particulate control for example. People are the dirtiest objects in clean rooms and there is therefore considerable incentive to replace them with something better. Robots have already been tried out in some pilot lines, but have yet to achieve significant use in production environments. Crucial steps toward this goal have been taken; microprocessor controlled cassette to cassette tools , in line equipment for photoresist processing and line balancing, inventory and process control from a central computer. Robot arms or fully automated wafers tracks for transporting from one process step to the next are already starting to appear in pilot sub micron lines. The fully automated line for complete wafer manufacture is not far away and will probably be with us by the end of the decade (see series on automation in solid State Technology, July 1984). The expense will be horrific but the alternatives would probably not permit the successful production of Ultra Large Scale ICs at sufficient yield levels to be profitable for main stream memory and microprocessor applications .

REFERENCES

Chapman B, 1980
" Glow Discharge Processes"
Published by Wiley, Interscience, New York, 1980

Cuthbertson A, Ashburn P, 1984
"Self Aligned Bipolar Transistors with Enhanced Efficiency Polysilicon Emitters"
Int Elect Dev Meeting - Digest, p 749, San Fransisco , Dec 1984

Dennard R H , 1984
"Evolution of the MOSFET Dynamic RAM - A personal view"
IEEE Trans on Elect Dev, vol ED-31, no 11, p 1549, Nov 1984

Eden R C , 1982
" Comparison of GaAs Device Approaches for Ultra High Speed VLSI"
Proc IEEE , vol 70, no 1, p5, Jan 1982

Kilby J S, 1976
"Invention of the Integrated Circuit"
IEEE Trans on Electron Dev , vol ED-23, no 7, p648, July 1976

Long D M , 1980
" State of the Art Review - Hardness of MOS & Bipolar ICs"
IEEE Trans Nucl Sci , vol NS-27, no 6, p1674, 1980

Long S I et al, 1982
" High Speed GaAs ICs"
Proc of IEEE , vol 70, no 1, p 35, Jan 1982

Meindl J D, 1984
" Ultra Large Scale Integration "
IEEE Trans Electr Dev , vol ED-31, no 11, p 1555, Nov 1984

Roberts D H, 1984
" Silicon Integrated Circuits - Apersonal view of the first 25 years

Electronics & Power, p282, April 1984

Rung R, 1984
" Trench Isolation Prospects for CMOS VLSI"
Int Elect Dev Meeting, San Fransisco, p 574, Dec 1984

Sakai T , Suzuki M, 1983
" Super Self Aligned Bipolar Technology"
1983 Symposium of VLSI Technology-Digest, p 16, Maui, Sept 1983

Shockley W, 1976
" The Path to the Conception of the Junction Transistor"
IEEE Trans on Elect Dev , vol ED-23, no 7, p 597, July 1976

Singer P H, 1984
"The Technology of Clean Room Design"
Semiconductor International, p 94, June 1984

Smith K, 1985
"Britons seek Tolerant Chips"
Electronics Week, p20, Feb 25, 1985

Soloman P M , 1982
" A Comparison of Semiconductor devices for High Speed Logic"
Proc IEEE, vol 70, no 5, p 489, May 1982

Yu K, 1983
" CHMOS - The Emerging VLSI Technology "
Symposium on VLSI Technology - Digest, Maui, p32, Sept 1983

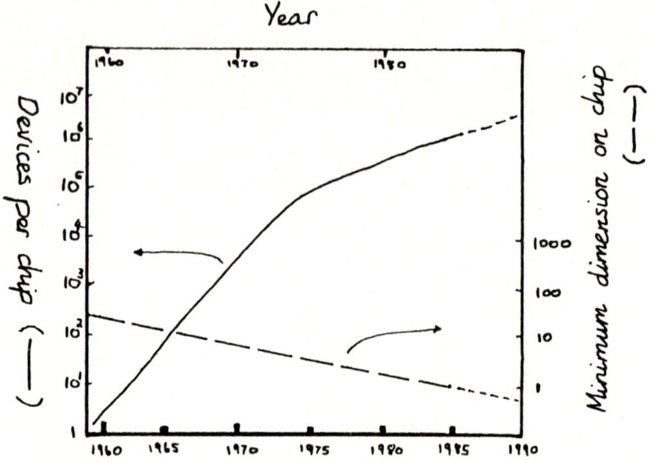

Advances in chip technology showing steady increase in component count brought about by decreasing feature size.

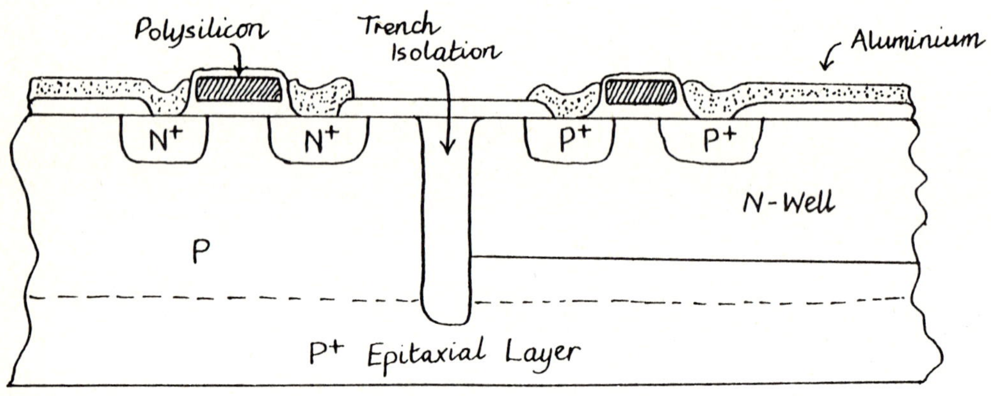

Trench isolation with epitaxial layer for sub-micron CMOS.

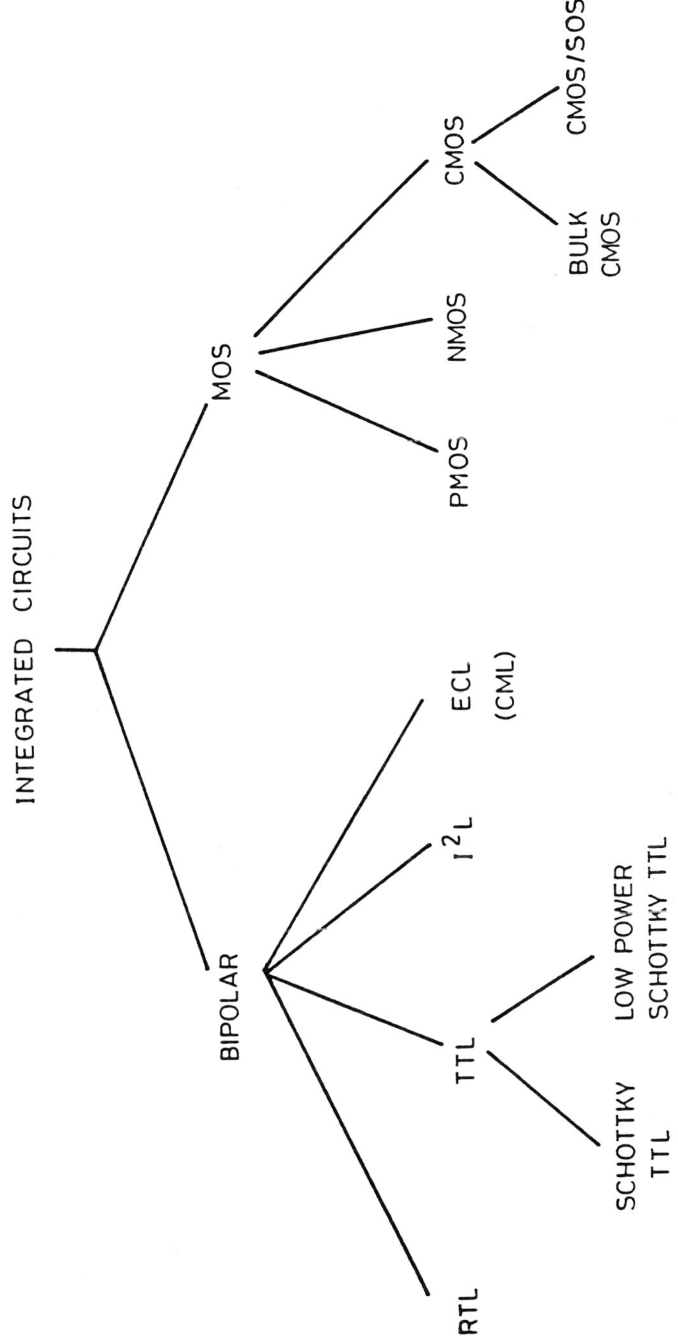
INTEGRATED CIRCUITS
MOS
BIPOLAR
CMOS
NMOS
PMOS
CMOS/SOS
BULK CMOS
ECL (CML)
I^2L
TTL
RTL
SCHOTTKY TTL
LOW POWER SCHOTTKY TTL
SUMMARY OF IMPORTANT TECHNOLOGIES

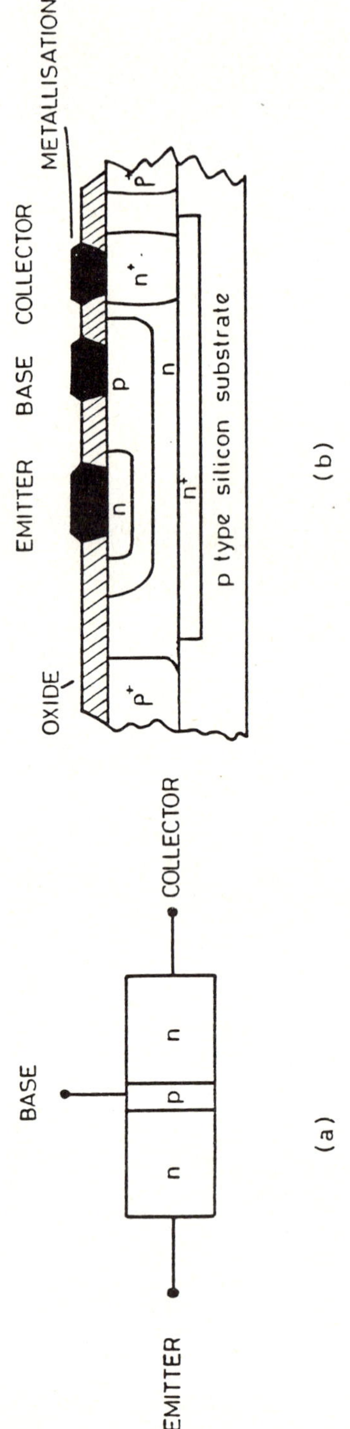

(a) BASIC BIPOLAR TRANSISTOR (b) TYPICAL INTEGRATED VERSION

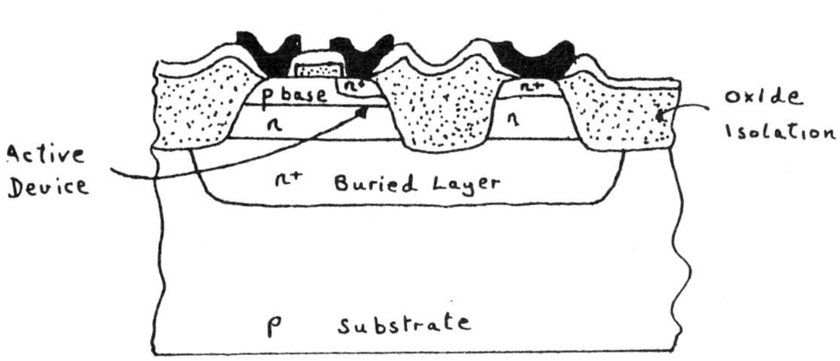

Oxide isolated bipolar transistor - giving high packing density and high speed.

CHAPTER 38.

NEW DEVELOPMENTS AND APPLICATIONS
OF MICROCOMPUTER HARDWARE AND SOFTWARE

DR. AMAR GUPTA
MIT, Cambridge, U.S.A.

INTRODUCTION

The microcomputer revolution has several interesting facets.
In a world of surging inflation, it is amazing to note that the
cost of computer logic devices has declined at 25% per year, and
the cost of computer memory units diminish by 40% each year.
If over the last 25 years the aircraft industry had witnessed an
equally spectacular evolution in terms of cost, speed, and energy
consumption, a supersonic Concord aircraft would today cost five
hundred dollars, and it would fly around the globe in twenty
minutes consuming just five gallons of fuel for the entire journey!

Advances in semiconductor technology have enabled tremendous
amounts of computing power to be generated at plummeting costs.
Whereas twenty years ago computers could be afforded only by
large organizations, the minicomputers of the seventies were
purchased by departments and groups within such organizations.
Now the personal computer is within the reach of every individual.
Within the last six years alone, there has been a hundred-fold
increase in the use of personal computers. At one end of the
spectrum there are general-purpose computers capable of performing
a broad range of functions, gradually taking over the role of
calculators. At the other end there is an increasing number of
microcomputers devoted to dedicated tasks such as in automobiles,
in household appliances, and in an array of industrial control

environments. Current projections indicate that the population
of microcomputers on this planet will outstrip the population
of human beings before the end of this century!

With microprocessors, microcomputers, and personal computers
becoming such ubiquitous aids, it is incredible that none of
these electronic wizards existed fifteen years back. The dawn
of the microprocessor era is marked by the introduction of the
Intel 4004, the first computer on a chip. This 4-bit 4004 CPU,
introduced in 1971, contained 23,000 transistors and could
execute 45 different instructions. The term "microprocessor,"
first used in 1972, connotes the central arithmetic and logic
unit of a computer scaled down in size to fit on a single silicon
chip (sometimes several chips) holding tens of thousands
(frequently, hundreds of thousands) of transistors, resistors,
and similar circuit elements. A microcomputer combines a
microprocessor with memory and input/output capabilities to
provide a fully operational computer.

Personal computers constitute an important sub-set of
microcomputers. A microcomputer can be dedicated to a single
task such as controlling a machine tool or metering the injection
of fuel into an automobile engine; it can be a word processor, a
video game or a "pocket computer" that is not quite a computer.
A personal computer, on the other hand, connotes a stand-alone
computer that puts a wide array of capabilities at the disposal
of an individual and meets <u>all</u> the following criteria:

   a) The price for the basic system is under $5,000;

   b) The system offers secondary memory capabilities in the
      form of floppy disks or a cassette tape;

   c) It has an address space of at least 64K bytes (K in

computer parlance denotes 2^{10} = 1,024 rather than 1,000);

   d) At least one high level language (Basic, Fortran, Cobol, Pascal, Ada, or C) is available;

   e) The operating system facilitates an interactive mode of operation rather than simple batch facility;

   f) The distribution is through mass marketing channels with major emphasis directed towards the neophyte computer user.

The evolution of the personal computer is a direct sequel to the evolution of the microprocessor. Based around an Intel microprocessor, Micro Instrumentation and Telementry Systems (MITS) Inc., an Albuquerque firm, developed the first computer in 1975. The basic system was sold for $395 in kit form and $621 in assembled form; the peripherals were extra. The Altair 8800 Advanced Accounting/Engineering Systems included sophisticated features and sold commercially for $10,500. The success of the MITS system was partly due to a cover article in the January 1975 issue of <u>Popular</u> <u>Electronics</u> and the system was purchased mostly by hobbyists. The system is no longer manufactured; however, its protocol to interconnect peripherals and the main computer has become an industry standard. In more recent years, too, evolution of microelectronics technology has continued to have lasting impact on the communications industry, particularly in the definition of networking protocols and standards.

The history of personal computers is interwoven with the evolution of microprocessor technology. Each provides an incentive for the development of the other technology. In order to comprehend trends in these fast-developing fields, it is pertinent to first analyze some of the key milestones in the domain of microprocessor hardware.

	4-bit	8-bit	16-bit	32-bit	64-bit (projected)
Year of First Chip	1971	1972	1974	1981	1986
Number of Devices	2,300	10,000	70,000	450,000	1,000,000
Function	Calculator	Dedicated Controller	Minicomputer	Micro-Mainframe	Maximicro-Mainframes
Clock Speed (in megahertz)	0.4	0.5	1	10	50
Prices (1984)	$1	$5	$50	$250	$1,250

Table I: Evolution of Microprocessors

TRENDS IN MICROPROCESSOR HARDWARE

The computational power of a microprocessor is determined
by two major factors: a) the frequency of the electronic clock,
which synchronizes the operations of the computer; and b) the
word-size, which governs the "width" of the computer's data path.
The trend in microprocessors is towards a higher frequency and
a larger word size. As the frequency increases, there are more
machine cycles per second; as the word size increases, an operation
can be completed in fewer cycles. In general, a larger word size
also brings the abilities to access a larger volume of memory
and to run larger programs.

During their fourteen years of existence, the overall
throughput of the microprocessor has increased by two to three
orders of magnitude. The clock frequency has increased by a
factor exceeding 50. Microprocessors embodying 4-bit, 8-bit,
16-bit, and 32-bit architectures were first introduced in 1971,
1972, 1974, and 1981, respectively (see Table I). We are
currently witnessing a spate of new products belonging to the
fourth generation of microprocessors. Even though microprocessors
with word sizes larger than 32-bits will be available soon, it
is unlikely that such fifth-generation products will ever become very
popular. Just as mainframe computers have generally adopted the
32-bit standard, it is logical to conclude that 32-bit microprocessors
will continue to be the industry standard for a long time.

Before discussing the highlights of some of the newer
advanced microprocessors, it is relevant to consider the complexities
involved in using word size as the single parameter for evaluating
microprocessors. Irrespective of its architecture, a microprocessor
contains the following:

    a) several registers to store operands and results of

       operations;

    b) internal pathways used to transfer instructions;

    c) internal pathways used to transfer data;

    d) external pathways that carry instructions from pins on

       the chip to inside the microprocessor; and

    e) external pathways that carry data from/to pins on the

       chip.

In some cases the same path may be used to carry both instructions
and data, though not simultaneously. In early microprocessors
the size of registers, the width of internal instruction paths
and data paths, and the width of external instruction paths
and data paths were almost always identical. This is less true
now. Larger external paths require the chip package to have a
large number of pins, which increases the total cost of packaging
and production. Thus, microprocessors nowadays tend to have
wider internal paths than external paths. For example, the
Motorola 68000 and the National NS 16032 have 32-bit internal
paths and 16-bit external paths. A true 32-bit microprocessor
has all paths and all internal units capable of communicating or
processing 32 bits in parallel; some of these paths may, in fact,
be still wider. For example, a multiply operation involving two
numbers each 32 bits wide results in a result which is 64 bits
long. Some 32-bit microprocessors are designed to store
intermediate results with higher accuracy.

Unlike the first microprocessor which contained only 2,300
transistors, contemporary microprocessors frequencly contain
hundreds of thousands of devices. The Hewlett-Packard 32-bit
microprocessor chip, the heart of the HP-9000 computer system,

has 450,000 transistors on a single chip. This increased density
of devices helps in two ways. First, functions previously
performed using auxiliary chips can now be performed by the main
microprocessor itself. These functions include: ability to
generate timing signals; on-chip primary memory for program and
data storage, and the ability to interface with peripheral units.
Second, the increased transistor density permits the implementation
of instruction repertoires that are much larger and much more
powerful than the ones on previous generation microprocessors.
On several systems a single instruction can control the transfer
of an entire block of data from the memory or manipulate several
registers simultaneously. Such single instructions replace
several instructions of earlier systems allowing programs to be
more compact. The instruction sets now bear a closer resemblance
to instructions of higher level languages. This facilitates the
compilation process. As instruction size and complexity have
increased, it now takes over 100 man-years of engineering time
to design a new chip. Hence, instead of designing new instruction
repertoires, one trend is towards supporting instruction sets with
an established base. The T-11 chip, manufactured by DEC, emulates
the PDP-11 instruction set and offers an execution speed comparable
to that of the PDP 11/34. This in turn closes the gap between
microcomputers and minicomputers and makes it easier to transport
programs and data across systems.

    In view of the large number of transistors, most
manufacturers have opted to fabricate microprocessors using MOS
(metal oxide semiconductor) technology in preference to bipolar
transistor technology. Currently, the most popular MOS technology
is n-channel MOS (NMOS) by virtue of its high packing density and
fast switching speeds. CMOS (complementary MOS) circuits provide

faster speed and lower power consumption than circuits implemented
with traditional PMOS and NMOS technology; the disadvantage of
CMOS lies in its lower packing density. Classical CMOS logic
designs have an equal number of n- and p-channel devices. Newer
CMOS designs use a higher number of n-channel devices than
p-channel devices in order to implement higher circuit densities.
High-density CMOS microprocessor circuits have been implemented
among others by Bell Laboratories, by Rockwell International,
and by Hewlett-Packard. In coming years CMOS will become the
most popular technology for fabricating microprocessors because
of the advantages offered by CMOS in terms of faster speed,
lower power consumption, and higher noise immunity.

All microprocessors support data in the form of bytes and
words. However, only some support data in the form of bits,
binary coded decimal words, floating-point numbers, words longer
than 4 bytes, and character strings. Floating-point capabilities
are useful for scientific work. Character string manipulation
capability is required for text editing applications. Auxiliary
chips, co-processors, or slave processors are sometimes used to
perform these functions. As technology improves, it will be
feasible to incorporate more functions on the main chip itself.

Single-chip microcomputers constitute an important subset
of microprocessors in which all functions, including memory,
are implemented on the same chip. In view of the chip area
devoted to auxiliary functions, there is always a time lag between
the introduction of a microprocessor chip of a given word size
and the introduction of a microcomputer chip of an equivalent word
size. For example, the first 8-bit single-chip microcomputer,
the Intel 8048, was introduced in 1976, four years after the

introduction of the first 8-bit microprocessor, the Intel 8008. At the other extreme of the spectrum, there are applications that require higher computing power or better accuracy than that provided by single-chip microprocessors. For such applications, <u>bit-sliced</u> <u>organization</u> enables linking several identical modular chips in parallel to achieve higher accuracy. Also, since these chips are implemented in either bipolar or emitter-coupled logic (ECL) technology, bit-sliced chips offer higher throughput than MOS chips. Thus by using multiple 4-bit chips of this kind, one can easily integrate systems offering an effective word size of 8, 12, 16 bits, or even more. The 2900 series of 4-bit chips manufactured by MOS Technology and Advanced Micro Devices has been very popular. Note, however, that although the Intel iAPX 432 uses a three-chip set, it does <u>not</u> represent an example of bit-sliced architectures, as the three chips are neither capable of operating individually, nor are they identical to each other. With the advent of wider word size, general-purpose microprocessors, the primary merit of using bit-sliced microprocessors for higher accuracy has gradually eroded over the years. For most applications, word sizes of 16 bits or 32 bits are more than adequate, permitting use of standard (nonbit-slice) 16-bit and 32-bit microprocessors.

In spite of the continuing trend towards use of 16-bit and 32-bit microprocessors, chips with small word sizes continue to be used in large numbers. The TMS-1000 series introduced in 1974 has made Texas Instruments the leading manufacturer of 4-bit processors used by millions in games, toys, calculators, and other low-end controller applications. The low price of less than $1 per chip is made possible by two major factors--first, the PMOS technology has become a mature technology and, second, the widespread usage of such chips has reduced production costs

through economies of scale. Equivalent microprocessors implemented
in CMOS (for low-power applications, for example, CMOS TMS 1000)
or bipolar technology (for higher performance) cost more. The
4-bit CMOS microprocessors are used in conjunction with liquid-crystal
displays (LCDs) for a wide array of hand-held products. Low-cost
microprocessors continue to have a tremendous potential use in
industrial (testing, process control, instrumentation,
manufacturing), commercial, and consumer applications.

There are three distinct areas in which 8-bit microprocessors
dominate the show. First, 8-bit microprocessors are used in
portable computers. The Radio Shack TRS-80 Model 10, for
example, uses an OKI 80C85, the CMOS equivalent of the Intel
8085 microprocessor. Since CMOS devices consume little power,
they are ideal for use in portable computers. Second, 8-bit
microprocessors are used for decoding keyboard depressions.
The 8-bit 8048 microcomputer is used in several personal computers
including the NEC PC-100. DEC personal computers use an 8051
microprocessor-driven keyboard. Since low power consumption is
important in a "cordless" environment, the IBM PCjr keyboard uses
a CMOS 80C48 microprocessor. Third, 8-bit microprocessors are
used as auxiliary microprocessors to execute the existing base
of 8-bit programs. The DEC Rainbow personal computer contains an
Intel 8088 microprocessor and a Z-80A 8-bit microprocessor.
Similarly, the DECmate II contains a custom designed CMOS 6120
12-bit microprocessor and a Z-80A 8-bit microprocessor. The use
of a popular 8-bit microprocessor in conjunction with a higher
performance 16/32-bit microprocessor allows a user to execute
existing application programs as well as to benefit from the
architectural sophistication of newer technology.

Table II: Families of 16-Bit Microprocessors

	TI 9900	Intel 8086	Zilog-Z8000	Motorola 68000	NS 16032
Year of Commercial Introduction	1976	1978	1979	1980	1982
No. of Basic Instructions	69	95	110	61	82
No. of General-Purpose Registers	16	14	16	16	8
Pin Count	40	40	48/40	64	48
Direct Address Range (Bytes)	64K	1M	48M*	16M/64M	16M
Number of Addressing Modes	8	24	6	14	9

*6 segments of 8M each

Table III: General Characteristics of 32-Bit Microprocessors

	Western Electric 32000	HP 32-Bit CPU	Intel IAPX 432
Year of Commercial Introduction	1982*	1982*	1981
Technology	2.5-μm Domino CMOS	1.5/1.0 μm NMOS	HMOS
No. of Transistors	146,000	450,000	219,000 on 3 Chips
Size of Chip	160,000 Mil^2	48,400 Mil^2	100,000 Mil^2 Each
Power Dissipation	0.7 Watt at 8 MHz	4 Watts	2.5 Watts/Chip
Pin Count	63 Active; 84 Total	83	64 per Chip
Basic Clock Frequency	10 MHz	18 MHz	8 MHz
Direct Address Range (Bytes)	2^{32}	2^{29} Real; 2^{41} Virtual	2^{24} Real; 2^{40} Virtual
No. of General-Purpose Registers	16 User-Visible	28 (Not All General-Purpose)	No Registers Visible To User
No. of Basic Instructions	169	230	221
No. of Addressing Modes	18	10	5

*Currently for internal use only.

The characteristics of leading 16-bit microprocessors, summarized in Table II, show the trend over the years of increasing functional capabilities, the addressing range, the diverse types of data supported, and clock speeds. Newer and more powerful chips, fully compatible with earlier 16-bit chips have become available. Upward compatibility often prohibits any major changes in chip architectures; this, in turn, restricts implementation or support of newer functions and data types. The five-fold increase in number of transistors between the Intel 8086 and the Intel 80286 has been used to increase performance six-fold, and to perform memory management and protection functions on the chip itself. Similarly, the Motorola MC 68010, introduced in 1982, retains the basic architecture of the original MC 68000 but provides additional support for virtual memory. This similarity of architectures enables many different 16-bit microprocessor chips to be studied through evaluation and comparison of a few families of chips.

Virtually all manufacturers of 16-bit chips have designed 32-bit chips which are compatible with the earlier 16-bit chips. The Motorola MC 68020 and the National NS 32032 are very similar in architecture to the MC 68000 and the NS 16032, respectively. However, Intel preferred to enter the 32-bit arena in 1981 with its iAPX 432 which is very different from its earlier chips. Table III summarizes the characteristics of three families of 32-bit microprocessors which possess no 16-bit equivalent. Overall, the performance of the newer microprocessors approaches the performance of mainframes. The Intel 432 at 8-MHz clock frequency takes 6.375 μs for a 32-bit integer multiply and 27.875 μs for an 80-bit floating-point multiply. The equivalent figures for the IBM 370/148 are 16.0 and 38.5 μs, respectively.

In terms of basic computational power, the iAPX 432 is superior
to an IBM 370/148, and the Western Electric 32000 and the
Hewlett-Packard processors are expected to be superior compared
to an IBM 370/158. However, whereas the IBM 370 family is
supported by extensive software in terms of compilers and
application programs, it would take some time for similar
facilities to be available on 32-bit microprocessors. A typical
end user has to decide among several options: wait for the
desired application software to become commercially available;
develop the software in house; or use an earlier generation
microprocessor that provides the software needed.

Concurrent with the development of basic processors,
manufacturers have developed sophisticated chips for auxiliary
functions--memory management, control of DMA operations, control
of peripherals, bus management and arbitration, control of
communications, and control of input and output functions.
However, a particular chip of this kind is designed to support
only a particular family of microprocessor chips of a particular
vendor. Exhaustive lists of chips are published annually in
several trade magazines. Usually there is a time lag between
the introduction of the processor chip itself and the introduction
of support chips. This results in extra effort in implementing
systems based on recently introduced microprocessors.

TRENDS IN MICROPROCESSOR SOFTWARE

In order to take over applications previously handled by
minicomputers and mainframes, users demand that microprocessor
based systems offer high throughput, ease of use, and friendliness

of the system. To optimize utilization of resources and to
minimize user effort, an <u>operating system</u> is used. It is used
for some or all of the following functions:

    a) processor management,

    b) memory management,

    c) peripheral management,

    d) file management,

    e) task scheduling and process management,

    f) user-oriented facilities like command-line interpreter,

    g) miscellaneous features to support networking, utilities,
       and high-level languages.

In order to fully comprehend the emerging trends in
microcomputer software, it is relevant to know a little about
the history of the popular operating systems.

The earliest uses of microprocessors were in embedded
control applications. Programs were written on mainframe
computers, cross-assembled for the micro, and loaded as object
code into the micro's memory for execution. To aid the writing
of such control programs, Intel, in 1972, hired MAA (Microcomputer
Application Associates, later to become Digital Research) to
design and implement a systems programming language. This
language, called PL/M (Programming Language for Microcomputers)
used ideas from PL/I, Algol, and XPL, the command-writing language.
PL/M became quite popular and is still used.

Along with PL/M, MAA proposed a small operating system,
called CP/M (Control Program for Microcomputers), to enable
applications to be written and compiled on the Intel 8080-based
microcomputer. As Intel was reluctant, MAA developed the product

independently in 1975. CP/M subsequently became the most popular
operating system for microcomputers; now there are 200,000
installations using a wide spectrum of hardware configurations.
It has become one of the de facto standards with most vendors in
both the United States and abroad supporting it on their 8-bit
and 16-bit microprocessors.

UNIX, developed during the 1970s at Bell Laboratories, is
the premier example of an operating system optimized for program
development by professional programmers in a multiuser
interactive environment. The popularity of UNIX can be judged
by the vast number of look-alike operating systems, such as:
Coherent and Xenix on the 8086, Zeus, Onix, and Xenix on the
Z-8000; Uniflex, Idris, Coherent, and Xenix on the 68000; Cromix,
UNIX, and Idris on the Z-80; and Idris, Xenix, and Coherent on
LSI-11 and PDP-11 systems.

According to Kenneth Thompson, the principal architect of
the UNIX operating system, "the UNIX kernel consists of about
10,000 lines of C code and about 1,000 lines of assembly code.
The assembly code can be further broken down into 200 lines
included for the sake of efficiency (they could have been written
in C) and 800 lines to perform hardware functions not possible in
C. The assembly code represents 5 to 10 percent of what has been
lumped into the broad expression the UNIX operating system. The
kernel is the only UNIX code that cannot be substituted by the
user to his own liking." Some companies like Microsoft have
adapted this hardware-dependent code for several microprocessors.
Others like Mark Williams Company have chosen to rewrite the entire
code based on the UNIX design.

Inspired by UNIX, Digital Research, the originator of CP/M, has developed the MP/M operating system. Similar to UNIX, MP/M is a multiuser, multitasking operating system. But unlike UNIX, MP/M has a real-time kernel that can be either interrupt-driven or dependent upon device polling. Also, MP/M uses multilevel directories rather than the tree structure provided by UNIX. In the UNIX environment, a fast disk file is used as a buffer to communicate between two processes. Such "pipes" are opened and closed as standard files, but are limited to character I/O only. MP/M permits variably sized messages to be written to and to be read from an unlimited number of processes, through buffers maintained in the memory. Each such "queue" has a name and is treated like other disk files. Further, queues can be optimized for message sizes. UNIX, on the other hand, offers a large array of excellent system development tools, and the ability to link utilities through a single command. The advent of personal computers has resulted in a growing popularity of the MS-DOS operating system developed by Microsoft. This operating system is supported on many leading computers of U.S. and Japanese make. Today, UNIX, MS-DOS and CP/M are the three standard operating systems which are popular in the realm of microcomputers.

Unfortunately in all these cases, even though the same operating system is supported on several computer systems, the differences in hardware make it essential to modify application programs to execute under the same operating system on different systems. New techniques are evolving that enable such differences to be transparant to end users. For example, the UCSD p-system, originally developed by the University of California at San Diego, permits maximum level of software portability through use of intermediate code, called p-code, into which all the high-level

languages are compiled. When a new processor is introduced, the
p-system is implemented simply by writing an interpreter that
translates p-code into the new processor's native code. The
penalty is in terms of reduced execution speed of interpreted
code. The advantage is in terms of ability to execute the same
program under different environments like 8086, Z8000, 68000,
TI 9900, and others. As microprocessors offer increased speeds,
and as programming costs continue to escalate, it is likely that
more users will accept the penalty of reduced execution speeds,
and opt for using such techniques of intermediate code to aid
conversion of programs to achieve software compatibility.

In the domain of large computer systems, Fortran and Cobol
became industry standards by virtue of their availability on a
large number of systems. This does not, however, imply that all
vendors offered identical languages. The transitional problem
of incompatible higher level languages has been carried over to
the microprocessor area. Although Basic is supported on almost
all systems, the different vendors offer significantly different
versions, depending on word size, memory addressing, and other
factors. Frequently, multiple versions of Basic are available
for the same machine (for example, on the IBM Personal Computer
alone there are three versions of Basic available). The current
trend in new operating systems is to support Pascal and Ada.
These two languages are likely to be major forces in coming
years. The increasing use of higher level languages will mitigate
the problems of soaring software development costs. The operating
systems themselves are also written entirely in higher level
languages.

TRENDS IN APPLICATION SOFTWARE

Application programs are comprised of two generic types:
i) programs for particular problems, e.g., a cardiac monitoring
program, a diet tracking program; and ii) generic tools that
facilitate solutions in a wide variety of areas, e.g., spreadsheet
programs, database, charting, and graphing programs. The latter
category is sometimes termed the fourth generation of programming
languages in recognition of the fact that such generic tools offer
greater programming functionality and a higher level of portability
than third-generation higher level languages such as Fortran and
Cobol. A VisiCalc environment on a personal computer, for example,
offers users a reasonably friendly environment to execute commands
that directly focus on the application problem.

Ten years ago a typical application used 3K bytes of memory
at a hardware cost of $100 to hold an application program of
1,000 lines of assembly language code. Considering productivity
in 1975 to be around 10 lines per day of finished, documented,
and debugged code and manpower costs of $40,000 including overhead,
this program would have taken less than one-half man-year to
complete at a cost of $20,000. By 1980 the software development
cost had escalated to nearly half a million dollars if done in
assembly language and to $100,000 if done in a higher level
language. Such costs now exceed $750,000 for a typical program
developed from scratch including runtime libraries and utilities.
These industry estimates (Table IV) reflect the underlying fact
that software development costs can be prohibitive. In 1980 the
development of a reasonably sophisticated spreadsheet package is
estimated to have consumed around $500,000 including all coding,
testing, documentation, and support necessary to bring the

Table IV: Software Development Costs for a Typical Microprocessor Application (Industry Estimates)

Year	Hardware Cost of Memory	Bytes of Memory	No. Lines of Finished Code[†]	Man Years	Software Development Expenditure
1975	$100	3K	1K	0.5*	$ 20,000
1980	$120	40–45K	13K ASL	6.5**	$450,000
			3K HLL	1.5**	$100,000
1985	$250	500K	20K HLL[††]	~7.0***	$875,000

  * ~10 lines/day; $40K/man year including overhead
  ** ~10 lines/day; $70K/man year including overhead
*** ~15 lines/day; $125K/man year including overhead; note that this assumes a 50-percent increase in programmer productivity over 1975 and 1980 figures.
[†] Lines refer to debugged, documented, finished lines of code that appear in the final product.
[††] Includes allowance for run-time libraries and utilities.

product to market. Because of these high costs, microcomputer
programs are geared towards activities with a large potential
customer base. Moreover, smaller organizations with lower overhead
structures than large organizations can develop microcomputer
applications for substantially smaller costs than shown in Table
IV. Consequently, an entire cottage industry of individual
entrepreneurs working out of their homes, or similar low-overhead
environments, has provided the lion's share of microcomputer
software development activity.

Whereas programs for specialized functions (and smaller
customer bases) are typically priced between $500 and $5,000,
home-oriented software usually is priced under $50. In between
these two extremes are the general business packages such as
VisiCalc, VisiPlot, and 1-2-3. It is products in this middle
range ($100-$500) that hold the potential for revolutionizing
the work environment altogether, of making "electronic cottages"
a reality, and of further nucleating the widespread use of
microcomputers. Newer software products are consciously designed
so as to provide a reasonably friendly user interface. Examples
include the orientation towards natural languages and the support
of speech input and output capabilities that dispense with the
need for good typing skills.

One good example of this phenomenon is the predominant
use of "menus" in microcomputers, while mainframes and
minicomputers continue to depend primarily on command languages.
Hierarchically organized menus permit users to do complex tasks
with efficiency and with no errors since the user is able to
select only a "valid" choice. Also, there is no longer any
requirement to memorize different options--one needs only to be

able to "recognize," rather than recall, an option. While menu
structures differ from program to program, microcomputers are
standardizing around menu-driven user interfaces. Menu-driven
interfaces are already standard in the case of spreadsheet packages
which are used for manipulating sets of numbers. Similar
techniques are becoming popular for database packages, too.

Unlike previous generation languages (Basic, Pascal, and
Fortran) which offered little support for transferring information
between alternative programming environments, fourth-generation
languages support such exchange through the concept of "windows."
These windows, which are simply separate areas or boxes on the
display screen, are used to facilitate the simultaneous display
of multiple programs on a microcomputer and to enable information
to be interchanged between such programs.

The concept of "windows" as an effective user interface was
pioneered by the Smalltalk system developed at the Xerox Palo
Alto Research Center. This graphics oriented interface presents
images of several overlapping pieces of paper on a grey electronic
desktop. Each piece of paper, or window, represents an activity
which can proceed independently of all others. A "mouse" is used
to select a window, to operate a scrolling mechanism that brings
the desired data into view in the window, and to invoke commands
from menus. The Apple Lisa uses this window concept, as well
as the concept of a menu bar containing up to twelve different
menu titles. The concept of visual _icons_, which originated in
the Xerox Star user interface, has been used in systems such as
the Apple Lisa/MacIntosh and the $200 Commodore 64 computer.
Instead of using words, the menu uses pictures of objects. For
example, to type, one points to the typewriter; to erase, one

points to the trash basket; and so on.

The use of pictorial information in the field of microcomputers was initially spearheaded by the myriad of game
packages on home computers. In such packages the entire picture
was designed in advance, and the user was given no flexibility
to alter the picture displayed. Then came business oriented
packages like VisiPlot, 1-2-3, Chartmaster, and Chartman which
allowed data to be displayed in the form of line diagrams, bar
charts, pie charts, and histograms. Currently, we are witnessing
the era of presentation graphics packages with emphasis on
creating pictures for meetings and presentations. Whereas a
two-dimensional representation suffices for business applications,
many engineering applications in the CAD/CAM areas need
three-dimensional graphics with shading and real-time simulation
capabilities. It has now become feasible to generate fairly
sophisticated graphic images using inexpensive software products
such as VCN ExecuVision.

Conversion of mainframe and minicomputer software to a
microcomputer environment represents an interesting development.
The limited capabilities of the microcomputer do not, in general,
allow for a mainframe software package to be transported in its
entirety to a microcomputer. Also, because of large centralized
databases it is not always desirable to move the entire mainframe
package. Most likely, the original mainframe software is
partially hosted to different degrees on both machines with
communications between them. The microcomputer provides terminal
emulation, screen handling and query preprocessing and
postprocessing capabilities. The mainframe retains responsibility
for its principal task of database access, security, and query

response. Thus a large number of tasks previously handled by
the mainframe alone are now split between the microcomputer and
the host. A system such as the IBM PC-XT/370 offers facilities
for better interfacing to the mainframe and for executing the
original programs with little or no modification. Depending on
the make of the mainframe or the minicomputer which is currently
being used in an organization, there are some advantages in
using a microcomputer of the same make or, alternatively, a
microcomputer which offers facilities for emulation of instruction
sets of the mainframe computer.

CONCLUSION

The ability to implement increasing numbers of devices on
the same chip has enabled microprocessors to offer increased
functional capabilities at diminishing costs over the years. The
enhanced capabilities are in the areas of processing power,
peripheral support, and in terms of software. These trends are
likely to continue. The domain of microprocessors constitutes
a dynamic world, and we can always expect newer and more
powerful chips.

The spectacular advances in microprocessor technology have
catalyzed the computer revolution. Fully functional computing
gadgets are now available at a price level comparable to that
of television sets and stereo systems. From being a novelty
item for organizations and institutions, microcomputers are now
perceived as consumer items for the masses. Like the contemporary
automobile which has replaced several traditional modes of
transportation, microcomputers are poised to become the
dominant category of computers!

ACKNOWLEDGEMENT

This chapter contains some material from two edited books
[1], [2] and a paper [3] published by the IEEE. The author thanks
the IEEE for giving permission to use this material.

FOR FURTHER READING

[1] Amar Gupta and H. D. Toong (eds.), <u>Insights Into Personal</u>
     <u>Computers</u>, IEEE Press, New York, 1985.

[2] Amar Gupta and H. D. Toong (eds.), <u>Advanced Microprocessors</u>,
     IEEE Press, New York, 1983.

[3] Amar Gupta and H. D. Toong, "Microprocessors--The First Twelve
     Years," <u>Proc. of the IEEE</u>, November 1983.

[4] Amar Gupta and H. D. Toong, "An Architectural Comparison of
     32-Bit Microprocessors," <u>IEEE Micro</u>, February 1983.

[5] H. D. Toong and Amar Gupta, "An Architectural Comparison of
     Contemporary 16-Bit Microprocessors," <u>IEEE Micro</u>, May 1981.

[6] H. D. Toong and Amar Gupta, "Evaluation Kernels for
     Microprocessor Performance Analyses," <u>Perform. Eval.</u>, North
     Holland Publishing Company, May 1982.

[7] K. Thomson, "The UNIX Operating System," <u>Bell System Technical</u>
     <u>Journal</u>, July-August 1978.

[8]   Paul M. Russo, "VLSI Impact on Microprocessor Evolution, Usage,
      and System Design," IEEE Trans. Electron. Devices, August 1980.

[9]   Dennis Moralee, "Microprocessor Architectures: Ten Years of
      Development," Electron. and Power, March 1981.

[10] R. Rice, VLSI Support Technologies--A Tutorial, IEEE Press,
      New York, 1982.

[11] D. J. McGreivy and K. A. Pickar, VLSI Technologies Through
      the 80s and Beyond, IEEE Press, New York, 1982.

CHAPTER 39.

DEVELOPMENTS IN LARGE COMPUTER SYSTEMS

DR. CHRIS NORRIE
The Amdahl Corporation, Sunnyvale, U.S.A.

> Supercomputers: the class of computer most
> suited to solving superproblems.

Many problems of both scientific and engineering basis require the solution of computationally very large problems in either a reasonable or critical time period. Often the resolution of the result depends on how much computation can be achieved within that time. Increasing need for finer resolution on larger and larger problems is causing the advent of:

1. faster and faster processors

2. more sophisticated, faster and finely tuned algorithms

This chapter takes a glimpse at various supercomputer architectures which are particularly suited to problems requiring the solution of mega, giga (and tera?) number of floating-point arithmetic operations. Such large problems are termed superproblems.

Before embarking on an investigation into developments in large computer systems two terms will need further definition:

1. superproblems

2. supercomputers

SUPERPROBLEMS

Large scale computing involves the solution of exceedingly many floating-point operations. These occur in problems which are not only exceptionally large and complex but also those which are more modest in size and are non-linear and/or time dependent.

Often the problems to be solved are continuous-field problems (i.e., problems that involve phenomina which act over a continuous region such as heat conduction in a rocket during atmospheric re-entry) and the solution is via a numerical approximation-technique. In this class of numerical technique the continuous field is approximated by a discrete and finite set of nodal points. The differential equations describing the physics of the the continuous field are then applied to the nodes and an approximate solution may thus be obtained. If the differential equations describing the physics of a node are a function of the values of neighbouring nodes then the numerical technique may require iteration in order to converge onto a steady-state solution. As the number of nodes is increased the continuous field is better approximated and, hence, the solution becomes more fully resolved but at the expense of an increase in computational requirements. If the problem involves geometric and/or material non-linearities, as well as for time-dependent problems, the entire approximation procedure must be repeated for each deformation increment or time slice, often a great many times in total. [Norrie[1]]

Continuous-field problems requiring numerical approximations arise in many diverse fields such as fluid dynamics, nuclear physics, astronomy, structural analysis, oil exploration, quantum physics, and meteorology. Consider the simulation of the aerodynamics around a jet aircraft. The partial-differential equations describing the fluid motion of air with the conservation of mass, energy and momentum are known as the Navier-Stokes equations. There exists a reduced set of these equations known as the Euler equations. (The Euler equations simplify the problem by neglecting various terms of the Navier-Stokes equations such as viscosity and flow perturbation induced by the aircraft). The application of these Euler equations in three dimensions on a complete jet aircraft may require well over 10^{10} floating-point operations. A full

Navier-Stokes solution (which is still not practical on present supercomputers) will require many more orders of computation than this. [Cray[2], Hankey[3]]

A further interesting example of a superproblem is found in the relatively new field known as digital scene simulation. Digital scene simulation is a process of generating life-like scenes via a computer. Its application is particularly useful for the commercial motion picture business. The recently released motion picture 2010 includes scenes produced by digital computers. TRON is another example of a motion picture that employed digital scene simulation. If each 70mm frame of a digitally produced scene is to have a resolution of 4,000 x 6,000 pixels and each pixel colour (red, blue, and green) requires 10 calculations to generate and the motion picture is to run at 24 frames per second then 1.728 x 10^{10} calculations are required to produce one second of animated scenery. In reality, various lighting and rendering requirements result in calculations to ranging anywhere between 1 and 10,000 per pixel. Therefore, one second of motion picture may typically demand anywhere between 1.7 x 10^{10} and 1.7 x 10^{14} arithmetic calculations. Although various shortcuts employed by graphics specialists may reduce these figures, there is still an enormous amount of processing required to produce even short periods of digitally generated motion scenes. In the case of the motion picture 2010, approximately three and a half minutes of Cray-XMP supercomputer time was required to produce each frame. The digital frames are a pseudo-spectral hydrodynamic simulation of the atmosphere of the planet Jupiter. Actual Jovian data was used as a basis for the simulation. [Cray[4], Demos[5]]

<u>SUPERCOMPUTERS</u>

Although no firm definition of supercomputers exist, they are basically the end of the computer range that are most suited to solving

superproblems. Typically they are capable of performing hundreds of millions of floating-point operations per second, have word lengths in the
order of 64 bits and main memory sizes measured in millions of words.
Quoting Neil Lincoln, "A supercomputer is a system that is only one generation behind the computing requirements of leading edge efforts in science and engineering" [Lincoln⁶]. Both past and present examples include
Control Data Corporation's CDC-6600, Star-100 and Cyber-205, Burrough's
Illiac IV and BSP (Burrough's Scientific Processor), Denelcor's HEP-1 and
HEP-2, Goodyear's STARAN, Texas Instruments ASC (A Scientific Computer)
and Cray Research's Cray-1 and Cray-XMP.

     Two principal divisions exist:

     1. special-purpose supercomputers

     2. general-purpose supercomputers

Special-purpose machines have their architecture designed around a
specific problem or type of problem. This makes them particularly well
suited for a reasonably fast solution of that problem. However, one of
their main objections is the development cost required to produce such
few machines for such a narrow spectrum of problems.   General-purpose
machines, on the other hand, allow a very wide range of problems to
easily be moulded onto the architecture.

     Both class of supercomputer are designed to exploit the type of pro-
cessing commonly found in superproblems. In essence, this is:

     1. matrix manipulations

     2. loop manipulations (of non-matrix processing)

     3. scalar manipulations (i.e., operations on single variables)

Generally, loop manipulations can be reduced to a set of matrix-like
operations. Consider the two synonomous program segments:

```
100  DO 300 I=1,N              400  READ (5,30) (A(I),B(I), I=1,N)

     READ (5,10) A,B                DO 500 I=1,N

200  C = A * B                 500  C(I) = A(I) * B(I)

300  WRITE (6,20) C            600  WRITE (6,40) (C(I), I=1,N)
```

Lines 100-300 involve a loop operation. Lines 400-600 have separated the I/0 statements from the processing loop and replaced the scalar computation of line 200 with a matrix operation. Although the loop could have been left as a loop of scalar and I/0 operations, supercomputer exploitation of matrix operations leads to execution that is faster than the equivalent scalar operations. Hence, problems are best described as manipulations of matrices in preference to manipulations of scalars.

The two most significant supercomputer architectures that presently exist for the efficient handling of matrices are array processors (also known as SIMD (single-instruction multiple-data) processors) and vector processors. These architectures may be incorporated into both special-purpose and general-purpose machines.

ARRAY PROCESSORS

These are single-instruction multiple-data (SIMD) machines. As the name implies, a single instruction may act on many sets of operands or data simultaneously. This necessitates the availability of many arithmetic units. Figure 1 shows a block diagram of an array processor.

The control processor is itself a computer. It has its own local memory, arithmetic unit, registers, control unit, etc. The crucial difference between the control processor and the arithmetic processors is that the arithmetic processors lack the ability to interpret conditional-branch instructions. Their mode of operation is to run as a slave to the control processor. It is often the case that array processors may supplement or even replace the local memories by a global and common memory with a suitable organisation.

Basically, the operation of this type of computer is for the control unit to fetch an instruction and determine whether or not it is a matrix operation. If it is, then the instruction is passed onto the arithmetic

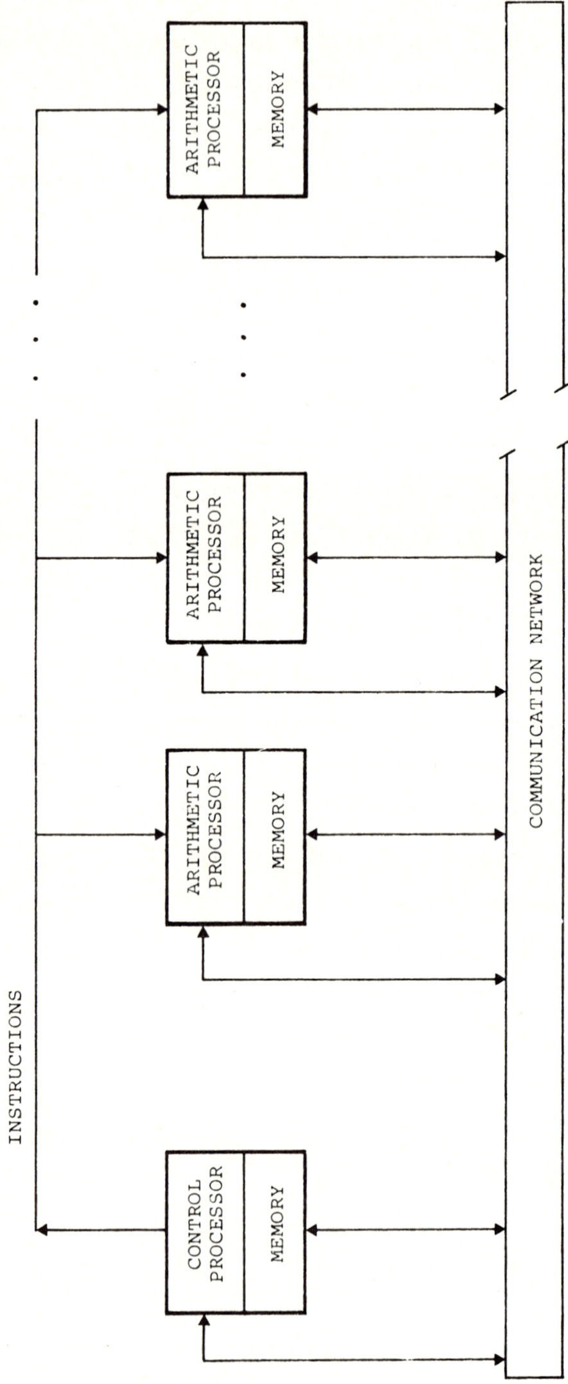

Figure 1. Block diagram for an array processor.

processors, each of which hold a partition of the matrix being operated on inside their own local memory. In the simplest case the arithmetic processors hold exactly one element of the matrix operands. However, if the size of the matrices exceeds the number of processors in the array then the processors may hold a row or a column or a sub-matrix of the operands. Since all of the arithmetic processors receive instructions from the control processor simultaneously, the entire matrix operation proceeds in parallel. If a fetched instruction is not a matrix operation then the control processor does not pass it onto the arithmetic processors but executes it itself.

Since array processors are generally designed for high processing rates, especially if they are to be classified in the supercomputer class, it is of critical importance that the system is designed such that a high flow of data and instructions can be maintained. More specifically, this means a high-bandwidth link to memory and a high-bandwidth link between the control processor and arithmetic processors. The instruction stream within the control processor should be highly buffered so as to minimise memory contention with other processors. Instruction fetching can be done in parallel with operations which do not require the use of common memory. Instruction throughput can be substantially enhanced by the use of techniques such as pipelining. Another option is multiple instruction-issuing for certain instruction pairs. This allows scalar operations in the control processor to be performed in parallel with matrix operations being performed within the arithmetic processors.

In order to get a greater appreciation of this type of computer, four modes of operation will be identified. It is solely up to the control processor to recognise these modes and take appropriate action.

<u>Mode 1:</u> Processor Independency.

Consider a matrix addition:

$$A(i,j) = B(i,j) + C(i,j) : i = 1,m; j = 1,n$$

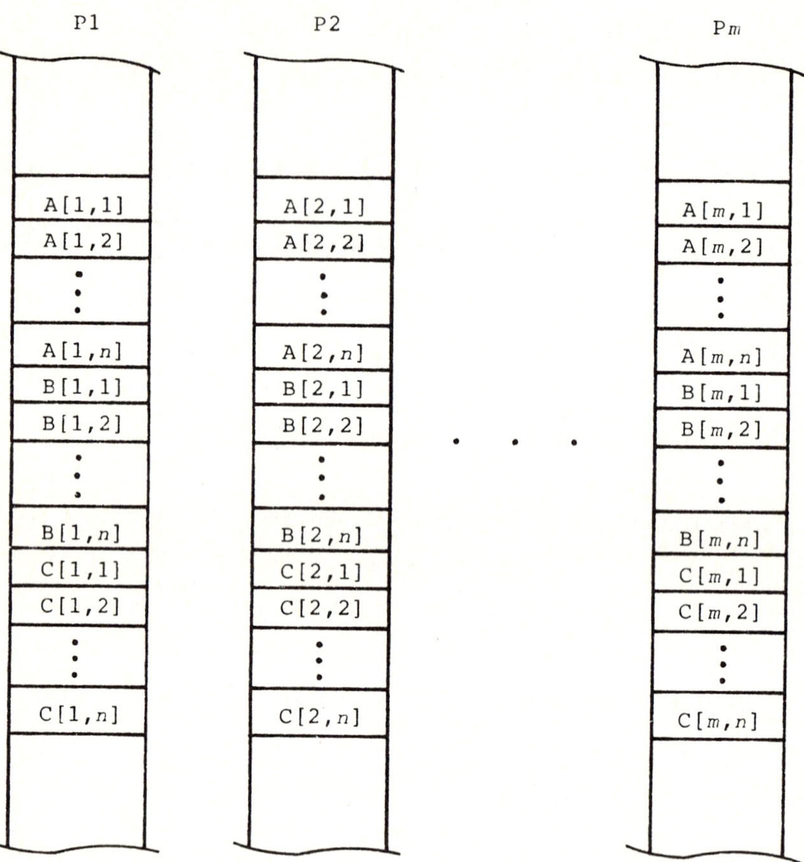

Figure 2.   Memory map for processors P1 to Pm each holding
a row from matrices A, B and C.

In the case where there are at least m x n processors, each processor can hold a particular subscript, (i,j), of the operands B and C. The control processor need only issue the command A = B + C in order to accomplish the matrix addition. In the case where there are less than m x n processors, each processor may hold a row of the operand matrices as depicted in Figure 2. Execution now requires the control processor to issue a loop of instructions of the form A(k) = B(k) + C(k) : k = 1,n. Depending on the structure of the problem it may be desirable that each processor hold a column or submatrix or a particular structure of the operand matrices instead. Nevertheless, the control processor will still need to issue a sequence of instructions or an instruction that automatically issues a sequence of operations within the arithmetic processors. Intuition suggests that index registers in an array processor are as important as index registers in any simple scalar-processor.

The similarities between simple general-purpose scalar processors and the arithmetic processors of the array processor are evident. Their instruction repertoirs obviously include the same kind of instructions, although the arithmetic processors may also include instructions that are specific to their working environment within the array-processor network.

Efficiency of this mode is high due to the large proportion of processors working in parallel.

Mode 2: Processor Dependency.

Consider the dot product of a vector:

C = sum(A(i)*B(i) : i=1,n)

Obviously, the A(i)*B(i) part of the calculation is analogous to the previous mode. However, the summation is a little more difficult. Interprocessor communication is required to pass the A(i)*B(i) products onto other processors so that they can be added as pairs of operands. Obviously, data buses external to the processors must be incorporated into the architecture.

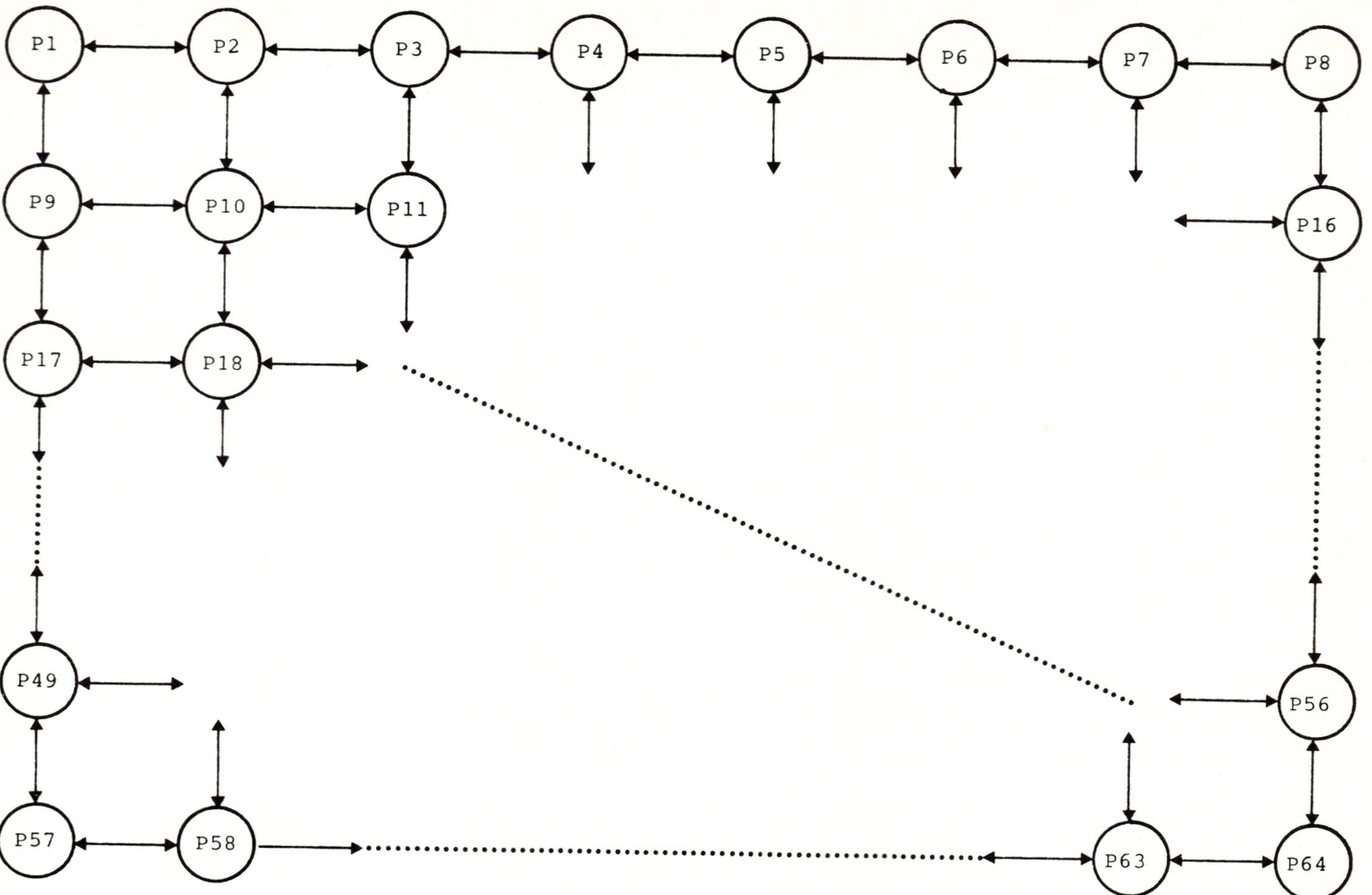

Figure 3.   The cyclic-shift interconnection on a 2-dimensional 64-element array-processor.

Ideally each processor would be directly connected to each other processor. Such a connection is known as a "complete-interconnection network". Due to both cost factors and physical complexity this is generally not a practical solution when the number of processors is anything above a dozen. It is not difficult to see that the expense of a complete-interconnection network is proportional to the square of the number of processors. Since the performance of array processors at best increases linearly with the number of processors in the array, it is not feasible to use complete-interconnection networks on large array processors. Instead, it is better to adopt an interconnection pattern that is suitable for a broad number of applications. Even this is not a simple problem - especially if the computer is to be a general-purpose machine.

A simple interconnection scheme is to join each processor to its nearest neighbours, as depicted in Figure 3. This, known as a two-dimensional cyclic-shift interconnection network, is particularly useful in problems that require interaction with neighbouring values, as does partial-differential equations. For example, an often executed statement could be of the form:

$A(I,J) = (A(I+1,J) + A(I-1,J) + A(I,J+1) + A(I,J-1)) / 4.$

The disadvantage of this type of interconnection scheme becomes apparent in algorithms that require non-cyclic data-permutations. Even algorithms that are cyclic in nature often require non-cyclic data-permutations. For example, dynamic models of continuous fields require periodic re-zoning in order for the model to conserve the laws of physics when the continuous-field approximation becomes distorted. The effectiveness of this interconnection scheme is drastically reduced in such circumstances.

A more innovative interconnection scheme is the bidirectional perfect-shuffle. Its name is derived from the perfect shuffle with a set of playing cards; the deck is split into two equal halves which are interlaced together with successive cards originating from alternate

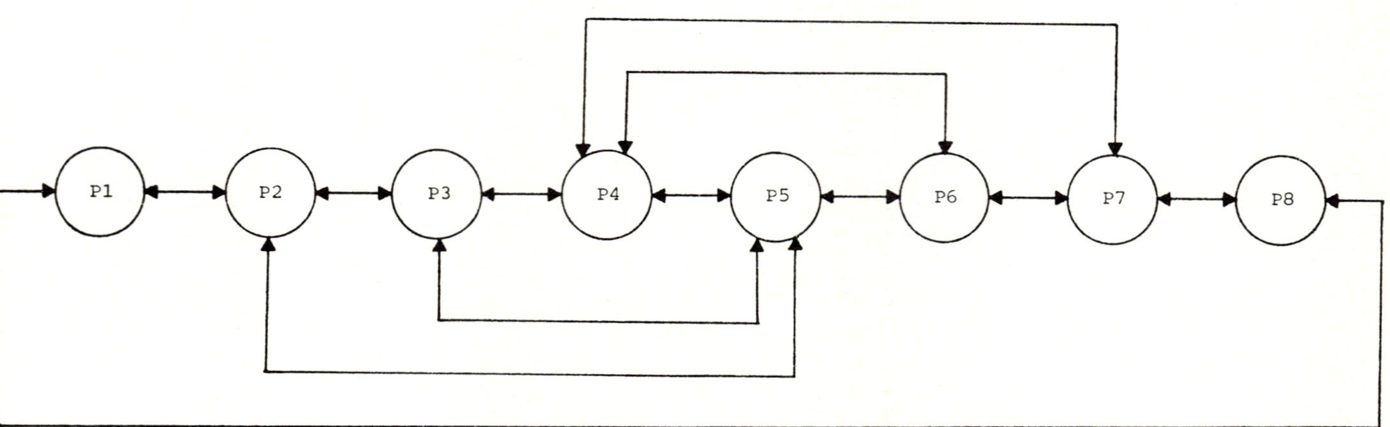

Figure 4.   A cyclic-shift interconnection network augmented with a perfect-shuffle interconnection network.

halves. The processors are connected such that the xth processor of the unshuffled deck is bidirectionally interconnected to the xth processor of the shuffled deck. At first this seems to be a rather odd interconnection scheme but upon analysis it is soon found that quite a collection of parallel algorithms can make use of it. These algorithms include sorting, matrix transposition, Fourier Transforms, etc. The power of such an interconnection scheme is greatly enhanced when it is incorporated with even just an elementary cyclic-shift interconnection network. In fact, it has been discovered that when the number of processors is a power of two and a perfect shuffle is augmented with a cyclic-shift interconnection network and particular data structures are used then some very efficient parallel algorithms can be derived for a whole host of problems [Lawrie[7]]. Although this subject is too involved to delve into here, Stone[8] gives an introduction to algorithms for interconnection networks and Stone[9] gives a more detailed analysis of this. Figure 4 shows the actual interconnections on an eight-processor machine with both a cyclic shift and perfect-shuffle interconnection network.

Efficiency of this second mode varies between mediocre and high, depending on the operation being performed. Some operations cause certain processors to stand idle while others continue on. Other operations can maintain coherency between processors despite their dependencies on each other. How well this is achieved is, of course, algorithm dependent where the algorithm in turn is relying on various processor interconnections. For example, the best algorithm working on a simple cyclic-shift interconnection can sum 64 elements from 64 processors in no less than 32 shifts. However, the same problem can be solved in as little as 6 shifts providing an interconnection scheme is available that supports the necessary binary-shifting process. (6 is the base two logarithm of 64).

<u>Mode 3:</u> Processor Idling.

This mode occurs when the control processor fetches a scalar instruction from memory. While one processor carries out the operation all others stand idle waiting for the next matrix operation. Obviously, efficiency is relatively very poor. For this reason, it is possible to find that the processor that executes the scalar instructions runs faster than all the other processors. It is also for the same reason why there is particular value in having a sophisticated instruction-streaming mechanism within the control processor. As already discussed, this sophistication may include extensive instruction buffering, instruction-stream pipelining (especially for instruction decoding) and multiple instruction-issuing hardware.

A similar condition to Mode 3 also exists when there may be n arithmetic processors but the problem is using matrices of size n + d where d is small compared to n. Two phases of operation are necessary to process the matrices. In the first phase, n processors process n elements of the matrices. In the second phase, d processors process the remaining matrice elements and n - d processors remain idle.

<u>Mode 4:</u> Conditional Processing.

Since all of the arithmetic processors receive the same sequence of instructions from the control processor, a problem arises as to the solution of a statement such as:

IF (A(I,J).LT.O.) A(I,J) = O.

Each processor can determine if its A(i,j) is less than zero but only some processors are allowed to execute A(i,j) = O. The difficulty is that if any A(i,j) is less than zero then the control processor is compelled to issue the operation A(i,j) = O. This results in all of the arithmetic processors receiving the A(i,j) = O commands, not just the applicable ones. The problem is overcome via a "processor-enable mask". Simply, a processor only listens to the instruction stream from the control processor while its associated bit in the processor-enable mask is set. In the above example, the IF statement is used to set the processor-enable mask. Therefore, only those processors that did not

switch themselves off by failing the IF test can execute $A(i,j) = 0$.   It
is up to the control processor to reset the mask at the appropriate time.

The mask also gives the control processor the ability to select particular rows and/or columns that a particular operation is to be performed on. This is important when the problem of having n processors and
$n + d$ matrice elements is reconsidered; in the second phase of the matrix
operation the control processor must switch off $n - d$ processors while
the remaining appropriate processors complete the operation.

It can be seen that the control processor should include in its
instruction repertoir a set of instructions that operate on the processor
enable mask. Instructions such as logical, shift, complement, test, set,
etc., would be of invaluable aid. Consider the following IF-THEN-ELSE
statement:

      IF condition

         THEN code_1

         ELSE code_2

The control processor will issue the corresponding operations:

      issue instructions to test condition

            (the condition code of each arithmetic processor

            will reflect the result of the evaluated condition)

      SET MASK according to the arithmetic processors' condition codes

      issue instructions for code_1

      COMPLEMENT MASK

      issue instructions for code_2

      SET MASK to turn all arithmetic processors on

It is immediately apparent that the control processor issues instructions
for both the THEN code and the ELSE code. Hence, the efficiency of conditional branching in an array processor is reduced.   This performance
degradation can be minimised by the ability to test the processor enable
mask. If the control processor does such a test and it recognises that
all of the arithmetic processors disabled themselves (i.e., they all

failed the test) then it may skip the pertinent section of code; there is
no value in broadcasting redundant code to the arithmetic processors.

One of the earlier and famous array processors was the Illiac IV and
this is discussed in Slotnik[11] for those who are interested. Although a
powerful machine, only one was ever put into production [Kozdrowicki[13]].
It resided at NASA Ames Research Center, Mountain View, California. Only
a few years back did it finally yield to the more modern Cray-1 supercomputer.

A present day example of an array processor is the Burrough's Scientific Processor (BSP). This has a scalar-processing unit to supplement
the parallel-processing unit that holds the array of arithmetic processors. This helps overcome the inefficiency of Mode 3 previously discussed. The scalar processor reads all instructions from main storage
and passes the "vectorised" instructions onto the parallel-processing
unit. The parallel processing unit consists of one control processor and
16 arithmetic processors. A hardware mechanism exists for the automatic
control of vectors that are not integral lengths of 16 elements. Memory
is not tied to particular processors but is arranged into 17 independent
banks. This permits arithmetic elements to simultaneously access up to
16 elements of a matrix row, column, or diagonal. The system clock runs
with a cycle time of 160ns (1 nanosecond = $1/10^9$ seconds) and two clock
cycles are required for basic arithmetic instructions. This allows a
maximum result rate of 50 megaflops (million floating-point operations
per second). Floating-point numbers are 48 bits wide (36-bit mantissa,
10-bit exponent, and 2 sign bits) but double precision hardware extends
this.

VECTOR PROCESSORS

These too are sometimes referred to as SIMD machines [Stone[8]] but
the reason is less obvious than that of the array processor. In essence,

a "vector instruction" operates on a sequence of operands (a vector) rather than on single operands. Vector processing implies the use of a technique known as pipelining, but pipelining does not necessarily imply vector processing.

Pipelining can be simply understood with reference to an assembly line. Consider a car manufacturing plant. It may be segmented into m stages where each stage carries out a particular operation on the evolving vehicle. If each stage requires no more than t minutes to complete then the assembly line can move at a rate of one stage per t minutes. Hence, tm minutes are required for any one particular car to be produced. Now consider a vehicle that has just finished stage 1 and is moving onto stage 2. Stage 1 is now free to carry out its particular operation on a new vehicle. At the end of a further t minutes, stage 2 can move onto stage 3, stage 1 onto stage 2 and stage 1 is again free to start on another vehicle. After tm minutes the first car has passed through the entire assembly line and is now ready for dispatch. Since there is also a vehicle following one stage behind, it too will be ready in a further t minutes. In fact, now that the assembly line is full, cars will be produced at a rate of one car per t minutes despite the fact that each car requires tm minutes to construct.

The same principle can be applied to computers. For example, a possible floating-point multiplication pipeline (cf., assembly line) is shown in Figure 5.

Presume each stage requires no more than t clock cycles to complete. The following conclusions can be drawn:

1. The startup time (i.e., the time between the first operand entering the pipeline and the first result appearing at the end of the pipeline) is 5t.

2. The total data movement to keep the pipeline saturated is three items (2 operands and 1 result) per t clock periods.

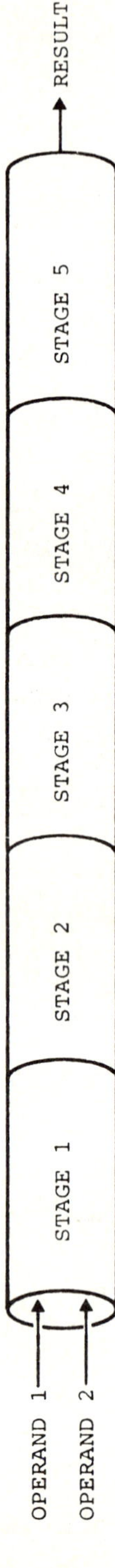

STAGE 1: COMPARE EXPONENTS

STAGE 2: ALIGN OPERANDS ACCORDINGLY

STAGE 3: ADD EXPONENTS AND MULTIPLY MANTISSAS

STAGE 4: DETERMINE NORMALISATION FACTOR

STAGE 5: NORMALISE RESULT

Figure 5. A simplistic pipeline for floating-point multiplication.

Three points are eminent:

1. The shorter t is, the faster results can be produced. (t = 1/result rate). Since computers cannot compute at or faster than the speed of light, t has a minimum of one clock cycle. If a floating-point multiplication requires at minimum k clock cycles then there must be at least k segments in the pipeline for t = 1.

2. The startup time of the pipeline is given by kt.

3. The shorter t is the greater the bandwidth for data movement outside the pipeline is. For t = 1, this is three data items per clock cycle per pipeline.

The high bandwidth has caused the advent of vector processing. This technique is designed to exploit the bandwidth in order to keep the pipelines saturated. The high throughput of vector processors is attributed to the level of saturation that can be maintained within the pipeline.

The vector processing technique requires an instruction set repertoir that includes "vector instructions". These vector instructions specify an operation that is to be performed on a selected set of operands. These operands are referred to as "vectors". When the control unit issues a vector instruction, the first element(s) of the vector(s) are sent to the appropriate pipeline via communication lines known as buses. After t clock cycles, the second element(s) of the vector(s) are sent to the same pipeline via the same buses. This continues until all the operands have been transmitted. Meanwhile, after the startup time of the pipeline, the first result appears and is transported via a further bus to its residing location. Every t clock cycles later the subsequent results are dealt with in a synonomous manner. The time to complete the vector instruction is given by:

startup_time + t * (vector_length-1)

Since the startup time is static for any one pipeline and independent of the length of the vector to be processed, the relative speed of a vector instruction (i.e., the number of operations per unit time that is achieved) is increased by:

1. minimising the startup time

2. optimising the length of the vector that can be processed

Minimising the startup time is a function of the computer designer. As for the vector length, this is a function of the programmer. The programmer needs to organise his problem such that the vector lengths maximise throughput on the computer architecture he is working on. This does not necessarily imply long vectors; there may be certain characteristics of the computer architecture that constrain optimal vector lengths.

Thus far emphasis to fast processing of vectors has been stressed. However, the importance of scalar execution capabilities in supercomputers is equally important. Nearly all vectorisable code still requires substantial volumes of scalar manipulation. A supercomputer with a fast vector-processing unit and a slow scalar-processing unit is poorly balanced and this will severely impinge upon instruction throughput. A simple analogy will illustrate: suppose a car drives one mile at 100 miles per hour (mph) then one mile at 1 mph. Although half the distance of the journey is at 100 mph and half is at 1 mph, the average speed of the car is not (100+1)/2 = 50.5 mph. In reality, the average speed of the car is less than 2 mph! The cost of traveling very fast for a short period of time then very slow for an extended period of time does not reap large benefits. Likewise for supercomputers; spending millions of dollars on fast vector-hardware is of little value if only poor scalar-processing support is provided.

Performance of pipelined processors depends greatly upon the order of instructions in the instruction stream. If consecutive instructions have data or control dependencies on each other or contend for resources then instruction issue will be retarded and "holes" will appear in the pipeline. To eliminate such performance degradation, code scheduling is in order. Compilers can statically schedule code to ensure that interdependent instructions are kept separated as best as possible. (Static code-scheduling means that instructions in the instruction stream retain their order during execution). Various dynamic code-scheduling techniques are also known. Dynamic code-scheduling is where a computer's instruction issue logic possesses the ability to issue instructions not necessarily in the order they appear in the instruction stream. Tomasulo's algorithm is one such dynamic code-scheduling technique. This is discussed with good detail in Tomasulo[14] and Weiss[15]. Dynamic code-scheduling has been used very little in the past but interest has been increasing recently, principally in academic circles.

Two present day examples of vector processors are CDC's Cyber-205 and Cray Research's Cray-1. The Cray-1 contains 13 totally independent pipelines referred to as functional units. Each functional unit is designed to carry out a specific task such as multiplication, addition, logical operation, etc. The functional units could be arbitrarily divided into four groups: address, scalar, vector and floating point. Of the 13 functional units, two are for address arithmetic (add/subtract and multiply), four for non-floating-point scalar processing (add/subtract, logical, shift and population/leading-zero-count), four for non-floating-point vector processing (add/subtract, logical, shift and population/leading-zero-count) and three for floating-point operations of either the scalar or vector variety (add/subtract, multiply and reciprocal approximation). The pipeline to main memory may also be considered a functional unit. The vector functional-units are fed from a set of eight vector registers. Each of these vector registers may contain up to 64 numeric quantities, each 64 bits wide. A vector operation must extract at least one of its operands from a vector register and no operands may come directly from memory. (One class of vector operation allows one of the operands to be repetitiously sent from a scalar register while a vector register supplies all of the conjugate operands). This is particularly useful when a vector is to be operated on by a constant.

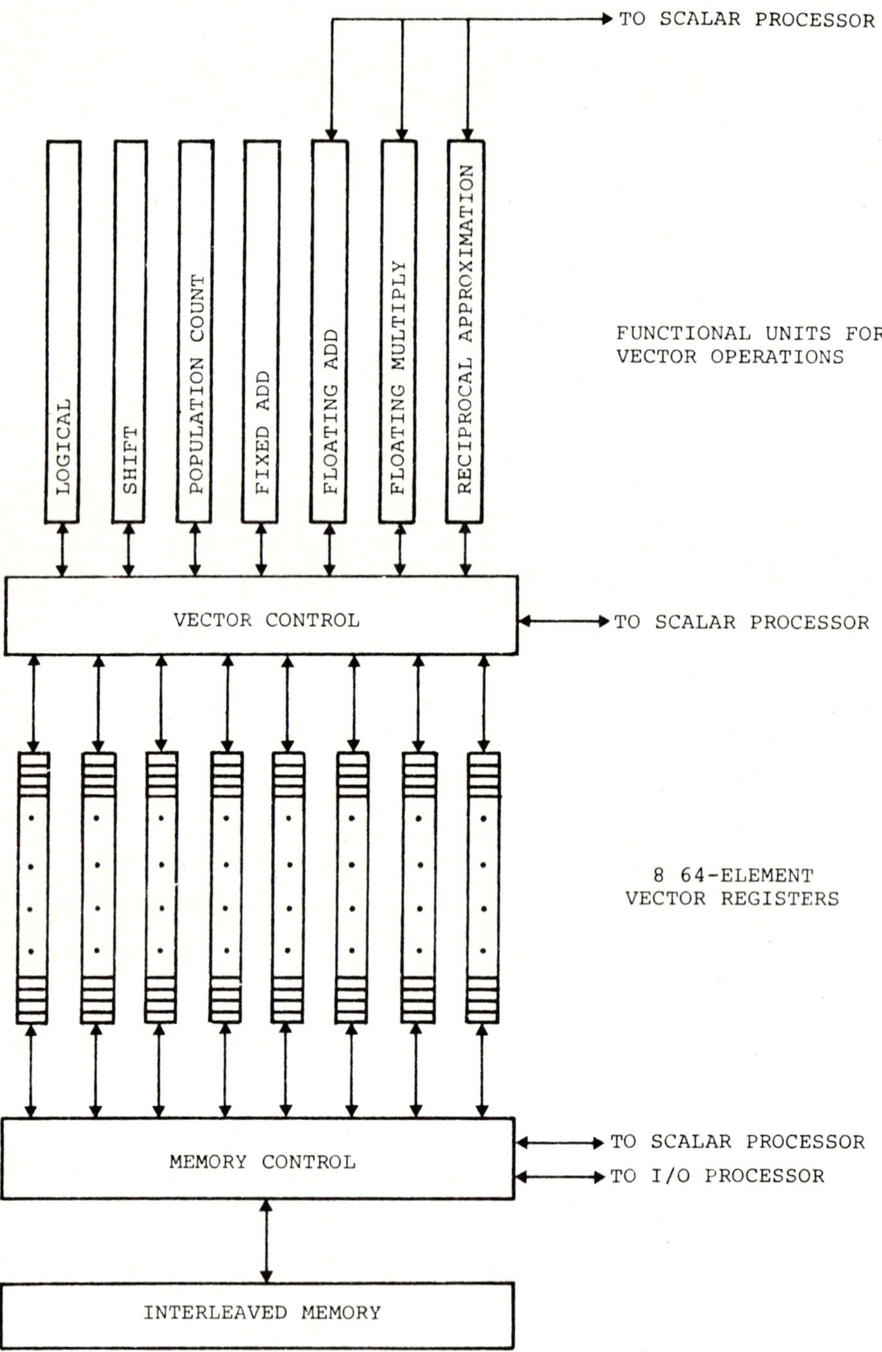

Figure 6. Block diagram of the Cray-1 vector-processing section.

Matrices too large to fit into a vector register require software fragmentation but this is automatically handled by the compiler. The run-time overhead due to matrix fragmentation is minimal since the code necessary for the fragmentation is executed by the scalar pipelines in parallel with the vector pipelines carrying out the matrix operation.

Figure 6 gives an overview of the vector processing side of the Cray-1 supercomputer.

The presence of the vector registers lead to some particularly good advantages. Not only do they reduce the traffic flow to and from the already heavily utilised main memory, but their fast access times assist in mimimising startup times for vector operations. In fact, vector-operation startup times are so erficient that speed advantages of vector processing over scalar processing can be realised for vectors as short as two or three operands.

The Cray-1 processor exploits the vector registers even further via the application of a technique known as "chaining". Consider two vector registers that are to have their corresponding elements multiplied together and the resultant vector added to another vector. Symbolically:

    V2 <= V1 * V0
    V4 <= V3 + V2

where V0 through V4 are five vector registers. After the startup time of the multiplication operation the first result of V2 appears. At this point the second vector operation may be initiated. As results appear out of the multiplication pipeline they are transported via V2 into the addition pipeline along with V3. The net effect is a merge of the two vector operations into one; the addition operation is initiated before the multiplication operation is completed. V2, the multiplication pipe-line and the addition pipeline are links in a chain of operations being being performed. The time required to execute these vector instructions is given by:

    startup_time_of_chain + t * (vector_length-1)

where startup_time_of_chain is equal ιο the summation of the startup
times of the multiplication pipeline and the addition pipeline plus any
inter-pipeline delay. It takes little mathematics to verify that the
speed advantage chaining has over non-chained sequential-processing is
given by the formula:

$$v * t * (vector\_length-1)$$

where v represents the number of pipelines in the chain.

The Cray-1 also includes a very fast address-processing section and
a scalar-processing section with pipelined functional-units that may
operate in parallel with each other as well as the vector-processing sub-
system. The address processor and scalar processor subsystems are complemented with their own sets of fast addressable register banks that
function as an intermediary between main memory and operating registers.
This also reduces traffic to and from the main memory. Since the main
memory runs at one quarter of the speed (50ns) of the CPU (12.5ns) it is
organised into a phased system consisting of 16 interleaved banks. Special pipeline hardware allows rapid access to blocks of data that are
distributed in memory with addresses that increase by units of 1, 2, 4,
8, or 16. (This is of significant value not only for general matrix processing but also for many parallel algorithms). The control unit maintains blocks of code in a set of up to four instruction buffers.
Instructions can be issued at a rate of up to one instruction per machine
cycle.

The Cyber-205 consists of either one, two, or four vector pipelines,
each of which may perform a variety of operations: floating-point
add/subtract and multiply/divide/square root; shift; logical/pack/unpack;
delay. They are fed from a vector-stream unit that is directly coupled
onto the memory. This vector-stream unit is designed to maintain the
data flow between the main memory and each of the pipelines. The pipelines are designed to work on only one operation at a time and the pairs
of operands are directed to the pipelines on a round robin basis. The

net effect of this approach is long vector startup times. This is attributed to the main memory running at a quarter of the speed (80ns) as the
CPU (20ns) plus the general purpose pipelines having a naturally long
startup period. However, once the pipelines are full, the ultra-high-
bandwidth memory can provide exceptionally large vectors in an uninter-
rupted manner. Due to the very large volume of traffic to and from the
main memory, one would expect a memory organisation that is correspondingly suitable. This is one instance where first impressions are quite
correct. Each million words of main memory contains 16 memory stacks
where each stack holds a half word (32 bits plus single-error correction
double-error detection parity bits). Any single memory operation may
access up to 16 stacks simultaneously. This corresponds to eight words
of data and the term "superword" is the appropriate CDC jargon. Since
the stacks are also eight-phase interleaved, a subsequent memory operation on that set of stacks may be initiated on the following machine
cycle.

Figure 7 gives an overview of the vector processing side of the
Cyber-205 supercomputer.

The Cyber-205 pipelines offer a further feature. That is the ability to perform half-precision arithmetic (32-bit operands) with a doubling in the result rate.

Included in the computer system is a string processor and a scalar
processor that also handles instruction fetching and issuing. Instruction issuing involves directing decoded instructions onto the unit they
are applicable to. i.e., vector instructions onto the vector processor,
string instructions onto the string processor and scalar instructions
onto the scalar-instruction control network. Since the scalar and vector
processors each contain independent instruction controls, the scalar processor can execute its instructions in parallel with the vector processor
executing its instructions, providing there is no conflict. (Conflicts
could be, for example, certain memory references or order-dependent

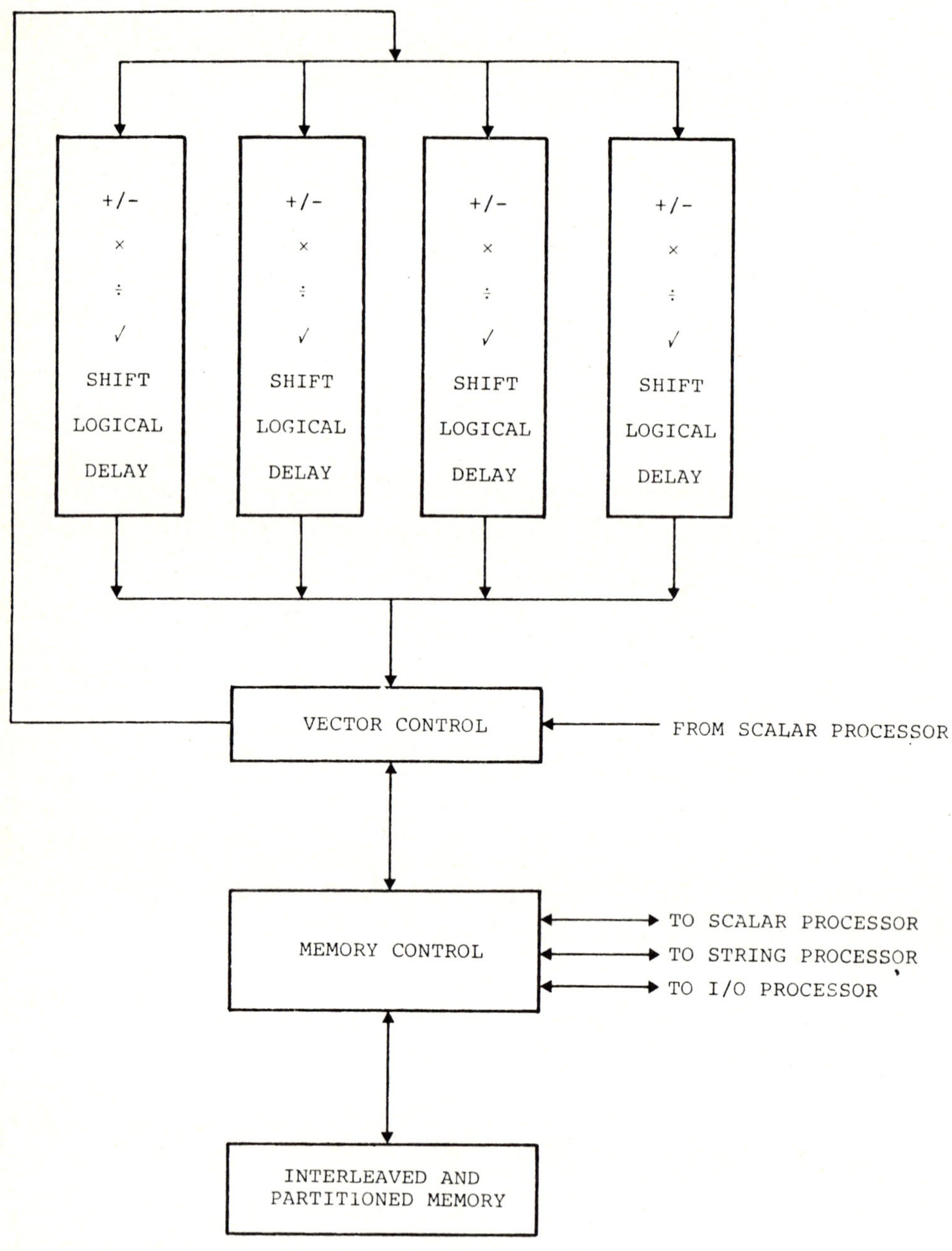

Figure 7. Block diagram of the Cyber-205 vector-processing section.

instructions). The string processor is an integral part of the vector processor and, hence, strings are processed as logical/shift/delay vector operations.

Another key feature of the Cyber-205 is its reasonably sophisticated virtual-addressing scheme. This includes lock and key memory protection, variable page sizes, user program/data sharing capability and an addressing capacity of 2^{42} (approximately 4×10^{12}) words.

FUTURE GENERAL-PURPOSE SUPERARCHITECTURES

Already the future superarchitectures are becoming the present superarchitectures. The progression of computers from SISD (single-instruction single-data) processors to SIMD (single-instruction multiple-data) processors leads to the logical conclusion that the new frontier may be a MIMD (multiple-instruction multiple-data) processor. This seems to be the case. One obvious way to create a MIMD processor is to link together a number of SIMD processors.

Cray Research Incorporated has done exactly this. Their latest and greatest announced machine is the Cray-XMP which consists of a number of redesigned versions of the Cray-1 supercomputer placed back-to-back, so to speak. Communication between the processors is via a cluster of very fast shared registers. The memory subsystem has been expanded from one read/write pipeline to one write pipeline and two read pipelines. Memory interleaving has been correspondingly increased. All of this leads to better chaining capabilities. The clock period has been reduced to 9.5 nanoseconds.

The Cray-2 supercomputer, which is getting ready for public announcement, is to be a four-processor MIMD machine where each processor is more powerful than the Cray-1. The clock period is 4 nanoseconds with an 8 nanosecond instruction decode.

                    The Leading Edge

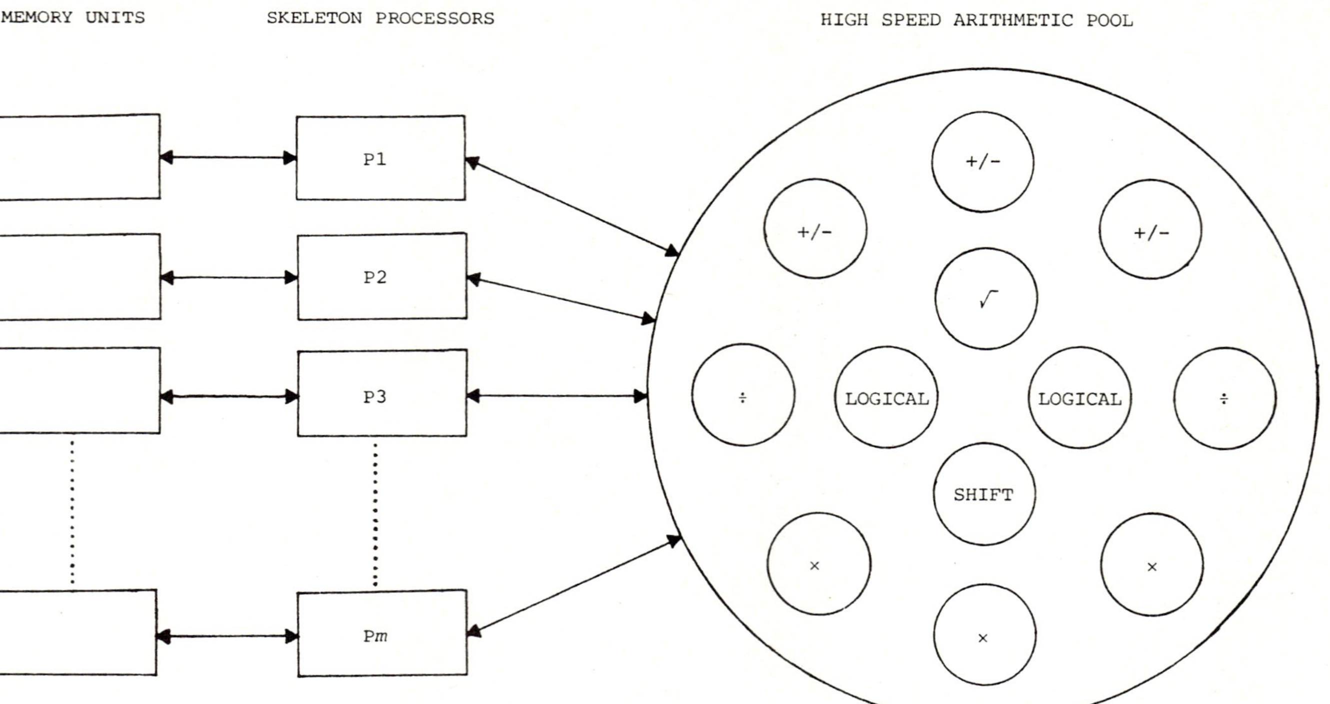

Figure 8. A possible MIMD-computer structure.

Further strategies for MIMD processor design have and are being considered (for example, Levine[16]), but their relative effectiveness for general problems is still rather doubtful. This does not imply that the SIMD multiprocessor setup for the MIMD architecture is necessarily a good one. In fact, one disadvantage is that the approximate linear increase in price for the number of SIMD processors in the multiprocessor leads to a relatively less increase in system performance. The reason for this is the communication overhead and inevitable inefficiencies in processor utilisation, which is chiefly algorithm dependent.

One of the greater struggles with MIMD architecture design is due to the little understanding of MIMD algorithms. That is, for a given problem what algorithm best utilises a particular multiprocessor architecture and what multiprocessor architectures lend themselves best to general MIMD algorithms. Until a better understanding of MIMD philosophy is attained, MIMD architecture is going to be a tough road.

From a simplistic understanding of multiprocessing, some intuitively sound proposals for MIMD processors have been put forward. One is to have an m processor system with n independent memory modules. The processors link themselves to the memory modules via a crossbar network and perhaps a memory mapping scheme as well. The crossbar network is essentially a switching network with the m processor buses crossed over the n memory buses in order to generate mn switches. The potential of this is to allow any combination of processors to be linked with any combination of memory modules. Generally, any one processor is exclusively linked to only one memory module at any one instant in time.

Another idea, which is rather novel but not to the point of being radical, is to connect a collection of independent processors that contain their own memory but lack an arithmetic unit to a common pool of very fast and pipelined arithmetic elements. These processors are aptly termed "skeleton processors". Figure 8 shows this multiprocessor structure. Without a doubt, this is a genuine MIMD machine but because the skeleton processors are independent the machine lacks the flexibility of the previously discussed MIMD architectures. Nevertheless, there are some particularly good advantages. One is the decreased interconnection complexity. No sophisticated memory mapping schemes are necessary and a crossbar network is not required for data communication. However, the high speed arithmetic pool must possess the logic to receive operands from and transmit results back to the appropriate skeleton processors. Another interesting advantage is best demonstrated by example. Consider the skeleton processors executing the same instruction stream on different data. Very quickly there is going to be contention for one of the pipelines in the high speed arithmetic pool. This can be minimised by having pipeline duplicates but this does not always eliminate the problem. Some skeleton processors are going to have to wait. As soon as this occurs they break synchronisation with each other and further contention due to this cause is removed.

SPECIAL-PURPOSE SUPERCOMPUTERS

This breed of machine is designed to solve a particular problem or class of problem. Due to the limited demand for a particular special-purpose supermachine, their developmental costs must be justified against the need to solve the problem in a time more acceptable than that of a general-purpose machine of similar cost. An example of this may be in weather forecasting. A special-purpose weather forecasting computer may be able to generate more accurate weather predictions in a given period of time than a general-purpose machine of the same cost. Fortunately, reducing logic costs, increasing reliability, new innovative architectures and very large scale integration (VLSI) are helping to bring the costs of special-purpose machines down and to make them more technically feasible. Nevertheless, special-purpose machines are still not too common. General-purpose supercomputers often suffice, principally because of their immediate availability and less expense.

Special-purpose computers can be subdivided into two categories. In the first of these categories the architecture is modelled to reflect the physical structure of the problem to be solved. An example of this is a finite-element solving computer being constructed at NASA-Langley Research Laboratory [Jordan[17]] which employs an array of microprocessors, one for each node in the finite-element model of the continuous field. The microprocessors are interconnected in a fashion that parallels the finite-element nodal interactions. This type of architecture lends itself to very fast results but has a severe difficulty when the physical structure of the problem is altered in any way.

In the second category of special-purpose machine, the architecture is designed to reflect the general solution method for that class of problem. An example of this type of special-purpose supercomputer is the Parallel Finite Element Machine (PARFEM) being developed within the Engineering Department, Calgary University, Canada [Norrie[1]]. PARFEM consists of three subsystems, each designed to handle a particular section of the Finite Element solution procedure. viz., generation of element stiffness-matrices, assembly of the system matrix, and solving of the system matrix. PARFEM employs a mixture of array processing and vector processing techniques.

SUMMARY

The necessity for fast processors has been demonstrated and their present inadequacy that exists (and may always exist) has been shown. A study of the hardware architectures of various supermachines and the ploys they apply for tackling a problem has now shed some light on the difficulties in solving large problems. Yet there are still further difficulties which have not been alluded to in this chapter. These include development cost versus demand, technological limits of electronic components, physical limitations of being able to compact so much hardware into a given volume of computer, the now very limiting speed of electricity and many other phenomena of physics, electronics, chemistry, and human attributes. However, changing human demands, rapidly evolving technology and innovative ideas are all in the battle to subdue these difficulties. Since no projected catastrophe will completely halt these "warriors", today's supermachines may be tomorrow's norm and possibly tomorrow's home computer!

For those readers who are further interested in this subject, the following references (not cited elsewhere in the chapter) are recommended: Lincoln[6], Johnson[19], Hwang[20], Chen[21], Russel[22], Higbie[23], Higbie[24], Theis[25], Cray[26], Cray[27], Control Data[28], Norrie[29].

Lincoln[6] gives an expose' on some of the practicalities and philosophies in designing the Cyber-205. Stone[8] gives an introduction on array processors, vector processors and MIMD machines. He also takes a glimpse at workload distribution on such machines. Stone[9] takes a deeper look at the perfect-shuffle interconnection network on array processors and Bhuyan[10] investigates the design of generalised interconnection networks. Slotnik[11] discusses some of the design criteria and philosophies as well as the overall architecture of the Illiac IV computer while Seban[12] studies two interconnection schemes for the Illiac IV. Tomasulo[14] presents Tomasulo's dynamic code-scheduling algorithm and Weiss[15] investigates instruction issue using Tomasulo's algorithm. Kozdrowicki[13] makes a simple but interesting comparison of the Burrough's BSP, the Cray-1, and Cyber-205. He also takes a look at some of their system software. Levine[16] gives an interesting talk on supercomputers. He concentrates not only on the Cray-1 and Cyber-205 but also on the Illiac IV and some MIMD machines that are currently being developed to fit into the supercomputer category, such as the S-1 Multiprocessor being developed at the Lawrence Livermore National Laboratory. Johnson[19] supplies an excellent introduction to vector processing and the Cray-1. Higbie[23] supplements this further with the application of vector processing. Hwang[20] takes a good look at vector processors, array processors and processing techniques. Chen[21] studies the pipelining principle and how it can be exploited. Russel[22] provides a concise and very readable document of the Cray-1 architecture. Cray[26] is Cray Research's hardware manual on the Cray-1. It too is very readable. Cray[27] is Cray Research's manual on the Cray-XMP. Control Data[28] is CDC's hardware manual on the Cyber-205.

Significant portions of this chapter have been based upon Norrie[29]. This is a good reference for an extension of some of the ideas presented in this chapter.

<u>REFERENCES</u>

[1]   D H Norrie and C I W Norrie, "Large Scale Computation: Architecture and Program Structure for Special Purpose Machines", Proceedings, Large Engineering Systems, 1982, pp 395-400

[2]   Cray Research Incorporated, "Computational Aerodynamics: Revolutionizing Aircraft Design Methods", Cray Channels, Vol 4, No 2, 1982, pp 2-6

[3]   W L Hankey and J S Shang, "Vector Processing and CFD (Computational Fluid Dynamics)", Proceedings, Science, Engineering and the Cray-1, Cray Research Incorporated, 1982, pp 49-66

[4]   Cray Research Incorporated, "Digital Productions - Blending Technology and Artistry", Cray Channels, Vol 5, No 1, 1983, pp 12-14

[5]   G Demos, M D Brown and R A Weinberg, "Digital Scene Simulation: The Synergy of Computer Technology and Human Creativity", Proceedings of the IEEE, Vol 72, No 1, Jan 1984, pp 22-31

[6]   N R Lincoln, "Supercomputers = Colossal Computations + Enormous Expectations + Renowned Risk", Computer, Vol 16, No 5, May 1983, pp 38-47

[7]   D H Lawrie, "Memory-Processor Connection Networks", Report No
      UIUCDCS-R-73-557, Department of Computer Science, University of
      Illinois, Urbana, February 1973

[8]   H S Stone, "Parallel Computers", Introduction to Computer Architec-
      ture, Science Research Associates, 1975, pp 318-374

[9]   H S Stone, "Parallel Processing with the Perfect Shuffle", IEEE
      Transactions on Computers, C-20, 1971, pp 153-161

[10] L N Bhuyan and D P Agrawal, "Design and Performance of Generalized
      Interconnection Networks", IEEE Transactions on Computers, C-32, No
      12, December, 1983, pp 1081-1090

[11] D L Slotnik, "The Fastest Computer", Scientific American, Vol 224,
      No 2, February 1971, pp 76-87

[12] R R Seban and H J Siegel, "Shuffling with the Illiac and PM21 SIMD
      Networks", IEEE Transactions on Computers, Vol C-33, No 7, July
      1984, pp 619-625

[13] E W Kozdrowicki and D J Theis, "Second Generation of Vector Super-
      computers", Computer, Vol 13, No 11, November 1980, pp 71-83

[14] R M Tomasulo, "An Efficient Algorithm for Expoiting Multiple Arith-
      metic Units", IBM Journal of Research and Development, Vol 11, No
      1, January 1967, pp 25-33

[15] S Weiss and J E Smith, "Instruction Issue Logic in Pipelined Super-
      computers", IEEE Transactions on Computers, Vol C-33, No 11,
      November 1984, pp 1013-1022

[16] R D Levine, "Supercomputers", Scientific American, Vol 246, No 1,
      January 1982, pp 118-135

[17] H F Jordan and P L Sawyer, "A Multiprocessor System for Finite Ele-
      ment Structural Analysis", Computers and Structures, Vol 10, 1979,
      pp 21-29

[18]   D H Norrie and C I W Norrie, "Architecture and Program Structures
        for a Special Purpose Finite Element Computer", EDF Bulletin de la
        Direction des Etudes et Recherches,   Serie C - Mathematiques Infor-
        matique, No 1, 1983, pp 103-108

[19]   P M Johnson, "An Introduction to Vector Processing", Computer
        Design, February 1978, pp 89-97

[20]   K Hwang S Su and L M Ni, "Vector Computer Architecture and Process-
        ing Techniques", Advances in Computers, Vol 20, Academic Press,
        1981, pp 115-197

[21]   T C Chen, "Overlap and Pipeline Processing", Introduction to Com-
        puter Architecture, Science Research Associates, 1975, pp 375-431

[22]   R M Russel, "The Cray-1 Computer System", Computer Structures:
        Principles and Examples, McGraw Hill, 1982, pp 743-752

[23]   L C Higbie, "Applications of Vector Processing", Computer Design,
        April 1978, pp 139-145

[24]   L C Higbie, "Supercomputer Architecture", Computer, Vol 6, No 12,
        December 1973, pp 48-58

[25]   D J Theis, "Vector Supercomputers", Computer, Vol 7, No 4, April
        1974, pp 52-61

[26]   Cray Research Incorporated, "Cray-1 Hardware Reference Manual",
        1982

[27]   Cray Research Incorporated, "Cray-XMP Mainframe Reference Manual",
        1982

[28]   Control Data Corporation, "CDC Cyber-205 Hardware Reference
        Manual", 1982

[29]   C I W Norrie, "Supercomputers for Superproblems: An Architectural
        Introduction:, Vol 17, No 3, Computer, Copyright March 1984, pp
        62-74

<u>CHAPTER 40.</u>

PUBLIC & PRIVATE DEVELOPMENTS IN SATELLITE & CABLE SYSTEMS

PROFESSOR R.LEDUC
University of Wisconsin, Madison, U.S.A.

Most of the excitement about communication satellites during the
past decade has been generated by proposals for new DBS delivered
mass entertainment services. Yet, while these projected systems
languish on the drawing board, advances in this field have actually
been occurring within the traditional realm of the communications
common carrier where constant, if unspectacular, improvement in design
and operation has resulted in the communication satellite emerging as
the dominant informational distribution network linking industrial
societies.

A. <u>THE WORLDWIDE EXPANSION IN DOMESTIC SATELLITE SERVICE</u>

Within the past three years, for example, the number of
communication satellites in operation throughout the world has more
than doubled, from 130 in 1981 to 271 as the year 1984 began, with the
global investment in such technology during this period exceeding $13
billion.# As significant, perhaps, in terms of the primary
communication functions of these satellites, is the fact that less
than 15 percent of these new units have the capacity to provide DBS
service on the high power 12/14 Ghz BBS (Broadcast Satellite Service)
channels, while nearly twice as many are equipped to transmit on
similar Ku band FSS (Fixed Satellite Service) frequencies. In other
words, satellite owners, during this period of great enthusiasm for

---

#These figures do not include communication satellite information
from the Soviet Union or its national telecommunication associates.

the potential of direct broadcast service have chosen by a margin of more than two to one to ignore the more glamorous entertainment service possibility and to invest instead in narrow beam channels for private business uses.

Although the number of domestic satellites and new satellite systems increased most rapidly in North America during these three years (from 38 satellites and 10 systems in 1981 to 108 satellites operated by 20 systems in 1984), expansion has been almost equally impressive in other parts of the world. In Western Europe, for example, where both narrowly defined national telecommunication interests and massive investment in terrestrial telephonic and data networks had effectively discouraged every effort to achieve regional cooperation in the development of a joint communication satellite system for more than a decade, Eutelsat, a consortium of some 20 national PTTs (Postal, Telegraph and Telephone) organizations, is now fully committed to the launching of a series of five Ku band communication satellites within the next ten years. These satellites, designated as "ECS" (European Community Satellites) 1-5, are designed to serve not only as a back up to existing land line facilities, but also as relays for direct broadcast services, either to the individual home or the cable headend; and from ECS-2 onward, to act as providers of a business service, called Multi-service Satellite System (SMS), offering a wide range of functions such as teleconferencing, data transfer between computers, remote printing, high-speed facsimile and teletex.

The first two of these ECS satellites have already joined other European national satellites now in operation, such as the French PTT's Telecom I and II, and will soon include as well the Swedish Tele-X in addition to numerous other satellites designed primarily to deliver DBS programming; the British Unisat, the Italian-EBU (European Broadcasting Union) L-Sat and perhaps even the "infamous" Coronet satellite of Luxembourgh.

As the competitive relationship between the European Space Agency's Ariance rocket launcher and NASA's shuttle continues to reduce the costs of satellite launching, it is entirely possible that additional European satellite projects postponed in the past because of the need to defray the initial $60-70 million charge to be put in orbit, can justify further development on the basis of new pricing policies that may reduce the magnitude of this expense by almost 50 percent. At the moment, it is projected that Western Europe will require at least ten large satellites to meet the continent's communication traffic demands by the end of this century, with at least four of these satellites being devoted exclusively to business communication traffic. Under these circumstances, it seems quite likely that the communication satellite boom in Western Europe is now only beginning to occur.

Communication satellite services appear to be expanding with almost equal rapidity in other parts of the world. In November 1984, for example, the European Space Agency is scheduled to launch Arabsat-A, the first stage of a three satellite regional system for the Arab League. At the same time, other developing nations such as India, Mexico, Brazil, Argentina, Nigeria and Pakistan are planning to follow the example set by Indonesia, which began operating its own domestic satellite system in 1979.

Among Western nations, Australia, the United Kingdom, West Germany and Italy, among others, are soon scheduled to join the once exclusive club of national satellite operators that now includes Canada, the United States, France and Japan. If each of these projects should be concluded successfully, there will be at least 20 national or regional satellite systems in operation by the end of this decade, without including the 110 national, regional and international satellite network of Intelsat, or the 14 nations connected to its

Eastern counterpart, Intersputnik.

Yet, despite the global nature of this trend towards broader satellite communication service it must be pointed out, in order to put this tendency in proper perspective, that 108 of the 271 domestic satellites now operating, or almost 40 percent of the world's total, are aimed directly toward the North American continent. Canada was clearly the early leader in this field, with its Anik A-1 becoming, in 1972, the first satellite in the world operating from a geostationary orbit for commercial domestic service, and in 1980, its Anik B becoming the first commercial satellite operation on the Ku or high powered 12/14 Ghz band.

Today, the Canadians, through Telesat, their domestic satellite corporation, operate both Anik A and B communication systems in the traditional 4 Ghz band, and also Anik C 1-3, transmitting on the higher powered Ku 12/14 Ghz band. Without question, though, it is the United States that is at the moment the largest single national domestic satellite user in the world. If the 19 new domestic satellites authorized by the FCC in April 1983 should join the 19 already in orbit by the end of 1987 as scheduled, a single nation would, in itself, have jurisdiction over between 10-15 percent of all of the communication satellites in the world.

B.   <u>AMERICAN DOMESTIC SATELLITE POLICY</u>

It was only a decade ago, in April 1974, that Western Union launched Westar I, America's first domestic satellite. The delay in inaugurating this service was due in large part to the difficult regulatory question the FCC raised for itself and finally answered before issuing licenses to satellite applicants. As it indicated it might do at the beginning of the proceeding, the Commission ultimately abandoned the traditional practice of granting an exclusive right of operation and management to a single communications common carrier entity, and supervising its performance in that role. Instead, the

FCC announced a revolutionary "Open Skies" policy, allowing every qualified applicant to operate its own domestic satellite system (except AT&T, barred by the FCC initially because of its dominant position in the field of terrestrial lines), with the marketplace to determine which particular satellite pricing and service policies were wise or unwise in terms of public demand or interests.

Soon after Westar I was launched, RCA's Satcom I joined it in orbit, and with Time-Life's HBO leasing transponder space to create a nationwide pay-TV service for its cable system affiliates, a new mass marketing phenomenon had emerged in the world. Turner Broadcasting followed HBO to Satcom I, and by 1979, all but four of Satcom I's transponders were devoted to carrying cable TV pay or ad supported channels on a full-time basis. When the FCC reduced its size and performance standards for domestic satellite antennas in the same year, thus dropping the price of these units drastically, broadcast stations began following cable operators to these new satellite delivered programming services.

Today, more than 60 percent of all American broadcast stations, and over 90 percent of all cable systems, are equipped for satellite transmission reception; all of the major radio and television networks are shifting over to satellite dissemination of their previously "land-locked" services, and new "ad hoc" regional and national networks are constantly being formed and then disbanded as the need arises and disappears. Thus, in the absence of any direct public policy guidance, economic incentives seen, in themselves, to have led program suppliers to new satellite networking services, generating substantial revenues both for these programming services and the satellite system owner, while at the same time providing the American public with a much broader range of programming options than had been available in the past.

However, while such electronic mass media related satellite

usages may be the most dramatic type of vindication for the FCC's

unusual "free market" approach to satellite common carrier service in

the United States, it must be pointed out that equally innovative

approaches to the designing and distributing of business related

information packages has been at least as successful during the past

few years, and often far more profitable than simple passive relay of

broadcast or cable programming. In fact, one justification the

Commission offered in authorizing the sale of, rather than the more

traditional leasing of, satellite transponders in 1982 was to allow

these specialized packagers to participate in satellite distribution

of their services at the lower "broker" rate the purchaser of the

transponder would charge, rather than the higher "occasional use"

tariff levied by the satellite system owner. The Court of Appeals for

the District of Columbia eventually sustained the FCC's decision to

adopt this unprecedented rule, furnishing the FCC with one more reason

to believe its _laissez faire_ approach to satellite regulation was

clearly the most enlightened one.

A recent study commissioned by Western Union has projected a

rather remarkable 900 percent increase in the use of domestic

satellite services in the United States by the end of this century.

Based upon the performance record of the American satellite industry

during the past decade under the stewardship of the FCC, this agency

is almost certain to remain committed to its unique competition based

common carrier policies in the future in order to encourage that

continued expansion in American satellite communication service

essential to meet this growing demand.

C. THE INTERNATIONAL TELECOMMUNICATIONS POLICY ARENA

Ironically, however, the very success the Commission has enjoyed

with its competitive domestic policies has now begun to erode those international connections every modern information system must have in order to operate effectively. This is because the Commission, firmly convinced of the wisdom of its "marketplace" approach to public policy in this field, has committed itself to extending to its international communication common carriers the same benefits of a competitive environment its domestic carriers now enjoy, without great concern for the impact such a drastic shift in policy would be likely to have upon the entire framework of international communications service throughout the world.

International communications, of necessity, must be based upon negotiated accommodations among national telecommunication organizations, for every message destined to travel beyond a nation's borders requires the complete cooperation of one or more foreign organizations for its delivery. Through the years elaborate "account and settlement" formulations have been negotiated among those organizations sending, relaying or receiving each international message, a mutually acceptable set of agreements which European PTTs at least have believed must be achieved within a tightly controlled regulatory environment.

Despite the preference of many of its European partners for the continuation of such an environment, the FCC, with the full support of the United States Congress, ruled in December 1979 that it was no longer bound by section 222 of the Communications Act of 1934 to distinguish between domestic and international carriers when adopting communications policy (FCC 79-841). On that basis, and without consulting with other national telecommunications authorities,the Commission began to encourage expansion in the number of competing American international carriers by ending or substantially reducing barriers to entry such as increasing the number of "gateway" cities, (points where foreign messages can enter the United States) lessening distinctions between "record" and "voice" carriers so that entities

could compete in both fields, allowing a domestic carrier, Western
Union, to become an international carrier, and holding that its
domestic "Computer II" decision was equally applicable to
international telecommunications.

At this point the U.S. Department of State entered the policy
arena to attempt to force the Commission to consult, if not negotiate,
with other national telecommunications authorities before moving any
further towards it objective of free competition in the field of
international communications. This intersession slowed the FCC for a
time, but then a new type of competitive initiative emerged, this one
challenging Intelsat's exclusive right to provide satellite
connections between North America and Western Europe.

In March 1983, Orion Satellite Corporation asked the FCC for
permission to construct, launch and operate two Ku band communication
satellites in order to sell its transponder space to large users of
telecommunications service, particularly American video syndicators
seeking to transmit programming to European cable TV systems. Within
the year four other companies were seeking similar approval from the
Commission, and an executive-branch report suggested that the FCC
authorize such competition.

To understand the degree of hostility these American proposals
stimulated throughout the world, it is necessary to consider briefly
both the importance of Intelsat in the field of international
satellite communications and the magnitude of the threat such
competition might pose for this organization. Founded only two
decades ago, Intelsat has emerged to become perhaps the most
successful example of international cooperation in the modern world.

Intelsat currently supplies more than two-thirds of the world's
intercontinental information services, through a satellite system
providing some 65,000 voice circuits, virtually all regional and
international television relays, and channels equipped to deliver

everything from 50 band telegraphy to 1.5 megabits per second data streams. The fourteen national telecommunications organizations that made up the original Intelsat in 1965 have become 110 national members today, served by a 15 satellite system representing an investment of almost $3 billion. During the past two decades, its regional and international tariffs have been reduced on twelve separate occasions, and its charges today are 18 times less, on an adjusted for world inflation basis, than they were in 1965.

As a non-governmental organization supported only by the communications revenues it generates, Intelsat has achieved an enviable record in the area of development communication, in effect drawing upon revenues generated from its lucrative North Atlantic route to subsidize expenses of operating the less heavily used networks serving Asia, South America and Africa. Opponents of those American satellite systems that would compete with Intelsat only for this Atlantic corridor traffic thus argue that authorizing such services would inevitably drive the costs of "Third World" communication service upward, either by forcing Intelsat to operate on an actual cost basis throughout the world, or by compelling it to abandon this most profitable route and thereby lose the revenues essential to underwrite communication networks in less developed regions of the world.

Adding to the magnitude of this competitive challenge, the FCC recently authorized the building of the world's first transoceanic fiber optics cable between North America and Western Europe, a project to be completed by 1988 that will add the digital equivalent of 37,800 new voice circuits in direct competition with the Intelsat's North Atlantic satellite channels. Intelsat has considered responding to this challenge by launching a massive Delta-class satellite in the North Atlantic, with spot beam coverage of Europe and North America, but although this would probably allow it to undercut its challengers,

it could do so only by resorting to an actual pricing policy that
would severely diminish the revenues available for the support of its
current "Third World" activities.

To complicate these arguments even further, it is interesting to
note that those European PTTs that have been most critical of the
American threat to Intelsat have conveniently overlooked the fact that
by forming the regional Eutelsat satellite network, they have also
played a part in eroding the financial foundation of Intelsat,
diverting from it those revenues Intelsat otherwise could have earned
from those satellite services the European PTTs will now provide for
themselves. In that same sense, almost all of those national or
regional satellite systems described earlier in this chapter have also
had some degree of adverse impact upon this international system as
well, denying it those charges it could have levied had it remained
the sole provider of the Western world's satellite services.

Just two decades ago it was the CEPT, the European PTT regional
organizations, that was suspicious of the newly formed Intelsat,
fearing that its communication satellite circuits might needlessly
complicate a placid telecommunications environment of terrestrial,
radio and submarine cable channels. Now that suitable accommodations
have been made, and Intelsat has become a respected institution within
international communications community, the same fears are being
expressed about those whose challenges might dislodge it from this
position.

What this seems to suggest more than anything else about
telecommunications public policy in general, and international
telecommunications policy in particular, is its inability to adapt
rapidly to advances in message delivery techniques. Lacking the
capacity to project the long term implications of such changes in
terms of national self interest, the instinctive administrative
response is to make every effort to discourage such advances. Only

after there has been ample opportunity to shape the new technological
advance to conform to traditional practices, and to modify those
practices as necessary to make this accommodation, is the new
technique, its competitive edge blunted as necessary to make it
compatible with existing practices, admitted to the international
communications community.

However, until this process is completed, the short term effect
of innovation in this field is generally to retard rather than to
increase the efficiency of message processing, because of the
preoccupation of each telecommunication institution with gaining a
tactical advantage in the global policy struggle to define its
ultimate role within the framework of regional and international
information and data exchange. Thus, for example, recent American
regulatory efforts to encourage high power Ku band satellite systems
to compete with Intelsat for North Atlantic communications traffic, or
to authorize domestically unregulated "enhanced" communication
services for European markets, will almost undoubtedly result in an
immediate decrease rather than an increase in the effectiveness of
telecommunications service between these continents, because it will
trigger a series of unpredictable retaliatory measures from European
PTTs that will seriously complicate the communication planning
strategies of carriers and their potential users.

Unfortunately, if it is true that every change or possible change
in international telecommunications traditional policy produces a
period of instability during which the efficiency of the message
delivery process may be reduced, then it is quite likely that the
remainder of this decade will not be a particularly inspiring era in
the overall history of international communications. Even if the
United States should eventually abandon its ambition to transform
telecommunications into a "free trade" area there are other major
changes looming ahead that no shift in national policy can avoid.

D.   THE EMERGENCE OF THE HIGH POWER SATELLITE

One of the most significant of these potential changes can be traced back to an international telecommunications policy decision in the year 1971, where at a World Administrative Radio Conference (WARC), the newly developed 12/14 Ghz band was divided between direct broadcast to home (BBS) television services and point to point private data services (FSS), with each of the world's three geographic regions given the task of making allotments of frequencies and orbital slots among the nations of that region. European PTTs moved rapidly to develop this BBS service, meeting in Geneva in 1977 to divide what are now generally known as direct broadcast satellite (DBS) allocations in order to encourage the establishing of such high technology systems in Europe in part to serve as showcases for the communications hardware they hoped to market in the "Third World". North America moved much more leisurely in this regard, not making its own regional allocation until mid-1983.

Despite the early lead that they had gained in the DBS development race, European PTTs found themselves unable to benefit from this advantage. Although skilled in the design and development of communication systems generally, these technical bodies had little knowledge of, or interest in the specific advantages or disadvantages inherent in satellite distribution of popular television programming to mass audiences. The "public service" broadcast organizations of the region, virtually shut out of the PTTs satellite policy planning process, were opposed to DBS distribution of their programming services from the beginning, contending that they would gain no advantage from paying the PTT's a substantially higher fee for satellite dissemination of programming their audiences were already receiving from existing terrestrial transmitters. In addition, they argued that by compelling them to use a far more expensive method of distribution, the only inescapable result would be to require the tax on television receivers (license fee) to be raised in order to compensate for this additional expense.

Perhaps the most compelling argument of all, however, was the one that caused each project to be delayed in hopes that some other system would surge ahead to become the first major DBS system in Western Europe. Facing that first system would be the prospect of commencing operation with massive investments in satellite, launching and programming, with virtually no audience capable of receiving its service. In the absence of any large scale DBS operation existing anywhere in the world, electronic manufacturers have had no inducement to develop home satellite antenna-converter equipment, much less to be capable of marketing it at the popular price that economies of scale would eventually allow. As a result, this initial DBS system operator would not only have to absorb start up expenses in excess of $150 million, but also months if not years of additional operating expenses before the size of the DBS audience might justify, if not compensate the operator fully for his continuing investment.

It is the same situation that recently had led all of the DBS applicants in the United States except the original one, Satellite Television Corporation, to pull back from the starting line so that some other corporate entity could have the honor of introducing direct broadcast service by satellite to this nation.

E. <u>THE MODERN BROADBAND COMMUNICATION SYSTEM</u>

In Europe, the pattern of satellite distribution of television programming that emerged through private initiative at the beginning of this decade has now been adopted by virtually every European government as official policy. Paralleling the Time-Life HBO pay-TV approach in the United States in 1975, a European consortium approached Eutelsat in 1979 with a request to lease a relatively low powered C band (4 Ghz) satellite in order to furnish European cable systems with advertising supported, popular appeal television

programming. Ignoring the protests of European broadcasters, the PTTs
agreed to lease this channel on a short term basis, and the service
now known as "Skychannel" began.

Shortly thereafter, several PTTs, seeking to stimulate the growth
of national broadband cable or fiber optic communication networks,
realized that popular entertainment programming would be necessary to
attract the subscribers essential for the short term financial
stability of systems eventually envisioned as becoming vast, interactive mass information networks. Such cable headend rather than DBS
distribution offers one special advantage in Western Europe, allowing
a single piece of equipment owned by the cable system to convert each
satellite channel it receives into the proper color standard, and in
some cases, even the proper language for local reception in that
particular nation being served by a pan-European satellite programmer.

Today ESC-1, a Eutelsat common carrier satellite, provides
"Skychannel", an advertising supported entertainment channel for cable
systems in the United Kingdom, "PKS", a West Germany cable delivered
ad supported entertainment channel, "TV-5" a French language cultural
service to France, Belgium and Switzerland, "Music Box", an
advertising supported pan-European music video channel for cable, and
pay-TV services such as "Teleclub", "EURO TV" and "Esselte." At the
same time, Intelsat leases a satellite channel for the transmission of
such cable delivered programming services as "Screen Sport", "Ten",
"Premiere" and "The Children's Hour" in the United Kingdom, with other
services such as "The Games Network", "The Key Channel", "Beta-
Premiere" and "Thames" planning to begin operation within the next
year.

Undoubtedly, each new cable delivered viewing alternative
introduced into Western Europe erodes still further that potential
audience once projected for DBS services on that continent. As cable
subscriber bases continue to expand in major nations such as France,

West Germany and the United Kingdom, particularly if combined in this regard with the 15-25 percent of all homes in these nations that already have the VCR viewing alternatives, the prospects for any successful DBS venture must be seen as diminishing to the same extent as those viewing alternatives expand.

In similar fashion in the United States, and possibly also in Canada, DBS may well have missed its crucial moment of opportunity, hesitating too long until cable, VCRs, and in the United States, LPTV, and MMDS as well, are already capable of performing those services that only a decade ago it seemed ultimately destined to provide. If this assumption should prove to be correct, it might have a significant influence upon evolutionary patterns in the field of information delivery by satellite, and upon the international policy process designed to control such evolution.

In terms of cable, freedom from the powerful competitive challenge of DBS might well furnish the degree of financial stability necessary to encourage the extending and expanding of the scope of those informational and transactional services these broadband systems already have the channel capacity to provide. Even though most modern cable systems are still not interactive, and lack the universality of telephone service, the long term potential is there for individual access to national and worldwide networks of a dimension now only available to the most sophisticated of corporate entities. Access of this type will not only have a profound effect upon retail sales, banking, investment and publishing, but could also have a significant impact upon the traditional relationship between the communication common carrier and its public.

It is true that recent American experience with metropolitan cable franchise holders has not been encouraging in this regard. Yet, it must be remembered that at the moment, the largest cable owners in the United States are still relatively small corporate entities,

undercapitalized for the massive task of wiring those urban areas they
have already committed themselves to serve. Once this initial drain
upon their investment capital had diminished, or mergers and
consolidations have strengthened the industry, it is very likely that
marketing and information service will be a high priority area for
development among the major urban franchises in the United States.

F.   FUTURE HIGH POWER SATELLITE SYSTEMS;   PUBLIC POLICY IMPLICATIONS

While this expansion of public access to informational and
transactional activities through broadband communication systems is
likely to be a very significant trend in the field of information by
the end of this decade, an even more important trend may emerge within
the next few years if the dominant function of the high power Ku band
(12/14 Ghz) communication satellites should become point to point
information delivery rather than broadcast service. As the odds
against successful DBS system operation, at least in the industrial
world, continue to lengthen, those relating to information service
(FFS) in this band look more and more favorable. Under these
circumstances, it is entirely possible that some future international
frequency allocation conference will release that segment of the band
and those orbital slots reserved for DBS to information services, at
least within those regions of the world that wish to make such an
adjustment. However, even if this should not occur in the immediate
future, new generations of hybred (multiple frequency-service) can
achieve almost the same level growth for such information services
through existing techniques such as high speed digital transmission to
increase their communications capacity.

The primary reason why these Ku band, FSS communication
satellites are so "revolutionary" in terms of private information
services is that because of their high powered transmission, and the
frequencies they have been allocated, they are capable of sending a
message directly from any location to any other location, even in the

midst of an urban area, requiring only modest uplink facilities and a small reception dish.

Use of the Ku band for satellite relayed data transfer, teleconferencing, and telephonic messages has already begun to emerge as an important domestic service, with 32 new FSS or hybred satellites with FSS Ku band capacity having been launched in 1984 alone. SBC, the former subsidiary of COMSAT, has been a pioneer in this field, and Intelsat now operates a digital service, IBS, a North Atlantic corridor channel that will become worldwide within the next two years. Yet, despite the best efforts of its promoters, these high power, high capacity delivery systems have not as yet won universal acceptance among the world's major business organizations, particularly for international information service.

At the moment a major reason for this lack of acceptance is that the international satellite carrier Intelsat's IBS downlink in the United States operates on the 11 Ghz band, shared with terrestrial microwave bands that are heavily used in North America, generating interference that limits its reception in urban areas. However, the advantages of Ku band usage are so obvious that a massive shift from traditional C band low power satellite earth station-terrestrial lines to high power direct user to receiver relay may well occur within a matter of a few short years. Once the lower cost, higher efficiency and greater flexibility of Ku band satellites for such functions as data transfer, full-motion teleconferencing, multiple-voice an slow-speed data delivery is firmly established, the next logical step would be to press for direct inter-satellite service between regional Ku satellites, an extremely high capacity radio communication link that would connect circuits directly, without need of relay through intervening satellite-earth station or submarine cable systems.

Now that the FCC, in its "authorized user" policy decision, has approved the ownership and operation of earth stations by organizations other than COMSAT and its earth station consortium, this type of proposal does not appear to be quite as unorthodox or as impossible to win approval in the United States as it would have seemed to be only a few years ago.

The potential advantages this type of global Ku band satellite system could offer are truly impressive. Each business could have access to such a network literally at its own doorstep, and through resale and shared use arrangements, could create its own unique national, regional or international communications channel instantaneously, for direct transmission of data, voice or teleconferencing service as it wished, at a far lower cost than is currently imposed for such services by intermediary telecommunications organizations at such times as they have appropriate circuits available. Permanent networks could be developed to connect each office of national and multi-national corporations far more cost-effectively than is the case today, and occasional networks could be created on command to meet any special business needs as they arise at the national or international level.

Yet despite the fact that such satellite systems are already technologically possible and economically feasible, describing them in terms of performing specific functions such as these will remain nothing more than an idle exercise in "blue sky" speculation until each of these functions has been shaped by international telecommunications policy to fit within existing institutional customs and practices. At the moment, "site to site" international satellite transmission exchanges would undoubtedly contravene precisely defined "collection" formulas for allocating international revenues among carriers; "shared usage" would probably violate CCITT leasing restrictions, and "inter-satellite relay" would almost certainly be in conflict with existing Intelsat satellite service agreements. In truth, these objections do no more than suggest only a few examples of

the many preliminary attacks that such proposals would not only have
to withstand, but surmount before the modifications they reflect in
existing communication service could ultimately be authorized.

Unfortunately, however, as recent American efforts to force
change unilaterally upon the international telecommunications
conclusively establish, no alternative exists to the deliberate and
cautious process of mutual accommodation at the international level,
reconciling conflicting interest through an elaborate series of
national and institutional trade-offs before any major policy
decisions can be made. In this particular instance the delay that is
an integral part of this process might seem particularly well
justified, since the changes being proposed could possibly imperil the
operations of Intelsat, an organization vital to all national
communication interests throughout the world. However, whether
justified or not, it would be safe to predict on the basis of the very
nature of this policy process, that while the long range prospect for
higher capacity, more flexible and less costly satellite services at
both the national and international levels appears to be very
promising, the short range outlook for these services must be
described as being far less encouraging.

FURTHER REFERENCES

Dizard, Wilson P. Jr., The Coming Information Age. Englewood Cliffs,
    N. J. Prentice Hall, 1983.

Federal Communications Commission, Allocation of Scarce Resources: An
    Analytical Framework and Its Specific Application to Orbital
    Slots, Satellite Transponders and Radio Interference. Charles
    Needy, Economic Division, Common Carrier Bureau, Sept. 1981.

Gandy, Oscar H. Jr. Beyond Agenda Setting: Information, Information
    Subsidies and Public Policy. Norwood, N.J. Ablex Press, 1982.

Hopkins, John et al (ed.). Satellite Broadcasting In Western Europe.
London, International Institute of Communications, 1982.

Le Duc, Don R. "Communication Satellites: Parallel Policy Patterns
in Europe and the United States", Journal of Broadcasting.
(27:2) Spring 1983, p.99.

Levy, Steven A., "The Quiet Revolution in International
Communications," Satellite Communication. January 1984, p. 58.

Oettinger, Anthony G., et al, High and Low Politics: Information
Resources for the 1980s. Cambridge, MA, Ballinger, 1978.

Robinson, Glen O. (ed.), Communications for Tomorrow. New York, N.Y.
Praeger, 1979.

Rubin, Michael Rogers, Information Economics and Policy in the United
States. Littleton, CO. Libraries Unlimited, 1983.

Rutkowski, A.M., "The Impact of New Technology Upon Satellite
Communications," Telecommunications. February 1983, p. 46.

Sterling, Christopher E. (ed.). International Telecommunications and
Information Policy. Washington, DC, Communication Press, 1983.

U.S. Congress. House. Committee on Energy and Commerce.
Subcommittee on Telecommunications, Consumer Protection, and
Finance. Status of Competition and Deregulation in the
Telecommunications Industry. 97th Cong., 1st sess., 1981, H.
Reprt. 29.

U.S. Congress. House. Committee on Energy and Commerce. A Report by
the Majority Staff of the Subcommittee on Telecommunications,
Consumer Protection, and Finance. Telecommunications in
Transition: The Status of Competition in the Telecommunications
Industry. 97th Cong., 1st sess., H. Rept. No. 97-V, 1981.

U.S. Government Accounting Office, FCC Needs to Monitor A Changing
International Telecommunications Market. GAO/RCED 83-92, March
14, 1983.

Whellon, Albert D., "The Future of Communication Satellites",

    Intermedia. March 1984, p. 40.

Wigand, Rolf T., "Broadcast Satellites In Europe," *Satellite*

    Communications, April 1983, p. 21.

Wiley, RIchard E., Neustadt, Richard, "U.S. Communications Policy in

    the New Decade," *Journal of Communication*, Spring 1982, p. 85.

<u>CHAPTER 41.</u>

DEVELOPMENTS IN SPEECH REGOGNITION SYSTEMS

DR. H. NEY
Philips Information Systems Laboratory, Hamburg, FRG.

1. INTRODUCTION

Automatic speech recognition is a general term describing the process of recognizing human speech by computer. Sometimes it is helpful to distinguish between speech recognition and speech understanding. The automatic dictation machine the goal of which is to accurately transcribe the spoken sentence into printed form would provide an example of speech recognition because it 'solely' requires an exact word-by-word transcription of the spoken utterance. Speech understanding requires the correct interpretation of the key words in the spoken utterance and the generation of an appropriate response or action, e.g. the retrieval of some stored information from a data base. Automatic speech recognition is still far from approaching human performance. Therefore it is appropriate to distinguish different tasks in automatic speech recognition: isolated word recognition where the words must be separated by distinct pauses, connected word recognition where the word strings are built up from a limited vocabulary and no pauses between the words are necessary, and continuous speech recognition, where grammatically complete sentences are spoken in a continuous and natural manner and the vocabulary is less restricted, typically more than 500 words. For the recognition of a small vocabulary of up to 100 words, usually whole words are the smallest units of recognition, whereas for larger vocabularies some sort of subword units is given the preference. Another aspect is whether the recognition system must be trained to each user's voice. Speaker dependent systems have to be trained by each individual speaker and guarantee reliable recognition only for this speaker. Speaker independent systems ideally require no training by the user, which is a much more ambitious and difficult goal.

The object of this paper is both to illustrate the recognition techniques and describe the state of the art in speech recognition with respect to research and commercial systems. In Section 2, we describe the knowledge sources involved in human and in automatic speech recognition. In Section 3, signal processing and feature extraction are considered. Section 4 deals with various types of subword units and segmentation. In Section 5, recognition techniques and statistical decisions technique are described. Section 6 deals with different system architectures for speech recognition. Section 7 provides an example of a particular algorithm for connected word recognition. In Section 8, isolated word recognition along with commercial products is described.

The primary sources of information in this area, in addition to the references, are the 'IEEE Transactions on Acoustics, Speech and Signal Processing' along with the conference proceedings of the corresponding IEEE International Conference on Acoustics, Speech and Signal Processing and, with respect to commercial products and applications, the journal 'Speech Technology' .

2. KNOWLEDGE SOURCES INVOLVED IN SPEECH RECOGNITION

Why is speech recognition by computer difficult ? Most people tend to take their own speech recognition capabilities for granted. However this point of view is likely to change immediately when they are faced with the problems of understanding spoken sentences of a foreign language. In their native language, they subconsciously make use of a number of so-called knowledge sources [Reddy 1976] that are not or only to a smaller extent available in the case of a foreign language. These knowledge sources are:

1. the characteristics of the speech sounds (phonetics),
2. the variability in the spoken system of the language (phonology), depending on speaking rate, speaker and dialect,
3. the stress and intonation pattern of speech (prosodics),
4. the vocabulary and its sound patterns (pronunciation lexicon),
5. the grammatical structure of language (syntax),
6. the meaning of word and word groups (semantics),
7. the context of conversation in a dialogue or talk (semantics).

Looking at these knowledge sources, the reader could get the impression that speech recognition amounts simply to recognizing the speech sounds (phonemes), group the phonemes into words, construct grammatical phrases and sentences and interpret the meaning of these sentences. However, considerable experience gained over the last 15 years demonstrates that such an approach is bound to end up in failure. There are several reasons for this. The speech is an extremely highly encoded signal that is generated in the speaker's mind. The underlying concept, namely the sequence of words or phonemes, may be discrete, but the acoustic signal is continuous with no clear boundaries between phonemes or words. Then, the speech signal is highly variable in a number of ways. The acoustic realization of the individual phonemes often depends on the surrounding phonemes and on the speaker as well. Obviously, one speaker's voice can be different to another's due to different sex, age or accent. But even for the same speaker, it is impossible to repeat the same word without causing differences in the speech waveform. As a result, it is not possible to reliably determine the identity of the individual phonemes from the acoustic signal alone, at least not by automatic techniques given today's state of the art. In order to increase the recognition reliability, the redundancy provided by the other knowledge sources must be heavily utilized. This is indirectly done by people in everyday conversations when they adjust their way of speaking to the situation, i.e. they put just enough cues into their speech to allow their listeners to reconstruct the message unmistakably.

Basically, an automatic system for speech recognition must try to make use of the same knowledge source as a human does. A typical system structure is shown in Fig. 1. It consists of a series of data converting stages. In the signal processing stage, each short time speech segment of 10-30 ms is analyzed and represented by an high dimensional acoustic vector. From these acoustic vectors, acoustic-phonetically relevant features are extracted. Then these features are used to segment the continuous speech signal into acoustically significant regions, called subword units, and are identified or labeled. These subword hypotheses serve as input to the lexical matching stage to form word hypotheses. The syntactic and semantic analysis stages produce hypotheses about word groups and the meaning of these word groups, respectively. The difference between syntactic and semantic constraints is illustrated by

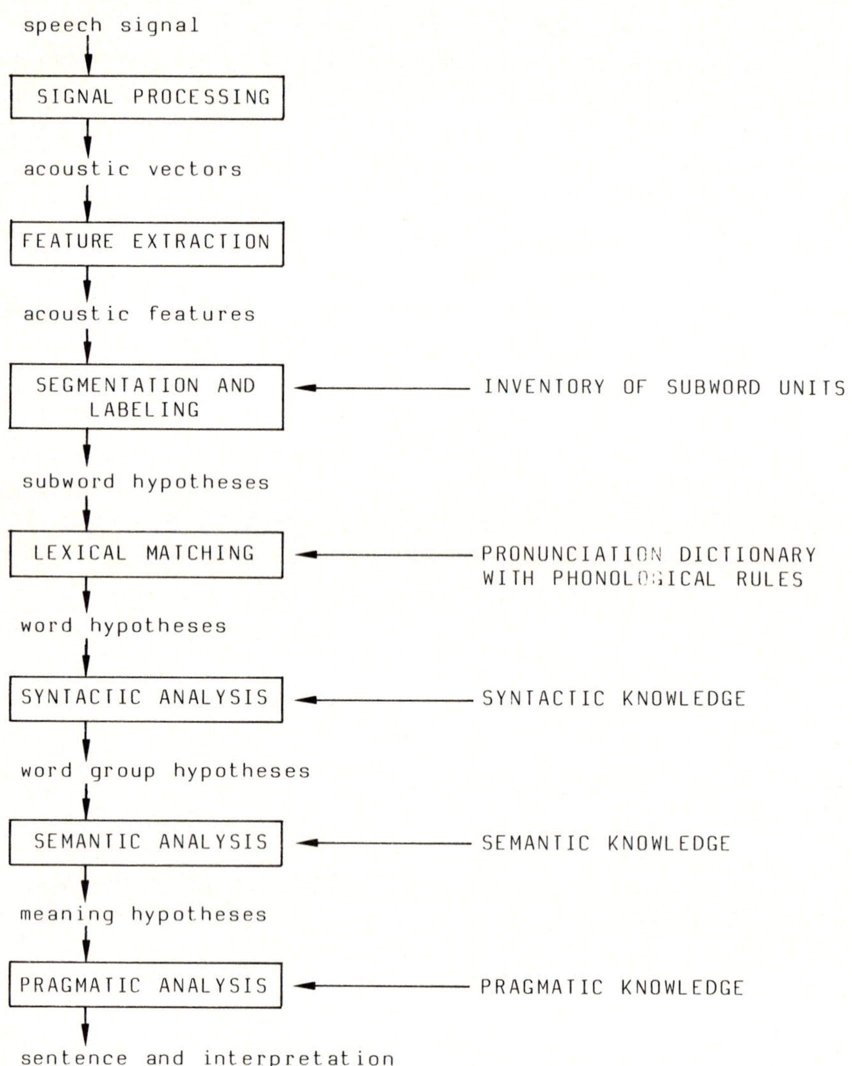

Fig. 1: Processes involved in speech recognition.

Chomsky's famous sentence 'Colorless green ideas sleep furiously', which is syntactically acceptable, but semantically incorrect. The final stage is the pragmatic analysis producing either the written sentence or the intended interpretation of the spoken utterance. These processing stages will be discussed in detail in the following sections.

Although the system structure in Fig 1. may look very straightforward, the reader should realize that the ambiguity in the results of each processing stage must be transmitted to the next stage in an appropriate way. The system structure and the processing stages have been chosen in such way that all relevant techniques in automatic speech processing are present and can be put into perspective. Thus in a real system, not all stages must be actually realized. A number of successful systems use directly the acoustic vector sequence, i.e. the output of the signal processing, as input to the lexical matching stage with no feature extraction or segmentation. The degree of abstraction, in terms of distance to the acoustic signal, is increased from stage to stage. A stage for processing prosodic information has been left out because it is difficult to use in practice and nearly no system has used it so far.

3. SIGNAL PROCESSING AND FEATURE EXTRACTION

In order to understand the technical realization of signal processing, it is useful to look at the human speech production [Fant 1960]. Physically, the speech signal is a sound pressure waveform that is radiated from the speaker's mouth and nose. The waveform is produced by an air stream coming from the lungs and passing through the vocal cords. The vocal cords are either tensed for voiced sounds and then vibrate like an relaxation oscillator producing a sequence of air pulses or spread apart for unvoiced sounds leaving the air stream unaffected. When passing through the vocal tract consisting of the pharynx and mouth and/or through the nasal tract, the frequence spectrum of the air stream is shaped by the spectral characteristics of the vocal and nasal tracts. The shape and position of these acoustic cavities change continually during the process of speaking. The speech signal typically covers a frequency range from 20 Hz to 10 kHz, but for recognition purposes an upper limit of 6 kHz is considered to be sufficient.

Most signal processing techniques can be viewed as special data reduction techniques that exploit the manner in which speech is produced. The underlying assumption of most signal processing techniques [Rabiner et al. 1978] is that the speech waveform remains relatively unchanged over a short time interval of 10-30 ms, which is usually referred as a frame. The most common way to analyse a speech signal is to measure its (short time) spectrum, i.e. the distribution of energy over frequency. One of the oldest and simplest methods for implementing a spectral analysis is a bank of analog bandpass filters. Nowadays analog filters are usually replaced by digital filters or by the digital Fourier transform [Rabiner et al. 1978]. The spacing of the bandpass filters is often chosen in analogy to the frequency response of the human ear, which is the basis of the mel-frequency scale. Also, the human ear is relatively insensitive to the phase spectrum information present in the speech signal. This is the reason why signal processing is usually confined to an analysis of the amplitude spectrum of the speech signal. The cepstral analysis provides an example of a theoretically exact technique under the assumption that speech is produced as a convolution of an excitation function with a vocal tract impulse response. In practice, it is calculated as the cosine transform of the log-power spectrum and its first few terms are used to form the acoustic vector. Linear predictive coding (LPC) is an analysis technique that tries to predict the samples of the speech waveform from preceding speech samples using a least squares fit. It can be shown to be equivalent to an parametric estimation of the speech spectrum. Another method of signal processing that is not so closely related to the energy spectrum of the speech signal is based on a direct analysis of the signal waveform and derives parameters from the the zero crossings and individual cycles of the signal waveform. Such parameters in general can provide a better time resolution, but they are computationally inconvenient due to the lack of a fixed frame rate. The output of the signal processing stage is thus a sequence of acoustic vectors of dimension 8-32 at a fixed frame period of 10-30 ms. These acoustic vectors may be strongly affected by the placement of the microphone, the room acoustics, the characteristics of the ambient noise and by speaker typical characteristics. Therefore normalization techniques are often employed to reduce these drawbacks [Reddy 1976].

The feature extraction stage attempts to further reduce the data rate and, at the same time, emphasize the relevant information conveyed by the signal. There are systems that do not perform any sort of feature extraction, but instead directly model the sequence of acoustic vectors as a probabilistic function of time by statistical methods [Baker 1975b; Bahl et al.1983]. Examples of features often used or recommended are the information whether the sound was voiced or not and, if so, the pitch frequency and the presence of high energy if fricative sounds are to be detected. The format frequencies as the acoustic resonances of the vocal tract resonances are particularly important. They are controlled by the position of the tongue, jaw and lips during the process of speaking and are interesting from the viewpoints of both speech production and perception.

Detailed acoustic characterizations of the phonemes have been given by Zue and Schwartz [1976]. A lot of phonetic knowledge about speech and acoustic features is available, but so far the efforts to transfer this knowledge to automatic system have been met with rather limited success. There is one research group [Zue 1982] that explicitly defines as research topic to concentrate on finding and quantifying knowledge about how the acoustic characteristics of speech sounds are affected by their phonetic context and to incorporate this knowledge into automatic recognition. The ultimate goal is to achieve better performance with respect to speaker independence, large vocabularies and continuous speech recognition.

4. SEGMENTATION AND SUBWORD UNITS

The primary motivation for segmentation is to reduce the computational expenditure of the recognition process. The segment boundaries are used as anchor points and restrict the size of the search space in the recognition phase. By the segmentation process, the speech signal is divided into acoustically distinctive regions which can correspond to one of several types of subword units.

The phonemes are the basic sounds that make up the acoustic realization of a language. Languages such as English, French and

German have typically 40 to 50 phonemes. The usual definition of phonemes is a functional one: phonemes are the smallest units of speech by which semantically different words are distinguished. Thus, the English words 'tap' and 'cap' differ in their first phoneme. Yet, phonemes are not speech sounds in an absolute sense. Their acoustic realization is often dependent on the phonetic surrounding. This phenomenon is called coarticulation: a speech sound is affected by the sounds that precede and follow it because the vocal tract apparatus starts from the position of the preceding phoneme and anticipates the position of the next phoneme. In addition, the system of phonemes is language dependent. For example, the sounds 'l' and 'r' do not correspond to different phonemes in Japanese.

To avoid such problems, larger subword units can be chosen so that the coarticulation effects are practically confined to the region within a single subword, such as diphones, demisyllables and syllables. The disadvantage of these types of subword units is that the number of basic units increases drastically. For a 50-phoneme language, we have already 50*(50-1) phoneme pairs, resulting in 2450 diphones.

Although segmentation at the subword level provides a higher degree of abstraction and reduces subsequent computations, this process is far from perfect. Faulty segmentation decisions can lead to insertion errors and deletion errors at the subword level. To enable the recognition system to recover from such errors, often a so-called segment or subword lattice is introduced as in HWIM [Lea 1980]. In such a subword lattice, alternative segmentation decisions and several subword candidates are retained in order to pass the ambiguity to the higher levels and delay the decision until sufficient evidence for a final decision is available. The difficulty with the recognition at the subword level is illustrated by the fact that recognition accuracies of only 50-70 % can be achieved for a subword set of 100-200 units without using additional knowledge sources. A more reliable method for segmentation is to avoid the explicit segmentation as such and incorporate it into the recognition stage, which, however, is computationally more costly.

5. RECOGNITION TECHNIQUES AND STATISTICAL DECISION TECHNIQUES

Each recognition strategy is faced with the problem of handling decisions in the presence of ambiguity and context. This is independent of the type of the decisions and of the details of the approach. If it were possible to recognize subword units with very high reliability, it would not be necessary to rely heavily on statistical methods. However, from the experience gained so far in subword and particularly phoneme recognition, we cannot expect any approximately accurate method for this problem. Statistical decision theory and classical pattern recognition tell us what is the best to do under those circumstances [Fukunaga 1972]. We first consider classical pattern recognition, then finite state machines to model decisions in context and finally the ideal criterion for speech recognition from the statistical point of view.

5.1 CLASSICAL PATTERN RECOGNITION

In classical pattern recognition, a set of several measurements is used to form a high dimensional pattern vector for each object to be classified. In the case of speech, these objects can be 10-ms frames, phonemes or larger subword units or even complete words. Usually the recognition task amounts to determining the most likely class according to the Bayes' decision rule [Fukunaga 1972]. This method requires a model of the probability distributions for each class. The method used most frequently is to assume a multivariate normal or Gaussian distribution for the pattern vectors. Such a distribution is completely defined by its mean vector and its covariance matrix [Fukunaga 1972]. If as an approximation we assume diagonal covariance matrices, such an probability density can be interpreted as equivalent to a weighted Euclidean distance by taking the negative logarithm of the probability density. If we further restrict the probability model to a diagonal covariance matrix with equal variance for all vector components and all classes, we obtain a comparatively simple classifier that is simply defined by the mean vector of each class. This classifier is often referred to as template matching technique, because the mean vector defines a typical template for each class. Although of course the above assumptions are not all true, such a template matching approach or distance classifier works surprisingly well and is used

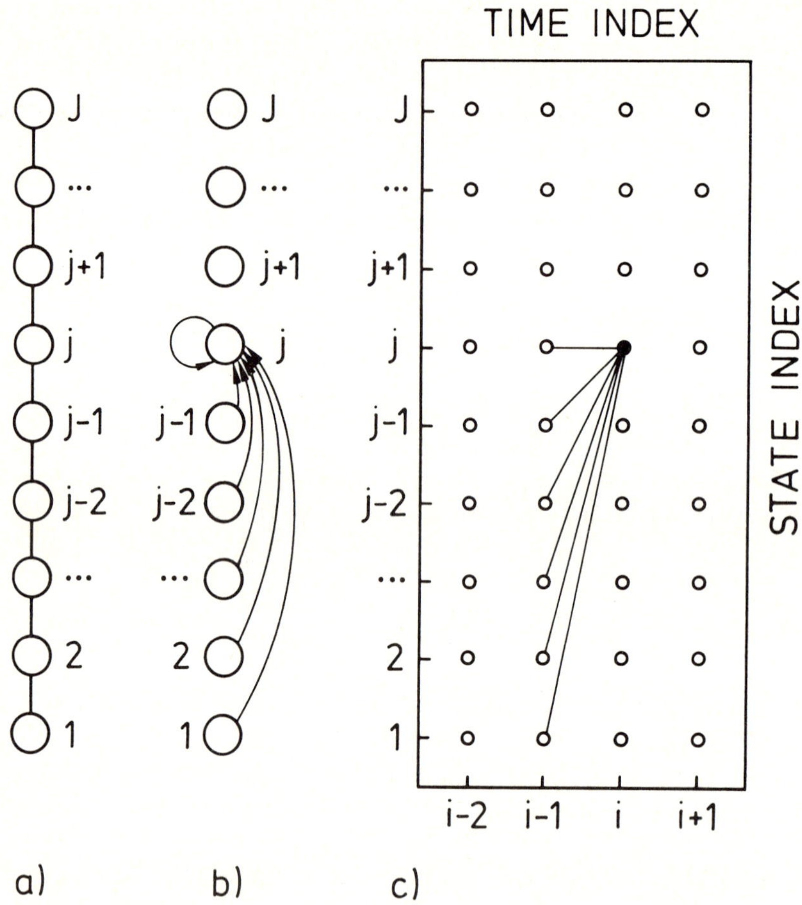

Fig. 2: Illustration of a finite state machine (Markov model):
a) linear arrangement of states,
b) transitions to state j,
c) search space and transition rules.

in many laboratorial and commercial systems [Lea 1980; Doddington et al. 1981]. A different technique is to reduce the intrinsically continuous pattern vectors to a finite set of labels or symbols, which is often referred to as clustering or vector quantization. Each class probability function is then defined by the expected number of occurrences of each symbol [Bahl et al. 1983]. A special variant of a mathematical probabilistic formalism is the so-called fuzzy set theory [de Mori 1983]. Another more heuristic technique for classification is to compare certain feature values against thresholds. The drawback is that no consistent framework is available. Template matching is implicit, because the class characteristics are contained in the data.

Another approach is to incorporate the knowledge explicitly in subroutines. Such an approach could be called 'rule' oriented in contrast to 'template matching'.

5.2 FINITE STATE OR MARKOV MODELS

To model context dependencies in a probabilistic framework, we introduce finite state machines or automata [Baker 1975 b]. The motivation for using such a model to describe the acoustic-phonetic probability functions can be seen from a simplified model of the human speech production. We can consider the human vocal tract to assume only a finite number of states representing articulatory configurations. During the process of speaking, the vocal tract changes from one state to another and a short time speech segment is generated. This process, however, is not deterministic. In principle, for a given transition from one state to another, quite a variety of speech segments can be generated or emitted with different probabilities. These emission probabilities are assumed to depend solely on the state pair or transition under consideration. In addition, there are transition probabilities for each state pair as well. These transition probabilities improve the finite state model by incorporating the expected frequency of occurences into the model. In principle, such finite machines can be used at different stages in recognition, e.g. at the 10-ms frame level, at the subword level and also at the word level. Fig. 2 shows an example. We have a linear arrangement of states

(Fig.2a). The transitions to a particular state j are shown (Fig.2b): several skip transitions, one forward transitions and one loop transition. Given a sequence of measured data over time, we have to look for the most likely state sequence that has caused the observed measurements.

To capture all combinatorial possibilities, we have to unfold the linear arrangement of states j along time axis i such that the new lattice of grid point (i,j) comprises the ensemble of all state sequences that could have generated the observed vector sequence up to time i and end in state j. A probability or distance score (Section 5.1) is assigned to each transition in the (i,j) lattice. To find the best explanation for the observed data, we simply have to look for the best path through the lattice. Such an optimization can be carried out very efficiently by dynamic programming [Bellman 1957]. Dynamic programming is very well tailored to such a type of optimization problem where only a small number of choices or decisions have to be taken at each optimization step [Ney 1982]. By dynamic programming, the overall optimization problem is broken down into a sequence of subproblems that are easier to solve. In the application considered here, it results in filling in a table of hypotheses scores by recursively evaluating the recurrence relation step by step. Thus the algorithm creates a table of solutions to all subproblems that might ever occur. Thus no preliminary decisions have to be taken. The dynamic programming algorithm permits a straightforward implementation without recourse to feedback or decision correcting strategies. Computing a hypothesis score amounts to evaluating the hypothesis that the observed data up to time i results from a state sequence ending in state j.

One attractive property of dynamic programming is that hypotheses are recombined at exactly the same rate that new hypotheses are formed. After the table of hypotheses has been filled, the globally optimal path is constructed by tracing back the decisions taken at each recursion step. The best path provides a mapping of the sequence of time indices along with the corresponding observations onto a state sequence. This mapping is also referred to as (time) registration path and plays an important role to account for speaking rate fluctuations [Vintsyuk 1971, Itakura 1976, Sakoe 1979]. This is evident by considering that skip transitions shorten and return transitions lengthen the real time axis. More details will be given in the sections on isolated and connected word recognition. A similar method is often used to segmentation errors at the lexical matching stage: the skip transitions correspond to segment deletion errors, the return transitions to segment insertion errors [Jelinek 1976].

5.3 THE STATISTICAL RECOGNITION CRITERION

Now, we formulate, from a statistical point of view, the ideal criterion for recognizing a spoken word sequence and discuss its implications on the design of speech recognition systems.   Similar considerations   apply if we have subword sequences rather than word sequences.

In order to minimize the probability of error according to the Bayes' decision rule [Fukunaga 1972], the task of a speech recognizer must be to determine that sequence of words $w(1),...,w(n),...,w(n)$:= $w[1:N]$ (of unknown length N) that has most probably caused the observed sequence of measurements $x(1),...,x(i),...,x(I)$:=$x[1:I]$.   Using the Bayes' theorem [Fukunaga 1972], we can cast it into the form:

Determine that sequence of words $w[1:N]$ that maximizes
$$Pr(w[1:N]) * Pr(x[1:I]|w[1:N]).$$

This is a very important equation. It highlights the interaction between the observed data and the knowledge sources of the system: the decision must lead to the best compromise between the observed data and the knowledge sources. At the same time, the equation allows a clear border line to be defined between the acoustic-phonetic knowledge sources and the higher level knowledge sources. The first term, $Pr(w[1:N])$, is the a priori probability of the word sequence $w[1:N]$. It is independent of the acoustic observations and completely specified by the higher level knowledge sources.   In other words, the high level knowledge sources syntax, semantics and pragmatics are equivalent to the knowledge of the a priori probabilities $Pr(w[1:N])$ of all word sequences $w[1:N]$. The second term, $Pr(x[1:I]|w[1:N])$, is the conditional probability of observing the sequence $x[1:I]$ when the word sequence $w[1:N]$ has been uttered. It must reflect the acoustic-phonetic and lexical knowledge sources. Once the probability functions of the language and of the acoustic-phonetics are known, it is in principle possible for a given sequence of measurements $x[1:I]$ to evaluate $Pr(w[1:N])*Pr(w[1:N]|x[1:I])$ for each word sequence $w[1:N]$ and to determine the most likely word sequence directly. However, the computational expenditure would be far too high. Therefore special search procedures have been developed, e.g. stack decoding [Bahl et al. 1983], dynamic programming [Baker 1975a,b], beam search [Lowerre 1976] and ordered search [Nilsson 1982]. In order to reduce the combinatorial complexity of the optimization problem, special approximations are often employed such as replacing the most likely word sequence by the most likely state sequence in the search space [Baker 1975 b].

An interesting property of the statistical approach is that it leads quite straightforward to an automatic training procedure to estimate the parameters of the statistical models. In the literature, these procedures are known as Baum-Welch algorithm, forward-backward algorithm and Viterbi training [Baker 1975 b; Bahl et al. 1983; Brown et al. 1984]. Such procedures provide a lot of advantages over man supervised procedures because they guarantee a consistency between the training and the recognition phase of the system. In this view, the successful design of a speech recognition method relies crucially on a skilful compromise between theoretical model assumptions and statistical parameter estimation.

6. SYSTEM ARCHITECTURES

Useful criteria to systematically classify system architectures are the way in which the ambiguity problem of the hypotheses is handled and the organization of the search procedure. Many of the system architectures still in use today have been developed during the 'Research Understanding Project' (SUR) sponsored by the U.S. Department of Defense's Advanced Research Project Agency (ARPA) [Lea 1980].
A number of details on system architectures can be found in the books by Lea [1980] and Haton [1982]. Often system architectures are classified according to whether hypotheses are constructed in a 'bottom-up' or 'top-down' manner. The attributes stem originally from the parsing of nonprobabilistic context free grammars [Hopcroft et al., 1979] In a 'bottom-up' approach, the recognition

at the subword or the word level operates independently of the high level components in order to produce subword word hypotheses. In a 'top-down' approach, the high level components predict certain subwords or words according to the portion of the input sentence already processed and to the knowledge about syntax, semantics and pragmatics and propose them to the acoustic level to evaluate their likelihoods. However, in the light of the statistical decision theory discussed in Section 5.3, the distinction between 'bottom-up' and 'top-down' becomes meaningless. What matters, is the quality of the search strategy to optimize the product of the probabilities.

A number of systems are based on a hierarchical structure that can be derived directly from the Fig. 1. A hierarchy of processing levels with corresponding knowledge sources is defined, and interactions take place only between adjacent level. Ideally, as many hypotheses as possible should be passed on from one level to the next in order to make sure that the correct hypothesis is not likely to be missed. A good approximation to a complete set of hypotheses could amount to a table depending on three parameters: the beginning and ending points of the sentence portion under consideration and the subword, word or word group being hypothesized. However due to memory and time limitations, usually a number of short cuts are applied, which effectively results in preliminary decisions that may be difficult to correct at later processing stages. Typically an explicit segmentation is performed to produce a comparatively small number of subword hypotheses for each segment portion. Examples of systems relying on a hierarchical structure are HWIM [Lea 1980], KEAL [Mercier 1980] and MYRTILLE [Haton et al. 1982].

A completely different approach was employed in the HEARSAY system [Lea 1980]. HEARSAY is based on a set of cooperating independent knowledge sources that communicate through a global data base called blackboard. This blackboard is basically made up of all hypotheses produced by the knowledge sources during the recognition process. Each knowledge source has access to the data base and can create, modify or complete hypotheses. Attempts are being made by many artificial intelligence groups to use this type of architecture for other knowledge based systems.

The other extreme of one single integrated knowledge representation was realized in the HARPY system [Lowerre 1976; Lea 1980]. A similar approach has been employed by Vintsyuk [1982]. The

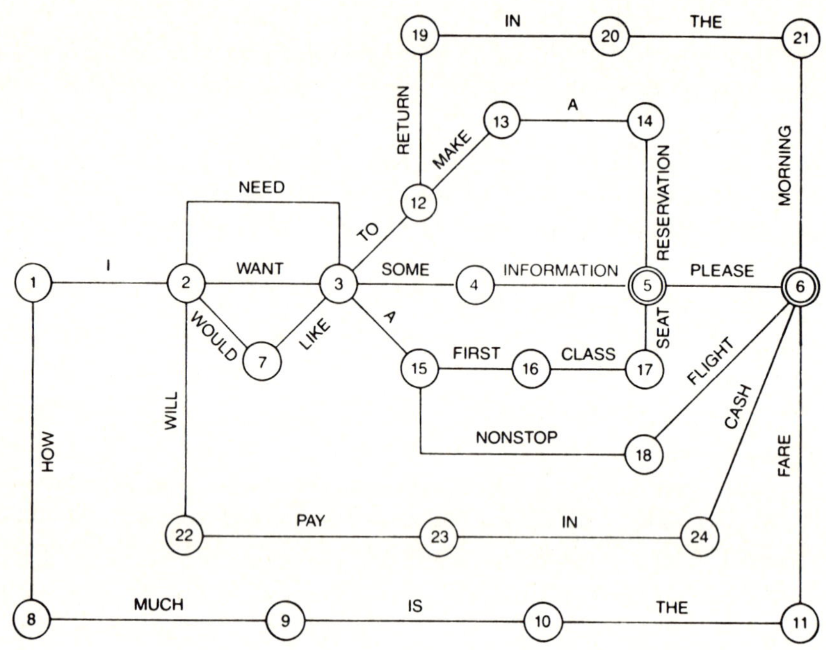

Fig. 3: Example of a finite state network for an artificial
language (after Levinson et. al, 1978).

theoretical foundations for the HARPY type of knowledge representation had been developed in the DRAGON system by Baker [1975a]. HARPY merges lexical knowledge, phonological rules, syntactic and semantic knowledge into a unified network. In addition, HARPY makes use of a very efficient graph search technique in which all except a beam of near-miss alternatives around the best paths are pruned from the search tree and thus the combinatorial explosion of possibilities is avoided. HARPY was the most successful system in the ARPA SUR project. For a 1011-word vocabulary, the word error rate was 3%. However, the complexity of a recognition task does not necessarily correlate with the size of the vocabulary. One way to measure the complexity of the recognition problem or, in other words, the degree of constraints imposed by the high level knowledge sources is the so-called branching factor, which is the average number of words that could appear next in an allowable sentence. An example of such an artificial language is shown in Fig. 3 for the flight reservation system of Bell [Rabiner et al. 1981]. Each path through the network results in a legal sentence. Thus such a task can be simpler than the recognition of digit strings if the average branching factor is smaller than 10. Techniques for setting up artificial language models designed by the experimenter and natural language models extracted from observed data are described in [Bahl et al. 1983]. Some models can be based on the stochastic variants of context free grammars [Hopcroft et al. 1979] or augmented transition network (ATN) grammars [Woods 1970].
The most consequent exponent of statistically based recognition is Jelinek's group at IBM [Bahl et al. 1983]. Their goal is the transcription of a limited natural language for the dictation of business letters. They take the probabilistic approach so far that nearly every piece of knowledge about both the speech signal and the language structure is extracted automatically from a sufficient amount of training data. A demonstration system is in operation that recognizes a 5000-word vocabulary. The words must be spoken with small pauses, the word error rate is reported to be 5%.

7. CONNECTED WORD RECOGNITION

In this section, an algorithm for connected word recognition will be presented. This algorithm will provide an example of

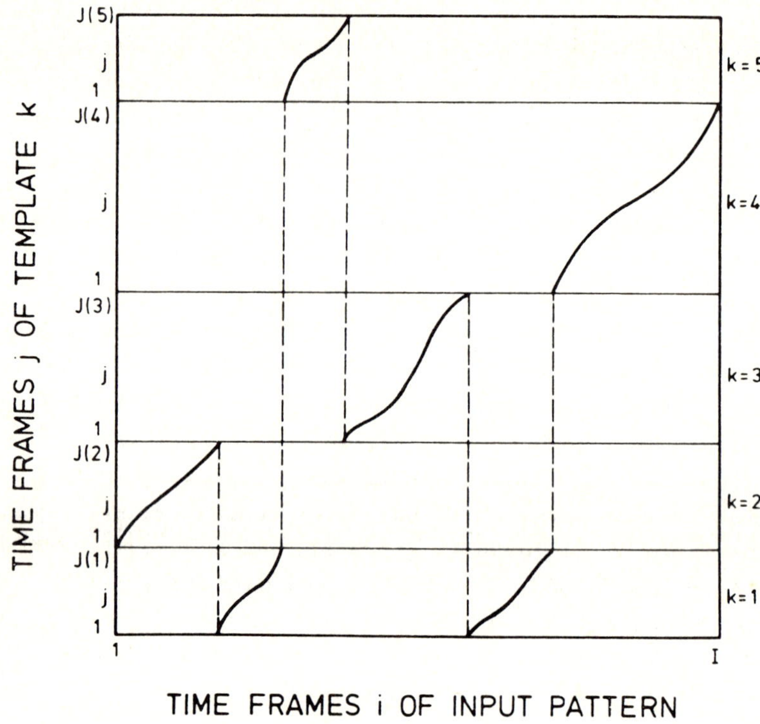

Fig. 4: Illustration of connected word recognition.

successful approach to speech recognition using only a few assumptions about speech.

In connected word recognition, the spoken input is a sequence of words from a vocabulary of small size, typically 10 to 100 words. Typical examples include connected digit strings where the vocabulary is the set of 10 digits or connected letter recognition where the vocabulary is the set of 26 letters. For such vocabulary sizes, whole word reference patterns is given the preference as compared with some sort of subword units. Most of the problems in connected word recognition arise from the difficulty in reliably determining the word boundaries. As a result, there is a large amount of interdependence between the word boundary detection, the nonlinear time alignment and the classification itself; e. g. an error in the word boundary detection is likely to lead to another error in the nonlinear time alignment and the word identification, and conversely.

The best method for dealing with the interdependence of several operations and to take decisions in context, is to define a global criterion as in Section 5.3, into which all the requirements of the three operations of word boundary detection, nonlinear time alignment and word identification are incorporated. Depending on the recognition task, it may be required to include a syntactic analysis as well. This formulation of the recognition problem for connected word recognition avoids any local or preliminary decisions and performs the word boundary detection, the nonlinear time alignment and the classification simultaneously in one stage, thus taking account of the interdependence of these operations. There have been a number of different search strategies based on dynamic programming to the problem of recognizing strings of words in concatenation [Vintsyuk 1971; Sakoe 1979, Spohrer et al. 1980, Myers et al. 1981, Bridle 1982]; a comparison is given in [Ney 1984]. A computationally most efficient algorithm will be considered now. The algorithm can be derived immediately using whole word reference patterns and the framework developed in Section 5. It is worthwhile reviewing its operation here in order to place the word boundary detection as part of the algorithm into evidence.

The unknown input or test pattern consists of $i = 1, \ldots, I$ time frames, each represented by an acoustic vector. The input pattern is known to be composed of individual words, which are chosen from a given vocabulary. The words of the vocabulary correspond to a set of K reference patterns or templates obtained from single word utterances spoken in isolation. The word templates are distinguished by the index k = 1,...,K. The time frames of the template k are denoted as j = 1,....,J(k). The basic idea is illustrated in Fig. 5. The time frames i of the test pattern and the time frames j of each template k define a set of grid points (i,j,k) (cf. Fig . 2). Each grid point (i,j,k) is associated with a local distance measure d(i,j,k). It can be considered as the negative logarithm of the emission probability function and defines a measure of dissimilarity between the corresponding speech segments. The connected word recognition problem can be viewed as one of finding that path through the set of grid points (i,j,k) which provides the best match between the test pattern and the unknown sequence of templates. This registration path, is given as a sequence of grid points [1,1,k(1)], ..., [i,j(i),k(i)], ..., [I,j(I),k(I)].

The frame index i of the input pattern is used as the path parameter for indexing the ordered set of path elements. For the path, there are certain continuity constraints or transition rules resulting from the problem under consideration. It is helpful to distinguish between two types of transitions: transitions within a word template and transitions at the word template boundaries. The within-template transition rules, i.e. the rules for path points with j > 1, are the same as in Fig. 2. (Section 5.2). The grid point (i,j,k) can be reached from any other grid point (i-1,j',k) with j'<j or j'=j in the same template k. The between-template transition rules,i.e. the rules for path points with j = 1, are that grid point (i,1,k) can be reached from the end (i-1,J(k'),k') of any preceding template k' or from grid point (i-1,1,k) in the same template k. The set of potential predecessor grid points {i-1,J(k'),k'} takes account of potential word boundaries. As an additional constraint, the path must start and end at template boundaries.

The recognition criterion described is able to tackle the problem of word boundary detection, although at word boundaries the match between template frames and input frames must be expected to be rather poor due to coarticulation effects. However, the algorithm is forced to match especially the central parts of the words, and as a by-product due to the continuity constraints of the time warping path, the word boundaries are determined as correctly as it is possible within the assumptions used.

Utilizing the technique of dynamic programming [Ney 1982], we define a minimum accumulated distance $D(i,j,k)$ along any path to the grid point (i,j,k). This minimum accumulated distance is also referred to as matching score. Due to the additivity of the accumulated distance and its minimum property, two recurrence relations are obtained, one from the within-template transition rules for $j > 1$ and another from the between-template transition rules for $j = 1$. The time distortion penalties $T(j-j')$ are defined using the transition probabilities as in Section 5.2. At the potential word boundaries, i.e. at the start of each reference pattern k with j=1, we have:

$$D(i,1,k) = d(i,1,k) + \min \{ D(i-1,1,k)+T(0);$$
$$D(i-1,J(k'),k')+T(1): k'=1,\ldots,K \}$$

In the word interior with j>1, we have:

$$D(i,j,k) = d(i,j,k) + \min \{ D(i-1,j',k)+T(j-j'): j'=1,\ldots,j \}$$

The recursive evaluation is carried out in three loops each over the input frames, the templates and the template frames. After the final input frame has been processed, the optimal path is constructed by tracing back the optimal decisions taken at each of the local optimization steps. Thus the word sequence that best matches the input pattern is determined.

The algorithm proceeds for all templates in parallel by moving along the time axis of the input pattern and thus performs a strict left-to-right search. This property is ideally suited for the purposes of book keeping and real time operation. The dynamic programming recursion can be implemented by using only one column from the whole $D(i,j,k)$ matrix which is propagated along the i time axis and two additional arrays indexed by the time index i for keeping track of the decisions at the potential word boundaries. The algorithm described so far allows a number of useful and interesting modifications which shall be mentioned here [Bridle et al. 1982]. It is possible to perform an online traceback before

the end of the utterance has been reached without sacrificing any
recognition accuracy. The syntactic analysis based on a regular
grammar can be included by a suitable modification of the word
transition rules. To take account of the context dependence of
each word, it may be necessary to have several independent copies
for each word. The endpoint detection can be incorporated into the
algorithm suitably both by introducing a silence template and
rejection class for nonvocabulary input. Finally, a considerable
reduction of the computational cost can be achieved by removing
unlikely path candidates in the recognition algorithm. The
technique of delayed decisions as described above and its efficient
algorithmic implementation both in software and hardware forms the
basis of the more advanced commercial systems for connected word
recognition. Examples are the NEC DP200 (the successor to the DP
100) of Nippon Electric Co. Ltd., Japan, the Verbex 3000 of Verbex
Corp., USA, the MSDS SR 128 of Marconi Space and Defense Systems,
England, and the Logica LOGOS of Logica Ltd., England. The word
error rates of these systems are typically in the range of 1% for
the digit vocabulary.

8. ISOLATED WORD RECOGNITION AND COMMERCIAL SYSTEMS

The number of commercial systems for isolated word
recognition increase steadily from month to month. Such systems
are now in regular use in quality control and inspection and in
goods and mail handling and similar data entry tasks requiring
hands or eyes busy activities. With the increasing capabilities of
speech recognition, more ambitious applications are becoming
feasible. Such applications could include computer programming,
computer aided design (CAD) and information retrieval from computer
databases. For most tasks, the vocabulary can be structured into
several subsets of the entire vocabulary by a suitable syntax tree.
The syntax tree determines which subset of the vocabulary is active
at different stages within the task procedure sequence according to
a 'menu' format. Thus the syntax tree helps reduce computation
time. The recognition can be increased by using longer
polysyllabic words instead of short ones and phonetically
dissimilar words.

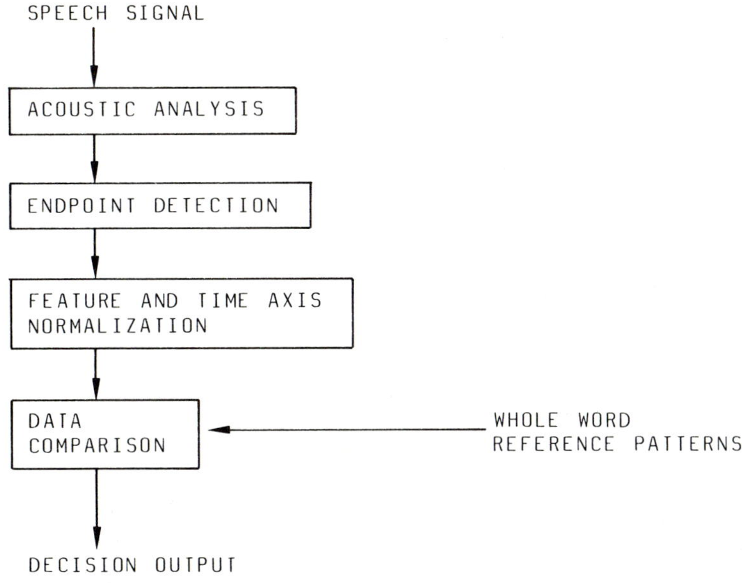

Fig. 5: Typical structure of a system for isolated word recognition.

In 1981, a comparative test of 7 commercial word recognizers was performed by Doddington and Schalk [1981] of Texas Instruments. The error rates for speaker dependent high quality word recognition varied from 0.2% to 12.6% for a 20-word vocabulary and correlated surprisingly well with the price of systems ranging from 500 to 65000 US-Dollars. Due to the progress in the technology of chip integration, prices have gone down drastically since then.

A typical structure of an isolated word recognizer is shown in Fig. 5. After the spectral analysis, the beginning and the ending point are determined, usually by some sort of comparison with energy thresholds. Then the input pattern of the utterance is constructed by dividing the utterance into a fixed number of time slices (12-16) and representing each time slice by a suitable set of acoustic parameters or features that have been normalized appropriately with respect to energy (loudness) and speaking rate. The input pattern is now ready for comparison. For each reference word, a distance measure serving as measure of dissimilarity is computed by comparing the data of each time slice of the input pattern with the corresponding data of the reference pattern. This can be viewed as a distance classifier described in Section 5.1. In many systems, the rough time normalization is refined by performing a nonlinear time alignment on the 16 time slices with a rather small adjustment window [Kuhn et al. 1983].

Most systems are speaker dependent, i.e. each user must train the system to his individual voice before using it. Speaker independent systems should ideally permit users to speak to the system without ever having previously trained the system. The reference patterns are usually extracted from a large data base for an entire population of speakers, typically about 100 speakers. Nevertheless, recognition accuracy decreases significantly in comparison with speaker dependent reference patterns, and the true speaker independent recognition capability could be considered as today's hardest problem is automatic speech recognition.

REFERENCES

L.R. BAHL, F. JELINEK ,R.L. MERCER: "A Maximum Likelihood Approach to Continuous Speech Recognition", IEEE Trans. on Pattern Analysis and Machine Intelligence, Vol. PAMI-5, No. 2, pp. 179-190, March 1983.

J.K. BAKER: "The DRAGON System - An Overview", IEEE Trans. on Acoustics, Speech and Signal Processing, Vol. ASSP-23, No. 1, pp. 24-29, February 1975 a.

J.K. BAKER: "Stochastic Modeling for Automatic Speech Understanding", in D.R. REDDY (ed.): 'Speech Recognition', Academic Press, New York, pp. 512-542, 1975 b.

R. BELLMAN: 'Dynamic Programming', Princeton University Press, Princeton, New Jersey 1957.

J.S. BRIDLE, M.D. BROWN, R.M. CHAMBERLAIN: "An Algorithm for Connected Word Recognition", Proc. 1982 IEEE Conf. on Acoustics, Speech and Signal Processing, Paris, France, pp. 899-902, May 1982.

P. F. BROWN, C.-H. LEE, J. C. SPOHRER: "Bayesian Adaptation in Speech Recognition", Proceedings, 1983 IEEE Int. Conf. on Acoustics, Speech and Signal Processing, Boston, Massachusetts, pp. 761-764, April 1984.

G.R. DODDINGTON, T.B. SCHALK: "Speech Recognition: Turning Theory to Practice", IEEE Spectrum, pp. 26-32, Sep. 1981.

G. FANT: 'Acoustic Theory of Speech Production', Mouton, The Hague, The Netherlands, 1960.

K. FUKUNAGA: 'Introduction to Statistical Pattern Recognition', Academic Press, New York, 1972.

J.-P. HATON (ed).: 'Automatic Speech Analysis and Recognition', Nato Advanced Study Institute Series, D.Reidel Publishing Company, Dordrecht, Holland, 1982.

J.-P. HATON, J.M. PIERREL, S. SABBAGH: "Semantic and Pragmatic Processing in Continuous Speech Understanding", in [Haton 1982], pp. 253-268, 1982.

J.E. HOPCROFT, J.D. ULLMAN: 'Introduction to Automata Theory, Languages and Computation', Addison-Wesley Publishing Company, Reading, Massachusetts 1979.

F. ITAKURA: "Minimum Prediction Residual Principle Applied to Speech Recognition", IEEE Trans. on Acoustics, Speech and Signal Processing, Vol. ASSP-23, pp.67-72, Feb. 1975.

F. JELINEK: "Continuous Speech Recognition by Statistical Methods", Proc. of the IEEE, Vol. 64, No. 10, pp. 532-556, April 1976.

M.H. KUHN, H. TOMASCHEWSKI: " Improvements in Isolated Word Recognition", IEEE Trans. on Acoustics, Speech and Signal Processing, Vol. ASSP-31, No. 1, pp. 157-167, Feb. 1983

W.A. LEA (ed): 'Trends in Speech Recognition', Prentice-Hall, Inc., Englewood Cliffs, New Jersey, 1980.

B.T. LOWERRE: "The HARPY Speech Recognition System", Ph.D Thesis, Carnegie Mellon University, Dept. Computer Science, Pittsburgh, Pennsylvania, April 1976.

G. MERCIER: "Acoustic-phonetic Decoding and Adaptation in Continuous Speech Recognition", in [Haton 1982], pp. 69-100, 1982.

R. DE MORI: 'Computer Models of Speech Using Fuzzy Algorithms', Plenum Press, New York, 1983.

C.S. MYERS, L.R. RABINER: "Connected Digit Recognition Using a Level-Building DTW Algorithm", IEEE Trans. on Acoustics, Speech and Signal Processing, Vol. ASSP-29, No. 3, pp. 351-363, June 1981.

H. NEY: "Dynamic Programming as a Technique for Pattern Recognition", Proc. 6th Int. Conf. on Pattern Recognition, Munich, Germany, pp. 1119-1125, Oct. 1982.

H. NEY: "The Use of a One-Stage Dynamic Programming Algorithm for Connected Word Recognition", IEEE Trans. on Acoustics, Speech and Signal, Vol. ASSP-32, No. 2, pp. 263-271, April 1984.

N.J. NILSSON: 'Principles of Artificial Intelligence', Springer-Verlag, New York, 1982.

L.R. RABINER, S.E. LEVINSON: "Isolated and Connected Word Recognition - Theory and Selected Applications", IEEE Trans. on Communications, Vol.COM-29, No. 5, pp. 621-659, May 1981.

L.R. RABINER, R.W. SCHAFER: 'Digital Processing of Speech Signals', Prentice Hall, Englewood Cliffs, New Jersey 1978.

D.R. REDDY: "Speech Recognition by Machine: A Review", Proc. of the IEEE, Vol. 64, No. 4, pp. 501-531, April 1976.

H. SAKOE: "Two-Level DP-Matching - A Dynamic Programming-Based Pattern Matching Algorithm for Connected Word Recognition", IEEE Trans. on Acoustics, Speech and Signal Processing, Vol. ASSP-27, No. 6, pp. 588-595, Dec. 1979.

J.C. SPOHRER, P.F. BROWN, P.H. HOCHSCHILD, J.K. BAKER: "Partial Traceback in Continuous Speech Recognition", Proc. Int. Conf. on Cybernetics and Society, Cambridge, Massachusetts, pp. 36-42, Oct. 1980.

T.K. VINTSYUK: "Element-wise Recognition of Continuous Speech Composed of Words from a Specified Dictionary", Kibernetika (Cybernetics), Vol. 7, No. 2, pp. 133-143, March-April 1971.

T.K. VINTSYUK: "Speech Recognition and Understanding", Kibernetika (Cybernetics), Vol. 18, No. 5, pp.101-105, Sept.-Oct. 1982.

W.A. WOODS: "Transition Network Grammars for Natural Language Analysis", Commun. of the ACM, Vol. 13, No. 10, pp. 591-606, Oct. 1970.

V.W.   ZUE: "Acoustic-phonetic   Knowledge   Representation:
Implications from Spectrogram Reading Experiments", in [Haton
1982], pp. 101-120, 1982.

V.W. ZUE, R.M.   SCHWARTZ: "Acoustic Processing and Phonetic
Analysis", in [Lea 1980], pp.   101-124, 1980.

CHAPTER 42.

CURRENT DEVELOPMENTS IN ARTIFICIAL
INTELLIGENCE AND EXPERT SYSTEMS

PROFESSOR DONALD MICHIE
The Turing Institute, Glasgow, Scotland.

The professional activity of the knowledge engineer is to develop expert
systems.   An expert system is a machine system which embodies useful human
knowledge in machine memory in such a way that it can give intelligent
advice and also can offer explanations and justifications of its decisions
on demand.   That is the key clause in the customer's specification.   A
system which gives good decisions but cannot explain itself in terms to
which the human expert can relate may be a software product of great value,
but it belongs to some other category: operations research, decision
support systems, automatic control, etc.   So the system must be capable
not only of emulating the expert in the quality of decisions, but also in
the ability to give reasons and justification.

From a structural point of view an expert system is a knowledge-based
inference engine (Figure 1).

The inference engine is an interpreter for a high-level language in which
the knowledge base is expressed.   The knowledge base itself is an
interconnected set of pattern-coded hypotheses, observations, and rules.
So we find a sharp contrast with classical, sequentially-driven programs.
The typical setup is a division between a body of situation-action rules
and what is called the data-base, which maintains an up-dated map of the
current state of the problem (Figure 2).

The driver of such a system is not the sequence in which the rules are
written down, but the matching process whereby a rule is "fired".   The
current state-description, or "situation", is something that may or may not
be satisfied in the data-base.   That is to say the left hand side, the
"if" part of each given rule, may or may not match with something in the
data-base.   An action is some process - it may be simply drawing a
conclusion, it may be putting out a message, it may be initiating a robotic
action.   But whatever it is, it is some process that possibly changes the
data-base.

In the simplest case control simply cycles through the rules in the
rule-base and in each cycle finds which rules have their situation part
satisfied, uses some criterion of conflict resolution to select one of the
candidate rules for firing and then performs the action part of that rule.
The action may have the form of offering advice or may even be asking a
question.   If the user responds by querying the selected action, then the
system will explain it, - for example, somewhat trivially but quite
effectively by displaying the sequence of rules which generated its
behaviour.   Figure 3 illustrates the "recognise-act cycle".

The tradition of knowledge engineering as it has evolved in the USA has
been based on a scenario in which the knowledge engineer, the computer
scientist who specialises in doing this kind of work, labours hand in hand
with a domain specialist whose knowledge it is desired to transfer.   The

EXPERT SYSTEM = KNOWLEDGE-BASE + INFERENCE ENGINE

Inference engine is the interpreter for a very high-level language

Knowledge-base is an interconnected set of pattern-coded observations, hypotheses and rules

Figure 1.   Structure of an expert system.

| DATABASE | | SITUATION-ACTION RULES |

SITUATION: SOMETHING THAT MAY OR MAY NOT BE SATISFIED IN THE DATABASE

ACTION: SOME PROCESS THAT POSSIBLY CHANGES THE DATABASE

Figure 2.   Partition of an expert system into "database" and "rulebase".

EACH CYCLE THE INFERENCE ENGINE

*** FINDS WHICH RULES HAVE THEIR SITUATION PART SATISFIED
IN THE 'DATABASE'**

*** SELECTS ONE OF THEM TO BE 'FIRED'**

*** PERFORMS THE ACTION PART OF THE SELECTED RULE
(THUS POSSIBLY CHANGING THE DATABASE)**

**THE "ACTION" MAY HAVE THE FORM OF OFFERING
ADVICE OR ASKING A QUESTION**

**IF THE USER RESPONDS BY QUERYING THE ACTION '
THE SYSTEM MAY "EXPLAIN" IT BY DISPLAYING
THE SEQUENCE OF RULES WHICH TRIGGERED IT.**

Figure 3.   The recognise-act cycle of an expert system.

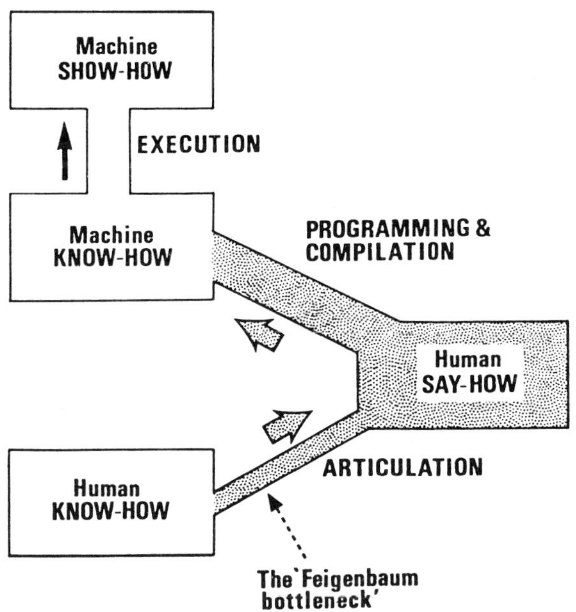

Figure 4.   Knowledge engineer's route map: old style.

<u>Figure 5.</u>   Human experts can occasionally find it
difficult to explain their reasoning.

engineer seeks to fish the required expertise out of the expert's head in the form of rules which can be encoded in the machine system. The so-called dialogue acquisition method is depicted in Figure 4 as an old-style knowledge engineer's route map.

His object is to convert human "know-how" into "say-how" through a process of articulation of which the expert is supposed to be capable. Once in this form, the traditional arts of programming and compiling can convert it into machine code. This code is the machine representation of the know-how. At run time it generates what I have called machine show-how, in other words the expert behaviour that the customer desires.

This seemed a promising way to go because experts in various domains such as chemistry or troubleshooting complex equipment or medical diagnosis, are surprisingly confident about their ability to access the large body of pattern-based rules which they have in their heads. It seemed a reasonable idea to take this confidence at its face value. However time has moved on, and this craft has been in existence for very nearly ten years since the original laboratory demonstrations. Yet the number of systems which are out in the market place actually earning money could, I think, be counted on the fingers of one hand. There must be a reason for this.

Edward Feigenbaum has put his finger on the trouble. Note the channel in the Figure which I have drawn as rather narrow. He called it "the bottleneck problem of applied artificial intelligence". If the narrowness of that channel is independent of the complexity of the task domain, then the situation is one which the technology could live with. We would have a hard time, and we would always have a hard time pushing or pulling expertise through the narrow channel, but it could at least be done. In the last few years at Edinburgh we thought it worthwhile to make an investigation to see if this hypothesis of independence is valid. There is an alternative possibility, namely, that the more complex the mental skill, the greater the proportion of it which is encoded in intuitive form and hence beyond access by anybody including the expert himself. The results of our quite extensive tests have been conclusive. Expert articulacy is **not** independent of complexity. One reaches the dark area of inaccessibility surprisingly soon as one moves up the complexity scale. In Figure 5 I have purloined a Thurber drawing to illustrate the point.

So one of two alternatives presents itself.
The first is that the knowledge engineering enterprise seemed like a good idea at the time, but has now reached the end of its useful life.

The alternative possibility is that this route map is incomplete and that there is some way of going from human know-how to machine know-how other than by the method of articulation.

The first indication that the latter might be the case comes from the elementary observation that when an expert is asked to perform a know-how transplant into a human apprentice rather than into machine memory, he does not in general proceed by articulating the precepts and rules of his craft. Most of the work is done by presenting a cleverly graded and sequenced series of **tutorial examples.**

It thus appears there is another way of moving this conceptualised material into another agent provided that that agent is in a suitably prepared state. In the human case the agent is the apprentice. By "suitably prepared" we mean that the agent should be capable of learning by example.

This blocked channel can thus be circumvented if and only if a means can be

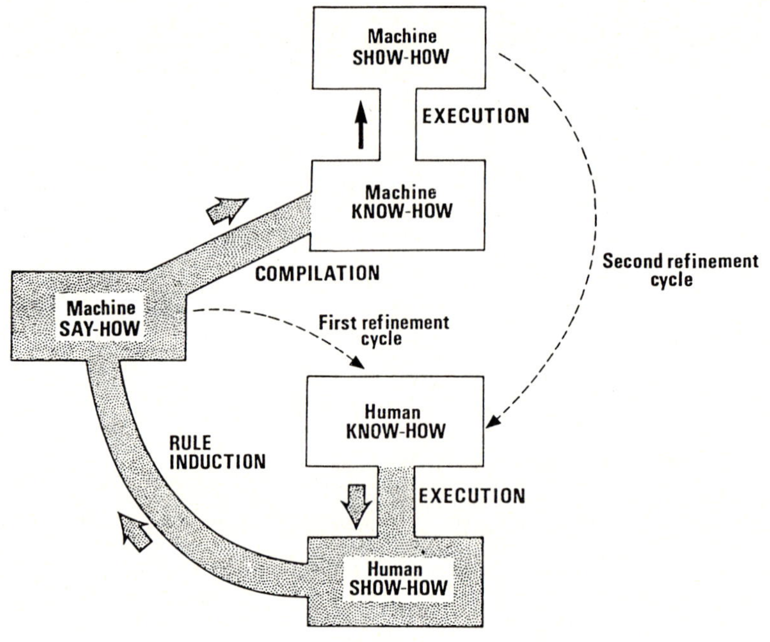

Figure 6.   Map of overall problem.

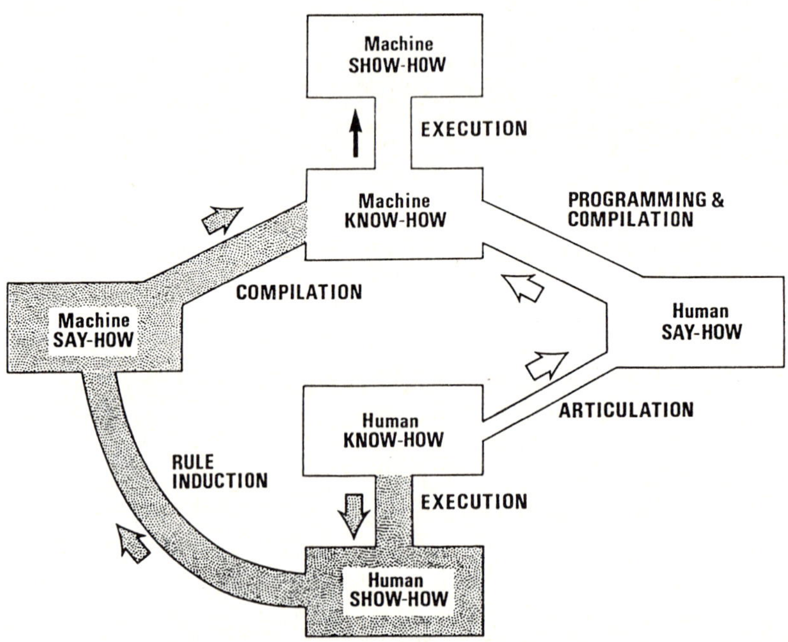

Figure 7.   Knowledge engineer's route map: new style.

found for moving the rules from the expert's head to machine memory via the language of examples rather than via the language of explicit articulation. For that we require effective algorithms for inductive inference to be executed by the recipient machine.   Such algorithms must simulate the apprentice's ability to reconstruct from the tutorial examples a mental model of the master's know-how.

Figure 6 depicts a map of the overall problem somewhat richer than the old-style map shown earlier.   In this case we propose that it is possible to proceed from human show-how, that is, human-supplied examples.   We know that the human can change his know-how into tutorial show-how.   We know this because an expert is usually hired by his employer for two things, not just one.   One task is to employ his skills on actual cases: the second task is to transmit his skills to new recruits.   Given that, then by computer induction we can have the machine acquire expert skills from tutorial examples of expert decisions presented to it.   A model of the expert's skill in explicit form can then be displayed on the screen as rules.   Those can be compiled into machine know-how.   If this can all be done then we have a Northwest Passage to circumvent the "bottleneck". Thanks to the fact that there are now some quite efficient inductive inference algorithms available it has been possible to engineer tool-kits for building expert systems from expert-supplied examples.   In our own laboratory we do not now do things any other way.

I do not want to suggest that we should make no use at all of expert articulation.   There is no matter of principle about it.   Rather, the question is where the main traffic should pass.   What is involved is a cyclic trial and error process.   The small refinement cycle in Figure 7 depicts how the expert with the help of the computer scientist generates tutorial examples so that incrementally the machine can display successively refined rules on the screen: the expert then has the freedom to say whether he likes the rules.   A vital criterion is, does he understand them? Do they make sense from his point of view? Secondly, can he mentally check them? If he can do both, he tends to be satisfied. If he is not satisfied, then he can use the rule-editor directly and edit the rules.   More often the domain specialist will go around the cycle and generate new examples in order to refine or correct by induction those parts of the rule-base that he does not like.   This design process is essentially iterative.   Finally the rule-base is perceived as good enough to install in the field.

Inevitably there is a second refinement cycle occasioned by run-time "bugs", not low-level bugs of the kind with which programmers are mostly familiar, but more conceptual bugs.   Customer complaints get reported back to the development laboratory.   In due course the knowledge engineer has to sit down with his own domain specialist, or borrow one from the customer, and get these bugs out.

All this depends on there being good, economically adequate induction algorithms.   There is quite a rich history of inductive inference work in artificial intelligence.   One of the most active centres has for a long time been Ryszard Michalski's group at the University of Illinois.   I shall not dwell on his work, interesting though it is.   Whether or not the Michalski algorithms, which are academically motivated, could be made into cost-effective software tools is an open question.   On the other hand, even earlier than Michalski's work, studies were reported in the 1960's which were overlooked by the artificial intelligence community and by the computer science community at large.   This was work by Earl Hunt, described in a book by Hunt, Marin and Stone called **Experiments in Induction**, published in 1966.   The algorithm is simple and was possibly neglected because Hunt is by profession a psychologist.   So the work was published in the wrong subculture.

ID3

Given: a collection of positive and negative <u>instances</u>, where each instance is the description of an object in terms of a fixed set of <u>attributes</u> or properties

Produces: a decision tree for differentiating positive and negative instances

<u>Figure 8.</u> The ID3 algorithm was conceived for operating on pre-existing collections of positive and negative instances of a concept.

A Q II in PLI 120K bytes of program space

SOY-BEAN DATA: 19 diseases

35 descriptors (domain sizes 2-7)

307 cases (descriptor sets with confirmed diagnoses)

Test set: 376 new cases

<u>machine</u> runs using rules of different origins

$\left\{\begin{array}{l}\end{array}\right.$

>99% accurate diagnosis with <u>machine</u> rules

83% accuracy with <u>Jacobsen's rules</u>

93% accuracy with interactively improved rule

<u>Figure 9.</u> Experiment by R. Chilansky, B. Jacobsen and R.S. Michalski.

In 1978 I was teaching a graduate course in artificial intelligence at Stanford University. A distinguished visiting professor, Ross Quinlan, from Sydney decided to try the programming exercise which I had given to the class. The task was to use an induction algorithm to solve a certificated hard problem which I had brought from Edinburgh. The problem was hard in the sense that as far as we could tell, it was too complex to be programmable by conventional means, and therefore needed something special. As a Ph.D. student in the 1960's in Sydney, Quinlan had assisted Hunt. At the end of term, he had a program running in Lisp which solved the hard problem. Back in Sydney he recoded it in Pascal and proceeded to do a sequence of extremely interesting experiments. Some of these are summarised in **Machine Learning: The Artificial Intelligence Approach** edited by Michalski, Carbonell and Mitchell, published by Tioga.

Quinlan's own considerable extension of Hunt's algorithm is called ID3 and is the basis of all commercially viable induction systems at the present time. It is given a training set of positive and negative instances, where each instance is represented as a fixed list of attributes or properties. Attributes can have either truth values or numerical values. It is required to produce a decision tree for differentiating positive and negative instances. Since a decision tree is logically equivalent to a conditional expression in a programming language, you can say that the output of the algorithm is a program. The synthesised expert program can then be run on new material, to test the level of skill induced by the particular examples used as the training set.

My Edinburgh laboratory subsequently developed an enhancement of ID3 to include the ability to handle numerical as well as logical attributes of the problem domain. A commercial version of this, Expert-Ease, is available on the IBM Personal Computer. Expert systems already developed with this approach include Dow Jones forecasting, error-message interpretation in UCSD Pascal, classification of lymphatic cancers, developing rules for high-school algebra and many others.

So far the source of the tutorial examples has been presented as being the human expert himself in interaction with the system, like a teacher with an apprentice. However, that was not the picture that Quinlan had in mind when he developed ID3. This point is brought out in Figure 8. To apply ID3 or any other algorithm which generates rules from examples, i.e. any algorithm for computer induction, a sufficient set of primitive attributes must have been identified. At present we do not know of any source other than the domain specialist himself that can say what primitives one ought to measure. However poorly developed the expert's powers of articulation of entire rules may be, he has no trouble in knowing what low-level measurements are relevant, although he commonly attributes relevance to additional measurements which may later be shown to be redundant.

This does not matter from the knowledge engineer's point of view. The induction algorithm simply leaves those attributes on one side and fails to incorporate them in the final rule. The expert may or may not then argue that it ought to have incorporated them. I am not implying that the dummy attributes are not performing some important task in the cognitive economy of the expert. I suspect that they may be, just as various superstitious beliefs play a useful role in many highly developed skills including even in athletics. But logically from the point of view of incorporation into the final rule-base, they appear to be redundant.

A further requirement is an oracle, a source of expert decisions for the system to work from. The oracle can be one of a number of things. It can be a human oracle, an expert. Or it can be a precomputed data-base. There is a well-known algorithm in two-person finite games with perfect

ID3 was designed to work with large numbers of instances. It starts by selecting a small subset of them (the working set) and at each cycle

1.   Forms a decision tree that is correct for the current working set

2.   Finds the exceptions to this decision tree among the other instances

3.   Constructs a new working set from the current window and the exceptions

<u>Figure 10.</u>   Iterative refinement by ID3 of a classification
                rule in the form of a decision tree.

information, which makes it possible to take some nontrivial endgame of only a few million legal positions in which chess masters flounder, and by exhaustive backwards computation develop a data-base, a lookup table, of positions paired with their game-theoretic values. By expending a great amount of computational labour, we end up with an oracle which is rather expensive to store. One application of computer induction is to take such giant lookup tables and squeeze them down into compact explanatory, descriptive and predictive rules.

Another kind of oracle may be the external world. I will give two examples. One is the task of predicting what the Dow-Jones Index is going to do in the next fourteen days. This was a student project at the University of Illinois and the student, Mr. Helmut Braun, selected it himself. He also located a professional group willing to act as certifiers of the quality of performance of the final system. In a graduate class we do not want expert systems which are only as good as human experts. That is for under-graduate students. In its run-time behaviour it is reasonable to demand of properly engineered knowledge bases that they do a little better. The only way to find out in a given case is by getting authentic experts to spend some of their time validating student exercises. Braun found a company in Indianapolis that make their money by publishing regular forecasts of the Dow-Jones Index. Their success is based on the expert skill of the founder of the company.

There were thus two possible oracles that the student could use. He could use the skilled forecaster himself, since he had available an archival file of the last few years of his expert decisions. Or he could take what would in general be expected to give a higher level of performance in the induced product, namely what actually happened, not what the expert predicted. Did the Index actually go up, or was it roughly stationary, or, did it go down? Mr. Braun did it both ways round and he got an "A" for that project. He also aroused interest in the Accountancy Department of the University, and the work is now being extended. My other example of taking events in the real world as an oracle, i.e. as a source of pre-classified instances, is from the realm of control. We tackled a task of this kind many years ago with extremely rudimentary induction methods compared with the present day. The task was that of balancing a pole on a motor-driven cart that goes back and forth on a track. It must not drop the pole, and it also must not run off either end of the track. It is not a trivial task. An even more complex task would be riding a bicycle. If one received a contract to develop a robot bicyclist, the first task, as always, would be to work out a good set of measurements to take and a frequency of sampling. The human is not able to sample more than perhaps ten times per second. But the important thing is that the only sample of expert decisions is that obtained by monitoring the real-time behaviour of a human bicyclist who is already able to perform this skill. This is what is meant by a real-world oracle.

Can an expert system be generated exclusively from examples? It has been done convincingly more than once, the first by Michalski in the middle 1970's in the case of diagnosing soybean diseases. This is a crop of considerable commercial interest to the state of Illinois. He chose nineteen common diseases suggested by plant pathologist colleagues. These formed the attributes, some yes-no, some with result sets containing as many as seven different values (Figure 9).
Michalski's training set comprised 307 cases, each presented as a list of 35 values paired with the name of the disease. He did the job both ways, i.e. using dialogue acquisition and using inductive acquisition. He worked with Dr. Barry Jacobsen, a plant pathologist who specialised in soybean diseases and who has already known for a taxonomy that he had developed himself. Between the two of them they got a rule-base by

dialogue acquisition which when tested on 376 new cases, gave 83% accuracy.
this would have been encouraging were it not for the fact that by merely
inducing rules from the data Michalski obtained a rule-base of more than
99% accuracy.   Only one plant out of the 376 was misclassified when the
rule was tested on new material.

When Jacobsen saw that, he worked hard in dialogue acquisition mode using
the computer facilities available, to see if he could improve his rules.
He got it finally to 93% accuracy.   He then decided to accept the
machine-generated rules in place of his own as reference material, and this
he uses to the present day.   It is a significant early event - an example
of a phenomenon that we will see more commonly.   The useful products to be
obtained from knowledge engineering have in the past been conceived
entirely in terms of the run-time behaviour of the program.   But if the
rule-base itself can be structured and constrained in such a way as to
remain intelligible and professionally useable by the experts then there is
a product of a different kind, namely new and improved codifications.
These have an independent value apart from whether they run on the machine.
Such codifications are positive contributions in themselves and are indeed
welcomed by the experts as new reference material.

Let us now consider Quinlan's induction system, ID3.   We start off with a
collection of instances which are already classified and then we proceed as
in Figure 10.   Details can be found in Quinlan's contribution to the work
on machine learning referenced earlier.

Having got a rule, the algorithm uses it to classify new material sampled
from the data-base.   Each example for which the rule gives the right
answer, the algorithm throws away.   But whenever it finds a refutation
example, it saves it, because that has "tutorial" value for creating a
better rule.   When the refutation file has grown to a preset limit then a
new file of exceptions is merged with the old working set to form a new
working set.   The entire rule is then thrown away, - rather shocking to
many people because we humans do not work that way.   We are conservative
about our theories and we try to hang on to them and patch them when we get
refutations.   But the economics of ID3 are such that it does better to
forget the old rule, work instead on the augmented example set, and induce
a new rule from scratch.   In a really hard case it may go round the
iteration loop 19 or 20 times in the style shown in Figure 10, until it has
tested the current version of the rule on a sufficiently large number of
new cases without finding a refutation - "sufficiently large" being a
user-defined parameter.   Then it terminates.   Unless the resulting rule
is tested on the entire universe of cases, there can be no guarantee that
the rule obtained will be 100% correct.   Quinlan's paper gives a technical
discussion of that point, with some rather surprising and encouraging
results concerning bounded error.   The main result seems
counter-intuitive: on the assumptions that Quinlan made in order to do the
theory, accuracy of the rule is only a function of the size of the training
set and is independent of the size of the universe.   Secondly, one finds
oneself also surprised at how accurate a rule can be obtained from how
small a number of examples.   Quinlan also reports systematic empirical
tests.   All of the results fall well within the bounds predicted by his
theory.

Two or three years ago Quinlan tackled an extension of the original problem
that I gave to the Stanford class.   The original problem was from the
chess endgame king-and-rook against king-and-knight.   Is the knight side
lost in two ply?   In other words, is the position such that whatever the
knight does, the rook side can either capture the knight or checkmate on
the next move.   This can be recognised more or less at a glance, certainly
in a few seconds by a master.   But if the object is to write a

pattern-based program which can do fast "at-a-glance" recognition it is an adverse programming problem. Quinlan then tackled the next level of complexity, knight lost in three ply. The rook side must spot whether there exists a move such that whatever the knight does, then the rook side kills him on the next move, either by capture or by checkmate. In terms of cognitive complexity, it is a substantial jump. Chess masters can take up to half a minute or so to classify such a position and in our experience just occasionally get it wrong. It is totally out of the question to build an expert system for this task in conventional style other than by reckless use of skilled manpower. Having elaborated a set of 49 primitive attributes, Quinlan generated a decision tree inductively using a training set of 715 instances. The decision tree had 177 nodes, that is 84 tests in the corresponding conditional expression. It was fairly cheap to manufacture, requiring only 34 seconds on the Cyber 172 computer. By contrast, the best expert system of the pattern-driven, production-rule that Quinlan could develop, using himself as both expert and knowledge engineer in internal dialogue, took him the best part of a year. That is not a reasonable use of human resources to manufacture a program, when an equally accurate program can be manufactured in 34 seconds on a Cyber 175. But the denouement was even more striking. The run-time performance of the machine-made decision tree was five times faster than the best specialised-search program that Quinlan could code.

On the face of it, that looks like a very useful breakthrough for the software technology industry. A semi-automatic process can apparently generate difficult programs which are actually five times more efficient than the best that programmers can code. There is no question that such programs and such ways of making programs will filter into software practice as soon as the industry becomes aware that these straightforward but powerful tools exist. However, there are grounds for unease. Quinlan's decision-tree program, although it ran fast and accurately on the machine, when shown to the chess master was completely opaque. It was not a question of a few glimmers of sense here and there scattered through a large obscure structure, but just a total black-out. We have repeatedly confirmed the phenomenon with other material in Edinburgh. If this method of manufacturing useful bits of software has a very attractive feature, commercially attractive, does it matter if such artificially generated materials are opaque? In some applications it does not matter and a black box can be tolerated. But in the very complex decision-making areas where there is the greatest market pull, problems like control software for nuclear power stations, or, shall we say, the U.S. NORAD nuclear warning system, matters stand differently. There are numerous areas where control software is already more opaque than is safe. We recently did a two-year study for the European Economic Commission. What we found concerning opacity in hand-programmed systems was worrying enough. But a source of rather cheap automatically generated code which is intrinsically doomed to add to that opacity, must be regarded as even more worrying.

For the user who needs transparency in the generated code, over very large and complex domains, a facility must be incorporated in the induction package for the well known strategy of "divide and conquer" common both to AI and to the structured programming school. I am referring to the decomposition of a large problem into sub-problems, sub-sub-problems etc., thus forming a procedural hierarchy. This facility is not explicitly provided in Quinlan's algorithm. It is however planned as a central feature of an inductively oriented expert systems language designed by Mr. Stephen Muggleton in Edinburgh. Version 1 is available under the commercial name RuleMaster (Intelligent Terminals Ltd. of Scotland and Radian Corporation of Austin, Texas). Preliminary results of its application to meteorological forecasting and to other problems are summarised below.

(1) WILLARD is an expert system which forecasts the likelihood of severe
thunderstorms occurring in the central United States. Examination and
interpretation of critical meteorological parameters (such as: temperature,
moisture, winds and pressure) by an experienced severe thunderstorm
forecaster yields clues on the temporal and spatial domain of severe
thunderstorms.   The WILLARD expert system consists of a hierarchy of
thirty modules, each of which contains a single decision rule.   This
hierarchy is on average four levels deep.   All modules' rules were
developed using inductive generalisation (although RuleMaster allows expert
authored rules).   About 140 examples out of a possible nine million
situations were used in building WILLARD.   WILLARD can operate in
interactive or batch forecast mode and gives a full explanation of
reasoning on demand.   WILLARD has been found to compare favourably with
the US National Severe Storm Forecast Centre over a number of test cases.

(2) EARL is an expert system for diagnosing faults in large distribution
transformers.   The repair or replacement costs of these large transformers
(> 10000 kva) range from \$150,000 to \$1,500,000.   A human expert has in
the past been employed in interpreting measurements of the amounts of
different gases dissolved in the cooling fluid of these transformers.   The
relative quantities of these gases gives strong indications of possible
problems in the transformer.   This expert system has been installed and is
being used by the Hartford Steam Boiler Insurance company.   A recent
comparison showed that the expert system made the same diagnosis as the
expert it was based on in all 30 different test cases.

(3) ARCH is a procedural expert system, built inductively, to carry out
robot plans in a blocks world.   The problem involved many of the facets of
procedural expert systems, such as design and scheduling.   ARCH, like the
more diagnostic expert systems (WILLARD and EARL), gives, on demand, a full
explanation of all decisions and actions made.

An account of the design features of RuleMaster, including back-chaining
and forward chaining and a 'finite state' formalism conducive to control
applications, is to appear in the Proceedings of the December 1984 joint
conference of IEEE and AAAI.

In conclusion, there is no compulsion on an information technololgist to
interest himself in this new field.   But when other methods fail he may
find something here to his advantage.

Relevant reading

Michalski, R.S. and Chilausky, R.L. (1980) Knowledge acquisition by
encoding expert rules versus computer induction from examples: a case study
involving soybean pathology.   Int. J. for Man-Machine Studies, 12, 63-87.

Michalski, R.S. and Chilausky, R.L. (1980) Learning by being told and
learning from examples: an experimental comparison of the two methods of
knowledge acquisition in the context of developing an expert system for
soybean disease diagnosis.   Policy Analysis and Information Systems, 4,
125-160.

Michie, D., Muggleton, S., Riese, C. and Zubrick, S. (1984)   RuleMaster:
a second generation knowledge-engineering facility.   Radian Technical
Report MI-R-623.   Austin, Texas: Radian Corp. (Proc. 1st Conf. on Art.
Int. Applns. sponsored by IEEE and AAAI).

Mozetic, I., Bratko, I. and Lavrac, N. The Derivation of Medical Knowledge
from a Qualitative Model of the Heart.   Monograph submitted to the Board
of the International School for the Synthesis of Expert Knowledge, Bled,
August 1984.

Shapiro, A. and Michie, D. (in press) A self-commenting facility for inductively synthesised endgame expertise.   **Advances in Computer Chess 4** (ed. D. Beal), Oxford: Pergamon.

Shapiro, A. and Niblett, T. (1982) Automatic induction of classification rules for a chess endgame.   **Advances in Computer Chess 3** (ed. M.R.B. Clarke), Oxford: Pergamon.

CHAPTER 43

ADVANCED INFORMATION SYSTEM STRUCTURES

Edwin J. Smura
The Xerox Corporation, El Segundo, USA

Technology is available that, incorporated into a single information system, enables voice, graphic, and textual data to be delivered to distant places in a single package. Factors which inhibit the development of these integrated information systems include cost and problems as operability, heterogeneous interfaces, and reliable delivery of information in a noisy environment. Most critical is the slow development of structures within which diverse forms of intellectual information--voice, graphics, and text--can be stored and communicated.

The first problem is the capture of information without loss of quality. As we use the term, *quality* means the accurate acquisition of character symbols and all of the sender's means of showing emphasis, e.g., underlining, annotation in a margin, signature, tone of voice, etc. The input device should be able to accomodate the full dynamic range of sounds for voice input and should have the resolution and color capabilities comensurate with the class of images to be processed. In addition, the system record structure should be able to indicate whether information missing in a transmission--such as pictures, verbal clarification, or signature--is or is not available. At present the physical and logical record structures of information do not exist that would permit this problem to be solved.

The second problem is the sheer number of hardware interfaces, software translations, and communications protocols found in the range of communication devices available today. For example, consider the television screens with Touchtone keyboards accessed via Viewdata facilities; home computers connected to the television set or via a modem to a network; personal computers connected to a company network; office equipment--teletypewriter, typewriter, word processor-- connected to a local network and mainframe computers with access to public and commercial networks. The connections differ because many of these technologies have arisen in different technology settlements. Overcoming these differences requires the intercession of the human element, and this element requires training. The result is that it takes time to communicate even very low quality "intellectual information" once it has been captured in a storage device.

The third problem is that existing storage systems have not incarnated the *time spirit of man*. Instead, we have libraries of information that lack a time tested system of reference numbers. We have gatherings of information in our storage systems, but we fail to satisfy the more subtle needs of users.

The human race struggled over thousands of years to create spoken language. The natural languages that survive today meet the needs of mankind: they are an incarnation of the *spirit of man over a long time*. Similarly, the development of paper-like materials--and eventually paper, pens, pencils, printing, and the reference library--took place over time. All were gradually shaped to meet the needs of the users. For example, the signature as the mark of identity, as a carrier of authority, and as a tool of verification was not a single creation: it is part of a system that meets many needs.

We need means for management to exercise control over information in storage. We need ways of making priority assignments. We need tools for the graceful transfer of data from working files to a library and then to archival storage. When users are a part of the design process to meet these needs and the system grows with them the outcome must eventually be a *living system*. When a system lives through its users, when it makes sense to them, only then may we say that it possesses architecture. In this view, not all gatherings of elements have architecture.

Our objective is not to define an architecture but to furthur consider the problems that have to be solved in attaining an eventual structure. While designed arrangements may be said to have *structure*, only the ones that have weathered the tests of the marketplace gain the status of *architecture*. Our objective is the satisfaction of user needs – a structure for processing and communicating all kinds of information. The ideas resulting from this study--for instance, a method for measuring the quality of information--may guide the design of overdue new systems and provide methods for evaluating alternative approaches.

Creating information systems

An information system may be defined as an input/output structure which acquires, stores, communicates, processes, rearranges, and/or distributes intellectual information in an organized manner. To achieve the status of architecture, it must serve objectives needed by mankind; it must over time settle into a stable pattern; and it must please its users.

Intellectual information. Intellectual information may be regarded as the external manifestation of knowledge resident in man. This knowledge evolves through successive generations and is characterized by historical styles. These styles also incarnate the time spirit of man.

To create new knowledge, man is dependent on information that is current, correct, and controlled.[1] To establish beliefs in common throughout large groups requires that knowledge be widely communicated. Thus, as men direct their energies to increasing knowledge, information systems evolve and achieve architectural status.

Structure scale. Information systems may be studied in relation to the characteristics of the social environment in which they are used. For our purpose, the way in which man relates to information systems ranges from unstructured at one end of the environment scale to structured at the other end, as shown in Figure 1. Information-communication and information-processing systems are at the opposite ends of this scale.

At the unstructured end, new knowledge is created and communicated among men. Since this process is not deterministic, progress in the creation of knowledge cannot be scheduled. With newly discovered knowledge it needs to be communicated, it is necessary to have preparation and distribution facilities which are convenient. Moreover, the indeterminate nature of the work surrounding the creation of new information requires an unstructured environment--perhaps we may term it *humanistic*.

At the structured environment end of the scale, the information or data processing environment is more impersonal. It is often repetitive. To maintain efficient production, a high degree of structure is necessary. In contrast to the "humanistic" unstructured environment, the structured environment is "mechanistic".

Advances in technology have led both to increased efficiency in the information-processing environment and to greater convenience in the communications environment. Improved methods and procedures within data processing centers, for example, assure data-base integrity. This increased structure increases system efficiency. In the generation of software for these systems, increased convenience brought on by technological advances has resulted in a growing cottage industry in the generation of new software. This increased convenience provides a natural setting for new knowledge development in the software area and illustrates the result of technology induced trends.

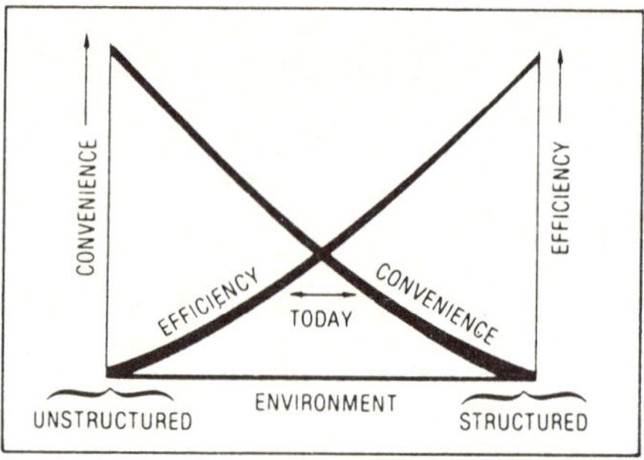

Figure 1. Information systems may be ranged on an environmental scale from unstructured to structured. For effective human communications a less structured environment appears to be convenient. A structured environment is necessary for machines to communicate with humans more efficiently.

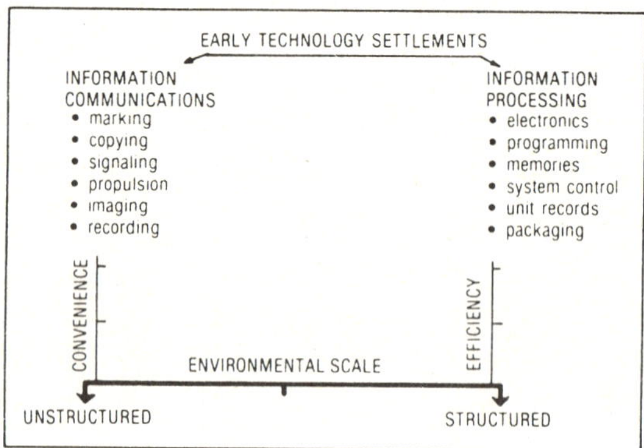

Figure 2. Historically, information-communication and information-processing systems have evolved on the basis of technologies more or less isolated in different settlements. Recently, system developers have been drawing on technology as required from the various settlements. A common technology base for information systems is developing.

System stability threatened. Since computers are compiling more data. networks are delivering more information. and copiers are producing more copies. the methods for distributing hard copies are becoming overburdened. Tremendous volumes of hard copies become less useful to their potential users. The inundation in papers is an example of a system that is becoming. in human terms. unstable. This instability is affecting transaction-based enterprises such as banking, credit. and transportation. It is also affecting knowledge-sharing systems in the technical and management communities. Here. the problem is that access to the vast amounts of existing information is not fast enough.

To solve problems as these. the knowledge resident in one technology settlement is being used to create systems which overlap the other technology settlements. as listed in Figure 2. For example. copier technology is being used to improve the output capability of information-processing systems by translating data into non-impact printed output. Telephone networks are providing host to host connections between information-processing systems. Digital electronics and storage technologies are automating functions involved in communications.

The mixing of technologies is leading to a pool of techniques that is being applied to both information-communications and information-processing tasks. As information systems spread widely. their existence tends to worsen an old problem. the interface between man and machine. This problem exists in the office. development laboratory. and elsewhere. The underlying problem is that basic communications capability of men--in the sense of knowledge--far exceeds that of current machines.

Consequently. in communicating from man to machine. information is lost. One example occurs in the world of transaction data processing. Each human being can impress his unique personal identity upon a check or credit card transaction with his signature. his way of writing numbers, etc. However. this special information is lost in the return statement from the computer system. The system can only process standard numerals and letters. Who has not been frustrated by having certain transactions turn sour that can be reconstructed only with the greatest effort from the meager information provided by the system.

A second example is taken from the increasingly systemetized world of business communications. As digital technology is incorporated into word processing equipment. office communications also become limited to a narrow range of characters. Lost are personal marks such as signatures. the ability to modify the format. or a choice of fonts. Each communicant is restricted by the options his particular equipment provides. If his addressee's equipment is different, the capabilities that overlap may be narrow indeed.

A third example refers to the often considerable specialized knowledge needed to operate a particular system. The user's ability to concentrate on content is diluted by the necessity to also pay attention to embedded commands, system responses, and even the level of electrical signals. When content matters are separated from matters of systems operation, the result is a new class of worker which we term "white-collar blue". Such people work in offices, but perform tasks of machine attendants.

Combining text and graphics

The nature of the solution to these problems is clear. To the abilities of data processing must be added those of graphic processing[2] and, in time, other forms of information, such as voice. Many systems today capture only data, usually through keyboard input or the equivalent. The gasoline credit card form, for example, represents an attempt to communicate different kinds of information for different reasons. In the data-processing community only numerals can be acquired at present. Unfortunately, for various other purposes, the signature of the customer is important. The script marks made by the station attendant may also be important. Without this kind of information, the customer, the merchant, and even the oil company are handicapped if independent validation of the transaction later becomes necessary.

Technology is available--at added cost--to extend this transactions-processing system. Now, hand marks and signature can be acquired by image capture techniques. The unstructured information is scanned, digitized, and stored as a bit map.

Programmable windows. To minimize the added cost, it is desirable to partition text from images. Thus, text can be acquired as characters and stored and processed in byte codes. Dealing with a character code in code form takes far less storage and communicating bandwidth than dealing with it as an image. Signatures, handwriting, diagrams, or photographs necessarily have to be acquired and processed as images, but cost can be somewhat reduced by adjusting the pixel density to the nature of the image. For this reason, we need a separate window for each type of material. The information system and its software have to be able to establish windows, keep track of their position, and define the quality of the image in each window.

The size, position and quality of each window is derived from each input form. This information is stored in the system where it may be accessed by window control software. Each input format requires a set of window characteristics to be placed in storage. By implementing this function in software. the system can adapt to variable input forms. The system user defines the characteristics for each new format he devises.

The operations required to make windows into storage are analogous to those performed on hard copy with a knife and straight edge--cut and paste. The windows are of many varieties, as shown in Figure 3. Perhaps the simplest category is white space--nothing need be stored but its position. The first category of windows shown in the figure contains marks on paper or a display screen that were created at the word processor. In this case. the byte code contains no redundant information. The second category of window holds marks that were preprinted on the form or prestored in the word processor. Characteristic of these marks are the different sizes and styles of type and the logos and the possible use of color. The third group contains line graphics--boxes. arrows. diagrams. and line art. These windows. like others, can contain a mixture of lines and text strings. The authenticating signature image is the last category on the typical business communication.

The graphics information beyond plain text makes communications more effective. It comes closer to communicating the full range of which man is capable.

In many business communications, photographs are not employed. From an information-systems standpoint, however, a category of window for this purpose is technically feasible. The equipment would have to have the capability to scan and store pixels at a density great enough to permit the photograph to be reproduced. Similarly, color is simply a matter of storing additional bits to encode the color of each pixel. Of course. the addition of photographic and color capability takes additional specialized equipment at added cost.

With this equipment, the sender can organize his communication to gain the attention by electronically cutting and pasting the different windows. A pointing device permits the user to arrange and rearrange the window contents until he is satisfied that his communication will be effective.

Forms distance. An information system must be capable of allocating space on all types of equipment to which it may be connected. These devices include typewriters, impact and non-impact printers, and display screens. Because each of these devices came out of a different technology

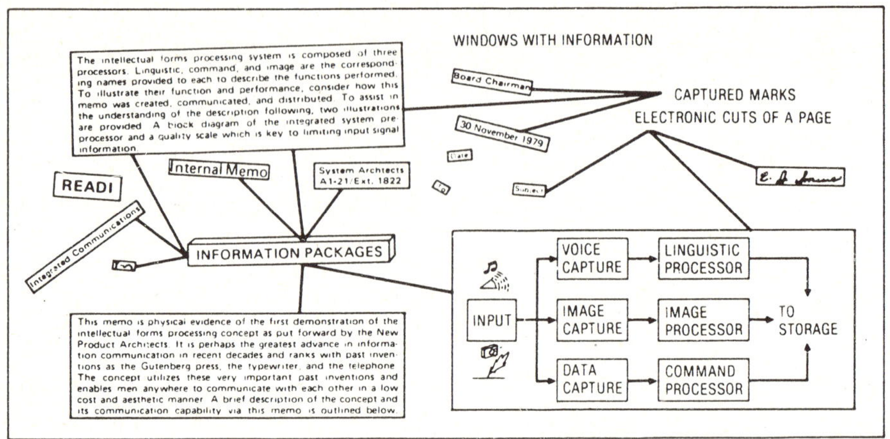

Figure 3. The text and graphics information system operates through the concept of windows. A display screen is divided into sections which, under software control, handle different text fonts, diagrams, or signatures.

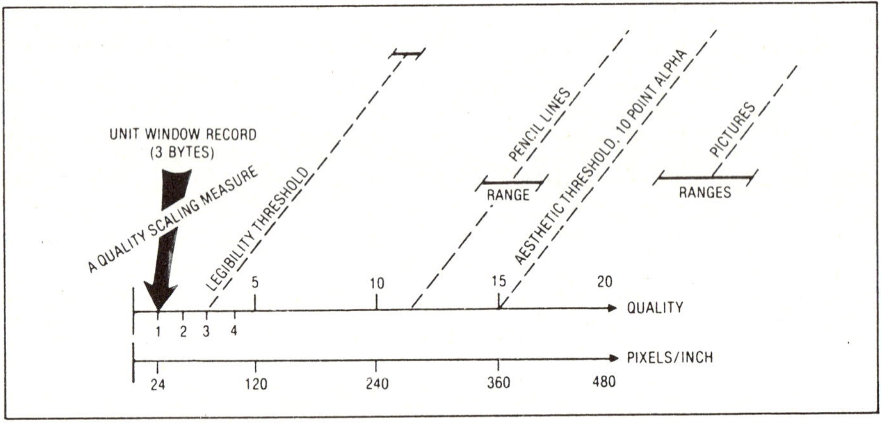

Figure 4. The quality scale provides a means to measure the quality of black and white images. Quality units (top) and pixels per inch (bottom) illustrate the different quality thresholds for the various types of images.

settlement at different points in historical time, they use different methods of measuring distance on a form or page.

Historically first, printing measures distance in points. A point is approximately 1/72-inch; 72 is a remarkable number, being divisible by 2, 3, 4, 6, 8, 9, and 12. Thus, type size can be expanded or reduced in a number of convenient integral multiples.

On the typewriter, space is measured horizontally in characters and vertically in lines--so many characters or lines per inch.

In the most recent technologies, display screens and non-impact printers, the devices produce information a picture element at a time. Distance is meassured in pixels per linear unit.

On a black and white display, a pixel is represented by a single bit in the bit map in storage. Storage is usually processed within the machine eight bits or a byte, at a time. Therefore, it is desirable that the pixels per unit of linear measure should be in integral numbers of bytes per linear unit.

The two principal units of linear measure at this scale level are the centimeter and the inch, related by the multiplier 2.54. If we take 24 bits, or three bytes, as our unit of distance, we get a display resolution of 24 pixels per inch or approvimately 10 pixels per centimeter. Multiples of 24 bits provide a number of distance relationships which are related by simple multiples, as shown for a range of values in Table 1. Thus, up-scaling or down-scaling the pixels per unit distance to accomodate a particular equipment or purpose becomes simpler.

Quality. Pixels per unit distance is not only a measure of distance on a display or a non-impact printer, it is also a measure of the device resolution. Moreover, resolution is, in general, directly proportional to the apparent quality of the output as perceived by the human eye. Consequently, this measure of distance may also be used to represent quality. We will take unit quality as 24 bits or three bytes of storage, equivalent to 24 pixels per inch or 10 pixels per centimeter. Table 1, therefore, is also a means of assessing the quality of a display. Figure 4 shows the quality unit laid out as a scale[3] in relation to several types of black and white images.

Shown on the scale is the approximate positions of the thresholds for several kinds of material. As the pixel density is reduced below the aesthetic level the legibility threshold is reached. At fewer pixels per inch, the storage requirement also falls. At quality levels below those legible to humans,

Table 1

In a digital environment, distance may be measured in pixels. Pixels may be considered equivalent to the bits that represent them in storage. Because most digital machines process information in units of one or more bytes, it is convenient to represent pixel values in multiples of three bytes.

MULTIPLE (Quality)	BITS	BYTES	PIXELS/INCH	PIXELS/CM (Approx.)
1	24	3	24	10
2	48	6	48	20
3	72	9	72	30
4	96	12	96	40
5	120	15	120	50
6	144	18	144	60
7	168	21	168	70
8	192	24	192	80
9	216	27	216	90
10	240	30	240	100

some special means would be required to comprehend the meaning of the image. When men agree upon a code, only a few bits are required to transmit the agreed upon image. In the ISO 646 seven bit code, for example, the entire alphabet of the English language may be transmitted.

While quality is related to resolution, the two concepts are not the same. If a system acquires an image at 300 pixels per inch and prints it at the same value, resolution and quality of the particular image are the same. However, if the acqusition is at 100 pixels per inch and the reproduction device operates at 300 pixels per inch, the quality is unchanged but the resolution has been tripled. The level of quality at which the various elements of a system can operate is limited by the resolution of the image capture equipment. Output devices with fewer pixels per inch than the capture device may reduce the quality, but the higher resolution output device cannot increase it.

In general, resolution and its related vartiable, quality, are inherently proportional to cost. The reason is that resolution is directly proportional to the number of bytes stored and processed. Hence, it is economic to limit the quality to the capability of the human eye. Smaller pixel areas than the eye can resolve have no value.

Moreover, quality is related to image type and usage. In text, a sans serif font requires less resolution to provide aesthetically pleasing print than a fine serif typeface such as Bodoni, which is used in books.

Certain types of images reproduce satisfactorily at lower resolution than other types. A block diagram, composed solely of horizontal and vertical lines, reproduces nicely on a scanning device at relatively low resolution, because scanning devices make good horizontal and vertical lines. At the same resolution a diagonal or curved line will exhibit a stairstep effect. The vernier acuity of the eye makes these small ragged edges very objectionable.

Image scaling. Since quality level needed varies, the design requirements of a single form can be satisfied by permitting the quality levels of the windows to vary. It is convenient to let them vary in multiples of the unit quality level. A unit graphic image area may be defined at any desired quality level.

A one inch square image area of 24 by 24 pixels per side represents a quality level of one, when the area is upscaled by multiplying the original bits by an integer (x), the quality remains the same.

An image may also be downscaled to a lower quality level. To display a picture for cropping, merging, or other picture composition function, it is   necessary to scale an image to the level at which current display technology operates. For a workstation display the resolution at the screen is about 96 pixels per inch (Q=4). the near minimum value for a user positioned close to the screen.

At a quality level of four. several times that of commercial TV. the system response time may be intolerable for a user. It may be desirable to first reblock to a quality level of one. thus improving the response time. For some purposes. such as locating the window oulines and initial image cropping. the process speed and operational efficiency improves.

At a quality level of one several advantages result: process speed increases by sixteen. the square of the quality ratios. and typewriter text is blurred to the point that text lines are forced solid black. Figure 5 illustrates this condition. A solid black image is quickly oulined by contouring software which determines window position and boundaries.

User interface. Information-communications systems consisted initially of the hardware that transmitted messages. With the addition of processing capability. these systems gained intelligence. This addition called for another subsystem--software. Since the entire system exists to serve users. we may conceptualize another subsystem, *liveware.*

Liveware consists of those elements of the system that serve the user directly, including the keyboard, pointing device, display, command language, procedures, and standard symbols. They enable the user to view and manipulate information in storage. If the hardware and software tools that serve the user are well organized. they make the user interface simple, pleasant, and friendly. The Xerox Star workstation is an example of a good *liveware* design.

Page addressing. Specifying locations on the form or page is an important issue to two classes of information system designers. The first class includes designers who are interested in quality and, consequently, in the resolution to achieve it. The second class includes the computer specialist and forms designer who must deal with issues of addressability. It is desirable that the scale used in storage be related to the scale used in in creating forms.

A problem that arises with high quality images is the large number of bytes required to specify distances. The solution is to make format instructions independent of the resolution of the image inside the window. In other words. the window can be located or addressed on a coarser scale, compared to the image within it.

At a quality level of one, an 81/2 inch by 11 inch sheet of paper can be addressed by 204 locations in the short direction and 264 locations in the long direction. These numbers can essentially be contained within one byte (256). A negligible margin at the top and/or bottom is unaddressable. Thus, the window itself can be located and sized by one-byte addresses, while the content of the window may be an image of as high a quality as desired.

Information communications

The societal goal of information-communications is to share information widely. The efficiency and productivity of modern society would be greatly diminished if the approach taken to the design and implementation of these systems were self-centered. Life would become ingrown, we would all have less information at out disposal, and dissatisfaction would mount.

To communicate widely, the most important requirement is to be able to share information between heterogeneous systems. A second, less widely recognized requirement is the need of users for information presentations that have *dignity*. Dignity means that the appropriate information--data, hand marks, signature, etc.--is present to convey the whole of the communicator's meaning. When dignity is present, the total transaction can be executed and verified without the irritating frustration that many of today's incomplete systems impose upon their "victims."

Fascimile. This method of communication is an example of a widely available system that transmits a complete record with dignity. Virtually everything that is on the paper at the sending terminal reaches the receiving unit. Unfortunately, facsimile has disdvantages. The chief one is cost, largely resulting from the fact that it transmits text by image-scanning techniques rather than by the more economic character code. Consequently, to hold down cost, the quality of the transmission is sometimes sacrificed. Other drawbacks are a significant amount of time and manual operation.

Non-pictorial text and graphics. Computer programs can also be used to generate representations of documents that are sent to printers, where the representation is processed to produce printed output. They can be used to represent program listings, tabular output, and other data traditionally printed on a printer. They can also be used to represent the hardcopy output from word processing equipment in the form of letters, reports, and modest sized documents. Graphical images normally printed on plotters, such as the output from computer-aided design programs, can also be represented for transmittal to a printer. Finally, computer programs can be used as the means of assembling together all of the text and graphics needed for printing of a book.

The advantage to not mimicking the interface to a printing press by presenting the printer with a fascimile picture is the enormous savings in storage space and communications cost--cost being

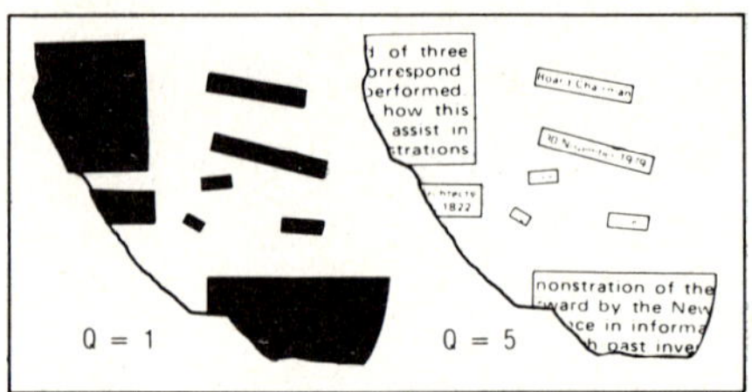

Figure 5. Typed material turns black at a quality level Q=1 under the condition of:
logic 0 - n X n matrix cell empty
logic 1 - n X n   matrix cell not empty.
Space between typed blocks stays white. If reading is required text must be displayed
at a higher level, 5 in the example.

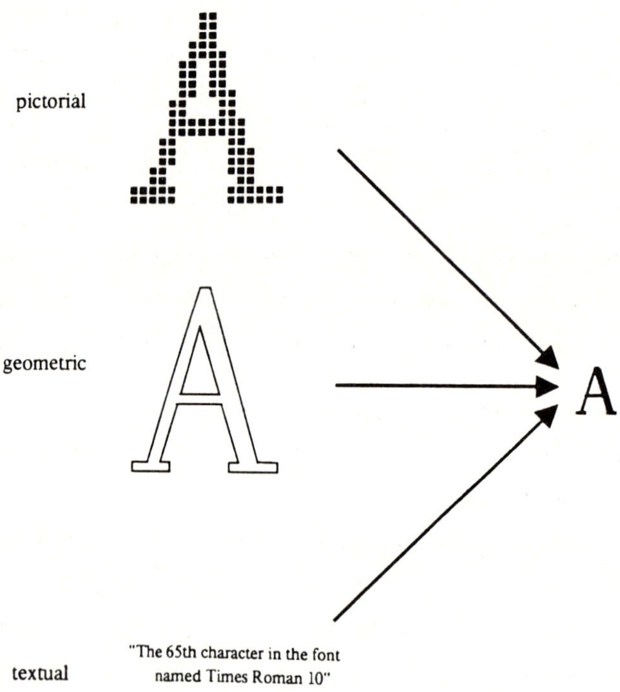

Figure 6 There are three ways to print a character on a page. 1500 bits are required to print the
"A" via a fascimile process. but only 500 bits to store vector oulines. The instruction method only
requires 16 bits to represent the character "A".

directly related to the number of bits in storage and which must be transmitted. To compare approaches. Figure 6 illustrates the several ways that a print representation could produce the same pattern on a page. The first row depicts a typical fascimile representation. which takes about 1500 bits to store at typical raster printer resolution. The second row shows a geometric representation. which takes about 500 bits to store the vectors in the outline. The third row shows a textual representation that instructs the printer to extract a character from a particular font: this method requires 16 bits to represent a character. The third approach is obviously preferred.

What is required to exchange information between a wide variety of computers and printers is a standard format. a standard interface between the creator of a document and the printer of a document. Standardization avoids a proliferation of special-purpose software. In the absence of an interchange standard. every workstation would be required to contain software for driving a wide range of printers--any printer that a customer wishes to attach to the workstation. either directly or indirectly through a communications network.

By standardizing the representation of documents each work station need only have a single interface. The documents generated by the workstation can be printed on a variety of printers. but each printer is responsible for interpreting the single interchange standard. The Xerox Interpress[TM] Electronic Printing Standard[4] is an interchange standard for connecting raster printers to digital computers.

The representation of a document in the Interpress standard is called a master, a term chosen by analogy with conventional printing reproduction techniques. Any computer program that generates an Interpress master is called a creator: any program that interprets a master to make an image is called a printer.

The master is actually a program coded in the Interpress language and represented digitally as a sequence of bytes. The procedural nature is entirely invisible to someone who is using an application program that generates Interpress output--a user is free to think of an Interpress master as a data file that. when sent to an Interpress printer. will produce printed output. To introduce files as scanned "picture data" into a master, the printing instruction *sequenceInsertFile* is used to insert names of "picture" files into a master.

Interpress permits documents to be represented in a way that is independent of any particular printing device. The representation of a document does not depend on the details of the printer. Whether the printer is color or black or white. high or low resolution. continuous tone or black-only. an attempt to print an Interpress document on that printer should yield a usable result. The goal of device independence is responsible for the complexity of the Interpress standard.

Information-sharing. If we are to share information beyond a small circle of compatible equipment. if we are to reach a nationwide or worldwide audience. we must make it possible for herterogeneous units to work off   a common digital store. Consider. first, the input at a user interface. After processing, the command input may cause an output to a transmission machine and an acknowledgement to the user.

An input from the transmission machine to the mark processing system is another example. A sending system might request a description of the resident facilities at the receiving location. This kind of information is not presently communicated. To process the various kinds of information that a window system may possess. the sending equipment would need to obtain facilities information from the remote site on distribution facilities. types of printers. graphic forms printing capability. quality printing resources. as well as audit and security provisions.

Protocol. The information needed may be defined within a protocol machine. Protocol is a set of agreements that permits communication between parties. This model is a problem requiring immediate attention if heterogeneous facilities are to be operated in an integrated manner in the near future. Formal techniques exist for specifying and verifying protocols. but little work has been accomplished on the service they provide[5]. Past activity has focused on the protocol itself.

The service requirements of the user are the basis for all protocol developments. A statement of the information requirements of the user interface is a necessity to resolving the protocol issues that affect the integration of networks. We may identify four aspects of this requirement.

Under the window concept. we may have a variety of marks--characters. handwriting. signatures. pictures. diagrams. and eventually voice--in digital storage. A means is needed to associate the bits stored for each window with the identity or attributes of the text or images of that window. Second is the need for a measurement standard with which to communicate information about the quality level at which the bits for each window are stored.

Third is the need for a means of communicating a set of instructions which will specify the way in which output printing is to be executed.

Fourth is the need for verification. We need to establish that the various windows have been routed to the receiver and that they are legible. A confirmation is also needed that the delivery has not been marred by noise.

The user service requirements coupled with the transmission machine requirements form the total input service requirement for integrated communications. The objective is to meet the graphic needs of the user.

Verification. In Figure 7 are shown all of the system elements involved in processing intellectual information. Voice capture, together with text and image capture, comprises the input capture system. The voice signal is processed into digital form suitable for digital storage and transmission. Also, a block has been added for down-scaling image information and is immediately followed by a data compressor function since image data is redundant.

The presence of noise during communication, the existence of flaws on the recording surface of rotating storage, and data compressor/decompressor problems are influences that can corrupt graphic information packages. If such factors interfere, the output image may not be readable. In addition, the user does not know where the problem lies: at home, at the receiver sites, or in the transport system. With highly compressed image data, one noise burst may destroy the ability to reconstitute the image. In any event, means of verification are necessary.

One method with which a user can verify that a highly compressed image has been delivered correctly is stitching. As shown in Figure 8, the sender cuts an image apart, stitches a line between the two parts, and requests its return. At the receiving end, the stitch may be erased by manual cut and paste (electronically) or by means of a preprogrammed electronic scissors, assumimg the location of the line is agreed upon in advance. In this connection, a standard means of measuring distance on various equipment would be an asset in reducing any ambiguity in the position of the stitched line.

Communications format. As a means of illustrating the variety of subjects we have considered, Figure 9 indicates the type of format required for integrated communications. In addition to the existing header required by the transmission protocol, the illustration contains additional header information related to this type of communication. This information is needed to assemble   and later use the package of bits and bytes which follows. The header contains the distribution information needed to sort mail in the internal communication network prior to hard-copy printing. Printing by mail stop or address is assumed.

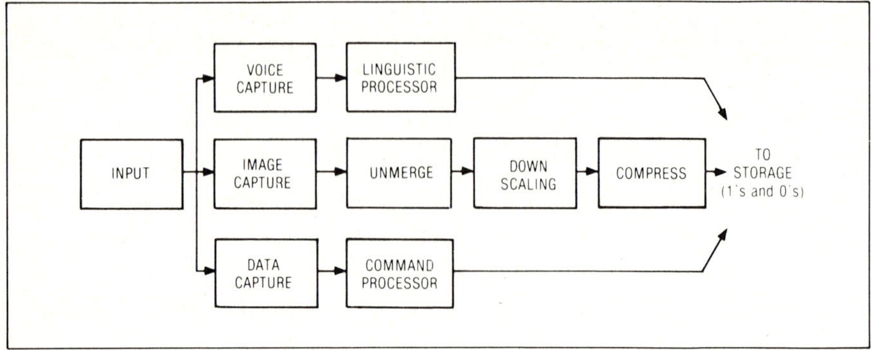

Figure 7. Voice has been added to the text and image capture mechanisms discussed. The captured voice signal has been converted to digital form so that it can be stored and treated in the same way as other information.

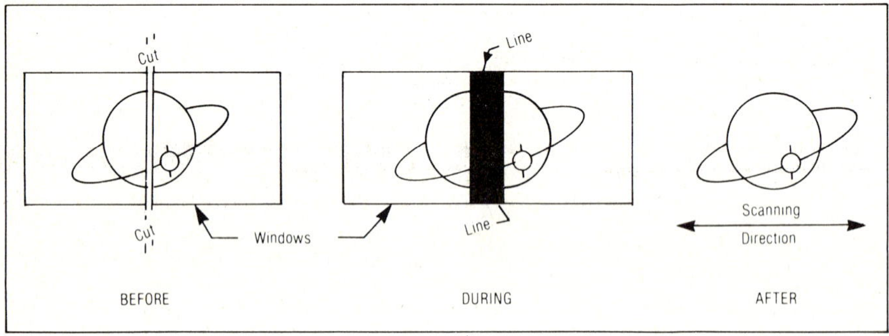

Figure 8. The correct transmission of a window may be verified by stitching a line into a picture and requesting its return.

Verification techniques may be buried in the graphic material. Trailing the graphic message are the standard byte check features such as cyclic checking. Also included in the trailing section may be a bit-map transmission check.

Planning the information system

In planning an information system. a first requirement is the service needs of all members of the organization and the service priorities that management assigns. This step permits a strategy to be developed for allocating resources and scheduling user access. The aim is to relate system utilization to the objectives of the organization's members. as controlled by management's actions.

A second requirement is a facilities statement listing the information-capturing services. transport services. and output capabilities at the sender location. This data. together with that gathered to meet the first requirement. makes it possible for intelligent machines to communicate to users the special tools and services at their disposal.

A final requirement is a statement of facilities and user access privileges at the receiving site. The ability of a sender to communicate information is limited not only by the quality and capability of the services at his site. but also by the capability of the equipment at the network terminations. However. this basic information is only part of what should be communicated.

Service objectives. We assume that the principal goals of an information system are to encourage progress. assure the continuity of business operations. and sustain the viability of established socioeconomic systems. In the light of these goals. a set of service objectives can be postulated.

The first objective is to accelerate the creation of new knowledge. The system's contribution to this purpose is accomplished by achieving friendly. convenient. and barrier-less communication. The creation of new knowledge leads to continuing progress in satisfying increasing needs.

A second objective is to facilitate the transfer of funds. and in this way to increase the productivity of capital.

A third objective is to provide the means of feeding information back to consumers. This task can be accomplished by providing consumers with a gateway to information services of interest to them. Teletext-like services are a harbinger of what is to come in this area. A satisfied customer. one whose information needs have been met. establishes the trust necessary to assure economic stability.

These objectives identify the second information package that is transmitted in a network

TRANMISSION MACHINE PROTOCOL	
DISTRIBUTION DATA (Name. address. mail stop. route)	
ECHO (ask. answer. forward)	BYTES
MATRIX TAGS (Quality. identity. priority. etc.)	
DOCUMENT NAME (File reference number)	
DOCUMENT FORMAT (Size. duplex. finishing. etc.)	
ALPHANUMERIC	
LINE AND SCRIPT	BITS AND BYTES
PICTURE	
VOICE	
IDENTITY (Machine. location. etc.)	BYTES
CHECKING (Bytes and bits)	

Figure 9. What is communicated is largely in the form of bytes and, hence, can be transmitted and processed economically. Bit maps are used only where quality requires this form.

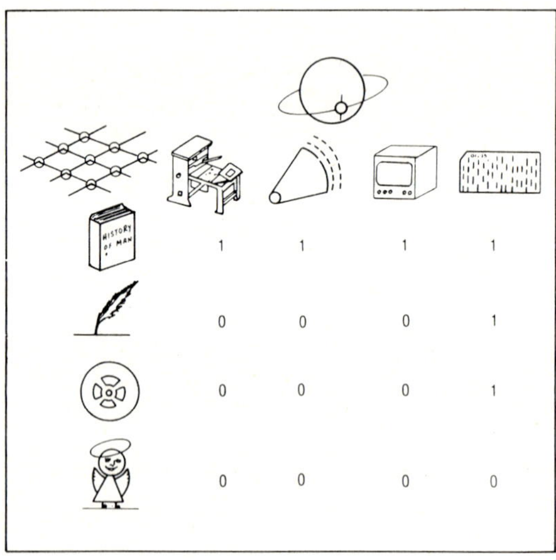

Figure 10. Information services are arrayed across the top. and various needs are symbolized in the first column. The notation "1" in the matrix indicates that service is available and accessible to serve the need indicated. while a "0" implies that the service is lacking or access is denied.

composed of many different communicants.

Matrix for integrated communication. To help visualize the different user services and the type of information communicated between sender and receiver sites, Figure 10 provides a matrix in glyphic notation. Across the top line are glyphics for storage (core memory), hard copy, voice copy, soft copy, and record copy. The second line indicates that all of these services are needed by those whose mission is the creation of new knowledge, symbolized by a book on the history of man.

On the third line, the quill pen stands for the transfer or commitment of funds. The fourth line represents the exchange of information, between an inquirer and a computer-controlled data base. On the last line, the angel foretells the need for a reference service to assist in resolving problems of interfaces, standards, and semantics if today's isolated systems are to share information in the future.

The book, pen, tape, and protocol representative (angel) also represent the control offices that monitor and manage information flow in an integrated office information system. The symbol indicates the type of control being exercised. In sequence these symbols may be interpreted as knowledge, transaction, data base, and reference. The address of the communicant is suggested by the core memory symbol. It points to a need for personal information resident in storage that will identify communicants, indicate their security level, and record the services available to different users. The satellite at the top signifies the electrical aspect of communications.

The graphic matrix provides only a first-level view of the information that may be communicated. Other levels exist, but they begin with the recognition that facilities exist. An example of second-level information is quality. Other levels may concern the message delivery schedule, distribution alternatives, acknowledgement, etc.

Evolving communications

Author guidelines. A standard for electronic manuscript preparation and exchange is being prepared by the Association of American Publishers. It will provide editors, publishers, designers, and others with the means to augment document content for their specific needs. Generalized tagging is the recommended basis for providing additional information in the manuscripts in order to facilitate exchange and processing.

The standard draws upon the work of many individuals and organizations. Principal among them are the American National Standards Institute committees X3J6 and X3V1, plus their International Standards Organization equivalent committees and others. One such standard[6] is the ongoing effort toward definition of a Standard Generalized Markup Language (SGML). in the final stages of development.

The first effort is a provisional standard. which together with companion author guidelines. will be tested and evaluated by a number of publishers. Validation will result in changes to the provisional standard and guidelines. a consequence of field testing. and following will be promulgation of the standard by the AAP.

Voice quality scale. Since information systems must eventually include voice. it is not premature to consider a voice-grade quality scale. The unit rate of of digital signal transmission may be taken as 64 kilobits per second. This would represent conversation at a quality of one. One second of written speech. communicated at a unit rate of 64 kilobits per second. would be comparable in quality to a telephone conversation.

Assuming this information is stored. the number of bits for a second of voice communication at a quality of one equals approximately the number of bits in an image at a quality level of 16. or 384 pixels per inch. The assumption made is that three words per second is a normal rate of speech between friends. At five characters per word. we have a means of comparing communication costs and storage requirements for two forms of communication--both utilizing a common store and communications media.

Recommended reading

1. Joseph D. Becker. "Multilingual Word Processing," Scientific American. Vol. 251. No. 1. July 1984. pp. 96-107.

2. Xerox Corporation. Introduction to Interscript. Xerox System Integration Guide. Stamford, Connecticut: 16 November 1984.

3. Jerry Mendelson. "Interpress 82 Reader's Guide." Xerox System Integration Guide. Stamford. Connecticut: 16 November 1984.

REFERENCES

1. Edwin J. Smura, "A Current. Correct. and Controlled Communication Process." IEEE Trans. Systems, Man, and Cybernetics. Vol. SMC-11. No. 2, Feb. 1981. pp. 168-176.

2. Edwin J. Smura, "Graphical Data Processing," AFIPS Conf. Proc.. vol. 32. pp. 111-118, 1968.

3. Edwin J. Smura, "A quality scaling measure for integrated communication." IEEE Trans. Consumer Electron, vol. CE-26, pp. 520-526. Aug. 1980.

4. Xerox Corporation. Introduction to Interpress. Xerox System Integration Guide. Stamford, Connecticut; 1984 April; XSIG 038304.

5. Theme articles on network protocols. Computer. Vol. 12. No. 9. Sept. 1979.

6. Information Processing Systems--Text Preparation and Interchange--Text Processing and Markup Languages. Part 6: Document Markup Metalanguage, ISO TC97/SC18/WG8 N8. International Standards Organization. 1984 Sep. 01. 109 pp.

CHAPTER 44

PROGRESS IN OFFICE SYSTEMS

Ian Young
The Economist Informatics Ltd

1.   A Sense of Perspective

To address a chapter of a book of the range and scope of
this book, and to call that chapter, "Progress in Office
Automation", begs a whole series of issues. The starting
point is to consider the concept of 'progress'.
Necessarily it requires a starting-point - the progress
measured from where? If we go back too far then we are in
danger of talking of progress in terms of truisms. How
may of the authors here, let alone the readers, can
imagine office life without the telephone, or to be more
recent and reasonable, the function of the office without
ready access to a photocopier. If progress is measured
from before the start of either of these two now universal
pieces of of office equipment, then we would conclude that
there has been substantial progress in office automation,
and this chapter would be drawn to a rapid conclusion.

Conversely, if we consider office automation to start only
at the edge of what is already practicable, then we are
immediately faced with the prospect of gloom and
despondency that is associated with the knowledge of yet
another prophecy being failed as concept or prototype
refuses to be turned into a mass produced item.

The first problem therefore is to adopt and accept a
starting point from which we are to assess the rate of
progress in office automation. It is a feature of the
printed media that the author is left free to adopt such a
criterion, while the reader can choose either to accept or
reject the author's choice. With that relationship
established, it is my proposal that this chapter should
consider the progress of office automation from a 'ground
zero' of the basic word

My choice of the word processor as a starting point is for
two reasons. Firstly it can be accepted as almost a
universal amongst the companies in which the readers find
themselves today. Indeed, I was recently visiting the
Head Office of a major UK retailing company, and while
seated in the reception area, I became aware of a vaguely
nostalgic sound - that of a multitude (my rough estimation
would be more than 50) of typewriters being operated by
secretaries and copy typists. Subsequently, as I was led
through the open plan working area of the secretarial
staff, my suspicions were confirmed, electric typewriters
were clearly evident by their visual presence as well as
their noise, but there was no sign of a word processor.

It was the experience of this exception to the rule that made me appreciate how well and rapidly the word processor had been accepted and assimilated into the working life of the normal company. Hence, we should consider the progress of office automation subsequent to the word processor.

Secondly the acceptance of the word processor as the starting point for measuring progress is appropriate because it brought and raised the concept of 'automation' to the environment of the white collar worker.

Before this time it had been accepted that there would be progress and 'automation' in the area of unskilled and semi-skilled jobs on the factory floor. Exceptionally, during the 1960's, the progress of modern technology started to reach into limited sections of the white collar professions, notably the introduction of computers to the banking world. But the word processor was the first broadly-based piece of technology to hit the office environment. That piece of technology was particularly significant because it truly brought with it the idea of 'automating' office practices. The major sales pitch of the WP (word processor/ing) salesman was that time and motion studies of secretarial activities had shown that only a relatively small proportion of the secretaries' day was spent on key strokes on the typewriter generating new (and final) text. Substantial, and previously unmeasured, time was spent lining up paper in the typewriter carriage, inserting carbon paper for copies, and correcting text either because of the typist's inaccuracies (usually a matter for correction paper or fluid), or the boss's indecision (a more serious matter, involving complete rekeying). By transferring many of these activities to the care of the word processor, the secretary would have more time to dedicate to the productive activity of entering new keystrokes, and hence new text into the memory of the word processor.

A natural result of this change would be that a single secretary would be able to handle more 'work' (this being defined only as productive when entering new keystrokes), and hence the number of secretarial staff required in an organisation of a given size, could be reduced without any detrimental effect. A further extension of the same principle was that even greater savings could be made on the administrative budget if the work load could be spread more evenly between the individual secretaries and typists. The shared logic word processor meant that any one of a group of typists could access a document to apply corrections or changes, it no longer had to be the originator of the text. By increasing the efficiency of the typist/secretary through changing her into one of a pool of word processing operators, the capital cost of word processing equipment could be met by savings in staff salaries following the reduction in secretarial numbers in little over a year.

This truly was the concept of automation – greater efficiency and less human error – but with it went the problems that had been encountered in the early days of

automation on the factory floor. Words like deskilling,
and alienation were heard for the first time around the
coffee machine in the office, and the reaction was
expressed in a variety of ways from simple increased staff
turnover, through more time spent off work with eyestrain
and headaches, to anxieties about cancer risks from too
much use of VDU screens. At the same time there was a
general decrease in the accuracy of first drafts of keyed
text.   The culprits were not just the typists themselves
(who naturally did not worry about the precision of their
typing now that it could be corrected so easily) but also
the text authors, who were more prepared to get half
considered ideas keyed up prior to an expected substantial
edit. The net result of these problems, not identified by
the WP salesman, is that most WP installations cannot be
shown to have resulted in any increased efficiency of
their company, or any directly attributable decrease in
operating costs. Even those that can legitimately claim
savings through the introduction of word processing, would
fall short of the scale of saving that was being held out
by the WP salesman of five years ago.

But if WP has not had the predicted effect on the bottom
line of the user organisations, and if it has raised all
the problems cited amongst the secretarial and typing
community, then why has it been adopted so widely as to
justify the earlier remark that it is notable by its
occasional absence from major companies? The answer is
that it has met the needs of business, but in ways other
than the simple reduction in staff through a more
efficient way of typing letters or reports.

Firstly there is the quality of the text presented in a
letter. Having gone to the trouble and expense of having
letterheaded stationery designed and printed, the image
conscious company does not want to ruin its presentation
with variable quality typing and inadequate layout.
Particularly when its competitors are all making use of
word processing, this company cannot be seen to lag
behind. So, letters that are uniformly spaced, and free
from encrusted layers of Snopake, become the standard, and
for a company to achieve that norm of presentation, it has
to follow the path of acquiring word processing
capability.

Secondly, there are new variations of ways of doing
business that have resulted from, and perpetuate the use
of the word processor. One example is the increased use
of the short mailing list.   Prior to the word processor,
a letter/information note could be typed individually,
typed with carbon copies, typed and photocopied, or
printed in some way. Typing and printing both produced
high quality results, but the former method was highly
inefficient for volumes of copies greater than ten or so,
while the latter did not become efficient until the number
of copies produced was several hundred. The middle route
of copying tended to lack quality, and it was impossible
to make the letter in any way personal.   Most word
processing facilities however can handle the merging of
standard text with a list of names and addresses (which
may themselves have been automatically selected form a

longer list by some identifying characteristic), to create
mailing lists of standard text, but high quality and
efficiently for runs as low as 15 - 20.

When we consider the progress that has been made in Office
Automation it needs to be set against the perspective
outlined above for the basic component of any office
automation system - word processing. Should we pay too
much attention to the success or otherwise in achieving
efficiency savings through a straight automation process?
I would suggest that we should not. However, if we are to
abandon the most obvious and easily quantified objective,
then what can we put in its place to be able to draw a
conclusion about the progress or failure of office
systems.

There are several features that could be considered, but I
will limit myself to two. The first of these is simple
technical progress. What advances have been made in the
development of systems or use in the office environment.
Secondly, but of equal importance, is how well those
advances have been accepted and integrated into the office
itself, and whether they have been able to address needs
of the organisation as a whole.

2.   Technical Progress

The progress of office systems in terms of their technical
capability can be measured on a number of dimensions:

*   capability and capacity

*   integration in workstations

*   communications

*   man-machine interface

2.1   Capability and Capacity

The ability of desk-top machines to handle large
quantities of data, and to process them at ever increasing
speeds is something that requires little in the way of
support for the assertion of its truth. In terms of
memory capacity we have already seen the development from
floppy discs to hard discs as a standard feature for
personal computers in the business environment. Other
developments include the move to the wafer as a means of
increasing RAM, and the introduction of the videodisc as a
mass storage device. This coupled with the continued
development of faster processors means that the terminal
placed on the desk of the secretary, clerical worker, or
executive is at least capable of operating at a pace equal
to that required by the user. Technical progress in
terms of the capabilities of the terminals and systems
that come under the rubric of office automation, is at
least equal to the demands of the user population.

At the same time as there has been an increase in the capability of the hardware of office technology, there has also been a corresponding and necessary development in the software. Whereas once upon a time only a small elite group of computer programmers knew how to make the hardware work for them, now software exists that allows even the busy novice to make at least limited use of the terminal on his desk.

Starting with word processing, it was necessary to develop software that allowed the user only a limited number of choices at any point, and to back these choices with prompts and support that the user could work from on-screen. In similar vein, the most popular software for business applications over recent years have been the spreadsheet calculation packages such as Visicalc, and its derivatives such as Lotus 1-2-3 and Symphony. With an added dash of a database package, virtually all requirements of the office can be met in a single terminal, and in a manner which is accessible to the professional worker without a degree in computer science.

2.2   Workstation Integration

A second area where there has been significant development is in the integration of functions to the individual workstation. Traditionally, these have been text based, with the possibility of incorporating (rather than integrating) a telephone handset alongside the screen. There has been a noticeable movement toward true integration of functions within a single workstation.
Desk top screen displays are now capable of handling basic text plus a reasonable quality of graphical presentation. However, more important is the bringing together of the telephone handset and the VDU terminal with access to databases and communication facilities. One example recently launched is the ICL OPD - standing for One Per Desk. The result of collaboration between UK computer manufacturer ICL, Sinclair Research, and British Telecom, the OPD is a stand-alone executive workstation with communications facility. It incorporates word processing, calculator and spreadsheet programmes, can be used as terminal for viewdata access, or as a terminal to a local or remote host computer, handles electronic mail between OPD terminals or through commercial electronic mail services, incorporates a telephone handset, and telephone directory which can be linked to provide autodial capability. A further touch of integration is the inclusion of a speech synthesiser with limited vocabulary that can be used to provide a range of different telephone answering messages, constructed by the user in text on the screen, for use when the person is away from his desk, or does not want to be disturbed. Finally, the whole operation of the OPD's functions can be run in a simulated multifunction manner, allowing the user to break off from one activity for a while, and then return to it when required at the point of departure.

The OPD is illustrative of the direction terminals are

taking.   For a while they may represent overkill to the
needs and expertise of the users, whether these are
'executives', or as the name of the OPD expects, all white
collar workers in an organisation.   However if costs are
kept close to those of standard dumb terminals, or a
simple business microcomputer, then the multifunction
workstation could look like a good buy, that will be
gradually taken up by more and more people in a company.

2.3   Communications

The early entrants to OA, as indicated earlier tended to
consider office functions in a stand-alone manner.
Keystrokes and text production could be seperated from the
origination, editing, and final presentation of the content
of the text.   This conceptualisation primarily put up a
barrier between the secretary-typist and the text generator.
Whilst the shared logic WP represented one form of
communication in that several operators could pick up the
same editing function, the more important step was that of
peer-to-peer communication both within the office system and
outside.

Within the office, most integrated Local Area Network based
office systems provide some form of text message facility
between workstation.   Some have moved toward voice messaging
and some (eg. Wang) provide for voice annotation to text,
particularly to meet the situation where text messages need
to be handed-off to others with a brief voice comment.
However we have to consider the practical value of such
facilities as demonstrated to date.

Messaging is however of greater value when it can leave the
confines of the immediate group defined by the LAN and
provide communication with a wider area.   Developments in
this sense have similarly shown progress.   In the text form
there are a variety of services providing person to person
text messaging via electronic mail boxes.   However at present
these electronic mail services do not generally communicate
with each other, and so undermine the full utility of the
service.   Being restricted in terms of whom one can
communicate with places the user in the position of having to
invest in the equivalent of several telephone services to
ensure being connected to a client.

Communication between office systems brings us directly to
the most problematic area to the continued development of
systems and services - that of establishing standards for
interconnection at a variety of levels.   At present the
question of standards for interconnection is being addressed
in two ways - major corporate muscle and international
committee.   The corporate muscle is being applied by IBM with
their Systems Network Architecture (SNA).   With the largest
installed DP base internationally, and a strong presence in
the OA market throught the IBM PC and other products, IBM
wants to set a de facto standard that other manufacturers
will have to meet if they are to interconnect with IBM
machines.

Ranged against SNA are a host of other manufacturers of DP and OA equipment, with a strong but not exclusive european flavour, who are supporting the 'Open Systems Interconnection' (OSI). OSI is a multi level set of standards and protocols to permit interconnection from the level of simple data transportation up to specific applications protocols. Whilst there is agreement on the benefits of establishing such a comprehensive set of standards, it is the intrinsic nature of any committee-based activity, that the rate of progress is not usually very great. OSI is no exception to this rule. To date agreement has been reached on interconnection protocols up to the fourth of the seven layers of OSI. As the upper levels are concerned with the all important applications area, it is crucial that agreement is reached soon and is not overtaken by proprietory services becoming established in the marketplace.

The discussion of inter-office communication here has so far only focused on text communication . Within the office function the tranference of data is equally of importance alongside text, and at this time suffers from precisely the same constraints due to standards limitations and text communication. The battle between IBM's SNA and OSI applies equally well to data systems interconnection. However, it should be recognised that within the office and even between offices, the most usual form of communication is by voice and personal discussion, and not by text and data. A review of office systems should therefore include, with more than just a passing nod, the developments in voice store and forward capabilites and the technological advances of teleconference systems.

Voice store and forward is the equivalent of an active rather than passive answerphone service. The call initiator on finding that the respondent is not at his or her desk can decide to leave a message which may be later picked up by the recipient (when they check into their voice mail system) or be forcibly delivered by repeatedly dialing a number until respondent is finally on hand to take the call. Store and forward voice systems can be an add-on to the telephone exchange of either the sender or receiver (though of course the functions vary with such placements) or they can be located as a facility in a telecommunications network. The strongest marketing device employed so far is the avoidance of "Telephone Tag" – that is the 'game' whereby an initial call finds the recipient not available to take the call so instead the originator leaves a message to return the call. This the recipient does, but the return call is met with an equal absence, so a message is left etc. etc. The term 'telephone tag' takes its name from the children's playground game of tag. Whoever is 'it' has to pass the responsibility off to someone else as rapidly as possible. However in the meantime no-one is actually achieving communication with the other person. With store and forward voice, or voicemail as it is sometimes called, the 'tag' element is not entirely removed but there is a prospect of more substantive messages being exchanged in non-real time compared with the curt 'while you were out' note.

Store and forward voice systems have shown substantial

technical development in the USA, though the installed base is still small.

Since all store and forward voice systems have to interconnect to the public switched telephone network of whatever country they operate in, at least part of the question of interconnection standards is automatically addressed. However in practice there remain problems both of a technical and an operational nature. Technically, most systems rely on the use of 'touch-tone' telephone handsets to send tone signals to control and direct the systems. In countries or companies which rely on rotary dials and pulse code signalling the opportunities for making full use of store and forward voice systems are very much reduced. Operationally, the different systems use differing number sequences as system commands (eg. commands such as play back messages, skip to next message, delete and so on). So far this does constitute a major problem as few users of systems will ever have experienced using more than one. However it can be anticipated that in the future there will be problems of transference which will in turn pose problems for the users. It remains to be seen whether this in due course will prove to be a substantive barrier to the widespread acceptance of store and forward voice systems.

The other area of office technology which needs to be included under this communications heading is that of teleconferencing - the linking together of two or more groups of people in different locations by a variety of telecommunications means. Teleconferencing is a generic term for a wide range of service types, and has been around in various forms for over fifteen years. In terms therefore of 'progress', I will restrict this discussion to developments in video-conferencing, that is teleconferencing which incorporates moving video images of the meeting participants.

Fifteen, and even just five, years ago the technology available for videoconferencing was precisely the same as that available for normal television services. Cameras were linked directly to TV screens, and signals carried between the two were at full broadcast standard bandwidth. In consequence the cost of such systems and services was extremely high, especially when long distances were involved.

The breakthrough for videoconferencing came with the development of Codecs (Coders-Decoders) which firstly digitize the video signal, and then apply rules of sampling and prediction to convey changes in the video images rather than the full image itself. The net result is that the use of codecs, permits the transmission of standard 'head and shoulders' images (ie. the upper part of the body that would normally be seen in a business discussion across a table or desk) at between 1.5 and 2 megabits per second, which requires only a thirtieth of the transmission capacity used by the full broadcast standard systems, and yet retains an adequate signal quality of value to the recipient.

The entry of codecs and video signal compression techniques encouraged some companies to build videoconference studios on their premises and use part of their data communication networks to carry videoconferences.

The cost of constructing studios, buying codecs and possibly increasing the private data circuit capacity still remains high though. The manufacturers of codecs have responded by constructing all-in-one cabinets containing TV camera and monitors plus the codec in a single unit that can be rolled into a normal conference room. At the same time experimental services in the UK provided by British Telecom and planned services by the German PTT have looked at ways of sharing the cost of both the codecs and the transmission by constructing a specific network incorporating the codecs, and into which participating companies can plug-in on a usage charge basis. Taken together the less expensive 'rollabout' videoconference unit and the shared facilities network should offer prospective user companies a low cost and low risk entry strategy to videoconferencing. However as yet it is too early to judge whether the approach is successful.

Again, with this area of video communications there is a standards issue. The earliest codecs were produced in the USA to a transmission speed of 1.5 Megabits per second. Different codecs by companies such as Compression Labs and NEC use different signal compression techniques and hence are incompatible. European manufacturers on the other hand have opted for a common interconnection standard called COST 211 which operates at 2 Megabits per second, to ensure that as networks are built up nationally they will be able to talk to each other. So far the question of interconnection in this area of office technology is asked only occassionally rather than regularly, but it will be one that becomes more pertinent as videoconferencing use begins to spread more widely.

Finally, the movement toward saving transmission costs continues with greater compression techniques that have taken videoconference facilities below 1.5 Mb/s. through various stages down to 56 kb/s. The significance of this level of compression is that future planned telecommunications networks are expected to integrate voice and data transmission at between 56 and 144 kb/s. transmission speeds. If and when these services are established then compressed image videoconferences could be common place.

2.4   Man-Machine Interface

The final area of technical development that I want to address is the point of contact between the user and the technology. Office systems having developed from computer technology suffer from two problems – the reliance on the keyboard as a means of communication with the system, an expectation that users will be familiar with standard computer jargon and procedures. The progress has been more marked on the first issue and slow but non-the-less continued on the second.

The keyboard is seen as a disadvantage to the widespread use of office systems firstly because the status conscious executive would not be prepared to use a device which he considered to be more appropriate to his secretary's role, and secondly because even if he was prepared to use it, the process would be slow reflecting his lack of training.

The first of these concerns has not been found to hold true
in the majority of cases. With the possible exception of
senior executives in terms of both status and age, the
businessman has adapted readily to using a keyboard, and does
not for the most part consider it to be a demeaning activity.

The second concern, on speed and ease of use rather than
willingness, is more real and overlaps with the aspect of the
language and procedures of interaction. Here progress has
been in the form of menu-driven routing procedures and the
use of diagramatic presentation of choices (eg. the Apple
Mackintosh) to make the task of selecting and taking action
more obvious and quicker for the user. In this way on-screen
information can be used to prompt and guide the user at all
times, and to make the response quicker. To achieve the
response (and in addition to the standard keyboard) there has
been increased use of touch-sensitive television screens and
of the device known as the 'mouse'. Both of these provide
ways of pointing to aspects of information or choices
displayed on the screen which are then acted upon.

The only area in which there has not been significant
development has been voice input. Whilst there has been some
improvement in voice-activated machinery responding to a
limited range of single-word commands, the development of
syntactic comprehending programs to detect and translate
verbal instructions into actions or first draft text still
appear some way off. Every so often there are press
announcements of a new product about to be launched, but
invariably there is a gap between promise and delivery.

3.   User Acceptance and Benefits

Having considered areas where there has been greater or less
progress on the technological front of office systems, we
need to return finally to the crucial question of whether
progress has been made in the introduction of these systems
into the office in such a way as to demonstrably improve the
operation of that office's function.

The problem with trying to answer such a question is that of
avoiding the setting up of anecdotal evidence in support of
sweeping conclusions. For instances where clear advantages
have been gained there can be others where expensive office
equipment lies underutilized. It was to circumvent the
reliance an anecdote and personal interpretation that a UK
government backed scheme to encourage the development and use
of advanced office systems in public sector organisations,
incorporated as part of its scope an evaluation exercise.

The scheme in question was launched in 1982 by the Department
of Trade and Industry with the intention of encouraging the
system suppliers to accelerate their development programmes
by providing them with an independent test bed, and at the
same time give public sector groups experience of advanced
 office systems which they could later expand into other
parts of their operation. The encouragement offered was part
(but substantial) payment of the capital costs of the
equipment which would be selected on the basis of a 'marriage

brokering' between user organisation requirements, and system capabilities (both current and to be developed). This brokerage service was carried out by a consortium of consultancies called the Office Automation Consulting Group - a subset of companies in the Computer Services Association.

The same consortium, under the guidance and management of The Economist Informatics then undertook a series of two year evaluation projects, on each of 20 plus trial systems. The evaluations constituted a series of snapshots of the organisations, at points before and after the introduction of the office systems, and undertook measurements and assessments both of standard office procedures and of the functional achievements of the whole office environment.

At the time of writing, the entire project is entering its final phase.

Data available at this time is not sufficient to draw final conclusions on progress in office systems, but it does show instances where they have been incorporated successfully into the operation of organisational practices. General trends show that where systems are introduced to serve identifiable needs in an organisation they can be readily assimilated. However, at this advanced level there needs to be a continued dialogue between the user organisations and the suppliers of the technology to tailor performance to the user's requirements. The policy of sell, deliver and run is not successful when advanced systems are being introduced to a wide user base.

Successful systems have so far been marked by a combination of:

* identifiable objectives
* implementation support for users
* feedback cycles to modify the system performance

There has not, by contrast, been any clear indication of groups of people too senior, old, innumerate or inept to accept new office technology if they could see or could be shown its relevance.

4.   Conclusions

This chapter posed, or was posed, the question of whether there had been progress in office automation. The conclusion is that measured from a starting point of the word processer there has been significant technical progress, and that in specific instances there has also been progress in introducing and gaining accceptance of office systems to a broad range of users.

However, two reservations exist:

(i)   The continued expansion of office technology will rely on there being significant progress in the near future on the interconnection of office systems both within and outside of a single organisation.

(ii)   The progress of office systems will depend on the
        support offered to user organisations to select and
        adapt technology to their own needs and business
        objectives.

Technology, however clever, developed in isolation of these
considerations will make slow progress, if any at all, in
gaining entry to the market place.

Bibliography

DTI Pilots   -   Office Automation Pilots
                                    Conference held on 21st - 22nd
                                    March, 1984, & 10th - 11th
                                    October, 1984. Papers for Days
                                    One, Two, Three & Four.

Pye & Young   -   Do Current Electronic Office
                                    Systems Meet User Needs.

                                    Paper presented at Stanford
                                    University   "International
                                    Symposiom on Office Automation".
                                    March 1980.   Published   in
                                    "Emerging Office Systems". Ablex
                                    Publishing Corporation, Norwood,
                                    NJ, 1982.

Teldok   -   Report   for   The   Economist
                                    Informatics.

                                    Review of Office Automation in
                                    Europe

CHAPTER 45. PROGRESS IN OFFICE SYSTEMS: ANOTHER VIEWPOINT

Jim Driscoll

Since you are reading this chapter you obviously want to know how to improve productivity through "office automation", however that may be defined. You may be a staff expert trekking monthly from office show to office show keeping up with the state of the art in office systems - hardware, software, and business applications, or you may be a line manager considering the purchase of office automation systems or faced with a higher-management decision to computerize some of your operations, or you may be a student/consultant/ seeking a career in this "hot" field. In every case, I assume you want to know how to improve the productivity of office workers - and how to use the stunning technical advances in computers as a means to that end.

First, the Bad News: Office Automation Doesn't Improve Productivity

The problem you face is the failure of office automation to improve productivity at all. Again and again, organizations invest millions of dollars in new office technology with <u>no</u> measurable net increase in productivity.

The Good News is Nobody Finds Out the Bad News

Fortunately for the peace of mind of managers - and especially for the career prospects of you readers of this chapter who are staking your professional lives on this office automation boondoggle, the vast majority of buyers of office automation conduct <u>no evaluation whatsoever</u>. Amidst the pressure of budget review, new products, and re-organization, who has the time to play "PhD", to gather the cost data, and to figure out what percentage of whose time goes to handling "exceptional cases" the computer system was designed to handle?

In those few cases where evaluations <u>are</u> carried out, the key decision maker who "championed" the system usually conducts the evaluation. In those cases, not surprisingly, the evaluations are favourable - but partial.

A simple dollars and sense approach is always foregone - do we spend more or less to do the same work than we did before the new computer system? In the long history of computer-based installations, I know of <u>no</u> computer system of any type that paid for itself in <u>reduced</u> payroll costs. Office automation is simply a specific application of the general rule.

Instead, such "evaluations" as are done typically focus on some narrow improvement in fuctioning, or a new capability that the computer system provides. The "evaluation" then lapses into fairly elaborate explanations of new capability, "enhanced functioning" is a pet phrase, and the original, tough, no-nonsense, "bottom line", did it pay for itself, orientation is gone forever.

Where Do I Get Off Saying These Things

As background for this claim of the failure of office automation, let me give a brief personal history. I began studying office automation in 1973 as a graduate student at Cornell University. Two of my Professors had been retained as part of a national, multi-disciplinary consulting team to find out why word processing systems failed so often to meet the manufacturer's productivity claims. For the next seven years, as an Assistant Professor at the Sloan School of Management at M.I.T., I continued my studies of word processing, electronic mail, and decision-support systems. In all, I reviewed over a hundred installations of computer-based equipment ranging from a small, stand-alone word processor to the nearly-completely-computerized office support of research centers employing more than one hundred professionals and associated support staff.

In <u>none</u> of these cases did a hard economic study demonstrate sufficient cost savings either from lower payrolls or other sources, to cover the costs of computer installation and operation. In <u>no</u> case did the computer add sufficient new business at margins which covered those costs.

In a <u>few</u> cases, for example, the application of centralized word processing to law offices handling large volumes of highly-repetitive typing, such as wills-offices that resembled small print shops, less rigorous calculations suggested the possibility of a simple economic justification of office automation. In no case was such hard economic analysis completed.

In another <u>few</u> cases, an ad-hoc evaluation was conducted, usually based on interviews, but occasionally quantifying some narrow measure of performance such as "per cent of professionals time spent in revising copy". Most of these studies were positive, justifying the expenditure on office automation equipment. In most cases of positive evaluation, the study was conducted by the "champion" of the computerization project. Apart from their limited value as indicators of productivity, these studies are useless given the myriad potential for bias by the "champion", whether intentional or not. Gerry Gordon and John Kimberley in the first <u>Annual Handbook of Sociology</u> summarized the reasons for ignoring such "champion" studies.

<u>So Why Do Folks Buy Office Automation Systems? A Political Aside</u>

What has been going on, then, is a <u>charade</u>. Lots of academics have postured in a ritual attending the advance of technology. The technology is driven by forces quite different than the competitive drive to improve productivity.

Some of these forces are obvious. "Office automation" is one of what John Kenneth Galbraith termed manufactured or created needs. Listen to the advertisements some time. if a manager doesn't have "the latest" in office automation, it's the career cemetery for certain. Of course, there are immense profits in this business for the manufacturing firms with the budgets to generate these advertising campaigns.

Office automation got its start in the large companies at the oligopolistic core of the Western economy, initially the United States, with the economic slack to invest in office automation, regardless of its economic advantage. Once underway, much like military contracting, careers are now at stake in these same companies. Apart from the internal "champions" the heads of "information systems" and the like, outside the firms, hordes of students, professors and consultants stand ready to recommend the latest round of technological sophistication.

The impact of this technology on society is, as I have argued elsewhere, unfortunate. While the technology, as always, is neutral, the particular direction, the "path" taken by invention, development, and application, has accentuated the tendency in post-industrial firms toward two social classes. The larger society in the U.S. has become increasingly stratified in the last fifteen years as fewer people earn and retain larger percentages of national income and wealth. The macro-forces obvious in the redistribution of wealth, the election of "conservative" governments, even the glorification of "yuppies", have been mirrored at the micro level in technological applications that concentrated information, power, and benefits in the hands of a narrowing elite in each organization.

Setting aside that political analysis, the serious student of improving productivity in offices is left in an empirical vacuum. On the one hand, manufacturers make extravagant claims of success with no serious empirical support. On the other hand, skeptics like myself, draw the opposite conclusions on almost equally flimsy evidence. We have, after all, published very few studies documenting the shortcomings of office automation from a hard economic stand point.

The reader should note here an important bias in the world of scholarly publication. It is infinitely harder to get a study published showing <u>no</u> impact from an innovation, than to publish even the most trivial of impacts. The alternative explanations for a finding of no impact are so many, that most serious scientific journals will not publish such studies, a bias not confined to this particular subject. If, however, the reader is willing to let me conclude from this absence of empirical demonstration, the lack of any beneficial impact of office automation on productivity, the obvious question is "Why no impact"?

<u>Why Office Automation Doesn't Improve Productivity</u>

The reason office automation has not improved productivity is definitional. Productivity is human. People, in the last analysis, <u>always</u> do the work of an organization. Whether it is a secretary keying in the words of a letter or a senior manager using a computer-based message system to communicate a message to her staff, computers aid, assist, supplement, multiply but simply do not do the work in the absence of people.

The last fifteen years of "office automation" have downplayed, if not ignored, the importance of human beings in the accomplishing of organizational objectives. The spate of seminars, articles and promotional blurbs about "the human factor" and "user-friendliness" remain solidly in this tradition. In a variety of ways, the design, implementation, and operationalization of office automation systems has contradicted what we know about human beings and how we behave: in our individual nature, in groups, and in organizations.

In the main body of this chapter, I will review what we know about human behavior, then lay out some principles for improving productivity in organizations with or without office automation, and then contrast that with the current picture of office automation. Finally, I will point out how office automation could be used as an opportunity to improve productivity.

Since I have already published my critique of office automation, what follows is my reason for writing this chapter. In 1982, I decided to quit my job as a college professor in part due to my reluctance to continue my part of this charade. I was making a handsome living flying all over the world carrying this critique more potent than the absence of empirical evidence of productivity from office automation, however.

Since 1982, I have been seeking to shape those societal forces more directly, albeit on a different topic. I have been setting up organizations all over the U.S. dedicated to stopping the nuclear arms race. The reasons for that focus as a father and a Vietnam veteran are obvious. I refuse to sit idly by as we prepare for species suicide. However, that is a different chapter.

In that organizational work, I have bought, programmed, and managed "office automation systems" ranging from my own personal computer up to multi-million dollar direct mail fundraising programs. I have had occasion to put into practice what I learned my in PhD program and what I had taught at M.I.T. some of it was useful; some of it was not.

From that experience, I have forged certain simple insights I wanted to share in my swan song to this field. For those of you who have come to know and trust me, I urge that you give these insights a try. The chances of increasing office productivity from their application looks great. Of course, we both know that I haven't measured these increses and that you probably won't. They are, however, a whole lot cheaper than a gross IBM PC/XTs.

What We Know About Human Behaviour in Organizations

There is little disagreement among psychologists about the positive side of
human nature. People are naturally intelligent, energetic, and cooperative.
Study after study in work organizations documents the importance of positive
motives. People work not just because they are paid and told what to do, but in
order to achieve feelings of accomplishment, challenge, and self worth.

What has puzzled psychologists for some time is the negative behaviour
exhibited by some of these "good" people. Why do some people loaf
systematically, occasionally undermine coworker's efforts and, in the extreme,
actually sabotage equipment? (There are occasions when work stoppages and
disruptions represent wholly rational, sometimes conscious, resistance to
exploitation in organizations. Even the most committed Marxist, especially if
given the responsibility for getting some work done, will admit that much of the
unproductive side of human behaviour in work organizations is personal, not
political). These rigid, unthinking and destructive acts are best conceived of
as old, bad habits, inappropriate to the current situation, but fallen into by
the person because something in the current situation reminds him or her of
something long ago when that bad habit was the best the person could do.

Psychologists from many schools are converging on this explanation of
unproductive, ineffective behaviour. Whether viewed in behaviourist terms as an
old "response" stimulated by something in the present, or in Freudian terms as a
"defence mechanism", a fixed way of coping with certain threatening situations
that is first developed during childhood.

I take the time to lay out this general theory of human behaviour because
every communication - book, speech, or sales pitch - has some set of assumptions
about human behaviour underlying their recommendations. It's much simpler to
evaluate the policy recommendation when its philosophical underpinnings are made
explicit.

The most general principle to guide any intervention is human organizations,
given these assumptions, is simply:

1.   <u>Tap into people's natural intelligence, energy, and cooperation as much
as possible</u>. This wonderful human nature is <u>always</u> available as a resource in
<u>any</u> organizational situation.

2.   <u>Trigger people's bad habits, their fears, worries, and insecurities, as
little as possible</u>. Since each person gets hurt in highly specific ways, it is
always necessary to identify the specific things for each person or group that
will bring back old memories and possibly set off an old, unproductive, and
ineffective way of behaving.

Some more specific principles of human behaviour relevant to organizational
intervention follow from this view of human nature:

3.   <u>Let people appraise their own performance</u>. To improve people's
performance, let them sit down, preferably with their peers, but also with their
supervisors, and review their <u>own</u> behaviour. First, have them describe what they
have done well. Second, how they could improve. After the focal person takes
his or her turn, then coworkers or the supervisor can follow the same format.

This approach engages a person's positive motivation, their natural interest
in doing better. By contrast, it is almost impossible for another person,
especially one with power over that person, to tell him or her what they think of
their behaviour without reminding them so much of parents, teachers, coaches, and
setting of old, closed, defensive feelings and responses.

Since the tangible differences in organizational reward - pay increases, promotional opportunities etc., - are embarrassingly trivial at all but the highest organizational level, the only reason for performance appraisal is the impact of the process itself on performance.

4. <u>Let every member of the group participate in every discussion</u>. Given the natural intelligence of each member of the group, it <u>always</u> makes sense for <u>everyone</u> to listen attentively to each person's views on an important subject. This can be done in a group meeting or the leader can go around individually and listen to the thinking of each person. Often, especially for people who have been ignored in work groups it will be necessary to wait patiently through a period of silence to get a contribution. Sometimes, the disussion will not shed light on the problem, but it is astonishing the pearls of wisdom that come from a "low status" member of the group.

5. <u>Take turns when talking one on one</u>. All the current training on communication skills boils down to taking turns. When it's your turn to listen, listen. Don't think of your response, don't second guess, don't sympathize. In fact, the easiest way to get good communication started is simply to divide the time available (in half for two people, thirds for three, more sections for larger groups). One person talks, the other(s) listens. Then you can switch roles, with the talker confident that the listener is paying attention, and the listener secure that he or she will get his or her turn.

6. <u>Build deep personal relationships at work</u>. Making friends goes on all the time at work, but it has a bad name in management circles (outside of Japan where such friendships are assumed). People naturally work better with people they know and trust. The only way to build good relationships is to spend time listening attentively to the other person's hopes and fears.

7. <u>Encourage the Physiological Processes of Tension Release - Crying, Laughing, Shaking, and Yawning</u>. A growing body of research and experience now documents the importance of the most basic physical processes in helping people get over tension, both from current distressing experiences and from things happened long ago which still cloud their thinking.

When people are sad, they need to cry. When they are embarrassed they need to laugh. When frightened they need to shake. Yawning seems to release all kinds of physical tension. Rather than trying to maintain rigid decorum at work, people need to be encouraged to "let off some of their steam" in these simple, non-disruptive processes. Indeed, when two people divide up a period of time and truly listen to one another, it is highly likely that they will be given to laugh a bit, sweat and even cry as they discuss what is really on their minds with someone they trust.

8. <u>Set Clear and Specific Expectation for All Relationships</u>. The commonsense of building effective working relationships is for <u>both</u> parties to know <u>all</u> the time <u>exactly</u> what each other expects. Periodically both parties need to tell each other what they expect and let the other respond. Some expectations can be met easily, others a person can try to meet. Still others, either by ability or preference may be out of the question. For example, when relationships get close, some people may expect constant attention, long hours of friendship on demand, overlooking errors in performance, etc. Clear expectations can prevent this potentially negative impact of close relationships on productivity.

Obviously, all expectations for performance should be high. It is, after all, human nature to seek excellence.

9.   <u>Always designate a Leader</u>. Someone has always got to be responsible for thinking about the group as a whole. Much of the "participative management" movement has floundered around "group" or "consensus" decisions. <u>Individual</u> people make decisions, not groups. Of course, a leader should always consult with group members in order to get their input. However, the unique contribution of the leader is to sift through that input, formulate an action proposal, as fully developed as possible, and present it clearly to the group. Such a proposal may always be modified or rejected by the group.

10,   <u>Organizations Don't Exist, Only People and Their Relationships</u>. All the trappings of organizations are meaningless exactly to the extent they go beyond the current relationships among organizational members as individuals, human beings, and their expectations of one another. Organizational charts, job descriptions, pay scales, long-range plans, budgets, and the like are useful <u>only</u> to the extent they help establish or summarize expectations among people. The focus on changing organizations should always be on specific people and their relationships, not meaningless paper abstractions.

<u>A Humanly Rational Approach to Office Automation</u>.

Having laid out what we know about organizations, let's review how office automation might be done more effectively and, in the process, contrast current practice with this ideal.

<u>System Design</u>. The current design practices in office automation ignore these principles of human behaviour. At the earliest stages of <u>product</u> design, a cohort of actual and user-secretaries, order clerks, insurance sellers, etc., should be brought together to help design the system. Their input should be continued throughout the product-design process Of course, a project manager retains responsibility for final decisions and synthesizing the end user input (along with technical, financial, and other considerations).

Current practices in office automation product design is abysmal. One manufacturer, after years of problems in designing office automation systems, finally hired an anthropologist to talk to secretaries about their jobs and watch what they actually did. Her report highlights almost all the problems encountered by the firm's word-processing products in the last 15 years - only 20% of a secretary's time is spent typing, lots of the job is non-standardized work, secretaries need hard copies close at hand, and a key element in a secretary's job is personal support from a boss. How much simpler it would have been 15 years ago for this and other manufacturers to listen carefully to a few secretaries at the beginning of the product-design process.

Such product design and end-user teams, like all the groups of people to be described below, <u>must</u> function by the equal time rule and require a leader committed to listening and following those equal time guidelines. Too often - usually because of sex, age, race, or economic status - certain members in an organization are ignored - female, young, low-paid, or third-world people. Too often, the leader is busy formulating her proposal, especially when she should be "listening" to these low-status groups.

<u>Implementation</u>. A similar end-users' group ought to be constituted for <u>every</u> installation. Remember, the specific "hot buttons" triggering old, rigid responses vary widely. Therefore, a system tailored for one group in a division or even a local department may flop completely next door. One manufacturer I consulted with (after this incident) actually painted "decision support" personal computers blue (for boys) and "word processing" personal computers pink (for girls). Needless to say, women with even a passing exposure to "women's liberation" were reminded of lots of other, productivity-destroying thoughts when these colours were introduced.

The project leader should be a "permanent" end user. Too often, a short-service, ambitious, staff specialist is put in charge of an office automation system. Not only is that person unlikely to understand the specific concerns of the particular users in a particular installation, he or she is usually long gone when problems inevitably arise. The project leader needs to build <u>relationships</u> that will carry the project through. Designation of another "staff specialist" as the new project leader is meaningless in the absence of real personal relationships.

<u>Operation</u>. An effective office automation system will allow the end user to initiate <u>private</u> performance feedback. Such information will allow the user to correct performance problems by providing information which the person is psychologically ready to use and without triggering off all the old defences against outside evaluation. The leader of the work unit also needs performance data, but such data should cover longer periods of time - hour, day week, and compare performance with particular circumstances - seasonal load, etc. Ideally such data would be used in a group's self-evaluation period apart from the pressure of doing the job.

Current systems respond to the designer's insecurity by giving maximum information possible to the supervisor. This simply encourages low performance reminding the workers of childhood and school experiences.

In my experience, job security is the best predictor of success with office automation. People do not respond well to change when they are afraid of losing their jobs or not meeting simple living expenses. Rather than rushing to make marginal job layoffs in order to justify an office automation system economically (which the careful reader will recall is a lost cause in any event), the project leader would be far better off <u>guaranteeing</u> the jobs of all people concerned and look to economic savings, if ever, down the road through attrition or voluntary transfers. The most likely payoff in office automation is always the creative <u>new</u> uses made possible by the system. These creative ideas come best from secure workers, not terrified ones.

Office Automation and Human Productivity

Office automation is only one of many innovations an effective organization may make to improve human productivity. Designing or choosing a product for purchase, implementing the new technological system, and operating it are routine tasks for an effective organization.

The mistake of office automation "experts" to date has been to attempt to isolate their one technological change from the ongoing work of the organization, and in so doing, to disrupt effective organizational processes. The purpose of this article has been to review office automation in the context of our best understanding or organzational functioning in order to provide a guide for better office automation practices in the future.

Many of the suggestions for improving office productivity offered in this chapter have been developed through a world-side network of unpaid <u>peer</u> counsellors known as Re-evaluation Counselling. I would be happy to put the interested reader in touch with its practitioners in almost any country.

FURTHER READING

Attewell, Paul; Rule, James.
   Communications of the ACM 27(120, 1184-1192, December 1984.
      Computing and organisations: what we know and what we don't know.
Boddy, David; Buchanan, David A.
   Omega 12(3),233-240, 1984.
      Information technology and productivity - myths and realities.
Caporael, Linnda R.
   J. Social Issues 40(3), 15-29, 1984.
      Computers, prophecy, and experience: a historical perspective.
Higgin, Gurth.
   Aslib Proc. 37(2), 91-98, February 1985.
      Information management: taking account of the human element.
Kanter, Moss.
   Counterpoint/Unwin, 1985.
      The change-masters. Entrepreneurs at work.
Kling, Rob.
   Computing Surveys, 12(1), 61-110, March 1980.
      Social analyses of computing: theoretical perspectives of recent
      empirical research.
Mumford, Enid.
   In Moneta J.(Ed). Information Technology. North Holland. 1978
      Human values and the introduction of technical change.
Robb, A.C.
   Proc IEE, 132(1) Part A, 67-73, January 1985.
      An essay in futurology: groups, networks, and complexity in the open
      society.
Steinmuller, Wilhelm.
   Information Age, 6(3), 163-171, July 1984.
      Consequences of information technology.
Weizenbaum, Joe.
   In Forester, Tom (Ed.). The Microelectronics Revolution. Basil Blackwell,
Oxford, 1980.
      Once more the computer revolution.

CHAPTER 46.

RECENT DEVELOPMENTS IN TELECONFERENCING AND RELATED TECHNOLOGY

DR. STARR ROXANNE HILTZ
New Jersey Institute of Technology, Newark, U.S.A.

The research on which this paper is based was partially supported by grants from the National Science Foundation (NSF-MCS-00519, MCS-77-27813, and MCS 812865). The opinions and conclusions are solely those of the author and do not necessarily represent those of the National Science Foundation.

The author would like to thank Murray Turoff, Elaine Kerr, and Kenneth Johnson for their collaboration in many of the studies which formed the basis for materials included here, and Ronald Rice for his helpful comments on the manuscript.

INTRODUCTION

The use of the computer to mediate human communication is reportedly advancing "like an avalanche"(Stockton, 1981). There is a confusing profusion of systems and terminology , and a few studies of its effects on individuals, groups and organizations. This review puts computer-mediated communication systems (CMCS) into perspective by summarizing how they compare to other forms of teleconferencing: audio, audiographic, and video systems. Then it focuses on some of the important issues related to current research on CMCS, including impacts on organizations, norms for effective computer-mediated interaction among humans, and structures which can help to avoid information overload among users.

COMPUTER-MEDIATED COMMUNICATION AND COMPUTERIZED CONFERENCING:
THEME AND VARIATIONS

In all of the various systems which currently harness the computer and telecommunications technologies for text-based human communication, there are certain constants:

.Communication occurs by typing into a keyboard and reading from a computer printout or CRT.

.The participants may be separated in time as well as in space. The communications are stored until the recipient(s) "sign in" for receipt.

.The computer can be used as an "active participant" and regulator of the communications structure, producing new forms of human communication.

It is this latter characteristic which is the essence of the allure and potential future developments for this technology. The computer can be much more than just a "store and forward" mechanism. It can be used to create tailored structures which are optimized for particular groups and applications, and to integrate other computer resources, such as data bases and computational capabilities, into a group communication

Among the many forms that computer-mediated communication takes are:

.Message Systems deliver discreet text communications from a sender to one or more recipients via computer networks, and may include extensive editing, filing, and retrieval capabilities.

.Computerized conferences are group discussion spaces set aside for a specific group to discuss a specific topic or task. They may have a basically "linear" and/or "branching" structure, and may include many features to aid the group in its work, such as voting.

.Bulletin Boards, generally microcomputer based, public and free, are common files where users can post "notices" for all to see.

.Knowledge Worker Augmentation Systems support specific types of tasks or functions, such as project management, joint composition of text, electronic journals, online educational delivery, or work with specific data bases or models.

Any one computer-mediated communication system may include more than one type of structure. For example, most computerized conferencing systems also include a message capability. To further confuse the terminology, message systems with extensive features including distribution lists and keyword retrieval may in fact be used like conferencing systems.

The first computerized conferencing system was developed by Murray Turoff while he was at the Office of Emergency Preparedness of the office of the U.S. President (see Turoff, 1972). At about the same time, Jacques Vallee and his colleagues at the Institute for the Future began work with a computerized conferencing system called Forum at first, later Planet. Turoff moved to the New Jersey Institute of Technology and headed the development of a system called EIES (Electronic Information Exchange System). Much of the evaluation research has taken place on users of EIES and Planet. Today there are dozens of computerized conferencing systems, most available commercially or used within single organizations. EIES remains unique in that it is a not-for-profit research and development system located within a university setting and conceived of as a "laboratory without walls" for developing and assessing the impact of many forms of computer-mediated communication. It will be featured prominently in this review because it represents not a single form of computer-mediated communication, but rather includes a high-level language which has been used to prototype and evaluate many different computer-mediated structures for different applications.

The BLEND-LINC project on electronic journals in Great Britain is involved with the development, application, and assessment of software "which involves using a computer to aid the normal procedures whereby an article is written, refereed, accepted and plublished" (Shackel, Pullinger, Maude, and Dodd, 1983, p. 247). Building on the experiences of the first electronic journals project on EIES from 1978-1980, they have developed a wide variety of structures for communication among the participating scientists, from informal "chit-chat" and work messages through an annotated abstracts journal, a "poster papers" (non-refereed) journal, to the formal refereed papers journal. An important difference between a regular paper journal and an electronic journal is that the latter provides structures for an orderly discussion and questions about papers, so that the author and the readers communicate about the text.

Another prominent center of development and research has been the COM system, under the leadership of Jacob Palme, now at the University of Stockholm. Palme has been particularly active in the development of "portable" software that will run on different hardware configurations, and in standards for allowing the interchange of messages among different computer networks (see Palme, 1984). Other conferencing systems for which there are published reports include Participate (which runs on the Source network in the U.S.), CONFER (developed at the University of Michigan but now marketed comercially as CONFER II), and the German KOMEX system.

Much of the early research on the social effects of CMCS involved attempts to reach generalizations about the impact of this new medium. For example, Johansen, Vallee, and Spangler (1979:180-181) summarize a number of studies with the statement that "computer conferencing promotes equality and flexibility of roles in the communication situation" by enhancing candor of opinions and by helping to bring about greater equality of participation. On the basis of early pilot studies comparing face-to-face and computerized conferences, Hiltz and Turoff (1978:124) conclude that more opinions tend to be requested and offered in computerized conferences, but that there is also less explicit reaction to the opinions and suggestions of others, whether agreement or disagreement. In terms of organizational impacts, Uhlig, Farber, and Bair (1979:306) state that "collaboration of groups of persons, whether on a report or a complex decision, is accelerated by the speed of communication, including distribution and feedback." (See Kerr and Hiltz, 1982, for a summary of the generalizations which emerge from the findings of eighteen research and development projects related to CMCS;a good recent review of research on all forms of teleconferencing is Rice, 1984).

The second generation, so to speak, of research on CMCS seeks a better understanding of the conditions under which the general tendencies of the medium are stronger weaker, or totally absent. Some of this research focuses on the structure or facilities of the computer-mediated communications system itself. For instance, recent work on CMCS at the Institute for the Future deals not with the general social effects of the PLANET system, but with the effects of adding three specific tools designed to support specific group tasks to the basic conferencing program: "graphical communication, ...communication focused on the running of computer programs through its program workspace, and communication focused on the creation and editing of a document" (Lipinski, Spang, and Tydeman, 1980:159).

Current work at the New Jersey Institute of Technology focuses on the development and evaluation of a variety of new capabilities for computer-mediated communication systems. The goal is to discover the interactions among task types, communications structures, and individual or group attributes that will allow the selection of

SUMMARY OF STRENGTHS AND WEAKNESSES
TELECONFERENCING MEDIA

STRENGTHS   WEAKNESSES

COMPUTERIZED CONFERENCING

STRENGTHS	WEAKNESSES
CONVENIENT- USER CHOOSES TIME AND PLACE TO PARTICIPATE	DIFFICULT TO ENFORCE REGULAR PARTICIPATION
ALLOWS EQUALITY OF PARTICIPATION	REQUIRES STRONG LEADERSHIP
GOOD FOR TECHNICAL INFORMATION EXCHANGE	REQUIRES CRITICAL MASS OF ABOUT TEN PARTICIPANTS TO SUSTAIN INTERACTION
ALLOWS TIME TO REFLECT ON TOPICS	REQUIRES EFFORT TO LEARN AND KEYBOARD SKILLS
LEAST EXPENSIVE TO USE PER HOUR	REQUIRES ACCESS TO EXPENSIVE (BUT MULTI-PURPOSE) TERMINALS

AUDIO CONFERENCING

STRENGTHS	WEAKNESSES
FAMILIAR-SEEMING MEDIUM, LEAST INTIMIDATING TO NEW USERS	ACTUALLY REQUIRES TRAINING FOR EFFECTIVE USE, THIS REQUIREMENT NOT OBVIOUS
SATISFACTORY FOR GAINING INITIAL PERCEPTIONS OF OTHERS, PERSUASION, INFORMATION SEEKING	"CAN CREATE AN IMPERSONAL, UNCOOPERATIVE COMMUNICATION ENVIRONMENT"
"MOST USEFUL WHEN SESSIONS ARE SHORT, REGULAR, AND INVOLVE SMALL GROUP"	BOREDOM AND FATIGUE SET IN QUICKLY (LESS THAN ONE HOUR)
REQUIRES NO SPECIAL EQUIPMENT	NO TABLES, GRAPHICS, ETC. UNLESS SEPARATELY DISTRIBUTED

AUDIOGRAPHIC TELECONFERENCING

STRENGTHS	WEAKNESSES
VISUAL SUPPORT FOR MEETINGS IMPORTANT IF THERE ARE CHARTS OR DRAWINGS	TENDS TO DISTRACT ATTENTION FROM THE PEOPLE AND THEIR INTERACTION
"NARROWBAND" CHANNELS MUCH LESS EXPENSIVE THAN FULL-SCREEN VIDEO	GRAPHICS EQUIPMENT OFTEN SLOW, AWKWARD, SUITABLE FOR ONLY LIMITED KINDS OF MATERIALS

VIDEO TELECONFERENCING

STRENGTHS	WEAKNESSES
MORE EFFECTIVE THAN NON-VISUAL MEDIA FOR TASKS WHICH STRESS INTERPERSONAL RELATIONS	VERY EXPENSIVE, THUS LIMITING ACCESS
GREATER FEELING OF "SOCIAL PRESENCE" AND "SOCIAL CONTACT" THAN AUDIO OR CC	ONLY MARGINALLY BETTER FOR MOST FUNCTIONS
NEW (FIRST TIME) USERS TEND TO RESPOND MOST POSITIVELY TO VIDEO	"HOLLYWOOD" SYNDROME (FORMALITY AND SELF-CONSCIOUSNESS)

****

Phrases in quotations from Johansen, Vallee, and Spangler, 1979; This summary also draws from Svenning and Rudenskas, 1984.

optimal system designs and implementation strategies to match variations in user group characteristics and types of tasks or applications. The research program involves a combination of field trials and controlled experiments. This report focuses on three selected and related issues being studied at NJIT and elsewhere: organizational impacts, emergent norms for CMCS, and avoid "information overload." The information overload section provides one illustration of what is meant by the concept of using the computer to provide software structures that can enable a group and organization to work together more productively.

ORGANIZATIONAL IMPACTS

Kerr and Hiltz (1982) list 32 impacts of computer-mediated communications on groups and organizations, based on reports from those who have done case studies of implementations. These include increases in the amount of communications within and between organizations, in the total number of active communication links sustained by individuals, and in the total size of effective working groups. The social structure of the organization itself is changed as a result, typically from a pyramidal or hierarchical system to a more equalitarian or "networked" organization. This organizational change is often unanticipated, and occurs gradually as more people spend a larger proportion of their total communication time on a teleconferencing system. As Johansen sums it up, "Basic changes in organizations are almost always slow, and it is organizational change that is the main event in a teleconferencing implementation, whether or not this is recognized by the implementors" (1984:7).

One example of the qualitative change that can take place in the organization's speed of reacting to opportunities is reported as follows by Kiesler, Siegel, and McGuire (1984:1127):

> Electronic communication differs from any other communication in time, space, speed, ease of use, fun, audience, and opportunity for feedback. For example, in one firm where someone posted a new product idea on the network, the proposition was sent in one minute to 300 colleagues in branches across the country, and, within two days, sufficient replies were received to launch a new long-distance joint project.

Sharp and Perkins (1981:132) list the following impacts on their organization from the extensive use of an internal system called MAILBOX:

> .MAILBOX makes nonsense of traditional pyramidical management structures and vastly increases the traditional "span of control."
>
> .It allows for the best qualified 20 or 50 or 100 people to discuss an issue in a manner that no face-to-face meeting could.
>
> .MAILBOX has obsoleted the concept of "management meetings" or committees. Pseudo-meetings are event-oriented rather than time-oriented.
>
> .It allows a lot of people to be in lots of different places all at the same time, without unduly disturbing their principal activities scheduled for that time.

The "bottom line" is whether computer-mediated communication increases the effectiveness of information workers (managers and professionals), and thus increases productivity. This is extremely difficult to measure and prove, and ultimately comes down to subjective evaluations by the participants. The difficulties in measuring increases in productivity of information workers have been summarized as follows:

> The quality and timeliness of information may be critical to its use; yet quality may be largely subjective and determined separately by the producer and the user. Overabundance may sap the scarce resource of managerial attention (Simon 1973). More efficient dissemination of information that is incorrect or unneeded will clearly harm the effectiveness of an organization. That is, the effectiveness or outcome of many information activities is more crucial than its efficiency... Organizations may die

> if they fail to reduce the amount of information that must
> be processed or fail to increase internal processing
> capability (Galbraith 1977). Handling information--
> filtering, abstracting, storing, retrieving, evaluating it
> (especially in unstructured situations), deciding how and
> when to perform information processing tasks, avoiding
> overload-- is a primary process of information workers...
> (Rice, 1984:187).

One important difference between computer-mediated communication and other forms of communication, including other modes of teleconferencing, is in the size of the communications network which can be sustained. All other forms of human group communication tend to start to limit the ability of people to fully participate once there are more than about a dozen people in the group, because only one speaker at a time can have a "turn." Because computer-mediated communication is asynchronous, and because recipients can filter and select among the available communication to focus attention on those which appear to contain new or useful information, this medium can sustain truly interactive groups that are quite large. However, the obverse is that a computerized conference seems to require a much larger number of active participants in order to sustain interaction. Hiltz and Turoff (1978) refer to this as the "critical mass" phenonenon, and set it at about ten active participants. In order for an exchange to be sustained, there must generally be new waiting communications whenever a person logs on. Receiving a new communication tends to stimulate the recipient to respond; receiving a notification that there are no items waiting tends to discourage new entries and to subsequently discourage participants from going to the trouble to dial up the computer and log on. Since many people do not log on every single day, and since at any time some members of a group may be ill or on vacation, it takes much more than three or four people to build up a self-sustaining mass of dialogue on a topic. In a two-year longitudinal study of several groups of information workers who were given the opportunity to use a computerized conferencing system, Hiltz (1984:197) summarizes the results related to productivity increases as follows:

> Exposure to a broader range of information and ideas than otherwise possible, and the availability of a much larger network of people who may be helpful when one does want information and assistance with a specific project, are among the benefits that are seen as increasing productivity... (However) Computer-mediated communication systems are not a technological magic wand that can be waved over an organization to achieve instantaneous transformations in productivity. It takes some time for new users to become comfortable with the medium and realize the potentials that it offers. It also takes the right "social implementation," from the initial choice of an application that will supply a "critical mass" for the online community, through constant attention to facilitating or managing the group's work online.

Whether the productivity-enhancing potentials of computerized conferencing are realized within a particular online community depends upon whether that community can adapt a mode of operation that increases its flow of useful information rather than burying it in an overload of irrelevant or trivial communications. This in turn depends upon whether they achieve a combination of social organization and software tools that prevents information overload.

Peter and Trudy Johnson-Lenz have written about means of structuring computer-mediated communication as "groupware." They assert that:

> For a group to use a computerized conferencing system effectively, it must have a set of explicit procedures to follow, which include the goals and tasks, who can communicate with whom and when, how decisions are made and disagreements resolved, and the sequence of activities to be followed... The most effective use of the medium occurs when a group uses processes and procedures specifically designed to meet its needs, plus software which supports and facilitates those procedures. The group process without computer support may be inefficient and cumbersome. Software without a group which can make effective use of it is a wasted resource.... This union of group process and software support we call groupware. (selection from Kerr and Hiltz, 1982: 46-47).

There are thus two main varieties of "structure." First, group interaction processes and procedures may be ordered by agreement on norms and roles. The computer may be used to help generate or support such norms or roles, but norms depend upon the group members for acceptance and enactment. Second, software support may be used to play an active part in the communication. The computer can regulate the flow of communications by, for instance, disallowing private messages among group members, so that all communications are visible to the entire group; enforcing the use of pen names or anonymity; or analyzing and displaying data or responses to surveys or votes.

NORMS FOR EFFECTIVE NETWORKING

Whenever a new technology emerges, a set of social beliefs and expected behavior in relation to that technology also evolves. The problem is that there is a period of "cultural lag" or disjunction when people struggle with how to use the technology without having integrated it into their culture by developing a set of normative and role expectations to regulate behavior which is related to the new technology. For instance, Kiesler, Siegel and McGuire assert that

> Although computer professionals have used electronic communication for over two decades, and they make up a subculture whose norms influence computer users and electronic communication... no strong etiquette as yet applies to how electronic communication should be used...There are few shared standards for salutations, for structuring formal versus informal messages, and for adapting content to achieve both impact and politeness (1984: 1125-1126).

Kiesler and her colleagues may have come to this conclusion from observing what might be termed a "socially immature" network: users who were relatively new to the technology and who did not have a pre-existing social structure to provide them with behavioral expectations toward one another. When a group has interacted for a

long   period of time (e.g., months or at least weeks), they develop a
set of understandings about what kinds of behavior on the network
will be effective in terms of allowing the technology to increase
rather than decrease their ability to work together productively.

New norms do evolve and are now frequently published as part of user
manuals or as stored online material for new users. The most
comprehensive I have seen is 240 lines of "netiquette" for USENET,
which runs on unix-based machines. Typical of the free-flowing
information of the networked world, this was passed to me by a
microcomputer user who downloaded it and then uploaded it to one of
the networks I use... and its original author has been lost in the
process.

> ### Excerpts from "Emily Post for Usenet"
>
> Usenet is a large, amorphous collection of machines (100s)
> and people (1000s)... The kinds of interaction that   occur
> in USENET are new to almost everyone... It takes aspects
> of formal and informal communications, and combines them in
> a new way. Use is enhanced when people follow the emerging
> "net etiquette." Users at new sites (those at which USENET
> has been available for less than 3 months) should be
> especially cautious until they have adjusted to this new
> form of communication.
>
> The following list of suggestions is long, but I plead with
> you to read it before submitting items.
>
> 1.   Try to find the appropriate group for any submission. .
> .
>
> 4.   Take   care   in   preparing   items.   While USENET
> interactions   sometimes   take   on   the   flavor of casual
> conversation, you should spend the time and effort to make
> your item readable and pertinent. That includes proper
> spelling and good grammar. And be sure you have something
> new to say. In particular, be sure you have understood
> earlier items. If you are in doubt
>
> about an author's intent, carry on a private interaction...
>
> 7.   Don't be rude or abusive...
>
> 8.   Be careful about sarcasm and facetious remarks.
> Without the voice inflection and body language of personal
> communication these are easily misinterpreted...
>
> 9.   Titles should be descriptive so that readers can decide
> whether to read or skip items based on the title.

For another example of norms made explicit, see the section on "Ethics and Conventions" in the COM manual (Palme and Albertsson, 1983: 33-34).

The social processes underlying effective computer-mediated communication can perhaps best be studied in controlled experiments rather than in field applications. The two main locations for formal experiments have been NJIT and Carnegie-Mellon (under the leadership of Sara Kiesler). Small group communication experimental results to date are summarized well in Rice (1984).

SOFTWARE FOR STRUCTURING HUMAN COMMUNICATION VIA COMPUTER: THE CASE OF INFORMATION OVERLOAD

"Information overload" or "communication overload" occurs when a CMCS makes available more communications than one can possibly read on a daily basis, let alone respond to. A variety of software options can help users to cope with the potential of information overload resulting from computer-mediated communication systems. These include segmentation of communication topics via a conference structure, length limitations, voting structures, and a variety of mechanisms to filter and organize information. Encouragement of the emergence of an online social system, with norms and sanctions about considerate communications behavior, is of course also important for preventing "junk mail" and similar impositions of unwanted material on users of these systems. A few of the software structures that have been employed to help users to deal with "information overload" are described below. (See Hiltz and Turoff, 1985, for a more complete discussion.)

Segmentation Via a Conference Structure

In a message system, communications from all sources and on all topics tend to get mixed together indiscriminantly. By segmenting communications exchange into topic-oriented discussion spaces with members who may join and leave as their interests change, we make a quantum leap in both screening capabilities and the probability of the emergence of online social groups with strong norms.

A conference is simply a topic-oriented discussion or information exchange space. An individual can belong to as many conferences as he or she chooses, each focused on a different subject or task, and each with self-selected memberships of people who are interested in following that discussion. All of the communications on a specific task or subject are collected together in one space, and the member chooses whether, when and how to receive them. For instance, automatic routines may be set to pick up the full text of all new items in a conference of high interest, but to select only the header lines of new items in other conferences. Unlike "distribution lists" in many electronic mail systems, it is the receiver, rather than the sender, who decides when and if he or she wishes to receive the communications on the topic.

When conferences exist, discussions assume some shape and continuity and social order. There is often social pressure exerted to encourage members of the network to put everything except urgent or personal communications into the conferences, so that members of the online groups do not become inundated with waiting messages on subjects with which they have no interest in dealing on a priority basis. Members also let one another know when entries seem completely "off the subject" of a conference.

Conferences may provide further segmentation internally. For instance, the PARTIcipate system has a tree-like structure in which new "subconferences" or subtopics are continuously branching off; the member decides whether or not to join each of these sub-conferences, depending on whether he or she is interested in that particular aspect of the topic.

Filtering and Scanning Features

David Morris, one of the principal designers of IBM's internal conferencing system, EQUAL, asserts that "An effective method of presenting each user with an overview of what is available and letting them pick what is of interest to pursue further is the single most important capability a CMCS can provide" (personal communication). Some systems allow users to scan limited portions of a conference or other pending communications to extract cues about their contents, and then decide whether or how much of each item to retrieve. For instance, EIES includes key words for each item and PARTICIPATE includes an "About" line in the header. On the COM system, a user can set a "scan" command to print out only the first N lines of pending items. One can then immediately give the command "read the rest" in order to read the rest of the entry which has just been scanned, or "mark" the item for later reading; later on you can ask for all the entries which you have "marked" (Palme and Albertson 1983).

Conferences can "organize themselves" with the cooperation of users who take advantage of key words and associations to other items. A reader can use search and retrieval functions to extract only those items of interest by asking for items with a particular key, or a series of items which are associated with one another as a kind of sub-topic or discussion thread in a conference. Automatic indexing routines can then be used on this information to produce an outline of the conference.

Just as software and user behavior conventions in combination may be used to filter communications by topic, filters by author are also possible with software designed for this purpose. If a particular person has been sending you "junk," you can have any future messages from that person automatically rejected without you even being bothered with a notification. The real problem here is not the software, but the social etiquette of how to word the notification to the would-be sender. Probably something like "Sorry, you do not have the privilege of sending messages to (name)" will come into vogue. On one conferencing system built in Canada, there were problems with anonymous messages of an unpleasant type being sent to some of the female members. Software was implemented so that a recipient could give a command that blocked that person from ever sending an anonymous message to him or her again, without blocking the possibility of sending a signed message.

Communications may take the form of an abstract, with additional pages of information or explanation delivered only if requested by the recipient. The delivery of a short item to another user becomes an access key to the receivers which they can use to trigger the retrieval of the longer item. On EIES this is accomplished with the +SUBMIT and the +READ commands. EIES text can contain programs as well as text. The "+submit" command takes the author through a program that allows the creation of a text item that carries the writer's privileges to access a specific longer item that may be in a normally private file. The receiver triggers the program by executing the "+READ" command.

Length Limitations

The length of individual items may be severely limited in order to force people to make their communications concise. Different lengths may be suitable for different functions and different groups.

The extreme in length limitations was probably achieved by a large group (about 75 members) of legislative science advisors and their resource persons on EIES, who decided to create a TOPICS system which limited the length of items that could be broadcast to the entire group, called "Inquiries," to only three lines. The group itself discussed and agreed upon this limitation before the software was implemented to impose it. Recipients had to actively "select" an inquiry to access the often voluminous material associated with it.

Survey and Voting Structures

With the use of numerical responses rather than text, many more people can exchange information in a more concise and precise way. The computer can be used to average, analyze, and display the results of the inputs of all group members on an issue. The PARTICIPATE system refers to this capability as "dialogue balloting," which is explained as "polling not to elect nor to sample but to facilitate participation" (Stevens, 1981). Such voting procedures can take the form of scales which indicate, for instance, degree of agreement with a statement or proposal on a one-to-five or one-to-ten basis; numerical estimates of items such as the proportion of a budget which should be devoted to research and development or advertising; or rank-ordering of alternatives.

Leaders or Moderators

When activity is segmented into topic-oriented conferences, software support can be provided for leadership or information management functions related to that specific activity. For instance, conference leaders are called "coordinators" on COM and "moderators" on EIES. Our controlled experiments with problem-solving discussions have demonstrated that a designated human leader for a computerized conference can be helpful in enabling a group to accomplish its task (Hiltz, Johnson, and Turoff, 1982). Software supports may empower a leader or moderator to edit items or keywords for clarity, or to delete or move items which are inappropriate or out of date. More importantly, a specified leadership role usually involves acceptance of organizing suggestions by that person, which serves to decrease the amount of irrelevant communications.

Evaluation Challenges

There are thousands of combinations of behavioral guidelines for participants, software mechanisms, and moderator actions which can be used in CMCS. Analysis of the comparative process and outcome of different system design choices within varying organizational contexts provides a rich area for future research. At the same time, CMCS offers some unique methodolgical tools and resources for the study of human communication (Kerr and Hiltz, 1982; Rice, 1984; Kiesler, Siegel and McGuire, 1984).

MODES OF TELECONFERENCING

Teleconferencing can be defined as interactive communication among three or more participants at two or more sites, mediated by telecommunications technology. (If we eliminate the latter requirement , note that American Indians using smoke signals teleconferenced).

> It comes in four modes (computer, audio, audiographic, and
> video) and a bewildering array of possible configurations
> within each of the modes... Depending on the choices the
> organization makes with respect to mode and facility
> configurations, teleconferecning will vary on important
> attributes such as utility, accessibility, convenience,
> ease of learning, and ease of use (Svenning and Ruchinskas,
> 1984:219).

It is unfortunate that organizations seem to think that they have to make one choice and stick with it for all remote meetings. In fact a mix of media options (including such non-teleconferencing modes as face-to face meetings and mailed documents) might be the optimal solution for most groups and organizations.

Audio-only teleconferencing can be as simple as using two speakerphones to allow multiple participants in an ordinary telephone conversation at two sites. However, this apparently inexpensive and easy solution is generally very disappointing. The audio quality sounds poor, there is a "line-grabbing" or voice-switching phenomenon that occurs when two or more speakerphones are used simultaneously, and other equipment in the vicinity can set up feedback loops and cause most unpleasant wailing sounds. As Johansen (1984:6) points out:

> One surprise for most new users is that audio presents the
> most technical difficulties of any component-- even in a
> video conferencing facility-- for reasons of acoustical
> engineering... The acceptable range in video quality is
> usually much broader than that of audio. Slightly fuzzy
> pictures of participants or less crisp letters in
> viewgraphs will not destroy a meeting. But the inability to
> hear clearly what is being said will.

One can also use the call-transfer feature of modern telephone switching equipment to add a third person to the basic two-party call; once again, this "simple" solution often degrades audio quality. More sophisticated, higher-quality and thus much more acceptable and effective systems include special conference rooms with microphones and acoustics designed for this function, or having everyone call a central conferencing number (a "meet-me bridge") at a specified time. The dynamics are very different than those in either a face-to-face meeting or a two-person telephone call, however, and effective audio conferences require training and self-discipline of participants and a skilled moderator.

Audiographic systems use one or more additional telephone lines to transmit a visual signal. For example, facsimile machines may transmit copies of a document in as little as ten seconds per page, depending on the price and thus speed of the machines; telewriting devices such as the AT&T "electronic blackboard" may transmit newly created material; computer displays or remotely controlled slide projectors may transmit images of three-dimensional objects; and slow-scan/freeze frame video can give "snapshot" images of most of these, refreshed every 10 to 60 seconds. However, note that all this special audiographic equipment means that there must be a fixed conferencing room set up for each site and that each room must have completely compatible equipment; thus audiographic meetings must be planned rather than spontaneous.

Video teleconferencing provides moving images for multi-location meetings; it requires both the most expensive equipment and the largest "bandwidth" requirement for transmission, which makes it expensive on a per-hour basis. It is probably as a consequence of this expense that it is the least used. There are two main subsets of video-conferencing. Point-multipoint uses a one-way video from the originating site and audio-only feedback from the receiving sites; it is essentially a closed-circuit television broadcast. Fully interactive two-way video systems allow two locations to both see and hear one another. Most systems use a small tv-sized screen at the two sites, so that the images are not anywhere near "life-size." One notable exception is the inhouse ARCO-VISION system, which uses a semi-circular screen facing a semi-circular table with six participant chairs; it provides life-sized projections and gives the feeling of really being "accross the table" from the group members at the other site.

Because of the very high cost of installing such a special video-conferencing room at each office location, many organizations would probably rather rent the use of publically available video-conferencing rooms. However, the only widely available system in the U.S. is AT&T's "Picturephone Meeting System." It is a voice-switched system. This means that rather than showing the entire group on the screen at all times ("continuous presence"), the camera switches to show just the person speaking. Evaluation research shows that users prefer the continuous presence version of videoconferencing, which feels much more like a meeting (Svenning and Ruchinskas, 1984: 222-224).

Fulk and Dutton (1984) report favorable results for two exploratory case studies of the organizational uses of video teleconferencing for business meetings. Among their tentative conclusions are that video meetings are more efficient than face-to-face meetings because they are more task-oriented. They also note that the medium changes organizational communication patterns, by allowing the inclusion of more lower-level participants at each site than would have been flown to a face-to-face meeting. Overall, it produces a "complex pattern of lines accross nodes" of the organization, including both hierarchical and horizontal links within and accross nodes (ibid., p. 117).

A number of studies have compared the effectiveness of the media for various kinds of tasks or communications, so that we can begin to know their relative strengths and weaknesses. These are summarized in the accompanying chart.

Audio, video, and computerized conferences can compete well with face-to-face conferences for such functions as exchanging information, exchanging opinions, giving and receiving "orders" (or assignments) and generating ideas. (See Hiltz and Turoff, 1978.) They are least satisfactory for "getting to know someone" and for resolving disagreements.

Computerized conferences are the only interactive medium in which participation can be asynchronous; each person can participate at the time and place she/he prefers, with the computer storing the waiting communications for each participant. One can also use the power of the computer to search, retrieve, and order the entries, and to add data bases and computational capabilities designed for the use of a group. Video conferences give the highest sense of "personal presence," next to actually "being there." Audio conferences can also give a sense of immediacy and of social contact, and are fairly simple to arrange and learn to use. Graphics capabilities added to audio-conferencing can greatly expand the number and types of meetings for which the audio mode can be effective.

Each of the media also has weaknesses. Video conferences are very expensive and require students to come to central locations. Video conferences, in addition to their high cost, often suffer from the

"Hollywood syndrome": self-conscious participants are more concerned with how they look on camera than with the topic of the meeting (Johansen, Vallee, and Spangler, 1979: 147). Most importantly, the increased costs do not seem to provide any appreciable increase in effectiveness as compared to audio or computerized conferences. There is also a problem with misleading or absent non-verbal cues, which can create misunderstandings and mis-cuing during the group interaction. Eye gaze is absent or misleading, gestures and facial expression lost or hard to see on the small screen.

In audio conferences among large groups, it is difficult to provide cues for turn-taking, so that people don't try to talk at the same time, or conversely, leave large gaps of silence politely waiting for one another to speak. In computer conferences, initial passivity – reading what others say without writing anything yourself – seems to be a problem. The audiographic systems are limited and contain often frustrating gadgets. For example, the "electronic blackboard" is blackboard-sized only at the sending end; the receiving end is a receive-only CRT. In order to send back an addition to a drawing or list, the receiving end would have to have a duplicate set of equipment; and re-draw the received material before adding to it. In trying to get a lot of different pieces of equipment working in a synchronized manner and watching what comes out of them, the group members tend to get diverted from interacting with one another and focused on the equipment instead.

Finally, all of the teleconferencing systems except for computerized conferencing tend to involve several persons at one site, and another sub-group at another site. This tends to create a we-they dynamics or splitting of the group (Short, Williams, and Christie, 1976).

CONCLUSION: THE PROGNOSIS

If one were to purchase a computer terminal or microcomputer just for participating in computerised conferencing, then the amortised per-hour cost for this form of communication would seem high. Moreover, familiarity with a keyboard is a precondition to comfortable interaction via computer and this seems like a formidable barrier to those who have never before used a computer. These conditions are now changing as information workers are acquiring microcomputers on their desks both in the office and at home. Once the equipment is within arm's reach and familiar, communicating via computer will seem like the most convenient and cheapest way to link together a dispersed group. We will see a great deal more use of the computer for human communication. Not only will it be used for computer conferences and computer based message systems, but it will also be used to provide graphics displays for audio and face-to-face meetings, and for "voice mail."

Applications of computer-mediated communication systems are liable to run ahead of evaluation research in the next decade. There is currently indeed an "avalanche" of new product announcements in both microcomputer hardware and in software to support computer-mediated communication. It will take considerable time for the marketplace to sort itself out and for user organizations to develop norms about how to employ the technologies effectively. One problem is that the very simple mail or conferencing systems which appeal to new users often become inadequate for handling a great deal of communication within a large group or organization, but people are reluctant to start over again with a different CMCS once they have become comfortable with a particular system. We can expect many failed implementations as well as many "success stories" and permanent adoptions of teleconferencing technology in the next decade. The failures will include not only systems which are rejected by prospective users, but also systems which are used heavily but produce negative impacts which do serious damage to the organizations which come to depend upon them.

Just as it is difficult to get the results of an experiment published when there is a finding of "no difference" between experimental and control conditions, it is too rare that we see full reports and analysis of failed implementations of teleconferencing. (A notable exception is Morris and Martin-Vegue, 1980. See also the analysis of differences between the most successful and least successful groups using EIES in Hiltz, 1984; and the extensive analysis of potential problems with missing social-emotional cues in computer-mediated communication in Kiesler et.al., 1984).

The systems which emerge as the standard inhouse organizational communication utilities are likely to represent new hybrids of communication and information systems, and a blending of some of the now-distinct modes of text, data, graphics, and voice. We are also likely to see more examples of groups making a judicious mix of face-to-face meetings, audio conferences, and computer-mediated communication to support cooperative work.

REFERENCES

Fulk, J. and Dutton, W. (1984). Videoconferencing as an organizational information system: Assessing the role of electronic meetings. Systems, Objectives, Solutions, 4: 105-118.

Galbraith, J. (1977). Organization Design. Reading, MA: Addison Wesley.

Hiltz, S.R. (1984). Online Communities: A Case Study of the Office of the Future. Norwood NJ: Ablex.

Hiltz, S.R., Johnson, K., and Turoff, M. (1982) The effects of formal human leadership and computer-generated decision aids on problem solving via computer: A controlled experiment. Newark, N.J., Computerized Conferencing and Communications Center, Res. Rep. 18.

Hiltz, S.R. and Turoff, M. (1978). The Network Nation: Human Communication via Computer. Reading, Mass.: Addison Wesley.

Hiltz, S.R. and Turoff, M. (1985). Structuring computer-mediated communication systems to avoid information overload. Ms. submitted to Communications of the ACM.

Johansen, R. (1984). Teleconferencing and Beyond. New York: McGraw Hill.

Johansen, R., Vallee, J., and Spangler, K. (1979). Electronic Meetings: Technical Alternatives and Social Choices. Reading, Mass.: Addison Wesley.

Kerr, E.B. and Hiltz, S.R. (1982). Computer-Mediated Communication: Status and Evaluation. New York: Academic Press.

Kiesler, S., Siegel, J. and McGuire, T.W. (1984). Social psychological aspects of computer-mediated communication. American Psychologist 39,4:1123-1134.

Kiesler, S., Zubrow, D., Moses, A.M., and Geller, V. (1984). "Affect in computer-mediated communication: An experiment in synchronous terminal-to-terminal discussion." Pittsburgh, Pa.: Carnegie Mellon U., unpublished paper.

Lipinski, H., Spang, S., and Tydeman, J. (1980). Supporting task-focussed communication." In Communicating Information: Proceedings of the 43rd ASIS Annual Meeting (A.R. Benenfeld and K.J. Kazlauskas, eds.,) pp. 158-160. White Plains NY, Knowledge Industries.

Morris, A.J. and Martin-Vegue, C. (1980). "MRC-TV: A large-scale video teleconferencing system-- Anatomy of a Failure." Proceedings, Teleconferencing and Interactive Media, Madison, Wisc.: U. of Wisconsin Center for Interactive Programs, pp. 74-86.

Palme, J. (1984). "Survey of computer-based message systems and experience with the COM computer conference system. In Proceedings of the INTERACT '84 IFIP Conference on Human-Computer Interaction.

Palme, J. and Albertson, E. (1983). COM-Teleconferencing System-Advanced Manual. Stockholm University Computing Center.

Rice, R.E. & Associates (1984). The New Media: Communication, Research, and Technology. Beverly Hills: Sage.

Shackel, B., Pullinger, D.J., Maude, T.I., and Dodd, W.P. (1983). The BLEND-LINC project on `electronic journals' after two years. The Computer Journal, 26,3: 247-254.

Sharp, I.P., and Perkins, F.J. (1981). "The impact of effective person-to-person telecommunications on established management structures." Proc Conf Business Telecoms, 127-133.

Short, J., Williams, E., and Christie, B. (1976). The Social Psychology of Telecommunications. London: John Wiley & Sons.

Simon, H. (1973). "Applying information technology to organizational design." Public Administration Review, 33,3: 268-278.

Stevens, C.H. (1981). Many-to-many communication. Boston, Mass., Center for Information Systems Research, MIT, CISR No. 72.

Stockton, W. (1981, June 28). The technology race. New York Times Magazine, p. 14.

Svenning, L.L., and Ruchinskas, S. E. (1984). "Organizational teleconferencing," in Rice, 217-248.

Turoff, M. (1972). "`Party line' and `discussion' computerized conferencing systems." In Computer Communication-- Impacts and Implications," S. Winkler, ed. Proceedings of the International Conference on Computer Communication, Washington D.C., pp. 161-170.

Uhlig, R.P., Farber, D.J. and Bair, J.H. (1979). The Office of the Future: Communication and Computers. Amsterdam: North-Holland Publishing Co.

CHAPTER 47.

CURRENT TRENDS AND ISSUES IN LIBRARIANSHIP AND INFORMATION SCIENCE

DR. MAURICE B.LINE & SUE HOWLEY

The British Library Lending Division, Boston Spa, England.

Introduction

This chapter does not aim to be comprehensive either in range or in geographical coverage. In particular, it is concerned with advanced capitalist economies, not with socialist countries nor with the Third World; and within the Western world it concentrates on the United States and the United Kingdom. The selection of trends and issues, and the emphasis placed on each, reflect the experience and the views of the authors.

"Trends" are defined simply as the way things are going. "Issues" are matters of concern or debate. Some trends are also issues. Not all of the trends and issues have received much attention in the literature, but a selection of relevant references is appended.

The views of the authors, both members of the staff of the British Library, do not necessarily represent those of the British Library.

Economic trends

In nearly all countries with capitalist economies there
has been a recession of varying degrees of seriousness
for the last eight or nine years, and the general trend
is still downwards. The effects are felt by all types
of library, whether funded from public or private
sources.

Libraries have reacted to economic constraints in
different ways. Academic libraries tended first to cut
book acquisitions until it became clear that their
entire acquisition budget would soon be spent on
journals. Public libraries have had a wider range of
choices: reducing opening hours, cutting services back,
eliminating whole activities (such as audiovisual
departments), and sometimes reducing materials
expenditure to very low levels. Some academic and
public libraries have implemented or extended charging
for various services - of which more later. Some
industries have contracted out the entire
library/information service to a private broker, or
have reduced it to a minimal unit - in both cases
placing greatly increased reliance on external sources
of material; some libraries have disappeared entirely
with the firms they serve.

Reductions in capital expenditure have meant that many
fewer libraries have been able to move into new
buildings or expand existing ones, and although in the
UK a report by the University Grants Committee

suggesting radical solutions was vehemently rejected by university librarians, the problem of inadequate space remains. Obvious alternatives are weeding, practised regularly in most public libraries but only to a much smaller extent in academic libraries; conversion to more compact forms such as microform, which is generally far too expensive unless microforms can be bought commercially; and low-use stores separate from the main building, possibly shared with other libraries, though a trend towards shared storage that could be detected 20 or so years ago seems to have been halted by a realization that the problems and costs of sharing tend to be greater than the benefits.

Responses to reduced resources

Reductions in resources have led to more general effects. One has been an increased emphasis on the optimal use of resources. Performance measurement is one key element in this, in particular output measures of a more sophisticated kind than numbers of books issued or readers visiting the library. Efforts have been made to determine optimal journal collections - both current subscriptions and retention, including binding policies - whether by conducting local use studies or using external data, including citation data. Efforts have similarly been made to calculate the optimal balance between availability on the premises and from external sources (interlibrary loan). Optimization of journal purchase is difficult, because of the data that need to be collected and analysed;

optimization of book purchase is almost impossible, since use is largely a function of the collection and so cannot serve as a guide to what the collection should be. Weeding is simpler both in principle and in practice, so long as there is an alternative source from which discarded books can be obtained.

Increased effort has also been put into costing library operations, in terms of both service costs and unit costs. Such figures are of much more value if they are carried out over a number of years, or if comparisons can be made with other libraries. Interlibrary comparisons have been carried out in both public and academic libraries in the UK, but the costs, particularly in staff time, of conducting such studies regularly are likely to make such comparative studies infrequent. Studies of this kind can serve as a partial guide to resource allocation within a given library, though of course they reveal nothing about the value of each service, nor even the value placed on it by users. Assessments of relative value can be carried out, but once again they are so difficult and costly that they are likely to be few. There is nevertheless a greatly increased awareness on the part of librarians, many more of whom must be doing automatic, perhaps semi-conscious, cost-effectiveness calculations as part of their regular thinking.

The provision and supply of materials

One conspicuous trend in the last forty years has been

increased use of external sources (the term 'interlibrary lending' is no longer adequate or accurate). In some countries the volume of demand on remote sources increased by a factor of four in twenty years, the rate of growth being affected more by the supply system than by demand and the ability of local libraries to supply. Even when libraries had sufficient money to keep up with the growth and cost of publications, greatly increased numbers of users, particularly in academic libraries, combined with a much greater exposure to references through on-line bibliographic databases, led to a growth in remote demand.

The pattern of more recent years, when local funds have not kept pace with the cost and growth in publications, is more complex. A greater need to rely on remote sources has been accompanied by a need or temptation to reduce costs by restraining extra-library demand. In the last four or five years remote demands have tended to decline, though one reason for this has been the reduction in the number of users in many academic institutions as staff and research have shrunk.

In many countries serious efforts have been made to improve interlibrary access. The most obvious way to do this has been by the development of automated union catalogues, preferably with both input and access on-line. This can greatly speed up notification of new entries to the catalogue and their incorporation in them, consultation of the catalogue, and, in more

advanced systems, requesting and switching of requests
between sources of supply.   Much the largest catalogue
of this kind is the one developed by OCLC, initially as
a bibliographic database (see below), but increasingly
as an interlibrary access tool.   The Research Libraries
Group (RLG) has another very large automated union
catalogue.   There is none on this scale in Europe,
though several European countries either have automated
union catalogues already or plan to have them soon.

Automated union catalogues do not in themselves improve
provision: access to external resources cannot be
effective unless the resources are there.   Some efforts
have been made to plan provision.   There are a few
examples in the world of centralized national document
centres, much the largest being the British Library
Lending Division.   This has been studied by several
countries, including the United States, as a possible
model, but has been either deliberately rejected as a
matter of policy or not implemented for financial or
operational reasons.   Two trends can now be detected:
dependence on existing resources, without any
deliberate national planning, as in the United States,
where there are so many and such large libraries that
such dependence is possible; and designation of
selected libraries as subject specialist collections,
following the example of the Federal Republic of
Germany.   Subject specialization is being planned with
more or less determination in nearly all the
Scandinavian countries.   France plans a combination of
central and subject specialist supply.

With the growth of interlibrary supply, more libraries have found, or felt, it necessary to put it on an economic basis. Charging is by no means universal, but it may well become so as it is recognized that a major and intrinsic element in library provision cannot be simply a grace and favour operation.

National acquisition plans do not exist in most countries, but a great deal of attention has been given to 'resource sharing'. This rather vague term can include dependence on a central resource, as in the UK; access to existing holdings, as in ordinary interlending; and deliberate attempts on the part of groups of libraries to optimize their acquisitions or holdings and so to extend (or prevent the reduction of) total provision. Unfortunately, the extensive literature on resource sharing contains very few real success stories. There are at least two reasons for this. The logistics of resource sharing are inevitably rather complex: libraries have to find out what other libraries already have or are planning to buy, and then decide who is to have what, and there also has to be a list of desiderata which are of interest to more than one library. Secondly, when libraries are short of funds, they cannot be expected to buy literature that may be wanted by remote libraries at the expense of locally needed material. Given several libraries of a similar type, the tighter their funds become the more similar their acquisitions are likely to be, since their 'core' collections will be much more similar than their collections of 'fringe' material.

The question also arises whether there is any real
benefit in cooperation with neighbouring libraries
compared with obtaining materials from anywhere in the
country, whether a single centre or a very large number
of libraries as in the OCLC system. There are obvious
advantages in very close proximity, which enables a
book to be collected and consulted the same day, and
the most successful resource sharing schemes may be
local rather than regional. Efforts in the UK to
collect harder information on the costs and benefits of
resource sharing of various kinds have so far yielded
little more guidance to future policy than a simple
paper analysis of the issue would provide. There is
however an increasing use of networks, often based on
microcomputers, to facilitate local cooperation, and
this may make it more attractive.

Another disappointing area is telefacsimile
transmission of documents. Machines and communications
are still relatively slow, and also expensive, in staff
time as well as other costs. There are no signs that
facsimile transmission will become a general method of
supply; rather, it will be used for particularly urgent
requests, and it may gradually be superseded by
transmission of electronically stored text, possibly by
satellite.

Document supply may be changed radically in the future
by electronic storage and transmission and an
increasing involvement of the private sector. These
issues are discussed below.

Bibliographic databases

One of the most widespread developments of recent years
has been the automation of library catalogues. At one
time it seemed as if the computer would be used mainly
to produce computer output microfilm (COM) catalogues,
but it now appears that these were an intermediate
phase between card catalogues and On-Line Public Access
Catalogues (OPACs). Fears that users would resist them
seem to have been exaggerated; indeed, younger
generations tend to prefer them, since many of them
have become familiar with computers at school and at
home.

Parallel with the trend to automate local catalogues
has been a trend towards obtaining catalogue records
from databases, whether specially created by national
centres or constructed by library cooperatives. Two
basic questions are unresolved: the length and nature
of catalogue entries that local libraries need, and,
connected with this, the relative cost-effectiveness of
constructing independent local entries and obtaining
entries from a remote database. In spite of research
that seems to show clearly that a short record is
adequate for nearly all libraries, the tendency of
academic libraries is still to prefer longer entries,
sometimes approaching full MARC entries, and this is
one factor that has led them to obtain their records
from elsewhere. Bibliographic databases are therefore
flourishing, in spite of occasional crises such as
RLG's Research Libraries Information Network (RLIN) has

experienced. There are likely to be, if not mergers, direct links between databases so that membership of one system gives access to others also. A further trend is to make database operation fully commercial (though not generally profit-making).

Another issue is whether the same file should serve the purposes of cataloguing and interlibrary access. The answer probably depends on the interlending system of the country in question. Where there is a central document supply facility there is less case for having a single file serve both purposes, though there is nothing to prevent libraries from using a catalogue file for interlibrary access if it has the locations of holding libraries on it, as has happened with the OCLC system.

Bibliographic databases may serve another function, that of information retrieval. Monograph databases are nearly all national, and offer much poorer subject access than the large machine-readable databases in science, which cover mainly journal literature, and are international in scope. Subject access to books is being increasingly recognized as in need of major improvement, and of much more interest to users than bibliographic details, but there are formidable obstacles - of cost, of the market, and of language.

Conservation

Conservation has always been a matter of concern to

librarians of valuable book collections, but interest in it has become rather more widespread in the last few years. Research libraries have realized that their holdings were decaying as fast as they were being added to, and that if drastic action were not taken many or most records of the past would disappear, sooner rather than later. The British Library, whose Reference Division Library now spends about as much each year on conservation as it does on new acquisitions, has set up a National Preservation Office, while the Library of Congress and the National Library of Canada have extensive conservation programmes. Techniques for deacidification of paper and protection for the future have been known for some time; the problem has been devising a system that can cope with books on a large enough scale to be really worthwhile. Even the mass deacidification systems being used by the Library of Congress cannot cope with more than a few thousand books a year.

In the last resort a decision will have to be made as to which books to preserve in their pristine state, which to preserve in another form, whether microform, optical digital disc or whatever, and which to destroy or leave to deteriorate into a state that is unusable. These basic issues still have to be faced squarely.

Private sector involvement and the economics of information provision

There has always been a huge private sector involvement

in information supply. The materials that libraries
buy are bought mostly from the private sector, and most
reading material is sold commercially to individuals.
In addition, huge quantities of financial and
commercial information are sold privately. The
information supplied by libraries, whether actively as
information services or passively as book collections,
forms only a tiny proportion of total information
transfer of printed text. Nevertheless, small though
the fraction may be in quantity, it has been very
important, partly because libraries have been the main
source of academic or professional reading material to
academic and special library users, partly because only
in libraries can wide ranges of reading material be
made accessible to (potentially) everyone. Publicly
funded libraries have served to equalize access to
information, and their services have presumably been
regarded as a public good like free art galleries,
museums or parks.

Publishers have been content with this because
libraries constitute the main market for many of their
products especially academic books and journals.
Whereas however they are happy to sell their material
to libraries, and content for it to be consulted or
borrowed, they are much less happy that it should be
photocopied without some recompense to them. Their
concern echoes that of authors of books, at least until
they were entitled to receive some payment for the
library loans of their books after the establishment of
Public Lending Right in the UK.

It is now being asked whether the private sector may have something to gain from carrying out at least some of the information activities commonly associated with libraries. One obvious activity is the information service many public libraries offer to local industries. Information brokers may offer such a service, including bibliographic searches and document supply. This example raises several of the issues involved. In the first place, the information broker has to charge and the public library normally does not; it may therefore be in unfair competition. If on the other hand the public library does charge, it may be breaking a more fundamental principle of free service; and its basis of charging may not be comparable with that of the information broker. On the other hand, the information broker has to obtain his materials somewhere, and for this he almost certainly uses a free library service (even if a public library might wish to charge an information broker in principle, in practice it could hardly distinguish him from other users). The issue becomes quite involved, both in economic and ethical terms.

More fundamentally, if publishers can supply, direct or through a commercial intermediary, literature to users, they can bypass libraries entirely. The reason they do not do this at present is because the 'packages' in which the literature is published (mainly journals) are too large to make it economic. If however, as is often the case, users only want an article from a journal or an excerpt from a book, possibly a reference work, the ability to bypass libraries could be beneficial to publishers. The capacity to do this is provided by electronic storage and transmission, whereby material is held in machine-readable form and made available on demand, whether printed out at source and provided as a hard copy or supplied on-line.

Such considerations have been behind recent efforts to achieve so-called 'electronic publishing'. One of the most widely known projects has been the ADONIS project developed by a consortium of major journal publishers, in consultation with the British Library Lending Division. The concept involves electronic data capture from printed text, conversion to optical digital disc, automatic scanning and printing out on demand, and supply of hard copies. Even this limited concept has so far proved difficult to realize, largely because of the large material investment required. While there is a substantial market for electronic transmission of the printed word, scientific and technical literature constitutes only a small fraction of it, and if a solution is found it is likely to involve shared use of facilities.

For shorter articles, 'newsletter'-type items, and 'popular' magazines, electronic storage and transmission is already with us, but it is not known how much use is being made of these files, and in any case they are too new for the figures to mean very much. Most of them are available also in printed form, and it remains to be seen whether there is a double

market, one for the printed version and one for the
electronic one.

A number of experiments involving electronic storage
and transmission are being carried out under the
auspices of the Commission of the European Communities.
Some of these are on a small scale, but schemes like
the APOLLO one of satellite transmission of documents
have much wider implications, particularly as initial
studies suggest that if they generate enough use the
total costs involved may compare favourably with
traditional transmission, while the speed of
transmission will of course be much greater.

The future system to which we seem to be moving is one
where many 'information units' (selected journal
articles) are not sold as printed packages, to be used
subsequently by any library user, but supplied on the
basis of payment for each use. This need not rule out
the involvement of libraries, but libraries would have
to pay for every use made, and this would raise the
same kind of issues as on-line searching of
bibliographic databases has done in the past, but on a
much larger scale. It could also have undesirable
consequences for scholarly publication: it would reveal
sharply for the first time how much, or how little,
many or most articles were used, and the result of this
might be that many articles that make some contribution
to knowledge but have only a small 'market' might
either not be published at all, or be relegated to a
kind of dump supported by the scholarly community on a

non-commercial basis.

A matter that has received some attention lately is the archiving of electronic text. With a text that may be subject to frequent change, which version is archived, where, in what form, and on what terms? How can it be ensured that some appropriate record is kept for future generations? And what sort of bibliographic control is appropriate for such material? The main questions have been identified, but not the answers, which can only be found by close cooperation between publishers, librarians, and possibly database hosts.

Meanwhile efforts are still being made by publishers to obtain payment for photocopies made by libraries. Publishers maintain, though they have not been able to prove, that their sales are damaged by photocopying, and that in any case they should be paid for what they consider to be 'republishing' in order to keep journals going. Libraries maintain that if copying fees had to be paid they would buy fewer journals. Publishers claim a moral right to payment for use of their material, while librarians hold by the principle of free access by their users to the material they have paid for, particularly as they pay about twice as much as individual subscribers for many journals. Such legislation as has been passed seems to have helped very little. Under the recent US Copyright Act, provision is made for payment under certain conditions - conditions that the publishers say are not nearly stringent enough, and that librarians say are so rare as not to be worth legislating for. The Copyright Clearance Center has so far barely succeeded in covering its operating costs.

The public/private sector debate was given an impetus in the United States by a report of the National Commission on Libraries and Information Science on _Public/private sector interaction in providing information services_, and in the UK by the report _Making a business of information_ prepared by the Government's Information Technology Advisory Panel (ITAP). The NCLIS report dealt with the principles of public versus private sector involvement, particularly in so far as they affect the supply of information emanating from or published by the Government. The ITAP report, which states as one of its express purposes a redressing of the balance between information and technology by taking information more into account, develops the concept of information as a 'tradeable commodity', of economic importance in Britain's future. Neither report touches very closely and directly on libraries, but both have large implications, since they implicitly raise the whole question of what should be provided by publicly funded libraries and what should be provided by the private sector.

Many libraries are behaving in more commercial ways, as is evidenced by the growing literature on marketing of library services. There seems little doubt that librarians will have to give much closer attention to whether their functions compete or conflict with the private sector, and to the justification for a free or subsidized service. In practice many of them are tempted to impose charges to compensate for their diminished funds. Many academic libraries make at least a nominal charge to their users for on-line bibliographic searches, and in some cases for interlibrary supply, while public libraries often charge for the loan of sound recordings or videotapes though not for books - in the UK it is illegal to charge for the latter. Librarians will surely need to clarify the principles on which they charge for some services and not for others. There is a range of possibilities: to charge for some services and not for others, to charge different prices for different services, to charge some categories of user and not others, to charge nominal fees to discourage irresponsible use, to recover marginal costs, and so on. The fundamental questions are why, if services offered by libraries are so valuable, they should not be paid for; and whether, if no-one wants to pay, they are valuable. The 'public good' argument might have been sufficient answer 10 or 20 years ago, but there has been a big shift in thinking among many western Governments in recent years about social and public services of all kinds.

The public/private sector issue is likely to be a major one for some years. The outcome will be determined by various pressures, whether financial within libraries or political from Governments or competitive from private operators; but it will be a pity if at the same time the full moral, social, political and economic aspects of it are not explored.

Roles and functions of libraries

For some time, largely independently of the trends considered above, libraries have been tending to evolve from collections of books to providers of information - user-oriented rather than book-oriented. Now, not only reductions in funds but changes in technology and in the political and social climate are persuading librarians to look even more deeply at their role and functions.

The most basic traditional function of libraries, the provision of literature, is threatened as electronic storage and transmission develop. Electronic publishers have several choices: to bypass libraries entirely; to transmit material for on-line use in libraries; to permit downloading, so that a library can build up its own text database on agreed terms; and to sell electronic databases to libraries, presumably with strict limits on the exploitation of the database (eg no secondary downloading). Agreement between publishers and libraries is essential if libraries are not to see their role diminished.

Some academic libraries, particularly large research collections, still see their future as ever-growing collections of material, which it is up to users to exploit as best they can. At the other extreme, smaller libraries, particularly in technological institutions, may aim to be primarily information services, with an emphasis on current stock, weeding of outdated stock, a wide range of services, including bibliographic searches and personal assistance, and a fairly heavy reliance on external sources of documents.

Many academic libraries now provide instructional sound and video recordings. A more radical step is to provide computer-assisted instruction, whether in the library itself or by the provision and loan of discs for use with personal computers - which may themselves be borrowed from the library. With home computers and telecommunication links, it may not be necessary to borrow discs at all, since instruction programs can be accessed directly from remote sources. Such a system (developed by TeleSystems Inc, and called the Electronic University) is already in operation in the United States.

An academic institution offering a wide range of services, including access to bibliographic and text databases, instructional materials, and expert personal information assistance could reach a much wider community. The possibilities of 'distance learning' add another dimension. Since continuing education is likely to become much more important in the future, with rapid changes in the knowledge required for every highly skilled job, this role might become a very important one. It could also be a substantial revenue earner, and thus attract the interest of the private sector.

The effect of the electronic revolution, if such it is, on many industrial libraries could be their virtual demise, since it may be more cost-effective to have a switching centre with minimal staffing than to have any library/information unit as such. In industries with big research and development departments, however, it might be desirable to build up their own electronic text databases in a similar way to academic institutions, though on a smaller scale.

The role of public libraries has never been absolutely clear cut. Whether they should aim to serve primarily the middle classes, not only _de facto_ but as a deliberate act of policy (after all, they provide indirectly most of the funds), or whether they should aim to reach out to the wider community, particularly the disadvantaged, seems likely to be a major issue, partly because reduced resources may make a choice necessary. So does the balance between the educational, social and information functions of the public library. Insofar as any trend can be detected, it is in the direction of community services, but this is demonstrated by a few libraries moving strongly in that direction rather than by a general trend.

The possibilities and problems of diversification that face academic libraries are more acute with public libraries. Some of them have gone beyond the provision of books and sound and video recordings to computer tapes, jigsaw puzzles and even garden tools. They may do this as a means to the end of attracting readers or as an end in itself, in effect redefining the library as a recreation centre with a range of social, cultural and related activities, of which books form only a small part.

There are three major underlying and related trends. Unoccupied time (a more neutral term than unemployment or leisure) is already a serious problem in many developed countries. It can be used harmfully and destructively or creatively and profitably, and the library could have a significant role to play. At the same time, there will be an increasing need to keep up with changing knowledge and develop new skills for those in work, and here too libraries, public as well as academic, could play a part.

Secondly, the growing realization that much of the future of developed countries rests on their becoming efficient 'information societies' has led to action to accelerate research in information technology and develop industries that use it, but not so far to a recognition that libraries have any real part to play, let alone to any assistance to help them plan for a future role.

Thirdly, changes in the communication chain are beginning to be brought about by technology. The term 'publication' will need to be redefined, since it is possible to produce a master from which items can be made available on demand, a master moreover that can be modified and adapted frequently, so that there is no definitive version of a text. There need be no permanent physical product like paper. Booksellers may find themselves not only selling a wider range of materials (such as computer tapes and discs) but offering a wider range of services, some of them perhaps overlapping with those at present given by libraries. Libraries already produce for their users copies of material on demand, and with electronic media this activity could greatly increase. Full text intermediaries will undoubtedly develop on similar lines to bibliographic database hosts, and these could take over some of the present functions of booksellers and libraries. Information brokers will make use of various other sectors to repackage material to customers' specifications. A redistribution of the various activities involved is already visible. What place libraries will occupy is not yet clear. If the term 'librarianship' is still used in 10 or 20 years' time, it may mean something very different from what it has done in the past.

Professional education

Discussion of the roles and functions of libraries leads inevitably to the roles and functions of librarians. Professional education is increasingly seen as being in need of a radical overhaul. One fundamental question is what professions or activities people are being educated for - traditional librarianship, information work, or, more ambitiously, the whole spectrum of communication from publishing to readership? Librarianship has become an almost totally graduate profession, but can or should it pretend to be an academic discipline? If it cannot, is a first degree in it 'respectable'? And is a degree in librarianship in any case too narrow in view of shifting boundaries? An alternative might be a fundamental course in communication studies, with a high academic content, topped up by diplomas in more specific activities.

Knowledge is changing even more rapidly in the field of communications than in other fields. Information workers must be flexible - willing to change and able to change - and they must be kept educated with changing knowledge. They receive at present very little help in this; continuing education has been much debated, but in many countries it still consists mainly of occasional short courses. Practical pressures from users, institutions and information workers themselves must surely force changes in the balance between first and continuing education, but the inbuilt conservation of the education system is likely to make change a slow process.

National library and information policy and planning

Whether a country should have a national library/information policy, and if so what form should it take, has certainly been an issue in recent years. There are two main reasons for this: the reduction in library resources, leading to calls for some national plan to ensure their more effective use (and if possible their expansion); and recognition of the importance of information to the economies of developed countries, which are likely to depend far less on basic manufacturing than on higher level skills, which in turn depend on information. The role of the state is perceived differently in different countries. In the United States, the general policy is one of minimal interference, on the principle that the less the public sector is involved in information provision the more the private sector is likely to exploit it, to the benefit both of the private sector and of the country at large. In Europe, the tendency is still for librarians to press for more state involvement, sometimes to the extent of direct allocation of resources to particular libraries or groups of libraries, the designation and special funding of 'centres of excellence', and a permanent national body with a greater or lesser degree of control over libraries. With a powerful central body like the British Library, or systems of subject specialization as in the Federal Republic of Germany, quite effective national provision and supply can be achieved with little more involvement by the state than continued funding of the centres concerned; other libraries can determine their own acquisition and retention policies accordingly. In most countries, however, such conditions do not exist.

There is probably a general recognition that without some kind of national plan, however loose or informal, the library system will be less effective than it might otherwise be. In principle librarians can cooperate to formulate their own policy and fulfil it themselves; in practice, it is not so simple. More commonly, a body of librarians, perhaps in company with educationalists, industrialists, etc, have prepared policy documents which they have then put to the government. Bodies such as the Library and Information Services Council in the UK and the National Commission on Libraries and Information Science in the US exist in quite a few countries, but they have little power and often, it seems, not much direct influence except on the thinking of librarians.

<u>Summary</u>

Among the main trends that can be detected are:

    Reduced funding for libraries

    Increased dependence on external sources

    Increase in automation of operations and records

    Increasing shortage of accommodation

    Conservation

    Charging for services

    Involvement of the private sector in some aspects of information provision

    Electronic storage and transmission of text.

Some of these trends are independent of politics: automation, conservation, and perhaps electronic

publishing. Others are the direct effect of political
or economic decisions: reduced funding and shortage of
accommodation.   Others are the indirect consequences
of political and economic policies: increased
dependence on external resources, and charging for
services.

Major issues include:

    Private/public sector balance in information
    provision

    Role and function of libraries and information
    services

    Changing boundaries in the production,
    transmission and communication of information

    Economic justification for libraries

    Professional education.

SELECT REFERENCES

The references that follow are a small selection from a
very large list of writings pertinent to the theme of
the article.

Economic trends

Harris, Colin and Gilder, Lesley (eds) The academic
library in times of retrenchment. Proceedings of a
conference of the Library and Information Research
Group, 1982. London, Rossendale, 1983.

Responses to reduced resources

Steele, Colin (ed). Steady-state, zero growth and the academic library. London, Bingley, 1978.

Centre for Interfirm Comparison. Inter-library comparisons in academic libraries. Wetherby, British Library, 1984 (BL R&D Report 5763).

Centre for Interfirm Comparison. Inter-library comparisons: pilot comparison with public libraries. Wetherby, British Library, 1981 (BL R&D Report 5638).

Blagden, John (ed). Do we really need libraries? Proceedings of the first joint Library Association/Cranfield Institute of Technology conference on performance assessment. Cranfield, Cranfield Press, 1983.

The provision and supply of materials

Line, Maurice B. Resource sharing: the present situation and the likely effect of electronic technology, in Fjällbrant, Nancy (ed) The future of serials: publication, automation and management. Proceedings of the tenth meeting of IATUL, 1983. Goteborg, IATUL, 1984, p. 1-11.

Line, Maurice B. Provision of serials in a time of stringency, in UK Serials Group

Bibliographic databases

Collier, Mel. Centralization and after: a review of the prospects for distributed processing in libraries. <u>Aslib Proceedings</u>, 34(6/7), June/July 1982, 295-300.

De Gennaro, Richard. Library automation and networking: perspectives on three decades. <u>Library Journal</u>, 108(7), April 1, 1983, 629-635.

Seal, Alan and others. <u>Full and short entry catalogues: library needs and uses</u>. Bath University Library, 1982. (BL R&D Report 5669).

Williamson, Nancy J. Subject access in the on-line environment. <u>Advances in Librarianship</u>, 13, 1984, 50-98.

Conservation

Ratcliffe, F W. <u>Preservation policies and conservation in British libraries: report of the Cambridge University Conservation Project</u>. Wetherby, British Library, 1984 (Library and Information Research Report 25).

<u>Private sector involvement and the economics of information provision</u>

McDonald, Dennis D. Public sector/private sector interaction in information services. <u>Annual Review of Information Science and Technology</u>, 17, 1982, 83-98.

Cronin, Blaise and Martyn, John.   Public/private sector
interaction: a review of issues, with particular
reference to document delivery and electronic
publishing.   Aslib Proceedings, 36(10), October 1984,
373-391.

[US] National Commission on Libraries and Information
Science.   Public sector/private sector interaction in
providing information services.   Washington, DC, US
GPO, 1982.

[UK] Cabinet Office - Information Technology Advisory
Panel. Making a business of information.   London,
HMSO, 1983.

[UK] Office of Arts and Libraries - Working Group on
Electronic Publishing.   The impact of electronic
publishing.   Electronic Publishing Review, 3(4),
December 1983, 283-302.

Cornish, Graham P.   Copyright law, reprography and
interlending: a round-the-world survey.   Interlending
and Document Supply, 11(4), October 1983, 131-139.

Wall, R A and Lewis, D A.   Photocopying and copyright:
a status report.   Aslib Information, October 1984,
217-219.

Roles and functions of libraries

Durrance, Joan C.   Community information services - an innovation at the beginning of its second decade. Advances in Librarianship, 13, 1984, 100-128.

Lancaster, F W and others.   The changing face of the library: a look at libraries and librarians in the year 2001.   Collection Management, 3(1), Spring 1979, 55-77.

Boss, Richard W.   Technology and the modern library. Library Journal, 109(11), June 15, 1984, 1183-1189.

De Gennaro, Richard.   Libraries, technology, and the information marketplace.   Library Journal, 107(11), June 1, 1982, 1045-1054.

Neavill, Gordon B.   Electronic publishing, libraries, and the survival of information.   Library Resources and Technical Services, 28(1), January/March 1983, 76-89.

Oakeshott, Priscilla.   The impact of the new technology on the publication chain.   London, BNB Research Fund Committee, 1983.   (BNB RF Report 11).

Professional education

Cronin, Blaise.   Post-industrial society: some manpower implications for the library/information profession. Journal of Information Science, 7(1), August 1983, 1-14.

McGarry, Kevin. Education for librarianship and information science: a retrospect and a revaluation. <u>Journal of Documentation</u>, 39(2), June 1983, 95-122.

<u>National library and information policy and planning</u>

Rosenberg, Victor. National information policies. <u>Annual Review of Information Science and Technology</u>, 17, 1982, 3-32.

[UK] Library and Information Services Council. <u>The future development of libraries: working together within a national framework</u>. London, HMSO, 1982 (Library Information Series 12).

Higham, Norman. Information in national planning - a developing role. <u>Aslib Proceedings</u>, 36(3), March 1984, 136-143.

CHAPTER 48. EVERYDAY PROBLEMS IN AN INFORMATION SOCIETY

Eugene Garfield
Institute for Scientific Information, Philadelphia

The information-conscious and the information literate society

While I think society as a whole has become very information conscious, unfortunately it is not yet information-literate. An "information-literate" is a person who knows the techniques and skills for using information tools in molding solutions to problems.

When people in all parts of society have rapid access to the information they want, we can say that the information conscious society has become the information society. Reduction in the cost and size of computers will accelerate the process. Of course, developments will depend on the technology available commercially. As memory becomes cheaper, it might be more economical to duplicate rather than centrally to store certain kinds of information. With such duplication a centralized World Brain wouldn't be necessary at all. This kind of decentralization would prevent government or industry from obtaining a monopoly on the flow of information.

Once large numbers of people have computers at home, we can expect them to have a great impact on education. It may be possible for people to continue being educated until the day they die. Many people will no doubt become self-taught in many subjects before their old age although some educators are unimpressed by Computer Aided Education (CAI).

The physically handicapped or shut-ins stand to benefit greatly from developments such as home journals. They could receive information about books, magazines, or journal articles and audiovisual materials, through home terminals. Conceivably home terminals could give them the information they need to order hard copies through conventional or electronic mail.

Home terminals could provide access to legal and medical information. This would certainly be a boon for everyone regardless of economic level. Women and minorities could use the legal information to help combat job discrimination. As for medicine, people may have access to enough information to treat simple diseases, or take steps to prevent major ones like heart disease or cancer.

But the movement towards computer systems and displays and away from print-on-paper is subject to some very human constraints.

Scanning on video display units is technically possible right now, but it does not take into account the real shortcomings of video display units for prolonged reading purposes. It also ignores the realities of typographical and other aesthetic considerations that make scanning pleasant. In the foreseeable future, perhaps in five to ten years, flatbed portable screens may become commercially available - a device using, say, Compact Disk storage could have an enormous impact. That may make it possible to substitute the printed page with electronic images. However, many of us will continue to browse on planes and other places where electronic access, even if developed to perfection, will not be readily available.

Information in print or on a machine?

Online searching of databases has greatly increased in the last few years but it should be remembered that online services and printed indexes are not equivalent. Each has unique advantages. To give up one is to give up certain advantages. The cost may be less, but search capabilities are also diminished.

I do not mean to criticize ISI's online files by this defense of print. Our online <u>Scisearch</u> and <u>Social Scisearch</u> files are very useful for performing a number of searches. For example, the files are extremely valuable for doing complex multiterm searches. Using Boolean logic, users can search with almost any number of terms and quickly retrieve documents on highly specific topics. Obviously, online capability is essential for performing this type of search. In addition <u>Scisearch</u> has the advantage of being able to print the list of references cited by a particular source paper. But despite online's low cost and importance in some search situations, it is still an immature technology which can be used only by trained search analysts. Therefore online enthusiasts have no right to deprive users of the benefits of printed indexes. The print versions of the <u>Science Citation Index</u> and <u>Social Sciences Citation Index</u> offer easy access to information for everyone - both library staff and library patrons.

The psychological reluctance with which many patrons approach a library is well documented in the literature. Many library users are not certain of the information they need. They have not carefully formulated a search question. And many have browsing needs rather than specific search needs. The absence of the printed index forces users to interface with the librarian and expose their feelings of ignorance and uncertainty about the information that they are seeking. The absence of a printed index means that they cannot begin to find answers themselves or browse to find information that will make their search a lot more specific. The probing reference interview is an abrasive process for people uncertain of the information they need. Not every user is an extrovert. Scholars often prefer to work alone unaided by librarians or others, well-intentioned as they may be.

Some online search services claim that online facilities are helping rather than hindering the development of printed indexes. We have not yet seen proof of that claim. On the other hand, we have seen proof that some subscribers, when given the option of online searching, will abandon their printed indexes to the detriment of a significant number of users. Since it is clear that one cannot raise the price of an online search to non-print subscribers to absurd levels, there may be no recourse other than to the policy of limiting online access to print-copy subscribers.

The late 1980's will be a period of transition and testing. Right now, online technology lacks many of the important display features of the printed index. Considering the speed and direction in which computer technology is moving, those shortcomings probably are not permanent ones. There is no doubt that the relationship between online and printed indexes is in a period of transition. Nor is there any doubt that much testing has to be done to finally define the pricing philosophy that will accurately reflect that relationship.

The transition will be made even more complex by the emerging microcomputer revolution. It is not unreasonable to expect that by the end of the decade, central online databases may be replaced by local databases stored on and manipulated by microcomputers. By that time we may be sending out floppy disks or whatever, instead of printed volumes. This will happen only when we have managed to develop software, sufficiently transparent to the user, that will make it possible to do everything, and more, on a computer that can be done now with a printed index. Until that time, print indexes will still be frequently consulted in most libraries.

<u>A new look at some "simple" problems</u>

How can we apply our expertise, developed during the post-Sputnik period, to solve the problems of an increasingly information-conscious, but still information-illiterate, society?

The problem is that we as information scientists are unable to identify the everyday information problems of society. Rather, we too often confuse complexity with erudition.

Indeed, our preoccupation with complex and sophisticated information-delivery systems has prevented us, even to this day, from thinking seriously about these problems. In 1970, I mentioned the telephone directory problem as one that epitomized this situation. Have we professional information scientists, supposedly experts in the arts and science of indexing, ever concerned ourselves with the mundane problems of ordinary people in the use of that most ubiquitous of indexes, the telephone book? Are we really aware that many people are actually afraid to use any type of index, and that their fear cuts them off from information - one of the most important resources available to them? While we have developed sophisticated methods for searching DNA sequences, have you noticed any significant improvement in phone books lately?

Clearly it is too soon to tell, but hopefully the divestiture of AT&T will result in a telecommunications industry that is not only less conservative, but more responsive to consumer needs. After watching twenty years of unprecedented developments in computer and telecommunications technology, it is depressing to realise how little of that knowhow is applied to everyday problems. Where are all the improvements we were promised to help us to locate a taxi, or even a public toilet? The information revolution is here but we have only begun to talk about using information to deal with these seemingly trivial problems.

I believe it is our responsibility as information scientists not only to instruct society in the technology that is available, but also to identify the problems that need to be solved. In short, every profession must have a conscience.

Information is more widely recognised as a natural resource in the post-industrial era, but we must not confuse our stockpiles of information riches with access to them. We have large pockets of information poverty and deprivation within an otherwise affluent society. We must ensure that the right access is maintained for everyone. We all, even the most destitute among us, have information <u>needs</u>.

Galbraith's term "the affluent society" is rarely heard anymore - possibly because of the series of recessions the US economy has suffered since the phrase was coined. Nor is it more comfortable for us to use terms like "the post-industrial society" of Bell, or the "knowledge-production society" of Machlup, or even the "information-conscious society" of Garfield. None of these terms connotes affluence. We all tacitly assumed, as we solved our information problems we would also have solved our economic problems. The advent of the information society implied an affluent society for all.

Information <u>does</u> have the potential for solving problems of poverty - not only because information is inherently economic in nature, but also because poverty is rooted in ignorance and lack of education. The poor and under-priviledged constitute a vast information market waiting to be exploited. They always have been. The information industry will undoubtedly respond to explicit request for proposals by the government or implicit suggestions to solve their problems, but the question remains "Who pays"? Like the medical profession who take the Hippocratic oath, we too must see to the information needs of our clients - a term that, today, encompasses all of humanity.

But even in an information-rich society like the United States, we are the only country in the world to neglect its statistical information activities. Wassily Leontief, the Nobel prize-winning economist, has said "We are living in an information age without information. Washington is gutting the government's statistics. They are cutting appropriations. Next year, we will know less about

the American economy that we knew last year. We cannot effectively take
advantage of modern computers, which enable us to deal with masses of
information, because we haven't got the information. Pieces of information are
like a pile of bricks, not a building. You don't collect information before you
know what to do with it. The United States is the only advanced industrial
country that does not have a real central statistical office to collect facts and
figures".

The shortcomings of everyday information requirements

I believe information, like education, is the key to individual and personal
survival. Of course, one can survive, after a fashion, without information. If
you want to toil on a cooperative, back-to-nature farm somewhere, you may not
miss today's hectic information environment; indeed, that is what you might be
attempting to escape. But this is survival of a special kind. You may soon
realise, like the migrant farm workers, that rural life in America and elsewhere
is not a garden of Eden. Even the poorest peasant today realises the value of
television to both private pleasure and information in his life.

Back in 1970, I demonstrated how difficult and painful it could be to obtain
information of even the most basic kind. I described the case of a poor woman in
Johnstown, Pa, who was trying to locate the local legal aid society. She could
not find the information in her directory because it was listed strictly
alphabetically under "Cambria County Legal Aid Society". Do you realise that in
14 years - and in spite of AT&T's claims to be listening - the appropriate
cross-reference has still not been created? You still cannot find a listing
under "Legal Aid Society". I tried myself just last week. If you look in the
yellow pages, you'll find thousands of lawyers but still no entry under "legal
aid". However, I did find a heading called "Lawyer Referral Service", which
leads to community legal services. I tried that number and received a recorded
message to call back on Tuesday, so I suggest you avoid trouble on Sunday or
Monday.

As a more up-to-date example of information frustration, I give you the case
of a recently arrived immigrant trying to find information about or instruction
in English as a second language. I recently spent over an hour one Sunday before
I could assemble the information needed for my foreign-born friend. Through
perseverence I eventually learned, via the YMHA, about a language tutorial
service provided by the Nationalities Service Center of Philadelphia. It is
unfortunate that they do not have the wisdom to include an ad in the yellow pages
alongside Berlitz & Interlingua.

But why was this service not known to the information people at the US
Immigration and Naturalization Service? How about the Adult Education division
of the Philadelphia School System? After all, they offer such courses
themselves. Why not tell the new immigrant that language instruction is not only
more immediately available through the Nationalities Service Center, but that the
International House of Philadelphia also organises tutorial services and courses
for the families of visiting foreign students and scholars?

We have arrived at the Information Conscious Society, in spite of our
failure to systematically identify the most basic information needs of society.
The ad-hoc methods of the entrepreneur have successfully identified many
important areas of need. But the information industry, in spite of billions of
dollars in revenues, has still only scratched the surface of what is to come, and
the information profession can be a stimulus to the even more prosperous
information society that is developing without sacrificing anyone along the way.

Information Education

Another area of serious neglect is our failure to provide educational programs in information and library science. In the early days of computer science there were only mathematicians or electrical engineers who taught the subject. First there were graduate courses, then undergraduate programs. Here in Philadelphia at the University of Pennsylvania's Moore School, I taught a graduate course in information retrieval myself in the early days. Now there are undergraduate programs in computer science in hundreds of institutions. That is what the information profession should aspire to, and when and if it happens, a graduate degree will earn far more respect than it does today.

It seems to me that our profession should welcome with open arms - indeed regard it as the arrival of the millenium - that undergraduate programs in information and library science in the US are being proposed and implemented. Whatever the rationalization in the past, it is absured to claim that more than four years is required to expose a student to the fundamentals of information science. I think it is significant that bachelor degree graduates from certain programs earn more as information technologists than do the graduates from one-year master's programs elsewhere. Yes, a B.S. graduate in information studies may find himself doing cataloging or indexing at first. But is this any different than the filtrations, titrations and viscosity measurements I did as a B.S. chemist?

The Right To Know

Finally there is the question of the Right To Know - well illustrated by the history of the right-to-know movement right here in my home city of Philadelphia. In 1970 the Philadelphia Area Project on Occupational Safety and Health (PHILAPOSH), a union-sponsored group, and Ralph Nader's Health Research Group (HRG) petitioned the Occupational Safety and Health Administration (OSHA) for a regulation to require employers to inform employees about the hazardous substances in the workplace.

The right-to-know remained a matter of unexercised bureaucratic discretion, however, until 1979, when a group of Philadelphia residents organised the Bridesburg Civic Council to improve the quality of the air in their heavily industrialised community. The Council organised community meetings to inform citizens of the possible connection between pollution and public health. The cancer death-rate in Bridesburg was twice that for the US as a whole.

A strong labor-environment-community coalition managed to overcome the opposition to right-to-know that was led by the Greater Philadelphia Chamber of Commerce. City Council hearings in October 1980 attracted hundreds of citizens, many of whom testified to the tragedies they suffered from exposure to toxic chemicals. The Philadelphia Right-to-Know Ordinance was enacted on January 22, 1981; its impact was national in scope. Approximately 18 states and 30 local communities have now enacted similar laws. Apparently the passage of so many local laws has forced the federal government to sit up and take notice. Last fall, OSHA issued its own form of right-to-known regulations, although in a weaker and more limited form than most local and state laws.

I think most of us are optimistic about the future. The future holds a great deal of excitement and fascination for all of us. I suggest that in the area of fundamental understanding of the basic laws of information science we have not progressed as far as we had expected since I entered this field about 25 years ago. It's time Information Scientists ventured beyond their small bit of turf into broader fields like the Right To Know, for example, where their professional skills could surely be of the greatest help in community projects.

CHAPTER **49**.

PROGRESS IN EDUCATIONAL INFORMATION TECHNOLOGY

PROFESSOR DAVID HAWKRIDGE
The Open University, Milton Keynes, England.

With Gallic vigour and hyperbole, the French call it 'Le mariage du siecle', the marriage of the century, the marrying of information technology and education.   Should we expect a long partnership or will there be a quick divorce?

Like many other people, I have long been aware of the potential of technology in education, but since 1979 I have been studying the impact, for good or ill, of new information technology (IT) on education (Hawkridge and Robinson, 1982; Eicher, Hawkridge, McAnany, Mariet and Orivel, 1982; Hawkridge, 1983; Hawkridge, Vincent and Hales, 1985). Here, I describe and analyse advances in seven sectors of education and training.

Advances in education of children outside school

Children's informal learning outside school is changing.   They are learning more, and what they are learning is different.   IT is in part responsible and is becoming more so.

Traditionally, children outside school hours are thought of as being out of education, unless they are doing homework, but IT alters the relationship between learning and playing.   Homes contain radios, television sets, telephones, audiocassette players and pocket

----

Although updated, this chapter is based on Hawkridge (1983), which contains many other examples and a large number of references for further reading.

calculators as standard items and children learn much from them, informally.   Teletext, microcomputers, videotex, videocassette recorders and players, and videodisc players are still fairly unusual in homes, but where they exist children learn from them also.   To observant adults, this informal learning appears extraordinarily random and episodic.

We know very little indeed about the impact of IT on children in their first three years, that is, up to the stage of speech development. By the age of two, children can safely operate some devices.   Touch-sensitive switches enable two-year-olds to turn television sets on and off, and to select channels, too.   They can start an audiocassette player to listen to a favourite story, song or piece of music.   These very young children respond to voices, music and moving pictures, but we do not know whether and in what ways their thinking is affected by the technology.

We do know that IT is increasing the variety and amount of informal learning parents provide for children in this age bracket.   A mother finds that her young child greatly enjoys Sesame Street.   She therefore records (illegally) the broadcasts, and promises her child Sesame Street as a reward.   Parents like the increased variety provided by the new technology because it enables them to exercise their own values rather than having only one or two old movies or 'talk shows', which often form a large part of daytime television.

Preschoolers (aged three to five) also have access to radios, television sets, audiocassette players, pocket calculators and the telephone, and many rapidly acquire manipulative skills required to operate them.   Even before they can read, young children in this age-group like to 'play' with microcomputers, teletext and videotext.   They learn to call up the weather map on teletext, and operating a videocassette player is not beyond them by any means.   They approach the machines with less trepidation than their elders, and by playing with the devices and systems they infer how to operate them, rather than reading instructions and deducing what they should do.

There is a discontinuity at present, a sharp and disturbing one, between what preschoolers are likely to learn at home through IT and what they learn in primary school. Homes with the technology may offer an environment that is much more information-rich than the average primary school classroom. Preschoolers spend enough of their waking hours in this rich environment to learn a great deal from it. Unfortunately, schools cannot easily take into account the unstandardised curriculum that preschoolers follow at home.

What is it that makes up this unstandardised curriculum, mediated by radio, television and even microcomputers? From the radio and audiocassettes, preschoolers hear music, songs and stories, like their younger siblings, and they learn more from them because they are a little older. The broadcasts, and more recently the cassettes, are about relatively familiar topics, often extensions of nursery songs and storybooks familiar to previous generations.

Television, however, is doing far more than translating the familiar into the televised medium: it is also bringing to preschoolers much that is unfamiliar. As a group, cartoon programmes are close to the familiar and so are programmes such as Story Time. Sesame Street is in quite a different category, as it presents a kaleidoscope of images in fast-moving short sequences, using techniques borrowed from television advertising. Some sequences aim to teach letters and numerals, which were very rarely taught at home through technology until this series was made. The same series brings a great variety of vicarious, mediated experience to the children who view it (Postman, 1983).

Breadth of experience distinguishes preschoolers today from those of the previous generation. They view broadcasts about nature, about the social world far outside their own community, about journeys of

exploration and adventure, and about war and violence.   Their
opportunities to choose these mediated experiences are far greater than
those of their younger siblings, because they do not need adults to
operate the television set and because their parents tend to exercise
less control over viewing habits as the children get older.   In fact,
children's choice of viewing converges on adults' choice rather rapidly.
These are significant changes in our society.   Among adults of the
1950s, how many would have thought that in 1968 millions of four-year-
olds would be watching astronauts landing on the moon?   How many would
have predicted that in America of the 1980s television sets in many
homes would be turned on each day, during the waking hours of
preschoolers, for as many hours as the length of the primary school day?

Not a few parents have realised the potential of microcomputers for
informal learning and have encouraged their preschoolers to begin with
games that teach familiarity with keyboard and screen, and go on to
others that teach basic skills and concepts.   Primary school age
children use games at home for reinforcing or even remedial purposes, to
help them to spell or learn arithmetic, but preschoolers are only at the
beginning of understanding what spelling is, or arithmetic.   A five-
year-old, perhaps impatient to get to primary school, may sit for hours
with a game, fascinated by the combination of spoken word and visual
display that is utterly at his or her command.   What is being learned?
Not necessarily how words should be spelled, nor even the number bonds
to twenty, although the child may well pick these up, especially if a
slightly older sibling is around to consult.   Rather, the child may be
learning at an intuitive level that letters are associated with sounds,
that together they make strings of sounds that are words, and,
similarly, that numbers have names and can be put together in several
ways. These fundamental principles will be useful the following year at
school.

Children's capacity to use and benefit from IT increases rapidly as they learn to read and as their manipulative skills improve.   On the other hand, primary education takes five hours of each day, leaving them with less time for informal learning, and parents widely believe that entertainment is the dominant function of equipment such as television, radio, audiocassette recorders and even microcomputers.

Children of school age have few problems in learning how to operate IT systems.   At a downtown Washington DC public library, students after school have no difficulty in learning, by trial-and-error, to use a keypad to operate a teletext system.   Even those without good reading skills find teletext interesting.   Adults nervously stand behind the youngsters, waiting for them to leave, then copy what they have seen the children do, rather than first trying for themselves.

Is it the case that children are acquiring new mental sets, as well as new manipulative skills, through using IT?   Television-like screens have long been the place for 'presentations' judged in terms of how attentive viewers were, and, occasionally, by how much they learned.   Information-providers have taken a similar view: all they had to do was present information.   Now children are learning to interact with screens.   Computer games tell us something about the appeal of interactivity.   Humans interact more eagerly with material that has been produced in much more complex ways than the presentations, which were linear like a story.   Games like Space Invaders engage interest by direct response, by being easily understood at the level needed to operate them and by offering a stake (in winning or scoring). But above all,they do so by offering control to the user, within certain limits.

Challenge, fantasy and curiosity are essential for intrinsically motivating teaching by computer games.   Challenge depends on goals with outcomes that are uncertain because the difficulty level is varied; it may also depend on the goals being multiple, on randomness existing

within the game or success following discovery of hidden information.
Fantasy, the opportunity for the player to fantasise, can be either
extrinsic or intrinsic to the game, depending on whether it is closely
related to skills demanded by the game.   Curiosity can be enhanced by
making learners believe their knowledge is incomplete, inconsistent or
not sufficiently parsimonious.

For children in computer clubs and at home, entertainment motivates
them to learn.   Soon, however, they begin to learn cooperatively.
Four or five children gather round an adult who demonstrates how the
computer works.   One child claims a turn and sits at the keyboard,
typing in what the others suggest.   The group discusses what to do
often without the adult.   In time, the size of the group dwindles down
to two, with more expert children starting to work alone.   Once a child
becomes expert in a particular area, other children call on him or her
before calling for the adult.

For adolescents, microcomputers hold a special fascination because
with one they can create a totally controllable world.   An electronics
fault may have to be repaired by a technician, but their own programming
errors they can detect and repair.   For those of logical, mathematical
and spatial bent, BASIC holds no terrors and requires little capacity to
express oneself in English.   Creative acts are now possible for them
that formerly were beyond all but those most articulate in their native
language.   Imaginative games programmed by adolescents on
microcomputers are witness to the fact.

More passively, adolescents learn informally from television and
radio, audio- and videocassettes, videotex in libraries and shop
windows, pocket calculators and cash tills, and electronic games such as
chess and Space Invaders.   They learn new mental sets from amusement
arcades, television and audiocassette recorders, all part of their out-
of-school world.

Advances in primary schools

At this level children acquire 'computer awareness' (knowing in general about computers) and 'computer literacy' (knowing broadly how they work and how to program them).   Computer literacy is acquired only by a minority, through actual experience and practice in programming (Maddison, 1982; Obrist, 1983).   An early stage in computer literacy consists of 'keyboard literacy', acquired through playing with the machine, usually with games programs, just to get the feel of the keyboard and screen, and to operate the various components.   Next, children use 'courseware', educational programs obtained by the teachers from a program exchange or from commercial suppliers, and some learn to program, usually in BASIC.

What can children learn of the formal curriculum from courseware?   Primary schools emphasise learning to read, to write in the mother tongue and to calculate.   Courseware to date has focused first on language and number, although programs for other topics do exist.   Courseware is of three main types: drill-and-practice routines, tutorials and simulations, all of which may require interaction between teacher, student and computer.

For learning the English language, there is no lack of drill-and-practice programs to improve reading, spelling, correct usage and so on. Many existing programs do little more than teach the accepted grammar or language usage in ways that probably inhibit creativity.   Few help children to develop their writing by planning a story for a particular audience, or to understand the structure of language.   Able teachers may and do adapt such programs to particular needs.   Word processing programs (see below) may also help.

Most programs for teaching arithmetic and mathematical skills are the drill-and-practice type.   If teachers want their children to perform such drills on a computer, the children will probably be entertained.   The chief evidence that these programs actually increase children's achievement is testimony of teachers who say, 'Staff and children gain from using them.'

Papert (1980), on the other hand, says that the computer provides a learning tool of great power because it enables young children to test their own theories about the physical or abstract worlds and to obtain rapid feedback. His turtle geometry enables children to create command sequences which generate pictures on the computer's screen just as if they were sitting on the pencil doing the drawing. The child must create a control program, and to do so must construct a model in his or her mind before seeing the result. If the model is right, the computer shows this clearly. If the picture turns out to be wrong, there is a strong motivation to correct the model and thence the program, to produce the right picture, says Papert. The language Papert uses for this programming is LOGO. With it, the child can work out the strategy involved in, say, adding two 2-digit numbers and write a program to do it. The language is simple enough for the emphasis to be on understanding the problem and thinking out the logical steps for solving it. LOGO expects children to program, and Papert says that children using LOGO are unconsciously using concepts of deep significance in logic and computing.

Pocket calculators, cheap IT devices, are recommended by educational professionals in the UK and the US. Yet many teachers and parents fear they 'rot the brain'. Calculators reinforce number bonds and help understanding of place value and decimals. They help children understand problem-solving processes, both in mathematics and everday matters requiring arithmetical solutions. Children grasp the concepts better, in, say, long multiplication, and calculators, strangely enough, help the teaching of these algorithms enormously, because children come to understand what they are doing instead of following routines blindly. Children may depend on calculators to build up their confidence, but they also become aware of calculators' limitations. In the past, few

children became fully proficient at long division and multiplication.
With the help of calculators, many more will become so.   The rest need
to know how to use a calculator.

Videodiscs, especially interactive ones, may offer some benefits to
primary school classrooms.   In an American series (SCHOOLDISCS) for
players without microprocessor control, children can locate the start of
particular segments.   Each disc has six 10-minute segments devoted to
six different subjects.   Each segment includes moving pictures, 90
stills and bibliographies referring students to readings.   In another
American videodisc, young Olympic gymnasts demonstrate tumbling skills,
including the forward roll, the handstand, etc.   The disc can be slowed
down or stopped to show particular movements for children to practice.

Videotex (Prestel) is in use in some British primary schools, but
it is essential for teachers to consult the relevant pages before
recommending them to students.   For example, African Weather may lead
on to pages and pages of information or it may merely offer the previous
day's maximum temperature in a small selection of African capitals.
The database is changing all the time (African Weather comes and goes!).
Teachers' opinions of videotex's usefulness to them as a source of
information are mixed (for telesoftware see below).   There has been
some interest, however, in using microcomputers to develop local
databases (Ross, 1984).

In general, primary teachers have not been trained to use IT and
their attitudes towards it vary: some see their students being
motivated; some see the machines adding to their authority.   But others
are critical: with the present poor quality programs they cannot justify
the outlay.   For instance, they question whether microcomputers are
what schools need most.   Attempts to assess whether microcomputers
actually raise primary schoolchildren's achievement more than other
methods are rare, and very seldom yield convincing data.

Advances in secondary schools

Western governments are recognising the importance of IT at this level, and so are the Japanese.   Microcomputers are entering secondary schools quickly, but there are not enough yet and they must be backed by software, courseware and training.   O'Shea and Self (1982) discuss this issue in detail.

As in primary schools, microcomputers with word processing programs are used in some schools to assist 'composition' or creative writing. Students write drafts, which teachers 'annotate' or comment upon, then students revise their drafts.   The final copy is clean and neat, giving students much satisfaction in their work.   In foreign languages, programs provide drill, say, in Spanish verb forms and Spanish vocabulary.   Students may enter at their own individual level.   If they make mistakes, they receive a good deal of help, ranging from simple correction to hints of various kinds to an offer to teach again that verb form.

Microcomputers are used to set up and analyse local history databases.   For a given period, local records may yield demographic statistics of religion, educational standard, occupation and workplace; average age, proportion of males to females, average number of persons per household; and specialised lists, such as the ages of working children, whether or not servants were illiterate, and so on. Such databases, either prepared elsewhere or built up by staff and students, may also provide bibliographic references, taking students to reprints, books and other documents within a research collection. Students learn on-line searching, a useful information skill.

Business Studies is suitable for secondary school microcomputer applications, including training games, balance sheets, market research, and so on.   Economics programs teach such topics as elasticity of demand, price fluctuations, agricultural commodity, price stabilisation, theory of the firm, the multiplier, fiscal policy, creation of credit, monetary policy and gains from trade.   Geography programs offer simulations and games: e.g., crop-planting, a joint stock companies trading game, simulations of drainage basin morphometry and human population growth, statistics for geographers, urban land use, land slopes, transport networks and location of settlements.   Transport networks are studied through planning and plotting communications in a developing country, while settlement is studied through simulation within two specimen landscapes.

Programs are available to help students to learn how to compose and play back their own electronic music, which can be reproduced on a stereo.   The music staves are on the display screen.   Other programs provide drills in musical skills, e.g., rhythm, ear training, melody memorising.

In biology, programs are available in genetics and inheritance, predator-prey relationships, pond ecology, transpiration, counter current systems, human energy expenditure, statistics for biologists and many other topics.   Chemistry programs include rates of reaction, manufacture of sulphuric acid, homogeneous equilibrium, lattice energy, electrochemical cells, gas chromatography and chemical elements.   In Physics, recent programs cover the photo-electric effect, mass spectrometers, gravitational fields, planetary motion, capacitor discharge, radioactive decay and gaseous diffusion.

Many good programs require the student to examine a problem, plan an investigation, respond to computer prompts and interpret computer-generated results.   Microcomputers may thus oblige students to engage in high-level intellectual activity.

Microcomputers can simulate use of expensive and sophisticated apparatus, or, in some cases, dangerous experiments, some conducted over a long time-span, longer than can be conveniently accommodated in school laboratories.   Students can vicariously experience the consequences of errors of judgement,   inappropriate experimental design and dangerous procedures.   Students may confuse a simulation with reality, of course. Computers do not allow students to perform genuine experiments.   It is dishonest to use a simulation as experimental evidence for theories and assumptions on which the simulation itself is based.

Computer science itself, including computer literacy, is now being taught in most secondary schools, using microcomputers.   British syllabuses are somewhat theoretical, not offering students enough hands-on experience.   By contrast, at some schools every student is introduced to BASIC then to word processing and data retrieval.   They go on to fundamentals of electronics, including circuit building.

Most mathematics programs at this level offer drill-and-practice routines, leaving the teacher to introduce concepts.   Unfortunately, many programs deal with wrong answers by giving the right answer after two or three tries, without remedial teaching.   Wrong answers disappear off the screen as students proceed, leaving little incentive for them to examine their errors.

A few videodiscs are available for use in secondary schools.   One well-known American disc teaches the physics of sympathetic vibrations through the example of the Tacoma Narows Bridge collapse.   It is able to provide several levels of explanation depending on the mathematics background of the student using it, up to and including university standard.

In the United Kingdom, educational telesoftware is sent by videotex (Prestel).   Computer programs stored on the central computer can be accessed, retrieved and stored by any school with the necessary equipment and membership of the system, which is fully automatic.   A 5K program can be transferred in about 2.5 minutes, at a cost of 15 pence at peak time, less at other times.   The system can be used to transmit software in any language and checks errors so that problems from line noise are eliminated.

Vocational guidance systems are available for use with terminals linked to mainframe computers.   An enquirer can ask sophisticated questions and receive full information in reply, and soon job placement information will also be provided.

Advances in higher education

University students have used mainframe computers to learn for about twenty years (Suppes, 1981).   Microcomputer applications are newer, as are computerised databases and interactive videodisc.   Little or no use is yet made in universities of videotex and teletext systems.

Computers, including microcomputers, are vitally important in higher education because they make possible a wide range of teaching simulations, many depending in some way on computer graphics.   These simulations have many advantages (see above), but are particularly useful for explaining complex relationships and for visualisations of complex biological, chemical or engineering systems (Wildenberg, 1981).

IT is now essential for teaching certain vocational subjects at university, such as architecture and engineering design, where computers' graphic and computational capabilities are now used very widely in related professions.   IT is also entering every other subject in the curriculum, whether statistics, economics, art, music or history.

For example, on one experimental videodisc are 1,000 black and white images of woodcuts and engravings by Albrecht Durer and Raimondi from the Bartsch collection in London.   To search the collection, users can either use the Bartsch number or select by artist, date, medium (woodcut or engraving), state (if the print was completed in stages), theme or words in the title.   Series can be found as well as individual images.   The system is not perfect, however, and users say they cannot compare two images at once (important in art history) and the image quality is poor compared with slides.   For some, 1,000 images are too few.

University libraries are leaders in using IT databases to assist students and researchers.   For example, some 2,400 North American

university and college libraries use the services of the Online Computer
Library Center.   Over 4,000 terminals in these institutions are
connected by a private network of 150,000 miles of telephone lines.
The central computer holds entries for more than 7 million titles,
attached to over 90 million locations, i.e., a title may be held by
several libraries, all of which are listed.   Every week, another 25,000
titles enter the system, mostly from member libraries, and 4,000
interlibrary loans are initiated within it.   Many of the loans are
between universities, which are provided with a centralised acquisition
and cataloguing service too.

Commercial computerised scientific database services such as DIALOG
are now firmly established and essential to higher education,
particularly for research but also for teaching.   The DIALOG databases,
located in California, are accessible from many countries by data
transmission lines, via cable and satellite, at relatively low cost.
France, Japan and other countries are struggling to keep up with the
American lead in these databases, which are very valuable to
universities.

In teaching at this level, IT is not only useful to developed
countries: the People's Republic of China is using IT extensively for
teaching in its new television universities, which have hundreds of
thousands of students (Hawkridge and McCormick, 1983).   Bates (1984)
provides examples from many other countries.

Advances in vocational and continuing education

'Vocational' education is education or training aimed particularly
at fitting an adult to pursue a livelihood.   'Continuing' education is
much broader, taking in education and training after first 'vocational'
qualifications have been obtained.

The widest use of microcomputers for vocational and continuing
education is in Business Studies.   Many packages are available to teach
basic business practice, including accounting.   Similarly, packages to

teach computer programming are widely available.   Computer-based
training is slow in coming to the fore, because of the heavy investment
required in courseware development.   Some companies use it to teach
skills, such as telephone installation, that can be simulated
graphically.

Simulation on computers is again a useful teaching strategy,
because many physical constraints inherent in an actual plant are
removed, time can be speeded up and slowed down, event sequences can be
replayed and casualty procedures too dangerous to attempt in a real
plant can be readily practised.   Ideally, a simulation is accompanied
by a computerised tutor to answer questions, provide hints and give
explanations required to develop a deep understanding of the system
and events being simulated.

For vocational and continuing education, videodisc and
microcomputer can combine powerfully.   'Flight Training' teaches
trainee pilots the landing procedures for a private light plane.
Segments cover visual cues, instruments, the approach and landing.   The
computer shows instrument readings and asks the trainee what part of the
landing he is in.   To go on to the next segment the trainee has to
answer correctly.   It is next best to a flight simulator, which is much
more expensive.

A new interactive videodisc developed by the American Heart
Association teaches cardo-pulmonary resuscitation (CPR).   Trainees
begin by watching a doctor on the screen, who tells them about CPR with
the help of stills and demonstrates the motor skills required.   They
answer a test at the end of the doctor's 'lesson', using a light pen to
spell out words (by pointing at selected letters on the screen) instead
of a keyboard.   Next, trainees use a manikin to practice CPR.   The
manikin has sensors, wired to the microcomputer, which 'tell the doctor'
whether the trainees are carrying out CPR correctly, and the doctor
coaches those who make mistakes.

The Association for Media-Based Continuing Education for Engineers, a consortium of 21 universities teaching engineering, with headquarters in Atlanta, Georgia, distributes over 500 engineering courses, particularly for continuing education, on videocassette.   Most of the cassettes were recorded during lectures in one of the universities; some were recorded specially in studios.

American experience is patchy in using mainframe computer-assisted instruction at the community college level, where much vocational and continuing education occurs.   Students often do not use the computer sufficiently for it to offer real benefit.   In one case, where mathematics students were obliged to use the system for 30-40 hours per term, those who completed the computerised course had higher scores than those taught conventionally.   Many made slow progress through the computerised lessons and did not complete the course.

Videotex is being used, occasionally, for vocational education. One group of British students were taught via Prestel.   The text dealt with lithographic printing techniques, in which retraining is often required.   It was modified to fit Prestel and to take advantage of Prestel's facilities such as colour graphics.   The students said they enjoyed learning via Prestel, and their test results show increased scores.

Many countries offer vocational and continuing education via broadcasting, as in the United Kingdom, the Netherlands, France, the Federal Republic of Germany, Japan and Canada (Neil, 1981).

Advances in informal learning by adults

Just as children learn informally at home, adults are learning informally at home, too, in libraries, at work or in some other place. Microcomputers are being used by adults to learn informally about many topics, not least computer programming.   Users can link them to a central computer, and learn, for example, about stocks and shares.   The Source, owned by The Reader's Digest, is an American computerised database offering subscribers computer programs in various programming languages, business and financial services, United Press International wire service (news), the New York Times consumer database, an electronic mail system to other users, cheap voice messages of up to a hundred words sent anywhere in the country, database search services (including abstracts from 27 leading business journals), health and medicine information, personal financial information services, travel and leisure pursuits information, a buying service (including an electronic book ordering service), games and educational programs that include French, German, Italian and Spanish vocabulary drills, Esperanto, algebra, geometry, social science, vocational guidance and business analysis and planning.　There are some disadvantages: microcomputer screens are usually rather small, requiring considerable pruning of information. Highly selected information is not always useful and costs are not low. Compuserve, another American service, offers microcomputer users the entire text of eight major newspapers, including The New York Times and the Washington Post, sports news, weather forecasts, an encyclopedia, electronic mail, securities quotations, etc.　In other countries, including the United Kingdom, similar databases are now available.

The stock brokers, Merrill Lynch, conducted a nationwide investment seminar televised from New York via satellite to 17,000 viewers gathered in thirty convention halls and seminar rooms, and possibly two million watched at home, being subscribers to certain cable systems.　The seminar was on the 1981 tax law, and included the President of the United States speaking live from the White House.　Viewers were able to phone in questions.

Television broadcasting over-the-air provides informal learning, too.　Educational series aimed at adults can be very successful, often combining print with television, or print with radio.　From the BBC, the recent Computer Literacy series is a typical example.　Broadcasting in the education of children and adults is analysed by Bates (1984a).

Advances in learning by disabled children and adults

Finally, IT is the basis for important advances in learning by children and adults who are physically-disabled, blind, deaf or speech-impaired.   Above all, IT improves communication for them, quickly transforming print into Braille or speech for blind students, speech into print for deaf students, keypresses into print or speech or pictures for physically-handicapped students, and so on.   Latest developments in this field are dealt with in detail by Hawkridge, Vincent and Hales (1985).

References

Bates, A.W. (ed.) (1984). The Role of Technology in Distance Education. London and New York: Croom Helm and St. Martin's Press.

Bates, A.W. (1984). Broadcasting in Education: An Evaluation. London: Constable.

Eicher, J.C., Hawkridge, D.G., McAnany, E., Mariet, F. and Orivel, F. (1983). The Economics of New Educational Media. Vol. 3. Paris: Unesco.

Hawkridge, David and Robinson, John (1982). Organizing Educational Broadcasting. London and Paris: Croom Helm and Unesco.

Hawkridge, David (1983). New Information Technology in Education. London and Baltimore: Croom Helm and Johns Hopkins University Press.

Hawkridge, David and McCormick, Bob (1983). China's television universities. British Journal of Educational Technology, Vol. 14, No.3.

Hawkridge, David, Vincent, Tom and Hales, Gerald (1985). New Information Technology in the Education of Disabled Children and Adults. London and San Diego: Croom Helm and College Hill Press.

Maddison, Alan (1982). Microcomputers in the Classroom. London: Hodder and Stoughton.

Neil, Michael W. (1981). Education of Adults at a Distance. London: Kogan Page.

Obrist, A.J. (1983). Microcomputers and the Primary School. London: Hodder and Stoughton.

O'Shea, T. and Self, J. (1982). Learning and Teaching with Computers. Brighton, Sussex: Harvester Press.

Papert, Seymour (1980). Mindstorms: Children, Computers and Powerful Ideas. Brighton, Sussex: Harvester Press.

Postman, Neil (1983). The Disappearance of Childhood. London: Allen.

Ross, Alistair (1984). Making Connections: Developing the Primary School Curriculum Using a Microcomputer for Information Retrieval. London: Council for Educational Technology.

Suppes, Patrick (ed.) (1981). University-level Computer-assisted Instruction at Stanford, 1968-1980. Stanford: Institute for Mathematical Studies in the Social Sciences, Stanford University.

Wildenberg, D. (ed.) (1981). Computer Simulation in University Teaching. Amsterdam: North Holland.

<u>CHAPTER 50</u>.

NEW DEVELOPMENTS IN BANKING TECHNOLOGY
AND RETAIL CASH TRANSFER SYSTEMS

MR. E.FOSTER
Spectra Services Ltd., Hurst, England.

1. <u>ELECTRONIC POINT OF SALE</u>

<u>THE DEVELOPMENT OF ELECTRONIC POINT OF SALE</u>

During the post-war years due to the expansion of merchandise
ranges it became increasingly desirable for retailers to collect
more detailed information on sales transactions. In response cash
registers became more and more sophisticated, larger and more
expensive. However, their capabilities remained limited by their
basic technology. Even the large and expensive machines were not
capable of providing enough detailed information. Retailers
compensated to a degree by employing large staffs to carry out
till roll analysis.

<u>Electronic Cash Registers</u> (ECR's)

These were electronic based equivalents of the previous
electro-mechanical cash registers. They offered a small number of
department, cash and void totals with no data storage other than
the audit roll. Subsequent development has been in parallel with
that of electronic point of sale (EPOS) systems and today there is
a high degree of convergence.

<u>Standalone Data Collection</u>

Data collection capabilities when first introduced, used audio
type cassettes which were rather insecure and were replaced first
by special digital cartridges, and then by more sophisticated
floppy discs, bubble memory and Winchester disc systems.
Collecting data over Public Switched Telephone lines has also been
a risky business. Early European services were largely aimed at

COMPARATIVE FACILITIES OF
DIFFERENT 'POINT OF SALE' TERMINALS

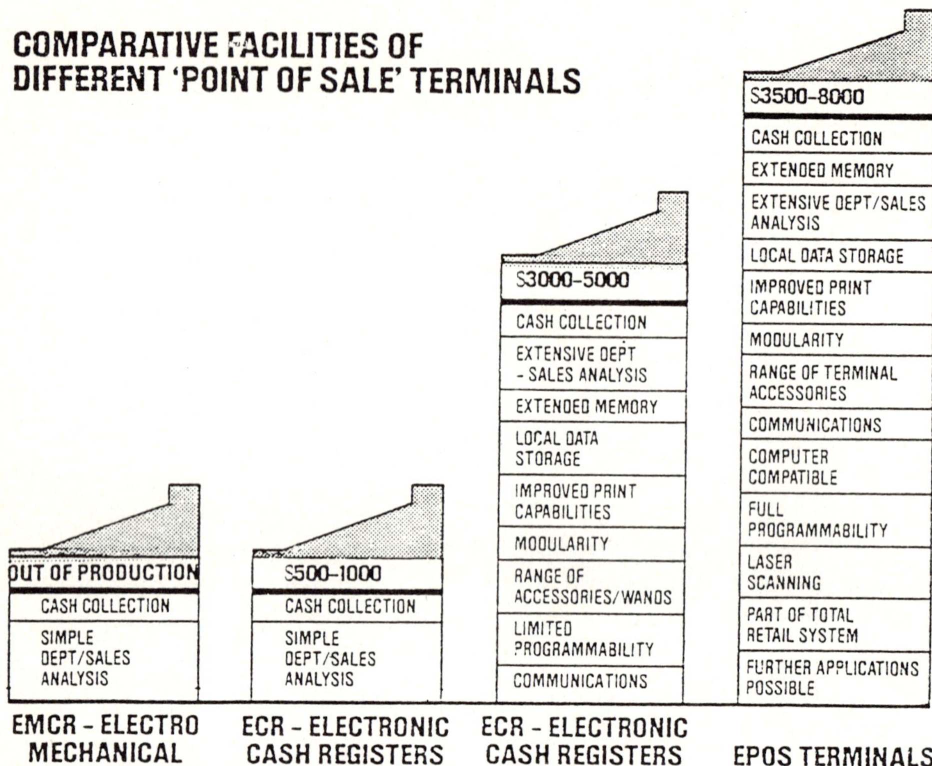

slow speed telex transmission, and there were serious problems of
line noise. More recently significant improvements have been made
and as a result there are an increasing number of 'networked'
systems being installed.

2.   AUTHORISATION TELEPHONES

Authorisation Telephones provide a convenient means of automating
and extending existing credit card authorisation procedures.

The devices, containing inbuilt CCITT V21 modems, are designed for
direct connection to the public telephone network, and are similar
in size and appearance to a conventional push button telephone.

In addition to use as an authorisation terminal, the phones can
also be used to make and receive normal telephone calls. A 16

character alphanumeric display is provided which leads the user
through the operation of the device, as well as displaying
response messages received from the card issuers host computer as
a normal part of the authorisation procedure.

How Authorisation Phones Work

The retailer's assistant passes the customer's card through a
magnetic stripe reader which records the account number and
validity date. The transaction value is entered from the
keyboard. The phone then dials automatically into the local
network entry point. The authorisation request is then passed to
the appropriate card company's computer where a response is
generated and returned to the phone and displayed. All
transactions are handled in a similar manner, with card issuers
being free to offer additional services for the benefit of their
retailers and card holders.

The device can be powered from an associated plug top power
supply; however, internal float charged batteries are provided
which allow normal operation for a limited period of several hours
in the event of mains failures. Primary telephone facilities are
however always available, regardless of the mains supply or state
of charge of the internal batteries.

The terminal will normally communicate with the card issuer's host
computer, using the Packet Switching Service. The terminal
obtains access to this service through a PSTN dial-up connection
into a Public or Private PAD located at a convenient local
exchange.

The Authorisation Phone prepared the message before transmission
to a format agreed by the major card issuers.

The message includes unique terminal identifying characters, a
retailer number, together with the card data as read from the
magnetic stripe, and the amount of the proposed transaction. This
is sent to the host computer, and if the transaction is
authorised, a response message is sent to the terminal and the
display indicates an authorisation code. The code number is

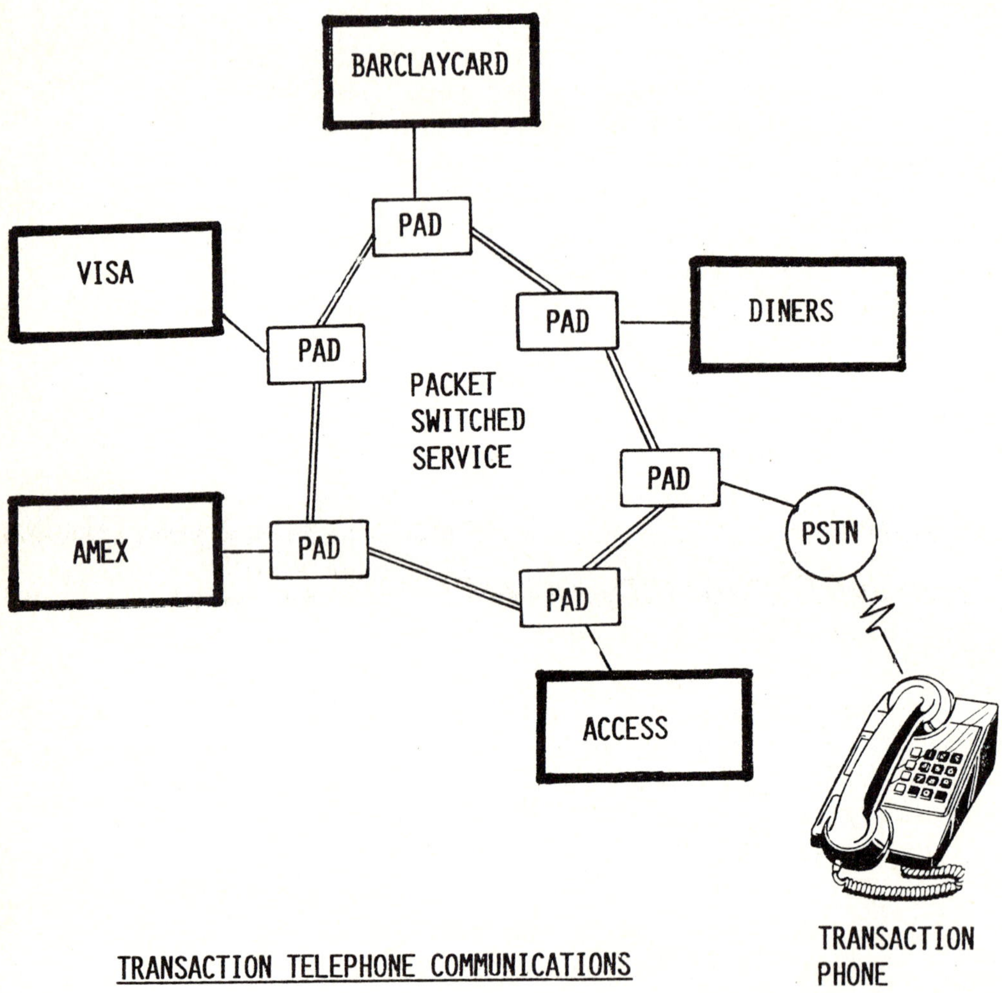

TRANSACTION TELEPHONE COMMUNICATIONS

written on the voucher by the retailer's assistant. Certain card
issuers may not wish to use the Packet Switching Service as the
communications system. In this case, the terminal can be set to
establish the call directly to the card issuer's host computer
using the PSTN dial-up service.

When terminals are installed on site, a set of cards, produced by
the card issuers, is used to preload the terminal with the
appropriate information it needs to establish calls to the card
issuer's computer. The terminal stores this information and uses
it to support the transactions from a given merchant's premises.

To assist this operation in the UK, British Telecom has made available a host computer system of its own which will carry out the initialising operation on the terminals, as they are installed. When the system is finalised, a special card, or manually entered account number will be used to allow the terminal to access a special British Telecom host. Having identified itself to the British Telecom host, the terminal will then receive down-line the instructions it needs to support the different card companies' transactions which have been agreed by that particular merchant.

This service is however, still under development, and Authorisation Phones have to date been installed using sets of plastic cards containing the necessary initialisation data.

3.　ELECTRONIC CHEQUE BOOKS - THE SMART CARD

As one of its many potential applications, the Smart Card can rightly claim to be the first truly electronic cheque book; it operates complete with the equivalent of 'stubs' for a fully reliable record of transactions - no human lapse of memory can jeopardise its accuracy - while there is an immediate display of 'balance in hand' each time it is used.

Specifically in the context of Electronic Money, it is of interest to trace the more recent evolution of financial services by categorising a series of technological 'waves' which have occurred over time, initially in the USA:

      1950's - magnetic character recognition emerged

      1960's - heralded the introduction of credit cards and
             ATM's

      1970's - saw the growth of Point of Sale and the
             appearance of debit cards

      1980's - has seen a growing convergence of these
             technologies leading in some respects to 'at
             home' banking along with the introduction of
             the Smart Card.

<u>Technical Principles</u>

Unlike the magnetic stripe card, the Smart Card is on a rising
curve of memory capacity having already passed 4K bits and reached
8K bits; nor is there a technical barrier to its expanding to 16K
bits - while still maintaining the ISO standard thickness for
credit and other bank cards.

Currently, three types of card exist:

(i)   'Memory only' which are low cost and disposable
when the memory of 512 bits is exhausted. A
typical application is for payphones and
similar low value transactions hence sometimes
referred to as the 'electronic purse'.

(ii)   'Wired logic' cards, on the other hand, contain
both memory and intelligence, but while the
intelligence is able to introduce more
stringent security checks than a memory only
card, the nature of the wired logic chip
requires that the application be programmed in
during manufacture and it can only handle the
one application.

(iii)   'Microprocessor' cards represent the ultimate
in Smart Card technology to date. They are
more versatile than wired logic versions and
can for example, use their superior technology
to handle more than one application on the same
card. Their security rating is also more
rigorous and one finds them used for the most
demanding applications.

The essential functions of these two latter versions of Smart Card
consist of recording and outputting information once a valid
personal identity number (PIN) has been keyed by the holder and
secondly, to perform calculations on data received from an
external source or already stored internally. These calculations
may take the form of financial balances or encryption/decryption
of complex codes.

THE SMART CARD

To accomplish these functions, the memory of the card is divided
typically into three zones - 'open' : to any authorised terminal;
'confidential' : only accessible on keying a correct PIN and
'closed zone' : not accessible by any external source including
the terminal. This latter area contains sensitive information
such as secret keys and confidential codes.

One final point - of marketing as well as technical significance -
is that by achieving the same dimensional standards as the
classical magnetic stripe based card, the means exist for the
Smart Card to combine both technologies on the one card vehicle;
this has been termed the 'Smart-Stripe Card'.

Credit Card Plans

In France, two large groups of credit cards exist - Carte Bleue
(Blue Card) which is associated with VISA and is jointly operated
by a majority of French banking interests, and Carte Verte (Green
Card) which is linked with the Eurocard/Mastercard system and is
wholly operated by Crédit Agricole - a federation of regional
banks originally serving the farming community but today much more
diversified in its customer base.

In December 1983, both organisations announced their intentions to combine Smart Card Technology with their existing magnetic stripe cards. These 'Smart Stripe Cards' as I have called them, will begin to be distributed in 1984. Using Bull technology, Carte Bleue will first be introduced in Blois as yet another Smart Card operation, while combined 'Smart Stripe' readers will be installed in POS locations. The ISO track 3 will not be used in this version. Subsequently, the plan is to distribute the cards in the same regional sequence as the Electronic Directory program for 1984/5 already announced by the Telecom Administration; this includes Brittany, Paris, Picardy in Northern France, Marseilles, etc. The projections are for 1m cards in 1984 and 10m by 1986.

4.   <u>AUTOMATED VENDING OF PETROL</u>

Card activated petrol vending is a service which enables cardholders to purchase petrol automatically on the garage forecourt using a magnetically striped plastic card.

The impetus for this technology emanates from Scandinavia and the Benelux countries. In 1975 Norol became the first oil company in the world to introduce automatic petrol dispensing by means of a credit card. Norol is one of Norway's largest oil companies with a network of nearly 500 service stations, and is the only Norwegian oil company with its own credit card. The Norol card was used exclusively in card activated pumps in Norol garages until 1981 when the system was expanded to facilitate the acceptance of a generic Norwegian bank card.

The Norol system now operates in an on-line mode for both bank and oil company cards. Connection is made automatically via the public data network to either Norol or the bank, whichever is applicable. While the customer types in his PIN code, customer data is validated against the central hot card files of either Norol or the Bank. The response is sent via the station computer to the pump, and the customer is informed by a visual display as to whether or not he is authorised to fill his tank. When the filling has been completed, the transaction data is stored on the station computer until the next card insertion. The data is transferred to the relevant host computer (Norol or the Bank) in

connection with validation of the following customer's card, thus
reducing the number of link-ups and keeping down telecommunication
costs.

Since 1975, card activated petrol vending has become universally
accepted throughout Scandinavia. One of the primary reasons is
because the major oil companies have their own credit cards and
card activiated vending offers opportunities for the provision of
enchanced service levels including unattended 24 hours a day
operation. A significant number of card activated pumps have now
been deployed successfully throughout Scandinavia and Belgium.

Counterspeed, the first UK retail Point of Sale trial started in
1979 using a debit card, involved six garages in the Norwich
area. Cards were accepted in the garage kiosks for petrol and
ancillary transactions. The magnetically encoded cards were read
by a terminal and the data collected using British Telecom's
overnight lines.

It was not until 1983 that the first card activiated terminal was
installed in the UK. Together with Amoco, Barclaycard launched a
Cardpump trial at two sites in Rochester (Kent). There were a
variety of reasons for the delayed implementation, not least the
problems associated with obtaining Weights and Measures approval
from the Department of Trade and Industry.

Despite the problems, a second trial commenced in 1984 in Winnersh
(Berkshire).

Both Rochester and Winnersh trials operate off-line for data
capture in addition to PIN verification. Details of all the
transactions are written to a cassette and subsequently processed
by a computer bureau on behalf of the oil companies. The
transactions are subsequently submitted to Barclaycard via BACS.
This approach enables oil companies to accept other cards in the
kiosk and use card reading terminals to capture the data serially
with card activated transactions.

Market research indicates that cardholders enjoy using Automated
Petrol Systems.

The machine automatically charges the amount to the relevant
Barclaycard account, and it will appear on the statement in the
usual way.

The service can operate 24 hours a day and offers many other
customer advantages:

* provides a combined VAT receipt, and credit
  card voucher on reques

* credit card transactions reduced from an
  average of 6 minutes to 2 minutes.

* accurate transaction details

* simple and easy to use

* no walking to the kiosk to complete tedious
  paperwork

5. <u>ELECTRONIC FUNDS TRANSFER - AT THE RETAIL POINT OF SALE</u>

A. <u>WHAT IS EFT?</u>

In the beginning payment for goods and services took the form of
bartering. Then, as man's mobility increased, the carrying of
"exchangeable" items became impracticable.

To alleviate that problem coins were invented, and they first
appeared in China and Greece during the 7th Century BC, almost
2700 years ago. It was nearly 500 years later, in the 2nd Century
BC, that coins were first used in England.

By 600 AD, it was found that coins were also too cumbersome, and
so the Chinese began using paper money.

In modern times it has even become rather dangerous to carry paper
money, and although cheques have been used since the 17th Century,
they have neither been entirely satisfactory nor convenient for
consumers and retailers.

For more than a decade it has been heralded that the payment method to solve all problems was "just around the corner". By the end of this century, plastic debit and credit cards, instead of cheques and vouchers, will be the most convenient method of payment for bankers, retailers and consumers.

This new method of payment is called EFTS.

One of the most unusual definitions of EFTS came from Richard Hill of the American Bankers Association. He defined an EFT as a newt, and he went on to explain that a newt is like a snake, and that as a snake is like a worm, EFTS could be called a can of worms!

Once this could have been a valid definition.

> "EFT SYSTEMS INVOLVE THE USE OF COMPUTERS AND TERMINALS, LINKED BY SECURE COMMUNICATION NETWORKS, TO HANDLE PAPERLESS MONEY TRANSACTIONS.
>
> SETTLEMENT OF THE ACCOUNTS NEED NOT BE IN REAL-TIME."

EFT Systems can be divided into three groups:

> Inter-Bank EFT
> Corporate EFT
> Consumer EFT

Inter-Bank EFT Systems are those dealing with the transfer of paperless money transactions electronically between financial institutions. BACS (Bankers Automated Clearing Services) and CHAPS (Clearing Houses Automated Payment System) are the two most well-known systems in the UK that fall into this group.

Corporate EFT systems are offered by BACS so that businesses can generate magnetic tapes, etc, for Salary Payments, Purchase Ledger Payments, and Pension Payments, and thereby eliminate the need to produce and distribute paper-based transactions.

Consumer EFT systems can be divided into three sub-categories:

>   EFT at the Bank
>   EFT at the Shop
>   EFT from the Home

EFT at the Bank is the group of systems involving the use of Cash
Dispensers and Automatic Teller Machines (ATMs) located both
inside and outside the banks.

Many of us have Bank Accounts and have been issued with plastic
cards containing magnetic stripes, and we are familiar with the
procedure of inserting the card into a reading slot, and of
verifying ourselves by way of a secret number, called a Personal
Identification Number (PIN).

It certainly appears that consumers have fully accepted the
convenience of "EFT at the Bank" because so many prefer to queue
at ATMs in the rain even when the Banks are open and there are no
queues at the counters.

EFT at the Shop (EFT-POS) enables consumers to pay for goods
purchased in shops using a plastic debit card rather than a
cheque. It also enables a plastic credit card to be used for a
"voucher-less" transaction.

EFT from the Home is beginning to emerge in this country. One
version is "Home-Banking" which allows consumers to pay bills
(such as Gas and Electricity) from a home terminal. Another
version is "Home Shopping" where, for example, consumers can
communicate with retailers via Prestel to order goods and charge
them to their Bank or Credit Card Accounts.

>   "EFT-POS IS THE VERSION OF EFT BETWEEN THE POINT-OF-SALE
>   IN RETAIL AND OTHER DISTRIBUTIVE AND SERVICE OUTLETS,
>   AND FINANCIAL INSTITUTIONS, SUCH AS BANKS AND OTHER CARD
>   ISSUERS, INVOLVING A MUTUAL CUSTOMER, SUCH AS THE
>   CONSUMER."

B. CONCEPTS OF EFT-POS SYSTEMS

Consumer Identification

In any EFT system it is necessary to IDENTIFY the card issuer and the account to which the customer wishes to charge the purchase.

Originally plastic cards with embossed data were used by retailers, and these were imprinted onto Sales Bills for Account Transactions.

With the advent of POS Terminals, many retailers started to key-enter the account numbers, and to capture the transaction electronically (Off-Line EFT).

The introduction of the Banks' Self-Service Cash Dispensers and ATMs brought along plastic cards with Magnetic Stripes which could be read automatically. Today, Debenhams in the UK and GIB in Belgium issue Magnetic Stripe Cards to their own account customers.

Plastic Card standards are well estabished and cover three main areas.

The International Standards Organisation (ISO) have a standard (ISO 2894) for embossed cards which defines the physical specifications of the card, type fonts, location and dimension of the embossed data, and an account numbering system. It further identifies the procedure by which card issuers should be registered and their identifier codes distributed for the information and use of all concerned. The standard has also been approved by the British Standards Institute (BSI 5132 Part 1).

In addition there is a standard (ISO 3354 and BS 5132 Part 2) which specifies the physical and magnetic characteristics for a magnetic stripe on a plastic card, the encoding technique, the coded character set, and the encoding formats.

The use of international standards means that it is relatively simple for cards issued by different organisations to be read and

processed in a shared system. The standards for magnetic stripes
define that they should have three recording tracks, though they
do not all have to be encoded.

Track 1 was originally developed for airline use by IATA. Data on
this track is permanently encoded and so can only be read. It
allows for up to 79 characters of alpha-numeric data, including
the card holders surname, initials, title, account number, and
expiry date.

Track 2 was developed by the American Bankers Association (ABA) on
behalf of its members, VISA and MASTERCARD. Again the data can
only be read after the initial encoding, but it only allows for up
to 40 digits of numeric data including the Primary Account Number
(PAN) and expiry date.

Track 3 was specifically designed for use by ATMs operating
off-line systems. After the initial encoding, the data can be
read and re-written during normal use. It contains up to 107
digits of numeric data which includes the Primary Account Number,
and discretionary data which can be used for off-line Personal
Identification Number (PIN) verification. Equally important is
that account balance and usage information can be updated each
time the account is used.

Unfortunately, magnetic stripes can easily be "skimmed"
(duplicated) and "counterfeited" (altered) for about £15 by
professional thieves. There are a number of techniques available
to make them more secure. One approach is to use the Malcro
double-layer technique, and another is to use the 3M watermark.

Another solution being tried out is to issue magnetic stripe cards
with a sealed photograph; the cards could just as easily have a
sealed signature as well.

However, in 1984 the UK Banks adopted the PMI Data Card which is
claimed to be the first card with full Bank-Note security
features.

There are two alternatives to Magnetic Stripe Cards which are under consideration.

The first is the Micro-chip card which was developed by a 29 year old French journalist called Roland C Moreno in 1974.

The second is the Drexon Laser Card which is gaining greater interest in Japan and the United States. They are wallet-sized cards which were first announced in 1981. They deploy optical modifications to a special surface rather than magnetic or semi-conductor techology. Each card can contain two million characters.

C.　SECURITY

Consumer Verification

Having identified the account to which the purchase is to be charged, it is essential to VERIFY that the customer is actually entitled to use the card.

Until recently the most common method of customer verification has been to compare their signature with an example on the plastic card. However, this is very much a question of cashier judgement, and it can not be used with a self-service terminal, such as an ATM.

The Banks issue their ATM card holders with secret 4-digit numbers, known as Personal Identification Numbers or PINs. These are far more effective than signatures because they are precise and do not rely upon human judgement.

PIN numbers can be verified either off-line or on-line. With off-line verification the PIN entered by the customer is put through a mathematical algorithm, the answer of which is held on the plastic card. In an on-line system, the PIN is verified by the card issuer's computer.

A well-developed PIN system is as secure as the user and card issuer allows. Unfortunately various studies indicate that well

over 50% of card holders write their PIN on the card, and over 70%
write them somewhere else in their wallet or purse.

However, the Magnetic Stripe Card used in conjunction with a PIN
is the most cost effective way to identify and verify the rightful
customer today. There are unlikely to be any significant changes
for many years to come.

A verification system based on memorised PINs can be transferred
from one person to another without the consent of the owner. One
way to minimise this problem is to use a unique physiological
trait of the card owner for verification such as Finger Prints,
Palm Prints, Voice Prints, Finger Lengths, Signature Dynamics, and
Retinal Blood Vessel Patterns. They are all being investigated by
scientists, but many of them are unlikely to meet with consumer
approval.

Authorisation

There are a number of approaches to authorisation.

Firstly there can be NEGATIVE AUTHORISATION where the Account
number is checked for validity. There can be further
consideration on credit or debit worthiness to determine whether
the authorisation request can be approved. Perhaps the most
sophisticated authorisation systems take into consideration the
pattern of usage from both the value and frequency angle, as well
as geographical use.

There are examples of all these types of system in use by various
Card Issuers around the world.

Settlement

Nearly everyone is under the belief that EFT-POS means the
real-time transfer of funds between the consumer and the
retailer. While that is certainly feasible, it is not always the
case.

In the Credit Agricole System, for example, the Consumer's account

is not debited for 3 days so that EFT-POS is no quicker than an
equivalent cheque.

In Salzburg, the system does involve real-time funds transfer.

In Iowa, funds transfer takes place at 8.00 on the following
morning.

What will happen in the UK is not certain, and is likely to vary
from one card issuer to another as they battle for a competitive
advantage over their rivals.

So, it is extremely important to realise that EFT-POS, while it
may make Real-Time Funds Transfer possible, does not necessarily
mean that it will happen.

Encryption

It is generally accepted that a totally secure computer system is
unobtainable in practice. A thoroughly determined person will
always find a way into any system, either for the purpose of
fraud, or as an intellectual challenge.

It is only when the cost of access to a system is increased by
security devices to the extent that it exceeds the value of the
data, that a fraudster is likely to be deterred, and data remains
secure.

Message Authentication is designed to ensure the integrity and the
origin of the data message, while the data message can be sent in
"cleartext". Data Encryption is designed to ensure that the data
message is sent in "cyphertext" so that it can only be understood
by approved people. It is not concerned with the integrity and
the origin of the message.

In Message Authentication, a value called the Message
Authentication Code (MAC) is created by the sender using a highly
sensitive algorithm. The algorithm is applied to all or part of
the Data Message and the resultant MAC is attached as an extra
field to the Data Message for transmission. The receiver,

obviously knowing the algorithm and the appropriate fields,
generates its own MAC and compares it with the senders MAC. If
the two MAC values are identical, then the message is assumed to
have come from a legitimate sender.

As can be seen it is important that the algorithm must incorporate
a feature that will ensure that a MAC cannot be duplicated by
unauthorised parties. This feature is known as a "Key".

The National Bureau of Standards (NBS) Data Encryption Standards
(DES) were developed over fifty years ago, and they are widely
used as "Keys" in Message Authentication. It works on the
principle of using an 8-byte "key" with over 72 quadrillion
(72,057,594,037,927,936) possible keys to create a "bit-sensitive"
MAC. A MAC generated using a particular key can only be recreated
using the same data and the same key. Anyone attempting to insert
a complete message must know how to create a MAC, and to do this,
the key must be known.

As can be realised, Message Authentication does not seek to stop a
person interrogating the data contained in a message; it only
seeks to stop extra messages being created and existing ones being
altered.

Data Encryption does attempt to stop messages being interrogated
by turning "clear-text" data into "cypher-text" data. Again the
NBS DES techiques are generally used. The data fields are divided
into 8-byte blocks which are crypted by, for example, an 8-byte
DES key.

In EFT, the following data is usually crypted:

        Transaction Type (Debit or Credit)
        Customers Card Issuer and Account Numbers
        Retailer
        Amount and Currency Type
        Date
        Message Identifier

For the purposes of EFT, the DES chips are usually contained in a

box that also contains a microprocessor some RAM, and PROM to
handle the MAC calculation. It is obviously desirable to be able
to change the keys, and this can be done as frequently or
infrequently as required. If there are a large number of
terminals in the system, then it is usual to transmit the keys
down to the Terminal, and this is another reason for choosing
on-line EFT systems.

D.   <u>COMMUNICATIONS</u>

<u>Networks</u>

In the past there have been two schools of thought as to whether
EFT systems should be either off-line or on-line. The UK Banks,
for example, have been divided with their ATM Networks. National
Westminster and Midland supporting off-line and Barclays and
Lloyds supporting on-line configurations.

However, if an EFT system is to be shared amongst a large number
of card issuers, EFT can only be really effective in an on-line
network. Further advantages include greater security and
increased flexibility of services that can be offered to
customers.

An EFT network consists of Processors connecting EFT Terminals
with the Card Issuer and the Retailer's Bank. Because the EFT
Terminals should be shared by all the Card Issuers, the main
function of the Processors is to identify the appropriate card
issuer and switch the Authorisation Request Messages accordingly.

Depending on a number of variables, there are two principal types
of EFT Switch Network.

The Switch-in-Front permits EFT Terminals to be connected directly
to the Card Issuer via the Switch. The Switch-Behind means that
all EFT Terminals are connected directly to the Retailer's Bank
which pass on all the other Card Issuer messages via the Switch.

In any EFT system, there must be a minimum of two messages for
each transaction. Firstly there is the Authorisation Request

Message from the Retailer to the Card Issuer, and secondly there
is the Authorisation Response Message back to the Retailer. If
the transaction has been authorised, the Retailer must send a
third Confirmation Message to the Card Issuer to confirm that the
transaction has been completed.

In addition to these minimum messages, there should obviously be
many others for Audit and Security purposes.

Switch-In-Front

The Switch-In-Front configuration permits terminals to be
connected directly to the Switch. The system is as follows:

1   Terminal sends Authorisation Request to the Switch. The
         Switch logs the message for Inter-bank settlements and
         for retail terminal balancing.

2   The Switch transfers the Authorisation Request to the
         Cardholder's Bank.

3   The Cardholder's Bank sends the Authorisation Response
         to the Switch.

4   The Switch returns the Authorisation Response to the
         Terminal. The Consumer receives a printed receipt.

5   The Terminal sends the Transaction Configuration to the
         Switch.

6   The Switch sends the Transaction Confirmation to the
         Retailer's Bank.

7   The Retailer's Bank requests the transfer of funds from
         the Cardholder's Bank, or vice versa.

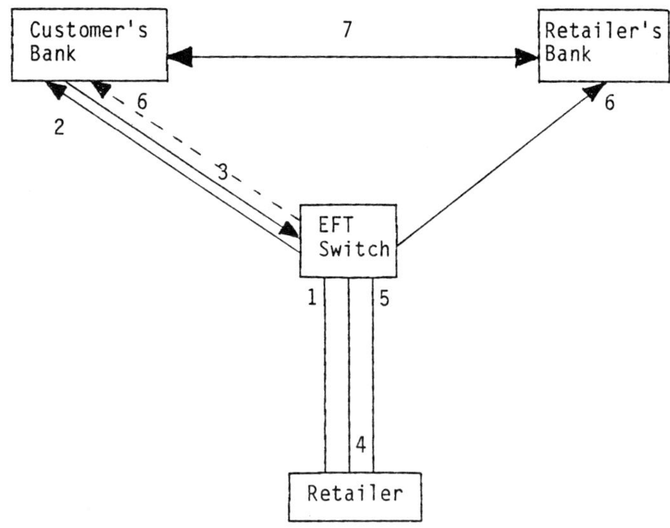

Switch-Behind

In the Switch-Behind configuration, terminals are connected directly to the Retailer's Bank.

1   Terminal sends Authorisation Request to the Retailer's Bank, which determines whether the Cardholder's Bank is the same or another Bank.

2   The Retailer's Bank transfers the Authorisation Request to the Switch.

3   The Switch transfers the Authorisation Request to the Cardholder's Bank.

4   The Cardholder's Bank sends the Authorisation Response to the Switch.

5   The Switch transfers the Authorisation Request to the Retailer's Bank.

6   The Retailer's Bank returns the Authorisation Request to the Terminal. The consumer receives a printed receipt.

7   The Terminal sends the Transaction Confirmation to the
         Retailer's Bank.

8   The Retailer's Bank requests the transfer of funds from
         the Cardholder's Bank, or vice versa.

If the Retailer's Bank and Cardholder's Bank are the same, then
steps 2-5 can be omitted.

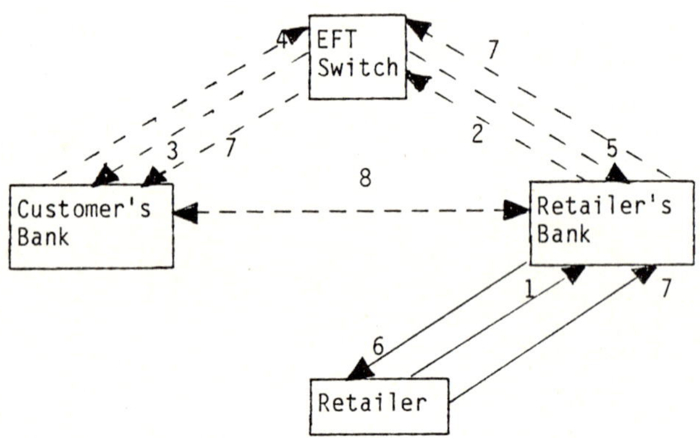

E.   BENEFITS OF EFT-POS

There are three parties involved in any EFT-POS transaction, the
Card Issuer, the Retailer, and the Customer. All the costs of
running an EFT-POS system must be borne by one or more of the
three parties, and likewise the benefits should be spread across
the parties involved.

In trying to identify and justify the benefits, the initial
assumption should be that, in time, all cheques will be replaced
by EFT Debit Card transactions, and that all Credit Card Voucher
transactions will be replaced by EFT Credit Card transactions.

Although there have been signs in France and Belgium that EFT-POS
reduces the volume of cash transactions in a shop, it is extremely
difficult to predict what will be the effect in the UK. On the one
hand, there are an increasing number of Automatic Teller Machines
being installed in Banks and now Building Societies, and soon they
will be common place in shops, factories and offices. This mean

that cash will be even easier to obtain than before. On another
hand the big unknown is how the card issuers will "market" EFT-POS
and how will the individual consumer be given an incentive to use
EFT-POS.

Benefits to Retailers

The most important thing to establish for any retailer is how much
do the existing methods of payment actually cost him?

> "Many retailers have no idea of the absolute or
> relative cost of accepting the different methods
> of payment, although all know that credit cards
> are the most expensive."

So, let us analyse the costs and benefit areas. The following is
only an example, and the benefits may be lesser or greater for an
individual retailer, but unless a retailer knows his own figures,
he has neither basis for claiming that there are insufficient
benefits in EFT-POS for his company nor the basis for
re-negotiating his bank and credit card company charges.

There are three stages to a "Cash Register" transaction. Firstly
there is the "Start" routine which establishes, amongst other
things, the assistant or cashier involved. Secondly there is the
"Merchandise" routine which itemises all the goods to be
purchased, and thirdly there is the "Payment" routine which
identifies and controls the method of payment. A retailer should
measure and know the average time elements for each of the three
stages. The second stage time will vary substantially according
to the number of items to be purchased, while the third stage time
will vary according to the payment type.

One of the reasons that supermarkets are installing scanning is to
reduce the time taken to itemise the goods being purchased
(merchandise routine) and this, because of the high average number
of items being purchased, has a significant effect on the total
transaction time. Scanning is of course, extremely beneficial in
shops with a "constant" queue of customers. Likewise, a reduction
in the payment times will also have, for many retailers,

POINT-OF-SALE PAYMENT TIMES & COSTS FOR A £20 SALE

* ESTIMATED

PAYMENT METHOD	1 POS PAYMENT TIMES	2 POS PAYMENT COSTS	3 BACK OFFICE COSTS	4 FRAUD THEFT INTEREST ETC	5 BANK & CARD ISSUER COSTS	6 EFT TERMINAL COSTS	7 TOTAL
CASH	30 SECS	1.7P	1.0P	10.0P	8.0P		20.7P
CHEQUE	90 SECS	5.0P	0.5P	2.0P	14.0P		21.5P
RETAIL CARD	60 SECS	3.3P	6.0P	45.0P			54.3P
CREDIT CARD	75 SECS	4.2P	0.5P	1.5P	50.0P		56.2P
T & E CARD	75 SECS	4.2P	0.5P	5.0P	80.0P		89.7P
EFT DEBIT CARD	15 SECS	0.8P	0.2P *		10.0P *	3.0P *	14.0P *
EFT RETAIL CARD	15 SECS	0.8P	0.2P *	45.0P		3.0P *	49.0P *
EFT CREDIT CARD	15 SECS	0.8P	0.2P *		40.0P *	3.0P *	44.0P *

a significant effect on the total transaction time. But
reductions in the payment times are only one aspect of the total
benefits that can be derived from EFT-POS, as there are further
benefits that can be achieved in the "back office".

POS Payment Times

A customer may wish to pay by either one tender type or several.
In this analysis the POS Payment Times are for a single tender
type, starting from the point in the transaction when the total is
established and ending when the receipt is printed.

The Payment Times used in this example are based upon the
experiences of many retailers, not only in this country, but also
in Europe and the USA. Payment Times do vary from one cashier to
another, even for an identical transaction, and so to even out
variations, the times have been rounded up to the nearest 15
seconds.

The analysis is based upon a £20 transaction.

The Cash Time assumes:

(a)   There is change to be given.
(b)   The cashier 'counts back' the change into the
         customer's hand.

The Cheque Time includes:

(a)   The customer writing the cheque.
(b)   The cashier ensuring that the cheque has been completed
         correctly.
(c)   The cashier referring to the Warning Notices.
(d)   The time taken to write the Cheque Guarantee Card
         details on the reverse of the Cheque.
(e)   The time taken to write the transaction reference
         details on the reverse of the cheque.
(f)   A contribution to the time taken to refer some
         transactions to a Floor Supervisor for a higher level of
         sanctioning.

The Credit Card and T & E Times include:

(a)   The customer signing the Voucher.

(b)   The cashier completing the Voucher.

(c)   The cashier referring to the Warning Notices.

(d)   A contribution to the time taken to refer some
           transactions by telephoning the Card Issuer for
           authorisation.

The Retail Card Time includes:

(a)   The customer signing the Sales Bill.

(b)   The cashier writing or imprinting the customer's name,
           address, and account number onto the Sales Bill.

The EFT Time includes:

(a)   The Cashier swiping the card through a Magnetic Card
           Reader.

(b)   The customer entering the secret PIN number.

(c)   Response time for authorisation from Card Issuer.

(d)   Printing of Receipt.

The following EFT-POS response times are being achieved:

Interspar, Austria to Savings Bank:	1+ seconds
Army & Navy Stores to American Express, USA:	5-6 seconds
Dahl's & Hy-Vee, USA to Iowa Banks:	7-10 seconds
"Counterplus", Scotland:	3-4 seconds

POS Payment Costs

The POS Payment Costs assume that the average cashier is paid
£2.00 per hour.

Back Office Costs

The following day, there are a number of clerical procedures in
the retailer's back office which must be followed. These will
vary according to the type of payment.

Cash for example, needs to be balanced and reconciled for each cash register, and "Floats" must be prepared for the next day.

Cheques need to be balanced and prepared for banking.

Credit Card Vouchers need to be balanced and sorted according to the Card Issuer. They must then be add-listed and balanced into controlled batches.

Retail Card Sales Bills need to be prepared for Sales Ledgers, and this may involve data preparation for the computer.

EFT cards will involve little or no back office costs, and so a nominal cost has been estimated.

<u>Fraud, Theft, Interest, etc.</u>

For Cash payments, the cost involved in insurance premiums to cover the cash held in the shop as well as the cost of employing security firms to move cash to and from the banks must be considered. It has been assumed that $\frac{1}{2}$% covers these costs.

For cheques, the retailer takes a risk when either accepting cheques without a cheque guarantee card, or cheques over the cheque guarantee card level. Included in this column must be the cost to the retailer of not receiving the money for the sale until the cheque has been cleared by the bank, typically three working days. It has been assumed that 0.1% covers the costs.

For Credit Cards, most retailers can receive the value of the vouchers when they are submitted to their banks, before they are cleared by the credit card companies. So, a lower cost of 0.07% has been used.

However, it is normal for retailers not to receive settlement for Travel and Entertainment Card Vouchers until they have been cleared by the Card Issuer, and so 0.25% has been used to cover the cost of delay in settlement.

Retailers have to cover themselves against all fraud and misuse of

their own Retail Card, as well as the fact that they will not
receive settlement for anything up to two months after the sale.
It has been estimated that 2.25% covers these costs.

EFT Debit and Credit Cards should not involve the retailer in any
costs in this section, but the costs will remain unaltered for EFT
Retail Cards.

Bank and Card Issuer Costs

Like individual consumers, retailers have to pay bank charges, and
their make-up is often the result of individual negotiations with
their bank managers.

One small retailer's charges were made up as follows:

Cash paid into bank	31p/£100
Cash paid out of bank	28p/£100
Cheques paid into bank	9p each
Debit entries	23p each
Credit entries	37p each
Statement requests	61p each

So the cost involved in banking excess cash and obtaining change
from the bank must be included in the calculations. The major
banks suggest that the fee is negotiated down from a "starting
point" of about 60p/£100, and that 40p/£100 is a typical figure.

There is a fee of between 10p - 15p for each cheque paid into the
bank, irrespective of its value.

Credit Card companies charge retailers about 2½% for each
transaction as a "Merchant Fee". As fraud is costing them about
0.33% and retailers are able to negotiate rebates for submitting
Claims Tapes instead of Vouchers, the Merchant Fees can probably
be reduced by about ½% for an equivalent transaction.

Travel and Entertainment Card companies traditionally have a
higher Merchant Fee to cover their greater overhead costs.

For EFT Debit Cards it has been assumed that the UK banks might
charge retailers a similar % fee to those charged in Europe,
instead of a flat fee for cheques. Typically these are between $\frac{1}{2}$%
- 1$\frac{1}{4}$%, and the justification for the charge could be that all
transactions, even though they may exceed the "Cheque Guarantee
Card" level, would be guaranteed.

Having established what are the cost elements, a Total Cost can be
easily derived, but in order to make the costs meaningful, it is
necessary to analyse the mix of payment methods. Supposing a
retailer has 1000 customers in a day or week, then he may find
that he has 650 transactions paid by cash, 300 by cheque, and 50
by credit card. If all Cheque transactions were replaced by EFT
Debit Card transactions, and all Credit Card transactions replaced
by EFT Credit Card transactions, then he would overall probably
find that he benefits by about 50% in Payment Time (about 7 hours)
and over 10% in Payment Costs (about £30).

So, having looked at the POS payment times and costs, let us study
some of the other areas of benefit.

Other Benefits to Retailers

There are a number of advantages for retailers if they can issue
their own Retail Card to customers. Retail Cards mean that
customers can make purchases without having the "cash" in their
pockets, and so they tend to spend more. Many retailers have
discovered that in fact, customers spend about twice as much per
visit than non-Retail Card customers. Besides spending more, they
also tend to be loyal and regular customers because it is less
convenient to shop anywhere else.

EFT-POS gives retailers the opportunities of operating a Retail
Card system at a lower cost than they could with a clerical
non-EFT version, and it will be about 60 seconds quicker at the
Point-of-Sale. It means that retailers such as Food Supermarkets
and Hypermarkets with low gross margins may now have the
opportunity to cost-justify the introduction of such a system.

The Belgian Hypermarket MAXI GB, which is part of the enormous GIB
organisation, has done just this by introducing an Option Account

POINT-OF-SALE PAYMENT TIMES & COSTS FOR A £20 SALE   * ESTIMATED

PAYMENT METHOD	WITHOUT EFT-POS		WITH EFT-POS		BENEFITS WITH EFT-POS	
	POS PAYMENT TIME	POS PAYMENT COST	POS PAYMENT TIME	POS PAYMENT COST	TIME ±%	COST ±%
CASH v CASH	30 SECS	20.7P				
CHEQUE v EFT DEBIT CARD	90 SECS	21.5P	15 SECS	14.0P *	83%	34%
RETAIL CARD v EFT RETAIL	60 SECS	54.3P	15 SECS	49.0P *	75%	9%
CREDIT CARD v EFT CREDIT	75 SECS	56.2P	15 SECS	44.0P *	80%	21%

Card. To overcome the low gross margins, they charge a
competitive interest rate from the date of purchase. At the end
of the month, the customer will receive a statement showing
details of all the purchases, interest, and repayments. To cut
down the costs, the customers when applying to open an account,
have to agree to MAXI GB automatically creating a Direct Debit for
either a minimum amount or one-twelfth of the outstanding balance,
whichever is the greatest.

Having established their own card, MAXI GB can now offer their
customers a number of benefits. As an alternative to writing out
a cheque at the Point-of-Sale, MAXI Card holders can use their
card to create a Direct Debit (Off-line EFT) via the retailer's
own computer and the Belgian Clearing Bank System. This is known
as Electronic Cash. With this system, the retailer can slow down
the EFT cycle by delaying submission of the EFT Claims Tapes to
the banks to encourage customers to use their cards.

In addition the retailer can offer discounts to MAXI Card holders
to boost sales and reduce stocks as and when he wishes.

Benefits to Card Issuers

The Card Issuers benefit by a reduction in the volume of cheque
and voucher processing, which means significantly reduced
transaction processing costs.

As the banks, for example, charge customers who have to pay bank
charges about half the price for processing an electronic ATM
transaction than for the same over-the-counter paper-cheque
transaction, it is not unreasonable to assume that this same
differential could not still apply to EFT-POS v. Cheques.
Furthermore, as retailers generally have to pay banks for the
cheques submitted for payment, surely the same approach should
apply for them.

EFT-POS will also mean the ability to control fraud significantly
better, especially with an on-line system. However, unless
consumers report stolen or missing cards immediately, there is
little that the card issuers can do unless the pattern of spending
was to change.

Many card issuers around the world are trying to take the
opportunity of the introduction of EFT-POS to making an annual
charge for the issue of cards to consumers. They are also trying
to introduce the concept that the on-line authorisation of
high-value transactions guaranteeing funds has a "value" or
"worth" to the retailers, and so perhaps, a small fee could be
introduced!

Benefits to Consumers

Customers will benefit by a quicker and more convenient method of
payment at the Point-of-Sale.

EFT-POS will save over a minute compared with a cheque, and will
be even quicker than a cash transaction requiring change to be
given.

Convenience will be the most significant benefit, because there
will no longer be the need to carry a cheque book and a cheque
guarantee card, nor will there be the need to carry out the
cumbersome task of writing a cheque.

Benefits to Network Owners

In the United States, there are a growing number of EFT Network
Owners who are in the business solely to make money from switching
EFT transactions between terminals and Card Issuers.

All the EFT-POS systems that have been installed have shown
conclusively that it is quicker and easier to pay by EFT-POS than
by cheque or even cash.

However, the success or failure of EFT-POS depends to a great
extent on how fairly the Card Issuers spread their benefits to the
other parties involved in the transaction.

The potential benefits of EFT give Card Issuers and Retailers
alike a powerful incentive to make it work, and improve the
service and convenience to their mutual customer, the consumer.

F. <u>WORLD-WIDE TRIALS OF EFT-POS</u>

COUNTRY	NAME	RETAILER	TOWN
AUSTRIA		INTERSPAR	SALZBURG
BELGIUM	"BANCONTACT"	PETROL	
	"MISTERCASH"	PETROL	
		MAXI GB	BRUSSELS ETC
DENMARK	"DANKORT"	VARIOUS	
FRANCE	* M.O.A.	VARIOUS	BOURG-EN-BRESSE
	"CREDIT AGRICOLE"	CARREFOUR	ECULLY
	"CREDIT AGRICOLE"	EUROMARCHE	LIMOGES
	"CREDIT AGRICOLE"	MAMMOUTH	CLERMONT FERRAND
	"CREDIT AGRICOLE"	MAMMOUTH	AGEN
	"CREDIT AGRICOLE"	CORA	VESOUL
	"CREDIT AGRICOLE"	RECORD	CHASSE-SUR-RHONE
	"CREDIT AGRICOLE"	LECLERC	VAULX-EN-VELIN
	"CREDIT AGRICOLE"	LECLERC	MEYZIEUX
	"CREDIT AGRICOLE"	SUPERCARDI	LONGUENESSE
	"CREDIT AGRICOLE"	AUCHAN	ORLEANS
	CARTE BLEUE	VARIOUS	
	CARTE A MEMOIRE	VARIOUS	BLOIS
	CARTE A MEMOIRE	VARIOUS	CAEN
	CARTE A MEMOIRE	VARIOUS	LYON

COUNTRY	NAME	RETAILER	TOWN
FRANCE		VARIOUS	AIX-EN-PROVENCE
	"POINT RUBIS"	VARIOUS	SAINT-ETIENNE
GERMANY		ELECTRICAL	HAMBURG
		VARIOUS	MUNICH
NORWAY	"MINIBANK"		
SPAIN		LA CAIXA	BARCELONA
SWEDEN	* "SPADAB"		BLEKINGE
	"BETA"		
UK	*	BROWNS	CHESTER
	* "COUNTERSPEED"	PETROL	NORWICH
		BENTALLS	KINGSTON ETC
	"COUNTERPLUS"	BP	SCOTLAND
		ARMY & NAVY	LONDON ETC
	"CARDPUMP"	AMOCO	ROCHESTER
	"PINPUMP"	TEXACO	WINNERSH
USA	"IOWA TRANSFER"	DAHL'S	DES MOINES, IOWA
	"IOWA TRANSFER"	HY-VEE	DES MOINES, IOWA
		KROGERS	CINCINNATI, OHIO
	"INTERLINK"		,CALIFORNIA
		PUBLIX	,FLORIDA

* WITHDRAWN

Section 7:   Classified Representative Product List and Supplier' Addresses

PRODUCT LIST

REPRESENTATIVE ELECTRONIC MAIL NETWORKS

US BASED

Name	Hardware needed	Software needed	Features	Prices
EASYLINK	Preferably IBM PC compatible micros with 250K disk drive and asynch. modem.	Easylink Mail Manager ($95)	Messages by phone telex or US ECOM	$25 minimum monthly. Mailbox message 30c/min at 300 bps, 45c/min at 1200 bps. 500 ch. 45c. Up to 7500 ch $1.
MCI MAIL	Preferably IBM PC or compatible micro with 256K disk drive and asynch modem.	MCI Mail access ($50)	Messages by phone telex mail or special delivery.	

UK BASED

Name	Hardware needed	Software needed	Features	Prices
EASYLINK (see also under "US BASED")	---	---	---	£25 registration + £5/user. Mail or rental £144 per annum. £36 min. monthly. 100 free messages per month.
COMET	Most PCs	Not supplied by COMET	Messages by phone or telex	Mailbox rental £30 per month.
TELECOM GOLD	Will run on a number of PCs	RAP (£145)	Messages by phone or telex	£40 per mailbox + 10p per minute.

<u>REPRESENTATIVE FACSIMILE MACHINES</u>

A = Pap.autofeed
L = Logs details
G = Grey scale
P = Polling

<u>Supplier</u>	<u>Type</u>	<u>Groups</u>	Max.Speed/ copy (secs) <u>(bps)</u>	<u>Features</u>
Canon	320E	2/3	20 9600	P A L
Canon	30	2	--	A
Canon	510	2/3	15 9600	P A L
Interscan	M7000	1/2/3	16 9600	P A L
Kalle Infotec	6500	2/3	20 9600	P A L
Muirhead	7850	2/3	14 9600	P A L
Muirhead	7600	2/3	35 4800	P A L
Plessey	PDF 3	2/3	30 9600	P A L G
Rank Xerox	495	1/2/3	60 9600	P A L
Rank Xerox	295	1/2/3	25 9600	P A L
Rank Xerox	485	1/2	--	- A -
Rank Xerox	455	1/2	--	- - -
Sharp	FO 2516	2/3	20 9600	P A L
Siemens	HF 2021	2/3	20 9600	P A L
STC (ex ITT)	3534	2/3	15 9600	P A L G
STC " "	3532	2/3	30 4800	P A L
STC " "	3535	2/3	20 9600	P A L G
U-Bix	IP 585	2/3	13 9600	P A L
U-Bix	IP 50	1/2	--	A
3M	9140	2/3	- 2400	- - -

<u>Approximate Prices</u>

<u>£</u>

Group 2/3, 9600 bps, comprehensive facilities	4000 – 9000
Group 2/3 slower, less comprehensive	2500 – 4000
Group 2 basic	1100 – 2500

SEE Chapter 9 for comments on this list.

REPRESENTATIVE LOCAL AREA NETWORKS (LANS)

Company	Network	Channel	Protocol	Max Stations/ Distance (ft)	Data Rate (bps)
BRIDGE	Ethernet	Baseband	CSMA/CD IEEE 802.3	100/8000	10M
CORVUS	Omninet	Baseband Twisted-pair	CSMA/CD	64/4000	1M
DATAPOINT	Arc Lan	Baseband	Token-passing	255/4 miles	2.5M
GANDALF	Pacxnet	Twisted-pair	Other	2048/unlimit.	19.2K
INTERLAN	Net/Plus	Baseband	CSMA/CD IEEE 802.	1024/8000	10M
NESTAR	Plan	Baseband Broadband Twisted-pair Optical	Token-passing	255/ 22,000	2.5M
NORTHERN	Digital PBX	Twisted-pair	--	30,000/40 miles	56K
PRIME	Primenet	Optical	Token-passing	164,000/ 50m	10M
RACAL	Planet	Baseband	Token-passing Other	500/13 miles	9.2M
TEXAS	Ethernet	Baseband	CSMA/CD	1024/8000	10M
UNGERMANN	Net/one	Baseband Coaxial	CSMA/CD	1024/9500	10M
	Net/one	Broadband	CSMA/CD	1500/10 miles	5M
WANG	Wangnet	Broadband	CSMA/CD IEEE 802.3 Token-passing Other	-- --	10M

Approximate prices

There are so many alternative ways of implementing a LAN and each supplier has so many options that no meaningful price data can be provided.

REPRESENTATIVE "BUSINESS" MICROCOMPUTERS

(M=multiuser with
max memory size)

MANUFACTURER/ MODEL	CPU	OP.SYSTEM	DISKS (Max Capac) Hard	Diskette
APPLE				
2E	6502	MSDOS,CP/M	5M	148K
3+	6502	MSDOS,CP/M	–	140K
Macintosh	68000	OTHER	–	800K
Lisa 2	68000	UNIX,CP/M	–	400K
ALPHA				
AM-1000(M 348K)	68000	UNIX,CP/M	10M	800K
AM01982(M 4M)	68000	UNIX,CP/M	400M	–
ALTOS				
580(M192K)	Z80A	MP/M,OASIS	20M	1M
986(M 1M)	8086	MP/M,XENIX	40M	1M
BURROUGHS				
822(M 640K)	8086	MSDOS,CP/M	10M	500K
CHARLES RIVER				
UV 68/05 (M 16M)	68000	UNIX	35M	1M
UV 68/67 (M 16M)	68000	UNIX	60M	–
CIFER				
2887	68000,Z80A	CP/M	10M	800K
Club	68000,Z80A	CP/M	21M	800K
9000 (M 1M)	68000	UNIX	–	800K
COMMODORE				
C8096	6502	OTHER	21M	170K
C Super Pet	6502,6809	OTHER	21M	170K
Vic 20	6502	OTHER	–	170K
Commodore 64	6510	OTHER	–	170K
Executive 64	6510	OTHER	–	170K
Pet 64	6510	OTHER	–	170K
Commodore 4032	6502	OTHER	21M	170K
C 8032	6502	OTHER	21M	170K
COMPAQ				
Compaq Plus	8088	OTHER	10M	360K
Compaq Portable	8088	OTHER	10M	360K
COMPUPRO				
816/10 (M 1M)	8088	MP/M	–	1600K
816/D (M 1M)	8086	CP/M,MP/M		2.4M
CONVERGENT				
AWS Turbo	8086	MSDOS,CP/M UNIX	40M	630K
AWS Color	8086	MSDOS,CP/M UNIX	40M	630K
IWS	8086	MSDOS,CP/M UNIX	40M	500K
MagaFrame (M 20M)	68010s	UNIX	100M	
CORVUS				
Concept (M 512K)	68000	OTHER	20M	622K
CROMEMCO				
C-10	Z80A	OTHER	5.9M	1200K
CS-1	Z80A	OTHER	60M	1200K
CS-2	Z80A	OTHER	60M	1200K
CS-3	Z80A	OTHER	60M	1200K
CS-3	68000,Z80A	OTHER		1.2M
DATA GENERAL				
30/SP	8086	OTHER	15M	–

```
(M=multiuser with
max memory size)
```

MANUFACTURER/ MODEL	CPU	OP.SYSTEM	DISKS (Max Capac) Hard	Diskette
DIGITAL				
Professional 325	F-11	OTHER	–	400K
" 350	F-11	OTHER	10M	400K
Decmate 11	6120	OTHER	10M	400K
Rainbow 100	8088,Z80	MSDOS,CP/M	10M	400K
Rainbow 100 Plus		MSDOS,CP/M	10M	400K
DURANGO				
800 (M 192K)	8085	OTHER		200K
Poppy 11 (M 1M)	80186,80286	MSDOS,CP/M XENIX	20M	–
EAGLE				
PC Plus-1	8088	MSDOS,CP/M	–	360K
PC Plus-2	8088	MSDOS,CP/M	–	360K
PC Plus-XL	8088	MSDOS,CP/M	10M	360K
Spirit-2	8088	MSDOS,CP/M	–	360K
Spirit-XL	8088	MSDOS,CP/M	10M	360K
GAVILAN				
Mobile	8088	MSDOS	–	360K
SC	8088	MSDOS	–	360K
GRID SYSTEMS				
1100	8086,8087	MSDOS	–	384K
1101	8086,8087	MSDOS	–	384K
1109	8086,8087	MSDOS	–	384K
HEWLETT-PACKARD				
HP 150	8088	MSDOS	15M	270K
HP-110 Portable	8086	MSDOS	–	270K
216S (M 768K)	68000	OTHER	–	–
236CS (M 2M)	68000	OTHER		512K
540 (M 5M)	NMOS 111	OTHER	65M	–
IBM				
IBM PC	8088	PCDOS,CP/M	–	160K
Portable PC	8088	PCDOS,CP/M	–	–
PCjr	8088	PCDOS,CP/M	–	–
IBM-PC/XT	8088	PCDOS,CP/M	10M	320K
3270-PC	–	PCDOS	10M	–
INTERTEC				
1000	8086,Z80A	MSDOS,CP/M	–	500K
MOMENTUM				
32/4 (M 1M)	68000	UNIX	5M	–
NCR				
NCR Personal	Z80A,8088	MSDOS,CP/M	30M	340K
DM V 8/16 10MB	Z80A,8088	MSDOS,CP/M	10M	500K
DM V 8/16 color	Z80A,8088	MSDOS,CP/M	1M	–
DM V 8/16 Flex	Z80A,8088	MSDOS,CP/M	1M	
NEC				
PC-8200 portable	80C85	OTHER	–	–
PC-8800	Z80A,8086	MSDOS,CP/M	15M	720K
ONYX				
186 (M 768K)	80186	OASIS	6M	
C8002M (M 1M)	Z8000	UNIX	20M	
OSBORNE				
Executive	Z80A	CP/M	–	200K
Osborne 1	Z80A	CP/M	–	200K
PERTEC				
4220 (M 1M)	68000	OTHER	100M	1M

(M=multiuser with
max memory size)

MANUFACTURER/ MODEL	CPU	OP.SYSTEM	DISKS (Max Capac) Hard	Diskette
PLESSEY				
6220 (M 256K)	LS1-11/23	UNIX	10.4M	1M
6245 (M 1M)	LS1-11/23	UNIX	20.8M	-
6742 (M 4M)	LS1-11/23	UNIX	70M	-
PRONTO				
Desktop 16/10	80186	MSDOS	-	800K
Graphics 16/25	80186	MSDOS	1.6M	800K
Color 16/30	80186	MSDOS	-	800K
Trans. 16/2020	80186	MSDOS	-	800K
RADIO SHACK/TANDY				
Personal Desktop	Z80A	OTHER	-	64K
4P "Transportable"	Z80A	OTHER	-	184K
Model 12	Z80A	OTHER	1.25M	-
TRS-80 model 16B	68000	OTHER	15M	-
2000 HD	80186	MSDOS	10M	
Tandy model 2000	80186	MSDOS	-	720K
TRX-XENIS (M 768K)	68000	OTHER	15M	-
RAIR				
Black Box (M 1M)	8088,8085	CP/M	19M	1M
SAGE				
Sage 4 (M 1M)	68000	OTHER	18M	640K
SANYO				
MBC 1100	Z80A	CP/M	10M	320K
MBC 1150	Z80A	CP/M	10M	320K
MBC 1200	Z80A	CP/M	10M	640K
MBC/250	Z80A	CP/M	10M	640K
MBC 550/555	-	MSDOS	10M	160K
MBC 4000/4050	-	CP/M	10M	640K
SONY				
SMC-70	Z80A	CP/M	20M	280K
SPERRY				
10	8088-2	MSDOS,CP/M	-	320K
30	8088-2	MSDOS,CP/M	-	320K
TELEVIDEO				
TS 803	Z80A	CP/M	-	360K
TPC1(portable)	Z80A	CP/M	-	360K
TS 803H	Z80A	CP/M	10M	360K
Tele PC	8088	MSDOS	-	360K
Tele XT	8088	MSDOS	10M	360K
TPL 11	8088	MSDOS	-	360K
TEXAS INSTRUMENTS				
Professional	8088	MSDOS,CP/M	10M	360K
Portable Prof.	8088	MSDOS,CP/M	10M	360K
VECTOR GRAPHICS				
SX-2000	Z80B,8086	MSDOS,CP/M	1.5M	-
WICAT				
160 (M 4.5M)	68000	UNIX	10M	630K
ZILOG				
11 (M 1M)	Z8000	UNIX,CP/M	19M	
31 (M 4M)	Z8000	UNIX,CP/M	80M	

<u>Aproximate prices</u>

	£
Small-medium without hard disk	1200-3000
Medium-large with hard disk	3000-6500

REPRESENTATIVE MICROCOMPUTER SOFTWARE

NAME	PURPOSE	SUPPLIERS	COMMENTS
VISICALC	Spreadsheet	Software Arts Visicomp	The first spreadsheet
MULTIPLAN	Spreadsheet	Microsoft	Easy to use spread-sheet.
SUPERCALC 3	Spreadsheet	Sorcim/ IUS	Large models. Graphics
LOTUS 1 2 3	Spreadsheet Database Graphics	Lotus	Large models. Easy to use. Comprehensive.
SYMPHONY	Spreadsheet Database Graphics Word processing Communications	Lotus	Very comprehensive. Very large models. Needs 320K excluding data space.
DBASE 11	Relational database management.	Ashton-Tate	Comprehensive. Hard to use.
DBASE 111	..	..	Hard to use. Runs on many machines.
FRAMEWORK	Database Management Word processing Graphics Spreadsheet	Ashton-Tate	Very comprehensive. Windows for IBM PC and compatibles.
SCIMATE	Database Management with off/online information retrieval	ISI	Personal information system with report generator and high speed searching.
INMAGIC	Database Management with off/online information retrieval	Inmaqic	Personal information system.
WORDSTAR	Word processing	Micropro	Runs on a very large number of machines.
MICROSOFT WORD	Word processing	Microsoft	Up-market Wordstar for 16 bit Machines.
SYSTAT	Statistical Analysis	Systat	Powerful analysis and statistical test pack.

<u>Approximate prices</u>

£200–£500

<u>REPRESENTATIVE MODEMS</u>

(to CCITT standards)

```
1=Synchronous
2=Asynchronous
3=Half Duplex
4=Full Duplex
5=Auto Answer
6=Auto Origina.
```

Manufacturer	Model	Speed (bps)	Channel	Other Functions
Alpha Datasystems	Datel 4123	300/600 1200	2/4 wire	2 3 4 5 6
CASE	460/22	1200	2 "	1 2 4 5
CASE	460/24	2400	2 "	1 2 4 5
CASE	4827	4800	4 "	2 4
CASE	Autoline 48	4800	4 "	1 4 5 6
General DataComm	D/C 4827	4800	2/4 "	1 2 3 4
General DataComm	D/C 2400 ASM	2400	4 "	1 2 4
General DataComm	TR 1200	1200	2/4 "	2 3 4 5
Infotron	DL 21/23	1200	2 "	2 4 5
Jaguar	Jaguar 7512	75/1200	2/4 "	2 4
Jaguar	Jaguar 1212	1200	2 "	1 2 4 5
Micom-Borer	M4024/LL	2400	2/4 "	1 3 4
Micom-Borer	M4048/V24+	4800	2/4 "	1 3 4
Micom-Borer	M3012/V21	300	2/4 "	2 4 5
Micom-Borer	M3012/V23	1200	2/4 "	2 3 5
Modular Technol.	M 321	300	2 "	2 4
Modular Technol.	M 7512	150/ 1200	2 "	2 4
Racal-Milgo	MPS 3021	300	2 "	2 4 5
Racal-Milgo	MPS 1222	1200	2 "	1 2 4 5
Transdata	307/307A	300	4 "	2 4 6

<u>Approximate price</u>

£200 – £650

Note 1. Cheap modems and acoustic couplers are now available in
the UK for less than £200.
Note 2. Modems on plug-in micro boards are available in the US
and will soon be available in the UK. All US modem prices are
up to 50% lower than UK.

<u>REPRESENTATIVE PRINTERS</u>

```
C.=Centronics
 C=Colour
CL=Current loop
GB=Bit mapped graphics
GD=Dot addrsd graphics
GL=Line graphics
IE=IEEE 488
IK=Inkjet
 R=RS232C
```

Company	Model	Type	Max. Charact. Per sec	Per line	Inter- face	Fea- tures
Anadex	DP-9000B	Impact	240	80	C.R	GD
..	DP-9725B	Impact	240	132	C.R	GD
Apple	Imagewriter	Impact	180	136	R	GB
..	.. (Wide)	Impact	180	136	R	GB
..	Scribe	Thermal	80	136	R	C GB
..	Daisywheel	Daisywheel	40	198	R	–
Brother	M1009	Impact	50	––	C.	–
..	2024L	Impact	160	––	C.	–
..	HR-15	Daisywheel	13	132	C.R	–
..	HR-35	Daisywheel	32	158	C.R	–
C.Itoh	1550B	Impact	120	136	C.R	GD
..	1550S	Impact	180	136	C.R	GD
..	8510B	Impact	180	80	C.R	GD
..	A-10-20	Daisywheel	20	100	C.R	–
Centro- nics	250	Impact	160	136	C.R	C GB
..	352	Impact	200	217	C.R CL	GD
..	358	Impact	400	217	C.R CL	GD

Company	Model	Type	Max Charact. Per sec	Per line	Inter-face	Fea-tures
Epson	RX--80	Impact	100	137	C.R IE	-
..	FX 80	Impact	160	80	C.R IE	-
..	LQ-1500	Impact	200	163	C.R IE	-
Facit	4510	Impact	120	80	C.R CL	GD
..	4528T	Impact	165	136	C.R	-
Hewlett	HP2225A/B	Ink Jet	150	96	-	GD IK
-Pack	2602A	Daisywheel	25	158	R IE	-
Honey-well	Model 30	Impact	100	132	R	GL
..	23 PRU	NEC thimble	55	136	R	-
NEC	PC-8027	Impact	120	136	P	GB
..	P2	Impact	180	136	C R	-
..	15 L Q	Daisywheel	14	151	P	-
Newbury	8905	Impact	180	211	C R	-
Okidata	Micro-line 82A	Impact	120	132	C R CL	-
..	Micro-line 84	Impact	200	231	C R CL	GD
Pana-sonic	KXP1091	Impact	120	132	C R	-
..	KXP3151	Daisywheel	22	198	C R	-
Texas	700, 703	Thermal	45	132	R CL	-
..	810	Impact	150	132	R CL	-
Wang	5577	Impact	192	132	-	GB
..	PC-PMO12	Daisywheel	20	198	R	-

Approximate prices

	$
Impact	200 - 3500
Thermal	300 - 800
Daisywheel	600 - 2200
Inkjet	500

REPRESENTATIVE BACK-UP 0.25" TAPE DRIVES

Company	Model	Mode Streaming Start/Stop	Max Capac. M/byte	Speed Ins.Sec	Trans. rate K/sec.	Interf.
ALLOY	PC	Start/stop	16.5	30	15	OTHER
ANALOG	DC300	Start/stop	12	30	6	OTHER
CIPHER	540	Streaming	60	90	87	OTHER
FEEDBACK	354	Start/stop	17.25	90	24	RS232C
NORTHERN	6112	Streaming	100	90	90	OTHER
RAYMOND	6449	Start/stop	4	90	6	RS232C
						IEEE488
SECONARY	6132	Start/stop	67	90	35	OTHER
WANGTEK	PC-36	Streaming	60	90	90	OTHER
	SCSI36	Streaming	60	90	90	OTHER

Aproximate prices

$800-$2000

REPRESENTATIVE TERMINALS

Company	Model	Type	Display (C=Colour)	Char/ lines	Emulation
ADDS/ DATATYPE	X5A	Intell/graph	CRT(C)	80x25	DEC
CIFER	3842	Edit/graph.	CRT(C)	132x25	DEC Tektronix
CYBERNEX	SA7800	Intell/graph	CRT	80x26	OTHER
DATA GENERAL	D211	Intell.	CRT	80x24	--
DATAPOINT	82	Editing	CRT	80x24	OTHER
DIGITAL	VT240	Intell/graph	CRT	132x24	DEC Tektronix
HEWLETT- PACKARD	2623A	Intell/graph	CRT	80x26	DEC Tektronix
	2627A	Intell/graph	CRT	80x26	DEC Tektronix
LEAR	ADM 5	Dumb	CRT	80x24	--
	ADM 11	Intell.	CRT	80x25	DEC
MILTOPE	TERO100	Edit/graph	Plasma	80x24	DEC
NCR	7900-111	Dumb	CRT	80x24	OTHER
	7910	Intell.	CRT	132x25	OTHER
PSITECH	GTC 314	Intell/graph	CRT(C)	132x48	DEC Tektronix
TELEVIDEO	910	Dumb	CRT	80x24	OTHER
	950	Intell/graph	CRT	80x25	---
TERMIFLEX	HT/1000E	Intell.	LCD	16x4	--

<u>Approximate prices</u>

$

	$
Simple	450 - 1000
General purpose	1000 - 2500
With very comprehensive facilities	2500 +

ADDRESSES OF PRODUCT SUPPLIERS

Adds Datatype
100 Marcus Blvd
Hauppauge
NY 11787
USA
516 231 5400

Alloy Computer Products Inc
100 Pennsylvania Ave
Framingham
MA 01701
USA
617 875 6100

Alpha Microsystems
17332 Von Karman
Irvine
CA 95008
USA
714 958 8500

Altos Computer Systems
2641 Orchard Parkway
San Jose
CA 91534
USA
408 946 6700

Anadex Inc
1001 Flynn Rd
Camarillo
CA 93010
USA
805 987 9660

Apple Computer Inc
20525 Mariani Ave
Cupertino
CA 95014
USA
408 973 2571

Apple Computer UK Ltd
Eastman Way
Hemel Hempstead
Herts.
England
0442 60244

Ashton—Tate
9929 West Jefferson Blvd
Culver City
CA 92030
USA
213 204 5570

Ashton—Tate
1 Lancaster Park
Richmond
Surrey
England
01 948 3111

Bridge Communications Inc
1345 Shorebird Way
Mountain View
CA 94043
USA
415 969 4400

Brother International Corp
8 Corporate Place
Piscataway
NJ 08854
USA
201 981 0300

Burroughs Corp
Burroughs Place
Detroit
MI 48232
USA
313 972 7000

Burroughs Ltd
Heathrow House
Bath Rd
Cranford
Middlesex TW5 9QL
01 750 1400

Canon Inc
7 Nishy—Shinauku
2—Chome Shinjuku—ku
Tokyo 160
Japan

Canon USA Inc
One Canon Plaza
Lake Success
Long Island NY 11042
USA

Canon UK Ltd
2 Manor Rd
Wallington
Surrey SM6 0BW
England

Case PLC
Caxton Way
Watford
Herts. WD1 8XH
England
0923 33500

Centronics Data Comp. Corp
1 Wall St
Hudson
NH 03051
USA
603 883 0111

Centronics Ltd
Petersham House
Harrington Rd
London SW7 3HA
England
01 581 1011

Charles River Data Systems
983 Concord St
Framingham
MA 01761
USA
617 626 1000

Cifer PLC
Avro Way
Bowerhill
Melksham
Wilts. SN12 6TP
England
0225 706361

Cipher Data Products Inc
10101 Old Grove Rd
San Diego
CA 92138
USA
619 578 9100

C. Itoh Electronic Inc
5301 Beethoven St
Los Angeles
CA 90066
USA
213 306 6700

Commodore Business Machines
1200 Wilson Dr
Brandywine Industrial Park
Westchester
PA 19380
USA
215 431 9100

Commodore Business Machines
675 Ajax Ave
Slough Trading Estate
Slough
Berks
0753 74111

Compaq Computer Corp
2033 FM 149
Houston
TX 77070
USA
713 370 7040

Compupro
3506 Breakwater Ct
Hayward
CA 94545
USA
415 786 0909

Convergent Technologies
3055 Patrick Henry Dr
Santa Clara
CA 95050
USA
408 980 0850

Corvus Systems Inc
2029 O'Toole Ave
San Jose
CA 95131
USA
408 946 7700

Cromemco Inc
280 Bernardo Ave, POB 7400
Mountain View
CA 94039
USA
415 964 7400

Cromemco
(UK Agent)
Comart Ltd
Eaton Socon
St. Neots
Cambs E19 3JG
0480 215005

Cybernex Ltd
1257 Algoma Rd
Ottawa
Ontario K1B 3W7
Canada
673 741 1540

Data General Corp
4400 Computer Dr
Westboro
MA 02158
USA
617 366 8911

Data General Ltd
724 London Rd
Hounslow
Middx TW3 1PD
England
01 572 7455

Datapoint Corp
9725 Datapoint Dr
San Antonio
TX 78284
USA
512 699 7000

Digital Equipment Corp
146 Main St
Maynard
MA 01654
USA
617 897 5111

Digital Equipment Co
Worton Grange
Imperial Way
Reading
Berks.
England
0734 868711

Durango Systems Inc
3003 North First St
San Jose
CA 95134
USA
408 946 5000

Eagle Computer Inc
983 University Ave
Los Gatos
CA 95030
USA
408 395 5005

Epson America Inc
23530 Hawthorne
Torrance
CA 90505
USA
213 373 9511

Epson Ltd
388 High Rd
Wembley
Middx HA9 6UH
England
01 900 0466

Facit Inc
235 Main Dunstable Rd
Nashua
NH 03061
USA
603 883 4157

Facit Ltd
Maidstone Rd
Rochester
Kent ME1 3QN
England
0634 401721

Feedback Data Ltd
Bell Lane,
Uckfield
East Sussex TN22 1PT
England
0825 6141

Gandalf Communications Ltd
19 Kingsland Range
Woolston
Warrington
Cheshire WA1 4RW
England
0925 818484

Gandalf Ltd
19 Kingsland Grange
Woolston
Warrington
Ches WA1 4RW
England
0925 818484

Gavilan Computer Corp
240 Hacienda Ave
Campbell
CA 95008
USA
408 379 8005

General Datacomm Ltd
Toutley Rd
Wokingham
Berks. RG11 5QN
England
0734 79144

Grid Systems Corp
2535 Garcia Ave
Mountain View
CA 94043
USA
415 961 4800

Hewlett-Packard Co
19447 Pruneridge Ave
Cupertino
CA 95014
USA
408 725 8111

Hewlett-Packard Ltd
9 Mile Ride
Easthampstead
Wokingham
Berks RG11 3LL
England
03446 3100

Honeywell Inf. Systems Inc
200 Smith St
Waltham
MA 02154
USA
617 895 6000

Honeywell Ltd
Great West Rd
Brentford
Middx TW8 9DH
England
01 568 9191

IBM Corp
900 King St
Rye
NY 10573
USA
914 934 4836

IBM (UK) Ltd
389 Chiswick High Rd
London W4 4AL
England
01 995 1441

IBM (UK) Ltd
Personal Computer Div
PO Box 32
Alencon Link
Basingstoke
Hants RG21 1EJ
England
0256 56144

Infotron Systems Ltd
Poundbury Rd
Dorchester
Dorset DT1 2PG
England
0305 66016

Inmagic Inc
238 Broadway
Cambridge
MA 02139
USA
617 661 8124

Inmagic
(UK agent)
Head Computers Ltd
Oxsted Mill
Spring Lane
Oxsted
Surrey RH8 9PB
England
08833 5580

Institute for Scientific
                Information
3501 Market St
University City Science Ctr
Philadelphia pa 19104
USA
215 386 0100

Institute for Scientific
                Information
132 High St
Uxbridge
Middx. UB8 1DP
England
0895 70016

Interlan Inc
3 Liberty Way
Westford
MA 01886
USA
617 692 3900

Interscan Ltd
39 Montrose Ave
Slough
Berks SL1 6BS
England
0753 70821

Intertec Data Systems
2300 Broad River Rd
Columbia
SC 209210
USA
803 498 9100

Jaguar Communications Ltd
Elton House
London Rd
St. Albans
Herts. AL1 1LJ
England
0727 32983

Kalle Infotec Ltd
Hoechst House
Salisbury Rd
Hounslow
Middx. TW4 6JH
01 577 5577

Lear Siegler Inc
901 E Ball Rd
Annaheim
CA 92805
USA
714 774 1010

Lotus Development Corp
55 Wheeler St
Cambridge
MA 02138
USA
617 492 7171

Micom Borer Ltd
15 Cradock Rd
Reading
Berks. RG1 0JT
England
0734 866801

Micropro International Corp
33 San Pablo Ave
San Rafael
CA 94903
USA
415 499 1200

Micropro International Corp
(UK supplier)
Microcomputer Products Ltd
Central House
Cambridge Rd
Barking
Essex
England

Microsoft
10700 Northup Way
Bellevue
WA 98004
USA
206 828 8088

Microsoft Europe Ltd
Bulbourne House
Gossoms End
Berkhamstead
Herts HP4 3LP
England
04427 75091

Miltope Corp
1770 Walt Whitman Rd
Melville
NY 11747
USA
516 420 0200

Modular Technology Ltd
Zygal House
Telford Rd
Bicester
Oxon. OX6 OXB
England
08692 3361

Momentum Computer Sys Int'l
2730 Junction Ave
San Jose
CA 95134
USA
408 942 0638

Muirhead Ltd
Beckenham
Kent BR3 4BE
England
01 650 4888

NCR Corp
1700 S. Patterson Blvd
Dayton
OH 45479
USA
800 543 4833

NCR Ltd
206 Marylebone Rd
London NW1 6LY
England
01 723 7070

NEC Information Systems Inc
1414 Mass. Ave
Boxborough
MA 01719
USA
617 264 8000

NEC Ltd
164 Drummond St
London NW1 3HP
England
01 388 6100

Nestar Systems Inc
2585 East Bayshore Rd
Palo Alto
CA 94303
USA
415 493 2223

Newbury Data Recording Ltd
Hawthorne Rd
The Causeway
Staines
Middlesex TW18 3BJ
England
0784 61500

Northern Telecom Inc
2100 Lakeside Blvd
Richardson
TX 75081
USA
615 885 3510

Northern Telecom Inc
100 Pheonix Dr
Ann Arbor
MI 48106
USA
313 973 4600

Okidata Corp
532 Fellowship Rd
Mt. Laurel
NJ 08054
USA
609 235 2600

Onyx Systems Inc
25 E. Trimble Rd
San Jose
CA 95131
USA
408 946 6330

Osborne Computer Corp
26538 Dante Ct
Hayward
CA 94545
USA
415 784 2291

Osborne Computer Ltd
28 Tanners Drive
Milton Keynes
Bucks MK14 5LL
England
0908 625274

Panasonic Industrial Co
1 Panasonic Way
Secaucus
NJ 07094
USA
800 222 0584

Racal Milgo Inc
6950 Cypress Rd
Plantation
FL 33318
USA
305 584 4242

Radio Shack Tandy
1500 One Tandy Center
Fort Worth
TX 76102
USA
817 390 3011

Rair Microcomputer Corp
4101 Burton Dr
Santa Clara
CA 95050
USA

Rank Xerox Ltd
Bridge House
Oxford Rd
Uxbridge
Middlesex
England
01 380 1418

Raymond Engineering Inc
217 Smith St
Middletown
CT 06457
USA
203 632 1000

Sage Computer Technology
4905 Energy Way
Reno
NV 89502
USA
702 322 6868

Sanyo Business Sys Corp
51 Joseph St
Moonachie
NJ 07074
USA
201 440 9300

Secondary Computer Storage
650 N Cannon Ave
Lansdale
PA 19446
USA
215 362 7050

Sharp Corp
Osaka
Japan

Sharp Electronics Ltd
Thorp Rd
Manchester M10 9BE
England
061 205 2333

Siemens Ltd
Windmill Rd
Sunbury on Thames
Middx. TW16 7HS
England
09327 85691

Panasonic Ltd
107 Whitby Rd
Slough
Middx SL1 3DR
England
0753 75841

Pertec Computer Corp
17112 Armstrong Ave
Irvine
CA 92714
USA
714 660 0488

Pertec Ltd
10 Portman Rd
Reading
Berks RG3 1DU
England
0734 591441

Plessey Ltd
Sopers Lane
Poole
Dorset BH17 7ER
England
0202 675161

Plessey Peripheral Sys Inc
17466 Daimler Ave
Irvine
CA 92714
USA
714 540 9945

Prime Computers Inc
Prime Park
Natick
MA 01760
USA
617 655 8000

Prime Computers Ltd
1 Lampton Rd
Hounslow
Middx. TW3 1JB
England
01 572 7400

Pronto Computers Inc.
3730 Skypark Dr
Torrance
CA 90505
USA
213 539 6400

Psitech Inc
16902 Von Karman
Irvine
CA 92714
USA
714 863 0981

Racal Milgo Ltd
Landata House
Station Rd
Hook
Hants. RG27 9UF
England
025672 3911

Software Arts Inc
27 Mica Lane Rd
Wellsley
MA 02181
USA
617 491 2100

Sony Information Products
1 Sony Dr
Park Ridge
NJ 07656
USA
210 930 6499

Sony (UK) Ltd
Pyrene House
Sunbury on Thames
Middx TW16 7AT
England
09327 81211

Sorcim Corp
2310 Lundy
San Jose
CA 95131
USA
408 942 1727

Sorcim Corp
(UK Agent)
Tamsys Ltd
Pilgrim House
2 William St
Windsor
Berks SL4 1BA
England
Windsor 56747

Sperry Corp
P.O.Box 500
Blue Bell
PA 19424
USA
215 542 4011

Sperry Ltd
Stonebridge Park
North Circular Rd
London NW10 8LS
England
01 965 0511

STC Business Systems
Diversey House
Cockfosters Rd
Cockfosters
Herts. EN4 9JE
England
01 440 4141

Telecom Gold Ltd
42 Weston St
London SE1
England
01 403 6777

Televideo Systems Inc
1170 Morse Ave
Sunnyvale
CA 94086
USA
408 745 7760

Termiflex Corp
18 Airport Rd
Nashua
NH 03063
USA
603 889 3883

Texas Instruments Inc
12501 Research Blvd
Austin
TX 78759
USA
713 895 3113

Texas Instruments Ltd
Manton Lane
Bedford MK41 7PA
England
0234 76466

Transdata Ltd
Battlebridge House
87 Tooley St
London SE1 2RA
England
01 403 5115

U-Bix Ltd
Theba House
49/50 Hatton Garden
London EC1N 8YS
England
01 242 3363

Ungermann Bass Inc
2560 Mission College Blvd
Santa Clara
CA 95050
USA
408 496 0111

Vector Graphic Inc
500 N. Ventu Park Rd
Thousand Oaks
CA 91320
USA
805 499 5831

Wang Laboratories Inc
1 Industrial Ave
Lowell
MA 01851
USA
617 459 5000

Wang UK Ltd
661 London Rd
Isleworth
Middx TW7 4EH
England
01 560 4151

Wangtek Inc
41 Moreland Rd
Simi Valley
CA 93065
USA
805 583 5255

Wicat Systems Inc
1875 South State St
PO Box 539
Orem
UT 84058
USA
801 224 6400

Zilog Inc
1315 Dell Ave
Campbell
CA 95008
USA
408 370 8000

Zilog Ltd
Moorbridge Rd
Maidenhead
Berks SL6 8PL
England
0628 39200

3M Co
3M Center, Bldg 225-5N-04
Box 33600
St. Paul
MN 55133
USA
612 736 2355

3M Ltd
Yeoman House
Croydon Rd
London SE20
England
01 659 2323

Section 8: Abbreviations, Glossary, Index

ABBREVIATIONS

ADPCM   Adaptive Differential Pulse
Code Modulation
AFIPS   American Federation of
Information Processing Societies
AI   Artificial Intelligence
ALU   Arithmetic Logic Unit
AM   Amplitude Modulaton
ANSI   American National Standards
Institute
APOLLO Article Delivery Over Network
System
ARPA   Advance Research Projects
Agency
ASCII   American Standard Code for In-
formation Interchange
ASLIB   Association of Special
Libraries & Information Bureaux
(new title The Association for
Information Management)
ASSASSIN A System for Storage and
Subsequent Selection of Information
AT&T   Automatic Telephone & Telegraph
Au   Angstrom Unit = 10^{-10} metres
Baud   Unit of signalling speed
1 Baud = 1 sig. element/sec.
BBC   British Broadcasting
Corporation.
BCPL   Basic Combined Programming
Language
BDLC   Burroughs Data Link Control.
Bit   Binary Digit: unit of
information content.
BLLD   British Library Lending
Division
BNB   British National Bibliography.
BMA   British Medical Associa-
tion.
Bpi   Bits per inch
BPO   British Post Office
Bps   Bits per second
BS   British Standard
BSC   Binary Synchronous Com-
munication.
BT   British Telecom
Byte   Usually 7 data bits plus
1 parity bit.
CAFS   Content Addressable File Store
CAV   Constant Angular Velocity.
CB   Citizen's Band
CCD   Charge Coupled Device
CCITT   Comite Consultatif Internation-
ale de Telegraphie et Telephone
CDROM   Compact Disk Read Only Memory.
CEC   Commission of the European
Community.
CEPT   Conference Européene des
Administrations des Postes et
des Telecommunications.
CGROM   Character Generator Read Only
Memory
CIM   Computer Input Microfilm
CLV   Constant Linear Velocity.
C-MAC   C(Sound) Multiple Analogue
Component.

CMOS   Complimentary Metal Oxide
CMOS   Complimentary Metal Oxide
Semiconductor
CNRS   Centre Nationale de la
Recherche Scientifique
COAX Co-axial cable.
COBOL   Common Business Oriented
Language
CODEC   Coder-Decoder.
COM   Computer Output Microfilm
CP/M   Control Programme for
Microprocessors.
CP/NET Control Program for Networks
Cps   Characters per second
CPU   Central Processing Unit
CR   Carriage Return
CRC   Communications Research
Centre
CRT   Cathode Ray Tube
CS   Circuit Switched OR Chip
Select
CSMA/CD Carrier Sense Multiple
Access/Collision Detection
CUG   Closed User Group
dB   Decibel
DBS   Direct Broadcast Satellite
DDC MP Digital Data Communications
Message Protocol
DEC   Digital Equipment Corp
DES   Data Encryption Standard
DIANE Direct Information Access
Network Europe
DIP   Dual in-line package
DMA   Direct Memory Access
DMS   Data Management System
DNA   Digital Network
Architecture
DOI   Department of Industry
DP   Data Protection OR Data
Processing.
DRAW   Direct Read After Write.
DRCS   Dynamically Redefinable
Character Set.
DSS   Decision Support System
DTL   Diode Transistor Logic
EBCDIC Extended Binary Coded
Decimal Interchange Code
ECL   Emitter Coupled Logic
ECOM   Electronic Computer
Originated Mail
ECS   European Communications
Satellite.
Ecu   European Currency Unit
EFT   Electronic Funds Transfer
EFTPOS Electronic Funds Transfer
from Point of Sale
EIA   Electronics Industry
Association
EIES   Electronic Information
Exchange System
EM   Electronic Mail
EMS   Electronic Message or
Mail System
EPC   Editorial Processing
Centre

EPROM   Erasable Programmable
  Read Only Memory
ESA   European Space Agency.
FAX   Facsimile
FCC   Federal Communications
  Commission
FDM   Frequency Division
  Multiplexing
FEP   Front End Processor
FET   Field Effect Transistor
FM   Frequency Modulation
FORTRAN FORmula TRANslator
FRG   Federal Republic of
  Germany
FSK   Frequency Shift Keying
FT   Financial Times
GAs   Gallium Arsenide
GHz   Gigahertz (thousand million Hz)
Giga-   Thousand million.
GNP   Gross National Product.
HDLC   High level Data Link Control
HEMT   High Electron Mobility
  Transistor
HEX   Hexadecimal
HIT   Retrieved item which
  matches query
HMOS   High Speed Metal Oxide
  Semiconductor
Hz   Hertz ("cycle")
IBA   Independent Broadcating
  Authority
IBM   International Business
  Machines.
IC   Integrated Circuit
ICI   Imperial Chemical Industries
ICL   International Computers Ltd
IEEE   Institute of Electrical
  & Electronics Engineers
IFIP   International Federation for
  Information Processing
IIS   Institute of Information
  Scientists
INRIA   Institut National de Recherche
  en Informatique et Automatique
INTREX Information TRansfer
  EXperiment
I/O   Input/Output
IPS   Instructions Per Second
IPSS   International Packet Switching
  System or Service
IR   Information Retrieval
ISBN   International Standard Book
  Number
ISDN   Integrated Services
  Digital Network
ISI   Institute for
  Scientific Information.
ISO   International Standards
  Organisation
ISPN   International Standard
  Program Number
I^2L Integrated Injection Logic
IT   Information Technology
ITA   Independent Television
  Authority
ITDM   Intelligent Time Division
  Multiplexing
ITT   International Telephone and
  Telegraph Co.

ITU   International Telecommunication
  Union
ITV   Independent Television
K   Thousand
Kbits   Thousand bits.
KWIC   Key Word In Context
KWOC   Key Word Out of Context
LAN   Local Area Network
Lc   Lower case
LCD   Liquid Crystal Display
LC/H   Lines of code per hour
LED   Light Emitting Diode
LPC   Linear Predictive Coding
Lpi   Lines per inch
LSI   Large Scale Integration
M   Million
MARC   MAchine Readable Catalogue
Mbits   Million bits.
Mbps   Million bits per sec.
Mbytes Million bytes.
MEDLARS MEDical Literature Analysis
  and Retrieval System
MEDLINE MEDLARS Online system
Mega-   Million
MESFET MEtal Semiconductor Field
  Effect Transistor
MHz   Megahertz. (million Hz)
Micro- Millionth
Mil   One thousandth of an inch
Milli- Thousandth
MIT   Massachusetts Institute for
  Technology
mm   Millimetres
Modem   Modulator/Demodulator
MODFET Modulation Doped Field Effect
  Transistor
MOS   Metal Oxide Semiconductor
MOSFET Metal Oxide Semiconductor
  Field Effect Transistor
MP/M   Multiprogramming Control
  Program for Microprocessors
ms   Millisecond
MS DOS Microsoft Disk Operating
  system
MTBF   Mean Time Between
  Failures
mu   Microsecond
Mux   Multiplexer
Nano-   Thousand Millionth
NAPLPS North American Presentation
  Local Protocol Syntax
NCC   National Computer Council
NCR   National Cash Register
NMOS   n-type Metal Oxide
  Semiconductor
NRZ   Non-Return to Zero
Ns   Nanosecond
NTSC   National Television
  System Committee.
NUI   Network User Identifier
OCLC   Ohio Computer Library Centre
OCR   Optical Character Recognition
ODBS   Optical Disk Based System
OEM   Original Equipment
  Manufacturer
OFTEL   Office of Telecommunications
OS   Operating System
OSC   Operating System Command
OSI   Open System Interconnections

OTS   Orbital Test Satellite
P   Pica (million Millionth)
PABX   Private Automatic Branch
  Exchange
PAD   Packet Assembler/Disassembler
PAL   Phase Alternation Line
Parity A zero or 1 added to a bit
  group to make the total always
  odd or always even
PC   Printed Circuit OR Personal
  Computer
PCM   Pulse Code Modulation
PCNET   Personal Computer NETwork
PDI   Picture Description
  Instructions
PDN   Public Data Network
Pel   Picture element
PIN   p-i-n photodiode
PIRA   Printing & Packaging Research
  Association
Pixel Picture element
PKA   Public Key Algorithm
PLP   Presentation Level Protocol
PMOS   p-type Metal Oxide Semi-
  conductor
Port   Point of entry or exit
  for data
PROM   Programmable Read Only
  Memory
PSI   Permuterm Subject Index
PSS   Packet Switching System/Service
PSTN   Public Switched Telephone
  Network
PTT   Post Telegraph & Telephone
  administration
RAM   Random Access Memory
R&D   Research & Development
RJE   Remote Job Entry
RLIN   Research Libraries Information
  Network
ROM   Read Only Memory
R/W   Read/Write
SBS   Satellite Business Systems
SCI   Science Citation Index
SDI   Selective Dissemination
  of Information
SDLC   Synchronous Data Link
  Control
SECAM   Sequential Couleur à Memoire
SLIC   Subscriber Line Interface
  Circuit
SNA   Systems Network Architecture
SPL   Sound Pressure Level.
STATDM Statistical Time Division
  Multiplexing

STD   Subscriber Trunk Dialling
STDM   Synchronous Time Division
  Multiplexing
STI   Scientific & Technical
  Information
STRING Contiguous symbols, characters
  and spaces
SURROGATE Short substitute
T   Tera (million million)
TDM   Time Division Multiplexing
Tera- Million million
THz   Terahertz (million million Hz)
TRE   Telecommunications Research
  Establishment
TTL   Transistor Transistor Logic
TTY   TeleTYpewriter
TV   Television
TVRO   TeleVision REceive Only
u   (Greek) Micro (millionth)
UART   Universal Asynchronous
  Receiver and Transmitter
UNESCO United Nations Educational
  Scientific and Cultural Organis.
UNISIST United Nations International
  Scientific Information SysTems
us   Microsecond
USART   Universal Synchronous/
  Asynchronous Receiver and
  Transmitter
USPS   United States Postal Service
VANS   Value Added Network Services
VAT   Value Added Tax
VCR   Video Casette Recorder
VDU   Visual Display Unit
VHD   Video High Density
VHSIC   Very High Speed Integrated
  Circuit
VLSI   Very Large Scale Integrated
  circuit
VME   Virtual Machine Environment
VSAM   Virtual Sequential Access
  Method
VTAM   Virtual Telecommunications
  Access Method
WARC   World Administrative Radio
  Conference
WATS   Wide Area Telephone Service
WFP   Wideband Flexibility Point
Word   A group of bits, usually
  7, 8, 16, or 32.
WP   Word Processing
WUI   Western Union International
X-OFF   Transmitter Off
X-ON   Transmitter On
XOR   Exclusive Or

GLOSSARY

ACOUSTIC COUPLER
    A modem incorporating receptacles for the microphone and earphone in a telephone handset. When the handset is placed on the acoustic coupler, which is connected to a computer communications port, tones representing data may be sent and received. Since the telephone is connected to a telephone line, no other direct connection to the telephone network is needed.

ALGORITHM
    A set of step-by-step rules for solving a problem.

ALPHA-GEOMETRIC CODING
    A scheme for transmitting control codes and displaying videotex frames, providing for a wider range of colours, character sizes, and character sets than are provided in alpha-mosaic coding.

ALPHA-MOSAIC CODING
    A scheme for transmitting control codes and displaying videotex frames built up from a repertoire of symbols stored in the receiver. The selection and positioning of the symbols in small areas on the CRT screen are controlled by coded data. The repertoire consists either of characters, occupying the whole of the small area, or smaller elements occupying all or part of the area, which can be combined together. A combination of small elements is used to construct graphics having a rather coarse structure. This method of coding, with variations, is used in most videotex systems, Telidon being a notable exception.

ALPHA-PHOTOGRAPHIC CODING
    A scheme used for controlling individual picture elements (Pels) with as much within-receiver storage as may be necessary to display high resolution pictures on all or part of the screen. See Picture Prestel.

ANISOTROPIC
    See ISOTROPIC.

ANTIOPE
    Generic name for French videotex systems e.g.Didon and Titan.

ARQ
    Automatic Request for Repeat. A method of error correction in which each block of data - a block is some fixed number of data elements - is checked at the receiver and if an error is detected a request for a repeat is automatically sent to the transmitter.

ASCII
    American Standard Code for Information Interchange - a code widely used for the transmission of text. It is a 7 bit (plus 1 parity bit) code providing for 128 alpha-numeric and other symbols.

ASSEMBLY LANGUAGE
    A computer language using symbols, often mnemonics, which is translated by the assembler conversion program into machine code. It enables a programmer to work in a language more like English instead of having to work with the bit patterns of machine code. For example if the assembly symbol for register C is C and the symbol for the ASCII code for K is "K", then the assembly language statement MV C, "K" would mean "Move the ASCII code for K to register C". In microcomputers each proprietary CPU has its own assembly language which takes account of the architecture - that is the resources and arrangement of the CPU.

Assembly language may appear to be "of higher level" than machine language and so qualify as a high level language, but it is not so regarded because it does not have all the features of higher languages. A single instruction in a high level language often translates into a series of sub-routine and/or machine code instructions.

A <u>Cross-Assembler</u> is a program which translates an assembly language program written for one type of microcomputer into a machine code for another computer.

AUTODIALLER
A device for automatically dialling telephone numbers, for instance by pressing one key, which may be under software control. Often many different numbers may be typed in by the user for permanent storage to be recalled by the software for single key "dialling".

AUTOMATIC SHIFT-DOWN
See Shift Down.

BACKUP
To make a copy of stored data in case the original data is lost because of a computer malfunction.

BANDWIDTH
The range of signalling frequencies which can be conveyed by a communications channel with some defined small amount of attenuation and distortion.

BASIC
Beginners All-purpose Symbolic Instruction Code. A high level language developed by Kemeny and Kurtz at Dartmouth College, USA in 1964. It was the first language to become very widely used in microcomputers and it still is very widely used.

BATCH MODE
Computer processing of data in one operation from start to finish.

BAUD
One signalling element per second.

BILDSCHIRMTEXT
A viewdata-type service in use in The Federal Republic of Germany.

BISTABLE MULTIVIBRATOR
A multivibrator in which one transistor is on and the other off until the states are changed over by a triggering pulse.

BIT MAP
A technique for providing high resolution computer displays in which every pixel on the CRT screen is addressable. A pixel may embody grey scale or colour information requiring more than the 1 bit required for on-off operation. In this case there must be as many "multiple plane memories" in parallel as may be necessary, each plane capable of simultaneously supplying one extra bit of information per pixel.

BLOCK
A contiguous sequence of bytes.

BUFFER
A storage unit organised to act as a reservoir for data being moved between a source and a destination which operate at different data rates.

BUS
    A set of electrically conducting lines between data sources and
destinations.

BYTE
    Usually 8 bits, which may include a parity bit, representing one character.

CACHE MEMORY
    A relatively small fast storage buffer unit organised to handle data called
from disk on a "probability of need" basis which can be transferred when needed
into main memory faster than from disk into main memory.

CAPTAINS
    A videotex system developed by Nippon Telegraph & Telephone (NTT) in Japan
capable of handling Kanji (Chinese) and Kana symbols which are reproduced by dot
patterns in 8 x 12 blocks. Control signal and dot patterns are transmitted. In
order to cope with the bandwidth/time problem a relatively high transmission rate
is used with data reduction techniques.

CEEFAX
    A teletext service offered by the British Broadcasting Corporation via its
television channels. Data is broadcast during an interval within each frame
unoccupied by "conventional" TV signal data.

CENTRAL PROCESSING UNIT (CPU).

    A set of computer circuits which interpret and execute instructions.

CHANNEL
    The electrical link between data communicating devices. The near synonym
"circuit" when used in this context is, perhaps, better reserved for individual
data-communication paths within the channel. A channel may contain one or more of
such "circuits".

CHARGED COUPLED DEVICE (CCD)
    A semi-conductor element in which data is stored as an electrical charge
which may be transferred to an adjacent element by a control pulse. In a CCD
image sensor, a charge is generated when light is focused upon it. Sensors may
be arranged in the form of a strip of CCD elements associated with an electronic
transport system. After a given light exposure time, the charges are shifted by
the transport system along to an output terminal where they represent a
bit-by-bit serial representation of the light reflected from a strip of the
image.
    Such an Image Sensor is manufactured like other integrated circuits, the
strip typically consisting of 1728 elements spaced at 0.127 mm, with about 8
elements per mm or about 200 per inch. The output from such a strip represents a
strip of the image 0.127 mm wide and about 21.9 cm long (0.005 x 8.6 inches).

CIRCUIT
    A set of interconnected electronic components or, in the communications
context, a telecommunications link (See CHANNEL).

CODE
    A system of symbols representing data. Thus a "7 bit binary code" could
represent up to 128 data elements. Sometimes coded data may be recoded. For
instance in facsimile systems, re-coding is used to transform data derived from
scanning the image into a suitable form for transmission, and to minimise the
effect of errors (for instance from line noise). In facsimile and other kinds of
image processing, codes may also be used for redundancy reduction, sometimes
called data reduction, or compression. A short code group is substituted for a
long succession of identical elements - e.g. "all black".

COMPILER
     A program which translates a program in a high level language into a
low-level one (usually in machine language).

COMPRESSION
     A method of reducing amounts of data. See also CODE.

CONCENTRATOR
     Generic name for devices which arrange for the transport of data from two or
more circuits within a single telecommunications channel without mutual
interference.

COUNTER
     An electronic circuit which generates an output pulse after receiving a
given number of input pulses.

CP/M
     Control Program Monitor, the most widely used microcomputer operating
system. It was developed by Gary Kidall of Digital Research in 1975. A large
number of versions of it have been written, CP/M 80 1.4 being well used for 8 bit
microcomputers but then moving on to other versions including CP/M 86 for 16 bit
machines (which is somewhat less successful), and a multi-user version
called MP/M.

DAISY WHEEL
     A type of impact printer printing-head comprising a rotating spoked wheel
with an embossed character at the end of each spoke. When printing, the required
spoke is positioned over the paper and pressed against a ribbon and the paper.

DATA
     Plural of Datum. A term loosely used to describe symbols assigned a meaning
so that "information" is conveyed.

DATAGRAM
     A message sent through a packet switching network without being separated
into packets.

DATA REDUCTION
     See COMPRESSION.

DEBUG
     Removing program errors.

DESCRIPTOR
     Synonym for TERM

DIDON
     French teletext system similar to British teletext but using a different
code and character repertoire requiring a degree of extra complexity.

DOWNLOADING
     Moving data from a source to a destination computer, usually through a
telecommunications link.

DRIVER
     A small program of routines for port input/output control.

DUOBINARY SIGNALLING
     A method of signalling in which two level impulses, 0, 1, are encoded into
three levels 0, +1, and -1. The signalling element rate remains the same but
more information is transmitted per element.

DUPLEX SIGNALLING
    Data transmission in both directions at once. A receiver can interrupt a transmitter without waiting for the conclusion of transmission.

DYNAMICALLY REDEFINABLE CHARACTER SET (DRCS)
    A scheme for transmitting control codes and diplaying videotex frames built up from a range of patterns transmitted or stored at the receiver either to form characters, or to be combined to form graphics with good resolution. The graphics are formed from combinations of patterns such as Line, Arc, Polygon, etc., or by specifying a shape pixel by pixel.

ECCLES-JORDAN CIRCUIT
    A bistable multivibrator.

ELECTRO-ETCH RECORDING
    A recording method in which a stylus scans the surface of sensitive paper in synchronism with the transmitter scanner. Contact is made when a "black" signal element is received, and a current passes across the contact point producing a mark on the paper.

ELECTROSTATIC RECORDING
    A recording method in which the basic principle is similar to electro-etch recording, but the stylus charges a point on the surface of non-conductive paper, corresponding to a "black signal" element. A liquid or particle "toner" then adheres to charged points and is fixed permanently by heat. It provides better quality than electro-etch recording.

EMULATOR
    A program to make a computer run programs written for a different type of computer OR (more widely) to make a computer behave as if it were another computer.

EQUALISING
    A method of compensating for distortion introduced by a communications channel by adjusting circuit elements externally connected to it.

EXPONENT
    The power to which the number base is raised e.g in 10^3 and 2^8, 3 and 8 are the exponents.

FIELD
    A part of a record designated for a particular kind of data. For example each record in a car part file might contain a field for the name of the part, a field for the manufacturer's name, a field for the part number, etc.

FILE
    A named collection of computer records, usually with common attributes – for example descriptions of car parts. The name enables the file to be stored and recalled as one unit.

FIRMWARE
    A program which is permanently stored in a computer hardware device, often as a circuit which always performs the same functions when triggered.

FLATBED SCANNING
    A scanning procedure in which an illuminated document is moved on rollers driven by a stepping motor past a photo-sensor strip so that it is flat when opposite the strip.

FLIP-FLOP
     A bistable multivibrator.

FLOATING POINT NUMBER
     The representation of a number by integer(s) multiplied by the radix raised
to a power e.g. 105 becomes 1.05×10^2. This form or representation is more
convenient for computer handling.

GATE
     An electronic circuit which generates an output pulse when a particular
combination of pulses are applied to its input.

GATEWAY
     A communications processor connected to at least two networks which enables
messages to pass between networks and therefore between stations connected to
different networks.

GREYSCALE
     The representation of a tone scale from black to white. For example each
of 256 shades could be represented by an 8-bit number.

HAMMING CODE
     A code in which extra bits are automatically inserted into a code group by a
transmitting device so that a receiving device capable of carrying out the
necessary checking procedures can detect and correct single bit errors.

HANDSHAKE
     An exchange of information between inter-communicating devices to establish
compatible operating conditions and procedures.

HIGH LEVEL LANGUAGE
     A language enabling programs to be written relatively quickly in which each
instruction embodies two or more instructions of a lower level language - e.g.
assembly or machine language. A programmer writing source programmes will usually
use a high level language, but parts, and occasionally all of a program will be
written in assembly language for special purposes. Instructions in a higher level
language take longer to execute than in assembly language.

HUFFMAN CODE
     A form of run length one dimensional code. A modification of it is
recommended by CCITT for data reduction in group 3 facsimile machines.

IMAGE SENSOR
     See SENSOR, IMAGE.

INFERENCE ENGINE
     Expert system software embodying a set of rules for solving problems using
data from the knowledge base.

INKJET PRINTER
     A printer in which a jet of ink is broken up into charged fine particles
which are steered on to paper by an electrostatic field.

INTERACTIVE MODE
     Computer processing which proceeds in steps with human intervention to
observe, modify, or input new data according to results or requirements.

INTERFACE
     The boundary between computer hardware devices or functions. The word may be
used to cover hardware details such as plug and socket pin connections or quite
complex software to control data in transit.

INTERPRETER
A program which fetches and executes an instruction in a high level language before proceeding to the next instruction.

INTERRUPT
A signal generated in a computer system to indicate a requirement to the CPU which has been assigned some priority rating. For example a signal may be received from a printer port to indicate that the printer is ready to receive data. The CPU may then interrupt the program currently running if the interrupt has a higher priority, supply the data, and then return to the program.

ISOTROPIC RADIATION
Radiation with equal intensity in all directions. A radio transmitting aerial (antenna) designed to provide a service to the area surrounding it would radiate isotropically. A satellite dish aerial beamed at some area of the earth is an example of anisotropic radiation.

KEYFAX
A teletext service introduced by Field Electronic Publishing, Chicago. It is transmitted via satellite to cable TV companies for distribution to their subscribers.

KEYPAD
A small device resembling a pocket calculator containing miniature keys. For example a keypad is used for controlling a television receiver. A videotex receiver keypad embodies keys numbered 0 to 9 and three or four control keys.

KNOWLEDGE BASE
The data base in an expert system input by a human subject expert .

MACHINE LANGUAGE
A set of binary-coded instructions for execution by a particular computer. Machine language instructions are directly executed by the computer so machine code may often be the object or target code which is produced by a higher level language (q.v.). These days it is unlikely that machine code will also be the source code - that is the code used by the programmer to write the program.

MACRO
A named series of source program lines which are inserted en bloc by an assembler program when named. A macro is a programmer's time-saving aid since a frequently used series of instructions can be added without the need to write out the full code.

MANTISSA
The significant integers of a number raised to a power. Thus in the floating point number 6.8×10^3, the mantissa is 6.8.

MENU
A computer-displayed page offering a number of choices. Typically each choice is numbered and a particular choice is executed by depressing a numbered key.

MESSAGE SWITCHING
A method for transmitting messages over a network, often implying a "store and forward" technique. For example a series of telex messages could be input to a message switching terminal which is already sending messages, to be stored and queued for transmission to addressees listed in headers.

MICROPROCESSOR
     The integrated circuit elements on one or more chips which form the Central
Processing Unit of a computer

MODULATION
     A method of converting data from the form in which it is generated into a
different form which enables it to be transmitted through a channel unable to
convey the data in its original form. For example data pulses may be changed into
audible tones which can be conveyed by the telephone network.

MP/M
     A multi-user operating system for microcomputers derived from CP/M

MS/DOS
     Microsoft Disk Operating System, a microcomputer operating system introduced
by Microsoft in 1982. It incorporates some improvements compared with CP/M
particularly in respect of transportability - that is the ease with which it can
be used on different types of machine. MS/DOS is being widely used with Programs
using "windows". A version of it - PC/DOS - is used on today's most popular
microcomputer - the IBM PC.

MULTIPLEXER
     1. A device which organises the data from two or more circuits to be
transported in a single telecommunications channel. The several different
techniques used in multiplexers are described in Chapter 5.
     2. An electronic switch used in computers successively to connect a number
of sources or destinations to a single bus. The switch may be multi-pole - for
example it may connect data from any of several 8-line sources to an 8-line bus.

MULTIVIBRATOR
     An electronic circuit consisting basically of two transistors with the
output of each coupled to the input of the other producing positive feedback. The
on-off states of the two transistors depend on the coupling method.

OBJECT CODE
     The machine code used for running programs on a computer. Programs are not
now written in the object code. They are automatically translated from a higher
level language written in a source code into the object code when a program is
run.

ONLINE
     Directly connected to a computer.

OPCODE
     An instruction for an operation to be carried out in a computer program.

OPERAND
     The quantity or function upon which an operation is performed in a computer
program.

OPERATING SYSTEM
     An operating system consists of a suite of utility programs which perform
computer management functions and organise and allocate the resources of the
machine to deal with Jobs. A job is simply a sequence of processes several of
which may be in progress concurrently - for example an overlapping of
computational and input/output processes. The operating system handles
peripherals and interrupts and deals with errors. It controls the computer
system, manages the memory, and provides for file operations and file
maintenance. Other important functions include management functions in a
microcomputer development system and in machines on which several programmers can
work simultaneously ("multi-user" machines).

ORACLE
A teletext system offered by Independent Television(ITV) companies in the UK via their television channels. Data is broadcast during an interval within each frame unoccupied by "conventional" TV signal data.

PACKET SWITCHING
A method of transmitting data through a network via computer-controlled store and forward nodes to ensure efficient error-free transmission. Nodes are usually interconnected by at least two telecom channels. A message is split into a number of relatively short blocks of data each comprising header, data, and checking tail. It is stored and despatched through any network path that may become available. Upon arrival at the node to which the addressee is connected the headers and tails are removed and the separate parts are re-constituted into the original message.

PARITY BIT
A form of error checking where a bit is added to a bit-group so that when all bits are added and the group is correct the total is always an odd number or an even number (as agreed between sender and recipient).

PARSER
Software used in natural language expert systems for breaking down a sentence into its component parts with reference to stored grammatical rules.

PASCAL
A high level language developed by Nicholas Wirth at the University of California (San Diego) in 1970 which became used increasingly in 1978 when compilers became available. It is gradually displacing Basic since it has a well defined standard and is designed specifically for programmers.

PEL
Picture element.

PHOTODIODE
A type of photosensor used in image scanners in a similar manner to a CCD element. A photodiode is a semiconductor device in which the reverse current varies according to the incident light.

PHOTOELECTRIC SCANNING
The original form of image scanning in which light reflected from the image is picked up by a photoelectric cell.

PHOTOSENSOR
A device which converts light energy into electrical energy.

PICTURE PRESTEL
A system developed by British Telecom for transmitting and receiving high resolution pictures. It exhibits various compromises in data transmission speeds, coding, receiver storage capacity, and percentage occupancy of the screen area by a high resolution picture.

PIPE-LINING
A method of speeding up the execution of a computer program by fetching and executing instructions in the same machine cycle.

PIXEL
Picture element.

POLLING
      A method of interrogating a number of transmitting devices with the intention of triggering data transmission if they have data to send. In facsimile, polling means one facsimile machine calling another and receiving a facsimile transmission from it having initiated the transmission with a password.

PORT
      The place provided on a computer for the connection of some peripheral device such as a printer, modem, etc.

PRAGMATICS
      The study of the useage of a language.

PRESTEL
      The viewdata service provided nationally in the UK by British Telecom. A network of interconnected geographically distributed computers are used so that local telephone call connection can be made by users. Page by page information is supplied by a number of information providers.

PREXTEND.
      A system developed by British Telecomm to demonstrate the feasibility of using more complex coding compatible with Prestel software.

PROGRAM
      A sequence of instructions to perform a computational process.

PROSODIC
      Patterns of stress and intonation in a language.

PROTOCOL
      A set of rules to control data handling in a communications system.

RASTER
      The pattern of scanning lines on a CRT screen produced by a spot which traces out a line and then rapidly flies back to trace another adjacent line.

READ CODE
      Relative Element Address Designate code – a two dimensional code of Japanese origin used in some facsimile machines.

RECORD
      A collection of items containing data with common attributes – for example descriptions of car components – together forming a file.

REDUNDANCY
      Information in a stream of meaningful data which may be excluded without affecting the meaning. Redundant information may be added to a message to make reception more certain. Data may be removed, possibly with some sacrifice in certainty, in order to permit greater efficiency during storage or transmission. For example much redundant information is present in human languages; if all the vowels are removed from a message in English, the meaning of the message may still be understood. Another example is the addition of codes to each code group before transmission to enable devices at a receiver to perform checking, and in some cases automatically to correct an erroneous code group. An increase in the probability of correctness has been achieved at the expense of an increase in redundancy.

REGISTER
      A computer storage circuit usually to store the bits in one word.

RESOLUTION, IMAGE
    The maximum number of discernible elements. Vertical resolution is usually specified in lines per inch or lines per millimetre, horizontal in Pels or lines per inch or millimetre. In facsimile systems when manufacturers specify resolution details, they may also specify the time taken to transmit average density text on A4 paper. More details are shown in the table.

Mode	Transmission Time	Vertical Resolution	Horizontal Resolution
High speed	15 secs	57 lpi(2.66 lines/mm)	200 lpi (7.94 lines/mm)
Standard	22 secs	100 lpi(3.97 lines/mm)	200 lpi
Fine detail	36 secs	200 lpi(7.94 lines/mm	200 lpi

    Note the trade-offs between resolution and transmission speed.

RS232
    EIA standard for terminal-modem serial data transmission interface, equivalent to CCITT V24. Current revision is RS232C.

RUN LENGTH CODING
    A code in which a sequence of identical data elements, each of which would normally be individually coded, are collectively coded. The net effect is a considerable reduction in the number of codes required.

SCANNING, IMAGE
    The operation of examining the reflected light from an image, usually on paper, point by point and line by line in an ordered sequence. This enables the image to be represented by a stream of data emanating from a photosensor which may be electrically communicated to a remote machine where the image may be reconstructed on paper by a synchronous scanning/printing process.

SEMANTICS
    The principles which govern meaning in a language.

SENSOR, IMAGE
    A device for detecting a change in light intensity and converting it into an electrical signal.

SHELL
    Inference engine software in an expert system which is domain independent - that is a general purpose set of rules which should be able to solve problems and derive conclusions from different kinds of knowledge data.

SHIFT DOWN
    The operation (which may be automatic) of changing the bit rate (transmission speed) to suit the quality of the communication channel (usually a telephone line). For example a facsimile machine might commence by attempting a rate of 9600 bps but shift down successively through 7200 and 4800 to 2400 bps, satisfactory transmission being impossible at faster speeds because of noise or insufficient bandwidth.

SIMPLEX
    Transmission in one direction only.

SINK
     Synonym for Destination.

SOFTWARE
     The collection of programs used on a computer including accompanying
paperwork such as instruction manuals and documentation for recording design,
coding etc.

SOURCE CODE
     The code of the high level language in which a program is written. It is
translated by a compiler program into the object code - the machine code in which
the program is actually run.

SPOOLING
     Queueing. A Spooler is a scheduling program for resources such as disk or
printer, whereby processes are queued and take their turn.

STORE AND FORWARD
     Any electronic device for storing data and transmitting it later. A facility
available on some facsimile machines for transmitting one or more documents to one
or more addresses automatically at a pre-chosen time. The transmitting and
receiving machines need not be attended during transmission and reception.

SYNCHRONOUS
     Occurring at the same instant.

SYNTAX
     The rules governing the grammar of a language.

TELESOFTWARE
     A system for storing programs on pages in a teletext database so they can be
captured by any user with the right equipment and fed into (downloaded)
microcomputer storage via a communications channel for execution.

TELETEL
     The national videotex service in France.

TELETEX
     An ill-chosen name used for a text transmission system which has nothing to
do with teletext. The system, comprising machines and protocols, is being
supported by PTTs to provide a faster and generally improved form of Telex.

TELETEXT
     A class of videotex system in which a sequence of numbered information pages
("Magazine") is broadcast cyclically usually over a shared television channel.
User interaction is limited to "frame grabbing" - the required page number is set
on a dial and the page is captured the next time it is transmitted, typically 12
to 20 seconds later on average, and "frozen" for viewing.

TELEX
     The public switched telegraph data network.

TELIDON
     A viewdata-type system developed by the Department of Communications,
Ottawa,Canada. It uses dynamically redefinable character sets (DRCS) which
enables finely structured graphics to be constructed and displayed with some
degree of extra cost and complication.

TELSET
     A videotex service being tested in Finland using the viewdata system.

TERM

A descriptive name, expression, or word. In information systems the label accorded to items in a record so that the record may be retrieved by using that label.

THERMAL PRINTER

A recording method in which a strip of transistor/resistor elements are heated and make marks on heat sensitive paper. It provides better quality than electro-etch recording. Faster better quality printing was later introduced by replacing these elements with thin film print heads capable of printing a page with 200 elements/inch in 15 seconds. Thermal transfer printing was introduced later still using a ribbon between heads and paper so that plain paper could be used. The ink melts on to the paper, but the cost of the ribbon offsets the cost of the cheaper paper. However colour printing becomes possible by using ribbon with colour bands.

TITAN

French videotex system similar to viewdata but using a different code and character repertoire accomodating accented and other special characters requiring a degree of extra complexity.

TRANSDUCER

A device which accepts signals in one form and changes them into another - for example optical to electrical, electrical to acoustical etc.

TREE STRUCTURED INDEX

An index designed to enable a user easily to locate particular information in a series of steps progressing from the general to the particular, usually by a succession of multiple choice "menus".

VIDEOTEX

Generic name for information storage and transmission systems enabling pages of information to be displayed in response to simple commands. Videotex systems are usually simpler to use and less expensive than other kinds of computer based information systems. The two main types of videotex systems are teletext and viewdata.

VIDEOTEX STANDARDS

The international videotex standards situation is complex. At present there seem to be two pseudo-standards. The first, CEPT, adopted by virtually all European PTTs under CCITT aegis, is a compromise solution to national differences in codes and character sets. It provides for a degree of standardisation leading to the possibility of mass producing receivers and terminals. The US situation seems to be in the hands of AT&T who have introduced a de facto standard, NAPLPS - an adaptation of Telidon.

VIEWDATA

The name chosen by the British Post Office (now British Telecom) for a videotex system which it developed. The components of viewdata are a central computer containing pages with a tree structured index, the PSTN, and modified television receiver "terminals". The TV receiver modifications include the means of connecting the receiver to a computer via a dial telephone line and a keypad. A menu command display and the tree structure of the index enable any page to be quickly and easily retrieved.

The viewdata service provided by the BPO was re-named Prestel, as "Viewdata" was found to be unregistrable. The word viewdata is still used as a generic word for describing systems of this type.

VIEWTEL
     A viewdata-type system developed and offered as a service by Online Computer
Library Center, in Columbus, Ohio, USA. It started as a home library service and
other services were added later. It is sometimes referred to as "Channel 2000" -
the number of the channel to which a user's modified TV receiver is tuned.

VIEWTRON
     A viewdata-type system developed by AT&T and introduced by the Knight-Ridder
publishing group for users in Coral Gables, Florida, USA.

VISTA
     An experimental viewdata-like system developed by Bell Northern, Canada.

V24
     CCITT recommendation for the terminal-modem interface for serial data
transmission. The only universally accepted and implemented CCITT recommendation.

WHITE SPACE SKIP
     A facility fitted on some facsimile machines (but not a part of the CCITT
standard) to substitute a short code for a succession of white elements within or
between lines. An appropriate code must be used to signify to a suitable
receiving machine that it must re-insert white space accordingly. The object of
white skip is to reduce transmission time.

WINDOW
     A program controlled bounded space displayed on a CRT screen to contain
information which may be manipulated independently or in association with
information contained within other windows which may be displayed at the same
time. In order to provide sufficient flexibility, bit-mapping is usually used to
construct windows within which text and graphics may be displayed.

X25
     A CCITT recommendation for the interface between data terminal equipment and
circuit terminating equipment operating in packet switched networks.

X400
     A series of CCITT recommendations for message handling protocols used when
interconnecting computer-based message handling systems.

INDEX TO CHAPTERS 1 TO 29